networks™
A Social Studies Learning System

**MEETS YOU ANYWHERE —
TAKES YOU EVERYWHERE**

WHO is in your network?

People Past and Present • Places • Events

networks™
A Social Studies Learning System

GO online

**MEETS YOU ANYWHERE —
TAKES YOU EVERYWHERE**

start **networking**

M2

networks
A Social Studies Learning System

**MEETS YOU ANYWHERE —
TAKES YOU EVERYWHERE**

It's **ALL** online

1. Go to *connected.mcgraw-hill.com.*

2. Get your User Name and Password from your teacher and enter them.

3. Click on your **Networks** book.

4. Select your chapter and lesson.

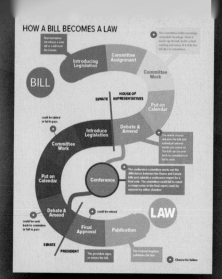

HOW do you learn?

Read • Reflect • Watch • Listen • Connect • Discover • Interact

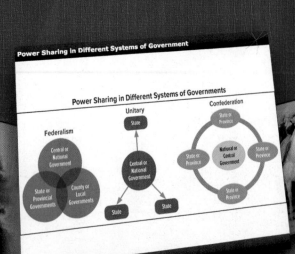

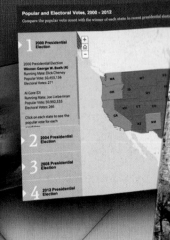

WHAT do you learn?

History • Geography • Economics • Government • Culture

start**network**ing

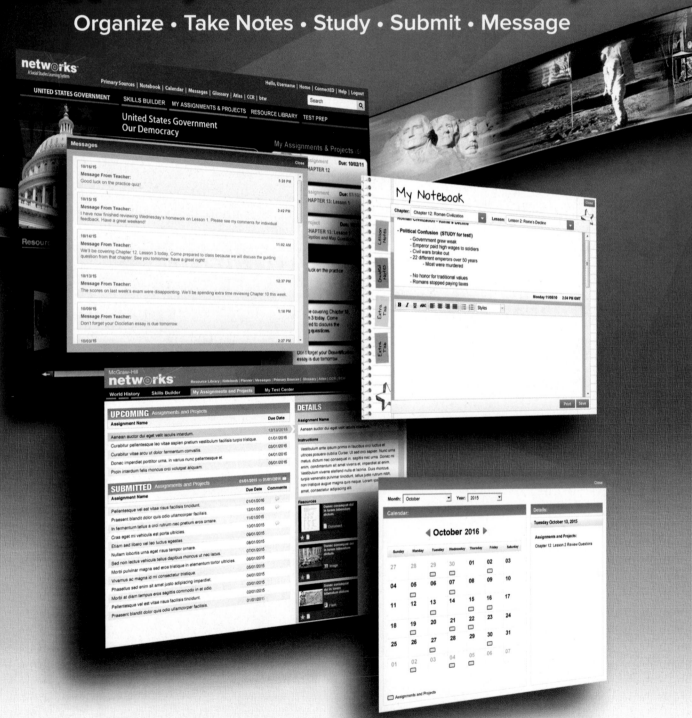

networks™
A Social Studies Learning System

MEETS YOU ANYWHERE — TAKES YOU EVERYWHERE

HOW do you make Networks yours?

Organize • Take Notes • Study • Submit • Message

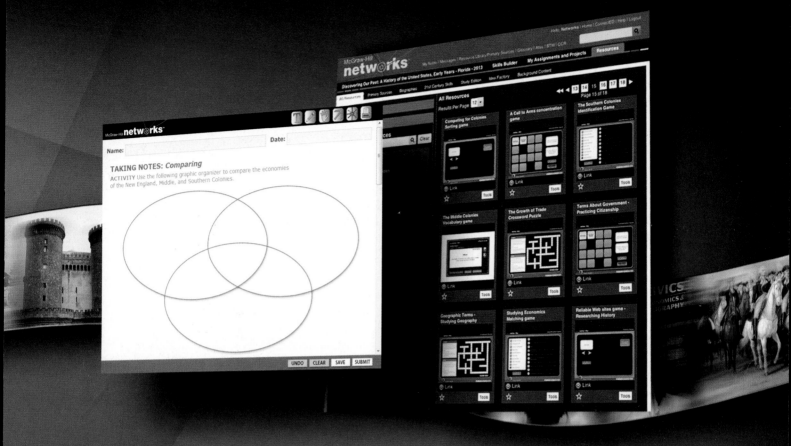

WHAT do you use?

Graphic Organizers • Primary Sources • Videos • Games • Photos

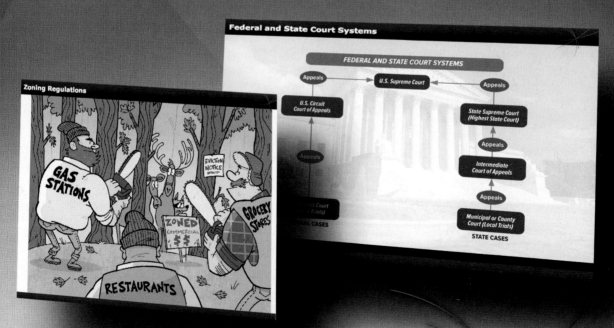

start **network**ing

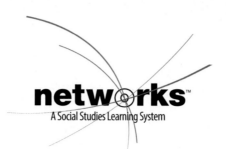

networks™
A Social Studies Learning System

UNITED STATES GOVERNMENT
OUR DEMOCRACY

Richard C. Remy, Ph.D.

Donald A. Ritchie, Ph.D.

STREET LAW™ INC

Lee Arbetman, Ed.M., J.D.

Megan L. Hanson, M.S.

Lena Morreale Scott, Ed.M.

Mc Graw Hill Education

McGraw-Hill Networks ™ meets you anywhere—takes you everywhere. It's ALL Online. 1. Go to <u>connected.mcgraw-hill.com.</u> 2. Get your User Name and Password from your teacher and enter them. 3. Click on your **Networks** book. 4. Select your chapter and lesson.

www.mheonline.com/networks

Send all inquiries to:
McGraw-Hill Education
8787 Orion Place
Columbus, OH 43240

ISBN: 978-0-07-663453-8
MHID: 0-07-663453-1

Printed in the United States of America.

7 8 9 10 11 DOW 20 19 18 17 16

AUTHORS

Richard C. Remy, Ph.D., is Professor Emeritus in the College of Education, The Ohio State University. He received his Ph.D. in political science from Northwestern University, taught in the Chicago public schools, and served as a consultant on civic education to numerous school systems, state departments of education, federal government agencies, and East European ministries of education. Dr. Remy has served on national advisory boards for the American Bar Association, the ERIC Clearinghouse for Social Studies/Social Science Education, and the James Madison Memorial Fellowship Foundation. His books include *Building Civic Education for Democracy in Poland, Teaching About International Conflict and Peace, Approaches to World Studies, Teaching About National Security, American Government and National Security, Civics for Americans, Lessons on the Constitution*, and *Citizenship Decision Making*. He is general editor for *American Government at Work,* a nine-volume encyclopedia for middle schools and high schools.

Donald A. Ritchie, Ph.D., is Historian of the United States Senate. Dr. Ritchie received his doctorate in American history from the University of Maryland after service in the U.S. Marine Corps. Dr. Ritchie has taught American history at various levels, from high school to university. He edits the Historical Series of the Senate Foreign Relations Committee and is the author of several books, including *Press Gallery: Congress and the Washington Correspondents*, which received the Organization of American Historians' Richard W. Leopold Prize. Dr. Ritchie has served as president of the Oral History Association and as a council member of the American Historical Association.

Lee Arbetman, M.Ed., J.D., is executive director of Street Law, Inc. and author of *Street Law: A Course in Practical Law* (McGraw Hill, 2010), as well as numerous articles about democracy and civic education. He has taught at the elementary, middle, and high school levels as well as in college and law school. Lee is a graduate of Grinnell College with a Master's Degree from the School of Education at the University of Massachusetts (Amherst) and a law degree with honors from George Washington University. He is the co-director of the Supreme Court Summer Institute for Teachers and an active member of the National Council for the Social Studies (NCSS).

Megan L. Hanson, M.S., is a Senior Program Director at Street Law, Inc. In that capacity, she provides professional development to secondary social studies teachers, trains legal professionals to volunteer in schools, and writes curricula. As co-director of the Supreme Court Summer Institute for Teachers, Megan specializes in writing and teaching about the U.S. Supreme Court, its cases, and constitutional law. She received her B.A. from Drew University, where she studied anthropology and human rights. She received an M.S. in Archaeology from the University of the Witwatersrand, South Africa.

Lena Morreale Scott, Ed.M., is Senior Program Director at Street Law, Inc. Lena has more than 25 years of experience in student-centered, experiential civic education. Lena taught government, history, humanities, and law at a public school in Maryland before joining Street Law's staff. She also was an instructor and outreach coordinator at the Close Up Foundation. Now, Lena writes curricula and provides training and technical assistance to educators, social workers, lawyers, judges, and others who teach and serve as mentors to young people. Lena's publications include the Teacher Manual that accompanies *Street Law: A Course in Practical Law* and lessons to accompany the PBS documentary *The Supreme Court*. Most recently, Lena was a writer and site director for Deliberating in a Democracy, a program that engages students around the world in deliberations about controversial public policy questions. Lena is a graduate of Northwestern University and Harvard, where she earned her master's degree in education.

STREETLAW is a global non profit that creates classroom and community programs that teach people about law, democracy, and human rights. Street Law is an outgrowth of a law school program at Georgetown University Law Center that began in 1972. In collaboration with the Supreme Court Historical Society, Street Law, Inc. has also developed the prestigious Supreme Court Summer Institute for High School Teachers. More than half the current members of the Court have participated directly in this program. Street Law is also a global leader in democracy and rule-of-law education, having worked in more than 40 countries overseas. Information about all programs and publications is available at www.streetlaw.org.

Contributing Authors

Jay McTighe has published articles in a number of leading educational journals and has coauthored ten books, including the best-selling *Understanding by Design* series with Grant Wiggins. Mr. McTighe also has an extensive background in professional development and is a featured speaker at national, state, and district conferences and workshops. He received his undergraduate degree from the College of William and Mary, earned a Masters degree from the University of Maryland, and completed postgraduate studies at Johns Hopkins University.

Laurel Singleton, M.S., is an associate with the Center for Education in Law and Democracy and consults with such other organizations as Street Law and PBS Learning Media. Laurel has worked in the field of social studies education for 35 years, developing curriculum materials, leading professional development programs for teachers, and conducting research. Among her publications are *A More Perfect Union: A Middle School Curriculum* and *Preparing Citizens: Linking Authentic Assessment and Instruction in Civic/Law-Related Education*. Laurel holds degrees in political science and journalism from the University of Illinois at Urbana-Champaign.

Dinah Zike, M. Ed., is an award-winning author, educator, and inventor known for designing three-dimensional hands-on manipulatives and graphic organizers known as Foldables™. Foldables™ are used nationally and internationally by teachers, parents, and educational publishing companies. Dinah has developed over 150 supplemental educational books and materials. She is the author of *The Big Book of Books and Activities*, which was awarded *Learning Magazine's* Teacher's Choice Award. In 2004 Dinah was honored with the CESI Science Advocacy Award. Dinah received her M.Ed. from Texas A&M, College Station, Texas.

ACADEMIC CONSULTANTS

Terri Bimes, Ph.D.
Lecturer, Charles and Louise Travers
  Department of Political Science
University of California at Berkeley
Berkeley, California

Glen Blankenship, Ph.D.
Associate Director and Chief Program
  Officer
Georgia Council on Economic
  Education
Georgia State University
Atlanta, Georgia

Gary E. Clayton, Ph.D.
Chair of Economics and Finance
Northern Kentucky University
Highland Heights, Kentucky

Margaret E. Fisher, J.D.
Distinguished Practitioner in
  Residence
School of Law
Seattle University
Seattle, Washington

John J. Patrick, Ph.D.
Professor Emeritus
School of Education
Indiana University
Bloomington, Indiana

David C. Saffell, Ph.D.
Professor of Political Science,
  Emeritus
Ohio Northern University
Ada, Ohio

Tom Daccord
Educational Technology Specialist
Co-Director, EdTechTeacher
Boston, Massachusetts

Justin Reich
Educational Technology Specialist
Co-Director, EdTechTeacher
Boston, Massachusetts

TEACHER REVIEWERS

Candee Collins
US Government Teacher
Pine Tree High School
Pine Tree Independent
    School District
Longview, Texas

Stephanie Doane
Social Studies Teacher
Casco Bay High School
Portland, Maine

Rose Durant
Government Teacher
Kashmere High School
Houston Independent
    School District
Houston, Texas

Janet Emond
Social Studies Teacher
Downers Grove North High
    School
Community High School
    District 99
Downers Grove, Illinois

Patricia Everett
Social Studies Teacher
Father Lopez Catholic High
    School
Daytona Beach, Florida

Tom Finnegan
Social Science Teacher
Lincoln-Way Central High
    School
New Lenox, Illinois

Michael Fox
Social Studies Teacher
Anderson High School
Anderson, Indiana

Cara Gallagher
Teacher
Evanston Township High
    School
Evanston, Illinois

Lane Halterman
Social Studies Department
    Facilitator
Westerville North High
    School
Westerville, Ohio

Loyd Henderson
Social Studies Teacher and
    Department Chair
Travelers Rest High School
Travelers Rest, South
    Carolina

Kristen Shappell Lockhart
Teacher and Social Studies
    Department Chair
Manchester High School
Midlothian, Virginia

Karen Staker
Social Studies Teacher
Pebblebrook High School
Marbleton, Georgia

Susan Strickland
AP Government Teacher
Friendly High School
Prince Georges County
    Public Schools
Fort Washington, Maryland

Mary D.P. Wagner
Social Studies Teacher
J. H. Blake High School
Montgomery County Public
    Schools
Silver Spring, Maryland

Alexia Weitzel
Government and Politics
    Teacher
Lindbergh High School
Lindbergh School District
Saint Louis, Missouri

Jean-Pierre De Mann/Alamy

CHAPTER 3

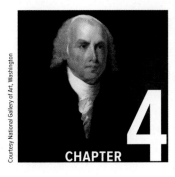

Courtesy National Gallery of Art, Washington

CHAPTER 4

CONTENTS

©Medioimages/Photodisc/Getty Images

CHAPTER 11

Library of Congress Prints and Photographs Division [LC-DIG-highsm-19318]

CHAPTER 12

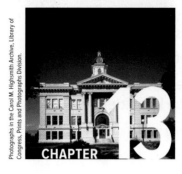

©Reed Kaestner/Corbis

CHAPTER 15

Constitutional Freedoms **437**

ESSENTIAL QUESTIONS

- *What restrictions, if any, should be placed on our constitutional rights and freedoms?*
- *Why are the freedoms in the Bill of Rights and later amendments essential to our democracy?*
- *How have citizen movements and social movements brought about political and social change?*

Photographer's Choice/Getty Images

CHAPTER 16

Constitutional Right to a Fair Trial **481**

ESSENTIAL QUESTIONS

- *How does our democracy protect the rights of individuals suspected, accused, convicted, or acquitted of crimes?*
- *How does our democracy balance the rights of the defendant and the search for truth?*

CONTENTS

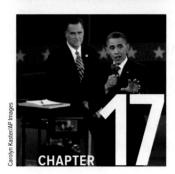

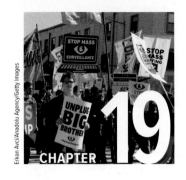

ANALYZING PRIMARY SOURCES

SUPREME COURT CASES

DEBATE

DELIBERATION

PARTICIPATING *IN* Your Government

FEATURES

C·I·V·I·C PARTICIPATION IN A DIGITAL AGE

GOVERNMENT *in your* COMMUNITY

Student Voices

We the People: Making a Difference

COMPARING

LANDMARK LAWS

SIMULATION

The Constitution

MAPS

TABLES

POLITICAL CARTOONS*

*There is a political cartoon in each Chapter Assessment.

netw⊙rks ONLINE RESOURCES

Analyzing Primary Sources

Every chapter has an interactive version of the Analyzing Primary Sources activity. Use these to take notes on the sources and analyze and synthesize the information, arguments, and counterarguments in several primary and secondary source documents. Some of the online activities have additional sources and longer excerpts!

Supreme Court Cases

Every chapter has an interactive version of the Supreme Court Case activity! There are four different types of activities: 1) **Unmarked Opinions**—decide which should be the majority opinion and which should be the dissenting opinion; 2) **Classifying Arguments**—read a list of arguments and classify each; 3) **Applying Precedents**—read a list of precedents and decide whether each should apply to the case before you; 4) **Moot Court**—prepare for a moot court in class.

Debates

There are interactive versions of the Debates online!

Deliberations

There are interactive versions of the Deliberations online!

Self-Check Quizzes

Every lesson has a self-check quiz to help you test your knowledge!

USG tv videos

Every unit has a USG tv animation to introduce you to the unit content!

Exploring the Essential Question Activities

Every lesson opens with an interactive version of the Exploring the Essential Question activity!

Interactive Features

In addition to the features available in the printed Student Edition, there are extra features online. These include Participating in Your Government, Civic Participation in a Digital Age, We the People: Making a Difference, Comparing, and more!

⌄ Infographics

Chapter 3
Lesson 2   Checks and Balances
Lesson 3   Amending the Constitution

Chapter 5
Lesson 1   Demographics of Congress

Chapter 6
Lesson 1   The Powers of Congress

Chapter 7
Lesson 1   How a Bill Becomes a Law

Chapter 8
Lesson 1   Comparing State Legislatures

Chapter 11
Lesson 2   The Size of the Executive Branch

Chapter 12
Lesson 2   Characteristics of Governors

Chapter 15
Lesson 4   Substantive Due Process
Lesson 5   Gender Pay Gap

Chapter 17
Lesson 1   Political Parties in the United States
Lesson 2   Political Party Demographics

Chapter 18
Lesson 2   Political Party Platforms

Chapter 22
Lesson 2   Farming in the United States

Chapter 23
Lesson 4   Technology and National Security

Chapter 24
Lesson 4   Global Supply Chain

networks

Interactive Charts, Graphs, and Tables

networks

Interactive Images and Slide Shows

Interactive Maps

TO THE STUDENT

Welcome to McGraw-Hill Education's **Networks** Online Student Learning Center. Here you will access your Online Student Edition as well as many other learning resources.

(1) LOGGING ON TO THE STUDENT LEARNING CENTER

Using your Internet browser, go to connected.mcgraw-hill.com

Enter your username and password or

Create a New Account using the redemption code your teacher gave you.

(2) SELECT YOUR PROGRAM

Click your program to launch the home page of your Online Student Learning Center.

Using Your Home Page

1 HOME PAGE

To return to your Home Page at any time, click the Networks logo in the top left corner of the page.

2 QUICK LINKS MENU

Use this menu to access:
- My Notes (your personal notepad)
- Messages
- The online Glossary
- The online Atlas
- BTW (current events website for social studies)
- College and Career Readiness materials

3 HELP

For videos and assistance with the various features of the Networks system, click Help.

4 MAIN MENU

Use the menu bar to access:
- The Online Student Edition
- Skills Builder (for activities to improve your skills)
- My Assignments and Projects
- Resource Library
- Test Prep
- Collaborate with Classmates

5 ONLINE STUDENT EDITION

Go to your Online Student Edition by selecting the chapter and lesson and then click Go.

6 ASSIGNMENTS

Recent assignments from your teacher will appear here. Click the assignment or click See All to see the details.

7 RESOURCE LIBRARY

Use the carousel to browse the Resource Library.

8 MESSAGES

Recent messages from your teacher will appear here.

Using Your Online Student Edition

SET TEXT SIZE

PRINT

HIGHLIGHT

1 LESSON MENU

• Use the tabs to open the different lessons and special features in a chapter or unit.

• Clicking on the unit or chapter title will open the table of contents.

2 AUDIO EDITION

Click on the headphones symbol to have the page read to you. MP3 files for downloading each lesson are also available in the Resource Library.

3 RESOURCES FOR THIS PAGE

Resources appear in the middle column to show that they go with the text on this page. Click the images to open them in the viewer.

4 LESSON RESOURCES

Use the carousel to browse the interactive resources available in this lesson. Click on a resource to open it in the viewer below.

5 CHANGE PAGES

Click here to move to the next page in the lesson.

6 RESOURCE VIEWER

Click on the image that appears in the viewer to launch an interactive resource, including:

• Lesson Videos

• Interactive Photos and Slide Shows

• Interactive Maps

• Interactive Charts amd Graphs

• Interactive Infographics

• Self-Check Quizzes for each lesson

Reading Support in the Online Student Edition

Your Online Student Edition contains several features to help improve your reading skills and understanding of the content.

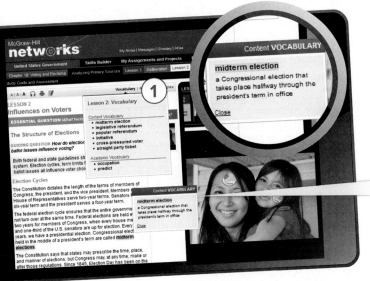

1 LESSON VOCABULARY

Click Vocabulary to bring up a list of terms introduced in this lesson.

VOCABULARY POP-UP

Click on any term highlighted in yellow to open a window with the term's definition.

2 MY NOTES

Click My Notes to open the note-taking tool. You can write and save any notes you want in the Lesson Notes tab.

Click on the Guided Notes tab to view the Guided Reading Questions. Answering these questions will help you build a set of notes about the lesson.

3 GRAPHIC ORGANIZER

Click Reading Strategies to open a note-taking activity using a graphic organizer.

Click the image of the graphic organizer to make it interactive. You can type directly into the graphic organizer and save or print your notes.

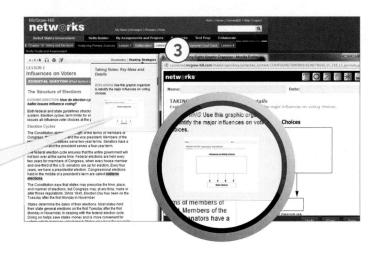

Using Interactive Resources in the Online Student Edition

Each lesson of your Online Student Edition contains many resources to help you learn the content and skills you need to know for this subject.

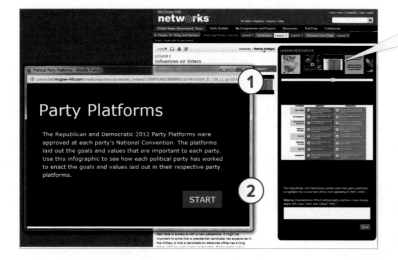

There are many kinds of resources. This is an interactive infographic.

1 LAUNCHING RESOURCES

Clicking a resource in the viewer launches an interactive resource.

2 QUESTIONS AND ACTIVITIES

When a resource appears in the viewer, there are usually one or two questions or activities beneath it. You can type and save your answers in the answer boxes and submit them to your teacher.

3 INTERACTIVE MAPS

When a map appears in the viewer, click on it to launch the interactive map. You can also zoom in and turn layers on and off to display different information. Many of the maps contain different layers of information and photographs and graphs. This map shows the percentage of the popular vote received by each presidential candidate by state.

4 CHAPTER OPENER FEATURE

Each chapter begins with an Analyzing Primary Sources feature that includes primary and secondary sources, including text, maps, graphs, political cartoons, and historical photographs. Analyze the sources and answer the Document-Based Questions.

You can write your own notes or highlight to copy text. You can save your work to access it later.

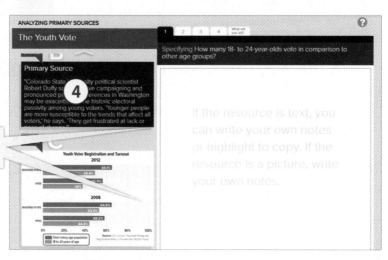

Study Guide and Assessment

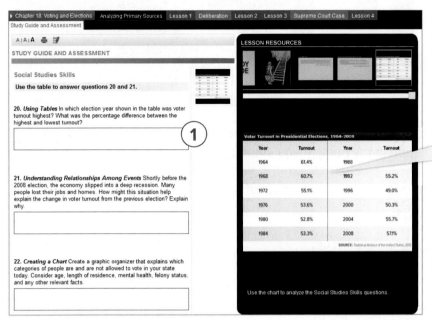

1 STUDY GUIDE AND CHAPTER ASSESSMENT

At the end of each chapter is the Study Guide and Assessment tab. Here you can test your understanding of what you have learned. You can type and save answers in the answer boxes and submit them to your teacher.

When a question or activity uses a political cartoon, a graph, a map, or a primary source, it will appear in the viewer.

Finding Other Resources

There are hundreds of additional resources available in the Resource Library. Click the Resources tab to enter the library.

2 RESOURCE LIBRARY

Click the Resource tabs to find collections of Videos, Supreme Court Cases, Charts/Graphs/Maps, Primary Sources, and Social Studies Skills activities.

You can search the Resource Library by Lesson or Keyword.

Click the star to mark a resource as a favorite.

SCAVENGER HUNT

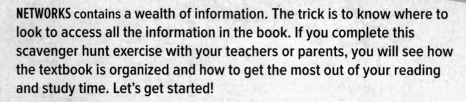

NETWORKS contains a wealth of information. The trick is to know where to look to access all the information in the book. If you complete this scavenger hunt exercise with your teachers or parents, you will see how the textbook is organized and how to get the most out of your reading and study time. Let's get started!

1 How many units, chapters, and lessons are in this book?

2 Where do you find the glossary and the index? What is the difference between them?

3 Where can you find primary sources in the textbook?

4 If you want to quickly find all the maps, charts, and graphs about the U.S. Congress, where do you look?

5 How can you find information about the U.S. Supreme Court case *Brown* v. *Board of Education of Topeka, Kansas*?

6 Where can you find a graphic organizer that lists the types of media that can influence voter choices discussed in Chapter 18?

7 Where and how do you find the content vocabulary for Chapter 2, Lesson 1?

8 What are the online resources listed for Chapter 9, Lesson 4?

9 You want to read the U.S. Constitution. Where would you find it?

10 What subject does Chapter 23 cover? How do you know?

UNIT 1
Foundations of American Government

IT MATTERS
BECAUSE . . .

Although there are different types of governments, in general governments exist to provide leadership, preserve order, provide public services, maintain national security, and provide economic security and assistance. The principles and origins of American government were influenced by the American colonists' experiences with the British, new political ideas, and the critical period of the American Revolution. The Founders of the United States of America created a lasting Constitution that remarkably still governs our nation today. The Constitution created three branches of government—legislative, executive, and judicial— where each branch checks and balances the power of the others. It also created a federal system where national and state governments divide and share power. This structure and the principles on which our nation was founded have endured. Today, the United States is a democracy, it has a federal system of government, and it is a constitutional republic. By understanding the origins and foundations of our American government, you can appreciate the continuity and change in our government throughout history.

How to
Interpret Political Cartoons

You have probably heard the saying "A picture is worth a thousand words." Political cartoonists agree. They use drawings to express opinions about public figures, political issues, or social conditions. Their goal is to convince readers of the cartoonist's or the publication's opinion in an amusing way.

Knowing how to interpret political cartoons is useful because it helps you put issues and candidates in perspective. Follow these steps to analyze the illustrations and words in a cartoon:

1. Read the title, caption, conversation balloons, and other text to identify the topic of the cartoon.

2. Identify the people, events, or symbols shown. Ask yourself: What action is occurring? Who is taking the action? What is the result of the action?

3. Determine the cartoonist's purpose: Is it to persuade, criticize, or make people think? What idea is the cartoonist trying to convey?

4. What is the point of view and frame of reference of the publication or the cartoonist? Is the publication or the cartoonist expressing bias? How can you tell?

Go online to interact with these digital activities and more in each chapter.

Chapter 1 Foundations of Government

Chapter 2 Origins of American Government

Chapter 3 The Constitution

Chapter 4 Federalism

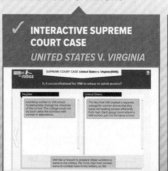
✓ **INTERACTIVE SUPREME COURT CASE**
UNITED STATES V. *VIRGINIA*

✓ **VIDEO**
THE BOSTON TEA PARTY AND THE AMERICAN REVOLUTION

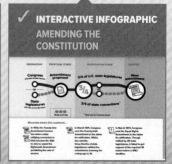
✓ **INTERACTIVE INFOGRAPHIC**
AMENDING THE CONSTITUTION

✓ **INTERACTIVE MAP**
FEDERAL AID TO STATE AND LOCAL GOVERNMENTS

BBC Worldwide Learning

2

Foundations of Government

networks
www.connected.mcgraw-hill.com
There's More Online about the foundations of government.

ESSENTIAL QUESTIONS

• What are the purposes of government? • What principles guide different types of government? • What is the role of government in different types of economic systems?

▲ Pericles, a leader of ancient Athens, described democracy as government "in the hands of not the few, but the many."

©iStockphoto.com/sedmak

ANALYZING PRIMARY SOURCES

THE STATE OF NATURE

The term *state of nature* describes what philosophers believe life would be like without laws and government. The idea of the state of nature has captured the imagination of novelists, filmmakers, readers, and moviegoers alike. Today, some observers believe that the way people interact in cyberspace is akin to the state of nature. Bullying, insults, and racist remarks, for example, are common. Many believe that the state of nature in cyberspace may even be causing our entire society to become less civil.

PRIMARY SOURCE A

This excerpt is from *Leviathan*, a political treatise written by the British philosopher Thomas Hobbes. An influential nonfiction book about the state of nature and the social contract, it was published in 1651 during the English Civil War.

"Whatsoever therefore is consequent to a time of Warre [war], where every man is Enemy to every man; the same is consequent to the time, wherein men live without other security, than what their own strength, and their own invention shall furnish them withall. . . . And the life of man, solitary, poore, nasty, brutish, and short."

—Thomas Hobbes, *Leviathan*, 1651

PRIMARY SOURCE B

This excerpt is from the 1985 novel by Cormac McCarthy, *Blood Meridian*. McCarthy's character Judge Holden discusses his view of the law.

"Moral law is an invention of mankind for the disenfranchisement of the powerful in favor of the weak. Historical law subverts it at every turn."

—Cormac McCarthy, *Blood Meridian, or the Evening Redness in the West*, 1985

PRIMARY SOURCE D

In the film *Mad Max 2: The Road Warrior*, society has collapsed following a global war. Gangs roam the countryside, looking for food and gas.

"On the roads it was a white-line nightmare. Only those mobile enough to scavenge, brutal enough to pillage would survive. The gangs took over the highways, ready to wage war for a tank of juice. And in this maelstrom of decay, ordinary men were battered and smashed."

—*Mad Max 2: The Road Warrior*, 1981

PRIMARY SOURCE C

In the 1954 novel *Lord of the Flies*, a group of British schoolboys are marooned on an island. Their attempts at self-government soon begin to break down. A boy named Jack paints his face as camouflage for hunting and finds that this "mask" frees him from the need to conform to social norms.

"Beside the pool his sinewy body held up a mask that drew their eyes and appalled them. He began to dance and his laughter became a bloodthirsty snarling. He capered toward Bill, and the mask was a thing on its own, behind which Jack hid, liberated from shame and self-consciousness."

—William Golding, *Lord of the Flies*, 1954

PRIMARY SOURCE D CREDIT: COMBINED AND UNEVEN APOCALYPSE by EVAN CALDER WILLIAMS Publ. April 2011, ZERO BOOKS, JOHN HUNT PUBLISHING, LTD.

In an op-ed to *The New York Times*, Christopher Wolf, an Internet and privacy attorney and leader of the Internet Task Force of the Anti-Defamation League, expressed his concerns with online anonymity.

"People who are able to post anonymously (or pseudonymously) are far more likely to say awful things, sometimes with awful consequences, such as the suicides of cyberbullied young people. The abuse extends to hate-filled and inflammatory comments appended to the online versions of newspaper articles—comments that hijack legitimate discussions of current events and discourage people from participating."

—Christopher Wolf, Letter to the Editor, *The New York Times,* November 20, 2011

PRIMARY SOURCE F

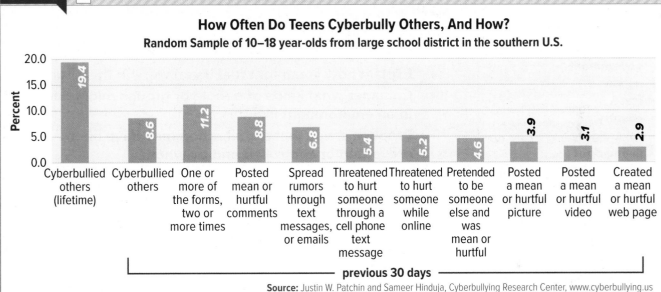

How Often Do Teens Cyberbully Others, And How?
Random Sample of 10–18 year-olds from large school district in the southern U.S.

Cyberbullied others (lifetime): 19.4
Cyberbullied others: 8.6
One or more of the forms, two or more times: 11.2
Posted mean or hurtful comments: 8.8
Spread rumors through text messages, or emails: 6.8
Threatened to hurt someone through a cell phone text message: 5.4
Threatened to hurt someone while online: 5.2
Pretended to be someone else and was mean or hurtful: 4.6
Posted a mean or hurtful picture: 3.9
Posted a mean or hurtful video: 3.1
Created a mean or hurtful web page: 2.9

previous 30 days

Source: Justin W. Patchin and Sameer Hinduja, Cyberbullying Research Center, www.cyberbullying.us

DBQ DOCUMENT-BASED QUESTIONS

1. **Defining** Create a list of phrases used to describe the state of nature. Use at least two of those terms to write a definition of *state of nature.*

2. **Applying** Does your definition of a state of nature apply to the types of Internet behavior that are illustrated or discussed in Sources E and F? Explain your answer.

3. **Evaluating** Do you believe that humans in a state of nature would show the worst aspects of their nature? Or do you see a more positive vision of the state of nature? How might your view of the state of nature influence your ideas about government?

WHAT WILL YOU DO?

A troll on a popular social networking site has been posting rude comments about you. How will you respond? Will you escalate, step back/not respond, or try to create a more civil society online? Will you look to government officials to help eliminate cyberbullying?

EXPLORE the interactive version of the analyzing primary sources feature on Networks.

LESSON 1
Purposes and Origins of Government

(l to r) Jill Braaten/McGraw-Hill Education; Library of Congress Prints and Photographs Division [LC-DIG-ppmsca-19301; Imagno/Hulton Archive/Getty Images; Rosenwald Collection/Courtesy National Gallery of Art, Washington; Apic/Hulton Archive/Getty Images

ReadingHelp Desk

Academic Vocabulary

- philosopher
- theory

Content Vocabulary

- anarchy
- government
- nation
- state
- country
- sovereignty
- divine right
- social contract

TAKING NOTES:

Key Ideas and Details

EXPLAINING Use the graphic organizer to explain the major theories on the origins of the state.

Theory	Explanation

ESSENTIAL QUESTION

What are the purposes of government?

Work with a partner to imagine each of the following situations. For each:

- **Suggest two adjectives that describe the situation.**
- **Explain how you might feel if you were in this situation.**
- **Consider what kinds of people or groups might "do well" in an environment like this.**
- **Propose a way that the situation may have been prevented or controlled and by whom.**

a. You arrive to school and settle into your desk, but there is no teacher. You and your classmates realize there are no teachers, no administrators, and no security—only other students. No one can communicate with anyone out of the building and the doors are locked so no one can leave. Some of the most rowdy students begin planning a "day of pandemonium." You do not know what they intend.

b. After a major hurricane, the power, phone, and Internet lines in your city have been out for more than a week. You hear a rumor that groups of armed gangsters are roaming the streets. You have spent four sleepless nights guarding your parents' store from looters.

c. Your country is in the midst of a devastating famine. Thousands of people have already died of starvation. A truck carrying flour, sugar, water, and medicine is scheduled to arrive in the center of your town today. As you wait, hundreds of people from another town show up. Fights break out when people cut in line. When the truck drivers see the hostile crowd, they are afraid and consider leaving.

The Functions of Government

GUIDING QUESTION *What is government, and what are its basic functions?*

Most humans cannot function and would not choose to live in chaos and turmoil, where mobs rule the land through might and violence. These conditions describe **anarchy**, or a state without government and laws. Some people believe governments exist to prevent situations like those described above. Legitimate and functioning governments create order, protect people, and give them ways to settle disagreements fairly and peacefully. **Government** is an institution through which leaders exercise power to make and enforce laws affecting the people under its control. People create governments for a variety of reasons. Governments provide leadership, order, security and defense, public services, and economic assistance and economic security.

To fulfill these purposes, governments make rules that everyone must follow—and they have the authority to punish those who do not follow them. These systems of laws create social, economic, and personal benefits for the people the government governs. All governments serve these purposes, whether those leaders are chosen by the people or take control for themselves.

Providing Leadership Government officials set priorities and make all sorts of decisions on behalf of the people. They decide what actions are crimes, make decisions about who has to pay taxes and how much they have to pay, and determine who benefits from natural resources like coal and natural gas. They can require that people do things they might not do voluntarily, such as pay taxes or serve in the army. Without leadership, no one and anyone can be in charge—creating anarchy.

Maintaining Order In nearly any group, people will disagree and some may take advantage of others. Two neighbors may argue about property lines. Parents may argue over a terrible call by a referee at their child's soccer game. Conflict is an inescapable part of life.

Governments try to control and contain conflict between people by placing limits on what individuals are permitted to do. Governments provide some sort of domestic security force—police or a national guard—to enforce laws and to keep peace. Governments provide courts and other ways for people to resolve their conflicts. They also punish people who break laws.

Without government, civilized life would be impossible. An effective government allows citizens to plan for the future, get an education, raise a family, and live orderly lives.

In the words of Abraham Lincoln,

 PRIMARY SOURCE

The legitimate object of government is to do for a community of people whatever they need to have done but cannot do at all, or cannot so well do for themselves in their separate and individual capacities. But in all that people can individually do for themselves, government ought not to interfere."

— Abraham Lincoln, 1854

anarchy a state without government and laws

government an institution through which leaders exercise power to make and enforce laws affecting the people under its control

Abraham Lincoln believed that the purpose of government is to do for people what they cannot do for themselves. ▼

EXPLORING THE ESSENTIAL QUESTION

Analyzing Point of View Do you agree or disagree with Lincoln's view of the proper role of government? Explain your answer.

Providing Public Services Governments create schools, build sewer systems, pave roads, and provide other services that individuals cannot or would not do on their own. Many other government services promote public health and safety. For example, most fire departments are funded (at least in part) by governments. In the United States, government officials enforce housing codes and inspect meat that is sold in markets. State governments pass laws that require drivers to pass a driving test before a license is issued.

Providing National Security

Another task of government is to protect the people against attack by another country or by terrorists. In today's world of nuclear weapons, spy satellites, international terrorists, and huge armies, it is a complex and demanding task to provide for the safety of a nation's citizens. The U.S. federal government is primarily responsible for this task. Some state governments have informal relations with other nations to increase their trade or cultural exchange, but the national government can place limitations on these relations.

Providing Economic Security and Economic Assistance

Governments protect the economic security of their people, just like they protect national security. Governments negotiate trade deals with other countries and they try to protect businesses that are important to their own economies.

Governments might intervene in the economic affairs of another nation to promote their own national security. For example, after World War II, the United States funded the Marshall Plan to help European nations rebuild their economies because of concern that high unemployment, food shortages, and economic depression could lead to communist revolutions.

Within their own countries, governments can also set policies to protect people's economic security. Governments usually try to stimulate economic growth and stability by encouraging trade and regulating the development of natural resources. They can enforce contracts between businesses or regulate the conditions under which banks can take control of homes when their owners fail to pay the mortgage.

Even in a wealthy country like the United States, many people lack enough food, necessary clothing, and adequate housing. The problem of scarcity is far greater in many other nations. Governments can provide assistance to people in need. This assistance might be in the form of food stamps or controls on how much rent landlords can charge in certain buildings. Governments vary greatly in their ability and determination to provide economic assistance to their citizens, and no country provides its citizens with everything they need or desire.

✓ **READING PROGRESS CHECK**

Listing What do governments provide their citizens?

Nation, State, and Country

GUIDING QUESTION *What is the difference between a nation and a state or a country?*

The terms *nation*, *country*, and *state* are sometimes used interchangeably. Technically, a **nation** is a sizable group of people who believe themselves united by common bonds of race, language, custom, or religion. For example, some groups, such as the Kurds, consider themselves a nation but do not have their own country.

Many people in the United States think about a state as a subdivision of the whole country, like the state of Texas. But the term *state* also means something larger. In the language of people who study governments, a **state** is a political community that occupies a definite territory and has an organized government. The term *country* has the same meaning. A state has **sovereignty**—that is, its government makes and enforces its own laws without approval from any other authority.

The term *state* likely came from the ancient Greek **philosopher** Aristotle, who believed a state was the territory of a town and its surrounding area where face-to-face communication was possible and where people could reasonably be governed.

> ## PRIMARY SOURCE
> **He who has the power to take part in the deliberative or judicial administration of any state is said by us to be a citizen of that state."**
>
> —*Politics II*, Aristotle

The states that make up today's political world share four essential features: population, territory, sovereignty, and government.

✓ READING PROGRESS CHECK

Defining How are the terms *nation*, *state*, and *country* defined?

nation a group of people united by bonds of race, language, custom, tradition, and sometimes religion

state a political community that occupies a definite territory and has an organized government

country a political community that occupies a definite territory and has an organized government

sovereignty the supreme and absolute authority within territorial boundaries

philosopher one who engages in the pursuit of wisdom

ESSENTIAL FEATURES OF A STATE

Population	States must have people. Without them, there is no one to govern and no reason for a state to exist. States and their populations have unique cultures, histories, traditions, and values.
Territory	A state has established boundaries. For example, the borders of the United States are recognized by its citizens, its neighbors, and the international community. The exact shape of political boundaries is often a source of conflict among states. Territorial boundaries may change as a result of war, negotiations, or purchase.
Sovereignty	The key characteristic of a state is sovereignty. Political sovereignty means the state has supreme and absolute authority within its boundaries. It has complete independence and power to make laws and foreign policy and determine its course of action. In theory, at least, no state has the right to interfere with the internal affairs of another state.
Government	States must have someone in charge. A government makes and enforces its own laws for its own people. Government provides leadership, maintains order, provides public services, offers defense and security, and makes decisions about how to establish economic security for its people.

EXPLORING THE ESSENTIAL QUESTION

Diagramming Draw a graphic representation of these four features and share your picture with a classmate. How do your drawings show the same concepts in different ways?

United States Acquisitions

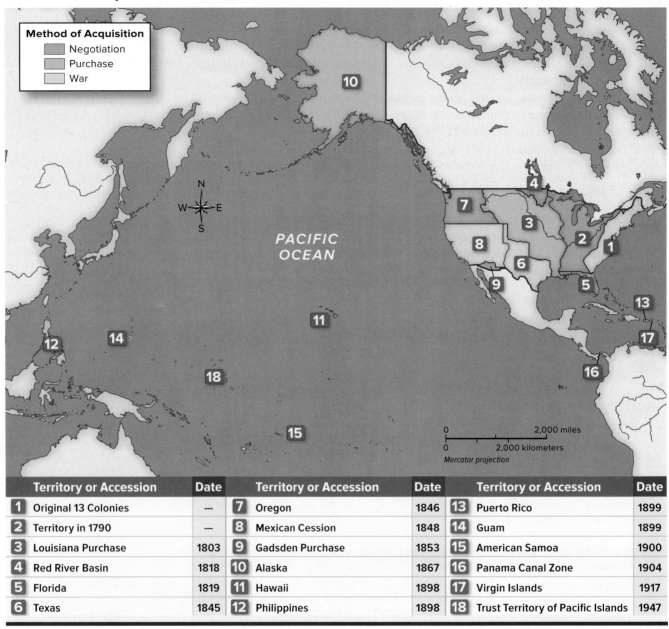

Method of Acquisition
- Negotiation
- Purchase
- War

PACIFIC OCEAN

0   2,000 miles
0   2,000 kilometers
Mercator projection

Territory or Accession	Date	Territory or Accession	Date	Territory or Accession	Date
1 Original 13 Colonies	—	7 Oregon	1846	13 Puerto Rico	1899
2 Territory in 1790	—	8 Mexican Cession	1848	14 Guam	1899
3 Louisiana Purchase	1803	9 Gadsden Purchase	1853	15 American Samoa	1900
4 Red River Basin	1818	10 Alaska	1867	16 Panama Canal Zone	1904
5 Florida	1819	11 Hawaii	1898	17 Virgin Islands	1917
6 Texas	1845	12 Philippines	1898	18 Trust Territory of Pacific Islands	1947

The territory of the United States has grown considerably since it declared independence. By purchase, negotiation, and war, the United States extended its territory.

▲ **CRITICAL THINKING**
Making Inferences Why do you think the United States acquired so many territories in the South Pacific?

theory speculation based on study

Origins of the State

GUIDING QUESTION *Why and how were governments created?*

No one knows precisely how or why people created the earliest governments, but scholars have constructed several **theories** to explain their origins.

Evolutionary Theory Some scholars believe that the notion of state evolved from the family. The heads of ancient families served as the authority over the group, and extended families might include hundreds of people. For example, according to Christian, Jewish, and Muslim religious beliefs, Abraham was a patriarch who became known as the "father to many nations." Supporters of this theory believe government came about because extended families needed more organization. Some modern Native American groups continue to be governed according to family and clan traditions.

Force Theory According to the force theory, states emerged when people needed to cooperate to survive but could become organized only when one or more people took control. For example, to keep out enemies, people needed to build walls around their city. The strongest leaders used violence and the threat of violence to control their own people to get the work done. A state emerged when everyone in an area was brought under the authority of one person or group by use of force.

Divine Right Theory The idea that certain people are chosen by a god or gods to rule is very old. For example, the ancient Egyptians, Chinese, Maya, and Aztec believed that their rulers were descendants of gods or chosen by them. The term *divine right*, however, refers particularly to European monarchs in the 1600s and 1700s who proclaimed that their right to rule came from God alone. The state existed to serve the demands of God. To oppose the monarch was to oppose God, and thus not only treasonous but sinful.

Social Contract Theory Some people believe states exist to protect and to serve their people. Without a state or government, people would live in a "state of nature" where life would be "nasty, brutish, and short." English philosopher Thomas Hobbes used this phrase in the 1650s when he wrote that without order and protection, no decent life of any kind would be possible. In the **social contract** that Hobbes envisioned, people surrendered their freedom to the state, and in return, they received order and security. Fellow Englishman John Locke had a different view on the terms of the social contract. He claimed the people had natural rights and the social contract was made between the people and a government that promised to preserve these rights. Locke's ideas about the social contract shaped the development of democratic governments, including the United States.

☑ **READING PROGRESS CHECK**

Summarizing What are the major theories of the origins of the state? Which do you find most convincing and why?

EXPLORING THE ESSENTIAL QUESTION

Defending Write a persuasive paragraph to convince a friend or relative why government is necessary. As you write, think about the origin of the state theories. Do you believe government exists to carry out God's will and leaders are chosen by God or gods? Do you believe governments exist to provide security and order for their people? Do you have a different theory? Explain your ideas thoroughly and share your paragraph with a friend or relative.

divine right the idea that people are chosen by a god or gods to rule

social contract theory that by contract, people surrender to the state the power needed to maintain order and the state, in turn, agrees to protect its citizens

---

LESSON 1 REVIEW

Reviewing Vocabulary

1. *Defining* What is *sovereignty*, and why is it an essential element of a state?

Using Your Graphic Organizer

2. *Applying* Using your graphic organizer, classify each of the following statements with the theory of origin that describes it.

   a. The emperor was chosen by God to rule China.

   b. A father or grandfather ruled over a family or tribe.

   c. A leader and some of his followers gained control by intimidating people to carry out important work.

   d. People hated anarchy, so they gave up their freedom for order.

Answering the Guiding Questions

3. *Defining* What is a government, and what are its basic functions?

4. *Contrasting* What is the difference between a nation and a state or a country?

5. *Explaining* Why and how were governments created?

Writing About Government

6. *Informative/Explanatory* Find several news articles about local, state, or national government in action. Write an essay that describes at least three different government actions and which purpose of government is demonstrated in each.

Interact with these digital
assets and others in lesson 2

✓ INTERACTIVE CHART
   Power Sharing in Different Systems
   of Government

✓ INTERACTIVE MAP
   Levels of Freedom

✓ SELF-CHECK QUIZ

✓ VIDEO
   Direct Democracy

netw☉rks
TRY IT YOURSELF ONLINE

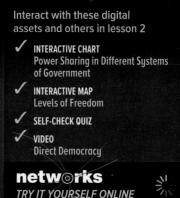

(l to r) Corporation for National and Community Service
Photo; State Department photo; Purestock

LESSON 2
Types of Government

Reading Help Desk

Academic Vocabulary

- assembly
- institution

Content Vocabulary

- unitary system
- confederacy
- federal system
- constitution
- constitutional government
- authoritarian
- totalitarian
- dictatorship
- oligarchy
- monarchy
- democracy
- republic

TAKING NOTES:

Key Ideas and Details

DESCRIBING Use the graphic organizer to describe the advantages and disadvantages of different systems of governments.

System of Government			
Description			
Advantages			
Disadvantages			

ESSENTIAL QUESTION

What principles guide different types of government?

The United States and many other countries around the world are democracies. What does the idea of democracy mean to you? What do you think are the most important characteristics of a democratic form of government? List them in order of importance.

Systems of Government

GUIDING QUESTION *How is a federal system of government different from a unitary or confederate one?*

All governments reflect their society's history and culture, and all societies must organize their governments to carry out important functions. Political scientists classify governments in a few different ways: according to how democratic they are and according to how power is divided between the larger society (like a country) and its smaller parts (like cities, counties, states, or provinces). There are three main systems of government: unitary, confederate, and federal. Each form has different advantages and disadvantages.

Unitary System A **unitary system** of government gives all key powers to the central government. This does not mean that only one level of government exists, but rather the only powers that states or local government have are those expressly given to them by the central government. While centralized power can be an advantage, there is less power given to localities, which can be a disadvantage. Japan, France, and Bolivia are examples of present-day unitary governments.

Confederate System When the United States first became independent from Great Britain, it formed a **confederacy**, or confederation—a loose union of independent and sovereign states. The new nation had many struggles under the Articles of Confederation. This weak central power was a disadvantage of this system. An advantage was the power it gave to the states. Consequently, the early leaders created a new form of government with comparatively more power resting with the national government.

The Constitution created a national government of limited and specific powers, leaving all other powers to the states. Today, few countries are a confederation. The Asian nation called Federated States of Micronesia is one example. It has a very weak central government and four independent states that maintain most authority, especially over their budgets.

Federal System A **federal system** of government divides the powers of government between the national and state or provincial government. Each level of government has sovereignty in some areas. The United States developed a federal system when it wrote its Constitution. There are many nations operating under a federal system, including Brazil. An advantage of the federal system is how it shares power among different levels of government while still having more centralized power than in a confederate system. A disadvantage may be that each level of government can make its own laws.

On a smaller scale, individual states in the United States may have their own structure of government. Some states are unitary and make almost all important decisions for the whole state. In other states, power is shared with cities or counties. For example, Maryland gives its counties much more authority to make their own decisions than most states.

☑ **READING PROGRESS CHECK**

Explaining What made the initial U.S. system of government a confederacy?

Constitutional Governments

GUIDING QUESTION *How is a constitutional government different than a country without a constitution?*

A **constitution** is a plan that provides the rules for government. A constitution serves several major purposes: (1) it sets out ideals that the people bound by the constitution believe in and share, (2) it establishes the basic structure of

unitary system a government that gives all key powers to the national or central government

confederacy a loose union of independent states

federal system a government that divides the powers of government between the national government and state or provincial governments

constitution a plan that provides the rules for government

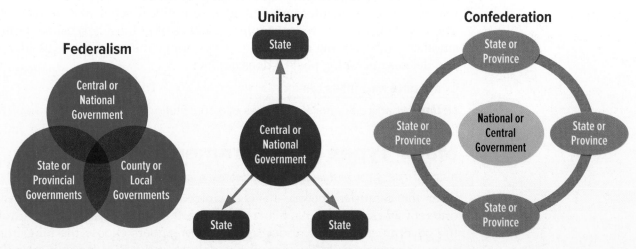

Power Sharing in Different Systems of Governments

Federalism
- Central or National Government
- State or Provincial Governments
- County or Local Governments

Unitary
- State
- Central or National Government
- State
- State

Confederation
- State or Province
- State or Province
- National or Central Government
- State or Province
- State or Province

Political scientists classify governments according to how power is shared among different levels of government.

▲ CRITICAL THINKING

1. *Comparing* What do federal, unitary, and confederate systems of government have in common?

2. *Analyzing* In which system of government does the central or national government have the most power? In which system does it have the least? Explain your answers.

Find a copy of your state's constitution or charter. Analyze how much power the state government has compared to counties or cities.

Analyzing Which level of government has the most say over budgets or law enforcement? Based on your analysis, would you say your state government is unitary, confederate, or federal? Explain your answer.

constitutional government a government in which a constitution has authority to place clearly recognized limits on the powers of those who govern

government and defines the government's powers and duties, and (3) it provides the supreme law for the country. Constitutions provide rules that shape the actions of government, much as the rules of soccer define the action in a soccer match.

Constitutions may be written or unwritten; however, in most modern states, constitutions are written. The United States Constitution, drawn up in 1787, is the oldest written constitution still serving a nation today. Other nations with written constitutions include France, Kenya, India, and Italy. Great Britain, on the other hand, has an unwritten constitution based on hundreds of years of legislative acts, court decisions, and customs.

The term **constitutional government** refers to a government in which a constitution has authority to place clearly recognized limits on the powers of those who govern. Thus, constitutional government is *limited* government. A country would not be called a constitutional government simply because it has a written constitution. It must operate according to the principles in that constitution.

Constitutions are important but incomplete guides to how a country is actually governed. They are incomplete for two reasons. First, no written constitution can possibly spell out all the laws, customs, and ideas that grow up around the document. In the United States, for example, until Franklin D. Roosevelt was elected president four times, it was custom, rather than law, that no person should be elected president more than twice. Only when the Twenty-second Amendment went into effect was a president limited by law to two elected terms.

Second, a constitution does not always reflect actual government practice. The People's Republic of China, for example, has a written constitution filled with statements about the basic rights, freedoms, and duties of citizens. Yet, the Chinese government does not uphold many of those rights and freedoms. For years, the Chinese government has maintained an extensive police force to spy on Chinese citizens that, in fact, has violated those rights. Citizens whose ideas are not acceptable to the state are sometimes punished. The Chinese government has also created a complex system of Internet firewalls that stop Chinese citizens from using websites that are available to people around the world. Twitter, Facebook, and YouTube—along with most sites that report news or information related to political activism—are blocked. The government also prevents online searches of politically sensitive terms, smothers embarrassing news stories, stops online messages from dissidents, and deletes microblog posts it does not like.

☑ **READING PROGRESS CHECK**

Listing What are the major purposes of a constitution?

Major Types of Government

GUIDING QUESTION *What are the differences between authoritarian and democratic governments?*

Over the centuries, people have organized their governments in many different ways. In Saudi Arabia, for example, the ruling royal family controls the government and its resources. Family members choose the king from among themselves. In Sweden, the people elect the Riksdag, which is the name for the Swedish national legislature. In turn, the Riksdag selects the prime minister to carry out the laws. In the Netherlands, the government consists of a queen and a cabinet of ministers. The cabinet ministers are elected by the people to make laws, while the queen reviews new laws and helps select cabinet ministers.

Governments can be classified in many ways. One way is based on how power and benefits are assigned. Who governs? Who or what gives the government its power? Who benefits from government? Imagine a continuum with one end labeled "authoritarian" and the other labeled "democratic." Governments that control all aspects of citizens' economic, political, and social lives are called **authoritarian**. Governments that give people economic, social, and political freedoms are democratic. In fact, democracy depends on citizen input to govern. All countries fall somewhere between those two labels.

authoritarian controlling all aspects of citizens' economic, political, and social lives

Authoritarian Governments Authoritarian governments are characterized by leadership that controls all aspects of its citizens' economic and social lives. These are sometimes referred to as **totalitarian** states because the government has total control. Both Adolf Hitler in Nazi Germany and Joseph Stalin in Soviet Russia tried to control every aspect of civilian life, not just government institutions. Power is concentrated in the hands of one or a few people, and opposition to the government is not allowed.

totalitarian a system of government in which the government has total control

Sometimes, authoritarian governments appear to have democratic features. They may hold elections, for example. However, if only one candidate appears on the ballot, or opponents to the current leaders are persecuted, the elections are a sham. Some authoritarian leaders have even been elected in a democratic election but once in office have seized and concentrated power to take total control.

We the People: Making a Difference

Aung San Suu Kyi

Aung San Suu Kyi is a Burmese political leader who has pushed for democracy and human rights in her country using nonviolent methods. In 1988 she founded the National League for Democracy and wrote letters to the government advocating for open multi-party elections, something that had not occurred since the military dictatorship took over the Burmese government in 1962. She made speeches about the importance of democracy and human rights to hundreds of thousands of people. In 1989 the military leaders offered her the chance to leave the country or be put under house arrest. She chose confinement. In 1991 Suu Kyi was awarded the Nobel Peace Prize. She spent most of the next two decades continuing her nonviolent protest and inspiring hundreds of other pro-democracy advocates in Burma while imprisoned in her home. In 2010 she was released from house arrest, and in 2012 she won a seat in the Burmese parliament.

EXPLORING THE ESSENTIAL QUESTION

Discuss the following questions and explain your answers.

a. **Gathering Information** The Burmese government that placed Aung San Suu Kyi under house arrest was an authoritarian government. Find two examples of the Burmese government's actions in this story that illustrate characteristics of authoritarian governments.

b. **Analyzing** How might citizen protests be treated differently in authoritarian governments than in democracies? Explain your answer.

c. **Explaining** Why would people like Aung San Suu Kyi advocate for multi-party elections?

d. **Making Connections** If you were in her shoes, do you think you would have chosen to leave the country or accept house arrest? Why or why not?

In authoritarian nations, there are few, if any, political freedoms such as the freedom of speech or freedom of **assembly**. The media—such as newspapers, television stations, and radio stations—are typically owned and controlled by the government. Because there are few restrictions on the power of government, it can often be difficult to contain corruption in authoritarian governments. Authoritarian governments use ruthless force or the threat of force to maintain order. Frequently, people in minority groups are oppressed.

For example, from 1947 to 1989, Romania had a brutal authoritarian government. In addition to the food and electricity rationing and other hardships caused by a devastated economy, the government maintained a secret police that coerced neighbors and family members to spy on each other. It is estimated that hundreds of thousands of citizens were tortured or killed by their government for political, economic, or unknown reasons. Minority groups such as the Roma and ethnic Hungarians were especially oppressed. In 1989 protesters revolted and executed their dictator, Nicolae Ceauşescu, ushering in a slow but steady move toward democracy.

Authoritarian governments can be further divided according to how many people have power. In a **dictatorship**, power is in the hands of one person and that ruler has total control. Romania's Ceauşescu and Cambodia's Pol Pot were dictators. An authoritarian government that gives power to a few people or a political party is called an **oligarchy**. Oligarchs derive their power from their wealth, social position, military power, or a combination of these factors. Examples include Vietnam and the Soviet Union under communism.

Monarchy **Monarchy** is another form of government in which one person has great power; a king, queen, or emperor inherits the throne and heads the state. This form of government originated in ancient times when rulers were considered sacred or sanctioned by religion. Monarchs who maintained power through intimidation or the force of an army or police are sometimes known as autocrats. The czars of Russia, who ruled until 1917 when the Russian Revolution occurred, were true autocrats. No group of nobles or church leaders had any power to check the czar's will.

Some monarchies are not authoritarian. In some cases, a monarch's power has been limited in some way by tradition or law. Medieval kings, for example, were expected to consult with a council of nobles. In France, a body of noble judges was supposed to review the king's laws to give them formal sanction.

Monarchies still exist. Swaziland is an absolute monarchy. Political parties are banned, the king shares little or no power, and protestors and reformers are targets of state police. Most monarchies, however, are constitutional monarchies, which means the king or queen is limited by the law. Examples include Great Britain, Sweden, Japan, and the Netherlands. Their rulers either share power with elected legislatures or serve merely as ceremonial figures.

Democratic Governments In contrast to authoritarian governments that derive their power from their ability to use force, democracies derive their power from the consent and trust of the people. Citizens in democratic states know that if their elected officials fail to respond to their interests, they can be voted out of office or legally removed from office.

A **democracy** is a system of government in which rule is by the people, either through representatives or directly. The word *democracy* comes from the Greek word *demos* (meaning "the people") and *kratia* (meaning "rule").

assembly a gathering

dictatorship a system of government in which power is in the hands of one person who has total control

oligarchy a system of government in which a small group holds power

monarchy a system of government in which a king, queen, or emperor exercises supreme powers of government

democracy government in which the people rule

The ancient Greeks used the term *democracy* to mean government by the many rather than by a small elite. Pericles, a great leader of ancient Athens, said, "Our constitution is named a democracy because it is in the hands not of the few, but of the many." This does not mean that everyone in Athens could vote. Only citizens could vote, and many people—including women, foreign residents, and slaves—were not considered citizens.

Thousands of years later, new democracies in Europe also excluded many people from voting. It was only in the early 1800s that some educated people in Western Europe began to believe that every adult should have the right to vote—and these people were often seen as radicals. Before that time, only a landowner, merchant, or professional person with significant wealth was able to vote. This was true even in the European country with the most progressive government, Great Britain. By degrees, however, modern governments became more democratic. First workers, and later minorities and women, were given the vote.

Democracies can be direct or representative. A direct democracy is a government in which all citizens cast a vote directly on government issues and laws. Such a government can exist only in a small society where it is practical for everyone to assemble, discuss, and vote. The ancient Athenians had a direct democracy, but in modern times one can find something like it only in some New England town meetings and the smaller states, or cantons, of Switzerland. In other democracies, people are allowed to vote directly on the passage of certain laws or policies through referenda, recalls, and other ballot initiatives.

In an indirect or representative democracy, the people elect representatives and give them the responsibility to make laws and conduct government. It is the most efficient way to ensure that the rights of individual citizens, who are part of a large group, are represented.

In the United States, we have a representative democracy that does not have a monarch in charge, which makes us a **republic**. Great Britain is a democracy but not a republic because Queen Elizabeth, a constitutional monarch, is the head of state.

republic a government in which voters hold sovereign power; elected representatives, responsible to the people, exercise that power

GOVERNMENT *in your* COMMUNITY

Community Building

AmeriCorps members serve through thousands of nonprofit groups, public agencies, and faith-based and other community organizations. They tutor and mentor youth, build affordable housing, teach older Americans computer skills, clean parks and streams, run after-school programs, or help communities respond to disasters.

AmeriCorps Service Corps members resurface a volleyball court in a park in West Virginia.

▶ CRITICAL THINKING

Making Connections Do you know anyone who has served through AmeriCorps? If so, write a brief paragraph explaining what he or she did.

Corporation for National and Community Service Photo

Democracy is more likely to succeed in countries where most people are educated, which is the motivation behind free public schools in most democratic nations. Democracy is not possible without a strong civil society. Civil society is made up of a complex network of voluntary associations—economic, political, charitable, religious, and many other kinds of civic groups.

The United States has thousands of such groups—the American Red Cross, the Humane Society, the Sierra Club, the National Rifle Association, churches and temples, labor unions, and business groups. These civic groups exist outside government, but government may support them in some way. It is through these organizations that citizens often organize and make their views known. Such groups give citizens a way to take responsibility for their communities, protect their rights, learn about democracy, and participate in it at the grassroots level.

✓ **READING PROGRESS CHECK**

Describing How do oligarchies differ from monarchies?

Principles of Democracy

GUIDING QUESTION *What principles are central to democracies?*

A number of countries call their governments "democratic" or "republics" when they are not. Their leaders may want to convey the idea that the people support those in power, but it is clear that their government **institutions** do not meet the definition of a democracy. The government of North Korea, for

institution establishment, practice, or social organization

MAP

LEVELS of FREEDOM

Freedom House does an annual assessment of countries to determine which are truly democratic.

▶ **CRITICAL THINKING**

1. *Reading Maps* Which continent is the "most free"? Which is the "least free"? What do you think accounts for the difference?

2. *Interpreting* Together with two other students, visit the website of Freedom House to find out what criteria they use. Then analyze their assessment of the United States and two other countries that interest your team. When you complete your research, create a continuum in your classroom with "democratic" on one end and "authoritarian" on the other. Choose one country you researched and stand along the line to show how democratic it is. Give reasons to support why you put the country where you did along the continuum.

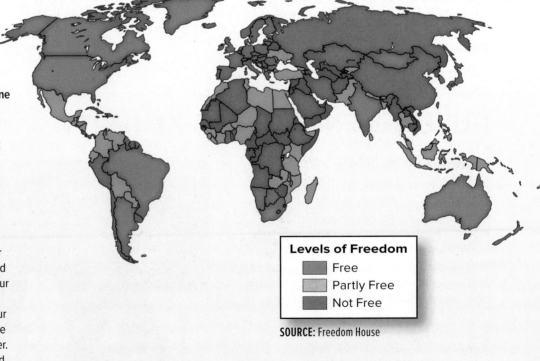

Levels of Freedom
- Free
- Partly Free
- Not Free

SOURCE: Freedom House

example, is called the Democratic People's Republic of Korea, but it is actually a totalitarian dictatorship. While no democracy is a perfect democracy, there are certain principles that guide them.

Citizen Participation One of the most basic principles of a democracy is citizen participation in government. Participation is more than just a right—it is a duty. Citizen participation may take many forms, including becoming informed, debating issues, voting in elections, attending community meetings, being members of private voluntary organizations, serving in the military or the national guard, paying taxes, serving on a jury, running for office, and even protesting. Effective citizen participation builds a stronger democracy.

Regular Free and Fair Elections One way citizens express their will is by electing officials to represent them in government. In a democracy, elections are held regularly, usually every few years. Elected officials must be chosen by the people in a free and fair manner. Most adult citizens should have the right to vote and to run for office—regardless of their race, gender, ethnicity, and level of wealth. All votes should be counted equally. Additionally, obstacles should not exist that make it difficult for people to vote. There should be no intimidation, corruption, or threats to citizens before or during an election.

Accepting the Results of Elections In elections, there are winners and losers. Occasionally, the losers believe so strongly that their party or candidate is the best that they refuse to accept that they lost an election. Assuming an election has been judged "free and fair," ignoring or rejecting election results violates democratic principles. Democracy depends on a peaceful transfer of power from one set of leaders to the next, so accepting the results of a free and fair election is essential.

The Rule of Law In a democracy, no one is above the law—not even a king, elected president, police officer, or member of the military. According to the rule of law, everyone must obey the law and will be held accountable if they violate it. Laws are known by the people and are equally, fairly, and consistently enforced.

Majority Rule With Minority Rights Democratic societies make most decisions according to what the majority of the people want. However, people in democracies are also concerned about the possibility of "the tyranny of the majority." This can occur when people in racial, ethnic, religious, or other minority groups do not agree with the dominant view and lack any power to influence government. If the people in the majority try to destroy the rights of people in minority groups or those with minority viewpoints, then they also destroy democracy. Consequently, democracies are politically tolerant. In democracies, people who are not in power are allowed to organize and speak out.

Accountability In a democracy, elected and appointed officials are responsible for their actions and have to be accountable to the people. Officials must make decisions and perform their duties according to the will and wishes of the people they represent, not for themselves or their friends.

Transparency For government to be accountable, the people must be aware of the actions their government is taking. A transparent government holds public meetings and allows citizens to attend or learn what happened in meetings. In a democracy, the press and the people are able to get information about what decisions are being made, by whom, and why.

PARTICIPATING
in Your Government

Deliberating

Deliberating is a way to understand and carefully consider both sides of a controversial issue and identify areas of agreement between opposing sides. During a deliberation, participants in groups first advocate for one side of an issue, explaining all of the best reasons to support that position. Then they switch roles and advocate for the other side of the issue by listing all of the best reasons to support that side. After both sides have received a fair hearing, participants drop their assigned roles and discuss the issue, trying to reach some consensus in their small group.

Purestock

EXPLORING THE ESSENTIAL QUESTION

a. **Determining Importance** Why is it important that people in a democracy are able to discuss controversial issues in a civil way?

b. **Making Connections** Think of an issue about which you disagree with a friend or family member. Are you able to list the reasons your friend or family member disagrees with you? The next time this issue comes up, try to listen to the other side carefully and understand the reasons given, even if you do not agree with them.

Limited Government and a Bill of Rights Most democratic countries have a list of citizens' rights and freedoms. Often called a "Bill of Rights," this document limits the power of government and explains the freedoms that are guaranteed to all people in the country. It protects people from a government that might abuse its powers. When a Bill of Rights becomes part of a country's constitution, it is easier for courts to enforce and harder for a government to take those rights away.

Control of the Abuse of Power One of the most common abuses of power is corruption, which occurs when government officials use public funds for their own benefit or exercise power in an illegal way. To protect against these abuses, democratic governments are often structured to limit the powers of government officials. For example, the executive, judicial, and legislative branches of government have distinct functions and can "check and balance" the powers of the other branches. In addition, independent agencies can investigate and impartial courts can punish government leaders and employees who abuse power.

Economic Freedom People in a democracy must have some form of economic freedom. This means that the government allows some private ownership of property and businesses. People are allowed to choose their own work and to join labor unions. The role the government should play in the economy is debated, but it is generally accepted that democratic government should not totally control the economy.

Equality In a democracy, all individuals should be valued equally and should be free from unreasonable discrimination. Individuals and groups maintain their rights to have different cultures, personalities, languages, and beliefs. All are equal before the law and are entitled to equal protection of the law. In democracies, individuals and groups have political rights to advocate for equal rights.

Individual or Human Rights Human rights are the rights all people have simply because they are human beings. Democracies respect and protect the dignity of all people. The Universal Declaration of Human Rights spells out many human rights. Many of these rights are reflected in the individual rights that democratic governments preserve, such as the U.S. Bill of Rights. Examples include, but are not limited to, the freedom of movement, religion, speech, and assembly.

Independent Judiciary In democracies, courts and the judicial system should be fair and impartial. Judges and the judicial branch must be free to act without influence or control from the executive and legislative branches of government. Judges should also not be corrupt or obligated to influential individuals, businesses, or political groups.

Competing Political Parties A political party is a group of individuals with broad common interests who organize to nominate candidates for office, win elections, conduct government, and determine public policy. To have a democracy, more than one political party must participate in elections and play a role in government. Rival parties make elections meaningful because they give voters a choice of candidates and policies.

✓ **READING PROGRESS CHECK**

Analyzing Why is citizen participation an important principle of democracy?

EXPLORING THE ESSENTIAL QUESTION

Applying Create a poster or multimedia presentation that explains and illustrates at least three principles of democracy. For each, include an image of that principle working or an image of that principle not working. For example, you could explain the idea of control of the abuse of power and show either a public official being impeached or in handcuffs or a picture of a government official accepting a bribe. Explain your choices.

LESSON 2 REVIEW

Reviewing Vocabulary

1. *Applying* Why is the United States a republic and a democracy?

Using Your Graphic Organizer

2. *Summarizing* Use your graphic organizer to write a paragraph analyzing the advantages and disadvantages of different systems of government, including unitary, confederate, and federal systems.

Answering the Guiding Questions

3. *Explaining* How is a federal system of government different from a unitary or confederate one?

4. *Contrasting* How is a constitutional government different than a country without a constitution?

5. *Contrasting* What are the differences between authoritarian and democratic governments?

6. *Identifying Central Issues* What principles are central to democracies?

Writing About Government

7. *Argument* Choose a principle of democracy that you feel is most essential to a democratic form of government. Write a paragraph explaining what this principle is and why it is essential. Include examples that support your choice.

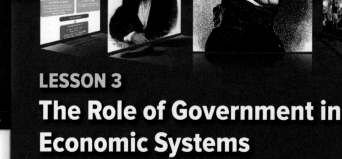

Interact with these digital assets and others in lesson 3

✓ INTERACTIVE IMAGE
  Socialist Protest

✓ SELF-CHECK QUIZ

✓ SLIDE SHOW
  Government Regulation: Then and Now

✓ VIDEO
  Hayek and Marx

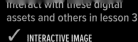

netw⊙rks
TRY IT YOURSELF ONLINE

ReadingHelp Desk

Academic Vocabulary

- **regulation**
- **consumers**

Content Vocabulary

- **economics**
- **capitalism**
- **free market**
- **free enterprise**
- **laissez-faire**
- **mixed economy**
- **socialism**
- **democratic socialist**
- **command economy**
- **bourgeoisie**
- **proletariat**
- **communism**

TAKING NOTES:

Integrating Knowledge and Ideas

CLASSIFYING Use the graphic organizer to explain the role of government in different types of economic systems.

Role of Government in Capitalism, Socialism, and Communism			
	Capitalism	Socialism	Communism
Government's role			
Government Involvement			
Example of countries with this type of economy			

LESSON 3
The Role of Government in Economic Systems

What is the role of government in different types of economic systems?

When is the last time you wanted to buy something you could not afford? Do you know people who can buy it and whatever else they want? How did they get enough money to buy it? Did they work hard? Did they save? Has their family always had plenty of money, going back for generations?

Now think about your needs instead of your wants. Can you or your family afford to pay for your basic needs like food, shelter, and clothing? Do you think the government has a responsibility to make sure you have all you need? Write a personal reflection answering these questions.

Fundamentals of Economics

GUIDING QUESTION *What are the basic factors of every economy?*

Like individuals and families, a country's resources are limited. There is not enough of anything for everyone to have everything they want. **Economics** is the study of how people and nations use their limited resources to attempt to satisfy wants and needs. In every society, governments guide economies. Some political systems let a free market, sometimes called a free enterprise system, determine how resources are used. Other political systems use government **regulation** or control to allocate resources.

A key function of government is to make essential decisions about the economy. Governments can exert almost total control over their economies or very little control. Either way, governments play significant roles in the economic lives of their people.

Every type of economy has these factors of production:
- Producers—people who make goods and services to sell
- Distributors—people who get products to buyers
- Consumers—people who purchase and use goods and services

- Labor—the work that people do or the workers themselves
- Resources—natural materials such as land and water, as well as human resources like knowledge and labor needed to make something
- Capital—the money or resources necessary to purchase or invest in production
- Entrepreneurs—risk-taking individuals who use or combine the other factors of production in search of profits

All economic systems must answer three key questions:

1. What and how much should be produced?
2. How should goods and services be produced?
3. Who gets the goods and services that are produced?

Economic systems are classified in two ways. One way looks at how economies actually work. The second way looks at the political ideology that is connected to an economy. Someone who classifies economies by how they work will use these three categories: traditional, market, and command. A traditional economy is one in which economic decisions are made according to customs, the economy is based in agriculture, hunting, gathering, and/or fishing, and where barter may be used instead of money. The other two types of economies are called market and command.

Someone who groups economies according to the related political beliefs identifies these major types of economies in the world: capitalism, socialism, and communism. There is also a blended economy called a mixed economy. These economies have different goals or principles and, therefore, the government plays a different role in each.

✓ READING PROGRESS CHECK

Explaining What are two different ways economic systems are classified? How are they different?

Capitalism

GUIDING QUESTION *What are the goals of capitalism?*

Capitalism is an economic system that emphasizes private ownership of the factors of production, freedom of choice, and individual incentives. These freedoms and incentives apply to workers, investors, **consumers**, and business owners. In pure capitalism, government does not interfere with the economy—the wages of workers, the prices of goods, what producers can make, the ways that businesses make or sell their goods and services, or any other regulations. Capitalism assumes that the best way to serve society is to let people own businesses and produce, sell, and buy goods and services as they wish.

The goal of capitalism is to create what is called a free market. In economic terms, a market is not literally just a market like a grocery store. A market or marketplace is wherever all sorts of goods and services can be sold and bought. In a **free market** or **free enterprise** economy like that under capitalism, government places no limits on the freedom of buyers and sellers to make their economic decisions.

Origins of Capitalism The basic theories about capitalism and free trade come from Adam Smith. Smith was a Scottish philosopher and economist who lived in the 1700s. In his famous book *The Wealth of Nations*, Smith suggested government take a **laissez-faire** approach to the economy. *Laissez-faire* is a French term meaning "to let alone."

economics the study of how people and nations use their limited resources to attempt to satisfy wants and needs

regulation rule or procedure that has the force of law

capitalism an economic system that emphasizes freedom of choice and individual incentive

consumer a person who purchases and uses goods and services

free market an economic system in which buyers and sellers make free choices in the marketplace

free enterprise the opportunity to control one's own economic decisions

Adam Smith, in his work *The Wealth of Nations*, advocated a hands-off policy that would allow market forces to guide the economy for the best possible outcome.

▼ CRITICAL THINKING
Making Connections How closely do you think the modern U.S. economy conforms to the ideas of Adam Smith? Explain your answer.

Capitalism, socialism, and communism are the three major types of economic systems. With each system, the government takes a different role in the economy.

▶ CRITICAL THINKING

1. Making Inferences How might private ownership and control of resources support competition among businesses?

2. Identifying In which economic system does the government assert the most control?

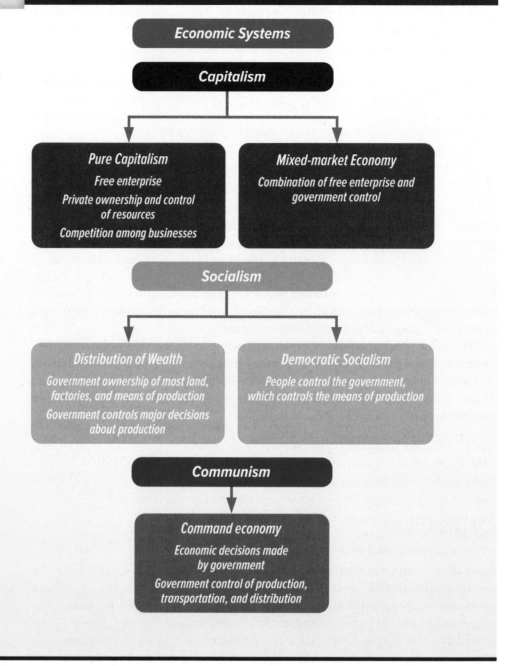

Economic Systems

Capitalism

Pure Capitalism

Free enterprise

Private ownership and control of resources

Competition among businesses

Mixed-market Economy

Combination of free enterprise and government control

Socialism

Distribution of Wealth

Government ownership of most land, factories, and means of production

Government controls major decisions about production

Democratic Socialism

People control the government, which controls the means of production

Communism

Command economy

Economic decisions made by government

Government control of production, transportation, and distribution

laissez-faire the philosophy that government should keep its hands off the economy

Smith thought the forces of the marketplace would act as an "invisible hand" guiding economic choices for the best possible results.

Competition plays a key role in a free-enterprise or free-market economy because sellers compete for resources to produce goods and services at the most reasonable price. If they are successful, they make more money. At the same time, consumers compete over limited products to buy what they want and need. Finally, these same consumers, now in their role as workers, compete to sell their skills and labor for the best wages or salaries they can get.

Pure capitalism has five characteristics: private ownership and control of property and economic resources, free enterprise, competition, freedom of choice, and the possibility of profits.

Free Enterprise in the United States A true and total capitalist system does not exist in reality. The United States, however, is a leading example of a capitalist system in which government plays a role. Our society is deeply rooted in the value of individual initiative—that each person knows what is best for himself or herself. We also respect the rights of all persons to own private property. Finally, our society recognizes individual freedom, including the freedom to make economic choices. However, because the United States government also regulates many aspects of the economy, it does not have a purely capitalistic economy.

✔ **READING PROGRESS CHECK**

Summarizing What are the five characteristics of pure capitalism? Be sure to define each in your response.

Mixed Economies

GUIDING QUESTION *What are mixed economies?*

Economists describe the economies in the United States and many other nations as mixed economies. **Mixed economies** combine elements of capitalism and socialism. Mexico is another example of a mixed economy. While primarily capitalistic, the government owns all natural resources and runs a giant oil company, Petrolero Mexicanos (PEMEX).

In its early history, the U.S. government played a very small role in the nation's economy. Since the early 1900s, however, the government's role in the economy has steadily increased in at least three ways.

First, as the federal government has grown, it has become the single largest buyer of goods and services. Second, the federal government has become more involved in regulating industries to protect consumer health and product safety. The Meat Inspection Act and the Pure Food and Drug Act—both passed in the early 1900s—were responses to public outcry over investigative reports showing grotesque conditions at meat packing plants and in food production. Since then, many other industries have become more regulated as well.

Third, the Great Depression of the 1930s created an economic emergency that propelled government action. With millions of Americans out of work, the government created programs to provide basic economic security. For example, it set up the Social Security system. It even set up a public corporation, the Tennessee Valley Authority, to provide electricity. Since then, many laws have been passed giving the government a role in such areas as labor management relations, environmental regulation, and control over financial institutions.

✔ **READING PROGRESS CHECK**

Explaining How does the U.S. economy differ from pure capitalism?

mixed economy a system in which the government regulates private enterprise

Beginning in the mid-1800s, many manufacturers sold "patent" medicines composed of various herbs but mostly alcohol. They claimed their special recipes would cure almost any ailment.

▼ CRITICAL THINKING
1. Making Connections What does the existence of regulatory agencies such as the U.S. Food and Drug Administration (USFDA) say about limits of capitalism?
2. Speculating What do you think would happen to our food supply if government agencies such as the USFDA were eliminated?

Socialism

GUIDING QUESTION *What are the goals of socialism?*

socialism an economic system in which the government owns the basic means of production, distributes the products and wages, and provides social services such as health care and welfare

Socialism is an economic system in which the government plays a significant role in the economy, but it does not completely control it. It owns most land, basic industries, and other means of production. Under socialism, government planners determine the use of resources and distribute the products and wages. The government also provides extensive social services such as education, health care, and welfare for its people. The goal of socialism is an equal distribution of wealth.

Early Socialism Socialism developed in the early 1800s along with the Industrial Revolution. Across Europe and the United States, industrialization resulted in modern economies that were vastly more productive and that generated a great deal of wealth for industrial leaders. However, it also created a great deal of suffering. Many workers, including children, lived in terrible poverty, working 12 hours per day, 6 days per week. In this time, before unions, workers had little or no power to bargain with employers for better wages or working conditions.

Reformers believed that no one should have to suffer or starve, especially as a few industrial leaders were making so much profit. They believed that under capitalism, there was no possible way for economic fairness. They wanted the government to take more control over the economy to distribute goods and wealth more equally. Some socialists believed that the people who profited from capitalism would never give up part of their wealth to share it with others so only a violent revolution would bring about change. Others believed reforms could be made peacefully and gradually by organizing the working class and voters. Still others tried to build ideal communities, known as communes, where people were supposed to share in all things.

Opponents of socialism say that it stifles individual initiative. They also say that under socialism, governments require very high taxes in order to pay for all their social services. These high tax rates hinder economic growth for the whole nation. Further, some people argue that because socialism requires increased governmental regulation, it helps create big government and thus can lead to dictatorship.

democratic socialist a socialist who is committed to democracy but wants government involvement in the distribution of wealth

Democratic Socialism Socialists who are committed to democracy in the political sphere but want government involvement in the distribution of wealth are called **democratic socialists**. Under a democratic socialist system, citizens have basic democratic rights such as freedom of speech and free and fair elections, but in the economic sphere, there is more government involvement. The government may own key industries in sectors such as defense, energy, transportation, and telecommunications. Also the government makes economic decisions designed to benefit the citizens of the country as whole. Some European nations practice forms of democratic socialism. For example, in 2012, France elected a president from the Socialist Party, and these democratic socialists gained a majority in parliament.

Socialist activists marched in protest during a meeting of the G20 in Toronto, Canada, on June 26, 2010.

▼ **CRITICAL THINKING**
Theorizing Do you think the protesters in the photo are proponents of laissez-faire capitalism? Why or why not?

☑ **READING PROGRESS CHECK**

Explaining Under socialism, who determines the use of resources?

Minor Political Parties and the Economy

Political parties and many political groups have web pages to explain and advocate for their views about the proper role of government in the economy. Visit the websites of several minor parties in the United States:

- **the Libertarian Party**
  www.lp.org
- **the Constitution Party**
  www.constitutionparty.com
- **the Socialist Party–USA**
  http://socialistparty-usa.net
- **the Communist Party USA**
  www.cpusa.org

CRITICAL THINKING
Comparing and Contrasting
Take notes about each group's slogan, motto, and mission. Compare and contrast the organizations and their visions.

Communism, a Command Economy

GUIDING QUESTION *How does a command economy work?*

In communist nations, the government decides how much to produce, what to produce, and how to distribute the goods and services produced. This system is called a **command economy** because decisions are made at the upper levels of government and handed down to the rest of the nation.

In purely communist countries, the state owns the land, natural resources, industry, banks, and transportation facilities. There is no private property, so no individual owns anything. The state controls mass communication, including newspapers, magazines, television, radio, the Internet, and the movie industry.

The basic theories about communism come from the German philosopher and reformer Karl Marx, who wrote in the mid-1800s about the suffering created by industrialization. He wrote that industrialization created deep divisions between the **bourgeoisie**—capitalists who owned the means of production, which is the factories, land, capital, and other resources necessary for making goods—and the **proletariat**—workers who produced the goods.

Marx predicted that workers would revolt against capitalists and that capitalism would collapse entirely. The goals of the revolution would be socialism at first, but he predicted that communism would be the end result. Under **communism**, there would be only one class, the working class. All property would be held in common and there would be no need for government at all. Ironically, communism has evolved into an economic system in which the government has total control.

During the Cold War, communist states existed in the Soviet Union, East Germany, and several countries in Eastern Europe. After the fall of the Berlin Wall in 1989 and the collapse of the Soviet Union in 1991 and its disintegration into independent republics, the number of communist states began to decline rapidly. Many of these states made the transition from communism to democracy. For example, many states in Eastern Europe have democratic governments.

Today only a handful of communist states exist in the world. North Korea is one. The North Korean government maintains strict control of the economy and individuals have no economic freedoms. The government sets wages and production levels and owns nearly all property.

command economy an economic system in which the government controls the factors of production

bourgeoisie capitalists who own the means of production

proletariat workers who produce the goods

communism an economic system in which the central government directs all major economic decisions

Like capitalist states, most communist states vary in how much of the economy is state controlled, and the role of government in the economy can change over time. For decades, in the People's Republic of China, the government had tight control of the economy. The Chinese government used five-year plans to set precise goals for every facet of production in the nation. It specified, for example, how many new housing units would be produced over the next five years, where houses would be built, who could live in them, and how much the rent would be. More recently, China has allowed many private investments and some free market practices. Political freedom is still very limited, however, and for that reason, economic freedom remains limited as well.

☑ **READING PROGRESS CHECK**

Describing What are the features of a purely communist country?

EXPLORING THE ESSENTIAL QUESTION

Problem-Solving Imagine your economy is in bad shape. Many people do not have jobs. Many people have had to sell or move out of their homes, and the number of people eating at soup kitchens and living in homeless shelters is increasing daily. Companies are failing and business owners are afraid to create new jobs because they do not know if they will make enough profit to afford the new workers, especially because it will cost them more to comply with new government regulations. Work with a group of students to prioritize the following strategies to improve the economy. Be prepared to explain your reasons.

a. The government should lower taxes on wealthy business owners so they will have an incentive to expand their business and hire more workers.

b. The government should lower taxes on poor and middle-class people so they have more money to spend on goods and services.

c. The government should not interfere with the economy.

d. The government should take over industries that employ a lot of people and make sure workers get a fair wage.

LESSON 3 REVIEW

Reviewing Vocabulary
1. *Contrasting* How do capitalism, socialism, and communism differ?

Using Your Graphic Organizer
2. *Summarizing* Use your completed graphic organizer to write a summary about the role of government in capitalism, socialism, and communism.

Answering the Guiding Questions
3. *Listing* What are the basic factors of every economy?

4. *Describing* What are the goals of capitalism?

5. *Defining* What are mixed economies?

6. *Describing* What are the goals of socialism?

7. *Explaining* How does a command economy work?

Writing About Government
8. *Narrative* Write a fictional story or draw a picture that illustrates the three major economic systems and how government is or is not involved in each. Your story or illustration should show the interactions among consumers, producers, workers, and government officials.

United States  Virginia (1996)

FACTS OF THE CASE Virginia Military Institute (VMI) is an all-male, taxpayer-supported state military college in Virginia. The school's mission is to produce citizen-soldiers, prepared for leadership in civilian life and military service. The school is well funded and well respected. VMI uses a system like military boot camp to instill physical and mental discipline in students. In recent years, the military role of the school has diminished. By 1995, about 15 percent of graduates were pursuing military careers.

After pressure from the government to admit women, VMI created a separate women's college. It used cooperative methods to train students and was not as well funded or well respected. The U.S. government sued VMI, arguing that the college was denying women equal treatment under the law, as required by the Fourteenth Amendment.

ISSUE

Is it unconstitutional for VMI to refuse to admit women?

ARGUMENTS

The following is a list of arguments made in the case of *United States* v. *Virginia*. Read each argument and categorize each based on whether it supports the U.S. government's side (that VMI's refusal to admit women is unconstitutional) or VMI's side (that the male-only admission policy is constitutional).

1. Admitting women to VMI would fundamentally change the character of the school. The college could not do boot camp-like activities with women in attendance.

2. The fact that VMI created a separate college for women shows that VMI was not treating women differently from men. Both men and women could attend a VMI school, just not the same school.

3. The college that VMI created for women was not the equal of the college for men. It used different methods and was not as well funded or well respected.

4. VMI has a mission to prepare citizen-soldiers to serve in the military. Far more men than women serve in combat roles in the military, so the school should be permitted to have an all-male training program.

5. VMI has strayed from its military mission and most graduates do not become soldiers. The college's argument that it needs to train men for combat no longer stands.

6. Many women attend military boot camps and serve in the military. They could certainly handle the training course at VMI.

7. VMI has an important network of graduates in leadership positions. That alumni network makes a degree from VMI more valuable than a degree from the new women's college.

EXPLORING THE ESSENTIAL QUESTION

Summarizing Once you have categorized the arguments, reread them. Research how the Court ruled and write a brief summary explaining the ruling. Highlight the arguments in your list that the Court found most compelling.

YOU BE the JUDGE

STUDY GUIDE

FUNCTIONS OF GOVERNMENT
LESSON 1

- ✓ Providing leadership
- ✓ Maintaining order
- ✓ Providing services
- ✓ Providing national security
- ✓ Providing economic security

PRINCIPLES OF DEMOCRACY
LESSON 2

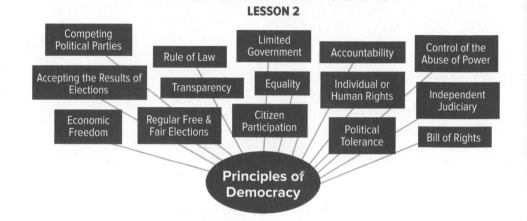

Competing Political Parties · Rule of Law · Limited Government · Accountability · Control of the Abuse of Power · Accepting the Results of Elections · Transparency · Equality · Individual or Human Rights · Independent Judiciary · Economic Freedom · Regular Free & Fair Elections · Citizen Participation · Political Tolerance · Bill of Rights · Principles of Democracy

TYPES OF GOVERNMENT
LESSON 2

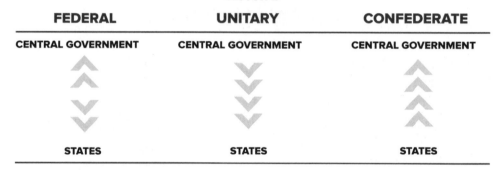

FEDERAL	UNITARY	CONFEDERATE
CENTRAL GOVERNMENT	CENTRAL GOVERNMENT	CENTRAL GOVERNMENT
STATES	STATES	STATES

THE ROLE OF GOVERNMENT IN ECONOMIC SYSTEMS
LESSON 3

ECONOMIC SYSTEM	CHARACTERISTICS
SOCIALISM	Government owns land, factories, and means of production. Government makes major decisions about production. Government decides how to use resources and distributes wealth more equally among people.
COMMUNISM	No recognized social classes, and all property is held in common Government controls means of production, transportation, and distribution. Command economy: economic decisions made by upper levels of government and handed down
CAPITALISM	Emphasis on freedom of choice and individual incentive Free enterprise Private ownership/control of resources Competition among businesses Mixed economy: Combines elements of capitalism (free enterprise) and socialism (government control of some resources)

Directions: On a separate sheet of paper, answer the questions below. Make sure you read carefully and answer all parts of the questions.

Lesson Review

Lesson 1

1 *Describing* What are the essential features of a state? Why is each necessary?

2 *Contrasting* What is the difference, if any, between a nation, a state, and a country? Give three examples of each.

3 *Explaining* What are the divine right of kings and social contract theories? How are these major political ideas different?

Lesson 2

4 *Analyzing* What are the advantages and disadvantages of federal systems of government? Do you believe the advantages outweigh the disadvantages? Explain.

5 *Comparing* Why is the United States a constitutional republic? Why is China, which has a constitution, not one? Compare the forms of government in the United States and China.

6 *Demonstrating* Name three principles of democracy. What makes each so important?

Lesson 3

7 *Identifying* What is a mixed economy? Give one example of why the United States is considered one.

8 *Differentiating* What are the similarities and differences between the role of the government in a free enterprise economic system and a socialist economic system? In which system is there more government involvement?

ANSWERING THE ESSENTIAL QUESTIONS

Review your answers to the introductory questions at the beginning of each lesson. Then answer the following Essential Questions based on what you learned in the chapter. Have your answers changed?

9 *Identifying Central Issues* What are the purposes of government?

10 *Explaining* What principles guide different types of governments?

11 *Examining* What is the role of government in different types of economic systems?

DBQ Interpreting Political Cartoons

Use the political cartoon to answer the following questions.

12 *Analyzing Visuals* What is the significance of the landscape and the man's appearance in this cartoon?

13 *Making Inferences* What does the little girl's response say about a difference between socialism and capitalism?

Critical Thinking

14 *Understanding Historical Interpretation* Why did the Founders adopt a federal system of government instead of a unitary system?

15 *Theorizing* Summarize the origins of the state theories described in this chapter. Then research other theories about the origins of the state. Which theories do you find least plausible? Explain.

16 *Predicting* How might our economy change if the government placed limits on free enterprise?

17 *Making Comparisons* Use a graphic organizer to explain how capitalism, democratic socialism, and communism are alike and different. Explain the graphic you chose.

Need Extra Help?

If You've Missed Question	1	2	3	4	5	6	7	8	9	10	11	12	13	14	15	16	17
Go to page	9	9	11	13	14	18	25	23	6	12	22	25	25	13	10	24	23

Directions: On a separate sheet of paper, answer the questions below. Make sure you read carefully and answer all parts of the questions.

DBQ Analyzing Primary Sources

Read the excerpts and answer the questions that follow.

PRIMARY SOURCE

"We hold these truths to be self-evident, that all men are created equal, that they are endowed by their Creator with certain unalienable Rights, that among these are Life, Liberty and the pursuit of Happiness . . . That whenever any Form of Government becomes destructive of these ends, it is the Right of the People to alter or to abolish it, and to institute new Government, . . . as to them shall seem most likely to effect their Safety and Happiness . . ."
—The Declaration of Independence

18 *Making Connections* What does the Declaration of Independence say about the peoples' rights with respect to destructive government? How did the colonists act on this promise?

19 *Identifying* What beliefs and principles are reflected in the Declaration of Independence? Explain how these beliefs and principles contributed to the national identity of the United States.

PRIMARY SOURCE

"The state of nature has a law of nature to govern it, which obliges every one: and reason, which is that law, teaches all mankind, who will but consult it, that being all equal and independent, no one ought to harm another in his life, health, liberty, or possessions . . ."

"I desire to know what kind of government that is, and how much better it is than the state of nature, where one man, commanding a multitude, has the liberty to be judge in his own case, and may do to all his subjects whatever he pleases, without the least liberty to any one to question or controul [archaic] those who execute his pleasure and in whatsoever he doth, whether led by reason, mistake or passion, must be submitted to."
—John Locke, *Two Treatises on Government*, 1821 version

20 *Interpreting* According to Locke, what is the law of nature?

21 *Comparing* How does the Declaration of Independence echo the ideas of John Locke?

Social Studies Skills

22 *Drawing Conclusions* In opposition to British rule, the Founders of the United States chose to set up a national government. Create a graphic organizer that lists the purposes of government in one column. In the second column, describe how our society might operate today without a government. Consider specific functions of government such as leadership, maintaining order, and providing public services, etc.

23 *Hypothesizing* Write a short essay discussing how today's society might have been affected if the Founders had chosen to adopt an authoritarian type of government.

Research and Presentation

24 *Researching* Research the classical republic in ancient Rome, the direct democracy in ancient Athens, and the French monarchy in the period before the French Revolution. Create a multimedia presentation in which you compare the U.S. system of government to these historical forms of government.

25 *Analyzing* Choose a country that claims to grant individual rights and freedoms to its citizens but does not deliver them. Conduct research on the Internet or in your school library. Then create a graphic organizer that lists the rights promised in one column and examples of the country violating those rights in the second column.

26 *Hypothesizing* The United States began as a confederation but replaced that form of government with the U.S. Constitution. Few nations are confederations. Choose a country that is a confederation, such as the Federated States of Micronesia, and, using it as an example, write an essay that hypothesizes why there are so few.

27 *Informative/Explanatory* Research the economic theories of Adam Smith and Karl Marx. With which economic theory is each associated? Why is each man influential? Write an essay contrasting the theories of Smith and Marx.

Need Extra Help?

If You've Missed Question	18	19	20	21	22	23	24	25	26	27
Go to page	14	11	11	11	7	15	16	18	12	23

Origins of American Government

netw⊙rks

www.connected.mcgraw-hill.com
There's More Online about the origins of American government.

ESSENTIAL QUESTIONS

- What influenced the development of our government institutions?
- Why and how did the colonists declare independence?

Courtesy National Gallery of Art, Washington

▲ George Washington, the first president of the United States, is often called "the father of our country."

COMPARING INDEPENDENCE MOVEMENTS

From the 1500s to the mid-1900s, European powers held colonies in Asia, Africa, and the Americas. The United States was one of the first countries to gain its independence from a colonial power. As other countries gained independence, new borders often put people with no shared history or even long-standing animosity into the same country. Explore these documents to compare the independence movements of the United States and South Sudan.

SECONDARY SOURCE

Background on South Sudan

Egypt gained its independence from British rule in 1922. Both South Sudan and Sudan were part of Egypt until 1956, when those two areas became one independent nation, Sudan. The people in South Sudan were promised political equality with the people in the northern part of the country. But that did not happen. Years of fighting between South Sudanese rebels and the Sudanese military followed. Groups within Sudan also argued about the distribution of resources and the role of religion in the state. Sudan's population was largely Sunni Muslim, while South Sudanese were Christians or practiced traditional religions. In 2005 peace was achieved when the southern part of the country was granted six years of autonomy, to be followed by a vote on secession. In 2011 more than 98 percent of the people in South Sudan voted for secession. South Sudan became an independent nation on July 9, 2011.

SOURCE: CIA, *The World Factbook,* 2013–2014

SECONDARY SOURCE   and

Comparing Sudan and South Sudan		
Characteristic	**Sudan**	**South Sudan**
Religion	Sunni Muslim, Christian minority	Christian, traditional religions
Resources	Petroleum, oil refineries and shipping facilities, small reserves of minerals	Hydropower, fertile agricultural land, gold, diamonds, petroleum (three times the production of Sudan)
GDP per capita	$2600	$1400

SOURCE: CIA, *The World Factbook,* 2013–2014

Comparing Great Britain and the American Colonies, 1770s		
Characteristic	**Great Britain**	**American Colonies**
Population	Est. 6.97 million (1771)	Est. 2.3–2.6 million (1775)
Religion	Official religion: Anglican	Varied Protestant denominations, Catholicism; some had official religions
Value of exports	From Britain to U.S., 1774: goods worth 2,590,437 pounds sterling	From U.S. to Britain, 1774: goods worth 1,373,846 pounds sterling

SOURCES: U.S. Census; Floud and McCloskey, eds., *The Economic History of Britain Since 1700, Volume I*

The South Sudanese felt they were treated unfairly by the Sudanese government. Their economy was not being developed at the same rate as that in the northern part of the country. They were also concerned about the prominent role of Islam in the government of Sudan. After a negotiated agreement with Sudan and a vote of the people, they declared independence on July 9, 2011:

"**RECALLING** the long and heroic struggle of our people for justice, freedom, equality, human dignity and political and economic emancipation;

CONSIDERING the years of conflict and the immeasurable sufferings of our people resulting from the conflict between North and Southern Sudan; . . .

RESOLVED to establish a system of governance that upholds the rule of law, justice, democracy, human rights and respect for diversity;"

—South Sudan Declaration of Independence

"The history of the present King of Great Britain is a history of repeated injuries and usurpations, all having in direct object the establishment of an absolute Tyranny over these States. To prove this, let Facts be submitted to a candid world.

He has refused his Assent to Laws, the most wholesome and necessary for the public good. . . .

He has refused to pass other Laws for the accommodation of large districts of people, unless those people would relinquish the right of Representation in the Legislature, a right inestimable to them and formidable to tyrants only. . . .

He has endeavoured to prevent the population of these States; for that purpose obstructing the Laws for Naturalization of Foreigners; refusing to pass others to encourage their migrations hither, and raising the conditions of new Appropriations of Lands. . . .

He has erected a multitude of New Offices, and sent hither swarms of Officers to harass our people and eat out their substance.

He has kept among us, in times of peace, Standing Armies without the Consent of our legislatures. . . ."

—The U.S. Declaration of Independence

DBQ DOCUMENT-BASED QUESTIONS

1. **Describing** Write descriptions of the American colonies and Great Britain that highlight their differences. Do the same for Sudan and South Sudan.

2. **Identifying** Identify reasons that American colonists and the South Sudanese people sought independence.

3. **Comparing** What similarities, if any, do you see between the South Sudanese independence movement and the American colonies' move toward independence?

WHAT WILL YOU DO?

As an American, do you favor U.S. involvement in independence movements in other parts of the world? What criteria would you use to decide which movements should be supported?

EXPLORE the interactive version of the analyzing primary sources feature on Networks.

Interact with these digital assets and others in lesson 1

✓ **INTERACTIVE CHART**
English Legal and Political Thought

✓ **INTERACTIVE IMAGE**
English Bill of Rights

✓ **INTERACTIVE MAP**
The Thirteen Colonies

✓ **VIDEO**
Magna Carta

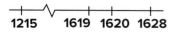
TRY IT YOURSELF ONLINE

LESSON 1
Government in Colonial America

Reading Help Desk

Academic Vocabulary

- establish
- levy
- vital

Content Vocabulary

- limited government
- representative government
- charter

TAKING NOTES:

Key Ideas and Details

SEQUENCING As you read, create a time line of influential European and colonial documents.

1215   1619 1620 1628

ESSENTIAL QUESTION

What influenced the development of our government institutions?

Read the list of rights below. Draw a table with two columns. In the first column, list each of the rights that you think Americans have today. In the second column, list each right that you think American colonists had before 1776. Highlight the four rights that you believe are the most important.

a. The right to a fair and speedy trial with a jury

b. The right to criticize the government

c. The right to be free from unjust punishments by the government

d. The right to practice one's own religion without government interference

e. The right to vote for representatives in the government

f. The right not to pay taxes if you disagree with the government

g. The right to be free from slavery

h. The right to ask the government to address a problem

i. The right to a job

Our Political Heritage

GUIDING QUESTION *Which historical events, documents, and philosophers influenced American colonists' ideas about government?*

During the 1600s, people from Europe migrated to North America, settling along the Atlantic Coast and inland. The great majority of the colonists were Christians familiar with both the Old and New Testament of the Christian Bible. They brought with them Judeo-Christian values and ideas derived from biblical law. For example, the Old Testament discusses how the law should apply equally to all people, even kings, and sets forth rules for a fair trial. These beliefs made an important contribution to the founding principles and documents of the United States.

36

Most of the early colonists were from England and considered themselves British. The English settlers formed thirteen colonies under charters from the King of England. Their ideas about the role and shape of government influenced the growth of the colonies, the American Revolution, and the system of government we have today. Many of their ideas about government had been developing in Europe for centuries, including the two basic principles of limited government and representative government.

Limited Government By the time the first European colonists settled North America, the idea of **limited government**—the concept that a government's power was not absolute—was accepted in England. Centuries earlier, in 1215, English nobles were upset with the oppressive policies of King John, including unfair taxation and cruel treatment of prisoners. They forced him to sign a document—the Magna Carta—recognizing their rights. The nobles did not think the Magna Carta **established** permanent principles of government, nor were they thinking of the rights of common people. As the centuries passed, however, the English people came to regard the Magna Carta as a guarantee of limited government. They believed it protected people from unjust punishment by the government and from the **levying** of taxes without popular consent.

English Bill of Rights Even after the signing of the Magna Carta, power struggles between the monarchy and Parliament (England's lawmaking body) persisted for more than 400 years. In 1688 Parliament removed King James II from the throne with little resistance. It chose two new monarchs who recognized Parliament as supreme—William III and Mary II.

In 1689 Parliament passed the English Bill of Rights, which set clear limits on the monarchy. It said:

- Monarchs do not have absolute authority but rule with the consent of the people's representatives in Parliament;
- Monarchs must have Parliament's consent to suspend laws, levy taxes, or maintain an army;
- Monarchs cannot interfere with parliamentary elections and debates;
- The people have a right to petition the government and to have a fair and speedy trial by a jury of their peers;
- The people should not be subject to cruel and unusual punishments or to excessive fines and bail.

The influence of the English Bill of Rights was felt directly in the American colonies. The colonists believed the document applied to them and that they had the same rights as people living in Britain. The king, however, had a different perspective—he saw colonists as subjects of the British Empire without the same rights as those living in Britain. These differing ideas were a major cause for the American Revolution.

English Law The English system of law had a major influence in the colonies, especially through the work of Sir William Blackstone. Blackstone's *Commentaries on the Laws of England* (1766) helped codify English common law and was widely followed by the Founders. Blackstone believed the source of all human law was derived from "the law of nature and the law of revelation [the Bible]" and that "no human laws should be suffered to contradict these."

Representative Government The colonists firmly believed in **representative government**, a

limited government the concept that a government's power was not absolute

establish to create or set up

levy to charge or impose

In 1688 Parliament offered the crown of Great Britain to William of Orange and his wife Mary, who, in turn, recognized the power of Parliament as supreme.

▼ CRITICAL THINKING
Summarizing How did the relationship between the monarch and Parliament change as a result of the English Bill of Rights?

representative government a government in which people elect delegates to make laws and conduct government

government in which people elect delegates to make laws and conduct government. This notion was familiar to the colonists because Britain's Parliament was a representative assembly with the power to enact laws. It had two chambers. The members of the upper chamber, the House of Lords, were the first sons of noble families and later members inherited their positions. The members of the lower chamber, the House of Commons, were elected. Since very few common or poor people were allowed to vote, members of the House of Commons were often the younger sons of noble families or wealthy commoners.

New Political Ideas: The Social Contract and Natural Rights

European philosophers and their ideas about government deeply influenced American colonists. During the late 1600s and 1700s, Europe experienced a major intellectual movement known as the Enlightenment. During the Enlightenment, Europeans challenged the rule of leaders who claimed to have power because of divine right, or by God-given authority, and began to consider different ideas about what makes government legitimate.

English philosopher Thomas Hobbes argued that people create a society by entering into a social contract. According to this theory, people need government to maintain order because they have not yet learned to live in groups without conflict. Under this social contract theory, people give up their individual sovereignty to the government. In exchange, the government provides peace and order. Like Hobbes, John Locke and Jean-Jacques Rousseau developed ideas about the purposes of government and the social contract.

John Locke, an English philosopher, reasoned that people have "natural rights," those rights people have simply because they are human beings. He named those natural rights as the right to life, liberty, and property. He theorized that people made a contract among themselves to create a government to protect their natural rights. If, however, a government failed

CHART

English Legal and Political Thought

Sir William Blackstone The law of nature, as found in the Bible, is perfect and supreme; no human law should be made to contradict it.	"THIS law of nature, . . . dictated by God himself, is of course superior in obligation to any other. It is binding over all the globe, in all countries, and at all times: no human laws are of any validity, if contrary to this; and much of them as are valid derive all their force, and all their authority, . . . from this original." —from *Commentaries on the Laws of England*, 1765
Thomas Hobbes The natural state of man is war. People live in fear of each other, which is why man is willing to trade individual liberty for the security of living in a society under a government.	"Hereby it is manifest that during the time men live without a common power to keep them all in awe, they are in that condition which is called war; and such a war as is of every man against every man." —from *Leviathan*, 1660
John Locke Men are born equal and given rights that cannot be denied. No man may be taken from his property, his life forfeit, and subjected to the authority of a government without his consent.	"Men being, as has been said, by nature, all free, equal, and independent, no one can be put out of this estate, and subjected to the political power of another, without his own consent." —from *The Second Treatise of Government*, 1690

EXPLORING THE ESSENTIAL QUESTION

1. **Identifying Points of View** How does Blackstone view the relationship of divine law and human law?
2. **Contrasting** How do Hobbes's and Locke's views on individual freedom and the purpose of laws differ?

to protect these rights, people were justified in rebelling and changing that government. For Locke, government was legitimate only as long as the people continued to consent to it.

Swiss-born political theorist Jean-Jacques Rousseau believed that property rights and other basic rights such as freedom of speech and religion came from people living together in a community. By working cooperatively, people created a social contract that allowed them to preserve their rights while at the same time creating law and government.

Charles-Louis de Montesquieu, a French Enlightenment thinker, wrote about the importance of separating the powers of government. In *The Spirit of the Laws*, he said, "There can be no liberty where the legislative and executive powers are united in the same person . . . [or] if the power of judging be not separated from the legislative and executive powers."

While the colonists' ideas about government were rooted in Christianity, educated colonists were familiar with the ideas of Blackstone, Hobbes, Locke, and other Enlightenment thinkers. The Declaration of Independence and the Constitution reflected these ideas.

☑ **READING PROGRESS CHECK**

Explaining How did the Magna Carta and the English Bill of Rights influence the American colonies?

▲ Thomas Hobbes believed that people entered into a social contract with government to maintain peace and order.

EXPLORING THE ESSENTIAL QUESTION

Outlining Choose one of these historical documents or thinkers:

- **Magna Carta**
- **English Bill of Rights**
- **John Locke**
- **Jean-Jacques Rousseau**
- **Charles-Louis de Montesquieu**

Read about your document or philosopher and create an outline of the main ideas presented. Research how the principles of laws and government institutions presented either in your document or by your philosopher affected the founding of the United States. Share your research in a group with students assigned to the other documents or philosophers. Together, create a list of concepts and rights suggested by these documents and philosophers that are also present in our government today.

Colonial Governments

GUIDING QUESTION *How were democratic ideals incorporated into colonial governments?*

Their English heritage and the political philosophers of the Enlightenment influenced the colonists' notions of representative government, republicanism, constitutionalism, and law. Each of the thirteen colonies had its own government consisting of a governor (usually appointed by the king), a legislature (elected at least in part), and a court system. These colonial institutions exercised some local authority, but the British believed that all colonists owed allegiance to the monarch.

The governments the colonists established were not democratic as we would define the term today. Democracy at that time meant that it was possible for a working farmer, for example, to have his views heard in local meetings or

THE THIRTEEN COLONIES

The population of the thirteen colonies varied.

▶ **CRITICAL THINKING**

1. Reading Maps Which colonies have the most people? Which have the fewest?

2. Analyzing Why might Georgia have had so few residents?

3. Making Inferences Think about these differences in population. How do you think these factors might influence the opinions about government held by residents of the different colonies?

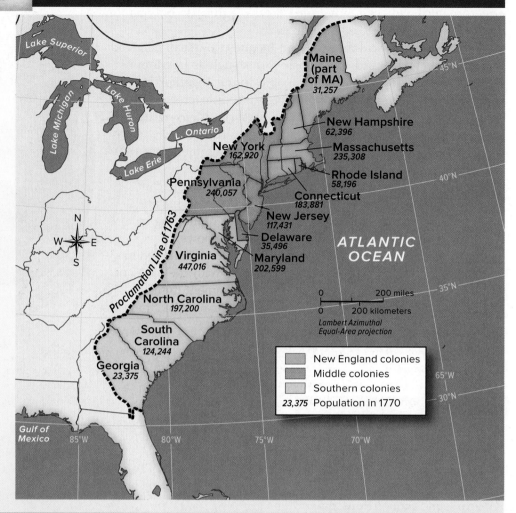

to vote on certain issues in some colonies. By contrast, women and enslaved people could not vote, and every colony had some type of property qualification for voting. Land was abundant and cheap, however, so compared to Europe, a relatively large percentage of the white, male population could vote.

Nine of the thirteen colonies had an official or established church, and many colonists remained intolerant of religious dissent. In Puritan town meetings, for example, voting was originally reserved for members of the community church. Despite such shortcomings, however, colonial governments established practices that later became a key part of the nation's system of government.

Written Constitutions A key feature of the colonial period was government according to a written plan. The Mayflower Compact that the Pilgrims signed in 1620 was the first of many colonial plans for self-government. Men of the Pilgrim families drew up the document in the tiny cabin of their ship, the *Mayflower*, anchored off the New England coast. The Pilgrim leaders realized they needed rules to govern themselves if they were to survive in the new land. Through the Mayflower Compact, they agreed to choose their own leaders and to make their own laws. Puritan immigrants established the Massachusetts Bay Colony, and in 1636 the colony adopted the first system of laws in the English colonies.

In 1639 colonists in Connecticut drew up America's first formal constitution, or **charter**. The Fundamental Orders of Connecticut gave the people the right to elect the governor, judges, and representatives to make laws. Soon after,

charter a written instrument from the authorities of a society granting rights or privileges

other English colonies created their own charters with similar provisions. The actions of colonial legislatures and courts could be reviewed (and rejected) by a committee of the king's Privy Council, but the colonies actually practiced a great deal of self-government.

Colonial charters divided the power of government among the governor, the legislative assembly, and the courts. The governor, the king's agent in the colonies, had executive power, while the legislative assembly had the power to pass laws. Colonial courts applied the law in court cases.

Colonial Legislatures The composition of the colonial legislatures varied. In some places, the king exercised his role as the head of the church and appointed bishops and clergy to serve in the colonial legislatures. In other places, especially where many American Puritans had settled, colonists rejected the tradition of the king acting as head of the church. The Puritans had migrated to America to gain the freedom to organize their churches as they chose and believed that each congregation should choose its ministers. They also believed that church members should elect their government. In 1636 Puritans in Massachusetts forced their leaders to allow each town to elect two members of the General Court, the colony's legislature.

By the mid-1700s, the legislative bodies of colonial government were dominant in political life. The rapidly growing colonies constantly needed new laws to cope with new circumstances. For example, they had to control the distribution of land and lay out plans for public buildings. They also had to build roads and ferries that were **vital** to the economy and set up schools and courts. By 1776, representative government was a well-established tradition in America. Most colonial legislatures had been operating for over 100 years, and they became the training grounds for the political leaders who wrote the Declaration of Independence and, later, the U.S. Constitution. The combination of their English heritage and colonial experience in representative self-government made them leaders in what one historian called "the seedtime of the republic."

The Virginia House of Burgesses, the first legislature in America, was established in 1619, only 12 years after the settlement of Jamestown. The burgesses made local laws for the colony.

▲ CRITICAL THINKING
Explaining Why did English political traditions influence colonial government?

vital essential, crucial

☑ **READING PROGRESS CHECK**

Defining What was a colonial charter and what was its purpose?

LESSON 1 REVIEW

Reviewing Vocabulary

1. ***Contrasting*** Explain the differences between a representative government and a limited government.

Using Your Graphic Organizer

2. ***Categorizing*** Use your completed time line to write two paragraphs—one on the influential European documents and another on the influential colonial documents.

Answering the Guiding Questions

3. ***Understanding Historical Interpretation*** Which historical events, documents, and philosophers influenced American colonists' ideas about government?

4. ***Synthesizing*** How were democratic ideals incorporated into colonial governments?

Writing About Government

5. ***Informative/Explanatory*** In what ways were colonial governments representative? List three examples and compare them to examples of representative government in America today.

(l to r) National Park Service; Working America of Columbus; Scott Dunlap/Getty Images

netw⬤rks
TRY IT YOURSELF ONLINE

LESSON 2
Uniting for Independence

ReadingHelp Desk

Academic Vocabulary
- **draft**
- **consent**

Content Vocabulary
- **revenue**
- **embargo**
- **boycott**
- **human rights**

TAKING NOTES:
Integrating Knowledge and Ideas

DETERMINING CAUSE AND EFFECT Use a graphic organizer like the one below to list the causes of the colonists' declaration of independence.

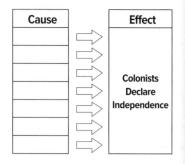

Cause		Effect
	⇨	
	⇨	
	⇨	Colonists
	⇨	Declare
	⇨	Independence
	⇨	
	⇨	

ESSENTIAL QUESTION

Why and how did the colonists declare independence?

Think about colonies, states, or groups of people that have sought independence. Select one of these examples, or choose an example of your own:

- India
- The Confederate States of America
- Romania
- South Sudan

Research your independence movement and answer the following questions:

a. Why did this group want to be independent?

b. What means did they employ to gain independence?

c. Was the independence movement successful?

The Colonies on Their Own

GUIDING QUESTION *What conditions prompted the American colonists to declare independence from Britain?*

For more than a century, relations between the colonies and Great Britain were peaceful. The colonists developed their political institutions without much interference. The colonists were British subjects, and as with other parts of the British Empire, the colonies were supposed to serve as a source of raw materials and a market for British goods. In the eyes of the British crown, the American colonies existed for the economic benefit of Great Britain.

In practice, the colonies in America did pretty much as they pleased. The colonies were more than 3,000 miles (4,828 km) from Great Britain. News from America and orders from the monarch took two months or more to travel across the Atlantic Ocean. Given this distance, only the governors of the colonies and the colonial legislatures were actually in a position to deal with the everyday problems facing the colonies. As a result, the colonists grew accustomed to governing themselves. Until the mid-1700s, the British government was generally satisfied with this political and economic arrangement.

Britain Tightens Control Two events changed the relationship between the colonies and Britain: the French and Indian War and the crowning of King George III.

The French and Indian War started as a struggle between the French and British over lands in what is now western Pennsylvania and Ohio. Many Native American tribes sided with the French and fought with them against British troops led by George Washington. By 1756, several other European countries had become involved. Great Britain won the war in 1763 and gained complete control of the eastern third of the continent, essentially eliminating French power in North America.

The war was very costly and Britain was left with a huge debt. The British believed the colonists had an obligation to pay that debt—after all, they were defending the colonies from the French. In order to defend against Indian rebellions after the war, Britain also maintained a standing army in the colonies, which was also a financial strain.

Taxing the Colonies George III became king in 1760. To help pay for the war, the king and his ministers levied taxes on tea, sugar, glass, paper, and other products. The Stamp Act of 1765 imposed the first direct tax on the colonists. It required them to pay a tax on legal documents, pamphlets, newspapers, and even dice and playing cards. The British Parliament also passed laws regulating colonial trade in ways that benefited Great Britain but not the colonies.

Britain's **revenue**—the money a government collects from taxes or other sources—from the colonies increased. Colonial resentment, however, grew too. Political protests began to spread throughout the colonies and many

We the People: Making a Difference

The Signers of the Declaration of Independence

Library of Congress Prints and Photographs Division [LC-DIG-pga-02322]

"With a firm reliance on the protection of divine Providence, we mutually pledge to each other our Lives, our Fortunes, and our Sacred Honor."

—The Declaration of Independence

With these words, the signers of the Declaration of Independence launched their nation's bid for freedom. For many, that goal came at great cost. Four signers were taken prisoner while fighting in South Carolina. Another signer, Richard Stockton of New Jersey, was taken prisoner, beaten, and held for several years. His health ruined, he died soon after being released. The New York home of signer Francis Lewis was plundered and his wife taken prisoner. Badly mistreated, she died a few years after her release.

Altogether 14 signers had their homes invaded and were forced to flee with their families. Carter Braxton of Virginia lost his merchant ships to the British. Robert Stockton was probably the only signer to die as a direct result of the Revolutionary War, but all of the signers were willing to risk everything for freedom. Without their courage, independence could not have been achieved.

EXPLORING THE ESSENTIAL QUESTION

Analyzing Think about what type of government action would prompt you to make a sacrifice like the signers of the Declaration did. What might a government do that would inspire you to risk your safety to protest?

colonists refused to buy British goods. The protests led to the repeal of the Stamp Act, but the British passed other tax laws and regulations to replace it, which came to be known as the Townshend Acts. The situation reached a boiling point in 1773. A group of colonists, dressed as Mohawk Indians, dumped 342 chests of British tea into Boston Harbor. This protest became known as the Boston Tea Party. In retaliation, Parliament passed the Coercive Acts, which the colonists called the Intolerable Acts. One of these acts closed Boston Harbor. Another withdrew the right of the Massachusetts colony to govern itself. By the early 1770s, revolution was not far off.

Colonial Unity The harsh new British policies spurred an American sense of community in a way that had not existed before. Prior to the Intolerable Acts, most colonists thought of themselves as British subjects. At the same time, each colony had developed largely on its own and had unique resources and economies. Residents therefore thought of themselves as Virginians or New Yorkers or Georgians. By the 1760s, however, a growing number of colonists began to think of themselves as Americans united by their hostility toward British authority. At the same time, colonial leaders began to work together to take political action against what they felt was British oppression.

revenue the money a government collects from taxes or other sources

Taking Action In 1765 nine colonies sent delegates to a meeting organized to protest the Stamp Act and King George's actions. They sent a petition to the king, arguing that only colonial legislatures could impose direct taxes like the Stamp Tax.

By 1773, colonists opposed to British rules were forming organizations to keep in touch with each other and to urge resistance to the British. These groups, called committees of correspondence, sprung up quickly. Within a few months after Samuel Adams formed the first committee in Boston, there were more than 80 such committees in Massachusetts alone. Virginia and other colonies soon joined this communication network, led by prominent members like Thomas Jefferson and Patrick Henry.

✓ **READING PROGRESS CHECK**

Describing How did the French and Indian War and the crowning of King George III change the relationship between the colonies and Great Britain?

C·I·V·I·C PARTICIPATION IN A DIGITAL AGE

Political Movements

The purpose of the colonists' committees of correspondence was to maintain contact with other opponents to British rule and to encourage and organize resistance to the British. How do members of social or political movements maintain contact and organize today?

Identify an issue in your state that is important to you. Use a search engine to find an online community or social networking group that is organized around this issue.

▶ **CRITICAL THINKING**
1. *Classifying* What is the group's purpose?
2. *Listing* Who are the members of the group? How many members are there?
3. *Summarizing* What information or ideas are expressed in the online group?
4. *Identifying* Can you identify any impact the online group has had on your issue?

PARTICIPATING IN Your Government

Advocacy

Identify an action or policy of your state government with which you disagree. Decide on a written format that would best express your disagreement, such as a letter to a newspaper editor, an e-mail to your state representative, a petition, or a complaint to a state agency.

EXPLORING THE ESSENTIAL QUESTION

Argument Write your complaint or grievance. How will you frame your argument to be most persuasive? Remember to suggest an alternative policy or action and to request a reply.

Working America of Columbus

Independence

GUIDING QUESTION *What complaints did the colonists list in the Declaration of Independence, and what freedoms did they want guaranteed?*

In the First and Second Continental Congress, the colonists passed a series of measures, culminating in their declaration of independence from Great Britain.

The First Continental Congress On September 5, 1774, delegates from every colony except Georgia met in Philadelphia for the First Continental Congress. Their purpose was to decide what to do about the relationship with Great Britain. Colonial leaders like Patrick Henry, Samuel Adams, Richard Henry Lee, and George Washington debated the merits of different proposals. They finally imposed an **embargo**, an agreement prohibiting trade, on Britain and agreed to **boycott** (not to buy) British goods. They proposed a second meeting the following year if Britain did not change its policies.

embargo an agreement prohibiting trade

boycott not to buy

Soon after, the king and British Parliament adopted stronger measures and events then moved quickly. "The New England governments are in a state of rebellion," George III firmly announced. "Blows must decide whether they are to be subject to this country or independent."

The first blow fell early on the morning of April 19, 1775, when British Redcoats clashed with colonial minutemen at Lexington and Concord in Massachusetts. This skirmish was the first battle of the Revolutionary War.

The Second Continental Congress Within three weeks, delegates from all thirteen colonies gathered in Philadelphia for the Second Continental Congress. The Continental Congress immediately assumed the powers of a central government and chose John Hancock of Massachusetts as president. Hancock was a well-known colonial leader, but he was also a wealthy merchant and thus well-placed for helping to raise funds for an army. The Congress also organized an army and navy, made plans to issue money, and appointed George Washington as commander of the Continental Army.

Delegates from the thirteen colonies gathered in this room at Independence Hall in Philadelphia on July 4, 1776 to approve the Declaration of Independence.

▲ **CRITICAL THINKING**
Explaining What gave the Continental Congress authority to declare independence?

The Second Continental Congress served as the acting government of the colonies throughout the war. It purchased supplies, negotiated treaties, and rallied support for the colonists' causes.

Declaring Independence At this point, the colonies had not yet declared their independence from Great Britain, but a movement for independence was growing rapidly. Thomas Paine, a onetime British corset maker, advocated for independence and influenced many colonists. In his pamphlet *Common Sense*, Paine argued that monarchy was a corrupt form of government and that George III was an enemy to liberty:

> **PRIMARY SOURCE**
> **The powers of governing still remaining in the hands of the [king], . . . And as he hath shown himself such an inveterate enemy to liberty, and discovered such a thirst for arbitrary power, is he, or is he not, a proper man to say to these colonies, 'You shall make no laws but what I please!'"**
>
> —Thomas Paine

Samuel Adams of Boston also influenced many colonists with his essays, letters, and articles on the struggle with the British. Adams was a natural-born politician with an independent mind. In April 1776, with the war almost a year old and no declaration of independence from the colonies, Adams was bewildered and frustrated. In a letter to a friend, he wrote:

> **PRIMARY SOURCE**
> **Is not America already independent? Why then not declare it? . . . Can Nations at War be said to be dependent either upon the other? . . . Upon what Terms will Britain be reconciled with America? . . . [S]he will be reconciled upon our abjectly submitting to Tyranny, and asking and receiving Pardon for resisting it. Will this redound to the Honor or the Safety of America? Surely no."**
>
> —Letter from Samuel Adams, April 3, 1776

In June 1776, Richard Henry Lee of Virginia introduced a resolution in the Continental Congress that "these United Colonies are, and of right ought to be, free and independent states." The Congress approved Lee's resolution on July 2 and the colonies officially broke with Great Britain.

After Lee's resolution, the Congress named a committee of John Adams, Benjamin Franklin, Thomas Jefferson, Robert Livingston, and Roger Sherman to prepare a written declaration of independence. The committee asked Thomas Jefferson, a Virginia planter known for his writing skills, to write the **draft**. When they reviewed his draft, there was considerable debate. A few passages were removed and some editorial changes were made. On July 4, the Congress approved the final draft. John Hancock, the president of the Congress, was the first to sign the document, which eventually held the signatures of all 56 delegates.

Key Parts of the Declaration The American Declaration of Independence is one of the most famous documents in history. It stirred the hearts of the American colonists. To that point, no government had been founded on the principles of human liberty and **consent** of the governed.

In the Declaration of Independence, Jefferson drew on the ideas of John Locke and other philosophers to explain the colonists' need for freedom. The

draft outline or first copy

consent permission or approval

Declaration explained the reasons the American colonies were angry with the British government and confirmed why revolution was justified.

The Declaration consists of four parts. The first paragraph, or Preamble, describes the source of the basic rights Americans enjoy as "the Laws of Nature" and "Nature's God." In philosophy, the law of nature, or natural law, is a system of moral principles regarded as the basis for all human conduct. For many, Jefferson's statement means that the rights set forth in the Declaration are not created by people but derive from higher powers and should never be violated.

The Preamble is followed by a statement of purpose and basic **human rights** derived from the laws of nature. This section on the declaration of natural rights defines and explains the unalienable rights that cannot be taken away and the right of people to resist illegitimate government and change or abolish it. It reads in part: "We hold these truths to be self-evident, that all men are created equal, that they are endowed by their Creator with certain unalienable Rights, that among these are Life, Liberty and the pursuit of Happiness. That to secure these rights, Governments are instituted among Men, deriving their just powers from the consent of the governed, That whenever any Form of Government becomes destructive of these ends, it is the Right of the People to alter or abolish it."

human rights rights that are believed to belong justifiably to every person

the DECLARATION of INDEPENDENCE

Read the following excerpts from the Declaration of Independence. Then complete the graphic organizer. Explain what each means in your own words and describe what influenced these ideas.

CRITICAL THINKING

1. Paraphrasing Restate each quote from the Declaration in your own words in the middle column.

2. Interpreting After you read this lesson, think about which thinkers and events influenced these different sections of the document. List those influences in the third column of your graphic organizer.

Text of the Declaration of Independence	In Your Own Words	Influences and Events
"When in the Course of human events, it becomes necessary for one people to dissolve the political bands which have connected them with another, and to assume among the powers of the earth, the separate and equal station to which the Laws of Nature and of Nature's God entitle them . . ."		
"We hold these truths to be self-evident, that all men are created equal, that they are endowed by their Creator with certain unalienable Rights, that among these are Life, Liberty, and pursuit of Happiness."		
"That to secure these rights, Governments are instituted among Men, deriving their just powers from the consent of the governed."		
"He has kept among us, in times of peace, Standing Armies without the Consent of our legislature."		
"For imposing Taxes on us without our Consent. . . For depriving us in many cases, of the benefits of Trial by Jury. . . For suspending our own Legislatures."		
"In every stage of these Oppressions We have Petitioned for Redress in the most humble terms. Our repeated Petitions have been answered only by repeated injury."		

The third section of the Declaration lists specific complaints or grievances against George III, and each item describes a violation of the colonists' political, civil, and economic liberties. These paragraphs were designed to justify the break with Great Britain.

The conclusion states the colonists' determination to separate from Great Britain. Their efforts to reach a peaceful solution had failed, leaving them no choice but to declare their independence.

The Declaration was rarely mentioned during the debates creating the Constitution. Yet, as time passed, the Declaration has come to be seen by many as the key guide to understanding the Constitution and the values embodied in it. This is a view shared with Abraham Lincoln, who declared the Declaration to be the foundation of his own political philosophy. In later years, Jefferson himself wrote: "I did not consider it any part of my charge to invent new ideas, but to place before mankind the common sense of the subject in terms so plain and firm as to command their assent. . . . It was intended to be an expression of the American mind."

The First States and the First State Constitutions The Declaration of Independence recognized the changes taking place in the colonies. One of the most important was the transformation into states subject to no higher authority. Thus, the states saw themselves as independent and sovereign.

About two months before the Declaration of Independence, the Second Continental Congress had instructed the colonies to form "such governments as shall . . . best conduce [lead] to the happiness and safety of their constituents." By the end of 1776, 10 states had adopted written constitutions. Within a few years, each state had a new constitution or had converted old colonial charters into a constitution.

Most of the new state constitutions contained a bill of rights defining citizens' personal liberties. All recognized the people as the sole source of authority in a limited government. There was not yet a formal government uniting all the states or a United States of America.

✓ **READING PROGRESS CHECK**

Identifying Central Issues What specific demands were outlined in the Declaration of Independence?

LESSON 2 REVIEW

Reviewing Vocabulary
1. *Making Connections* How are the terms *revenue* and *levy* related in the text? Be sure to define both terms in your answer.

Using Your Graphic Organizer
2. *Determining Cause and Effect* Use your completed graphic organizer to summarize the causes of the American independence movement.

Answering the Guiding Questions
3. *Describing* What conditions prompted the American colonists to declare independence from Britain?

4. *Identifying* What complaints did the colonists list in the Declaration of Independence, and what freedoms did they want guaranteed?

Writing About Government
5. *Informative/Explanatory* What is the right of resistance to illegitimate government and why is it important to American values? Give two examples of American colonists' activities to oppose British policies. Compare and contrast those to modern protest movements.

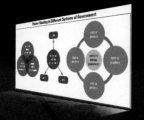

(c) Northwind/North Wind Picture Archives

LESSON 3
The Articles of Confederation

Reading Help Desk

Academic Vocabulary

- ratify
- furious
- discontent

Content Vocabulary

- unicameral
- currency
- tariff
- creditor
- treaty

TAKING NOTES:

Integration of Knowledge and Ideas

PROBLEM SOLVING Use the problem-solution chart to list the problems with the Articles of Confederation. Then list possible solutions to these problems.

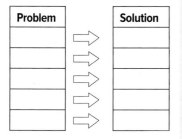

Problem		Solution
	⇨	
	⇨	
	⇨	
	⇨	
	⇨	

ESSENTIAL QUESTION

What influenced the development of our government institutions?

Under the Articles of Confederation, each state collected its own tax money and chose how to spend it. The national government could not collect taxes at all.

Today, Americans pay taxes to federal, state, and local governments. The federal government collects a lot of money in taxes and distributes much of it among the states as aid. The states do not receive the same amount of money, nor do they receive funding in proportion to their population or to the amount of federal taxes their citizens pay. For example, a study by the Tax Foundation found New Mexico received $2.03 in aid for every dollar its citizens paid in federal taxes, while Minnesota received $0.72 in aid for every dollar its citizens paid.

Consider these two different systems of taxation—the system under the Articles of Confederation and the system today.

   a. What are the possible benefits and drawbacks of the system of taxation under the Articles of Confederation?

   b. What are the possible benefits and drawbacks of today's system of taxation?

   c. Which do you think is most fair? Why?

Government Under the Articles of Confederation

GUIDING QUESTION *How did the Articles of Confederation reflect colonists' experiences with government?*

As Thomas Jefferson, Benjamin Franklin, John Adams, Robert Livingston, and Roger Sherman drafted the Declaration of Independence, another committee of the Second Continental Congress, chaired by John Dickinson, drafted a plan for the form government would take after independence. They needed to make rules about how the government would work and how the states would relate to one another. Their draft plan was debated for months, as some delegates believed the national government needed to be strong, and others favored stronger local and state governments. In the end, those who favored state powers won the debate.

The plan created a confederation, or "league of friendship," among the thirteen states, in which each retained significant independence and there was no strong central government. It was essentially a set of rules about what the national government could and could not do.

The plan, authored primarily by John Dickinson and called the Articles of Confederation, was not adopted immediately because each of the states had to approve it before it could take effect. By March 1781, all thirteen states had **ratified**, or approved, the Articles.

The plan for the central, national government was simple. It included no national court system, no president or king, and a **unicameral**, or single-chamber, legislature. Each state could send between two and seven delegates to Congress, but each state's delegates had to vote as a unit. Therefore, each state had one vote in Congress, no matter what its population. The Congress ran all aspects of the central government and had only those powers specifically mentioned in the Articles. State governments could do everything that was not specifically mentioned in the Articles.

ratify to approve

unicameral a single-chamber legislature

☑ **READING PROGRESS CHECK**

Describing What was the structure of the U.S. government under the Articles of Confederation?

ARTICLES OF CONFEDERATION

Congress and the National Government Could . . .	Congress and the National Government Could Not . . .
• Borrow or request money from the states	• Establish an executive branch, president, or king
• Declare war and peace	• Establish a national court system
• Maintain an army and navy (if states chose to contribute troops)	• Levy or collect taxes
• Make treaties and alliances with other nations	• Require states to provide money for running the national government
• Regulate affairs with Native Americans	• Regulate trade
• Establish post offices	• Force anyone to abide by the law
• Decide certain disputes between states	• Pass any law without the consent of nine states
• Coin money (though states could also create their own)	• Amend the Articles without the consent of all thirteen states

EXPLORING THE ESSENTIAL QUESTION

Remember the complaints the colonists had against the king and the relationship between the colonies and England. Look at the list of actions the national government could not take under the Articles of Confederation. Then discuss each of the questions below.

1. **Identifying Central Issues** Why do you think the leaders of the new nation did not want a president or king?
2. **Making Connections** Why do you think they did not want the national government to be able to collect taxes?
3. **Identifying** What objections would they have had to the national government regulating trade?
4. **Making Inferences** Why do you think they made it so difficult to pass national laws or to amend the Articles of Confederation?

Problems in the Confederation Period

GUIDING QUESTION *What were the strengths and weaknesses of our nation's first government?*

After the Revolutionary War, the new nation faced serious money problems. By 1787, the national government owed $40 million to foreign governments and to American soldiers who were still unpaid after the war. States, too, were financially strapped, as many had accumulated considerable debt during the war years and owed money to foreign governments.

Thirteen Sovereign States After the Revolutionary War, the thirteen states saw themselves as independent—not just from England, but from each other. People identified themselves more as "Virginians" or "South Carolinians" than as "Americans"; so, in a sense, the states were not united at all.

States created different **currencies**, which made trade among them extremely difficult. Some states also charged merchants in rival states a **tariff**, a tax on imported goods usually reserved for regulating trade with foreign countries. So, for example, farmers in New Jersey had to pay a tax to sell their vegetables in New York. States also made independent trade agreements with other countries, which caused conflict among them.

Many states ignored requests from the Congress to help fund the national government and to help repay war debts to other countries after the Revolution. The states did not consider the national debt their problem. Each respective state could decide whether to tax its own citizens and turn that money over to the national treasury. Some states owed a lot of money from the war. Others, like Virginia, had paid off their war debts and did not want to have to contribute extra money to help other states pay their **creditors**, or people to whom money is owed.

A Weak National Government The new national government faced huge problems and had little power to solve them. Congress could do little if a state refused its request to provide money. With no standing army and no power to regulate trade, it appeared weak in the eyes of foreign countries. These problems were exacerbated when the Congress issued paper money that was considered worthless because its value was highly inflated.

Congress passed very few laws because each bill could become law only if delegates from nine of the thirteen states voted for it. Since each state had only a single vote, the votes of any five of the smaller states could block a measure the larger states wanted. Congress could not even force anyone to obey the laws it did pass and could only advise and request that the states comply.

Finally, the government had no national court system and relied on state courts to enforce and interpret national laws. The lack of a court system made it difficult for the central government to settle disputes among the states, which threatened the peace and tranquility of the union.

After a few years, it had become clear that the Confederation could not effectively deal with many of the young nation's problems. The constraints on the central government meant that it simply could not effectively coordinate the actions of the states.

Achievements Despite its weaknesses, the Confederation made some important contributions to the new nation. In 1783 the Confederation signed a peace **treaty** with Britain, which recognized American independence. Land acquired from Britain—including all land from the Atlantic coast to the Mississippi River and from the Great Lakes and Canada to what is now the northern boundary of Florida—greatly enlarged the size of the young nation.

The Confederation's greatest success was in establishing a fair and consistent policy for settling and developing the lands west of the Appalachian

currency a system of money in general use in a particular country

tariff a tax on imported goods usually reserved for regulating trade with foreign countries

creditor a person to whom money is owed

treaty a formally concluded and ratified agreement between countries

THE EUROZONE

The Eurozone is an economic and political union of 17 European countries that all use the same currency, the Euro. The member countries each have their own governments, laws, and traditions, but have ceded some of their fiscal sovereignty to the European Union.

▶ **CRITICAL THINKING**

Researching Investigate the similarities and differences between the United States during the Articles of Confederation and the Eurozone today. Pay attention to issues of trade barriers, currency, monetary policy, and what happens when one state or country faces economic crisis. Based on your findings, predict whether the Eurozone will divide or unify its member countries in the future.

Mountains, one of the most hotly debated issues of the era. Congress passed two important laws that set out how the lands would be organized.

The first of these laws, the Land Ordinance of 1785, allowed the government to survey and divide the Northwest Territory into townships of equal acreage. One section of each township was reserved for public education and the other sections would be sold at auction, providing much needed revenue. The second law, the Northwest Ordinance of 1787, said that once these areas reached certain population levels, they could appoint a governor and judges, elect legislators, and achieve statehood on an equal basis with the original thirteen states.

Congress also set up the departments of Foreign Affairs, War, Marine, and the Treasury, each under a single permanent secretary. This development set a precedent for the creation of cabinet departments under the Constitution of 1787.

✓ **READING PROGRESS CHECK**

Evaluating What problems were created by the Articles of Confederation? What were the achievements of the Articles of Confederation?

Need for a Stronger National Government

GUIDING QUESTION *What events led to the dismantling of the Articles of Confederation and the call for a Constitutional Convention?*

The problems caused by a weak national government eventually led to the dismantling of the Articles of Confederation. A citizens' rebellion in Massachusetts known as Shays's Rebellion soon led to a Constitutional Convention.

Shays's Rebellion In Massachusetts, the state government increased taxes on the citizens to pay the state's war debts. At the same time, an economic depression and bad harvests left many farmers and merchants angry and in debt. Some creditors refused to accept payments in currency they thought was worthless. Some farmers were forced to give their property to the government. Others were sent to debtor's prison.

In 1786 armed groups of farmers marched to several courts and closed them down, preventing them from hearing foreclosure proceedings. Daniel Shays, a former captain in the Revolutionary Army, led a group of men that closed the Massachusetts state Supreme Court and advanced on a federal arsenal in Springfield.

The Massachusetts militia confronted and fired on the uprising, ending the rebellion. However, the rebellion spread to several states. In some places, states required creditors to forgive or excuse debts, which made creditors **furious**. The unrest frightened American leaders, who saw the weak national government as vulnerable to anarchy. To the **discontented** farmers, the government seemed unresponsive to the will of the people. Many Americans were now ready to see a strong national government. As Henry Knox expressed in a letter to George Washington: "This dreadful situation has alarmed every man of principle and property in New England. . . . What [will] give us security against the violence of lawless men? Our government must be [strengthened], changed, or altered to secure our lives and property."

A Move to Revise the Articles In 1787, a few months after Shays's Rebellion, delegates from the states began meeting to propose changes to the Articles of Confederation to help regulate trade and to make the national government more effective. They called for a convention of all states in Philadelphia.

Congress gave its consent to the meeting for the sole purpose of revising the Articles of Confederation. After months of debate, however, they abandoned the Articles of Confederation and decided to create an entirely new government, with a new guiding document, the Constitution.

☑ **READING PROGRESS CHECK**

Interpreting Significance What was the importance of Shays's Rebellion? To what change did it lead?

In the 1780s, Massachusetts government authorities jailed debtor farmers or seized their property. Daniel Shays led armed men to capture and close the courts, stopping land confiscations.

▲ CRITICAL THINKING
Speculating Why might the states have been reluctant to give up some sovereignty to a central government?

furious angry

discontent unhappiness

Northwind/North Wind Picture Archives

LESSON 3 REVIEW

Reviewing Vocabulary
1. *Defining* Restate the following sentence, defining the terms *currencies* and *tariffs* in your answer. "Under the Articles of Confederation, states had different currencies and charged rival states tariffs."

Using Your Graphic Organizer
2. *Outlining* Using your completed graphic organizer, outline a new plan of government that remedies the problems of the Articles of Confederation.

Answering the Guiding Questions
3. *Analyzing* How did the Articles of Confederation reflect colonists' experiences with government?

4. *Classifying* What were the strengths and weaknesses of our nation's first government?

5. *Identifying Cause and Effect* What events led to the dismantling of the Articles of Confederation and the call for a Constitutional Convention?

Writing About Government
6. *Informative/Explanatory* What experiences and conditions led the colonists to structure the Articles of Confederation as they did?

(l to r) BBC Worldwide Learning; ©North Wind Picture Archives; Independence National Historical Park/National Park Services

Interact with these digital assets and others in lesson 4

✓ **INTERACTIVE CHART**
Articles of Confederation Provisions

✓ **INTERACTIVE IMAGE**
Rising Sun Chair

✓ **SELF-CHECK QUIZ**

✓ **VIDEO**
Arguments over Ratification

netw⊙rks
TRY IT YOURSELF ONLINE

ReadingHelp Desk

Academic Vocabulary

- **populous**
- **export**

Content Vocabulary

- **bicameral**
- **interstate commerce**
- **extralegal**

TAKING NOTES:

Key Ideas and Details

CONTRASTING Use a graphic organizer like the one below to contrast the interests of the small states and the large states.

STATE INTERESTS

Small States   Large States

LESSON 4
Creating the Constitution

ESSENTIAL QUESTION

What influenced the development of our government institutions?

Assume that you move to an island that has never been inhabited before now. Several thousand other people have also moved there in the past year. Everyone agrees that the island needs to have some rules and someone needs to be in charge. You must create a plan to choose the leaders in the fairest way possible. Consider the following questions as you create your plan:

a. Who should get to decide what the rules should be? Options include: only the people who have been there the longest and know the island well, only the most educated people, only those above a certain age, or everyone.

b. Should families vote as a unit, or can each person in the family get his or her own vote?

c. Should all families get one vote, regardless of their size? Or should families with six children get more votes than families with two kids?

Once you have developed a plan that you think is fair, discuss it with your classmates. Try to reach a consensus about how to chose the island's leaders will be chosen.

The Constitutional Convention: Agreements and Compromises

GUIDING QUESTION *How did the Constitutional Convention reflect compromises between the states' competing interests?*

In May 1787, the Constitutional Convention began the daunting task of crafting a new system of government. The state legislatures sent 55 delegates to Philadelphia, many of whom had a great deal of practical experience in politics and government. George Washington and Benjamin Franklin both played active roles in the debates at the convention. Two other Pennsylvanians made important contributions, too. Gouverneur Morris wrote the final draft of the Constitution, and James Wilson did important work on the details of the document. James Madison of Virginia was the author of the basic plan of government that the convention eventually adopted. His careful notes are our major source of information about the convention's work.

The convention began by unanimously choosing George Washington to preside over the meetings. It was decided that each state would have one vote on all questions, and a simple majority of the states present would make decisions. The public and press were prevented from attending the sessions, in the hope that the private setting would enable the delegates to talk freely.

After deciding to abandon the Articles of Confederation, the delegates reached a consensus on many basic issues of forming a new government. They all favored the ideas of limited and representative government and agreed that the powers of the national government should be divided among legislative, executive, and judicial branches. They all believed it was necessary to limit the power of the states to coin money or interfere with creditors' rights. And all of them agreed that they should strengthen the national government.

The great debates and compromises of the convention were not over these fundamental questions—rather, they dealt with how to put these ideas into practice.

The Virginia Plan The debates opened with a proposal from the Virginia delegation, which laid out a plan for a strong national government. The plan proposed a government based on three principles. First, the government would have a strong national legislature with two chambers— the lower one to be chosen by the people and the upper chamber to be chosen by the lower. The number of legislators would vary from state to state and would be determined by how many people lived in the state. Furthermore, the legislature would have the power to bar any state laws it found unconstitutional. Second, a strong executive would be chosen by the national legislature. Third, a national judiciary would be appointed by the legislature.

The delegates debated the Virginia Plan for more than two weeks. Delegates from the smaller states quickly realized that the larger, more **populous** states would be in control of a strong national government under this plan. The smaller states wanted a less powerful government with more independence for the states.

populous having a large population

CHART

ARTICLES of CONFEDERATION PROVISIONS

After deciding to abandon the Articles of Confederation, the delegates at the Constitutional Convention reached a consensus on many basic issues of forming a new government.

Provision from Articles of Confederation	Replacement from the Convention
Delegates to Congress shall be annually appointed by each state.	
Each state shall have one vote.	
The treasury of the United States shall be supplied by the several states in proportion to the value of their land and property. Only the states may levy taxes.	
A president shall be elected annually by the members of Congress.	

CRITICAL THINKING
Analyzing Read each of the provisions from the Articles of Confederation in the table. In the right column, explain the agreement reached during the Constitutional Convention that replaced this feature of government under the Articles. Why did the Constitutional Convention replace these provisions?

The New Jersey Plan The delegates for the small states made a counterproposal. The New Jersey Plan called for keeping two major features of the Articles of Confederation. First, the government would have a unicameral legislature with one vote for each state. This made all states equally powerful, regardless of their population. Second, the nation would continue as a confederation of sovereign states.

Congress, however, would be strengthened by having the power to impose taxes and regulate trade. A weak executive, consisting of more than one person, would be elected by Congress, and a national judiciary with limited power would be appointed by the executive.

As the summer wore on, the convention became deadlocked over the question of the representation of states in Congress. The debate was bitter, and the convention was in danger of dissolving.

The Connecticut Compromise Finally, a special committee designed a compromise. Called the Connecticut Compromise, or the Great Compromise, this plan was adopted after a long debate. The compromise suggested that the legislative branch be **bicameral**, or have two houses—a House of Representatives, with the number of representatives based on each state's population, and a Senate, with two members from each state. The larger states would have an advantage in the House of Representatives, where representation would be based on population. Congress would be able to impose taxes, and all laws concerning taxing and spending would originate in the House. The smaller states would be protected in the Senate, with equal representation and state legislatures electing the senators.

Compromises About the Presidency There was further disagreement over whether the president should be elected directly by the people, by the Congress, or by state legislatures. As a compromise, the delegates finally settled on the Electoral College system, which is still used today. In this system, voters from each state select electors to choose the president. The president's four-year term was a compromise between those who wanted a longer term and those who feared a long term would give a president too much power.

☑ **READING PROGRESS CHECK**

Explaining What was the Connecticut Compromise? Which elements of the Virginia Plan and the New Jersey Plan were incorporated into the compromise?

Disputes Over Slavery

GUIDING QUESTION *How did the Constitutional Convention deal with slavery, one of the most divisive issues of the period?*

James Madison's notes tell us that the delegates disagreed about how to handle slavery. At the time of the convention, several Northern states were working on plans to abolish slavery. Many delegates were opposed to slavery and some wanted it abolished, but it was clear that the Southern states would never accept the Constitution if it interfered with slavery. In the end, the delegates did not deal with the issue. The Constitution mentions the slave trade and escaped enslaved persons but does not address the legality of owning slaves. In fact, the Constitution doesn't include the word *slave* anywhere. Instead of saying "slave" or "slavery," the Constitution refers to the "importation" of people, and "persons held to service or labor."

The delegates were under no illusions that their compromises on slavery had permanently solved the question. While they compromised in order to

bicameral relative to a two-house legislative body

Political Philosophies of the Founders

John Adams	• Opposed taxation without representation • Promoted the establishment of representative state governments • Framed a three-branch government in the Massachusetts Constitution that served as a model for the federal system • Believed that the government should use the power given it to meet the needs of the individual
Alexander Hamilton	• Ideas on a strong central government helped with the shaping and ratification of the Constitution • Distrustful of the masses, Hamilton ensured that state power did not trump federal authority. • Instrumental in establishing a stable financial system for the new nation
Thomas Jefferson	• Wrote the Declaration of Independence, challenging British rule as a violation of natural law and human rights • A champion of limited government and religious freedom, Jefferson provided influential support for a bill of rights.
James Madison	• The "Father of the Constitution," Madison promoted the three-branch system of government with separation of powers and checks and balances. • His arguments helped build support for a Constitution with a strong central government. • After ratification, he wrote the amendments that became the Bill of Rights.
John Jay	• Conservative supporter of a strong central government • Helped write the Federalist Papers, promoting ratification of the Constitution • As first Chief Justice, established protocols for the Supreme Court
George Mason	• Outspoken advocate of individual freedoms • Wrote the Virginia Declaration of Rights, a precursor to the national Bill of Rights
Roger Sherman	• Conservative supporter of independence • Concerned with the process of electing officials and how to balance power within government, Sherman proposed a compromise at the Constitutional Convention that led to the adoption of a bicameral legislature with a Senate and House of Representatives.
James Wilson	• Advocated a strong federal government with three independent branches • Favored the direct election of members of Congress by the people • Argued effectively for ratification of the Constitution

CRITICAL THINKING

1. Comparing What did John Adams, James Madison, and James Wilson have in common?

2. Synthesizing Choose two Founders with different philosophies or focuses, and explain how their contributions combined to improve the U.S. government.

create the new government, their refusal to deal with slavery left it to later generations of Americans to resolve.

The Three-Fifths Compromise There was profound disagreement about how to count enslaved persons in matters of representation and taxation. Almost one-third of the people living in the Southern states were enslaved African Americans. Delegates from these states wanted enslaved persons to be counted the same as free people to give the South more representation in Congress. At the same time, the Southern states did not want enslaved persons counted at all for the purpose of levying taxes. Because few enslaved persons lived in the North, Northern states took the opposite position. They wanted enslaved persons counted for tax purposes but not for representation.

The Three-Fifths Compromise settled this deadlock. Instead of counting all of the enslaved people, only three-fifths were to be counted for both tax purposes and for representation. Enslaved people were counted in this manner until 1868. By that date, the three-fifths provision had been nullified by the passage of the Thirteenth Amendment abolishing slavery and the Fourteenth Amendment, which required counting a state's entire population for purposes of representation.

Commerce and the Slave Trade A third compromise resolved a dispute over commerce and the slave trade—not slavery itself, but the continuing trade of enslaved people. The Northern states wanted the federal government to have complete control over trade with other nations, but the Southern states were afraid that the federal government would interfere with the slave trade. Depending heavily on agricultural **exports**, the Southern states also feared that business interests in the North would have enough votes in Congress to impose export taxes or ratify trade agreements that would hurt the South.

exports a commodity, article, or service sold to another country

To compromise, the delegates determined that Congress would have the power to regulate both **interstate commerce** (trade between the states) and commerce with foreign countries, but Congress could not ban the slave trade before 1808. To protect the South's exports, Congress was also prohibited from imposing export taxes. As a result, the United States is one of the few nations in the world today that does not directly tax the goods that it exports.

interstate commerce trade between the states

☑ **READING PROGRESS CHECK**

Describing What was the Three-Fifths Compromise? Why did it satisfy states in the North and the South?

★ ***We the People:*** Making a Difference

GEORGE MASON

George Mason refused to sign the draft Constitution, in part because it included a clause that prohibited the government from restricting the slave trade for at least 20 years. While Mason often spoke strongly against slavery, he held many enslaved persons and did not set any free. His stand against the Constitution and statements against slavery cost him many relationships, including his friendship with George Washington.

In 1787, Mason delivered these remarks to the Constitutional Convention:

"Every master of slaves is born a petty tyrant. [Enslaved persons] bring the judgment of heaven on a Country. As nations cannot be rewarded or punished in the next world they must be in this. By an inevitable chain of causes & effects, providence punishes national sins, by national calamities. [It is] essential in every point of view that the Genl. Govt. should have power to prevent the increase of slavery."

EXPLORING THE ESSENTIAL QUESTION

1. **Making Connections** Do you know anyone who has taken an unpopular stand on an important issue? What did that person risk by taking a stand?

2. **Researching** Investigate George Mason's objections to the Constitution and how he took action to oppose its adoption. Write a brief essay explaining what you have learned.

Ratifying the Constitution

GUIDING QUESTION *How did supporters and opponents of the Constitution argue for and against its adoption?*

By September 17, 1787, the Constitution was complete. Thirty-nine delegates signed the document, including the aging Ben Franklin, who had to be helped to the table to sign. Before the new Constitution could become law, however, it had to be ratified by 9 of the 13 states.

The political debate over ratification lasted until May 29, 1790, when Rhode Island became the last state to ratify the Constitution, even though the Constitution went into effect in June 1788 when New Hampshire became the ninth state to ratify it.

The Federalists and Anti-Federalists The question of ratification quickly divided the people in the states. One group, known as the Federalists, favored the Constitution and was led by many of the Founders. Their support typically came from merchants and others in the cities and coastal regions. The other group, called the Anti-Federalists, opposed the new Constitution and drew much of their support from the inland farmers and laborers, who feared a strong national government. The Anti-Federalists criticized the Constitution for having been drafted in secret. They claimed the document was **extralegal**, not sanctioned by law, because Congress had authorized the convention only to revise the old Articles of Confederation and not to form a new government. They further argued that the Constitution took important powers from the states.

extralegal not sanctioned by law

The Anti-Federalists' strongest argument, however, was that the Constitution lacked a bill of rights to protect citizens from their own government. The convention had, in fact, considered adding a list of people's rights. In their discussions, they concluded logically that it was not necessary to have a bill of rights, reasoning that the Constitution did not authorize the government to violate the rights of the people.

This was not good enough for the Anti-Federalists, who warned that without a bill of rights, a strong national government might take away the rights that were won in the Revolution. They demanded that the new Constitution clearly guarantee the people's freedoms. One of the strongest opponents of the Constitution was Patrick Henry, the passionate delegate from Virginia. He voiced his position eloquently:

> ### PRIMARY SOURCE
> **The necessity of a Bill of Rights appears to me to be greater in this government than ever it was in any government before. . . . All rights not expressly and unequivocally reserved to the people are impliedly and incidentally relinquished to rulers. . . . If you intend to reserve your unalienable rights, you must have the most express stipulation; for . . . If the people do not think it necessary to reserve them, they will be supposed to be given up."**
> —Patrick Henry, 1788

The Federalists, on the other hand, claimed that only a strong national government could protect the nation from enemies abroad and solve the country's internal problems. The Federalists also pointed out that eight states already had bills of rights in their state constitutions. Eventually, however, the

Ben Franklin remarked that during the long debates at the Constitutional Convention he looked at the sun on the back of George Washington's chair and wondered whether it was rising or setting, the latter signifying a possible end to the new nation. He commented that by end of the meetings, he was convinced it was a rising sun.

▶ **CRITICAL THINKING**
Analyzing Why did Ben Franklin say that the sun on the chair was rising? What made him optimistic?

Federalists promised to add a bill of rights as the first order of business when the new government met.

Progress Toward Ratification
With the promise of a bill of rights, the tide turned in favor of the Constitution, as many small states ratified it quickly because they were pleased with equal representation in the new Senate. By 1788, the legislatures in Virginia and New York had not yet held a vote on the new Constitution. Everyone knew that without the support of those two large and powerful states, the Constitution would not succeed. The Federalists won in a close vote in Virginia on June 25, 1788.

To help win the battle in New York, vocal supporters published more than 80 essays defending the new Constitution. Alexander Hamilton and James Madison wrote most of the essays, called *The Federalist Papers*. In *The Federalist* No. 39, Madison defined a republic as "a government which derives all its powers directly or indirectly from the great body of the people, and is administered by persons holding their offices. . . for a limited period." Madison brilliantly answered the opposition's fears that a republic had to be a small government. In *The Federalist* No. 10, he wrote: "Extend the sphere, and you take in a greater variety of parties and interests; you make it less probable that a majority of the whole will have a common motive to invade the rights of other citizens." On July 26, 1788, the Federalists in New York won by three votes.

The New Government Begins Its Work Once the new government was established, George Washington was elected president and John Adams vice president. Voters also elected senators and representatives. On March 4, 1789, Congress met for the first time in Federal Hall in New York City, the temporary capital. To fulfill the promises made during the fight for ratification, James Madison introduced a set of amendments during the first session. Congress approved 12 amendments and the states ratified 10 of them in 1791, which became known as the Bill of Rights.

☑ **READING PROGRESS CHECK**
Assessing Do you think having a bill of rights was necessary? Why or why not?

LESSON 4 REVIEW

Reviewing Vocabulary
1. ***Defining*** Explain what the power to regulate interstate commerce means.

Using Your Graphic Organizer
2. ***Contrasting*** Using your completed graphic organizer, make a multimedia presentation that contrasts the interests of the small states and the interests of the large states during the Constitutional Convention.

Answering the Guiding Questions
3. ***Analyzing*** How did the Constitutional Convention reflect compromises between the states' competing interests?

4. ***Explaining*** How did the Constitutional Convention deal with slavery, one of the most divisive issues of the period?

5. ***Comparing*** How did supporters and opponents of the Constitution argue for and against its adoption?

Writing About Government
6. ***Argument*** In your opinion, what were the Anti-Federalists' strongest arguments? Put yourself in the Federalists' shoes—how would you respond? Write a paragraph in response to the Anti-Federalists.

Texas  Johnson (1989)

During the Republican National Convention in 1984, Gregory Lee Johnson participated in a group political demonstration. The demonstrators were opposed to nuclear weapons. One demonstrator took an American flag from a flagpole and gave it to Johnson. The demonstration ended in front of the Dallas, Texas, city hall, where Johnson set fire to the American flag. While the flag burned, protesters chanted "America, the red, white, and blue, we spit on you." There were no injuries or threats of injury during the demonstration.

Johnson was arrested and charged with violating a Texas state law that banned the desecration of the American flag in a way that would seriously offend one or more persons likely to observe his action. Several people were offended by the flag burning and said so in court. Johnson was convicted, but he appealed, saying that the Texas law violated the First Amendment, which protects free speech.

ISSUE

Does a law banning the burning of the flag violate the First Amendment?

OPINION A Johnson's actions in this case are not protected by the First Amendment, and the state of Texas should be able to punish him for burning the flag. For 200 years, the American flag has occupied a unique position as the symbol of the nation. Congress and many states have enacted laws prohibiting the misuse and mutilation of the American flag. Even if the action of flag burning can be interpreted as speech, we do not have to allow all speech. There must be reasonable limits. There are other ways that Johnson could have expressed his views.

Texas did not punish Johnson's message, just the means he used to convey it. The flag symbolizes more than national unity. It has strong significance for war veterans and their families. It symbolizes our shared values of freedom, equal opportunity, and religious tolerance. It is in the government's interest to protect this important American symbol. It is not too much to ask that protesters use other means of speech to express their ideas. Johnson's conviction should be affirmed.

OPINION B Johnson's actions in this case should be protected as free speech. While the First Amendment literally protects speech, the Supreme Court has long recognized that speech can be more than the spoken or written word. Actions are symbolic speech when the actor intends to convey a particular message and there is a great likelihood that those watching would understand the message. Johnson burned the flag to express an idea—his dissatisfaction with the country's policies.

Johnson's actions did not incite violence or disrupt the peace. While it is important for the government to preserve the flag as a symbol, it is more important to ensure Americans' rights to protest when they disagree with the government. The government may not prohibit expression simply because society finds the ideas presented offensive. In this case, the government has not provided enough justification for punishing Johnson's speech. His conviction should be overturned.

EXPLORING THE ESSENTIAL QUESTION

Evaluating Read each of the two sample opinions in this case. Decide which one you think should be the majority (winning) opinion, and which one you think should be the dissenting opinion. Explain your choice.

STUDY GUIDE

GOVERNMENT IN COLONIAL AMERICA
LESSON 1

English Bill of Rights and English Law

Limited and representative government

Enlightenment ideas: Social Contract and Natural Rights

Colonial Governments
• Written constitutions
• Colonial legislatures

UNITING FOR INDEPENDENCE LESSON 2

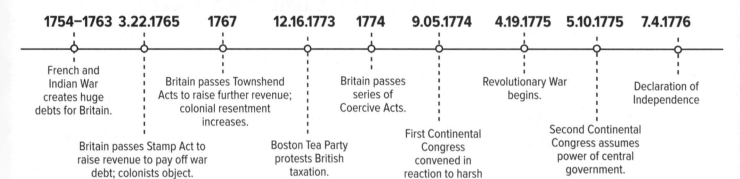

| 1754–1763 | 3.22.1765 | 1767 | 12.16.1773 | 1774 | 9.05.1774 | 4.19.1775 | 5.10.1775 | 7.4.1776 |

French and Indian War creates huge debts for Britain.

Britain passes Stamp Act to raise revenue to pay off war debt; colonists object.

Britain passes Townshend Acts to raise further revenue; colonial resentment increases.

Boston Tea Party protests British taxation.

Britain passes series of Coercive Acts.

First Continental Congress convened in reaction to harsh British policies.

Revolutionary War begins.

Second Continental Congress assumes power of central government.

Declaration of Independence

THE ARTICLES OF CONFEDERATION LESSON 3

| Created a weak national government | Congress cannot tax or regulate interstate commerce. | No common currency | Each state gets one vote in Congress, no matter its size. | No national executive or judicial branch |

CREATING THE CONSTITUTION LESSON 4

VIRGINIA PLAN

Bicameral legislature

Number of legislators varies according to state population

NEW JERSEY PLAN

Unicameral legislature

Each state gets one vote regardless of population.

CONNECTICUT COMPROMISE

Bicameral legislature

Representation in House of Representatives based on state population

Equal representation in Senate, with two members from each state

Directions: On a separate sheet of paper, answer the questions below. Make sure you read carefully and answer all parts of the questions.

Lesson Review

Lesson 1

1 ***Identifying*** What are three key ideas found in the English Bill of Rights? Explain the importance of each to America's founding.

2 ***Describing*** What practices established by colonial governments became a basic part of our current system of government?

Lesson 2

3 ***Summarizing*** What tasks did the Second Continental Congress accomplish?

4 ***Describing*** Which unalienable rights are included in the Declaration of Independence? Describe each.

Lesson 3

5 ***Examining*** What achievements were made under the Articles of Confederation?

6 ***Identifying*** What were some things Congress and the national government could not do under the Articles of Confederation?

Lesson 4

7 ***Stating*** State the position of the Federalists and Anti-Federalists. What were the differences between them?

8 ***Examining*** What were the major debates and compromises that affected the creation of the U.S. Constitution?

9 ***Analyzing*** Why was the U.S. Constitution amended to include a bill of rights? Why was a bill of rights not included initially?

Library of Congress, Prints & Photographs Division [LC-USZC4-5286]

ANSWERING THE ESSENTIAL QUESTIONS

Review your answers to the introductory questions at the beginning of each lesson. Then answer the Essential Questions based on what you learned in the chapter. Have your answers changed?

10 ***Identifying Central Issues*** What influenced the development of our government institutions?

11 ***Explaining*** Why and how did the colonists declare independence?

DBQ Interpreting Political Cartoons

Use the political cartoon to answer the following questions.

THE HORSE AMERICA, *throwing his Master.*

12 ***Analyzing Visuals*** What symbol represents the colonies in this 1779 cartoon? Who do you think the rider on the horse is?

13 ***Supporting Perspectives*** What is the message of this cartoon?

Critical Thinking

14 ***Drawing Conclusions*** Europe experienced an intellectual movement known as the Enlightenment during the late 1600s and early 1700s. What effect did the Enlightenment and Enlightenment thinkers such as Charles-Louis de Montesquieu have on the American Revolution and the founding of the United States?

Need Extra Help?

If You've Missed Question	1	2	3	4	5	6	7	8	9	10	11	12	13	14
Go to page	37	39	45	47	50	50	58	55	59	36	45	46	46	38

Directions: On a separate sheet of paper, answer the questions below. Make sure you read carefully and answer all parts of the questions.

15 *Identifying* Consider the English political and legal heritage, including English common law and constitutionalism, republicanism, the Magna Carta, and the English Bill of Rights, and identify at least three reasons it was important to the Declaration of Independence and the founding of the United States.

16 *Interpreting* In the Declaration of Independence, Thomas Jefferson wrote of the "Laws of Nature" and "Nature's God." Explain what Jefferson meant by these phrases.

17 *Considering Perspectives* In your opinion, why were the Articles of Confederation an unworkable or unrealistic plan of government? Discuss at least two articles and explain your reasons.

18 *Synthesizing* How do you account for the contradiction between the constitutional acceptance of slavery and the ideals set forth in both the Declaration of Independence and the Constitution?

19 *Evaluating* The Constitutional Convention served to create a new system of government. James Madison and Alexander Hamilton were coauthors of the *Federalist Papers*, a collection of essays that defended the new Constitution. Evaluate the impact of the political philosophies of Madison and Hamilton as explained in the *Federalist Papers*.

DBQ Analyzing Primary Sources

Read the excerpts and answer the questions that follow.

PRIMARY SOURCE

"It is time now to recollect that the powers were merely advisory and recommendatory; that they were so meant by the States and so understood by the convention; and that the latter have accordingly planned and proposed a Constitution which is to be of no more consequence than the paper on which it is written, unless it be stamped with the approbation of those to whom it is addressed."
— *The Federalist* No. 40, James Madison

"The important distinction so well understood in America between a Constitution established by the people and unalterable by the government, and a law established by the government and alterable by the government, seems to have been little understood and less observed in any other country."
— *The Federalist* No. 53, James Madison

20 *Analyzing Historical Documents* How do these quotes support James Madison's desire to see the Constitution ratified in the states?

Social Studies Skills

21 *Technology* Use the Library of Congress website to research political cartoons. Then create a political cartoon that might have appeared in a colonial newspaper.

22 *Presentation Skills* Find an editorial or letter to the editor in a newspaper or magazine that expresses a point of view about a political issue. Examples might be a country seeking independence or experiencing revolution. Write a paragraph analyzing the author's point of view and comparing it to your own. Explain why you agree or disagree with the author. Present your findings in class.

Research and Presentation

23 *Identifying* Create a multimedia presentation about the Founders. Be sure to include the following individuals in your presentation: John Adams, Alexander Hamilton, John Jay, Thomas Jefferson, James Madison, George Mason, Roger Sherman, George Washington, and James Wilson. Your presentation should include a brief biography, a photograph, and a description of the political philosophy and key accomplishments of each Founder.

24 *Narrative* The English system of law had a major influence in the colonies, especially through the ideas of Sir William Blackstone. Research Blackstone on the Internet or at your local library and write an essay that summarizes his ideas.

Need Extra Help?

If You've Missed Question	**15**	**16**	**17**	**18**	**19**	**20**	**21**	**22**	**23**	**24**
Go to page	37	47	50	57	58	58	64	64	57	37

The Constitution

ESSENTIAL QUESTIONS

- How does the U.S. Constitution structure government and divide power between the national and state governments? • Why and how has the U.S. Constitution been amended and interpreted throughout our history? • How do state constitutions and local charters structure government and protect individual rights?

Jean-Pierre De Mann/Alamy

▲ The Hall of Statues, in the National Constitution Center, includes statues of 42 delegates to the Constitutional Convention.

DEMOCRATIC VALUES

Democratic values like individual liberty, equality, limited government, consent of the governed, and justice serve as foundations for the U.S. Constitution and the government based on that Constitution. These shared values are also spelled out in documents like the Declaration of Independence and the Pledge of Allegiance. But different Americans cherish some values more highly than others. Presidential candidates often refer to the values they hold dearly and believe will connect them with voters. What values appeal most strongly to Americans? Analyze the sources and answer the questions that follow.

PRIMARY SOURCE A

Pledge of Allegiance, as modified in 1954

"I pledge allegiance to the Flag of the United States of America, and to the Republic for which it stands, one Nation under God, indivisible, with liberty and justice for all."

PRIMARY SOURCE B

▲ Eisenhower campaign button, 1956

PRIMARY SOURCE C

▲ Obama campaign button, 2008

PRIMARY SOURCE D

"We have reached a time for hope. This young century will be liberty's century. By promoting liberty abroad, we will build a safer world. By encouraging liberty at home, we will build a more hopeful America. Like generations before us, we have a calling from beyond the stars to stand for freedom. This is the everlasting dream of America and, in this place, that dream is renewed. Now we go forward grateful for our freedom, faithful to our cause, and confident in the future of the greatest nation on earth."

—George W. Bush, 2004 Republican National Convention

"As Americans, we believe we are endowed by our Creator with certain inalienable rights, rights that no man or government can take away. We insist on personal responsibility, and we celebrate individual initiative. We're not entitled to success. We have to earn it. We honor the strivers, the dreamers, the risk-takers, the entrepreneurs who have always been the driving force behind our free enterprise system, the greatest engine of growth and prosperity that the world's ever known.

But we also believe in something called citizenship—citizenship, a word at the very heart of our founding, a word at the very essence of our democracy, the idea that this country only works when we accept certain obligations to one another and to future generations."

—Barack Obama, 2012 Democratic National Convention

Source F CREDIT: Rasmussen Reports. RasmussenReports.com

SECONDARY SOURCE **F**

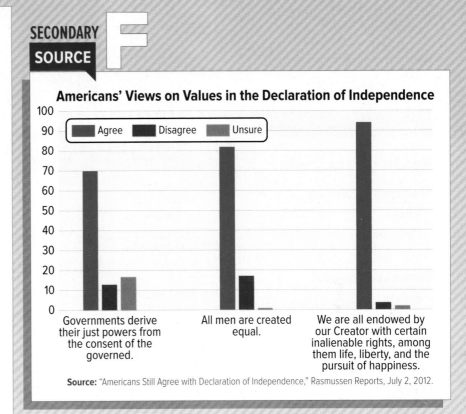

Americans' Views on Values in the Declaration of Independence

Legend: Agree · Disagree · Unsure

- Governments derive their just powers from the consent of the governed.
- All men are created equal.
- We are all endowed by our Creator with certain inalienable rights, among them life, liberty, and the pursuit of happiness.

Source: "Americans Still Agree with Declaration of Independence," Rasmussen Reports, July 2, 2012.

DBQ DOCUMENT-BASED QUESTIONS

1. **Identifying** What values are reflected in these documents?

2. **Comparing** How do the values expressed on the 1956 campaign button compare to the values expressed on the 2008 button? Do you consider all of these to be democratic values?

3. **Analyzing** What inferences, if any, can you make about American attitudes toward democratic values based on the polling data?

4. **Synthesizing** Using these sources and your own knowledge, describe how democratic values are invoked by presidential candidates and for what purpose.

5. **Evaluating** Based on your evaluation of the information provided here, what questions would you like to ask Americans about their commitment to the values on which the Constitution is based? Why would you ask those questions?

WHAT WILL YOU DO?

Imagine you are a member of a campaign team. Which value would you stress? Why? Design a campaign button using the value you selected to appeal to voters.

EXPLORE the interactive version of the analyzing primary sources feature on **Networks**.

(t to r) Jean-Pierre De Mann/Alamy; BBC Worldwide Learning

ReadingHelp Desk

Academic Vocabulary

- affect
- dynamic

Content Vocabulary

- article
- amendment

TAKING NOTES:

Key Ideas and Details

LISTING List the major principles reflected in the U.S. Constitution and briefly define each.

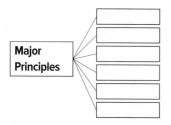

Major Principles

LESSON 1

Structure and Principles of the Constitution

ESSENTIAL QUESTION

How does the U.S. Constitution structure government and divide power between the national and state governments?

The first words of the U.S. Constitution are "We the people. . . ." The document goes on to explain why the Constitution was written and why the government is structured as it is. It also lays out rights "the people" have to be protected from the government. The Constitution was written in 1787 and became the law of the land in 1789.

a. Which "people" do you think the Founders had in mind when they created and enacted the Constitution? Explain your answers.

b. Which "people" do you think the Constitution applies to and protects now? Consider factors such as religion, race, ethnicity, gender, ability, age, nationality, citizenship, and others in your answer.

Structure of the U.S. Constitution

GUIDING QUESTION *What is the structure of the U.S. Constitution?*

When the Constitutional Convention was convened in 1787, the men who gathered to create a new system of government for the United States had been through a Revolutionary War with Britain and six years as a nation under the Articles of Confederation. Their experiences with the British monarchy and the confederation informed both their hopes and concerns for the young country.

The government under the Articles of Confederation had not worked well, partly because the Articles created a weak central government. The Founders' experiences with King George of Britain, however, made them worry that any government institution with too much power would become tyrannical. Nevertheless, although people in the thirteen individual states wanted to maintain their sovereignty, they came to understand that a central government could achieve some things more effectively than the individual states.

The solution the Founders agreed upon was a central government with limited power, where the government would be divided into three branches, with each branch exercising some control and restraint over the other two.

Furthermore, power would be divided between the central government and the states. The Constitution is a framework for our government. It presents the government's purposes, principles, powers, and limitations and tells how the government is both empowered and limited to protect the people of the nation.

Compared to the constitutions of some other countries, the United States Constitution is brief. It sets out the structure and powers of the government but does not spell out every detail of how the government should work. It is divided into three sections—the Preamble, the Articles, and the Amendments.

Preamble The Preamble, or introduction, explains why the Constitution was written and spells out the purposes of the government. You are probably familiar with the first words of the Constitution: "We the People of the United States, in Order to form a more perfect Union, establish Justice, insure domestic Tranquility, provide for the common defence, promote the general Welfare, and secure the Blessings of Liberty to ourselves and our Posterity, do ordain and establish this Constitution for the United States of America."

Articles The Constitution includes seven main sections called **articles**, each of which covers a different topic about how the government is structured. Most of the articles are divided into sections. Articles I, II, and III create the three branches of the national government—the legislative, executive, and judicial branches, respectively. Article IV explains the relationship of the states to one another and to the national government. Article V explains how the Constitution can be amended, or changed. Article VI establishes the Constitution as "the supreme Law of the Land," and Article VII addresses ratification.

article one of seven main divisions of the body of the Constitution

THE ARTICLES
of the
CONSTITUTION

◀ CRITICAL THINKING
Identifying Which article of the Constitution describes the structure of the presidency?

Article I **THE LEGISLATIVE BRANCH**
Establishes the legislative branch to make laws
- creates the Congress and describes the two houses of Congress
- describes who can serve in Congress and gives the general rules for passing laws

Article II **THE EXECUTIVE BRANCH**
Establishes an executive branch to carry out the laws that Congress passes
- describes the powers and duties of the president
- says who can become president and explains how the president and vice president are elected

Article III **THE JUDICIAL BRANCH**
Establishes the judicial branch and the Supreme Court to head it
- gives Congress the power to create lower federal courts
- describes the jurisdiction, or authority, of the Supreme Court and other federal courts

Article IV **RELATIONSHIPS AMONG THE STATES**
Describes the relationship of the states to the national government and to one another
- each state must give citizens of other states the same rights as citizens of their own state
- the national government will protect the states from foreign invasion or from unrest
- explains how new states can join the country

Article V **THE AMENDMENT PROCESS**
Explains how the Constitution can be amended, or changed

Article VI **NATIONAL SUPREMACY**
Contains the Supremacy Clause
- the Constitution, federal laws, and treaties shall be the "supreme Law of the Land"

Article VII **RATIFICATION OF THE CONSTITUTION**
Addresses the ratification of the Constitution

THE CONSTITUTIONS
OF INDIA AND THE U.S.

Compare the Preamble to the Constitution of India to the Preamble to the U.S. Constitution:

INDIA

"We, the people of India, having solemnly resolved to constitute India into a sovereign socialist secular democratic republic and to secure to all its citizens: justice, social, economic and political; liberty of thought, expression, belief, faith and worship; equality of status and of opportunity; and to promote among them all fraternity assuring the dignity of the individual and the unity and integrity of the nation; in our constituent assembly this twenty-sixth day of November, 1949, do hereby adopt, enact and give to ourselves this constitution."
—Preamble to the Constitution of India, 1949

UNITED STATES

"We the People of the United States, in Order to form a more perfect Union, establish Justice, insure domestic Tranquility, provide for the common defence, promote the general Welfare, and secure the Blessings of Liberty to ourselves and our Posterity, do ordain and establish this Constitution for the United States of America."
—The Preamble to the U.S. Constitution, 1787

India has the largest democracy in the world. It created its constitution in 1949.

The United States has the oldest written national constitution still in use.

▲ CRITICAL THINKING
Comparing and Contrasting Read both the preamble to the U.S. Constitution and to the Indian Constitution.
a. Make a list of unfamiliar words and find their definitions.
b. List which words appear in both documents.
c. With a partner, discuss which type of graphic organizer would best show how the preambles are the same and how they are different. Then create that graphic organizer.
d. Write a summary sentence or two comparing and contrasting the preambles.

amendment a change to the Constitution

Amendments The third part of the Constitution consists of **amendments**, or changes to the original document. The Constitution has been amended 27 times since it was ratified; some amendments describe the people's individual rights, while others modify some of the rules or structure for government. Several amendments extend the right to vote.

☑ READING PROGRESS CHECK

Specifying What are the purposes of Article I, Article II, and Article III?

Principles of the U.S. Constitution

GUIDING QUESTION *What principles are reflected in the U.S. Constitution?*

The Constitution is based on several fundamental principles—that the government will be limited, that power will be shared between the national government and the states, and that within the national government, power will be divided among three branches that can keep one another in check. Another fundamental principle of the Constitution is that it protects individual rights and balances those rights with pursuit of the public good. These underlying principles, as revealed in such documents as the Declaration of Independence, reflect the Founders' strongly held beliefs about the purpose of government and rights of the governed. They also reflect their experiences with Britain, the American Revolution, and the Articles of Confederation.

Popular Sovereignty and Republicanism The Constitution is based on the concept of popular sovereignty—rule by the people. The U.S. government is based upon the consent of the governed; the authority for government flows from the people. In a republican system of government, the people elect representatives to rule on their behalf.

Limited Government The principle of limited government is fundamental and essential to a democracy. One way the Constitution limits the power of the national government is by specifying not only the powers of government but also those things that the government is prohibited from doing.

Federalism The terms *federalism* and *federal system* describe the structure of American government. In this structure, power is divided between the federal, or national, government and the state governments. Within each state, the local governments are under the authority of the state government.

All levels of government pass their own laws, have their own agencies and officials to implement these laws, and have court systems to interpret laws.

Federalism creates a union while limiting central power. This system is flexible and allows the national government to act on issues that **affect** the country as a whole, while allowing state and local governments to act on local matters.

Separation of Powers In addition to creating a federal system, the Constitution also limits the national government by dividing power among the legislative, executive, and judicial branches. Under the separation of powers, each branch has specific duties in the government. This system prevents any single government institution from becoming too powerful.

affect to influence

Checks and Balances The three separate branches of the national government also have a system of checks and balances, through which each branch exercises some control over the other two. For example, Congress passes laws, but the president can check that power by vetoing (rejecting) legislation. That veto power is balanced by the power of Congress to override a veto by a two-thirds vote of each chamber. The judicial branch checks the power of Congress and the executive by ruling on the constitutionality of laws and actions of the other two branches, but the judicial branch's power can be checked by the Article V procedures for amending the Constitution.

Individual Rights The Constitution also protects the rights of individuals from government overreach. The first ten amendments to the Constitution, called the Bill of Rights, list the rights of Americans to speak and worship freely, bear arms, be free from unjustified government searches, and have fair criminal trials, among others. These rights are not unlimited, however, as all individual rights are balanced with the government's need to provide for the public good. For example, to maintain order, the government can place some restrictions on when and how people exercise their free speech rights.

Beliefs and Principles Today Although the Constitution and the principles on which it rests have existed for more than 200 years, it still forms the basis for our government today and remains a flexible and **dynamic** instrument for meeting the changing needs of people in our democracy. These underlying beliefs and principles, such as limited government, shared power between national government and the states, individual rights, and commitment to the rule of law, remain important in the United States today.

dynamic forceful, energetic

☑ **READING PROGRESS CHECK**

Monitoring What do the terms *federalism*, *separation of powers*, and *checks and balances* mean?

LESSON 1 REVIEW

Reviewing Vocabulary
1. *Describing* What are the articles and amendments to the Constitution?

Using Your Graphic Organizer
2. *Categorizing* Write a paragraph explaining one of the major principles reflected in the U.S. Constitution.

Answering the Guiding Questions
3. *Identifying* What is the structure of the U.S. Constitution?
4. *Specifying* What principles are reflected in the U.S. Constitution?

Writing About Government
5. *Informative/Explanatory* How are the major principles of the U.S. Constitution related to one another? Write a brief essay in which you define each and show how they are interrelated.

6. *Argument* Reread the Preamble to the U.S. Constitution. Then evaluate how well the federal government serves each of the purposes of government described in the Preamble.

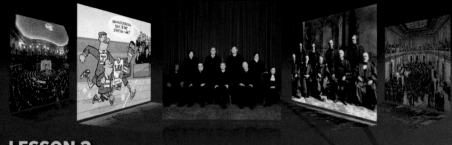

Interact with these digital assets and others in lesson 2

✓ **INTERACTIVE INFOGRAPHIC**
Checks and Balances

✓ **SELF-CHECK QUIZ**

✓ **SLIDE SHOW**
U.S. Government Then and Now

✓ **VIDEO**
Presidential Power

netw⊚rks
TRY IT YOURSELF ONLINE

ReadingHelp Desk

Academic Vocabulary
- contrast
- goal

Content Vocabulary
- **enumerated powers**
- **elastic clause**
- **jurisdiction**
- **judicial review**

TAKING NOTES:
Key Ideas and Details

SPECIFYING Describe the powers of the three branches of government.

Legislative Branch	Executive Branch	Judicial Branch

LESSON 2
The Three Branches of Government

How does the U.S. Constitution structure government and divide power between the national and state governments?

In 1887, British historian Lord Acton wrote, "All power tends to corrupt, and absolute power corrupts absolutely."

One hundred years earlier, American Founder James Madison wrote in *The Federalist* No. 51: "If men were angels, no government would be necessary. If angels were to govern men, neither external nor internal controls on government would be necessary. In framing a government which is to be administered by men over men, the great difficulty lies in this: you must first enable the government to control the governed; and in the next place oblige it to control itself."

a. What is your opinion of Lord Acton's assessment of power? Do you agree or disagree?

b. Discuss examples of famous people and people you know who have used their power in ways that support your point of view.

c. What do you think Madison meant by "if men were angels, no government would be necessary"?

d. Using ideas from Acton and Madison, create a speech, poster, or script that shows why our nation must be governed under a set of rules.

The National Government

GUIDING QUESTION *What is the structure of the national government?*

In 1787, after much conflict and compromise, the Constitution was drafted, but before it could become law it had to be ratified, or approved, by nine of the thirteen states. Supporters of the draft Constitution had to convince others that the Constitution would not create a government that was too strong, so James Madison, Alexander Hamilton, and John Jay rallied support for it by publishing essays called *The Federalist Papers*. One of their most persuasive arguments was that the Constitution balanced power between states and the national government and created three separate branches of government to divide its powers. The structure and functions of government as laid out in the Constitution made it impossible for one person—or even a small group—to have absolute power.

The Constitution creates three branches of the national government: the legislative branch (Congress), the executive branch (the president and administrative departments and agencies), and the judicial branch (the federal courts). The exact nature, roles, and responsibilities of the three branches were hotly debated by the Founders at the Constitutional Convention. In order to create a limited government, the Founders assigned different powers to each branch and gave each ways to check the power of the others.

☑ READING PROGRESS CHECK

Analyzing Why do you think having three separate branches of government was a persuasive argument for ratifying the Constitution?

Legislative Branch

GUIDING QUESTION *How is the U.S. Congress structured and what are its powers?*

The legislature is responsible for passing laws and is divided into two houses: the House of Representatives and the Senate. The House is the voice of the people, directly elected by popular vote; representation in the House is based on each state's population. By contrast, the Senate has the same number of representatives from each state. Initially, senators were elected by state legislatures, but in 1913 the Seventeenth Amendment was ratified, which called for the direct election of senators by popular vote. While the Seventeenth Amendment increased the power of the people, some have argued that it also increased the power of the federal government at the expense of the states. The Founders knew that the legislative branch would be very important, but they also feared that it might abuse its power; therefore, they gave Congress limited and expressed powers, or powers directly stated in the Constitution.

Thomas Jefferson on the Organization of the U.S. Government

"I like the organization of the government into Legislative, Judiciary & Executive. I like the power given the Legislature to levy taxes, and for that reason solely approve of the greater house being chosen by the people directly. For tho' I think a house chosen by them will be very illy qualified to legislate for the Union, for foreign nations &c. yet this evil does not weigh against the good of preserving inviolate the fundamental principle that the people are not to be taxed but by representatives chosen immediately by themselves."

—Letter from Thomas Jefferson, December 1787

While the Constitution was being drafted and approved, Thomas Jefferson was in Paris, serving as U.S. Minister to France. In 1787, he wrote a letter to James Madison expressing his opinions about the draft of the Constitution he had received.

◀ CRITICAL THINKING

1. *Explaining* Why does Thomas Jefferson think that the members of the House of Representatives should be directly elected by the people?

2. *Making Connections* What previous experiences made the Founders believe in a "fundamental principle" that people should be taxed only by those they directly elect?

enumerated powers a list of items, found in Article I, Section 8 of the Constitution, that set forth the authoritative capacity of Congress

elastic clause clause in Article I, Section 8 of the Constitution that gives Congress the right to "make all laws which shall be necessary and proper" to carry out the powers expressed in the other clauses of Article I

Enumerated and Expressed Powers Most of the powers of Congress are listed in Article 1, Section 8, and explain what kinds of laws Congress can make. These are called **enumerated powers**, because the Constitution lists them by number, 1 through 18. These enumerated powers include economic matters—the powers to levy taxes, borrow money, coin money, punish counterfeiting, and regulate commerce. They also include issues of national defense, including the power to declare war, raise and support armed forces, and organize the militia. Congress is also given the power to naturalize citizens and establish post offices and courts.

The Elastic Clause The final enumerated power says that Congress has the authority to "make all laws which shall be necessary and proper for carrying into Execution the foregoing Powers. . . ." This clause is sometimes called the **elastic clause**, because it lets Congress stretch its powers to meet situations that the Founders could not anticipate. The meaning of "necessary and proper" quickly became the subject of dispute, however. How far could Congress stretch its powers? The Supreme Court addressed this question in 1819 in the case of *McCulloch* v. *Maryland*, which was about Congress's power to create a national bank.

The Supreme Court determined that the elastic clause allowed Congress to create a national bank, even though the Constitution did not explicitly state that power. Because Congress had the power to create the bank, Maryland's taxing of its branches was unconstitutional.

Since *McCulloch* v. *Maryland*, Congress has used its power under the elastic clause in many ways. For example, Congress may allocate money to test a missile-defense system (something not specifically listed in the Constitution) based on the necessary and proper execution of its power to "raise and support Armies."

✓ **READING PROGRESS CHECK**

Explaining What are the enumerated powers of Congress?

Executive Branch

GUIDING QUESTION *How is the executive branch structured and what are its powers?*

Under the rule of King George, American colonists resented the way he exerted his extensive powers. After achieving independence, therefore, the new nation gave nearly all power to states and did not even allow for an independent executive branch at the national level. In just a few years, however, it became clear that the structure of government under the Articles of Confederation was not working. The country needed a national government with an executive function that could act in the interests of the United States as a whole, but the nation's leaders wanted to make sure the executive's powers were limited.

Role of the Executive Branch The president is the head of the executive branch, which includes numerous executive departments that carry out or enforce the laws passed by Congress. The Constitution does not specify how many departments there should be. There are currently 15 executive departments, including the Department of Justice, the Department of Education, the Department of the Treasury, and many others. The leaders of these departments report to the president and advise him or her about their areas of responsibility.

The executive branch also includes numerous federal agencies, boards, commissions, government corporations, and advisory boards that carry out

C·I·V·I·C PARTICIPATION IN A DIGITAL AGE

The Executive Branch Online

Executive branch agencies and departments impact Americans' everyday lives in many ways. For example, Medicare provides health insurance for Americans over age 65. The Department of Education provides grants, loans, and work-study funds for students in college, and the State Department provides passports for Americans who want to travel abroad. Many people interact with the federal executive branch through the U.S. Government's official web portal, www.usa.gov. This website serves as a clearinghouse of information and services.

USA.gov
Government Made Easy

▶ **CRITICAL THINKING**

a. **Using Digital Tools** Think about the everyday things that prompt Americans to interact with the federal government. Then find five things that someone can do using this website.

b. **Making Connections** Think about life in the United States before the Internet. How would Americans have completed the same tasks you identified in a pre-digital age? How would these federal agencies have publicized information and services?

specific executive functions. These include, for example, the Consumer Product Safety Commission, the Environmental Protection Agency (EPA), the National Aeronautics and Space Administration (NASA), and the Corporation for National and Community Service.

Powers of the President Most of the specific powers of the president are defined in Article II, Sections 2 and 3. The Constitution says the president has the power to grant pardons, make treaties, and appoint ambassadors, Supreme Court justices, and other government officials. A president can also fire officials in the executive branch, make agreements with foreign nations, or take emergency actions to save the nation.

The Founders recognized the need for a strong army to protect the United States. At the same time, they realized that if the military was not limited, it could be used to seize control of the government and threaten our democracy. Their solution was to make the military subject to civilian authority and to divide control over the military between different branches of the government. The Constitution names the president commander in chief and gives Congress the sole authority to declare war and to fund the military.

☑ **READING PROGRESS CHECK**

Identifying What powers does the Constitution give to the president?

Judicial Branch

GUIDING QUESTION *How is the judiciary structured and what are its powers?*

Article III of the Constitution establishes the federal court system. It names the Supreme Court and then gives Congress the authority to establish "inferior" courts. The Constitution says that federal judges "shall hold their office during good Behaviour. . . ," meaning that judges hold office for life unless they commit a crime.

Speech bubble: UNCONSTITUTIONAL. BACK TO THE STARTING LINE!

Labels: HOUSE OF REPS, SENATE, LAW, PRES, SUPREME COURT

jurisdiction the limits or territory within which authority may be exercised

judicial review the power of the Supreme Court to declare laws and actions of local, state, or national governments unconstitutional

contrast the difference between things that are of similar natures

When the Constitution was adopted, every state already had its own court system that heard cases and disputes about their state laws or the state constitution. The Constitution created the federal court system, which hears cases about the U.S. Constitution, federal law, foreign treaties, international law, and bankruptcies. In this dual-court system, each court has the authority to hear certain kinds of cases, which is known as the court's **jurisdiction**.

Much of the judicial branch's power comes from the courts' ability to interpret the Constitution and overturn laws that violate the Constitution. This process is called **judicial review**. It is not specifically mentioned in the Constitution, which says that "the judicial Power shall extend to all Cases . . . arising under this Constitution."*The Federalist* No. 78 discusses the power of judicial review:

▌▌ PRIMARY SOURCE

A constitution is, in fact, and must be regarded by the judges, as a fundamental law. It therefore belongs to them to ascertain its meaning, as well as the meaning of any particular act proceeding from the legislative body."

—*The Federalist* No. 78

The Supreme Court first exercised judicial review in 1803, in its decision in the case of *Marbury* v. *Madison*, which concerned the Judiciary Act of 1789. The Court decided that this law gave the Court more power than the Constitution allowed, so the law was unconstitutional. Chief Justice John Marshall wrote the opinion for a unanimous court, which held that the law was unconstitutional, and it remains one of the most important rulings in the history of the Supreme Court. By asserting judicial review, the judicial branch was elevated to a status equal to the other two branches of government.

☑ **READING PROGRESS CHECK**

Determining Importance Why is *Marbury* v. *Madison* considered one of the most important rulings of the Supreme Court?

American Government: Then and Now

GUIDING QUESTION *How has the work of the three branches of government changed over time?*

All three branches of government have changed significantly over the past 200 years. Early presidents would hardly recognize the office today. President Washington had so little to do on some days that he advertised in the newspaper the times when he would entertain visitors. He held tea parties for anyone "properly attired" on Friday evenings and had only a handful of advisers and staff. By **contrast**, modern presidents' schedules are timed by the minute. They have a White House staff numbering in the hundreds, a military force of millions, and a vast federal bureaucracy of all executive branch employees. A fleet of airplanes and helicopters stands ready to carry the president and close advisers to any part of the nation or the world.

In the first Congress, the Senate introduced only 24 bills, and the House introduced only 143. Attendance in legislative sessions was merely a part-time job for many years, as members had other jobs or were wealthy enough not to work. Congress did not sit in continuous session until the mid-twentieth century. Today members of Congress live and work nearly year-round in Washington, D.C., and about 10,000 bills are introduced annually.

Supreme Court justices also had much less to do in the early days. For the first three years, the Court heard almost no cases. Justices were assigned to "ride circuit"—when the Supreme Court was not in session, they traveled by horseback to hear appeals in different district courts. It was such an exhausting job that the first chief justice declined an invitation to serve again. It was not until 1891 that Congress created the modern federal court system.

☑ **READING PROGRESS CHECK**

Analyzing Based on the preceding description, which of the three branches do you think has changed the most? Why?

Relations Among the Branches

GUIDING QUESTION *How do the three branches share, check, and balance power?*

By creating three branches of government and dividing power between them, the Constitution assured that the branches would need to cooperate to take many important actions. The division of power and checks and balances also creates conflict among the branches as they limit one another.

Sharing Power So that the president does not become too powerful, many of the executive powers require cooperation with Congress. For example, the president (and the Secretary of State, the head of the State Department) has the power to negotiate treaties with foreign countries, but he or she needs the Senate to approve those treaties before they become law. Likewise, the power of Congress is limited by the need for presidential approval. Congress passes laws, but those laws generally must be signed by the president. If the president vetoes a bill, Congress needs a two-thirds majority to override it. Once a bill becomes law, the executive branch must carry it out and enforce it.

In practice, the executive branch often provides plans for the laws that Congress considers. A great deal of the president's power comes from the

▼ CRITICAL THINKING
Describing Use the photographs to describe at least one way the Supreme Court has changed since the late nineteenth century. Describe one way the Supreme Court has stayed the same.

The U.S. Supreme Court in 1892

The U.S. Supreme Court in 2010

CHECKS AND BALANCES

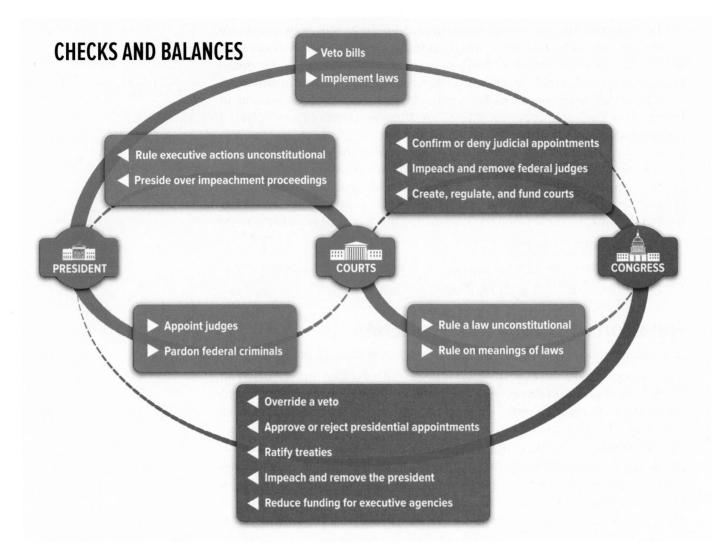

▶ Veto bills

▶ Implement laws

◀ Rule executive actions unconstitutional

◀ Preside over impeachment proceedings

◀ Confirm or deny judicial appointments

◀ Impeach and remove federal judges

◀ Create, regulate, and fund courts

PRESIDENT

COURTS

CONGRESS

▶ Appoint judges

▶ Pardon federal criminals

▶ Rule a law unconstitutional

▶ Rule on meanings of laws

◀ Override a veto

◀ Approve or reject presidential appointments

◀ Ratify treaties

◀ Impeach and remove the president

◀ Reduce funding for executive agencies

Each branch can check the power of the other two.

▲ CRITICAL THINKING

Summarizing In what ways does Congress check the Supreme Court?

fact that the voters elect a president based on what they believe he or she will accomplish in office. Quite often, the president proposes a legislative agenda and works with legislators to have it enacted. Congress appropriates funds for the government to function, but the executive branch spends the money.

Checks and Balances Each branch can check, or control, the power of the other two. The president can veto bills passed by Congress, but Congress can override the veto and impeach the president or federal judges. The courts can determine what federal laws mean and overturn them if they are unconstitutional. Congress can respond to a Supreme Court ruling by passing a new law that clarifies meaning or by proposing an amendment to the Constitution. The courts can also rule actions of the executive branch unconstitutional, but they often need the president to enforce their rulings.

The ability of the branches to limit one another results in a certain amount of conflict. One source of conflict stems from the congressional responsibility to monitor how the executive branch enforces the laws. Sometimes the two branches quarrel over the way the president interprets the will of Congress in the bills it has passed, and when this happens, the federal courts may be called upon to interpret the intent of Congress on a case-by-case basis.

Presidents have charged Congress with trying to encroach upon the proper powers of the executive to lead and protect the nation. Occasionally, Congress has been accused of yielding too much power to the president.

Political parties have also been a source of conflict. Obviously, if the executive office is controlled by one party and the legislature is controlled by another, cooperation will be difficult. Each party tends to have different **goals**, different constituents to please, and a different philosophy of government. At best, different parties in each branch can craft careful compromises; at worst, there is "gridlock"—a political traffic jam in which all forward progress comes to a halt.

Both the executive and legislative branches sometimes come into conflict with the judicial branch. The Constitution allows Congress to limit the Supreme Court's jurisdiction, but Congress does not often use that authority because it would challenge the independence of the judiciary. When the Supreme Court ruled in *Baker* v. *Carr* (1964) that state legislatures must reapportion seats according to population, some members of Congress were outraged. The House passed a bill to strip federal courts of jurisdiction in such matters and, ultimately, the Senate killed the bill.

In some rare cases, a president has refused to enforce a Supreme Court decision. In 1832 the Cherokee in Georgia were living on land that had been guaranteed to them by treaty. The state of Georgia wanted this land and tried to subject the Cherokee to state law. A non-Native American missionary who was arrested for living in the Cherokee nation without a license sued. In *Worcester* v. *Georgia*, the Supreme Court ruled in favor of the Cherokee. The Court's decision was written by the Chief Justice, John Marshall. Reputedly, President Andrew Jackson's angry reaction to its decision was: "John Marshall has made his opinion. Now let him enforce it."

This conflict underscores the kinds of power the two branches have—the judiciary has great authority, but the executive commands the military. The Georgia Cherokees were forcibly relocated in 1838 to what is now Oklahoma, a journey that became known as the Trail of Tears for the thousands of Cherokee who died of cold, hunger, and disease on the journey.

☑ **READING PROGRESS CHECK**

Analyzing Why do the three branches sometimes come into conflict with one another?

EXPLORING THE ESSENTIAL QUESTION

Read the government actions below. For each, describe how the three branches are involved.

a. A Supreme Court justice retires and a new justice is needed to replace her.

b. The president is caught stealing money from the treasury.

c. A foreign country attacks a U.S. military base overseas and Americans want to respond immediately and with force.

goal aim, purpose

LESSON 2 REVIEW

Reviewing Vocabulary

1. *Describing* What is judicial review? When did the Supreme Court first exercise this power?

Using Your Graphic Organizer

2. *Categorizing* Using your completed graphic organizer, choose one of the three branches of government and create an outline of that branch's powers.

Answering the Guiding Questions

3. *Identifying* What is the structure of the national government?

4. *Explaining* How is the U.S. Congress structured and what are its powers?

5. *Explaining* How is the executive branch structured and what are its powers?

6. *Explaining* How is the judiciary structured and what are its powers?

7. *Making Connections* How has the work of the three branches of government changed over time?

8. *Analyzing* How do the three branches share, check, and balance power?

Writing About Government

9. *Argument* The Constitution gives Congress the authority over the power of taxation. Why do you think the Founders gave this power to the legislative branch as opposed to the executive branch? Which branch do you think should have the power to levy and collect taxes? Write a persuasive essay to support your point of view. Be sure to provide concrete examples to support your points.

McCulloch v Maryland (1819)

FACTS OF THE CASE The case of *McCulloch* v. *Maryland* is about Congress's power to create a national bank. After Congress created such a bank, Maryland tried to make the Baltimore branch of the bank pay a large tax. The Bank refused to pay the tax, and the state of Maryland sued.

ISSUE

Does the Constitution give Congress the power to create a national bank?

The following is a list of arguments made in the case of *McCulloch v. Maryland*. Divide a blank piece of paper in half, and label one half McCulloch and the other Maryland. Read each argument and assign each based on whether it supports McCulloch's side (that Congress has the power to create a national bank and Maryland cannot tax it) or Maryland's side (that Congress is not allowed to create a national bank and Maryland can tax such a bank).

1. Creating a bank was not specifically stated in the Constitution, so Congress did not have the authority to do so.

2. The "elastic" clause of the Constitution says that Congress can make laws that are "necessary and proper" to the exercise of its other, enumerated powers.

3. Creating banks is a power that is reserved for the states.

4. The Constitution expressly gives Congress the powers to "lay and collect taxes; to borrow money; and to regulate commerce." A national bank would be "necessary and proper" to allow Congress to exercise these enumerated powers.

5. Maryland did not have the authority to levy the tax, because doing so interfered with the workings of the federal government. If Maryland can tax the bank, the taxes could be so high that the bank would go out of business.

6. Because states are sovereign, they have the authority to tax institutions and businesses within their borders.

7. A national bank might be an unfair competitor for Maryland's banks, which can operate only in Maryland.

8. The Constitution is the supreme law of the land. If the United States Congress passed a law within its authority under the Constitution, a state legislature could not pass a law to interfere with that action.

9. There is nothing in the Constitution restricting the powers of Congress to those specifically enumerated.

EXPLORING THE ESSENTIAL QUESTION

Categorizing After you have categorized the arguments, choose one that you think is the most persuasive and explain why you found that argument compelling.

Interact with these digital assets and others in lesson 3

✓ **INTERACTIVE INFOGRAPHIC**
Amending the Constitution

✓ **INTERACTIVE IMAGE**
Equal Rights Amendment Activists

✓ **SELF-CHECK QUIZ**

✓ **VIDEO**
The Equal Rights Amendment

netw⊙rks
TRY IT YOURSELF ONLINE

ReadingHelp Desk

Academic Vocabulary

- **desecrate**
- **assurance**

Content Vocabulary

- **convention**
- **repeal**
- **incorporation doctrine**
- **militia**
- **probable cause**
- **eminent domain**
- **impeach**

TAKING NOTES:

Key Ideas and Details

CATEGORIZING Categorize each of the amendments as those that extend individual rights, introduce structural changes, or extend government power.

Extends Individual Rights	Structural Changes	Extends Government Power

---

LESSON 3
Amendments

ESSENTIAL QUESTION

Why and how has the U.S. Constitution been amended and interpreted throughout our history?

The U.S. Constitution has been the law of the land for more than 225 years, but only 27 amendments have been made to it. Answer the following questions and explain your reasons.

a. In your opinion, what makes the Constitution relevant today?

b. Does the fact that the Constitution can be amended make it well-suited for changes in our economy, society, history, culture, and government? Explain.

c. Does the fact that the Constitution has been amended only 27 times imply that it was nearly perfect from the start? Explain.

Amending the Constitution

GUIDING QUESTION *What is the process for amending the Constitution?*

In 1787, the year the Constitution was written, the nation consisted of fewer than 4 million people living in thirteen agricultural states along the Atlantic Coast. More than two centuries later, the Constitution is the basis for governing an advanced nation of more than 300 million people in 50 states with varied geographies, resources, and economies. The Constitution has met the needs of a changing society and, at the same time, preserved the basic institutions and principles of the government the Framers created in 1787. As long ago as 1819, the Chief Justice of the United States, John Marshall, stated his conviction that the Constitution's flexibility was necessary and something that the Framers intended:

 PRIMARY SOURCE
We must never forget that it is . . . a Constitution intended to endure for ages to come, and, consequently, to be adapted to the various crises of human affairs."

—John Marshall, 1819

One of the ways that the Constitution can be adapted to changing times is through amending the document; the amendment process is explained in Article V. There are two steps to amending the Constitution.

An amendment must first be proposed, and then it must be ratified. In a reflection of our federal system of government, amendments are proposed at the national level and ratified in a state-by-state process.

Proposing and Ratifying Amendments There are two ways to propose amendments and two ways to ratify them. One method of proposing an amendment is by a two-thirds vote in the House and Senate. The other way to propose an amendment is for two-thirds of the states to ask Congress to call a **convention** to debate and then vote on the proposed amendment.

All of the current amendments—27 in total—were proposed using the congressional vote method. Dozens of new proposals are introduced in Congress every year. In recent years, suggestions have been made to limit income taxes, limit the tenure of Supreme Court justices, and give states complete control of oil deposits in their borders, but none of these have won the necessary two-thirds vote in the House and Senate.

When an amendment is proposed, Congress chooses one of two methods for obtaining state approval. The legislatures in three-fourths of the states can ratify the amendment. The other method is for the states to hold special conventions and then to have three-fourths of the conventions approve it.

Almost all of the amendments have been ratified using the state legislature method. The other ratification method—state-ratifying conventions—has been used only once: for the Twenty-first Amendment (1933), which **repealed**

convention a meeting held for the purpose of proposing and voting on amendments

Amending the Constitution requires two steps: proposal and ratification.

▼ CRITICAL THINKING
1. Summarizing Which process for amending the Constitution was used only once? Which process has never been used?
2. Analyzing Why do you think it is so difficult to amend the Constitution?

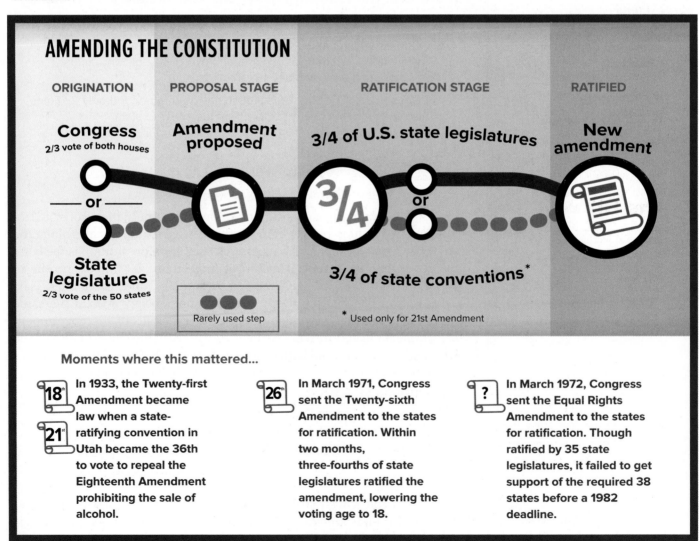

AMENDING THE CONSTITUTION

| ORIGINATION | PROPOSAL STAGE | RATIFICATION STAGE | RATIFIED |

Congress
2/3 vote of both houses

— or —

State legislatures
2/3 vote of the 50 states

Amendment proposed

Rarely used step

3/4 of U.S. state legislatures

3/4

or

3/4 of state conventions*

* Used only for 21st Amendment

New amendment

Moments where this mattered...

18th 21st In 1933, the Twenty-first Amendment became law when a state-ratifying convention in Utah became the 36th to vote to repeal the Eighteenth Amendment prohibiting the sale of alcohol.

26th In March 1971, Congress sent the Twenty-sixth Amendment to the states for ratification. Within two months, three-fourths of state legislatures ratified the amendment, lowering the voting age to 18.

? In March 1972, Congress sent the Equal Rights Amendment to the states for ratification. Though ratified by 35 state legislatures, it failed to get support of the required 38 states before a 1982 deadline.

the Eighteenth Amendment (1919) banning the sale of alcoholic beverages. For the Twenty-first Amendment, Congress let each state legislature determine how delegates would be elected to the ratifying conventions. Delegates ran for election on a pledge to support the amendment or reject it; at the conventions, the elected delegates voted as they had pledged to do. This method gave the people a direct voice in the amending process.

Congress sets a number of other rules that apply to the ratification process. A key rule is setting a time limit for states to ratify an amendment. Most recent amendments have had a limit of seven years. Time limits have a large influence on whether an amendment can get the necessary number of states to pass.

More than 11,000 amendments have been proposed over time, but only 27 have been ratified. Why so few? Amending the Constitution is an extremely complicated process; an amendment is adopted only when there is a broad national consensus on the issue. The Founders wanted to make the procedure difficult because they believed that most issues should be resolved by the ordinary political process; they wanted permanent changes to the Constitution to reflect an extraordinary consensus.

Sometimes, proposals to amend the Constitution reflect deep political division among the branches of government. For example, in 1989, the Supreme Court heard a case involving a man who set an American flag on fire as part of a public protest. He was arrested and convicted for violating a Texas law that prohibited **desecrating** the flag. In *Texas* v. *Johnson* (1989), the Supreme Court ruled that flag burning in the context of a political protest is symbolic speech protected by the First Amendment, so the Texas law was unconstitutional. Many people were outraged. The next day, a member of Congress introduced an amendment to ban any form of flag desecration. The amendment did not pass, but it has been proposed again many times since.

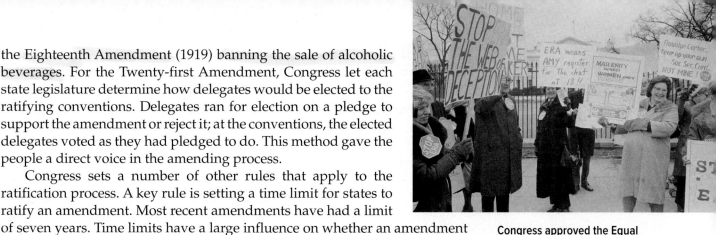

Congress approved the Equal Rights Amendment (ERA) in 1972, but it ran into opposition when it was sent to the states for ratification.

▲ CRITICAL THINKING
Applying Do you think the Framers of the Constitution made it too difficult to amend the Constitution? Explain.

✓ READING PROGRESS CHECK

Sequencing What are the steps to amend the Constitution?

The Bill of Rights

GUIDING QUESTION *What rights are guaranteed in the Bill of Rights?*

In 1788 political leaders in Massachusetts and Virginia refused to support the new Constitution without a bill of rights limiting the power of the new federal government. One of the Anti-Federalists' complaints about the Constitution was that it lacked any **assurances** that the new national government would not infringe upon people's rights. To help ensure ratification, supporters of the Constitution promised to add a list of basic, unalienable rights, and in 1791 the states ratified ten amendments, which became known as the Bill of Rights.

The Bill of Rights protects individual rights by limiting government powers. Originally the Bill of Rights applied only to the national government, but almost all of its provisions have been "incorporated" into the states through court decisions, meaning its protections cover state laws. This is known as the **incorporation doctrine**, an interpretation of the Constitution that means the due process clause of the Fourteenth Amendment requires state and local governments to guarantee their citizens the rights stated in the Bill of Rights.

The First Amendment One of the most well-known amendments to the Constitution, the First Amendment, states: "Congress shall make no law

repeal to revoke by legislative enactment

desecrate to treat disrespectfully

assurance full confidence, freedom from doubt

incorporation doctrine the adding of the Bill of Rights protections into the states through court decisions

Protesters fear that proposed legislation aimed at curbing media piracy would support censorship and inhibit their right to free speech under the First Amendment.

▲ CRITICAL THINKING

Identifying Which amendment is concerned with the right of free speech?

EXPLORING THE ESSENTIAL QUESTION

Depicting Create a collage that depicts the five freedoms protected in the First Amendment. Look for pictures for your collage in newspapers, magazines, on the Internet, or draw your own. Create a caption for the collage that describes how the images portray First Amendment rights.

militia local group of armed citizens

respecting an establishment of religion, or prohibiting the free exercise thereof; or abridging the freedom of speech, or of the press; or the right of the people peaceably to assemble, and to petition the Government for a redress of grievances."

The First Amendment protects the right of Americans to worship as they please or, if they prefer, to have no religion at all. The first part of the amendment, which prohibits Congress from establishing a national religion, is called the Establishment Clause. The very next portion, which says Congress cannot prevent people from practicing their religion, is called the Free Exercise Clause. These principles are known as separation of church and state (the Establishment Clause) and freedom of religion (the Free Exercise Clause). The First Amendment also protects freedom of speech and freedom of the press. The government cannot unreasonably prevent individuals from freely expressing their opinions, as they have the right to criticize the government and to spread unpopular ideas.

The First Amendment also generally protects the expression of ideas in newspapers, books, radio, television, and, to some extent, movies and the Internet. Unlike in some countries, the American press is seldom subject to prior restraint—that is, government usually cannot censor information before it is published or broadcast.

Freedom of speech is not unlimited, however. The right to free speech does not extend to lies told with the intent to damage a person's reputation (defamation) or to speech that endangers the nation by giving away military secrets. The government can also punish speech calling for the violent overthrow of the government without violating the First Amendment.

The First Amendment protects the right to assemble in groups and hold demonstrations. People may pass out pamphlets, hold meetings, and peaceably advertise their beliefs; however, courts have ruled that the government can require a group to obtain a permit before holding meetings or demonstrations.

Finally, the First Amendment protects the right to sign petitions in support of an idea, to present those petitions to government officials, and to send letters or e-mails to those officials.

The Second Amendment This amendment ensures citizens and the nation the right to security. It states: "A well regulated Militia, being necessary to the security of a free State, the right of the people to keep and bear Arms, shall not be infringed."

Prior to the American Revolution, the British attempted to disarm local groups of armed citizens, known as **militias**. Remembering this while drafting the Bill of Rights, the Framers included the Second Amendment to outlaw such kinds of forceful disarming of the people in the future. Whether the amendment intended to protect individual Americans' right to keep weapons unrelated to service in a militia has been a matter of debate for decades.

In 2008 the Supreme Court clarified the Second Amendment, ruling in a 5-to-4 decision (*District of Columbia* v. *Heller*) that the amendment protected Americans' rights to use handguns for legitimate, lawful purposes such as defending their homes. That said, the Supreme Court pointed out that, like the First Amendment's right of free speech, the Second Amendment's right to bear arms was not unlimited, and guns could still be reasonably regulated. In 2010 the Supreme Court extended the Second Amendment's protections to apply to states as well as the federal government in *McDonald* v. *Chicago*.

The Third Amendment This amendment prohibits the government from forcing people to provide shelter for soldiers in their homes, another British practice before the Revolution. In times of war, however, Congress may require a homeowner to house soldiers—but only under conditions clearly spelled out by law.

The Fourth Amendment This amendment reflects the early Americans' desire to protect their privacy. Britain used writs of assistance—general search warrants—to enter private residences in search of smuggled goods. The Fourth Amendment limits the government's power to conduct searches and seizures by protecting the right to privacy; it states that authorities must have a specific reason for a search or to seize evidence or people. With some notable exceptions, the police cannot conduct a search or seizure hoping to find evidence or arrest people on the chance they might have committed a crime.

To be lawful, a search must usually be based on **probable cause**—a reasonable basis to believe a person or premises is linked to a crime. A search of a home, for example, also typically requires a search warrant. These are orders signed by a judge describing the place to be searched and the items to be seized. The Fourth Amendment and its probable cause requirement also applies to seizures of a person, that is, an arrest.

probable cause a reasonable basis to believe a person or premises are linked to a crime

eminent domain the power of government to take private property for public use

The Fifth Amendment This amendment contains four important protections for people accused of crimes:

- No one can be tried for a serious crime unless a grand jury has decided there is enough evidence to justify a trial.
- A person found innocent may not be tried again for the same offense.
- No one may be forced to testify against himself or herself. People questioned by the police, standing trial, or testifying before a congressional hearing can refuse to answer questions if their answers would connect them with a crime. The burden of conviction is on the government; people cannot be forced to convict themselves.
- No one can be deprived of life, liberty, or property without due process of the law. Thus the government must follow constitutional procedures in all actions against individuals.

The Fifth Amendment also defines the government's right of **eminent domain**—the power to take private property for public use. The government must pay a fair price for the property and must use it to benefit the public.

The Sixth Amendment This amendment gives an accused person several important rights, including the right to a speedy, public trial by an impartial jury. Because of the Sixth Amendment, authorities cannot purposely hold a person for an unreasonably long time while awaiting trial. This protection prevents the government from silencing its critics, as often happens under dictatorships. A public trial assures that justice is carried out in full view of the people.

The Sixth Amendment provides for trial by jury, although an accused person could ask to be tried by a judge alone—that is a constitutional right, too. This amendment gives accused persons the right to know the charges against them so that they can prepare a defense. They also have the right to hear and question all witnesses against them, to compel witnesses to testify in court for them, and to be defended by a lawyer.

The Seventh Amendment This amendment provides for the right to a jury trial in federal courts to settle all disputes about property

The Fifth Amendment defines the government's right to eminent domain, often used for projects such as highways and other public works such as these freeways in Los Angeles.

▼ CRITICAL THINKING
Defining What is meant by the power of eminent domain?

Read the amendments below. They are all ideas that have actually been proposed to amend the U.S. Constitution. For each amendment, decide whether you agree or disagree with the idea.

After you have examined the proposals, choose one to explore further. Research when it was proposed, who supported it, who opposed it, and what happened to the amendment. (Did Congress ever vote on it? Did the states?) Prepare a two-minute presentation to share your findings with your other classmates.

a. An amendment defining marriage as a union between one man and one woman

b. An amendment prohibiting interracial marriage

c. An amendment to abolish the Electoral College

d. An amendment to give residents of the District of Columbia a representative with full voting rights equal to other members of Congress

e. An amendment to limit the number of terms that senators and representatives can serve in Congress

f. An amendment to repeal the Twenty-second Amendment, which limits a president to two terms in office

g. An amendment to abolish the death penalty

h. An amendment to outlaw all abortions

i. An amendment to declare that women have equal rights under the law

worth more than $20. When both parties in a conflict agree, however, a judge rather than a jury may hear evidence and decide the case.

The Eighth Amendment This amendment prohibits excessive bail—money or property that the accused deposits with the court to gain release from jail until the trial. The judge sets bail in an amount that ensures the accused will appear for trial; when the trial ends, bail is returned. If the accused does not appear, bail is forfeited.

The Eighth Amendment also prevents judges from ordering someone convicted of a crime to pay an excessive fine. Fines for serious crimes may be higher than those for less serious ones. If someone is too poor to pay the fine, he or she cannot be imprisoned for longer than the maximum sentence to "work off" the fine.

Finally, the Eighth Amendment bans "cruel and unusual punishment" for crimes. These are punishments that are grossly out of proportion to the crime committed. For example, life in prison for stealing a candy bar would be cruel and unusual punishment. The Eighth Amendment also has been used to limit the use of the death penalty in some circumstances.

The Ninth Amendment This amendment states that all other rights not spelled out in the Constitution are "retained by the people." The Ninth Amendment prevents government from claiming that the only rights people have are those listed in the Bill of Rights.

The Tenth Amendment Unlike the other amendments, the Tenth Amendment did not add any new rights. It says that "powers not delegated to the United States . . . nor prohibited . . . to the States, are reserved to the States respectively, or to the people." In other words, powers not given to the federal government were retained by the states or the people.

☑ **READING PROGRESS CHECK**

Explaining What protections are guaranteed by the First Amendment?

The Later Amendments

GUIDING QUESTION *How have amendments changed the Constitution?*

The remaining amendments to the Constitution can be divided into three groups: amendments that make structural changes, amendments that extend government power, and amendments that extend individual rights.

Structural Changes to the Constitution Several amendments modify the structure of the government or the powers of the branches.

Article III, Section 1, of the Constitution gives the federal courts jurisdiction in cases arising between states, between citizens of different states, or between a state and the citizens of another state. The Eleventh Amendment was ratified to prohibit a state from being sued in federal court by citizens of another state or of another nation. This amendment was added in response to the Supreme Court's ruling in *Chisholm* v. *Georgia* (1793). This case said that citizens of South Carolina were allowed to sue the state of Georgia in a federal court.

- **The Twelfth Amendment (1804)** calls for the Electoral College to use separate ballots in voting for president and vice president.
- **The Seventeenth Amendment (1913)** says that the people—not state legislatures—elect United States senators directly. Congress tried to pass this amendment several times, but in 1912, scandals involving charges of vote buying in state legislatures finally helped the amendment pass.

- **The Twentieth Amendment (1933)** sets new dates for when the president and vice president are inaugurated (January 20 of the year following the election) and when Congress begins its term (January 3 of every other year).
- **The Twenty-second Amendment (1951)** limits presidents to a maximum of two elected terms. It was passed in reaction to Franklin D. Roosevelt's election to four terms between 1933 and 1945.
- **The Twenty-fifth Amendment (1967)** establishes a process for the vice president to take over the office of president if the president is disabled. The amendment also establishes the process for filling the vice presidency if that office becomes vacant.
- **The Twenty-seventh Amendment (1992)** makes congressional pay raises effective during the term following their passage. Originally proposed as part of the Bill of Rights in 1789, it did not have sufficient votes for ratification. A campaign to pass it began in the 1980s, and it finally became law in 1992.

Extensions of Government Power Two amendments gave the government more power, but one was repealed just 14 years after it was enacted. In 1895 the Supreme Court reversed a previous decision and declared a federal income tax unconstitutional. This remained law until the Sixteenth Amendment (1913) gave Congress the power to levy individual income taxes.

The Eighteenth Amendment (1919) prohibited the manufacture, sale, or transport of alcoholic beverages. The Twenty-first Amendment (1933) repeals the Eighteenth Amendment. The Twenty-first Amendment, however, continued to ban the transport of alcohol into any state where its possession violated state law.

The Twenty-seventh Amendment

National Archives and Records Administration

While researching a paper, a 20-year-old student at the University of Texas discovered a constitutional amendment that James Madison proposed in 1789. The student, Greg Watson, thought the idea sounded like a good one. Madison proposed that members of Congress should not be able to raise their own pay. Several states had ratified the amendment when it was proposed, and it had no deadline for ratification.

In 1982 Watson began a campaign to get the remaining states to ratify the amendment. Over the course of ten years, the legislatures of many states were persuaded to ratify Madison's original proposal. The Twenty-seventh Amendment to the Constitution was ratified by Michigan, the necessary 38th state, in May 1992, more than 203 years after it was first proposed.

"I can still recall standing there . . . and feeling a strong impulse physically come over me that this 1789 congressional compensation amendment not only made imminent good sense but, also, that it was still technically pending before the state legislatures."

—Greg Watson wrote in an e-mail

EXPLORING THE ESSENTIAL QUESTION

Making Connections If you wanted to get an amendment passed, what steps would you take? Who would you talk to and how could you persuade enough influential people to back your idea? What strategies would you use?

In 1971 President Richard Nixon signed the Twenty-sixth Amendment giving 18-, 19-, and 20-year-olds the right to vote in all elections.

▲ CRITICAL THINKING

Explaining What was the basic argument behind the passage of the Twenty-sixth Amendment?

Extensions of Individual Rights Many Constitutional amendments extend individual rights. The Thirteenth, Fourteenth, and Fifteenth Amendments are often called the Civil War amendments because they resulted from that conflict. The Thirteenth Amendment (1865) outlaws slavery, and the Fourteenth Amendment (1868) prohibits a state from depriving a person of life, liberty, or property without "due process of law." The Fourteenth Amendment also says that all citizens have the right to equal protection of the law in all states. It was intended to protect the legal rights of the freed enslaved people and their descendants. The Fifteenth Amendment (1870) prohibits the government from denying a person's right to vote on the basis of race.

The Nineteenth Amendment (1920) guarantees women the right to vote. By 1920, women had already won the right to vote in many state elections, but the constitutional amendment established their right to vote in all state and national elections.

Before the Twenty-third Amendment (1961) was passed, citizens living in Washington, D.C., the nation's capital, were denied the right to vote for president and vice president because they did not live in a state. This amendment gives the District of Columbia three presidential electors to represent them in the Electoral College, the number to which it would be entitled if it were a state. Residents of D.C. still do not have full representation in Congress. They have a nonvoting delegate.

After the Civil War, some Southern states created poll taxes, which required people to pay a tax before they could vote. The tax was intended to keep poor people, especially poor African Americans, from voting. The Twenty-fourth Amendment (1964) prohibits poll taxes in federal elections.

The Twenty-sixth Amendment (1971) lowers the voting age in federal and state elections to 18.

☑ READING PROGRESS CHECK

Classifying Which amendments extended individual rights? To whom were rights extended?

Changes to Our Understanding of the Constitution

GUIDING QUESTION *How has our understanding of the Constitution changed over time?*

While amending the Constitution is the only way to change the content of the document, our understanding of the meaning of that content has evolved over time in several ways.

Practices and Customs When a branch of government exercises its powers in a new way and succeeds, it sets an example that influences future government officials. For example, the Constitution gives the House of Representatives the power to **impeach**, or formally accuse, federal officials—including the president—while it is up to the Senate to conduct an impeachment trial.

Article II of the Constitution states that an official can be removed from office if he or she is convicted of "treason, bribery, or other high Crimes and Misdemeanors." The meanings of treason and bribery are clear, but what is meant by "high crimes and misdemeanors"?

impeach to formally accuse

The actions of presidents have also affected interpretation of the Constitution, particularly the powers of the presidency and the workings of the executive branch. Modern presidents often conduct foreign affairs by executive agreement—an agreement between heads of state—rather than by treaty, as specified in the Constitution. A treaty, as an agreement between nations, must be ratified by the Senate, while an executive agreement does not. Additionally, presidents today are much more aggressive in requesting legislation from Congress, which has made the president's role in the government much larger than most of the Founders would have imagined.

Judicial Review When federal courts decide cases, they are often interpreting the meanings of words and phrases in the Constitution that are imprecise. The courts have the power to review federal laws or government actions to determine whether they violate the Constitution. In doing so, they decide what parts of the document mean. For example, in *Wisconsin* v. *Yoder* (1972), the Supreme Court ruled that the First Amendment's right to freedom of religion allows Amish families to keep their children home after eighth grade despite a state law that required school attendance to a later age.

Changes in the membership on the courts and in social and political conditions affect how the courts interpret the Constitution. In *Plessy* v. *Ferguson* (1896), the Supreme Court ruled that separate but equal facilities for African Americans did not violate the Constitution. Almost 60 years later, the Supreme Court reversed its position in *Brown* v. *Board of Education* (1954). In the *Brown* case, the Supreme Court said that "separate educational facilities were inherently unequal" and therefore unconstitutional.

The fact that some of the text of the Constitution is written using broad language leaves room for interpretation and adaptation, which has helped the document survive as the foundation for our government for more than 200 years. The Supreme Court is able to interpret the language in the Constitution and apply it to technologies and situations the Founders could never have imagined. Along with the formal amendment process, this has allowed the basic structure of government to remain intact since 1787.

☑ READING PROGRESS CHECK

Summarizing What are the formal and informal ways the Constitution has changed over time?

LESSON 3 REVIEW

Reviewing Vocabulary

1. *Explaining* What does it mean for law enforcement to have probable cause?

Using Your Graphic Organizer

2. *Calculating* Use your completed graphic organizer to create a graph showing the number of amendments in each category. Which category has the most? The least? Why do you think this is so?

Answering the Guiding Questions

3. *Identifying* What is the process for amending the Constitution?

4. *Stating* What rights are guaranteed in the Bill of Rights?

5. *Explaining* How have amendments changed the Constitution?

6. *Drawing Conclusions* How has our understanding of the Constitution changed over time?

Writing About Government

7. *Argument* What amendment to the Constitution would you like to propose? Write a newspaper editorial in which you describe the amendment and try to convince your fellow Americans of the merits of your proposal.

Should gun laws be looser or stricter?

DEBATING DEMOCRATIC PRINCIPLES

In 2008 the Supreme Court ruled that the Second Amendment protects a long-standing natural right to self-defense, in addition to prohibiting the disarming of militias. This means the government cannot ban the possession of handguns. However, the Supreme Court pointed out that reasonable regulation of guns is allowed. Although the Court did not explain which restrictions were allowed, it gave examples such as banning weapons not typically possessed by law-abiding citizens, prohibiting the possession of guns by felons and the mentally ill, and forbidding the carrying of firearms in places such as schools.

TEAM A — Gun Laws Should Be Stricter

Each year, more than 8,000 murders are committed with guns. There are too many guns in our society, and they are too easy to buy. Since guns are more lethal than other weapons, we need to regulate them more strictly. A criminal with a gun can do much more harm to many more people than someone with another type of weapon.

Moreover, guns are more likely to harm the owner or his family than to harm a criminal. Guns can fall into the wrong hands, and children with access to guns can cause horrible accidents. It is a tragedy when innocent lives are lost due to gun violence. The Constitution allows for reasonable restrictions.

TEAM B — Gun Laws Should Be Looser

Gun control infringes on a basic Constitutional right to protect oneself. Guns are used by law-abiding citizens for self-defense and protection. The police cannot protect everyone all the time and citizens must be prepared to protect themselves. Criminals may be deterred from robbing or harming someone if the potential victim has a gun.

Criminals will always get guns even if we make them illegal. Outlawing guns could even open up a large new black market where criminals buy and sell illegal guns. Guns are not responsible for injuries and deaths; the people who misuse them are. We should hold those people responsible.

EXPLORING THE ESSENTIAL QUESTION

Evaluating Arguments and Counterarguments Consider each proposal below. Think about the arguments, the Constitution, and your personal experiences. Do you think that these proposals should become law? Draw a line across your paper, with one end labeled YES and the other labeled NO. Place the number of the proposal along your line to indicate whether you want the proposal to become law. Note the reasons that support your position. Your teacher will ask you and your classmates to indicate your support for each proposal by standing along a virtual continuum in the classroom. Be prepared to defend your position.

1. Ban all assault weapons.
2. Allow people to carry concealed weapons more easily.
3. Require all guns to be registered to their owner.
4. Require biometric technology that allows only the owner to operate a gun.
5. Allow people to bring guns into schools and government buildings.
6. Ban high-capacity magazines that allow guns to fire many times without reloading.
7. Add a tax to bullets that would make them very expensive.

Interact with these digital assets and others in lesson 4

✓ **GOVERNMENT IN YOUR COMMUNITY**
Your Local Government Charter

✓ **INTERACTIVE GRAPHIC ORGANIZER**
State Constitutions and Local Charters Graphic Organizer

✓ **SELF-CHECK QUIZ**

✓ **VIDEO**
Power of Governors

netw⊙rks
TRY IT YOURSELF ONLINE

Reading Help Desk

Academic Vocabulary
• violation
• logic

Content Vocabulary
• **Supremacy Clause**

TAKING NOTES:
Integrating Knowledge and Ideas

COMPARING AND CONTRASTING Use the Venn diagram to compare and contrast the U.S. Constitution and state constitutions.

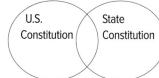

U.S. Constitution | State Constitution

LESSON 4
State Constitutions and Local Charters

ESSENTIAL QUESTION

How do state constitutions and local charters structure government and protect individual rights?

Constitutions can vary from state to state, but they cannot conflict with the U.S. Constitution. Imagine your school's discipline policies are like the U.S. Constitution and your teachers' expectations are like state constitutions as you complete this activity.

a. Make a list of three or more rules that your government teacher expects you to follow above and beyond the school rules. (For example, are you required to write in pen for quizzes and tests? May you chew gum? Must you sit in assigned seating?)

b. Do all of your teachers have the same classroom expectations? If not, how do your teachers' expectations differ?

c. In your opinion, why do teachers' expectations often go beyond school rules and differ from your school's expectations?

The Structures of State Governments

GUIDING QUESTION *How does the structure of state governments compare to the federal government?*

The United States is made up of 50 states, as well as unincorporated territories and commonwealths such as the District of Columbia, Puerto Rico, the U.S. Virgin Islands, American Samoa, Northern Marianas, and Guam. While everyone lives under the U.S. Constitution, most people also live in a place where there is a state constitution or local charter. In addition, people who live on Native American or Alaska Native lands have their own unique legal framework. Living under a national constitution as well as a state constitution is a fundamental aspect of political life in America.

The Three Branches in State and Local Government State constitutions create the structure of state government. Like the federal Constitution, every state constitution provides for separation of powers among three branches of government—legislative, executive, and judicial.

GOVERNMENT *in your* COMMUNITY

Your State Constitution

Step 1: The Organization of Our State Constitution

You and your classmates will prepare a classroom guide to your state constitution. Divide the work so that one small group of students takes the lead on each step. Each group will then teach the others about what they learned. Follow the steps in this lesson to complete your guide.

For Step 1, find a copy of your state constitution and complete the Exploring the Essential Question activity.

> **EXPLORING THE ESSENTIAL QUESTION**
>
> **a.** When was your constitution ratified?
> **b.** How is your constitution organized? Does it have a preamble? Articles? A list of rights? Amendments? How many articles, rights, and amendments does it have?
> **c.** Are there other notable aspects of the way your constitution is organized?
> **d.** Create a one- to two-page report to show what you learned.

Like the national government, each branch has the ability to check the power of the others. State constitutions outline the organization of each branch, the powers and terms of various offices, and the method of election for state officials.

The Legislative Branch State legislatures pass laws that deal with a variety of matters, including health, crime, labor, education, and transportation, and they have the power to tax and to spend and borrow money. In some areas—like public welfare and public safety—state legislatures have more power than the U.S. Congress, which is limited to the lawmaking powers described in Article 1, Section 8 of the U.S. Constitution.

Almost every state has a bicameral state legislature—one with two houses, like the U.S. Congress. The upper house is always called the senate, and the lower house is usually called the house of representatives, but some states refer to it as the general assembly, the house of delegates, the legislative assembly, or the general court. Nebraska has the only unicameral, or one-chambered, state legislature in the country.

The Executive Branch Every state has an executive branch headed by a governor, who has the power to carry out, or execute, state laws. The governor's responsibilities include proposing and signing legislation, budgeting, appointing officials, planning for economic growth, and coordinating the work of executive departments.

The amount of control that a governor has over the executive branch varies widely from state to state. At the national level, a candidate who is campaigning to become president chooses his or her vice presidential running mate. Voters choose the president and vice president, who in turn select cabinet members who share their vision and priorities to help lead the executive branch. This arrangement is true for many states, too, although some state constitutions divide executive branch power. In more than half the states, for example, the people elect the governor, the lieutenant governor, the attorney general (the state's top legal officer), and the secretary of state (the chief clerk of state government) separately. Each of these officers has specific and separate responsibilities defined by the state constitution, and the governor in these states has no power to select or remove these officials.

Governors often try to obtain grants from the national government for their state's schools, highways, and urban areas. They represent their states when they seek cooperation from other states in such areas as transportation and pollution control; more recently, governors have also begun representing their states internationally. For example, governors attempt to encourage foreign businesses to locate in their states and have sought foreign markets for products their states produce.

All state constitutions give governors the role of commander in chief over the state's National Guard. Governors can use the guard members in their states to maintain law and order during state emergencies.

The Judicial Branch Like the U.S. Constitution, state constitutions establish courts to uphold and interpret state laws. Those courts help resolve conflicts such as business disagreements and grievances that citizens might have against each other. State courts also punish criminals who violate state laws.

Every state has minor courts, trial courts, and appellate courts. Minor courts usually handle minor **violations** of law or private disputes, perform marriages, or legalize documents. Trial courts hear many different types of cases—whether a violation of the law or a dispute between individuals. Appeals courts review cases that a lower court has already decided. Each state's highest court is usually called its *supreme court*. The highest court also interprets the state's constitution and laws.

> **violation** an act of disregard or disrespect

Finally, state constitutions establish independent state agencies, boards, and commissions that have power in areas that affect citizens' lives directly. These include, for example, public utility commissions that regulate rates for gas and electricity and boards of education that help administer public schools throughout the state.

As the basic law of the state, the state constitution is supreme and trumps all other laws made within the state. At the same time, the state constitution cannot contain provisions that clash with the U.S. Constitution. Under the U.S. Constitution's **supremacy clause**, if a federal court decides that a provision or amendment of a state's constitution is in conflict with the U.S. Constitution, that provision or amendment must be removed.

> **supremacy clause** statement in Article VI of the Constitution establishing that the Constitution, laws passed by Congress, and treaties of the United States "shall be the supreme Law of the Land"

✅ **READING PROGRESS CHECK**

Comparing How is the structure of the national government similar to the structure of state governments?

GOVERNMENT *in your* COMMUNITY

Your State Constitution

Step 2. Three Branches of Government Under Our State Constitution
Using your state constitution, analyze the three branches of your state government.

EXPLORING THE ESSENTIAL QUESTION
   a. What is the name of your state's legislature?
   b. What are the names of the two legislative bodies? How many elected officials serve in each house? (If you live in Nebraska, answer for your one house.)
   c. What are your state lawmakers called? (Delegates? Representatives?)
   d. Describe at least two powers given to your governor by the state constitution.
   e. List the other offices that make up the executive branch of your state.
   f. Summarize your state court system. What are the names of the courts, from lowest to highest?
   g. Are judges in your state elected, appointed, or chosen another way?
   h. Prepare a one- to two-page report to show what you learned.

Rights and Amendments in State Constitutions

GUIDING QUESTIONS *How does the process for amending state constitutions compare to that of the U.S. Constitution?*

Besides a provision for separation of powers among the three branches of state government, all state constitutions contain a bill of rights. This section includes all or most of the protections of the Bill of Rights in the Constitution of the United States. Many state constitutions contain additional protections not found in the U.S. Constitution. In a sense, the U.S. Constitution creates a "ground floor"—everyone must get at least the rights contained in the U.S. Constitution. But that document is not a "ceiling" and states can provide additional rights. Examples of these protections are a worker's right to join a union, a ban on discrimination based on gender or race, and certain protections for the physically challenged.

Amending State Constitutions Compared to the U.S. Constitution, state constitutions tend to have an enormous number of amendments. The average state constitution has been amended 115 times. Alabamans have amended their constitution 770 times. These amendments might change the structure of the state government, redefine the powers allocated to different parts of government, or expand or restrict individual rights in the state.

How are state constitutions amended? In all states, there are multiple methods to amending the constitution, though the specific methods vary greatly from state to state.

Many states allow people to propose amendments directly through ballot initiatives. In these states, if enough eligible voters sign an official petition, the proposed amendment will appear on a ballot, and then voters can decide. In 2010 alone, 123 proposals to amend state constitutions appeared on state ballots and 89 passed.

All states allow their state legislature to propose constitutional amendments. In Delaware, amendments approved by the state legislature become law, without input from voters. In every other state, if the proposal gets enough votes in the legislature, the amendment is sent to voters for their approval or disapproval.

Most states have the option of convening a statewide constitutional convention, which is a gathering of citizens who are usually elected by popular vote and who meet to consider changing or replacing a constitution. Again, whether voters can call for a convention or whether state legislatures must agree to the convention varies from state to state.

GOVERNMENT *in your* COMMUNITY

Your State Constitution

Step 3. Amendments and Individual Rights Protected by Our Constitution

EXPLORING THE ESSENTIAL QUESTION

a. Look at the list of individual rights protected in your state constitution. Are they similar to those in the Bill of Rights of the U.S. Constitution? Does your state constitution grant additional rights? To all people? To certain groups of people? Explain.

b. How many times has your state constitution been amended? When was the most recent amendment and what did it do?

c. If you and your friends thought your state constitution could be improved, what steps could you take to get it amended? What is the process (or methods) for amending the constitution in your state?

A constitutional commission is a group of experts who are appointed to study the state constitution and recommend changes. Florida and New Mexico are the only states that offer this method for constitutional amendments.

☑ **READING PROGRESS CHECK**

Describing Describe the different processes for amending state constitutions.

Local Governments and Charters

GUIDING QUESTIONS *What are local charters?*

Although the United States has a strong tradition of local self-government, local governments exist only if a state constitution creates them and gives them local authority. State constitutions establish different types of local government, usually based on their size and population. State constitutions might create cities, counties, townships, municipalities, special districts, parishes, and boroughs. They also define the organization, powers, and duties of local governments.

State Constitutions State constitutions regulate the ways local governments can raise and spend money. In many states, the state constitution limits the taxing power of local governments by creating rules about the kinds of taxes local governments can levy and how revenue must be spent. A state government might, for example, assume control over a local school district that is in financial trouble.

Local Charters Charters are documents that state governments issue to local governments. A charter grants the community a legal status and allows it to have a separate local government. Charters specify the type of government the community will have, the powers and responsibilities of the local government, and the procedure for electing officials to the local government.

Most charters establish three branches of local government along with the powers and duties of each branch. Charters usually contain a bill of rights, which may include more protections and rights than the state or national constitution; a charter cannot contain fewer rights than the state and national constitutions, however. For example, the charter for Montgomery County, Maryland, gives firefighters the right to a union, although the State of Maryland does not provide this right.

Following the **logic** of national supremacy, local charters and laws passed by local legislatures cannot conflict with state constitutions, which cannot conflict with the U.S. Constitution.

☑ **READING PROGRESS CHECK**

Understanding Relationships What is the relationship between local charters and state governments?

logic the science of the formal principles of reasoning

EXPLORING THE ESSENTIAL QUESTION

Create a classroom guide to your local government's charter. Be sure to cover the following points. Then prepare a one- to two-page report to show what you learned.

a. When was your local government's charter created?

b. How is your local government structured?

c. Does your local government have the power to levy taxes?

d. Does your charter extend individual rights beyond those in the U.S. Bill of Rights? If so, how?

e. If you wanted to amend your local charter, what steps could you take?

LESSON 4 REVIEW

Reviewing Vocabulary
1. *Defining* How do bicameral and unicameral legislatures differ?

Using Your Graphic Organizer
2. *Contrasting* Using your completed graphic organizer, write a paragraph explaining how state constitutions and the U.S. Constitution differ.

Answering the Guiding Questions
3. *Comparing* How does the structure of state governments compare to the federal government?

4. *Comparing* How does the process for amending state constitutions compare to that of the U.S. Constitution?

5. *Defining* What are local charters?

Writing About Government
6. *Informative/Explanatory* Write a brief essay in which you explain the different processes for amending the various state constitutions. Conclude by explaining which one you would recommend to others based on what you have learned.

STUDY GUIDE

STRUCTURE AND PRINCIPLES OF THE CONSTITUTION
LESSON 1

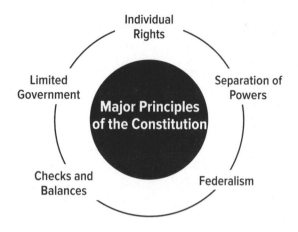

Individual Rights

Limited Government

Major Principles of the Constitution

Separation of Powers

Checks and Balances

Federalism

THE THREE BRANCHES OF GOVERNMENT
LESSON 2

Legislative Branch passes the laws.

Judicial Branch interprets the Constitution and laws.

Executive Branch carries out and enforces laws passed by Congress.

PROCESS FOR AMENDING THE CONSTITUTION
LESSON 3

Amendment Proposal

- Two-thirds vote by both houses of Congress *or*
- Convention called by Congress at request of two-thirds of the states

Amendment Ratification

- Three-fourths of the state legislatures *or*
- Three-fourths of special constitutional conventions called by the states

New Amendment

NATIONAL SUPREMACY
LESSON 4

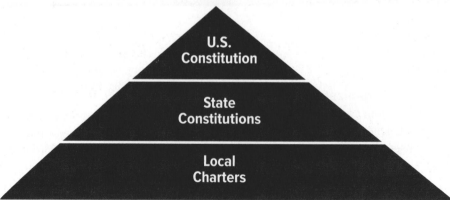

U.S. Constitution

State Constitutions

Local Charters

Directions: On a separate sheet of paper, answer the questions below. Make sure you read carefully and answer all parts of the questions.

Lesson Review

Lesson 1

1 ***Making Connections*** How does the basic structure of the Constitution demonstrate the principle of separation of power?

2 ***Evaluating*** Describe the Bill of Rights and explain why it was needed.

Lesson 2

3 ***Explaining*** Describe an action taken by the U.S. Congress in the past few months that is an enumerated power and explain why it is an enumerated power.

4 ***Explaining*** Explain how certain provisions of the Constitution provide checks and balances among the three branches of government.

Lesson 3

5 ***Organizing*** For the Bill of Rights, list the freedoms and individual rights protected in each amendment.

6 ***Analyzing*** Analyze the impact of the passage of the Seventeenth Amendment.

Lesson 4

7 ***Defining*** Define the phrase *national supremacy* and explain how this affects state and local governments.

8 ***Comparing and Contrasting*** Compare and contrast the U.S. Constitution with the constitution for your state government.

ANSWERING THE ESSENTIAL QUESTIONS

Review your answers to the introductory questions at the beginning of each lesson. Then answer the Essential Questions based on what you learned in the chapter. Have your answers changed?

9 ***Comparing*** How does the U.S. Constitution structure government and divide power between the national and state governments?

10 ***Analyzing*** Why and how has the U.S. Constitution been amended and interpreted throughout our history?

11 ***Classifying*** How do state constitutions and local charters structure government and protect individual rights?

DBQ Interpreting Political Cartoons

Use the political cartoon to answer the following questions.

12 ***Interpreting*** Identify and describe parts of the image representing major principles of the Constitution.

13 ***Identifying Perspectives*** What concepts are supported by this image? Explain your answer.

Critical Thinking

14 ***Finding the Main Idea*** In *The Federalist* No. 51, James Madison wrote, "you must first enable the government to control the governed; and in the next place oblige it to control itself." Give an example of a provision in the Constitution that reflects the ideas in this statement and explain how it carries out Madison's idea.

15 ***Identifying Cause and Effect*** Describe why limited government and the rule of law are necessary to protect individual rights.

Need Extra Help?

If You've Missed Question	1	2	3	4	5	6	7	8	9	10	11	12	13	14	15
Go to page	68	71	73	77	83	85	93	91	68	81	91	70	70	70	70

Directions: On a separate sheet of paper, answer the questions below. Make sure you read carefully and answer all parts of the questions.

16 *Defending* Does the U.S. Constitution guarantee the unalienable rights used in the Declaration of Independence as a justification to form an independent nation? Identify and define unalienable rights and defend your answer with text from the Constitution.

DBQ Analyzing Primary Sources

Read the excerpt and answer the questions that follow.

James Madison wrote several articles, known as *The Federalist Papers*, published in New York in support of ratification of the Constitution.

PRIMARY SOURCE

"If we resort for a criterion to the different principles on which different forms of government are established, we may define a republic to be, or at least may bestow that name on, a government which derives all its powers directly or indirectly from the great body of the people, and is administered by persons holding their offices during pleasure, for a limited period, or during good behavior."

—James Madison, *The Federalist* No. 39

17 *Identifying the Main Idea* What is Madison defining in this excerpt and what is his definition?

18 *Analyzing* Analyze how *The Federalist* No. 39 explains the principles of the American constitutional system of government.

Social Studies Skills

19 *Understanding Relationships Among Events* Review information about the background of the participants at the Constitutional Convention and explain why a written constitution is important.

20 *Making Connections* Describe the inherent tensions that exist between the states and national government. How does the Constitution address those tensions and balance the needs to the states and national government?

Use the table to answer questions 21 and 22.

RATIFICATION OF THE U.S. CONSTITUTION

State	Date
Delaware	December 1787
Pennsylvania	December 1787
New Jersey	December 1787
Georgia	January 1788
Connecticut	January 1788
Massachusetts	February 1788
Maryland	April 1788
South Carolina	May 1788
New Hampshire	June 1788
Virginia	June 1788
New York	July 1788
North Carolina	November 1789
Rhode Island	May 1790

21 *Creating and Using Charts and Tables* Create a time line using the information contained in the table.

22 *Time, Chronology, and Sequencing* Identify states that ratified the Constitution following the Bill of Rights amendments being sent to states for ratification.

Research and Presentation

23 *Evaluating* Describe the following constitutional provisions: republicanism, checks and balances, federalism, separation of powers, popular sovereignty, and individual rights. Evaluate whether these provisions have been effective in limiting the role of government. Provide examples to support your opinions.

24 *Making Connections* Identify how the American beliefs and principles reflected in the Constitution contribute to both a national identity and federal identity and are embodied in the United States today.

25 *Informative/Explanatory* Create a multimedia presentation that demonstrates five of the principles of democracy that are most evident to you in the U.S. Constitution.

Need Extra Help?

If You've Missed Question	**16**	**17**	**18**	**19**	**20**	**21**	**22**	**23**	**24**	**25**
Go to page	70	71	70	68	71	96	96	70	76	70

Federalism

ESSENTIAL QUESTIONS

- Why and how is power divided and shared among national, state, and local governments?
- How does federalism promote democracy and civic participation?

networks
www.connected.mcgraw-hill.com
There's More Online about federalism.

CHAPTER 4

Courtesy National Gallery of Art, Washington

▲ James Madison was called the "Father of the Constitution" due to his defense of the U.S. Constitution in the *Federalist Papers*.

ANALYZING PRIMARY SOURCES

FEDERALISM & EDUCATION

Who should make the critical decisions about education in the United States? Many different people and groups are interested in deciding what American students will learn, from students and parents to colleges, employers, and government leaders. Should all students study the same curriculum? What level of government should make decisions about what is taught or fund the schools? Explore the sources here and reach your own conclusion about whether education decisions should be made by federal, state, or local governments.

PRIMARY SOURCE A

The U.S. Constitution

"The Congress shall have the Power . . . to make all Laws which shall be necessary and proper for carrying into Execution the foregoing Powers, and all other Powers vested by the Constitution in the Government of the United States or in any Department or Officer thereof."

—Article I, Section 8

"The powers not delegated to the United States by the Constitution, nor prohibited by it to the States, are reserved to the States respectively, or to the people."

—Amendment X

PRIMARY SOURCE B

In 1859 President James Buchanan vetoed a bill donating public lands to the states to create colleges for agriculture and engineering.

"I presume the general proposition is undeniable that Congress does not possess the power to appropriate money in the Treasury, raised by taxes on the people of the United States, for the purpose of educating the people of the respective States. It will not be pretended that any such power is to be found among the specific powers granted to Congress nor that 'it is necessary and proper for carrying into execution' any one of these powers. Should Congress exercise such a power, this would be to break down the barriers which have been so carefully constructed in the Constitution to separate Federal from State authority."

—President Buchanan's Veto Message to Congress, February 24, 1859

PRIMARY SOURCE C

"What this Goals 2000 bill does, believe it or not, for the first time in the entire history of the United States of America, is to set world-class education standards for what every child in every American school should know in order to win when he or she becomes an adult. We have never done it before; we are going to do it now because of this bill."

—President Clinton's Remarks on Signing the Goals 2000: Educate America Act, March 31, 1994

PRIMARY SOURCE D

"In a perfect world where state and local administrators kept the best interests of students and taxpayers front and center, I'd be all for it. But the world isn't perfect, and in far too many places, state and local control means excuses, inaction, complacency, and union control. Our children, particularly those who most need us to have their backs, deserve better than that."

—Margaret Spellings, former U.S. Secretary of Education, 2011

"'Local control' does not mean sustaining the status quo. Rather, it recognizes that mandates from Washington do not achieve the same results in every community across the nation. States and school districts understand that strategies must be tailored to address the unique circumstances of students, and that is not something that can be done effectively without local control."

—Anne L. Bryant, Executive Director, National School Boards Association

SECONDARY SOURCE **F**

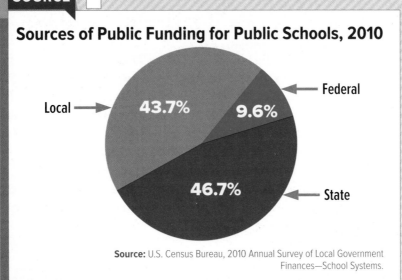

Sources of Public Funding for Public Schools, 2010

Local — 43.7%
Federal — 9.6%
State — 46.7%

Source: U.S. Census Bureau, 2010 Annual Survey of Local Government Finances—School Systems.

WHAT WILL YOU DO?

Imagine two candidates for the U.S. House of Representatives have very different ideas about education. Candidate A favors a strong federal role in education. Candidate B believes the important decisions about education should be made at the state and local level. Which candidate would you vote for? Why?

DBQ DOCUMENT-BASED QUESTIONS

1. **Analyzing Graphs** Which sources provide most of the funding for public schools?

2. **Explaining** In your own words, explain the argument that congressional involvement in funding and legislating about education is unconstitutional.

3. **Evaluating Arguments** List one good argument for a large federal role in education and one argument for local/state control. Which argument is stronger? Explain your answer.

EXPLORE the interactive version of the analyzing primary sources feature on Networks.

LESSON 1
Dividing and Sharing Power

Reading Help Desk

Academic Vocabulary

- authority
- contradict

Content Vocabulary

- **federalism**
- **delegated powers**
- **expressed powers**
- **implied powers**
- **reserved powers**
- **concurrent powers**
- **supremacy clause**

TAKING NOTES:

Key Ideas and Details

IDENTIFYING Use the table to list national powers, state and local powers, concurrent powers, and denied powers.

National Powers	State and Local Powers	Concurrent Powers	Denied Powers

ESSENTIAL QUESTION

Why and how is power divided and shared among national, state, and local governments?

Imagine you are in each of the situations below and you want someone in government to help you address it. Would you contact someone at the local, state, or national level? Are there any instances in which you might contact someone at more than one level? Once you have decided which level(s) of government could be involved, create a chart to record your information. As an example, the first answer depends on the road—some roads are maintained by states, others by local government.

a. There is a huge pothole in the road in front of your house.

b. You think someone is stealing the mail from your mailbox.

c. When you were looking for an apartment, you feel sure a property manager turned you down because of your race or national origin.

d. You live within a mile of a nuclear weapons plant and you just learned that a fifth neighbor has become very ill.

e. You want to get married.

f. You want to object to how high your taxes are.

g. You think one of your coworkers is actually a foreign spy.

h. Your supervisor has threatened to fire you if you do not work on Saturdays, but that is your religion's day of rest.

i. You want to get a pilot's license.

j. You want to enlist in the army.

Why Federalism

GUIDING QUESTION *Why does the Constitution divide power between the national and state governments?*

The Framers meeting in Philadelphia in 1787 faced a dilemma: How could they create one nation out of thirteen independent states in a way that would protect citizens' liberties from an all-powerful central government?

Their response was to create an entirely new approach to governing—**federalism**. In federalism, two or more governments exercise power over the same people and the same territory. In our federal system the central, or national, government has some special powers over all citizens, the states have certain powers reserved for them, and the two share some powers.

The roles of state and national government officials in our federal system have developed over two centuries of American government and history. Before the Constitution became the law of the land, it had to be approved by the states, and many leaders in state governments were apprehensive about sharing power with a new national government. Would the new national government ignore the sovereignty of the states and establish unfair taxes like the British monarch had done? Supporters of federalism like John Jay and Alexander Hamilton had to convince state leaders that the Constitution set up a power-sharing arrangement that was reasonable.

In *The Federalist* No. 9, Hamilton assured doubters that the Constitution would respect the power of state governments:

PRIMARY SOURCE

The proposed Constitution, so far from implying an abolition of the State governments, makes them constituent parts of the national sovereignty, by allowing them a direct representation in the Senate, and leaves in their possession certain exclusive and very important portions of sovereign power. This fully corresponds . . . with the idea of a federal government."

—Alexander Hamilton, 1787

EXPLORING THE ESSENTIAL QUESTION

Drawing Conclusions Many people today still disagree about the relative roles of local, state, and federal governments. Review each problem described here and decide whether you think this problem should be addressed by the local, state, and/or national government. Write down your answer and a list of criteria you used to make your decisions.

a. Only 75 percent of U.S. high school students graduate on time. Among those who graduate, a significant percentage is not prepared for the workforce or will need remedial course work in college.

b. Many American cities experience violent crime. In 2010, for example, there was an average of 428 violent crimes per 100,000 residents in cities.

c. More than 48 million Americans under age 65 did not have health insurance in 2011. Many people in the United States cannot afford health care when they get sick, and costs are growing rapidly.

d. American and European leaders believe that Iran is developing nuclear weapons. A nuclear Iran could threaten the United States or our allies in the Middle East.

e. Residents of a city are concerned that too many bars and dance clubs are opening downtown. Late at night, the patrons are noisy and the police are often called to keep the peace.

federalism a system of government in which two or more governments exercise power over the same people and the same territory

The Constitution was ratified and our government was established based on a federal model for dividing and sharing power among different levels of government. Even today, however, many people, political parties, and officials at all levels of government still disagree about the right formula for dividing and sharing power.

✓ **READING PROGRESS CHECK**

Speculating Why do you think people disagree about how different levels of government should divide power?

authority the right to command or lead

Federalism in the Constitution

GUIDING QUESTION *How does the Constitution divide power between national and state governments?*

The Constitution divides government **authority** by giving the national government certain specified powers, reserving all other powers to the states or to the people. In addition, the national and state governments share some powers, and finally, the Constitution specifically denies some powers to each level of government.

National Powers The Constitution grants both expressed powers and implied powers to the national government. Collectively, these powers are known as **delegated powers**, powers the Constitution grants or delegates to the national government.

The **expressed powers**, also called enumerated powers, are those powers directly expressed or stated in the Constitution by the Founders. Most of these powers are found in the first three articles of the Constitution. This constitutional authority includes the power to levy and collect taxes, to coin money, to make war, to raise an army and navy, and to regulate commerce among the states.

Some of the national government's powers are not stated specifically in the Constitution. They are **implied powers**. So, for example, even though the Constitution does not say anything about space exploration or nuclear weapons, it does state that the national government has the power to regulate interstate commerce and to defend the country. These programs were created to carry out those expressed powers. The basis for the implied powers is in the Constitution.

State and Local Powers While the national government has many powers under federalism, states have even more. The Constitution says that the states will have any powers not delegated to the national government, as long as they are not also prohibited to the states. These are called **reserved powers** because they are reserved for states. The Constitution does not list these powers specifically. Instead, it says:

PRIMARY SOURCE
. . . the powers not delegated to the United States by the Constitution, nor prohibited by it to the states, are reserved to the states respectively, or to the people."

—Amendment X

The delegated powers of Congress include both expressed and implied powers. One of the expressed powers is the power to raise an army and navy. Expeditionary Strike Group 2, shown here, is a naval group that uses amphibious expertise in operations around the world.

▼ **CRITICAL THINKING**
Analyzing In carrying out the expressed power of building an army and navy, Congress passed the Selective Service Act in 1917, requiring all men of 18 years old to register their names so that they may be drafted into the military if necessary. Do you think it is fair that women are not required to register, even though they are allowed to serve in combat? Explain your reasoning.

Purestock/Superstock

Division of Federal and State Powers

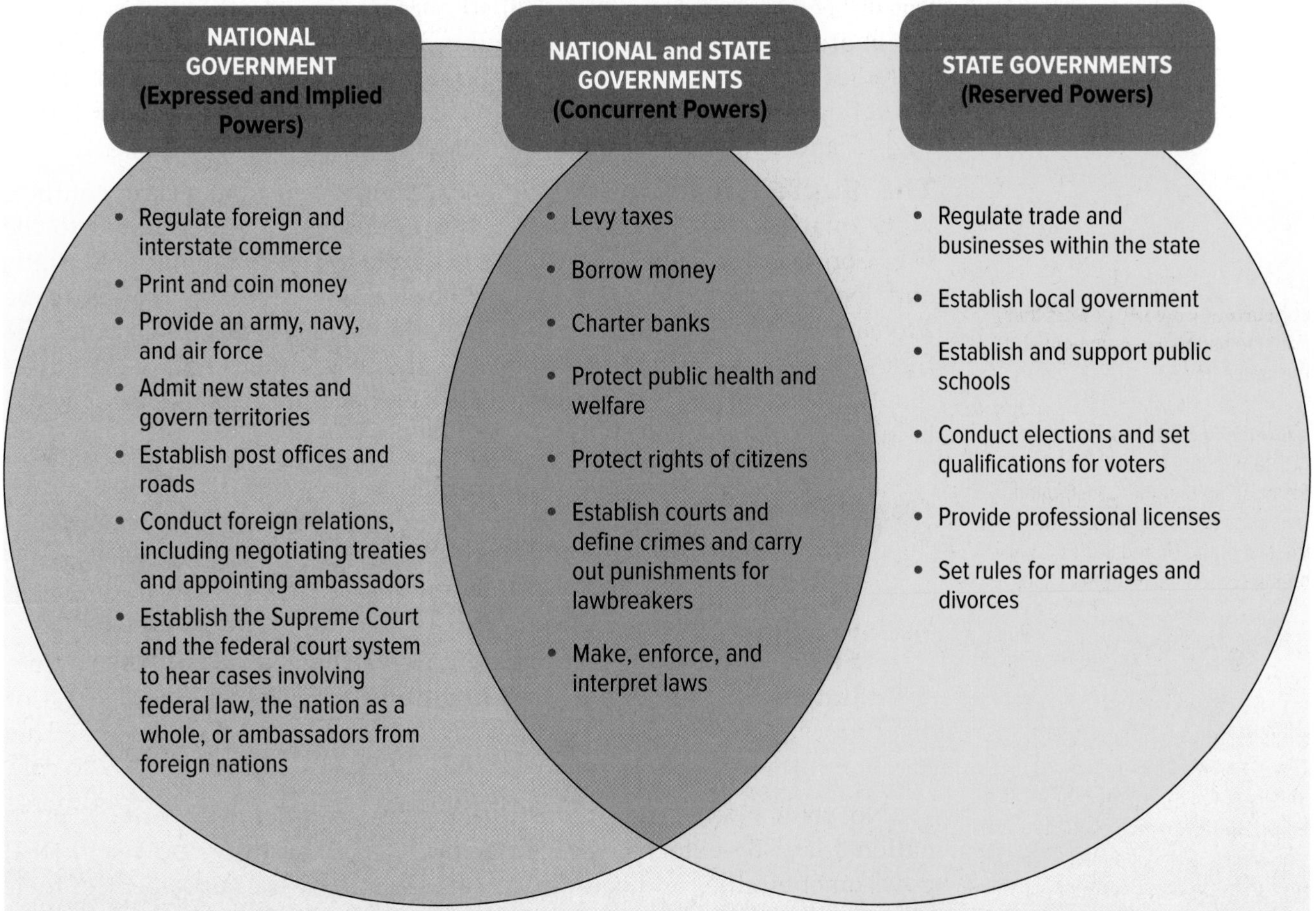

NATIONAL GOVERNMENT (Expressed and Implied Powers)	NATIONAL and STATE GOVERNMENTS (Concurrent Powers)	STATE GOVERNMENTS (Reserved Powers)
• Regulate foreign and interstate commerce • Print and coin money • Provide an army, navy, and air force • Admit new states and govern territories • Establish post offices and roads • Conduct foreign relations, including negotiating treaties and appointing ambassadors • Establish the Supreme Court and the federal court system to hear cases involving federal law, the nation as a whole, or ambassadors from foreign nations	• Levy taxes • Borrow money • Charter banks • Protect public health and welfare • Protect rights of citizens • Establish courts and define crimes and carry out punishments for lawbreakers • Make, enforce, and interpret laws	• Regulate trade and businesses within the state • Establish local government • Establish and support public schools • Conduct elections and set qualifications for voters • Provide professional licenses • Set rules for marriages and divorces

Thus, the states have authority over matters not found in the Constitution. Traditionally, reserved powers include states' powers to conduct elections, establish and support local schools, and regulate businesses and trade within the state.

Concurrent Powers The federal government and the states also have certain powers that they share, called **concurrent powers**, and each level of government exercises these powers independently. Examples of concurrent powers are the power to tax, to maintain courts and define crimes, and to take private property for public use. Concurrently with the national government, the states may exercise any power not reserved by the Constitution for the national government; however, state actions must not conflict with any national laws.

Denied Powers Finally, the Constitution specifically denies some powers to all levels of government. Article I, Sections 9 and 10, enumerate those things neither the national government nor state governments can do. For example, neither government can
- Pass retroactive laws (that punish actions that occurred before the law passed)
- Tax exports
- Hold or sentence a person to jail without a fair trial
- Pass any law that violates the Constitution
- Grant titles of nobility

▲ CRITICAL THINKING

Categorizing Write each of the powers listed in the graph on a separate note card or slip of paper. Shuffle them. Then, without using your book, try to put each card into one of three categories: national (delegated) powers, concurrent powers, and state (reserved) powers. Compare your chart to the one here and review powers and terms that were unclear to you.

delegated powers powers the Constitution grants or delegates to the national government

expressed powers powers directly stated in the Constitution

implied powers powers the government requires to carry out its expressed constitutional powers

reserved powers powers that belong strictly to the states

States cannot make treaties or alliances with foreign governments or coin money or make any laws that interfere with contracts. Unless they have permission from the Congress, states cannot collect duties on exports or imports, or make agreements—called *compacts*—with other states.

In order to protect individual rights and liberties, the Constitution also provides other limits on both national and state governments. These limitations are found in several places, including Article I, the Bill of Rights, and other Amendments.

The Supremacy Clause What happens when a state law conflicts with a national law? For example, the Twenty-sixth Amendment to the U.S. Constitution makes 18-year-olds eligible to vote in all national, state, and local elections. A state cannot pass a law requiring voters to be 21 years of age, but it could pass a law allowing 16-year-olds to vote. The first law conflicts with the national law; the second does not.

Article VI makes the acts and treaties of the United States supreme and is called the **supremacy clause**.

concurrent powers powers that both the national government and the states have

supremacy clause statement in Article VI of the Constitution establishing that the Constitution, laws passed by Congress, and treaties of the United States "shall be the supreme Law of the Land"

> **PRIMARY SOURCE**
>
> **This Constitution, and the Laws of the United States which shall be made in Pursuance thereof, and all treaties made . . . under the Authority of the United States, shall be the supreme Law of the Land; and the Judges in every State shall be bound thereby."**
>
> —Article VI

No state law or state constitution may conflict with any form of national law. By extension, because states create and give power to local governments, cities and counties are also bound by the supremacy of their state constitutions as well as by the supremacy of the U.S. Constitution. They cannot pass laws that **contradict** their own state constitution or the U.S. Constitution.

contradict to assert the contrary of, to imply the opposite of

✔ **READING PROGRESS CHECK**

Specifying Which powers are shared by the federal and state governments?

LESSON 1 REVIEW

Reviewing Vocabulary

1. *Defining* What are the expressed powers and implied powers of the national government?

Using Your Graphic Organizer

2. *Summarizing* Choose one of the columns in your completed graphic organizer and write two paragraphs summarizing the information.

Answering the Guiding Questions

3. *Drawing Conclusions* Why does the Constitution divide power between the national and state governments?

4. *Differentiating* How does the Constitution divide power between national and state governments?

Writing About Government

5. *Argument* Review the powers that are denied to government. Are there any powers that you think should be added or removed from this list? Write an essay explaining your reasoning.

Interact with these digital
assets and others in lesson 2

✓ INTERACTIVE MAP
  Federal Aid to State Governments

✓ SELF-CHECK QUIZ

✓ SLIDE SHOW
  Land-Grant Colleges and Universities

✓ VIDEO
  Arizona Immigration

netw⊙rks
TRY IT YOURSELF ONLINE

ReadingHelp Desk

Academic Vocabulary

- integrity
- alter
- allocate

Content Vocabulary

- enabling act
- federal grant
- mandate
- restraint
- preemption

TAKING NOTES:

Key Ideas and Details

IDENTIFYING Use the table to list national obligations and state obligations.

National Obligations	State Obligations

LESSON 2

Relations Between the National and State Governments

ESSENTIAL QUESTION

How is power divided and shared among national, state, and local governments?

Imagine that there has been an outbreak of a highly infectious and potentially deadly disease. Doctors and scientists have said that, at least for the moment, the disease is mostly clustered in an area of the country where three states share borders. Many people live in one state, work in another, and cross state lines on public transportation daily. However, hospitals in neighboring states have also reported incidents and the disease seems to be spreading fast.

Imagine you are the governor of one of the states at the center of the outbreak. You know you need a coordinated response to stop its spread. You decide to arrange a conference call to bring together people who can help. Who would you want to be involved in creating a plan for a smart response to the crisis? These people or groups are known as *stakeholders* because they have a stake in making sure the policies work and are fair.

a. Work with two other classmates to brainstorm a list of stakeholders you want to invite to the meeting. These are people with whom you will collaborate to make a plan to deal with this problem.

b. Predict which responses or strategies each group of stakeholders might propose.

c. Decide who should pay for all the activities that make up the response.

d. Now imagine the conference call has happened and you need to decide your plan. Write it down. What criteria did you use to pick the best response?

e. Imagine you need to present your plan at a news conference. Which key talking points would you include in your presentation?

The *Constitution*

WHAT DOES IT MEAN TO YOU?

The Constitution obliges the national government to do three things for the states. These duties are described in Article IV, Section 4.

"The United States shall guarantee to every State in this Union a Republican Form of Government, and shall protect each of them against Invasion; and on Application of the Legislature, or of the Executive (when the Legislature cannot be convened) against domestic Violence."

—Article IV, Section 4

DBQ

1. *Paraphrasing* Examine the text of Article IV, Section 4. What does it say the national government must do? Restate the text in your own words. If you do not know the terms, look them up. (In this context, *domestic violence* refers to civil unrest.)

2. *Applying* Give two examples of the national government's responsibilities to the states. Do you think this part of the Constitution requires the national government to help states where an infectious disease has broken out?

Guarantees to and Obligations of the States

GUIDING QUESTIONS *What does the national government guarantee to the state governments? What obligations do the state governments have to the national government?*

During times of crisis, as well as for many other mundane government tasks, local, regional, and state governments must sometimes work together. The relationships among national, state, and local governments are critical to the everyday workings of our system of government. Those relationships have been developed and refined through conflict, compromise, and cooperation.

Republican Form of Government and Protection Federal protections for the states are guaranteed in Article IV, Section 4. First, the national government must guarantee each state a republican form of government, where the voters hold sovereign power. Elected representatives who are responsible to the people exercise that power. Congress has the responsibility for enforcing this guarantee. When Congress allows senators and representatives from a state to take their seat in Congress, it is in effect ruling that the state has a republican form of government.

Second, the national government must protect states from invasion and unrest within the United States; an attack by a foreign power on one state is considered an attack on the entire country.

Third, Congress has given the president authority to send federal troops to a state where there is civil unrest and the governor or state legislature has requested help. When national laws are violated, federal property is threatened, or federal responsibilities are interfered with, the president may send troops to a state without the request of local authorities—or even over local objections. In 1894, for example, President Grover Cleveland sent federal troops to Chicago to restore order during a strike of railroad workers even though the governor of Illinois objected. During the strike, rioters had threatened federal property and interfered with mail delivery.

During the 1950s and 1960s, presidents Dwight D. Eisenhower and John F. Kennedy used this power to stop state officials from blocking the integration of Southern schools and universities. Eisenhower sent troops to Little Rock, Arkansas, in 1957 when local officials failed to integrate public schools. Kennedy used troops at the University of Mississippi in 1962 and the University of Alabama in 1963.

The national government also intervenes in states in the aftermath of natural disasters such as earthquakes, floods, hurricanes, and tornadoes. When one of these disasters strikes, the president may order federal troops to aid disaster victims. The government also provides low-cost loans to help people repair damages.

Territorial Integrity and Admission of New States Article IV, Section 3, says that the national government has the duty to respect the territorial **integrity** of each state.

integrity wholeness or unity

The Constitution gives Congress the power to pass laws that allow new states to join the nation, although Congress cannot make a state out of territory belonging to a state without its consent. Like all other laws, the admission of new states is subject to presidential veto.

Before a territory can become a state, Congress must pass an **enabling act**, which allows the people of the territory interested in becoming a state to prepare a constitution. If voters in those areas approve the constitution by popular vote, Congress can choose to take a vote on whether to accept the proposed state constitution and whether to admit the territory as a state.

enabling act an act that allows the people of a territory interested in becoming a state to prepare a constitution

Student VOICES

Building Support
for Statehood

▲ William-José Velez

William-José Velez and Markus Batchelor were leaders in different student groups rallying to build support for statehood for Puerto Rico and Washington, D.C. Among their many grievances is that their representatives in Congress do not have full voting rights.

To gain support for their causes, the student groups in the District of Columbia and Puerto Rico have created blogs and Facebook pages where supporters have exchanged ideas and strategies, staged protests and marches, arranged "teach-ins," and established chapters (like clubs) at various high schools and colleges. They have collaborated with other groups, hung posters around town saying "the last colony," and even asked the president to use the District's license plate ("Taxation Without Representation") in the presidential motorcade.

"I like to tell people that D.C. statehood should be and can be the leading civil rights issue in our nation right now."

— Markus Batchelor

CRITICAL THINKING
1. Determining Importance If a fellow student like William-José or Markus wanted you to join them for a cause they believe in (no matter what the cause), what strategies would get your attention the most? A march? A protest? A Facebook page? Something else?
2. Evaluating How would you evaluate which community organizing strategies are the most effective at reaching young people?

FEDERAL AID to STATE GOVERNMENTS

Federal aid to state governments varies across the country. This map shows federal aid dollars per capita.

▶ **CRITICAL THINKING**

Analyzing Is this system of federal aid fair?

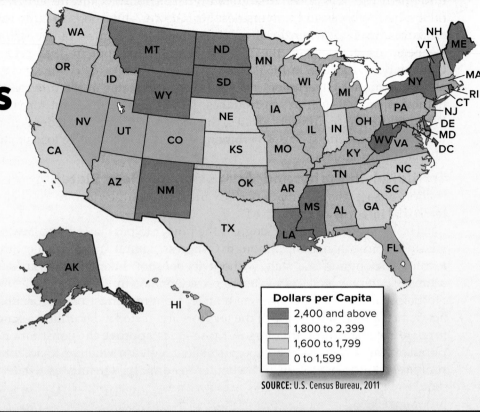

Dollars per Capita
- 2,400 and above
- 1,800 to 2,399
- 1,600 to 1,799
- 0 to 1,599

SOURCE: U.S. Census Bureau, 2011

alter to make different without changing into something else

Obligations of the States The states perform two important functions for the national government. First, state and local governments conduct and pay for elections of all national government officials—senators, representatives, and presidential electors. The Constitution gives state legislatures the power to fix the "times, places, and manner" of election of senators and representatives, though Congress can **alter** state election laws, too.

In addition, the states play a key role in the process of amending the Constitution. According to the Constitution, no amendment can be added to it unless three-fourths of the states approve it.

☑ **READING PROGRESS CHECK**

Defining What is a republican form of government?

Federal Aid and Mandates

GUIDING QUESTION *How does the federal government influence state and local governments?*

As the national government has grown and enlarged its powers over the years, Congress has developed two major ways to influence the policies of state and local governments. It provides **federal grants** of money to states and passes mandates that require state and local governments to follow certain policies.

federal grant a sum of money given to a state or local government for a specific purpose

Federal Aid The national government has always provided different types of aid to the states. In 1862, for instance, Congress passed a law giving nearly 6 million acres of public land to the states for support of colleges. Since the 1950s federal aid to state and local governments has increased tremendously.

The main way the national government provides money to the states is through federal grants—sums of money given to state or local governments for specific purposes. For example, federal money might go to a city to help improve airport runways or to a state to build new roads.

Federal grants redistribute income among the states. Taxes are collected by the federal government from citizens in all 50 states. This money is then **allocated** through grants to people in many states. Much of the federal money to states comes in block grants that are based on the population of the state.

allocate to assign a portion of something

Funds come at a price, however, as state and local governments have learned that along with aid comes federal control and red tape—federal money is granted only if the state and localities are willing to meet certain conditions.

Mandates and Preemption Since the mid-1960s, Congress has taken over some functions that used to be controlled by state governments by passing **mandates**. A mandate is a law that requires states to take on an activity or provide a service that meets minimum national standards. For example, states—not the federal government—issue driver's licenses. States have always set their own rules for the identification an applicant needs to obtain a driver's license, what is shown on the license, and what facts about the license holder are kept in its database. In 2005, however, Congress passed the Real ID Act, which requires the states to meet federal standards for issuing driver's licenses and sharing their databases. New requirements include proof of citizenship, such as a birth certificate, and proof of residence, such as a utility or mortgage bill.

mandate a formal order given by a higher authority

restraint an act that limits a state's ability to regulate an area

preemption the federal government's ability to take over a state government function

Nationally, congressional mandates have dealt with many issues. They have protected the civil rights of women and African Americans, set environmental standards, required state and local governments to make sidewalks more accessible to people with disabilities, and required the nation's schools to meet testing standards in math and reading.

Congress created land-grant colleges to give more Americans access to a college education. Michigan State University was the first land-grant university.

▼ **CRITICAL THINKING**
Identifying Which colleges or universities in your state are land-grant schools?

EXPLORING THE ESSENTIAL QUESTION

Researching Conduct Internet research about the 2005 Real ID Act. Find out how your state has complied with the legislation. A good source for this information is the National Conference of State Legislatures website.

Congress may also pass a **restraint**, which is an act that limits a state's ability to regulate an area. For example, when Congress passed the 1990 Nutritional Labeling and Education Act, states were no longer allowed to set their own food labeling standards, even if they were higher than the new national standards. This law restrained the states from acting.

The power of Congress to pass laws that allow the national government to assume responsibility for a state government function is called **preemption**. Some people argue that it is important for the entire country to have national standards for education, environmental laws, or safe food. Advocates of states' rights, however, dislike preemption

▲ The 1990 Nutritional Labeling and Education Act specified that most food should have nutrition labels. This legislation preempted the power of the states to establish their own food labeling standards.

because it takes away state and local authority to make their own laws and policies. In the process, preemption can interfere with the ability of local and state governments to set priorities for their own budgets. From this perspective, the worst kind of preemption law is one that provides no federal funds to carry out a policy—Congress is not required to pay for new mandates and can pass the burden of paying for them to the states. These are sometimes called "unfunded mandates" and are very unpopular with state leaders.

☑ **READING PROGRESS CHECK**

Summarizing What are some areas where the federal government has used mandates to influence policy?

Conflicts

GUIDING QUESTION *What role has the Supreme Court played in settling disputes between the federal and state governments?*

Because federalism divides the powers of government, conflicts often arise between national and state governments. By settling such disputes, the federal court system, particularly the Supreme Court, plays a key role of umpire for our federal system.

The question of national versus state power arose early in our history. In 1819, in the landmark case of *McCulloch* v. *Maryland*, the Supreme Court ruled on a conflict between a state government and the national government, concluding that when the national government and a state government come into conflict, the national government is supreme.

Since *McCulloch*, the Supreme Court has ruled many times on the constitutional issue of how powers should be divided between state and national governments. Through the years, the Court's view has shifted—sometimes giving more power to the national government, and other times giving more power to state governments.

☑ **READING PROGRESS CHECK**

Stating What did the Supreme Court rule in *McCulloch* v. *Maryland*?

LESSON 2 REVIEW

Reviewing Vocabulary
1. *Analyzing* What is preemption, and why is it often unpopular with advocates of states' rights?

Using Your Graphic Organizer
2. *Comparing* Use your completed graphic organizer to compare the obligations of the national government and state governments to each other.

Answering the Guiding Questions
3. *Stating* What does the national government guarantee to the state governments?

4. *Specifying* What obligations do the state governments have to the national government?

5. *Explaining* How does the federal government influence state and local governments?

6. *Identifying* What role has the Supreme Court played in settling disputes between the federal and state governments?

Writing About Government
7. *Argument* Write an opinion paper stating your position on the following question: Should the national government distribute money to states with "no strings attached," or should the grant have stipulations? Explain your position.

Should individual states be allowed to pass laws that regulate and enforce some aspects of immigration?

DELIBERATING DEMOCRATIC PRINCIPLES

Recently, several states have passed laws intended to affect the flow of undocumented immigrants into their states. Some individuals have come without visas, while others have stayed longer than their visas allowed. The federal government is responsible for immigration laws. Several states contend that the federal government is not doing enough to enforce laws about immigration and that states "bear the burden" of providing education and social services to people here illegally. Some counties and states have passed laws making it much more difficult for undocumented individuals to live and work there.

YES

TEAM A — States Should Regulate Immigration

The problems of illegal immigration disproportionately impact border states such as Arizona, California, New Mexico, and Texas. The influx of undocumented immigrants and human smuggling operations has created severe economic problems and safety hazards that demand a response. The federal government has not been doing its job enforcing immigration laws. States should be allowed to pass their own laws that help enforce federal immigration law and make the states less attractive to undocumented immigrants.

States do not want to conflict with existing federal immigration law or decide who is allowed to immigrate lawfully to the United States. They simply want to be able to enforce the laws. If federal enforcement is failing at its mandate to protect the people of a state, the people of that state are certainly entitled to protect themselves.

NO

TEAM B — States Should Not Regulate Immigration

Immigration is a national issue that requires a uniform national policy. If one state made its own immigration policies, it would, consequently, affect every state and therefore the whole country. The Constitution gives the national government the power "To establish a uniform Rule of Naturalization." The federal government has very few explicit powers, so where the Framers specifically name a national power, we respect that. Immigration is a highly complex and delicate subject. By making their own laws and enforcement strategies, states could harm national diplomatic efforts. Congress has spoken clearly on this issue and has crafted comprehensive national immigration laws. The Department of Homeland Security has placed a priority on removing undocumented immigrants that have been convicted of crimes in order to protect public safety. The United States should allocate its immigration enforcement resources according to a national scheme.

EXPLORING THE ESSENTIAL QUESTION

Deliberating With a partner, review the main arguments for either side. Decide which points are most compelling. Then paraphrase those arguments to a pair of students who were assigned to the other viewpoint. Listen to their strongest arguments. Switch sides and repeat the best arguments and add another compelling argument the other pair may not have thought of or presented. Then drop your roles and have a free discussion about which policy you support and why. Can you find any areas of common ground between the two views? How might a sensible policy address that common ground? What do you think is the best answer? Why?

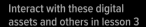

Interact with these digital assets and others in lesson 3

✓ **INTERACTIVE CHART**
Interstate Compacts

✓ **INTERACTIVE GRAPHIC ORGANIZER**
State Powers and Interstate Relations Graphic Organizer

✓ **SELF-CHECK QUIZ**

✓ **VIDEO**
Water Wars

netwrks
TRY IT YOURSELF ONLINE

ReadingHelp Desk

Academic Vocabulary

- administer
- license
- residency

Content Vocabulary

- extradite
- interstate compact

TAKING NOTES:

Integrating Knowledge and Ideas

PROBLEM SOLVING As you read, list the problems or issues that lead states to make interstate compacts.

Problem	Solution: Interstate Compact

LESSON 3

State Powers and Interstate Relations

ESSENTIAL QUESTION

How is power divided and shared among national, state, and local governments?

Imagine you own an ecotourism business that attracts customers by offering expeditions to remote mountains and whitewater rafting trips. Lately, some of your long-time, repeat customers have complained that the water has been too low for great rafting and is polluted. You are starting to lose business. You blame the problems on businesses in another state that "your" river runs through. You think that the other state has not done enough to hold businesses responsible for dumping. You also think that the other state has given too many business licenses to golf course operators, which, in your opinion, use and waste too much water.

What can you do? What role, if any, should your state play in resolving your concerns? How do you expect business owners and government officials in the other state will respond to your concerns? What is the best resolution to this conflict?

State Powers

GUIDING QUESTION *Under federalism, what powers are held by state governments?*

States can make laws about anything that is not prohibited by the Constitution or by national law. States are involved in many day-to-day concerns of their residents. They regulate and promote business, preserve natural resources, make and enforce criminal laws, protect individual rights, and provide for public health, education, and welfare.

States regulate corporations within their borders and promote those businesses; they have an interest in having local businesses succeed to benefit the state economy and provide employment for state residents. States also regulate businesses to protect consumers. States make and enforce laws to address unfair advertising, interest rates on credit cards, landlord-tenant relations, and more. States also regulate the safety and sanitary conditions for workers. States might provide for a minimum

114

wage that businesses must pay to employees and will provide payments to people who are injured on the job or to people who lose their jobs.

For the most part, protecting life and property is the responsibility of state and local governments. Laws prohibiting crimes such as murder, rape, assault, burglary, and the sale and use of dangerous weapons or drugs are all part of the state laws called the *criminal code*. Each state sets its own system of punishment. Local governments typically enforce these state laws through their local police forces.

State courts handle the great majority of all criminal cases in the United States. State prisons, county and municipal jails, and other detention facilities make up the states' correction systems.

Education, health, and welfare account for the largest portion of state spending. In education, local governments traditionally controlled and financed public schools, but today, states finance about half of education costs and the federal government about 10 percent. State governments establish local school districts and give them the power to **administer** schools, but the states establish rules about how much the local district can tax residents. States also establish policies that the school districts must follow.

In the area of health, states **license** doctors and dentists, require vaccines for children, and support public hospitals. State health agencies create programs and initiatives to care for mothers and children, treat contagious diseases, provide mental health care, and more. Governments provide aid to needy families with children, to people with disabilities, and to people who cannot afford health care.

States try to preserve their natural resources by regulating air and water pollution. Environmental regulation impacts the health of residents and state economy. For example, when the state of Maryland wanted to build a new road to ease terrible traffic, it would allow funding for construction only after it conducted an environmental impact report. As a result, the state rerouted the road to minimize negative impact on marshes and wildlife.

Federalism permits considerable freedom to each state in setting its own laws, regulations, taxes, criminal codes, and budget priorities, which results in important economic and political differences among the states.

administer to manage or supervise the execution, use, or conduct of

license give official permission to operate in a certain occupation

✓ **READING PROGRESS CHECK**

Expressing How do federal, state, and local governments share responsibility for education?

GOVERNMENT *in your* COMMUNITY

State Budgets

State budgets reveal much about the relative wealth, problems, and priorities of states. Find a copy of your state's most recent fiscal year budget. Find out how your state plans to distribute spending among different programs. You might find a circle graph or bar graph with this information. Review your state's budget and determine what your state's biggest challenges and priorities are.

▶ CRITICAL THINKING

Analyzing Do you agree with the way spending is distributed in your state? Explain your answer.

Delaware Governor Jack Markell signs the 2013 state budget.

Office of Governor Jack Markell

Relations Among States

GUIDING QUESTION *How do states cooperate and resolve conflicts with one another?*

Under federalism and the Constitution, states must honor other states' laws and court orders, even if their own laws are different. For example, if an individual has a driver's license issued in Florida and drives into Georgia, the state of Georgia must recognize the Florida license as valid. Or, if a person in Texas loses a lawsuit requiring a specific payment and then moves to Illinois to avoid paying the money, Illinois courts will enforce the Texas decision.

extradite to return a fugitive who flees across state lines back to the original state

While states set and enforce their own criminal laws, the Constitution requires that governors **extradite** or return to a state a criminal or fugitive who flees across state lines. If a governor refuses an extradition request from another governor, the federal government may intervene.

Privileges and Immunities The Founders knew that when citizens traveled between states, they might face problems. Someone from Delaware, for example, might be treated as less than a full citizen in Virginia or Maryland. To solve this problem, the Constitution provides that "the Citizens of each State shall be entitled to all Privileges and Immunities of Citizens in the several States." This means that one state cannot discriminate unreasonably against citizens of another state—they must give the same fundamental rights to people from other states that they give their own citizens.

The courts have never given a complete listing of all possible "privileges and immunities." Examples include the right to pass through or live in any state, use the courts, make contracts, and buy, sell, and hold property.

residency determined as where one lives and is legally eligible to vote

Whether a person is considered a resident depends on how a state defines **residency**. Some states require someone to live in a state for a certain period of time before being able to vote there. States can also require people to establish residency before they can practice a profession like law, medicine, or dentistry there.

PARTICIPATING
in Your Government

Research

The problem of hazardous waste disposal has become increasingly serious. Hazardous waste is waste that is dangerous or potentially very harmful to the environment and to people's health. These can include battery acid, cleaning solvents, pesticides, wastewater and sludge, and pharmaceuticals that end up in sewers. The federal government, state governments, and local governments all have interests in safely disposing and storing hazardous wastes. However, they do not always agree about the best methods.

Kent Knudson/PhotoLink/Getty Images

EXPLORING THE ESSENTIAL QUESTION

Researching Complete each of the tasks below with one partner or divide the tasks among several partners to create one group report. Then report your findings to your classmates.

   a. Research which hazardous wastes are created by the residents and businesses in your community and state. Make a list and note why each is dangerous or potentially dangerous.

   b. Find out the rules your community and state have to safely dispose those wastes.

   c. What role does your state environmental protection agency play? Has your state has entered into an interstate compact dealing with the disposal of hazardous waste?

States can treat out-of-state residents differently if the distinction is reasonable. It is reasonable for states to require people to be residents if they are to vote in a state, serve on its juries, or use public institutions that are supported by state taxes. Nonresidents, for example, do not have the same access to state colleges or public hospitals as residents do. State colleges and universities can, and usually do, charge higher tuition to students from other states than they do to in-state students.

Interstate Compacts The Constitution requires the states to settle their differences with one another peacefully. The principal way states settle disagreements is by negotiating **interstate compacts**, which are written agreements between two or more states. Congress must approve interstate compacts. This requirement prevents states from threatening the Union by making alliances among themselves. Once a compact has been signed and approved by Congress, it is binding; its terms are enforceable by the Supreme Court.

Before 1900, only 13 interstate compacts had received congressional approval. Most involved boundary disputes. Today nearly 200 interstate compacts are in force.

States use compacts to deal with issues regarding air and water pollution, pest control, toll bridges, and transportation. For example, New Jersey and New York started this trend in 1921 when they created the Port of New York Authority to develop and manage harbor facilities in the area. Many compacts today deal with natural resources; others deal with how hazardous waste should be transported and disposed of. Interstate compacts have become an important way for the states to deal with regional problems.

Lawsuits Between States Sometimes states are unable to resolve their disputes through negotiation or interstate compacts. In such cases, they may resort to lawsuits. Since 1789, nearly 200 disputes between states have been resolved in court. Suits among two or more states are heard in the U.S. Supreme Court—the only court where one state can sue another.

States bring one another to court for a variety of reasons. Cases in the West often involve water rights. Arizona, California, and Colorado have gone to the Court in disputes over water from the Colorado River. Other cases have involved state conflict over the sewage from one state polluting the water of another. Still other cases are disputes over boundary lines. Arkansas and Tennessee had such a dispute as recently as 1970.

✓ **READING PROGRESS CHECK**

Identifying What resources and tools do states use to manage their relations with one another?

Interstate compacts are written agreements between two or more states that are approved by Congress.

▲ CRITICAL THINKING
Making Generalizations Why are waterways and forests likely subjects for interstate compacts?

interstate compact a written agreement between two or more states

---

LESSON 3 REVIEW

Reviewing Vocabulary

1. *Defining* What does *extradite* mean, and why does the Constitution require states to comply with extradition requests from other states?

Using Your Graphic Organizer

2. *Problem Solving* Using your completed graphic organizer, write a paragraph explaining the types of issues that result in the formation of interstate compacts. What are some ways, other than interstate compacts, of resolving these issues?

Answering the Guiding Questions

3. *Classifying* Under federalism, what powers are held by state governments?

4. *Synthesizing* How do states cooperate and resolve conflicts with one another?

Writing About Government

5. *Informative/Explanatory* Research at least three ways your state treats residents and nonresidents differently. Then write an essay comparing and contrasting the treatment of residents and nonresidents.

Interact with these digital assets and others in lesson 4

✓ **INTERACTIVE GRAPHIC ORGANIZER**
Differing Views About Federalism
Graphic Organizer

✓ **INTERACTIVE IMAGE**
Homelessness

✓ **SELF-CHECK QUIZ**

✓ **VIDEO**
South Carolina Voter ID Law

netw⊙rks
TRY IT YOURSELF ONLINE

LESSON 4
Differing Views About Federalism

ReadingHelp Desk

Academic Vocabulary

- policy
- accommodation

Content Vocabulary

- public policy
- sunset law
- sunshine law
- states' rights position
- nationalist position

TAKING NOTES:

Key Ideas and Details

OUTLINING As you read, create an outline of the content in this lesson that includes the main ideas.

I.	Federalism and Public Policy
	A.
	B.
II.	Federalism and Political Parties
III.	Federalism and Political Participation

ESSENTIAL QUESTION

How does federalism promote democracy and civic participation?

Many people in the United States believe that our environment is being polluted and that the government should take action to preserve the environment. Read each proposed solution below and decide whether the proposal would best be implemented by the federal, state, or local governments.

a. Create drop-off centers near residential areas where people can recycle different types of materials

b. Place limits on the amount of pollution that factories can emit

c. Require car manufacturers to build vehicles that pollute less

d. Encourage charities to clean up rivers and parklands

e. Ban the use of certain chemicals that pollute drinking water

f. Create rules that developers must follow to minimize the impact of new buildings on the environment

Would you actively support or oppose government implementation of any of these proposals? What would you do to support or oppose these proposals? How might your involvement change based on whether the federal, state, or local government was primarily responsible? Write an editorial for your school or local newspaper describing your position and how, if at all, you plan to get involved to support or oppose one of these proposals. Be sure to use persuasive words and compelling arguments to support your position.

Federalism and Public Policy

GUIDING QUESTION *How is public policy created at different levels of government?*

Since the founding of the country, there has been constant debate about the proper division of powers between the national government and the states. The balance of power evolves in response to new issues.

For example, Congress has given states more power to control how they spend money for development in rural areas; however, Congress has also asked states to take on more responsibility for social welfare programs.

Congress has strengthened national control of food safety standards and the regulation of telecommunications. In 2001 Congress also passed the No Child Left Behind Act, which requires states to test students' basic skills in order to receive federal school funding, while allowing states to choose their own academic standards.

Defining Policies What do we mean exactly when we talk about a policy? A **policy** is a stated course of action for addressing certain problems or issues. A high school principal may say, "It's our policy that students not park in the teachers' parking lot." A sign in a local store often reads: "It's our policy to prosecute all shoplifters." In both cases, people are defining the actions they will take in response to a recurring problem or situation. When a government settles on a course of action, we call it **public policy**.

State and Local Policies The United States has many different units of government—50 state governments and thousands of local governments. States and localities are well positioned to develop and test new policies.

Georgia, for example, was the first state to allow 18-year-olds to vote. Colorado pioneered the use of the sunset laws now found in many states. A **sunset law** is a provision in a law that sets an automatic end date for that law: Lawmakers are forced to review the need for continuing the law beyond that date. In California, local groups pressured the state to pass laws to control air pollution. Their laws became models for federal air-pollution laws. In 1967 Florida legislators were the first in the nation to pass a **sunshine law**, which prohibits public officials from holding official meetings that are closed to the public. Since then, many states have adopted sunshine laws.

National Policies At other times, public policy is created at the national level and states follow. Occasionally, the national government has imposed policies on states if it believed those states were infringing on a group's basic rights. This happened most dramatically in the 1950s and 1960s during the African American struggle for civil rights. Remember that in most cases, states set their own rules for voting and elections. Before 1964, many states had rules and policies that made it difficult and even dangerous for African Americans to vote. After much debate and deep disagreements, the national government outlawed those discriminatory practices with the passage of the 1964 Voting Rights Act. Gradually, the civil rights movement attracted substantial media attention and public support.

National Power and the Commerce Clause In recent decades, Supreme Court decisions have expanded the constitutional power of the national government to regulate interstate commerce. The Court has interpreted the term *commerce* to mean almost any activity connected with producing, buying, selling, and transporting goods across state lines. For example, Congress used the commerce clause for the authority behind the Civil Rights Act of 1964 that prohibited racial discrimination in hotels, restaurants, and other public **accommodations**. In upholding the law, the Court reasoned as follows:

- If restaurants and hotels discriminate against African Americans or any group of Americans, it restricts interstate commerce.
- Congress has the power to regulate commerce.
- Therefore, Congress may pass laws against racial discrimination.

Recently, the Supreme Court has issued a few rulings that limit the legislative powers that the commerce clause grants to the federal government. In *Lopez* v. *United States* (1995), the Court asserted that a law must regulate an economic activity in order to be justified under the commerce clause.

policy a plan that includes general goals and procedures

public policy the stated course of action the government takes to address problems or issues

sunset law a law that requires periodic checks of laws or of government agencies to see if they are still needed

sunshine law a law prohibiting public officials from holding meetings not open to the public

accommodation a place where people can work, stay, or live

The
Constitution

"3. To regulate Commerce with foreign Nations, and among the several States, and with the Indian Tribes;"

—Article I, Section 8

▲ DBQ *Defining* Look up the word *commerce* in the dictionary. In what ways, if any, does this differ from how the Supreme Court has interpreted the word *commerce*?

In *National Federation of Independent Business* v. *Sebelius* (2012), the Court said that the 2010 Affordable Care Act's requirement that Americans purchase health insurance was not a constitutional exercise of Congress's commerce power, because it was trying to force people into economic activity, not simply regulate it. The law was upheld, however, because a majority of the justices agreed that it was constitutional under Congress's taxing power.

✅ **READING PROGRESS CHECK**

Identifying Central Issues What are some examples of states or the federal government taking the lead in making public policy?

Federalism and Political Parties

GUIDING QUESTION *What are different political parties' views on the proper balance of power between national and state governments?*

Rival political parties are a key element of democratic government. Federalism makes it possible for different parties to be victorious in state, local, and federal elections. Furthermore, federalism lessens the risk of one party having a monopoly of political power at all levels of government.

In the history of the United States, there have been two quite different views of how federalism should operate. One view favors state and local governments taking the lead on dealing with public policy problems. This is sometimes known as a **states' rights position**. A second view favors national action in dealing with these matters. This view is also known as a **nationalist position**. However, it is rare that anyone, even politicians or leaders of political parties, will be 100 percent consistent in their view that public policy problems should be solved only in Washington, D.C., or settled entirely at the state level.

states' rights position a position that favors state and local action in dealing with problems

nationalist position a position that favors national action in dealing with problems

Supporters of Stronger State and Local Government Powers

For the most part, twenty-first-century conservatives, who generally include Republican Party members, Tea Party members, and libertarians, believe the Constitution sets clear limits on the power of the national government. To support their argument, they point to the Tenth Amendment and its language about states retaining powers not specifically given to Congress in the Constitution. They believe that any doubt about whether a power belongs to the national government or is reserved to the states should be settled in favor of the states.

Supporters of stronger state governments believe state and local governments are closer to the people and better reflect the unique needs and wishes of their residents. They tend to see "big government" (as in a national government that interferes too much) as heavy-handed and a threat to individual liberty. These individuals are more likely to oppose broad federal laws and regulations that limit states' authority to legislate as they wish. In part, they argue that public policy needs to be tailored to challenges faced by individual states and that "one size doesn't fit all."

Supporters of Stronger National Government Powers
For the most part, twenty-first-century liberals, who generally include Democratic Party members and progressives, believe the Constitution confirms the Founders' belief in the need for a strong national government. They point to the supremacy clause to argue that the national government should be supreme in matters of public policy. They believe that under the elastic clause, the powers expressly delegated to the national government should be expanded as necessary to carry out the will of the people.

Supporters of a strong national government believe that the national government is better equipped to solve some major social and economic problems facing the nation. They are more likely to support national government standards and regulations in areas such as education, housing, and consumer and environmental protection. They tend to see the national government as important to ensuring that no matter what state a person lives in, he or she receives the same treatment and enjoys the same opportunities as citizens in other states.

✓ **READING PROGRESS CHECK**

Comparing and Contrasting Which parts of the Constitution appear to support a nationalist position? Which appear to support a states' rights position?

COMPARING STATE GOVERNMENTS

Compare Wyoming and Connecticut:

Wetzel and Company

Wyoming is located in the Mountain West, and is very sparsely populated (only 5.8 people per square mile). The state's main industries are ranching, mining, and tourism.

Laws and Policies, 2014

- No income tax, no corporate tax, low sales tax (4%); receives a lot of revenue from taxes on mineral, oil, and gas production

- State minimum wage is $5.15 per hour

- Children must attend school from ages 7–16 (or until completing 10th grade)

- Maximum posted speed limit on interstate highways is 75 mph

- Has many laws regulating hydraulic fracturing, a type of natural gas extraction

- In 2008, Wyoming spent $4.68 per person on public transit

Connecticut is located on the East Coast, and is densely populated (738.1 people per square mile). The state's main industries are manufacturing, insurance, and tourism.

Laws and Policies, 2014

- Receives revenue from an income tax (3–6.7%), a corporate income tax (7.5%), and a sales tax (6.35%)

- State minimum wage is $8.70 per hour

- Children must attend school from ages 5–18 (or until graduating high school)

- Maximum posted speed limit on interstate highways is 65 mph

- There is no natural gas extraction taking place in Connecticut

- In 2008 Connecticut spent $76.36 per person on public transit

EXPLORING THE ESSENTIAL QUESTION

Differentiating Examine the information above, then answer the following questions.

a. Describe the similarities and differences between Wyoming and Connecticut and their laws.

b. What characteristics of these two states might lead them to have different priorities? Where might the two states have the same priorities?

c. How does our system of federalism give states flexibility in meeting their citizens' needs?

d. Research laws and policies in your state (or another state you are interested in) and compare it to Wyoming and Connecticut. How is your state similar to or different from these two?

Federalism and Political Participation

GUIDING QUESTION *Why does federalism increase opportunities for political participation?*

Federalism increases opportunities for American citizens to participate in politics. A citizen can choose to run for local office, to lobby the state government, or to campaign for a candidate for national office.

American federalism gives citizens many points of access to government leaders and increases their opportunities for influencing public policy. Americans have the chance to vote on a regular basis. They elect governors, state lawmakers, mayors, council members, school board members, county prosecutors, and many other state and local officials, such as the judges who sit on the municipal, county, and state courts. They also vote on specific local issues—whether to build a mass transit system in their city, whether to outlaw smoking in public places, or whether to increase property taxes for schools.

Citizens may also work with special interest groups to influence national policies and state and local government agencies. For example, a group of concerned neighbors can petition the county zoning board to set aside nearby land for a public playground, or members of a local labor union may work together to support their union's efforts to influence passage of a law in the state legislature.

A related effect of federalism is an increased chance that one's political participation will have some practical impact on policy. And because that is true, people are more likely to become involved in political activity. In a campaign for city council in a smaller town, for example, someone working in the campaign has to persuade relatively few voters to elect the candidate of his or her choice.

☑ **READING PROGRESS CHECK**

Hypothesizing Why might it be easier to influence policy on the local level than on the national level?

Through participating in local politics, citizens can have a direct impact on their community.

▲ CRITICAL THINKING

Explaining What protects citizens' rights to express their political beliefs by putting up signs like this one? Do you think these signs have any influence on other citizens' opinions or actions? Explain your answer.

LESSON 4 REVIEW

Reviewing Vocabulary
1. *Contrasting* What is the difference between a sunset law and a sunshine law?

Using Your Graphic Organizer
2. *Finding the Main Idea* Use your completed graphic organizer to create a summary of the main ideas in this lesson.

Answering the Guiding Questions
3. *Explaining* How is public policy created at different levels of government?

4. *Differentiating* What are different political parties' views on the proper balance of power between national and state governments?

5. *Identifying Cause and Effect* Why does federalism increase opportunities for political participation?

Writing About Government
6. *Informative/Explanatory* How does one's view about the purposes of government relate to his or her beliefs about the proper division of power between states and the national government? Include specific examples in your response.

United States v Windsor (2013)

FACTS OF THE CASE Two women from New York, Edith Windsor and Thea Spyer, were recognized as married by the state of New York. When Thea died, she left her entire estate to Edith. One federal law allowed spouses to pass their estates on to their husbands or wives without any taxes. However, another federal law—the Defense of Marriage Act (DOMA)—said that the word *marriage* in federal laws could mean only a legal union between one man and one woman. When Edith filed for the estate tax refund, her application was denied because her marriage was not recognized under DOMA. Edith had to pay $363,053 in taxes from Thea's estate. She sued the federal government, arguing that DOMA's definition of marriage violated her right to equal protection of the law.

Does the Defense of Marriage Act (DOMA) violate the Fourteenth Amendment?

The following is a list of arguments made in the case of *United States* v. *Windsor*. Read each argument and categorize each based on whether it supports the government's side (that DOMA is constitutional) or Windsor's side (that DOMA is unconstitutional).

1. The Fourteenth Amendment guarantees equal protection of the laws, and DOMA does not apply to all marriages equally.

2. This law takes away a fundamental right for same-sex couples—the right to marry.

3. The Supreme Court has never said that laws must treat people equally based on their sexual orientation. Sexual orientation is not a classification like race or gender because gay and lesbian people have not suffered the same long history of discrimination. They have political power, as there is growing support for same-sex marriage.

4. This law's purpose is to promote traditional marriage and to set a uniform federal standard for marriage. It allows states to pass their own laws defining marriage.

5. Despite the government's stated purpose, DOMA does not promote traditional marriage. It only excludes lawfully married same-sex couples from federal marriage benefits. A law's sole purpose cannot be to discriminate against a disadvantaged group.

6. DOMA was passed by a bipartisan majority of Congress in 1996 and thus represents the will of the people.

7. The federal government should leave laws about marriage up to the states. States license couples to get married, not the federal government. DOMA does not respect the states that permit same-sex marriages.

8. DOMA is an appropriate use of federal power, because there are also other standards the federal government has in place that regulate marriage.

EXPLORING THE ESSENTIAL QUESTION

Classifying After you have classified the arguments, choose one for each side that you think is most persuasive and explain why you found those arguments compelling.

YOU BE the JUDGE

STUDY GUIDE

FEDERALISM
LESSON 1

National Government

State Governments

Local Governments

RESERVED STATE POWERS
LESSON 3

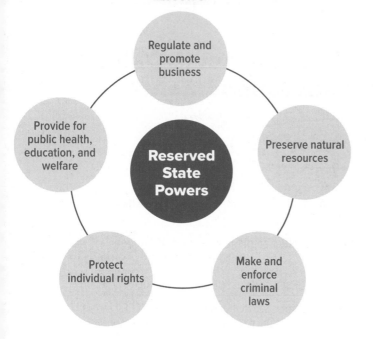

Regulate and promote business

Provide for public health, education, and welfare

Reserved State Powers

Preserve natural resources

Protect individual rights

Make and enforce criminal laws

GUARANTEES AND OBLIGATIONS OF THE STATES
LESSON 2

Guarantees to States	Obligations of States
Maintain a republican form of government	Conduct and pay for elections of all national government officials
Protects states from invasion and domestic unrest	Participate in the process of amending the Constitution
Respect the territorial integrity of each state	

FEDERALISM INCREASES OPPORTUNITIES FOR POLITICAL PARTICIPATION
LESSON 4

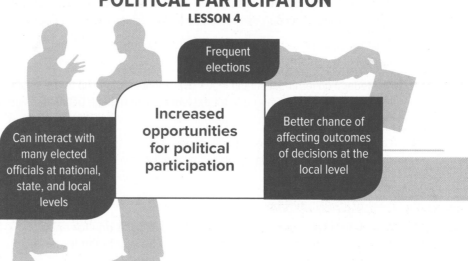

Frequent elections

Can interact with many elected officials at national, state, and local levels

Increased opportunities for political participation

Better chance of affecting outcomes of decisions at the local level

124

Directions: On a separate sheet of paper, answer the questions below. Make sure you read carefully and answer all parts of the questions.

Lesson Review

Lesson 1

1 *Explaining* Explain why the Founders created a distinctly new form of federalism.

2 *Describing* Describe the Supremacy Clause and explain why it is important for the federal system.

Lesson 2

3 *Listing* What guarantees does the federal government make to the states?

4 *Explaining* Explain the main method used to provide assistance to the states.

Lesson 3

5 *Describing* Describe the purpose of and process for establishing an interstate compact.

6 *Classifying* Which powers are reserved for state governments?

Lesson 4

7 *Analyzing* Analyze contemporary conflicts between the major political parties over the respective roles of national and state government.

8 *Identifying* Identify public policy areas where state governments and the national government have had conflicts. Give specific examples.

ANSWERING THE ESSENTIAL QUESTIONS

Review your answers to the introductory questions at the beginning of each lesson. Then answer the following Essential Questions based on what you learned in the chapter. Have your answers changed?

9 *Evaluating* Why and how is power divided and shared among national, state, and local governments?

10 *Analyzing* How does federalism promote democracy and civic participation?

DBQ Interpreting Political Cartoons

Use the political cartoon to answer the following questions.

11 *Analyzing Visuals* What does the plane represent and what is it doing?

12 *Identifying Perspectives* Is the cartoonist's view of federal mandates positive or negative? Explain.

Critical Thinking

13 *Interpreting* Explain why the Founders used the term *reserved* in the Tenth Amendment.

14 *Making Connections* Explain why the Founders adopted a federal system of government instead of a unitary system.

15 *Exploring Issues* Research the measures the federal government uses to establish a uniform drinking age across the country. Describe what measures were used to establish the drinking age at 21 and if they have been effective.

16 *Diagramming* Create a graphic organizer displaying the limits on the national and state governments in the U.S. federal system of government.

Need Extra Help?

If You've Missed Question	**1**	**2**	**3**	**4**	**5**	**6**	**7**	**8**	**9**	**10**	**11**	**12**	**13**	**14**	**15**	**16**
Go to page	102	106	108	110	117	114	120	119	104	122	119	119	104	102	106	108

Directions: On a separate sheet of paper, answer the questions below. Make sure you read carefully and answer all parts of the questions.

DBQ Analyzing Primary Sources

Read the excerpts and answer the questions that follow.

PRIMARY SOURCE

"A FIRM Union will be of the utmost moment to the peace and liberty of the States, as a barrier against domestic faction and insurrection. It is impossible to read the history of the petty republics of Greece and Italy without feeling sensations of horror and disgust at the distractions with which they were continually agitated, and at the rapid succession of revolutions by which they were kept in a state of perpetual vibration between the extremes of tyranny and anarchy."

— *The Federalist* No. 9, Alexander Hamilton

In *Coyle* v. *Smith*, 1911, the Supreme Court ruled on whether Congress could restrict the powers given to a state as a condition of being admitted to the Union.

PRIMARY SOURCE

"To maintain otherwise would be to say that the Union, through the power of Congress to admit new states, might come to be a union of states unequal in power, as including states whose powers were restricted only by the Constitution, with others whose powers had been further restricted by an act of Congress accepted as a condition of admission."

— Justice Horace Lurton, *Coyle* v. *Smith*, 1911 *Opinion of the Court*

17 *Historical Interpretation* Describe Hamilton's interpretation of the history of the classical republics, and explain how he is applying this information to his contemporary world.

18 *Finding the Main Idea* Describe the main idea being expressed in the opinion by Justice Lurton.

Social Studies Skills

Use the table to answer questions 20 and 21.

19 *Creating and Using Diagrams* Create a diagram to categorize government powers as national, state, or shared.

ESTIMATED STATE AND LOCAL GOVERNMENT EXPENDITURES BY FUNCTION (2010–2011)

Function	Expenditure (in millions)
Direct general expenditures*	**$2,583,101**
Education	$861,131
Highways	$153,005
Hospitals	$148,136
Interest on general debt	$108,658
Police protection	$96,332
Sanitation and sewerage	$78,746
Housing and community development	$56,121
Financial administration	$39,689
Parks and recreation	$38,694
Fire protection	$42,252
Natural resources	$29,071
Utilities and liquor stores	**$213,830**
Insurance trust expenditures	**$361,402**
TOTAL	**$3,158,333**

Source: United States Census Bureau * Not all categories are listed

20 *Creating and Analyzing Arguments* What is a top policy priority for state and local governments? What information supports your argument?

21 *Economics* What percentage of state and local budgets is spent on paying interest on general debt?

Research and Presentation

22 *Comparing* Write an essay that compares the structures, functions, and processes of the national government, your state government, and your local government in the U.S. federal system.

23 *Evaluating* Write an essay describing the *McCulloch* v. *Maryland* case and Supreme Court decision. Do you agree with the Court's decision regarding the conflict between national and state power? Support your argument.

Need Extra Help?

If You've Missed Question	**17**	**18**	**19**	**20**	**21**	**22**	**23**
Go to page	102	104	104	115	110	108	112

UNIT 2
The Legislative Branch

IT MATTERS
BECAUSE . . .

The legislative branch plays a variety of important roles in governing communities, states, and the nation. At each level of government, the legislative branch represents the interests of the voters and should reflect the makeup of the population it serves. Perhaps the most important function of the legislative branch is its power to pass, amend, and repeal laws. Legislators must balance competing interests so that a law is fair. Each part of the legislative branch has its own responsibilities in creating laws. At all levels, the laws our legislatures enact protect and endorse our rights and help us understand the "rules" we need to follow so society runs smoothly. The work of the legislative branch also plays an important role in overseeing the executive and his or her administration. Raising revenue—primarily through the use of taxes—and approving government spending are also the responsibilities of the legislative branch. In all of these functions, legislators are influenced by a great many factors: voters, staff members, political parties, and special interest groups. By understanding the roles and functions of the legislative branch, you can better understand how and why the laws that affect your daily life are made.

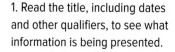
How to

Interpret Graphs, Charts, and Tables

Graphs, charts, and tables can be used to show government data and statistics in a visual format that makes it easy to understand how categories of information relate to each other. You will need to use mathematical skills to interpret numerical information and statistics in graphs, charts, and tables. Being able to interpret and evaluate government data in graphs, charts, and tables is essential for understanding and evaluating statistics about government and public policy. Follow these steps:

1. Read the title, including dates and other qualifiers, to see what information is being presented.

2. Read the headings and subheadings to see which categories are being presented.

3. Notice the source or sources of the data. Evaluate the validity and reliability of the source or sources.

4. Use statistical skills to evaluate the data. Is the data in the graph, chart, or table being presented in a misleading fashion?

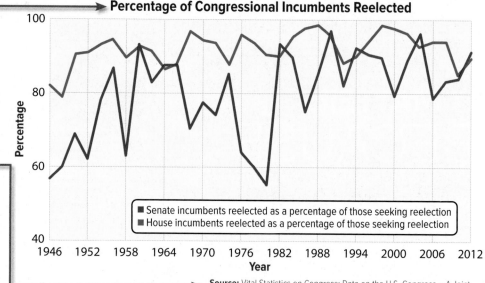

Percentage of Congressional Incumbents Reelected

■ Senate incumbents reelected as a percentage of those seeking reelection
■ House incumbents reelected as a percentage of those seeking reelection

Source: Vital Statistics on Congress: Data on the U.S. Congress – A Joint Effort from Brookings and the American Enterprise Institute, 2014

5. State in sentences what trend or relationships the graph, chart, or table shows.

6. Think of another way of presenting the data. Would a different type of graph or another format do a better job of conveying the key information? Transfer the information in the graph, chart, or table into another format.

---

netw⚙rks

TRY IT YOURSELF ONLINE

Go online to interact with these digital activities and more in each chapter.

Chapter 5 The Structure of Congress

Chapter 6 Congressional Powers

Chapter 7 Congress at Work

Chapter 8 State and Local Legislative Branches

✓ **VIDEO**
LIFE ON THE HILL

✓ **INTERACTIVE SLIDE SHOW**
MILITARY ACTIONS WITHOUT A DECLARATION OF WAR

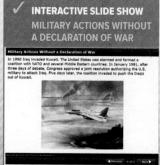

✓ **INTERACTIVE INFOGRAPHIC**
HOW A BILL BECOMES A LAW

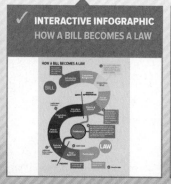

✓ **INTERACTIVE DELIBERATION**
JUVENILE OFFENDERS

The Structure of Congress

ESSENTIAL QUESTION

What is the structure and organization of Congress?

Photographs in the Carol M. Highsmith Archive, Library of Congress, Prints and Photographs Division.

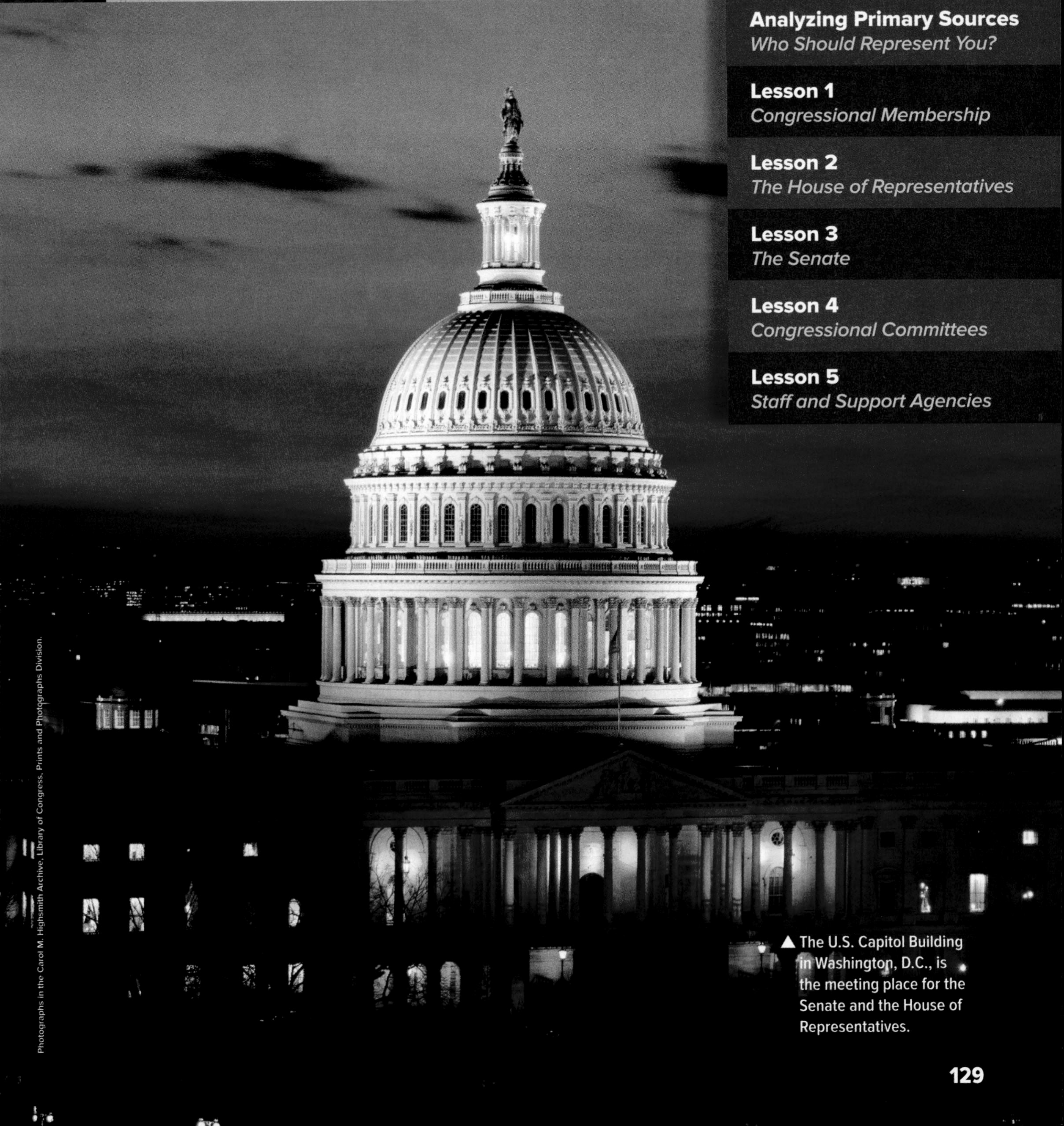

▲ The U.S. Capitol Building
in Washington, D.C., is
the meeting place for the
Senate and the House of
Representatives.

129

WHO SHOULD REPRESENT YOU?

Congress is the branch of government linked most closely to the people. Each member of the House and Senate is directly elected by the people of one state or one district within a state. Each member then represents those same people. But what do voters look for in a representative—someone who shares their views? Someone who has the wisdom to serve their interests well? Someone who has had similar life experiences? Develop your understanding of representation by analyzing the sources below and answering the questions that follow.

SECONDARY SOURCE A

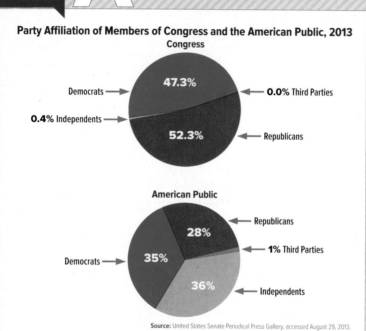

Party Affiliation of Members of Congress and the American Public, 2013

Congress

- Democrats → 47.3%
- 0.4% Independents
- 52.3% → Republicans
- 0.0% Third Parties

American Public

- Democrats → 35%
- 36% → Independents
- 28% → Republicans
- 1% Third Parties

Source: United States Senate Periodical Press Gallery, accessed August 29, 2013.

SECONDARY SOURCE C

Political scientists call people who are the same ethnicity as the people represented *descriptive representatives*.

"Descriptive representatives can affect the extent to which communities of color engage in the political system, which is a quality deemed important to democratic theorists. They can also lead to higher feelings of efficacy, which has been linked to an increase in political participation and empowerment. Finally, having a descriptive representative leads to more positive evaluations of one's incumbent representative which arguably enhances the extent to which one feels represented in government."

—Derek J. Fowler, Jennifer L. Merolla, and Abbylin H. Sellers, "The Effects of Descriptive Representation on Political Attitude and Behaviors," 2012

SECONDARY SOURCE B

Gender of Public and Members of Congress, 2013

	Male	Female
U.S. Public	49%	51%
Congress	81.6%	18.4%
House	82%	18%
Senate	80%	20%

Ethnicity of Public and Members of Congress, 2013

	African American	Hispanic/ Latino	Asian/ Pacific Islander	Native American
U.S. Public	12.6%	16.7%	5.0%	0.9%
Congress	8.1%	7%	2.4%	0.4%
House	9.4%	7.4%	2.3%	0.5%
Senate	1%	4%	1%	0%

SOURCE: Congressional Research Service, 2013

Religious Affiliation, Members of Congress and American Public, 2013

Religion	Congress	U.S. Public
Protestant	56.1%	48%
Catholic	30.6%	22%
Mormon	2.8%	2%
Orthodox Christian	0.9%	1%
Jewish	6.2%	2%
Buddhist	0.6%	1%
Muslim	0.4%	1%
Hindu	0.2%	1%
Other faiths	0.2%	2%
Unaffiliated	0.2%	20%
Don't Know/ Refused to Answer	1.9%	2%

According to the Pew Forum on Religion and Public Life, Congress is much more religiously diverse than it was 50 years ago, when about 75% of its members were Protestants.

SOURCE: Data from Pew Research Center, "Faith on the Hill: The Religious Composition of the 113th Congress," November 16, 2013, http://www.pewforum.org/2012/11/16/faith-on-the-hill-the-religious-composition-of-the-113th-congress/.

PRIMARY SOURCE F

Commenting on a study that showed legislators elected to Congress for the first time in 2012 had a net worth of almost exactly $1 million more than the average American ($1,066,515 compared to $66,740), Sheila Krumholz, executive director of the Center for Responsive Politics, said the following:

"While America continues to claw its way back to economic stability, voters have nevertheless chosen to elect new members of Congress who have already made it big. Apparently, on the whole, we don't want people who look like us, financially speaking. What's harder to measure is whether these new legislators appreciate the financial pain people face and can effectively represent them despite the fact that they themselves are well off."

—Sheila Krumholz, 2013

DBQ DOCUMENT-BASED QUESTIONS

1. **Explaining** In three different documents, find disparities between the members of Congress and the American public. Which of these disparities seems most important to you? Why?

2. **Hypothesizing** Which chamber of Congress has the higher percentages of members who are African American, Latino, Asian/Pacific Islander, and Native American? Why might this be the case?

3. **Evaluating** What questions does Krumholz raise? Do you think these questions are important to consider in deciding for whom to vote? Why or why not?

WHAT WILL YOU DO?

When you vote for members of the U.S. House and Senate, what will you be looking for in a representative? How important, if at all, will it be that your representative shares some of your life experiences?

EXPLORE the interactive version of the analyzing primary sources feature on Networks.

Interact with these digital assets and others in lesson 1

✓ **INTERACTIVE INFOGRAPHIC**
Demographics of Congress

✓ **INTERACTIVE GRAPH**
The Increase of Congressional Minority Members Over Time

✓ **INTERACTIVE MAP**
Congressional Apportionment

✓ **VIDEO**
Gridlock Gerrymandering

netw⚙rks
TRY IT YOURSELF ONLINE

LESSON 1
Congressional Membership

ReadingHelp Desk

Academic Vocabulary

- **formulate**
- **occur**
- **trace**

Content Vocabulary

- **bicameral legislature**
- **session**
- **census**
- **reapportionment**
- **redistrict**
- **gerrymander**
- **at-large**
- **censure**
- **incumbent**

TAKING NOTES:

Key Ideas and Details

COMPARING Use the graphic organizer to compare the qualifications for representatives and senators.

Qualifications	
Representatives	Senators

ESSENTIAL QUESTION

What is the structure and organization of Congress?

Imagine that you were among the delegates to the Constitutional Convention in 1787. Which of the following topics would you want to see addressed in the part of the Constitution that covers the legislative branch? What criteria would you use to decide what should be included?

- What the legislature should be called
- How legislators should be chosen
- Qualifications for legislators
- How long legislators should serve
- How much legislators should be paid
- The help legislators should have available to aid them in their work
- When and where the legislature should meet
- What the legislature can and cannot do
- The process of enacting a law
- Ethical guidelines for conducting legislative business
- Other details (name the details you think should be included)

Organization of Congress

GUIDING QUESTION *What is the structure of Congress?*

The Founders gave more power to Congress than to any other branch. The Constitution emphasized the importance of the lawmaking branch by describing Congress in the first main part of the Constitution, Article I. As James Madison said, Congress is "the First Branch of the Government."

Bicameral Legislature While the Constitution assigned great power to the legislators, it also made Congress a **bicameral legislature**, meaning that it is made up of two very different parts of the Congress, called *houses*—the Senate and the House of Representatives. In 1787 most Constitutional Convention delegates supported a bicameral legislature.

Senators serve six-year terms of office and represent their entire state, while representatives have two-year terms and are elected from districts. The Constitution also allows each house to write its own rules of procedure. The larger House of Representatives sets rules to limit debate and promote majority rule. The smaller Senate sets rules that gave more muscle to the minority, whether that be a party, a faction, or an individual senator.

It is quite common for the House to pass one bill and the Senate to pass a similar bill on the same subject, but with some variations. Before either version can be sent to the president, the House and Senate must work together to agree on the exact wording of the bill. This is an additional check on power because neither the House nor Senate can pass laws without the other. Congress's division into two houses has resulted in much friction because they often approach issues very differently. At best, the differences produce compromise and national consensus. At worst, they result in legislative gridlock, or the failure to get critical legislative work done.

Today, Congress plays a central role in **formulating** national policies. It initiates and approves laws on everything from health care to taxes.

Congressional Sessions Each term of Congress begins on January 3 in years ending in an odd number and lasts for two years. For example, the 112th Congress began its term in January 2011, and the 113th Congress began in January 2013. Each congressional term is two **sessions**, or meetings. A session lasts one year and includes breaks for holidays and vacations. Until the Twentieth Amendment was ratified in 1933, congressional sessions began in March, which left a four-month period between the November elections and when new members began to serve. This time delay was shortened when the Twentieth Amendment moved the session start date to January.

Congress remains in session until its members vote to adjourn. Neither the House nor the Senate can adjourn for more than three days without the approval of the other house. If the Congress does adjourn, the president has the authority to call it back for a special session if necessary.

bicameral legislature a two-chamber legislature

formulate to devise or develop

session meeting

☑ READING PROGRESS CHECK

Contrasting What are some of the differences between the House of Representatives and the Senate?

Membership of the House

GUIDING QUESTION *How is the House of Representatives organized?*

With 435 members, the House of Representatives is much larger than the Senate. The Constitution does not set the number of representatives in the House. It states that House seats must be apportioned, or divided, among the states on the basis of population. Each state is entitled to at least one seat in the House of Representatives, no matter how small its population.

Qualifications and Term of Office The Constitution sets the qualifications for election to the House of Representatives. Representatives must be at least 25 years old, be citizens of the United States for at least seven years, and be legal residents of the state that elects them. Traditionally, members of the House of Representatives also live in the district they represent.

Congress comes together in the U.S. Capitol to discuss national policy and make the nation's laws.

▼ CRITICAL THINKING
Identifying Which branch of the U.S. government meets in this building? Name the two houses that make up this branch of government.

The Constitution

"The House of Representatives shall be composed of Members chosen every second year by the People...."

—Article I, Section 2, Clause 1

"No person shall be a Representative who shall not have attained to the Age of twenty five Years, and been seven Years a Citizen of the United States, and who shall not, when elected, be an Inhabitant of that State in which he shall be chosen."

—Article I, Section 2, Clause 2

EXPLORING THE ESSENTIAL QUESTION

1. **Summarizing** Rephrase the constitutional requirements for someone to be elected to the U.S. House of Representatives.

2. **Understanding Historical Interpretation** These qualifications were set in 1787. Do you think they are still appropriate? If so, how do these qualifications help to ensure better government? If not, which qualifications might you change and why?

Members of the House of Representatives are elected for two-year terms. Elections are held in November of even-numbered years—for example, 2010, 2012, and 2014. Representatives begin their term of office on January 3 following the November election. This means that every two years, all 435 members of the House must run for reelection. It also means that the House reorganizes itself every two years. Because more than 90 percent of all representatives are reelected, however, the House has great continuity. If a representative dies or resigns in the first session of Congress, the state must hold a special election to fill that vacancy. Procedures for filling vacancies that **occur** during the second session vary from state to state.

occur to happen

Representation and Reapportionment In order to assign representatives on the basis of population, the Census Bureau takes a national **census**, or population count, every 10 years. The first census was taken in 1790, and each state was apportioned its representatives. The next census will be in 2020. Each state's population determines the number of representatives it will have for the next 10 years—a process called **reapportionment**. States with slow growth or a population decrease can lose representatives, while states with strong population growth can gain seats. For example, Illinois, Iowa, Michigan, and Missouri lost seats after the 2010 census, thus lessening Midwestern influence on lawmaking.

census a population count

reapportionment the process of reassigning representation based on population, after every census

Originally the House had only 64 members. As the population of the nation grew, the number of representatives increased. After the 1810 census, the House had 186 members; by 1911, that number had grown to 435 members. In 1929 Congress capped the number of House members at 435. Now each census decides how these seats will be divided among the states.

Congressional Redistricting After the states find out their new representation for the next 10 years, each state legislature draws the boundaries for the congressional districts—one for each representative. Representatives are elected from these districts. If a state is entitled to only one representative, it has one congressional district. The process of redrawing district lines after reapportionment has been completed is called **redistricting**.

redistrict to set up new district lines after reapportionment is complete

134

In 2006 the Supreme Court decided a case that allowed states to modify this time-honored procedure. In *League of United Latin American Citizens, et al.* v. *Perry*, the Court ruled that state legislators may redraw congressional districts in the middle of a decade rather than only after a U.S. census.

Over the years, some state legislatures abused the redistricting power in one of two ways. Sometimes a state would create congressional districts of very unequal populations. During the early 1960s, for example, there were some states in which the largest district in the state had twice the population of the smallest district. More often, states would draw district boundaries to give one political party an electoral advantage. This process is called **gerrymandering**.

gerrymander to draw a district's boundaries to gain an advantage in elections

Redistricting Cases In a series of decisions in the 1960s, the Supreme Court ruled on redistricting issues in three different states: Tennessee, Georgia, and Alabama. In a 1962 Tennessee case, *Baker* v. *Carr*, the Court held that federal courts could decide conflicts over drawing district boundaries.

Two years later, in *Reynolds* v. *Sims*, the Court held that the equal protection clause of the Fourteenth Amendment required that seats in both houses of the Alabama state legislature be apportioned on a population basis. In a 1964 Georgia case, *Wesberry* v. *Sanders*, the Court ruled that the Constitution clearly intended that a vote in one congressional district was to be worth as much as a vote in another district. This principle has come to be known as the "one-person, one-vote" rule. Today, each congressional district contains about 710,700 people. After the 1990 census, several states drew new district lines to increase the voting power of ethnic or racial minorities. This approach increased minority representation, but it also tended to concentrate the Democratic vote, leaving neighboring districts more Republican.

This apportionment map is based on the 2010 census. Congressional apportionment will be readjusted after the census of 2020.

▼ CRITICAL THINKING
Analyzing What is the general trend of reapportionment due to population shifts?

MAP

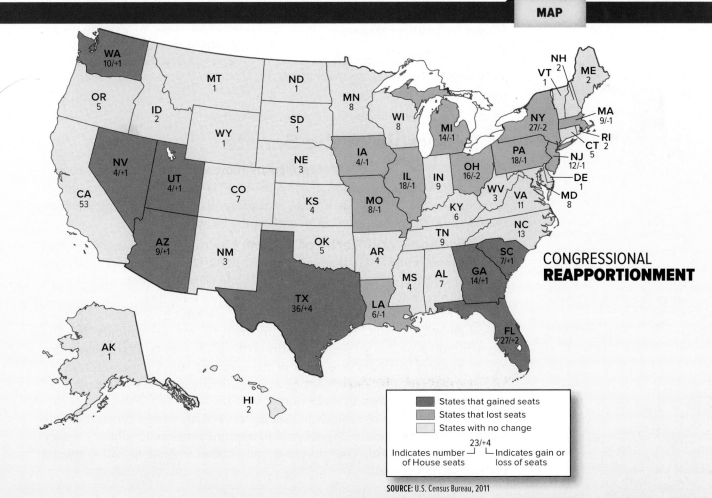

CONGRESSIONAL **REAPPORTIONMENT**

WA 10/+1
MT 1
ND 1
MN 8
OR 5
ID 2
WY 1
SD 1
WI 8
MI 14/-1
NH 2
VT 1
ME 2
NY 27/-2
MA 9/-1
RI 2
CT 5
PA 18/-1
NJ 12/-1
DE 1
MD 8
NV 4/+1
UT 4/+1
CO 7
NE 3
IA 4/-1
IL 18/-1
IN 9
OH 16/-2
WV 3
VA 11
CA 53
KS 4
MO 8/-1
KY 6
TN 9
NC 13
AZ 9/+1
NM 3
OK 5
AR 4
SC 7/+1
MS 4
AL 7
GA 14/+1
TX 36/+4
LA 6/-1
FL 27/+2
AK 1
HI 2

Legend:
States that gained seats
States that lost seats
States with no change

23/+4
Indicates number ⌐ ⌐ Indicates gain or
of House seats   loss of seats

SOURCE: U.S. Census Bureau, 2011

POLITICAL CARTOON

Gerrymandering is when a dominant state political party draws district boundaries to ensure victory in future elections.

▲ CRITICAL THINKING

Explaining How did the phrase "gerrymander" become popularized by the Federalists?

trace to discover by going backward over the evidence

at-large as a whole; for example, statewide

This was the case in North Carolina, where the Supreme Court ruled that the state's 1992 redistricting map violated the equal protection clause of the Fourteenth Amendment. In *Shaw* v. *Reno* (1993), the Court said that the plan used race as the predominant factor in drawing districts. The state redrew the districts in 1997 but was challenged again. Finally, in 2000 and 2001, the Court upheld the new redistricting plan. Because no clear guidelines are written for states on this issue, the Court has ruled on a case-by-case basis.

Gerrymandering When one party dominates the state legislature, it often tries to draw boundaries to ensure victory in future elections, resulting in oddly shaped districts. The term *gerrymandering* has been **traced** to Elbridge Gerry, an early Massachusetts governor who signed a redistricting plan that gave his party an advantage over the Federalists. Artist Gilbert Stuart thought the outline of one irregular district looked like a salamander. He added a head, wings, and claws and a newspaper published it as a cartoon labeled "Gerrymander."

"Packing" and "cracking" are ways to gerrymander. Packing a district means drawing the lines so they include as many of the opposing party's voters as possible. Crowding the opposition's voters into one district makes the remaining districts safe for the majority party's candidates. Cracking means dividing an opponent's voters into other districts to weaken the opponent's voter base.

The Supreme Court has issued several decisions that have cut down on some of the worst examples of gerrymandering. Nevertheless, the competitive struggle of the two-party system continues to fuel the practice of gerrymandering. Many districts today are still drawn in very irregular shapes for political reasons.

✓ **READING PROGRESS CHECK**

Describing What are some ways that political parties at the state level can gerrymander districts?

Membership of the Senate

GUIDING QUESTION *How is the Senate organized?*

According to the Constitution, the Senate "shall be composed of two senators from each state." Thus, each state is represented equally. Today's Senate includes 100 members—two from each of the 50 states.

Qualifications and Term of Office The Constitution provides that senators must be at least 30 years old, citizens of the United States for nine years before election, and legal residents of the state they represent. All voters of each state elect senators **at-large**, or statewide—they have no particular district.

Like those of the House, Senate elections are held in November during even-numbered years. Senators begin their terms on January 3. The Constitution provides for Senate continuity by giving senators six-year terms and providing that only one-third of the senators run for reelection every two years. In fact, the Senate has more continuity than the Founders planned because most senators win reelection.

If a senator dies or resigns before the end of his or her term, the state legislature can authorize the governor to appoint a person to fill the vacancy until the next election. The governor can choose instead to call a special election to fill the seat.

Salary and Benefits The Senate and the House set their own salaries. In 1789 salaries were $6 per day. Over the years, Congress has voted itself periodic salary increases. In 1991 it voted for a pay hike of $23,000, but it also included a provision that prohibited honoraria—money paid for speeches. A constitutional amendment on salaries for legislators changed these practices. Originally proposed by James Madison in 1789, the Twenty-seventh Amendment (1992) says that Congress cannot give itself a pay raise; the raise becomes effective only after another election.

With the new amendment on the books, a group of plaintiffs then challenged the cost-of-living increases in salary that Congress members regularly received. These plaintiffs argued that even a cost-of-living increase was prohibited by the new amendment. A U.S. district court judge, however, ruled that salary increases to match the cost of living were allowed.

> **PRIMARY SOURCE**
> **Automatic annual adjustments to congressional salaries meet both the language and the spirit of the 27th Amendment. . . . One way to maintain high-quality government is to provide our elected officials with a living wage that automatically changes to reflect changed economic conditions."**
>
> — Judge Stanley Sporkin, 1992

Since 2009, most members of Congress have earned $174,000 a year. In addition to their salary, members enjoy a number of benefits and resources. These include stationery, postage for official business (called the *franking privilege*), a medical clinic, and a gymnasium. They also receive large allowances to pay for staff, trips home, telephones, and newsletters. All members are entitled to an income tax deduction to help keep up two residences, one in their home state and one in the capital. In addition, senators and representatives may be eligible for pensions of up to 80 percent of their final salaries and have a generous 401(k) plan.

Privileges of Members The Constitution provides members of Congress with certain protections so they can carry out their public duties. For example, when they are attending Congress or on the way to or from Congress, they are free from arrest "in all cases except treason, felony, and breach of the peace."

Members also cannot be sued for anything they say on the House or Senate floor. This privilege does not cover what members say outside of Congress, however. This fact was established in a 1979 court case when the Court ruled that members of Congress can be sued for libel for statements in news releases or newsletters.

Another privilege of members of Congress is that both the Senate and the House may judge the qualifications of new members and decide whether to seat them. Each house may refuse to seat an elected member by a majority vote if the member-elect fails to meet the constitutional requirements of age, residence, or citizenship. Finally, each house may punish its own members for disorderly behavior by a majority vote and expel a legislator by a two-thirds vote. Only the most serious offenses, such as treason or accepting bribes, are grounds for expulsion. Members guilty of lesser offenses may be censured. **Censure** is a vote of formal disapproval of a member's actions.

censure a vote of formal disapproval of a member's actions

✓ READING PROGRESS CHECK

Identifying What salary and benefits do current members of Congress enjoy?

The Members of Congress

GUIDING QUESTIONS *How have the characteristics of members of Congress changed over time?*

Congress includes 535 voting members—100 senators and 435 representatives. In addition, there are five delegates in the House—one each from the District of Columbia, Guam, American Samoa, Northern Marianas, and the Virgin Islands—and one resident commissioner from Puerto Rico. None of these delegates can vote on the final passage of a bill, but they can attend sessions, introduce bills, speak in debates on the House floor, and vote in committees.

Characteristics Nearly half the members of Congress are lawyers. Lawyers are well prepared to understand the complex legal issues that may affect legislation. Many other Congress members come from the fields of business, banking, or education.

Historically, senators and representatives have been white, middle-aged males, but Congress has slowly begun to reflect more racial, ethnic, and gender diversity. The increase in the number of women representatives in the House, for example, has come about only in recent times. In the 85th Congress (1957–1959), there were only 15 women representatives (3 percent); by 2013, however, 100 women were serving in the House of Representatives (19 percent).

Reelection to Congress Membership in Congress tends to change slowly because officeholders seldom lose reelection. One representative put it simply: "All members of Congress have a primary interest in being re-elected." Beginning with Franklin D. Roosevelt's landslide presidential victories in the 1930s, incumbency helped Democrats dominate Congress in all but a few years until 1990.

We the People: Making a Difference

Even as she was attending college and graduate school, Eleanor Holmes Norton made time to contribute to the civil rights movement. In 1963 she helped organize the historic March on Washington for Jobs and Freedom, organizing buses from other cities and giving speeches about why people were marching.

Nearly 30 years later, Ms. Norton came to Congress as the Delegate for the District of Columbia. She had been a law professor, chairman of the New York Human Rights Commission, assistant legal director of the American Civil Liberties Union, and the first woman to chair the Equal Employment Opportunity Commission.

Norton has championed legislation that focuses on economic opportunities and economic development for her constituents. Her work has led to college scholarships for D.C. high school graduates, tax credits for businesses that employ district residents, incentives for homebuyers, and the relocation of several federal agencies to the district, creating tens of thousands of local jobs. She continues to work for full congressional voting representation and D.C. statehood.

ELEANOR HOLMES NORTON

Saul Loeb/AFP/Getty Images

EXPLORING THE ESSENTIAL QUESTION

Analyzing Point of View As a member of Congress, Norton has focused much of her efforts on economic opportunities. In your opinion, how does her focus relate to her commitment to civil rights and human rights?

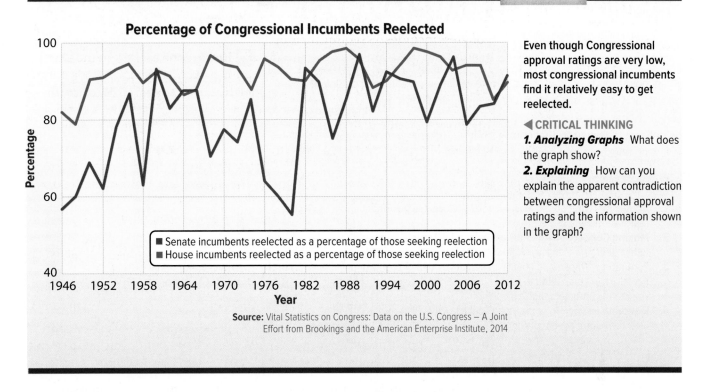

Percentage of Congressional Incumbents Reelected

■ Senate incumbents reelected as a percentage of those seeking reelection
■ House incumbents reelected as a percentage of those seeking reelection

Source: Vital Statistics on Congress: Data on the U.S. Congress – A Joint Effort from Brookings and the American Enterprise Institute, 2014

Even though Congressional approval ratings are very low, most congressional incumbents find it relatively easy to get reelected.

◄ CRITICAL THINKING
1. Analyzing Graphs What does the graph show?
2. Explaining How can you explain the apparent contradiction between congressional approval ratings and the information shown in the graph?

Between 1946 and 2012, more than 90 percent of all **incumbents**, members who were already in office, won reelection. In some elections, many seats went unchallenged because opponents knew that they would have little or no chance of winning. One analyst said that winning an election to Congress for most members was like removing olives from a bottle—"after the first one, the rest come easy."

There are many reasons why it is relatively easy for incumbents to be reelected. For example, incumbents can raise campaign funds more easily through personal contacts they make while representing their district. Second, many districts have been gerrymandered in the incumbent party's favor. Third, incumbents are better known to voters, who see them on television and read about them regularly in news stories. Fourth, incumbents use their position to solve the problems of voters, who are then grateful. Finally, incumbents may win simply because most voters believe they best represent their views.

Campaigning Online While candidates, parties, and political action committees continue to advertise heavily on radio and television, they have increasingly turned to the Internet and social media to influence elections. Candidates create websites that serve as electronic brochures. A typical campaign website offers a biography of the candidate, press releases, upcoming campaign events, and positions on hot issues. Websites are also used to recruit volunteers and raise campaign funds. In addition, candidates can use their websites to broadcast campaign events such as speeches.

The Internet also allows candidates to interact with voters more easily and effectively. Candidates can conduct town hall meetings for voters on the web. They use web technologies—search engines, portals, and e-mail lists—to identify voters who are interested in specific issues such as gun control or health care. Once they have this information, candidates can contact these voters with specifically targeted messages on any given issue.

incumbent elected official who is already in office

C·I·V·I·C PARTICIPATION IN A DIGITAL AGE

Twitter and Congress

Elected officials strive to stay current with trends in technology, especially when those tools help them communicate with their constituents, potential donors, and voters. Analyze the Twitter communications of your congressional representative. The address is likely to begin https://twitter.com/ followed by that person's name. Then answer each of the following questions and explain your responses.

EXPLORING THE ESSENTIAL QUESTION

1. **Analyzing** What do the most recent 20 tweets tell you about your representative?
2. **Making Connections** Are the tweets interesting to you? Would you follow your representative if you also had a Twitter account?
3. **Evaluating** What could your representative do to make his or her tweets more compelling to people like you? What can elected officials say in 140 characters that is meaningful?
4. **Exploring Issues** Do voters need special skills to interpret this kind of brief but nearly continual contact?

Increasingly, candidates use Twitter to send a string of short messages of 140 characters or less—known as *tweets*—to reach their supporters and motivate voters to go to the polls.

But candidates have found that almost anything they say, even at nonpublic events, is subject to being recorded and broadcast online. Campaign blunders may appear in text or video and "go viral"—spreading widely through Internet sharing. The Internet has also allowed more citizens to post their opinions in blogs, opening the political process to more voices and making it more democratic.

✓ READING PROGRESS CHECK

Determining Importance How has the Internet changed the way that congressional candidates interact with voters?

LESSON 1 REVIEW

Reviewing Vocabulary
1. ***Contrasting*** What is the difference between redistricting and reapportionment?

Using Your Graphic Organizer
2. ***Summarizing*** Use your completed graphic organizer to write a paragraph summarizing the qualifications for representatives and senators.

Answering the Guiding Questions
3. ***Describing*** What is the structure of Congress?
4. ***Explaining*** How is the House of Representatives organized?

5. ***Explaining*** How is the Senate organized?
6. ***Analyzing*** How have the characteristics of members of Congress changed over time?

Writing About Government
7. ***Informative/Explanatory*** Why did the Founders establish a bicameral legislature? What are the advantages of a bicameral as opposed to a unicameral legislature? Explain.
8. ***Informative/Explanatory*** Explain the process of redistricting. How have Supreme Court decisions such as *Baker* v. *Carr* and *Shaw* v. *Reno* affected the drawing of U.S. districts?

U.S. Term Limits, Inc. Ⓥ Thornton (1995)

FACTS OF THE CASE Article I of the United States Constitution includes the qualifications necessary to be a member of Congress.

Section 2, Clause 2: "No Person shall be a Representative who shall not have attained to the Age of twenty five Years, and been seven Years a Citizen of the United States, and who shall not, when elected, be an Inhabitant of that State in which he shall be chosen."

Section 3, Clause 3: "No Person shall be a Senator who shall not have attained to the Age of thirty Years, and been nine Years a Citizen of the United States, and who shall not, when elected, be an Inhabitant of that State for which he shall be chosen."

In 1992 the voters of Arkansas adopted an amendment to their state constitution to limit the number of times that a person can serve as a representative of Arkansas in the United States Congress. It said that any person elected to represent Arkansas cannot serve more than two terms in the U.S. Senate and more than three terms in the U.S. House of Representatives. Several citizens of Arkansas sued, saying that this state law was unconstitutional.

ISSUE

Does a state have the power to place limits on the terms of its federal representatives in Congress?

ARGUMENTS

OPINION A The only qualifications that can be in place for representatives in Congress are those that are included in the Constitution because these are the only qualifications that were ratified by all the people. The Constitution is very clear, so the only way that these qualifications could be changed is through a constitutional amendment.

Similarly, the power to change or modify these qualifications does not belong to the states. As the Supreme Court decided in *McCulloch* v. *Maryland*, the Constitution is supreme. It controls the laws of states and "cannot be controlled by them." States have never been able to regulate the term limits of persons serving in federal office. Therefore, the Arkansas law is unconstitutional.

OPINION B More than any other part of government, the legislative branch is set up to directly reflect the wishes of the people. A majority of the voters of Arkansas exercised their right to limit the time their representatives can serve.

Article I sets the minimal standards for terms and qualifications, but it does not prohibit states from adding extra qualifications. The people of Arkansas believe they are best represented when elected officials cannot stay in office for longer than a given period of time. Their desire to be represented effectively must be respected.

EXPLORING THE ESSENTIAL QUESTION

Evaluating Read each of the two sample opinions in this case. Decide which one you think should be the majority (winning) opinion, and which one you think should be the dissenting opinion. Explain your choice.

YOU BE the JUDGE

LESSON 2
The House of Representatives

ReadingHelp Desk

Academic Vocabulary

- **succession**
- **parallel**
- **constitute**

Content Vocabulary

- **constituent**
- **caucus**
- **majority leader**
- **whip**
- **bill**
- **calendar**
- **concurrent jurisdiction**
- **quorum**

TAKING NOTES:

Key Ideas and Details

IDENTIFYING Use a graphic organizer to identify and describe the House leadership.

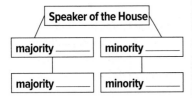

ESSENTIAL QUESTION

What is the structure and organization of Congress?

If the president dies or is unable to perform his or her duties, the vice president steps in. If the vice president is unable to perform, the next person in the line of succession is the Speaker of the House, the most powerful person in the House of Representatives.

Before a person can become Speaker, he or she must already be a member of the House of Representatives, elected by voters to represent them. The Speaker also must be a member of the political party that holds the most seats in Congress, called the majority, or majority party. The Speaker is chosen behind closed doors by the other elected representatives from the majority party.

What do you think about the Speaker's place in the line of succession? Why is the person who holds this position a good choice or a bad choice to take over the leadership of the country? Explain your answer.

Rules in the House

GUIDING QUESTION *What rules govern lawmaking in the House?*

Political divisions are unavoidable in a democracy; political debates have always stirred strong passions. Tempers have flared and angry words— even physical blows at times—have been exchanged over political disagreements. Legislators must be free to express their opinions, but rules are needed to help ensure fairness and to protect the minority. Article I, Section 51 of the Constitution says: "Each House may determine the Rules of its Proceedings." Thomas Jefferson stressed the importance of rules when he was vice president.

❝❝ PRIMARY SOURCE

It is much more material that there be a rule to go by, than what that rule is; that there may be a uniformity of proceeding in business not subject to the caprice [whims] of the Speaker or captiousness [criticisms] of the members."

— Thomas Jefferson, 1797

Jefferson spent much of his four years as vice president writing Congress's first rules manual. To avoid angry confrontations and foster reasonable debate, the manual instructed members not to address each other directly but to speak to the presiding officer. Members could disagree strongly on the issues but were not to question each other's motives or criticize each other's states. Above all, members were to maintain decorum—polite behavior—in the chamber. More than 200 years later, Jefferson's admonitions still influence congressional language and conduct during legislative debates.

Complex Rules Each chamber has scores of precedents based on past rulings that serve as a guide to conducting business. The House and Senate each print their rules every two years. House rules are generally aimed at defining the actions an individual representative can take, such as limiting representatives to speaking for five minutes or less during a debate.

The complex rules in the House are geared toward moving legislation quickly once it reaches the floor; consequently, House debates rarely last more than one day. Moreover, leaders of the House of Representatives have more power than leaders in the Senate. For example, the rules of the House allow its leaders to make key decisions about legislative work without consulting other House members.

Committee Work The committees of Congress perform most legislative activity. Because of the size of the House, committee work is even more important than in the Senate. Membership in the House is so large that organizing members into committees allows representatives to have more influence than on the House floor; committee work also gives representatives the time to study and shape bills. Finally, because members represent districts, they serve on committees that are important to their **constituents**.

Importance of Party Affiliation Political parties are important to many procedures in Congress. Party distinctions are physically obvious: In both the House and Senate, the Republicans and Democrats sit on opposite sides of the center aisle from each other. In each house, the majority party has the power to select the leaders of that body, to control the flow of legislative work, and to appoint the chairs of all the committees.

When an election produces a change in majority in the House, the incoming majority party can make sweeping changes. For example, in 1994 Republicans won a significant number of congressional seats that had been held by Democrats for years. The Republicans' new rules concentrated more power in the Speaker's office, provided for fewer committees and fewer staff members, and limited the terms of committee chairs. Absentee voting in committees was also ended.

The Republican majority pushed through these rules changes over objection from the Democrats. Yet when Democrats returned to the majority after the 2006 elections, they continued many of these practices. Nancy Pelosi, the first woman to serve as Speaker, concentrated authority in the Speaker's office at the expense of committees. Like Speakers before her, she used the powers of her office to maintain unity within her party and to promote its legislative agenda.

☑ READING PROGRESS CHECK

Determining Importance How do committees and party affiliation influence lawmaking in the House?

constituent a person whom a member of Congress has been elected to represent

Speaker of the House John Boehner spoke on April 6, 2011 about an impending government shutdown.

▼ **CRITICAL THINKING**
Explaining Why is the Speaker of the House a powerful position?

Mark Wilson/Getty Images News/Getty Images

LEGISLATURES IN MULTI-PARTY SYSTEMS

Many democracies have legislatures that include members of multiple parties. This can force collaboration among parties—when no party has a majority in the legislature, parties must work together to get legislation passed. There is no guarantee that will happen, however, and gridlock can thus result in multi-party systems as well as two-party systems.

ISRAEL

Israel's Parliament, known as the Knesset, meets in this building in Jerusalem.

INDIA

The Indian Parliament in New Delhi has two houses: Lok Sabha and Rajya Sabha.

At any one time, about a dozen parties are represented among the 120 members of Israel's Knesset.

The government (a coalition of parties working together to operate as a majority) introduces most legislation, but any member of the Knesset can present a bill. Most bills can be passed with a simple majority.

Every day that the Knesset is in session, time is reserved for members to question government ministers about matters for which they are responsible. Members will ask questions about policies or actions that concern them. Sometimes, the members of the Knesset will heckle, or shout, boo, or cheer, while the minister is speaking, to express their opinions about the policy being discussed.

In India, nearly 40 parties are represented in its 790-member Parliament—although one party, the Indian National Congress, has dominated the country since its independence.

The Indian Parliament has two houses—Rajya Sabha (Council of States) and Lok Sabha (House of the People). Every bill has to be passed by both houses and assented to by the president before it becomes law.

The members of Parliament (MPs) of Lok Sabha are directly elected by the Indian public. The MPs of Rajya Sabha are elected by the members of the State Legislative Assemblies. Several seats are reserved for representatives from groups that have been historically discriminated against.

EXPLORING THE ESSENTIAL QUESTION

1. **Contrasting** What key differences do you see between the U.S. Congress and the legislatures in these two multi-party systems?
2. **Evaluating** Are there any customs or rules from Israel's Knesset or India's Parliament that you would recommend the U.S. Congress adopt? If so, explain how that custom or rule aligns with the principles of democracy.

House Leadership

GUIDING QUESTION *Who makes up the House leadership?*

Leaders of the House coordinate the work of this large body of 435 individual members. It is helpful to think of the work of the leadership as meeting six kinds of goals:

- Organizing and unifying party members
- Scheduling work
- Making certain that lawmakers are present for key floor votes
- Distributing and collecting information
- Keeping the House in touch with the president
- Influencing lawmakers to support their party's positions

The Speaker of the House The Speaker of the House is the presiding officer and its most powerful leader. The Constitution states that the House "shall choose their Speaker and other officers." A **caucus**, or closed meeting, of the majority party chooses the Speaker of the House at the start of each session of Congress, and the entire House membership approves the choice of Speaker.

As both the presiding officer of the House and the leader of the majority party, the Speaker has great power. Presiding over the sessions of the House, the Speaker can influence proceedings by deciding which members to recognize first. The Speaker also appoints the members of some committees, schedules bills for action, and refers bills to the proper House committee. Finally, the Speaker of the House follows the vice president in the line of **succession** to the presidency.

Today, Speakers rely as much on persuasion as on their formal powers to influence other members. On a typical day, the Speaker may talk with dozens of members; the Speaker frequently does this just to hear their requests for a favor. As former Speaker Thomas P. "Tip" O'Neill once put it, "The world is full of little things you can do for people." In return, the Speaker expects representatives' support on important issues.

House Floor Leaders The Speaker's top assistant is the **majority leader**. The majority leader's job is to help plan the party's legislative program, steer important bills through the House, and make sure the chairpersons of the many committees finish work on bills that are important to the party. The majority leader is the floor leader of his or her political party in the House and, like the Speaker, is elected by the majority party. Thus, the majority leader is not a House official but rather a party official.

The majority leader has help from the majority **whip** and deputy whips, who serve as assistant floor leaders in the House. The majority whip's job is to watch how majority-party members intend to vote on **bills**, to persuade them to vote as the party wishes, and to see that party members are present to vote.

The minority party in the House elects its own leaders—the minority leader and the minority whip. Their responsibilities **parallel** the duties of the majority party, except that they have no power over scheduling work in the House.

caucus a private meeting of party leaders to choose candidates for office

succession the action or process of inheriting a title or office

majority leader the Speaker's top assistant whose job is to help plan the majority party's legislative program and to steer important bills through the House

whip an assistant to the party floor leader in the legislature

bill a proposed law

parallel to correspond to

✓ **READING PROGRESS CHECK**

Listing What are the main responsibilities of the Speaker, majority leader, and majority whip?

EXPLORING THE ESSENTIAL QUESTION

Analyzing After serving as a representative for 16 years, in 2006 Congressman John Boehner, a Republican from Ohio, was chosen as the House Majority Leader. Five years later, he became the Speaker of the House and was reelected to that position by his caucus in 2013. What skills do you think House majority and minority leaders must develop and demonstrate? Make a list and rank them. How might this work and experience help them ascend to the job of Speaker? Do you possess any similar skills or experiences? What could you do to develop your leadership abilities?

Lawmaking in the House

GUIDING QUESTION *How does the House conduct business?*

On a typical day, the House of Representatives might look a bit disorganized. Representatives are talking in small groups, reading newspapers, or constantly walking in and out of the chamber. Most representatives are not even on the floor but are in committee meetings, talking with voters, or in

PARTICIPATING
IN Your Government

their offices. Representatives reach the floor quickly, however, when it is time for debate or a vote on proposed bills.

Usually, the House starts its floor sessions at noon or earlier. Buzzers ring in members' offices in the House office buildings, committee rooms, and in the Capitol to call representatives to the chamber. The House is normally in session from Monday through Friday. Mondays are for routine work, and not much is done on Friday because many representatives leave to go to their home districts over the weekend. Thus, most of the House's important work is done from Tuesday through Thursday.

How House Bills Move Through Committees to a Vote All laws start as bills. A proposed law is called a bill until both houses of Congress pass it and the president signs it. According to the procedure that is currently in place, to introduce a bill in the House, representatives drop it into the hopper, a mahogany box that is accessible to all near the front of the chamber.

After a bill is introduced, the Speaker of the House sends it to the appropriate committee for study, discussion, and review. Of the thousands of bills and resolutions that are introduced during each legislative term of Congress, only about 10 to 20 percent ever go to the full House for a vote. Bills that survive the committee process are put on one of the House calendars. **Calendars** list bills that are up for consideration.

calendar a schedule that lists the order in which bills will be considered in Congress

The House Rules Committee The Rules Committee is extremely important because it is a "traffic officer," helping to direct the flow of major legislation. It is one of the oldest and the most powerful House committees. The representative who chairs this committee has great influence over legislative activity and how bills progress through Congress. After a committee has considered and approved a major bill, it usually goes to the Rules Committee. The Rules Committee can move bills ahead quickly, hold them back, or stop them completely. As a result, the power of the Rules Committee has often been the focus of political battles.

From 1858 to 1910, the Speaker of the House chaired this committee and dominated the flow of legislation. In 1911 the House revolted against Speaker Cannon's authoritarian leadership and removed him from the Rules Committee.

Party battles over the Speaker's power also have arisen in relatively recent times. In 1975 Democratic majorities in the House once again placed the Rules Committee under the control of the Speaker. The Democratic Caucus gave the Speaker the power to appoint all majority members of the Rules Committee, subject to caucus ratification. The Republican Caucus continued with this process when they gained majority control of the House in 1995. They appointed nine members and gave the Democrats the remaining four slots on the committee. While the members of the Rules Committee are usually senior representatives, in 2011 Republicans broke with tradition by selecting four freshmen representatives to serve on the committee.

Function of the Rules Committee

Major bills that reach the floor of the House do so by a rule—or special order—from the Rules Committee. As major bills come out of committee, they are entered on the calendar in the order in which they are received.

Calendars have so many bills on them that if they were taken up in calendar order, many would never reach the floor before the session ended. To solve this problem, the chairperson of the committee that sent the bill to the Rules Committee can ask for it to move ahead of other bills. The Rules Committee can also say how long the bill can be debated and revised.

The Rules Committee also settles disputes among other House committees. For example, the Armed Services Committee may consider a bill that involves a subject that is covered by the Veterans' Affairs Committee. Sometimes sections of a bill will be sent to two or more committees, a practice known as **concurrent jurisdiction**.

Finally, the Rules Committee often delays or blocks bills that representatives and House leaders do not want to come to a vote on the floor. In this way, it can draw criticism away from members who might have to take an unpopular stand on a bill if it did reach the floor.

concurrent jurisdiction authority shared by two or more committees

A Quorum for Business

A **quorum** is the minimum number of members needed for official legislative action. For a regular session, a quorum requires a majority of 218 members. When the House meets to debate and amend legislation, it often sits as a Committee of the Whole. In that case, 100 members **constitute** a quorum. This procedure helps speed consideration of important bills, but the Committee of the Whole cannot pass a bill. Instead, it reports the measure back to the full House with any revisions it makes. The House then passes or rejects the bill.

quorum the minimum number of members who must be present to permit a legislative body to take official action

constitute to make up, form, compose

☑ **READING PROGRESS CHECK**

Determining Importance What is the function of the House Rules Committee?

LESSON 2 REVIEW

Reviewing Vocabulary

1. ***Defining*** Who are constituents and why are they important to members of Congress?

Using Your Graphic Organizer

2. ***Summarizing*** Use your completed graphic organizer to write a short description of each House leadership position.

Answering the Guiding Questions

3. ***Describing*** What rules govern lawmaking in the House?

4. ***Identifying*** Who makes up the House leadership?

5. ***Explaining*** How does the House conduct business?

Writing About Government

6. ***Informative/Explanatory*** How does a bill move through the committee process and what is the role of the Rules Committee? Write a brief fact sheet explaining the process of getting a bill created and out of committee.

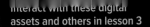

LESSON 3
The Senate

ReadingHelp Desk

Academic Vocabulary

- **specific**
- **assistant**
- **flexible**
- **devote**

Content Vocabulary

- **president pro tempore**
- **unanimous consent**
- **hold**
- **filibuster**
- **cloture resolution**

TAKING NOTES:

Key Ideas and Details

COMPARING AND CONTRASTING Use the Venn diagram to record the similarities and differences between the everyday operations of the House and the Senate.

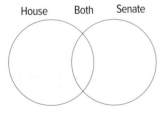

House   Both   Senate

continued on the next page

148

What is the structure and organization of Congress?

As you know, the House of Representatives has 435 members. The Senate, on the other hand, has only 100 members. Imagine trying to get work done in a group with 435 people. How would it be different from working with a group of 100 people? What rules might help each group be productive?

Below are some rules or procedures that apply either to the House only or the Senate only. Decide whether each would work best in the larger House or the smaller Senate. Explain your reasons.

- Debate on bills is usually unlimited.

- A Rules Committee provides strict procedures for moving a bill through the chamber.

- The atmosphere in the chamber is less formal.

- The chamber needs five calendars to keep track of all the bills introduced by members.

The Senate at Work

GUIDING QUESTION *What rules govern lawmaking in the Senate?*

All states are equal in the Senate. California, with the largest population, and Wyoming, with the smallest population, each has two senators. Unlike the House, where the majority of members represent a majority of the population, a majority of senators represent a small minority of the population.

The Senate is called a deliberative body because it deliberates, or formally discusses, public policies. Senators handle issues that are of **specific** interest to their committees, but they may address other issues, too. Because two senators represent an entire state, they are expected to be knowledgeable about many issues from national defense to farming.

Visitors going from the House to the Senate are often startled by the difference between the two chambers. The Senate is smaller, and usually only a few senators attend sessions. The Senate chamber has 100 desks (one per senator) facing a raised platform where the president pro tempore and another senator preside. Party leaders or their **assistants** stay in or near the Senate chamber at all times to keep the work moving and to look after their party's interests. In the Senate, the rules are more **flexible** than in the House to give all senators maximum freedom to express their ideas. For example, because the Senate usually allows unlimited debate on bills, senators can debate a proposal on and off for weeks or even months.

☑ **READING PROGRESS CHECK**

Explaining How is the Senate different from the House of Representatives?

specific having distinct or particular characteristics

assistant a helper

flexible capable of readily adapting to change

Leadership in the Senate

GUIDING QUESTION *Who makes up the Senate leadership?*

Leadership in the Senate closely parallels leadership in the House, but the Senate has no Speaker. The vice president presides over the Senate but cannot vote except to break a tie. Senate procedures also allow senators more freedom. Thus, Senate party leaders do not usually have as much influence over members as their counterparts in the House.

The Vice President The Constitution names the vice president as the Senate's president, but he or she does not have the same role or power as the Speaker of the House. The vice president may recognize members and put questions to a vote, but he or she is not an elected senator, so this person may not take part in Senate debates or cast a vote except in the event of a tie.

C·I·V·I·C PARTICIPATION IN A DIGITAL AGE

C-SPAN

C-SPAN (Cable-Satellite Public Affairs Network) is a nonprofit and nonpartisan organization dedicated to providing unedited coverage of the work of government. It receives no government funding. What began in 1979 as "gavel-to-gavel" television coverage of the House of Representatives has grown into multiple programming options where viewers and listeners can tune into TV, radio, satellite radio, and the web to access the day-to-day operations of the House and Senate as well as coverage of major national events.

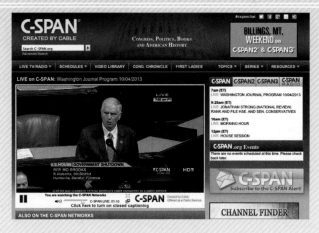

C-SPAN

EXPLORING THE ESSENTIAL QUESTION

1. ***Observing*** Tune in to C-SPAN's coverage of the U.S. Senate on your smartphone, television, radio, or satellite radio. Take notes about what you observe. How do senators address each other? How do rules about debate and votes affect their work? What is the style and function of the senator who is leading the group? What political party does he or she represent? What is the bill or issue under consideration? What else do you observe that is noteworthy?

2. ***Summarizing*** Summarize your observations in a news story about the Senate's work for that portion of the day.

PARTICIPATING
(IN) Your Government

devote to commit to an activity

president pro tempore the Senate member, elected by the Senate, who stands in as president of the Senate in the absence of the vice president

The vice president may, however, influence members through personal contact. Most vice presidents find Senate duties unchallenging and **devote** more time to executive duties. In the absence of the vice president, the **president pro tempore**—"pro tem" for short—presides. (The term means "for the time being.") The Senate elects this leader from the majority party. Historically, it is that party's longest-serving member.

Majority and Minority Leaders The Senate's most important officers are the majority and minority leaders. Elected by party members, these are officials of the party, not of the Senate. The job of the majority leader is to steer the party's bills through the Senate, which is done by planning the work schedule and agenda in consultation with the minority leader. The majority leader also makes sure that party members attend important sessions and gets support for key bills.

The minority leader has a different job—critiquing the majority party's bills and keeping his or her own party united. As in the House, whips and assistant whips are very important because they do the detailed work that supports leaders. A key job is making sure that legislators are present in the chamber when key votes come up.

✓ **READING PROGRESS CHECK**

Contrasting How are the roles of the Senate majority leader and the Senate minority leader different?

Lawmaking in the Senate

GUIDING QUESTION *How does the Senate conduct business?*

The Constitution requires a supermajority of two-thirds of the Senate to approve treaties, overturn presidential vetoes, and remove federal officials from office if they have been impeached in the House. Technically, the vote of a simple majority, fifty senators plus one, is required to pass a proposed bill.

As in the House, any senator can introduce a bill, but procedures for moving a bill through the Senate are less formal than in the House. Because it is smaller, the Senate has never needed a committee like the House Rules Committee. Instead, Senate leaders control the flow of bills to committees and to the floor. They do this by consulting closely with one another. The Senate has only two calendars—the Calendar of General Orders, which lists all the bills the Senate will consider, and the Executive Calendar, which schedules treaties and nominations.

Unanimous Consent The Senate brings bills to the floor by **unanimous consent**, a motion by all members present to set aside formal rules and consider a bill from the calendar. This procedure has not changed much through the years and the Senate does much of its daily business this way. Unanimous consent agreements mean the two parties have agreed and no one objects.

But a single senator can object to a unanimous consent agreement and slow down or even stop the pending business. Senators can place **holds** on a bill, alerting their party leaders that if unanimous consent was sought, they would object. Holds signal to the leaders that there is not yet agreement, and they should hold the bill back from debate. Holds and the ability to object to unanimous consent agreements empower every senator, senior or junior, majority or minority.

The Filibuster Today many important bills really need the votes of sixty senators to pass the Senate. The reason is a tactic called the **filibuster**. This is any number of actions taken by a senator or group of senators to prevent a bill from coming to a final vote. Because Senate rules usually allow unlimited debate on any bill, the classic filibuster tactic was to "talk the bill to death" by speaking continuously, thereby not allowing other senators to take action on the bill.

Since the 1960s, however, Senate rules allow a variety of ways to filibuster that do not require a senator to occupy the floor and speak nonstop, and do not prevent action on other bills. Instead, a bill that is filibustered is temporarily set aside and the Senate moves on to other business. As a result, filibusters have become very common and much easier to maintain. Today the mere threat of a filibuster is often used to stop action on bills.

unanimous consent a motion by all members of the Senate who are present to set aside formal rules and consider a bill from the calendar

hold a motion placed on a bill in the Senate that alerts party leaders that if unanimous consent were to be sought, they would object

filibuster a method of defeating a bill in the Senate by stalling the legislative process and preventing a vote

▼ CRITICAL THINKING
1. Defining What does it mean to say that the U.S. Congress is a *bicameral* legislature?
2. Assessing What are some differences between Senate and House leadership? In which house do party leaders have more influence?

The Senate chamber is a rectangular, two-story room located in the north wing of the U.S. Capitol. Senators sit at assigned desks in front of a raised platform below a visitor's gallery.

The House of Representatives chamber is in the south wing of the U.S. Capitol. House members, in unassigned seats, face the Speaker—Democrats to the Speaker's right and Republicans to the left.

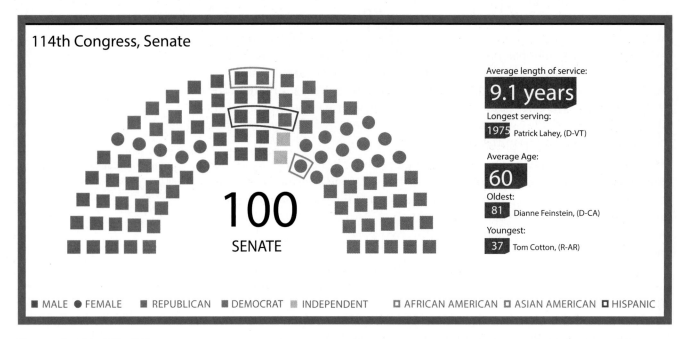

114th Congress, Senate

Average length of service:
9.1 years

Longest serving:
1975 Patrick Lahey, (D-VT)

Average Age:
60

Oldest:
81 Dianne Feinstein, (D-CA)

Youngest:
37 Tom Cotton, (R-AR)

100
SENATE

■ MALE ● FEMALE   ■ REPUBLICAN   ■ DEMOCRAT   ■ INDEPENDENT   □ AFRICAN AMERICAN   □ ASIAN AMERICAN   □ HISPANIC

The membership of the U.S. Senate is slowly changing to reflect the nation's diverse population.

▲ **CRITICAL THINKING**
Describing How many women serve in the U.S. Senate in the 114th Congress?

cloture resolution a procedure that allows each senator to speak only one hour on a bill under debate

Senators can end a filibuster by voting for a **cloture resolution**. Sixty senators must vote for cloture. This means that for all practical purposes any major bill can pass the Senate only if it can get the 60 votes needed to end a filibuster. Getting 60 votes can be very difficult, especially in a Senate where neither party has a large majority. It can force the majority party to negotiate with the minority to find consensus and build a coalition behind the bill.

The polarization of the parties during the last two decades has meant that many occasions arose when filibusters were threatened to prevent action on bills and cloture motions were attempted to stop them. One scholar has called this the era of the "60-vote Senate." Opinion polls have shown that citizens are upset at this degree of congressional gridlock where it seems impossible to enact proposals or reforms. Some observers view extensive use of the filibuster as a violation of the principle of majority rule.

Several senators have called for reform of the filibuster, including abolishing it altogether. In November 2013, the Senate instituted a rule change that prevented the need for a 60-vote majority for all presidential nominees except nominees to the Supreme Court. However, for other Senate business, the basic rules remain in place.

☑ **READING PROGRESS CHECK**

Stating How is the filibuster or threat of a filibuster used in the Senate?

LESSON 3 REVIEW

Reviewing Vocabulary
1. ***Understanding Relationships*** How are the terms *filibuster* and *cloture* related?

Using Your Graphic Organizer
2. ***Outlining*** Use your completed graphic organizer to write an outline describing the differences between the everyday operations of the House and the Senate.

Answering the Guiding Questions
3. ***Describing*** What rules govern lawmaking in the Senate?

4. ***Identifying*** Who makes up the Senate leadership?

5. ***Explaining*** How does the Senate conduct business?

Writing About Government
6. ***Informative/Explanatory*** Congress has a bicameral structure with two very different chambers. Write an essay analyzing how lawmaking is different in the Senate as compared to the House of Representatives.

Should the filibuster be abolished?

DELIBERATING DEMOCRATIC PRINCIPLES

In May 2013, Twitter announced that more than a million tweets about Senator Rand Paul had been sent during a 13-hour period. Paul was filibustering President Obama's nominee to head the CIA. By preventing a vote on the nomination, Paul hoped President Obama would guarantee that unmanned drones would not be used in the United States against U.S. citizens. Paul's effort was one of the longer filibusters in U.S. history, and it fed the debate on whether the filibuster is a useful strategy or a tactic that prevents the Senate from doing its job.

 YES

 **NO**

TEAM A — The Filibuster Should Be Abolished

The filibuster violates the principle of majority rule; in short, it is undemocratic. By the time a bill gets to the floor, it has already been through many steps that give opponents a chance to make changes or to reach compromises. The filibuster allows one or a few senators to prevent the majority of senators from taking a vote. It gives someone with a minority viewpoint control over the process that majority supports. The filibuster can block or delay important legislation from being passed. In the event of national emergency, this could be disastrous.

The filibuster originated as a means of ensuring that all issues would receive thorough debate in the Senate. Now, it serves as nothing but a block to debate an action. The way the filibuster is used, virtually no bill can pass without a 60-vote majority. This was not the intent of the Founders. The Constitution gives the Senate power to make its own rules. It does not grant the specific power of the filibuster, so the Senate can vote to end its use anytime. Reforms, such as lowering the number of votes needed to end the filibuster, would help. But it would be more effective to simply eliminate this undemocratic practice.

TEAM B — The Filibuster Should Not Be Abolished

The filibuster is a useful tool to protect the rights and interests of people with minority viewpoints. While democracy operates on the principle of majority rule, it also guarantees that the minority will be protected. The filibuster prevents the majority from forcing through legislation that may not be beneficial to the United States. The filibuster can also bring important questions or concerns to the attention of the public. The public can then become involved in the debate, and the Senate will be more aware of what citizens want.

The filibuster serves as an internal check on the power of the Senate. A filibuster against a president's nominations can be seen as a check on the power of the executive. Thus, it is well-aligned with the Founders' desire for a limited government. Because the Constitution allows the Senate to set its own rules, the filibuster is certainly constitutional. The filibuster procedures have been changed several times in the past. If necessary, they can again be changed. But the filibuster should not be abolished because of its important role in protecting Americans from the tyranny of the majority.

EXPLORING THE ESSENTIAL QUESTION

Deliberating With a partner, review the main arguments for either side of the question. Decide which points are most compelling. Then paraphrase those arguments to a pair of students who were assigned to the other viewpoint. Listen to their strongest arguments. Switch sides and repeat the best arguments and add another compelling argument the other pair may not have thought about or presented. Then drop your roles and have a free discussion about which policy you support and why. Can you find any areas of common ground between the two views? How might a sensible policy address that common ground? What do you think is the best answer? Why?

(l to r) U.S. Air Force photo by Tech. Sgt. Cherie A. Thurlby; Kevin Focht/www.kevinfocht.com; BBC Worldwide Learning

LESSON 4
Congressional Committees

ReadingHelp Desk

Academic Vocabulary

- issue
- temporary

Content Vocabulary

- **standing committee**
- **subcommittee**
- **select committee**
- **joint committee**
- **conference committee**
- **seniority system**

TAKING NOTES:
Key Ideas and Details

CATEGORIZING Use the graphic organizer to categorize and explain the roles of different types of committees in Congress.

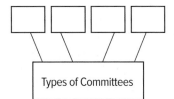

Types of Committees

ESSENTIAL QUESTION

What is the structure and organization of Congress?

Make a list of the five most pressing issues facing our nation. Look at the list of either House or Senate committees. Assign each issue to the committee most likely to work on it.

Choose one committee that interests you the most. What do you want to know about its work? Where could you go or with whom could you talk to find answers to your questions? In what types of laws and policy do you think it might specialize? Find out who is on that committee and how to contact at least one of those senators or representatives.

Purpose of Committees

GUIDING QUESTION *What purpose do congressional committees serve?*

At dawn on some mornings, college students and others line up outside Senate and House committee rooms. Sitting on the marble floors, they work on school assignments, read newspapers, or nap until just before the committees are due to meet. About then, lobbyists arrive who have hired them to reserve places in line. "Line sitting" has developed into a business to meet the demand for the limited number of seats in a congressional committee room. Lobbyists for various interests attend committee hearings because that is where the largest share of legislation will be shaped.

Although public attention usually focuses on the debates that take place in the Senate and House chambers, the real work of crafting bills takes place in the committee rooms. There, the members of Congress hear testimony from experts on different sides of an issue, propose amendments, and vote on whether to send the bill to the full House or Senate. While bills can still be amended on the floor, most of the final language will resemble what the committee members wrote.

Both the House and Senate depend upon committees to consider the thousands of bills that are proposed each session. Committees help ease the workload and are the key power centers in Congress.

The committee system serves several important purposes. First, it allows members of Congress to divide their work among many smaller groups. Lawmakers can become specialists, over their years of service, on the **issues** that their committees consider. This system is the only practical way for Congress to operate because no lawmaker can possibly know the details of each of the thousands of bills that are introduced in each term of Congress.

Second, from the huge number of bills that are introduced in Congress, committees select those few that are to receive further consideration. Committees are the places in which lawmakers listen to supporters and opponents of a bill. It is in committees where they work out compromises and decide which bills will or will not have a chance to become law. Most bills never get beyond the committee stage.

Third, by holding public hearings and investigations, committees help the public learn about key problems and issues facing the nation. Congressional committees have called the public's attention to such issues as organized crime, environmental protection, the safety of prescription drugs, hunger in America, airline safety, and many other concerns.

☑ **READING PROGRESS CHECK**

Explaining Why do the House and Senate organize themselves into committees?

issue an important topic or problem for debate or discussion

Kinds of Committees

GUIDING QUESTION *What are the different types of congressional committees?*

Congress has four basic kinds of committees: (1) standing committees, (2) select committees, (3) joint committees, and (4) conference committees. Congress always has the right, however, to change the method of committee organization and the number of committees.

Testifying Before the Human Rights Commission of Congress

At age 14, after seeing a news clip that showed video surveillance of a young girl being kidnapped and learning that one in four girls has been a victim of sexual assault, Dallas Jessup designed a service project. Dallas held a black belt in martial arts and recruited actors, videographers, police officers, and her martial arts instructors to make a film called *Just Yell Fire* to teach self-defense. She posted the film so anyone could see it for free on YouTube. She also created an organization to raise money to make the film available to people without Internet access.

When she was a freshman in college, Congress invited her to testify at a hearing on Human Rights. She told them: " . . . the average 14-year-old . . . could walk through a room filled with leopards and not notice because she is text messaging. . . . If you make self-defense, personal rights awareness, and danger avoidance a mandatory part of health class and PE. . . [you will] put these predators out of business."

Now a young woman, Dallas continues her work. Her organization has developed curricula and training programs that are used in high schools and colleges, crisis shelters, and community centers around the world.

"Substitute self defense for dodge ball in America's schools and you change the world."
— Dallas Jessup

CRITICAL THINKING

1. *Identifying Perspectives* Dallas was invited to share her concerns and solutions with Congress. Do young adults offer a unique perspective on this and other social problems? If so, which ones?

2. *Making Connections* What social problem bothers you the most? What film could you make or what steps could you take to inspire others to help solve that problem?

Standing Committees Early in its history, Congress set up permanent groups to oversee bills that dealt with certain kinds of issues. These are called **standing committees**—they stand, or continue, from one legislative session to the next. The House and Senate each create their own standing committees and control their areas of jurisdiction, occasionally adding or eliminating a standing committee when necessary.

The majority party has the power to write the rules in Congress. Republicans made changes in the structure and titles of several committees when they became the majority in 1995. The last major realignment of standing committees in the Senate took place in 1977.

The majority party controls the standing committees and selects chairpersons from among its members. The majority of the members of each standing committee are also members of the majority party. Party membership on committees is usually divided in direct proportion to each party's strength in each house. For example, if 60 percent of the members of the House are Republicans, then 60 percent of the members of each House standing committee will be Republicans. Thus, a ten-member committee would have six Republicans and four Democrats. However, the party in power in the House will often have a supermajority on the most important committees.

Subcommittees Nearly all standing committees have several **subcommittees**. Each subcommittee specializes in a subcategory of its standing committee's responsibility. Like committees, they usually continue from one

CHART

STANDING COMMITTEES of CONGRESS

The House and Senate have their own standing committees that continue from one legislative session to the next.

▶ CRITICAL THINKING

Comparing and Contrasting
Which committees are the same in the House and the Senate? Which committees are unique to each chamber? Why do you think the House and Senate have some different standing committees?

House Committees
Agriculture
Appropriations
Armed Services
Budget
Education and the Workforce
Energy and Commerce
Ethics
Financial Services
Foreign Affairs
Homeland Security
House Administration
Judiciary
Natural Resources
Oversight and Government Reform
Rules
Science, Space, and Technology
Small Business
Transportation and Infrastructure
Veterans' Affairs
Ways and Means

Senate Committees
Agriculture, Nutrition, and Forestry
Appropriations
Armed Services
Banking, Housing, and Urban Affairs
Budget
Commerce, Science, and Transportation
Energy and Natural Resources
Environment and Public Works
Finance
Foreign Relations
Health, Education, Labor, and Pensions
Homeland Security and Governmental Affairs
Judiciary
Rules and Administration
Small Business and Entrepreneurship
Veterans' Affairs

legislative session to the next, although the majority party can make changes. For example, House Republicans in the 113th Congress limited most committees to no more than 6 subcommittees. The exceptions were Appropriations (12 subcommittees), Armed Services (7 subcommittees), and Oversight and Government Reform (7 subcommittees).

Select Committees From time to time, each house has created **temporary** committees. Usually, these committees, called **select committees**, study one specific issue and report their findings to the Senate or the House. Select committees have been created to address matters of great public concern at a given time, such as energy independence and climate change, as well as the reorganization and reform of Congress. Select committees usually cannot submit bills to their parent chamber, however.

Select committees were set up to last for no more than one term of Congress. In practice, however, select committees may be renewed and continue to meet for several terms of Congress. For this reason, both the House and Senate have reclassified several select committees, such as the Permanent Select Intelligence Committee, as standing committees.

Joint Committees Made up of members from both the House and Senate, **joint committees** can be temporary or permanent. Both parties are represented on them, just like other committees. These committees usually act as a kind of study group that reports back to the House and Senate on a topic or bill. For example, the Joint Economic Committee might report on the economic impact of the war in Iraq or the income trends for average Americans.

In theory, joint committees coordinate the work of the two houses of Congress, but they do not have the authority to deal directly with bills or to propose laws to Congress. In practice, lawmakers usually limit joint committees to handling routine matters. Some joint committees study more volatile matters, such as atomic energy, defense, or tax reform.

Conference Committees No bill can be sent from Congress to the president until both houses have passed it in identical form. A **conference committee** is a temporary committee that is set up when the House and Senate have passed different versions of a bill. Its members, called *conferees*, usually come from the House and Senate standing committees that handled the bill. Democrats and Republicans are represented in the same way as on other committees.

The job of the conference committee is to resolve the differences between the two versions of the bill. Conference committees play a key legislative role because they work out a bill that both houses will accept and can then send to the president to be signed. To get such a bill, the conferees bargain over each section of the bill. A majority of the conferees from each house must accept the final compromise bill—called a *conference report*—before it can be sent to the floor of the House and Senate. When the conference committee's report reaches the floor of each house, it must be considered as a whole and cannot be amended. It must be accepted or rejected as it is.

✓ **READING PROGRESS CHECK**

Describing What is the role of a conference committee?

The Senate Armed Services Committee is a powerful committee charged with dealing with issues relating to the U.S. military.

▲ **CRITICAL THINKING**
Drawing Conclusions Do you think the Senate Armed Services Committee is a standing committee or a select committee? Explain your answer.

temporary lasting a short amount of time

select committee a temporary committee formed to study one specific issue and report its findings to the House or Senate

joint committee a committee that consists of members from both the House and Senate, formed to act as a study group that reports back to the House and Senate on a topic or bill

EXPLORING THE ESSENTIAL QUESTION

Analyzing Create a graphic organizer that shows the types of committees and how they differ from each other. Before you sketch it out, think about how you could show the relationships between them. Then compare your organizer to two of your classmates' organizers. How does yours compare? Which is most instructive? Why?

PARTICIPATING
IN Your Government

Becoming Informed About Your Elected Officials, Part 3

In this lesson and the next, you will continue developing the "My Representation in Congress" profile you began in Lessons 2 and 3 of this chapter.

- On which committees and subcommittees do your representative and senators serve?
- Do they hold leadership positions on those committees? If so, which positions on which committees?
- How might those committee assignments reflect the needs of your congressional district and state? In other words, how could your district or state benefit from these committees?
- How might those assignments be politically advantageous to those officials when they run for reelection?

CRITICAL THINKING

Using Technology Add this information to your profile using the same format you used in the previous lessons.

conference committee a temporary joint committee set up when the House and the Senate have passed different versions of the same bill

Choosing Committee Members

GUIDING QUESTION *How are senators and representatives assigned to committees?*

A freshman senator once consulted with a senior member about what committee assignments to seek. "What you want is a seat on the Appropriations Committee," the senior member advised, "where things happen."

Assignment to Committees The career of a member of Congress can be greatly influenced by the committees he or she is assigned. Assignment to the "right" committee can help a member's career in several ways. First, membership on some committees can increase a lawmaker's chances for reelection because it puts a congressperson in position to act on bills that are important to their constituents. A freshmen representative from a farm state, for example, might be eager to serve on the House Committee on Agriculture.

Second, membership on some committees can mean the lawmaker will be able to influence national policies. Committees that often help formulate national policies include those dealing with education, the budget, health, the judiciary, and foreign policy. Third, some committees allow a member to influence many other members because they affect matters that are important to everyone in Congress. The House Rules Committee is an obvious example of a committee with wide powers.

House members tend to serve on fewer committees than senators. Since committees generally meet at the same time, senators cannot physically attend all of their committees' hearings and will come and go during the hearings. Senators have sought to reform the committee process to reduce the number of their assignments. But the need to raise campaign funds encourages members to serve on as many committees as possible since each committee has its own constituency from whom funds can be raised.

In both the House and Senate, the parties have the job of assigning members to the standing committees. Newly elected members of Congress approach party leaders to express their interest in serving on a certain committee. Returning representatives who want to change committees can do the same. Each member can serve on only a limited number of standing committees and subcommittees.

The Role of the Committee Chair Along with the Speaker, president pro tem, majority and minority party leaders and whips, the chairpersons of standing committees are the most powerful people in Congress. They make the key decisions about the work of committees, such as when the committees will meet, which bills they will consider, and for how long. They decide when hearings will be held and which witnesses will be called to testify for or against a bill. Chairpersons also hire staff members for committees and control their budgets. Finally, chairs manage floor debates that take place on the bills that come from their committees.

Since the 1970s, the powers of committee chairpersons have been limited somewhat. The Legislative Reorganization Act of 1970 made a number of changes that made the committee system more democratic by reducing the power of committee chairs. A majority of committee members can call a meeting without the chair's approval. Committee members who disagree with the chair must be given time to present their views. Reasonable notice must be given for all committee hearings. Changes in 1995 carried this democratic trend further by prohibiting the chair from casting an absent vote, requiring committees to publish all members' votes, and setting six-year term limits for chairpersons.

The Seniority System The unwritten rule of seniority has guided the selection of chairpersons in the past. This meant that the majority party member with the longest uninterrupted service on a committee was appointed leader of that committee.

The **seniority system** has been criticized for giving a few members of Congress too much power. As a result, changes were made so that chairs are elected through a secret ballot. There have been notable exceptions, but for the most part, members tend to cast their ballots for the longest-serving members to chair committees.

☑ **READING PROGRESS CHECK**

Determining Importance Why is being assigned to the "right" committees so important to members of Congress?

EXPLORING THE ESSENTIAL QUESTION

Analyzing What are the advantages and disadvantages of using the seniority system? Should Congress give leadership positions to the longest-serving members? Is your answer the same for committee leadership and for general leadership such as the positions of Speaker or minority party whip? Explain your answers.

seniority system a system that gives the member of the majority party with the longest uninterrupted service on a particular committee the leadership of that committee

---

LESSON 4 REVIEW

Reviewing Vocabulary

1. ***Comparing and Contrasting*** How are the roles of a conference committee and a joint committee alike? How are they different?

Using Your Graphic Organizer

2. ***Analyzing*** Use your completed graphic organizer to analyze the roles of different types of committees in Congress.

Answering the Guiding Questions

3. ***Analyzing*** What purpose do congressional committees serve?

4. ***Classifying*** What are the different types of congressional committees?

5. ***Specifying*** How are senators and representatives assigned to committees?

Writing About Government

6. ***Narrative*** Imagine you are a member in the House of Representatives for your district. To what committees would you want to be assigned? Why? Think about such things as your constituents' interests, the power of the committee, and your own personal interests and expertise. Then write a memo to the House leadership requesting these committee assignments.

BBC Worldwide Learning; Office of U.S. Senator Chris Coons

LESSON 5
Staff and Support Agencies

ESSENTIAL QUESTION

What is the structure and organization of Congress?

Examine a recent daily schedule for Senator Max Baucus of Montana:

APRIL 24, 2014
Sen. Baucus

8:15 AM	Coffee with Senator Tester and Montana Constituents
9:00 AM	Meeting with Senior Staff
9:30 AM	Meeting with Finance Committee Staff
10:30 AM	Meeting with representatives from the Association of School Business Officials and Indian Impact Schools of Montana
11:45 AM	Lunch with Senator Jon Tester and Congressman Denny Rehberg
12:45 PM	Meeting with Finance Committee Staff
1:15 PM	Meeting with Senator Evan Bayh, Senator Bill Nelson, Senator Jeanne Shaheen, Senator Mark Udall, Senator Michael Bennet, Senator Joe Lieberman, Senator Blanche Lincoln, Senator Mark Warner
2:30 PM	Meeting with Staff
3:45 PM	Meeting with Congressman Charlie Rangel
4:30 PM	Remarks on Senate Floor
5:30 PM	Meeting with Senior Staff
6:00 PM	Votes on Senate Floor
7:30 PM	Meeting with Finance Committee Staff

In addition to the activities depicted here, a senator might also hold press conferences or media interviews, attend campaign events, and more. During a typical day, a senator might receive more than 300 calls, e-mails, and letters from constituents. When the public is focused on a divisive issue in the Senate, that number could double.

If you were a senator or representative, what kind of assistance would you want? What tasks could you delegate? If you had the opportunity to hire several staff members, what skills or experiences would you consider important?

Congressional Staff Role

GUIDING QUESTION *What role does congressional staff play in the work of Congress?*

Ted Kennedy of Massachusetts served more than 46 years in the Senate. When he first arrived in 1963, he had one staff member who worked on his two major committee assignments. Senators handled most of the committee business themselves, and mark-up sessions, when committee bills were being prepared to send to the Senate floor, would last for days as senators went over the bill line by line. By the end of his long career, Kennedy's staff had expanded considerably and mark-up sessions had become brief affairs because staff had already negotiated all of the revisions to the bill. Although Kennedy himself was famous for devoting attention to the bills he sponsored, he lamented that 95 percent of the "nitty-gritty work" of negotiating and drafting bills was now being done by staff.

The work of Congress is so extensive and **complex** that lawmakers have many resources to meet their obligations, including supporting agencies like the Library of Congress. The key resource of Congress, however, is trained staff that can help legislators draw up bills, stay informed on issues, and represent their constituents. Members rely heavily on staff in their committee work. Staff members research issues and topics on the committees' agenda and schedule witnesses for hearings.

complex involved, not simple

When Lowell Weicker of Connecticut was in the Senate, a woman wrote to him complaining about the way an airline had handled her dog. The dog, shipped as animal cargo, died during the flight. One of the senator's secretaries mentioned the letter to Weicker's press secretary, who thought that the incident had news value. He phoned the Federal Aviation Agency and other government offices and found many similar cases. After informing the senator, the secretary wrote a draft of a bill to authorize the Transportation Department to regulate air transport of animals. Senator Weicker later introduced the legislation on the floor of the Senate. The story became headlines in Weicker's home state, and he received many letters of appreciation.

This story illustrates that staffers do much of the important legislative work of Congress. Lawmakers rely on staffers to help them handle their ever-expanding workload, communicate with voters, run committee hearings and floor sessions, draft new bills, write committee reports, and attend committee meetings. Staffers also help lawmakers get reelected. Staffers help members of Congress get publicity, keep an eye on political developments back home, and write speeches and newsletters.

✔ **READING PROGRESS CHECK**

Describing What are the myriad tasks that congressional staff perform?

Congressional Staff Growth

GUIDING QUESTION *Why has congressional staff increased over time?*

Congress has not always relied on staff to accomplish its work. For almost 100 years, senators and representatives had no personal aides. Occasionally they might hire assistants out of personal funds, but Congress provided no paid staff. But inadequate staffing had become an urgent complaint among lawmakers by the time Congress considered the 1946 Legislative Reorganization Act. After passage of the act, the number of staff members increased dramatically. The House and Senate employed 2,000 personal staff

Congressional staffs help lawmakers see to the needs of constituents in their states or districts. Here members of Senator Coons's staff register attendees at a job fair.

▲ CRITICAL THINKING
Speculating How might congressional staffers influence the legislative process?

expert a person who has special knowledge in an area

personal staff the people who work directly for individual senators and representatives

committee staff the people who work for House and Senate committees

administrative assistant a member of a lawmaker's personal staff who runs the lawmaker's office, supervises the schedule, and gives advice

legislative assistant a member of a lawmaker's personal staff who makes certain that the lawmaker is well informed about proposed legislation

Office of U.S. Senator Chris Coons

members in 1947, but that number had grown to more than 10,600 by 2009. Committee staff increased from 400 to more than 2,200 in that same period.

Congressional staffs grew more as lawmaking became more complex in the 1970s. Lawmakers could not be **experts** on all the issues that came before their committees or that they needed to vote on in Congress. The demands that constituents placed on lawmakers also increased over the years. Members of Congress needed a large office staff simply to deal with the many letters, faxes, and e-mails from people in their states or congressional districts. Between 1977 and 2009, staff grew by over 11 percent in the House and 80 percent in the Senate.

Congressional staff are divided into two basic types: **personal staff** and **committee staff**. Personal staff members work directly for individual senators and representatives. Committee staff members work for the many House and Senate committees.

☑ READING PROGRESS CHECK

Explaining What are some of the reasons for the growth of congressional staff over time?

Personal Staff

GUIDING QUESTION *What roles are fulfilled by personal staff members?*

The size of each senator's personal staff varies because the allowances to pay for them are based on the population of the senator's state and distance from the capital. Senators each receive a yearly budget to operate their offices. Most of this goes for staff salaries. About one-third of personal staffers work in the legislators' home states; the rest work in Washington, D.C.

Administrative Assistants Lawmakers usually have several types of personal staff members in their offices. The **administrative assistant**, called an AA, serves as the chief of staff. The AA runs the lawmaker's office, supervises the lawmaker's schedule, and gives advice on political matters. A good AA also deals with influential people from the lawmaker's congressional district or state, which may influence the lawmaker's reelection.

Legislative Directors After the AA, the staff member with the most authority is the legislative director, or LD. The LD typically establishes the legislative agenda and briefs the lawmaker on all legislative matters. The LD supervises and serves as a resource person for the more junior legislative staff members. Some LDs also review constituent mail and the work of legislative clerks who handle the requests or e-mails to and from the lawmaker.

Legislative Assistants Supervised by the LD, **legislative assistants**, or LAs, make certain the lawmaker is well informed about the many bills with which she or he must deal. An LA does research, drafts bills, studies bills that are currently in Congress, and writes speeches and articles for the lawmaker.

Other important parts of the LA's job are to assist the lawmaker in committee meetings and to attend meetings when the lawmaker cannot be present. The LA who has followed the meeting and studied the bill in question may have prepared a short speech for the lawmaker or made up a list of questions for the lawmaker to ask witnesses.

LAs keep track of what is happening on the floor of Congress and of any bills that are in committee. While lawmakers may be in committee meetings or talking with voters, they may be interrupted by a buzzer signaling a vote.

Lawmakers rush to the floor of the Senate and House. They might not know what the vote is about, unless it involves a major bill and has been scheduled in advance. As they walk to the chamber floor, they look for their LAs.

In his book *In the Shadow of the Dome*, Mark Bisnow, a former legislative assistant, described the scene:

 PRIMARY SOURCE

> As the door of the "Senators Only" elevator opened, their bosses would pour out having come up from the tram in the basement that carried them from their offices. If they did not know what they were voting on (votes occurred frequently throughout the day, and it was hard to keep track), and if an aide had not already intercepted them en route, they would glance to the side to see if someone were waiting. A staffer might wave and run up for a huddled conference behind a pillar; or if the senator were in a hurry to make a fifteen minute deadline for voting, he might simply expect a quick thumbs-up or thumbs-down gesture."
>
> —Mark Bisnow, 1990

Press Secretaries Lawmakers' chances of reelection and of running for higher office depend heavily on the media coverage they receive. They want their constituents to know that they are serving their interests, and they also want to avoid negative publicity. As a result, almost every member of Congress employs a press secretary or communications director. Frequently former journalists themselves, press secretaries know how the media works and how to attract attention. Press secretaries draft press releases, schedule press conferences, and answer questions from the media.

With the development of social media, press secretaries also assist senators and representatives with their websites, videos, blogs, tweets, and other electronic communication. These help shape the lawmakers' public images, publicize their policy positions, and help citizens follow their legislative activities. Aided by their press secretaries, lawmakers can also conduct town meetings and press conferences by telecommunications, reaching extensive audiences in their home states and districts.

Caseworkers A large part of a congressional staff consists of **caseworkers**, a term borrowed from the social services field, because they handle the many requests for help from a member's constituents. In addition to their offices in Washington, D.C., lawmakers have offices in key cities in their home states and districts. Caseworkers usually staff these offices.

✓ **READING PROGRESS CHECK**

Identifying What do legislative assistants and caseworkers do? How are their roles different?

Committee Staff

GUIDING QUESTION *What is the role of committee and subcommittee staff?*

Every committee and subcommittee in Congress has a staff. The larger a committee, the more staff people it usually has. The committee chairperson and the senior minority party member of the committee hire and supervise staff members who support the committee as a whole, such as press

caseworker a member of a lawmaker's personal staff who handles requests for help from constituents

Becoming Informed About Your Elected Officials, Part 4

Continue to develop the profiles you began in previous lessons called "My Representation in Congress."

- What is the address and phone number for your representative's and senators' offices in Washington, D.C.? What are their e-mail addresses?
- What are the addresses and phone numbers for their offices close to your home? (Many representatives and senators have multiple "district" offices. Choose the one closest to you.)

CRITICAL THINKING

Using Technology Add this information to the profiles you began previously. Prepare a class presentation of the final, complete profile.

EXPLORING THE ESSENTIAL QUESTION

Analyzing Look at the web page of your Representative or one of your Senators. Does it show the names, titles, and contact information of staff? If so, what can you learn about the staff's expertise and responsibilities? If not, why do you think some or all of the staff might be "invisible"?

secretaries, clerks, and office managers. In addition, individual members of Congress who are assigned to that committee also designate their own staff to work specifically on those issues and will loan other staff when needed. Committee staffers draft bills, study issues, collect information, plan committee hearings, write memos, prepare committee reports, and negotiate with other staff on the pending legislation. They are largely responsible for the work involved in making laws but are much fewer in number than personal staff.

Some senior committee staff members are very experienced and are experts in the area their committee covers, whether it is tax policy, foreign affairs, or health care. Laurence Woodworth, who spent 32 years on staff of the Joint Committee on Internal Revenue Taxation, is a good example of such an expert. As the committee's staff director for 14 years, he was largely responsible for all changes in the tax laws. Later, Woodworth left the committee to become assistant secretary of the treasury.

✓ READING PROGRESS CHECK

Contrasting How do personal staff and committee staff differ?

Support Agencies

GUIDING QUESTION *What is the role of congressional support agencies?*

Several agencies in the legislative branch of government provide services that support the Congress. Some of their services are available to the other two branches of government and to American citizens, too. The four important support agencies created by Congress are discussed below.

The Library of Congress The Library of Congress is the largest library in the world, containing more than 100 million books, journals, music pieces, films, photographs, and maps. The Library is the administrator of the copyright law. As a result, it receives two free copies of most published works copyrighted in the United States. In 2010 it acquired a collection of all public tweets housed in a new Twitter Archive.

The Library of Congress has a Congressional Research Service (CRS) with hundreds of employees. Every year, the CRS answers thousands of requests for information from lawmakers, congressional staff, and committees. The CRS researches a broad range of topics for Congress.

Congress members use the CRS to research matters related to bills that are before Congress and to answer requests from voters.

Congressional Budget Office (CBO) Congress established the CBO in 1974 to **coordinate** the budget work of Congress, to study the budget proposals put forward by the president each year, and to project the costs of proposed programs. The CBO counterbalances the president's elaborate budget organization, the Office of Management and Budget (OMB). CBO staffers study economic trends, track how much congressional committees are spending, and report on the budget each April. They also calculate how budget decisions might affect the economy.

coordinate to arrange and organize

Government Accountability Office (GAO) Established in 1921, this agency is the nation's watchdog over how the funds Congress appropriates are spent. A comptroller general appointed to a 15-year term directs the GAO. The agency has a professional staff of about 3,000 people, who review the financial management of government programs that Congress creates, collect government debts, settle claims, and provide legal service.

Many GAO staff members answer requests for information about specific programs from lawmakers and congressional committees. They also prepare reports on various federal programs for lawmakers, testify before committees, develop questions for committee hearings, and provide legal opinions on bills that are under consideration. Almost one-third of the GAO's work now comes from congressional requests for information.

Government Printing Office (GPO) The GPO began in the era of printing presses. In the digital era, it now makes the Congressional Record, House and Senate bills, committee hearings, reports, and other publications available online as well as through web-based apps. The GPO promotes transparency in government by providing these publications over the Internet at no charge. It also shares its legislative information databases with the Library of Congress's THOMAS information services to track Congress's legislative activities, past and present.

☑ **READING PROGRESS CHECK**

Defining What do the acronyms CRS, CBO, GAO, and GPO stand for? How does each support the work of the Congress?

LESSON 5 REVIEW

Reviewing Vocabulary
1. *Specifying* What are the roles of an administrative assistant and a legislative assistant in the U.S. Congress?

Using Your Graphic Organizer
2. *Analyzing* Use your completed graphic organizer to analyze the functions of congressional personal staff and committee staff. How do their roles and functions differ?

Answering the Guiding Questions
3. *Identifying* What role does congressional staff play in the work of Congress?

4. *Explaining* Why has congressional staff increased over time?

5. *Stating* What roles are fulfilled by personal staff members?

6. *Specifying* What is the role of committee and subcommittee staff?

7. *Describing* What is the role of congressional support agencies?

Writing About Government
8. *Informative/Explanatory* How do you think the Internet has transformed the work of Congress and congressional support agencies? Do some research to find out more, and then write a brief essay explaining the transformation.

STUDY GUIDE

CONGRESSIONAL MEMBERSHIP
LESSON 1

Representative
- ✓ At least 25 years old
- ✓ U.S. citizen at least 7 years
- ✓ Legal resident of the state
- ✓ Two-year term
- ✓ Elected by a district
- ✓ Representation apportioned by population

Senator
- ✓ At least 30 years old
- ✓ U.S. citizen at least 9 years
- ✓ Legal resident of the state
- ✓ Six-year term
- ✓ Elected at-large
- ✓ Two from each state

HOUSE LEADERSHIP
LESSON 2

Speaker of the House

Majority Leader	Minority Leader
Majority Whip	Minority Whip
Deputy Whips	Deputy Whips

LAWMAKING IN THE SENATE
LESSON 3

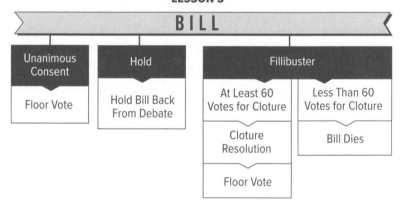

BILL

Unanimous Consent → Floor Vote

Hold → Hold Bill Back From Debate

Fillibuster
- At Least 60 Votes for Cloture → Cloture Resolution → Floor Vote
- Less Than 60 Votes for Cloture → Bill Dies

KINDS OF COMMITTEES
LESSON 4

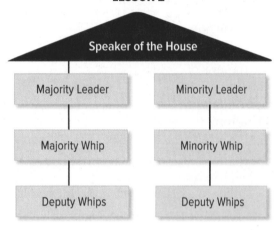

Types of Committees

Standing Committees
- permanent
- House and Senate create their own

Select Committees
- temporary
- study one specific issue
- House and Senate create their own

Joint Committees
- temporary or permanent
- acts as a study group on a topic or bill
- made up of members from both houses

Conference Committees
- temporary
- resolve differences between versions of a bill passed in each house
- made up of members from both houses

CONGRESSIONAL STAFF AND SUPPORT AGENCIES
LESSON 5

Personal Staff
- Administrative Assistant
- Legislative Directors
- Legislative Assistants
- Press Secretaries
- Caseworkers

Committee Staff
- Press Secretaries
- Clerks
- Office Managers
- Some Personal Staff

Support Agencies
- Library of Congress
- Congressional Budget Office
- Government Accountability Office
- Government Printing Office

Directions: On a separate sheet of paper, answer the questions below. Make sure you read carefully and answer all parts of the questions.

Lesson Review

Lesson 1

1 **Explaining** When the Senate and House of Representatives pass similar but not identical bills on the same subject, what must occur before the bill goes to the president?

2 **Contrasting** What key function can members of the House of Representatives perform that the delegate from the District of Columbia cannot?

Lesson 2

3 **Contrasting** The majority party chooses both the majority leader and the Speaker. What are some ways that these positions differ?

4 **Identifying** At what point in the legislative process does a bill go on the House calendar?

Lesson 3

5 **Comparing and Contrasting** How are the roles of the vice president in the Senate and the Speaker of the House similar? How are they different?

6 **Differentiating** Why do small states have equal power with large states in the Senate?

Lesson 4

7 **Applying** Suppose the Senate is composed of 70 Democrats and 30 Republicans. How many members of each party would you expect to be on a ten-member Senate standing committee?

8 **Identifying Trends** How has the role of committee chairpersons changed since the 1970s?

Lesson 5

9 **Identifying** Which personal staff members attend committee meetings when their lawmaker cannot?

10 **Applying** Suppose lawmakers wanted a report on how funds appropriated for the Head Start program were being spent. What legislative support agency should the lawmakers consult?

ANSWERING THE ESSENTIAL QUESTIONS

Review your answers to the introductory questions at the beginning of each lesson. Then answer the Essential Question based on what you learned in the chapter. Have your answers changed?

11 **Organizing** What is the structure and organization of Congress?

DBQ Interpreting Political Cartoons

Use the political cartoon to answer the following questions.

12 **Analyzing Visuals** What do the expressions on the faces of the audience suggest about the speaker?

13 **Identifying Cause and Effect** What will happen if rain comes from the cloud?

Critical Thinking

14 **Exploring Issues** During redistricting, why might the majority party in a state's legislature want to pack a district? Do you think this practice should be lawful or unlawful? Explain.

15 **Explaining** Why do major bills often require 60 votes to pass the Senate instead of a simple majority of 51?

Need Extra Help?

If You've Missed Question	1	2	3	4	5	6	7	8	9	10	11	12	13	14	15
Go to page	133	138	145	146	149	148	156	159	162	165	133	151	151	136	151

Directions: On a separate sheet of paper, answer the questions below. Make sure you read carefully and answer all parts of the questions.

16 *Analyzing Cause and Effect* Electronic communications, such as tweets, online petitions, and e-mail, have made it easier for constituents to voice their concerns to their members of Congress. How do you think easier communication has affected congressional staffing?

17 *Drawing Inferences* In both houses of Congress, Republicans sit on one side of the center aisle and Democrats sit on the other. In 2011, in a break with tradition, lawmakers crossed the aisle to sit with members of the opposing party to listen to the State of the Union Address. What message do you think this gesture was intended to convey?

DBQ Analyzing Primary Sources

Read the excerpt and answer the questions that follow.

PRIMARY SOURCE

"Every individual who participated in the redistricting process knew that incumbency protection was a critical factor in producing the bizarre lines. . . . Many of the oddest twists and turns of the Texas districts would never have been created if the Legislature had not been so intent on protecting party and incumbents."

—Justice John Paul Stevens, *Bush v. Vera*, June 13, 1996

18 *Identifying* What type of redistricting does this excerpt describe?

19 *Finding the Main Idea* According to the speaker, what was the goal of those doing the redistricting?

20 *Expressing* Based on this excerpt, what do the newly drawn lines of Texas districts look like?

Social Studies Skills

Use the table to answer the questions that follow.

Year	TOTAL GOVERNMENT EMPLOYMENT (numbers in thousands)			
	Executive Branch Civilians	Uniformed Military Personnel	Legislative and Judicial Branch Personnel	Total Federal Personnel
1962	2,485	2,840	30	5,354
1972	2,823	2,360	42	5,225
1982	2,770	2,147	55	4,972
1992	3,017	1,848	66	4,931
2002	2,630	1,456	66	4,152
2011	2,756	1,583	64	4,403

Source: U.S. Office of Personnel Management

21 *Using Tables* Describe the trends you see in each employment category in the table.

22 *Explaining Continuity and Change* Which category of employment most accounts for the trend in total federal personnel? Explain.

Research and Presentation

23 *Researching* Choose one congressional committee. Do research to learn about the work of this committee. Create a presentation summarizing the committee's key responsibilities. Include a discussion of a current issue before the committee.

24 *Analyzing* One of the Senate's most effective majority leaders was Lyndon B. Johnson. Consult several sources to find out why. Write a brief description of Johnson's leadership style that made him so effective. Cite your sources.

25 *Evaluating* Go to the website of Opportunities in Public Affairs, www.opajobs.com, and select "Capitol Hill jobs." Read the descriptions of job openings in the federal government. Which job most appeals to you? Explain why.

26 *Making Inferences* Based on information in the chapter about voters and political boundaries, what can you infer about the distribution of political power?

Need Extra Help?

If You've Missed Question	16	17	18	19	20	21	22	23	24	25	26
Go to page	161	143	135	136	136	162	162	155	150	161	136

Congressional Powers

ESSENTIAL QUESTIONS

- How have the powers of Congress changed over time?
- How does the separation of powers influence the work of Congress?

Joshua Roberts/Bloomberg/Getty Images

▲ Nancy Pelosi served as
Speaker of the House
from 2007 to 2011, when
she turned the gavel
over to the next Speaker,
John Boehner.

169

ANALYZING PRIMARY SOURCES

THE POWER TO INVESTIGATE: HURRICANE KATRINA

On August 29, 2005, Hurricane Katrina hit the Gulf Coast of the United States, causing extensive damage. More than 1,500 people in Louisiana were killed, and hundreds of thousands lost their homes. The immediate government response to the storm was criticized and a select committee of the U.S. House of Representatives was established to investigate. Examine these findings from the congressional investigation published in the 2006 report *A Failure of Initiative: Final Report of the Select Bipartisan Committee to Investigate the Preparation for and Response to Hurricane Katrina*.

PRIMARY SOURCE A

The Select Committee found that the predictions of the National Weather Service and National Hurricane Center were mostly accurate.

"Storm-track projections released to the public 56 hours before Katrina came ashore were off by only 15 miles.

The Hurricane Center's predicted strength for Katrina at landfall, two days before the storm hit, was off the mark by only 10 miles per hour. . . .

The day before Katrina hit, the NWS office in Slidell, Louisiana issued a warning saying, 'MOST OF THE AREA WILL BE UNINHABITABLE FOR WEEKS . . . PERHAPS LONGER . . . HUMAN SUFFERING INCREDIBLE BY MODERN STANDARDS.'"

PRIMARY SOURCE B

"Hundreds of miles of levees were constructed to defend metropolitan New Orleans against storm events. These levees were not designed to protect New Orleans from a category 4 or 5 monster hurricane, and all the key players knew this."

PRIMARY SOURCE C

"While the Mayor and the Governor recognized the dangers and expressed them to the public, they did not implement evacuation procedures for all of the citizens of New Orleans that reflected the seriousness of the threat. The results demonstrate the flaw of the evacuation—tens of thousands of citizens did not get out of harm's way. . . .

Despite the New Orleans [Evacuation] Plan's acknowledgement that there are people who cannot evacuate by themselves, the city did not make arrangements for their evacuation. . . .

In addition, New Orleans preparations for sheltering these people were woefully inadequate."

PRIMARY SOURCE D

"According to Scott Wells, Deputy FCO [FEMA official] for Louisiana . . . 'We did not have the people. We did not have the expertise. We did not have the operational training folks that we needed to do our mission.' . . .

According to the Director of the Mississippi Emergency Management Agency, Robert Latham, the federal logistics system failed in the days immediately following Hurricane Katrina, leaving state officials without adequate supplies of food, water, and ice for emergency shelters."

PRIMARY SOURCE E

▲ New Orleans residents whose homes became uninhabitable because of Katrina line up for emergency shelter at the Superdome.

PRIMARY SOURCE F

"The extent of destruction and damage to the communications infrastructure and services caused by Katrina exceeded that of any other natural disaster experienced by the Gulf Coast states. Simply put, Katrina's devastation overwhelmed government resources at all levels. The loss of power and the failure of various levels of government to adequately prepare for the ensuing and inevitable loss of communications hindered the response effort . . ."

PRIMARY SOURCE G

"Contributions by charitable organizations assisted many in need, but the American Red Cross and others faced challenges due to the size of the mission, inadequate logistics capacity, and a disorganized shelter process. . . . As much as any organization, public or private, the Red Cross played a substantial role in the immediate response to Hurricane Katrina. In what became a $2 billion, 220,000-person enterprise, the relief efforts undertaken by the Red Cross include the provision of financial assistance to 1.2 million families, encompassing more than 2.7 million hurricane survivors. . . . The Red Cross was dependent on FEMA and DOD to provide certain supplies—particularly food in the form of MREs [meals ready to eat]."

DBQ DOCUMENT-BASED QUESTIONS

1. **Identifying** Which agency or agencies did a good job before, during, and/or immediately after Hurricane Katrina hit New Orleans?

2. **Comprehending** List three problems that the investigative committee identified in the preparation for and initial response to Hurricane Katrina. How could these problems be fixed?

3. **Planning** Suggest three ways that Congress or the executive branch could act to address the problems uncovered in this investigation.

WHAT WILL YOU DO?

How would you find out if recommendations from an investigation like this were implemented? How would you work to influence your representatives in Congress to follow up on the findings from an important investigation?

EXPLORE the interactive version of the analyzing primary sources feature on Networks.

Interact with these digital assets and others in lesson 1

✓ **INTERACTIVE IMAGE**
The Debt Clock

✓ **INTERACTIVE INFOGRAPHIC**
The Powers of Congress

✓ **SLIDE SHOW**
Military Actions Without a Declaration of War

✓ **VIDEO**
Impeachment

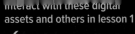
netw⊙rks
TRY IT YOURSELF ONLINE

LESSON 1
Constitutional Powers

Reading Help Desk

Academic Vocabulary

- major
- bond

Content Vocabulary

- expressed powers
- necessary and proper clause
- implied powers
- revenue bill
- appropriations bill
- authorization bill
- interstate commerce
- copyright
- patent
- impeachment

TAKING NOTES:
Key Ideas and Details

CLASSIFYING Classify the powers of Congress as either legislative or nonlegislative.

Legislative	Nonlegislative

ESSENTIAL QUESTION

How have the powers of Congress changed over time?

Article I, Section 8, of the Constitution lists (or enumerates) the powers of Congress. The last clause is especially interesting, as it says that Congress has the power to enact any laws "necessary and proper" to carry out the 17 enumerated powers listed in that same section. Decide whether you think the laws listed below are necessary and proper to carry out congressional powers. (Use your copy of the Constitution to identify the powers of Congress listed in Article I, Section 8.)

- A law making certain drugs illegal nationwide

- A law requiring states to lower their speed limits or lose federal highway funds

- A law taking farm properties owned by banks and turning them over to farmers

- A law establishing a new government agency to fight terrorism

- A law requiring people to purchase health insurance if they do not have coverage

- A law banning picketing at the funerals of servicemen and -women killed in action

- A law giving the president the power to veto individual items in spending bills

Constitutional Provisions

GUIDING QUESTION *What powers of Congress are listed in the Constitution?*

The Constitution lays down many important principles, but it is not an exact blueprint. In fact, the Constitution is unclear on many questions about how the president and Congress share power. Nearly half of its text, however, concerns the legislative branch in Article I, suggesting that the Framers wanted Congress, the branch that directly represents the people, to play a central role in American government.

THE POWERS OF CONGRESS

EXPRESSED VS. IMPLIED

In Article 1, Section 8, of the Constitution, the enumerated powers of Congress are listed. Each clause explains a power granted to Congress, including the ability to carry out powers that have become known as implied powers.

 Money & Commerce Powers

 Military & Foreign Policy Powers

 Social & Domestic Powers

E X P R E S S E D   P O W E R S

Lay and collect taxes to provide for the defense and general welfare of the United States
(Clause 1)

Establish bankruptcy laws
(Clause 4)

Borrow money
(Clause 2)

Coin, print, and regulate money
(Clause 5)

Regulate foreign and interstate commerce
(Clause 3)

Punish counterfeiters of American currency
(Clause 6)

Declare war
(Clause 11)

Raise, support, and regulate an army and navy
(Clause 12, 13, 14)

Provide, regulate and call into service a militia, known as the National Guard
(Clause 15 & 16)

Punish acts committed on international waters and against the laws of nations
(Clause 10)

Establish laws of naturalization
(Clause 4)

Establish post offices and post roads
(Clause 7)

Grant copyrights and patents
(Clause 8)

Create lower federal courts
(Clause 9)

Govern Washington, D.C., and federal property in the States
(Clause 17)

Clause 18 - "The Elastic Clause"

 To make all Laws which shall be necessary and proper for carrying into Execution the foregoing Powers, and all other Powers vested by this Constitution in the Government of the United States, or in any Department or Officer thereof.

I M P L I E D   P O W E R S

The power to support public schools, welfare programs, public housing, etc.

The power to prohibit discrimination in restaurants, hotels, and other public accommodations.

The power to draft people into the armed services.

The power to raise, support, and regulate an air force.

The power to limit the number of immigrants to the United States.

The power to collect and deliver mail.

The Constitution describes the legislative powers of Congress in Article I, Section 8, Clauses 1–18. These **expressed powers** of Congress are sometimes called the *enumerated powers*. The last clause (18) of Section 8 gives Congress power to do whatever is "necessary and proper" to carry out its enumerated powers. This **necessary and proper clause** implies that Congress has powers beyond those in the first 17 clauses. Because these **implied powers** have allowed Congress to expand its role to meet the nation's needs, the "necessary and proper clause" has often been called the *elastic clause*.

▲ **CRITICAL THINKING**

Applying Do you agree that the implied powers in the chart above are necessary to achieve the goals of the expressed powers? Pick one of the expressed powers from the chart and think of another power implied by that expressed power. Why is this example necessary to achieving the goal of the expressed power?

Because of the far-reaching implications of the expanding power of Congress, the Supreme Court has often needed to resolve conflicts over what is "necessary and proper" legislation. The first **major** conflict was between supporters of "strict construction," or interpretation, of the Constitution and those who believed in a "loose construction."

McCulloch* v. *Maryland When the Second Bank of the United States was created in 1816, the strict constructionists said that Congress had no right to charter the Bank. They backed the state of Maryland when it taxed the notes of the Bank. A federal bank teller named James McCulloch then issued notes without paying the state tax, and Maryland sued. When the state won in its own courts, the U.S. government appealed to the Supreme Court. In the landmark case of *McCulloch* v. *Maryland*, Chief Justice John Marshall, writing for the majority, supported the position of the loose constructionists by giving a very broad interpretation to the "necessary and proper" clause. This decision helped greatly expand the powers of Congress.

Limits on Congress The powers of Congress, like those of the other government branches, have limits. One very important constitutional limit is the Bill of Rights, but Article I, Section 9, of the Constitution also denies certain powers to Congress. One power specifically denied to Congress relates to a writ of *habeas corpus*—a court order to release a person accused of a crime to court to determine whether he or she has been legally detained. Congress may not suspend the writ of *habeas corpus* except in cases of rebellion or invasion when public safety requires it. In addition, Congress may not pass bills of attainder—laws that establish guilt and punish people without a trial. Congress is also prohibited from passing *ex post facto* laws; that is, they cannot criminalize an act that was legal when it was committed. Article I, Section 9, also denies Congress a number of other powers, including the power to tax exports.

☑ **READING PROGRESS CHECK**

Contrasting How do the expressed powers and implied powers of Congress differ?

> **EXPLORING THE ESSENTIAL QUESTION**
>
> **Making Generalizations** Make a list of the constitutional limits on the power of Congress. Can you find a common thread among these limits that relates to liberties? Based on this common thread, state a generalization about why the Framers created a limited government.

Legislative Powers

GUIDING QUESTION *What are the legislative powers of Congress?*

Congress has both legislative and nonlegislative powers. Nonlegislative powers include the power to confirm or deny presidential appointments, which is a power of the Senate. Congress has expanded the domain of its legislative powers—the power to pass laws—as the nation has grown. The most significant expansion of legislative power is in its control over the economy—taxing, spending, and regulating interstate commerce.

The Taxing and Spending Power Perhaps the most important power that Congress has is the power to levy taxes and control spending to provide for the general welfare found in Article I, Section 8, of the Constitution.

expressed powers powers directly stated in the Constitution

necessary and proper clause Article I, Section 8, of the Constitution, which gives Congress the power to make all laws that are necessary and proper for carrying out its duties

implied powers powers the government requires to carry out its expressed constitutional powers

major prominent or significant in size, amount, or degree

Sometimes this is called "the power of the purse." This power allows Congress to influence policy because no government agency can spend money without its authorization. This broad authority to provide for the general welfare allows Congress to impose many taxes. For example, taxes on narcotics are meant to protect public health.

Article I, Section 7, says, "All Bills for raising Revenue shall originate in the House of Representatives." **Revenue bills**, or proposed laws for raising money, start in the House and then go to the Senate. This provision was adopted at the Constitutional Convention because the more populous states, such as Virginia and Pennsylvania, insisted on having a greater voice in tax policy than the smaller states. Because representation in the House was to be based on population, the Founders agreed that any revenue bills introduced in Congress would originate there.

The legislative process for **appropriations bills**—meaning laws proposed to authorizing spending money—is not spelled out in the Constitution. Instead, the process has developed through usage. Article I, Section 9, merely requires that "No Money shall be drawn from the Treasury, but in Consequence of Appropriations made by Law." Congress uses a two-step process for approving expenditures. First, it passes an **authorization bill** that establishes a program and says how much can be spent on the program. Second, it passes an appropriations bill actually approving the funds for the program. Spending requests generally come from the executive branch. Today, most are presented to Congress in the president's annual budget proposal. Often, however, Congress does not follow exactly the president's requests in deciding what funds to appropriate.

revenue bill a proposed law for raising money

appropriations bill a proposed law to authorize spending money

authorization bill a bill that establishes a program and says how much can be spent on the program

GOVERNMENT *in your* COMMUNITY

Federal Funding for State and Local Government

The federal government is a significant source of funding for state and local government programs. The National Priorities Project is a national nonprofit, nonpartisan research organization that works to make federal budget information transparent and accessible. Visit the group's website at nationalpriorities.org. Search for federal spending in your state. Use the information you find to answer these questions:

- What federal programs provide grant money to the states? How much federal money does your state receive for some of these programs?

- Look at your state's budget for its programs that can also receive federal funding. Can you find out what percentage of the total program budget comes from federal grant money?

- What else can you learn from this information?

©Dennis MacDonald/Alamy

The federal government is a source of funding for many state and local government projects, such as road construction.

▲ CRITICAL THINKING

Determining Importance Decide how to convey what you learned from this research. In your final product, answer this question: How important do you think Congress's "power of the purse" is?

The government adds to the national debt when it borrows by issuing Treasury bills to meet operating expenses.

▲ **CRITICAL THINKING**

Theorizing Do you think the size of the national debt is meaningful to average citizens? Explain your response.

bond a government security

interstate commerce trade among the states

Over the years, Congress has used its taxing and spending authority to expand its regulatory powers. For example, when Congress authorizes money for state or local governments, it frequently requires them to follow specific federal regulations. Congress can also levy taxes in a way that encourages or discourages manufacturers to create a product or consumers to buy a product. For instance, heavy taxes on gasoline are meant to discourage its use, while tax breaks to farmers who sell their corn to producers of ethanol, an alternative fuel, are meant to encourage the development of ethanol.

Congress also uses its taxing and spending powers to regulate the economy. Cutting individual income taxes may encourage more personal spending, thus stimulating economic growth. Conversely, when Congress is worried about the national debt, it may try to reduce federal spending.

Other Money Powers Under Article I, Congress has other money powers, a significant one of which is to borrow to pay for government costs. Congress does this in various ways. The most common method is by authorizing the sale of government securities—**bonds** or notes. When people buy savings bonds, Treasury bills, or Treasury notes, they are lending the government money. In return, the government promises to repay buyers with interest at the end of a specified period of time—3 months to 30 years, depending on the type of security. Foreign governments are among those that invest in U.S. bonds.

Whenever it borrows to meet operating expenses, the government adds to the national debt—the total amount the government owes at any given time. This debt, almost $1 trillion in 1980, was more than $16 trillion in 2013. The Constitution does not restrict government borrowing, but Congress tries to set limits. When the debt exceeds the set amount, Congress must vote to raise the debt ceiling so that the government can continue to borrow to pay its bills.

As part of Congress's money powers, the Constitution gives the legislative branch the power to coin money and to regulate its value. All currency issued by the federal government is legal tender, meaning that it must be accepted as payment.

The Commerce Power Article I, Section 8, Clause 3, the so-called "commerce clause" of the Constitution, authorizes Congress to regulate foreign commerce and **interstate commerce**, or commerce among the states. In this clause, the Founders provided what has become one of the most sweeping powers of government. Over time, the Supreme Court has decided many cases about the meaning of this clause. At different times, the Court has interpreted this clause both narrowly and broadly. Since the Great Depression, this clause has given Congress great power to regulate many things. The Supreme Court has ruled that the meaning of *commerce*—whether international or interstate—far exceeds the mere buying and selling of goods and services.

The first decision on the breadth of the commerce powers did not come until 1824 when the Court decided the landmark case *Gibbons* v. *Ogden*. The case came about because American inventor Robert Fulton and his business partner got a license from the state of New York to be the exclusive operator of a steamboat in New York waters. In 1807 the steamboat began carrying passengers regularly between New York City and Albany, New York. The company then granted Aaron Ogden a permit for steamboat operation across the Hudson River between New York state and New Jersey.

Controversy began in the following years as others challenged this monopoly. One entrepreneur, Thomas Gibbons, started a competing line that operated boats between New York and New Jersey. Gibbons had no New York permit, but he had received a license from the federal government. An angry Ogden then sued Gibbons. New York upheld Ogden's position.

Gibbons, who believed his federal license gave him a solid claim, appealed the case. He argued that Congress, not New York, had the power to regulate commerce between the states. New York, meanwhile, argued that federal commerce powers covered only the regulation of products, not navigation. In a unanimous opinion, the Supreme Court disagreed:

PRIMARY SOURCE

The subject to be regulated is commerce; . . . it becomes necessary to settle the meaning of the word. The counsel for the appellee [Ogden] would limit it to traffic, to buying and selling, or the interchange of commodities, and do not admit that it comprehends navigation . . . . Commerce, undoubtedly, is traffic, but it is something more: it is intercourse . . . . The mind can scarcely conceive a system for regulating commerce between nations, which shall exclude all laws concerning navigation . . . ."

—John Marshall, 1824

Over the years, the Supreme Court has further expanded its definition of commerce. Many activities have been considered interstate commerce and made subject to federal control, including broadcasting, banking and finance, and air and water pollution.

This broad interpretation of commerce has allowed Congress to set policy in many areas. For example, Congress has required businesses engaged in interstate commerce to pay their employees a minimum wage. Because almost all businesses deal in some way with another state, Congress has been able to regulate working conditions across the nation.

One of the most significant applications of the commerce clause has been in the area of civil rights. In the Civil Rights Act of 1964, Congress used its powers under the commerce clause to prohibit discrimination in restaurants, hotels, and motels.

Businesses in many southern states resisted the goals of this legislation. A Georgia motel owner refused to serve African Americans as required by the new law. He claimed that his motel was a local business and therefore not part of interstate commerce. The Supreme Court disagreed with the motel owner. In *Heart of Atlanta Motel* v. *United States* (1964), the Court noted that places of accommodation served travelers who crossed state boundaries. If African Americans were unable to find decent places to stay or to eat, how would interstate commerce be able to take place?

EXPLORING THE ESSENTIAL QUESTION

Analyzing Review each proposed law. Determine whether Congress has the power to make that law under the commerce clause.

- a law that requires all states to use uniform warning signs and signals for trains; Congress hopes this law will prevent freight train crashes.

- a law that bans factories that make products that are sold in other states from employing children under the age of 18; Congress hopes this law will protect children from working too much.

- a law that prohibits all U.S. farmers who sell vegetables from growing more than 500 pounds of tomatoes each, even for their own consumption; Congress hopes that this law will boost falling tomato prices by reducing the number of tomatoes on the market.

We, therefore, conclude that the action of Congress in the adoption of the Act as applied here to a motel which concededly serves interstate travelers is within the power granted it by the Commerce Clause of the Constitution, as interpreted by this Court for 140 years."

— Justice Tom C. Clark, 1964

The Court clearly supported Congress's use of the commerce powers when the economic issue was not the motive in the case. Since then, the commerce power has been used to support federal laws aimed at racketeering and arson, too. However, the commerce clause power has limits.

In a more recent case, President Obama's new health care program—the Affordable Care Act—was challenged in court in 2012. The challengers believed the law's requirement that certain individuals purchase health care exceeded Congress's commerce clause power. The law was upheld in a 5-to-4 vote, but the deciding vote was based on the taxation power, not the commerce clause.

Foreign Policy Powers Congress shares power with the president to make foreign and national defense policy. Congress has the power to approve treaties, to declare war, to create and maintain an army and navy, to make rules governing land and naval forces, and to regulate foreign commerce.

Historically, Congress generally has let the president take the lead in these areas. As commander in chief, the president often sends troops on missions around the world without a declaration of war. Congress has declared war only five times, but the president has used troops in more than 200 international conflicts. Two major conflicts in the twentieth century, the Korean War and the Vietnam War, were fought without a declaration of war.

Because the Vietnam War was costly and lost public support over time, Congress looked closely at how the United States was drawn into the Southeast Asian conflict. Specifically, it focused on the actions of President Lyndon Johnson that led to American troops being sent to Vietnam. Congress concluded that the Constitution did not intend the president to have this kind of power.

In 1973, over President Richard Nixon's veto, Congress passed the War Powers Act. Under this law, the president must notify Congress within 48 hours of any commitment of troops abroad and must withdraw them in 60 to 90 days unless Congress explicitly approves the action. Since the act was passed, both Republican and Democratic presidents have protested its constitutionality.

Even with the passage of the War Powers Act, presidents have continued to send American troops abroad without a declaration of war by Congress. Troops were sent to Cambodia in 1975; to Iran, Lebanon, Grenada, Libya, the Persian Gulf, and Panama in the 1980s; to the Balkans and Somalia in the 1990s; and to Afghanistan and Iraq in the 2000s. Many of these incidents were not sustained actions, but in most cases the president adhered to the provisions of the War Powers Act.

There are countless other examples where the president did not send troops but still intervened militarily. For example, the United States gave limited military support to Libyan rebels in 2011, sending arms and providing air strikes. These were military actions, but did they constitute acts of "war"? President Obama argued that the U.S. military operations did not constitute

Military Actions Without a Declaration of War

The Constitution gives Congress the sole power to declare war, a provision that provides a check on the president's role as commander in chief. Sometimes, however, the United States has taken military action without a declaration of war. As you read, decide in which, if any, of the cases Congress should have asserted its power to declare war before any military action was taken.

In 1950 Communist North Korea invaded South Korea. The United Nations Security Council, of which the United States was a member, passed a resolution authorizing military action in Korea. The United States provided nearly 90 percent of the UN force.

In 1983 a military coup overthrew the government of the Caribbean island nation of Grenada. Officials were worried about threats to U.S. security due to Soviet and Cuban backing of the new regime and the safety of American medical students in Grenada. U.S. troops invaded Grenada without a congressional declaration of war.

In 1990 Iraq invaded Kuwait. The United States was alarmed and formed a coalition with NATO and several Middle Eastern countries. In January 1991, after three days of debate, Congress approved a joint resolution authorizing the U.S. military to attack Iraq. Five days later, the coalition invaded to push the Iraqis out of Kuwait.

In 2011 Libyan rebels were attempting to overthrow the government of longtime dictator Muammar al-Gaddafi. A UN resolution authorized member nations to establish a no-fly zone over Libya and to take action to prevent the government from attacking civilians. NATO, of which the United States is a member, took charge of the no-fly zone.

▲ CRITICAL THINKING

Analyzing In which, if any, of the cases do you think Congress should have asserted its power to declare war before any military action was taken? Be sure to justify each decision. If Congress should have declared war, what should it have considered in making that decision?

"hostilities" and that he was not required to seek authorization from Congress. There remains reasoned debate over when the War Powers Act should apply.

Providing for the Nation's Growth The Constitution gives Congress power over naturalization, the process by which immigrants become citizens. Under Article IV, Section 3, Congress also has the power to admit new states and govern any territories. Today, American territories such as Puerto Rico, Guam, the U.S. Virgin Islands, Northern Mariana Islands, American Samoa, and other islands such as Wake Island fall under this provision. Finally, Article I and Article IV give Congress the power to pass laws to govern federal property. When the Constitution was written, the Founders were thinking of military bases and government buildings, but today federal property also includes national parks, historic sites, and public lands.

Other Legislative Powers Article I, Section 8, Clause 8, gives Congress the power to grant copyrights and patents. A **copyright** is the exclusive right to publish and sell a literary, musical, or artistic work for a specified period of time. Under the present law, this period is the lifetime of the creator plus 70 years. A **patent** is the exclusive right of an inventor to manufacture, use, and sell his or her invention for a specific period, which, in most cases, is 20 years. These constitutional protections were established to protect intellectual property and foster creativity, entrepreneurship, and economic competition.

copyright the exclusive right to publish and sell a literary, musical, or artistic work for a specified period of time

patent the exclusive right of an inventor to manufacture, use, and sell his or her invention for a specific period, currently 20 years

In 1998 President Bill Clinton was impeached by a narrow margin in the House of Representatives.

▲ CRITICAL THINKING

Expressing Why did the Senate fail to convict Clinton of the charges brought against him?

impeachment the formal accusation of misconduct in office

Article I, Section 8, grants Congress the power to establish a post office and federal courts. Congress has also used its postal power to combat criminal activity; using the mail for any illegal act is a federal crime.

☑ READING PROGRESS CHECK

Summarizing What are the economic powers of Congress?

Nonlegislative Powers

GUIDING QUESTION *What are the nonlegislative powers of Congress?*

In carrying out their legislative powers, the two houses of Congress perform the same basic tasks—considering, amending, and voting on bills. Most nonlegislative functions require cooperation between the houses, but each house usually plays a distinct role in exercising these powers.

The Constitution requires Congress to hold a joint session to count the Electoral College votes for a new president. If no candidate has a majority, the House chooses the president from the three candidates with the most electoral votes. Each state has one vote in the House. For the vice presidency, a tie would be broken by a majority vote in the Senate from the top two vote-getters. It is, therefore, possible that the vice president could be from a different party than the president.

Only twice in American history has no presidential candidate captured a majority of electoral votes, requiring the election to be settled by these rules. In 1800 the House elected Thomas Jefferson over Aaron Burr, and in 1824 it chose John Quincy Adams over Andrew Jackson.

The Removal Power The Constitution gives Congress the power to remove any federal official from office. The House is the chamber with power over **impeachment**—the formal accusation of misconduct in office. If a majority of the House votes to impeach an official, the Senate then conducts a trial. The chief justice of the United States presides over the trial. A two-thirds vote of the senators present is required to convict and thus remove someone from office.

Since 1789, several federal judges, a Supreme Court justice, a cabinet secretary, and two presidents have been impeached. Several officials have been convicted by the Senate, but no presidents have been convicted. President Andrew Johnson came the closest, escaping conviction by only one vote.

In 1974 two reporters, Bob Woodward and Carl Bernstein, published a series of stories linking President Richard Nixon's administration to burglars who broke into Democratic Party offices in the Watergate Hotel in Washington, D.C. A Senate committee investigating the incident discovered other illegal activities, as well as evidence that the president had helped to cover up the crimes. When it was clear he would be impeached, Nixon resigned—the first president in American history to do so.

In 1998 President Bill Clinton was impeached by a narrow margin in the House. Clinton was charged with perjury and obstruction of justice because he lied under oath about his relationship with a White House intern. The Senate votes on the charges were well short of the two-thirds majority needed to remove the president from office. For many senators, the charges simply did not meet the criteria of "Treason, Bribery, or other high Crimes and Misdemeanors."

The Confirmation Power The Senate must approve presidential appointments to office. Often, Senate action is only a formality, but the Senate looks more closely at several hundred nominations to cabinet positions for regulatory agencies and major diplomatic and military posts. If appointed, these nominees typically serve for just the term of the president. Nominations for federal judges, including Supreme Court nominees, receive the most scrutiny, perhaps because those positions are lifetime appointments. The Senate has rejected about 20 percent of Supreme Court nominations.

The Ratification Power The Senate must also ratify formal treaties with other nations. To ratify a treaty, two-thirds of the senators present must vote for it. Senate action on treaties has usually not been a major factor in American foreign policy. In recent years, presidents have often bypassed the need for a treaty. Instead, they have negotiated executive agreements that do not require Senate approval.

The Amendment Power Congress and state legislatures share the power to propose amendments to the Constitution. Amendments can be proposed by a two-thirds vote of both houses of Congress, or by a convention called by the legislatures of two-thirds of the states.

The second method has never been used, but it raises this constitutional question: Can a constitutional convention called to propose a certain amendment then propose other amendments in addition to the one in the states' original petition? Some people fear that once delegates meet, they might propose revisions on long-established provisions. Congress has considered, but not acted on, measures to prevent this from happening. Finally, Congress also has the power to determine whether state conventions or state legislatures will ratify a proposed amendment.

To date, all of the constitutional amendments added to the Constitution have started in Congress. The states have approved 27 proposed amendments and have failed to ratify only six. Congress has required all amendments—except the Twenty-first Amendment (1933), which repealed the Eighteenth Amendment on prohibition—to be ratified by state legislatures. Advocates of the Twenty-first Amendment believed they would have better support in conventions than in state legislatures because many of these bodies were dominated by "Drys"—representatives who favored Prohibition.

☑ **READING PROGRESS CHECK**

Classifying What nonlegislative powers does the Senate have?

LESSON 1 REVIEW

Reviewing Vocabulary

1. *Contrasting* What is the difference between an authorization bill and an appropriations bill?

Using Your Graphic Organizer

2. *Analyzing* Choose one of Congress's legislative and nonlegislative powers and provide an example of how Congress has exercised those powers.

Answering the Guiding Questions

3. *Identifying* What powers of Congress are listed in the Constitution?

4. *Specifying* What are the legislative powers of Congress?

5. *Specifying* What are the nonlegislative powers of Congress?

Writing About Government

6. *Informative/Explanatory* The U.S. Congress has both legislative and nonlegislative functions. Write a brief essay in which you analyze the relative importance of each of the nonlegislative functions discussed in the text.

United States V Lopez (1995)

FACTS OF THE CASE In 1990 Congress passed the Gun Free School Zones Act. This law prohibited people from knowingly carrying a gun in a school zone. A person who was convicted of possessing a gun in a school asked the court to reverse his conviction, arguing that Congress never had the authority to pass the Gun Free School Zones Act.

Congress said its authority to pass the law came from the commerce clause. The government argued that regulating the possession of guns near schools is related to interstate commerce because the costs associated with violent crime are substantial and affect many people across the country. The government also argued that the presence of guns near schools negatively affects students' ability to learn, which will impact their future success, and thus the economy of the nation. The opponents of the law argued that the law was not at all related to interstate commerce. Since Congress did not have that power, it was up to states to decide whether people could carry guns near schools.

ISSUE

Did Congress have the power to pass the Gun Free School Zones Act?

ARGUMENTS

Arguments in a Supreme Court case are often based on precedents—previous cases the Court has decided about similar issues. Both sides argue that a particular precedent does or does not apply to the present case. The Supreme Court of the United States has ruled in several earlier cases about the commerce clause.

WICKARD V. FILBURN (1942) In an effort to increase wheat prices during the Great Depression, Congress passed a law limiting the amount of wheat that some farmers could grow. One farmer argued that Congress could not use the commerce clause to stop him from growing wheat for personal consumption because that wheat would not be sold and therefore would not be part of interstate commerce. The Supreme Court said that Congress could pass this law. Congress could regulate intrastate activity that, if taken all together, would substantially affect interstate commerce. If many farmers decided to grow their own wheat and not buy it on the market, their actions would substantially affect interstate commerce.

HEART OF ATLANTA MOTEL V. U.S. (1964) The Civil Rights Act of 1964 made racial discrimination in public places, including hotels, illegal. An Atlanta hotel refused to serve black customers. The hotel argued that Congress did not have the power to pass the law under the commerce clause. The Supreme Court ruled against the hotel, concluding that "commerce" includes travel from state to state and that racial discrimination in hotels can affect travel from state to state. Congress can therefore prohibit discrimination in hotels because, in the aggregate, it affects interstate commerce.

EXPLORING THE ESSENTIAL QUESTION

Analyzing For each precedent listed, answer these questions:
1. How is this precedent similar to the current case?
2. How is this precedent different from the current case?
3. In your opinion, does this precedent apply to the current case?

After analyzing the possible precedents, determine how the case before you should be decided and give your reasons.

YOU BE the JUDGE

Interact with these digital assets and others in lesson 2

✓ **INTERACTIVE IMAGE**
Titanic Investigation

✓ **PARTICIPATING IN YOUR GOVERNMENT**
Differentiating Between Fact and Opinion

✓ **SELF-CHECK QUIZ**

✓ **VIDEO**
Goldman Sachs Investigation

netw⊙rks
TRY IT YOURSELF ONLINE

r) Serial and Government Publications Division, Library of Congress; Arbogast/Getty Images; BBC Worldwide Learning

LESSON 2
Investigations and Oversight

ReadingHelp Desk

Academic Vocabulary

- schedule
- scheme

Content Vocabulary

- subpoena
- perjury
- contempt
- immunity
- legislative oversight
- legislative veto

TAKING NOTES:

Integration of Knowledge and Ideas

IDENTIFYING CAUSE AND EFFECT Use the graphic organizer to list the possible outcomes of congressional investigations.

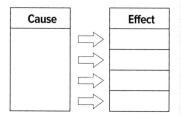

Cause		Effect
	⇒	
	⇒	
	⇒	
	⇒	

ESSENTIAL QUESTION

How does the separation of powers influence the work of Congress?

Congress has the power to investigate whether government officials have adequately, fairly, and legally carried out their responsibilities. Congress cannot investigate every allegation of misconduct or government inefficiency. Other institutions, including the media, "watchdog" groups, and executive branch inspectors general, can also perform these functions. Imagine yourself as a member of Congress. Which of the following scenarios warrant a congressional investigation? Why? Which deserves the highest priority?

- Constituents in your home district are outraged by allegations that the National Security Agency (NSA) has acquired data on cell phone usage and Internet searches by millions of Americans without search warrants. Congress and special national security courts may have given secret permission for the NSA to do so.

- A reporter names a covert CIA agent in a news story. It is alleged that the vice president gave the reporter the agent's identity after her husband, a former ambassador, publicly and vehemently criticized the foreign policies of the president. You are concerned that the reporter's revelation jeopardized other CIA agents. You are also concerned that more media attention may take an even bigger toll on national security.

- Your constituents complain about excessive government spending all the time. Allegations have surfaced that several government agencies have spent millions of dollars on conferences in extravagant places and their staff has accepted lavish gifts in violation of ethics rules. Your political party controls the executive branch, including these agencies.

The Power to Investigate

GUIDING QUESTION *How does Congress exercise its power to investigate government agencies?*

The ability to investigate social and economic misconduct and to oversee the performance of government agencies is a critical power of Congress. Congressional investigations into government failures and scandals have had a very long history in American politics.

Serial and Government Publications Division, Library of Congress.

The Senate investigation of the sinking of the *Titanic* brought about new safety practices on the high seas.

▲ **CRITICAL THINKING**

Analyzing How does Congress's power to investigate strengthen the system of checks and balances?

schedule to plan to occur at a specific time

scheme a plan of action, especially a crafty or secret one

The Founders neither granted nor denied Congress the power to conduct investigations. One of the first investigations involved the military. In 1792 the U.S. Army fought against a confederation of Native American groups over control of the Northwest Territory. The U.S. Army was defeated so soundly that Congress launched an investigation into what happened, who was to blame, and the general capacity of the military. Many congressional investigations have occurred since—into the sinking of the *Titanic* in 1912, into organized crime in the 1950s (the first televised congressional hearings), into the activities of the Environmental Protection Agency in the 1980s, and into the misuse of informants by the FBI in the early 2000s.

Congressional Investigations A standing or select committee may conduct investigations, which can last for days or go on for months. Committee staffers often travel around the country to collect evidence and **schedule** witnesses. Dozens of witnesses may be called to testify, sometimes under oath, at committee hearings.

Congressional investigations occur for many reasons; most get little notice, but a few have become media events. In 2013 a top official at the Internal Revenue Service (IRS) revealed that employees at her own agency had more closely scrutinized conservative groups that applied for special nonexempt status than they had scrutinized other groups. Many people were outraged, especially Republicans, Tea Party members, and other conservatives. Within days, two separate House committees launched investigations, both controlled by Republican leadership. The Senate Finance Committee, controlled by Democrats, launched an investigation as well.

More than once in the 1990s and 2000s, Congress investigated allegations against its own members. While some complaints were politically motivated, several members were indicted and one senator resigned to avoid expulsion.

One of the biggest congressional investigations in recent years concerned the activities of Jack Abramoff, a lobbyist convicted of bribing public officials. Others were convicted as a result of Abramoff's **schemes**, including the deputy of a cabinet member and Representative Bob Ney (R-OH). In federal court, Ney admitted that he had done favors for lobbyists in exchange for campaign contributions, expensive meals, expensive travel, and sports tickets.

Other times, Congress leads investigations that result in new legislation. For example, the U.S. Senate's Permanent Subcommittee on Investigations conducted a two-year bipartisan investigation into some of the leading investment banks and their possible role in the U.S. economic meltdown in 2008. The committee obtained millions of pages of memos, documents, and e-mails from the banks on computer disks. The subcommittee was "not just overturning some rocks," said its chairman, Michigan Senator Carl Levin. "Success is when we lead to reforms or lead to justice and accountability."

At the end of the investigation, the subcommittee concluded that the banks had seriously misled their clients on the risk in their investments. The publicity that this investigation generated helped Congress pass the Dodd-Frank bill to reform banking practices. It encouraged federal regulators and law-enforcement agencies to consider penalties for some of the banks' actions. It also showed how congressional investigations work best, burrowing into issues, subpoenaing witnesses and documents, spending long periods of time poring through the documents, and then taking the evidence into public hearings that draw the attention of the media. Congressional investigations can have additional clout by producing legislation designed to prevent future wrongdoing.

Rights of Congressional Witnesses Although congressional investigations are not trials, Congress has several powers that help committees collect evidence. Like courts, congressional committees have the power to **subpoena** witnesses. A subpoena is a legal order that requires a person to appear or produce requested documents. Congress uses this power frequently.

Like courts, congressional committees can require witnesses to testify under oath. Witnesses who do not tell the truth can be criminally prosecuted for **perjury**, or lying under oath. Committees may also punish those who refuse to testify or otherwise will not cooperate by holding them in **contempt** of Congress, meaning that they are willfully obstructing its work. Persons found in contempt of Congress can be arrested and jailed. The Constitution does not grant this power to Congress, but court decisions have generally upheld it.

Until the mid-twentieth century, witnesses who testified before a congressional committee had few rights. In 1948, for example, the chairperson of a House committee told one witness: "The rights you have are the rights given you by this committee. We will determine what rights you have and what rights you do not have before the committee."

The situation today is very different, and witnesses before congressional committees have important rights. In the case of *Watkins* v. *United States* (1957), the Supreme Court ruled that Congress must respect witnesses' constitutional rights just as a court does. In the Court's words:

> **PRIMARY SOURCE**
> **Witnesses cannot be compelled to give evidence against themselves. They cannot be subjected to unreasonable search and seizure. Nor can the First Amendment freedoms of speech, press, religion, or political belief and association be abridged."**
>
> —Chief Justice Earl Warren, 1957

subpoena a legal order that a person appear or produce requested documents

perjury lying under oath

contempt willful obstruction of justice

PARTICIPATING

Your Government

Differentiating Between Fact and Opinion

Congressional investigations can strengthen democracy or they can undermine it, depending on how they are conducted by Congress and perceived by the public.

Identify a current or very recent congressional investigation. (The website of the House Oversight Committee may help you identify an investigation.) Read two or three news reports about it. If possible, try to obtain stories from sources you consider politically neutral as well as from sources that you believe show political bias.

Take notes about the subject of the investigation. Compare the coverage of the hearings and or investigations. What bias, if any, does each news source demonstrate? Do the congressional investigators and witnesses focus on facts or opinions? How do you know? What conclusions can you draw about whether the investigation is fair and worthwhile? Can you suggest a better way to "get to the truth"?

▶ CRITICAL THINKING

Argument Express your findings and opinions in a persuasive essay or article about the relationship between this investigation and better democracy. Be sure to explain your thinking and cite your sources.

Jim Arbogast/Getty Images

One way congressional committees have gotten around this requirement to observe Fifth Amendment rights is by giving witnesses **immunity**. Immunity is freedom from prosecution for people whose testimony ties them to criminal acts. Of course, the Fifth Amendment states that people cannot be forced to testify against themselves. If witnesses are granted immunity, however, they can be required to testify; those who refuse may be held in contempt and jailed.

A 1987 case illustrates how immunity works. A Senate committee investigated charges against officials in the Reagan administration who were charged with selling arms to Iran and using the money to finance a war in Nicaragua. The committee granted immunity to Colonel Oliver North and compelled him to testify. North, who worked for the National Security Council, implicated the national security adviser as well as others. North was tried and convicted. His conviction was later overturned because the evidence was obtained only as a result of testimony he gave while under immunity.

☑ **READING PROGRESS CHECK**

Identifying Central Issues Why do you think the power to investigate is a critical power of Congress?

The Power of Oversight

GUIDING QUESTION *How does Congress oversee the executive branch?*

Most congressional investigations are related to another power that Congress has developed over the years—the power of **legislative oversight**. As the word suggests, legislative oversight is the power to review executive branch activities on an ongoing basis. In modern American government, the executive carries out those laws through a huge bureaucracy of multiple agencies and hundreds of public officials. Thus, the oversight power of Congress can be focused on a wide array of programs and officials.

Oversight and Checks and Balances Legislative oversight is a good example of how checks and balances work. Congress makes the laws, and the executive branch carries them out. As it does so, the executive branch interprets what the laws mean in a practical sense. Later Congress can check how the executive branch has administered the law and decide whether it met the law's goals.

Although lawmakers have broad oversight powers, they use them inconsistently. Vice President Hubert Humphrey once said that Congress "sometimes gets in the habit of 'pass it and forget it' lawmaking." Legislative oversight tends to occur on a "hit-and-miss" basis as congressional staffs and committees go about their business. Why?

First, lawmakers do not have enough staff, time, or money to keep track of everything going on in the executive branch. Second, lawmakers know that oversight does not interest many voters, unless it uncovers a scandal or major problem. Third, some legislation and regulations are so vague that it is difficult to know exactly what they mean. Without clear objectives, lawmakers have little means of judging whether the executive branch is doing its job.

▼ CRITICAL THINKING

Analyzing Which of these functions would you consider "oversight"? Explain.

LANDMARK LAWS
LEGISLATIVE REORGANIZATION ACTS

Congress has defined oversight functions in several laws.

1946 Legislative Reorganization Act

★ asked Congress to exercise "continuous watchfulness" over executive agencies

★ reduced the number of House committees from 48 to 19

★ reduced the number of Senate committees from 35 to 15

1970 Legislative Reorganization Act

★ gave each standing committee oversight authority for the areas of its responsibility and required them to issue biennial reports

★ made all committee hearings (excluding national security meetings and appropriations) public

★ permitted televised broadcasts of many committee hearings

★ created an electronic voting system in the House Chamber

Finally, committees sometimes come to favor the federal agencies they are supposed to oversee. Lawmakers and the officials who work for a federal agency often become well-acquainted because they spend long hours working together. This creates the possibility that committee members will not be objective when assessing the performance of people who work at the agency.

How Congress Limits the Executive Congress exercises oversight in several ways. It requires executive agencies to report to it. The 1946 Employment Act, for example, requires the president to send Congress an annual report on the nation's economy. During a recent congressional term, federal agencies submitted more than 1,000 reports to Congress. Keeping up with the reports, especially those that relate to a member's committee assignment, is an important job.

A second oversight technique is for Congress to ask one of its support agencies, such as the Government Accountability Office (GAO), to study an agency's work. The GAO typically examines the finances of federal agencies to see if public money is being spent appropriately and legally.

Obviously, the power of the purse gives Congress another means of overseeing the executive branch. Each year Congress reviews the budgets of all agencies in the executive branch. Congress can then decide to expand, reduce, or eliminate certain programs in the budget.

For years, Congress exercised oversight power by using the **legislative veto**. Congress put provisions into some laws that allowed it to review and cancel actions of the executive agencies carrying out those laws. In effect, Congress was claiming authority over officials who worked in the executive branch. In 1983 the Supreme Court ruled in *Immigration and Naturalization Service* v. *Chadha* that the legislative veto was unconstitutional because it violated the separation of powers.

Independent Counsel In 1978 Congress passed a law that allowed it to demand the appointment of a special prosecutor, called the independent counsel, to conduct certain investigations. In 1999 Congress let the law expire and gave the attorney general sole power to conduct ethics investigations of top officials.

☑ **READING PROGRESS CHECK**

Explaining How does Congress limit the power of the executive branch?

EXPLORING THE ESSENTIAL QUESTION

Analyzing Review the following principles of democracy. How does legislative oversight over the programs carried out by the executive branch relate to each of the following principles of democracy?

• rule of law

• accountability

• transparency

• control of the abuse of power

legislative veto a provision that Congress wrote into some laws that allowed it to review and cancel actions of executive agencies

---

LESSON 2 REVIEW

Reviewing Vocabulary

1. *Describing* What is the legislative veto and why was it declared unconstitutional?

Using Your Graphic Organizer

2. *Making Connections* Using your completed graphic organizer, choose an example of a congressional investigation and explain what outcomes it produced.

Answering the Guiding Questions

3. *Expressing* How does Congress exercise its power to investigate government agencies?

4. *Identifying* How does Congress oversee the executive branch?

Writing About Government

5. *Informative/Explanatory* How does congressional oversight reflect the principle of checks and balances in American government? Explain.

Should Congress stop regulating the Post Office?

DEBATING DEMOCRATIC PRINCIPLES

The U.S. Postal Service (USPS) is in financial trouble. Americans are using the Internet and cell phones and at the same time, commercial companies are handling a large share of business shipping. In the 1970s, the Postal Service became an "independent agency" of the government, tasked with operating like a business. Congress, however, retains the authority to approve or disapprove of business decisions made by the Postal Service. For example, Congress must approve postage rate hikes and changes to service. The Postal Service has proposed closing small post offices and discontinuing Tuesday or Saturday delivery. Residents in communities whose post offices are threatened with closure often rally around what they see as a center of community life. Members of Congress feel pressured to fight for the post offices in their districts. One proposed solution is for Congress to give up its power to regulate Postal Service activities.

 YES

 NO

TEAM A **Congress Should Stop Regulating the Post Office**	TEAM B **Congress Should Not Stop Regulating the Post Office**
The financial pressures on the Postal Service are significant. If Congress truly allowed the Postal Service to act like a business, it could make decisions that would help it get back on its feet. It could decide which assets to retain. It could decide what rates to charge, just as commercial shippers like FedEx and UPS do. It could stop making excess payments into the health insurance account for retirees.	Taking away Congress's power to regulate the Postal Service is not the solution. Post offices in small towns are much more than simply places where you go to mail a letter. They are centers of community, where people gather to talk about local concerns. Constituents can lobby Congress to keep post offices open. Decisions made on a strictly business basis would not take these intangible benefits into account.
The Postal Service needs to think about new ideas that will help it be successful. Digital technologies have changed the needs of individuals and businesses. Postal Service leaders need the freedom—and the motivation—to think innovatively. They need to think of ways not just to cut costs but to enhance service.	Furthermore, many Postal Service proposals are bad ideas. The Postal Service will not become more successful by providing worse service at higher cost. Congress's regulatory authority keeps pressure on the Postal Service to improve service, not cut it. Congress has made some mistakes, but they can change the law regarding health insurance payments. But they should keep their regulatory power—the Constitution gives them power to "establish Post Offices and post Roads."
Many nations have successfully privatized their postal services. That may be the ultimate solution for the United States Postal Service. While the Constitution gives Congress the power to create a post office, it does not mandate that post offices be a government service forever.	Other countries have privatized mail service. But are these countries as big as the United States? And is their service as good as ours?

EXPLORING THE ESSENTIAL QUESTION

Analyzing Read the evidence provided, and prepare to debate one side or the other.
1. Identify the best reasons to support your side of the debate question.
2. Draft a compelling opening statement that sets out your position in the debate and summarizes your argument.
3. Anticipate the strongest arguments to support the other position. How could you respond to those points?

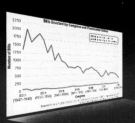

(l to r) US Dept. of the Treasury; LBJ Library photo by Yoichi Okamoto/ White House Photo Office

LESSON 3
Congress and the President

ReadingHelp Desk

Academic Vocabulary
- revise
- period

Content Vocabulary
- **divided government**
- **national budget**
- **impoundment**
- **line-item veto**

TAKING NOTES:

Integration of Knowledge and Ideas

CATEGORIZING Use the graphic to list legislation, events, and court cases that have shifted the balance of power to either the president or the Congress.

Balance of Power

Congress   President

ESSENTIAL QUESTION

How does the separation of powers influence the work of Congress?

At the end of 2012, the U.S. economy was recovering from a deep recession. Federal budget deficits were soaring, and tax cuts for Americans of all economic levels were due to expire. Economists warned that letting the cuts expire could push the economy "off a fiscal cliff."

President Obama pushed to continue the tax cuts for all but the wealthiest citizens. Congressional Republicans objected to any increase in taxes and called for deeper cuts in government spending.

President Obama and the Speaker of the House, John Boehner, were unable to reach an agreement that would satisfy conservative House Republicans. When these negotiations failed, the Senate Republican leader met with the vice president and crafted a compromise: Only Americans with incomes over $400,000 would face an increase in income taxes. A payroll tax cut for taxes that fund Social Security would be allowed to expire; federal unemployment benefits would be extended; and massive spending cuts would be delayed.

This compromise passed both the House and Senate, though most House Republicans refused to support it. On January 2, 2013, President Obama signed the American Taxpayer Relief Act into law.

- What was the conflict between the president and Congress?

- Do you think the underlying cause of the conflict was more philosophical or political? In your opinion, which type of conflict would be harder to resolve?

- What steps were taken to resolve the conflict? Why do you think negotiations between the Senate Republican leader and the vice president were more successful than talks between the president and the Speaker?

- How might this case help you understand presidential-congressional conflicts?

Sources of Tension

GUIDING QUESTION *What factors cause tension between Congress and the president?*

Tension between Congress and the president goes back to the origins of American government. Tension is inevitable as each branch guards its powers and tries to hold the other in check. The main source of tension is the checks and balances built into our system of separation of powers, but other factors are also involved.

1. Analyzing Graphs What does the data suggest about how frequently the Congress and president cooperate?

2. Researching Do some more research to learn on which policies the Congress and the president were able to reach an agreement.

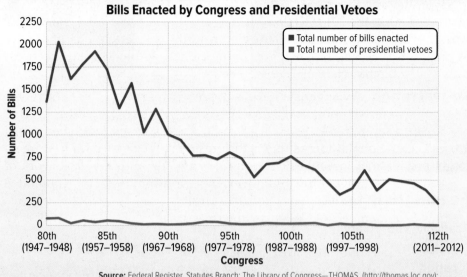

Bills Enacted by Congress and Presidential Vetoes

■ Total number of bills enacted
■ Total number of presidential vetoes

Source: Federal Register, Statutes Branch; The Library of Congress—THOMAS, (http://thomas.loc.gov); United States Statutes at Large, Government Printing Office

Checks and Balances The Constitution has been called "an invitation to struggle." The system of checks and balances that the Constitution created gives all three branches of government powers to counteract one another. Presidents share their most important duties with Congress, including making treaties, appointing federal officials and judges, and paying the expenses of the government.

Likewise, all the bills Congress passes require the executive's cooperation—the president must sign them before they become law. The president can veto a bill or threaten to veto it. For Congress to override a presidential veto, it requires a two-thirds majority in each house of Congress, which is usually difficult to obtain. This gives the president a major role in legislation. When either side refuses to cooperate, the other may be frustrated.

The system of checks and balances gives Congress and the president several tools to counteract each other. For example, the president may threaten a veto, arguing that a bill spends too much money and would spur inflation, which is harmful to the national economy. Some members of Congress may cooperate in attempting to amend the bill or override a veto because their states or districts would benefit from the bill. Historian James MacGregor Burns argues that the system is "designed for deadlock and inaction" and that it is really "President versus Congress" in our government.

Different Constituencies Upon election, the president is expected to represent all the people of the United States. Members of Congress represent only their constituents, people who live and vote in their state or local district. Thus, members of Congress will often have a more narrow view on a given issue than the president, who will take a national perspective. Even when a lawmaker wants to agree with the president's ideas, he or she must think about what will please the voters back home.

Party Politics Most elected leaders are loyal to their political party and to their party's philosophies. Partisan politics (politics driven mostly by party loyalty) can also affect relations between the president and Congress. This is most obvious if one party controls the White House and the other controls the House and Senate, a situation known as **divided government**. In recent decades, the president's party has rarely controlled both houses of Congress. This has increased conflict between the president and Congress. Divided government was pronounced in the 1990s when President Clinton, a

divided government when one party controls the White House and the other controls the House and Senate

Democrat, faced Republican majorities in Congress, and again after 2006, when Republican President George W. Bush had a Congress with Democratic majorities. After the 2010 election, Democratic President Barack Obama dealt with Democrats who controlled the majority in the Senate and with Republicans who held the majority in the House. As the legislative process slowed, the media often referred to "gridlock."

Organization The organization of Congress gives many tools to members who want to resist a proposal of the president. Rules of procedure, such as the Senate's unlimited debate rule, can be used to block legislation. Even when congressional leaders support the president, they may have to struggle to get presidential initiatives through Congress. Because the basic work of legislation is conducted in committees and subcommittees, the committee system also may be a weapon against the president. Committee chairpersons are powerful members of Congress, and they use their positions to influence bills. Conflicts in government occur when a president wants a major proposal approved and a committee tries to delay, **revise**, or defeat it.

revise to correct or improve

Different Political Timetables Conflicts may also occur because the president and Congress have different political timetables. Before any of these elected officials face voters again, they want to show they have accomplished what the voters asked them to do. Presidents have a little more than three years to develop, present, and move their programs through Congress before they must busy themselves running for reelection; at best, they have only eight years to accomplish their agendas.

By contrast, senators and representatives are not limited to two terms in office. Most members can look forward to being reelected for several terms. Thus, they have a much longer political timetable than the president. Representatives, who serve two-year terms, are always running for reelection. Senators, whose terms are six years, can be more patient in handling controversial bills. For various reasons, then, lawmakers in both houses may not be eager to act on legislation that does not benefit their constituents directly.

☑ **READING PROGRESS CHECK**

Interpreting Why do party politics and the election cycle often create conflict between Congress and the president?

PARTICIPATING
🅝 Your Government

Collaborating

Form a group with three other students. Together, brainstorm the causes of homelessness in the U.S. Assign two students to act as staff for members of Congress and two students to act as staff for the president and executive branch. Separately, each pair of students should list ideas to prevent homelessness. Think about these questions as you work:

- What role should the federal government play in addressing homelessness? What role should state and local governments play?
- What role should private individuals and voluntary organizations play in addressing homelessness? How might your proposals affect your community?

EXPLORING THE ESSENTIAL QUESTION

Synthesizing After each pair has generated at least three ideas, return to the group of four. Each pair should share their ideas. Can the four of you agree on any or all of the ideas? Does your perspective on these proposals change if you are representing a congressional district or if you are representing a whole nation?

President Lyndon B. Johnson was effective at exerting influence over members of Congress, as shown here in an encounter with Senator Richard Russell in the Cabinet Room of the White House in 1963.

▲ **CRITICAL THINKING**

Analyzing Visuals What does this photograph tell you about Lyndon Johnson's approach toward shaping legislation?

period a series of events, as in time

LBJ Library photo by Yoichi Okamoto/White House Photo Office

The Balance of Power

GUIDING QUESTION *What events and legislation have shifted the balance of power between Congress and the president?*

The system of checks and balances makes it likely that the president and Congress will always compete for power. Which branch will dominate in a specific **period** of time depends on many factors, including the political issues of the day, the political savvy of congressional leaders, and the popularity of the president.

The balance of power between the two branches has varied throughout our history. Prior to the Civil War, presidents looked to Congress to take the lead in proposing legislation, sometimes working behind the scenes with lawmakers to promote their ideas. During the Civil War, President Lincoln assumed vast executive powers to deal with the crisis and Congress went along. By contrast, the post-Civil War Congress nearly impeached Lincoln's successor, Andrew Johnson; over time, Congress again became the center of power in the federal government.

Starting in the early 1900s, the balance of power began to shift again. Strong presidents such as Theodore Roosevelt, Franklin Roosevelt, and Lyndon B. Johnson assumed leadership roles in proposing legislation as they dealt with changing social, political, and economic conditions. Public expectations of what the president should accomplish also grew enormously.

After the Watergate crisis, many members of Congress concluded that President Nixon tried to create an "imperial presidency" and that the executive was too strong. Congress worked to regain power and influence related to war making and budget policy. Today, Congress grants the president a leadership role in proposing legislation. At the same time, members of Congress feel free to debate, modify, and pass or defeat anything a president proposes. Any president who proposes major new programs will almost surely come into conflict with the legislative branch.

Emergency Powers In times of crisis, Congress has given extra powers to the president. Presidents have declared martial law, seized property, and controlled transportation and communications systems.

President Franklin D. Roosevelt had vast authority during the Depression and World War II. In 1933 Congress empowered him to close the nation's banks. When Pearl Harbor was bombed in 1941, another national emergency was proclaimed, giving Roosevelt broader control over the economy. In 1950 President Truman proclaimed a national emergency in response to the Korean conflict. President Nixon exercised this authority twice in the 1970s.

During the Vietnam War, congressional leaders came to believe that the president's emergency powers had helped deepen the nation's involvement in Asia. Before this time, many members of Congress were not aware that, legally, many emergency powers had been on the books since the 1930s. To correct this situation, Congress passed an act in 1976 to restrict the president's emergency powers. The National Emergencies Act established procedures for how and when a state of emergency exists. Under the act, presidents must notify Congress when they intend to declare a national emergency. In 2001 after the September 11, 2001, attacks, President George W. Bush used his authority under this act to suspend the law that permitted a military officer to retire.

Balancing Budget Powers For many years, presidents have assumed more responsibility for planning the **national budget**, the yearly financial plan for the national government. Because of this, by the early 1970s Congress had slipped into the role of merely reacting to budget proposals.

national budget the yearly financial plan for the federal government

To increase its role in budgeting, Congress passed the Congressional Budget and Impoundment Control Act in 1974. The act did several things: It established a permanent budget committee for each house; it set up the Congressional Budget Office (CBO) to provide financial expertise for Congress; and it limited the president's ability to impound funds. **Impoundment** is the president's refusal to spend money Congress has voted to fund a program. This law required the president to spend appropriated funds unless Congress agreed that the monies should be impounded.

impoundment the president's refusal to spend money Congress has voted to fund a program

The powers to budget and to tax have continued as an area of struggle in recent times. The U.S. government stood on the edge of a so-called "fiscal cliff" at the end of 2012. Eventually, compromise between both political parties in the Senate and House and the president led to the passage of the American Taxpayer Relief Act, which the president then signed into law.

Legislative and Line-Item Vetoes At times, Congress has wielded a legislative veto to invalidate actions by the executive branch. In the 1970s, when members of Congress felt the executive branch had grown too powerful, they began using legislative vetoes more frequently on a wider range of issues. Presidents objected that this infringed on their constitutional authority. In 1983 the Supreme Court struck down the legislative veto as unconstitutional. Despite this ruling, Congress has continued to require executive branch agencies to submit budget requests to Senate and House committees for approval, which has the effect of giving Congress a veto.

In order to get more control over federal spending, many presidents asked Congress for a **line-item veto** to reject part of a bill. This is a power that many state governments have, but the Constitution only provides for presidents to veto an entire bill. In 1996 Congress passed a bill authorizing the president to veto parts of spending bills and tax breaks. Such line-item vetoes would still be subject to a two-thirds vote in both houses of Congress to override. President Bill Clinton soon began exercising this power. Supporters of the line-item veto said it would help the president curb spending. Opponents said that Congress, not the president, should control spending. In 1998 the Supreme Court ruled that the line-item veto was unconstitutional and that Congress could not, in effect, give away its constitutional powers through legislation. In the words of Justice John Paul Stevens: "If there is to be a new procedure in which the President will play a different role . . . such a change must come not by legislation but through the amendment procedures set forth in Article V of the Constitution."

line-item veto the power of an executive to reject one or more items in a bill without vetoing the entire bill

☑ **READING PROGRESS CHECK**

Explaining What legislation helped to shift power back to Congress in 1974?

LESSON 3 REVIEW

Reviewing Vocabulary
1. *Constructing Arguments* What is divided government and how might it create partisan gridlock?

Using Your Graphic Organizer
2. *Evaluating* Write an essay explaining whether you think the president or Congress has gained more power in recent years.

Answering the Guiding Questions
3. *Making Generalizations* What factors cause conflict between Congress and the president?

4. *Analyzing* What events and legislation have shifted the balance of power between Congress and the president?

Writing About Government
5. *Argument* Both the legislative veto and the line-item veto have been declared unconstitutional. Choose one of these and write a speech defending its use. Be sure to anticipate and refute counterarguments in your speech.

STUDY GUIDE

CONGRESSIONAL POWERS
LESSON 1

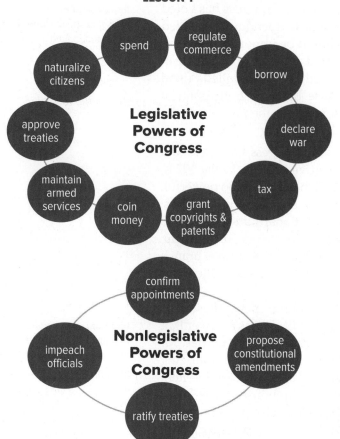

Legislative Powers of Congress

- spend
- regulate commerce
- borrow
- naturalize citizens
- approve treaties
- maintain armed services
- coin money
- grant copyrights & patents
- tax
- declare war

Nonlegislative Powers of Congress

- confirm appointments
- impeach officials
- propose constitutional amendments
- ratify treaties

CONGRESSIONAL INVESTIGATIONS
LESSON 2

Collect Information
- subpoena witnesses and documents
- require testimony under oath
- punish witnesses who lie or refuse to testify
- grant immunity to encourage testimony

Possible Outcomes
- new laws
- reforms
- firings and resignations
- criminal convictions
- damaged reputations

CONGRESSIONAL OVERSIGHT
LESSON 2

Checks and Balances
Congress oversees implementation of laws by executive branch

Separation of Powers
Congress may not cancel actions of or claim authority over executive agencies

CONGRESS AND THE PRESIDENT
LESSON 3

TENSION

- Different Electoral Timetables
- Party Loyalties
- System of Checks and Balances
- Different Constituencies
- Congressional Rules and Committee Organization

BALANCE OF POWER
LESSON 3

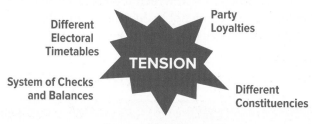

PRESIDENT
- leads in proposing legislation
- proposes budget
- has emergency powers
- legislative veto unconstitutional

CONGRESS
- placed curbs on emergency powers
- line-item veto unconstitutional
- can modify, pass, or defeat president's proposals
- increased budgetary role and limited impoundment

Directions: On a separate sheet of paper, answer the questions below. Make sure you read carefully and answer all parts of the questions.

Lesson Review

Lesson 1

1 *Specifying* What does the "necessary and proper" clause in the Constitution imply about the powers of Congress?

2 *Describing* What process does Congress use for approving expenditures?

3 *Defining* What is the confirmation power and which house exercises it?

Lesson 2

4 *Defining* What crime has a person convicted of lying under oath committed?

5 *Summarizing* What powers help congressional committees collect evidence in an investigation?

6 *Identifying* What principle of U.S. government prevents Congress from voiding actions of an executive agency?

Lesson 3

7 *Analyzing Cause and Effect* How do differences in the constituencies create conflicts between the president and members of Congress?

8 *Analyzing Cause and Effect* What effect does a divided government usually have on the work of Congress? Explain why.

9 *Explaining* If the line-item veto were constitutional, how would it affect the balance of power? Explain.

ANSWERING THE ESSENTIAL QUESTIONS

Review your answers to the introductory questions at the beginning of each lesson. Then answer the following Essential Questions based on what you learned in the chapter. Have your answers changed?

10 *Analyzing* How have the powers of Congress changed over time?

11 *Explaining* How does the separation of powers influence the work of Congress?

DBQ Interpreting Political Cartoons

Use the political cartoon to answer the following questions.

12 *Contrasting* Based on this cartoon, how do Republicans and Democrats feel about the Affordable Care Act?

13 *Making Inferences* Which branch of government does this cartoon illustrate? How do you know?

Critical Thinking

14 *Analyzing* Assume Congress wants to stimulate a sluggish economy. How could it use its taxing power to do this? Explain.

15 *Hypothesizing* Congress authorizes money to aid local schools. How might Congress use this spending power to encourage better education?

16 *Making Inferences* How might party politics affect congressional investigations?

17 *Evaluating* According to historian James MacGregor Burns, the system of checks and balances is "designed for deadlock and inaction." Do you agree? Explain.

Need Extra Help?

If You've Missed Question	1	2	3	4	5	6	7	8	9	10	11	12	13	14	15	16	17
Go to page	173	175	181	185	185	187	190	190	193	175	190	178	174	174	175	184	190

Directions: On a separate sheet of paper, answer the questions below. Make sure you read carefully and answer all parts of the questions.

DBQ Analyzing Primary Sources

Read the excerpt and answer the questions that follow.

PRIMARY SOURCE

"The result of the most careful and attentive consideration bestowed upon this clause is that, if it does not enlarge, it cannot be construed to restrain the powers of Congress, or to impair the right of the legislature to exercise its best judgment in the selection of measures to carry into execution the Constitutional powers of the Government."

—Chief Justice John Marshall,
McCulloch v. *Maryland* (1819)

18 *Interpreting* To what clause does this passage refer? How do you know?

19 *Identifying Perspectives* How is Chief Justice Marshall interpreting this clause?

Social Studies Skills

Study the table and answer the questions that follow.

Total Government Receipts and Outlays
(in millions of dollars)

Year	Receipts	Outlays	Surplus or Deficit (−)
2005	2,153,611	2,471,957	−318,346
2006	2,406,869	2,655,050	−248,181
2007	2,567,985	2,728,686	−160,701
2008	2,523,991	2,982,544	−458,553
2009	2,104,989	3,517,677	−1,412,688
2010	2,162,706	3,457,079	−1,294,373
2011	2,303,466	3,603,059	−1,299,593
2012	2,450,164	3,537,127	−1,086,963
2013*	2,712,045	3,684,947	−972,902
2014*	3,033,618	3,777,807	−744,189

*estimate
Source: Government Printing Office, Budget of the United States, Fiscal Year 2014.

20 *Comparing and Contrasting* What does the last column tell you about the relationship between receipts and outlays for the years shown? Explain.

21 *Economics* Based on the numbers in the table, between which two years did a severe recession begin in the United States? How do you know?

22 *Identifying Continuity and Change* Describe the trend in surplus or deficit after 2011.

Research and Presentation

23 *Identifying Perspectives* Immigration policy has been a thorny issue for Congress. Do research about recent proposals for immigration reform. Create a multimedia presentation of different reform options to present to the class.

24 *Drawing Conclusions* Research this question: Should Congress further limit the power of the president to conduct military actions abroad without congressional approval? Take a position and prepare to defend it in a class debate.

25 *Gathering Information* Lesson 2 began with three scenarios describing real events: NSA surveillance, the leaking of a covert CIA agent's name, and extravagant spending by government agencies. Choose one to research. Write a report describing how Congress went about investigating this issue and the result. Be prepared to present your report to the class.

Need Extra Help?

If You've Missed Question	**18**	**19**	**20**	**21**	**22**	**23**	**24**	**25**
Go to page	173	173	174	174	174	196	178	183

Congress at Work

netw⊙rks
www.connected.mcgraw-hill.com
There's More Online about
Congress at work.

CHAPTER 7

ESSENTIAL QUESTIONS

• How does a bill become a law? • How does the government raise and allocate money? • What factors influence congressional decision making?

▲ Candidate for Senate Ed Markey greets voters during a visit to a Worcester, MA, restaurant.

EPA/Alamy

ANALYZING PRIMARY SOURCES

RATING
CONGRESS

In summer 2013, the number of voters who thought Congress was doing a good or excellent job went up—to 10 percent. Two-thirds of those polled said Congress was doing a poor job. What criteria should be used to evaluate Congress? The polls do not provide an answer to that question. Use the primary and secondary sources to explore this issue.

PRIMARY SOURCE A

Appearing on the Sunday morning CBS program *Face the Nation* on July 21, 2013, Speaker Boehner said:

". . . we should not be judged on how many new laws we create. We ought to be judged on how many laws we repeal. We've got more laws than the administration could ever enforce. And so we don't do commemorative bills on the floor. We don't do all that nonsense. We deal with what the American people want us to deal with."

—Speaker of the House, John Boehner (R-Ohio)

PRIMARY SOURCE B

The Government Accountability Office (GAO) is often called the "congressional watchdog" because its primary job is to investigate how the federal government spends money. This excerpt from the agency's mission statement suggests some ways of looking at Congress's work.

"Our Mission is to support the Congress in meeting its constitutional responsibilities and to help improve the performance and ensure the accountability of the federal government for the benefit of the American people. . . . Our core values of accountability, integrity, and reliability are reflected in all of the work we do. . . . We advise Congress and the heads of executive agencies about ways to make government more efficient, effective, ethical, equitable and responsive."

—Mission of the U.S. Government Accountability Office (GAO)

PRIMARY SOURCE C

After retiring from Congress, Lee Hamilton established the Center on Congress at Indiana University. Here are some of his thoughts on how to evaluate Congress:

". . . dispute and dysfunction are two very different things . . . results are what count. The issues that Members of Congress have to deal with are difficult and complex, and because the system was set up to accommodate diverse points of view, disagreement and delay are a natural part of the legislative process. Intense debate doesn't mean that issues cannot be resolved — just that resolving them can be frustrating and time-consuming. I remember many conversations with disgruntled constituents over the years when I urged patience, and suggested that they judge Congress by the results, not by the untidy process."

—Former Congressman Lee Hamilton (D-Indiana)

SECONDARY SOURCE D

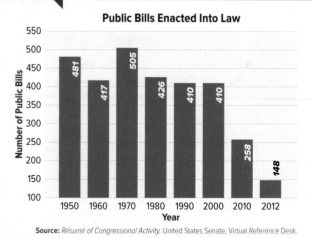

Public Bills Enacted Into Law

Source: *Résumé of Congressional Activity.* United States Senate, Virtual Reference Desk.

PRIMARY SOURCE E

Political scientists Ornstein and Mann are two of the most respected observers of Congress. In 2012 they wrote:

"Civic leaders also need to engage the public, especially to make it clear that nothing gets done in the American political system without having elected officials who revere their institutions, respect the regular order of parliamentary process, work to find constructive solutions that involve engagement—even compromise—with the opposition, and rely on facts to devise pragmatic answers to vexing problems—in other words, politicians, just like our Framers."

—Thomas E. Mann and Norman J. Ornstein, "The Election and the Future," *Democracy: A Journal of Ideas,* Fall 2012

PRIMARY SOURCE F

THEY CAN'T DO THEIR WORK, THEY DON'T PLAY WELL WITH OTHERS...

...THESE GUYS WOULDN'T LAST A DAY IN KINDERGARTEN.

DBQ DOCUMENT-BASED QUESTIONS

1. **Identifying** List terms from the sources that suggest criteria—standards—by which the performance of Congress might be judged. Circle three of the terms that are important to you.

2. **Making Inferences** What does the quote from Speaker Boehner reveal about his political philosophy? What might someone with a different view on the size of government say about how to judge Congress?

3. **Comparing** How do the sources differ in what they imply about the process of lawmaking? Do you see an "untidy process" as problematic? Why or why not?

4. **Evaluating** How might Speaker Boehner respond to the information in the bar graph? Lee Hamilton? Is this information important to you? Explain your answer.

WHAT WILL YOU DO?

How will you judge the work of Congress? Create a checklist that you will use now and in the future to evaluate how well Congress is doing its job. Then create a checklist to use to evaluate your representatives and senators.

EXPLORE the interactive version of the analyzing primary sources feature on Networks.

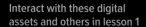

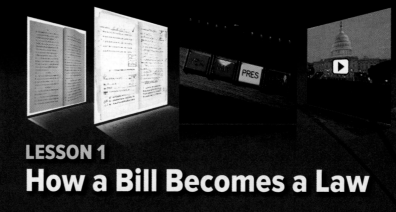

LESSON 1
How a Bill Becomes a Law

Reading Help Desk

Academic Vocabulary

- amend
- interactive

Content Vocabulary

- private bill
- public bill
- joint resolution
- simple resolution
- concurrent resolution
- rider
- hearing
- veto
- pocket veto

TAKING NOTES:

Key Ideas and Details

SEQUENCING Use a flowchart to show the major stages by which a bill becomes a law.

How a Bill Becomes Law

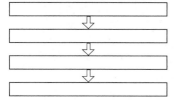

ESSENTIAL QUESTION

How does a bill become a law?

Have you ever thought, "There ought to be a law!" when observing something that was just not right? Some laws begin with ideas from private individuals or groups. If you had the chance to make a new law, get rid of an old one, or change one that exists, what would you want? Tell your idea to ten classmates. Persuade them why this law should exist, be thrown out, or changed. Listen to their ideas. Then vote on each. Did any of the ideas get six or more votes? Do you think those ideas could get support from 269 other people? Why or why not?

Types of Bills and Resolutions

GUIDING QUESTION *What are the different types of congressional bills and resolutions?*

Of the thousands of bills introduced in each session of Congress, only a few hundred become law; most die in Congress, and some are vetoed by the president. If a bill is not passed before the end of that congressional session (two years), it must be introduced again in the next session to be given further consideration.

It usually takes a long time for a bill to be enacted into law. Laws are complicated and their impact can be enormous; this is one reason why the process is deliberative. There are times when Congress can act with speed, though: When a crisis occurs, and when public protests grow loud enough, members of Congress can put aside their differences and act speedily to solve the problem.

Two types of bills are introduced in Congress: private bills and public bills. Private bills deal with individual people or places; they frequently involve claims against the government or an individual person's immigration problem. **Private bills** used to make up a significant percentage of congressional bills, but not lately. In the 112th Congress, fewer than 100 of the close to 7,000 bills introduced were private ones.

On the other hand, the vast majority of bills are **public bills**—they involve general matters and apply to the entire nation. They are often controversial since it is hard to shape policies that touch many people. Public bills might address tax cuts, national health insurance, gun control, civil rights, or abortion. The press covers major bills heavily and they may be debated for months before becoming law. Major public bills like these account for a large number of all bills passed.

Resolutions Besides passing laws, Congress can also pass resolutions to make policy on an unusual or temporary matter. Resolutions can range from expressing congressional opinion on an issue—such as a Sense of the Senate resolution on a foreign policy issue—to a resolution commemorating an achievement or honoring some group effort—such as Cancer Prevention Month. There are three kinds of resolutions: joint, simple, and concurrent.

A **joint resolution** is a resolution passed in the same form by both houses. When a joint resolution is signed by the president, it has the force of law; in that way it is very similar to a bill. Joint resolutions are often used to correct an error in an earlier law or to appropriate money for a special purpose. The joint resolution is also used if Congress wants to propose a constitutional amendment, but this does not require the president's signature.

A **simple resolution** covers matters affecting only one house of Congress and is passed by that house alone. If a new rule or procedure is needed, for example, it is adopted as a resolution. Because it is an internal matter, it does not have the force of law and is not sent to the president for signature.

Concurrent resolutions cover matters requiring the action of the House and Senate but on which a law is not needed. For example, a concurrent resolution might set the date for adjourning Congress or express Congress's opinion on an issue. Both houses of Congress must pass concurrent resolutions, but they do not require the president's signature, and they do not have the force of law.

Riders Bills and resolutions usually deal with only one subject. However, sometimes a rider is attached to a bill. A **rider** is a provision on a subject other than the one covered in the bill. Lawmakers attach riders to bills that are likely to pass. Presidents sometimes veto or threaten to veto bills because of a rider they oppose. Lawmakers sometimes attach many riders to a bill for a variety of constituents—the bill then resembles a Christmas tree loaded with ornaments.

Congress passes both bills and resolutions to make public policy.

CRITICAL THINKING

1. Categorizing Which bills and resolutions are used to pass laws? Which are not?

2. Applying Go to Congress.gov and find an example of each type of bill and resolution and summarize their purpose.

BILLS AND RESOLUTIONS

	Description	Examples of when it is used
Bill	• Used to pass a law • Must be passed by both chambers and presented to the president	• Authorization of federal programs • Appropriations • Establishment of new federal agencies • Revenue legislation
Joint Resolution	• Like a bill, can be used to pass a law • Must be passed by both chambers and presented to the president	• Appropriations for a special purpose • Propose a constitutional amendment • Declaration of war • Adjustment of the debt limit
Simple Resolution	• No law is necessary • Covers matters affecting only one house of Congress	To regulate the internal affairs of the House or Senate • Chamber rules • Election of committee members • Creation of a select committee • Censure of a member
Concurrent Resolution	• No law is necessary • Covers matters requiring the action of both the House and Senate	To regulate the internal affairs of Congress as a whole • Congressional budget resolution • "Sense of Congress" resolution • Creation of a joint committee • Congressional recess

HOW A BILL BECOMES A LAW

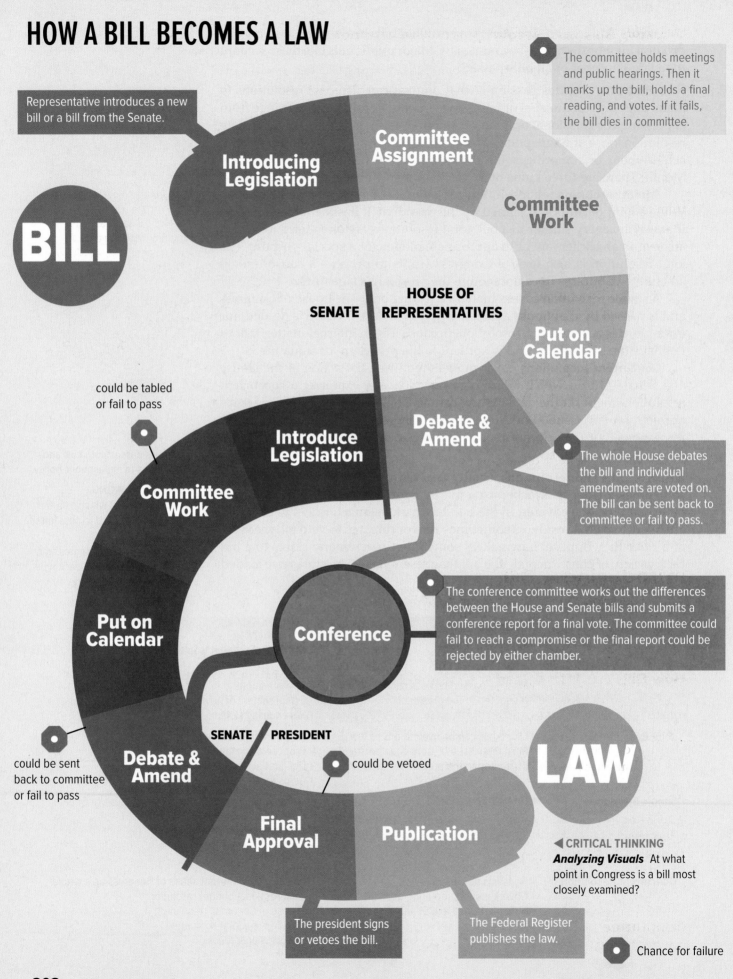

Representative introduces a new bill or a bill from the Senate.

Introducing Legislation

Committee Assignment

The committee holds meetings and public hearings. Then it marks up the bill, holds a final reading, and votes. If it fails, the bill dies in committee.

Committee Work

BILL

SENATE | **HOUSE OF REPRESENTATIVES**

Put on Calendar

could be tabled or fail to pass

Introduce Legislation

Debate & Amend

The whole House debates the bill and individual amendments are voted on. The bill can be sent back to committee or fail to pass.

Committee Work

Put on Calendar

Conference

The conference committee works out the differences between the House and Senate bills and submits a conference report for a final vote. The committee could fail to reach a compromise or the final report could be rejected by either chamber.

could be sent back to committee or fail to pass

Debate & Amend

SENATE | **PRESIDENT**

could be vetoed

LAW

Final Approval

Publication

The president signs or vetoes the bill.

The Federal Register publishes the law.

◀ **CRITICAL THINKING**
Analyzing Visuals At what point in Congress is a bill most closely examined?

⬡ Chance for failure

202

Tracking Bills and Resolutions on the Internet To find out about all legislation Congress is considering, citizens can access several free sources that are nonpartisan and funded by the government. One resource is Congress.gov, which is a website that allows those who are interested to search by either the bill number or a subject keyword; this will call up the full text or all versions of House and Senate bills. Another section of the database shows the full text of the Congressional Record, committee reports, summaries of bills, and updates on their status as they move through the legislative process. The history of bills is also searchable.

The website includes brief videos that explain the legislative process, from introducing a bill to holding committee hearings and floor debates, to presidential action. Congress.gov is designed to open up the complex lawmaking process to citizens, who can then voice their opinions, offsetting the power of lobbyists and special interests. Senator Charles Schumer, chairman of the Senate Rules and Administration Committee, hailed the new service when it was launched in 2012, saying, "Congress.gov will allow people at all levels of experience and expertise to follow legislative developments, access and compare policy proposals, and connect with their senators and representatives."

There are also private websites that provide information on Congress. The Congressional Quarterly (CQ) is a private nonprofit company that publishes books, magazines, and newsletters about Congress. It has a large staff of reporters and researchers who supply the information for its various publications. *Roll Call* is a newspaper widely read by members of Congress and their staff. Its website requires a subscription and provides news and commentary on whatever is happening on Capitol Hill.

☑ **READING PROGRESS CHECK**

Contrasting How do private bills and public bills differ?

EXPLORING THE ESSENTIAL QUESTION

Researching Explore one of the websites that covers the U.S. Congress. Take notes about how it is organized, how easy or difficult it is to navigate, and how clearly concepts are explained. Then choose one piece of legislation that was introduced in this session of Congress. It could be from the House or the Senate. Record the title and bill number and the date it was first introduced. Then try to summarize what the bill is about. (Do not worry if you have difficulty summarizing it now.) You will follow this bill throughout this lesson.

Introducing a Bill

GUIDING QUESTION *How do bills make their way through committees?*

The Constitution sets forth only a few of the many steps a bill must go through to become law. The remaining steps have developed as Congress has grown and the number of bills has increased.

How Bills Are Introduced The first step in the process is to write a bill. Ideas for bills come from citizens, lobbyists or other representatives of interest groups, or the executive branch. The executive branch suggests roughly half of all bills passed. Bills may be drafted by legislators, their staffs, lawyers for a Senate or House committee, or a representative from an interest group, but only a member of Congress can actually introduce a bill. Lawmakers who sponsor a major bill usually find cosponsors to show that the bill has wide support.

To introduce a bill in the House, a member drops the bill into the hopper, a box near the clerk's desk. In the Senate, the presiding officer must first recognize the senator, who then formally presents the bill. As soon as a bill is introduced, it is given a title and number and then printed and distributed to lawmakers. (The first bill in a Senate session is S.1, and the first bill in the House is H.R.1.) These steps make up the first reading of the bill.

Committee Action For both houses of Congress, bills are sent to the committees that deal with the subject. Sometimes, complex issues are divided between several committees with jurisdiction over some part of the bill. Committee chairs may then send a bill to a subcommittee. If a committee wants to reject a bill, it can ignore it and let the bill "die," a process called "pigeonholing," or the committee can "kill" it by a majority vote. A committee can completely rewrite a bill, **amend** it, or recommend that it be adopted as is before sending it back to the House or Senate. Committee members and staff are considered experts in their areas. If they reject a bill, other lawmakers will usually agree with them. Time is also a factor. Lawmakers have heavy workloads and depend on the judgment of their peers.

amend to change, alter

Committee Hearings
When a committee decides to act on a bill, it holds hearings. During a **hearing**, the committee listens to testimony from experts on the bill's subject, from government officials, and from interest groups that are concerned with the bill. Hearings allow a committee to gather information, but most information usually comes from their staff research.

hearing a session at which a committee listens to testimony from people interested in the bill

Hearings can be very important in their own right. Skillful committee chairs can use hearings to influence public opinion or to test its political acceptability. Hearings can also focus public attention on a problem or give interest groups a chance to present their perspective. Finally, hearings are often the best time for outside groups to influence the bill. Citizens can write letters, make phone calls, or send e-mails to express their opinions.

To improve the legislation process, many congressional committees have begun using the Internet in connection with hearings on a bill. The Internet has been used for the following:

- **interactive** hearings using expert witnesses
- to broadcast hearings, thus giving citizens the chance to e-mail questions to committee members
- to report on a bill's contents or status on their websites
- to make information available in a second language

interactive relating to a two-way electronic communication system

Markup Session
After the hearings are over, the committee meets in a markup session—marking up the bill—to decide what changes, if any, to make to the bill. Committee members go through the bill section by section, making any changes they think the bill needs. A majority vote of the committee is required for all changes made to the bill.

Reporting a Bill
When all the changes have been made, the committee votes either to kill the bill or to report it. To report the bill means to send it to the full House or Senate for action. Along with the revised bill, the committee will send to the House or Senate a written report prepared by the committee

Passing the Civil Rights Act of 1964 was not a simple task for Congress. As with many bills, it went through much revision. The first image shows what two pages of the bill looked like after going through markup by a congressional committee. The second image shows the same two pages of the final bill.

▼ **CRITICAL THINKING**
Sequencing What was the chain of events that the bill passed through on its way to becoming the Civil Rights Act of 1964?

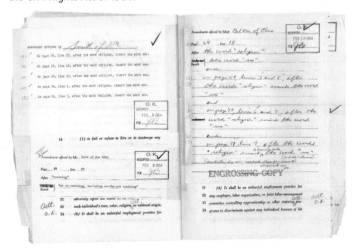

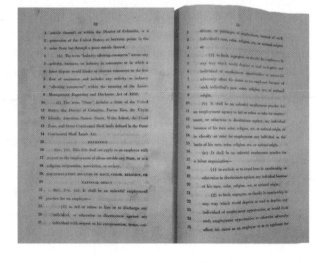

staff. This report is important. It explains the committee's actions, describes the bill, lists the major changes the committee has made, and gives opinions on the bill. The report is often the only document available to lawmakers or their staffs as they decide how to vote on a bill. The committee report may recommend passage, or it may report the bill unfavorably.

Why would a committee report a bill, but not recommend passage? This happens very rarely. A committee may believe the full House should have the opportunity to consider a bill even if the committee does not support it.

☑ **READING PROGRESS CHECK**

Summarizing What steps must lawmakers take to introduce a bill?

Floor Action

GUIDING QUESTION *What is the process for debating, amending, and voting on bills on the floor?*

The next important step in the lawmaking process is the debate on the floor of the House and Senate. Voting on the bill follows the debate. As you may recall, both houses have special procedures to schedule bills for debates and votes that involve the whole House or Senate, which is known as floor action.

Debating and Amending Bills Usually, only a few lawmakers take part in floor debates. The pros and cons of the bill have already been argued in the committee hearings and are already well-known to those with a strong interest. The floor debate, however, is the point where amendments can be added to a bill unless the House has adopted a closed rule—meaning no amendments can be adopted. During the floor debate, the bill receives its second reading. A clerk reads the bill section by section. After each section is read, amendments may be offered. Any lawmaker can propose an amendment during the floor debate.

Amendments range from the introduction of major changes to the correction of typographical errors. Opponents sometimes propose amendments to slow a bill's progress through Congress or to kill it. One strategy that opponents use is to load a bill down with so many objectionable amendments that it dies. In both the House and the Senate, it takes a majority vote of members present to amend a bill.

Voting on Bills After the floor debate, the bill, including any proposed changes, is ready for a vote. A quorum, or a majority, of the members must be present. The House or Senate now receives the third reading of the bill, and the vote is then taken. Passage of a bill requires a majority vote of all members present.

House and Senate members can vote on a bill in one of three ways:

- Voice vote—together members call out "Aye" or "No";
- A standing vote, or division vote—the "Ayes" stand to be counted, and the "Nos" stand to be counted; or,
- A roll-call vote—each member says "Aye" or "No" as names are called in alphabetical order.

The House uses a fourth method, the recorded vote, where votes are recorded electronically and displayed on panels. This method saves the House the many hours it would take to roll-call 435 members.

☑ **READING PROGRESS CHECK**

Explaining What is floor action? Why is it important to the process of voting on a bill?

EXPLORING THE ESSENTIAL QUESTION

Summarizing Continue your report about the bill you are monitoring. Where is it now? Was it assigned to a committee? Was there a hearing? A mark-up? Has it made it to a floor vote? Or does it appear your bill has been stalled, "pigeonholed," or "killed" since it was first introduced? Check news sources to find out if the media has covered it. If so, what do they say about it? If passed, what impact might the bill have on you or your community? Summarize what you have learned about the bill and the process of its becoming a law.

Negotiating

Puppy mills are commercial dog-breeding operations that care more about profits than the welfare of the animals in their care. Imagine that a bill about puppy mills has passed both houses of Congress—but the two bills have some key differences:

- The Senate bill limits the number of litters for females to two every 18 months. The House bill does not limit the number of litters but requires proof that all pregnant dogs have been examined by a veterinarian.
- The House bill requires that all new cages must have non-wire floors by four years from the date of the law. The Senate bill requires the elimination of wire floors in just two years.
- The Senate bill requires that dogs be allowed to spend time with other dogs and people to make sure the dogs will be suitable pets when sold. The House bill contains no such provision but does say that dogs that are no longer breeding must be treated humanely.

Imagine you and three of your classmates must negotiate the differences between the two bills in a conference committee. (Two of you will represent the House, the other two the Senate.) You must think about creating a bill that could pass both chambers. You may need to make concessions on some points to get what you want on others. Once you have reached your compromise, write it down.

◀ **CRITICAL THINKING**

Simulating What did you learn from taking part in this activity? Did it change your thinking about compromise? What's the difference between compromise and "caving in" to pressure? How is compromise necessary to the lawmaking process?

Final Steps in Passing Bills

GUIDING QUESTION *What are the final steps for a bill to become a law?*

To become law, a bill must pass both houses of Congress in *identical form*. A bill passed in the House of Representatives often differs at first from a Senate's bill on the same subject.

Conference Committee Action If one house will not accept the version passed by the other house, a conference committee must work out the differences the two chambers have. Members of the conference committee are called *conferees* or *managers*. They usually come from the House and Senate committee members that handled the bill originally.

The conferees work out the differences by finding compromises, supposedly only on the parts of the bill where the two houses disagree. But sometimes the conference committee will make changes that neither chamber has considered before. Finally, a majority of the conferees from each house drafts the final bill, called a *conference report*. Once accepted, it can be submitted to each house of Congress for final action.

Presidential Action Article I, Section 7 states that "Every Bill which shall have passed the House of Representatives and the Senate, shall, before it becomes a Law, be presented to the President." After both houses have approved an identical bill, it is sent to the president. If he or she signs the bill, it becomes law. The president can also keep the bill for 10 days without signing it. If Congress is in session, the bill then becomes law without the president's signature. Usually, however, presidents sign the bills that are sent to them.

The president can also reject a bill by using the **veto**. If a president vetoes a bill, it returns to the house where it originated, along with an explanation

veto rejection of a bill by the president

of why the president vetoed it. The president can also kill a bill using the so-called **pocket veto**. This means that the president refuses to act on a bill passed during the last 10 days of the session. By failing to send it back before the session ends, the president effectively kills the bill for that session.

pocket veto when a president kills a bill passed during the last 10 days Congress is in session by simply refusing to act on it

Congressional Override of a Veto Congress can override a president's veto with a two-thirds vote in both houses. If this happens, the bill becomes law. However, Congress seldom overrides presidential vetoes.

Registering Laws After a bill becomes law, it is registered with the National Archives and Records Service. The law is assigned a number that identifies the Congress that passed it and the number of the law for that term. For example, Public Law 194 under the 112th Congress is registered as PL 112-194—it was the 194th bill passed by the 112th Congress. The law is then added to the U.S. Code of current federal laws.

Why So Few Bills Become Law Fewer than 10 percent of all bills introduced in Congress become public laws. Why is this true? One reason is that creating law is a long and complicated process—as many as 100 steps can be involved. There are many points at which a bill can be delayed, killed, or amended. Thus a bill's opponents have many opportunities to defeat a bill.

Second, because there are so many steps, a bill's sponsors must be willing to bargain and compromise with others. Compromise is the only way to get enough support to move a bill from one step to the next—major bills have little chance of passage without strong support. Bills opposed by powerful interest groups are not likely to pass.

Another reason so few bills "make it" is that some members introduce bills as a symbolic gesture. A member might introduce a bill to show support for a policy, to attract media attention to an issue, or to satisfy an important group of voters. When reelection comes around, legislators can say they have taken action and they can blame others in Congress for the bill's failure to pass.

Finally, many bills are very complicated because they are intended to address complicated problems. It can be very difficult for even the most effective and determined leaders to convince a majority of senators and representatives to agree with every word of a bill that is hundreds of pages long.

✓ **READING PROGRESS CHECK**

Questioning Why is it so difficult for a bill to become a law?

EXPLORING THE ESSENTIAL QUESTION

Designing Working with one or two other students, create a board game about how a bill becomes a law.

- Choose a name for the game.
- Draw a background on which to play.
- Design a route for players to follow.
- Write down the rules of the game.
- Create playing pieces and, if necessary, wild cards to influence the process.
- Practice playing the game and modify it if necessary.
- Once your game is ready, share it with another group and play their game.

In your opinion, why is it so difficult for a bill to become a law? Is the fact that it is difficult "good" for democracy? Can you suggest improvements to the process? Explain your ideas.

LESSON 1 REVIEW

Reviewing Vocabulary

1. *Discussing* What is a congressional hearing? How are congressional hearings used by members of Congress?

Using Your Graphic Organizer

2. *Sequencing* Use your completed graphic organizer to create an outline that shows the process whereby a bill becomes a law.

Answering the Guiding Questions

3. *Classifying* What are the different types of congressional bills and resolutions?

4. *Sequencing Information* How do bills make their way through committees?

5. *Specifying* What is the process for debating, amending, and voting on bills on the floor?

6. *Explaining* What are the final steps for a bill to become a law?

Writing About Government

7. *Informative/Explanatory* Imagine you are a member of the House of Representatives and you want to pass a law reforming education. Explain the steps that you would take to create a bill and make it into a law. Be sure to explain the different points at which your bill could fail to become a law.

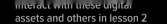

interact with these digital
assets and others in lesson 2

✓ **INTERACTIVE GRAPH**
Tax Revenue as a Percent of GDP

✓ **INTERACTIVE IMAGE**
Hurricane Sandy and Congress

✓ **SELF-CHECK QUIZ**

✓ **VIDEO**
Earmarks

netw☉rks
TRY IT YOURSELF ONLINE

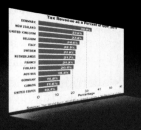

LESSON 2
Taxing and Spending Bills

ReadingHelp Desk

Academic Vocabulary

- consequence
- strategy

Content Vocabulary

- tax
- closed rule
- open rule
- appropriation
- authorization bill
- appropriations bill
- continuing resolution
- earmark
- entitlement

TAKING NOTES:

Key Ideas and Details

COMPARING AND CONTRASTING Use the Venn diagram to compare and contrast the roles of the House and Senate in making and passing tax laws.

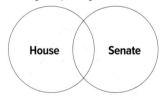

House   Senate

ESSENTIAL QUESTION

How does the government raise and allocate money?

"No Taxation without Representation" was one of the battle cries of the American Revolution. More than 200 years later, tax policy still generates controversy. What taxes do you and your family pay? What do your tax dollars pay for? Why is taxation necessary? Do you trust your representative to make decisions about taxing and spending your money? Explain your reasons.

Making Decisions About Taxes

GUIDING QUESTION *What role does Congress play in raising money?*

Passing laws to raise and spend money is one of the most important jobs Congress has. The government could not operate without money to carry out its programs and provide services. The national government gets most of its revenues from taxes. **Taxes** are money that people and businesses pay to support the government. The Constitution states:

> **PRIMARY SOURCE**
> The Congress shall have the power to lay and collect taxes, duties, imposts and excises, to pay the debts and provide for the common defense and general welfare of the United States. . . ."
>
> —Article I, Section 8

House Power Over Revenue Bills The Constitution gives the House of Representatives the exclusive power to start all bills that deal with revenue. Almost all important work on tax laws occurs in the House Ways and Means Committee, which decides whether to go along with presidential requests for tax cuts or increases and makes the numerous rules and regulations that determine who will pay how much tax. Some of these rulings are very simple, while others are more complex. The Ways and Means Committee, for example, influences how much of a tax deduction parents are allowed on their income tax for each child living at home. It also decides what kind of tax benefit businesses can claim for building new factories.

The committee's tax bills are usually debated on the House floor under a **closed rule**, which forbids members from offering any amendments to a bill from the floor. This rule means that only members of the Ways and Means Committee have a direct hand in writing a tax bill. Regardless of political party, supporters of a bill prefer a closed rule in order to speed the bill to passage. By contrast, opponents want an **open rule**, which permits floor debate and the addition of amendments to the bill. Such debate and amendments give opponents the chance to stop a bill or weaken its chances of success.

In recent Congresses, the leaders of both parties have brought almost every tax measure to the floor under closed or effectively closed rules. Other House members have largely accepted this procedure on tax bills for several reasons. House leaders claim that tax bills are too complicated to be easily understood outside the committee and that tax legislation is often controversial and usually involves highly complex deals arranged between the Ways and Means Committee and powerful special interest groups. Representatives who were not part of crafting these deals could upset them with floor amendments that derail the legislation. Such members might also come under great pressure from powerful special interest groups.

The Senate Role in Tax Laws All tax bills start in the House. Article I, Section 7, of the Constitution, however, says, "The Senate may propose . . . amendments. . . ." This provision gives the Senate the authority to amend tax bills passed by the House, which is why many people view the Senate as the place where special interest groups are able to get tax provisions they oppose taken out of a House bill.

In the Senate, the Committee on Finance has primary responsibility for tax matters. Like the House Ways and Means Committee, this committee is exceptionally powerful. Although the Senate Finance Committee has subcommittees, the full committee does most of the work. This makes the committee chair an extremely important figure.

tax the money that people and businesses pay to support the activities of the government

closed rule rule that forbids members of Congress to offer amendments to a bill from the floor

open rule rule that permits floor debate and the addition of amendments to the bill

GRAPH

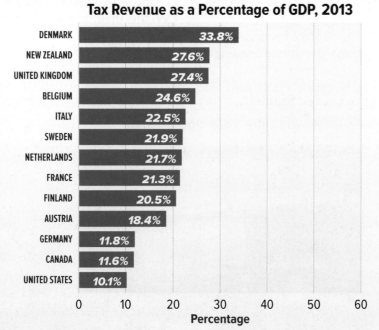

Tax Revenue as a Percentage of GDP, 2013

Country	Percentage
DENMARK	33.8%
NEW ZEALAND	27.6%
UNITED KINGDOM	27.4%
BELGIUM	24.6%
ITALY	22.5%
SWEDEN	21.9%
NETHERLANDS	21.7%
FRANCE	21.3%
FINLAND	20.5%
AUSTRIA	18.4%
GERMANY	11.8%
CANADA	11.6%
UNITED STATES	10.1%

Source: The World Bank, World Development Indicators, *Tax Revenue (% of GDP)*

Use the bar graph to compare the taxes paid by the United States and twelve other industrialized nations as a percentage of GDP.

◀ **CRITICAL THINKING**
Analyzing Countries in which people pay more in taxes also tend to have stronger support systems. What American economic belief works against such a system?

In the Senate, no closed rule exists, and tax bills often do become collections of amendments. Similar to appropriations bills, many tax bills become magnets for amendments dealing with particular interests in the members' states.

☑ **READING PROGRESS CHECK**

Understanding Relationships What role does the House of Representatives play in proposing revenue bills? What role does the Senate play?

Spending Money

GUIDING QUESTION *What role does Congress play in spending money?*

Besides passing revenue bills, Congress has another important power over government spending. The power of **appropriation**, or approval of government spending, belongs to Congress. In Article I, Section 9, the Constitution states, "No money shall be drawn from the Treasury, but in **consequence** of appropriations made by law." Thus, Congress must pass laws to appropriate money for the federal government. Congress must approve spending before the departments and agencies of the executive branch can actually spend money.

How Congress Appropriates Money Congress follows a two-step procedure in appropriating money—an authorization bill and an appropriations bill. Suppose Congress considers a bill to build recreational facilities in inner cities. The first step in the legislative process is an **authorization bill**, which sets up a federal program and specifies how much money can be used for it. For example, the law has a provision limiting the amount of money that can be spent to $30 million per year. The recreation bill also states that the Department of Housing and Urban Development (HUD) will administer the program. HUD, however, does not yet actually have any money to carry out the program.

The second step in the appropriations process comes when HUD requests that Congress provide the $30 million it authorized. Congress does this with an **appropriations bill**, a legislative grant of money to pay for a government program. Appropriations committees decide how much to actually give an agency or program. HUD's request for the $30 million will be only one small item in the multibillion-dollar budget HUD will send to Congress for that year. HUD's budget, in turn, will be part of the president's total annual budget for the executive branch.

Each year the president presents a proposed budget to Congress. The appropriations committees create their own appropriations bills. Congress might decide to grant HUD only $15 million to carry out the building program; in the following year, HUD would need to request another appropriation in order to continue the program.

appropriation approval of government spending

consequence something produced by a cause or action

authorization bill a bill that sets up a federal program and specifies how much money may be appropriated for the program

appropriations bill a proposed law to authorize spending money

Congress must pass an appropriations bill in order to provide relief to communities that are victims of natural disasters.

▶ **CRITICAL THINKING**

Exploring Issues Why might it be difficult for Congress to pass a bill to distribute aid to victims of a national disaster, even though the situation is an emergency?

Patsy Lynch/FEMA

Congressional Hearing Simulation

A bill has been introduced in the U.S. House to cut the federal budget by doing away with public funding of presidential campaigns. That funding is provided by taxpayers who voluntarily agree that $3 of their federal taxes should go into the presidential campaign fund. Candidates who take federal funds agree to certain limitations on their spending. The bill has been referred to the House Ways and Means Committee, which deals with all tax-related legislation.

Arguments for a presidential campaign fund	Arguments against a presidential campaign fund
The idea behind public financing is to limit the role of private money and the possibility for corruption that accompanies private donations. Supporters also believe it can equalize the resources available to candidates and allow candidates to spend more time getting their ideas, rather than raising money.	Several recent candidates have not accepted public funds. They have been able to raise more money from private sources than they could get from the public financing system. Third-party or independent candidates have difficulty accessing the funds. Doing away with public campaign financing would allow the taxes set aside for that purpose to be used to support other programs.

EXPLORING THE ESSENTIAL QUESTION

Simulating You will be taking part in a simulated committee hearing on the bill. Some students in your class will play the roles of committee members; others will be witnesses who testify on the bill.

- **Witnesses** If you are testifying, decide whether you support or oppose the bill. Prepare a two-minute statement advocating for that position. When you begin to testify, clearly state your position. Then give evidence and arguments to support your view. Finish your statement by restating your position and asking committee members to vote with your position.
- **Committee Members** If you are a member of the committee, develop questions to ask the witnesses. After all the witnesses have testified, you will vote with other committee members, explain which testimony was most persuasive, and clarify the reason for your vote.

In a Congress where the majorities in the House and Senate are controlled by different parties, the two may not be able to agree on appropriations bills. The alternative is for Congress to pass **continuing resolutions** that will keep the government open and operating under previous levels of appropriations. Even if the recreation facilities have been authorized, the funding for it may not be included in the continuing resolution.

continuing resolution a resolution that keeps the government open and operating under the previous level of appropriation during times when Congress cannot agree on a new appropriation

The Appropriations Committees The House and the Senate have committees dedicated to appropriations bills. These committees have a powerful influence on government agencies' budgets. Both the House and Senate appropriations committees have 12 subcommittees covering the same policy areas. Thus, the same appropriations subcommittees in both chambers would review the HUD budget, including its recreational facility program. Every year, department heads and program directors answer questions about their budgets in hearings of the appropriations subcommittees. These officials explain why they need the money they have requested. Each year, officials must return to Congress to request the money they need to operate in the coming year. In this way, lawmakers become familiar with federal programs.

Appropriations subcommittees often develop close relationships with certain agencies and tend to favor them in appropriating funds. Powerful special interest groups also try to exercise influence with the appropriations subcommittees. For example, a private aeronautics firm might try to influence an appropriations subcommittee so that the Defense Department has money in its budget to have a certain kind of aircraft built.

Earmarks Members of Congress can specify that some part of a funding bill will go toward a certain purpose in their state or congressional district. These are known as **earmarks**. Sometimes earmarks are included in the text of a bill, but many earmarks appear only in the committee reports explaining a measure. An earmark might say that as part of a much larger general appropriations bill, $490,000 will be set aside for the Los Angeles County Fire Museum.

Critics see earmarks as allowing members of Congress to direct money to pet projects or to satisfy their constituents. Further, they argue that earmarks increase federal spending and add to the national debt. Others defend earmarks. One member said earmarks are acceptable because they allow Congress to direct the spending of funds. Otherwise, she said, "the [executive] agencies allocate the dollars rather than members of Congress."

In recent years, there have been many attempts to reform earmarks. Information about earmark requests is now widely available to the public. In March 2008 Congress defeated a proposal to put a one-year moratorium on earmarks. Since then, leaders from both parties in the House and Senate have voluntarily implemented several **strategies** to limit earmarks. For example, starting with the 110th Congress, lawmakers were required to post all earmark requests on their websites and sign a letter (then put online) stating they and their spouses have no financial interest in the request.

Uncontrollable Expenditures The House and Senate appropriations committees do not have a voice in all current federal government spending. Earlier legislation, such as the laws establishing Medicare, represents about 70 percent of federal spending each year. Since the government is already committed to these expenditures, neither the president nor the Congress can alter them without a change in the law. Economists call these expenses *uncontrollables*. Such required spending includes interest on the national debt and federal contracts that are already in force. Some of these expenditures are known as **entitlements** because they are social programs that entitle individuals to a certain program or monetary benefits—veterans' pensions and Social Security payments, for example, are entitlements.

earmark part of a funding bill that will go toward a certain purpose

strategy a plan or method for achieving a goal

entitlement a required government expenditure that continues from one year to the next

☑ **READING PROGRESS CHECK**

Defining What is an appropriations committee? How does it relate to Congress's role in spending money?

LESSON 2 REVIEW

Reviewing Vocabulary
1. *Contrasting* What is the difference between a closed rule and an open rule?

Using Your Graphic Organizer
2. *Summarizing* Write a paragraph explaining the roles of the House and the Senate in taxing.

Answering the Guiding Questions
3. *Expressing* What role does Congress play in raising money?

4. *Specifying* What role does Congress play in spending money?

Writing About Government
5. *Informative/Explanatory* Research the major categories of revenues and expenditures in the current federal budget. Find out what amounts of money the government plans to raise and spend in each category. Based on what you learned, write a report explaining the priorities of the federal government. You may want to include charts and graphs to illustrate your report.

National Federation of Independent Business v Sebelius (2012)

FACTS OF THE CASE In 2010 Congress passed the Patient Protection and Affordable Care Act. This law included several components designed to make health insurance more available and to reduce the costs of health insurance and health care. One of these components required almost all Americans to maintain a minimum level of health insurance. Anyone who didn't have the minimum level of insurance would have to pay a penalty (except for people below a certain income level), starting in 2014. The law also prohibited insurance companies from denying coverage to sick people and from charging them more than others in their communities.

Individuals and several states sued, arguing that Congress did not have the constitutional power to require individuals to buy health insurance. The federal government said that Congress had the power to pass the law under the Commerce Clause, which allows Congress to regulate interstate commerce. Opponents of the law argued that choosing not to purchase health insurance is a noneconomic, intrastate activity.

Under the Commerce Clause, can Congress require individuals to purchase health insurance?

OPINION A We rule for the federal government—the Affordable Care Act is constitutional. Under the Commerce Clause, Congress may regulate "activities that substantially affect interstate commerce." The health care market is huge and nationwide. The decision not to buy health insurance is a form of economic activity. Almost all Americans will inevitably need medical services at some point in their lives, and hospitals are required to treat sick people, even when they cannot pay.

As a group, uninsured people consume and cannot pay for billions of dollars' worth of health care every year. The costs of that unpaid care are shifted onto the rest of society and have a substantial effect on interstate commerce.

Upholding this law will not allow Congress to force people to buy other things. Buying health insurance is a unique economic activity. Everyone consumes health care, but no one knows when and how much they will need.

OPINION B We rule that the requirement that Americans purchase health insurance is unconstitutional. This law is not regulating people who are engaged in commerce. It is forcing people to engage in commerce against their will. People who do not have health insurance are not engaging in economic activity.

If this law were upheld, there would be no limit on Congress's Commerce Clause power. If Congress can force people to buy insurance, it could force people to buy anything. Whether we buy something will always affect the national market for things, so Congress could use the same logic to force individuals to purchase cars to improve the auto industry.

The states are traditionally responsible for protecting the health and safety of their citizens, and that division of powers is designed to limit the federal government's ability to interfere with issues central to individual liberty.

EXPLORING THE ESSENTIAL QUESTION

Evaluating Read each of the two sample opinions in this case. First, explain how this case illustrates the question of how powers should be divided among different levels of government. Next, decide which opinion you think should be the majority (winning) opinion and which one you think should be the dissenting opinion. Explain your choice.

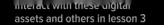

(l to r) U.S. Marine Corps photo by Sgt. Alvin D. Parson; ©ImageState/age fotostock; Win McNamee/Getty Images News/Getty Images; Library of Congress Prints and Photographs Division [LC-DIG-ggbain-23837]

Reading Help Desk

Academic Vocabulary

- aware
- contribute

Content Vocabulary

- interest group
- lobbyist
- lobbying

TAKING NOTES:

Key Ideas and Details

CATEGORIZING Use the graphic organizer to record who and what influences Congress.

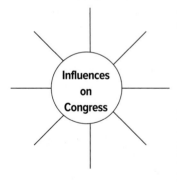

Influences on Congress

LESSON 3

Influencing Congress

ESSENTIAL QUESTION

What factors influence congressional decision making?

Imagine you are a U.S. Representative. Before being elected to public office, you were a research scientist. A member of your party has proposed a bill about genetically modified foods, which are foods that have been genetically engineered for human consumption. Many other members of your party plan to vote in favor of it, and a majority of your constituents support the bill. However, your experience as a scientist tells you this bill is not a good idea. Several of your scientific colleagues have e-mailed or texted you asking you to oppose the bill.

- What will you do? Will you vote for the bill because your constituents support it or vote against it because your own knowledge tells you it is bad policy? Would it matter if your party strongly supported the bill? What if an interest group that contributed to your campaign supported the bill?

- Whatever you decide, some people will be unhappy with you. What steps would you take to explain your vote and minimize conflict? Below are some options, but you may have better ideas of your own:

  ○ Hold town meetings in your district to gather views and inform people about the issue.

  ○ Send out a newsletter explaining your vote.

  ○ Hold a press conference to explain your vote.

Influences on Lawmakers

GUIDING QUESTION *Who influences members of Congress?*

Members of Congress make hard decisions every day. They decide which policies they will support and when to yield to political pressure from their constituents, their party, or the president. They must also decide when to make speeches explaining their views. In a single session, members may cast votes on a thousand issues. Their speeches and actions influence government policy and shape the public's views on bills and issues before Congress. What are the forces that influence lawmakers?

A great many factors influence how a lawmaker votes. One is the lawmaker's personal temperament. Some members are more willing to compromise for the "sake of the greater good"; others stick to their original positions as a matter of principle. Some leaders are more willing to take risks; others might "play it safe" or follow their party leaders. The nature of the issue also plays a role in how a lawmaker votes. For example, on a controversial issue, such as gun control, lawmakers might adhere closely to the positions of the voters back home or of their party, no matter what their own personal beliefs may be. On an issue that has little direct effect on their constituents, however, lawmakers tend to rely on their own beliefs or the advice of other lawmakers or experts they trust.

Congressional staffers also influence decisions. Staffers research issues and present them to members of Congress prior to a meeting, hearing, or vote. In addition, staffers set their member's daily calendar, which means they influence who he or she will meet with and which committee meetings the member attends. They may also influence which issues a member chooses to present or comment on in committee meetings.

Many factors affect lawmakers' decisions. They are especially attuned to the concerns of their constituents, who will cast votes to reelect or defeat them. They usually try to align themselves with their party's position on the issues. They may be influenced by appeals from the president. They also hear from special interest groups seeking their support.

☑ READING PROGRESS CHECK

Discussing What are the major influences on members of Congress? How do those influences affect how they vote?

The Influence of Voters

GUIDING QUESTION *How do voters influence members of Congress?*

The political careers of all lawmakers depend upon how the voters back home feel about the lawmaker's job performance. Only very unusual lawmakers would regularly vote against the wishes of the people in their home states or districts.

What Voters Expect Experienced lawmakers know that their constituents expect them to pay a great deal of attention to their needs. Voters usually expect their representatives to put the needs of their district ahead of nationwide needs. But what if a conflict arises between what the lawmaker thinks is needed and what constituents want? In a national opinion survey, most people still said their lawmaker should "follow what people in the district want."

It is not surprising that most members' votes often reflect their constituents' opinions. Especially on issues that affect constituents' daily lives, such as civil rights and social welfare, lawmakers usually go along with voter preferences. In contrast, on issues where constituents have less information or interest, such as foreign affairs, lawmakers often make up their own minds.

Despite the fact that voters have said that they want and expect their representatives to follow their wishes, most voters do not take the time to find out how members actually vote. Voters may not even be **aware** of all the issues lawmakers are considering. Why, then, do voting records count in a reelection?

aware knowing

Sometimes, local and national interests collide. Addressing a national problem may create health, safety, or economic problems at the state and local levels. Think about how you would respond to the following situations as a representative of your state in Congress.

a. The United States needs somewhere to dispose of waste from nuclear power plants. Experts say the site will be completely safe. It will not threaten public health. But people cannot help worrying. The proposed disposal site is in your state, about 200 miles from where you live.

b. Worldwide opinion about the United States would improve if the prison at Guantanamo Bay, Cuba, were closed. The president has proposed moving ten of the remaining suspected terrorists at the prison to a federal penitentiary in your state.

c. The U.S. debt is huge. To get the debt under control, all government agencies must reduce spending. The Defense Department has proposed closing several large military bases. One base is located in your community. You and many of your friends have civilian jobs on the base.

Was your response to these dilemmas different when you thought as a member of Congress? Should it be? Can you think of a strategy for dealing with problems that put national and local/state interests in conflict?

The answer is that in an election campaign, candidates will bring up their opponent's record and may demand that their opponent explain the votes that turned out to be unpopular. A good example of this is congressional support for the Iraq war. In October 2002, by a margin of roughly two-to-one, Congress passed a joint resolution to authorize military force against Iraq. When support for the war faded, Hillary Clinton, a Democratic presidential candidate in the 2008 primaries, had to defend her Iraq vote many times on the campaign trail. The opposite is also true: If a legislator has voted for measures important to some group, he or she will remind those voters about that during a campaign.

In this way, campaigns inform voters about their representative's voting record. Lawmakers know this will happen. Thus, well before they run for reelection, they work to find out what voters back home are concerned about.

Visits to the District Most lawmakers use several methods to try to keep track of their constituents' opinions. One method is making frequent trips home to learn the local voters' concerns. Senators and representatives make dozens of trips to their home districts each year. During their visits, they try to speak with as many voters as possible about issues of concern.

Messages From Home Lawmakers also pay attention to the messages pouring into their offices every day. Staff members screen the mail to learn what issues concern voters most—for example, the closing of a plant in a community would probably get a lawmaker's attention.

Not all messages carry equal weight. Lawmakers are usually interested only in messages from their constituents or from special interest groups relevant to their district or state. The form of the message is also important. Phone calls and meetings with staff members or lawmakers are usually very effective. For many years, personal letters were one of the best ways to make one's point of view known. Now, however, all mail and packages sent through the U.S. Postal Service or other delivery services must pass through a strict X-ray security process; this screening process can take months. Because of increased security and the speed and ease of use of electronic communications, most people today use e-mail to send written comments or requests to their representatives in Congress.

Surveys Many lawmakers send questionnaires to their constituents asking for their opinions on various issues. Increasingly, lawmakers use websites and e-mail to get feedback on key issues. Before an election, lawmakers will often hire professional pollsters to conduct opinion surveys on issues.

Key Supporters Finally, all lawmakers pay close attention to the ideas of their rain-or-shine supporters—people who regularly work in their campaigns and **contribute** money to win their reelection. As one lawmaker put it, "Everybody needs some groups which are strongly for him." These supporters also help lawmakers keep in touch with events back home.

✅ **READING PROGRESS CHECK**

Listing How do members of Congress keep in contact with their constituents?

The Influence of Parties

GUIDING QUESTION *How do political parties influence members of Congress?*

Almost every member of Congress is either a Republican or a Democrat. Both political parties take stands on major issues and come out for or against certain legislation. Party identification is one of the most important influences

contribute to give or supply in company with others

on a lawmaker's voting behavior. Knowing which political party a member belongs to often predicts how he or she will vote.

Party Voting Both Democrats and Republicans tend to vote with their parties. While party unity scores vary from year to year, in both parties and in both houses, members of Congress voted with their party more than 80 percent of the time. However, party voting is much stronger on some issues than others. On economic issues, for example, party members tend to vote together; party voting is also strong on social welfare issues. It is usually weaker on foreign policy because the parties do not often have fixed positions in this area.

The Importance of Parties Why do parties often vote together? The obvious answer is that party members tend to share the same political outlook. As a group, Democrats are more likely to favor social welfare programs, job programs, tax laws that help people with lower incomes, and government regulation of business. In general, Republicans are likely to support lower taxes, less social welfare spending, less business regulation, and limited intervention in the economy.

Another reason for party voting is that many lawmakers do not have strong opinions on every issue. Since they cannot know enough to make informed decisions on every bill, they will get advice from party members.

On some issues, party leaders put pressure on members to vote according to the party position. If the president is of the same party, a party leader will urge members to support the president's program. Likewise, leaders of the opposing party often vote against the president's program and seek to make their opposition a political issue. The party leaders, the Senate majority

---

We the People: Making a Difference

JEANNETTE RANKIN

Jeannette Rankin did not follow the crowd. Born in Montana in 1880, the oldest of 11 children, she graduated from college in 1902 and pursued several careers before becoming involved in the movement to give women the right to vote. In 1916 she became the first woman elected to Congress. Just four days after taking office, Rankin voted against U.S. entry into World War I, saying "I want to stand by my country, but I cannot vote for war."

The vote against the war cost Rankin her seat in Congress. Before the next election, Montana redrew its congressional districts, and Rankin was placed in a heavily Democratic district (she was a Republican). She launched a race for the Senate but was defeated.

Rankin won election to Congress in 1940; by this time, there were six women in the House. Once again, however, her antiwar views meant her career would not be a long one. Following the Japanese attack on Pearl Harbor, Rankin was the only member of the House who voted against the declaration of war, saying, "As a woman I can't go to war, and I refuse to send anyone else." Knowing she would be defeated, Rankin chose not to run for reelection.

◀ CRITICAL THINKING
1. *Evaluating* What one adjective would you choose to describe Rankin's decision? Explain why you picked that descriptor.
2. *Identifying Perspectives* What was the greatest influence on Rankin when she cast her votes on U.S. entry into World Wars I and II?

PARTY UNITY SCORES

Members of Congress tend to vote with their party more than 80 percent of the time.

▶ CRITICAL THINKING

1. Identifying Which party has generally been more unified in the House of Representatives?

2. Interpreting Why do you think unity scores have risen in the past decade?

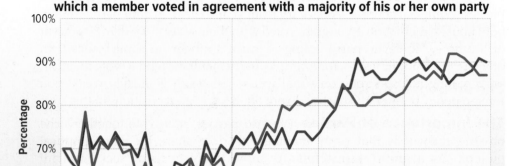

Average House unity scores: Percentage of House party unity votes on which a member voted in agreement with a majority of his or her own party

- ■ Republicans
- ■ Democrats

leader, and the Speaker of the House usually use the power of persuasion and work hard to influence lawmakers to support the party's position. Gaining party members' support is one of the main jobs of a party leader. Very few issues are unaffected by party identity.

☑ READING PROGRESS CHECK

Predicting How does knowing which political party a member of Congress belongs to often serve as a predictor of how he or she will vote?

Other Influences on Congress

GUIDING QUESTION *How do the president and interest groups influence members of Congress?*

Other than voter preferences and parties, there are two other influences on Congress—the president and various interest groups.

The Influence of the President Every president tries to influence Congress to pass the bills he or she supports. Some presidents work harder than others at this task—and some are more successful in getting programs passed.

Members of Congress often complain that presidents have more ways to influence legislation and policy than they do. Through White House speeches or television appearances, the president has the best stage for influencing public opinion. In 1990, for example, when Iraq invaded the small nation of Kuwait, President George H.W. Bush sent U.S. troops to nearby Saudi Arabia. A military buildup followed as the U.S. government tried to force Iraq out of Kuwait. The president frequently expressed his belief that military action against Iraq was necessary. With public support growing, Congress did vote for military action in the Persian Gulf. In the spring, summer, and fall of 2009, President Obama worked hard to rally public opinion and support in Congress around his proposal called The Patient Protection and Affordable Care Act. It was passed by Congress in 2010. However, at the time, Obama had substantial Democratic majorities in Congress. The law was passed without a single Republican vote in either the House or Senate.

Presidents can also influence individual members of Congress by supporting or opposing their legislative goals. In the 1960s, for example, Senator Frank Church of Idaho criticized President Lyndon Johnson's conduct of the Vietnam War. To support his viewpoint, Church showed President Johnson a newspaper column written by journalist Walter Lippmann criticizing the war. "All right," Johnson said, "the next time you need a dam for Idaho, you go ask Walter Lippmann."

The Influence of Interest Groups The paid representatives of **interest groups**, called **lobbyists**, are another important influence on Congress. Lobbyists try to convince members of Congress to support policies favored by the groups they represent. Their efforts to persuade officials to support their points of view are called **lobbying**. The largest and most powerful lobbying groups have their own buildings and full-time professional staffs in the nation's capital.

Lobbyists represent a wide variety of interests such as business and environmental organizations, labor unions, doctors, lawyers, education groups, and minority groups. Some lobbyists work for groups that sometimes form to support or to oppose a specific issue or short-term concern.

Lobbyists use many methods to influence members of Congress. They draft legislation and give it to lawmakers or their staff and offer lawmakers data and case studies on policies they support or oppose. They visit lawmakers in their offices or in the lobbies of the Capitol to try to persuade them to support their positions. They encourage citizens to contact members of Congress on the issues they favor or oppose. Lobbyists also use advertising to persuade people and leaders, and they help generate publicity and media coverage for their causes.

Interest groups and lobbyists also focus their attention on congressional committees. For example, farm groups concentrate their attention on influencing the committees responsible for laws on agriculture. Labor unions focus their effort on committees dealing with labor legislation and the economy. Lobbying represents freedom of speech in a very basic form—speaking out for the political interests of a group of like-minded people. The Constitution guarantees free speech as well as the right to petition—to ask your elected official to represent your views. Congress depends on information that lobbyists provide, and many groups have legitimate reasons for lobbying Congress. Lobbyists are often experts on specific policy matters, whereas members of Congress and their staff have to know about many issues.

Is it legitimate for a former senator or representative, or a former congressional staff member, to try to lobby Congress? When senators or representatives retire or are defeated for reelection, many of them become congressional lobbyists. So do veteran staff members of the Senate and House. This raises complaints about a "revolving door" by which former members can use their past friendships and privileges to gain special access to Congress. As a result, Congress has created a "cooling off" period in which members, staff, and former executive branch officials are prohibited from lobbying the government. These regulations aim to prevent corruption and the abuse of power.

interest group a group of people who share common goals and organize to influence government and policy

lobbyist a paid representative of an interest group who contacts government officials on behalf of these interest groups

lobbying direct contact made by lobbyists to persuade government officials to support the policies their interest groups favor

Lobbyists try to persuade members of Congress to support policies favored by the groups they represent.

▼ CRITICAL THINKING
Assessing Should lobbying be banned from politics? Why or why not?

Win McNamee/Getty Images News/Getty Images

Evaluating What types of regulations would control corruption related to lobbying? That has been a subject of much discussion on Capitol Hill and beyond. Which of the following regulations would you support?

a. Banning all paid lobbying

b. Banning anyone who benefits from government funding from lobbying

c. Requiring all paid lobbyists to register with the government and to reveal on which issues they are lobbying and how much they are being paid

d. Preventing lobbyists from giving members of Congress and their staffs any gifts worth more than $40

e. Mandating that earmarks be identified in all spending bills

f. Preventing groups that lobby from contributing to political campaigns

g. Banning lobbyists from hosting events at political parties' conventions

h. Prohibiting former members of Congress and their staffs from lobbying Congress for one or two years after they leave their jobs on the Hill

The House of Representatives prohibits its former members from making any appearance of communication with the intent to influence the legislative branch for a year after they leave office. The Senate extends that ban to two years. Likewise, former members of the executive branch cannot lobby executive agencies for a year after they leave the agency. But executive branch officials face no restriction on lobbying Congress.

Former lawmakers and staff have experience and expertise in dealing with legislative matters that make them effective lobbyists. But critics have complained about the "cozy relationships" that develop between legislators and lobbyists. The ethics laws seek to avoid the appearance of improper behavior and special privilege without excluding former members from lobbying the institution where they once served.

Political Action Committees As the cost of campaigning for Congress has increased, members of Congress and their challengers spend a great deal of time and effort raising campaign funds. Lobbyists are large contributors both to individual candidates and to political action committees (PACs).

PACs are political fund-raising organizations established by corporations, labor unions, and other special interests and ideological groups. They can donate money to individual candidates and to party organizations. PACs use the money they raise to support those lawmakers who agree with their specific positions on certain issues.

After the Supreme Court struck down many restrictions on PACs in 2010 in the case *Citizens United* v. *Federal Election Commission*, a new type of "super" PAC emerged that has no limits on the sources of funds it can raise. These SuperPACs do not contribute to candidates or parties but run their own advertisements, by mail or through the media. While they cannot support or oppose any specific candidate, they can raise issues that clearly favor one side or another in any political debate.

✓ **READING PROGRESS CHECK**

Defining What is a lobbyist? How do lobbyists attempt to influence members of Congress?

LESSON 3 REVIEW

Reviewing Vocabulary

1. *Making Inferences* What is lobbying and why does the term have negative connotations?

Using Your Graphic Organizer

2. *Interpreting Significance* Use your completed graphic organizer to create two rankings of the influences on Congress. For the first, explain which influences you think are the most to the least important in affecting members and their priorities. For the second, explain which influences you think should be the most to the least important in affecting members and their priorities.

Answering the Guiding Questions

3. *Stating* Who influences members of Congress?

4. *Discussing* How do voters influence members of Congress?

5. *Explaining* How do political parties influence members of Congress?

6. *Examining* How do the president and interest groups influence members of Congress?

Writing About Government

7. *Informative/Explanatory* Choose an interest group whose goals you support. Then conduct Internet research to learn more about the group's purpose and activities. Write a report summarizing how the group attempts to influence legislators.

LESSON 4
Helping Constituents

Interact with these digital assets and others in lesson 4

✓ **PARTICIPATING IN YOUR GOVERNMENT**
E-Mailing Your Representative or Senator

✓ **SELF-CHECK QUIZ**

✓ **STUDENT VOICES**
Arlys Endres Raises the Statue

✓ **VIDEO**
Spending Bill

netw⊙rks
TRY IT YOURSELF ONLINE

Reading Help Desk

Academic Vocabulary

- involve
- source
- assign

Content Vocabulary

- casework
- pork-barrel legislation
- logrolling

TAKING NOTES:

Key Ideas and Details

LISTING Use the graphic organizer to list the nonlegislative duties of Congress.

Nonlegislative Duties

ESSENTIAL QUESTION

What factors influence congressional decision making?

Imagine you work for a senator and part of your job involves reading requests from constituents and responding to them appropriately. You quickly learn that some requests and responses are very complicated, while others can easily be handled in a standard reply. You also learn that some requests are strange or misguided—often from people who do not understand what is or is not a government issue. Alternatively, they may not understand what requests should be directed to city or state officials, who can better handle the problem.

Read the list of requests below. Should the senator's office help this person? If not, can you suggest someone who could?

1. Dear Sir, I'm offended by the inappropriate things that get broadcast on television these days. Can't you do anything about it?

2. Dear Madam, My garbage did not get picked up today. Can you take care of it?

3. Dear Senator, My niece is missing in a foreign country. We think she has been arrested, but no one can tell us what she is charged with or where she is. Can you help?

4. Dear Senator, I have been waiting for my IRS refund for 13 months. They are not returning my calls or e-mails. Can you help?

5. Dear Senator, Can I work in your office as an intern this summer?

Handling Problems

GUIDING QUESTION *How do members of Congress help their constituents?*

Veteran lawmakers have described three elements to representation in Congress. The most obvious is passing or opposing legislation. The second is educating the public—particularly their constituents—on what the issues are. Third, they have a duty of advocacy, to plead their constituents' interests.

casework the work a lawmaker does to help constituents with problems

involve to engage as a participant

Advocacy often consumes a great deal of the members' personal and staff attention. These can be issues as large as an appeal from a mayor for help in getting federal funds to replace a decaying bridge to a single person seeking help in getting a veterans' benefit that has become stalled somewhere in the government bureaucracy.

Lawmakers have learned that they are expected to do more in Congress for their constituents than debate great issues. To be reelected, they must spend much of their time solving problems for voters who had difficulties with federal agencies. They must also make sure their district or state gets its share of federal money for projects such as new post offices, highways, and contracts.

These nonlegislative duties are not new, but as the national electorate has grown they have become a very time-consuming part of a lawmaker's job. However, these duties can be very satisfying. As one senator commented, "It does make a difference when you walk down the street and have someone come up, recognize you, and say, 'You helped.'"

Helping constituents with problems is called **casework**, and all lawmakers today are **involved** with it. One House member put it this way: "Rightly or wrongly, we have become the link between the frustrated citizen and the very involved federal government in citizens' lives. . . . We continually use more and more of our staff time to handle citizens' complaints."

Many Different Requests Lawmakers respond to thousands of requests from voters for help in dealing with executive agencies. Here are some typical requests: A soldier would like the Army to move him to a base close to home because his parents are ill; a local businessperson claims the Federal Trade Commission (FTC) is treating her business unfairly and she wants to meet with top FTC officials; a veteran has had his GI life insurance policy canceled by a government agency, which states that the veteran failed to fill out a certain form (the veteran says he never got the form); a new high school graduate wants help in finding a government job in Washington.

Many lawmakers complain that voters claim to want less government in their lives, but, in fact, they demand more and more from their representatives. Sometimes voters make unreasonable requests or ask for help a lawmaker is unwilling to deliver. A representative from New York, for example, was asked to fix a speeding ticket; another member received a call from a constituent asking what the lawmaker was going to do about the shortage of snow shovels at a local hardware store during a blizzard.

Who Handles Casework All lawmakers have staff members called caseworkers to handle constituent problems. Most caseworkers live and work in the lawmaker's congressional district. This makes the caseworkers more accessible to constituents. Usually, the caseworkers can handle the requests on their own—the problem can be solved simply by having a caseworker clarify matters with the agency involved. At other times, however, the senator or representative may need to become directly involved.

Purposes of Casework Why do lawmakers spend so much time on casework? Casework serves three important purposes. Perhaps most importantly, it helps get lawmakers reelected. "I learned soon after coming to Washington," a Missouri legislator once said, "that it was just as important to get a certain document for somebody back home as for some European diplomat—really, more important, because that little guy back home votes."

As a result, many lawmakers actually look for casework. One lawmaker, for example, regularly sent invitations to almost 7,000 voters in his district asking them to bring their problems to a town meeting that his staff runs. Today legislators may encourage voters to visit their websites and communicate with them by e-mail. In addition, many representatives have vans that staff members drive through their districts as mobile offices to keep watch on problems back home.

Second, casework is one way Congress monitors the performance of the executive branch. Casework brings problems with federal programs to the attention of Congress. Through casework, lawmakers and their staffs can better understand how well executive agencies handle such federal programs as Social Security and veterans' benefits. These types of programs are very important to constituents.

Third, helping voters with problems is part of what lawmakers are supposed to do. Casework provides a way for the average citizen to navigate the huge national government and the attendant bureaucracy. Before the national government grew so large, most citizens with a problem turned to their local politicians—called ward heelers—for help. Sam Rayburn, a former long-time lawmaker and Speaker of the House, explained, "In the old days, you had the ward heeler who cemented himself in the community by taking care of everyone. Now the Congressman plays the role of ward heeler—wending his way through bureaucracy, helping to cut through red tape and confusion."

✓ **READING PROGRESS CHECK**

Explaining What is casework? What purpose does it serve?

PARTICIPATING
(IN) Your Government

E-Mailing Your Representative or Senator

A fundamental political right is the right to ask your elected officials to work for you—to solve a problem, to vote a certain way, or to explain their actions. Think about what you expect from your representative or senator. Write an e-mail to him or her to: ask what his position is on a particular bill or issue facing Congress (learn about these at www. congress.gov), state your position on an issue or bill and ask her to vote a certain way, or request assistance resolving a personal problem that involves the government. A few points to remember:

1. Address your lawmaker formally, as in *Dear Rep. Matthews,*
2. When possible, try to identify the bill number that concerns you.
3. Present your views succinctly. Remember, if you must disagree, you should still be polite. That will likely be more persuasive.
4. Ask for a response. Include your return e-mail under your signature. Keep in mind that your senator and representative receive thousands of e-mails and calls. They cannot reply to them all personally, so their staff will likely reply to you.

To: Representative Matthews
From: Emily.Harris@anytown.org
Subject: H.R. 1947

Dear Representative Matthews,

My name is Emily Harris, and I am in the twelfth grade at Anytown High School.

I am writing to ask you about your positions on H.R.1947. I hope that you will support this bill. I believe that H.R.1947 will help the people in our district with the problems that we face. I also believe this bill will be beneficial to the country as a whole.

I appreciate your taking the time to consider my request and look forward to hearing your thoughts on this bill.

Sincerely,
Emily Harris
1234 Main Street
Anytown U.S.A.

EXPLORING THE ESSENTIAL QUESTION

When you receive a response, evaluate it. Was the reply timely? Did it answer your question or respond to your specific request? Was the reply clear and well-written? What is the outcome of your communication? Share and describe your experience with your family.

Arlys Endres
"Raises the Statue"

While she is not a lobbyist or a member of a political action committee, Arlys Endres of Phoenix, Arizona, has already made her mark in Congress. In 1996, when she was 10 years old, Endres wrote a school report on suffragist Susan B. Anthony. Endres later discovered that a statue of Anthony and two other famous suffragists was given to Congress in 1921. It was briefly displayed in the Capitol Rotunda but then moved permanently to the first floor below the Rotunda.

"I was furious about this," the precocious girl told an interviewer. She decided to campaign to have the statue moved back to a place of prominence. "If it weren't for her, I wouldn't have the right to vote, the right to hold public office, the right to own property, or the right to keep my children after a divorce."

She discovered that women in the Congress were already working on the issue, but money was needed for the move. Endres mailed at least 2,000 letters and raised almost $2,000. Her efforts also took her to Washington, D.C., to see the statue and speak at a "Raise the Statue" rally.

Her campaign did not go unnoticed by national legislators. The U.S. Congress unanimously voted to reinstall the statue in the Capitol Rotunda in 1996.

"If it weren't for her, I wouldn't have the right to vote. . . "

— Arlys Endres

▲ **CRITICAL THINKING**
Making Connections Do you know anyone in your neighborhood, school, or community who took a stand for something they believed in and communicated with government at any level to advocate for change? Have you similarly advocated for change for something you believe in? How does this advocacy make you feel about the power of a few to make a difference? Explain.

Helping the District or State

GUIDING QUESTION *How do members of Congress help bring federal projects to their districts and states?*

Besides providing constituent services, members try to bring federal projects to their districts and states. They do this in three ways: through legislation that directs spending to their districts and states, by winning federal grants and contracts, and by working to keep existing federal projects.

Public Works Legislation Every year, through public works bills, Congress appropriates billions of dollars for local projects. Examples include post offices, dams, military bases, river improvements, federally funded highways, veterans' hospitals, pollution-treatment centers, and mass-transit system projects.

Public works projects such as these bring jobs and money into a state or district. For example, Senator Robert Byrd's pet project, the Appalachian Regional Commission, oversaw more than a billion dollars' worth of government spending in its first three years. In 1989 Byrd used his position as chair of the Appropriations Committee to relocate federal agencies to his home state of West Virginia. Agencies or divisions of the FBI, CIA, Internal Revenue Service, and even the Coast Guard were moved from Washington to Byrd's state. When Congress passes laws to appropriate money for such local federal projects, it is sometimes called **pork-barrel legislation**. The idea is that a member of Congress has dipped into the "pork barrel," meaning the federal treasury, and pulled out a piece of "fat," a federal project for his or her district. This kind of legislation often draws criticism.

pork-barrel legislation laws that are passed by Congress to appropriate money for local federal projects

More often, lawmakers take the view that if "you scratch my back, I'll scratch yours." They share the belief that getting federal projects for the home state is a key part of their job, so they often help each other. When two or more lawmakers agree to support each other's bills, it is called **logrolling**.

Like many issues in politics, spending is a matter of perspective. What one person considers "pork" another might consider "targeted spending," looking out for the people who elect them, or simply creating or preserving an important project for the whole nation that happens to be in their district.

Grants and Contracts Lawmakers also try to make sure their districts or states get their fair share of the federal grants and contracts that are funded through the national budget. A senator from Colorado put it this way: "If a program is to be established, the state of Colorado should get its fair share."

Federal grants and contracts are very important to lawmakers and their districts or states. These contracts are a vital **source** of money and jobs and can radically affect the economy of a state. Every year, federal agencies like the Department of Defense spend billions of dollars to carry out hundreds of government projects and programs. For example, when the Air Force decided to locate a new project at one of its bases in Utah, almost 1,000 jobs and millions of dollars came into the state. Lawmakers compete for such valuable federal grants and contracts: Several states wanted the Air Force project, but Utah's lawmakers got the prize.

Members of Congress do not vote on grants and contracts as they do on pork-barrel legislation. Instead, executive branch agencies like the Defense Department or the Department of Labor award them. Lawmakers, however, try to influence agency decisions in several ways. They may pressure agency officials to give a favorable hearing to their state's request for a grant or encourage their constituents to write, telephone, or e-mail agency officials with their requests. If problems come up when someone from the state is competing for a grant or contract, lawmakers may step in to help.

Many lawmakers **assign** one or more staffers to act as specialists in this area. These staff members become experts on how individuals, businesses, and local governments can qualify for federal money. They help constituents apply for contracts and grants because the lawmaker wants to make sure they continue to flow to their state or district.

logrolling an agreement by two or more lawmakers to support each other's bills

source origin, point of procurement

assign to appoint to a duty

✔ **READING PROGRESS CHECK**

Applying How does pork-barrel legislation help members of Congress support their states?

LESSON 4 REVIEW

Reviewing Vocabulary
1. *Making Connections* Define pork-barrel legislation and provide at least two examples.

Using Your Graphic Organizer
2. *Summarizing* Use your completed graphic organizer to write a paragraph summarizing the nonlegislative duties of Congress.

Answering the Guiding Questions
3. *Identifying* How do members of Congress help their constituents?

4. *Explaining* How do members of Congress help bring federal projects to their districts and states?

Writing About Government
5. *Argument* Why do lawmakers get involved in casework? What percentage of time do you think lawmakers should devote to casework as compared to their legislative duties? Write an essay defending your point of view.

STUDY GUIDE

HOW A BILL BECOMES LAW
LESSON 1

INTRODUCE
Write bill

Submit bill

Bill given title and number and distributed to lawmakers

COMMITTEE WORK
Rewrite, amend, recommend as is, or kill

Hold hearings

Mark up

Report to full House or Senate

FLOOR ACTION
Debate and amend

Vote

CONFERENCE COMMITTEE
Reconcile differences in versions

Draft final bill and submit to each house for final vote

PRESIDENTIAL ACTION
Sign, veto, or pocket veto

Override requires two-thirds vote of both houses

LAW
Successful bills registered

Unsuccessful bills die

TAX BILLS
LESSON 2

HOUSE
- starts all revenue bills
- Ways and Means Committee shapes bill
- debated on floor under closed rule

SENATE
- offers amendments
- Finance Committee primarily responsible
- debated under open rule

PASSES BOTH HOUSES

TAX LAW

SPENDING BILLS
LESSON 2

AUTHORIZATION BILL → APPROPRIATIONS BILL → SPEND MONEY

ongoing appropriations to continue programs

INFLUENCES ON CONGRESS
LESSON 3

- POLLS
- POLITICAL ACTION COMMITTEES
- PERSONAL BELIEFS AND TEMPERAMENT
- SPECIAL-INTEREST GROUPS
- SURVEYS
- LOBBYISTS
- STAFFERS
- KEY SUPPORTERS
- POLITICAL PARTY
- PRESIDENT
- CONSTITUENTS

needs ← problems ← requests for grants and contracts ← Constituents

HELPING CONSTITUENTS
LESSON 4

Members of Congress → casework → advocacy → issue education → legislation

Directions: On a separate sheet of paper, answer the questions below. Make sure you read carefully and answer all parts of the questions.

Lesson Review

Lesson 1

1 *Differentiating* Which type of congressional resolution has the force of law?

2 *Specifying* When does a committee hold a markup session? What is the purpose of this session?

Lesson 2

3 *Identifying Cause and Effect* In what situation might Congress pass a continuing resolution? What does this resolution do?

4 *Explaining* Why do economists call entitlements "uncontrollable expenditures"?

Lesson 3

5 *Explaining* Most voters are unaware of how their representatives vote, yet representatives still typically vote according to their constituents' wishes. Explain why this is true.

6 *Explaining* Why do members of Congress often vote along party lines?

Lesson 4

7 *Explaining* Why is casework an important part of a lawmaker's job?

8 *Differentiating* How is pork-barrel legislation different from federal grants and contracts?

ANSWERING THE ESSENTIAL QUESTIONS

Review your answers to the introductory questions at the beginning of each lesson. Then answer the following Essential Questions based on what you learned in the chapter. Have your answers changed?

9 *Sequencing* How does a bill become a law?

10 *Explaining* How does the government raise and allocate money?

11 *Analyzing Cause and Effect* What factors influence congressional decision making?

DBQ Interpreting Political Cartoons

Use the political cartoon to answer the following questions.

12 *Making Inferences* What does the ladder in this cartoon represent?

13 *Interpreting Significance* What is the significance of the congressman's statement?

Critical Thinking

14 *Making Inferences* Most of the debate on a bill occurs in committee, not on the House or Senate floor. Why do you think this is so?

15 *Exploring Issues* In recent years, some groups have advocated for reducing the size of government. Explain what this means in terms of taxes and spending and possible effects on government programs and the national debt.

16 *Analyzing* How can a website help members of Congress stay in touch with their constituents?

17 *Interpreting* Former Speaker of the House Tip O'Neill once stated: "All politics is local." What do you think he meant?

Need Extra Help?

If You've Missed Question	1	2	3	4	5	6	7	8	9	10	11	12	13	14	15	16	17
Go to page	201	204	211	212	215	215	222	224	202	208	214	224	224	204	210	216	222

Directions: On a separate sheet of paper, answer the questions below. Make sure you read carefully and answer all parts of the questions.

DBQ Analyzing Primary Sources

Read the excerpt and answer the questions that follow.

PRIMARY SOURCE

"I have long spoken about the broken appropriations process and the corruption it breeds. . . . Just look at the scandals in the last five years alone. Former U.S. Representative Randy Cunningham sits in a Federal penitentiary today for selling earmarks. Among the many bribes Cunningham admitted receiving were . . . Persian rugs, jewelry. . . . In return, he earmarked untold millions of dollars and pressured the Department of Defense to award contracts to his co-conspirators. . . . Now we have multiple pay-to-play scandals unfolding before our eyes. . . . Earmarks breed corruption, pure and simple. . . . So I ask my colleagues, how many more scandals must we suffer before we enact meaningful earmark reform?"

—Senator John McCain, Floor Statement, July 23, 2009

18 ***Identifying Perspectives*** What is Senator McCain's purpose in making this statement?

19 ***Finding the Main Idea*** Why does Senator McCain object to the current earmark system?

20 ***Making Connections*** Based on this passage, describe how earmarks can lead to trouble.

Social Studies Skills

21 ***Defending*** Do research to identify an issue currently before Congress. Then locate news articles that present differing opinions on what Congress should do. Summarize the main points from each point of view. Take a side and explain why this point of view most appeals to you.

22 ***Citizenship*** Imagine that you are part of a local committee that has requested a federal grant to build a park in your area. Write a simulated e-mail to your member of Congress, urging him or her to support the request. Be specific about your vision for the park and why your area needs it.

23 ***Identifying Differing Interpretations*** Consider this statement from the textbook: "What one person considers 'pork' another person might consider ... 'looking out for the people who elect them'. . . ." Is pork-barrel legislation good or bad? Take a position and prepare to defend it in a class debate. Do research to inform your position.

Research and Presentation

24 ***Simulating*** Go to Congress.gov and skim a few simple congressional resolutions to get a sense of topics handled in this type of resolution and the writing style. Then devise a resolution that you would like to see adopted. Use wording similar to that used in the resolutions you skimmed. Be prepared to promote your resolution to the class.

25 ***Using Technology*** Identify a cause or an issue on which you have a strong opinion. Imagine that you are forming an interest group to promote your view on this topic. Look at several interest group websites to see the kinds of information they include. Then design a hypothetical website for your new organization. Use computer software to create the layout for your home page. Create some graphics and links you would include.

Need Extra Help?

If You've Missed Question	18	19	20	21	22	23	24	25
Go to page	212	212	212	203	223	224	201	219

State and Local Legislative Branches

networks

www.connected.mcgraw-hill.com
There's More Online about
state and local legislative branches.

CHAPTER 8

ESSENTIAL QUESTIONS

- How are state and local legislative branches structured?
- How can citizens participate in state and local government?
- How are laws created at the state and local levels?

©Mike Norton/Purestock/SuperStock

▲ The Texas Capitol is the
meeting place for the
legislature of the state
of Texas.

ANALYZING REDISTRICTING

Every ten years, the federal government counts all Americans and records where they live. After each census, political district boundaries must be adjusted so that residents are equally represented no matter where they live. States are responsible for redrawing the district boundaries for the U.S. House of Representatives and the state legislatures. Explore the evidence here about how states draw district boundaries.

PRIMARY SOURCE A

"Whether the way that districts are currently drawn in any given state is good or bad depends on what you believe the goals of the process to be. Some stress objectivity; some independence; some transparency, or equality, or regularity, or other goals entirely. There is ample debate among scholars, activists, and practitioners about the role of political insiders, the nature of protection for minority rights, the degree of partisan competition or partisan inequity, and the ability to preserve established or burgeoning communities."

—Justin Levitt, *A Citizen's Guide to Redistricting,* 2010 Edition, the Brennan Center for Justice, NYU School of Law

SECONDARY SOURCE B

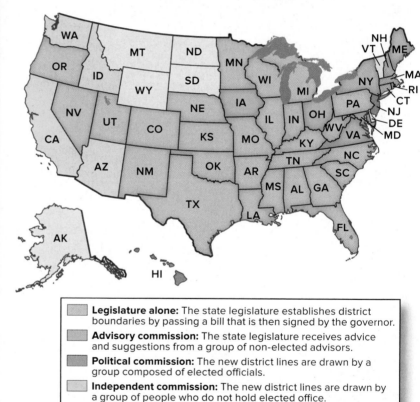

Methods Used to Draw Congressional Districts, by State

Legislature alone: The state legislature establishes district boundaries by passing a bill that is then signed by the governor.

Advisory commission: The state legislature receives advice and suggestions from a group of non-elected advisors.

Political commission: The new district lines are drawn by a group composed of elected officials.

Independent commission: The new district lines are drawn by a group of people who do not hold elected office.

*States with a single congressional district are shaded gray.

PRIMARY SOURCE C

"Here is a telling statistic: 153 of California's congressional and legislative seats were up in the last election and not one changed parties. What kind of democracy is that?"

—California Governor Arnold Schwarzenegger, 2005 State of the State Address

Former Justice Department Official Gerald Hebert spoke about nonpartisan or bipartisan districting commissions:

"Hebert believes that such commissions 'are ultimately the only solution. Trying to take the redistricting decision out of the henhouse so the foxes can't do it and promote their own self-interest, and putting it in the hands of people who don't have their own political careers at stake, may be the only way to take some of this excessive partisan gerrymandering out of the arena and produce more competitive seats. Right now the House is as noncompetitive as it has ever been in our history.'"

—Robert Pack, "Land Grab: The Pros and Cons of Congressional Redistricting," April 2004

"The evils of gerrymandering cannot be cured simply by drawing districts that follow county or municipal boundaries, or by increasing the geometric compactness of district shapes, or even by transferring the power to redraw lines from politicians to an independent commission. Rather, it requires a careful effort to create districts that will be fair and competitive."

—Sam Hirsch and Thomas E. Mann, "For Election Reform, a Heartening Defeat," *New York Times*, November 11, 2005

Often, redistricting maps are challenged in court—either by the party who feels disadvantaged by the maps, or by voters who argue that the maps discriminate in some way.

"We say once again what has been said on many occasions: reapportionment is primarily the duty and responsibility of the State through its legislature or other body, rather than of a federal court."

—Majority Opinion of the Supreme Court, *Chapman* v. *Meier*, 1975

DBQ DOCUMENT-BASED QUESTIONS

1. **Identifying** What methods do states use to redraw district boundaries? Who might support each method?

2. **Hypothesizing** How might different goals for redistricting affect the methods employed for drawing the lines? How might these goals affect the shapes of the resulting districts?

3. **Synthesizing** What are the arguments for and against each method? Which is the strongest argument presented in the source material? Explain your answer.

WHAT WILL YOU DO?

How do you think your state should draw its political districts? Which method will you advocate for, and why?

EXPLORE the interactive version of the analyzing primary sources feature on Networks.

LESSON 1
State Legislatures

r) BBC Worldwide Learning; ©Mike Norton/Purestock/SuperStock; hael Sohn/AP Images

Reading Help Desk

Academic Vocabulary

• advocate
• adjust

Content Vocabulary

• unicameral
• bicameral
• lieutenant governor
• special session
• blanket primary

TAKING NOTES:

Integrating Knowledge and Ideas

SUMMARIZING Use the graphic organizer to take notes about different aspects of state legislatures and their work.

State Legislative Organization	State Legislative Elections	Making State Laws

ESSENTIAL QUESTION

How are state and local legislative branches structured?

Every state has a state legislature, which passes laws, sets the state budget, establishes state taxes and spending priorities, and acts as a check on the power of the governor and the bureaucracy.

Most state legislatures meet for only part of the year. Some meet once every other year. Most state legislators are not paid a high salary; thus, many state legislators also have other jobs.

With a classmate, brainstorm advantages and disadvantages of having a part-time legislature made up of people who hold other jobs as well. On balance, would you prefer that your state have a part-time or full-time legislature? Why?

State Legislative Powers and Structure

GUIDING QUESTION *What are the powers and organization of state legislative branches?*

State legislatures derive their powers from the state constitution. Legislatures are empowered to pass laws for the state about almost any topic—from crimes to education to business regulation to transportation. Legislatures also check and balance the executive and judicial branches. In many states, the legislature confirms some executive appointments, has the power to impeach executive and judicial officials, and oversees the work of state executive agencies and commissions. The governor, the head of a state's executive branch, places an important check on state legislatures' lawmaking. In every state, the governor can veto legislation, and the legislature can override the veto if enough legislators vote to do so.

While the Tenth Amendment of the U.S. Constitution limits Congress's power to pass certain kinds of laws, most state constitutions do not have extensive limits on the types of laws that their legislatures may pass. State lawmaking is limited by a principle of federalism—state laws cannot conflict with federal laws. If a state and the federal government both pass laws that are in conflict with each other, then federal law is usually supreme.

While it is not usually dictated by the state constitution, many state lawmakers also spend time helping their constituents navigate state bureaucracy, locate resources, or **advocate** for solutions to their problems.

Organization of Legislatures Most state legislatures are organized like Congress. Nebraska is unique because it is **unicameral**, meaning it has only one house. Every other state has a **bicameral** state legislature—one with two houses, like the U.S. Congress. In every case, the upper house is called the senate and has fewer members than the lower house. In many cases, the lower house is called the House of Representatives, although in some states it is referred to as the House of Delegates, State Assembly, or the Legislative Assembly. In the lower house, the presiding officer is usually called the speaker of the house. As in the U.S. Congress, the majority party in this body usually chooses the speaker. The speaker then appoints all the members and chairpersons of the house committees.

States vary considerably in who presides over the senate. In some states, the majority party leader is in charge; in other states, the president pro tempore is in charge. **Lieutenant governors** are often figurehead leaders who can cast tie-breaking votes, much like the vice president.

The size of state legislatures varies widely and is not determined by the size of the state. Because of its unicameral nature, the smallest state legislature in the country is Nebraska's, with 49 members. In the bicameral legislatures, senates have smaller memberships than houses, with a range from 20 senators in Alaska to 400 house members in New Hampshire. Most state senators, and house members in five states, serve four-year terms. In the remaining state houses, members serve two years.

advocate to support or speak in favor of

unicameral a single-chamber legislature

bicameral relative to a two-house legislative body

lieutenant governor elected official serving as deputy to the governor

▼ CRITICAL THINKING
Hypothesizing Why might a state's citizens prefer that their legislative branch be a hybrid or part-time legislature?

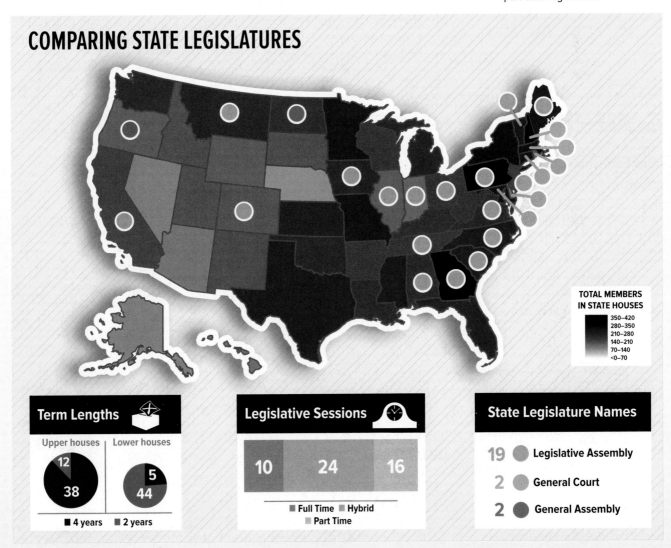

COMPARING STATE LEGISLATURES

TOTAL MEMBERS IN STATE HOUSES
- 350–420
- 280–350
- 210–280
- 140–210
- 70–140
- <0–70

Term Lengths

Upper houses	Lower houses
12 / 38	5 / 44

■ 4 years ■ 2 years

Legislative Sessions

| 10 | 24 | 16 |

■ Full Time ■ Hybrid ■ Part Time

State Legislature Names

19 ● Legislative Assembly

2 ● General Court

2 ● General Assembly

Legislative Sessions There are two types of legislative sessions: regular and special (sometimes called extraordinary). The regular session is the annual or biennial—every-other-year—gathering of the legislature. The start date and length of session are typically set by the state constitution or by a law. A **special session** is a specially called meeting of the legislature, typically to deal with pressing problems. Special sessions may be called by the governor or the legislature, depending on the state. Once the lawmakers meet in special session, they are often allowed to consider only the issues specifically described in the call for the special session.

Fifty years ago, more than half of the state legislatures met only every other year. By the mid-1970s, however, many state legislatures began meeting more frequently to handle their growing workload. Today, almost all states hold annual sessions.

Qualifications The legal qualifications for state legislators are defined in a state's constitution. In most states, a person must be a resident of the district that he or she wants to represent. To serve as a senator, a person must usually be at least 25 years old and a resident of the state for some specified time. To serve in the lower house, a person must usually be at least 21 years old and meet residency requirements. While the age requirement is fairly young in most states, less than 4 percent of state lawmakers are under the age of 34.

Legal qualifications aside, the office of state legislator seems to attract certain kinds of professional people. Many state legislators are lawyers. A sizable number of state legislators also come from professions that state laws directly affect, such as real estate and insurance. Unlike members of the U.S. Congress, most state legislators work only part time at their offices and are paid much less for their service.

GOVERNMENT *in your* COMMUNITY

Your Legislative District

Research your state legislative district and representatives to answer the following questions. (In some states, the senate district lines are drawn differently than the lower house boundaries. If that is true in your state, answer these questions separately for the senate and lower house.) You can find many of the answers by starting at your state legislature's website.

- In what legislative district is your school? Do you live in the same district?
- How large is your district?
- What are the geographic boundaries of your district?
- How many people live in your district?
- Who are your state legislator(s)?
- How long have your legislators served in their offices?
- Of what parties are they members?
- What issues are important to your legislators?

Using your answers, design a poster that conveys information to the residents of your legislative district.

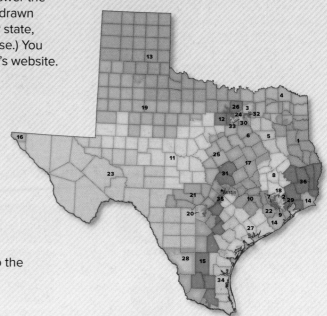

Texas State Legislative Districts, 2014

While many states continue to have part-time "citizen legislatures," others have moved to more professional legislatures marked by full-time service, higher pay, and more staff.

State legislators are becoming a more diverse group. About one quarter of state legislators are women, and just over 10 percent are African American or Latino.

☑ **READING PROGRESS CHECK**

Describing What are the formal and informal qualifications to be a state legislator?

State Legislative Elections

GUIDING QUESTION *How are state legislators elected to public office?*

Members of the state legislature are elected from legislative districts of relatively equal population. Until 1964, states were divided into districts based on geographic areas, regardless of population. Most states used the county as the basic voting district for the upper house. When population growth occurred, it was, of course, not uniform in all counties. As a result, striking differences arose in legislative representation. A county with 1,500 people and a county with 800,000 people were both entitled to one senator. In practice, this meant that legislators from rural or sparsely populated areas often represented fewer people than legislators from urban areas. In many states, a city-dweller's vote had less influence on the makeup of the state senate than a rural person's did.

In a 1964 case called *Reynolds* v. *Sims*, the Supreme Court ruled that such uneven districts violated the Fourteenth Amendment to the U.S. Constitution, which promises "equal protection of the laws." The Court said that the districts for both houses of state legislatures had to be based on roughly equal populations. States then redrew their districts to comply with the Court's ruling. In general, large cities and their suburbs gained seats, while rural areas lost seats.

Primary Elections All state senators and representatives are directly elected by the people in their voting districts. In a majority of states, this process looks very similar to congressional elections, but on a smaller scale. Candidates will typically take part in a primary in order to be put on the general election ballot, and the candidate will then have to win a plurality of the votes during the general election. In some nonpartisan primaries, if a candidate receives enough votes (usually 50 percent or more), he or she will be automatically elected and will not need to run in a general election.

Most states require a two-part process consisting of a closed or semi-closed primary during which only voters registered to a certain party can choose candidates to go on to represent that party in a general election. In other states, any voter may vote in either party's primary, regardless of registered affiliation. In California, Louisiana, and Washington, aspiring state representatives and senators compete in a **blanket primary** in which all candidates are placed on the same primary ballot, and the top two candidates, regardless of political party, move on to the general election.

blanket primary a primary in which all candidates are placed on the same primary ballot, regardless of party

Campaign Finance Some candidates for state legislatures spend millions of dollars trying to get elected, while others spend very little. While the total amount spent on state house and senate elections in 2012 was almost $1 billion, this amount represents what was spent in more than 7,000 separate elections for state senators and representatives. In comparison, almost $2 billion was spent during the 2012 presidential campaign on a handful of candidates.

PARTICIPATING
ⓘ Your Government

Weighing Alternatives and Making Decisions

Many state legislatures have considered allowing self-driving cars on their states' roads. Proponents claim that self-driving cars could prevent some of the 30,000 highway deaths each year. Opponents worry that the technology is untested and that there are many legal hurdles to overcome—from what auto insurance should cover to who should be authorized to build and test such cars.

Michael Sohn/AP Images

You will participate in a legislative committee hearing about a bill that would allow driverless cars in your state.

State Legislature: You are a state legislator. Learn more about the issue and prepare to question the interest group representatives.

Interest Groups: You represent one of these groups. Learn more about the issue and prepare a two-minute opening statement to the legislative committee that explains whether the bill should become law. Anticipate questions that legislators are likely to ask and prepare to answer them.

- **Technology Companies:** You represent several companies that make self-driving technology. They want the law to pass because business will grow. Research conducted by this industry shows driverless cars are safer than human drivers and can reduce accidents.

- **Traffic Safety Group:** You represent a group that is concerned about traffic accidents and traffic safety. They worry that there is no good evidence showing that driverless cars would reduce the number of accidents.

- **Car Insurance Companies:** You represent car insurance companies. They want the state to study the issue more before passing this bill. They are concerned that the bill does not address many legal issues like who is responsible if a self-driving car has an accident.

▲ **CRITICAL THINKING**

Identifying Points of View
Conduct the legislative committee hearing. The chairperson will call the committee to order and each interest group will make a two-minute opening statement. The legislators will question the interest groups about their position and then vote on whether to pass the proposal out of committee.

Generally, the amount of money spent on a state election depends on the political importance of the district in question and the party affiliations of its voters. For example, a district in which 90 percent of the voters belong to one party will not likely see much campaign spending because candidates know that a district with such a one-sided majority will almost always elect the candidate supported by the majority party.

On the other hand, some state legislative elections attract quite a bit of national attention. This is especially true when a state is preparing to redraw its congressional boundaries. Every 10 years after the national census, states must **adjust** their district boundaries to reflect population shifts. State legislatures typically control the process for redrawing districts, and they could draw the lines so one party has a better chance of winning. National parties often provide more funding for legislative elections in years where redistricting will take place.

☑ **READING PROGRESS CHECK**

Specifying What are the different types of primary elections that states hold to elect members of the legislature?

Passing Laws and Influencing the Legislature

GUIDING QUESTION *How do state legislatures make bills and pass laws?*

The ideas for laws come from many sources, such as someone who works for the governor or other state executive branch official. Other times, a bill may be suggested by constituents or by representatives of interest groups.

Regardless of who suggested or drafted a bill, it must be introduced by a member of the legislature. A bill can be introduced in either house, although many states require bills that raise revenue or spend tax dollars to be introduced in the lower house. The presiding officer sends the bill to the committee that specializes in the bill's subject matter. The committee discusses the bill and may hold public hearings. During the public hearings, people who are interested in the issue may testify to the committee members.

The committee may rewrite the bill or modify it and then send it back to the full house with a recommendation to be passed or not passed. If one house passes a bill, it must go through a similar process in the other. Sometimes the second house changes a bill. In this case, a conference committee of both houses must meet to draft an acceptable version, on which both houses vote. If it is passed, it goes to the governor for signature or veto. Of bills that are introduced, fewer than one-quarter become law.

State legislators have support from their staffs. Staff members handle policy research, drafting bills, writing legal opinions, evaluating programs, and assessing the state's budget. They help constituents, handle public relations, and campaign for legislators. Each state legislature typically has one to ten staff members for each legislator.

State legislators and their staffs often look to the public for input on issues. Residents of the state can send letters, e-mails, and social network communications and make phone calls. Legislators meet with constituents, both at their office in the state capital and in their districts. They hold public meetings in their districts to share information about their work and to hear the views of citizens. These sessions, often called town hall meetings, may be general in nature or designed to address a specific problem or piece of legislation. Meetings are announced well in advance through mailings, public notices, and advertisements.

☑ **READING PROGRESS CHECK**

Explaining What roles do staff members play in supporting state legislators?

EXPLORING THE ESSENTIAL QUESTION

Analyzing What background and types of experiences do you believe would help make someone a good legislator in your state? Write a resume for an ideal state legislative candidate. Consider education, age, job experience, where the person has lived, experiences in government or private industry, skills, and interests.

adjust to adapt to or conform

LESSON 1 REVIEW

Reviewing Vocabulary
1. *Defining* What is a blanket primary?

Using Your Graphic Organizer
2. *Formulating Questions* Use your completed graphic organizer to write three questions about things you would still like to know about state legislatures. Then do some research to locate the answers to your questions.

Answering the Guiding Questions
3. *Identifying* What are the powers and organization of state legislative branches?

4. *Explaining* How are state legislators elected to public office?

5. *Sequencing* How do state legislatures make bills and pass laws?

Writing About Government
6. *Informative/Explanatory* In what ways is lawmaking similar at the state levels and national levels of government? In what ways is it different? Write an essay comparing the process for making laws at the federal and state levels.

ReadingHelp Desk

Academic Vocabulary

- maintenance
- disposal

Content Vocabulary

- county
- county board
- zoning code
- municipality
- ordinance
- township
- town meeting
- direct democracy
- special district

TAKING NOTES:

Key Ideas and Details

CATEGORIZING Use the graphic organizer to describe the different types of local governments.

Type of Local Government	Description
County	
City	
Township	
Municipality	
Special District	
Tribal Government	

LESSON 2
Local Legislatures

ESSENTIAL QUESTION

How can citizens participate in state and local government?

Create a simple but artistic representation of your city or town. It should show the best and worst of your community. It could be a picture, poem, sculpture, or other representation of your choice.

Then, think about what would make it an ideal city or town. Write a short answer to the following questions and include it with your creation.

- What could your local government do to make your community better?
- What can you and other members of your community do to make it better?

Civic Participation in Local Government

GUIDING QUESTION *How can citizens participate in the political process at the local level?*

Americans have relatively more power and influence at the local level of government than at any other level, and there are many avenues for citizens to participate in the political process.

Participating in local government is easier than it is at other levels of government. The reason is proximity. It is relatively easy for most people to observe and participate in a local school board meeting or a meeting of the county government. Most local civic groups, neighborhood associations, and citizen advisory groups welcome input and participation from members of the community. In turn, these groups of community members, acting in concert, armed with petitions, and speaking with one voice, can have a big influence.

Sometimes, local government officials do not wait for the motivated citizens to "come to them." Elected leaders (and their staff) visit local coffee houses, initiate telephone or e-mail surveys, or even offer a "listening" booth at the county fair to get input.

Many public and private groups make it their mission to educate people about how to be informed, engaged, and involved in local government. Some are even geared to inspire high school students by giving them real experiences making a difference. For example, the MIKVA Challenge in Chicago gets students active in the political process

238

through involvement in city wide elections and community organizing. Its slogan is "Democracy is a VERB." In Street Law's Youth Act! Program, some Washington, D.C., students advocated on behalf of homeless families after learning that the wait list for homeless teens and families seeking emergency shelters was often more than six months. The students conducted surveys, circulated petitions, coordinated a clothing drive, and spoke at a rally. Finally, they testified before the D.C. City Council and persuaded its members to revise their budget to make more services available to homeless families.

✓ **READING PROGRESS CHECK**

Describing Why is participating in local government easier than at other levels of government?

Government Structure and Lawmaking

GUIDING QUESTION *How are local governments structured and how do they make laws?*

The United States has four common types of local government: counties, townships, municipalities, and special districts, plus tribal governments that enact laws for their Native American populations. It is important to understand which of these types are found in your state and how legislative bodies in those local governments create laws.

GOVERNMENT *in your* COMMUNITY

County Government

Lubbock is a county of nearly 300,000 people in northwestern Texas. Its legislative body is called the Commissioner's Court, and it is made up of the elected county judge and four commissioners elected from precincts within the county. The Commissioner's Court has executive powers as well, which it shares with several other elected officials.

At a recent meeting, the Commissioners Court dealt with a broad array of topics, including the following:

- Considered a resolution to conduct joint elections with other governmental units

- Considered recommendations from the committee that hires and supervises county employees

- Considered a resolution to authorize Lubbock County to participate in a pilot program established by the Department of Public Safety

- Heard a report on the status of county road projects

- Accepted the resignation of the Precinct 4 constable, an elected official who has some police powers to keep the peace and some minor judicial powers

County governments around the country have different names. Cook County, Illinois, has a Board of Commissioners.

EXPLORING THE ESSENTIAL QUESTION

Researching In Lubbock, the commissioners deal with some areas that are typically part of the executive branch, such as how employees are hired and supervised. Find out if your county board has both legislative and executive powers. How is your county government structured? Is the system of checks and balances as important on the county level as it is on the national level? Explain your answers.

HOW A BILL
Becomes an
ORDINANCE

Many local governments require an opportunity for community members to give input before an ordinance, or a law at the local level, is passed. Here is an example of the process in Montgomery County, Maryland.

▶ CRITICAL THINKING

Specifying At what points might members of the public be able to voice their opinions before a bill is voted on?

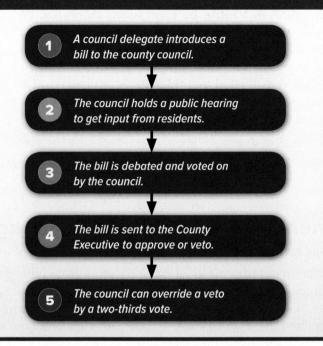

1 A council delegate introduces a bill to the county council.

2 The council holds a public hearing to get input from residents.

3 The bill is debated and voted on by the council.

4 The bill is sent to the County Executive to approve or veto.

5 The council can override a veto by a two-thirds vote.

---

county the largest political subdivision of a state

county board the governing body of most counties

zoning code a rule that specifies how land in particular parts of a city or county can be used

Perhaps the truest thing that can be said about legislative bodies at the local level is that they are diverse. Look for differences as you read about lawmaking in counties, municipalities, townships, and special districts.

Counties Counties are normally the largest territorial and political subdivision within a state. Every state except Connecticut and Rhode Island has a system of county governments. In Louisiana, counties are called *parishes*, and in Alaska they are called *boroughs*. Counties of the United States vary tremendously. The number of counties within a state varies from state to state, and counties differ in size and population. County governments also vary considerably in power and influence.

In some metropolitan areas, county governments have recently grown in importance as they have assumed some of the functions that municipalities once handled. For example, the government of Miami-Dade County, Florida, now administers transportation, the water supply, and other services for the Miami area.

A **county board** has the authority to govern most counties. The name of this board varies from state to state. It may be called the county board of supervisors, the county council, the board of county commissioners, or the board of freeholders. Board members are almost always popularly elected. State law strictly limits the legislative powers of county boards. For the most part, county boards decide on the county budget, taxes, and **zoning codes**, which are rules that specify how land in particular parts of a city or county can be used. In other words, they decide what types of buildings can be built and where, which lands are reserved for parks, and so forth.

In most counties, the legislative branch is separate from the executive branch. However, in some counties, the county board has both executive and legislative powers. Board members often divide executive power, with each member being responsible for a different county department. In many counties, the county board shares executive power with other officials who are usually elected.

Cities and Municipalities States decide what is called a city and what is called a municipality. In most cases, cities have a certain size population and geographic area. The term *municipality* is a bit more generic and can be any subdivision of a state—besides a county—and can have any number of residents and any geographic area.

municipality an urban unit of government chartered by a state

States also decide what powers their cities and municipalities have. They are spelled out in charters (local constitutions) that also spell out how laws are made and what powers that level of government has and does not have. State legislatures can change the powers granted to cities and municipal government at any time.

In the United States, the three basic forms of city and municipal government are the mayor-council form, the council-manager form, and the commission form. In the mayor-council and council-manager forms, an elected city council serves as the legislative body for the city. Executive power rests with the mayor or city manager. In the commission form, the elected commission has both legislative and executive power, with commission members serving as the heads of city departments.

Most city councils have fewer than 10 members, who usually serve four-year terms, although some larger cities exceed that number—Chicago, for example, has a 50-member council, the largest in the nation. In most cities, council members are elected from the city at large, but individual wards or districts sometimes elect members, too.

City councils pass **ordinances** in many policy areas. These areas include zoning or land use, mass transit, violence prevention, economic and workforce development, homelessness, and many more.

ordinance a law at the local level

township a unit of local government found in some states, usually a subdivision of a county

Townships **Townships** exist as units of local government in 20 states—mostly in New England and the Midwest. In the 1600s, the early settlers

PARTICIPATING
in Your Government

Decision Making at Town Meetings

Many politicians hold "town meetings" where the particpants gather to give input to their elected officials.

At times, town meetings can become very heated, as citizens may disagree vehemently with each other or their elected officials. In other cases, people who disagree, even deeply, do so respectfully and civilly.

Imagine that you are a local politician hosting a town meeting about a "hot" issue in your community. What rules will you put in place to keep the conversation productive and civil? Think about:

- How people should address each other
- How the order of speaking will be determined
- How long each person will be allowed to speak
- How questions will be handled

Toby Talbot/AP Images

EXPLORING THE ESSENTIAL QUESTION

Exploring Issues Attend a meeting of a local legislative body or town meeting and take notes on the rules they use to keep order and to promote civility. Observe how people express their ideas and disagreements. In your opinion, would different rules have resulted in a better meeting? Why or why not? Summarize your notes and opinions in a brief report.

in New England established the first townships in America. Typically, townships are created as divisions of counties, and their size and jurisdiction vary greatly from one state to another. In New Jersey, a township may cover a large area that includes several municipalities.

The services of township governments vary from state to state, too. In Nebraska and Missouri, the primary function of township government is road building and **maintenance**. In Pennsylvania, townships provide many government services, including police and fire protection. In some urban areas, such as those in Michigan and New Jersey that have grown rapidly, townships have assumed some functions of city government, such as providing water, sewage **disposal**, and police protection.

Historically, townships were governed with very direct participation of their residents. **Town meetings** were the centerpiece of local government in New England and an example of true **direct democracy** wherein citizens rule themselves rather than electing representatives to govern on their behalf. Town meetings were open to all voters, and citizens participated in lawmaking, decided on taxes, and approved money for public projects they believed were needed. Citizens elected "selectmen," who were responsible only for administering the government between town meetings—not for making laws. Thomas Jefferson once described politics in the typical New England town as "the perfect exercise of self-government." With the strong community spirit fostered by their founders, these towns were models of citizen participation in local government because they embodied the key elements of direct democracy: universal participation, political equality, and majority rule.

As towns grew, this town meeting form of direct democracy became impractical in most communities, though they still exist in some smaller towns.

maintenance the upkeep of property or equipment

disposal the act of getting rid of

town meeting a meeting called by an elected official to get input from his or her constituents

direct democracy a form of government wherein citizens rule themselves rather than electing representatives to govern on their behalf

Serving on the School Board

Loudoun County Public Schools

The Loudoun County, Virginia, School Board has a unique approach. It selects one representative, a senior, from each high school in the district. Each representative serves on the board for one month. While they cannot vote, they advocate for the interests of students and teachers.

One student, Katherine Knobloch, identified several issues of concern to students in her school: "I want to raise the issue of Wi-Fi access, the need for more stop signs in the school parking lots, and possible exemption policies for underclassmen, not just seniors." The 13 students selected as school board representatives collaborate to advance issues of concern to all the high schools.

Pablo Rivera, who served as a student representative to the school board in 2012–2013, reported he learned a lot about how a meeting is run using *Robert's Rules of Order*, a well-known guide to meeting procedures. Being a board representative, he said, "showed me a new perspective on how to act, how to listen to other people's insight, and how to be smart with what you say."

"[I learned] how to listen to other people's insight, and how to be smart with what you say."

— Pablo Rivera

▲ CRITICAL THINKING

1. Considering Advantages and Disadvantages What might be the advantages of having a different student serve on the school board each month? A disadvantage?

2. Analyzing What do you think Pablo Rivera meant by saying he learned "how to be smart with what you say"?

3. Making Connections Does your school district include student representatives on the board? If so, how are they selected and what are their responsibilities? If not, how does the board ensure they receive student input?

Now, in most towns, as with our national government, voters elect representatives to make decisions on their behalf. Today, the term *town meeting* usually describes a meeting called by an elected official to get input from his or her constituents. They can also be arranged by people who think their elected leaders need to hear what they have to say.

Special Districts Local governments establish special districts that are better able to respond to specific problems than a more general unit of local government. **Special districts** are units of local government that deal with a specific function, such as education, firefighting, trash removal, water purity and supply, or transportation. Special districts are the most common type of local government, and they deal with a variety of special services.

Most state governments limit the taxing and borrowing powers of local governments. Some states also have laws that limit how much these local governments may spend. Creating a special district that is not subject to such limitations becomes a practical solution for local leaders whose budgets are strained. Many special districts make their own policies, levy taxes, and borrow money. More than 37,000 special districts exist.

School Districts Local school districts are usually governed by an elected local body, the school board. School boards are responsible for hiring and firing superintendents, leaders who run the day-to-day operations of schools. School boards determine the budget for the school system and decide on new school programs and facilities. They set school policies and may have the final decision about hiring teachers and supervisory staff. In some places, school boards also decide on the amount of school taxes to levy.

The past 40 years have seen a trend toward including student representatives on school boards. In some cases, student representatives do not have a vote on the board, but in others they are full voting members.

Tribal Governments In over half the states, a separate level of government serves the Native American population—tribal government. More than 500 tribes are recognized by the federal government, which has an official policy of encouraging Native American self-government. Tribal governments levy taxes, pass their own laws, and operate their own court system. Some tribal governments have three branches of government similar to the U.S. government, with a Tribal Council serving as the legislative body. Others vest executive and legislative powers within a Tribal Council led by a Tribal Chair.

☑ **READING PROGRESS CHECK**

Describing What are counties, cities, municipalities, and townships?

The federal government encourages Native American self-government and self-determination. This photograph shows new delegates for a legislature of the Tlingit and Haida Tribes of Alaska.

▲ CRITICAL THINKING
Identifying In what areas of law might tribal laws conflict with state laws?

special district a unit of local government that deals with a specific function, such as education, water supply, or transportation

---

LESSON 2 REVIEW

Reviewing Vocabulary
1. *Comparing* What is an ordinance and how does it compare to a national law?

Using Your Graphic Organizer
2. *Summarizing* Use your completed graphic organizer to write a summary of each type of local government.

Answering the Guiding Questions
3. *Gathering Information* How can citizens participate in the political process at the local level?

4. *Explaining* How are local governments structured and how do they make laws?

Writing About Government
5. *Informative/Explanatory* How does the legislative structure of local government compare to the legislative structure of state governments and the federal government? Write an essay drawing comparisons about the legislative structure at all three levels of government in the U.S. federal system.

Board of Education v Earls (2001)

FACTS OF THE CASE Most students at Tecumseh High School participated in a variety of extracurricular activities. School district policy required each student that participated in any of the school's extracurricular activities to agree to be tested for drug use. Tecumseh High School did not have a serious drug problem, but officials adopted this policy to prevent a drug problem from developing.

There were no academic penalties for refusing to take the test or for testing positive. Results of the tests were not shared with law enforcement authorities. In two school years, only four students tested positive. Two students who participated in extracurricular activities but not athletics sued the school district, saying this policy was like a "search" of their body and therefore a violation of their right to privacy.

ISSUE

Does a mandatory drug test for students who participate in any extracurricular school activity violate those students' Fourth Amendment right to privacy?

ARGUMENTS

OPINION A The school is responsible for the care and education of the children and has an interest in keeping them safe. Students do not have the same expectations of privacy at school as adults do. Students are often required to submit to physical examinations to play sports or to receive vaccinations to attend school. The school does not have to suspect that an individual student is using drugs. The need to promote the health and safety of all students outweighs an individual student's privacy interests.

As the Court said in a previous case about student drug testing, these are reasonable searches. In this school, students can choose not to participate in extracurricular activities. No student is tested without his or her consent. The searches are not conducted to punish anyone—there is no police involvement. Finally, if a student tests positive, he or she has an opportunity to dispute the test results.

OPINION B Students have the right to be free from unreasonable searches. In order for a search to be reasonable, authorities must have some suspicion that the person they are searching will have the thing for which they are looking. In a previous case about student drug testing, that school district had a known drug problem among athletes and they were the only students tested. In this case, students could be tested whether they were athletes, chess players, or members of the choir—none of whom were suspected of having a drug problem. The desire to participate in extracurricular activities should not be enough to make school officials suspicious.

The school district's goal of preventing drug use does not outweigh students' constitutional right to privacy, particularly where there is little evidence of a drug problem. The claim that the testing was voluntary is not legitimate when students need extracurricular involvement for college admissions and scholarships. In order to challenge a positive test, students must disclose more confidential information—including use of prescription medication—which further violates their right to privacy.

EXPLORING THE ESSENTIAL QUESTION

Applying Read the two sample opinions in this case. First, explain how this case illustrates the importance of the role local governments play in daily life. Then decide which opinion you think should be the majority (winning) opinion, and which you think should be the dissenting opinion. Explain your choice.

interact with these digital assets and others in lesson 3

✓ **INTERACTIVE GRAPH**
Crime Rates

✓ **INTERACTIVE MAP**
Per Pupil Education Spending

✓ **SELF-CHECK QUIZ**

✓ **VIDEO**
Soda Wars

netw⚙rks
TRY IT YOURSELF ONLINE

ReadingHelp Desk

Academic Vocabulary

- incorporate
- restrict
- prohibit

Content Vocabulary

- public policy
- mass transit

TAKING NOTES:

Key Ideas and Details

SUMMARIZING Use the graphic organizer to list policy issues that are of concern to state and local lawmakers. Include a brief description of each policy area.

State Policy Issues	Description

Local Policy Issues	Description

LESSON 3
State and Local Legislative Policy

ESSENTIAL QUESTION

How are laws created at the state and local levels?

Below are some of the policy areas on which state and local legislatures work. Give each policy area two ratings—one to show how important this area is to you and one to show how knowledgeable you are about issues in the area. Use a scale of 1 to 5, with 1 being not at all important or not at all knowledgeable and 5 being very important or very knowledgeable.

Policy Area	Level of Importance	Level of Knowledge
Voting		
Environment		
Education		
Public Safety: Crime Prevention and Corrections		
Economic Development		
Transportation: Highways and Mass Transit		
Land Use/Zoning		

Are there areas that you think are important but you know little about? How could you become more knowledgeable about issues in these policy areas?

Public Policy Concerns of State Legislatures

GUIDING QUESTION *What public policy issues are addressed by state legislatures?*

State and local governments enact laws that specify public policy in many areas, including business regulation, controlling and regulating natural resources, protecting individual rights, and implementing health, education, and public welfare programs. **Public policy** is a plan of action adopted by government decision makers to solve a problem or reach a goal. Like national legislatures, state and local legislatures can make policy by writing new laws, taking old laws off the books, or changing laws.

Compare and contrast these points of view about voter identification laws.

▲ CRITICAL THINKING

Analyzing Political Cartoons Identify the viewpoints expressed in each cartoon. Which do you most agree with? Why?

public policy a plan of action adopted by government decision makers to solve a problem or reach a goal

Voting Laws Many states have moved to add more stringent requirements related to voting. Citing the problem of voter fraud, lawmakers in these states have introduced a range of measures designed to prevent unauthorized people from voting. The first voter-ID laws were enacted in 2003. In 2008 an Indiana law requiring voters to show photo identification was upheld by the Supreme Court in the case of *Crawford* v. *Marion County Election Board.* Within the next four years, 11 states had enacted voter-ID laws.

Opponents of these laws have argued that they disproportionately impact poor, minority voters who are less likely to have a photo ID. They point out that obtaining the required ID can be expensive and difficult for poor or elderly people. They also cite low numbers of voter fraud prosecutions as evidence that the laws are unnecessary. Proponents, however, claim that voter fraud is a real problem that must be stopped to ensure the integrity of the voting process. In response, some states have worked to make it easier to obtain a photo ID where one is required.

Some state legislatures that wanted to enact voter-ID laws were blocked from doing so by the federal government. Because of a long history of voting discrimination, this group of states had been required to ask the federal government for permission to make any changes to their voting laws. In 2013 the Supreme Court struck down parts of the Voting Rights Act, making it possible for those states and counties to enact photo ID requirements without first getting permission from the federal government (*Shelby County* v. *Holder*). The Attorney General for the State of Texas announced on the day of the Court's decision that his state's strict voter-ID law would be put into effect immediately; four other states followed suit within 24 hours. In response, the federal Department of Justice quickly sued to stop Texas and North Carolina from implementing their new voter-ID laws.

While voter-ID laws are controversial, they are certainly not the only election-related policies state legislatures have enacted recently. In the twenty-first century, numerous states have passed laws allowing early voting, all-mail voting, and "no-excuse required" absentee voting. The year after a presidential election, when turnout is high and any problems with the election system become apparent, many state legislatures take action to avoid those problems in the future.

Environment States have taken the lead on legislating about environmental use and protection. Many states are attempting to balance their energy needs with the need to protect the environment by carefully regulating the use of energy sources. Energy companies have devised new methods, including hydraulic fracturing, or "fracking," to access fossil fuels more efficiently. In fracking, water, sand, and chemicals are injected into rock to release natural gas and oil supplies. While some see this method as an opportunity for states and the nation to gain energy independence, others believe the process has negative environmental consequences. In 2012, 24 state legislatures proposed a combined total of more than 130 bills related to fracking.

Traditional sources of oil and gas are also regulated by the states. In 2013 the Alaska state legislature appropriated $355 million to spend on an in-state gas pipeline. States in the Midwest passed new regulations regarding interstate oil pipelines that connect oil fields in the interior with ports in the Gulf of Mexico. These states want more oversight over the development of such pipelines, requiring developers to get permission from the state before building interstate systems.

The states regulate other issues affecting the environment, including the size and location of landfills, the protection of state parks, and the preservation of wildlife refuges. For instance, North Carolina requires a buffer zone between landfills and state parks and wildlife refuges. Oregon bans billboards and disposable bottles. Nearly half of the states have passed laws to control strip-mining, a form of mining that removes topsoil.

Education States continue to wrestle with the challenge of making sure that schools and education programs are providing the best outcomes for students. Some states have passed laws allowing for public charter schools, schools that do not have to follow all state regulations and can experiment with new ideas for teaching children. Other states have authorized vouchers for students to attend private schools. Under a voucher system, students are able to apply the funding that the state would have paid for their education in a public school to the tuition at a private school. Many states have adopted new standards and curricula and policies that **incorporate** technology into the classroom.

States are also exploring ways to assess and evaluate teacher quality, often by creating evaluation systems that rely in part upon students' standardized test scores. If students in a school are doing poorly on standardized tests, some states require those schools to make significant changes in how they teach. California recently passed a "parent trigger" law. This law says that if half the parents of children in a school with low test scores sign a petition, the school must either close, become a charter school, or put other major reforms in place.

incorporate to blend into or combine

MAP

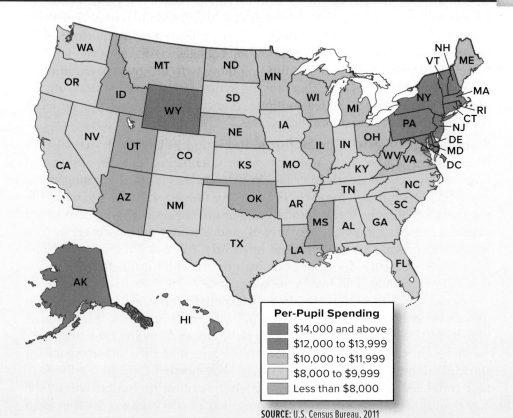

Per-Pupil Spending
- $14,000 and above
- $12,000 to $13,999
- $10,000 to $11,999
- $8,000 to $9,999
- Less than $8,000

SOURCE: U.S. Census Bureau, 2011

Per-Pupil EDUCATION SPENDING

Per-pupil education spending varies from state to state.

◀ **CRITICAL THINKING**

1. *Analyzing Maps* Which states spend the most and least per pupil?

2. *Speculating* What might account for the differences in state spending levels?

GOVERNMENT *in your* COMMUNITY

Influencing Public Policy in Your State

Find out what your state legislature has been doing in different policy areas. What new laws have they passed? What existing laws have they amended? What laws have they taken off the books? Then choose a policy area that you are passionate about. How could you influence lawmakers to change policy in this area, whether by passing a new law, amending an existing law, or rescinding a law you do not like? Which of the following strategies would you use? Why?

- A petition

- A letter-writing campaign

- A peaceful protest or demonstration

- Testifying at a public hearing

- Involving the media

- Meeting with legislators

- Setting up a town hall meeting

- Your own ideas

A letter-writing campaign is one of many ways to influence public policy.

EXPLORING THE ESSENTIAL QUESTION

Making Decisions Make a plan that uses at least two strategies. Your plan should include drafts for each strategy, such as a poster, petition, letter, invitation to the town hall meeting, questions you would ask your state lawmaker, talking points you would use when speaking with reporters, and so forth. Ask your teacher or another student to give you feedback on your plan, and then implement it.

States are also challenged to fund higher education—colleges, universities, technical colleges, and community colleges. State-supported institutions of higher education have always been seen as an affordable option for students who could not pay the high tuition at private colleges. But costs for higher education have soared, while most states faced decreased revenue and sharp budget reductions. Ten states have already moved toward performance-based funding—providing support to colleges with proven student achievement, rather than simply funding those with the greatest enrollment. Two dozen other states are either moving in that direction or are studying the merits of the program. States continue to encourage partnerships between community colleges and local businesses.

Public Safety and Corrections Protecting public safety has always been a major goal of state and local governments. Legislatures often enact laws in response to trends in crime. In response to a period of rising crime from the 1960s through the early 1990s, many states passed laws to make life tougher for those who break the law. Legislatures required lengthy mandatory prison sentences for a variety of crimes, and prison populations grew. As a result, the prison population grew by nearly 800 percent in the last few decades. That figure does not even include the significant increase in the number of juveniles held in detention centers.

Housing all these inmates is very expensive. The estimated cost per inmate for one year is approximately $30,000. In some states, the cost is as high as $60,000 or $80,000 depending on the age and health of the prisoner.

In recent years, many states decided to prioritize their prison space for the most dangerous offenders. To do so, they needed to improve the way that convicted felons are supervised while serving probation within the community. They also needed to strengthen re-entry programs that help felons make the move from prison back into the community. These "justice reinvention" programs have been found to reduce crime and recidivism rates (the number of people committing new crimes after completing their sentences), while also saving money. In addition, many states are reducing the mandatory minimum penalties for low-level drug crimes, opting to offer drug offenders treatment instead.

☑ READING PROGRESS CHECK

Describing What role do state governments play in educating children and environmental regulation and protection?

Public Policy Concerns in Local Legislatures

GUIDING QUESTION *What public policy issues are addressed by local legislatures?*

Many of the public policy concerns addressed by state legislatures are also worked on by local legislatures. However, there are some additional public policy areas that are particularly important to local governments.

Land Use and Zoning One of the goals of local governments is to create livable cities—good places for people to live and work. Regulating land use using such tools as zoning is one way local governments try to achieve that goal. Most large cities and many smaller ones have zoning ordinances. Zoning ordinances specify how land in particular parts of the city can be used. Generally, four types of use are defined in zoning ordinances: residential, commercial (offices and stores), mixed residential-commercial, and industrial.

Zoning ordinances may also specify such factors as how big a building can be, how close to the street it can be built, and, for commercial or industrial buildings, where off-street parking will be provided. Zoning ordinances—or regulations developed by the zoning boards who implement zoning ordinances—can be very detailed.

City councils are also concerned with other land use issues, too. These include how public land will be used, how much land should be set aside for open space and parks, and how much is needed for city government buildings.

Land use issues can be controversial. Because zoning ordinances **restrict** how people can use their own property, some people believe they violate their property rights. If, for example, a family wants to keep chickens in their backyard, they may believe they should be allowed to do so. At the same time, their neighbors may be happy that zoning ordinances **prohibit** raising chickens within the city. People also disagree about how public land should be used. When the city buys an open field in the heart of the city, should it be used for soccer fields, open space where people can walk and enjoy nature, or a new jail?

Transportation and Mass Transit Getting people where they're going more efficiently and in a more environmentally sound manner is a goal for state and local governments.

One way that state and local governments address this goal is by providing **mass transit** systems—trains or buses that transport large numbers of people on a route system around the city. But many of the cities with the worst traffic problems also have mass transit systems. What other policies can be put in place to make the transportation system work better?

Some state or local governments provide incentives for carpooling, such as high-occupancy vehicle (HOV) lanes that move faster than the regular traffic lanes, carpool arrangements, and cheaper parking for carpoolers.

restrict to limit

prohibit to forbid

mass transit a public transportation network, consisting of buses, trains, subways, or other forms of public transportation

Some governments provide incentives for carpooling such as special high-occupancy vehicle traffic lanes and reduced parking costs.

▼ CRITICAL THINKING

Exploring Issues Do HOV lanes exist on any highways in or near your community? If so, do you think they help improve the flow of local traffic? If not, do you think providing such lanes would be beneficial? Explain your answer.

◇ CARPOOLS ONLY
2 OR MORE PERSONS PER VEHICLE ↖

©iStockphoto.com/MCCAIG

Exploring Issues You are a homeowner. The city council is considering a proposal to turn a branch library that was closed due to budget cuts into a homeless shelter. As a teacher who has taught several homeless students, you are sympathetic to the problems of homeless families. On the other hand, as a homeowner, you are concerned about the safety of the neighborhood and property values. A neighbor has asked you to protest against the proposal by doing three things: sign a petition, put a sign in your yard, and attend a city council meeting where it will be debated. What will you do? Will you talk to your neighbor about your perspective?

Other local governments encourage bicycle commuting by designating bike lanes and making "loaner" bikes available. Local governments also sometimes provide tax breaks to companies that encourage telecommuting—working from home with the aid of computers.

Economic Development State and local governments are typically quite concerned about the health of their community's economy. Sometimes they design targeted measures to attract or retain business. These often include tax breaks or credits to businesses that locate their companies within the state or city or to those that create more jobs. For example, the state of Maryland designated 28 "enterprise zones" in 2012. These were geographic areas in which employers could locate their businesses for lower taxes and reduced regulations. These enterprise zones were targeted to help grow areas of the state in need, from a large portion of a rural county to underdeveloped neighborhoods in its largest city.

Smaller cities are competing for businesses, too. The city of Grand Island, Nebraska, explains on its website the incentives it offers businesses who locate there. The incentives include a cash payment to businesses based on the number of jobs created. The city of Waco, Texas, offers tax abatements for projects that would result in a significant investment in real estate or personal property, that is, new equipment and machinery.

These types of programs are increasing in frequency, as every state and many cities now offer incentives. It is estimated that states and cities spend billions of dollars each year on these incentives. Some people have doubts that these programs work, while others believe they are an effective way to improve a struggling area. Economic experts continue to research the best ways for these policies to be effective, and caution state lawmakers and city councils to be thoughtful with decisions about how these tax incentives will affect their communities.

City and state governments also work on improving their community's economic well-being through workforce development. They adopt policies that provide support to people who need jobs, whether by operating job placement centers or offering retraining for people whose jobs have been eliminated.

☑ **READING PROGRESS CHECK**

Explaining Why are land use issues often contentious?

LESSON 3 REVIEW

Reviewing Vocabulary
1. **Defining** What is public policy and how is it made at the state and local levels of government?

Using Your Graphic Organizer
2. **Exploring Issues** Using your completed graphic organizer, explain which policy areas are of greatest concern at the state and local levels. Then select one policy area and learn more about recent developments in your state or community.

Answering the Guiding Questions
3. **Identifying** What public policy issues are addressed by state legislatures?

4. **Identifying** What public policy issues are addressed by local legislatures?

Writing About Government
5. **Informative/Explanatory** States, municipalities, and cities often work on many of the same policy issues. Why do you think that is so? Select one or two issue areas that are of great concern to state and local governments. Then explain what each level of government does to address the issue. How are their roles similar and different?

Should our state punish juvenile offenders as adults?

DELIBERATING DEMOCRATIC PRINCIPLES

What should happen to children who commit violent crimes? Should they be punished like adults? Or should they be treated differently? Should the fact that a young person suffered a traumatic childhood excuse him or her from being tried as an adult for committing a violent crime?

These are some of the questions state lawmakers consider when setting policy on violent juvenile offenders. In most U.S. states, an 18-year-old is automatically sent to the adult criminal system. Younger offenders are usually handled in the juvenile court system, which has a greater emphasis on rehabilitation and treatment. But all states and the District of Columbia allow some juvenile offenders to be transferred to adult courts. Is this a good idea?

 **YES**

TEAM A — The State Should Punish Violent Juvenile Offenders as Adults

One purpose of punishment is retribution. Punishing offenders in proportion to their crimes gives victims a sense of justice. Effective punishments also deter future crime. People who know they could be sent to adult prison might be discouraged from committing serious crimes.

Punishment is also designed to keep society safe. If criminals are in jail, they cannot hurt the rest of society. In the juvenile system, young criminals get back on the streets between the ages of 18 and 21 regardless of how much time they served.

The juvenile justice system is more expensive. While the idea of rehabilitation is laudable, many juvenile facilities do not have the supportive programs they are supposed to have. In difficult economic times, governments cannot afford to sentence older teens to facilities that are already underfunded.

 NO

TEAM B — The State Should Not Punish Violent Juvenile Offenders as Adults

Young offenders tried as adults end up in prison with a variety of violent and career criminals. The research shows that youth punished in the adult system are twice as likely to reoffend upon release.

Young offenders can get better education and therapy in the juvenile justice system. Through rehabilitation, young people can reenter society and lead productive lives.

Scientists say the human brain does not fully mature until the age of about 25. The parts of the brain that control anger and anticipate consequences are slow to develop. For most purposes, young people are not considered adults until age 18. They cannot vote, serve in the military, or take out bank loans. So why would they be considered mature enough to be punished as an adult when they have not yet reached the established legal age of adulthood?

EXPLORING THE ESSENTIAL QUESTION

Deliberating With a partner, review the main arguments for either side. Decide which points are most compelling. Then paraphrase those arguments to a pair of students who were assigned to the other viewpoint. Listen to their strongest arguments. Switch sides and repeat the best arguments and add another compelling argument the other pair may not have thought about or presented. Then drop your roles and have a free discussion about which policy you support and why. Can you find any areas of common ground between the two viewpoints? If so, how might a sensible policy address that common ground? What do you think is the best answer? Why?

STUDY GUIDE

STRUCTURE AND FUNCTIONS OF STATE LEGISLATURES
LESSON 1

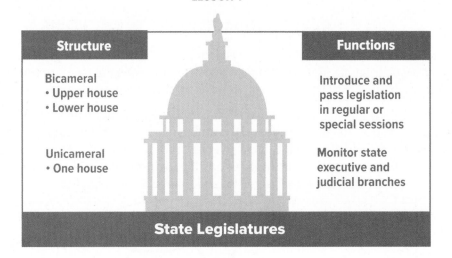

Structure		Functions
Bicameral • Upper house • Lower house		Introduce and pass legislation in regular or special sessions
Unicameral • One house		Monitor state executive and judicial branches

State Legislatures

TYPES OF LOCAL GOVERNMENTS
LESSON 2

Local Governments					
Cities and Municipalities • Mayor-council • Council-manager • Commission	**Townships** • Provide basic government services	**Tribal Governments** • Tribal council • Native American self-government	**Special Districts** • Deal with a specific function such as firefighting	**School Districts** • School board	**Counties** • County board • Largest form of local government

STATE AND LOCAL PUBLIC POLICY
LESSON 3

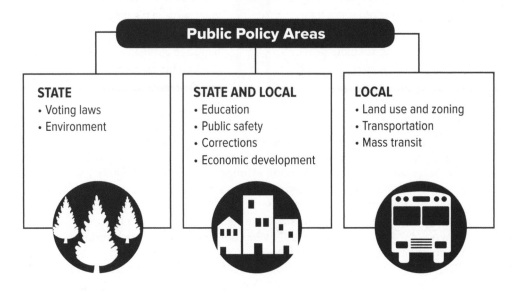

Public Policy Areas

STATE
• Voting laws
• Environment

STATE AND LOCAL
• Education
• Public safety
• Corrections
• Economic development

LOCAL
• Land use and zoning
• Transportation
• Mass transit

Directions: On a separate sheet of paper, answer the questions below. Make sure you read carefully and answer all parts of the questions.

Lesson Review

Lesson 1

1 *Contrasting* Describe the two types of legislative sessions and the differences between them.

2 *Describing* Describe the methods of participation in the lawmaking process in your state legislative branch. Explain the effectiveness of the methods you describe.

3 *Discussing* Discuss how state senators and representatives are elected.

Lesson 2

4 *Evaluating* Describe why political participation at the local level is often more effective than at the state and national levels.

5 *Identifying* What are special districts and why are they formed?

6 *Explaining* Describe the different meanings of the term *town meetings* in local politics.

Lesson 3

7 *Defining* What is a zoning ordinance and why are they used?

8 *Identifying Central Issues* State why voter-ID law proponents want increased regulation and why voter-ID law opponents are against increased regulation.

9 *Listing* What are some public policies being implemented to reduce the number of inmates held in state prisons?

ANSWERING THE ESSENTIAL QUESTIONS

Review your answers to the introductory questions at the beginning of each lesson. Then answer the following Essential Questions based on what you learned in the chapter. Have your answers changed?

10 *Differentiating* How are state and local legislative branches structured?

11 *Evaluating* How can citizens participate in state and local government?

12 *Analyzing* How are laws created at the state and local levels?

DBQ Interpreting Political Cartoons

Use the political cartoon to answer the following questions.

13 *Analyzing Visuals* What is happening in this cartoon?

14 *Making Inferences* What does this cartoon say about the tradeoffs that local government officials must consider when making zoning decisions?

Critical Thinking

15 *Making Connections* Identify similarities in the functions of national, state, and local governments in the United States federal system.

16 *Assessing* How did the *Reynolds* v. *Sims* Supreme Court decision affect how state legislative representatives are elected?

17 *Evaluating* Describe the reasons local governments create special districts and discuss whether this makes local governments more or less effective.

Need Extra Help?

If You've Missed Question	**1**	**2**	**3**	**4**	**5**	**6**	**7**	**8**	**9**	**10**	**11**	**12**	**13**	**14**	**15**	**16**	**17**
Go to page	234	237	235	238	243	242	249	246	248	233	235	237	249	249	232	235	243

Directions: On a separate sheet of paper, answer the questions below. Make sure you read carefully and answer all parts of the questions.

DBQ Analyzing Primary Sources

Read the excerpts and answer the questions that follow.

In *Kelo* v. *New London*, 2005, the Supreme Court was asked to decide if the City of New London had the authority to force owners to sell their property to a private developer using the power of eminent domain.

PRIMARY SOURCE

"*In assembling the land needed for this project, the city's development agent has purchased property from willing sellers and proposes to use the power of eminent domain to acquire the remainder of the property from unwilling owners in exchange for just compensation. The question presented is whether the city's proposed disposition of this property qualifies as a 'public use' within the meaning of the Takings Clause of the Fifth Amendment to the Constitution.*"
—Justice John Stevens, *Susette Kelo, et al., Petitioners v. City of New London, Connecticut, et al., Opinion of the Court*, 2005

18 **Finding the Main Idea** What does Justice Stevens say is the question the Court looked at in the case?

In *Reynolds* v. *Sims*, 1964, the Supreme Court was asked to decide if Alabama's voting districts met requirements in the U.S. Constitution. Alabama's system used county borders and 1900 U.S. census results to establish voting districts following the 1960 U.S. census.

PRIMARY SOURCE

"*Legislators represent people, not trees or acres. Legislators are elected by voters, not farms or cities or economic interests. As long as ours is a representative form of government, and our legislatures are those instruments of government elected directly by and directly representative of the people, the right to elect legislators in a free and unimpaired fashion is a bedrock of our political system.*"
—Chief Justice Earl Warren, *Reynolds* v. *Sims, Opinion of the Court*, 1964

19 **Interpreting Significance** Describe how this ruling could affect how legislative representatives are selected in your state.

Social Studies Skills

20 **Citizenship** Describe the accepted forms of identification for a registered voter to cast a ballot in your state.

Use this bar graph to help answer questions 21 and 22.

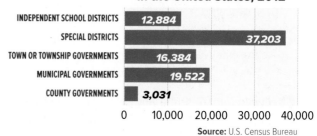

Numbers of Local Governments in the United States, 2012

INDEPENDENT SCHOOL DISTRICTS	12,884
SPECIAL DISTRICTS	37,203
TOWN OR TOWNSHIP GOVERNMENTS	16,384
MUNICIPAL GOVERNMENTS	19,522
COUNTY GOVERNMENTS	3,031

0   10,000   20,000   30,000   40,000

Source: U.S. Census Bureau

21 **Geography Skills** Refer to the bar graph. Compare the number of county and municipal governments by explaining the ratio between them.

22 **Creating and Using Graphs, Charts, Diagrams, and Tables** Which is the most common type of local government shown on the graph? Explain why this is the case.

Research and Presentation

23 **Comparing** Create a multimedia presentation comparing the different methods of filling public offices in the legislature at the local, state, and national levels.

24 **Assessing** Write an essay analyzing the effectiveness of various methods of participation in the political process at the state and local levels. Is participation at the state level more effective than participation at the local level? Support your answer.

25 **Evaluating** Research policies your local government has taken to promote economic growth and development. Write an essay describing the policies and evaluating whether the policies are effective.

Need Extra Help?

If You've Missed Question	18	19	20	21	22	23	24	25
Go to page	254	235	246	240	241	235	238	250

UNIT 3
The Executive Branch

IT MATTERS
BECAUSE . . .

As the country's only nationally elected office, presidents today have much greater power and responsibility than presidents who served earlier in our nation's history. The president is the head of state, chief executive, commander in chief, chief diplomat, legislative leader, economic leader, and party leader. Successful executives are in tune with the public, possess good communication skills and a sense of timing, are willing to compromise with competing factions, and demonstrate political courage. Many federal departments, agencies, boards, commissions, government corporations, and advisory committees make up the executive branch of the U.S. government. All of these bodies help carry out the president's policies and the laws passed by Congress. The function of the executive branch on the state and local levels is much the same as on the federal level: State and local executives administer and enforce the laws passed by the legislative branch. By understanding how the executive branch operates, you will more clearly see how the actions of federal, state, and local bureaucracies affect your daily life.

How to
Interpret Election Maps

Election maps show various kinds of government data and information about an election. For example, a national election map might show the popular vote or the Electoral College vote in a presidential election by identifying the states that voted for each candidate. Other maps might show the outcome of a congressional election, district by district, or the results of local bond issues by neighborhood.

Being able to interpret and evaluate government data using maps is useful for analyzing political trends and understanding how your state, city, county, or region fits into these trends. Being able to read an election map makes it easy to quickly determine how various states voted. To read an election map, follow these steps:

1. Read the map title to determine what election information is being shown.

2. Read the map key to determine how the information is being presented.

3. Based on this information, decide what kinds of questions the map is intended to answer.

4. State in sentences what trend or other important information the map shows.

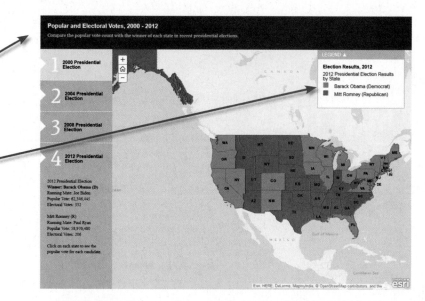

5. Think of another way of presenting the data. Would a graph, text, table, or another format do a better job of conveying the key information? Transfer the information in the map into another format.

---

netw⚡rks

TRY IT YOURSELF ONLINE

Go online to interact with these digital activities and more in each chapter.

| **Chapter 9** The Presidency | **Chapter 10** Choosing the President | **Chapter 11** Structure and Functions of the Executive Branch | **Chapter 12** State and Local Executive Branches |

✓ **INTERACTIVE DEBATE**
IS THE WAR POWERS ACT CONSTITUTIONAL?

✓ **VIDEO**
PRESIDENTIAL COMMUNICATION STYLES

✓ **INTERACTIVE IMAGE**
THE CABINET

✓ **INTERACTIVE INFOGRAPHIC**
CHARACTERISTICS OF GOVERNORS

The Presidency

networks
www.connected.mcgraw-hill.com
There's More Online about
the presidency.

CHAPTER 9

ESSENTIAL QUESTION

- What are the powers and roles of the president and how have they changed over time?

▲ The White House is
the official residence
of the president of
the United States.

Pixtal/AGE Fotostock

PRESIDENTIAL DECISION MAKING: THE CUBAN MISSILE CRISIS

Presidents must make decisions about military action quickly, and with changing information. After World War II, the United States and the Soviet Union possessed nuclear weapons that could destroy the other nation. They formed competing international alliances and fought for global influence. Many people feared the possibility of another world war—one that might result in nuclear annihilation.

In 1962 President John F. Kennedy learned that the Soviet Union was putting nuclear missiles in Cuba, a country less than 100 miles from the United States. For 13 days during the Cuban Missile Crisis, it seemed the world was on the brink of nuclear war.

SECONDARY SOURCE A

THE EVENTS OF THE CUBAN MISSILE CRISIS

October 14	An American spy plane flying over western Cuba took pictures of Soviet missiles.
October 16	Kennedy was informed that there were nuclear missiles in Cuba and assembled a team of advisors to work on the crisis.
October 22	The public learns of the Soviet missiles when Kennedy announces on television that the U.S. Navy will block ships carrying military cargo from entering Cuba.
October 25	At an emergency meeting of the United Nations Security Council, the United States presented photos of the missile sites to counter Soviet claims that there were no missiles in Cuba.
October 26	In a private letter to Kennedy, the Soviet premier Nikita Khrushchev said he would remove the nuclear missiles from Cuba if Americans pledged never to invade Cuba.
October 27	In a public letter, the Soviets demanded that the United States pledge to never invade Cuba and withdraw U.S. missiles from Turkey.
October 28	Khrushchev publicly announced it would withdraw its missiles from Cuba in exchange for an American offer to never invade Cuba. Kennedy and Khrushchev made a secret deal: the Americans would also remove their missiles from Turkey.
November 5–9	Disassembled missiles leave Cuba.

SOURCE: The World on the Brink, John F. Kennedy Presidential Library and Museum

PRIMARY SOURCE B

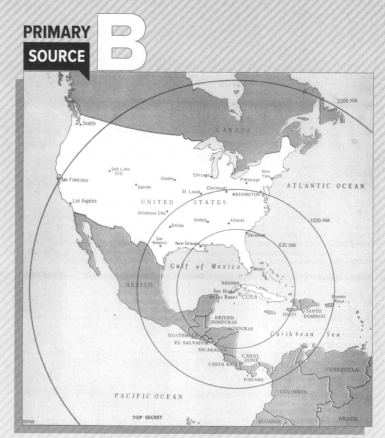

▲ This map shows the range of the nuclear missiles being built in Cuba in 1962. This is the actual map used in White House talks on the crisis.

On October 18, Theodore Sorenson, a special advisor to the president, wrote a memo laying out the actions being considered and identifying who among the president's close advisors supported each.

"Two big questions must be answered, and in conjunction with each other:

1. Which military action, if any:
   — Limited air strike: Rusk, probably Ball and Johnson, Acheson originally
   — Fuller air strike: McNamara and Taylor (who convinced Acheson) Bohlen's 2nd choice
   — Blockade: Bohlen, Thompson, probably Martin, probably McNamara and Taylor 2nd choice
   — Invasion: McCone, maybe Nitze

2. Should political action — in particular a letter of warning to Khrushchev — precede military action?
   — If blockade or invasion, everyone says yes
   — If air strike
     — Yes: Bohlen, Thompson (also K. O'Donnell)
     — No: Taylor, McNamara, presumably Acheson
     — Undecided: Rusk

These questions could be focused upon by considering either the Rusk or the Bohlen approaches."

—Memo from Theodore Sorenson, October 18, 1962

On October 22, President Kennedy gave a televised speech explaining the problem and the actions the United States was taking.

"I have directed that the following initial steps be taken immediately:

First: To halt this offensive buildup a strict quarantine on all offensive military equipment under shipment to Cuba is being initiated. All ships of any kind bound for Cuba from whatever nation or port will, if found to contain cargoes of offensive weapons, be turned back. . . . We are not at this time, however, denying the necessities of life as the Soviets attempted to do in their Berlin blockade of 1948.

Second: I have directed the continued and increased close surveillance of Cuba and its military buildup. . . .

Third: It shall be the policy of this nation to regard any nuclear missile launched from Cuba against any nation in the Western Hemisphere as an attack by the Soviet Union on the United States, requiring a full retaliatory response upon the Soviet Union.

The path we have chosen for the present is full of hazards, as all paths are; but it is the one most consistent with our character and courage as a nation and our commitments around the world."

—President Kennedy's October 22, 1962 speech

DBQ DOCUMENT-BASED QUESTIONS

1. **Identifying** On the time line of the Cuban Missile Crisis, identify points where President Kennedy had to make important decisions.

2. **Analyzing** Use the primary source documents to identify options available to President Kennedy at each decision point. What might have been the consequences of each option?

3. **Evaluating** How effectively do you think President Kennedy handled the Cuban Missile Crisis? Explain your answer.

WHAT WILL YOU DO?

How will you evaluate presidential decision making in future international crises? How will you determine whether the president is making good decisions? What information would you need to have in order to make your evaluation?

EXPLORE the interactive version of the analyzing primary sources feature on Networks.

 net**w**rks *TRY IT YOURSELF* ONLINE   www.connected.mcgraw-hill.com   *The Presidency* **259**

LESSON 1
Sources of Presidential Power

Reading Help Desk

Academic Vocabulary
- **contemporary**
- **investigation**

Content Vocabulary
- **inherent powers**
- **executive privilege**
- **mandate**
- **impeach**

TAKING NOTES:
Key Ideas and Details

CATEGORIZING Use the graphic organizer to list the presidential powers granted by the Constitution as well as other inherent powers.

Powers of the President	
Constitutional Powers	Inherent Powers

ESSENTIAL QUESTION

What are the powers and roles of the president and how have they changed over time?

Read about each of the actions below. Decide whether you believe the president should be able to take each action. Explain your reasons for each decision.

a. A group of rebels in a foreign country overthrows its president and surrounds the American Embassy. The U.S. president declares war on the rebel government.

b. The president has nominated a new federal judge, but the Senate has not yet approved the appointment. It seems unlikely that the Senate will vote to confirm the new judge. When the Senate goes on a holiday break, the president appoints the judge without the Senate's approval.

c. The president meets with the leader of a foreign country. Together, the two leaders agree not to charge tariffs (taxes on imports) on each other's cars and trucks.

d. Congress passes a law that bans possession of certain drugs. The president instructs the Drug Enforcement Agency to focus their enforcement efforts on suspects who appear to be selling large amounts of the illegal drugs and not to worry much about people who are caught with small amounts.

e. A staff member from the vice president's office is sentenced to prison time for tampering with an election. The president pardons the staffer, releasing her from prison.

Constitutional Powers

GUIDING QUESTION *What powers does the Constitution grant to the executive branch and the president?*

The Constitution is broad but vague when it comes to the powers of the president: It says that the executive power of the nation will be vested in a president. The nature of that power and the roles of the president were matters of debate during the Constitutional Convention more than 200 years ago and remain so today.

Need for a Strong Executive Having fought a revolution against the king of Britain, the Framers of the Constitution did not want the leader of the new executive branch to become a tyrant. Despite these concerns, they had two reasons for creating a strong executive.

First, the Founders had seen the problems caused by the Articles of Confederation's failure to provide for an independent executive. Without an executive, the national government had no one to carry out the acts of Congress. Moreover, the government had difficulty responding quickly to problems and enforcing laws.

Second, many of the Founders distrusted direct participation by the people in decision making. They feared that mass democratic movements might try to redistribute personal wealth and threaten private property. Consequently, they wanted a strong executive branch that would protect liberty, private property, and businesses. A strong executive would hold the legislature (the branch that directly represents popular opinion) in check. The Founders believed the legislative branch could be the most powerful of the three branches. Thus, checks on its power would be necessary. For example, in Article I, the Founders gave the president power to sign bills passed by Congress into law or to veto them.

Powers Defined in the Constitution Article II of the Constitution says that the executive power is vested in a president. It also outlines several key presidential powers, including the power to execute laws, veto legislation, command the military, and engage with foreign leaders. With Senate approval, the president can make treaties with foreign nations and appoint ambassadors and federal judges.

☑ **READING PROGRESS CHECK**

Explaining Why did the Founders create a strong executive?

Growth of Presidential Power

GUIDING QUESTION *What are informal sources of presidential power?*

The constitutional duties of the nation's first president, George Washington, and those of a modern president are much the same. Even so, today's presidents have much greater power and responsibility than past presidents.

The Constitution

WHAT DOES IT MEAN TO YOU?

"The executive Power shall be vested in a President of the United States of America ..."

—Article II, Section 1

"The President shall be Commander in Chief of the Army and Navy of the United States ... he shall have Power to Grant Reprieves and Pardons for Offenses against the United States, except in Cases of Impeachment."

—Article II, Section 2

"He shall from time to time give to the Congress Information of the State of the Union, and recommend to their Consideration such Measures as he shall judge necessary and expedient ... he shall take Care that the Laws be faithfully executed ..."

—Article II, Section 3

DBQ

a. *Listing* List the presidential powers that are specifically named in these excerpts from Article II of the Constitution.

b. *Using Context Clues* What does the phrase "shall take care that the laws be faithfully executed" mean?

c. *Identifying* Refer to the full text of the Constitution and look for Article II. Besides those listed here, what other powers does the president have?

inherent powers powers not described in the Constitution, but that have been claimed by presidents

Inherent Powers Throughout our history, presidents have enlarged presidential authority by justifying their actions in terms of **inherent powers**. Inherent powers are those claimed by the president that are not clearly expressed in the Constitution. Presidents assert that these powers can be inferred from loosely worded phrases in the Constitution such as "the executive power shall be vested in a President" and from the very nature of the president's job. In 1803, for example, Thomas Jefferson decided to purchase the Louisiana Territory from France. Nothing in the Constitution, however, stated that a president had the power to acquire territory. Jefferson decided that such a power was attached to the office itself. The Senate agreed with Jefferson and ratified the Louisiana Purchase treaty.

Theodore Roosevelt expressed the broad view of presidential power, explaining that it was both the president's right and duty to "do anything that the needs of the Nation demanded, unless such action was forbidden by the Constitution or by the laws." He took actions unlike earlier presidents, including aggressive "trust-busting" and intervention in labor disputes. In a letter to a **contemporary** historian, Roosevelt explained:

contemporary happening, existing, living, or coming into being during the same period of time

> ### PRIMARY SOURCE
> **I have used every ounce of power there was in the office and I have not cared a rap for the criticisms of those who spoke of my 'usurpation of power'; . . . I believe that the efficiency of this Government depends upon its possessing a strong central executive . . . ."**
>
> —Theodore Roosevelt, 1908

When a president exercises an inherent power not stated in the Constitution, Congress and the courts may either try to limit the power or go along with it. During the Korean War, for example, President Harry S. Truman took over the nation's steel mills during a strike in order to prevent a disruption of steel production. In 1952 the Supreme Court declared Truman's action unconstitutional because the president's power to seize private property was not listed in Article II of the Constitution.

Immediate Needs of the Nation Presidents have often used their inherent powers during war or other times of emergency. During the Civil War, Abraham Lincoln took many actions that exceeded accepted limits of presidential authority. He suspended the writ of habeas corpus and jailed opponents of the Union without a trial or the legal authority to do so. He raised an army before getting Congress's approval and took illegal action against the South by blockading its ports. Lincoln claimed the inherent powers of his office gave him the authority to do what was necessary to preserve the Union.

President Franklin Delano Roosevelt took office in 1933 during the economic crisis known as the Great Depression. He took more leadership in steering the economy than any previous president by convincing Congress to create a vast number of programs known as the New Deal to improve the economy. As a result, the executive branch expanded to carry out those programs. Roosevelt enlarged the role of government in American life and left his successors the modern presidency.

Following the September 11, 2001, terrorist attacks, President George W. Bush declared a "war on terrorism" and claimed substantially expanded powers to fight terrorism. Congress granted President Bush significant intelligence-gathering powers through the Patriot Act. His administration

President Theodore Roosevelt expressed a broad view of presidential power.

▼ CRITICAL THINKING
Explaining How did Theodore Roosevelt's "trust-busting" activities reveal his view of presidential power?

Library of Congress Prints and Photographs Division [LC-DIG-stereo-1s0197]

COMPARING
PRESIDENTIAL POWERS

CONSTITUTIONAL POWERS

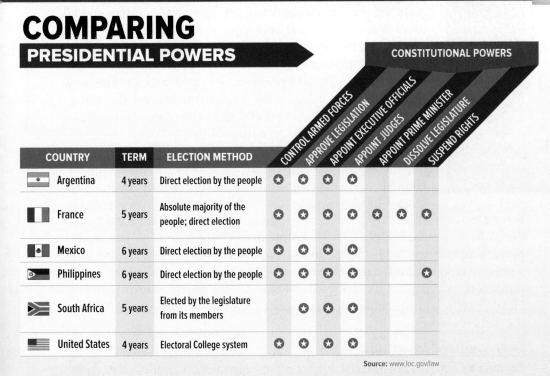

COUNTRY	TERM	ELECTION METHOD	CONTROL ARMED FORCES	APPROVE LEGISLATION	APPOINT EXECUTIVE OFFICIALS	APPOINT JUDGES	APPOINT PRIME MINISTER	DISSOLVE LEGISLATURE	SUSPEND RIGHTS
Argentina	4 years	Direct election by the people	★	★	★	★			
France	5 years	Absolute majority of the people; direct election	★	★	★	★	★	★	★
Mexico	6 years	Direct election by the people	★	★	★	★			
Philippines	6 years	Direct election by the people	★	★	★	★			★
South Africa	5 years	Elected by the legislature from its members		★	★	★			
United States	4 years	Electoral College system	★	★	★	★			

Source: www.loc.gov/law

◀ CRITICAL THINKING
1. *Identifying* Which powers are shared by presidents in all of the countries in this chart?
2. *Evaluating* Which presidents do you think are most powerful? Why?

collected intelligence on people both outside and within the United States and responded to the terrorist attacks with military force.

Executive Privilege The power of **executive privilege** is not named in the Constitution. Nonetheless, presidents since George Washington have claimed it. This is the right to withhold from Congress or the courts information about communications between the president and his or her advisers. The Supreme Court has ruled that with certain qualifications, executive privilege is a part of the separation of powers.

executive privilege the right of the president and other high-ranking executive officers to refuse to testify before Congress or a court

Popular Opinion All presidents claim that their ideas and policies represent a **mandate** from the people. They say that since they won the election, the people agree with their plans and priorities. A mandate, or a perceived mandate, can be an informal source of presidential power. The president's popularity ratings can change very quickly, however. Modern presidents use the mass media to communicate their message and to gain popular support for what they want to do even after elections. President Ronald Reagan's skillful use of the media led some to dub him the "Great Communicator."

mandate an authorization to act given to a representative

Public opinion can also limit a president. In 1968 public dissatisfaction with President Lyndon Johnson's conduct of the Vietnam War convinced him not to run for reelection. Without favorable public opinion, no president can carry out a political program. For example, in 1993 President Bill Clinton proposed major changes to the nation's health care system. Various interest groups, including insurance companies and doctors, campaigned against the president's proposal. When public opinion turned against the plan, Congress decided not to act on Clinton's proposal. When public opinion shifted during the Obama presidency, however, Congress passed a new health care law.

Checks and Balances on Presidential Powers The Founders built safeguards into the Constitution against potential presidential abuse of their lawful powers. The judicial and legislative branches limit the president's authority. The Supreme Court can rule executive actions unconstitutional.

President Ronald Reagan was well known for his skillful use of the media.

▲ CRITICAL THINKING

Assessing How would good communication skills help someone carry out the duties of the presidency?

impeach to accuse a public official of misconduct in office

investigation an observation or study by close examination

Congress can pass legislation even if a president vetoes it, and the Senate must confirm a president's appointees and all treaties. Congress must also approve the budget.

The House and Senate can also **impeach** the president. The term *impeach* means to formally accuse a public official of misconduct. When a president is impeached, the House of Representatives initiates the impeachment, and the Senate investigates the accusation and then votes about whether or not to remove the president from office.

In the nation's history, two presidents have been impeached. In 1868, just after the end of the Civil War, the House impeached President Andrew Johnson over issues related to how southern states would be reconstructed. The Senate acquitted him by one vote, so he remained in office. In 1998 the House voted to impeach President Bill Clinton over charges that he committed perjury and obstructed justice in an **investigation** about his relationship with someone who worked in the White House. The Senate acquitted him and he remained in office. In 1974 President Nixon was nearly impeached—the House prepared impeachment charges against him—but he resigned before the full House vote.

✓ READING PROGRESS CHECK

Explaining Why do presidential powers often expand during war or other times of emergency?

Presidential Roles

GUIDING QUESTION *What are the main roles that modern presidents fulfill?*

Today, the president has seven main roles. The president is the head of state, chief executive, commander in chief, chief diplomat, legislative leader, economic planner, and party leader.

- **Head of State**—the president serves as a ceremonial figure representing the United States.
- **Chief Executive**—the president leads the executive branch of government, which implements the laws that Congress passes. The president also appoints (with Senate confirmation) federal judges and the heads of executive departments and agencies.
- **Commander in Chief**—the president is responsible for the nation's security and is in charge of the military.
- **Chief Diplomat**—the president meets with foreign leaders, appoints ambassadors, and makes treaties (with Senate approval).
- **Legislative Leader**—the president delivers an annual State of the Union message to Congress, proposes legislation, signs or vetoes laws passed by Congress, and can call Congress into special session when necessary.
- **Economic Planner**—the president appoints economic advisors, meets with business leaders, prepares an annual budget request, and submits economic reports to Congress.
- **Party Leader**—the president leads his or her political party, rewarding party supporters with positions in government, and helps to elect other party members by raising money and campaigning for party members.

✓ READING PROGRESS CHECK

Applying What are the seven presidential roles? Provide an actual or hypothetical example of a president fulfilling each of these roles.

The President's Schedule

September 14 –20, 2014

(M)	(T)	(W)	(T)	(F)
10:00 A.M. The President and the Vice President receive the Presidential Daily Briefing	**9:15 A.M.** The President meets with Special Presidential Envoy for the Global Coalition to Counter ISIL General John Allen and Deputy Special Presidential Envoy Brett McGurk	**9:45 A.M.** The President participates in a briefing at U.S. Central Command in Tampa, Florida	**10:00 A.M.** The President receives the Presidential Daily Briefing	**10:30 A.M.** The President and the Vice President receive the Presidential Daily Briefing
11:30 A.M. The President meets with Secretary of Education Duncan		**10:50 A.M.** The President tours the Joint Operations Center at U.S. Central Command in Tampa, Florida	**10:45 A.M.** The President participates in an Ambassador Credentialing Ceremony	**11:45 A.M.** The President delivers remarks at the launch of the "It's On Us" Campaign
12:30 P.M. The President and the Vice President meet for lunch	**2:35 P.M.** The President participates in a briefing at the Centers for Disease Control & Prevention in Atlanta, Georgia	**11:50 A.M.** The President delivers remarks in Tampa, Florida	**2:00 P.M.** The President holds a bilateral meeting with President Petro Poroshenko of Ukraine	**3:35 P.M.** The President delivers remarks at the DNC's annual Women's Leadership Forum
1:50 P.M. The President awards Army Command Sergeant Major Bennie G. Adkins and Army Specialist Four Donald P. Sloat, the Medal of Honor	**3:25 P.M.** The President meets with Emory University doctors and healthcare professionals	**6:30 P.M.** The President delivers remarks at a picnic for Members of Congress in Washington, D.C.	**3:55 P.M.** The President attends a DNC roundtable	**4:30 P.M.** The President holds a bill signing
5:20 P.M. The President attends a DSCC event	**4:05 P.M.** The President delivers remarks		**7:00 P.M.** The President delivers a statement on Congressional passage of the Continuing Resolution	

Use the schedule of President Obama's activities the week of September 14, 2014, to answer the critical thinking questions.

▲ **CRITICAL THINKING**

1. *Analyzing* What roles do you think the president was fulfilling in each activity?
2. *Making Connections* What principles of democracy are illustrated by the fact that this schedule is made public?

LESSON 1 REVIEW

Reviewing Vocabulary

1. *Discussing* What does it mean to impeach a president? Which presidents have been impeached?

Using Your Graphic Organizer

2. *Summarizing* Use your completed graphic organizer to summarize the constitutional and inherent powers of the president.

Answering the Guiding Questions

3. *Identifying* What powers does the Constitution grant to the executive branch and the president?

4. *Describing* What are informal sources of presidential power?

5. *Explaining* What are the main roles that modern presidents fulfill?

Writing About Government

6. *Argument* Review the list of roles that presidents fulfill. Rank them from most important to least important. Then decide what percentage of a given week a president should spend on each of these roles. Last, write a memorandum explaining your choices to the president. Provide reasons for your arguments.

7. *Informative/Explanatory* Compare the contributions of presidents Abraham Lincoln, Theodore Roosevelt, Harry Truman, and George W. Bush during their terms of office. Be sure to include important historical events and how each president used the powers of his office in order to respond to them.

netw⚙rks
TRY IT YOURSELF ONLINE

LESSON 2
Head of State and Chief Executive

Reading Help Desk

Academic Vocabulary

• fund

Content Vocabulary

• executive order
• impound
• reprieve
• pardon
• amnesty

TAKING NOTES:

Integration of Knowledge and Ideas

DESCRIBING As you read this lesson, fill in the columns for each role. Describe at least two examples of actions the president takes in that role, find a news story that relates to that role and summarize the article, and draw a symbol that represents this role.

Presidential Roles	Examples of Actions	Summary of News Story	Symbol to Represent This Role
Head of State			
Chief Executive			

ESSENTIAL QUESTION

What are the powers and roles of the president and how have they changed over time?

Read the following examples of government actions. Which activities fulfill the president's role as head of state? Which as chief executive? Rank the presidential activities in each role in order from most to least important. Explain your reasoning.

• Gives a Presidential Medal of Freedom to British Prime Minister Tony Blair

• Issues an Executive Order creating a National Economics Council

• Advocates for a new health care law in the U.S. Congress

• Throws out the first pitch at the first game of the World Series

• Appoints Janet Napolitano as the Secretary of Homeland Security

• Meets with the cabinet to discuss presidential priorities for this term

Head of State

GUIDING QUESTION *How does the president fulfill the role of head of state?*

The U.S. president is both head of state and chief executive. (In this context, the term *head of state* refers to the leader of a nation or country.) As head of state, the president represents the nation and performs many ceremonial roles. As chief executive, the president directs the activities of the thousands of executive branch employees who carry out the laws. In many countries, different people perform these two duties. One person, such as a king, queen, or emperor, is the ceremonial head of state, while another person, such as a prime minister or premier, directs the government.

Some of the president's duties as head of state are specifically mentioned in Article II of the Constitution. For example, the Constitution says the president shall "receive Ambassadors and other public Ministers." To fulfill that duty, the president hosts such dignitaries as kings, queens, and heads of foreign governments.

266

Modern presidents play an important role when a natural disaster such as a hurricane strikes or a tragedy like a mass shooting or bombing occurs. Victims look to the president to visit the scene and provide words of comfort on behalf of all citizens across the country.

Other ceremonial duties are less serious but also widely covered in the press. Many presidents throw out the first pitch to begin the baseball season, light the nation's Christmas tree and Menorah on the Ellipse—a grassy area near the White House lawn—meet public figures such as U.S. Olympic athletes, or give awards to distinguished business leaders, actors, or artists.

Much of the mystique of the presidency exists because presidents are more than politicians. To millions around the world and at home, the president is the symbol for the United States.

☑ READING PROGRESS CHECK

Determining Importance Why are the president's ceremonial roles important?

Chief Executive

GUIDING QUESTION *How does the president fulfill the role of chief executive?*

The president leads the executive branch of government that carries out the laws that Congress passes and runs the programs Congress creates. These laws and programs range over a great many areas of public concern from Social Security, taxes, housing, flood control, and energy to civil rights, health care, education, and environmental protection.

There are more than 150 departments and agencies that take responsibility for implementing laws in different areas. More than 2 million people work for the federal government, from FBI agents to air traffic controllers to clerks for the Social Security Administration. The president is in charge of these employees and the federal departments and agencies for which they work.

Source of President's Executive Power The president's executive power is described in the Constitution, but the document does not provide much detail about the components of this power. Article II, Section 1, simply says "the executive Power shall be vested in a President of the United States of America. . . ." Section 3 of the same article says ". . . he shall take Care that the Laws be faithfully executed."

What does it mean to "faithfully execute" the laws? When Congress passes a law, it is the president's responsibility to put that law into action. Congress cannot provide enough details in every law to explain exactly how it should be implemented. The president must make some decisions about how to put the law into effect but must also work within the boundaries provided in the law; that is, the law must be implemented in a faithful way.

Consider a 2012 law that required the Department of Homeland Security (DHS) to develop special airport security screening procedures to help Armed Forces members traveling on official orders clear security more quickly. The DHS could decide exactly how to screen members of the military. However, for the law to be faithfully executed, the DHS would have to develop a system that would help military personnel get through those airport security lines faster than the average traveler.

One of the many roles of the president is to perform ceremonial duties, as shown in this photo of President Obama presenting former Senator and astronaut John Glenn with a Presidential Medal of Freedom.

▼ CRITICAL THINKING
Identifying In which presidential role is Barack Obama acting here?

NASA/Bill Ingalls

The requirement that the laws must be faithfully executed can be a limit on the president's executive power. Additionally, funding to administer laws is controlled by Congress, which authorizes and appropriates **funds**. The president is also limited in this power by the judicial branch. Federal courts can decide whether the actions a president takes to implement laws are constitutional.

The Appointment Power No president could directly supervise the daily activities of the many agencies in the executive branch. Instead, the president appoints about 2,200 top-level federal officials who run the executive branch. Key among these are the 15 people who will lead the cabinet departments—the major agencies of the executive branch. This authority to appoint top officials in the administration is one important tool a president has to influence how legislation is implemented. Presidents try to appoint officials who share their political beliefs because they will be committed to carrying out their goals. Selecting the right people can be one of a president's most important tasks. This power is partially limited by the Senate, however, which must confirm many top-level appointments.

Presidents can also control the implementation of the laws by firing officials they have appointed. For example, President Nixon fired his secretary of the interior for opposing his Vietnam policies. It is not always easy, however, to remove a popular official who has congressional and public support.

The president also appoints all federal judges, including the justices of the Supreme Court. All judicial appointments must be approved by the Senate. Judicial nominations tend to be among the most contentious conflicts between the legislative and executive branches, particularly when the White House and Congress are controlled by different parties. By appointing justices with particular points of view on the Constitution and other issues, presidents can exert broad influence on government and society. Since federal judges may hold their positions for life terms, the impact of judicial appointments can be seen for years or even decades after a president leaves office.

The president leads the executive branch that consists of more than 150 departments and agencies and employs more than 2 million people.

▼ CRITICAL THINKING

Identifying Explain how the president hand picks many of the officials who serve at each of these levels within the executive branch.

Organization of the Executive Branch

THE PRESIDENT
THE VICE PRESIDENT
THE EXECUTIVE OFFICE OF THE PRESIDENT (EOP)

EXECUTIVE BRANCH (OR CABINET)
DEPARTMENTS
Department of Agriculture
Department of Commerce
Department of Defense
Department of Education
Department of Energy
Department of Health and Human Services
Department of Homeland Security
Department of Housing and Urban Development
Department of Interior
Department of Justice
Department of Labor
Department of State
Department of Transportation
Department of Treasury
Department of Veterans Affairs

INDEPENDENT AGENCIES AND
GOVERNMENT CORPORATIONS

Executive Orders In addition to staffing and leading the executive branch, presidents issue **executive orders**, which are presidential directives that have the force of law without the approval of Congress. This power is implied by the Constitution because Article II grants the president "executive power" and charges him or her with making certain that "the laws be faithfully executed." President Dwight D. Eisenhower did this when he used an executive order to put the Arkansas National Guard under federal control in order to force the Little Rock, Arkansas, public schools to desegregate.

Executive orders may be issued to detail the specific actions federal agencies must take to implement a law. For example, President Jimmy Carter used an executive order to put thousands of acres of land in Alaska under the control of the National Park Service.

Executive orders have also been used to make dramatic new policy. President Abraham Lincoln issued the Emancipation Proclamation with an executive order; President Harry S. Truman used an executive order in

FIRST-YEAR **EXECUTIVE ORDERS**

President George W. Bush (2001)	President Barack H. Obama (2009)
• Sets out executive branch responsibilities related to faith-based initiatives	• Revokes 2001 executive order about executive privilege
• Establishes White House Office of Faith-Based and Community Initiatives	• Establishes ethical guidelines and requires ethics pledge for executive branch appointees
• Extends the President's Information Technology Advisory Committee	• Requires interrogations to comply with U.S. and international law
• Makes changes to federal contracting rules providing that employees of federal contractors must be informed that they cannot be forced to join a union or pay union dues (four separate executive orders on this topic)	• Calls for review of detention practices for people held in war on terror
	• Calls for closing of Guantanamo Bay detention facility
	• Makes changes to federal contracting rules providing that employees of federal contractors must be informed of their right to collective bargaining

Presidents often issue executive orders that implement their campaign promises and repeat their priorities.

◀ CRITICAL THINKING

1. *Making Inferences* What does the information in the chart suggest about the campaign promises or priorities of these two presidents?

2. *Considering Advantages and Disadvantages* What does this information suggest about the advantages and disadvantages of executive orders?

1948 to racially integrate the armed forces; and President Franklin D. Roosevelt used one to place Japanese Americans in internment camps during World War II. Some recent presidents have used executive orders to bypass the U.S. Congress and legislate in areas such as environmental protection where the Congress has been unable or unwilling to pass a law.

At the same time, presidents cannot issue all executive orders they would like. Such orders must be related in some way to either powers given to the president in the Constitution or delegated to him or her by Congress. Presidents usually spell out the constitutional or statutory basis for their executive orders. Given the president's constitutional role as a commander in chief, the courts usually give presidents especially broad limits when it comes to orders relating to foreign policy and the military.

Presidents can readily issue executive orders, but their successors may just as easily reverse them. In 1984 President Ronald Reagan issued an executive order restricting federal funding for family-planning groups who performed or actively promoted abortions in other countries. President Bill Clinton reversed this order when he took office. President George W. Bush then reinstated the limits on funding first ordered by President Reagan. With the stroke of a pen, President Barack Obama again renewed funding.

Impoundment of Funds When the president has deep disagreements with Congress about what programs should exist or how they should be run, he or she may **impound** the funds Congress had approved to carry out those programs. For example, in 1803 President Thomas Jefferson did not spend money Congress set aside for new gunboats because he believed they were no longer needed.

impound to refuse to spend

Supporters of impoundment argue that it is an inherent power of the executive branch. Opponents may argue that impoundments undermine the will of the people who have chosen the legislators who created and funded the programs.

This word cloud displays the words occurring most frequently in President George W. Bush's 2005 inaugural address.

▶ **CRITICAL THINKING**

Analyzing What might this tell you about how President Bush hoped to address his second term as president?

A president's power to impound funds is limited, though. After President Richard Nixon impounded huge sums—billions in a single year—for programs he opposed, groups that would have benefited from the programs took Nixon to court. The court then ordered the president to spend the appropriated money. Congress later passed legislation to prevent such large-scale impounding without congressional approval and strengthen the budget authority of Congress.

Reprieves, Pardons, and Amnesty As chief executive, the president also can grant reprieves and pardons for federal crimes. A **reprieve** postpones legal punishment. A **pardon** releases a person from legal punishment. People who receive them have usually been convicted of a federal crime. An exception was in 1974 when President Gerald Ford granted Richard Nixon a full pardon before he could be indicted for any crimes he might have committed during the Watergate scandal. The pardon was very controversial, but it was fully within President Ford's power to grant it.

The president may also grant **amnesty**. Amnesty is a pardon for a group of people who have committed an offense against the government. President Jimmy Carter granted amnesty to young men who evaded the draft during the Vietnam War.

reprieve a presidential order that postpones legal punishment

pardon a presidential order that releases a person from legal punishment

amnesty a presidential order that pardons a group of people who have committed an offense against the government

☑ **READING PROGRESS CHECK**

Explaining What are the different ways that executive orders are used by presidents?

LESSON 2 REVIEW

Reviewing Vocabulary

1. ***Defining*** What are the similarities and differences between reprieves and pardons?

Using Your Graphic Organizer

2. ***Contrasting*** Use your completed graphic organizer to contrast the president's roles as head of state and chief executive.

Answering the Guiding Questions

3. ***Explaining*** How does the president fulfill the role of head of state?

4. ***Explaining*** How does the president fulfill the role of chief executive?

Writing About Government

5. ***Informative/Explanatory*** Explain how the president's role as chief executive is limited by the legislative and judicial branches.

Interact with these digital assets and others in lesson 3

✓ **INTERACTIVE CHART**
Official Declarations of War

✓ **INTERACTIVE IMAGE**
The USA Patriot Act

✓ **SELF-CHECK QUIZ**

✓ **VIDEO**
Defense Budget Cuts

networks
TRY IT YOURSELF ONLINE

LESSON 3
Commander in Chief and Chief Diplomat

ReadingHelp Desk

Academic Vocabulary

- **deny**
- **access**

Content Vocabulary

- **civilian**
- **national security**
- **reauthorize**
- **military tribunal**
- **treaty**
- **executive agreement**

TAKING NOTES:

Integration of Knowledge and Ideas

DESCRIBING As you read this lesson, fill in the columns for each role. Describe at least two examples of actions the president takes in that role, find a news story that relates to that role and summarize the article, and draw a symbol that represents this role.

Presidential Roles	Examples of Actions	Summary of News Story	Symbol to Represent this Role
Commander in Chief			
Chief Diplomat			

ESSENTIAL QUESTION

What are the powers and roles of the president and how have they changed over time?

The following situations represent actual presidential actions during war. Recall what the Constitution says about power and authority over the military. Read each situation below and discuss whether or not the president should be able to exercise this power. What are the advantages and disadvantages of the president having this power?

a. An American citizen protesting a war is arrested, held in jail for a long time without charges, and then put on trial before a U.S. military tribunal. Should the president have the power to hold someone in jail without charges? Should the president be able to prosecute a civilian in military courts?

b. The United States is involved in a war overseas, fighting against a terrorist organization. U.S. troops capture an individual who is a U.S. citizen and was fighting against the U.S. The U.S. designates this person as an "unlawful combatant," which means he is not entitled to access the court system or have a lawyer, rights guaranteed to most Americans. Should the president have the power during wartime to label U.S. citizens as unlawful combatants, to hold them indefinitely, and to deny them a lawyer?

c. The United States has been attacked by a foreign country. The government rounds up all immigrants from the enemy country and anyone who has ancestors who were born in the enemy country and makes them live in concentration camps for the duration of the war. Should the president have the power during wartime to detain a group of people based on their race and ancestry?

Commander in Chief

GUIDING QUESTIONS *How does the president fulfill the role of commander in chief? How is the president limited in this role?*

The Constitution makes the president commander in chief of the armed forces of the United States. The Constitution does not provide many details about what powers are included in this role. Because of this lack of detail, presidents have been able to argue that they possess all the powers needed to defend the nation or help it wage war against an enemy, as long as they do not interfere with the power of other branches or violate the law. The president may also use the military to control serious turmoil in the nation. For example, presidents have used federal troops to control rioting in American cities. In case of a natural disaster, such as a flood, the president may send needed supplies or troops to help keep order.

Power to Make War Congress provides an important limitation on the president's role as commander in chief. Congress retains the power to declare war, as well as the power to provide the funds to pay for the military. Even so, presidents have sent American forces into action many times without a formal declaration of war.

In the early 1900s, several presidents sent military forces into countries in Latin America and Asia to support leaders who were friendly to the United States. President Theodore Roosevelt sent the American troops on the USS *Nashville* to support Panamanian rebels in their revolution for independence from Colombia.

President Lyndon Johnson deployed forces to Vietnam without an official declaration of war. Instead Congress passed the Gulf of Tonkin resolution, which authorized the president to use troops in Vietnam. As the conflict in Vietnam dragged on, however, Congress decided that the continued use of American troops in Vietnam was a result of an abuse of presidential power. It passed the War Powers Act in 1973 to limit the president's ability to wage war without a formal declaration by Congress. The War Powers Act prevented presidents from committing troops to combat for more than 60 days without congressional approval. It also allowed Congress to order the president to disengage troops involved in an undeclared war. President Nixon vetoed the law, but Congress mustered enough votes to override his veto. The law has not substantially changed presidential engagement in war making, however.

Since passage of the War Powers Act, there have been many instances where a president has engaged in military operations; debates have ensued over what constitutes combat troops and whether the War Powers Act should apply. For example, when President George H.W. Bush ordered an invasion of Panama to overthrow the dictator Manuel Noriega, he did not seek congressional approval. Was approval required?

In 2001 President George W. Bush began the "war on terrorism" by sending troops to Afghanistan. Congress passed an Authorization to Use Military Force in Afghanistan by overwhelming margins. Later Bush asked for congressional approval for a much larger military action against Iraq. In October 2002 Congress passed a resolution that authorized the president to use the U.S. armed forces in Iraq "as he deems necessary and appropriate."

CHART

OFFICIAL DECLARATIONS OF WAR

▶ **CRITICAL THINKING**

Drawing Conclusions The Vietnam War lasted from 1956 to 1975. Did Congress declare war on Vietnam? How do you know?

War	Date War Declared	House Vote	Senate Vote
The War of 1812	June 17, 1812	79–49	19–13
The Mexican-American War	May 12, 1846	174–14	40–2
The Spanish-American War	April 25, 1898	By voice votes	By voice votes
World War I (Germany)	April 6, 1917	373–50	82–6
World War II (Japan)	December 8, 1941	388–1	82–0

Will You Send American Military Support to Libya? Imagine you are the president. A civil war has begun in Libya, and rebels are fighting against the longtime dictator, Muammar al-Qaddafi. For many years, Qaddafi funded terrorist groups that attacked the United States. Qaddafi's government denied many basic human rights to Libyans, but Qaddafi had begun to cooperate more with the United States and said that he intended to remove many dangerous weapons from Libya. If the rebels overthrow Qaddafi, their new government might be friendlier to the United States, but it is hard to know what type of government they would create.

The Libyan rebels have asked the United States to send military support. They want the United States to patrol Libyan airspace with fighter jets and bomb government radar and missile launching sites. Some Americans believe it would not cost much to support the rebels, and it is the right thing to do. Others point out that American soldiers could get injured or killed, and they worry the war could drag on for years. Congress is equally split on the issue.

As president, you must decide whether or not to commit American military resources.

Making Decisions Will you send American military support to Libya? To help you decide, make a list of the most persuasive reasons you can identify for each side. Weigh the evidence and make a decision. Explain your decision.

In 2011 President Obama did not receive congressional approval for NATO airstrikes in Libya by the 60-day deadline.

Military Operations and Strategy As commander in chief, the president is responsible for key military decisions that define military policy and strategy. The president is a **civilian**, not an active member of the military, although historically many presidents have had military experience and leadership. Generals, admirals, and other military leaders run the armed forces on a day-to-day basis. The president receives regular reports from military and national security leaders that help him or her know about national security threats and developments around the world.

Shadow War For hundreds of years, the U.S. engaged in conventional wars fought with large numbers of troops in foreign countries in full public view. For the last 15 years, however, the U.S. has also been conducting a new kind of war, a "shadow war." This is fought in secret by special operations troops, hired private contractors, and armed drones—remote-controlled, pilotless aircraft firing missiles. It is aimed at tracking down and killing terrorists in places like Pakistan, Yemen, and Somalia. These new technologies are seen by many as lower-cost, lower-risk alternatives to messy wars of occupation.

President Bush started this shadow warfare following the September 11, 2001, attacks, and President Obama greatly increased these activities. The Central Intelligence Agency (CIA) and the Pentagon have the primary responsibility for such operations under the overall direction and authority of the president. Osama bin Laden was killed in Pakistan by Navy SEALs as part of this program. In at least one case, two American citizens known to be engaged in terrorist activities were killed by CIA drones.

Many shadow war activities are classified—information about them is not made public. The Obama administration has gone to court to fight efforts to make this information public. Some observers worry that secrecy makes it

civilian one not on active duty in the armed services or not on a police or firefighting force

President George W. Bush expanded presidential powers with the USA Patriot Act as a means of fighting terrorism following the attacks of September 11, 2001.

▲ CRITICAL THINKING
Formulating Questions Write a question you would want to have answered in order to decide whether or not to support the USA Patriot Act.

national security protection of a nation—its lands and people—from foreign threats, whether from governments, organized groups, or individual terrorists

reauthorize the act of passing legislation into law again

military tribunal a military court designed to try members of enemy forces during wartime, operating outside the scope of conventional criminal and civil proceedings

difficult to hold public officials accountable for this kind of "shadow" warfare. Some are concerned that shadow war has changed the CIA from an intelligence service to a high-tech paramilitary organization. Nevertheless, experts predict such activities are likely not only to continue, but to increase.

The Presidency in Times of War During a war, presidents often claim increased powers to protect the nation. Congress is also more likely to give the president special powers at home as well as abroad. During World War II, Franklin D. Roosevelt demanded and received from Congress power to control prices, ration gas and food, and manage the industries needed to produce tanks, guns, and other war materials.

Following the attacks of September 11, 2001, President George W. Bush expanded presidential powers as a way to fight terrorism. Just weeks after the attacks, Congress passed the USA Patriot Act. The act gave the president and executive branch broad powers to gather information about possible suspects and to detain people suspected of terrorism. For example, the act made it much easier for law enforcement to conduct wire taps and searches, including secret searches of the homes and records of U.S. citizens that can be carried out without a customary search warrant.

Civil liberties groups and others have challenged the Patriot Act and other post-9/11 executive actions, charging that they unnecessarily strip fundamental constitutional protections at a time when the U.S. is not really at war. They also claim the Patriot Act is unconstitutional. Supporters say there are times and circumstances—such as the threat of terrorism—that justify a stronger focus on **national security**. They say the Patriot Act and other executive actions strike the right balance between protecting national security and constitutional freedoms. Since its initial passage, the law has been **reauthorized** in 2005 and 2010, with slight modifications to address critics' concerns.

President Bush also took other actions to fight terrorism. In 2002 he persuaded Congress to create a new federal department, the Department of Homeland Security, to better coordinate antiterrorism activities across the government. Bush also put into place a practice to indefinitely detain foreigners and U.S. citizens who were captured on the battlefield. In 2004, however, the Supreme Court ruled in *Hamdi* v. *Rumsfeld* that the president cannot indefinitely lock up foreigners or U.S. citizens without giving them a chance to challenge their detention in court. In 2006 the justices rejected the Bush administration's use of specially created courts called **military tribunals** to try suspected terrorists.

☑ READING PROGRESS CHECK

Analyzing How has the presidential power to make war changed over time?

Chief Diplomat

GUIDING QUESTIONS *How does the president fulfill the role of chief diplomat? How is the president limited in this role?*

The president directs the foreign policy of the United States, making key decisions about the relations the United States has with other countries in the world. In this role, the president is the nation's chief diplomat. The president can negotiate and sign treaties, sign executive agreements with foreign heads of state, and recognize foreign governments. However, the president is limited in this role by the Congress.

Treaties and Diplomatic Resolutions As chief diplomat, the president has sole power to negotiate and sign **treaties**. As part of the constitutional system of checks and balances, however, two-thirds of the Senate must approve all treaties before they can go into effect.

The Senate takes its constitutional responsibility about treaties very seriously. Sometimes the Senate has refused to approve a treaty. After World War I, President Wilson was one of the three international leaders to create and propose the Treaty of Versailles. That treaty set terms to end the war and made the United States a member of the League of Nations. Despite Wilson's role internationally, the U.S. Senate refused to ratify the treaty. More recently, in 1977 President Carter signed two treaties giving control of the Panama Canal to the government of that country, but the Senate took months to debate and ratify the controversial treaties.

In addition to its power over treaties, Congress can enact foreign policy legislation. It also can restrict or **deny** funds for foreign policy initiatives through its power of appropriations. Congress can also pass diplomatic resolutions. While these resolutions are not legally binding, they can exert influence on the president and U.S. relationships with other countries.

In the struggle for control over foreign policy, presidents have two key advantages over Congress: **access** to information and decisive ability. Presidents have access to more information about foreign affairs than most members of Congress do. The administration sometimes classifies this information as secret. The Central Intelligence Agency (CIA), the State Department, the Defense Department, and the National Security Council

treaty a formal agreement between the governments of two or more countries

deny to refuse to admit or acknowledge

access freedom or ability to obtain or make use of something

PARTICIPATING
(IN) Your Government

Negotiating

For more than 20 years, the United States has tried to stop Iran from enriching uranium. Iran maintains that it wants to fuel nuclear power plants, but the United States suspects that Iran is secretly developing nuclear weapons. Iran argues that it has the right to develop nuclear fuels. The United States and its allies are concerned about Iran having nuclear weapons or such weapons falling into terrorists' hands. The UN Security Council has passed many resolutions against Iran's nuclear program, and the member countries have imposed economic sanctions.

New negotiations are set to begin. Iran wants the West to recognize its right to develop nuclear fuel and wants to build new facilities. The United States wants to emphasize peace and security and for Iran's program to be transparent and open to international monitoring. It would prefer that Iran not enrich uranium itself but rather receive enriched uranium fuel from Europe. The United States wants Iran to commit to not developing weapons of mass destruction. Iran wants economic sanctions to end and wants to receive new technology for civil aviation and agriculture from the West. Both countries want to cooperate to combat terrorism.

TOPICS	Starting Point: What Is Your Ideal Outcome?	Negotiation: Where Is There Flexibility in Your Ideal?	Bottom Line: Which Points Are Non-negotiable?
Iran's Enrichment Facilities			
Monitoring and Transparency			
Sanctions and Cooperation			

EXPLORING THE ESSENTIAL QUESTION

Making Decisions Imagine that you are part of a group helping the president prepare for UN Security Council negotiations. Identify what you think the U.S. approach should be. Then consider which points are negotiable and where you will draw the line and cannot compromise further. Use the table to plan a negotiating strategy.

U.S. Secretary of State John Kerry meets with South Sudanese President Salva Kiir in 2013.

executive agreement legally binding pact between the president and the head of a foreign government that does not require Senate approval

(NSC) give the president the latest information needed to make key foreign-policy decisions. Presidents use this information to plan and justify actions they want to take. Members of Congress who lack this information often find it difficult to challenge the president's decisions. The ability to take decisive action has added to the power of the presidency in foreign affairs. Unlike Congress, the executive branch is headed by a single person who can act swiftly. In an international emergency, the responsibility for action rests with the president.

Executive Agreements The president also has the authority to make **executive agreements** with other countries. These agreements have the same legal status as treaties, but they do not require Senate consent. Most diplomatic executive agreements involve routine matters, but some presidents have used executive agreements to conclude more serious arrangements. During World War II, Franklin D. Roosevelt lent American ships to the British in exchange for leases on British military bases. Roosevelt knew that he could not persuade the Senate to ratify a treaty, so he negotiated an executive agreement.

Some presidents have kept executive agreements secret. In 1969 Congress discovered that several presidents had kept secret many executive agreements giving military aid to South Vietnam, Laos, Thailand, and the Philippines. To prevent this, Congress passed a law in 1972 requiring the president to make public all executive agreements signed each year.

Recognition of Foreign Governments As chief diplomat, the president decides whether the United States will recognize governments of other countries. The president determines whether the government will acknowledge the legal existence of another government and have official dealings with that government.

Presidents sometimes use recognition as a foreign-policy tool. For example, since 1961, presidents have refused to recognize the Communist government of Cuba. This action indicates American opposition to the policies of the Cuban government. In 2011 the United States officially recognized the Libyan opposition group that controlled a region of that country as the legitimate government of the whole country.

☑ **READING PROGRESS CHECK**

Comparing and Contrasting How are *treaties* and *executive agreements* similar? How are they different?

LESSON 3 REVIEW

Reviewing Vocabulary
1. ***Defining*** Why is the commander in chief a civilian?

Using Your Graphic Organizer
2. ***Summarizing*** Use your completed graphic organizer to summarize the types of actions a president can take in his or her roles as commander in chief and chief diplomat.

Answering the Guiding Questions
3. ***Explaining*** How does the president fulfill the role of commander in chief? How is the president limited in this role?

4. ***Explaining*** How does the president fulfill the role of chief diplomat? How is the president limited in this role?

Writing About Government
5. ***Informative/Explanatory*** What advantages does the president have over Congress when it comes to foreign and defense policy? Explain.

Is the War Powers Act constitutional?

DEBATING DEMOCRATIC PRINCIPLES

The War Powers Act of 1973 was inspired by the Vietnam War. Many believed the president should not have sent so many American soldiers to Vietnam without a formal declaration of war. Congress wanted to prevent this from happening again. The act sets various deadlines for the president to notify and get congressional approval for sending troops abroad. Since the Constitution gives both the president and Congress war-making powers, the act remains controversial.

TEAM A — **The War Powers Act Is Constitutional**

The War Powers Act was necessary to maintain a proper balance of power between the executive and legislative branches. The Framers of the Constitution gave Congress the power to declare war or to ultimately decide whether to enter a war. As commander in chief, the president has the power to lead U.S. forces when the decision to wage war has been made by Congress. It is dangerous to encourage presidents to act alone, assuming that Congress will rally around the president after he or she has committed a sufficient number of troops to combat. The president can commit troops in an emergency, but the Framers never intended them to be committed indefinitely—or for so long that war is inevitable. The War Powers Act provides some real control for Congress by setting clear time limits and improves communication between the president and Congress in a crisis. The War Powers Act also promotes stability because it moderates a president's response to a crisis since he or she knows that actions may ultimately be vetoed by Congress.

TEAM B — **The War Powers Act Is Not Constitutional**

The War Powers Act interferes with the president's authority as commander in chief. It restricts the president's effectiveness in foreign policy and should be repealed. The act restricts a president's power to send troops into action in an international crisis. If the president wants to conduct the best foreign policy—and use American military superiority to help solve world crises—he or she needs flexibility. The time limits in the War Powers Act highlight the fact that the law is unconstitutional as well as impractical. Further, the obligation of a deadline presents the image of a divided nation to the world. It gives the enemy hope that the president will be forced by domestic pressure to withdraw troops after a short period. This can actually increase the risk to American soldiers who are sent into action. As stated in the Constitution, the president is meant to command the armed forces, thus he or she must be able to commit troops without interference.

EXPLORING THE ESSENTIAL QUESTION

Evaluating Arguments How does the War Powers Act attempt to balance power between the Congress and the president? Identify the most compelling reasons to support each side of the issue. With which side do you tend to agree? Explain your reasoning.

Interact with these digital assets and others in lesson 4

✓ **INTERACTIVE GRAPH**
Presidential Vetoes Overridden by Congress

✓ **INTERACTIVE IMAGE**
The President as Party Leader

✓ **SELF-CHECK QUIZ**

✓ **VIDEO**
The State of the Union Address

networks
TRY IT YOURSELF ONLINE

  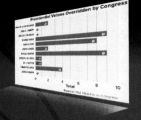

LESSON 4
Legislative, Economic, and Party Leader

ReadingHelp Desk

Academic Vocabulary

• annual
• ensure

Content Vocabulary

• Federal Reserve System
• Council of Economic Advisers
• political patronage

TAKING NOTES:
Integration of Knowledge and Ideas

DESCRIBING As you read this lesson, fill in the columns for each role. Describe at least two examples of actions the president takes in that role, find a news story that relates to that role and summarize the article, and draw a symbol that represents this role.

	Presidential Roles		
	Legislative Leader	Economic Leader	Party Leader
Examples			
News Story			
Symbol			

ESSENTIAL QUESTION

What are the powers and roles of the president and how have they changed over time?

The president acts as a legislative, economic, and political party leader and has different tools available at his or her disposal to use in these roles. Explore the list of hypothetical events and situations. Categorize each as involving the president's role as legislative, economic, or political party leader. As you read, think of tools or powers that the president could use to advance his or her agenda.

1. The Congress passes a law that the president disagrees with.

2. There is a recession in the country and the unemployment rate has climbed to 10 percent.

3. The Senate is evenly split between Democrats and Republicans and congressional elections are coming up. There is a chance that the president's party could gain a majority if they do well in the election.

4. The president has a proposal for U.S. immigration reform and would like Congress to pass a new law.

Influencing Legislation

GUIDING QUESTION *How does the president influence the legislative process?*

The Constitution gives Congress—not the president—the power and responsibility to make laws. However, the vast majority of bills become laws only if they are signed by the president. (A small number of bills become laws despite presidential opposition.)

Most presidents have significant influence over the types of laws that are proposed and how those laws are crafted. The Constitution refers to the president's role in influencing Congress. Article II, Section 3, says the president "shall from time to time give to the Congress information of the State of the Union, and recommend to their consideration such measures as he shall judge necessary and expedient."

Usually the president describes legislative priorities in the **annual** State of the Union address to Congress. The address calls attention to the president's ideas about how to solve key problems facing the country.

The president can suggest legislation, and Congress may adopt those ideas, but it may also reject or significantly revise the president's proposals. The president's power to influence legislation is also limited by the judiciary, as the federal courts can rule that laws are unconstitutional.

Tools to Influence Congress The president works to influence Congress in several ways—from drafting and negotiating about legislation to submitting a suggested annual budget and economic reports. The president has a large staff to help with these activities. When the president and the majority in Congress are from the same party, the president's ambitious legislative goals are more likely to be met.

A standard measure of presidential success with Congress is how frequently presidents get their way on congressional roll call votes they support. President George W. Bush's success rate was about 75 percent during the six years there was a Republican majority in Congress. When Democrats gained control of Congress in the 2006 elections, Bush's success rate declined to 38 percent.

A president's relationship with members of Congress and external events might also influence the degree of cooperation. President George W. Bush pushed for legislation to fight terrorism, including the USA Patriot Act, in the weeks after the terrorist attacks of September 11, 2001. Many provisions were quickly passed with large majorities. Support for the president among members of Congress and the public soared after the attacks.

When the president and the majority in Congress are from different political parties, the president must work harder to influence Congress to support the administration's programs. Presidents often meet with party leadership and members of Congress from both parties to share their views.

annual happening once per year

President Lyndon B. Johnson's 1964 State of the Union Address

"This administration today, here and now, declares unconditional war on poverty in America. I urge this Congress and all Americans to join with me in that effort. . . . The richest Nation on earth can afford to win it. We cannot afford to lose it . . .

The program I shall propose will emphasize this cooperative approach to help that one-fifth of all American families with incomes too small to even meet their basic needs. Our chief weapons in a more pinpointed attack will be better schools, and better health, and better homes, and better training, and better job opportunities to help more Americans, especially young Americans, escape from squalor and misery and unemployment rolls where other citizens help to carry them."

—President Lyndon B. Johnson, State of the Union Address, January 8, 1964

Use the excerpt from President Lyndon B. Johnson's 1964 State of the Union Address to answer the questions.

◄ CRITICAL THINKING

1. *Analyzing* What does this excerpt tell you about President Johnson's legislative goals for 1964?

2. *Describing* List three types of programs that the President intends to propose to Congress. How does he say these programs will help Americans?

3. *Explaining* Whenever the government creates a new program, it must be authorized and funded by Congress and run by the executive branch. How does Johnson begin to justify the expense of the proposed programs?

4. *Informative/Explanatory* Choose one of the following programs created during the "War on Poverty" that still exists today: Medicare, Medicaid, food stamps, and Head Start. Write a brief summary of the program. Explain who is eligible for the program, what it aims to do, the current cost of the program, and which executive branch agency runs it.

PRESIDENTIAL VETOES OVERRIDDEN BY CONGRESS

A president's veto may be overriden by a two-thirds vote of both houses of Congress.

▶ CRITICAL THINKING

Analyzing Graphs Which three presidents had the most vetoes overridden by Congress? What conclusions can you draw about the makeup of Congress during the administrations of these presidents?

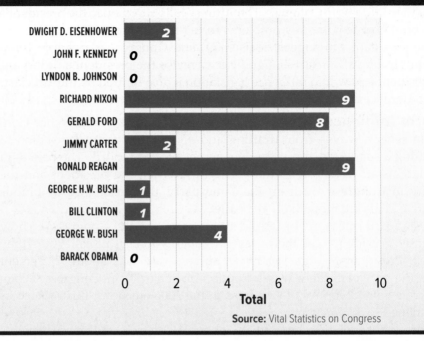

President	Total
DWIGHT D. EISENHOWER	2
JOHN F. KENNEDY	0
LYNDON B. JOHNSON	0
RICHARD NIXON	9
GERALD FORD	8
JIMMY CARTER	2
RONALD REAGAN	9
GEORGE H.W. BUSH	1
BILL CLINTON	1
GEORGE W. BUSH	4
BARACK OBAMA	0

Source: Vital Statistics on Congress

Both sides must often compromise in order to get any significant legislation passed. For example, in 1983 President Ronald Reagan worked with House Speaker Tip O'Neill to create a bipartisan plan to fund Social Security that required compromises from both parties.

One of the key features of President Lyndon B. Johnson's presidency was his leadership in pushing Congress to pass legislation he called the "War on Poverty." Having served in both the House of Representatives and the Senate before becoming president, Johnson was friendly with many legislators. He was also known for his keen political and persuasive skills.

Presidents may hand out political favors to get congressional support. They may visit the home state of a member of Congress to support his or her reelection. Or a president may start a new federal project that will bring money and jobs to a member's home state or district.

In general, public support can give a president real leverage in influencing lawmakers. Since Congress is a representative body, it is very sensitive to the amount of public support a president can generate. When a president is popular, presidential proposals and policies are better received by Congress than when the public holds a president in low regard.

When Lyndon B. Johnson succeeded to the office of president, Congress passed his War on Poverty legislation. However, when Johnson became unpopular during the Vietnam War, he encountered fierce opposition in Congress. His effectiveness as a leader was almost destroyed.

The Veto Presidents possess an important tool in lawmaking known as the veto. Each bill Congress passes is sent to the president for approval and signature. According to the Constitution, the president has 10 days to sign or veto (reject) the bill. If the president takes no action in 10 days, the bill becomes a law without his or her signature. However, if the president takes no action and the Congress adjourns during that 10-day period, the bill does not become a law. This is known as a pocket veto. Congress can override the president's veto if two-thirds of both houses vote to do so. If the Congress is able to muster enough votes to override the veto, the bill becomes a law despite the president's objections.

Presidents sometimes use the threat of a veto to force Congress to stop a bill or change it. The threat of a veto may succeed because Congress generally finds it very difficult to gather enough votes to override a veto.

Unlike most state governors, the president does not have the power to veto selected items in a bill. This type of veto is called a line-item veto. Congress attempted to give the president some power over individual items by passing the Line Item Veto Act in 1996. President Clinton began to use the new power almost immediately, but the law was challenged as soon as it went into effect. In *Clinton* v. *City of New York* (1998), the Supreme Court struck down the law as unconstitutional, ruling that Congress could not give the president power to alter laws without changing the Constitution.

☑ **READING PROGRESS CHECK**

Analyzing Why is the veto considered such an important legislative tool for the president?

Economic Planning

GUIDING QUESTION *How does the president fulfill the role of chief economic planner?*

The president's role as chief economic planner was not set out in the Constitution but developed over time. The role has grown rapidly since President Franklin D. Roosevelt's New Deal. During Roosevelt's presidency, the Great Depression caused a severe economic crisis in the United States, leaving 25 percent of the population without jobs. Roosevelt persuaded Congress to create many new programs to provide income for the elderly, supply people with jobs, regulate banks, and set up the federal agencies to run these programs. This "New Deal" greatly expanded the role of the federal government in the economy. After Roosevelt, Americans expected their presidents to take a firm hand in directing the nation's economy.

In 1935 Congress passed the Banking Act, which gives the president the authority to appoint the seven members that direct the nation's central banking system known as the **Federal Reserve System,** or simply "the Fed." The president can also appoint the group's chairman when there is a vacancy in that position. The Fed is an independent agency, which is structured to be less subject to political pressures than most federal agencies. Still, presidents nominate individuals who share their views about the best way to stabilize the banking system and to grow the economy. The president's nominees must be confirmed by the Senate.

In 1946 Congress passed the Employment Act, giving new duties to the president. This law directed the president to submit an annual economic report to Congress. The law also created a **Council of Economic Advisers** to study the economy and to advise the president on domestic and international economic policies. The law declared for the first time that the federal government was responsible for promoting high employment, production, and purchasing power.

Since 1946, Congress has continued to pass laws giving presidents the power to deal with economic problems, though the executive and legislative branches sometimes do not agree on policies.

Budgeting One of the president's economic duties is to prepare an annual budget. The president supervises this work and spends many months with budget officials deciding which government programs to support and which to cut back. These decisions about spending reflect the president's priorities—programs the president favors will receive more funding than those the president does not.

Federal Reserve System the central banking system of the United States

Council of Economic Advisers presidential advisers who study the economy and advise the president on domestic and international economic policies

The Federal Reserve Board building in Washington, D.C., is where the Board of Governors of the Fed meets.
▼ CRITICAL THINKING
Speculating Why do you think the Fed is an independent agency?

President Obama campaigning for U.S. Senate candidate Democrat Martha Coakley in Boston

▲ CRITICAL THINKING

Hypothesizing Under what circumstances might a candidate not want a president to help with campaigning?

ensure to make sure, certain, or safe

political patronage appointment to political office, usually as a reward for helping get a president elected

The annual budget proposal is submitted to the House of Representatives, where it is modified and debated. Ultimately, Congress passes a law that creates the budget and the president can sign or veto that law.

☑ **READING PROGRESS CHECK**

Comparing How does the president use the Federal Reserve System and the Council of Economic Advisers to plan and manage the United States economy?

Political Party Leader

GUIDING QUESTION *What is the president's role as party leader?*

The president's political party expects the chief executive to be a party leader. The president may give speeches to help party members who are running for office or may attend fund-raising activities to help raise money for the party. The president also selects the party's national chair and often helps plan future election strategies.

Presidents are expected to appoint members of their party to government jobs. These appointments **ensure** that supporters will remain committed to a president's programs. **Political patronage**, or appointment to political office, rewards the people who have helped get a president elected. Being a political party leader can be a difficult role for a president. People expect a president, as head of the government, to represent all Americans. Political parties, however, expect presidents to provide leadership for their own political party. Sometimes these conflicting roles cause problems. When President Bill Clinton compromised with the Republican Congress to enact legislation that cut back federal funding for welfare programs in 1996, he was criticized by the more liberal members of his party. If a president appears to act in a partisan way, that is, in a way that favors his or her party, the media and the public can be critical.

☑ **READING PROGRESS CHECK**

Making Inferences Why might a president's role as leader of the nation and leader of a political party conflict?

LESSON 4 REVIEW

Reviewing Vocabulary

1. *Applying* What is political patronage? Give at least one example of a president using political patronage.

Using Your Graphic Organizer

2. *Summarizing* Write a brief summary of the actions presidents take in their roles as legislative, economic, and party leader.

Answering the Guiding Questions

3. *Explaining* How does the president influence the legislative process?

4. *Stating* How does the president fulfill the role of chief economic planner?

5. *Describing* What is the president's role as party leader?

Writing About Government

6. *Argument* While Congress has the responsibility and constitutional authority to make laws, the president still has significant power to influence legislation. Some observers believe that Congress has relinquished too much control over the legislative process to the president and the executive branch. Write an essay either agreeing or disagreeing with this observation.

Youngstown Sheet & Tube Co.
v Sawyer (1952)

FACTS OF THE CASE In December of 1950, the United States officially entered the Korean War. Fighting this war required the continuous production of weapons, planes, ships, and other materials. Many of these materials were made out of steel. In 1951, a dispute arose between many of the nation's largest steel mills and their employees. The workers' unions called for a strike to begin several months later if their demands were not met by then. President Harry Truman met with Congress to express his concerns that a strike would endanger the production of war materials and, therefore, the nation's defense. However, Congress did not take any action or provide for any procedures that might keep the steel mills running during a strike. On April 8, the day before the strike was to begin, President Truman issued an executive order that directed his Secretary of Commerce to take direct control of all the steel mills that would be affected by the strike so that they would continue producing steel.

The steel companies resisted a government takeover of their mills by suing the Secretary of Commerce, Charles Sawyer. The case reached the Supreme Court in less than a month.

May the president use a power that is constitutionally delegated to Congress if Congress fails to act?

SAWYER The president's actions were reasonable because as commander in chief of the armed forces, he has the constitutional right to take any actions necessary to keep the armed forces operational. Though this case involved taking private property, there are many other examples throughout history of presidents taking similar action. For example, Abraham Lincoln freed all enslaved persons in the Confederacy even though these individuals were considered property at the time. In 1941, right before America entered World War II, Franklin Roosevelt ordered the army to take control of the North American Aviation plant after its workers went on strike. If these actions were acceptable, then so is the seizure of the steel mills.

YOUNGSTOWN SHEET & TUBE CO. At the time this case came before the Supreme Court, Congress had not declared war against Korea, so President Truman could not take over steel plants on behalf of an unauthorized war effort. The president had no authority to take private property unless Congress authorized such an action. Just because Congress does not use its power does not mean the president has the authority to do so. The Constitution is very clear on the powers of the three branches of government. Those powers do not change just because one branch makes a bad decision or refuses to act.

EXPLORING THE ESSENTIAL QUESTION

Moot Court You will be assigned to one of three groups: lawyers for Sawyer, lawyers for Youngstown Sheet & Tube Co., or Supreme Court justices. You will prepare for a moot court of this case. The lawyers for each side should develop arguments and prepare to answer questions from the justices. The justices should prepare questions to ask the lawyers. Each team will have five minutes to present its side during oral arguments, and the justices will be allowed to ask the lawyers questions. The justices will then vote and explain their decision. Next, write an essay or blog that reflects your personal opinion about this issue.

STUDY GUIDE

POWERS OF THE PRESIDENT
LESSON 1

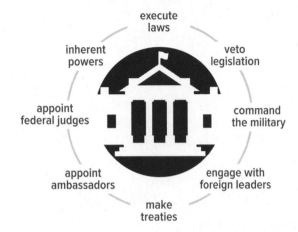

- execute laws
- veto legislation
- command the military
- engage with foreign leaders
- make treaties
- appoint ambassadors
- appoint federal judges
- inherent powers

ROLES OF THE PRESIDENT
LESSON 1

THE PRESIDENT WEARS MANY HATS:

Head of State

Chief Executive

Commander in Chief

Chief Diplomat

Legislative Leader

Economic Planner

Party Leader

HEAD OF STATE AND CHIEF EXECUTIVE
LESSON 2

HEAD OF STATE	CHIEF EXECUTIVE
performs ceremonial functions	carries out the laws
comforts citizens in times of crisis	appoints cabinet and other agency heads
hosts dignitaries	appoints federal judges and Supreme Court justices
	issues executive orders
gives awards to distinguished citizens	grants reprieves, pardons, and amnesty

LEGISLATIVE LEADER, ECONOMIC PLANNER, AND PARTY LEADER
LESSON 4

LEGISLATIVE LEADER
gives annual State of the Union address
drafts and negotiates bills
signs or vetoes laws passed by Congress
can call a congressional special session

ECONOMIC PLANNER
submits annual budget to Congress
submits economic reports to Congress
appoints heads of Federal Reserve System

PARTY LEADER
gives speeches and attends fund-raisers to support party candidates
selects party's national chair
helps plan election strategies
appoints party members to political office

COMMANDER IN CHIEF AND CHIEF DIPLOMAT
LESSON 3

COMMANDER IN CHIEF As civilian commander of the armed forces, can use the military to	CHIEF DIPLOMAT
defend the nation	directs U.S. foreign policy
engage in overseas operations	makes decisions about U.S. relations with other countries
control serious turmoil in the United States	negotiates and signs treaties
aid in natural disasters in the United States	signs executive agreements with other countries
	recognizes foreign governments

Directions: On a separate sheet of paper, answer the questions below. Make sure you read carefully and answer all parts of the questions.

Lesson Review

Lesson 1

1 *Identifying* What positions can the president fill by appointment, and what check does the Constitution place on the power of appointment?

2 *Identifying Cause and Effect* What are inherent powers, and how have these influenced presidential authority over time?

Lesson 2

3 *Explaining* What is the role of executive departments and agencies?

4 *Identifying* What is the role of the cabinet and how do cabinet members get their jobs?

Lesson 3

5 *Specifying* Explain how the federal government makes treaties.

6 *Contrasting* What is "shadow war," and how is it different from previous forms of warfare?

Lesson 4

7 *Identifying* What is the purpose of the Council of Economic Advisers?

8 *Differentiating* How does a pocket veto differ from a veto?

ANSWERING THE ESSENTIAL QUESTIONS

Review your answers to the introductory questions at the beginning of each lesson. Then answer the following Essential Question based on what you learned in the chapter. Have your answers changed?

9 *Analyzing* What are the powers and roles of the president and how have they changed over time?

DBQ Interpreting Political Cartoons

Use the political cartoon to answer the following questions.

10 *Drawing Inferences* Why do you think the cartoonist depicted President Theodore Roosevelt much larger than the other people in the cartoon?

11 *Interpreting* Who do the other people in the cartoon represent?

12 *Analyzing Visuals* Based on this cartoon, how would you describe "The New Diplomacy"?

Critical Thinking

13 *Analyzing Cause and Effect* How did experience with the Articles of Confederation influence the way the Founders set up the executive branch?

14 *Analyzing* Why is the appointment of federal judges a source of contention between the legislative and executive branches, especially in a divided government?

15 *Making Inferences* How has the president's power as commander in chief changed over time? Why do you think this is so?

16 *Sequencing* Describe the process used to create the national budget.

Need Extra Help?

If You've Missed Question	1	2	3	4	5	6	7	8	9	10	11	12	13	14	15	16
Go to page	261	262	266	268	275	273	281	280	260	272	272	272	261	268	271	281

Directions: On a separate sheet of paper, answer the questions below. Make sure you read carefully and answer all parts of the questions.

DBQ Analyzing Primary Sources

Read the excerpt and answer the questions that follow.

In 1972 police caught five burglars planting listening devices in Democratic Party offices at the Watergate Hotel. The unfolding scandal roiled the nation as investigations pointed to the White House. Facing impeachment and possible criminal charges, President Richard Nixon resigned in 1974. Vice President Gerald Ford assumed the presidency.

PRIMARY SOURCE

"*After years of bitter controversy and divisive national debate, . . . I am compelled to conclude that many months and perhaps more years will have to pass before Richard Nixon could obtain a fair trial. . . . During this long period of delay and potential litigation, ugly passions would again be aroused. And our people would again be polarized in their opinions. . . . My conscience tells me clearly and certainly that I cannot prolong the bad dreams that continue to reopen a chapter that is closed. My conscience tells me that only I, as President, have the constitutional power to firmly shut and seal this book. . . . I feel that Richard Nixon and his loved ones have suffered enough. . . . Now, therefore, I, Gerald R. Ford, . . . do grant a full, free, and absolute pardon unto Richard Nixon. . . .*"
—President Gerald Ford, Sept. 8, 1974

17 *Interpreting* What constitutional power is President Ford referring to in this passage?

18 *Finding the Main Idea* What reasons does President Ford give for his action?

19 *Identifying Central Issues* What does President Ford say will happen to the nation if he does not take action?

20 *Making Connections* What does President Ford's action mean for Richard Nixon? Do you agree with Ford's decision? Why or why not?

Social Studies Skills

21 *Creating a Chart* Use computer software to create a chart listing each presidential role. Search online for articles about activities of the current president. In your chart, list one specific activity that the president performed in each role. Cite your sources.

22 *Explaining Continuity and Change* President Franklin Roosevelt pushed the envelope of presidential power during the Great Depression. Research and write a report about how Franklin Roosevelt expanded presidential power in domestic policy during this crisis.

Research and Presentation

23 *Researching* Go to whitehouse.gov and identify the cabinet-level departments. Form small groups, with each group taking one department. With your group, research and prepare a multimedia presentation about what the department does. Include a profile of the current department head.

24 *Acquiring Information* Research a treaty in which the United States is a party. Prepare a class presentation on this treaty. Identify the parties to the negotiation, describe the treaty's purpose, and discuss controversies. Describe key outcomes.

25 *Exploring Issues* The USA Patriot Act has stirred controversy in recent years. Do research to learn what supporters and opponents are saying. Take a stand for or against this law and prepare to defend your position in a class debate.

Need Extra Help?

If You've Missed Question	17	18	19	20	21	22	23	24	25
Go to page	270	270	270	270	264	262	268	275	274

Choosing the President

networks
www.connected.mcgraw-hill.com
There's More Online about choosing the president.

CHAPTER 10

ESSENTIAL QUESTIONS

• What are the key components of presidential leadership? • How has the role of vice president and the process for presidential succession changed over time? • Why and how has the process for nominating and electing presidents changed over time?

Official White House Photo by Chuck Kennedy

▲ President Barack Obama walks through the White House with former President George W. Bush while First Lady Michelle Obama accompanies former First Lady Laura Bush.

PRESIDENTIAL **QUALIFICATIONS**

Every president has a unique style of leadership. The success of a president in pursuing his agenda depends in some part on his leadership skills. Political scientist Fred I. Greenstein has identified six essential characteristics a president must have to succeed: public communication skills, organizational capacity, political skill, vision, cognitive style, and emotional intelligence. Examine these sources to explore types of presidential leadership.

PRIMARY SOURCE

"I sit here all day trying to persuade people to do the things they ought to have sense enough to do without my persuading them. . . . That's all the powers of the President amount to."

—President Harry Truman

PRIMARY SOURCE

"He would pick the basic trajectory, and he was pretty resolute then about sticking with the policies it required. He never thought about reversing course."

—Mitchell E. Daniels, Jr.,
President George W. Bush's first budget director

PRIMARY SOURCE

"Any given decision you make you'll wind up with a 30 to 40 percent chance that it isn't going to work. You have to own that and feel comfortable with the way you made the decision. You can't be paralyzed by the fact that it might not work out."

—President Barack Obama, 2012

SECONDARY SOURCE

Presidents Reagan and Carter had different approaches to the details of their policies. During a negotiating session over tax cuts, President Ronald Reagan stopped by. His Treasury Secretary asked, "Would you like to join us?" The President replied, "Heck no. I'm going to leave this to you experts. I'm not going to get involved in details." President Carter, on the other hand, spent many hours studying policy details and often became directly involved with his assistants to sort through them.

—Summary: Steven R. Weisman, "Reagan's Style: Focusing on 'The Big Picture,'"
The New York Times, August 8, 1981

▲ President Obama and his senior advisers receive an update on the mission against Osama bin Laden in May 2011.

▲ President George W. Bush meets with senior advisers on September 11, 2001.

SECONDARY SOURCE G

Top Five Qualities Partisans Are Looking For in Next President March 26–29, 2007	
Republicans/Lean Republican	**Democrats/Lean Democratic**
Honesty/straightforward (30%)	Honesty/straightforward (34%)
Leadership/strength (22%)	Listen to people/not special interests (13%)
Integrity (13%)	Put U.S. first/focus on domestic issues (13%)
Competent/govern effectively (11%)	Leadership/strength (12%)
Good moral character/family values (8%)	Competent/govern effectively (10%)

SOURCE: Gallup, 2007

DBQ DOCUMENT-BASED QUESTIONS

1. **Making Inferences** Come up with a word or phrase describing a leadership quality implied in each of the presidential quotes or anecdotes.

2. **Comparing** What do the two photographs have in common? Are special qualities required to be a successful leader in a time of crisis?

3. **Analyzing** In the Gallup Poll, which qualities are prized by both Republicans and Democrats? Can you write a definition of leadership qualities with which members of both parties could agree?

WHAT WILL YOU DO?

What leadership qualities will you look for in a potential president? How will you be able to tell if a person has the qualities of leadership?

EXPLORE the interactive version of the analyzing primary sources feature on Networks.

ReadingHelp Desk

Academic Vocabulary

- **survey**
- **generate**

Content Vocabulary

- **landslide**

TAKING NOTES:
Key Ideas and Details

LISTING Use the graphic organizer to list and define the presidential leadership skills described in this lesson.

Leadership Skills

LESSON 1
Presidential Qualifications and Leadership

ESSENTIAL QUESTION

What are the key components of presidential leadership?

Think about someone you know who is a leader. This might be an adult at school or in your community or place of worship, or a student who is a leader at school or on a team. What qualities does this person possess that make him or her a good leader?

Make a list of personality traits, skills, and experiences that can make someone a good leader. Highlight the items on your list that might also apply to good presidential leadership. Explain your choices.

Qualifications for the Presidency

GUIDING QUESTION *What are the formal and informal qualifications to be president?*

In order to be elected and serve successfully as president of the United States, a person must possess a variety of skills, talents, experiences, and personal qualities. Most of these are not required by the Constitution; instead, these qualifications are determined by the voters, who expect a president to meet certain standards.

Constitutional Requirements In Article II, Section 1, the Constitution defines the formal requirements for the presidency. The president must be a natural-born citizen of the United States, at least 35 years old, and a resident of the United States for at least 14 years before taking office. The same requirements apply to the vice president.

Informal Requirements Many other qualifications and experiences are necessary for a person to have a real chance of being elected president, though. One important qualification is experience in government. Every president in American history has served in one of these roles before becoming president: vice president, U.S. senator or representative, cabinet secretary, governor of a state, or general in the U.S. Army.

Since 1900, candidates who have served as U.S. senators or state governors have won the major parties' presidential nominations the most often. A political career gives someone experience in lawmaking, compromise, and understanding how government functions. Prior

(l t) www.whitehouse.gov; BBC Worldwide Learning

government experience also gives presidential candidates the chance to form the alliances necessary to be nominated within their own political party, as well as the name recognition that is necessary to win votes.

Political Beliefs Extremely liberal or conservative candidates have little chance of being elected, and the major parties usually choose candidates who are moderate. Exceptions do occur, however. In 1964 Barry Goldwater, a very conservative Republican, became his party's nominee for the presidency. In 1972 a very liberal Democrat, George McGovern, won his party's nomination. Both men were defeated in the general election.

Personal Characteristics What kind of person becomes president? Historically, most presidents have come from northern European backgrounds. A few have been from poor families—Abraham Lincoln, Harry S. Truman, and Bill Clinton, for example. Several presidents—such as Franklin D. Roosevelt, John F. Kennedy, George H.W. Bush, and George W. Bush—have come from wealthy families, but most have been middle class. Most presidents have been white, married, and financially successful.

Barack Obama was the nation's first African American president. The election of President Obama in 2008 represented a major change in American politics. Only 50 years earlier, African Americans faced oppressive, state-sanctioned discrimination. In his campaign, Obama stressed the need for unity among all ethnic, racial, and religious groups. In a speech at the Constitution Center in March 2008, then-candidate Obama said:

❝❞ PRIMARY SOURCE

I have never been so naïve as to believe that we can get beyond our racial divisions in a single election cycle, or with a single candidacy—particularly a candidacy as imperfect as my own. But I have asserted a firm conviction—a conviction rooted in my faith in God and my faith in the American people—that working together we can move beyond some of our old racial wounds, and that in fact we have no choice if we are to continue on the path of a more perfect union.❞

—Barack Obama, March 2008

To date, every president has been a man and each has identified as Christian. John F. Kennedy, elected in 1960, was the first Roman Catholic president; previously, voters had always elected a Protestant candidate. Still, presidential and vice-presidential nominees and presidential candidates are becoming more diverse. Several women have been candidates for president and vice president. For example, Republican Sarah Palin and Democrat Geraldine Ferraro were vice-presidential candidates. In 2008 Hillary Clinton came close to becoming the first female presidential nominee from a major party. Joe Lieberman, Al Gore's running mate, was the first Jewish American vice-presidential nominee. In 2012 Mitt Romney was the first Mormon candidate from a major party.

EXPLORING THE ESSENTIAL QUESTION

Identifying Think about the different roles the president fills and the qualifications you have read about. Which skills and experiences are needed to fill those many roles? Write a job advertisement that could be used to hire a new president of the United States. Include the following sections: **1)** Overview of the position; **2)** Major responsibilities; **3)** Required qualifications: education, experiences, and skills.

PRESIDENTIAL **CAMPAIGN** Contributions, 2012

Presidential campaign contributions tend to come from the states with the largest populations.

▶ **CRITICAL THINKING**

Applying Do greater campaign contributions necessarily lead to a candidate winning in a particular state? How do you know?

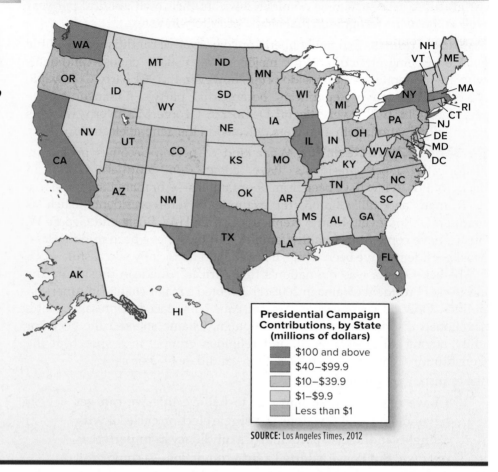

Presidential Campaign Contributions, by State (millions of dollars)

- $100 and above
- $40–$99.9
- $10–$39.9
- $1–$9.9
- Less than $1

SOURCE: Los Angeles Times, 2012

Financial Backing Running for the presidency costs tens of millions of dollars. Candidates pay for advertising, salaries of campaign staff and consultants, and travel; they also spend millions of dollars to reach out to voters by mail, e-mail, Internet, and phone.

The figures for expenditures for the 2012 presidential campaign demonstrate how important it is for a candidate to have access to huge sums of money. The Federal Election Commission (FEC) tracks campaign spending based on reports required by the candidates. According to the FEC, all of the presidential candidates from both parties during the primaries and general election spent more than $1.3 billion.

In order to raise the vast sums of money needed to be competitive, presidential candidates must have strong financial support from many people. Personal wealth is a great asset for any candidate as well. Presidential candidates can accept public financing for their campaigns, but they must limit how much money they spend to specific dollar amounts. For the 2012 presidential election, the overall primary limit was $45.6 million and the general election spending limit was $91.2 million.

Candidates who forgo public financing can spend as much as they can collect. In 2008 then-candidate Barack Obama was the first major presidential candidate to forgo public financing for the general election. In 2012 both Mitt Romney and Barack Obama turned down public financing. Obama raised $722.4 million and Romney raised $447.6 million.

✓ **READING PROGRESS CHECK**

Applying What makes a candidate more likely to win the office of the president?

Leadership Skills

GUIDING QUESTION *What kinds of leadership qualities do successful presidents have?*

When the Founders wrote the Constitution, they thought that Congress, not the president, would lead the nation. At best, the president was to be the nation's chief administrator and, in time of war, its commander in chief. Instead, the powers and duties of the president have grown steadily over the years. Public opinion **surveys** clearly show that Americans look to the president to keep the peace and to solve economic and social problems.

survey a poll; a collection of data

Every president has a unique style of leadership. Sometimes presidents demonstrate leadership by introducing bold new policies; President Truman did this in 1948 when he announced measures to end discrimination against African Americans in the military. More often, presidents demonstrate leadership by responding to crises, problems, or opportunities as they occur.

Understanding the Public A president must know and understand the American people. The most successful presidents have a genuine feel for the hopes, fears, and moods of the nation. Understanding the people is necessary to gain and hold their support.

Public support, in turn, can give a president real leverage in influencing lawmakers. Since Congress is a representative body, it is very sensitive to the amount of public support a president can **generate**. When a president is popular, presidential proposals and policies are better received by Congress than when the public holds a president in low regard. Failure to understand the public mood can prove disastrous for a president. In 1932, when the nation was mired in the Great Depression, President Herbert Hoover believed that the public did not want government to take an active role in confronting the nation's economic problems. Actually, with millions out of work, Americans wanted their problems solved by any means, including federal intervention. President Hoover's failure to understand people's attitude cost him the presidency. In 1932 he lost the presidential election to the Democratic candidate, Franklin D. Roosevelt, by a large majority of votes, a **landslide**.

generate to produce; to be the cause of

landslide a great majority of votes for one side

Ability to Communicate A leading expert has said, "Presidential power is the power to persuade." Successful presidents must be able to communicate effectively and to present their ideas in a way that inspires public support. President Hoover was considered "out of touch" with the people as the economy started to crumble at the beginning of the Great Depression. He met infrequently with the press and answered only questions that were written in advance. In contrast, President Roosevelt was a master at communicating with the public. He held weekly press conferences during which he answered all questions. After his famous "fireside chats" over the radio, Roosevelt received as many as 50,000 letters of public support per week.

Modern presidents often use a strategy of "going public" to appeal directly to voters. President Ronald Reagan became known as "the Great Communicator" because of his ability to sell his ideas to the public. A former actor, he had a very relaxed demeanor, soothing voice, and practiced sense of timing during speeches and debates. Reagan also had a keen sense of humor and spoke optimistically and simply about his vision for America. He made the public feel as if they knew him. These communication skills were essential to his success as a candidate and a president, especially in times of crisis.

Sense of Timing A successful president must know when to introduce a new policy, make a key decision, or delay action. During the crisis in the former Soviet Union in the early 1990s, President George H.W. Bush agreed that American economic aid would encourage democratic reforms there.

Tracking Presidential Communications

At the time of Franklin D. Roosevelt's presidency, radio was a relatively new phenomenon. Roosevelt used it masterfully to communicate his ideas to the general public. In a similar way, Ronald Reagan was skilled at communicating through televised speeches and debates. Today's presidents also use newer technologies to communicate with the people.

Explore the president's presence on social media and on the White House webpage. Note what digital technologies the president uses to convey ideas and to elicit support for programs and policies.

EXPLORING THE ESSENTIAL QUESTION

Examining Track a variety of posts and feeds in those forums and report about the president's use of technology over the course of two or three days. What issues or public policies receive priority? What does the president want you to know or think about these issues? Do you think the president is an effective communicator? Give examples to support your reasons.

www.whitehouse.gov

President Bush decided to delay acting on this policy, however, until the Soviet political situation was clearer and more stable. On the other hand, when some former Soviet republics declared their independence, Bush was quick to recognize their sovereignty.

Skillful presidents often use their assistants or cabinet secretaries to test the timing of new policy initiatives. They might deliberately leak information or have a cabinet secretary or an aide make a statement about a policy under consideration. Public response to the issue may influence whether the president pursues, delays, or quietly drops a policy initiative.

Ability to Compromise Good leadership requires the capacity to be flexible and open to new ideas. A successful president must also be able to compromise. The nature of politics is such that even the president must be willing to give up something to get something in return. Presidents who are successful leaders are able to recognize that sometimes they must settle for legislation that provides only part of the programs they want. Presidents who will not compromise risk accomplishing nothing at all.

A famous dispute at the end of World War I between President Woodrow Wilson and the Congress is often cited as an example of a president refusing to compromise and losing everything in the end.

Wilson had represented the nation at the Paris Peace Conference negotiations to end the war. He lobbied the other nations involved with the treaty to include a plan for a League of Nations, a global organization whose goal was to prevent war. When the treaty came before the Senate for ratification, many senators opposed it. They did not want permanent ties of any kind to Europe and its problems. They specifically objected that the League of Nations plan would take away the right of Congress to declare war. (The League called for members to take collective action against any aggressor nation.)

Faced with these objections, President Wilson still refused to modify the treaty. Wilson faced a significant problem, however: If changes were made to the treaty to please the Senate, it would also have to be renegotiated with foreign powers. An angry Wilson decided to go on a public speaking tour to build support for the treaty. The tour ended suddenly when Wilson suffered a stroke. The Senate rejected the treaty, and the United States never joined the League of Nations. It did join the successor organization, the United Nations, in 1945.

Political Courage Successful presidents need political courage because sometimes they must go against public opinion to do what they think is best. It takes courage to make decisions that will be unpopular.

President Abraham Lincoln made this kind of decision during the Civil War. The early years of the war went very badly for the North—despite some Union victories, casualties were very high, and the war's end seemed nowhere in sight. As time passed, the war became increasingly unpopular, and the president came under intense public and political pressure to negotiate peace. Despite his belief that his decision would mean his defeat in the 1864 election, however, Lincoln chose to continue the war to preserve the Union.

At times, presidents have shown leadership and courage by going against the traditional views of their own political parties. For example, prior to becoming president, Republican Richard Nixon's congressional career and term as Dwight D. Eisenhower's vice president were built around being an ardent anti-Communist. In that context, it was amazing that Nixon became the first president to visit the communist nation of People's Republic of China. His efforts to open diplomatic relations with China surprised many people, especially members of his own party. Similarly, many people did not expect President Bill Clinton, a Democrat, to initiate efforts to reform the welfare system, a program often defended by Democrats and criticized by Republicans.

✓ **READING PROGRESS CHECK**

Evaluating Which leadership skills are most important for a president to have? Explain your reasoning.

EXPLORING THE ESSENTIAL QUESTION

Summarizing Look for a news story about a current event that required the president to display political courage or the ability to compromise. Give a proper citation for the article and then summarize it by answering these questions:

a. When was the article written?

b. What event, legislation, or decision does the article describe?

c. What did the president do or what decision was made?

d. How did this action reflect political courage or the ability to compromise?

e. What could be the negative and positive consequences of the president's action or decision?

LESSON 1 REVIEW

Reviewing Vocabulary
1. *Defining* What does *landslide* mean in the context of elections? What is another meaning of *landslide*?

Using Your Graphic Organizer
2. *Listing* Using your completed graphic organizer, rank the presidential leadership skills in order from most important to least important. Explain your decisions.

Answering the Guiding Questions
3. *Describing* What are the formal and informal qualifications to be president?

4. *Explaining* What kinds of leadership qualities do successful presidents have?

Writing About Government
5. *Narrative* If you wanted to be president, what decisions can you make now and in the next few years to help you get elected later? What type of education, work experience, and leadership skills can you work toward? Do you have any personal characteristics that could help you win the election and do a good job? Write a personal reflection that answers these questions.

Bush  *Gore* (2000)

FACTS OF THE CASE In 2000, after all the popular votes were counted in other states, the presidential election hinged on Florida. It appeared George W. Bush had won by about 1,800 votes. Because the vote was so close, Florida election law required an automatic recount of all the ballots in the state.

The ballots in Florida required voters to punch out a hole next to the name of the candidate of their choice, and then the ballots were scanned by a machine. Thousands of ballots were rejected by the machines because the paper square had not been completely punched through. Al Gore, Bush's opponent, requested that several counties perform recounts by hand. The manual recounts began but were time-consuming and controversial. The process required a group of officials to look at each ballot to determine what the voter had *intended* to do. Different officials could use different criteria to identify the voters' intentions. Bush sued to stop the recount, arguing that it was unconstitutional to use different standards to review different votes. The Florida Supreme Court and a federal court ordered the recounts to continue. Bush appealed the decisions. Election officials in some counties requested an extension for more time to count the ballots. The Secretary of State in Florida denied their requests and certified the election results with Bush as the winner.

ISSUE

Does recounting ballots using similar but different methods violate the Fourteenth Amendment's Equal Protection Clause?

ARGUMENTS

The following is a list of arguments made in the case of *Bush* v. *Gore*. Read each argument and categorize each based on whether it supports Bush's side (that Florida's recount is unconstitutional and should be stopped) or Gore's side (that Florida's recount is constitutional and should proceed).

1. The recount violates the Fourteenth Amendment because different voters' ballots are treated differently when recounted.

2. Many counties in the states have different voting methods, and yet no court says that violates the Fourteenth Amendment.

3. Each county in Florida has different standards for doing manual recounts. Some ballots that would be accepted as legitimate in one county may not be accepted in another.

4. There is not enough time for Florida to change its vote counting procedures before the new president is due to take office. If the election was still undecided, chaos could ensue.

5. In our system of government, states run elections. The federal government should respect the states' decisions related to ballot recounts and let the court-ordered manual recount continue in Florida.

6. Regardless of the exact rules used for recounts in each county, they all work to figure out which hole the voters meant to punch, which is treating all the ballots equally.

7. There should be no time limit when constitutional rights are at stake, and the voters of Florida have a right to have their votes count. Florida should find a way to count the ballots that treats them all equally, even if it delays the election results.

EXPLORING THE ESSENTIAL QUESTION

Evaluating After you have classified the arguments, evaluate the arguments presented by Bush and Gore. Choose a side in the case and explain your reasoning.

YOU BE the JUDGE

Interact with these digital assets and others in lesson 2

✓ **INTERACTIVE CHART**
The Line of Presidential Succession

✓ **INTERACTIVE IMAGE**
Presidential Benefits

✓ **SELF-CHECK QUIZ**

✓ **VIDEO**
Role of Vice President

networks
TRY IT YOURSELF ONLINE

Reading Help Desk

Academic Vocabulary
- decline
- successor

Content Vocabulary
- compensation
- presidential succession

TAKING NOTES:
Key Ideas and Details

UNDERSTANDING CAUSE AND EFFECT Describe these amendments to the Constitution, explain the historical circumstances that led to their passage, and describe the effects they have had on the political process.

	Twenty-second Amendment	Twenty-fifth Amendment
Description		
Historical Background		
Effects		

LESSON 2
Presidential Salary, the Vice President, and Succession

ESSENTIAL QUESTION

How has the role of vice president and the process for presidential succession changed over time?

The vice president could—at any moment—become the leader of the United States.

Make one list detailing what you know about the vice president and a second list showing what you think you should know about the person who holds that office. Consider these and other details you think are important: name, age, prior work experiences, areas of expertise, political party, relative health, home state, and education.

Terms, Salary, and Benefits

GUIDING QUESTION *What are the terms of office and compensation for the president?*

Originally, the Constitution did not specify how many four-year terms a president could serve. George Washington set a long-held precedent when he served for eight years and then **declined** to run for a third term. When the next president took office, the peaceful transfer of power from Washington to John Adams showed that democracy had taken root in this country. Washington had not grabbed power and refused to let it go.

The tradition of presidents serving only two terms lasted for 150 years. Then in 1940 and in 1944, President Franklin D. Roosevelt ran for an unprecedented third and fourth terms. Many were outraged that Roosevelt wanted to keep power, but the voters kept electing him. They wanted to "carry on" with the president who had led them through the Great Depression and was leading them through World War II.

Reaction to Roosevelt's four terms in office and concern over too much executive power led to passage of the Twenty-second Amendment in 1951. This amendment established that a president would be limited to two terms in office; it also allowed a vice president who takes over in the middle of a presidency and serves no more than two years to serve two more terms. Thus, one person could be president for 10 years but no more.

Special transportation is provided to the president to help maintain his personal security.

▲ CRITICAL THINKING
Explaining Why would the Secret Service discourage the president's use of public transportation?

decline to refuse to undertake

compensation something given or received as an equivalent for services

Salary and Benefits The Constitutional Convention determined that presidents should receive compensation but left it up to Congress to decide the amount of **compensation**, or salary. The president currently earns $400,000 per year. The Executive Office of the President also provides a nontaxable travel allowance of up to $100,000 per year and a $50,000 expense account. Congress cannot increase or decrease the salary during a president's term.

Other benefits, some necessary for security reasons, are also provided to the president. For example, *Air Force One*, a specially equipped jet, as well as other planes, helicopters, and limousines, are made available to the president and top assistants. Presidents receive free medical, dental, and health care. They live in the White House where the White House domestic staff does the cooking, shopping, and cleaning. The government pays to operate the White House and to hold official events, but the president's family must pay for their own food, dry-cleaning, personal parties, and other expenses—adding up to thousands of dollars every month.

When presidents retire, they receive a lifetime pension that is equal to the pay for cabinet secretaries; the amount of a president's pension is currently $199,700 per year. They also have free office space, free mailing services, lifetime Secret Service protection for themselves and their children, and up to $96,000 per year for office help. When presidents die, their spouses are eligible for a pension of $20,000 per year.

☑ **READING PROGRESS CHECK**

Analyzing Why are there presidential term limits? Do you think they are necessary? Explain.

The Vice President

GUIDING QUESTION *What are the roles and responsibilities of the vice president?*

The roles and responsibilities of vice presidents have changed significantly since the founding of the nation. At one time, the president and vice president were elected separately. They did not even have to be from the same political party, which was a source of tension in the White House. Now, vice presidents and presidents are typically allies loyal to the same priorities.

Constitutional Responsibilities The Constitution gives the vice president three duties. First, the vice president takes over the presidency in case of presidential death, disability, impeachment, or resignation. Second, the vice president presides over the Senate and votes in case of a tie; most vice presidents spend very little time in this part of the job. Third, under the Twenty-fifth Amendment, the vice president helps decide whether the president is unable to carry out his or her duties and acts as president should that happen. Nine vice presidents have succeeded to the presidency upon the death or resignation of the president. Another five have been elected president after their terms as vice president.

Modern Responsibilities For many years, the vice presidency was almost a purely ceremonial office, with vice presidents attending events in place of the president and making goodwill tours to foreign countries. Today, a vice president's role is more significant.

Depending upon the duties the president assigns, a vice president's work and power can be much greater than those mentioned in the Constitution. Modern vice presidents have had greater access to the president, participated frequently in policy meetings, and undertaken urgent special assignments. For example, President Obama assigned Vice President Joseph Biden to develop new proposals for gun control after a mass shooting in Connecticut in 2012.

Vice presidents have also become more involved in serious foreign policy efforts. Vice presidents are members of the National Security Council and take part in its policy deliberations. During the Bush administration, Vice President Richard Cheney played a leading role in developing the administration's war on terror policies. As a veteran of the Senate Foreign Relations Committee, Joe Biden has been a key foreign policy adviser to President Obama.

Presidential candidates select their vice-presidential running mates carefully. They are often looking to add expertise or voter appeal to the campaign and the future administration. Presidential candidates also look for someone who will appeal to voters from a particular geographic region or demographic group to balance out their own qualities in the eyes of voters.

EXPLORING THE ESSENTIAL QUESTION

Applying Of the three hypothetical vice presidents below, who would you advise the candidate to select? Why?

COMPARING
VICE PRESIDENTIAL CANDIDATES

Imagine that you are an adviser to a presidential candidate who has just received the Republican Party nomination. Your candidate is from Virginia, previously served as that state's governor, and is a former businessperson. The candidate is well known for innovative economic policies and championing reduced regulation of businesses but does not have much experience in foreign policy. The presidential candidate must now announce a running mate—a candidate for vice president. Review the resumes of these three hypothetical candidates.

OPTION 1
Current senator from Georgia

OPTION 2
Former governor of Arizona

OPTION 3
Former mayor of New York City

This candidate has been in the Senate for 18 years and was recently elected to a fourth term. He has served on the Foreign Affairs Committee and the Appropriations Committee. At age 72, he is the oldest of the candidates under consideration, and he was recently treated for a heart condition.

This candidate was a popular but controversial governor, as she fought for stricter immigration laws in her state. She strongly supports your candidate's economic policies and modeled recent initiatives in Arizona on them. Her fiery personality and outspoken nature lead to controversy in the media.

This candidate served two terms as mayor of New York City and presided over an overhaul of the city's school system. He is more moderate than your candidate and does not always agree with your candidate's business policies. He has lots of supporters in New England.

The Line of PRESIDENTIAL SUCCESSION

CRITICAL THINKING

Evaluating Together with two other students, think about who you believe should run the country if the president and vice president are unable to do so. If you believe the current line of succession is good, explain why you think so. If not, propose a new line of succession and explain your reasons.

1.	Vice President	10.	Secretary of Commerce
2.	Speaker of the House of Representatives	11.	Secretary of Labor
3.	President pro tempore of the Senate	12.	Secretary of Health and Human Services
4.	Secretary of State	13.	Secretary of Housing and Urban Development
5.	Secretary of the Treasury	14.	Secretary of Transportation
6.	Secretary of Defense	15.	Secretary of Energy
7.	Attorney General	16.	Secretary of Education
8.	Secretary of the Interior	17.	Secretary of Veterans Affairs
9.	Secretary of Agriculture	18.	Secretary of Homeland Security

successor one that follows

Sometimes voters have reacted negatively to a vice-presidential candidate who did not appear well prepared to serve as vice president and a possible **successor** to the president.

✓ **READING PROGRESS CHECK**

Discussing What are the constitutional duties of the vice president?

Succession

GUIDING QUESTION *What is the process for presidential succession?*

Eight presidents have died in office. Four were assassinated, and four died of natural causes. In 1967 the Twenty-fifth Amendment was ratified to clarify the succession to the presidency and the vice presidency.

❝❝ **PRIMARY SOURCE**

Section 1. In case of the removal of the President from office or of his death or resignation, the Vice President shall become President.

Section 2. Whenever there is a vacancy in the office of the Vice President, the President shall nominate a Vice President who shall take office upon confirmation by a majority vote of both Houses of Congress."

—Twenty-fifth Amendment, 1967

The amendment was first applied in 1973 when Spiro Agnew resigned as President Richard Nixon's vice president. Nixon then nominated Gerald Ford as vice president, and Congress approved the nomination. Less than a year later, when President Nixon resigned due to the Watergate scandal, Ford became president. Ford then nominated Nelson Rockefeller as vice president, and Congress again approved the nomination.

These events from 1973 onward marked the only time in American history that neither the president nor the vice president was elected to those offices.

What would happen if the offices of president and vice president both become vacant at the same time? The Succession Act of 1947 established the order of **presidential succession** for such instances. According to this law, after the vice president, the next in line for the presidency is the Speaker of the House. The president pro tempore of the Senate follows the Speaker. Next in line are the cabinet officers, starting with the secretary of state. The other 14 department heads follow in the order in which Congress created the departments.

What happens if a president becomes seriously disabled, or unable to fulfill the duties of the president, while in office? In fact, several presidents have experienced health problems and have been unable to execute their responsibilities. President James Garfield lingered between life and death for 80 days after he was shot in 1881, but no one was officially named to fulfill his duties. Just after World War I, a stroke disabled President Woodrow Wilson—his wife often performed his duties. In 1955 President Dwight D. Eisenhower had a heart attack, was completely disabled for several days, and had limited energy for several months; during that time, his assistants ran the executive branch.

The Twenty-fifth Amendment describes what should be done when a president is disabled. It provides that the vice president becomes acting president under one of two conditions: if the president informs Congress of an inability to perform in office and, second, if the vice president and a majority of the cabinet or a body authorized by Congress inform the Congress of this condition. This second provision takes effect when the president is unwilling or unable to inform Congress of a disabling condition.

The Twenty-fifth Amendment also spells out how a president can resume the powers and duties of the office. This can happen at any time the president informs Congress that a disability no longer exists.

On November 22, 1963, after President Kennedy was shot, Vice President Lyndon B. Johnson was sworn into the presidency aboard *Air Force One*.

▲ CRITICAL THINKING
Identifying After the vice president, who is next in the order of presidential succession?

presidential succession the order in which officials fill the office of president in case of a vacancy

☑ READING PROGRESS CHECK

Explaining What happens if a president is unable to carry out the duties of the office?

LESSON 2 REVIEW

Reviewing Vocabulary
1. ***Defining*** What is presidential succession? How is it determined?

Using Your Graphic Organizer
2. ***Comparing*** Use your completed graphic organizer to write a summary comparing the effects of the Twenty-second Amendment and the Twenty-fifth Amendment.

Answering the Guiding Questions
3. ***Identifying*** What are the terms of office and compensation for the president?

4. ***Specifying*** What are the roles and responsibilities of the vice president?

5. ***Identifying Central Issues*** What is the process for presidential succession?

Writing About Government
6. ***Informative/Explanatory*** Choose two vice presidents who have served in the past 25 years. Research each to learn about their areas of expertise and the special projects they pursued while in the vice presidency. Compare the two, examining similarities and differences in their backgrounds, policy interests, and projects they led during their terms.

Interact with these digital
assets and others in lesson 3

✓ INTERACTIVE IMAGE
  Campaigning for President

✓ INTERACTIVE MAP
  2012 Presidential Election

✓ SLIDE SHOW
  Presidential Inauguration

✓ VIDEO
  Electoral College Crash Course

netw⊙rks
TRY IT YOURSELF ONLINE

ReadingHelp Desk

Academic Vocabulary

- margin
- media
- alternative

Content Vocabulary

- elector
- Electoral College
- winner-take-all system
- political action committee (PAC)
- Federal Election Commission (FEC)
- primary
- caucus
- convention
- third-party candidate

TAKING NOTES:

Integration of Knowledge and Ideas

EXPLAINING Complete a graphic organizer about the Electoral College system.

The Electoral College System

Why was it created?	What does it do?	What are some criticisms?

LESSON 3
Electing the President

ESSENTIAL QUESTION

Why and how has the process for nominating and electing presidents changed over time?

Imagine that your school is having an election for student government president. What strategies do you suggest the candidates should take to win the majority of votes? Should they spend their time and energy "shoring up" votes from people who know them and are likely to agree with them? Should they spend more time and energy earning the confidence of people they do not know well? Should the candidates reach out to school clubs, sports teams, and other groups at school?

Road to the White House

GUIDING QUESTION *How do Americans choose their president?*

The system of electing the U.S. president is unique. Unlike elections for members of Congress, governors, and many other officials, the president and vice president are not directly elected by voters. While the presidential candidates' names appear on the ballot, voters are actually voting for **electors**, people who promise they will officially elect the president several weeks later. Thus, a vote for the Democratic candidate is a vote for the Democratic electors, and a vote for the Republican candidate is a vote for the Republican electors. These electors are known collectively as the **Electoral College**.

The Role of the Electoral College The Constitution sets the basic rules for electing a president, including the role of the Electoral College. As they were drafting Article II of the Constitution, the Framers argued about whether or not the president should be elected directly by the people. Many of them did not trust an average person's judgment about such an important matter. They also thought it would be difficult for average citizens to become informed enough about the candidates to make a wise choice. They doubted an average person living in one corner of the country could learn enough about a candidate from another part of the country could learn enough about a candidate from another part of the country. On the other hand, many Framers were concerned about giving someone else the responsibility to choose, namely the Congress. That would give Congress too much control over another branch of government. They compromised by creating a system of electors for each state.

Less than 20 years after the Constitution was adopted and the electoral system was put in place, it was amended to fix problems unforeseen by the Framers. Under the original system, a candidate for vice president could actually receive more votes than a candidate for president. The Twelfth Amendment (1804) required presidential electors to vote separately for president and vice president to solve this problem.

Today, the Electoral College includes 538 electors. Each state has as many electors as it has senators and representatives in Congress. With 1 representative and 2 senators, Wyoming has 3 electoral votes. California, the most populous state, has 55 electoral votes (53 representatives and 2 senators). Washington, D.C., has 3 electors, even though it has no voting representation in Congress.

To be elected president or vice president, a candidate must win at least 270 of the 538 votes. The Electoral College is a **winner-take-all system** in almost every state. That means the candidate who receives the most popular votes in a given state wins all the electoral votes for that state—even if the **margin** of victory is only a single popular vote!

Only Maine and Nebraska do not use the winner-take-all system. They allocate their electoral votes by congressional district. Whichever candidate receives the most popular votes in each district gets that district's electoral vote. The remaining two electoral votes in those states are awarded to the candidate who wins the popular vote statewide.

The Electoral College meets a few weeks after the general election to record the electors' votes. If no presidential candidate receives the majority of the electoral votes, the House of Representatives chooses from the three candidates who have the largest number of votes.

This Electoral College system (and the winner-take-all system, specifically) impacts the entire election process, from who becomes a candidate to how and where they campaign.

Preparing to Run for President Years before a presidential election, potential candidates begin to plan their campaigns. They often begin by forming a **political action committee (PAC)**, an organization of supporters. PACs can gather like-minded individuals to test whether a potential candidate has enough national appeal to win. PACs also begin raising large sums of money that would be needed for a campaign.

Candidates also form exploratory committees who meet with potential supporters and find well-respected public figures to endorse them. These committees help candidates solidify their positions on important issues, develop campaign slogans, and recruit others who might work on the campaign.

If the political scene looks favorable, prospective candidates might make their candidacy official by registering with the **Federal Election Commission (FEC)**, an independent regulatory agency created by Congress to enforce federal election laws. Once a candidate begins to raise and spend money on a campaign, he or she must report all fundraising and expenditures to the FEC.

elector a member of a political party chosen in each state to formally elect the president and vice president

Electoral College the institution that is composed of a set of electors who are chosen to elect a president and vice president into office every four years

winner-take-all system the candidate who receives the most popular votes in a given state wins all the electoral votes for that state

margin the amount by which something is won or lost

2012 Republican presidential candidate Mitt Romney campaigns in Iowa.

▼ CRITICAL THINKING
Naming Why do presidential candidates spend a lot of time campaigning in Iowa?

© Aaron Roeth Photography

Primaries, Caucuses, and National Party Conventions In the first phase of presidential campaigns, candidates must convince members of their own political party to choose them instead of another candidate from the same party. So, Democrats run against Democrats and Republicans run against Republicans in a series of **primaries** or **caucuses**.

In a primary, members of the party go to the polls and vote on which candidate they want to see earn their party's nomination. In some states, non-party members can vote in a primary, but in most states, primary voters are party members. Delegates to the national party convention will cast votes for their state's primary winner. During a caucus, members of a political party gather together to discuss candidates and select delegates to send to the national party convention, where they will also vote to nominate a candidate.

Each state runs its own primary or caucus, and the dates and rules for these vary from state to state. New Hampshire historically holds the first primary, and Iowa holds the first caucus, both during the winter, more than 10 months before the national presidential election. Throughout the spring, other states hold their primaries and caucuses.

As candidates travel from state to state for different primaries, they tend to focus on issues that are important to the party's active members. Republicans might seem more conservative, and Democrats more liberal, as they campaign to win the votes of the party leaders and loyal party members.

In addition, candidates often focus on issues important to party voters in a particular region. For example, a candidate might spend more time talking about water rights in the West, where water rights are most contentious. During debates and campaign appearances, candidates might work to make their primary opponents appear far from the party's values, or they might tout their own electability in the general election.

By late summer, when all the states have held their primaries and caucuses, the major political parties host national nominating **conventions**. At these conventions, loyal party members who have been chosen as delegates from each state vote for the candidate supported by their state's voters. Delegates to the conventions represent all 50 states, the District of Columbia, and all U.S. territories. The delegates vote to nominate a candidate based on the outcome of their states' primary elections and caucuses.

PARTICIPATING
ⓘ Your Government

Investigating

Find out if your state has a primary or a caucus to help select the president. Then find out when the next one is scheduled. The websites of the following organizations will help you find that information:

- The League of Women Voters' Vote 411 project
- The Democratic National Committee
- The Republican National Committee

▶ CRITICAL THINKING

Listing Make a list of what you will need to know by the primary date so you can choose the best candidate.

DEMOCRATS

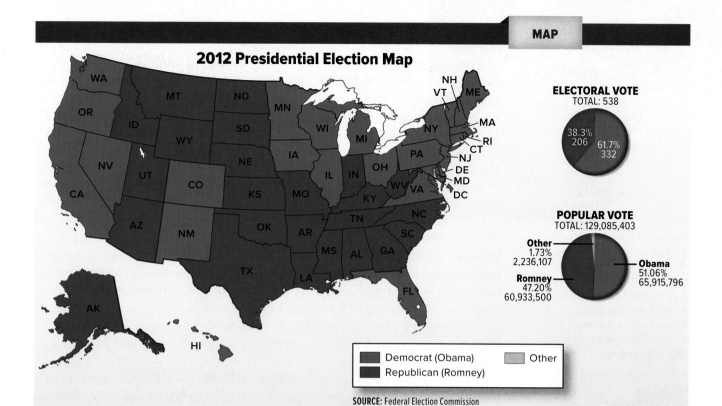

2012 Presidential Election Map

ELECTORAL VOTE
TOTAL: 538

38.3%
206   61.7%
332

POPULAR VOTE
TOTAL: 129,085,403

Other
1.73%
2,236,107

Obama
51.06%
65,915,796

Romney
47.20%
60,933,500

■ Democrat (Obama)   ■ Other
■ Republican (Romney)

SOURCE: Federal Election Commission

General Election After securing the endorsement of a national party, candidates try to appeal to a wider circle of potential voters—people who are less loyal to a party or who are undecided.

Campaigns will spend vast amounts of money on commercials, and candidates will travel extensively around the states that they believe are most necessary to win the national election. Campaign advisers study electoral maps to predict which states' electoral votes a candidate has a chance to win. Campaigning will often be concentrated in "swing states" where polls show voters closely divided. For example, in states like Florida, Pennsylvania, Nevada, and Ohio, voters have been less predictable, so candidates from either major party may win there. In recent presidential elections, these states have been bombarded with campaign ads, canvassers, phone calls, rallies, and public appearances by the candidates.

It is customary for presidential candidates to debate one another in the run-up to an election. These debates are typically held in large auditoriums and are also televised and broadcast by radio, drawing very large national audiences. The formats of the debates are worked out beforehand by the two campaigns.

On a presidential election day, millions of Americans go to the polls and cast their votes for president and vice president. The campaigns have been carrying out extensive "get out the vote" efforts for months aimed at persuading as many of their supporters to vote as possible. The **media** report on the results of the election as soon as the polls close in the evening and often project a winner by midnight.

In December, a few weeks after the general election, the electors meet to cast their official votes for president and vice president.

✓ **READING PROGRESS CHECK**

Sequencing What are the steps that a presidential candidate takes starting with preparing to run through to Election Day?

In the 2012 election, Obama overwhelmingly won the electoral vote, while the popular vote was much closer.

▲ CRITICAL THINKING

1. *Applying* Visit the website of 270toWin.com to find your state's voting history and trends. How has your state allocated its votes in the last five presidential elections? How predictable is your state in choosing candidates from one party or the other?

2. *Explaining* Did many states change the political party to which they gave their electoral votes over the course of four presidential elections? What factors do you think may lead some states to change their dominant party frequently while others tend to stay the same over long periods of time? What was the trend in your home state?

media a source of information including television, print, and the Internet

Broward County, Florida, election workers scrutinized ballots during the presidential contest of 2000. The race was so close that election officials in several Florida counties manually recounted the ballots in an effort to make sure that the count was accurate.

▲ CRITICAL THINKING
Identifying Who selects the president and vice president if no candidate receives a majority of the electoral votes?

third-party candidate someone who represents a political party that is neither Democrat nor Republican

Electoral College Issues

GUIDING QUESTION *What are the weaknesses of the Electoral College system?*

In most presidential elections, the Electoral College system works without controversy or even much attention from the general public. The system does support the principle of federalism because it gives small states more weight since they have two senators just as large states do. Further, it allows the states to decide how they will choose their electors.

Calls for reforming the system, however, are heard after every closely contested election. Critics often point to three major weaknesses in the system that could affect the outcome of an election.

Winner Takes All In all but two states, if a candidate wins the largest number of popular votes, that person receives all the state's electoral votes. Critics argue that this system is unfair to those who voted for a losing candidate. For example, in 2012 more than 3 million Texans voted for Barack Obama, but he did not receive any of Texas's electoral votes. Likewise, Mitt Romney received more than 4 million votes from Californians but none of California's electoral votes.

The winner-take-all system makes it possible for a candidate who loses the popular vote to win the electoral vote. This usually happens when a candidate wins several large states by narrow margins. Four times in American history, the candidate who lost the popular vote won the election: in the elections of John Quincy Adams in 1824, Rutherford B. Hayes in 1876, Benjamin Harrison in 1888, and George W. Bush in 2000. In the 2000 election, for example, Democrat Al Gore won about 500,000 more popular votes than Republican George W. Bush. Bush, however, received 271 electoral votes to 266 for Gore.

Third-Party Candidates When a **third-party candidate**—someone who represents a political party that is not the Democrats or Republicans—is a strong presidential contender, other problems can arise in the Electoral College. A third-party candidate could win enough electoral votes to prevent either major-party candidate from receiving a majority of the votes. The third party could then bargain to release electoral votes to one of the two major-party candidates.

Election by the House When neither presidential candidate wins 270 electoral votes, the House of Representatives must decide the winner. Each state casts one vote. The candidate who receives 26 or more votes is elected.

Election by the House raises three issues. First, states with small populations, such as Alaska and Wyoming, have as much weight as populous states, such as New York and California. Second, under the rules, if a majority of a state's representatives cannot agree on a candidate, the state loses its vote. Third, if some House members favor a strong third-party candidate, it could be difficult for any candidate to get the 26 votes needed to win.

Ideas for Electoral College Reform Many changes to the Electoral College have been proposed. One idea is to choose electors from congressional districts as is already done in Maine and Nebraska. The candidate with the most votes in a congressional district would win its electoral vote; then the candidate with the most districts in a state would receive the two statewide electoral votes.

C·I·V·I·C PARTICIPATION IN A DIGITAL AGE

Get Out the Vote

Young people are less likely to vote than any other age group. They are also more likely than other age groups to use social media and the Internet to learn about presidential candidates and campaigns. Campaign staffs know this and have developed strategies to reach young voters. Besides campaign organizations, many nonpartisan groups work to draw more young people into the political process.

Conduct research about Kids Voting USA and Rock the Vote. Compare their social media outreach and online initiatives for youth. Note the information each provides about presidential candidates.

EXPLORING THE ESSENTIAL QUESTION

Evaluating Prepare a brief post for your own (real or imaginary) social media account to endorse the group you think is most effective at encouraging and preparing young people to vote. Be sure to include a link to the group and a brief explanation about why your friends or followers should check it out.

Another idea is to assign electoral votes based on the winner of the nationwide popular vote. Supporters of this idea want to change the process by passing laws in each state to award that state's electoral votes to the candidate who wins the most popular votes in the whole country. This method would not require amending the Constitution. Instead, the new rules would take effect when states possessing 270 electoral votes enact this type of law. So far, 10 states and the District of Columbia (possessing 165 electoral votes) have enacted that bill.

A third plan proposes that the presidential candidates would win the same share of a state's electoral vote as they received of the state's popular vote. If a candidate captured 60 percent of the popular vote, for example, the candidate would earn 60 percent of the state's electoral votes. This plan would remove the very rare possibility of electors voting for someone they are not pledged to support. Critics of the plan point out that it could possibly expand the role of third parties and complicate the election process. Third-party candidates could get at least part of the electoral vote in each election, and they might be more likely to force a presidential election to be decided in the House of Representatives.

Others argue for the elimination of the Electoral College. Instead, the people would directly elect the president and vice president. While this **alternative** might seem obvious, it may drive up the cost of elections because candidates would have to campaign in all the major media markets across the country. Or, candidates might concentrate their campaign efforts on densely populated areas and ignore more rural communities. Others say eliminating the Electoral College would undermine federalism. With no electors, states would lose their role in the choice of a president.

alternative a different option

☑ READING PROGRESS CHECK

Classifying What reforms have been proposed for the Electoral College system? Briefly describe each one.

First Lady Nancy Reagan and President Ronald Reagan dance at his inaugural ball, January 21, 1985.

▲ CRITICAL THINKING
Speculating What do you think is the purpose of the Inaugural Ball?

The Inauguration

GUIDING QUESTION *How is the president inaugurated?*

Until the inauguration in late January, the new president is referred to as the president-elect. The new president takes office at noon on January 20 in the year following the presidential election. (Until 1933, the inauguration occurred in March.) The Constitution requires the president to take this oath:

📖 PRIMARY SOURCE

I do solemnly swear (or affirm) that I will faithfully execute the Office of President of the United States, and will to the best of my Ability, preserve, protect, and defend the Constitution of the United States."

—Article II, Section 8

By custom, the incoming president rides with the outgoing president from the White House to the Capitol for the inauguration when the chief justice of the Supreme Court administers the oath of office. The new president then gives an inaugural address.

Several inaugural addresses have become part of the nation's heritage. During the Great Depression, Franklin D. Roosevelt lifted American spirits with the words: "The only thing we have to fear is fear itself." In 1961 John F. Kennedy inspired a generation when he said: "Ask not what your country can do for you—ask what you can do for your country."

Members of Congress, foreign diplomats, and thousands of citizens attend the inauguration. After the speech, a parade goes from the Capitol to the White House. The tradition of the inaugural parade began with George Washington's inauguration. Today, thousands of people participate in the inaugural parade. The evening of the inauguration, parties are held to celebrate the new administration and to thank political supporters. The inaugural ball also has a long history and dates back to 1809. Recent presidents have attended multiple balls the evening of the inauguration. For example, President George W. Bush attended nine for his second inauguration, and President Barack Obama attended ten for his first inauguration.

☑ READING PROGRESS CHECK

Paraphrasing How would you paraphrase the oath of office?

LESSON 3 REVIEW

Reviewing Vocabulary
1. *Explaining* What is the Electoral College and what is the role of electors?

Using Your Graphic Organizer
2. *Summarizing* Use your completed graphic organizer to write a one-page fact sheet about the Electoral College system.

Answering the Guiding Questions
3. *Explaining* How do Americans choose their president?

4. *Analyzing* What are the weaknesses of the Electoral College system?

5. *Describing* How is the president inaugurated?

Writing About Government
6. *Informative/Explanatory* Locate a copy of the most recent inaugural address. Then write a short analysis of the address. In your analysis, include a description of any major policy pronouncements. Also include any key phrases or ideas that you find memorable.

Should the Electoral College system be amended?

DEBATING DEMOCRATIC PRINCIPLES

Americans do not vote directly for the president. Instead, voters choose a number of representatives to the Electoral College, who then cast their votes for president. Is this system fair, or should the Electoral College system be replaced?

 YES

TEAM A — The Electoral College System Should Be Amended

The Electoral College should be abolished. It is undemocratic because a candidate can win even if he or she did not get a majority of the popular vote. In addition, a third-party candidate could receive a significant number of votes nationally yet not have a single electoral vote to show for it. This weakens the multiparty system, which is an important principle in democracy because it allows the expression of alternative views on good government.

Today, presidential candidates typically focus most of their campaigning in a few "swing" states. States that are strongly Republican or Democratic do not receive much attention, even if they have millions of voters. If we did away with the winner-take-all Electoral College, candidates would have an incentive to campaign everywhere, because every vote would add to their total. Finally, most states do not legally require electors to vote for the candidate who wins the popular vote. There have been at least 10 instances where electors have broken with this custom, demeaning the purpose of the popular election.

 NO

TEAM B — The Electoral College System Should Not Be Amended

We should keep the Electoral College because it does what the Founders intended—it balances the interests of different regions and prevents a few large states or urban areas from choosing the president. The electoral system gives the 12 states of the Plains and the Southwest 66 votes—more than California (55 votes) or Texas (38 votes), and more than Florida and New York together (58 votes). By contrast, under a direct election system, the voting power of these 12 states would be smaller than the single state of California or Texas or of Florida and New York. The voting-age population in the 12 states is more than 25 million, while the voting-age population in California is more than 27 million. The Electoral College encourages candidates to pay attention to smaller states and to all regions of the United States.

The Electoral College has worked well for more than 200 years, and there are procedures in place in case no candidate wins 270 electoral votes.

EXPLORING THE ESSENTIAL QUESTION

Identifying Perspectives Together with two other students, choose which of the following groups you will represent. Consider how your group's perspective might be different from that of other groups. Then prepare to debate this question from the perspective of your chosen group. Be sure to use the arguments here as well as the material in lesson 3.

Group A: small state

Group B: large state with many urban areas

Group C: large state with an agriculture-based economy and a small population

STUDY GUIDE

PRESIDENTIAL LEADERSHIP SKILLS
LESSON 1

Leadership qualities of successful presidents

- Keen sense of timing
- Political courage
- Ability to compromise
- Understands American public
- Effective communicator

PRESIDENTIAL SUCCESSION
LESSON 2

The president is unable to carry out the duties of office because of death, resignation, or disability.

Congress is notified by either the president or the vice president and a majority of cabinet members.

A successor, as specified in the Constitution, becomes the acting president.

If the president recovers from the disability, he or she may resume office by notifying Congress that he or she is able to carry out the duties of office.

THE PATH TO THE PRESIDENCY
LESSON 3

Candidates officially declare their candidacy.

Party primaries and caucuses are held in states to assign delegates to a nominating convention.

Parties hold nominating conventions to select presidential and vice-presidential candidates for general election.

General election is held to assign Electoral College electors to the candidates.

Electoral College meets and a winner is declared if a candidate receives 270 votes.

If no candidate receives 270 votes at the Electoral College, Congress votes to determine which candidate becomes president.

Directions: On a separate sheet of paper, answer the questions below. Make sure you read carefully and answer all parts of the questions.

Lesson Review

Lesson 1

1 **Differentiating** Explain the difference between the constitutional and informal requirements to become president and why they are important.

2 **Identifying** Who was Abraham Lincoln and how did he display political courage as president?

3 **Listing** List which leadership skills are important to be successful as a president.

Lesson 2

4 **Explaining** Why was an amendment added to the Constitution establishing term limits for the office of president?

5 **Describing** Describe what happens if the president is unable to perform the duties of the office.

6 **Classifying** Distinguish the constitutional responsibilities and the modern responsibilities of vice presidents.

Lesson 3

7 **Contrasting** Describe how using the Electoral College system is different than using the majority of votes cast to determine the winner of a presidential race.

8 **Differentiating** Describe the differences between primaries and caucuses.

9 **Describing** Describe how a president would be selected if no candidate were able to reach the needed votes in the Electoral College.

ANSWERING THE ESSENTIAL QUESTIONS

Review your answers to the introductory questions at the beginning of each lesson. Then answer the Essential Questions based on what you learned in the chapter. Have your answers changed?

10 **Describing** What are the key components of presidential leadership?

11 **Explaining** How has the role of vice president and the process for presidential succession changed over time?

12 **Analyzing** Why and how has the process for nominating and electing presidents changed over time?

DBQ Interpreting Political Cartoons

Use the political cartoon to answer the following questions.

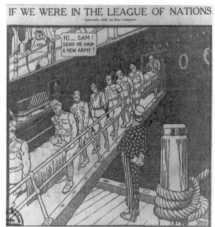

13 **Identifying Point of View** Is this cartoonist arguing for or against joining the League of Nations?

14 **Finding the Main Idea** According to the cartoonist, what could result from U.S. membership in the League of Nations?

Critical Thinking

15 **Comparing and Contrasting** Compare different methods of filling the public offices of president, senator, and representative at the national level.

16 **Considering Advantages and Disadvantages** Explain the advantages and disadvantages of the Electoral College system and discuss whether it is a good system for electing a president today.

17 **Making Connections** Explain why Ronald Reagan is described as being a "great communicator" and why it was important during his presidency.

Need Extra Help?

If You've Missed Question	1	2	3	4	5	6	7	8	9	10	11	12	13	14	15	16	17
Go to page	290	295	293	297	298	298	302	304	306	293	297	302	294	294	302	306	293

Directions: On a separate sheet of paper, answer the questions below. Make sure you read carefully and answer all parts of the questions.

DBQ Analyzing Primary Sources

Read the excerpts and answer the questions that follow.

When Franklin Roosevelt sought a third term as president in 1940, he faced strong criticism that he was abandoning the two-term precedent established by George Washington.

PRIMARY SOURCE

"*I know and you know that any man who is in an office of great responsibility today faces a heavier responsibility, perhaps, than any man has ever faced before in this country. Therefore, to be a candidate of either great political party is a very serious and solemn thing.*

You cannot treat it as you would treat an ordinary nomination in an ordinary time. We people in the United States have got to realize today that we face a grave and serious situation."

—Eleanor Roosevelt,
Address to the 1940 Democratic Convention

PRIMARY SOURCE

"*The strength of my inclination to [retire], previous to the last election, had even led to the preparation of an address to declare it to you; but mature reflection on the then perplexed and critical posture of our affairs with foreign nations, and the unanimous advice of persons entitled to my confidence, impelled me to abandon the idea. I . . . am persuaded, whatever partiality may be retained for my services, that in the present circumstances of our country you will not disapprove my determination to retire.*"

—George Washington, *Washington's Farewell Address to the People of the United States,* 1796

18 ***Finding the Main Idea*** Identify the main idea being expressed by Eleanor Roosevelt in this excerpt.

19 ***Interpreting*** Identify statements in Washington's address that would support or be against Roosevelt's decision to seek a third term as president.

Social Studies Skills

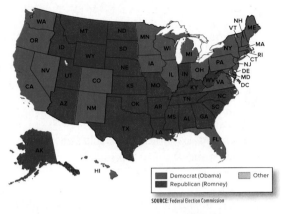

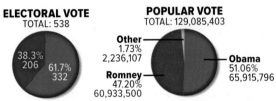

ELECTORAL VOTE
TOTAL: 538

38.3% 206   61.7% 332

POPULAR VOTE
TOTAL: 129,085,403

Other
1.73%
2,236,107

Obama
51.06%
65,915,796

Romney
47.20%
60,933,500

20 ***Understanding Relationships Among Events*** Create a time line showing primary and caucus dates and results for both the Democratic Party and Republican Party for a recent presidential election.

21 ***Interpreting Maps and Graphs*** Refer to the election map. Describe the results of the popular vote and the Electoral College vote shown in the map and graphs.

22 ***Understanding Relationships Among Events*** Explain how a third-party candidate can affect the outcome of an Electoral College vote.

Research and Presentation

23 ***Analyzing*** Write an essay analyzing how the popular vote in a presidential election and the Electoral College work together to determine who becomes president.

24 ***Evaluating*** Write an essay describing the most important qualities and experiences a person needs to have a successful presidential campaign and presidency. Are the qualities the same for both?

Need Extra Help?

If You've Missed Question	**18**	**19**	**20**	**21**	**22**	**23**	**24**
Go to page	297	297	304	305	306	302	290

Structure and Functions of the Executive Branch

networks

www.connected.mcgraw-hill.com
There's More Online about the structure and functions of the executive branch.

CHAPTER 11

ESSENTIAL QUESTIONS

- What are the structure and functions of the executive branch? • How does the federal bureaucracy regulate individuals, communities, and businesses?

©MediaImages/Photodisc/Getty Images

▲ The Eisenhower Executive Office Building, behind the First Division Monument, houses offices for the White House staff.

IMPLEMENTING A NEW LAW

About 48 million people annually get sick from foods they have eaten in the United States. Approximately 3,000 die each year as a result of these food-borne illnesses. Concerned about the safety of food, in 2010 Congress passed the FDA Food Safety Modernization Act; President Obama signed it into law in early 2011. The law has many parts, including a requirement for more inspections of farms and food processing plants, especially those places that have a high risk of distributing contaminated food. The challenging job of implementing this new law falls to the Food and Drug Administration (FDA). Implementation is a multi-year process. Use these sources to explore the process of implementing a law.

PRIMARY SOURCE A

Deadliest Outbreaks of Food-Borne Illness		
Event	Food	People affected
Listeria, 2011	Cantaloupe	147 sickened, 33 died
Listeria, 1998	Hot dog	101 sickened, 21 died
Salmonella, 2008	Peanut butter and paste	714 sickened, 9 died
Listeria, 2002	Deli meat, sliced turkey	54 sickened, 8 died
Listeria, 2000	Deli meat, sliced turkey	29 sickened, 7 died

SOURCE: CDC, Foodborne Outbreak Online Database

PRIMARY SOURCE B

PRIMARY SOURCE C

The day after President Obama signed the Food Safety Modernization Act into law, the head of the FDA blogged about the law:

"Here's a quick look at some of the provisions in the new law:

- **Issuing recalls:** For the first time, FDA will have the authority to order a recall of food products. Up to now, with the exception of infant formula, the FDA has had to rely on food manufacturers and distributors to recall food voluntarily.

- **Conducting inspections:** The law calls for more frequent inspections and for those inspections to be based on risk. Foods and facilities that pose a greater risk to food safety will get the most attention.

- **Importing food:** The law provides significant enhancements to FDA's ability to oversee food produced in foreign countries and imported into the United States. Also, FDA has the authority to prevent a food from entering this country if the facility has refused U.S. inspection.

- **Preventing problems:** Food facilities must have a written plan that spells out the possible problems that could affect the safety of their products. The plan would outline steps that the facility would take to help prevent those problems from occurring.

- **Focusing on science and risk:** The law establishes science-based standards for the safe production and harvesting of fruits and vegetables. This is an important step forward. These standards will consider both natural and man-made risks to the safety of fresh produce.

- **Respecting the role of small businesses and farms:** The law also provides some flexibility, such as exemptions from the produce safety standards for small farms that sell directly to consumers at a roadside stand or farmer's market as well as through a community supported agriculture program (CSA)."

—FDA Commissioner Margaret A. Hamburg, M.D., 2011

Since the law was passed, the FDA has issued monthly reports on the progress the agency has made toward implementation of the law. Below are just a few of the steps reported on in the first two years following the law's passage:

- Eight major speeches on the new law were given at food safety conferences.
- Four public meetings were held to gather input on various requirements of the law.
- A variety of enhancements to the FDA website were made, including launching of a better search engine to allow consumers to identify recalled foods, posting of videos and a webcast about the new law, and providing numerous FAQs about the law.
- Seven sets of guidelines for industry were written/updated and published.
- Three major sets of rules were put in place and work on many other rules was begun.
- Two pilot projects were launched.
- Four reports were submitted to Congress.
- Procedures for identifying high-risk facilities (those that will be inspected more often) were developed and published.
- Staff worked to create agreements with other countries, and an agreement with New Zealand was signed.

—FSMA Progress Reports, U.S. Food and Drug Administration

The ink on the Food Safety Modernization Act was barely dry when the head of the FDA mentioned the importance of the funding needed to implement the law:

"The funding we get each year, which affects our staffing and our vital and far-ranging operations, will also affect how this legislation is implemented. For example, the inspection schedule in the legislation would increase the burden on FDA's inspection functions. Without more funding, we will be challenged to implement the law fully without compromising other key functions. We look forward to working with Congress and our partners to ensure that FDA is funded sufficiently to achieve our food safety and food defense goals."

—FDA Commissioner Margaret A. Hamburg, M.D., 2011

Several organizations representing farmers and food producers sent a letter to members of the Appropriations and Agriculture committees about possible fee increases as a result of the law :

"Imposing new fees on food facilities would represent a food safety tax on consumers. As food companies and consumers continue to cope with a period of prolonged economic turbulence, the creation of a new food tax would mean higher costs for businesses and higher food prices for consumers. We urge Congress to reaffirm its stated opposition to imposing new user fees on food producers and stand ready to work with Congress and the administration to find a better and less burdensome solution."

—Letter to congressmen from industry groups, UnitedFresh.org

DBQ DOCUMENT-BASED QUESTIONS

1. **Describing** What problems with food safety does the new law attempt to solve?
2. **Making Inferences** How is the new law impacting the work of the FDA? Take one provision of the law and think of as many decisions as you can that must be made in implementing just that one piece.
3. **Evaluating** Why is the budget of the FDA critical to implementation of the new law? Why do you think Commissioner Hamburg mentioned this issue the day after the bill was signed into law?

WHAT WILL YOU DO?

Has examining these sources helped you understand what it means to implement a law? How will this understanding influence the way you analyze proposed pieces of legislation?

EXPLORE the interactive version of the analyzing primary sources feature on **Networks**.

Interact with these digital assets and others in lesson 1

✓ **INTERACTIVE GRAPH**
Size of the Executive Office of the President

✓ **INTERACTIVE IMAGE**
National Security Council

✓ **SELF-CHECK QUIZ**

✓ **VIDEO**
Clinton Cabinet Appointments

netw⦿rks
TRY IT YOURSELF ONLINE

Reading Help Desk

Academic Vocabulary

- **federal**
- **reaction**

Content Vocabulary

- **cabinet**
- **leak**
- **National Security Advisor**
- **White House chief of staff**
- **press secretary**

TAKING NOTES:

Integration of Knowledge and Ideas

COMPARING AND CONTRASTING Use the Venn diagram to compare and contrast the structure and functions of the cabinet and the Executive Office of the President.

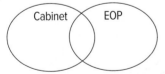

Cabinet   EOP

LESSON 1
The Cabinet and the Executive Office of the President

ESSENTIAL QUESTION

What are the structure and functions of the executive branch?

The president relies on key advisers to recommend government policies and to carry out his or her vision for the presidency. Imagine you have just been elected to lead the nation. Rank the following characteristics according to which would be the most important as you choose your closest advisers.

- Someone with experience running a company with a big budget
- Someone with experience in the executive branch of government
- Someone with experience as an academic expert on a specific policy subject
- Someone who raised a huge amount of money for your campaign
- Someone who will be easily approved by those who must approve of your advisers
- Someone who represents a racial minority or ethnic group
- Someone who agrees with your basic ideas about how to run the government
- Someone who has very different opinions than yours about government but who is well-respected
- Someone you have known for a long time and trust

The Cabinet

GUIDING QUESTION *How is the president's cabinet selected and what is its role?*

One of the first responsibilities of a president is to select his or her **cabinet**, people who serve as some of the president's closest advisers. The cabinet includes the secretaries of each of the 15 executive departments, the vice president, and other key officials. In addition to advising the president, the cabinet secretaries also run the executive departments for which they have responsibility.

The Nomination and Confirmation of Cabinet Officials As a reflection of the importance of the cabinet—and as an illustration of checks and balances—the president cannot simply choose his or her cabinet. The Senate must confirm each person the president nominates to be cabinet secretary.

The selection process for a new president's cabinet begins long before Inauguration Day. The president-elect draws up a list of candidates after consulting with campaign advisers, congressional leaders, and representatives of interest groups. Key campaign staffers meet with potential candidates to discuss the issues facing the department they may be asked to head. Before making final decisions, members of the president-elect's team may **leak**, or deliberately disclose, some candidates' names to the news media. They do this to test the reaction of Congress, interest groups, and the public to their nominations.

The selection of a president's cabinet is largely a political process. In selecting their department heads, presidents must balance a great many political, social, and management considerations.

- **Experience in a Particular Policy Area**—Secretaries should have expertise in the policy areas their departments will manage. The secretary of the interior, for example, typically is someone from a western state who has experience in land policy and conservation issues. Generally, the secretary of housing and urban development (HUD) is from a large city and the secretary of agriculture is from a farm state.

- **Administrative and Supervisory Experience**—Cabinet officers are responsible for huge departments that employ thousands of people and spend billions of dollars each year. They must be able to adequately manage and supervise the many programs run by the executive branch.

- **Support for the President's Goals and Plans**—Many presidents reserve some number of cabinet positions for people loyal to the president's political party and who have been most helpful in getting them elected.

- **Support from Various Groups that Hold Political Power**—The president needs to satisfy powerful interest groups that have a stake in a department's policies. The secretary of labor, therefore, generally is someone who is acceptable to labor unions. The secretary of commerce will have a good reputation with business and industry. The secretary of the treasury will often be a banker or someone with close ties to the financial community.

- **Demographic Diversity**—Today, presidents typically try to assemble a cabinet that includes women as well as representatives from different geographic, racial, and ethnic groups.

Even after people are selected, obstacles can arise. Some people chosen by the president have turned down the opportunity. Faced with giving up a secure career for a possible short-term appointment, many qualified candidates find the pay, the work, or life in Washington politics unattractive. Cabinet secretaries earn $199,700 per year. For many, this salary represents far less than they could earn in the private sector. As public officials, their private lives become public and they are under constant scrutiny from the press and pressure from interest groups.

The Senate holds confirmation hearings on the president's nominees for cabinet posts. Nominees answer questions about their views and background before the Senate committee that is relevant to the cabinet position. In many cases, the Senate is willing to routinely confirm the president's nominees. Of more than 500 cabinet appointments since the time of George Washington, the Senate has rejected only a handful.

Appointments are not automatic, however. For example, the Senate rejected President George H.W. Bush's nomination of John Tower as secretary of defense. During his confirmation, allegations surfaced that he had shared secrets about negotiations with the Soviet Union with defense contractors who could profit from that information.

cabinet the president's closest advisers, consisting of the vice president, the secretaries of each of the 15 executive departments, and other top government officials who help the president make decisions and policy

leak to release secret information to the media by anonymous government officials

EXPLORING THE ESSENTIAL QUESTION

Narrative Recall the 15 executive departments and choose a department that interests you. If you want more information about it, visit the department's website at www.usa.gov. Imagine the president has asked if you would like to run the department and become a member of the cabinet. Write a letter accepting or rejecting the president's offer, explaining which factors influenced your decision.

The cabinet includes the secretaries of each of the 15 executive departments, the vice president, and other key officials. In addition to advising the president, the cabinet secretaries also run the executive departments for which they have responsibility.

▲ **CRITICAL THINKING**

Describing Choose two members of the cabinet and describe the different roles they fill.

In some cases, a president has withdrawn a nomination after it became clear that the Senate or the public did not support the nominee. In one case, in 2008 President Obama nominated Tom Daschle to be secretary of health and human services. Daschle had a distinguished career in both the House and Senate and was an expert on Obama's new health care plan. However, he was forced to withdraw his nomination when a controversy developed over his failure to properly report and pay his income taxes.

Still other nominees have received just enough votes to be confirmed, but the process illustrated conflicts among the executive and legislative branches over the right course of policy. This was the case in 2013, when President Obama nominated Chuck Hagel to be secretary of defense. Hagel had earned two Purple Hearts for his military service in Vietnam and went on to become a senator. He narrowly earned enough votes to be confirmed, but only after Senate opponents issued scathing criticisms of his policies on Iran and Israel and on his views regarding the reduction of the number of troops in the war in Afghanistan.

The Constitution and its system of checks and balances give the Senate the power to confirm or reject a president's choice for cabinet secretary. However, the Constitution does not require the president to get congressional approval to fire a cabinet member or any other executive employee. The Supreme Court clarified this in a 1926 case called *Myers* v. *United States*.

The Functions and Changing Role of the Cabinet The purpose of the cabinet is to advise the president and to lead executive branch departments. The cabinet meets when the president calls it together. Meetings might be held once a week or more or less frequently depending on the preference and the needs of a president. Meetings take place in the cabinet room of the White House and are usually closed to the public and the press.

From the beginning, the cabinet's role in decision making depended on the president's wishes. Some presidents paid little attention to their cabinet. Andrew Jackson, known for giving jobs to his friends and supporters, relied on a small group of friends for advice. Since they often met in the White House kitchen, they became known as the Kitchen Cabinet.

Secretary of State William Seward had this to say about how Abraham Lincoln viewed his cabinet: "There is only one vote in the cabinet, and it belongs to him." Before he issued the Emancipation Proclamation, Lincoln simply called his cabinet together to inform them that he intended to end slavery: "I have got you together to hear what I have written down. I do not wish you to advise about the main matter for that I have determined myself."

During the Great Depression, Franklin Roosevelt often relied on people who were not in the official cabinet. They were a group of university professors and outside experts nicknamed the "brain trust." His wife, Eleanor, was also a frequent adviser.

Following the death of President Kennedy, Lyndon Johnson kept much of Kennedy's cabinet in place. However, over time he replaced those advisers with people more loyal to himself. Some scholars claim that Johnson was less interested in the advice of his cabinet than in their willingness to carry out his directions. When a meeting occurred, it was generally to give department heads what one assistant called their "marching orders."

Other presidents have relied more heavily on their cabinets for advice. President Kennedy, for example, held his cabinet (as well as Thomas Jefferson) in very high regard. He is known for saying, "I think this is the most extraordinary collection of talent, of human knowledge, that has ever been gathered at the White House—with the possible exception of when Thomas Jefferson dined alone."

Some cabinet members have greater influence because their departments are concerned with the most sensitive national issues. This would include the secretaries of state, defense, and the treasury, as well as the attorney general in most administrations.

Factors Limiting the Influence of the Cabinet There are several factors that limit the president's use of the cabinet and the cabinet's influence. No president commands the complete loyalty of cabinet members. Even though the president appoints them, cabinet officials have loyalties to three other constituencies: long-term officials in their own department, members of Congress, and special interest groups. Each of these groups has a stake in the department's programs. Each may push the secretary in directions that do not always agree with the president's plans and policies—or with each other.

Sometimes disagreements arise among different cabinet secretaries. These might be a result of loyalty to their department's programs, to its constituent groups, or to personal animosity. During George W. Bush's first term, for example, notable disagreements arose between Colin Powell, the secretary of state, and Donald Rumsfeld, the secretary of defense. Their disagreements created some confusion about national security policy and eventually led to Powell's resignation.

Presidents naturally prefer to discuss tough problems with people they know and trust. Yet because of the political factors that must be considered, presidents can end up appointing relative strangers to their cabinets. President Kennedy, for example, had never met his secretary of defense and secretary of the treasury before he appointed them. For these reasons, presidents have increasingly turned to the Executive Office of the President and to their White House staff for help.

☑ **READING PROGRESS CHECK**

Analyzing How has the role of the cabinet changed over time?

The Executive Office of the President

GUIDING QUESTION *What are the roles and responsibilities of the staff in the Executive Office of the President?*

In addition to the cabinet, the president looks to the experts in his or her Executive Office of the President, or EOP. This group is supervised by the White House chief of staff and has become the president's closest group of advisers. Staff in the EOP gather information, develop policy, and advise the president. Many of the staff gain their positions due to their political support for the president's policies. EOP agency staffs include attorneys, scientists, social scientists, and other highly technical or professional personnel. The EOP currently has more than 1,500 full-time employees, many of whom work in the west wing of the White House.

The History of the EOP Franklin D. Roosevelt, who took office during the Great Depression, immediately proposed many **federal** programs to deal with the country's serious economic problems. As Congress passed one special program after another, the size of the national government grew rapidly.

federal pertaining to the union of states under a central government distinct from the individual governments of the separate states

The Executive Office of the President

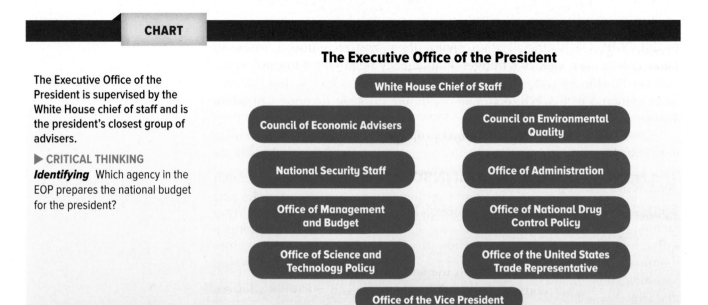

The Executive Office of the President is supervised by the White House chief of staff and is the president's closest group of advisers.

▶ CRITICAL THINKING

Identifying Which agency in the EOP prepares the national budget for the president?

By the mid-1930s, Roosevelt and his few White House assistants were unable to coordinate all the programs or gather all the information he needed to make decisions quickly and effectively. A special committee studied the issue and recommended that a personal staff be installed to assist the president in:

PRIMARY SOURCE

Obtaining quickly and without delay all pertinent information ... so as to guide him in making his responsible decisions; and then when decisions have been made, to assist him in seeing to it that every administrative department and agency affected is promptly informed."

—The President's Committee on Administrative Management, 1937

In response, Congress passed the Reorganization Act of 1939, which created the Executive Office of the President, which has since grown dramatically under subsequent presidents. Roosevelt also established the White House Office, a smaller group of advisers who work directly with the president on day-to-day matters.

Many of today's huge federal programs require that several executive departments and agencies work together. EOP staff members have been added to coordinate these efforts. For example, President Ronald Reagan created the Office of National Drug Control Policy in 1988. This department coordinated the activities of more than 50 federal agencies involved in the war on drugs.

Three of the oldest agencies in the EOP have played the greatest role in presidential decision making. They are the Office of Management and Budget, the National Security Council, and the Council of Economic Advisers.

The Office of Management and Budget (OMB) The OMB is the largest agency within the Executive Office of the President. It prepares the national budget for the president, who then presents it to Congress.

Budgets reflect spending priorities. The OMB's budget reflects what the federal government will spend money on and how much. A president's influence over the budget is thus one important way that the president can influence government policy.

Each year all executive departments and agencies submit their budgets to the OMB. OMB officials then review them and recommend where to make cuts in each agency's budget. If an agency head wants to challenge a cut, he or she must appeal directly to the president or a top adviser. This system gives OMB real and continuing influence over executive agencies. After the OMB reviews the separate executive department budget proposals, it creates an overall budget proposal for the president to submit to Congress.

The National Security Council (NSC) The National Security Council (NSC) is composed of the president's senior national security advisers and cabinet officials. They advise the president and coordinate American military and foreign policy. They also coordinate the government's planning for and response to domestic terrorism and catastrophes. Besides the president, the council includes the vice president, the secretary of state, secretary of the treasury, and the secretary of defense. The president can ask other advisers to participate in NSC meetings, such as the CIA director or the chairperson of the Joint Chiefs of Staff of the military.

A special assistant, the **National Security Advisor**, directs the NSC staff. Perhaps more than most other advisory groups, the importance of the NSC has varied with the president's use of it.

The responsibilities and composition of the current NSC illustrate how EOP can change under different presidential administrations. Shortly after the September 11, 2001, terror attacks on the United States, President George W. Bush created the National Homeland Security Council, a cross-governmental group that wanted to improve the way different parts of the government investigate and respond to natural disasters, terrorism, and other catastrophes on U.S. soil. In 2009 President Obama folded this group into the NSC, expanding the role of that EOP agency significantly. Obama's NSC includes the secretary of homeland security, the attorney general; the directors of the FBI, CIA, and Federal Emergency Management Agency (FEMA); and the secretaries of defense, treasury, transportation, and health and human services.

The Council of Economic Advisers Since the Great Depression, the president has been the nation's chief economic planner, formulating the nation's economic policy. In this role, the president relies on the Council of Economic Advisers. By law, the Council is composed of three members who must be confirmed by the Senate. The council is supported by a team of economists, statisticians, and research assistants.

The Council assesses the nation's economic health, predicts future economic conditions, and supports other executive agencies that are involved in economic planning. It also proposes solutions to specific problems, such as unemployment or inflation. It has access to any information a federal agency gathers on the American economy. The Council also prepares an annual report that the president gives Congress on the state of the economy.

National Security Advisor the director of the National Security Council (NSC)

The National Security Council advises the president and coordinates American military and foreign policy.

▼ CRITICAL THINKING
Identifying Is the National Security Council a cabinet-level department?

Size of the Executive Office of the President

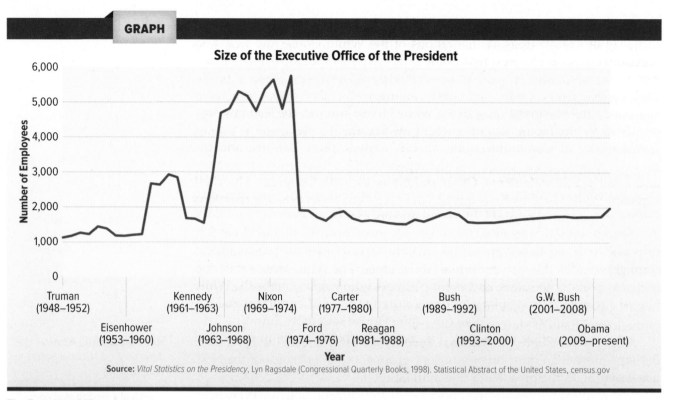

Source: *Vital Statistics on the Presidency*, Lyn Ragsdale (Congressional Quarterly Books, 1998). Statistical Abstract of the United States, census.gov

The Executive Office of the President currently has more than 1,500 employees who gather information, develop policy, and advise the president.

▲ CRITICAL THINKING

Drawing Conclusions What possible factors affect the number of Executive Office employees?

Other EOP Agencies The number and size of EOP agencies can vary because presidents can have different priorities. For example, President Lyndon B. Johnson's War on Poverty involved many different programs to fight unemployment and other social problems in the inner cities and among all Americans. He therefore set up an Office of Economic Opportunity to track some of these programs. His successor, President Richard Nixon, opposed many of Johnson's policies, so Nixon eliminated this office.

Currently, the Office of Environmental Policy advises the president on environmental issues and works closely with the Environmental Protection Agency and the departments of Interior, Agriculture, and Energy. The Office of Science and Technology Policy advises the president on all scientific and technological matters that can affect the nation. The Office of the United States Trade Representative works to negotiate trade agreements with other nations.

The White House Office The nation's first presidents had no personal staff. George Washington hired his nephew at his own expense to be his personal secretary. In fact, most early presidents had few people working for them or helping them to run the executive branch. When James Polk was president from 1845 to 1849, his wife, Sarah, was his secretary. During the 1890s, two presidents, Grover Cleveland and William McKinley, personally answered the White House telephone. As late as the 1930s, Herbert Hoover's personal staff consisted of a few secretaries, several administrative assistants, and a cook.

Today, the EOP also includes a special unit called the White House Office. It is yet another set of key advisers and assistants for the president. They gather information, advise the president about policy and political strategy, communicate on behalf of the president, and run the day-to-day operations of the White House.

Unlike cabinet members, most White House staff can be chosen without Senate confirmation. They are often long-time supporters and personal friends of the president, vice president, and the president's spouse. These top assistants become a kind of inner circle around the president.

The president's most trusted adviser is usually the **White House chief of staff**. He or she oversees the operations of the White House and EOP and regulates access to the president. Some staff members specialize in particular policy areas. Others focus on political strategy, analyzing how a policy decision will affect voters and members of Congress. For the legal consequences of a policy, the president looks to the White House counsel, the lead lawyer.

Other White House staffers present the president's views to the public. In the Office of Communications, speech writers, press liaisons, and the **press secretary** handle relations with the press corps, set up press conferences, and issue public statements. Other staffers work with Congress. The chief assistant for legislative affairs advises the president about possible **reactions** in Congress to a policy and lobbies lawmakers to win support.

Meanwhile, a steady stream of people from inside and outside government want to see the president. Which people and which issues get through is decided largely by White House aides. The White House staff also includes chefs, schedulers, and event planners who work to make the White House a special meeting place for foreign dignitaries and important guests.

Recent presidents have given top White House staff more authority over policy making. Today, more policy decisions are being made in the White House than in executive agencies.

Executive Privilege Presidents do not want information from their advisers to become public while they are still deciding on policies. Presidents sometimes assert a right of executive privilege to keep this information confidential. Executive privilege means the president can refuse to provide documents or other records to the legislative and judicial branches. Although executive privilege is not mentioned in the Constitution, the concept comes from the separation of powers. Courts have ruled that presidents have some right to executive privilege, but that it is not absolute.

In 2012 President Obama invoked executive privilege when his attorney general refused to turn over documents to Congress related to a gun-trafficking sting operation known as "Fast and Furious." His predecessor, President George W. Bush, used executive privilege six times, including to avoid giving Congress information on the use of FBI mob informants.

✓ **READING PROGRESS CHECK**

Determining Importance Why are the positions of White House chief of staff and press secretary key roles in the modern presidency?

EXPLORING THE ESSENTIAL QUESTION

Drawing Inferences Go online to find a video or transcript of a recent press conference or press briefing. Take notes about the message the White House press secretary is trying to convey. Also take notes about the questions reporters ask and how the press secretary answers them. If possible, note whether the press secretary seems to have a friendly or contentious relationship with the members of the press. Based on your notes and observations, what skills do you think a person needs to be a successful White House press secretary? Do you think your answer would change if you were a reporter? Explain your answers.

White House chief of staff the president's most trusted adviser and the overseer of the work and operations of the White House and the Executive Office of the President (EOP)

press secretary one of the president's top assistants who is in charge of media relations

reaction a response to a situation or stimulus

LESSON 1 REVIEW

Reviewing Vocabulary
1. *Defining* What is the cabinet and what is its relationship, if any, to the White House Office?

Using Your Graphic Organizer
2. *Summarizing* Use your completed graphic organizer to summarize the different roles of the cabinet and the EOP.

Answering the Guiding Questions
3. *Explaining* How is the president's cabinet selected and what is its role?

4. *Describing* What are the roles and responsibilities of the staff in the Executive Office of the President?

Writing About Government
5. *Argument* Most presidents reserve some cabinet positions for loyal partisans who helped with their election campaign. Some people see this as improper, while others think it makes sense for a president to choose a trusted individual to serve in this role. What do you think? How should a president select the members of his cabinet? Write a persuasive essay in which you present your argument and refute possible counterarguments.

United States Ⓥ Nixon (1974)

FACTS OF THE CASE In 1972 the Democratic Party headquarters was located in a Washington, D.C., office complex called Watergate. There, party leaders made decisions relating to political campaigns and fund-raising.

Five burglars were caught breaking into the party's office. Later, investigators discovered that Republican President Richard Nixon and his aides had hired people to burglarize the offices. Nixon and his associates had hoped to gather information that would help Nixon get reelected.

Investigators also learned that President Nixon secretly taped most of the conversations that took place in his office. The prosecutor in the case believed that the tapes had information about the illegal things President Nixon and his aides had allegedly done. He asked President Nixon to turn over the tapes. Nixon said no, claiming that executive privilege protected him from being required to turn over the tapes.

ISSUE

Did executive privilege allow the president to withhold evidence of tape-recorded conversations from a prosecutor?

ARGUMENTS

Read each argument and identify whether it supports President Nixon's view or that of the prosecutors (United States).

1. Compelling the president to turn over the tapes would be an unconstitutional intrusion into the functioning of the executive branch. This would violate the separation of powers provided for in the U.S. Constitution.

2. No one is above the law. If the president is allowed to commit a crime and hide evidence from the prosecutors, then the principle of the rule of law means nothing.

3. The president must be allowed to keep conversations with his aides confidential. Privacy is required so that advisers can be honest without worrying about being criticized by other people. Their honest opinions help the president make decisions.

4. Sometimes a president's discussions with aides need to be private to protect the country.

5. The tapes being requested did not involve matters of national security. Thus, justice in the criminal case was more important than protecting the privacy of the president and his aides.

EXPLORING THE ESSENTIAL QUESTION

Evaluating After you have classified the arguments, think about which arguments are strongest. Then decide whether executive privilege should apply to the following situations:

1. The first lady forms a task force on health care. When Congress asks for records of her meetings with government officials and health care providers, she insists they remain secret.
2. Accused of lying to prosecutors, the president claims his aides cannot be called to testify before a grand jury.
3. After pardoning several people, the president refuses to allow his staff to testify before a House panel investigating the pardons.

Interact with these digital assets and others in lesson 2

✓ **INTERACTIVE INFOGRAPHIC**
The Size of the Executive Branch

✓ **INTERACTIVE TIME LINE**
The Cabinet Departments

✓ **SELF-CHECK QUIZ**

✓ **VIDEO**
NASA Lands Curiosity

netw⚡rks
TRY IT YOURSELF ONLINE

ReadingHelp Desk

Academic Vocabulary

- **data**
- **innovative**

Content Vocabulary

- **ambassador**
- **embassy**
- **government corporation**

TAKING NOTES:
Key Ideas and Details

DESCRIBING Use the chart to list details about the departments, agencies, corporations, and commissions within the federal bureaucracy.

Cabinet Departments
Independent Agencies
Government Corporations
Regulatory Commissions

LESSON 2

Cabinet Departments and Independent Agencies

ESSENTIAL QUESTION

What are the structure and functions of the executive branch?

Choose one cabinet-level department that interests you and locate a few news stories about the department to learn more about its mission, programs, size, and clout. Based on what you have learned, answer the following questions:

- In general terms, what is the department responsible for?
- Which of the department's programs do you think are most valuable to society? Least valuable to society?
- Do you think the department is too large, too small, or the proper size?
- What queries do you have about the department that would help you better answer these questions?

Cabinet Departments

GUIDING QUESTION *What are the functions of the 15 cabinet departments in the executive branch?*

The president's cabinet includes the heads of the 15 executive branch departments. In addition to advising the president in matters related to their specific department, these individuals run their departments. They oversee all the programs, services, and people that carry out their mission.

The Founders anticipated the need for creating federal agencies to carry out the day-to-day business of government. The Constitution establishes the executive departments and the role of those who lead each. Article II, Section 2, states that, "He [the president] may require the opinion, in writing, of the principal Officer in each of the executive Departments, upon any subject relating to the Duties of their respective Offices, . . ."

Today, nearly 2.8 million civilians work for the federal government. The government owns about 900,000 buildings scattered across the nation and around the world. Much of the federal government's work is associated with the 15 executive departments. The earliest departments were created in 1789, soon after President George Washington's election: the Department of State, the Department of War, the Department of the

Treasury, and the attorney general's office. Since 1789, eleven additional departments have been created.

The title for the person who heads each executive department is "secretary," except for the head of the Department of Justice, who is the attorney general. Departments usually have a second-in-command, called the deputy secretary or undersecretary. In addition, departments have assistant secretaries. The president appoints all these officials who are subject to Senate confirmation.

Below these top officials are the directors of the major units of the cabinet department, along with their assistants. These units have various names, including bureau, agency, office, administration, or division. Overall policy is set by the top officials in each department—secretaries, directors, deputy directors, and their assistants. These high-level leaders rely on ideas and information from career officials who are specialists and business managers in each department. Often, these career civil servants, who have many years of experience, do the research on the policy options that leaders will consider.

State The Department of State is responsible for developing and implementing the foreign policy of the United States. It represents the United States to the United Nations (UN) and to more than 180 other countries through its network of **ambassadors** and civilian Foreign Service employees who work at **embassies** and consulates around the world. The department also assists U.S. citizens living abroad and foreign nationals who wish to enter the United States. The range of department activities is vast, from countering international crime, to providing aid to other countries, to promoting democracy and cultural exchanges.

Treasury The Department of Treasury manages the monetary resources of the country. It includes the U.S. Mint, which manufactures coins, and the Bureau of Engraving and Printing, which produces paper money. The largest bureau in the department is the Internal Revenue Service (IRS). The IRS collects taxes paid by American citizens and businesses each year. The Treasury Department is also responsible for making payments to the public and for borrowing any money needed to operate the federal government. The Treasury

ambassador an official of the government who represents the nation in diplomatic matters

embassy the official residence and offices of the ambassador and his or her staff; the primary function of an embassy is to make diplomatic communication between governments easier

---

We the People: Making a Difference

Nilesh Shah, Foreign Service Officer

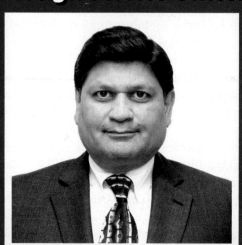

Nilesh Shah represents the U.S. government by working at the American Embassy in India. After a career in finance, Nilesh wanted to get involved in an area where he could make an on-the-ground impact. He joined the U.S. Foreign Service—where employees represent the U.S. government, serve and protect American citizens, promote trade and investment, and facilitate greater cooperation among governments, businesses, and citizens. Nilesh helped organize a group in India that created a system for village-level entrepreneurs to deliver safe drinking water to residents. He also helped facilitate a partnership between U.S. and Indian technology developers that created low-cost, low-energy farm produce chillers to reduce spoilage of food on the way to grocery stores. Nilesh remarked, "Foreign Service employees serve in some of the most dangerous and challenging places around the world. For me, the best thing is being able make a difference and help people."

▲ CRITICAL THINKING

Analyzing What role do Foreign Service employees play in the U.S. government?

Health and Human Services **$700**

Defense **$527.5**

Agriculture **$95**

Education **$68.6**

Transportation **$70**

Homeland Security **$60.6**

Housing and Urban Development **$40**

State **$35**

Veterans Affairs **$90**

Justice **$25**

Interior **$16**

Labor **$50**

Energy **$23**

Treasury **$13**

Commerce **$6.5**

Department budgets in billions of dollars, 2013

The size of each department's budget varies dramatically.

▲ CRITICAL THINKING

1. Reading Graphs Which three executive departments have the largest budgets?

2. Drawing Conclusions What conclusions can you draw about how important they are (and to whom)?

3. Evaluating Do you think those departments should be largest and the bottom three should be the smallest? Explain your answer.

4. Collaborating Work with three other students to rank the 15 executive departments from what you believe should be the most to least important. Explain how your new order demonstrates your group's ideas about government priorities.

Department also coordinates with other agencies to protect the nation's financial and banking institutions from foreign threats or economic crisis.

Interior The Department of the Interior executes federal policy and programs to protect natural resources including public lands and minerals. It supports research to protect fish, wildlife, and endangered species. It maintains the extensive national park system and hundreds of national dams and reservoirs. It issues recreation permits and leases to companies who use national resources for energy, minerals, grazing, and timber. The Interior Department also carries out our nation's responsibilities to Native Americans, Alaskan Natives, and Pacific Islanders through programs to support tribal education, health, job training and employment, law enforcement, resource management, and government infrastructure.

Agriculture The U.S. Department of Agriculture (USDA) develops and executes policy on farming, agriculture, and food. It consists of 17 agencies that carry out laws to support farmers and ranchers, protect our national forests, promote agricultural trade, assure food safety, and provide nutrition assistance and programs to end hunger in America and abroad.

Justice The Department of Justice (DOJ) enforces federal laws designed to protect public safety, reduce crime, punish people who break laws, enforce civil rights, and ensure justice for all Americans. It includes the Drug Enforcement Administration (DEA), the Federal Bureau of Investigation (FBI), the U.S. Marshals, and the Federal Bureau of Prisons and the Civil Rights Division.

▲ The Department of Housing and Urban Development was created in 1966 in response to concern with the condition of inner cities during the War on Poverty.

data factual information used as a basis for reasoning, discussion, or calculation

In addition, the head of the department, the attorney general, represents the United States in legal matters, and advises the president and the heads of the executive departments.

Commerce The Department of Commerce supports the economy by developing and executing policies to promote American businesses and industries. It promotes exports and enforces international trade agreements with other countries. It issues patents and trademarks and administers laws relating to scientific and technical standards, telecommunications, and technology. It monitors data about our oceans and weather and administers the census, which counts the population and analyzes demographic trends.

Labor The Department of Labor administers federal programs to protect and improve the productivity of workers. It runs programs to address job training, minimum hourly wage and overtime pay, employment discrimination, and unemployment insurance. It also protects workers' retirement benefits and enforces laws involving interactions between labor unions and managers. The Labor Department also works to protect workers' safety through its Occupational Safety and Health Administration (OSHA). In addition, the Bureau of Labor Statistics analyzes **data** on employment, prices, wages, and other economic indicators.

Defense The Department of Defense (DOD) protects the security of our country. It consists of the U.S. Army, U.S. Navy, U.S. Marines, and U.S. Air Force as well as the Joint Chiefs of Staff and 17 defense agencies. The DOD's work is carried out by millions of active duty personnel, hundreds of thousands of civilian employees, and more than a million people who serve in the National Guard and Reserve forces. In addition to fighting wars and providing national security, the DOD is involved in efforts to deter war, assist in disasters, and provide humanitarian aid.

HHS The Department of Health and Human Services (HHS) is concerned with protecting public health and providing social services to those least able to support themselves. It provides health insurance and administers programs such as Medicare and Medicaid. It funds medical research to improve public health and to prevent disease. The department administers the Centers for Disease Control and Prevention (CDC) and the Public Health Service. The Food and Drug Administration (FDA) inspects food- and drug-processing plants and must approve all new drugs before they can be sold.

HUD The Department of Housing and Urban Development (HUD) is responsible for national policies and programs that address America's housing needs, improve and develop the nation's communities, and enforce fair housing laws. HUD supports home ownership for lower- and moderate-income families through its mortgage and loan insurance programs. It provides rent subsidies and administers public housing and assistance programs for people who are homeless. HUD also manages programs that help communities with economic development and tries to ensure equal access to housing opportunities for all.

Transportation The Department of Transportation (DOT) develops policy and administers a variety of programs relating to transportation. Its programs oversee the nation's mass transit systems, railroads, bridges, and waterways. The Federal Highway Administration (FHWA) runs programs to improve driver and pedestrian safety as well as to reduce distracted driving and driving under the influence of alcohol or drugs. The Federal Aviation Administration (FAA) regulates air travel and works to ensure air safety.

Energy The Department of Energy (DOE) executes law and policies about the nation's energy. It administers funding for research and innovation in science and engineering, including programs to promote affordable and clean energy to protect the environment. It runs programs to increase our country's energy independence. The department's work includes overseeing the nation's nuclear energy and nuclear weapons programs.

Education The Department of Education provides assistance to public and private schools, collects data from schools, distributes research results, and administers federal financial aid programs. It works with state and local school systems to set high standards for students and schools. The department also administers policies designed to prohibit discrimination in education and ensure equal access for students regardless of their race, ethnicity, national origin, physical disabilities, and level of proficiency in English.

Veterans Affairs (VA) The VA administers benefit programs for veterans and their families and survivors. These benefits include pension, education, disability compensation, home loans, life insurance, vocational rehabilitation, survivor support, medical care, and burial benefits.

Homeland Security The Department of Homeland Security (DHS) coordinates national efforts to protect against acts of terrorism that would jeopardize the American people, key resources, and critical infrastructure. If an incident does occur, it leads the efforts to respond and to recover. It administers immigration laws and responds to national disasters. Its work is carried out by employees, including those of the U.S. Customs and Border Protection, the U.S. Coast Guard, the U.S. Secret Service, the Transportation Security Administration (TSA), the Federal Emergency Management Agency (FEMA), and the U.S. Immigration and Customs Enforcement.

☑ **READING PROGRESS CHECK**

Classifying Which executive branch departments are involved in foreign policy and defense? Explain the specific role of each.

Independent Agencies, Government Corporations, and Regulatory Commissions

GUIDING QUESTION *What are the purposes of the independent agencies, government corporations, and regulatory commissions of the executive branch?*

In addition to the 15 cabinet departments, there are also independent agencies, government corporations, and regulatory commissions that are part of the federal bureaucracy.

Independent Agencies The federal bureaucracy includes more than 100 independent organizations that are not part of the executive departments. The president appoints the heads of these agencies. A few of these agencies—like the National Aeronautics and Space Administration (NASA)—are almost as large and well-known as cabinet departments. NASA conducts missions relating to space exploration, technologies, and potential economic opportunities in the field of space, such as commercial space flight. One technological innovation currently under development is NASA's Low-Density Supersonic Decelerator (LDSD), a major advancement in deep space exploration that will allow large payloads to be landed on other planets.

▼ The Department of Veterans' Affairs was created in 1988 in recognition that the Veterans' Administration, one of the largest federal agencies, deserved cabinet status.

Andrew Harrer/Bloomberg/Getty Images

C·I·V·I·C PARTICIPATION IN A DIGITAL AGE

Executive Branch Websites

Each of the executive departments and agencies has its own website.
To find a link to each, go to www.usa.gov.

1. **Choose an agency or department that interests you.**

2. **Analyze its website.**

   a. What news is featured on the home page today?

   b. Leave the home page and explore the site. Is the site easy to navigate?

   c. Does it have a kids' page? If so, what topics or activities does it offer? Do you have any suggestions to make the kids' page more engaging?

   d. Does the agency or department have a blog? A Twitter account? If so, who writes it and what topics do they cover? Would you consider following the blog or tweets? Why or why not?

3. **Choose a second department, agency, or federal corporation. Compare and contrast its website to the one you analyzed first.**

EXPLORING THE ESSENTIAL QUESTION

Summarizing Using what you have learned from the two executive branch websites, write a summary of your analysis.

NASA also explores ways to use data gathered in space to solve problems on the ground, such as air traffic congestion. In addition to space exploration and data collection, NASA scientists continually work to develop new technologies to improve the quality of life on Earth. For example, government-assisted NASA research and development has produced life-saving medical technologies such as hand-held devices that can test and monitor critical body processes from any location. These devices are being used in the U.S. military and also in patients' homes. Consumer products developed by NASA include home air purifiers, water-purification bottles, and even clothing made of fabrics developed for use in space suits.

Some independent agencies perform services for the executive branch. The General Services Administration (GSA) is responsible for constructing and maintaining all government buildings and supplying equipment for federal offices. The primary mission of the Central Intelligence Agency (CIA) has been to gather and evaluate information about what is going on in other countries. The CIA uses its own secret agents, paid informers, foreign news sources, and friendly governments to collect information.

Government Corporations The federal government runs approximately 60 **government corporations**. They are organized somewhat like private businesses. Each has a board of directors and executive officers who direct the day-to-day operations. The Tennessee Valley Authority (TVA) builds and maintains dams and supplies electric power for an eight-state area. The Federal Deposit Insurance Corporation (FDIC) insures bank accounts up to a certain amount. If a bank fails, the FDIC takes it over and repays the depositors. AMTRAK is a government corporation that runs passenger rail service. The United States Postal Service (USPS) accepts, sorts, and delivers mail and is probably the best known government corporation.

Government corporations are supposed to be more flexible than regular government agencies. They are more likely to take risks and to find **innovative** solutions to the challenges they confront. Unlike private businesses, however, money from Congress supports government corporations.

government corporation a business that the federal government runs

innovative characterized by a new idea or method

Regulatory Commissions Regulatory commissions occupy a special place in the federal bureaucracy. They are independent agencies that have the government's authority to issue licenses and punish people and groups that violate the laws under their authority. They make and enforce rules for large industries that affect many people. Examples include:

- The Federal Communications Commission (FCC) regulates communication by television, cable, radio, satellite, and wire.
- The Nuclear Regulatory Commission (NRC) seeks to ensure the safe use and disposal of radioactive materials for nonmilitary purposes. It licenses and monitors the safety of nuclear power plants.
- The Environmental Protection Agency (EPA) works to protect human health and the environment. The EPA evaluates pesticides and air and water quality, and cleans up toxic waste sites.
- The Federal Trade Commission (FTC) enforces antitrust and consumer protection laws. The FTC investigates claims of unfair or deceptive sales practices.
- The Federal Election Commission (FEC), which enforces campaign financing laws for all federal elections.

While funded by Congress, the commissions are independent of all three branches of the national government. To keep the regulatory commissions impartial, Congress has tried to protect them from political pressure. Each commission has from 5 to 11 commissioners, whom the president appoints with Senate consent. The terms of office of these board members are long—in some cases, as long as 14 years—and the starting dates for terms are staggered. Unlike other bureaucrats, these commissioners do not report to the president, nor can the president fire them.

These regulatory commissions were created to make rules for large industries and businesses that affect the public. They also regulate the conduct of these businesses and industries. Regulatory agencies decide such questions as who will receive a government license to operate a radio station or to build a natural gas pipeline to serve a large city. The commissions can also act as a kind of court investigating businesses, holding hearings, and setting penalties for businesses that may have violated the rules.

☑ **READING PROGRESS CHECK**

Contrasting How are regulatory commissions different from independent agencies?

LESSON 2 REVIEW

Reviewing Vocabulary

1. *Describing* What is a government corporation and in what ways is it similar to a for-profit corporation?

Using Your Graphic Organizer

2. *Creating Visuals* Create a presentation about the structure of the executive branch.

Answering the Guiding Questions

3. *Describing* What are the functions of the 15 cabinet departments in the executive branch?

4. *Explaining* What are the purposes of the independent agencies, government corporations, and regulatory commissions of the executive branch?

Writing About Government

5. *Informative/Explanatory* Select one of the independent agencies or regulatory commissions that interests you. Write a fact sheet explaining its purpose at its inception and its purpose today.

Interact with these digital assets and others in lesson 3

✓ **INTERACTIVE IMAGE**
Political Appointees

✓ **LANDMARK ACTIVITY**
The Pendleton Act, 1883

✓ **SELF-CHECK QUIZ**

✓ **VIDEO**
Whistleblower

netw☼rks
TRY IT YOURSELF ONLINE

ReadingHelp Desk

Academic Vocabulary

- ignore
- neutral

Content Vocabulary

- spoils system
- civil service system
- whistleblower
- recuse

TAKING NOTES:

Key Ideas and Details

LISTING Use the graphic organizer to list details about the civil service and political appointees.

Civil Service	Political Appointees

LESSON 3
The Federal Workforce and Civil Service

ESSENTIAL QUESTION

How does the federal bureaucracy regulate individuals, communities, and businesses?

If you were an employer, what would you see as the advantages and disadvantages of retaining workers in their jobs for a long time and through numerous bosses?

If you were a newly appointed cabinet secretary, what percentage of your staff would you want to be people who have previously demonstrated their loyalty to you?

How do the hiring and promotion processes support or diminish the quality of our government and our democracy?

Origins

GUIDING QUESTION *What are the origins of the civil service system?*

Federal employees are vital to the smooth and efficient functioning of the U.S. government. About a third of federal government employees are administrative workers. The government also employs doctors, veterinarians, lawyers, cartographers, scientists, engineers, accountants, and many other professionals. Today over 70 percent of all federal jobs are filled through a competitive process based on job skills and experience, but this method was not used when our government was established.

The Spoils System George Washington declared that he appointed government officials according to "fitness of character." At the same time, however, he favored members of the Federalist Party. When Thomas Jefferson entered the White House, he found most federal workers already working there opposed him and his political ideas. Consequently, Jefferson fired hundreds of workers who were members of the Federalist Party. He replaced these workers with people from his own political party, the Democratic-Republican Party.

By the time Andrew Jackson became president in 1829, the federal government had begun to grow. Jackson fired about 1,000 federal workers and gave their jobs to his own political supporters. Jackson defended his actions by arguing that rotation in office was more democratic.

Long service in the same jobs by any group of workers, he claimed, would only promote tyranny.

A New York senator defended Jackson's actions by stating, "To the victor belong the spoils." The **spoils system** became the phrase used to describe Jackson's method of appointing federal workers. Today, the term *spoils system* refers to the practice of victorious politicians rewarding their supporters with government jobs.

For the next 50 years, national, state, and local politicians used the spoils system to fill bureaucratic positions. Political supporters of candidates expected to be rewarded with jobs if their candidate won. As the federal government grew larger, the spoils system flourished.

Calls for Reform The spoils system fostered inefficiency and corruption. Inefficiency grew because, as government became more complex, many jobs required specific skills. Yet most federal workers were not experts in their jobs; their skills were in working in election campaigns to secure victory for their candidates.

Corruption developed as people used their jobs for personal gain. Government employees did special favors for special interest groups in return for political support for their candidates. Jobs were often bought and sold, and people made large profits from government contracts. Bureaucrats regularly gave jobs to friends rather than to the lowest bidder.

Calls for reform began in the 1850s when newspapers and magazines described the problems with the spoils system. In 1871 Ulysses S. Grant, whose own administration was filled with corruption, persuaded Congress to set up the first Civil Service Commission. In 1875, however, reform efforts faltered when Congress failed to appropriate money for the new commission.

It took a tragedy to restart reforms. In 1881 President James A. Garfield **ignored** Charles Guiteau's requests for a job in the diplomatic service. Infuriated, Guiteau shot Garfield, who eventually died from his wounds. Chester A. Arthur, who succeeded Garfield as president, pushed for reforms, as did the outraged general public. In 1883 Congress passed the Pendleton Act, creating the present federal **civil service system**.

The Pendleton Act transformed the nature of public service. It diminished the power of political parties and the president by putting most of the responsibility for running the day-to-day functions of executing and enforcing laws in the hands of people without close political ties to the government or department secretaries. Today many well-educated and well-trained professionals work for the federal government. When the Pendleton Act went into effect, only 10 percent of the federal government's 132,000 employees were covered. Today, more than 90 percent of the 2.7 million federal employees are covered.

☑ **READING PROGRESS CHECK**

Analyzing How did the spoils system lead to the civil service system for federal workers?

The Civil Service Today

GUIDING QUESTION *How does the civil service function today?*

Today, the Office of Personnel Management handles recruitment, pay, retirement policy, and exams for federal workers. The Merit System Protection Board settles job disputes and investigates complaints from federal workers.

spoils system victorious politicians rewarding their supporters with government jobs

ignore to refuse to take notice of

civil service system government employment based on competitive examinations and merit

▼ CRITICAL THINKING
Explaining How does the civil service system try to take political considerations out of the hiring and promotion process for most federal employees?

LANDMARK LAWS
THE PENDLETON ACT, 1883

In 1883, Congress passed the Pendleton Act creating the present civil service system. The Pendleton Act:

★ created the civil service system that hires, employs, and promotes workers based on open, competitive exams and merit

★ made it illegal to fire or demote employees covered by the law for political reasons

★ forbade covered employees from giving political service or contributions

★ created the Civil Service Commission to administer exams and supervise the operation of the new civil service system

Getting a Job Competition for federal jobs today is stiff. In recent years, every job opening has had about 80 applicants. The Office of Personnel Management, along with individual agencies, is responsible for filling federal jobs. Job notices for most "career" or civil servant jobs are posted in post offices, newspapers, and online at USAJOBS (www.usajobs.gov). Most secretarial and clerical jobs require the applicant to take a written examination. For other jobs such as accountants, social workers, and project managers, applicants are evaluated on their training and experience. Veterans are given special preference.

Government jobs are attractive because of the many benefits they offer. Salaries for most federal workers are competitive with those in private industry, and benefits include paid vacation days, sick leave days, health insurance, and a retirement package.

Protections for Civil Servants All civil service workers have job security. They may be fired, but only for specific reasons and only after a very long, complex series of hearings.

According to law, most executive branch employees of the federal government can join unions but may not be forced to do so. Numerous federal employee unions and associations represent civil servants' interests in improving working conditions and other job factors. Unlike most private sector unions, these unions do not negotiate for pay. While union membership has declined in the general public, membership in federal employee unions grew significantly between 2000 and 2012.

whistleblower a federal employee who reports corruption or wrongdoing by the government

Federal employees who report corruption or wrongdoing by the government are known as **whistleblowers**, because they call attention to misconduct. In some instances, whistleblowers have lost their jobs or been demoted. Individuals and groups such as the Government Accountability Project worked for more than a decade to increase legal and First Amendment protections for those employees. In 2012 Congress passed and President Obama signed into law the Whistleblower Protection Enhancement Act; the act passed both the House and Senate unanimously.

Restrictions for Civil Servants In 1939, amidst concerns about the ethical implications of federal employees working on political campaigns,

GOVERNMENT *in your* COMMUNITY

Finding Government Positions

You can find internships, summer jobs, part-time work, and full-time employment at all levels of the federal government. You might think most federal jobs would require you to work in Washington, D.C., but nearly 85 percent of federal jobs are in other parts of the country and the world.

Go to www.usajobs.gov and search for job openings in your community or region. Take notes about two jobs that interest you. If you prefer, you can conduct the same search for two different internships. Information about some federal internships will be posted on the Pathways Program portion of the same usajobs.gov website. Other positions will be posted on the websites of individual federal departments and agencies.

US Department of Energy

▶ **CRITICAL THINKING**

Displaying Create a poster or pamphlet that features two internships or jobs. For each, summarize:

  a. the type of work
  b. whether the position is full-time, part-time, or seasonal
  c. the application process including who to contact
  d. qualifications required
  e. salaries and benefits

Congress passed the Hatch Act, which prevents federal workers from participating in election campaigns.

The law has been controversial since its passage, and its constitutionality has been the subject of two Supreme Court cases. Opponents argue that the law violates freedom of speech for federal workers. They also claim that it discourages political participation by people who may be well informed about political issues.

Supporters of the Hatch Act believe it is needed to keep the federal civil service politically **neutral**. They argue that the act protects workers from political pressure from superiors and that it prevents employees from using their government positions to punish or influence people for political reasons. A high-profile example of how political prejudice can affect bureaucratic decisions occurred in 2008. Charges were made that Secretary of Housing and Urban Development Alphonso Jackson canceled a housing grant to someone who said he did not like President George W. Bush. Secretary Jackson resigned following press reports of the charges.

In 1993 Congress revised the Hatch Act to address criticisms. The amended law prohibits federal workers from engaging in political activities during work hours, including wearing a campaign button. When they are not at work, though, they are permitted to hold office in a political party, participate in political campaigns and rallies, publicly endorse candidates, and raise funds from within their government agency's political action committee. They cannot run for an elective office, however, or solicit public contributions.

IRS and Treasury officials testify before Congress in 2013, after allegations that the IRS was unfairly scrutinizing conservative organizations' applications for tax-exempt status. In response, Congress created a whistleblower website for people to provide information about IRS abuses.

▲ CRITICAL THINKING
Exploring Issues Do you think laws such as the Whistleblower Protection Enhancement Act are necessary? Explain.

☑ **READING PROGRESS CHECK**

Describing What protections do civil servants possess?

Political Appointees in Government

GUIDING QUESTION *What role do presidential appointees play in the executive branch?*

In each presidential election year, the House or Senate publishes a book known by Washington, D.C., insiders as the *Plum Book*. The word *plum* can mean something good—a tasty sweet—given in return for a favor. When we are talking about government, it means a political plum, that is, a job the new president can award to supporters. The *Plum Book* lists all such jobs.

On taking office, every president has the chance to fill about 3,700 jobs in the federal bureaucracy that are outside the civil service system, meaning that a person does not take a civil service exam to win the position.

The president appoints close to 800 top-level jobs that require Senate approval. These jobs include very important, high-profile posts, such as the 15 cabinet secretaries, about 300 top-level bureau and agency heads, and more than 170 ambassadors to foreign countries. There are also over 300 appointees that do not require Senate approval. The number of such appointments almost doubled after the passage of the Presidential Appointment Efficiency and Streamlining Act of 2011, which eliminated the need for Senate approval on 163 nominations. Also about 10 percent of the jobs in the Senior Executive Service in the executive branch are filled by presidential appointees. There are also lower-level political appointments that include about 1,400 aide and assistant positions known as "Schedule C" appointees.

Filling these jobs gives presidents a chance to put loyal supporters into critical positions. These political appointees head agencies, offices, and bureaus and will make key political decisions. They are expected to try to implement the president's policies. Unlike career civil service workers, their employment usually ends when a new president is elected.

neutral not favoring either side in a debate, contest, or war; not aligned with a political or ideological group

Douglas Graham/CQ-Roll Call Group/Getty Images

▲ Gina McCarthy being sworn in as administrator of the U.S. Environmental Protection Agency (EPA)

USEPA Photo by Eric Vance

recuse to remove oneself from participation to avoid a conflict of interest

Many people, in and out of government, would find it very difficult to learn and excel in their jobs in just a few years. Political appointees face this challenge. They also face the complexities of government agencies, which have multiple departments, divisions, programs, issues, and procedures. The result of these short tenures is that much of the real power over daily operations stays with the career civil service officials. Their day-to-day decisions do not often make headlines or the nightly newscast, but they do shape the national policy on crucial problems.

Political appointees are subject to more ethics restrictions than career civil servants. Since the enactment of a 1989 executive order, the vast majority of full-time political appointees have been prohibited from earning income outside their work duties. The law requires them to report all income, including investment income, each year. This information is then made public.

In addition, a 2009 executive order requires all full-time political appointees to sign an ethics pledge in which they commit not to accept gifts from lobbyists or lobbying organizations. They must also **recuse** themselves from any decisions or issues that involve former employers or clients. Political appointees who were lobbyists within two years of their appointments must make additional pledges to recuse themselves from assignments on issues they lobbied for the previous two years.

People at the Top The people appointed to leadership and political positions are first and foremost the president's political supporters. Most are well educated. Nearly all are college graduates. The majority have advanced degrees, and a significant percentage are usually lawyers. Others are successful businesspeople or other professionals. Some of the people in these positions have expertise in the specialized work of the agency they are appointed to, but many do not. They may or may not have served in government before. Almost certainly they will have administrative or managerial experience. When the president leaves office, most of them return to jobs outside the government.

☑ **READING PROGRESS CHECK**

Considering Advantages and Disadvantages What are the advantages and disadvantages of having presidential appointees serve in high-level and lower-level government positions?

LESSON 3 REVIEW

Reviewing Vocabulary
1. *Defining* What does a whistleblower do?

Using Your Graphic Organizer
2. *Comparing and Contrasting* Use your completed graphic organizer to compare and contrast civil service employees and presidential political appointees.

Answering the Guiding Questions
3. *Understanding Historical Interpretation* What are the origins of the civil service system?

4. *Explaining* How does the civil service function today?

5. *Identifying* What role do presidential appointees play in the executive branch?

Writing About Government
6. *Informative/Explanatory* How did the spoils system foster inefficiency and corruption? How did the civil service system solve the problems with the spoils system? Write an essay in which you explain the advantages and disadvantages of each system. Are there any reforms you would make to our current civil service system? If so, what problems with the current system are you trying to solve?

Interact with these digital assets and others in lesson 4

✓ **INTERACTIVE IMAGE**
Getting Public Input

✓ **INTERACTIVE POLITICAL CARTOON**
The Nature of Bureaucracy

✓ **WE THE PEOPLE**
Heidi Landgraf, DEA agent

✓ **VIDEO**
Tobacco Regulation

netw⊕rks
TRY IT YOURSELF ONLINE

LESSON 4
The Executive Branch at Work

Reading Help Desk

Academic Vocabulary

- implement
- so-called

Content Vocabulary

- public policy
- bureaucrat
- liaison officer
- stakeholder
- injunction
- client group
- iron triangle
- deregulate
- red tape

TAKING NOTES:

Integrating Knowledge and Ideas

ANALYZING Use the graphic organizer to analyze the advantages and disadvantages of government regulation.

Government Regulation	
Advantages	Disadvantages

ESSENTIAL QUESTION

How does the federal bureaucracy regulate individuals, communities, and businesses?

Nearly all new tobacco users are under the age of 18. Many will be addicted before they are mature enough to make an informed decision about the use of tobacco products. To address this problem, the Tobacco Control Act was passed and signed into law in 2009. Among its many provisions, the law restricts advertising tobacco products to youth under the age of 18, including banning tobacco sponsorship for sporting events or concerts. It requires larger and more prominent warning labels on tobacco products and bans most flavored cigarettes. All tobacco companies must register and be subject to inspection every two years to make sure they are following the law. They cannot keep secret the results of any research about the effects of tobacco use.

Imagine that you and two other classmates work for the agency responsible for implementing this law, the Food and Drug Administration (FDA). Your team should discuss the following questions and then write a memorandum to your supervisor that outlines your recommendations about how your agency should implement the law:

- Who will perform inspections of tobacco companies and how often?
- How will they decide which companies to inspect?
- What will inspectors look for?
- What will happen to companies that fail inspection?
- How will your agency inform tobacco companies of what they'll be looking for and how to comply with the law?
- How will your agency know if their inspections are making a difference in reducing smoking among youth?
- What could be the negative consequences of your recommendations? How should the FDA best handle those potential problems?

Public Policy, Rules, and Regulations

GUIDING QUESTION *How does the federal bureaucracy make, interpret, and implement public policy?*

Public policy is the stated course of action that the government takes to address problems or issues. Public policy might include actions the government requires or forbids. If Congress decides to increase the number of inspections of meatpacking plants or to increase the size of FDA staff so it can investigate foreign imports like Chinese toothpaste, that is a public-policy decision. A president's decision to refuse to send military aid to a Latin American country is also public policy. Requiring federal contractors to submit certain kinds of reports is also public policy.

The entire complement of agencies and departments that **implement** laws and make related policy is called the *bureaucracy*. People who work for these agencies and departments are called **bureaucrats**. Federal bureaucrats help make policy in several ways. The most important of these involves administering the hundreds of programs that affect almost all aspects of national life. Administering these programs requires federal bureaucrats to write rules and regulations and to set standards to implement laws.

Bureaucratic Involvement in Lawmaking Before a law is even passed by Congress, executive department staff have likely been watching its development and considering its implications. Each cabinet department has **liaison officers** who develop relationships with the elected officials and congressional staff members who have authority over the work of their departments. Liaison officers keep track of bills moving through Congress. They also supply information to lawmakers, who may request an analysis of bills. Liaison officers promote communication and good relations with Congress.

Sometimes, the executive branch takes a more active role in lawmaking. Executive liaison officers may help draft new bills for Congress as well as testify about legislation. Lawmakers know that it can be difficult to pass major bills unless they have gotten the advice of the federal agencies that will administer the laws.

Often, the ideas for new laws come from within the bureaucracy. For example, studies by the Public Health Service on the effects of smoking led Congress to pass new laws designed to cut down on the use of cigarettes.

Making Rules and Policy In the simplest terms, federal bureaucrats carry out the policies the Congress makes and the president signs. However, when Congress does pass a law, it cannot spell out exactly how to enforce it. The bureaucracy shapes what the law actually means. The main way federal agencies do this is by issuing rules and regulations designed to translate the law into action. The bureaucracy formulates rules or regulations to carry out each law. Complex laws contain many more rules and regulations than the average law. For example, the Dodd-Frank Wall Street Reform and Consumer Protection Act is more than 800 pages long and the federal government has created approximately 400 rules in order to implement the law.

Consider the Social Security Program. In 1935 Congress passed the Social Security Act. The act makes it possible for disabled workers to receive payments from the government, but it left certain questions unanswered. What does the word *disabled* mean? Are workers considered to be disabled if they can work only part-time? Are they disabled if they can work, but not at the job they had?

public policy a plan of action adopted by government decision makers to solve a problem or reach a goal

implement to put into effect and ensure fulfillment by concrete measures

bureaucrat one who works for a department or agency of the federal government; a civil servant

liaison officer an officer who develops relationships with the elected officials and congressional staff members who have authority over the work of his or her department

Over time, the Social Security Administration has developed many specific rules and regulations describing disability. Someone who is "visually impaired" is defined, for example, as someone with no better than 20/70 vision in his or her better eye (with correction). The measure for being considered "legally blind" is corrected vision of 20/200 or lower in the better eye. Rules help ensure that only eligible people receive benefits.

Rules made by federal agencies have the force and effect of law. For example, the Department of Housing and Urban Development (HUD) has created guidelines for building contractors who hire minority employees. Unless contractors follow these guidelines, they cannot bid on federally-funded construction projects. If building companies ignore regulations or rules, they can be fined. So, in effect, the HUD guidelines—and other rules and regulations—have the force of law.

This means that, in practice, the bureaucracy makes public policy. By deciding who qualifies as disabled, or setting guidelines about federal building contractors' hiring policies, these agencies are making public policy. Other examples include safety requirements for nuclear power plants (by the Nuclear Regulatory Commission, an independent agency) and fuel-efficiency targets for automakers (by the Department of Transportation).

Executive branch employees often play key roles in setting specific goals and making rules for government programs. Some people are concerned that people who were not elected make policy. Others say that the complexity of federal law and federal programs demands that they do.

Public Input Executive agencies and staff cannot and do not make rules and regulations in a vacuum. They seek input from private citizens and others who will be affected by potential rules and regulations. These people are sometimes called **stakeholders**. In addition to getting feedback from private citizens, official lobbying groups also attempt to influence the ways rules and regulations are written.

> **stakeholder** a private citizen or other who will be affected by potential rules and regulations

When agencies draft new rules, they must publish drafts of those rules and allow the public to see and comment on them before they go into effect. Americans can comment on proposed rules and regulations online, by e-mail, by postal mail, or at public meetings.

The process for getting public input varies by agency, but the procedures are very specific and must be followed. Typically, an agency will publish

PARTICIPATING
in Your Government

U.S. Environmental Protection Agency

Identifying Stakeholders

On a particular date in 2013, the *Federal Register's* website listed nine proposed rules. Two of those proposed rules are summarized below. For each, consider which individuals and groups would be most interested in the new rule or regulation. Name at least three possible stakeholders for each.

a. The Environmental Protection Agency is proposing to approve separate requests from three different states that would revise the rules about the level of motor vehicle emissions allowed under the Clean Air Act.

b. The Federal Aviation Administration proposes changes in regulations requiring inspections of defective planes made by Hawker Beechcraft Corporation. It would also prohibit the use of specific spare parts on those planes.

CRITICAL THINKING
Interpreting Explore the website of the *Federal Register* and do the same task for two rules proposed today.

The federal bureaucracy seeks input from private citizens who will be affected by new projects, rules, or regulations. Here a representative from the U.S. Army Corps of Engineers speaks with a resident during a public information meeting about a levee project along the American River.

▲ **CRITICAL THINKING**

Defining Who do you think the stakeholders are in the levee project along the American River?

injunction an order that will stop an action or enforce a rule or regulation

draft rules in the *Federal Register* and then give the public 60 days to comment on each. Occasionally, after the initial comment period, an agency may publish a second draft and ask for comments again. After this time, the agency then prepares the final version of the rule or regulation and publishes it in the *Federal Register* or the *Code of Federal Regulations.*

The Influence of Interest Groups The right to provide input is not just for individuals. Interest groups use various strategies to encourage their members to weigh in on rules that might affect them. For example, if the Environmental Protection Agency (EPA) is going to issue new rules about what types of pollution power plants are allowed to emit, groups like the Chamber of Commerce and the Sierra Club will encourage their members to attend meetings, send letters, or sign petitions to the EPA.

Checks and Balances on the Bureaucracy When citizens or interest groups are not satisfied with a rule or regulation, they can take their case (and the agency that wrote the rule) to court. They may ask a federal court to issue an **injunction**—an order that will stop an action or enforce a rule or regulation. In this way, federal courts can have an important impact on policy making. Citizens do not often win such cases, however. Courts rarely reverse decisions of federal regulatory commissions—they uphold approximately two-thirds of the agency actions they review. Congress can check the power of executive agencies and departments in three ways. Lawmakers can pass laws to alter the rules or regulations a federal agency establishes. They can also hold agencies more accountable for what they do. For example, Congress passed the Government Performance and Results Act, which requires federal agencies to write strategic plans, set annual performance goals, and then collect data to measure how well the goals are being met. Starting in 2000, each agency began publishing reports on their performance. Lawmakers can use these reports to make sure the executive branch is carrying out laws as they were expected to do. Over time, lawmakers and taxpayers can also use these reports to determine which programs produce the best results for the money spent. Congress can also increase or decrease funding for an agency to send a message about what it believes the agency's priorities should be. Of course, Congress can also eliminate an agency or department altogether.

☑ **READING PROGRESS CHECK**

Explaining What tools do bureaucrats use to shape public policy?

Debates About the Size of Bureaucracy

GUIDING QUESTION *What has contributed to the growth of the federal bureaucracy? How might the bureaucracy be reduced in size?*

People have different views about the federal bureaucracy. In some ways, those differences can be traced all the way back to the Federalists and Anti-Federalists who debated how the executive branch of government would work when the Founders wrote the Constitution. Some people today worry that the national government is too big, too inefficient, and too costly. Others believe that federal government programs are vital to the nation and should be maintained or expanded. Leaders with both points of view have tried to make the large bureaucracy more effective.

Factors Contributing to Growth in the Bureaucracy There is little doubt that the size of the federal bureaucracy has grown since the founding of the country and the signing of the Constitution. Several forces have driven the growth in size and importance of the federal bureaucracy.

Population Growth The sheer number of people living in America requires government to grow. The number of government officials who ran a country of 4 million people cannot govern a country of more than 300 million people.

Industrial and Technological Advances Americans now live in a much more urban, industrial, and technological society. Presidents and executive branch staff of 100 years ago could have never imagined the existence or ramifications of nuclear power, laser surgery for cancer, space exploration, the Internet, or solar-powered cars.

Growing Global Economy Over time the strengths and weaknesses of the U.S. economy has become more entwined with world financial markets, complex trade relationships, and global competition over resources and markets. The government's role in protecting and growing American business has increased as well.

Threats to National Security Bureaucracy expanded rapidly after World War II. The United States was in a race against the Soviet Union to build weapons and to persuade other countries to join our side. Several agencies were created to help us succeed: the Central Intelligence Agency, the Arms Control and Disarmament Agency, the United States Information Agency, and the Peace Corps. The Korean and Vietnam Wars involved millions of American soldiers and required significant spending. The Department of Veterans Affairs has become one of the largest federal agencies.

After the terrorist attacks of 2001, President George W. Bush created the Department of Homeland Security to consolidate and improve the government's ability to deal with the threat of international terrorism. The wars in Iraq and Afghanistan led to an even greater need for veterans services.

We the People: Making a Difference

Heidi Landgraf, DEA agent

Paul Harris/Hulton Archive/Getty Images

Hearing the words, "My name is Heidi Landgraf. I'm an agent with the DEA," two drug cartel bosses stared in disbelief. The drug bosses were the victims of a sting operation of the Drug Enforcement Administration (DEA). Landgraf was at the center of Operation Green Ice, playing the part of a drug lord's daughter for two years. Green Ice involved Landgraf and more than 100 other federal agents worldwide. The operation led to the arrest of about 140 suspects and a seizure of $50 million.

With the use of tax returns, credit cards, and a passport, Landgraf was turned into "Heidi Herrera." Although she was watched by fellow agents, she was in constant danger. From a phony business location, she collected cash from drug dealers around the country and laundered it through banks. After two years of collecting evidence, the DEA scheduled the "takedown."

When press stories identified her, Landgraf had to give up being an undercover agent. She continued to work within the DEA, however, in media relations and drug prevention.

CRITICAL THINKING
1. **Identifying** What executive branch goals and policies was Heidi Landgraf helping to carry out?
2. **Explaining** Why did Heidi Landgraf have to give up being an undercover agent?

Economic Crises During the Great Depression and the presidency of Franklin D. Roosevelt, the number of federal workers nearly doubled. The government had created numerous programs to provide economic relief, to put people back to work, and to stimulate the economy.

When Lyndon Johnson became president, nearly a quarter of Americans lived below the poverty line. He rallied the country around his vision for a "Great Society" in which the government did more to promote racial equality, reinvigorate cities, and so forth. A centerpiece of his Great Society was what he called the "War on Poverty." Johnson pushed for (and Congress funded) government programs to reduce poverty and improve the living standards for America's poor, such as Head Start, food stamps, work study, and Medicare and Medicaid, all of which still exist today.

In 2008 Americans faced an economic crisis; many demanded that the government bail out large employers like automakers and financial institutions that could cause worldwide damage if they went bankrupt. Many also called on the government to regulate the mortgage industry as significant numbers of people were losing their homes. In its wake, the Dodd-Frank Act of 2010 created the Consumer Financial Protection Bureau to protect Americans in financial transactions, especially mortgages, credit cards, and student loans.

Critics of big government say all of this growth is unsustainable, costly, and an overextension of the proper role of the federal government. Some argue that these tasks are best accomplished at the state and local levels of government, where elected officials and the bureaucracy are closer to the people.

Efforts to Reduce Size of Bureaucracy and the Federal Workforce
Many elected officials and public figures have proposed ways to reduce the size of the federal bureaucracy. Under President Bill Clinton's

---

President Bush's **War on Terror**

▶ CRITICAL THINKING

1. Identifying What does President Bush say is his first priority? How do his budget proposals reflect that priority?

2. Speculating Why do you think President Bush used the phrase "war against terror"? Do you agree with this usage?

3. Analyzing President Bush acknowledges that he is asking for the largest increase in defense spending in two decades. What effect do you think this will have on the federal bureaucracy?

"What we have found in Afghanistan confirms that, far from ending there, our war against terror is only beginning. . . .

Our first priority must always be the security of our Nation, and that will be reflected in the budget I send to Congress. My budget supports three great goals for America: We will win this war; we will protect our homeland; and we will revive our economy. . . .

My budget includes the largest increase in defense spending in two decades, because while the price of freedom and security is high, it is never too high. . . . The next priority of my budget is to do everything possible to protect our citizens and strengthen our Nation against the ongoing threat of another attack. . . . My budget nearly doubles funding for a sustained strategy of homeland security, focused on four key areas: bioterrorism, emergency response, airport and border security, and improved intelligence. . . .

Homeland security will make America not only stronger but, in many ways, better."

—President George W. Bush, *Address Before a Joint Session of the Congress on the State of the Union*, January 29, 2002

administration, Vice President Al Gore led a massive effort called "reinventing government." Its mission was to reform the way the federal government works by creating a government that "works better, costs less, and gets results Americans care about." At the same time, under the leadership of Newt Gingrich, Republicans in Congress embraced a "Contract With America" that targeted government waste.

One way to reduce the size of government is to reduce the number of government employees. Another is to cut or freeze their pay, or to require them to take unpaid days off, called *furlough*. In 2013, after the president and Congress could not agree to a general budget plan, they put into place automatic budget cuts that affected all federal programs that became known as *sequestration*. Agencies handled their budget cuts in different ways. Some placed a freeze on all new hiring, leaving the work to be done by existing staff. Others stopped offering certain services. For example, the Department of Health and Human Services cut the number of children who could enroll in federally subsidized early childhood education programs. Other agencies instituted furloughs. Various interest groups and different segments of the public were very unhappy with the cuts.

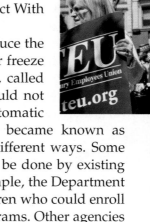

In 2013 automatic budget cuts furloughed thousands of federal employees as Congress debated the budget plan.

▲ CRITICAL THINKING
Stating What impact does sequestration have on the federal bureaucracy?

READING PROGRESS CHECK

Determining Cause and Effect How have economic crises caused the federal bureaucracy to increase?

Influence of Interest Groups on the Bureaucracy

GUIDING QUESTION *What is the relationship between interest groups and the federal bureaucracy?*

Each agency has **client groups** made up of individuals and groups who work with the agency and are most affected by its decisions. The client groups of the Department of Defense, for example, include the contractors who make equipment, weapons, and supplies for the armed forces.

Client groups often attempt to influence agency decisions through lobbyists. Lobbyists may testify at agency hearings, write letters, meet with agency staff, track agency decisions and report them to their clients, and take many other steps to support or oppose government regulations according to their groups' interests.

Congressional committees, client groups, and a federal department or agency often cooperate closely to make public policy. When these groups continually work together, such cooperation creates what analysts have called an **iron triangle**. The term is used because the three groups rely so heavily on each other. For example, the Department of Veterans Affairs (VA) provides important services to men and women who have served the nation, especially hospital care provided through veterans' hospitals. The VA needs Congress to approve its budget every year. Members of Congress know that veterans and groups like the American Legion are important constituents, vocal and reliable voters. They are also the beneficiaries of VA services. Similar iron triangles operate in many policy areas such as agriculture, business, labor, and national defense.

Critics say that iron triangles make it difficult for outside groups to make their voices heard. They also say that because the bonds of iron triangles are so strong, it is difficult for the government to eliminate agencies or reduce

client group individuals and groups who work with a government agency and are most affected by its decisions

iron triangle a relationship formed among government agencies, congressional committees, and client groups that work together

Iron Triangles

Department of Veterans Affairs

The American Legion

GOVERNMENT AGENCY OR DEPARTMENT

INTEREST GROUPS

CONGRESS

House Committee on Veterans' Affairs

Because of iron-triangle alliances, it is often difficult to change agency policies or eliminate government agencies.

▲ CRITICAL THINKING

Analyzing Why do some people consider iron triangles a threat to democracy? Could such triangles promote democracy? Why?

deregulate to remove regulation

their funding. There are also concerns that people often move from one side of the triangle to another. In the area of national defense, for example, a general might retire and become a lobbyist for a defense contractor that sells weapons to the Department of Defense. A congressional staff member on the Armed Services Committee might take a civilian job at the Pentagon or as a defense contractor. Critics believe that iron triangles and the revolving door of people in them allow interest groups undue influence outside the control of the executive branch.

To address these concerns, many presidents have initiated ethics requirements and rules for lobbyists. For example, key executive employees may not become a lobbyist within a certain period of time, usually two years. Lobbyists who become top executive employees may not be a part of decisions that involve their former clients or employers.

While few would give lobbyists or interest groups unlimited influence on the bureaucracy, there are a few arguments against tighter restrictions. In some cases, lobbyists are experts in their field with technical knowledge and experiences that can provide valuable information on complicated issues. In addition, good government requires people engaging with government. The constitutional freedoms of speech and petition are based on this requirement.

☑ **READING PROGRESS CHECK**

Explaining What are iron triangles and how do they work?

Government Regulation

GUIDING QUESTION *What are the costs and benefits of government regulation?*

In our mixed economy, we Americans tolerate some government interference with the marketplace but do not want too much. We tolerate some government hand in owning and managing natural resources but not too much. We accept some government regulations but do not like too many.

The Costs and Benefits of Regulation Typically, business owners and manufacturers disdain regulation, arguing that they drive up prices and higher prices hurt consumers. When customers do not buy their products, companies lay off workers. Some larger companies hire lawyers to follow, implement, and comply with regulations. Regulations sometimes hurt profits, which in turn hurts consumers and workers. Business leaders and conservatives often call on government to **deregulate**.

On the other hand, many regulations are designed to protect workers, consumers, and the environment. The Occupational Safety and Health Administration (OSHA) holds employers accountable for providing a safe and healthy workplace. It also gives employees a process to report concerns. Labor unions, environmentalists, many liberals, and some business experts often point out the need for regulations.

This difference in viewpoints played out when President Obama proposed a new federal agency called the Consumer Financial Protection Bureau. Those in favor of the agency believed the government needed to do more to protect families from unfair or deceptive practices by credit card companies, banks, and businesses that provide home loans. Republicans who opposed the creation of this new agency argued that the bureau would be too powerful and would harm banks and consumers.

"Red Tape" and Paperwork The term **red tape** is used to refer to overly burdensome regulations and requirements. Red tape occurs when large and unwieldy organizations put so many convoluted procedures in place that it is difficult to get anything done. Politicians often campaign on promises of cutting red tape and making government more efficient and responsive.

red tape overly burdensome regulations and requirements

One aspect of red tape is paperwork. To carry out their functions, government agencies ask businesses and individuals to provide information by filling out forms—including applications for licenses, permits, benefits, and grants. More than 2 billion forms are filled out and submitted to the federal government each year.

If this paperwork is confusing, unnecessary, or difficult to complete, it is a burden on businesses and individuals. The Small Business Administration estimated that companies spent at least 1 billion hours per year filling out forms—at a cost of about $100 billion annually. The Paperwork Reduction Act of 1995 was passed to reduce this burden. Under the law, federal departments and agencies must try to streamline and simplify their forms and requests for information. Since that time, many government agencies have simplified their forms and put essential forms online for easier access.

The general goal to reduce red tape is shared by people in both political parties and across government. However, collecting information helps the government keep track of their programs and make sure they work. Forms can also help agencies ensure that people who interact with government are treated in a fairly uniform way. In a way, these justifications relate to the principle of democracy known as *transparency*, which means that citizens and the press must have access to information about the way government conducts itself. **So-called** "paper trails" can support that.

so-called commonly named

✓ **READING PROGRESS CHECK**

Describing Why are critics of a large federal bureaucracy concerned about red tape and paperwork?

LESSON 4 REVIEW

Reviewing Vocabulary

1. *Making Connections* What is the definition of a bureaucrat? Provide several concrete examples.

Using Your Graphic Organizer

2. *Analyzing* Using your completed graphic organizer, summarize whether you think the benefits of government regulation outweigh the costs.

Answering the Guiding Questions

3. *Explaining* How does the federal bureaucracy make, interpret, and implement public policy?

4. *Summarizing* What has contributed to the growth of the federal bureaucracy?

5. *Drawing Inferences* How might the bureaucracy be reduced in size?

6. *Exploring Issues* What is the relationship between interest groups and the federal bureaucracy?

7. *Evaluating* What are the costs and benefits of government regulation?

Writing About Government

8. *Informative/Explanatory* Federal agencies regulate or shape policy for groups in the private sector. As a result, these groups lobby agencies to influence policy and regulations that affect them. Research two or three client groups of one federal agency. Write a short report that explains the client groups' interests in the agency and the client groups' probable messages to the agency.

9. *Informative/Explanatory* Select an issue area and compare and contrast how government regulatory policies in this issue area influence the economy at the national, state, and local levels.

STUDY GUIDE

THE CABINET AND EXECUTIVE OFFICE OF THE PRESIDENT
LESSON 1

Cabinet
Secretaries of each of the 15 executive departments advise the president and lead the departments.

Executive Office of the President (EOP)
Gathers information, develops policy, and advises the president

Office of Management and Budget	National Security Council	Council of Economic Advisers	Other EOP Agencies	White House Office

CABINET DEPARTMENTS
LESSON 2

EXECUTIVE DEPARTMENTS

Agriculture Farming, agriculture, and food	**Commerce** Business and trade	**Defense** Armed forces and national security	**Education** Assistance to schools	**Energy** Energy policy
Health and Human Services Public health, social services	**Homeland Security** Guards against terrorism	**Housing and Urban Development** Addresses housing needs	**Interior** Manages parks and natural resources	**Justice** Enforces federal laws
Labor Workers and the workplace	**State** Conducts foreign policy	**Transportation** Mass transit, roads, air travel	**Treasury** Manages monetary resources	**Veterans Affairs** Benefit programs

THE FEDERAL WORKFORCE AND CIVIL SERVICE
LESSON 3

Political Appointees
- Jobs given to the president's supporters
- Outside the civil service system

Federal Workforce

Civil Service Workers
- Compete for jobs
- Protected by civil service system

THE EXECUTIVE BRANCH AT WORK
LESSON 4

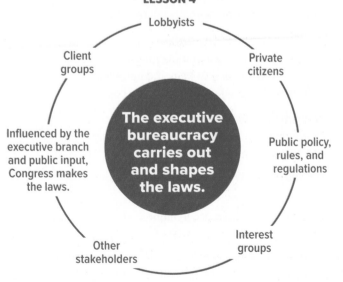

Lobbyists

Client groups

Private citizens

Influenced by the executive branch and public input, Congress makes the laws.

The executive bureaucracy carries out and shapes the laws.

Public policy, rules, and regulations

Other stakeholders

Interest groups

Directions: On a separate sheet of paper, answer the questions below. Make sure you read carefully and answer all parts of the questions.

Lesson Review

Lesson 1

1 *Explaining* Why does the Constitution give the Senate the power to confirm or reject the president's choices for cabinet secretaries?

2 *Analyzing* Why was the Executive Office of the President created in 1939? How did this increase presidential power?

Lesson 2

3 *Identifying* What were the first four executive departments that were created in 1789? What was the role of each department?

4 *Understanding Relationships* Why is it helpful for commissioners of regulatory commissions to have long terms?

Lesson 3

5 *Explaining* How were most candidates chosen to fill government jobs in the period before the Pendleton Act of 1883?

6 *Stating* What did the Pendleton Act accomplish?

Lesson 4

7 *Describing* What role does the executive branch play after a law has been passed by Congress and signed by the president?

8 *Explaining* How does a government agency seek public input when it drafts new rules?

ANSWERING THE ESSENTIAL QUESTIONS

Review your answers to the introductory questions at the beginning of each lesson. Then answer the Essential Questions based on what you learned in the chapter. Have your answers changed?

9 *Evaluating* What are the structure and functions of the executive branch?

10 *Explaining* How does the federal bureaucracy regulate individuals, communities, and businesses?

DBQ Interpreting Political Cartoons

Use the political cartoon to answer the following questions.

The engraving on the statue says, "To the Victors Belong the Spoils." —A. Jackson.

11 *Identifying* Who is Andrew Jackson? How is he depicted in this cartoon? Is it a flattering or an unflattering depiction? Explain.

12 *Analyzing Visuals* What is the point of view of this cartoon regarding the spoils system? Provide details to support your answer.

Critical Thinking

13 *Analyzing* Explain why the president needs a staff to run the Executive Office of the President (EOP).

14 *Hypothesizing* Congress created the Department of Homeland Security shortly after the terrorist attacks of September 11, 2001. How do you think this department and others might have grown since the attacks? Explain your reasoning.

15 *Defending* Why might a government agency try to influence the language of a law before it is passed?

16 *Hypothesizing* Government regulations are often unpopular with businesses because they impose a burden. Take the examples of food inspections and workplace safety. What might happen if the government stopped regulating businesses? Why?

Need Extra Help?

If You've Missed Question	1	2	3	4	5	6	7	8	9	10	11	12	13	14	15	16
Go to page	316	319	325	331	333	333	338	339	316	338	332	333	319	329	338	344

Directions: On a separate sheet of paper, answer the questions below. Make sure you read carefully and answer all parts of the questions.

DBQ Analyzing Primary Sources

Read the excerpt and answer the questions that follow.

This excerpt is from Senator Chuck Hagel's confirmation hearing as secretary of defense.

PRIMARY SOURCE

"*Senator CRUZ: All right. Well, let's move on to your record then. And you stated in your prepared remarks, quote: 'My overall world view has never changed.' I have to admit I find that difficult to reconcile with statements and positions you've taken for over a decade and what seems to me a fairly significant shift since you've been nominated for Secretary of Defense. . . .*

Beginning with number one. 2001, you voted against legislation sanctioning Iran. Now, am I correct you no longer agree with that position; you think sanctions against Iran are a good policy today?"
—Confirmation hearing in the U.S. Senate Committee on Armed Services, Jan. 31, 2013

17 *Classifying* What is the manner of Senator Cruz's questioning? How is Senator Cruz fulfilling the constitutional goal of maintaining checks and balances? Is there any other possible motivation for Senator Cruz's questions?

This excerpt is from Hillary Clinton's confirmation hearing as President Obama's first secretary of state.

PRIMARY SOURCE

"*BOXER: So I'll stop there and just say how much I appreciate your comments, not only on this subject but everything you've spoken about. It shows your breadth of understanding, in the same way with my chairman, who—I mean, I think we have a team that's just extraordinary. And I'm proud. I hope to play a small role in that team. Thank you.*

CLINTON: Thank you."
—Confirmation hearing in the U.S. Senate Committee on Foreign Relations, Jan. 13, 2009

18 *Comparing and Contrasting* Compare the tone of this questioning to the Cruz-Hagel interview. What do you think explains the difference?

Social Studies Skills

19 *Identifying Cause and Effect* The size of the federal government has increased dramatically several times during the country's history. For each of the following periods of expansion, list the causes of those expansions: (1) the New Deal, (2) military spending in the 1940s, and (3) the Great Society.

20 *Decision Making* How would you prefer to get a job: under a spoils system or under a civil service system? Describe the pros and cons of each system.

Use the table to answer questions 21 and 22.

Spending of Selected Independent Agencies	
Agency	**Estimated Spending, 2014 (in millions of dollars)**
Corps of Engineers—Civil Works	$7,078
Environmental Protection Agency	$8,637
Executive Office of the President	$412
General Services Administration	$361
NASA	$17,936
National Science Foundation	$7,479
Office of Personnel Management	$96,922

SOURCE: Office of Management and Budget, 2013

21 *Using Tables* Using the information in this table, create a bar graph showing independent agency spending.

22 *Economics* How much more money does the National Science Foundation (NSF) spend than the Executive Office of the President? Why do you think the NSF budget is larger?

Research and Presentation

23 *Researching* Research several different independent executive agencies and regulatory commissions. Use software to create a table identifying the purposes of NASA, the EPA, OSHA, the FDA, and the FCC.

Need Extra Help?

If You've Missed Question	**17**	**18**	**19**	**20**	**21**	**22**	**23**
Go to page	316	316	340	332	348	348	329

State and Local Executive Branches

network
www.connected.mcgraw-hill.com
There's More Online about
state and local executive branches.

CHAPTER 12

ESSENTIAL QUESTIONS

- How are state and local executive branches structured?
- What are the characteristics of effective governors and mayors?

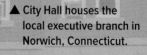

▲ City Hall houses the local executive branch in Norwich, Connecticut.

Library of Congress Prints and Photographs Division [LC-DIG-highsm-19318]

349

CITY GOVERNMENT BUDGETS

The nationwide recession that began in 2007 put a strain on already-tight city budgets. For several years, revenues in many cities fell. Additional strain was created by ballooning pension and health care costs for civil servants, police, and firefighters. Cities assumed that a strong economy and good investments would support these plans, but many now face shortfalls since the employees have retired and investment income has lagged. Examine these sources to evaluate cities' budget decisions.

SECONDARY SOURCE A

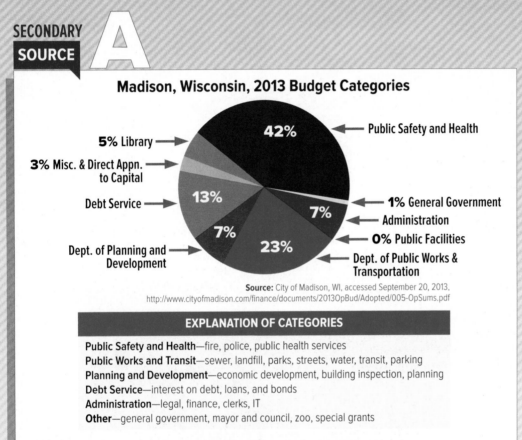

Madison, Wisconsin, 2013 Budget Categories

- 42% Public Safety and Health
- 5% Library
- 3% Misc. & Direct Appn. to Capital
- 13% Debt Service
- 7% Dept. of Planning and Development
- 7%
- 23% Dept. of Public Works & Transportation
- 0% Public Facilities
- Administration
- 1% General Government

Source: City of Madison, WI, accessed September 20, 2013, http://www.cityofmadison.com/finance/documents/2013OpBud/Adopted/005-OpSums.pdf

EXPLANATION OF CATEGORIES

Public Safety and Health—fire, police, public health services
Public Works and Transit—sewer, landfill, parks, streets, water, transit, parking
Planning and Development—economic development, building inspection, planning
Debt Service—interest on debt, loans, and bonds
Administration—legal, finance, clerks, IT
Other—general government, mayor and council, zoo, special grants

PRIMARY SOURCE B

In his introductory letter to a report about how cities are dealing with budget shortfalls, Tom Cochran noted several ways cities are making ends meet, including:

- "Hiring freezes, hiring deferrals, elimination of positions, employee layoffs and furloughs, early retirement programs, elimination of overtime;
- Wage and benefit cuts, elimination of benefits for new hires and other employee categories;
- Increased employee contributions (and lower city contributions) to personnel benefits;"

—Tom Cochran, CEO and Executive Director, U.S. Conference of Mayors, "City Responses to Recession-Driven Budget Shortfalls," June 12, 2009

SECONDARY SOURCE C

By 2014, Knoxville, TN, had faced years of flat revenues and increasing costs.

"I am recommending a tax increase of 34 cents, which will bring the tax rate to $2.7257 ($2.73 rounded). When adjusted for the impact of inflation and countywide reappraisals, the proposed tax rate is actually lower than it was ten years ago. This rate assures that we can meet our pension obligations, provide sufficient operating and capital budgets, maintain a reasonable fund balance, and not put our bond ratings in jeopardy. For a house appraised at $100,000, this is an increase of $85 per year or roughly $7 per month."

—Mayor Madeline Rogero's speech on the proposed budget, City of Knoxville's fiscal year 2014–2015

PRIMARY SOURCE D

"Let me offer a few thoughts about how we build great communities . . . it's not just about our physical infrastructure in our neighborhoods, it's about our social infrastructure. Public safety, human services, job training, arts classes are as important as sidewalks, parks, and streets to knitting a neighborhood together. . . . little things add up. Crosswalks, sidewalks, greenways, neighborhood parks add up to big differences in health, quality of life and our environment. They deserve to be priorities."

—2013 State of the City Address by Seattle Mayor Mike McGinn

SECONDARY SOURCE E

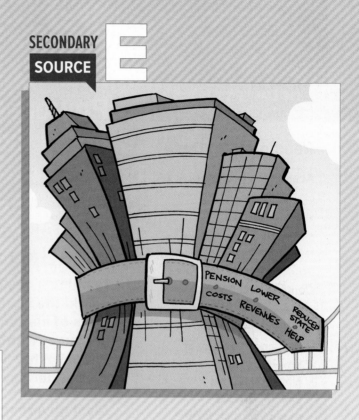

PENSION COSTS LOWER REVENUES REDUCED STATE HELP

DBQ DOCUMENT-BASED QUESTIONS

1. **Comparing** Compare the different ideas for cutting city budgets presented in the sources. What are the most commonly suggested ways of saving budgets?

2. **Making Inferences** How do you think Mike McGinn balanced the Seattle budget—by increasing revenues, cutting spending, or both? Explain your reasoning.

3. **Drawing Conclusions** Choose one of the common ways that cities have cut their budgets. How would this cut in the budget affect the lives of city residents?

WHAT WILL YOU DO?

If you were the mayor of a medium-sized city facing a 10 percent budget shortfall, what would you do? Would you raise revenues, cut spending, or both? What priorities would you have in mind as you decided?

EXPLORE the interactive version of the analyzing primary sources feature on Networks.

Interact with these digital
assets and others in lesson 1

✓ **INTERACTIVE IMAGE**
   The Pardon Power

✓ **INTERACTIVE MAP**
   Types of Municipal Systems

✓ **SELF-CHECK QUIZ**

✓ **VIDEO**
   Roles of Mayors

netw○rks
TRY IT YOURSELF ONLINE

Reading Help Desk

Academic Vocabulary

- **resource**
- **administrator**
- **modify**
- **principle**

Content Vocabulary

- **governor**
- **gubernatorial**
- **lieutenant governor**
- **line-item veto**
- **National Guard**
- **special district**
- **mayor-council form**
- **strong-mayor system**
- **weak-mayor system**
- **municipality**

TAKING NOTES:

Key Ideas and Details

COMPARING Use the graphic organizer to compare the powers and roles of the U.S. president to the powers and roles of a state governor. Complete the president portion and then complete the governor portion as you read the rest of this lesson.

Powers and Roles	President	Governor

LESSON 1

Powers and Roles of State and Local Executives

ESSENTIAL QUESTION

How are state and local executive branches structured?

Imagine a day in the life of a governor or a mayor. How early would the work day begin and what time would it end? What sorts of meetings or events would she attend? Who would she meet with? What problems would she work on and with whom? What is likely to be the most interesting or important part of her day?

Most governors and some mayors have an assistant to help them prioritize and schedule their invitations and meetings. Imagine you are that assistant. You have the task of writing up your boss's schedule for tomorrow. You need to show who she will meet with, the topics for those meetings, and how long they will last. Remember to include ceremonial functions.

Responsibilities, Roles, and Powers of Governors

GUIDING QUESTION *What are the responsibilities, roles, and powers of governors?*

Every state has an executive branch headed by a **governor**. In colonial times, governors were appointed by the British monarch; they reported to him and carried out his laws. Because they were not chosen by the people they governed, governors were not well trusted by their constituents. After the colonies won independence, governors still had few powers, and most had very short terms in office.

Over the past 100 years, states have made changes to the structure of the executive, and now governors are very powerful. Since 1965, more than half the states have amended their constitutions to give their governors more power. Some states have lengthened their governors' term of office; others have given their governors more power to make appointments to departments and agencies.

All states have constitutions that establish the powers and responsibilities of their governors. These constitutions also explain the limits on **gubernatorial** power. Governors' power and influence vary because of differences in population, area, and needs of each state.

The major roles of most state governors mirror those of the president of the United States. Governors tend to be responsible for running the executive branch, influencing the legislature, acting as head of state and head of their political party, leading the state's National Guard, and serving as a liaison to the national and other state governments.

Governors do not take on the presidential role as chief diplomat, though, because diplomacy is reserved as a national power. However, governors do often host important foreign visitors and travel overseas. Governors often consider these visits as ways to find new opportunities for people and businesses in their states.

All but seven states have a **lieutenant governor**, a "second in command," whose responsibilities are similar to the vice president of the United States. The lieutenant governor is the first in line to succeed the governor if a vacancy should occur. About half of the nation's lieutenant governors also serve as the presiding officer in the state senate. In many cases, governors and lieutenant governors run for election as a team.

Head of State and Party Leader
Like presidents, governors have important ceremonial functions. They represent their states at important events, state fairs, press conferences, and ribbon-cutting events for new state buildings or highways. Governors are also "the face" of their states at national and international meetings.

As heads of their own states, governors address the people of their states in times of emergency or celebration. For example, Governor Chris Christie of New Jersey implored residents to stay safe during Hurricane Sandy in 2012. After the storm, he held numerous town hall meetings to address the rebuilding of towns and homes.

Governors are also leaders of their state-level political parties. Governors attend political party dinners, speak at party functions, and may campaign for party candidates in local elections. In addition, governors participate in national political party events.

Chief Executive
Governors' executive powers include two basic components: the power to carry out the law and the power to supervise the executive branch of state government. Governors have many tools and powers to implement laws. For example, they direct the work of executive departments and agencies; they also direct spending that is in line with the state's budget and laws.

Governors can issue executive orders that create a task force to study issues or to address a variety of immediate concerns. Governors can also declare a "state of emergency" after a natural or man-made disaster. Such a declaration enables the governor to take emergency actions like mobilizing **resources**, ordering evacuations, restricting access to some areas, or implementing curfews.

In contrast to the national executive branch, the constitutions of many states have created a divided executive branch, making many executive officials politically and legally independent of one another. In more than half the states, for example, the people

governor the leader of the executive branch of a state

gubernatorial from the Latin *gubernare*, meaning of or relating to the governor

lieutenant governor elected official serving as deputy to the governor

resource a source of supply or support; available goods or means

Governors are leaders of their state political parties, and they participate in political party events such as national conventions.

▼ CRITICAL THINKING
Making Inferences How might governors use their role as party leaders to advance their policy agendas?

separately elect the governor, the lieutenant governor, the attorney general, and the secretary of state. These elected executive leaders may serve for different terms of office, and, as a result, leaders of those states' executive branches may be members of different political parties with very different ideas about government and conflicting political ambitions. Cooperation can be difficult under such circumstances, leaving the governor with limited control over the executive branch.

Some states, such as Hawaii and New Jersey, give the governor considerable control over the executive branch. The constitutions of these states have created an executive branch with only one elected official or only a few such officials.

State citizens communicate with the executive branch through the departments and agencies as well as the governor's office. Interest groups form in states to lobby the governor or executive departments about issues that matter to their members.

Governors typically have the power to appoint the top officials for executive departments and agencies. Even in states that separately elect many executive officers, governors still appoint dozens of executive branch officials. In Arizona, for example, the governor appoints almost 20 executive branch **administrators** and more than 250 board and commission leaders.

Most governors have the power to appoint some state court judges. Unlike the president, some governors must choose judicial candidates from a list of names prepared by a nominating committee made of other government leaders, law groups, and citizens. These appointments are usually subject to confirmation by the state legislature. In other states, many court judges are elected to their positions.

In most states, governors have the power to issue pardons for state crimes. (They cannot pardon people convicted of federal crimes.) In some states, the governor and legislature must agree to pardon someone; in other states, governors may pardon only individuals recommended for pardon by state clemency boards. Some governors may also reduce sentences, dismiss fines, or release prisoners on parole.

To avoid public criticism, governors tend to issue pardons in the final days of their terms. Advocates for pardons argue that they are an essential safeguard for correcting mistakes made by overworked courts.

administrator one who performs executive duties or manages

In most states, governors have the power to issue pardons for state crimes. In this photograph, North Carolina Governor Beverly Perdue signs pardons.

▼ CRITICAL THINKING

Naming In addition to issuing pardons, what other judicial powers do governors generally have?

Legislative Leader Like the nation's president, governors have legislative power without being part of the legislative branch. People look to their governors for leadership, including setting legislative agendas and proposing solutions to state problems.

Governors can propose legislation to the state legislature, send messages to the state legislature, or present new programs as part of the state budget. In addition, governors can rouse public opinion to support these legislative proposals.

Governors also have the power to call a special session of the legislature. Legislatures meet at regularly scheduled times, but the governor can call a special session to deal with legislation that he or she believes is vital to the state.

GOVERNMENT *in your* COMMUNITY

The Role of the Governor

Consult your state constitution or the website of the National Governors Association. Research the role of the governor in your state. Does your governor have the power to . . .

a. Veto legislation? If so, how many votes does the legislature need to override a veto?

b. Use a line-item veto? If so, can it be used for any bills or only for spending bills?

c. Issue pardons? Does anyone else need to approve a pardon or commutation?

d. Issue executive orders?

e. Make executive branch appointments? If so, which officials does your governor appoint?

f. Appoint judges? If so, which ones? Must the governor choose from a list of qualified appointees?

g. Take extraordinary actions during a state of emergency? If so, how?

h. Call the legislature into special session? If so, under what circumstances?

Craig F. Walker/The Denver Post/Getty Images

▲ **CRITICAL THINKING**

Applying Create a poster or presentation that illustrates the powers of your state's governor.

All governors have veto power over an entire bill passed by their state legislatures. In all but six states, governors also have a special veto power called the **line-item veto**. Those governors can veto one section of a bill without rejecting the entire bill. In some cases, governors may issue a line-item veto only on a spending bill.

Some governors have the power to veto a bill and send it back to the legislature with recommended amendments. State legislatures can override their governors' vetoes under certain conditions. Usually a two-thirds vote of all the legislators in each house is required to override a governor's veto. In four states (Alabama, Indiana, Kentucky, and Tennessee), the legislature can override a veto with a simple majority vote. In those states, the governor's veto power is quite weak.

Guardian of the State Economy Governors try to steer their state's economy to increase employment and revenue. They do this by promoting tourism and other key industries for their states.

Most governors try to obtain grants from the national government for their states' schools, highways, and urban areas. They also represent their states when they seek cooperation from other states in such areas as transportation and pollution control. More recently, governors have begun representing their states internationally. For example, they have tried to encourage foreign businesses to locate in their states and have sought foreign markets for products their states produce.

In all but eight states, governors have full responsibility for preparing the state budget. After it is prepared, governors submit their budgets to the state legislature for approval. The power to make up the budget allows a governor to push or reduce certain programs and policies.

line-item veto the power of an executive to reject one or more items in a bill without vetoing the entire bill

In states that allow a line-item veto on spending bills, governors can remove unnecessary spending from budget legislation. In practice, it is a way that governors can have influence over policies by deciding which items receive funding. This issue has created conflict between state legislatures and their governors for several decades, with each claiming the other has too much influence.

Commander in Chief of the State National Guard All governors can exercise military powers through their role as commander in chief of the state **National Guard**. All states and territories have both Army National Guards and Air National Guards. State constitutions allow the governor to use the National Guard to maintain law and order during state emergencies. Most members of the National Guard are part-time soldiers, also holding full-time civilian jobs; when they are called up, they leave those jobs and go where they are needed. A state's National Guard is often called out to keep the peace during civil disturbances or to keep order and provide emergency relief during natural disasters. The Guard can provide a rapid military response from within the state.

In case of war or another national emergency, the president can activate the National Guard. The Guard are then under the president's command and fall under the control of either the U.S. Army or the U.S. Air Force. Guard units have been activated in every major conflict since World War II.

National Guard a rapid-response military body responsible for maintaining order during state emergencies and civil disturbances and providing emergency relief during natural disasters

We the People: Making a Difference

In his 13 years in the Guard, Jim LeFavor has been deployed to Saudi Arabia, Iraq, Iceland, Israel, and Canada. In all of these deployments, he flew F-15 jets, enforcing no-fly zones and training with U.S. allies.

His unit has also provided a wide variety of services during domestic events. They have helped with debris clearing, power production, communications, transportation, medical support, the handling of hazardous materials, security, chaplain services, mortuary services, food preparation, and wellness checks, to name several. In emergency situations, they also help first responders collect information and assess damage to help state leaders, including the governor.

Colonel LeFavor sees the Guard's "citizen soldiers" as critical to the U.S. military. Says LeFavor, "This 'citizen soldier' concept is a tried and true method of maintaining low-cost armed forces and has been an instrumental part of America since the very first Guard unit mustered in the town of Salem, MA, in 1636 . . . the first organized military in our history." Working with great people—"a very focused and fine-tuned force"—has been the best part of Colonel LeFavor's time in the Guard. The hardest part? Long hours and few days off. But, he says, "Serving in any of our armed forces is a noble cause" that provides "a lifetime of experience in a short period of time."

CRITICAL THINKING

1. Analyzing How does the National Guard play an important role in the U.S. military and in states?

2. Making Connections If you were in the Guard, what leadership qualities would you expect to see in your commander in chief? In what ways can you imagine yourself serving your community, state, or nation? What sacrifices are you willing to make to give back?

COLONEL JIM LeFAVOR

Jim LeFavor/United States National Guard

The U.S. military increasingly depends on National Guard units to supplement active duty military forces. More than 300,000 National Guard troops were deployed to Iraq or Afghanistan during those wars.

☑ READING PROGRESS CHECK

Comparing and Contrasting How is the role of governor similar to the role of president? How is it different?

Federalism and Gubernatorial Powers

GUIDING QUESTION *How does federalism limit the powers of a governor?*

Like the president, state executives have limited power. Their actions are checked and balanced by their states' legislative and judicial branches. In some states, for instance, the legislature must approve gubernatorial pardons and appointments of executive officials or judges. All state legislatures can override a governor's veto, though the number of votes it takes to do so varies from state to state. In addition, all state legislatures must approve a budget proposed by a governor; they also have the power to **modify** it before approval.

modify to alter, change, or revise

The judicial branch interprets the executive's actions in light of the state constitution. State courts can rule on whether the executive's programs, policies, or actions violate the state or federal constitution.

The **principle** of federalism also limits some state powers and, therefore, some powers of the governors. The national government has an impact on what states can and must do. The federal government contributes funds to the states to fulfill a variety of purposes, and governors must often administer programs that use those funds in line with federal requirements. For example, the federal government provides funding for states to administer Medicaid, a health insurance program for low-income Americans. To qualify for the federal money, however, states must include certain groups in their Medicaid programs.

principle an underlying doctrine or assumption

In 2009 the federal government began a competitive grant program called Race to the Top. The program made more than $4 billion in education funding available to states. In order to win a grant, states had to make certain reforms to their education policies and standards.

Governors advance their agendas together through their membership in the National Governors Association (NGA). This nonprofit group represents the governors of the 50 states as well as the five U.S. territories. It meets annually to provide a forum in which governors can share and improve upon their individual policy initiatives. The NGA represents states' interests in Washington, D.C., as the "collective voice of the nation's governors." It also exists to provide management and technical assistance to both new and incumbent governors.

☑ READING PROGRESS CHECK

Explaining How are governors limited in their powers?

Roles and Powers of Local Executives

GUIDING QUESTION *How do local executives exercise power?*

Although the United States has a strong tradition of local self-government, local governments have no legal independence. Established by the state, they are entirely dependent on the state governments under which they exist. The state can assume control over them or even abolish them. State constitutions usually set forth the powers and duties of local governments. They also might describe the form of government a locality can adopt based on its size and population.

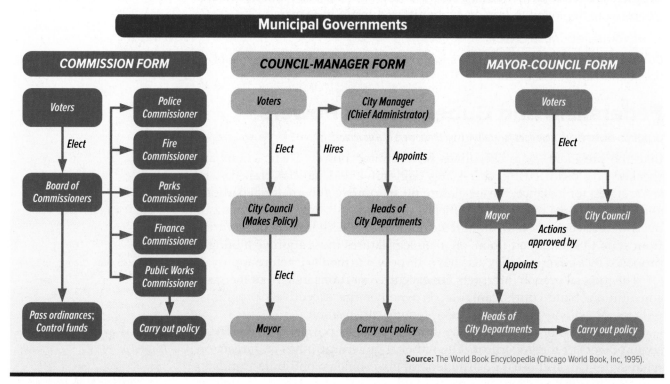

Municipal Governments

COMMISSION FORM

Voters — Elect → Board of Commissioners

Police Commissioner
Fire Commissioner
Parks Commissioner
Finance Commissioner
Public Works Commissioner

Pass ordinances; Control funds

Carry out policy

COUNCIL-MANAGER FORM

Voters — Elect → City Council (Makes Policy)
Hires → City Manager (Chief Administrator)
Appoints → Heads of City Departments
Elect → Mayor
Carry out policy

MAYOR-COUNCIL FORM

Voters — Elect → Mayor / City Council
Actions approved by
Appoints → Heads of City Departments → Carry out policy

Source: The World Book Encyclopedia (Chicago World Book, Inc, 1995).

State constitutions usually set forth the powers and duties of local governments and may describe the form of government that a locality can adopt.

▲ **CRITICAL THINKING**

Identifying Which form of municipal government most closely mirrors the structure of federal and state executive branches? Which type of city is most likely to use that form of government?

special district a unit of local government that deals with a specific function, such as education, water supply, or transportation

mayor-council form a system in which executive power belongs to an elected mayor and legislative power belongs to an elected council; in this system, mayors may have extensive executive powers or few executive powers

The roles that local executive branch leaders play are similar to those of presidents and governors. They carry out ceremonial functions as head of state. As chief executive, they oversee a staff that carries out laws passed by the legislature. They are the leaders of their political parties on a local level. In other ways, local executives often play very different roles than presidents and governors.

Local governments have even more variety than state governments when it comes to the powers and role of the executive. The powers of local executives are usually set forth in their city or county charters. Local governments usually have two tiers: counties (also called boroughs or parishes) and municipalities (also called cities, towns, villages, townships, or boroughs). Local governments also include **special districts** such as school districts or fire protection districts that stretch across county or municipal boundaries. Some municipalities have an elected mayor, others have an appointed city manager, while still others have an elected panel of commissioners with some executive powers.

Mayors in the Mayor-Council System The oldest and most widely used form of municipal government is the **mayor-council form**. Today about half the cities in the United States use it, and it is preferred by the largest cities. The mayor-council form follows the traditional concept of separation of powers. Executive power belongs to an elected mayor, and legislative power belongs to an elected council.

Under this system, mayors can either have extensive executive powers (known as the strong-mayor system) or relatively few executive powers (known as the weak-mayor system). In the **strong-mayor system**, the mayor usually has the power to veto measures that the city council passes, and many of his or her actions might not require council approval. The mayor can appoint and fire department heads and high-ranking members of the municipal bureaucracy. In addition, a strong mayor can prepare the municipal budget, subject to council approval, and propose legislation to the city council. The mayor usually serves a four-year term. The strong-mayor system is most often found in large cities.

Many small cities, especially in New England, use the **weak-mayor system**. In this form, the mayor has limited powers. The mayor has little control over the budget or the hiring and firing of municipal personnel. The city council makes most policy decisions, and the mayor's veto power is limited. The mayor usually serves only a two-year term. In some small municipalities, the office of the mayor is only a part-time position.

The success of the mayor-council form of government depends to a large extent on the individual who serves as mayor. In the strong-mayor system, a politically skillful mayor can provide effective leadership. Under the weak-mayor plan, because official responsibility is in many hands, success depends upon the cooperation of the mayor and the council. Seeking to improve management under both weak- and strong-mayor systems, some cities have added a chief administrative officer, whose role is similar to that of a city manager.

City Managers in the Council-Manager System
Under a council-manager form of government, legislative and executive powers are also separated. The council of between five and nine members acts as a legislative body and makes policy for the **municipality**. A city manager carries out the council's policies and serves as chief administrator. More than half of cities with more than 100,000 residents use this form.

strong-mayor system a mayoral system in which the mayor usually has the power to veto measures that the city council passes, appoint department heads, prepare the municipal budget, and propose legislation

weak-mayor system a mayoral system in which the mayor has limited powers and the city council makes most decisions

municipality an urban unit of government chartered by a state

In the 30 largest cities in the United States, the mayor-council form of municipal government is most common.

▼ CRITICAL THINKING
1. *Interpreting* In what region is the mayor-council form of government most common?
2. *Hypothesizing* What does this geographical distribution indicate about the age of the mayor-council form in relation to the other forms?

MAP

Types of Municipal Systems

Type of Municipal Government
- ● Commission
- ● Council-Manager
- ● Mayor-Council

SOURCE: National League of Cities, 2013

Researching The United States Conference of Mayors (USCM) is an organization similar to the National Governors Association. Its primary mission is to be "the voice of America's mayors in Washington, D.C." Membership is open to the mayor of any city that has a population greater than 30,000, and the USCM holds at least two meetings per year. At its meetings, mayors share ideas, take part in lessons on leadership and management, and voice their opinions on national policies in order to strengthen federal-city relationships.

Investigate the group's website at http://usmayors.org/. Read about its legislative agenda, programs, and task forces. What can you deduce about the priorities of local executives? In your opinion, which issues are important in your community? Explain your answer.

The city manager is appointed by the council and acts as chief executive. He or she appoints and fires municipal workers, prepares the budget, and runs the day-to-day affairs of the city. The city manager also may make policy recommendations to the council. Most city managers are professionals who are trained in public administration. They must answer to the council and are subject to dismissal by the council.

The council-manager form usually includes a mayor with limited powers. Many political experts believe the council-manager form brings better management and business procedures to the government. Executive and legislative powers are clearly separated, and it is easy for the voters to assign praise or blame for what the government has done. Some critics, however, point out disadvantages associated with council-manager government. For example, citizens do not elect the city manager, who might not be a city resident. In addition, this form of government might not provide the political leadership that is necessary in large cities with a diverse population. Therefore, many manager systems have moved to directly elect a mayor with increased powers to function along with the manager. Over time, both mayor-council and manager systems have moved closer to each other.

Commissioners The commission form of government combines executive and legislative powers in an elected commission. This commission is usually made up of five to seven members.

Each commissioner heads a specific department and performs all the executive duties related to that department. The most common departments are police, fire, public works, finance, and parks. The commissioners also meet as a legislative body to pass laws and make policy decisions. One of the commissioners usually has the title of mayor. The mayor has no substantial additional powers, however. Usually he or she merely carries out ceremonial functions like greeting important visitors to the city or officiating at the dedication or opening of hospitals and other public institutions.

Tribal Government Some states have a separate level of government that serves the Native American population. In New Mexico, for example, the Pueblo Native American culture is divided into 22 governing units operating on New Mexico's 19 Pueblo land formations. Each tribal office has a governor and a lieutenant governor.

✓ **READING PROGRESS CHECK**

Comparing and Contrasting What are the most common forms of leadership in local government? How are they alike? How are they different?

LESSON 1 REVIEW

Reviewing Vocabulary

1. *Contrasting* How do the strong-mayor system and weak-mayor system differ?

Using Your Graphic Organizer

2. *Comparing* Use your completed graphic organizer to create a digital slide show to compare the powers and roles of the U.S. president to the powers and roles of state governors.

Answering the Guiding Questions

3. *Describing* What are the responsibilities, roles, and powers of governors?

4. *Analyzing* How does federalism limit the powers of a governor?

5. *Explaining* How do local executives exercise power?

Writing About Government

6. *Argument* Who do you think has more executive power—the president or the governor of your state? Explain your answer.

Interact with these digital assets and others in lesson 2

✓ **INTERACTIVE INFOGRAPHIC**
Characteristics of Governors

✓ **SELF-CHECK QUIZ**

✓ **STUDENT VOICES**
Interning at the Governor's Office

✓ **VIDEO**
Ex-Governors Seeking Reelection

netw⊙rks
TRY IT YOURSELF ONLINE

LESSON 2
Choosing Governors and Mayors

Reading Help Desk

Academic Vocabulary

- obtain
- misconduct

Content Vocabulary

- plurality
- recall

TAKING NOTES:

Integration of Knowledge and Ideas

COMPARING AND CONTRASTING Use the Venn diagram to compare and contrast how governors and mayors are selected.

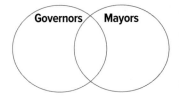

ESSENTIAL QUESTION

What are the characteristics of effective governors and mayors?

We expect our local elected officials to know us so they can serve us well. Perhaps they do not literally need to know our names, but they need to understand the demographics of the people they represent. They should also know the geography, resources, challenges, and attractions of the states or communities they lead. Create a presentation that includes what you think your governor and mayor should know about you and your community.

Qualifications of State and Local Executives

GUIDING QUESTION *How do state and local executive branch leaders qualify for their positions?*

Many voters pay more attention to the campaigns and elections of national leaders than state and local leaders. Yet in many ways, the people who lead closer to home—on the state and local levels—make decisions that affect voters more directly. Governors, county executives, mayors, and city managers and commissioners enforce decisions about education, recreation, housing, public safety, emergency response, social services, and even where new shopping centers can be built. Consequently, voters should choose their state and local leaders very carefully.

Qualifications of Governors State constitutions spell out the few legal or formal qualifications for becoming governor. In most states, a governor must be at least 30 years old, an American citizen, and a state resident for five or more years; however, citizenship and residency requirements differ widely among the states. Some states, like Kansas, have no formal qualifications for their governors. Others, like Mississippi, require a gubernatorial candidate to have been a U.S. citizen for 20 years and a resident of the state for five years. The qualifications to become lieutenant governor are usually identical to those for governor.

In addition to these legal qualifications, governors must also possess certain political credentials and leadership experience. Most governors have served in state and local government before running for governor;

many have also served as lieutenant governor or as the state attorney general. Among the exceptions, Ronald Reagan and George W. Bush were elected governors of the nation's two largest states without previous experience in any elected office. Roughly half of recently elected governors were lawyers, and almost all held college degrees. In most recent years, between five and ten states have elected women to be their governors; voters in a small handful of states have also elected racial or ethnic minorities to the post.

A variety of personal characteristics can help governors to be successful. For example, some governors are skilled at managing complex state governments, while others are effective at negotiating, which is essential for working closely with the state legislature. A good personal relationship with legislators may help governors achieve their goals, and being popular with voters can give the governor's proposals extra weight.

The average salary for governors is $133,348. Most governors live in the state's governor's mansion during their time in office.

Qualifications of Mayors or City Managers There are as many different sets of qualifications for mayor or city manager as there are cities in the United States. Typically, cities, or the states in which they are located, set a minimum age for mayor at somewhere between 18 and 25. Mayoral candidates are typically required to live for at least one year in the town or city, and if they are elected, they must continue living there for the duration of their term in office. The average age of U.S. mayors is about 45 years old.

State governors come from a variety of backgrounds.

▼ **CRITICAL THINKING**

1. Analyzing How many states have women governors? Minority governors? Do the demographics of the country's governors in terms of number of women and minorities in office seem representative of the population? If not, why might this be?

2. Evaluating Does the distribution of Republican and Democratic governors seem to match the political party you would expect to be dominant in each state based on the results of the last presidential election? Can you explain any discrepancies?

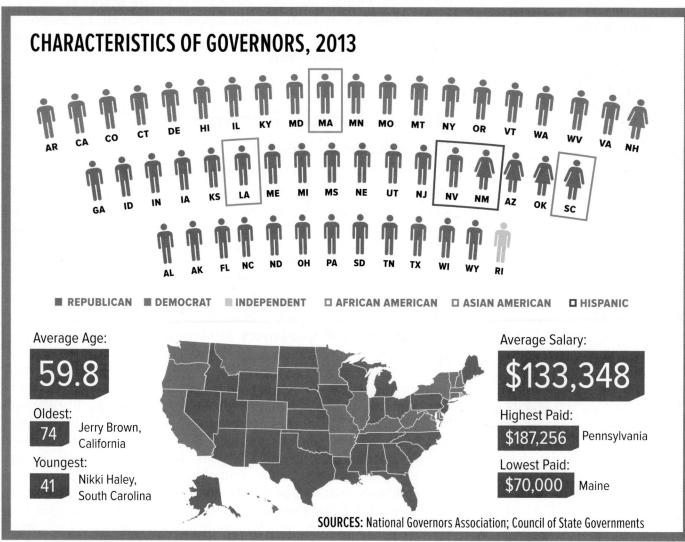

CHARACTERISTICS OF GOVERNORS, 2013

AR CA CO CT DE HI IL KY MD MA MN MO MT NY OR VT WA WV VA NH

GA ID IN IA KS LA ME MI MS NE UT NJ NV NM AZ OK SC

AL AK FL NC ND OH PA SD TN TX WI WY RI

■ REPUBLICAN   ■ DEMOCRAT   ■ INDEPENDENT   ❑ AFRICAN AMERICAN   ❑ ASIAN AMERICAN   ❑ HISPANIC

Average Age:

59.8

Oldest:
74 Jerry Brown, California

Youngest:
41 Nikki Haley, South Carolina

Average Salary:

$133,348

Highest Paid:
$187,256 Pennsylvania

Lowest Paid:
$70,000 Maine

SOURCES: National Governors Association; Council of State Governments

PARTICIPATING
Your Government

Government Response to Natural Disasters

During natural disasters, agencies at the local, state, and federal levels must work together and coordinate their responses. Wildfires, which are prevalent in the western United States, are one such natural disaster.

Consider the challenges posed by just one small fire, known as the Acton wildfire. Acton, California, a small mountain community in the Los Angeles metropolitan area, had experienced a major fire in 2009 and another small fire earlier in 2012. This fire broke out in northern Los Angeles County on May 8. High winds and low humidity allowed the fire to spread rapidly. Up to 400 firefighters from Los Angeles County, the city of Los Angeles, and the U.S. Forest Service battled the blaze, with help from five aircraft. Residents of the area—including many animals—were evacuated, a county road was closed, and the train system linking outlying areas with Los Angeles stopped service temporarily. Although the fire was quickly controlled, 125 acres, one mobile home, and several ranch buildings were burned. Once the fire was extinguished, cleanup began, with volunteers soliciting donations to help ranch owners rebuild.

▲ CRITICAL THINKING

Problem Solving Create a web diagram with the Los Angeles County chief executive officer (CEO) in the center. On one side, show the CEO's connections to all the Los Angeles County government departments that might have been involved in fighting the Acton fire or in the cleanup afterwards. On the other side, show links to other governments or private individuals or organizations that were involved in the response.

    a. What does your web diagram suggest about government response to disasters?

    b. Given that this was a fairly small fire, how do you think the web diagram would change with a larger fire or disaster? Would the person in the center change?

    c. What technology and technology skills could help this CEO respond effectively?

    d. What other skills would a leader of the executive branch need to coordinate with so many different departments and governments?

Most mayors serve two or four years in office. Sometimes their duties are largely ceremonial; other times they have a big hand in shaping the policies of their cities. They may appoint people to city council, advisory boards, committees, and commissions. Some mayors even get to set their towns' annual budgets.

The average salary for a mayor is $56,000, but many jurisdictions pay their mayors little or nothing at all.

Term of Office and Succession Most governors serve four-year terms. In two states, Vermont and New Hampshire, the term of office is only two years. Many states also limit the number of terms a governor may serve in office. Twenty-seven states have a two-term limit. Governors in Virginia may serve only one term.

In most states, the lieutenant governor takes over if the governor dies, resigns, or is no longer able to serve. In five states and Puerto Rico, other officials succeed the governor if he or she leaves office.

Interning at the Governor's Office

Summer Cook

Summer Cook began thinking about a career in politics in middle school. She decided to investigate possible jobs by interning in Colorado state government. She spent one summer working for then-Governor Bill Ritter and another summer interning with Lieutenant Governor Joe Garcia. Summer helped plan events, drafted various forms of communication, assisted at events and meetings, and researched and compiled information for projects.

"There is a huge focus on working with people to create policies that will benefit the most people. It is impossible to make everybody happy, but it is nonetheless critical to find out where people stand on certain issues and how important those issues are to them."

"There is a misperception that all interns do is sharpen pencils and fetch coffee. In my experience that is not the case at all."
—Summer Cook

▲ **CRITICAL THINKING**

Analyzing In what ways did Summer's work as an intern develop the skills she will need in a career in political communications? What other career skills might interning in the executive branch help a person develop? How might the work of an intern in a governor's office help people of that state?

There is a wide variation in the term length for mayors and other chief executives at the local level. Few local charters impose term limits on their chief executives. For example, Hilmar Moore, the mayor of Richmond, Texas, died in office in 2012 after serving as mayor of that town for 63 years.

☑ **READING PROGRESS CHECK**

Listing What are the qualifications to become a governor? To become a mayor?

Elections of State and Local Executives

GUIDING QUESTION *How are state and local executives elected?*

Today, all governors are directly elected. This gives citizens a direct influence over the governors' plans, policies, and actions.

Elections In most states, the process of electing a governor has two basic steps. First, an individual must gain the nomination of a major political party, usually by winning a party primary. Only three states—Connecticut, Utah, and Virginia—still use the older convention method to nominate candidates for governor. In nearly every case, the major candidates for governor run for office as nominees of either the Democratic or Republican parties.

Second, after he or she is chosen, the nominee runs in the general election. In most states, the candidate who wins a **plurality** vote is elected governor. A plurality is the largest number of votes in an election. For example, in the 2006 gubernatorial election in Texas, candidate Rick Perry won the election with 39 percent of the vote, a plurality, but not a majority.

In five states, however, a majority is needed to be elected. In Arizona, Georgia, and Louisiana, if no one receives a majority, a runoff election is held between the two candidates who received the most votes in the general

plurality the largest number of votes in an election

election. In Mississippi, the lower house of the state legislature chooses the governor if no candidate **obtains** a majority. In Vermont, the house and senate choose.

Most states' lieutenant governors are also elected by the voters. In the largest number of states, the governor and lieutenant governor run as a ticket, while in other states, separate elections are held. In Tennessee and West Virginia, the president of the senate serves as the lieutenant governor.

In the United States, there are about 3,000 counties, 20,000 municipalities, 16,000 townships, and 37,000 special districts, each with its own rules on which positions will be in charge and how those positions will be elected. Most officers are elected by direct vote. In addition to the mayor, commonly elected offices include judge, sheriff, and city council.

obtain to get, acquire, or procure, as through an effort or by a request

Impeachment and Recalls All states except for Oregon allow for impeachment proceedings against a governor. The procedures for impeaching a state official vary, as do the grounds for impeachment. Some state constitutions specify what can cause a governor to be impeached; these grounds typically include corruption, bribery, or other crimes. In 2009 Governor Rod Blagojevich of Illinois was impeached for abusing the power of his office. He was subsequently convicted of federal corruption charges, including soliciting bribes, and sentenced to 14 years in prison.

Another factor that can influence the governor's term of office is **recall**, which is the process of voting to remove state officials from office. In 19 states, voters can go to the polls and vote for a governor to be removed from office. Some states allow for recalls only in specific circumstances, such as criminal behavior or serious **misconduct** on the part of the elected official. Throughout U.S. history, only two governors have been removed from office through the recall. In 1921 the governor of North Dakota was recalled, along with the attorney general and the commissioner of agriculture. In 2003 California voters recalled their governor, Gray Davis. In 2012 voters in Wisconsin attempted to recall Governor Scott Walker, but he survived the recall and remained in office.

recall the procedure by which an elected official may be removed from office by popular vote

misconduct deliberate violation of a law or standard especially by a government official

Recall of local officials is much more common than recall of state officials. In 2011, for instance, Mayor Carlos Alvarez of Miami, Florida, was recalled by voters shortly after raising taxes while giving his aides salary increases.

☑ **READING PROGRESS CHECK**

Defining What is recall and how can it affect a governor's term of office?

LESSON 2 REVIEW

Reviewing Vocabulary
1. *Defining* What does it mean for a candidate to win a plurality vote?

Using Your Graphic Organizer
2. *Describing* Use your completed graphic organizer to create a digital slide show about the similarities and differences between governors and mayors.

Answering the Guiding Questions
3. *Analyzing* How do state and local executive branch leaders qualify for their positions?

4. *Explaining* How are state and local executives elected?

Writing About Government
5. *Informative/Explanatory* Research and write a biography of your mayor, city manager, or commissioner. It should include his or her education, prior work experiences, priorities in office, and basic information about his or her family. Try to learn about his or her personality and working style.

DEBATING DEMOCRATIC PRINCIPLES

The recall is a tool of direct democracy. It allows voters to remove elected officials from office before their terms are up. Most recalls occur at the local level, involving city council or school board members.

However, 19 states also provide for recall of state officials. Eight of the states that allow recalls list specific grounds for recall. These include such offenses as incompetence, misconduct, misuse of public funds, or conviction of a felony. In the other 11 states, a recall petition can be started for any reason. In most states, a citizen or group of citizens circulate a petition, gathering a required number of signatures from voters. They submit the petitions to election officials, who determine if enough valid signatures are included. If so, a special recall election is held.

 YES

 NO

TEAM A — **Voters Should Be Able to Recall Officials**

The recall keeps power in the hands of voters. In a democracy, citizens should have not just the right to elect officials but to remove them as well. The recall also provides a "safety valve" for people who are very unhappy with an official's action, providing an outlet for their disapproval.

Elected state officials know they can be recalled if they do not work in the best interests of their constituents. Thus, they will work harder to do a good job and represent their constituents well. The ability to recall elected officials will hold them to their campaign promises.

The possibility of a recall election raises interest in government. When more people are paying attention to what the government is doing, the government must be more responsive.

TEAM B — **Voters Should Not Be Able to Recall Officials**

The recall is an expensive example of too much democracy. Policies do not always work immediately. Elected officials must have time to put policies in place and allow those policies to take effect. The threat of a recall also discourages officials from considering all viewpoints and making tough decisions.

As voters, we agree to live with the results of elections, as long as those elections are free and fair. Officials who are doing a bad job can be held accountable at the next election.

Special interests with a lot of money can manipulate the recall process. They can hire people to collect signatures on a petition. They can buy advertising to influence voters. Political parties can also use recalls to advance their interests rather than to promote better government.

EXPLORING THE ESSENTIAL QUESTION

Analyzing Should our state laws make it possible for citizens to use recalls to remove governors and other state officials from office for any reason? Read the evidence provided, and prepare to debate one side or the other.

1. Identify the best reasons to support your side of the debate question.
2. Draft a compelling opening statement that sets out your position in the debate and summarizes your argument.
3. Anticipate the strongest arguments to support the other position. How could you respond to those points?

Interact with these digital
assets and others in lesson 3

✓ **INTERACTIVE GRAPH**
How Americans Get to Work

✓ **INTERACTIVE MAP**
Municipal Zoning

✓ **SELF-CHECK QUIZ**

✓ **VIDEO**
Eminent Domain

netw⊚rks
TRY IT YOURSELF ONLINE

ReadingHelp Desk

Academic Vocabulary

- **finance**
- **inadequate**

Content Vocabulary

- **block grant**
- **public utility**
- **workers' compensation**
- **unemployment compensation**
- **zoning**
- **suburb**
- **infrastructure**
- **mass transit**

TAKING NOTES:

Key Ideas and Details

LISTING Use the graphic organizer
to list the different services provided
by state and local governments.

Government Services

State Government	Local Government

LESSON 3
State and Local Executive Branches at Work

ESSENTIAL QUESTION

How are state and local executive branches structured?

Which government services benefit you? Create a list of at least five government services that you have taken advantage of in the past month. Identify what level of government provided each service. As you work through this section, you can make corrections to your list as you learn more about state and local government services.

The Structure of State and Local Executive Branches

GUIDING QUESTION *How do state and local executive branches function?*

In addition to governors, mayors, and other local leaders, executive branch staff implement laws and policies at the state and local levels.

State Executive Branch Officers No state gives its governor power to appoint an entire executive team. Instead, they must work with some elected, appointed, and hired individuals. In all but four states—Maine, New Hampshire, New Jersey, and Tennessee—other elected officials are part of the executive branch. Less visible than the governor, these executives often hold important positions.

Forty-four states have a lieutenant governor, a position similar to that of the vice president of the United States. The lieutenant governor becomes governor when the office is vacated. The lieutenant governor also usually presides over the state senate.

In all but eight states, the people elect the attorney general, who is the top legal officer in state government; in those eight states, the governor usually appoints the attorney general. The attorney general supervises the legal activities of all state agencies, gives legal advice to the governor, and acts as a lawyer for the state in cases in which it is involved. Probably the most significant power of the attorney general is the power to issue opinions, or written interpretations of the state constitution or laws. These opinions carry legal authority unless a court overturns them.

In state government, the role of secretary of state is not at all like that of the federal secretary of state, which deals with foreign relations. Although responsibilities vary from state to state, common duties of the secretary of state include licensing businesses, various professionals, and drivers. The secretary of state is also responsible for state records and documents. In addition to these duties, the position often manages state elections. Consequently, many secretaries of state play an active role in initiating programs that may directly impact voter participation and civic education.

The state treasurer manages the money that a state government collects and pays out. He or she pays the bills of state government and often serves as the state tax collector. In most states, the state treasurer also has the power to invest state funds.

Many other executive officers work in state governments. Some of the more important offices commonly found in states are the state comptroller or auditor, the superintendent of public instruction, and the insurance commissioner.

Much like the national government, state and local executive branches are divided into numerous departments and agencies to implement different laws. Each department or agency works to help the public in a specific area, such as public safety, agriculture, or education. The following sections highlight some of the areas in which state and local agencies work.

GOVERNMENT *in your* COMMUNITY

Crime

Most crimes fall under state jurisdiction. This means that criminal justice issues are among the most important—and expensive—problems that state and local governments deal with. After decades of rising prison populations and costs, many states began to look for innovative ways to combat crime, protect victims, and reduce prison populations.

Which of these approaches would you favor? Rank the following policy choices in order of which ones you would most want to direct additional state funding to.

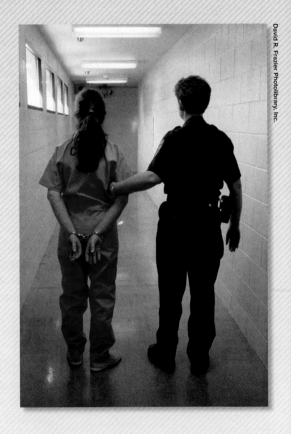

David R. Frazier Photolibrary, Inc.

- Hire more police officers.

- Create rehabilitation programs for people addicted to drugs.

- Build more prisons.

- Pass stricter mandatory sentences for violent crimes.

- Create community policing programs where officers spend more time getting to know individuals in the community.

- Create training and education programs to help reintroduce prisoners to society.

- Build databases to better track all crimes and criminal suspects.

- Create programs and community centers for young people to keep them from joining violent groups.

EXPLORING THE ESSENTIAL QUESTION

Comparing What actions has your state taken to address crime, prison populations, or recidivism lately? Create a list and compare it to the policy choices above. How do your state's recent actions compare with your priorities?

Local Executive Branch Structures Whether a local government is organized in a mayor-council, council-manager, or commissioner form, executive power is often shared between multiple individuals. These might include the sheriff, attorney, clerk, treasurer, auditor, coroner, surveyor, and school superintendent.

Local executive branches can be arranged in a number of ways. Some towns are run like businesses, where a board of directors makes all of the big decisions. Some smaller cities may have only a handful of employees to carry out the city's work. Larger cities, such as Chicago, have more than 20 executive departments and nearly a hundred agencies.

☑ **READING PROGRESS CHECK**

Listing What are some of the offices of the state executive branch?

Public Safety

GUIDING QUESTION *How do state and local governments protect communities?*

For the most part, protecting life and property is the responsibility of state and local governments, rather than the federal government. Laws dealing with most common crimes come from the state. Local governments usually do not make criminal laws, but they enforce state laws that protect life and property. Police and fire services are expensive and make up a large part of most municipal budgets.

Police and Criminal Corrections State police are normally limited in their functions. Most are highway patrol units. The state police have investigative powers in many states, but they possess broad police responsibilities in only a few states. Local police departments handle most day-to-day patrolling, emergency response, and investigation of crimes. Police protection is the second-largest expense of many American cities, after public utilities.

State courts handle the great majority of all criminal cases in the United States. State prisons, county and municipal jails, and other houses of detention throughout a state make up a state's correction system.

Fire Protection Fire protection is a local function that varies with the size of the community. In small towns, volunteers usually staff the fire department. In large cities, professional, full-time fire departments provide the necessary protection. Professional fire departments also serve some small towns that have many factories and businesses.

☑ **READING PROGRESS CHECK**

Explaining What types of things do the local police typically handle? What is the main function of the state police?

Education, Health, and Welfare

GUIDING QUESTION *How do state and local governments maintain public schools and provide health and social services to residents?*

Both state and local governments have some control over public schools and provide a range of health services and social services for low-income residents.

Education Providing education is one of the most important functions of government. State governments establish local school districts and give them the power to administer the schools, but the state regulates the taxes that

It is generally the responsibility of state and local governments to protect life and property by providing emergency services.

▲ **CRITICAL THINKING**
Identifying Which level of government is generally responsible for public safety?

Identifying Central Issues The quality of schools across any given state can vary dramatically. Should all schools in the state follow the same curriculum? Should all schools receive the same amount of state or national funding per pupil? Is it better to allow local communities to fund their own schools as well as they can? Should local schools have more control over what students learn? Explain your reasons for each of your answers to the preceding questions. Which principles of democracy inform your opinions about this topic?

finance to provide necessary funds for

block grant a grant of money to a state or local government to be used for a general purpose

school districts can levy or the amount of money they can borrow. The federal government provides about 10 percent of funding for public schools. Local school districts generally provide about half of the money and make many key decisions on public school policy. Local funding and local control of schools go hand in hand. However, local funding also contributes to inequality of education across the many districts of a state. Wealthier districts can provide much better educational opportunities. As a result, some states and state courts have begun to address this issue, raising questions about the way education is **financed**.

States also set some standards for public schools throughout the state. For example, about half of the states require a minimum competency test for graduation.

Health In the area of health, states license doctors and dentists, regulate the sale of drugs, and require vaccines for schoolchildren. State health agencies provide care for mothers and their newborn children, treatment of contagious diseases and chronic illnesses, mental health care, public dental clinics, and immunization against communicable and other diseases. State agencies also provide laboratory services to local health departments that cannot afford separate facilities. State governments often pay the bill for public health services that local authorities deliver and administer.

Medicaid, a program that provides medical and health services to low-income people, is a program that is jointly funded by the state and federal governments. The federal government establishes guidelines for Medicaid, but each state can work within these guidelines to shape the program to fit its needs. Groups that receive Medicaid services include low-income elderly people, low-income families, and the visually and physically impaired.

Social Services State and local governments offer important services to citizens who cannot afford them. States both administer federal programs and finance and administer state-level programs with some support from local governments. For example, states administer the federal Temporary Assistance for Needy Families (TANF) program. TANF provides federal payments, or **block grants**, to states to help needy families, but the emphasis is on short-term assistance. States can shape their TANF programs as long as they target four goals:

- to support needy families so their children can be cared for at home
- to help parents in need by training them for jobs and successful parenting
- to reduce the incidence of out-of-wedlock pregnancy
- to support two-parent families overall

States also have their own social welfare programs, which vary widely. Heavily urbanized states such as New York, California, Michigan, and Massachusetts tend to have more generous programs. Since the early 1930s, state governments have spent more on general assistance programs in line with increases in public health, education, welfare, and environmental spending.

Normally, local governments provide services to people who have special needs that result from unemployment, low income, ill health, or permanent disabilities. One type of social service provides aid to people who are temporarily unemployed. This aid consists of cash payments and help with finding new jobs. A second program is hospital care for people who need medical attention and cannot afford it. The third program is direct assistance to needy people in the form of cash payments. This type of social service is often referred to as *public welfare.*

Recreation and Cultural Activities As the amount of Americans' leisure time increases, local governments have responded with recreational and cultural programs. Some local communities offer swimming, dancing, and arts and crafts programs. In addition, many localities provide baseball, football, and other sports programs. The maintenance of parks, zoos, and libraries is also a function of local government. Many cities and counties have helped build stadiums, arenas, and convention centers that are used for sports and entertainment.

☑ **READING PROGRESS CHECK**

Specifying How do state and local governments finance education?

PARTICIPATING
ⓘⓝ Your Government

Identifying and Contacting Government Services

Imagine that you are confused about an assignment in your government class. Where would you go for help? Would you ask the girl who sits next to you in math? The principal? Your third-grade teacher?

While the example above is obvious, knowing who to ask when you want the government to take action is a key to your success. First, you need to identify whether the problem requires national, state, or local action. Next, you need to think about who in government can help.

PROBLEM	LEVEL OF GOVERNMENT	GOVERNMENT AGENCY

Consider these examples. Which government agency should you contact to help with these problems?

- A state highway and city street intersect near your school. Several students walking or skateboarding across the intersection have been hit by cars making illegal turns.

- Your family is considering buying a house several miles outside town. Because the area has been in a drought for several years, your mother is worried about how fast firefighters could get to the house if a fire occurred.

EXPLORING THE ESSENTIAL QUESTION

Problem Solving With a group of three or four students, brainstorm a list of issues or problems in your community. As a group, pick the three issues or problems most important to you. For each problem, identify the correct level of government and which agency at that level of government could help. Use the graphic organizer to record this information.

As individuals, choose the problem that is most important to you. If others pick the same problem, work with them; otherwise, work on your own. Find out who is working on this problem in your community. This could include other individuals or organizations. Contact them to find out what they are doing and how you could help in the effort to solve the problem.

Business and Labor

GUIDING QUESTION *How do state governments regulate businesses?*

State governments regulate businesses, industries, and unions that operate in their state.

Business Regulation State governments have a special obligation to regulate certain kinds of business. Their regulatory power in these kinds of industries is broader than the power of the federal government. Regulations affect many kinds of corporations, but laws regulating banks, insurance companies, and public utilities are especially rigorous. A **public utility** is an organization, either privately or publicly owned, that supplies such necessities as electricity, gas, telephone service, or transportation service. In the United States, most public utility companies are owned by private stockholders. States can give public utility companies the right to supply service in the state or in a part of the state. In return for granting a company the right to provide a service, the state assumes the right to regulate the company. Beginning in the 1980s, many states worked to reduce their regulation in order to encourage competition, but since the early 2000s, there has been less enthusiasm for deregulation.

Labor Laws States also provide **workers' compensation**—payments to people who are unable to work as a result of job-related injury or ill health. Workers who lose their jobs may receive **unemployment compensation** under programs that are set up and regulated by their states.

Workers in all states have the right to join unions, but some states protect workers from being forced to join. More than one-third of the states have passed laws (often called *right-to-work laws*) that prohibit union shops. A union shop is an agreement between a union and an employer that all workers must join a union, usually within 30 days of being hired.

Business Development State governments are active in trying to attract new business and industry. Governors often travel in this country or abroad to bring businesses to their states, using television ads, billboards, brochures, and newspaper ads to promote travel or business opportunities. Today, states and cities often give businesses short-term incentives such as a reduced tax rate in the hopes that the company will create new jobs and stimulate other business growth—both of which will result in more tax revenue to the state in the long term.

✅ **READING PROGRESS CHECK**

Discussing What is a public utility and how are public utility companies regulated?

Land Use, Infrastructure, and Environment

GUIDING QUESTION *What are the responsibilities of local government in regard to land use, infrastructure, and environment?*

As the population in an area increases, available land becomes more scarce and, hence, more costly. Local governments often have to decide whether available land should be used for new housing, industry, stores, office buildings, or open space.

Municipal governments attempt to manage land use to provide an environment for orderly growth. What action should be taken when an area begins to deteriorate?

New York Governor Andrew M. Cuomo speaking at the launch of a new campaign to promote tourism throughout the state

▲ **CRITICAL THINKING**
Making Connections The commercials are being unveiled following the one-year anniversary of Hurricane Sandy. What connection does this have to tourism?

public utility an organization, either privately or publicly owned, that supplies such necessities as electricity, gas, telephone service, or transportation service

workers' compensation payments to people who are unable to work as a result of job-related injury or ill health

unemployment compensation payments to people who lose their jobs

MUNICIPAL ZONING

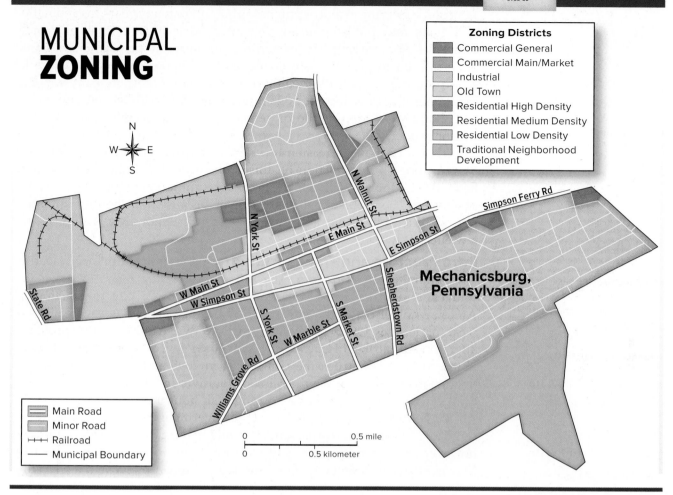

Zoning Districts
- Commercial General
- Commercial Main/Market
- Industrial
- Old Town
- Residential High Density
- Residential Medium Density
- Residential Low Density
- Traditional Neighborhood Development

Mechanicsburg, Pennsylvania

- Main Road
- Minor Road
- Railroad
- Municipal Boundary

0   0.5 mile
0   0.5 kilometer

Zoning

Zoning Local governments use **zoning** to regulate the way land and buildings are used, thus shaping how a community develops. Zoning boards can regulate growth, preserve neighborhoods, and prevent the decline of land values. They can rule that certain districts (zones) be used only for homes, businesses, or parks. In some cases, mixed zoning permits residences and certain types of businesses to occupy the same areas.

Some critics claim that zoning is an excessive use of government power because it limits how people can use their property. Some criticize zoning laws that make it difficult for certain people, often minorities or families with children, to move into particular neighborhoods. Critics call this *restrictive zoning*. Advocates of zoning claim that without zoning, a community might develop in ways that would lower property values and make it an unpleasant place to live.

Housing Shortages

Housing Shortages Many major cities, including Atlanta and Philadelphia, have responded to housing shortages by renovating older housing. In Baltimore, Maryland, and Des Moines, Iowa, funds from the city government along with federal, state, and private funds have made some highly successful renovation programs possible. In contrast, large numbers of unsafe, unoccupied houses in Detroit have been torn down by the city.

The federal government has also provided low-interest loans to local housing authorities. The loans have been used to help build housing for low-income residents. Local housing authorities received federal aid to maintain rents at affordable levels.

Municipal governments use zoning maps like this one to help plan the layout of the city.

▲ **CRITICAL THINKING**

1. Drawing Inferences How might the locations of commercial general zones benefit a new business?

2. Identifying What kind of transportation for supplies and products would be available to businesses in the industrial zones and to those in the commercial general zones?

zoning the means a local government uses to regulate the way land and buildings may be used in order to shape community development

Housing Discrimination Many Americans have been discriminated against when trying to rent or purchase a home. For many years, a combination of private and public policies prevented African Americans and other minorities from buying houses and renting in many parts of cities. Banks often refused to provide bank loans, and ordinances mandating large lot sizes prevented all but the wealthy from building homes in many **suburbs**. Many cities kept low-income housing separate from middle- and upper-class neighborhoods. Often landlords refused to rent to people based on their race or gender.

The courts have consistently ruled that discrimination in housing is illegal. Congress took action on this problem in 1968 when it passed the Federal Fair Housing Act, which barred discrimination in the sale and rental of housing. The problem persists, however, because housing discrimination can be difficult to prove, and the government has not always enforced the law effectively.

Infrastructure and Transportation One essential duty for city leaders is maintaining **infrastructure**. The term *infrastructure* refers to the roads, bridges, and water and sewer systems that allow a city to function. In America's older cities, the infrastructure has been showing severe signs of wear for decades. Often, public attention is drawn to infrastructure problems after tragedy strikes. Issues with **inadequate** levees were exposed when Hurricane Katrina struck the Gulf Coast in 2005 and when severe storms flooded many towns along the Mississippi River in 2007 and 2008. In 2007 a bridge in Minneapolis collapsed during rush-hour traffic.

By the 1990s, spending at all levels of government for airports, highways, railroads, and transit surpassed $100 billion per year. To many mayors, however, the federal government was not doing its share. New York City Mayor Michael Bloomberg said, "the federal government is not investing enough in our infrastructure, and when it does, it's not investing wisely."

Maintaining a sound transportation network is a serious challenge for local governments. Chronic traffic jams and air pollution have resulted from

suburb an outlying part of a city or town

infrastructure the basic facilities of a city, such as roads, bridges, water and sewage pipes, and public buildings

inadequate insufficient

GRAPH

Most Americans drive to work. Due to Americans' dependence on the automobile, local governments spend millions of dollars each year to maintain more than 3 million miles of streets.

▶ CRITICAL THINKING

1. *Calculating* What percentage of Americans drive alone to work?

2. *Problem Solving* What do you think local governments can do to encourage people to use mass transit or even to walk or bike to work?

How Americans Get to Work, 2011

- Cycling, Walking, Other → 5%
- Using Public Transportation → 5%
- 80% ← Driving Alone
- 10%
- Carpooling →

Source: American Community Survey, 2013; U.S. Census Bureau, www.census.gov

the millions of Americans who use their automobiles to commute to work. Local governments spend millions of dollars each year to maintain more than 3 million miles of streets. In recent years, local governments have tried to encourage people to use **mass transit** rather than their own automobiles. Mass transit moves large numbers of people, produces less pollution by consuming less fuel than automobiles, and uses less energy. Despite all the advantages of mass transit, however, most Americans prefer to drive to work in their automobiles. So far, higher gas prices have made only a modest impact on this cultural preference.

Many local leaders believe that more people would use mass-transit facilities if they were cleaner, faster, and more efficient. Elaborate mass-transit systems have been built in Washington, D.C., Atlanta, and in the San Francisco–Oakland area. San Francisco's Bay Area Rapid Transit (BART) system cost twice its original estimate to build. High costs discourage planners in other cities from taking on such projects.

Some communities have adopted policies to encourage commuters to bike to work. Bicycles are obviously easier on roads, do not burn carbon-based fuels, and lead to healthier communities. Communities may create zoning rules that allow new apartment buildings or housing developments to be put only in areas that are close to public transportation or that are particularly "walkable."

Water Supply Local governments make vital decisions regarding water service. Smaller communities may contract with privately owned companies to supply water. The threat of water pollution and water shortages has prompted some local governments to create special water district arrangements. In case of a water shortage, such districts or local governments may attempt to limit the amount of water that is consumed.

Sewage and Sanitation Local government is responsible for sewage disposal. Untreated sewage, if it is allowed to return to the natural water supply, can endanger life and property. Many local governments maintain sewage-treatment plants to deal with this problem. High costs have forced some smaller communities to contract with private companies to provide their sewage and sanitation services.

Because of environmental concerns, landfills are no longer the simple solution to sanitation that they once were. Some local governments use garbage-processing plants to dispose of the community's solid wastes.

Sewage and sanitation issues also often require that officials make difficult political decisions. For example, where should sewage-treatment plants be located? Although such plants are necessary, people are often opposed to having them near their homes. Another difficult decision involves how to pay for these services. While people want a clean and healthy community, they often object to paying taxes to improve sewage and sanitation services.

Environmental Issues State governments are also involved in many activities related to the environmental health of their citizens. For example, states monitor air and water quality and manage the disposal of hazardous wastes.

Today, state governments are very concerned about pollution and most now require environmental impact statements for major governmental or

In recent years, local governments have encouraged commuters to use mass transit as an alternative to driving their own automobiles in order to reduce pollution and traffic congestion.

▲ CRITICAL THINKING
Assessing What are some other ways local governments might try to reduce pollution and traffic congestion?

mass transit a public transportation network, consisting of buses, trains, subways, or other forms of public transportation

private projects, describing how the project is likely to affect the environment. Many states require industries to secure permits if their wastes pollute the air or water. Often such permits are so costly that the industry finds it cheaper to install antipollution devices. Most have developed waste-management systems. Most regulate the disposal of radioactive wastes.

With huge concentrations of people, large cities across the nation could be drastically affected by air pollution and climate change. Mayors are playing an important role in finding ways for city governments to cut their power use and to encourage citizens and businesses to do the same. For example, in 2005 Seattle Mayor Greg Nickels drafted a document called the U.S. Mayors Climate Protection Agreement.

Boston Mayor Thomas M. Menino plans to reduce Boston's greenhouse gas emissions 25 percent by 2020 and 80 percent by 2050. The city is piloting a residential composting program, is encouraging the use of hybrid taxis, and has implemented an energy management system to track municipal energy use.

Philadelphia's Greenworks initiative has weatherized more than 9,000 homes with insulation, air sealing, and cool roofs. The city has diverted 70 percent of its solid waste from its landfills, either to be recycled or to produce energy. The city of Philadelphia reduced the municipal government's greenhouse gas emissions 13 percent between 2006 and 2012 and planned to reduce them further by 2015. Nashville, Tennessee, Mayor Karl Dean created the Office of Environment and Sustainability, which coordinated electronics recycling events, promoted green spaces, and created a bike-sharing program. San Francisco officials are using recycled fat, oil, and grease from restaurants to make biodiesel fuel for the city's garbage trucks.

✓ **READING PROGRESS CHECK**

Differentiating What roles do state and local governments play in providing water and sanitation services?

LESSON 3 REVIEW

Reviewing Vocabulary

1. ***Defining*** What is a block grant and how can it provide assistance for families in need?

Using Your Graphic Organizer

2. ***Describing*** Use your completed graphic organizer to write a summary of the different services provided by state and local government.

Answering the Guiding Questions

3. ***Analyzing*** How do state and local executive branches function?

4. ***Explaining*** How do state and local governments protect communities?

5. ***Identifying*** How do state and local governments maintain public schools and provide health and social services to residents?

6. ***Questioning*** How do state governments regulate businesses?

7. ***Summarizing*** What are the responsibilities of local government in regard to land use, infrastructure, and environment?

Writing About Government

8. ***Argument*** Mayors of large cities need strong arguments to get federal funding to address their problems. What could a mayor say to the president and Congress to support the city's cause? Research the types of projects that would benefit your community. Write a proposal explaining the need for federal money for a project in your community.

Kelo  New London (2005)

FACTS OF THE CASE The city of New London, Connecticut, experienced a significant economic decline after the closure of a military base. The city formed the **New London Development Corporation (NLDC)**, which allowed the city to lease properties in one neighborhood to a private developer to build hotels, office spaces, and some high-end residential units. The development plan for the property would require the current residents to move out. The City of New London forced the homeowners to sell their property using eminent domain. Eminent domain is the ability of a local government, under the Fifth Amendment, to take over private property for "public use" as long as the owners are given due process and just compensation.

Typically, eminent domain is used when a local government needs to build or expand a road, build a bridge, or otherwise provide for public use and benefit. The Kelos refused to move out of their home.

ISSUE

May a local government take private property for economic development purposes?

ARGUMENTS

KELO The property in this case is not in a run-down area, and it is not hazardous. The city wants this property only because it could receive more tax revenue if the property were developed differently. If states are allowed to take property in order to promote economic development, there would be no limit to what would qualify as "public use." Without limits, states could essentially control all property.

Moreover, the state should not be allowed to take private property and give it to another private entity. Traditionally, when states use eminent domain, the property taken is used by the government to build some type of infrastructure project. The public purpose served should be direct and immediate.

NEW LONDON The city of New London was suffering from an economic downturn, and the tax revenue to be gained would substantially benefit the public. Economic development can be as important to a community as an infrastructure project. An area should not have to be in shambles before a city can step in and take property to create economic development.

The Fifth Amendment simply says that property should not be taken without due process and just compensation. The city followed required procedures, and the homeowners in this case were paid enough for their property. Additionally, in this case the property would be owned by the city and leased to the developer. A basic premise of federalism allows localities to make decisions based on their situations—what works in Connecticut might not work in Utah.

EXPLORING THE ESSENTIAL QUESTION

Moot Court You will be assigned to one of three groups: lawyers for Kelo, lawyers for New London, or Supreme Court justices. You will prepare for a moot court of this case. The lawyers for each side should develop arguments to present during oral argument and prepare to answer questions from the justices. The justices should prepare questions to ask the lawyers during oral argument. When you argue the case, each team will have five minutes to present its side, and the justices will be allowed to ask the lawyers questions throughout their five minutes. The justices will then vote and announce their decision explaining their reasons. After the moot court is complete, write a persuasive essay or blog that reflects your personal opinion about this issue.

YOU BE the JUDGE

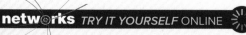

STUDY GUIDE

ROLES OF GOVERNOR
LESSON 1

- Legislative leader
- Chief executive
- Guardian of the state economy
- Party leader
- Commander in chief of state National Guard
- Head of state

ROLES OF GOVERNOR

FORMS OF LOCAL GOVERNMENT
LESSON 1

Commission
- commissioners head specific departments

Council-Manager
- city manager is chief administrator

FORMS OF LOCAL GOVERNMENT

Mayor-Council

Strong-mayor	Weak-mayor
• power to veto	• limited powers
• four-year term	• two-year term

WORK OF STATE AND LOCAL EXECUTIVE BRANCHES
LESSON 3

Functions of State and Local Executive Branches

 Public safety

 Education, health, and welfare

 Business and labor

 Land use, infrastructure, and the environment

GUBERNATORIAL ELECTION PROCESS
LESSON 2

Primary Election
- Convention
- Nomination by political party

General Election
- In 45 states, must win with plurality vote

or

- In 5 states, must win with majority vote. In 3 of these 5 states, a runoff election is held if no one receives a majority.

Lesson Review

Lesson 1

❶ Contrasting What is a divided executive branch in state government? How is it different than the national executive branch?

❷ Making Connections How does the federal government use grants and funding to limit some state powers?

❸ Comparing and Contrasting Compare and contrast the mayor-council and council-manager systems of local government.

Lesson 2

❹ Describing Describe the legal or formal qualifications and term in office for governors in most states.

❺ Differentiating Describe the similarities and differences between recall and impeachment processes for governors.

Lesson 3

❻ Comparing and Contrasting Examine how national and state executive branches are organized, identifying similarities and differences.

❼ Naming Name the services local governments provide to protect life and property.

❽ Describing Describe how state and local governments manage the use of resources.

ANSWERING THE ESSENTIAL QUESTIONS

Review your answers to the introductory questions at the beginning of each lesson. Then answer the Essential Questions based on what you learned in the chapter. Have your answers changed?

❾ Making Generalizations How are state and local executive branches structured?

❿ Analyzing What are the characteristics of effective governors and mayors?

DBQ Interpreting Political Cartoons

Use the political cartoon to answer the following questions.

⓫ Analyzing Does this political cartoon portray governors seeking reelection in a positive or negative light? Explain your answer.

⓬ Evaluating When deciding which gubernatorial candidate to vote for, how might you judge an incumbent candidate differently than a candidate who has never served before?

Critical Thinking

⓭ Exploring Issues Research and describe activities your governor has carried out in the past year to fulfill the role of state political party leader. How could citizens participate in these events?

⓮ Considering Advantages and Disadvantages Describe the advantages and disadvantages of requiring a plurality of votes and of requiring a majority of votes to win a gubernatorial election.

⓯ Gathering Information Research who provides water, sewage, and sanitation services in your community. Describe how these groups are related to your local government.

⓰ Making Connections Describe a governor's role as legislative leader and compare it with formal legislative powers assigned to the office.

Need Extra Help?

If You've Missed Question	❶	❷	❸	❹	❺	❻	❼	❽	❾	❿	⓫	⓬	⓭	⓮	⓯	⓰
Go to page	353	357	358	361	365	367	369	372	352	361	352	361	353	364	375	354

DBQ Analyzing Primary Sources

Read the excerpts and answer the questions that follow.

Formal requirements for holding the office of governor are included in state constitutions. Refer to the excerpts from the California and Texas constitutions.

PRIMARY SOURCE

"ARTICLE 5 EXECUTIVE SEC. 2. The Governor shall be elected every fourth year at the same time and places as members of the Assembly and hold office from the Monday after January 1 following the election until a successor qualifies. The Governor shall be an elector who has been a citizen of the United States and a resident of this State for 5 years immediately preceding the Governor's election. The Governor may not hold other public office. No Governor may serve more than 2 terms."

—California Constitution, January 8, 1964

PRIMARY SOURCE

"ARTICLE 4. EXECUTIVE DEPARTMENT

INSTALLATION OF GOVERNOR; TERM; ELIGIBILITY. The Governor elected at the general election in 1974, and thereafter, shall be installed on the first Tuesday after the organization of the Legislature, or as soon thereafter as practicable, and shall hold his office for the term of four years, or until his successor shall be duly installed. He shall be at least thirty years of age, a citizen of the United States, and shall have resided in this State at least five years immediately preceding his election."

—The Texas Constitution

17 *Comparing and Contrasting* Create a Venn diagram comparing and contrasting the formal requirements for governor in California and Texas.

18 *Analyzing Primary Sources* When does a governor take office in California and Texas? Why would this be included in a constitution?

19 *Research Skills* Create a table displaying the method of selection, term of office, formal requirements, and general responsibilities for public offices in your state's executive branch.

Social Studies Skills

Use the table to answer questions 20 and 21.

Women, African American, and Hispanic Governors Since the Civil War			
	Women	African Americans	Hispanic
Before 1960	3 in WY & TX	1 in LA	4 in CA, NM, & SC
1960–1979	3 in AL, CT, & WA	—	2 in AZ & NM
1980–1999	12 in AZ, KS, KY, NE, NH, NJ, OH, OR, TX, & VT	1 in VA	2 in FL & NM
2000–2012	18 in AK, AZ, CT, DE, HI, KS, LA, MA, MI, MT, NC, NH, NM, OK, SC, UT, & WA	2 in MA & NY	2 in NM

20 *Drawing Conclusions* Which group above has been most successful at winning the governor's office?

21 *Geography Skills* Identify and explain patterns in the characteristics of states where Hispanics have held the office of governor.

Research and Presentation

22 *Gathering Information* Research and describe the process for electing the governor in your state.

23 *Diagramming* Create a diagram highlighting the roles the governor and executive departments play in creating the budget in your state. Include planning and proposal, legislative action, review and approval, and implementation and monitoring.

24 *Researching* Write an essay describing the form of municipal government and the process of selecting officeholders in your community.

25 *Gathering Information* Interview someone who participated in the last election for governor or local executive. Describe how effective his or her participation was in the election.

26 *Comparing and Contrasting* Compare and contrast how executive branch officials are appointed at the national, state, and local levels.

Need Extra Help?

If You've Missed Question	17	18	19	20	21	22	23	24	25	26
Go to page	361	361	361	364	364	364	355	364	364	354

UNIT 4
The Judicial Branch

IT MATTERS
BECAUSE . . .

Although all Americans agree that the Constitution is the law of the land, not everyone agrees on what various parts of the Constitution actually mean. When questions concerning a particular law arise in lower courts, the nine justices of the Supreme Court may interpret the law's meaning and constitutionality. Decisions made by the Supreme Court usually impact the entire nation. It is important to remember, however, that although the Supreme Court is the most powerful and important institution of the judicial branch, many other courts operate below the Supreme Court within the federal judiciary. Federal appeals courts review lower court rulings and sometimes pass cases on to the Supreme Court. State and local courts—like family, traffic, or small claims courts—interpret and apply state and local laws. The right of due process, the right to a fair trial, and the right to appeal—as well as the process of judicial review—are fundamental safeguards that help ensure that our rights and freedoms are not unlawfully taken from us. Knowing how the judicial branch works will help you understand that the judicial process is clearly defined and is structured to safeguard your rights.

How to
Analyze Primary and Secondary Sources

To analyze and evaluate primary and secondary sources, you must determine the accuracy, validity, and reliability of the information. Understanding the point of view of the author and his or her frame of reference will help you analyze and evaluate the arguments or counterarguments made by the author. Primary and secondary sources include text materials such as letters, diaries, official records, and books; audio materials such as speeches and interviews; and visual materials such as political cartoons, photographs, paintings, graphs, charts, and data. Biased information may contain factual errors, be incomplete, or be distorted by propaganda techniques. Follow these steps when analyzing and evaluating primary and secondary sources:

1. Determine the purpose and nature of the information.

2. Determine if the information is from a primary or secondary source.

3. Evaluate the validity and reliability of the source.

4. Determine the point of view and frame of reference of the author.

5. Evaluate the arguments the author presents.

6. If you do not understand some of the terminology used in an excerpt, use a dictionary. This will help you understand the term and use it correctly in the future.

7. When analyzing several primary and secondary sources, compare the arguments with counterarguments or information in other sources. See if they support or contradict each other. Synthesize the information you have learned from these sources.

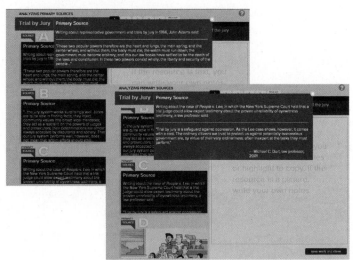

8. Use these steps when analyzing the primary and secondary sources in this program. In responding to document-based questions that accompany the Analyzing Primary Sources features, be sure to use social studies terms correctly. Use standard grammar, spelling, sentence structure, and punctuation in your written responses to the questions.

---

netw⊙rks *TRY IT YOURSELF* ONLINE

Go online to interact with these digital activities and more in each chapter.

Chapter 13 Federal and State Court Systems

Chapter 14 The Supreme Court of the United States

Chapter 15 Constitutional Freedoms

Chapter 16 Constitutional Right to a Fair Trial

✓ **INTERACTIVE IMAGE**
EARLY SYSTEMS OF LAW

✓ **INTERACTIVE GRAPH**
SUPREME COURT STATISTICS

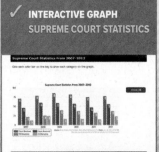

✓ **INTERACTIVE TIME LINE**
CIVIL RIGHTS LEGISLATION

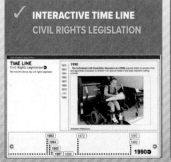

✓ **INTERACTIVE SUPREME COURT CASE**
YARBOROUGH V. ALVARADO

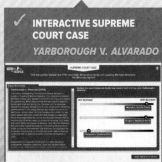

Federal and State Court Systems

ESSENTIAL QUESTIONS

- What is the role of the judicial system in our democracy?
- What are the purposes of trials and appeals in our court systems?
- How are federal, state, and local courts organized?

networks

www.connected.mcgraw-hill.com

There's More Online about federal and state court systems.

CHAPTER 13

▲ Local courts, such as this county courthouse in Missoula, Montana, are part of the state court system.

ANALYZING PRIMARY SOURCES

TRIAL BY JURY

Juries are a central component of the American legal system. While the Framers disagreed on many points, they consistently agreed on the need to protect the right to trial by jury in the Constitution. The right to a jury trial helps guarantee judgment by one's peers and provides a check on government power. However, in recent decades the role of the jury has been the subject of much debate. Many people believe that juries are not the fairest and most effective way to decide legal cases. Explore the sources here to learn more about the benefits and drawbacks of trial by jury.

PRIMARY SOURCE A

Writing about representative government and trials by jury in 1766, John Adams said:

"These two popular powers therefore are the heart and lungs, the main spring, and the center wheel, and without them, the body must die; the watch must run down; the government must become arbitrary, and this our law books have settled to be the death of the laws and constitution. In these two powers consist wholly, the liberty and security of the people . . ."

—John Adams, January 27, 1766

PRIMARY SOURCE C

Writing about the case of *People* v. *Lee*, in which the New York Supreme Court held that a trial judge could allow expert testimony about the proven unreliability of eyewitness testimony, a law professor said:

"Trial by jury is a safeguard against oppression. As the Lee case shows, however, it comes with a cost. The ordinary citizens we trust to protect us against potentially overzealous government are, by virtue of their very ordinariness, often inexpert at the tasks they must perform."

—Michael C. Dorf, law professor, 2001

PRIMARY SOURCE B

". . . the jury system works surprisingly well. Juries are quite able in finding facts; they inject community values into broad legal mandates; they act as a restraint on the powers of judges and prosecutors; their determinations are almost always accepted by disputants and society. That our jury system performs well, however, does not mean that reform efforts should stop. . . .

. . . the evidence is the prime determinant of a jury's verdict. Because jurors are most influenced by the quality of information presented to them, the best way to improve jury verdicts is to improve the information the jury receives to consider."

—Randolph N. Jonakait, law professor and author, 2003

PRIMARY SOURCE D

Jury Trial Innovations

Some people think that jury trials are not the best method. They argue that jurors do not understand everything that happens in court and are vulnerable to emotional appeals. Those who want to reform the jury system have recommended several modifications. These include giving jurors more guidance about the law or the process of deliberation and allowing jurors to ask questions, among others. This graph shows how often these reforms are used in U.S. courtrooms.

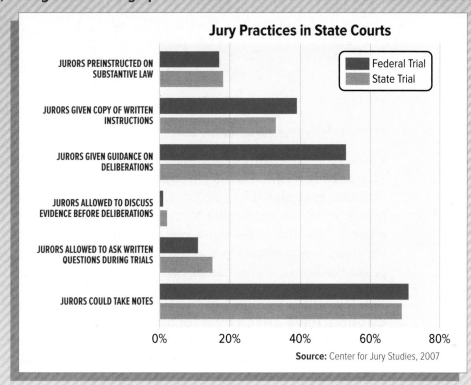

Jury Practices in State Courts

Legend: Federal Trial / State Trial

- JURORS PREINSTRUCTED ON SUBSTANTIVE LAW
- JURORS GIVEN COPY OF WRITTEN INSTRUCTIONS
- JURORS GIVEN GUIDANCE ON DELIBERATIONS
- JURORS ALLOWED TO DISCUSS EVIDENCE BEFORE DELIBERATIONS
- JURORS ALLOWED TO ASK WRITTEN QUESTIONS DURING TRIALS
- JURORS COULD TAKE NOTES

0%   20%   40%   60%   80%

Source: Center for Jury Studies, 2007

DBQ DOCUMENT-BASED QUESTIONS

1. **Identifying** List two arguments that support the use of the jury system. List two flaws of the jury system.

2. **Explaining** How do the innovations listed in Source E address the flaws in the jury system you listed in the previous question?

3. **Evaluating** What conflicts do you see between the views of Professor Jonakait and Professor Dorf?

4. **Synthesizing** What innovation or jury reform—either one from Source E or one you think of yourself—do you think would be most important in helping the jury system function as John Adams believed it should?

5. **Making Connections** If you were falsely accused of a crime, would you want a jury trial or a bench trial (one in which a judge renders the verdict)? If you were found guilty, would you want to be sentenced by a jury or only a judge? Explain your thinking.

WHAT WILL YOU DO?

If you are picked to serve on a jury, how could you be sure that you were doing a good job?

EXPLORE the interactive version of the analyzing primary sources feature on Networks.

Interact with these digital
assets and others in lesson 1

✓ **EXPLORING THE ESSENTIAL QUESTION**
  Judicial Independence

✓ **INTERACTIVE IMAGE**
  Early Systems of Law

✓ **SELF-CHECK QUIZ**

✓ **VIDEO**
  The 12 Tables of Rome

netw⊙rks
TRY IT YOURSELF ONLINE

Reading Help Desk

Academic Vocabulary

- interpretation
- entity
- clarify

Content Vocabulary

- law
- judicial review
- unconstitutional
- impartial

TAKING NOTES:

Integration of Knowledge and Ideas

CONSIDERING ADVANTAGES AND DISADVANTAGES Use the graphic organizer to record the pros and cons of the two systems of selecting judges.

	PROS	CONS
Appointing Judges		
Electing Judges		

LESSON 1
The Judicial System in Our Democracy

ESSENTIAL QUESTION

What is the role of the judicial system in our democracy?

The city of Beautifica has established a lovely park in the city. The park is a place where people can find grass, trees, flowers, and quiet. In addition, there are playgrounds and picnic areas. A road runs through the park. Now the road is closed. The city legislators passed a law saying that no vehicles are allowed in the park. The city legislators wish to preserve some elements of nature undisturbed.

The law—"No Vehicles in the Park"—seems clear, but some disputes have arisen over its meaning as police begin to enforce the law. Interpret the law in the following situations, keeping in mind what the law says as well as what the lawmakers intended. Examine each situation and decide whether you will uphold the ticket that each person received for having a vehicle in the park. Explain the reasons for your choices.

a. Tony lives on one side of the city and works on the other. He drove through the park to save 10 minutes and received a ticket.

b. To keep the park clean, trash barrels are located throughout the area. The sanitation department drove a truck into the park to collect the trash from the barrels and received a ticket.

c. Juanita decides to ride her bicycle through the park. She is given a ticket.

d. Amul visited the park. He received a ticket while rolling along in his wheelchair.

e. An ambulance drove through the park on the way to the hospital with a dying patient. The shortest route was through the park. The ambulance driver received a ticket.

f. Elena took her baby to the park in a stroller and received a ticket while pushing the stroller along the path.

Early Systems of Law

GUIDING QUESTION *What are early systems of law and how did they influence the American system of law?*

Law is the set of rules and standards by which a society governs itself. In democratic societies, law resolves conflict between and among individuals and groups and protects individuals against government power. It defines criminal acts and determines the punishments for them. These are only some of its many functions.

The earliest known written laws or rules were based on practices in tribal societies. The most well known is the Code of Hammurabi, laws collected by Hammurabi, king of Babylonia from 1792 to 1750 B.C. The code categorized crimes and provided 282 examples and their punishments. Today we would refer to these categories as criminal law, property law, and family law, to name a few examples.

The Ten Commandments were one of the sources of law for the ancient Israelites. According to the Hebrew Bible, Moses received these commandments from God on Mount Sinai. The Ten Commandments' emphasis on social justice and individual and communal responsibility have become a model for ethical laws.

Roman law is another early source of law. Ancient Romans made their laws by writing them down. The government published the Twelve Tables (for the tablets on which they were written) in about 450 B.C. The tables focused on different areas of law, such as family law or criminal law.

As the Roman Empire spread, laws were continuously added so that the body of law became very complex and difficult to follow. Emperor Justinian had scholars reorganize and simplify the laws into a final Roman legal code, the Justinian Code, which was completed in A.D. 534.

Perhaps the single most important basis of the American legal system is English common law, which originated in eleventh-century England. Common law is made by judges as they resolve individual cases. In the American colonies, English colonists used the common law they were familiar with. When they studied law, colonial lawyers also studied English sources, especially the important four-volume work by William Blackstone, *Commentaries on the Laws.*

law the set of rules and standards by which a society governs itself

interpretation explanation

This photograph shows a part of a wall frieze of the U.S. Supreme Court that depicts lawgivers throughout history. Both Moses and Hammurabi are pictured.

▼ **CRITICAL THINKING**
Identifying What laws are associated with Moses?

✔ **READING PROGRESS CHECK**

Summarizing What areas of law were found in the Code of Hammurabi and the Twelve Tables?

Principles of Democracy in the Judiciary

GUIDING QUESTION *Which principles of democracy are integral to the judicial branch?*

According to our democratic principles, every person should have a free and equal opportunity to pursue individual goals and desires. So that one person's pursuit of happiness does not infringe upon another's, we have agreed upon certain guidelines for our behavior. We do this by voting for elected representatives who then write our laws. Sometimes the meaning of a law passed by a legislature and enforced by the executive branch is unclear. When that happens, the judicial branch provides an **interpretation** of the law.

When individuals have conflict in spite of the laws, or when people deliberately choose to break laws, our courts provide a solution. The solution might be determining right and wrong, or guilt and innocence.

Steve Petteway, Collection of the Supreme Court of the United States

GOVERNMENT *in your* COMMUNITY

Police Accountability

One aspect of the rule of law is that everyone must obey the law and be held accountable if they violate it. Sometimes, police officers are accused of breaking the law. These are two ways to promote police accountability and make sure that even law enforcement officers are obeying the law:

- Internal Affairs Units allow the police to investigate misconduct within the department.

- Civilian Review Boards are independent outside groups that investigate police conduct.

CRITICAL THINKING

Researching Contact your local law enforcement agencies to determine whether your community uses Internal Affairs Units or Civilian Review Boards to investigate alleged police misconduct. If your community uses Internal Affairs units, interview law enforcement personnel in that department to learn more. If your community uses Civilian Review Boards, learn how citizens can participate in that process.

A court might direct one person to pay money to make up for harming someone else, or even pay a fine or serve time in a jail or prison as punishment for breaking the law.

The court system—the judicial branch of government—helps people resolve conflicts without resorting to violence. It is extremely important that people have confidence in all aspects of the court system—from selection of judges to the process for deciding cases—so that its decisions will be trusted, respected, and obeyed.

Courts also determine what the laws mean. As you can see from the activity at the beginning of this lesson, even a law as simple as "No Vehicles in the Park" might need to be interpreted.

Rule of Law A central purpose of the courts is to promote the rule of law. The idea behind the rule of law is that no individual, group, organization, or governmental **entity** is above the law. Everyone must obey the law and be held accountable if they violate it. Laws must be clear and known to all. Laws must be equally, fairly, and consistently enforced.

entity something that has separate and distinct existence

Controls on the Abuse of Power The judicial branch plays an important role in our system of checks and balances. The judiciary may limit the executive and legislative branches through its ability to declare laws and government actions unconstitutional. **Judicial review** is the power of courts to say that laws and actions of local, state, or national governments are invalid because they conflict with the Constitution. If a court declares a law **unconstitutional**, then the law cannot be enforced. Judicial review also gives courts the power to declare an action of the executive or legislative branch to be unconstitutional. For example, courts can rule that law enforcement officers acted unconstitutionally if they violated an individual's rights during an investigation or arrest.

judicial review the power of the Supreme Court to declare laws and actions of local, state, or national governments unconstitutional

unconstitutional not consistent with a nation's constitution

The power of the judicial branch, on the other hand, is checked by the legislative and executive branches. The executive branches of government enforce the decisions of the courts. The president appoints federal judges with the advice and consent of the Senate. The state and federal legislative branches have the power to create some courts, set judges' salaries, and change laws to **clarify** their meanings.

clarify to make clear

The power of the judiciary is further limited by the rules of our legal system. According to the Constitution, courts can only decide issues that are brought to them in the form of cases. A judge cannot decide that someone has violated the law and sentence them, for example, unless the individual is first arrested and prosecuted for a crime. Federal courts are also prevented from giving "advisory" opinions. This means that the executive or legislative branch cannot ask a federal court for advice on whether or not a certain law would be constitutional if it were to be passed. Courts are also limited in the types of cases they can hear.

✓ READING PROGRESS CHECK

Determining Importance Why is it crucial that people have confidence in the U.S. court system?

Judicial Independence

GUIDING QUESTION *Why is an independent judiciary a key element of a democracy?*

A key element of a democracy is that courts must act **impartially** and make fair decisions without undue influence by outside forces. The fair selection of judges, fair procedures, the power of judicial review, and the benefit of an executive branch that will enforce court orders all contribute to judicial independence.

impartial unbiased

In the federal court system, and in a few states, judges are appointed for life terms. People who favor life terms believe that this system allows judges to make decisions without being concerned about how it might affect their chances for reelection. In most states, however, judges are either elected or initially appointed and then must face voters from time to time in retention elections. Some believe that the need to raise funds for elections can result in a judge being biased, especially when deciding cases related to campaign donors' interests. Others believe that a system of electing judges ensures accountability to citizens and is appropriate in a democracy. Many people disagree about whether judicial election or appointment is more likely to prevent corruption in the judiciary.

✓ READING PROGRESS CHECK

Comparing Advantages and Disadvantages What are the arguments for and against appointing judges to life terms?

LESSON 1 REVIEW

Reviewing Vocabulary

1. ***Explaining*** Why is the power of judicial review key to the system of checks and balances?

Using Your Graphic Organizer

2. ***Defending*** Using your completed graphic organizer, write a brief essay arguing for either the election or appointment of judges. Which do you think is least likely to lead to corruption?

Answering the Guiding Questions

3. ***Understanding Historical Interpretation*** What are early systems of law and how did they influence the American system of law?

4. ***Analyzing*** Which principles of democracy are integral to the judicial branch?

5. ***Determining Importance*** Why is an independent judiciary a key element of a democracy?

Writing About Government

6. ***Informative/Explanatory*** Choose a principle of democracy related to the judiciary. Find examples of that principle in current events and explain how they demonstrate that principle.

LESSON 2
Trials

Interact with these digital assets and others in lesson 2

✓ **INTERACTIVE CHART**
Comparing Trial Systems

✓ **SELF-CHECK QUIZ**

✓ **STUDENT VOICES**
You Can Be a Juror

✓ **VIDEO**
Jurors for Enron Case

netw⊙rks
TRY IT YOURSELF ONLINE

ReadingHelp Desk

Academic Vocabulary

- obvious
- sufficient

Content Vocabulary

- criminal trial court
- civil trial court
- original jurisdiction
- adversarial system
- inquisitorial system
- plaintiff
- prosecutor
- defendant
- jury
- public defender
- plea bargain
- grand jury
- indictment

TAKING NOTES:

Integration of Knowledge and Ideas

COMPARING Use the Venn diagram to compare and contrast criminal and civil trial courts.

Civil Trial   Criminal
Courts   Trial Courts

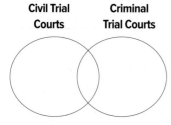

ESSENTIAL QUESTION

What are the purposes of trials and appeals in our court systems?

Imagine that a student in your class just had his phone stolen. He accuses another student in the class of stealing the phone. The accused student claims that she did not take the phone. Review the following options for resolving this conflict:

a. The principal of the school will listen to both students' stories and decide who is telling the truth.

b. The police will be called and require everyone in the class to (publicly) empty their purses, backpacks, and pockets.

c. The teacher will decide who is telling the truth based on her own experiences with how cooperative the accuser and accused have been in class this semester.

d. All of the students in your class will take a vote right away on who they believe.

e. The two students will have a competition to decide who is telling the truth—the person who can run a mile the fastest will win.

f. Both the victim and the accused thief will get a lawyer to represent them. The lawyers will interview the class and gather evidence, and then present their evidence and the best reasons to support their case to a group of unbiased students from another class. That group will decide who is telling the truth.

Which option would you choose if you were the victim of the theft? Which option would you choose if you were the student who was accused of stealing the phone? Which option seems fairest to both sides? Does a trial seem necessary?

The Function of Trial Courts

GUIDING QUESTION *How do criminal and civil trial courts function?*

In theory, trial courts are the places where the truth comes out about whether someone has committed a crime or has caused some sort of damage to someone else's reputation, property, or body. **Criminal trial courts** can hear cases about crimes, like burglary, murder, or driving under the influence of alcohol or drugs. **Civil trial courts** hear cases where one person or group thinks another person or group should pay for causing harm. In both types of trial courts, judges or juries determine the facts of the case and then apply the relevant law to decide the outcome of the case. There are both federal trial courts (called U.S. district courts) and state trial courts (which go by many different names, depending on the state).

Jurisdiction Trial courts have **original jurisdiction** over criminal cases and civil disputes. This means that cases originate in trial courts—these courts are the first place where most cases are tried. Before a case can get to court, someone must be formally accused of a crime or of causing damage to another person in violation of civil law. A trial court cannot try a case where there is no harm or alleged violation of the law. For example, Betsy cannot sue Jake for causing a car accident unless she was actually harmed in some way by the car accident.

Adversarial and Inquisitorial Systems The trial system in the United States is an **adversarial system**. This means it is a contest between opposing sides, or adversaries. Lawyers argue their cases and present witnesses and evidence to support their claims. Judges and juries listen, but do not question the witnesses or gather their own evidence. The judge is impartial, serving as sort of a referee to ensure that the rules are followed. The adversarial process, however, is not the only method for handling legal disputes. Many countries have different trial systems. Some countries use the **inquisitorial system**, in which the judge plays a more active role in gathering and presenting evidence.

Supporters of the adversarial system believe it is the best way for the truth to come out. They claim that the judge or jury will be able to determine the truth if opposing parties present their best arguments and show the weaknesses of the other side's case. On the other hand, critics of the adversarial process say that it is not the best method for discovering the truth

criminal trial court hears cases about crimes like burglary, murder, or driving under the influence of alcohol or drugs

civil trial court hears cases where one person or group thinks another person or group should pay for causing harm

original jurisdiction the authority of a trial court to be the first to hear a case

COMPARING TRIAL SYSTEMS

Adversarial System	Inquisitorial System
A contest between opposing sides with each side trying to present the most persuasive argument	Seeks the truth through examining the evidence and investigation
The defense and the prosecutor and police conduct investigations, argue their case, and present witnesses and the evidence that benefits their argument.	The judge may supervise investigations and decide whether a case should proceed to trial. Evidence is made available in advance to both prosecution and defense.
Judges and juries listen but do not question the witnesses or gather evidence.	A judge questions the witnesses and may gather evidence.
A judge's role is to be impartial, like a referee, and ensure that due process and other rules and guidelines are observed.	The judge assumes the main role in conducting the trial.
Any criminal case may go to a jury trial.	Juries are only used in very serious cases.
Prejudicial evidence is not presented to juries.	More lenient rules on the admissibility of evidence
The accused is not required to answer questions.	A judge can require the accused to answer questions.

The adversarial and inquisitorial systems both have the same goal—determining truth—but the pathway to justice can look different. The differences are greatest in criminal cases.

◄ CRITICAL THINKING
Comparing and Contrasting
Compare and contrast the adversarial system and the inquisitiorial system. Which system seems fairer to you? Why?

adversarial system a trial system that is a contest between opposing sides

inquisitorial system a trial system where the judge plays an active role in gathering evidence

about what happened and who is at fault. They compare the adversarial process to a battle in which lawyers act as enemies, making every effort not to present all of the evidence. According to this view, the goal of trial is "victory, not truth or justice."

✓ **READING PROGRESS CHECK**

Comparing Advantages and Disadvantages What are the advantages and disadvantages of the U.S. trial system?

The Trial Process

GUIDING QUESTION *How do trial courts resolve conflict?*

Trial courts listen to testimony, consider evidence, and decide the facts in disputed situations. To make sure that the process is fair, certain legal principles govern the way the two sides present their evidence and how the judge or jury considers that evidence and makes a decision. For example, in a criminal case, the judge or jury must be convinced beyond a reasonable doubt that a crime occurred and that the accused person committed the crime.

Roles in a Trial In a trial there are two parties, or sides, to each case. In a civil trial, the party accusing someone of causing damage is called the **plaintiff**. In a criminal trial, the government, rather than the victim of the crime, initiates the case and serves as the **prosecutor**. In both civil and criminal trials, the party responding to the plaintiff (for civil trials) or prosecution (for criminal trials) is called the **defendant**.

plaintiff in a civil trial, the person who brings suit in court

prosecutor an attorney who represents the government in a criminal case

defendant the person against whom a civil or criminal suit is brought in court

jury a group of citizens who hear evidence during a trial and give a verdict

Judges and juries are essential parts of our legal system. The judge presides over the trial, protecting the rights of those involved. Judges also make sure that attorneys follow the rules of evidence and trial procedure. In trials without juries, the judge determines the facts of the case and reaches a verdict or decision. A **jury** is a group of citizens who are sworn to give a verdict based on evidence presented to them in a court. In jury trials, the judge instructs the jury as to the law involved in the case and the jury renders a judgment. Finally, in criminal trials in most states, judges sentence individuals convicted of committing crimes.

Each party in a case may have attorneys, who represent the plaintiff and defendant. They collect all of the evidence that supports their side of the case and decide how to present the evidence at the trial. In criminal cases, the prosecutor is an attorney who works for the government. Defense attorneys represent civil and criminal defendants. The Sixth Amendment to the U.S. Constitution guarantees the defendant the right to have "assistance of counsel."

GOVERNMENT *in your* COMMUNITY

Juries

Choose one of the following activities to learn about juries in your community:

a. Attend a criminal or civil trial in which a jury is used and write a description of what you observe about jurors during the trial.

b. Research how jurors are chosen in your community. Be sure to explain whether potential jurors where you live are identified by drivers' license lists or voter registration lists, whether jurors are paid for their service, and whether child care is provided. Write a public service announcement about the process.

STEPS IN A TRIAL

Step 1	Opening Statement by Plaintiff or Prosecutor	The plaintiff's attorney (in civil cases) or the prosecutor (in criminal cases) explains to the trier of fact (the judge or jury) the evidence to be presented as proof of the allegations (unproven statements) in the written papers filed with the court.
Step 2	Opening Statement by Defense	The defendant's attorney explains evidence to be presented to disprove the allegations made by the plaintiff or prosecutor.
Step 3	Direct Examination by Plaintiff or Prosecutor	Each witness for the plaintiff or prosecution is questioned. Other evidence in favor of the plaintiff or prosecution is presented.
Step 4	Cross-Examination by Defense	The defense has the opportunity to question each witness. Questioning is designed to break down the story or to discredit the witness.
Step 5	Motions	If the prosecution's or plaintiff's basic case has not been established from the evidence introduced, the judge can end the case by granting a motion (oral request) made by the defendant's attorney.
Step 6	Direct Examination by Defense	Each defense witness is questioned.
Step 7	Cross-Examination by Plaintiff or Prosecutor	Each defense witness is cross-examined.
Step 8	Closing Statement by Plaintiff or Prosecutor	The prosecutor or plaintiff's attorney reviews all the evidence presented and asks for a finding of guilty (in criminal cases) or a finding for the plaintiff (in civil cases).
Step 9	Closing Statement by Defense	This is the same as the closing statement by the prosecution or plaintiff. The defense asks for a finding of not guilty (in criminal cases) or for finding for, or in favor of, the defendant (in civil cases).
Step 10	Rebuttal Arguments	The prosecutor or plaintiff may have the right to make additional closing arguments that respond to points made by the defense in its closing statement.
Step 11	Jury Instructions	The judge instructs the jury as to the law that applies in the case.
Step 12	Verdict	In most states, a unanimous decision by the jury is required for a verdict. If the jury cannot reach a unanimous decision, it is called a *hung jury*, and the case may be tried again by a new judge or a jury.

But what do those words mean? For example, does it simply mean that the defendant may have a lawyer if he or she can afford one? Does it mean that a defendant who wants to represent himself must instead hire a lawyer? Like many phrases in the Constitution, the precise meaning is not always **obvious**.

By the 1960s, the Supreme Court had already ruled that the federal government had to provide a free lawyer to defendants who could not afford one and were charged with a serious crime in federal court. In the case of *Gideon* v. *Wainwright* (1963), the Supreme Court ruled that states must do the same for those tried in state court. This decision was controversial because it was one of the early cases in which the Court imposed national rules on criminal trials in state courts. Some people believed this advanced the concept of equal justice, while others viewed this as a violation of the principle of federalism and states' rights.

Public defenders are attorneys who work for the state and defend people who cannot afford a private attorney. Some states have public defender systems, while other states have a system where the trial judge appoints a lawyer to represent an indigent defendant who cannot afford a lawyer.

obvious easily discovered, seen, or understood

public defender attorney who works for the state and defends people who cannot afford a private attorney

In these states, the appointed lawyer might not have as much experience as a public defender in handling criminal cases.

Witnesses are people with knowledge about the facts of the case. They provide evidence through sworn testimony during the trial—they take an oath promising to tell the truth. A witness can tell the court what he or she saw, heard, did, or experienced in relation to the incident in question.

Settling Cases Without a Trial Most legal cases never go to trial. Civil cases usually result in out-of-court settlements—agreements between the two parties about how to resolve the issue. Criminal cases rarely go to trial. Instead, a **plea bargain**, or pretrial agreement between the prosecutor and the defendant, disposes of the case without a trial. Typically, the defendant pleads guilty to a lesser crime (or fewer crimes) in return for the government not prosecuting the more serious crime with which the defendant was originally charged.

Supporters of plea bargains claim that they are efficient and save the state the cost of a trial in situations where the defendant's guilt is obvious, as well as those where the government's case is weak. Courts have a tremendous volume of cases to process every year, and plea bargains reduce their workload. Opponents argue that plea bargains allow some criminals to get off lightly, or that it encourages people to give up their rights to a fair trial.

plea bargain an agreement whereby a defendant pleads guilty to a lesser crime than the one with which a defendant was originally charged and in return the government agrees not to prosecute the defendant for the more serious crime

☑ **READING PROGRESS CHECK**

Summarizing What roles do different individuals play in a trial?

Juries

GUIDING QUESTION *Why are juries an important component of our legal system?*

Juries are an integral part of our democracy, and the right to a trial by jury in many cases is guaranteed by the Constitution. When private citizens serve on juries, they are able to participate in creating justice and overseeing the judicial branch of government. Juries serve to protect the rights of the parties and make it more likely that justice is impartial.

The Constitution

"In all criminal prosecutions, the accused shall enjoy the right to a speedy and public trial, by an impartial jury of the State and district wherein the crime shall have been committed, which district shall have been previously ascertained by law, and to be informed of the nature and cause of the accusation; to be confronted with the witnesses against him; to have compulsory process for obtaining witnesses in his favor, and to have the Assistance of Counsel for his defence."

—Amendment VI

"In Suits at common law, where the value in controversy shall exceed twenty dollars, the right of trial by jury shall be preserved, and no fact tried by a jury, shall be otherwise re-examined in any Court of the United States, than according to the rules of the common law."

—Amendment VII

DBQ *Comparing* In what ways are the Sixth Amendment and the Seventh Amendment similar?

You Can Be a Juror

There are opportunities for high school students to experience what it is like to sit on a jury. Many communities and some schools have teen courts where young people accused of minor crimes may have their sentences determined by peers instead of entering the official court system. These programs—sometimes called *peer courts* or *youth courts*—are often looking for volunteers. Torren Broussard-Boston has served on a youth court in Seattle, Washington, and has enjoyed "every aspect of it." To find out if there is a teen court in your community, go to: www.youthcourt.net.

In addition to teen courts, your high school may be located near a law school, where mock trials are conducted to help law students prepare for the practice of law. Bar associations (professional groups of lawyers) also have trial practice programs. These programs often need people to play the role of jurors. Contact your local law school or bar association to find out if you can participate.

"There isn't anything that I don't enjoy about Youth Court . . . I've learned about the legal system, I've learned how to better communicate with other students, and I've gained more self-confidence. I don't know if it has truly changed my ideas about justice, but I have a better grasp of the justice system."

—Torren Broussard-Boston

CRITICAL THINKING

Summarizing Write a paragraph summarizing what you learned about the youth courts and mock trials in your community. If you decided to participate in one, write your summary about your experience instead.

Juries also give people a voice in government, which makes trials more democratic. They promote a sense of fairness, since regular people determine whether or not a crime was committed or a law broken.

Some states and the federal government use a **grand jury** to determine whether or not the government can go forward with a serious criminal prosecution. A grand jury is a group of 16 to 23 people charged with determining whether there is **sufficient** cause to believe that a person has committed a crime and should stand trial. The Fifth Amendment to the U.S. Constitution requires that before anyone can be tried for a serious crime in federal court, there must be a grand jury **indictment**, or formal charge of criminal action. About half of the states also use grand juries. Historically, the grand jury was seen as a guardian of the rights of the innocent. Citizens serving on juries and grand juries play important roles in our democracy.

grand jury a group that hears charges against a suspect and decides whether there is sufficient evidence to bring the person to trial

sufficient enough to meet the needs of a situation or a proposed end

indictment a formal charge of criminal action by a grand jury

Right to a Jury The Sixth Amendment to the U.S. Constitution guarantees the right to trial by jury in criminal cases. This right applies in both federal and state courts. The Seventh Amendment guarantees a right to trial by jury in civil cases in federal courts. This right has not been extended to state courts, but many state constitutions provide a right to a jury trial in civil cases heard in their own courts.

The Constitution protects the right to trial by jury, but this does not mean that a jury is required in every case. Juries are not used as often as one might think. In civil cases, either the plaintiff or the defendant may request a jury trial. In criminal cases, the defendant decides whether the case will be heard by a jury or a judge.

Jury Service Serving on a jury is one of the most powerful actions that citizens take in a democracy. Juries represent people's opportunity to participate directly in government. Because juries are so central to our democracy, citizens have a civic duty to serve on juries when called upon. To serve on a jury, you must be a U.S. citizen, at least 18 years old, able to speak and understand English, and a resident of the state where the trial is taking place. In most states, convicted felons are ineligible for jury service. People who are not exempt and are called for jury duty are sometimes excused if they can show "undue hardship or extreme inconvenience."

Americans believe they have a right to a "jury of their peers." This right is not specifically mentioned in the Constitution, though it does say that people have the right to a jury that is impartial and from the state or district where the crime was allegedly committed. A "jury of your peers" does not mean that every juror in every case must be the same age as the defendant, be of the same gender or race, or have the same characteristics or life experiences. However, it does mean that the jury system as a whole should generally reflect the diversity of the community in which the trial is taking place.

When the jury system first began in the United States, only white men who owned property were allowed to serve. The Civil Rights Act of 1875, passed by Congress in the years after the Civil War, gave basic civil rights, including the right to participate on juries, to African Americans. But in the years that followed, the Supreme Court ruled inconsistently in interpreting this law, sometimes allowing defendants from minority groups to be tried before all-white juries. The legal battle over racial and gender exclusion in jury selection continued for decades.

In 1954 the U.S. Supreme Court heard a case in which Pedro Hernandez, a Mexican agricultural worker, had been convicted of murder. His legal team showed that no Mexican Americans had served on a trial jury in this county for more than 25 years. In other words, Mexican Americans had been systematically excluded from jury service. In *Hernandez* v. *Texas* (1954), the Court ruled unanimously in favor of Hernandez and required that he be retried with a jury that did not intentionally exclude Mexican Americans. In *Hernandez* and subsequent cases, the Court made it clear that eliminating a juror solely based on race, ethnicity, or gender in either a civil or criminal trial is unconstitutional.

✔ **READING PROGRESS CHECK**

Describing What are the qualifications for serving on a jury?

LESSON 2 REVIEW

Reviewing Vocabulary

1. *Contrasting* What is the difference between a jury and a grand jury?

Using Your Graphic Organizer

2. *Summarizing* Using your completed Venn diagram, create a multimedia presentation about criminal trial courts and civil trial courts.

Answering the Guiding Questions

3. *Discussing* How do criminal and civil trial courts function?

4. *Examining* How do trial courts resolve conflict?

5. *Determining Importance* Why are juries an important component of our legal system?

Writing About Government

6. *Narrative* What do you think are the most important qualities of an effective juror? These might be skills, values, experiences, or other qualities. Make a list, and then compare it to a classmate's list. Together, plan and write a description of your ideal juror. This person should be the kind of juror you would want if you or someone you care about had to face a jury in the future.

Interact with these digital assets and others in lesson 3

✓ **INTERACTIVE CHART**
How a Case Travels Through the Court System

✓ **INTERACTIVE IMAGE**
Following Precedents

✓ **SELF-CHECK QUIZ**

✓ **VIDEO**
Juvenile Offenders Appeal Their Sentences

netw⊙rks
TRY IT YOURSELF ONLINE

LESSON 3
Appeals

Reading Help Desk

Academic Vocabulary

- arbitrary
- circumstance

Content Vocabulary

- error of law
- procedural due process
- majority opinion
- dissenting opinion
- concurring opinion
- precedent
- stare decisis

TAKING NOTES:

Key Ideas and Details

SUMMARIZING Use the three-column table to summarize the information about appeals courts.

Types of cases that are appealed	Procedures at an appeals court	Precedent and stare decisis

ESSENTIAL QUESTION

What are the purposes of trials and appeals in our court systems?

James's neighbor Sally, who owned a large pasture full of horses, offered to pay James to catch and then sell the horses for her. While catching horses, James accidentally wandered into another pasture full of horses that were not owned by Sally. James caught and sold some of these horses, thinking that they belonged to Sally.

At trial, the jury did not believe that James had stolen the horses knowingly, but the judge told the jury that the crime of horse thievery required only that James took the horses without permission. The jury convicted James of horse theft. In fact, the horse theft law says that a person stealing horses has to take the horses knowing that they do not belong to him or her.

What do you think? Did James get a fair trial? Should James have the opportunity to appeal his conviction? What is the likelihood that his appeal would be heard or be successful in overturning his conviction?

Types of Cases That Are Appealed

GUIDING QUESTION *Which cases can be appealed, and to which courts?*

An individual who loses a case in a trial may wish to appeal that decision. In a criminal case, someone convicted can appeal the verdict or the sentence imposed; however, not every case can be appealed. Generally, a successful appeal is possible only when the losing party can claim that the trial court did not apply the law correctly or that the trial was not fair.

Errors of Law In our legal system, questions about the facts of a case are decided at trial. Trial judges and juries hear testimony, review evidence, and are in the best position to determine the credibility of the witnesses. For this reason, appellate courts seldom reconsider a trial court's determination of the facts; instead, appellate courts focus on deciding legal questions that arise in a trial.

The highest court in a state is usually referred to as the supreme court. Shown here is the Indiana Supreme Court in the state capitol.

▲ CRITICAL THINKING

Identifying Is the Indiana Supreme Court a federal or state court?

error of law a mistake by a judge as to the applicable law in a case

procedural due process the fair administration of justice

arbitrary existing or coming about seemingly at random or by chance

Appeals are possible when the losing party can claim that the trial court made an **error of law**. An error of law occurs when the judge makes a mistake about the law applicable in the case. For example, the judge at James's trial gave the wrong instruction to the jury. Another error of law might occur if a judge permits evidence to be shown to a jury that should not be allowed. A judge's error is considered minor as long as it does not affect the outcome of the trial; in these cases involving minor errors of law, the trial court decision will not be reversed. In James's case, however, the error of law did affect the outcome of the trial; consequently, he could appeal his case and should win.

Procedural Due Process The fair administration of justice is called **procedural due process**. Fair procedures help prevent **arbitrary**, unreasonable decisions. Due process also ensures that police, lawyers, judges, and jurors must follow the same basic procedures regardless of the specific defendant. The U.S. Constitution provides several guarantees to ensure that trials are fair. If a constitutional guarantee is violated, the case can be appealed. According to the U.S. Constitution, defendants in criminal cases have several procedural due process rights. Many of these rights are included in the Fourth, Fifth, Sixth, and Eighth Amendments of the U.S. Bill of Rights. These due process rights include the right to be notified of charges against oneself, the right to a speedy trial, the right to an impartial jury of one's peers, the right to confront witnesses, the right not to be tried for the same crime twice (known as double jeopardy), and the right to be free from self-incrimination, among others.

✓ READING PROGRESS CHECK

Explaining What is procedural due process and how is it guaranteed in the Constitution?

HOW A CASE TRAVELS THROUGH THE COURT SYSTEM

Supreme Courts

Have **appellate** jurisdiction. In rare cases, the U.S. Supreme Court and states' highest courts have original jurisdiction.
They review claims that a lower court did not interpret the law correctly.

↑

Appeals Courts

Have **appellate** jurisdiction.
They review claims that an error of law was made at trial.

↑

Trial Courts

Have **original** jurisdiction. Some states have several types of trial courts.
They hear evidence and determine guilt in criminal cases or liability in civil cases.

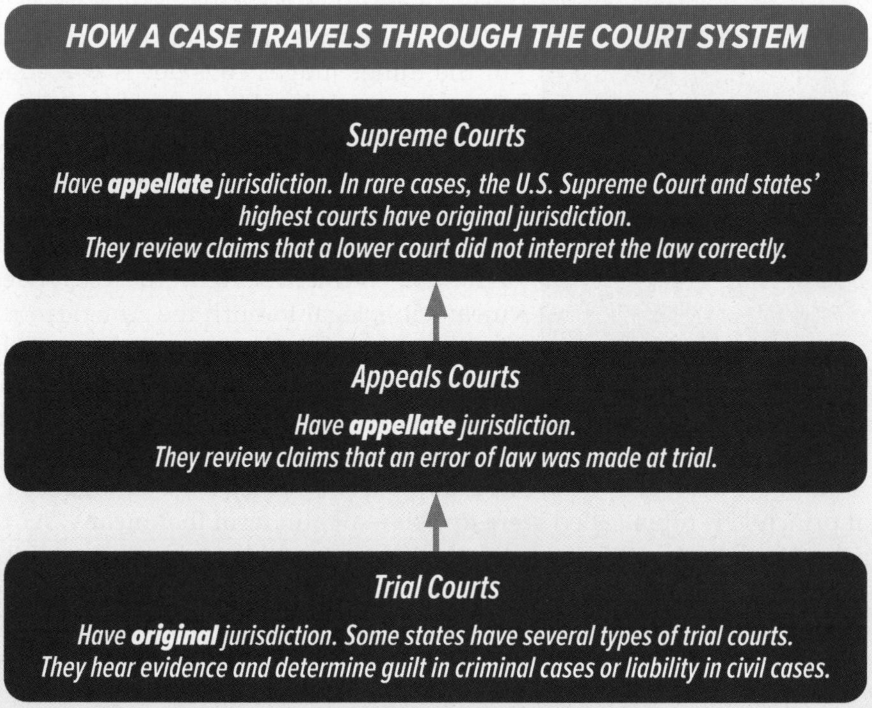

This chart shows the general progression of cases through trial, appeals, and supreme courts. Note that each state has its own particular system.

◀ CRITICAL THINKING
Creating Visuals Search the Internet for your state supreme court's website. At this site, you will be able to find out how your state court system is organized. Then, using this chart as a general guide, draw a chart to show the hierarchy of courts in your state. Which ones have original jurisdiction and which have appellate jurisdiction?

Procedures at an Appeals Court

GUIDING QUESTION *How are cases appealed?*

In an appeals court, one party presents arguments asking the court to review the decision of the trial court; the other party presents arguments supporting the decision of the trial court and the procedures it followed. There are no juries or witnesses in an appeals court, and no new evidence is presented. Only lawyers appear before the judges to make legal arguments about the validity of decisions made by the trial court.

Typically, a panel of judges—or justices, as appellate judges are sometimes called—decide appeals. The panel may consist of three or more judges. A court of appeals may decide an appeal in one of three ways: it may uphold the trial court's decision, it could reverse the trial court's decision, or it could send the case back to the lower court to be tried again. When appeals courts decide a case, they usually issue a written opinion explaining their ruling.

If the judges on a panel disagree about a decision, two or more written opinions may be issued in the same case. The **majority opinion** states the decision of the court. Judges who disagree with the majority opinion may issue a separate document called a **dissenting opinion**, which states the reasons for the disagreement. In some instances, judges who agree with the majority's outcome, but for reasons different from those used to support the majority opinion, may write a **concurring opinion**.

Unless appealed to the highest court in the state, or to the U.S. Supreme Court, decisions of an appeals court are final.

☑ READING PROGRESS CHECK

Making Connections How are procedures at appeals courts different from those at trial courts?

majority opinion states the decision of the court

dissenting opinion a document issued by judges who disagree with the majority opinion

concurring opinion a document issued by judges who agree with the majority opinion, but for different reasons than those used to support the majority opinion

This court of common pleas must follow precedents established by higher state courts including courts of appeals and the state supreme court.

▲ CRITICAL THINKING

Defining Does a court of common pleas have original or appellate jurisdiction? Explain your answer.

precedent a legal principle created by an appellate court decision that lower court judges must follow when deciding similar cases

circumstance a modifying or influencing factor

stare decisis a Latin term meaning "let the decision stand"; refers to the principle that courts should follow precedent

Precedent and Stare Decisis

GUIDING QUESTION *Why do courts follow precedent?*

When an appeals court decides a case, one of the things judges consider is **precedent**. Precedents are legal principles created by an appellate court decision that lower court judges must follow when deciding similar cases. For example, the U.S. Supreme Court decided in *Texas* v. *Johnson* (1989) that the First Amendment's right to free speech means it is legal to burn the American flag as part of a political protest. Because of this ruling, lower courts throughout the land must rule that laws prohibiting flag burning in similar **circumstances** are not allowed.

Following precedent is an important part of our legal system. This basic legal principle is often called **stare decisis**—a Latin term that means "let the decision stand." Stare decisis makes the law predictable and leads to stability in our society. People know what the law means and that it will not change every time a court decides a new case.

Precedents apply to all the courts below the court that rules in the case. For example, when a state supreme court creates a precedent, all the lower courts in that state must follow that precedent. When a federal court of appeals creates a precedent, all the federal trial courts in that circuit must follow the precedent. However, that precedent is not binding on federal trial courts in a different circuit. By contrast, when the U.S. Supreme Court creates a precedent, all lower courts throughout the land must follow it.

Appellate courts have the power to overrule one of their earlier precedents, but this does not happen often. From time to time, courts overrule precedents because the law must have some degree of flexibility and be able to adapt to changing times and circumstances. Sometimes judges change their minds about legal issues over time, and sometimes new judges are elected or appointed who bring different legal views.

✓ **READING PROGRESS CHECK**

Applying If a state supreme court creates a precedent, must federal trial courts follow it? Explain.

LESSON 3 REVIEW

Reviewing Vocabulary
1. ***Defining*** What are the differences among a majority opinion, a dissenting opinion, and a concurring opinion?

Using Your Graphic Organizer
2. ***Outlining*** Using your completed graphic organizer, create an outline about appeals courts.

Answering the Guiding Questions
3. ***Classifying*** Which cases can be appealed, and to which courts?

4. ***Explaining*** How are cases appealed?
5. ***Finding the Main Idea*** Why do courts follow precedent?

Writing About Government
6. ***Argument*** Write an essay either supporting or criticizing the appeals system. Explain whether you do or do not believe due process is a fair administration of justice. Use facts from the lesson to support your argument.

Morse V *Frederick* (2007)

FACTS OF THE CASE A group of high school students were watching the Olympic torch being carried through their town from a street near their school. One student held up a sign referencing illegal drugs, and the principal took the sign away and suspended him. The student said that the sign did not mean anything—he just wanted to get on TV. After he was punished, he filed a lawsuit in federal court, accusing the school of violating his right to free speech.

ISSUE

Does the First Amendment allow public schools to prohibit students from displaying messages promoting the use of illegal drugs at school-supervised events?

ARGUMENTS

Arguments in a Supreme Court case are often based on precedents—previous cases the Court has decided about similar issues. Both sides argue that a particular precedent does or does not apply to the present case. The Supreme Court of the United States has ruled in three earlier cases about free speech at schools:

1. ***Tinker* v. *Des Moines* (1969)** In this case, two students wore black armbands to their public school to protest the Vietnam War and were punished for doing so. The Supreme Court ruled that students in public schools have a right to free speech, as long as that speech does not substantially disrupt the school's work or interfere with the rights of others.

2. ***Bethel School District* v. *Fraser* (1986)** In this case, a student made a speech to an assembly endorsing a candidate for a student government position. In the speech, the student used lewd, suggestive language. The Supreme Court ruled that schools can restrict students' speech if it is lewd, indecent, or plainly offensive. Schools have an interest in preventing speech that is inconsistent with their "basic educational mission."

3. ***Hazelwood School District et. al.* v. *Kuhlmeier* (1988)** In this case, a principal prevented students from publishing some stories in their school newspaper that he felt dealt with inappropriate themes. The Supreme Court ruled that schools could restrict students' speech when that speech is part of a school-sponsored activity and could be reasonably interpreted to represent the school's opinion on an issue.

EXPLORING THE ESSENTIAL QUESTION

Analyzing Take on the role of a Supreme Court justice to determine whether these precedents apply to the case of *Morse* v. *Frederick*. For each precedent listed, answer these questions:

  a. How is this precedent similar to the current case?
  b. How is this precedent different from the current case?
  c. In your opinion, does this precedent apply to the current case?

After analyzing the possible precedents, determine how the case should be decided and explain your reasons.

YOU BE the JUDGE

Interact with these digital
assets and others in lesson 4

✓ **INTERACTIVE CHART**
Jurisdiction of State and
Federal Courts

✓ **INTERACTIVE MAP**
The Federal Judicial Circuits

✓ **SELF-CHECK QUIZ**

✓ **VIDEO**
State and Local Court Systems

netw⊙rks
TRY IT YOURSELF ONLINE

LESSON 4
Local, State, and Federal Courts

ReadingHelp Desk

Academic Vocabulary

- retention
- expertise

Content Vocabulary

- statute
- general jurisdiction
- limited jurisdiction
- regional circuit
- court-martial
- reservation
- tribal courts

TAKING NOTES:

Key Ideas and Details

LISTING Use the graphic
organizer to list the types of courts
and the kinds of cases they can hear.

Type of Court	Kinds of Cases

ESSENTIAL QUESTION

How are federal, state, and local courts organized?

Imagine you are considering a career in law. You know it would be helpful to see lawyers, judges, court reporters, bailiffs, and others in action, so you decide to observe a court in session. But you do not want to see just any kind of trial. You want to observe a specific type of case. Look at each of the types of cases below and determine whether you are most likely to see them in a state court, a federal court, or either court.

   a. An adoption hearing

   b. A case involving someone accused with tampering with U.S. mail

   c. A lawsuit involving an amusement park ride that broke

   d. A trial about murder that may have been motivated by hatred toward a specific group

   e. A case in which a foreign government is accused of hacking into the computers of a major U.S. bank

Jurisdiction

GUIDING QUESTION *Which courts hear which cases?*

Most people think of discrete political units when they think of the word *jurisdiction*. For example, the cities of Minneapolis and St. Paul are located next to each other but are separate jurisdictions. However, in the context of courts, the word *jurisdiction* is best understood as meaning "power," as in the power or authority of the court to decide a case. Each court system has jurisdiction to decide certain kinds of cases.

The United States has many courts. Each state and the District of Columbia has a court system; there is a federal court system, military courts, as well as tribal justice systems. Each state and federal court system has a trial court (and in some cases multiple trial courts) as well as an appeals court. Cases must start in trial courts with original jurisdiction. Decisions in trial courts can be appealed to courts with appellate jurisdiction, which include courts of appeals and supreme courts.

(l to r) ©iStockphoto.com/Chmiel; ©Brand X Pictures/
PunchStock; BBC Worldwide Learning

The federal courts are considered to be courts of limited jurisdiction, just as the federal government is a government of limited, enumerated powers. Federal courts can generally hear cases that raise questions about a federal law (called a **statute**) or the federal constitution. Federal courts can also hear certain state law disputes when the litigants are from different states.

State courts are considered to be courts of general jurisdiction, able to hear a wide variety of cases that deal with state or local law, the state constitution, or federal law or the federal constitution. There are a few types of federal cases—primarily bankruptcy and maritime—that can only be heard in federal court.

✓ **READING PROGRESS CHECK**

Discussing How are federal courts limited in their jurisdiction?

State and Local Courts

GUIDING QUESTION *How do state and local courts operate?*

State and local courts interpret and apply state and local laws. State courts decide most cases involving state law, which include most criminal, family, contract, and juvenile law cases. Local courts are part of their state court system and decide cases involving local laws, like those concerning littering or parking violations. Cases involving many—but not all—federal laws can also be tried in the state court system.

Jurisdiction Each state has its own court system and most of the legal cases in the United States are resolved in state courts. State courts can hear a wide variety of cases involving state and local laws, the state or federal constitution, and some federal laws. This makes them courts of **general jurisdiction**. State court systems handle about 103 million cases per year. In 2010 about 55 percent of the cases involved traffic offenses and about 20 percent involved criminal offenses. The rest were civil cases.

State Trial and Appeals Courts State court systems vary in their structure but generally have three types of courts: minor courts, general trial courts, and appeals courts. The names of these courts often vary.

Minor courts are often called justice courts, municipal courts, magistrate courts, or inferior trial courts. They are often specialized to deal with specific types of legal issues. For example, family courts deal only with issues of family law, like divorce, adoption, or custody. Traffic courts hear driving violations. Cases involving juveniles are usually heard in a special juvenile court.

Small claims courts hear lawsuits involving small amounts of money. Probate courts handle cases involving wills and claims against estates of persons who die with or without a will.

General trial courts go by different names in different states. These include superior court, county court, district court, or the court of common pleas. General trial courts can hear a wide range of cases—civil or criminal.

Imagine you have lost your case at a general trial court. You may be able to appeal to an intermediate court of appeals or, in some states, directly to your state's highest court. These appeals courts go by different names in different states, including supreme court, court of appeals, or supreme judicial court.

Judges There are about 30,000 state court judges in the United States. These judges are selected in four different ways: popular election, election by the legislature, appointment by the governor, or by a combination of appointment and popular election. In most states, judges are elected. In all states, judges serve a limited term, though they may be reelected or reappointed when their term expires.

statute a federal law; a law written by a legislative branch

general jurisdiction courts that are able to hear a wide variety of cases that deal with state or local law, the state constitution, or federal law or the federal constitution

GOVERNMENT *in your* COMMUNITY

Learn About Your State and Local Courts

The National Center for State Courts has information about and links to the court system in every state. Visit their website, www.ncsc.org, and learn as much as you can about the courts in your community. Then answer the following questions.

EXPLORING THE ESSENTIAL QUESTION

1. **Identifying** What courts exist in your community and state? What kinds of cases do they handle?

2. **Locating** Which court is closest to your home or school?

3. **Explaining** What is the process for visiting a local court or observing a trial?

4. **Specifying** What is the highest court in your state? (It is sometimes called the court of last resort.) Where is it located?

The U.S. judiciary consists of parallel systems of federal and state courts. Because state court systems differ, the chart shows a general representation of a state court system.

▶ **CRITICAL THINKING**
Comparing and Contrasting How are the federal court system and state court system similar? How are they different?

retention the act of continuing to hold or have, as in a political position

limited jurisdiction courts that generally hear cases that raise questions about a federal law or the federal constitution

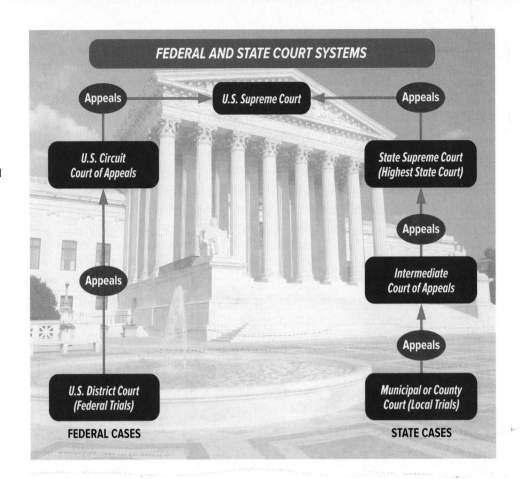

FEDERAL AND STATE COURT SYSTEMS

Appeals → U.S. Supreme Court ← Appeals

U.S. Circuit Court of Appeals

State Supreme Court (Highest State Court)

Appeals

Appeals

Intermediate Court of Appeals

Appeals

U.S. District Court (Federal Trials)

Municipal or County Court (Local Trials)

FEDERAL CASES

STATE CASES

The **Constitution**

"The judicial Power of the United States, shall be vested in one supreme Court, and in such inferior courts as the Congress may from time to time ordain and establish. The judges, both of the supreme and inferior Courts, shall hold their Offices during good Behaviour, and shall, at stated Times, received for their Services, a Compensation, which shall not be diminished during their Continuance in Office."

—Article III, Section 1

DBQ ***Paraphrasing*** Explain Article III, Section 1, in your own words.

People disagree over the best method for selecting judges. Those who favor popular election believe that it is important in a democracy for people to be able to choose their judges directly. They believe it ensures accountability. By contrast, others believe that the need to raise funds for elections can result in a judge's being biased when deciding a particular case.

Some states choose judges in a method known as *merit selection*. Using this approach, a judicial commission made up of lawyers, judges, and sometimes laypeople either decides who will be a judge or sends names of judicial candidates to the governor, who then chooses judges from the list. Some states also have a blended system in which judges are initially appointed and then stand for **retention** in periodic elections.

☑ **READING PROGRESS CHECK**

Explaining In state court systems, what are the differences among minor courts, general trial courts, and appeals courts?

Federal Courts

GUIDING QUESTION *How is the federal court system structured?*

Article III of the U.S. Constitution sets out the basic structure of the federal court system. The Constitution creates a Supreme Court and gives Congress the power to create lower courts. These courts include the federal district courts, the federal courts of appeals, and the United States Court of International Trade.

Jurisdiction The federal courts are considered to be courts of **limited jurisdiction**, just as the federal government is a government of limited, enumerated powers. Federal courts can generally hear cases that raise questions about a federal law or the federal constitution.

In addition, federal courts can sometimes decide cases that deal with state law if the parties to the case are from different states and a large amount of money is in question. Assume, for example, that Jack from Indiana is seriously hurt in a car accident with Jill from Ohio while driving through Ohio. It makes sense that Ohio motor vehicle laws apply to a lawsuit about a serious car accident that happens in Ohio. But Jack might fear that Ohio state courts would favor their resident, Jill. So the federal court in Ohio can decide this case, providing a more neutral forum, applying Ohio law.

Overall, federal courts handle more than 375,000 cases per year; this figure does not include the more than 1 million bankruptcy petitions federal courts handle annually.

Federal Trials and Appeals Courts Congress has divided the United States into 94 federal judicial districts, with a trial court known as a federal district court in each district. These federal trial courts handle both criminal and civil cases.

There are also federal bankruptcy and tax courts that handle only certain kinds of cases. Some federal judicial districts cover an entire state, while other states have several districts within its boundaries.

The trial courts are grouped into 12 **regional circuits**, each of which has a federal court of appeals, also called a U.S. Circuit Court. Court of appeals judges handle appeals of trial court decisions from within their circuits to determine whether district court judges applied the law correctly. There is also a special Court of Appeals for the Federal Circuit that hears only appeals dealing with specific legal topics, primarily international trade, patent law, money claims against the federal government, and veterans' issues.

regional circuit the divisions under the United States Federal Courts system, grouped into 12 regional circuits, each of which has a federal court of appeals, also called a U.S. Circuit Court

Congress created district courts to serve as trial courts for federal cases.

▼ CRITICAL THINKING
1. Applying Which federal judicial circuit hears cases from the state where you live? How many district courts are in the state where you live?
2. Analyzing Maps Which federal judicial circuit covers the greatest land area?

MAP

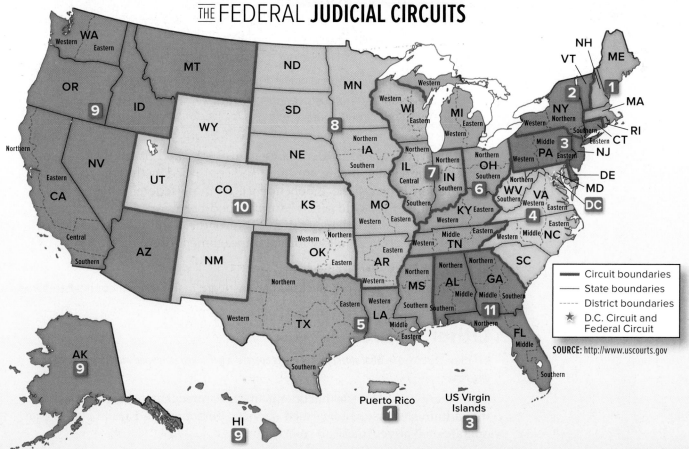

THE FEDERAL JUDICIAL CIRCUITS

Circuit boundaries
State boundaries
District boundaries
★ D.C. Circuit and Federal Circuit

SOURCE: http://www.uscourts.gov

CHART

JURISDICTION OF STATE AND FEDERAL COURTS

▶ CRITICAL THINKING

Classifying Review the chart. Then write three short case scenarios. Describe one example of a case that will be heard in state court, one that will be heard in federal court, and one that could be heard in either court. After you draft your case scenarios, explain why each would be heard in the court system you assigned it to.

Jurisdiction of State Courts	Jurisdiction of Federal Courts	Concurrent Jurisdiction

• Crimes under state laws
• State constitutional issues
• Cases involving state laws and regulations, including:
  ○ Family law
  ○ Probate and inheritance
  ○ Contract disputes
  ○ Personal injury
  ○ Property
  ○ Most traffic violations and registration of motor vehicles
• Most cases involving federal law
	• Federal crimes
	• Issues involving federal law, including the U.S. Constitution
	• Disputes between states
	• Treaties with foreign nations
	• Bankruptcy
	• Admiralty and maritime
	• Antitrust
	• Securities and banking regulation
	• Foreign diplomats or foreign governments
		• Crimes punishable under both federal and state law
		• Issues involving the U.S. Constitution
		• Certain civil rights claims
		• Environmental regulations
		• Certain civil disputes involving federal law

expertise special skill or knowledge in a particular field

Appeals come to this court from all over the country. These issues are dealt with in a special court because they are complex, and Congress believed that the Federal Circuit judges would develop special **expertise** in these complex cases.

EXPLORING THE ESSENTIAL QUESTION

Researching Visit the U.S. Supreme Court's website at www.supremecourt.gov.

- What information is available at that site?
- What is happening this week at the Court?

Locating Visit the website maintained by the federal courts at www.uscourts.gov.

- Where is your federal district court located?
- Where is your circuit court of appeals located?

Judges There are 852 federal judges in the United States. Federal court judges are appointed by the president and confirmed by the Senate. The U.S. Constitution protects the independence of these federal court judges by providing that they hold office "during good behavior." For the most part, federal judges serve until they resign, retire, or die. Removal of federal judges requires that Congress follow formal impeachment procedures.

✓ READING PROGRESS CHECK

Differentiating What types of cases can be heard in the federal court system?

Other Courts

GUIDING QUESTION *What other types of courts operate in the United States and what types of cases do they hear?*

Two other types of courts that operate in the United States are military courts that administer justice for armed services personnel and tribal courts that operate on Native American reservations.

Military Courts Article I, Section 8, of the U.S. Constitution gives Congress the authority to "make rules for the government and regulation of the land and naval forces." This allowed Congress to develop a separate justice system specifically for the U.S. military that is overseen by the president as the commander in chief of the armed forces. Though there have been several sets of rules developed for the military, the current regulation is known as the Uniform Code of Military Justice (UCMJ). The UCMJ is very similar to criminal codes found in many of the states, but also contains punishments for specific military conduct such as failure to perform an official duty, conduct unbecoming a soldier, and refusing to obey a lawful order.

Violations of the UCMJ are heard in proceedings called **courts-martial**, which are like criminal trials but consist of judges and attorneys drawn from legal officers of the military branch in which the violation occurred. Each military branch also has its own court of appeals. If a judgment is appealed from any of these courts of appeals, the case comes before the U.S. Court of Appeals for the Armed Forces, which is a panel of five civilian judges appointed by the president for terms of 15 years. Cases from this court can be appealed to the Supreme Court of the United States.

Tribal Courts Several hundred Native American tribal groups govern **reservations** in the United States. Most of these groups have tribal justice systems. **Tribal courts** hear a broad range of both criminal and civil cases involving both Native Americans and non-Native Americans. The work of tribal courts strongly reflects the culture of the people they serve.

The jurisdiction of such courts varies based on such factors as the location of the offense (on or off the reservation) and the status of both the defendant and the plaintiff (Native American or non-Native American).

Federal courts have jurisdiction over many felonies committed by Native Americans on the reservation. Tribal groups can choose which actions to make crimes, but the criminal sentencing authority of tribal courts is limited to imprisonment for no longer than one year and a fine of no more than $5,000. Tribal courts cannot prosecute non-Native Americans for crimes committed on the reservation. The power of a tribal court to hear civil matters on the reservation is very broad. Tribal courts are essential to the preservation of contemporary tribal self-government.

☑ **READING PROGRESS CHECK**

Comparing What are tribal courts and military courts? Why do they fall outside the federal and state court systems?

A courtroom facility at the U.S. Army Fort Bragg military base

▲ CRITICAL THINKING
Stating What constitutional provision allowed Congress to develop a separate justice system for the U.S. military?

court-martial similar to criminal trials, but consists of judges and attorneys drawn from legal officers of the military branch in which the violation occurred

reservation a tract of public land set aside for use by Native Americans, on which most of these groups have their own tribal justice systems

tribal court a court that hears criminal and civil cases operating within the tribal justice system

---

LESSON 4 REVIEW

Reviewing Vocabulary

1. ***Making Connections*** What are tribal courts and what do they have to do with reservations?

Using Your Graphic Organizer

2. ***Applying*** Use your completed graphic organizer to create a hypothetical list of cases that could be tried before the different courts listed in your graphic organizer.

Answering the Guiding Questions

3. ***Categorizing*** Which courts hear which cases?

4. ***Explaining*** How do state and local courts operate?

5. ***Summarizing*** How is the federal court system structured?

6. ***Stating*** Besides federal and state courts, what other types of courts operate in the United States and what types of cases do they hear?

Writing About Government

7. ***Informative/Explanatory*** Write a one-page memo that explains the concept of *jurisdiction* and describes the four different types of jurisdiction.

STUDY GUIDE

PRINCIPLES OF DEMOCRACY IN THE JUDICIARY
LESSON 1

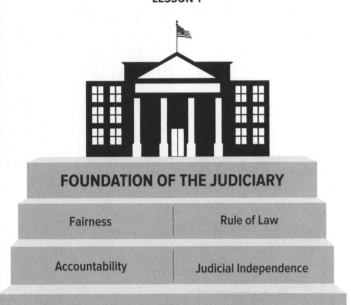

FOUNDATION OF THE JUDICIARY

Fairness	Rule of Law

Accountability	Judicial Independence

Controls on Abuse of Power (Judicial Review)

ROLES IN A TRIAL
LESSON 2

Plaintiff

Person who brought civil suit in court

Prosecutor

Attorney for the government in criminal cases

Defendant

Person against whom the civil or criminal suit was brought

Defense Lawyer or Public Defender

Lawyer for the defendant. If the defendant cannot afford a lawyer in a criminal case, the state hires a public defender.

Jury

Citizens who hear evidence and give a verdict

Witness

Person called to provide evidence through sworn testimony

Judge

Person who presides over the trial, instructs the jury, and determines sentences

APPEALS PROCESS
LESSON 3

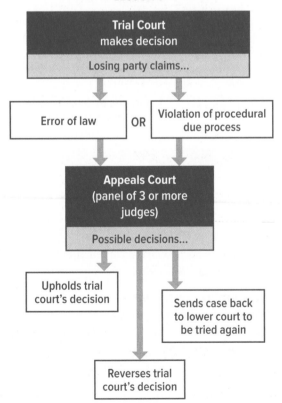

Trial Court
makes decision

Losing party claims...

Error of law   OR   Violation of procedural due process

Appeals Court
(panel of 3 or more judges)

Possible decisions...

Upholds trial court's decision

Sends case back to lower court to be tried again

Reverses trial court's decision

TYPES OF JURISDICTION
LESSON 4

General Jurisdiction
- State and local courts
- Authority to decide wide variety of cases

Original Jurisdiction
- Trial courts
- Authority to decide cases first

Jurisdiction
Power or authority to decide a case

Limited Jurisdiction
- Federal courts
- Authority limited to cases involving federal law or U.S. Constitution

Appellate Jurisdiction
- Appeals courts and supreme courts
- Authority to decide appeals

Directions: On a separate sheet of paper, answer the questions below. Make sure you read carefully and answer all parts of the questions.

Lesson Review

Lesson 1

1 *Drawing Inferences* Why do you think English common law became the most important basis of the American legal system?

2 *Identifying Cause and Effect* If the courts rule a law unconstitutional, what is the effect?

Lesson 2

3 *Defining* What is original jurisdiction and which courts have it?

4 *Explaining* What is the function of a grand jury?

Lesson 3

5 *Identifying* What is the principle of stare decisis and why is it important?

6 *Specifying* An appeals court can make one of three decisions. What are the three decisions?

Lesson 4

7 *Explaining* Which courts have limited jurisdiction and what does this mean?

8 *Identifying* How are judges chosen for state courts?

ANSWERING THE ESSENTIAL QUESTIONS

Review your answers to the introductory questions at the beginning of each lesson. Then answer the following Essential Questions based on what you learned in the chapter. Have your answers changed?

9 *Analyzing* What is the role of the judicial system in our democracy?

10 *Explaining* What are the purposes of trials and appeals in our court systems?

11 *Differentiating* How are federal, state, and local courts organized?

DBQ Interpreting Political Cartoons

Use the political cartoon to answer the following questions.

Federal Court

12 *Activating Prior Knowledge* To what term in office is a federal judge appointed?

13 *Interpreting Visuals* What comment is the cartoonist making about the term of federal court judges?

Critical Thinking

14 *Interpreting Significance* Why is it extremely important that people have confidence in the court system?

15 *Comparing and Contrasting* In what ways does our adversarial trial system differ from the inquisitorial system? In what ways are the systems similar?

16 *Sequencing* Describe the route a case follows through the federal court system and state court systems.

17 *Drawing Inferences* Why do we have a military court system, rather than trying military cases in federal or state courts?

Need Extra Help?

If You've Missed Question	1	2	3	4	5	6	7	8	9	10	11	12	13	14	15	16	17
Go to page	387	388	391	395	400	399	404	403	387	390	402	406	406	387	391	404	407

Directions: On a separate sheet of paper, answer the questions below. Make sure you read carefully and answer all parts of the questions.

DBQ Analyzing Primary Sources

Read the excerpt and answer the questions that follow.

In *Hernandez* v. *Texas*, Pedro Hernandez appealed his conviction on grounds that his jury included no Mexican Americans. His lawyers showed that no Mexican Americans had served on a trial jury in Jackson County, Texas, for more than 25 years.

PRIMARY SOURCE

"In numerous decisions, this Court has held that it is a denial of the equal protection of the laws to try a defendant of a particular race or color . . . before a . . . jury, from which all persons of his race or color have, solely because of that race or color, been excluded. . . . The State of Texas would have us hold that there are only two classes—white and Negro—within the contemplation of the Fourteenth Amendment. The decisions of this Court do not support that view. . . . [C]ommunity prejudices are not static, and, from time to time, other differences from the community norm may define other groups which need the same protection. . . . [I]t taxes our credulity to say that mere chance resulted in there being no members of this class among the over six thousand jurors called in the past 25 years. The result bespeaks discrimination, whether or not it was a conscious decision. . . ."

—Chief Justice Earl Warren,
opinion in *Hernandez* v. *Texas*, May 3, 1954

18 *Identifying Perspectives* What argument did Texas make in this case?

19 *Identifying Perspectives* Why did the Supreme Court disagree with the Texas argument?

20 *Finding the Main Idea* What view did the Supreme Court express about the fact that no Mexican Americans had served on a trial jury in the past 25 years in Jackson County?

Social Studies Skills

Use the graph to answer the following questions.

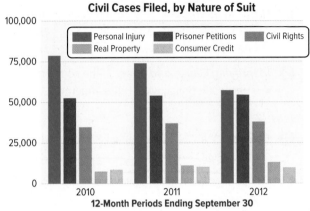

Civil Cases Filed, by Nature of Suit

Source: *Judicial Business of the United States Courts: 2012 Annual Report of the Director, U.S. District Courts; www.uscourts.gov*

21 *Using Graphs* Which type of civil case appears to be declining? At its highest point, about how many of these cases were filed?

22 *Using Graphs* Describe the trend of civil rights cases filed between 2010 and 2012.

Research and Presentation

23 *Understanding Historical Interpretation* Select one of these early systems of law: Code of Hammurabi, Ten Commandments, Twelve Tables, Justinian Code, English common law. Research and prepare a multimedia presentation about the system's key elements and how they relate to the American legal system.

24 *Sequencing* Do research to find a case that was appealed to the U.S. Supreme Court. Create a time line showing the sequence of legal steps the case went through on its way to the Supreme Court. Be prepared to explain your time line to the class.

25 *Researching* Select one minor court in your state or local area, such as probate, juvenile justice, or small claims. Do research to learn the types of cases this court handles, its processes, and possible outcomes. Prepare a multimedia presentation to teach the class about this court.

Need Extra Help?

If You've Missed Question	18	19	20	21	22	23	24	25
Go to page	396	396	396	391	391	387	399	403

The Supreme Court of the United States

ESSENTIAL QUESTIONS

- What influences how the Supreme Court selects cases, decides cases, and interprets the Constitution? • What affects the selection process for Supreme Court justices?

networks

www.connected.mcgraw-hill.com
There's More Online about the Supreme Court of the United States.

CHAPTER **14**

▲ From this iconic building, the Supreme Court hears important cases involving constitutional or federal law.

EQUAL JUSTICE UNDER LAW

Above the entrance to the Supreme Court building in Washington, D.C., are carved the words "Equal Justice Under Law." These inspiring words express important democratic values—equality, justice, rule of law—that represent the mission of the Supreme Court. Those values echo through many of the Court's landmark decisions. Yet many observers would argue that equal justice under law has not been achieved and must remain a goal the United States continues to work toward.

PRIMARY SOURCE A

"Today, education is perhaps the most important function of state and local governments. Compulsory school attendance laws and the great expenditures for education both demonstrate our recognition of the importance of education to our democratic society. . . . In these days, it is doubtful that any child may reasonably be expected to succeed in life if he is denied the opportunity of an education. Such an opportunity, where the state has undertaken to provide it, is a right which must be made available to all on equal terms. . . .

We conclude that in the field of public education the doctrine of "separate but equal" has no place. Separate educational facilities are inherently unequal. Therefore, we hold that the plaintiffs and other similarly situated . . . are . . . deprived of the equal protection of the laws guaranteed by the Fourteenth Amendment."

—Chief Justice Earl Warren for the Court, *Brown* v. *Board of Education*, 347 U.S. 483 (1954)

PRIMARY SOURCE B

"That government hires lawyers to prosecute and defendants who have the money hire lawyers to defend are the strongest indications of the widespread belief that lawyers in criminal courts are necessities, not luxuries. The right of one charged with crime to counsel may not be deemed fundamental and essential to fair trials in some countries, but it is in ours. From the very beginning, our state and national constitutions and laws have laid great emphasis on procedural and substantive safeguards designed to assure fair trials before impartial tribunals in which every defendant stands equal before the law. This noble ideal cannot be realized if the poor man charged with crime has to face his accusers without a lawyer to assist him."

—Justice Hugo Black for the Court, *Gideon* v. *Wainwright*, 372 U.S. 335 (1963)

PRIMARY SOURCE C

". . . First Amendment rights, applied in light of the special characteristics of the school environment, are available to teachers and students. It can hardly be argued that either students or teachers shed their constitutional rights to freedom of speech or expression at the schoolhouse gate. . . .

. . . The Fourteenth Amendment, as now applied to the States, protects the citizen against the State itself and all of its creatures—Boards of Education not excepted. These have, of course, important, delicate, and highly discretionary functions, but none that they may not perform within the limits of the Bill of Rights. That they are educating the young for citizenship is reason for scrupulous protection of Constitutional freedoms of the individual, if we are not to strangle the free mind at its source and teach youth to discount important principles of our government as mere platitudes. . . ."

—Justice Abe Fortas for the Court, *Tinker* v. *Des Moines Independent Community School District*, 393 U.S. 503 (1969)

Criminal defense lawyers appointed for poor people and civil lawyers who provide free services are often called legal aid lawyers. This graphic compares the prevalence of private lawyers to legal aid lawyers.

1 private lawyer for every

429 people in general population

1 legal aid lawyer for every

6,415

people in poverty

Source: Legal Services Corporation, "Documenting the Justice Gap in America," September 2009.

DBQ DOCUMENT-BASED QUESTIONS

1. **Recognizing** In each of the excerpts from landmark Supreme Court cases, find words or phrases that link the decision to the idea of "equal justice under law."

2. **Interpreting** What do you think the cartoonist is saying about "equal justice under law"? If the cartoon were to become a series supporting the cartoonist's view, what figures might you add on the steps of the Supreme Court building?

3. **Explaining** Explain what the graphic shows in words. What is the relationship between the graphic and equal justice?

4. **Synthesizing** Taken together, what do the documents on these pages suggest about "equal justice under law"?

WHAT WILL YOU DO?

How will you assess whether the U.S. Supreme Court and the judicial system more generally are achieving the goal of "equal justice under law"? What can you do if that goal is not being met?

EXPLORE the interactive version of the analyzing primary sources feature on Networks.

interact with these digital
assets and others in lesson 1

✓ **INTERACTIVE CHART**
Three Ways Cases Reach
the Supreme Court

✓ **INTERACTIVE IMAGE**
Justice Clarence Thomas with His Clerks

✓ **SELF-CHECK QUIZ**

✓ **VIDEO**
On the Docket

netw⊙rks
TRY IT YOURSELF ONLINE

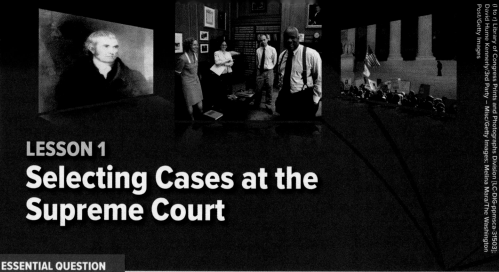

LESSON 1
Selecting Cases at the Supreme Court

ReadingHelp Desk

Academic Vocabulary

• **primary**
• **uniform**

Content Vocabulary

• **advisory opinion**
• **writ of certiorari**
• **law clerk**
• **rule of four**

TAKING NOTES:

Key Ideas and Details

SEQUENCING Use the flowchart
to show the process whereby Supreme
Court cases get selected.

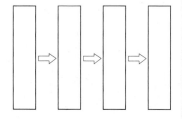

ESSENTIAL QUESTION

What influences how the Supreme Court selects cases, decides cases, and interprets the Constitution?

Imagine a state has a law that requires all children to attend school until age 16. In that state there is also a religious group that believes children between the ages of 14 and 16 should stay at home, studying the Bible and learning farmwork. State officials prosecuted several sets of parents for not sending their children to school. The parents were convicted and fined.

The parents believed that the state was violating their rights. The state believed it had the authority to compel attendance at school (or an equivalent educational activity) until age 16.

Should the Supreme Court hear this case and resolve this conflict or should it allow the state to determine the final outcome? Give your reasons.

The Function of the Supreme Court

GUIDING QUESTION *What is the role of the Supreme Court in our democracy?*

The Supreme Court is the highest court in the land and as such sits at the top of the judicial branch in our democracy. The Court's **primary** function is to resolve disputes that arise over the meaning of federal law and the U.S. Constitution. The Court tries to make sure that federal law is **uniform** and means the same thing everywhere in the country.

One of the Supreme Court's most important powers is judicial review. Judicial review is the power the Court has to examine the laws and actions of local, state, and national governments and to overturn them if they violate the Constitution. This power is not specifically mentioned in the Constitution. The Supreme Court first exercised this power in 1803, in the case of *Marbury* v. *Madison*, when the justices unanimously ruled a federal law unconstitutional.

The Supreme Court can decide what a federal law means or whether any law (a local, state, or federal law, judicial opinion, or agency decision) is unconstitutional. However, the nine justices on the Court cannot simply

414

see a law that is confusing or perhaps unconstitutional and issue an opinion about what the law means. Instead, they must usually wait for a trial to be held and for the losing party at the trial to appeal the case to at least one higher court. Then the losing party from the appeal may be able to seek Supreme Court review. This is different in some other countries where their highest courts can issue **advisory opinions**—a ruling on a law or action that has not yet been challenged in court.

Almost 9,000 cases are appealed to the Supreme Court every year. The justices only decide about 80 cases each term. This number is less than 1 percent of the cases that are appealed to them.

primary first in order of time or development

uniform consistent in conduct or opinion

advisory opinion a ruling on a law that has not yet been challenged in court

We the People: Making a Difference

CHIEF JUSTICE
JOHN MARSHALL

Library of Congress Prints and Photographs Division [LC-DIG-ppmsca-31503]

John Marshall served as chief justice from 1801 to 1835. In a series of decisions starting in 1803, he helped shape a strong national government and established the Court's power of judicial review. By 1825, the Marshall Court had declared at least one law in each of 10 states unconstitutional. What to some observers had appeared to be the weakest branch of the new national government was now clearly an influential, independent branch equal to the legislative and executive branches. In addition to his development of judicial review, he confirmed the supremacy of federal law over state law and supported a broad reading of the enumerated powers in the Constitution. Here are a few cases of the Marshall Court:

Marbury v. *Madison* (1803)
In 1803, the Supreme Court asserted its power of judicial review for the first time. Some of the Founders argued for judicial review in the *Federalist Papers*, especially Alexander Hamilton's *The Federalist* No. 80, but until this court case, judicial review had not been clearly established. The Court unanimously ruled that a section of the Judiciary Act of 1789 was unconstitutional. In this law, Congress had given the Supreme Court some powers that exceeded the powers provided by the Constitution.

McCulloch v. *Maryland* (1819)
In this case, the Court established that the federal government was "supreme in its sphere of action." The State of Maryland had tried to tax the Bank of the United States, but Marshall said a state could not interfere with federal actions that were "necessary and proper." Creating a national bank was "necessary and proper" because Congress had the power to borrow money, collect taxes, and raise an army. In addition, because the bank was a federal institution, Maryland could not tax it.

Gibbons v. *Ogden* (1824)
In this case, the Court used the Constitution's commerce clause to deliver a strong message about the power of the national government. In a conflict between two steamboat operators, one licensed by the state of New York and one licensed by the federal government, the Court ruled that the federal government's regulation of interstate commerce trumped inconsistent state regulation of commerce.

▲ CRITICAL THINKING
Analyzing How did these three cases support the power of the national government?

With few exceptions (such as federal voting rights cases), the Court is not required to hear the cases appealed to it. So exactly how does the Court decide which cases to take?

☑ **READING PROGRESS CHECK**

Summarizing Under what conditions can the Supreme Court hear a case?

Choosing Cases

GUIDING QUESTION *How does the Court decide which cases to hear?*

You may have heard of people who lose a trial claiming, "I am going to take my case all the way to the Supreme Court!" While they might try, it is far from guaranteed that the Supreme Court will ever decide their case. The Supreme Court decides which cases it will hear and rule on.

Jurisdiction The Supreme Court has both original and appellate jurisdiction. Article III, Section 2 of the Constitution sets the Court's original jurisdiction. It addresses two types of cases: (1) cases involving representatives of foreign governments and (2) certain cases in which a state is a party. The Court's original jurisdiction may only be changed by constitutional amendment.

Many original jurisdiction cases have involved two states or a state and the federal government. When Maryland and Virginia argued over oyster fishing rights, and when a dispute broke out between California and Arizona over the control of water from the Colorado River, the Supreme Court had original jurisdiction.

The Supreme Court's original jurisdiction cases form a very small part of its yearly workload—an average of less than one case per year. Most of the cases the Court decides fall under the Court's appellate jurisdiction—*appellate* comes from the word *appeal*. Under its appellate jurisdiction, the Court hears cases appealed from lower courts of appeal, or it may hear cases from federal district courts where an act of Congress was held unconstitutional.

The Supreme Court can also hear cases appealed from the highest court of a state if claims under federal law or the Constitution are involved. In such cases, however, the Supreme Court has the authority to rule only on the federal issue involved, not on issues of state law.

CHART

SUPREME COURT JURISDICTION

Three Ways Cases Reach the Supreme Court
1. Original Jurisdiction
2. Appeals Through State Court Systems
3. Appeals Through Federal Court Systems

CRITICAL THINKING

Applying Which of the following situations fall within the Supreme Court's jurisdiction? In other words, if these issues were brought to the Supreme Court, which ones would the justices be allowed to decide?

a. The president calls the chief justice to ask whether a proposed law restricting campaign contributions to national candidates for office is constitutional.

b. A man gets a speeding ticket and thinks the officer ticketed him because he was driving a Toyota and the police like Fords. The man appeals directly to the Supreme Court.

c. A student who wears a religious necklace to school is told she must remove the religious symbol while at school. She thinks her First Amendment rights were violated, and sues the school. She loses at the trial, and at the appeals court. She appeals the ruling to the Supreme Court.

d. The Supreme Court justices are concerned about a new law Congress passed. They worry that it is unconstitutional and decide to review it.

Conflicts and Importance

The justices are looking for several things when they choose which cases to hear each year. First, they may choose cases where lower courts have decided the same issue in different ways.

For the most part, however, the Court does not view its job as correcting errors from lower courts. Instead, the Supreme Court is concerned about ensuring uniformity in decisions about the meaning of the Constitution and the interpretation of federal laws.

They also choose cases that raise major questions about the law that will have a national impact—questions that they believe must be answered for the good of the country. This includes controversial issues like abortion, privacy, or the death penalty, as well as politically charged topics like campaign finance. The Court also hears a large number of business cases. While not grabbing headlines like cases involving social issues, these cases can involve billions of dollars and directly affect many people's lives.

More than half of the cases appealed to the Supreme Court each year come from people in prison who are appealing their criminal convictions. In order to have their cases accepted, these people must usually show that their case raises a question about a federal law or the U.S. Constitution, and that the question has been answered differently by lower courts. In a typical year, the Supreme Court hears a handful of such cases. For example, in 1963 Clarence Gideon appealed his conviction from a Florida state prison. He argued that the Sixth Amendment to the U.S. Constitution guaranteed him a right to a lawyer at his trial—a right that he had been denied. The Court accepted his case and ruled in his favor.

Petitions for Certiorari

The party that appeals to the Supreme Court is generally the party who lost in a lower court—either in a federal circuit court of appeals or a state supreme court.

To appeal, the losing party sends the Court a petition for a **writ of certiorari**. In this document, the Supreme Court is asked to hear the case and given reasons it should do so. At this stage, the petition does not suggest *how* the Court should decide the case—just *that* it should decide the case. For example, the petitioner might argue that two or more federal courts of appeal have ruled that the federal law means two different things, and that the Court must step in to assure national uniformity. In order to emphasize the importance of the case, the petitioner might also encourage others to file a "friend of the court" or amicus brief, urging the Court to accept the case.

Solicitor General

Often, the U.S. government is involved in the case, too—either because the government is being sued or because a federal law is

---

The Supreme Court chooses cases that raise major questions about the law and are often controversial. This photograph shows activists protesting outside the Supreme Court in Washington D.C. in 2012 while the Court considered the legality of President Obama's Affordable Care Act.

▲ CRITICAL THINKING
Identifying Central Issues In what way do social forces influence the Supreme Court?

writ of certiorari an order from the Supreme Court to a lower court to send up the records on a case for review

▲ U.S. Supreme Court Justice Clarence Thomas (right) meets with three of his law clerks in his chambers.

law clerk an attorney who assists a justice in reviewing cases

at issue in the case. The solicitor general is the government official most often responsible for representing the federal government in court.

The solicitor general decides which cases to appeal to the Supreme Court and how to respond when others appeal a case involving the federal government. Sometimes, when the justices are considering whether to accept a case, they will ask the solicitor general to submit the government's views about whether or not they should accept the case. When the solicitor general recommends that the justices accept a case, they often do.

Selecting Cases to Hear The process of dealing with 9,000 petitions for certiorari is extremely time consuming for the Court. It would be impossible for the justices to carefully review all these petitions on their own and do all their other work. So the justices' law clerks—each justice usually has four—assume a major role in reviewing the petitions. The **law clerks** are typically recent law school graduates who have done exceptional work as law students and have already clerked for one year at a federal court of appeals.

The law clerks read every petition. They look for cases that clearly present a federal legal issue that is important and that has divided the lower courts. They do not simply look for a decision that should be reversed or overturned. The law clerks from most of the justices' chambers work together in a "cert pool" and divide up the task of reviewing the petitions and writing summaries. Some justices do not participate in the pool. These justices and their law clerks review all the petitions.

The law clerks' summaries of the cases give the justices a recommendation as to whether or not each petition should be granted. The justices meet to decide which cases they will hear. If four of the nine justices agree to hear a case, then the petition for certiorari is granted, and the case is scheduled for argument. This unwritten rule is called the **rule of four**.

rule of four an unwritten rule declaring that if four of the nine justices agree to hear a case, it will be scheduled for argument

For most cases, though, certiorari is denied. In fact, more than 99 percent of the petitions are denied. When the Supreme Court refuses to hear a case, the decision of the lower court stands. This does not mean that the Supreme Court necessarily agrees with the lower court—just that they did not choose to hear the case.

☑ **READING PROGRESS CHECK**

Describing What are the different ways that a case can reach the Supreme Court? Which is least common? Why?

LESSON 1 REVIEW

Reviewing Vocabulary
1. ***Identifying*** Who are Supreme Court law clerks and what role do they play?

Using Your Graphic Organizer
2. ***Summarizing*** Use your completed graphic organizer to create a digital slideshow summarizing how the Supreme Court selects its cases.

Answering the Guiding Questions
3. ***Analyzing*** What is the role of the Supreme Court in our democracy?

4. ***Explaining*** How does the Court decide which cases to hear?

Writing About Government
5. ***Informative/Explanatory*** Find a newspaper article about a case the Supreme Court recently decided to hear. Write a summary of the case, describing who appealed the case, what issue it raises, and when the Supreme Court will hear it. Why might the Supreme Court have agreed to hear this case?

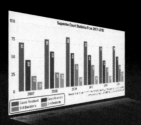

Interact with these digital assets and others in lesson 2

✓ CIVIC PARTICIPATION IN A DIGITAL AGE
Advocacy Groups and Amicus Curiae Briefs

✓ INTERACTIVE GRAPH
Supreme Court Statistics, 2007–2011

✓ SELF-CHECK QUIZ

✓ VIDEO
Arizona Immigration Ruling

netw⊙rks
TRY IT YOURSELF ONLINE

LESSON 2
Deciding Cases

ReadingHelp Desk

Academic Vocabulary

- **preliminary**
- **revise**

Content Vocabulary

- **brief**
- **amicus curiae**
- **unanimous ruling**

TAKING NOTES:

Key Ideas and Details

LISTING Use a flowchart or other graphic organizer to describe the process whereby the Supreme Court decides cases.

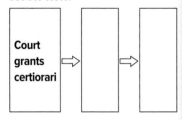

What influences how the Supreme Court selects cases, decides cases, and interprets the Constitution?

Find a news article about a recent Supreme Court case. Read the article and highlight portions of the article that describe the following components of the case:

- The name of the case
- The issue in the case: What is the Supreme Court being asked to decide?
- The date the case was argued in the Supreme Court, if arguments have taken place
- The date the case was decided, if it has been decided

Arguing and Deciding Cases

GUIDING QUESTION *How are cases argued and decided by the Supreme Court?*

Compared to most trials, the Supreme Court hearings are typically quite short. Unlike a trial court, the Supreme Court does not hear witness testimony, accept evidence, or have a jury. The nine justices read written arguments from the parties and notes from their clerks, and participate in one hour of oral argument for each case.

Briefing Once the Court decides to hear a case (i.e., grants certiorari), each side submits a written **brief**, explaining how they want the Court to decide their case and the best arguments in support of that decision. The lawyers who craft the brief provide arguments they hope will convince the justices. An important part of their legal brief involves pointing out similar cases the Court has already decided and noting how the decisions in those cases (precedents) support their argument.

Interest groups may also submit **amicus curiae** briefs, explaining why the case is important to their members and how they want it decided. *Amicus curiae* means "friend of the court," and the justices find these amicus briefs helpful in understanding how their decision will affect all sorts of people. For example, in a case about the death penalty for juvenile offenders, a coalition of juvenile justice professionals may submit a brief explaining how the decision would affect thousands of young criminals on death row.

Sometimes individuals or groups of people with special expertise file amicus briefs. For example, experts on the brain development of young people might file a brief on the juvenile death penalty, too. Controversial cases can generate dozens of amicus briefs on each side.

The solicitor general can also submit a brief on behalf of the federal government to explain the United States's perspective on the issues in the case. The justices and their clerks read the briefs and then have meetings to discuss them. Typically, the justices do not discuss the case with one another until after oral arguments.

brief a written statement setting forth the legal arguments, relevant facts, and precedents supporting one side of a case

amicus curiae Latin for "friend of the court"; a written brief from an individual or group claiming to have information useful to a court's consideration of a case

preliminary something that precedes or is introductory or preparatory

unanimous ruling issued when the justices all agree on the outcome and the reasons for a decision in a case

Oral Argument During this hour-long argument, which is open to the public, each side has 30 minutes to present its case to the justices. The justices, who have already read the briefs and studied the case, ask many tough questions that take up most of the allotted time.

In cases where the federal government is a party, a lawyer from the solicitor general's office will usually present the oral argument for the United States. In cases where the United States is not a party but has an interest in the case, the solicitor general's office might also participate in the oral argument, presenting the federal government's views during some of the time allotted to the party whose side the government supports.

Deciding the Case Once the oral argument is completed, the justices meet in conference to discuss their ideas about the case. At the conference, the justices take a **preliminary** vote to either uphold or reverse the lower court decision. This is also an opportunity for them to discuss their reasoning. If the justices all agree on the outcome and the reasons, they issue a **unanimous ruling**. If they disagree on the case, they issue a majority opinion and a dissenting opinion. Either way, the majority or unanimous opinion is the ruling of the Court and becomes law. Sometimes, some justices agree with the outcome, but not with all the reasoning. In that case, those justices might issue a separate, concurring opinion.

One justice is assigned to draft each opinion, or ruling in the case. The most senior justice in the majority—either the chief justice (who by custom is considered the senior justice) or the person who has been serving on the Court the longest—decides who will write the Court's opinion. If there are dissenters, the most senior justice among them assigns someone to write a dissenting opinion.

C·I·V·I·C PARTICIPATION IN A DIGITAL AGE

Advocacy Groups and Amicus Curiae Briefs

California passed a law banning the sale of violent video games to minors unless they had a parent's permission to purchase them. Video game makers challenged the law, arguing that it violated the First Amendment's protection of free speech. The case made it to the Supreme Court.

Choose one of the interest groups that advocates about this issue—Common Sense Media or The First Amendment Coalition—and learn about this group by visiting its website.

CRITICAL THINKING

1. Identifying What does this interest group think about the issue of regulating the sale of violent video games to minors?

2. Making Connections If you were to submit an amicus curiae brief on behalf of the group, how would you ask the justices to rule? Why?

Supreme Court Statistics From 2007–2012

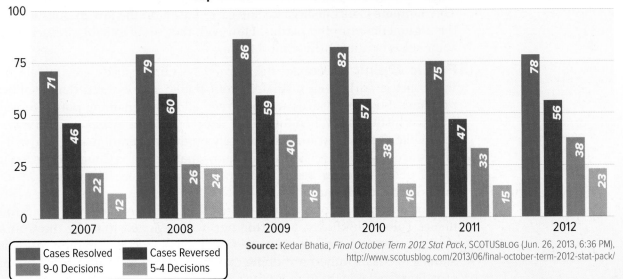

Cases Resolved · **Cases Reversed** · **9-0 Decisions** · **5-4 Decisions**

2007: 71, 46, 22, 12
2008: 79, 60, 26, 24
2009: 86, 59, 40, 16
2010: 82, 57, 38, 16
2011: 75, 47, 33, 15
2012: 78, 56, 38, 23

Source: Kedar Bhatia, *Final October Term 2012 Stat Pack*, SCOTUSBLOG (Jun. 26, 2013, 6:36 PM), http://www.scotusblog.com/2013/06/final-october-term-2012-stat-pack/

Once the opinions are drafted, circulated, **revised**, and put in final form, they are announced in court. They are released to the public via the Court's website and in printed copies. The Court's written opinions are its way to communicate with Congress, the president, interest groups, and the public.

Enforcing Decisions Decisions of the Supreme Court become the law. Lower courts are expected to follow its rulings, and if a law is overturned as unconstitutional, the executive branch must stop implementing that law. However, the Court does not have the power to enforce its decisions. There is no army waiting to carry out Supreme Court decisions. Sometimes, lower court judges or the executive branch refuse to enforce a decision. President Andrew Jackson once refused to carry out a Court ruling barring the removal of the Cherokee Indians from Georgia. In the 1960s, many state court judges and state officials sought ways to avoid enforcing the Court's rulings on integrating schools.

✓ **READING PROGRESS CHECK**

Describing What are written briefs and oral arguments and how are they used in deciding Supreme Court cases?

In all Supreme Court cases, the majority opinion becomes law.

▲ **CRITICAL THINKING**
1. *Calculating* How many cases, on average, does the Supreme Court decide each year?
2. *Contrasting* Does the Court reverse more cases than it upholds? Does the answer surprise you? Explain.

revise to alter something already written or printed, in order to make corrections, improve, or update

EXPLORING THE ESSENTIAL QUESTION

Researching The Supreme Court reports all of its decisions on its website—www.supremecourt.gov. But there are many other websites that offer information and commentary about the Court's work. A particularly comprehensive website about all aspects of the Court is found at www.scotusblog.com.

Research the Supreme Court's current term using these websites.
a. How many cases have been granted review?
b. How many cases have been argued so far this term?
c. How many cases have been decided?
d. Select one case that has been decided and write an analysis explaining what you think about the decision. Is this case relevant to you directly? Be prepared to share your analysis with the class.

Influences on the Court

GUIDING QUESTION *What influences the Supreme Court justices' opinions on cases?*

The Supreme Court justices decide cases based on the law in question and the arguments from the parties. However, they are inevitably influenced in some ways by the world around them.

Public Opinion Because the Supreme Court justices are not elected, the Court is fairly well insulated from public opinion and daily political pressures. Still, the justices are concerned about maintaining public support for their institution. When they issue decisions that may be unpopular with the public, they are aware that they rely on the cooperation and goodwill of others to enforce its decisions. They know that when the Court moves too far ahead or lags too far behind public opinion, it risks losing support and diminishing its own authority.

For example, in one ruling against voter discrimination in the South, Justice Felix Frankfurter, a Northerner, was assigned to write the Court's opinion. After thinking it over, the Court reassigned the opinion to Justice Stanley Reed, a Southerner, hoping that this would produce an opinion more broadly acceptable throughout the country.

Values of Society As society changes, attitudes and practices that were acceptable in one era may become unacceptable in another. In time, the Supreme Court's decisions will usually reflect changes in American society. Some of the Court's decisions on racial segregation provide an example of how the Court changes with the times. In 1896, in *Plessy* v. *Ferguson*, the Court ruled that it was legal for Louisiana to require "separate but equal" treatment in a public accommodation (a railway car).

By the 1950s, however, society's attitudes toward race relations were changing. African Americans had fought courageously in World War II, and civil rights groups were demanding an end to racial discrimination. Researchers began to document the damaging effects segregation had on African American children. These social forces helped persuade the Supreme Court to overturn the precedent established in the Plessy case. In *Brown* v. *Board of Education of Topeka* (1954), the Court ruled unanimously that "separate but equal" educational facilities were unconstitutional.

☑ **READING PROGRESS CHECK**

Analyzing To what extent do you think the Court is affected by the public's opinion and societal values? Explain.

LESSON 2 REVIEW

Reviewing Vocabulary
1. *Comparing and Contrasting* What are unanimous rulings, majority opinions, and dissenting opinions? How do they differ?

Using Your Graphic Organizer
2. *Outlining* Use your completed graphic organizer to create an outline describing how the Supreme Court decides its cases.

Answering the Guiding Questions
3. *Explaining* How are cases argued and decided by the Supreme Court?

4. *Analyzing* What influences the Supreme Court justices' opinions on cases?

Writing About Government
5. *Informative/Explanatory* Explain the role that precedent plays in Supreme Court decisions and how precedents can change. Include specific examples in your response.

Interact with these digital assets and others in lesson 3

✔ **INTERACTIVE CHART**
Justices of the Supreme Court

✔ **INTERACTIVE IMAGE**
Confirming Justices

✔ **SELF-CHECK QUIZ**

✔ **VIDEO**
Sotomayor Supreme Court Hearing

netw⊙rks
TRY IT YOURSELF ONLINE

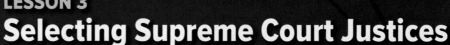

LESSON 3
Selecting Supreme Court Justices

Reading Help Desk

Academic Vocabulary

- professional
- ideological

Content Vocabulary

- Supreme Court justice
- contentious
- appellate litigation

TAKING NOTES:

Integration of Knowledge and Ideas

DESCRIBING Use the graphic organizer to describe the formal requirements and informal qualifications for a Supreme Court justice.

Formal Requirements	Informal Qualifications

ESSENTIAL QUESTION

What affects the selection process for Supreme Court justices?

Think about the role of a federal judge. What qualities might help make someone a good judge? Rank the following factors in order of their importance. Explain your ranking and reasons.

a. Understanding of the law

b. Good education

c. Ability to listen carefully

d. Problem solving skills

e. Ability to write and speak clearly

f. Understanding of U.S. history

g. Success in overcoming personal challenges

h. A sense of fairness

i. Ability to compromise

j. Honesty

The Nomination and Confirmation Process

GUIDING QUESTION *How are Supreme Court justices nominated and confirmed?*

There is little question that U.S. Supreme Court decisions have wide-ranging impact on people throughout the country. The justices are not elected, nor are they accountable to anyone—just to the law. Supreme Court justices may keep their jobs for life, unless they are impeached, which is very, very rare. Lifetime appointments to the Court are designed to ensure a fair and impartial judiciary. Given these factors, there is much debate and discussion about who should be appointed to the Court.

The processes for nominating and confirming **Supreme Court justices** are the same as those for other federal judges. In both cases, there are few constitutional requirements and a large number of political considerations involved.

Chief Justice John Roberts administers the Constitutional Oath to Elena Kagan as she becomes an associate justice of the Supreme Court.

▲ **CRITICAL THINKING**

Stating In what ways can Congress try to influence and/or check the power of the Supreme Court?

Supreme Court justice a member of the Supreme Court of the United States, the highest court in the nation

contentious likely to cause disagreement or argument

professional relating to job experience that requires special education, training, or skill

Constitutional Requirements The Constitution does not say much about who should serve as a federal judge. The Constitution does not have an age, citizenship, or education requirement for Supreme Court justices. There are only two requirements: the person must be nominated by the president and receive Senate consent. Article II, Section 2, of the Constitution, in listing the powers of the presidency, explains the process of choosing federal judges, including Supreme Court justices. The president ". . . shall nominate, and by and with the Advice and Consent of the Senate, shall appoint . . . Judges of the supreme Court . . ."

Confirmation by the Senate The Senate has confirmed about 80 percent of presidential Supreme Court nominations. Until the early part of the twentieth century, the Senate usually held hearings to learn about a nominee and then voted on the nominee within a week of receiving the president's submission. That started to change in the 1980s. Today, we expect a Supreme Court nomination to be a major political and media event. Now, confirmations are neither fast nor easy and are usually **contentious**.

The Process and Politics As soon as a sitting justice announces his or her retirement, or if a justice dies, both the White House and the Senate Judiciary Committee begin working on the nomination process. White House and Senate staff members conduct extensive research about the personal and judicial backgrounds of multiple candidates. Presidents get a tremendous amount of advice from staff and advocacy groups and often interview a short list of candidates before announcing the nominee.

Interest groups also advocate for candidates of their choice. Interest groups will lobby the White House and members of the Senate Judiciary Committee to try to get appointees who might agree with their positions.

The choice made by the president is a political decision: the president selects a nominee who is confirmable by the Senate. This is an example of a check on the power of the executive by the legislative branch.

Once the president has chosen a candidate, he or she will be introduced to the public and announced as the nominee. The nominee begins working to get confirmed by the Senate, first by meeting with many senators, including typically, all those on the Senate Judiciary Committee. At the same time, staff from the White House begins to prepare the nominee for the confirmation hearing. At the hearing, senators ask the nominee questions about his or her qualifications and experiences for the job. They want to ensure that the nominee is qualified in a personal and **professional** sense.

Senators are also interested in the approach the nominee will take to deciding controversial issues. Once the senators complete their questioning—which takes place over a period of several days—the committee votes on whether or not to send the nomination forward to the entire Senate. If the nominee is not voted out of committee, the nomination dies there. If voted out of committee, the entire Senate then votes. A nominee who gets a majority of the votes cast in the Senate has received consent and will be sworn in as a new justice. While there is careful review of the nominee's record, some observers believe that the most important factor in whether the nominee gets confirmed is the political popularity and strength of the president. In other words, confirmation may turn on the nominator as much as the nominee.

☑ **READING PROGRESS CHECK**

Specifying What are the constitutional requirements to be a federal judge?

Steve Petteway, Collection of the Supreme Court of the United States

COMPARING
SUPREME
COURT
NOMINEES

You are legal adviser to the president. One of the current Supreme Court justices has just announced her resignation. You need to advise the president on whom to nominate as a replacement. Consider this information about the president: The president is a Republican in his second term. He is concerned about increasing criminal activity across the country as well as national security threats. After the resignation, there are six men and two women serving on the Court. You have narrowed the choice down to three nominees. Review the information about each and decide which one to recommend to the president.

CANDIDATE #1

- 45-year-old, Hispanic American female
- Graduated first in class from a top law school
- Worked as a prosecutor
- Respected trial court judge

CANDIDATE #2

- 66-year-old, white female
- Graduated near the top of her class in law school
- Worked as a district attorney
- Served as a federal district court judge and as a federal appeals court judge

CANDIDATE #3

- 55-year-old, African American male
- Graduated from a good state law school
- Practiced law as a corporate attorney
- Was elected as a state representative, and then a state senator

Candidate #1 has not spoken publicly or written much about her views on the Constitution. As a trial judge, she was known for strict sentencing of convicted criminals. Lawyers have called her "tough, but fair." She often speaks to groups of young people about the challenges she faced growing up.

Candidate #2 has issued many opinions about constitutional issues. She has expressed concern about sentencing guidelines that do not allow judges enough flexibility to consider the facts of the case before them. She has repeatedly upheld the power of the government to restrict some freedoms in the interest of national security.

Candidate #3 was originally elected as a Democrat, but he switched parties before running for the state senate. In his state legislature, he was known for crafting compromises between the parties. He voted to impose stricter mandatory sentencing guidelines in his state. He is well-liked by his colleagues on both sides of the aisle.

The Selection of Supreme Court Justices

GUIDING QUESTION *What characteristics make someone an ideal nominee for the Supreme Court?*

Presidents consider several factors when nominating a justice. These considerations also weigh on senators' minds when they are deciding whether to vote to confirm a nominee.

Merit and Ideology Supreme Court justices will hear the most difficult and divisive legal issues in the country. Presidents typically want someone with extraordinary personal integrity and professional expertise. All Supreme Court justices have been trained as lawyers and demonstrate thorough understanding of the law. Some presidents want justices with extensive experience as a judge; others might want justices with experience prosecuting criminals or dealing with Americans' everyday concerns. Presidents want nominees who are intelligent, with an excellent education and training, including outstanding oral and written communication skills.

A nominee's judicial temperament—which means being open minded, courteous, patient, and committed to equal justice under the law—is also important, as is a demonstration of his or her understanding of the judicial role in our constitutional order. One way the president can have an impact well beyond the term of the presidency is by placing someone on the Court who shares the president's **ideological** perspective. It can be hard to determine how a person will vote on controversial issues once he or she becomes a

▲ CRITICAL THINKING
Argument Write a memo to the president identifying your choice and explaining the reasons for your recommendation. If you want additional information about one or more candidates, identify that information.

ideological of or pertaining to the body of beliefs that guide an individual, political system, or nation

SUPREME COURT JUSTICES

A president can have a lasting impact by placing justices on the Supreme Court who share the president's ideological perspective.

CRITICAL THINKING

Analyzing What does it mean for the Supreme Court to be representative today? Should the Supreme Court mirror the diversity of the country?

CURRENTLY SERVING SUPREME COURT JUSTICES		
Name	**Date of Appointment**	**Appointing President**
Antonin Scalia	1986	Ronald Reagan
Anthony Kennedy	1988	Ronald Reagan
Clarence Thomas	1991	George H.W. Bush
Ruth Bader Ginsburg	1993	Bill Clinton
Stephen Breyer	1994	Bill Clinton
John G. Roberts	2005	George W. Bush
Samuel Alito	2006	George W. Bush
Sonia Sotomayor	2009	Barack Obama
Elena Kagan	2010	Barack Obama

justice. Some presidents nominate judges with long public records of deciding cases that they can look to; others, by contrast, nominate candidates with little or no judicial record to investigate.

Representativeness Presidents often want a group of justices who are somewhat representative of the country. Historically, presidents were concerned with geographic representativeness and sometimes with religious representativeness, even while all of the justices were white men. Today, however, gender and racial representation appear to be important to presidents. As of 2014, there were six men and three women on the Court, including one African American justice and one Latina justice.

The justices on the Supreme Court as of 2014 had remarkably similar law backgrounds. All attended either Harvard or Yale law schools and spent most of their professional lives either as law school professors or involved in **appellate litigation** (as lawyers or judges). These justices spent less time as lawyers in private practice, trial judges, or elected politicians than any previous Court.

appellate litigation a lawsuit occurring at the appeals level of the court system

☑ READING PROGRESS CHECK

Explaining What characteristics do presidents look for in a Supreme Court nominee?

LESSON 3 REVIEW

Reviewing Vocabulary

1. *Discussing* Why is the process of nominating a Supreme Court justice often contentious? Be sure to define *Supreme Court justice* and *contentious* in your response.

Using Your Graphic Organizer

2. *Analyzing* Explain whether you think there should be additional formal requirements for an individual to be a Supreme Court justice. If so, what requirements would you add? If not, why do you think the existing requirements are sufficient?

Answering the Guiding Questions

3. *Explaining* How are Supreme Court justices nominated and confirmed?

4. *Describing* What characteristics make someone an ideal nominee for the Supreme Court?

Writing About Government

5. *Informative/Explanatory* What process must a Supreme Court nominee go through in order to become a justice? What makes a nominee more likely to be confirmed? Explain.

Should justices have lifetime tenures?

DEBATING DEMOCRATIC PRINCIPLES

Unless they are impeached for bad behavior, Supreme Court justices are appointed for life. Some law professors and scholars argue that the Court's justices should serve a limited term. Justices are now living longer and critics question whether it is a good thing to have elderly justices. In 2005, when Chief Justice William Rehnquist died in office at the age of 81, the issue seemed more relevant than ever. Diagnosed with cancer in 2004, Rehnquist was reluctant to retire. Although he continued to work from his home, he missed more than 40 oral arguments over a several-month period.

 YES

 NO

TEAM A — Justices Should Have Life Terms

In *The Federalist* No. 78, Alexander Hamilton quoted a great French thinker, Charles-Louis de Montesquieu, who understood the importance of an independent judiciary: "There is no liberty if the power of judging be not separated from the legislative and executive powers." Anything less than life tenure will make a justice vulnerable to political influence. Supreme Court justices are living longer, but so is the population in general. Critics have not pointed to any specific Supreme Court decisions as flawed because a justice was incompetent due to advanced age. The confirmation process is highly politicized, it is true, but it could be just as politicized under a new system. The real key to the confirmation process is how well the two parties can cooperate, not how often vacancies occur. The current system has stood the test of time, and there is no good reason to change it.

TEAM B — Justices Should Have Limited Terms

We need to limit the terms Supreme Court justices serve for several reasons. First, the length of their term in office has grown: According to one study, from 1789 to 1970, justices served terms of about 15 years on average. Since 1970, however, justices have served an average of 26 years. With increasingly longer terms, it becomes more likely that a president will serve an entire term without being able to nominate a justice, thus eroding an important power of the executive.

It is likely that some justices stay on the Court even when their mental and physical powers are weakened, relying on the assistance of talented law clerks. There is an even more important reason for establishing term limits, however. When vacancies occur so infrequently due to the long tenures, the battles over appointments to the Court tend to become bitter and divisive to the nation. Finally, because such long tenures are possible, a president may be tempted to appoint a relatively young justice with less experience.

EXPLORING THE ESSENTIAL QUESTION

Analyzing Arguments Read the evidence provided and prepare to debate one side or the other. Identify the best reasons to support your side of the debate question. Draft a compelling opening statement that sets out your position in the debate and summarizes your argument. Do you think that the way judges are selected influences whether they are trustworthy and independent? Explain how your answer to this question affected which side of the debate you chose.

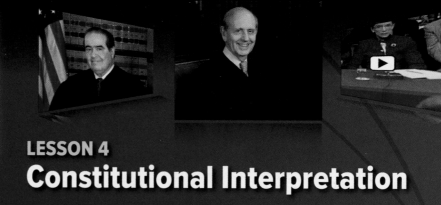

Interact with these digital assets and others in lesson 4

✓ INTERACTIVE CHART
   Landmark Supreme Court Cases: Overturning Precedents

✓ COMPARING
   Comparing Judicial Philosophies

✓ SELF-CHECK QUIZ

✓ VIDEO
   Justice Ginsburg

networks
TRY IT YOURSELF ONLINE

ReadingHelp Desk

Academic Vocabulary

- amend
- reject

Content Vocabulary

- judicial restraint
- judicial activism
- originalism
- "living" constitution

TAKING NOTES:

Key Ideas and Details

DEFINING Use the table to explain different terms in the lesson.

Term	Definition
Judicial activism	
Judicial restraint	
Originalism	
"Living" constitution	

LESSON 4
Constitutional Interpretation

What influences how the Supreme Court selects cases, decides cases, and interprets the Constitution?

The Eighth Amendment to the Constitution says that "excessive bail shall not be required, nor excessive fines imposed, nor cruel and unusual punishment inflicted." For each case described below, decide whether you think the sentence imposed constitutes "cruel and unusual punishment." Explain your reasoning.

a. A person who is convicted of shoplifting $50 worth of goods from a store and has no criminal history is sentenced to 10 years in prison.

b. A person who is convicted of arson for the third time in three years is sentenced to life in prison. No people died as a result of the arson, but millions of dollars' worth of property was destroyed.

c. A fifteen-year-old who committed murder was sentenced to death.

d. A person who drove a vehicle while intoxicated and hit a stop sign is sentenced to stand on the corner for two days holding a sign that says "I was stupid. I drove drunk."

Interpreting the Constitution

GUIDING QUESTION *How do judges decide what the Constitution means?*

Citizens, interest groups, businesses, and many others have different opinions about the role the Supreme Court should play in our federal system when it uses the power of judicial review. Some advocate judicial restraint; others argue for judicial activism. What do those phrases mean?

Judicial Restraint and Judicial Activism Those who support **judicial restraint** believe that the Court should avoid overturning laws passed by democratically elected bodies, like Congress or state legislatures. They believe that overturning such laws causes the Court to become too involved in social and political issues. They believe the Court should uphold acts of Congress unless the acts clearly violate a constitutional provision. In other words, the Court should leave policy making to elected officials.

Those who support **judicial activism** believe the opposite: that the Court must step in when Americans' rights are violated. This means the Court would actively help settle the difficult social and political questions of the day. Under Earl Warren, chief justice from 1953 to 1969, for example, the Court overturned many laws limiting the civil rights of minorities.

Because of the kinds of cases the Warren Court decided, people tend to think that judicial activism means the Court is active on civil rights or social issues. But judicial activism can also serve conservative goals. In the 1930s, for example, conservative justices often took activist positions against New Deal programs intended to regulate the economy. Historically, liberals have been more likely to support judicial activism, and conservatives have been more likely to support judicial restraint. However, this generalization has not held true in recent years. Furthermore, the justices themselves do not typically embrace the labels of *activism* or *restraint*.

Influences on Decision Making The justices must decide how to determine what the text of the Constitution means when the words are unclear. Many portions of the Constitution are written using very general language. When justices are reviewing cases, how can they decide what "cruel and unusual punishment" (from the Eighth Amendment) or "unreasonable search and seizure" (from the Fourth Amendment) means today? Two major influences on the decisions justices make are precedents and judicial philosophy.

Precedent and Stare Decisis One of the basic principles of law in making judicial decisions is stare decisis ("let the decision stand"). Under this principle, once the Court rules on a case, its decision serves as a precedent, or model, on which to base other decisions in cases that raise the same legal issue.

judicial restraint the philosophy that courts should generally avoid overturning laws passed or actions taken by democratically elected bodies

judicial activism the philosophy that courts must sometimes step into political and social controversies in order to protect Constitutional rights

LANDMARK SUPREME COURT CASES: OVERTURNING PRECEDENTS

Here are some landmark Supreme Court cases where the Supreme Court overturned a previous precedent.

FORMER PRECEDENT	CURRENT PRECEDENT
***Betts* v. *Brady* (1942)** The Supreme Court ruled that the right to counsel does not compel states to provide legal representation to defendants if they cannot afford a lawyer.	***Gideon* v. *Wainwright* (1963)** The Supreme Court ruled that state governments must provide free legal representation to people who are charged with a felony and cannot afford a lawyer.
***Whitney* v. *California* (1927)** The Supreme Court ruled that speech "tending to incite crime, disturb the public peace, or endanger the foundations of organized government and threaten its overthrow" was not protected.	***Brandenburg* v. *Ohio* (1969)** The Supreme Court ruled that the government cannot punish speech just because it might tend to incite crime—instead, it must directly incite imminent lawless action.
***Stanford* v. *Kentucky* (1989)** The Supreme Court ruled that it is not cruel and unusual punishment to execute defendants who were under age 18 when they committed their crime.	***Roper* v. *Simmons* (2005)** The Supreme Court ruled that it is unconstitutional to execute defendants who were under age 18 when they committed their crime.
***Austin* v. *Michigan Chamber of Commerce* (1990)** The Supreme Court ruled that a law prohibiting corporations from using corporate money to support or oppose candidates during an election was constitutional.	***Citizens United* v. *Federal Election Commission* (2010)** The Supreme Court ruled that corporations may use corporate money to support or oppose candidates during an election.

CRITICAL THINKING
Evaluating Under what circumstances might the Court overturn a previous precedent?

COMPARING
JUDICIAL PHILOSOPHIES

JUSTICE BREYER

JUSTICE SCALIA

"[Judges must] look at what the basic *values* were that underlie the First Amendment, free expression, religion, etc. . . . those don't change. You have to follow . . . the *value* underlying the Constitutional provision, applying it to circumstances that [the Framers] thought might not even exist."

—Justice Breyer

"The only way to preserve [constitutional] values the way The People voted to maintain them is to give the words the meaning they were understood to have when The People ratified them."

—Justice Scalia

▲ CRITICAL THINKING

a. *Comparing and Contrasting* Justice Breyer talks about the need to apply the values of the Framers to new circumstances, while Justice Scalia talks of giving the words of the Constitution the same meaning as the people at the time understood them to have. How are these two views similar and different?

b. *Making Inferences* How might these different views lead these two justices to interpret the same words in the Constitution differently?

The principle of stare decisis is important because it makes the law predictable. If judges' decisions were unpredictable from one case to another, what is legal one day could be illegal the next, and respect for the law would diminish.

In most cases, Supreme Court justices give great weight to existing precedent when deciding a case. However, sometimes society changes so dramatically over time that a precedent becomes unworkable. In those instances, following precedent would reduce respect for the law. For example, the Court allowed the "separate but equal" doctrine to survive constitutional scrutiny in *Plessy* v. *Ferguson* in 1896. But when this issue came back to the Court in 1954 in *Brown* v. *Board of Education*, the Court ordered the desegregation of public schools and refused to be bound by their ruling in *Plessy*.

On occasion, a justice may also advocate for not adhering to precedent when he or she believes the original precedent was wrongly decided. In these instances, the justice makes a "why continue down the wrong road" argument.

Judicial Philosophy Supreme Court justices explain their decisions in terms of law and precedents. However, it is the justices themselves who determine what laws mean and what precedents are important based upon their judicial philosophy. This is their idea about what guidelines to use when interpreting the Constitution. Judicial philosophies have evolved throughout our history.

Because every Supreme Court decision is explained in a written opinion, people who study the Court have developed some ideas about the different philosophies of today's justices. In addition, some of the justices have written books or articles about their approach to interpreting the Constitution.

Originalists believe that the best way to figure out what the Constitution means today is to look at the original understanding of the people who ratified the Constitution or its amendments. They argue that this approach leads to a fixed meaning. For example, originalists would assert that whatever "cruel and unusual punishment" meant when the Eighth Amendment was adopted in 1791 is what it means today. With a fixed meaning, there is stability and predictability in the legal system. Since the people give the government authority and power, then the people's understanding of the text at the time of ratification must continue to govern.

Additionally, they say, if you do not have a fixed meaning for the provisions in the Constitution, then unelected judges are just choosing their own meanings, which is not democratic. If there is a need to change the meaning of the Constitution, then originalists believe that change should come through the democratic process—by **amending** the document.

Critics of this approach say that we cannot always determine what the people understood the Constitution to mean at the time of its ratification. Moreover, it is impractical to have the views of people from 200 years ago govern us today. It is also difficult to figure out how their understandings of the document apply to new technologies such as the Internet or drone aircraft.

A different approach is what might be called the **"living" constitution** or what one justice has called the "active liberty" philosophy. This view holds that historical analyses cannot provide all the answers for modern situations and that, where they do not, judges must apply the values of the Constitution in light of modern circumstances. Justices who follow this approach look to multiple sources in order to apply the values in the Constitution to modern problems. Like originalists, they begin their analysis of a constitutional provision with a careful reading of the text, followed by consideration of the historical record. Where the text is unclear and history does not provide answers, the justices go on to consider the Constitution's underlying values and the likely consequences of various interpretations.

Supporters of this philosophy believe that the meaning of the Constitution must evolve because it is a living document. This flexibility has allowed it to be used as our basis of government for more than 200 years. They think such an approach may also result in greater public support for decisions because interpretation of the Constitution can align with contemporary values and standards. They point out that it is very difficult to amend the Constitution and that the document cannot be amended every time a new technology is invented or a new situation arises. The Constitution must be applicable to conditions that the people of the 1780s never imagined.

Critics of the living constitution say that it is an invitation for judges to make up the law. If the Constitution's meaning changes over time, then it is not fixed and is not really law. It is dangerous and undemocratic for unelected judges to create meaning in the Constitution.

originalism a judicial philosophy that interprets the Constitution by exploring understanding of the text that people had when they adopted the Constitution

amend to change

"living" constitution a concept that claims that the Constitution is dynamic and that modern society should be considered when interpreting key constitutional text

☑ **READING PROGRESS CHECK**

Analyzing Which approach do you think is better when interpreting the Constitution—originalism or the "living" constitution viewpoint? Explain.

a. *Roper* v. *Simmons* (2005) Simmons was sentenced to death for a murder committed when he was 17 years old. He argued that the death penalty was a cruel and unusual punishment for a juvenile. The Supreme Court agreed, saying that a national consensus had developed among the states that this was cruel and unusual punishment.

b. *U.S.* v. *Jones* (2011) Without a warrant, federal agents placed a GPS device on Jones's car in order to track his activities. Jones argued that this was a search the Fourth Amendment forbids. The Supreme Court agreed, comparing the GPS use to a policeman hiding in a carriage in the 1700s, an activity which Americans who ratified the Constitution would have thought required a warrant.

reject to refuse to grant

Checks and Balances on the Supreme Court

GUIDING QUESTION *How is the Supreme Court's power limited and balanced by the other branches of government?*

While Supreme Court opinions affect millions of Americans' lives, set law, and sometimes change national policies, the Court is not all-powerful. The executive and legislative branches have important checks on the Supreme Court's power.

The president has the power to appoint justices to the Supreme Court, while the Senate has the power to approve or **reject** those appointments. Congress has the power to impeach and remove justices from the bench. Congress even decides how many justices will be on the Supreme Court and sets their salaries.

If the American people do not like a Supreme Court ruling, they can (through their elected representatives) change the law or the part of the Constitution that the Supreme Court interpreted. For example, think about a federal law that bans discrimination against people with disabilities. If the Supreme Court decides that the law means that private clubs need to install wheelchair ramps—but Americans disagree with that decision—then Congress can amend the law to exclude private clubs.

If the people do not like a Supreme Court ruling about the Constitution, however, they must go through the more difficult process of amending the Constitution. This has happened several times in the past; there are twenty-seven amendments to the Constitution. For example, in an 1895 case, *Pollock v. Farmers' Loan & Trust Company*, the Supreme Court ruled that a tax on incomes was unconstitutional. In response, the Sixteenth Amendment was ratified in 1913. It granted Congress the power to levy an income tax.

In addition to these checks on the Supreme Court's power, remember that the justices cannot decide on any and all issues. The justices can only decide issues that come to them through the court system in the form of legal cases. Those issues are limited to determining what a federal law means or deciding whether a law or government action is constitutional.

✓ **READING PROGRESS CHECK**

Discussing What are ways that the legislative branch can check the power of the Supreme Court?

LESSON 4 REVIEW

Reviewing Vocabulary
1. *Analyzing* What do the terms *judicial activism* and *judicial restraint* mean?

Using Your Graphic Organizer
2. *Categorizing* Use your completed graphic organizer to create a guide to Supreme Court interpretation.

Answering the Guiding Questions
3. *Drawing Conclusions* How do judges decide what the Constitution means?

4. *Explaining* How is the Supreme Court's power limited and balanced by the other branches of government?

Writing About Government
5. *Informative/Explanatory* How do the justices interpret the Constitution in order to determine its meaning in contested cases?

Brown v Board of Education (1954)

FACTS OF THE CASE In 1896, the Supreme Court decided a case called *Plessy* v. *Ferguson*. The Court said that segregation was legal when the facilities for whites and African Americans (trains, bathrooms, restaurants, etc.) were similar in quality. By the early 1950s, many schools were segregated by race.

However, under segregation, usually the buildings and buses for the all-African American schools were significantly lower in quality. Often, African American children had to travel far to get to their school.

The family of Linda Brown, an African American student who had to attend a segregated school, sued the Board of Education of Topeka, Kansas. The Brown family believed that the school system violated the Fourteenth Amendment, which guarantees that people will receive the equal protection of the law.

ISSUE

Does the segregation of children in public schools by race violate the Fourteenth Amendment?

ARGUMENTS

The following is a list of arguments in the case of *Brown* v. *Board of Education*. Read each argument and categorize each based on whether it supports Brown's side against segregation or the Board of Education of Topeka's position in favor of segregation.

1. Racial segregation in public schools reduces the benefits of public education to one group solely on the basis of race and is unconstitutional.

2. The Fourteenth Amendment states that people should be treated equally; it does not state that people should be treated the same. Students do not have to attend the same schools to be treated equally under the law; they must simply be given an equal environment for learning.

3. Psychological studies have shown that segregation has negative effects on African American children. By segregating white students from African American students, a badge of inferiority is placed on the African American students.

4. In the 1896 case of *Plessy* v. *Ferguson*, the Supreme Court declared that segregation was legal as long as facilities provided to each race were equal.

5. In 1950 the Supreme Court of the United States decided the case of *Sweatt* v. *Painter*. In this case, the Supreme Court determined that the facilities, curricula, and faculty of two Texas law schools for different races were not equal.

6. The United States has a federal system of government that leaves educational decision making to state and local legislatures.

7. At the time the Fourteenth Amendment of the Constitution was drafted, most African American children received no education at all. It is unlikely that those involved with passing the Fourteenth Amendment thought about its implications for education.

EXPLORING THE ESSENTIAL QUESTION

Summarizing Once you have categorized the arguments, reread them. Research how the Court ruled and write a brief summary explaining the ruling. Highlight the arguments in your list that the Court found most compelling.

YOU BE the JUDGE

STUDY GUIDE

U.S. SUPREME COURT
LESSON 1

The U.S. Supreme Court:

- Interprets meaning of federal law and U.S. Constitution
- Ensures uniformity in decisions about meaning of U.S. Constitution and federal law

Original Jurisdiction	Appellate Jurisdiction
• Cases involving representatives of foreign governments • Certain cases in which a state is a party • Average of fewer than one case per year	• Cases from lower courts of appeal • Cases from federal district courts where a law was held unconstitutional • Cases from highest state courts involving federal law or U.S. Constitution

PRESIDENTIAL SUPREME COURT NOMINEE
LESSON 3

Senate Judiciary Committee hearing

Full Senate majority vote needed to confirm

Supreme Court Justice lifetime appointment

loses vote

nomination ends

DECIDING CASES
LESSON 2

Briefs
- From lawyers for each side
- Cite precedents

Amicus Curiae Briefs
- "Friend of the court" briefs
- From interest groups or experts in the field

Solicitor General's Brief
- Explains federal government's view

Information Submitted to Supreme Court

Oral Argument
- By lawyers for each side
- 30-minute limit for each side
- Solicitor general's office may participate

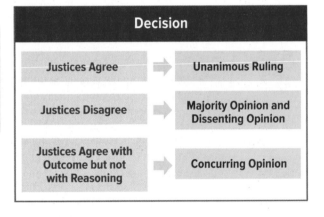

Decision	
Justices Agree	⇒ Unanimous Ruling
Justices Disagree	⇒ Majority Opinion and Dissenting Opinion
Justices Agree with Outcome but not with Reasoning	⇒ Concurring Opinion

INTERPRETING THE CONSTITUTION
LESSON 4

Judicial Restraint	or	Judicial Activism
Supreme Court should avoid overturning laws passed by democratically elected bodies		Supreme Court must sometimes step into a social or political controversy when rights are being violated by the government

Constitution

All justices begin their analysis with: • Careful reading of text • Consideration of precedents	Originalist Philosophy Interpret according to the understanding of the people who ratified the Constitution	or	"Living" Constitution Philosophy Interpret using enduring Constitutional values in the context of modern society

Directions: On a separate sheet of paper, answer the questions below. Make sure you read carefully and answer all parts of the questions.

Lesson Review

Lesson 1

1 **Describing** Describe the primary function of the United States Supreme Court.

2 **Explaining** Explain the three ways cases can reach the Supreme Court.

Lesson 2

3 **Sequencing** Name and describe the sequence of steps for cases heard at the Supreme Court.

4 **Discussing** Discuss how public opinion affects actions of the Supreme Court justices.

Lesson 3

5 **Making Connections** Describe how political differences between the major parties affect the nomination and confirmation of justices.

6 **Explaining** Explain why having justices that represent the population of the country is important in selecting nominees.

Lesson 4

7 **Describing** Describe why precedent is important for judicial decisions.

8 **Specifying** Specify how a Court ruling can be altered by the American people.

ANSWERING THE ESSENTIAL QUESTIONS

Review your answers to the introductory questions at the beginning of each lesson. Then answer the following Essential Questions based on what you learned in the chapter. Have your answers changed?

9 **Making Generalizations** What influences how the Supreme Court selects cases, decides cases, and interprets the Constitution?

10 **Analyzing** What affects the selection process for Supreme Court justices?

DBQ Interpreting Political Cartoons

Use the political cartoon to answer the following questions.

11 **Analyzing Visuals** Why do you think the cartoonist showed the Supreme Court in the background?

12 **Making Connections** What individuals and groups do you know of that have fought for equal justice through the courts?

Critical Thinking

13 **Making Connections** Describe the ruling in the 2010 case *Citizens United* v. *Federal Election Commission*. What precedent did it overturn?

14 **Evaluating** Explain the changes in American culture brought about by the 1954 *Brown* v. *Board of Education* ruling.

15 **Explaining** Who files amicus curiae briefs? Describe ways an amicus curiae brief can be helpful at the Supreme Court.

16 **Differentiating** Describe the advantages and disadvantages of the originalist and "living" Constitution judicial philosophies.

Need Extra Help?

If You've Missed Question	**1**	**2**	**3**	**4**	**5**	**6**	**7**	**8**	**9**	**10**	**11**	**12**	**13**	**14**	**15**	**16**
Go to page	414	416	419	422	424	426	429	432	416	423	432	432	429	422	419	431

Directions: On a separate sheet of paper, answer the questions below. Make sure you read carefully and answer all parts of the questions.

DBQ Analyzing Primary Sources

Read the excerpt and answer the questions that follow.

Decisions in the *Marbury* v. *Madison* case helped define the role of the Supreme Court in government.

PRIMARY SOURCE

"*It is also not entirely unworthy of observation that, in declaring what shall be the supreme law of the land, the Constitution itself is first mentioned, and not the laws of the United States generally, but those only which shall be made in pursuance of the Constitution, have that rank.*

Thus, the particular phraseology of the Constitution of the United States confirms and strengthens the principle, supposed to be essential to all written Constitutions, that a law repugnant to the Constitution is void, and that courts, as well as other departments, are bound by that instrument."
—Chief Justice John Marshall, *Marbury* v. *Madison* Opinion, 1803

17 *Identifying* Who wrote the opinion? State the main idea expressed in the excerpt from the *Marbury* v. *Madison* opinion.

18 *Making Connections* Explain the connection between the Court's ruling in *Marbury* v. *Madison* and judicial review. Why is this case significant?

Social Studies Skills

19 *Creating Diagrams* Create a diagram listing and defining the jurisdictions of the Supreme Court.

20 *Citizenship* Give an example of a Supreme Court decision that exhibited judicial restraint. Explain why it demonstrated the concept of judicial restraint.

Use the graph to answer the questions 21 and 22.

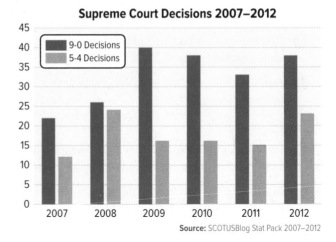

Supreme Court Decisions 2007–2012

■ 9-0 Decisions
■ 5-4 Decisions

Source: SCOTUSBlog Stat Pack 2007–2012

21 *Understanding Relationships* Describe the relationship between the number of unanimous decisions versus 5-4 decisions shown in the graph, and give an explanation for this relationship.

22 *Using Graphs* Using the graph, list the two terms that had the highest number of 5-4 decisions. What, if anything, might that say about the Court and the cases it heard during those sessions?

Research and Presentation

23 *Informative/Explanatory* Write an essay analyzing how judicial activism helped promote civil rights during the 1950s and 1960s.

24 *Informative/Explanatory* Write an essay explaining how the ruling in *Gideon* v. *Wainwright* provided protection of individual rights and limited the powers of government. Which rights from the Bill of Rights were applied to the states in this case?

25 *Argument* Describe the rights applied to the states in the Court's *Roper* v. *Simmons* (2005) ruling. Analyze the impact of this ruling on the scope of federalism.

Need Extra Help?

If You've Missed Question	**17**	**18**	**19**	**20**	**21**	**22**	**23**	**24**	**25**
Go to page	415	415	416	428	430	430	429	429	432

Constitutional Freedoms

networks
www.connected.mcgraw-hill.com
There's More Online about constitutional freedoms.

CHAPTER 15

ESSENTIAL QUESTIONS

- What restrictions, if any, should be placed on our constitutional rights and freedoms? • Why are the freedoms in the Bill of Rights and later amendments essential to our democracy? • How have citizen movements and social movements brought about political and social change?

▲ Since its dedication and opening in 1886, the Statue of Liberty has been a symbol of the freedom secured by the U.S. Constitution.

©Reed Kaestner/Corbis

THE STRENGTH OF OUR LIBERTY

The First Amendment says that "Congress shall make no law . . . abridging the freedom of speech . . . or the right of the people peaceably to assemble." For hundreds of years, Americans have been speaking out—about policy and politics, social issues, and everyday life. Many believe that the foundation of our democratic system of government depends on the free exercise of our right to speech. Why might this be so? Consider the following primary sources as you try to answer that question.

PRIMARY SOURCE A

Writing for the U.S. District Court in the case of *ACLU* v. *Reno*, Judge Stewart Dalzell wrote,

". . . the strength of our liberty depends upon the chaos and cacophony of the unfettered speech the First Amendment protects."

—Judge Stewart Dalzell

PRIMARY SOURCE B

"Congress shall make no law respecting an establishment of religion, or prohibiting the free exercise thereof; or abridging the freedom of speech, or of the press; or the right of the people peaceably to assembly, and to petition the Government for a redress of grievances."

—The First Amendment

PRIMARY SOURCE C

▲ As part of the suffrage movement, women picketed outside the White House in 1917.

PRIMARY SOURCE E

▲ Student-led protests against the Vietnam War occurred on many college and university campuses in the 1960s and 1970s.

PRIMARY SOURCE D

▲ In August 1963, the March on Washington for Jobs and Freedom brought citizens and activists in the Civil Rights Movement together from all over the nation.

PRIMARY SOURCE F

▲ Unhappy with the direction government was taking, the Tea Party movement in the 2000s focused on cutting taxes and federal spending.

DBQ DOCUMENT-BASED QUESTIONS

1. **Identifying** For each photograph, identify in what issue or issues the people depicted are interested. What forms of expression are depicted in each?

2. **Making Connections** How, if at all, do these photographs illustrate the idea of "chaos and cacophony"? Do they help you understand both problems and benefits associated with the chaos and cacophony of free speech?

3. **Evaluating** Do these sources help you better understand the quotation from Judge Stewart Dalzell in Primary Source A? Do you agree that the "strength of our liberty" depends on free speech?

WHAT WILL YOU DO?

As a citizen, what issues do you care strongly enough about to make your voice heard in the public discussion? What forms of expression will you be most likely to use? Why?

EXPLORE the interactive version of the analyzing primary sources feature on Networks.

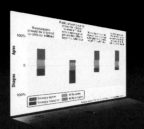

INNOVATION because you're not just changing lanes...

(l to r) Manuel Balce Ceneta/AP Images; Jill Braaten/McGraw-Hill Education

ReadingHelp Desk

Academic Vocabulary

• category
• require

Content Vocabulary

• pure speech
• symbolic speech
• obscenity
• defamation
• slander
• libel
• "fighting words"
• commercial speech
• seditious speech

TAKING NOTES:

Integrating Knowledge and Ideas

CATEGORIZING Use the table to categorize different types of speech and expression as protected or not protected by the freedom of speech in the First Amendment.

Protected Speech	Not Protected Speech

LESSON 1
Freedom of Speech

ESSENTIAL QUESTION

What restrictions, if any, should be placed on our constitutional rights and freedoms?

Free speech is guaranteed by the First Amendment to the Constitution, though that freedom is not absolute. Some speech can be prohibited or restricted in some circumstances. Think about the purpose of free speech in a democracy and then read the actions described below. For each, decide if the "speaker" should be allowed to say or do this.

a. A student writes an article for a public school newspaper that calls the principal names.

b. A uniformed military officer silently burns the U.S. flag at a protest rally.

c. A person gives a speech at a public meeting that encourages people to volunteer in their communities.

d. A band performs a song at a concert that includes offensive racial slurs.

e. An American citizen gives money to a mayoral candidate's campaign.

f. A pharmaceutical company exaggerates its claims about how effective a prescription drug is.

g. Some people who are angry with the U.S. tax system construct a barricade in front of the IRS so the employees of the agency cannot get in to work.

h. A person posts a review on a website that claims a restaurant has a rat problem, but it does not.

Free Speech in a Democracy

GUIDING QUESTION *Why is free speech essential in a democracy?*

The belief in fundamental freedoms of expression and religion lies at the heart of the American political system. Citizens and noncitizens alike have the right to speak freely, to read and write what they choose, and to worship as they wish or not worship at all. The Bill of Rights—the first ten amendments to the U.S. Constitution—protect those rights and others.

The First Amendment protects people's freedom of religion, speech, press, assembly, and petition. The last four rights protect political expression.

They protect people's right to express themselves without interference from the government and to be able to hold the government accountable.

The First Amendment's protection of speech and expression is central to U.S. democracy. The essential, core political purpose of the First Amendment is self-governance: enabling people to obtain information from a diversity of sources, make decisions, and communicate these decisions to the government. In this sense, the First Amendment's protection of speech lies at the heart of an open, democratic society.

In authoritarian countries, the government controls the media and restricts free speech to maintain control and power. In a democracy, freedom of speech enables the truth to emerge from diverse opinions. People determine the truth by seeing which ideas have the power to be accepted in the "marketplace of ideas." This underscores the democratic principle of trusting the will of the people. Like any marketplace, there may be products (ideas) that are popular, unpopular, and even offensive to some people.

Originally, the First Amendment was intended to protect people from having their speech punished by the federal government. Over the past 100 years, however, courts have ruled that other government officials—in state or local governments, for example—may not make laws abridging free speech either. This process of applying Bill of Rights protections to state and local levels of government is called *incorporation* and is discussed later in this chapter.

The Bill of Rights protects people from actions by the government and from those acting with the authority of the government. For example, the First Amendment prevents the government from punishing you if you speak publicly in opposition to a government policy. It does not prevent your parents from punishing you for shouting at your brother.

The **Constitution**

"Congress shall make no law respecting an establishment of religion or prohibiting the free exercise thereof; or abridging the freedom of speech, or of the press; or the right of the people peaceably to assemble, and to petition the government for a redress of grievances."

—The First Amendment

▲ DBQ **Identifying** Who is protected by the First Amendment, and from whom are they protected?

PRIMARY SOURCES

FREE SPEECH IN A DEMOCRACY

a. *"... the ultimate good desired is better reached by free trade in ideas—that the best test of truth is the power of the thought to get itself accepted in the competition of the market. ..."*

—Justice Holmes, dissent in *Abrams* v. *U.S.* (1919)

b. *"... if there is any principle of the Constitution that more imperatively calls for attachment than any other, it is the principle of free thought—not free thought for those who agree with us, but freedom for the thought that we hate."*

—Justice Holmes, dissent in *U.S.* v. *Schwimmer* (1929)

c. *"... that right of freely examining public characters and measures, and of free communication among the people ... has ever been justly deemed, the only effectual guardian of every other right."*

—Virginia's resolution against the Sedition Act of 1798

EXPLORING THE ESSENTIAL QUESTION

Analyzing Read each of the quotations about the importance of free speech. Then, in your own words, explain what each speaker meant. Finally, rank the quotations in order of importance. Which do you think are the most important reasons for the freedom of speech? Why?

The First Amendment exists to protect ideas that may be unpopular or different from those of the majority. Freedom of speech protects everyone, including people who criticize the government or express unconventional views. The U.S. Constitution protects not only the person making the communication but also the person receiving it. Therefore, the First Amendment includes the right to hear, to see, to read, and in general to be exposed to different messages and points of view.

Types of Speech

Pure speech refers to verbal expression to an audience that has chosen to listen. This is the most common form of speech and what most people think of when they hear the word *speech*. It might be talking with friends at home or giving a passionate address to a crowd.

You may be surprised to learn that the freedom of speech protects not only the spoken word, but all forms of verbal and nonverbal communication: books, art, dance, film, photographs, and telecommunications and other media.

Expression may be symbolic as well as verbal or nonverbal. **Symbolic speech** is conduct that expresses an idea. Sit-ins, flag waving, demonstrations, and wearing armbands or protest buttons are examples of symbolic speech. Because symbolic speech involves actions, the government can sometimes restrict it in ways that do not apply to pure speech—for example, if it endangers public safety.

pure speech verbal expression before an audience that has chosen to listen

symbolic speech the use of actions and symbols, in addition to or instead of words, to express ideas

☑ **READING PROGRESS CHECK**

Explaining How does pure speech differ from symbolic speech?

PARTICIPATING
ⓘⓝ Your Government

Conducting Polls and Analyzing Poll Data

Each year, the First Amendment Center conducts polls to learn what Americans think about the First Amendment. Examine these results in the bar graph from recent State of the First Amendment reports.

EXPLORING THE ESSENTIAL QUESTION

To learn more about how your peers feel about the First Amendment, design and implement your own poll with at least five questions. Be sure the questions are clear and understandable. Consider multiple-choice, yes/no, or scaled questions so that you can easily compare answers. You might use the *State of the First Amendment* surveys as a guideline.

Administer your poll to at least 10 students. Create a graph of your results and write a paragraph summarizing your findings.

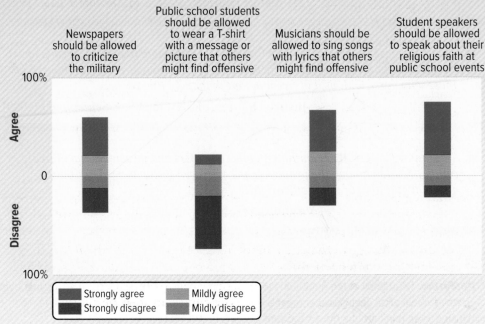

Source: *State of the First Amendment*, First Amendment Center

SYMBOLIC SPEECH

The Supreme Court has ruled several times on what constitutes symbolic speech and when it can be restricted by the government.

Stromberg v. *California* (1931) A California state law prohibited the public display of a red flag (associated with communism) as a symbol of opposition to organized government. The Supreme Court said the law was unconstitutional, because it could punish legal opposition to government.

U.S. v. *O'Brien* (1968) Four young men burned their draft cards to protest the Vietnam War. They were arrested for violating a law that required them to keep their draft cards in their possession at all times. The Supreme Court ruled that the law did not violate the First Amendment because it served a valid government interest and was not intended to suppress speech. The men could have sent the same message in other formats.

Tinker v. *Des Moines* (1969) Students wore black armbands to school to protest the Vietnam War. They were suspended, but the Supreme Court ruled that the school could not punish the students for this symbolic speech. It said students do not "shed their constitutional rights to freedom of speech or expression at the schoolhouse gate" and this particular symbolic speech did not substantially disrupt the school's educational environment.

Texas v. *Johnson* (1989) A protester burned the American flag, which was against the law in Texas. The Supreme Court said the law banning flag burning was unconstitutional because it infringed on the right to free speech.

◀ CRITICAL THINKING
1. Differentiating What is the difference between pure speech and symbolic speech?
2. Making Connections What methods of symbolic speech are used today?

Content Restrictions on Speech

GUIDING QUESTION *What content restrictions may be placed on the freedom of speech?*

While our freedom of speech is important, it is not unlimited. Like other constitutional rights, the government can place some restrictions on the freedom of speech. For example, imagine if someone yells "Fire!" in a crowded place when there is not a fire. This joke could lead to a panic and injuries as people rush for the doors. The government might be able to protect public safety by restricting the speech of the person shouting "Fire!"

Conflicts involving freedom of expression are among the most difficult ones that courts are asked to resolve. Free speech cases frequently involve a clash of fundamental values. For example, how should the law respond to a speaker who makes an unpopular statement to which the listeners react violently? Courts must consider the need for peace and public order against the fundamental right of an individual to express his or her point of view. They call this the "balancing test." They weigh the danger to the public against the benefit of an individual of being able to choose what to say and where to say it.

Because speech is such a fundamental freedom in our country, courts have ruled that laws governing free speech must be clear and specific. This is so that a reasonable person can understand what expression is allowed and what is prohibited. Laws also need to be clear so that they can be enforced in a uniform and nondiscriminatory way.

Generally, the government cannot restrict speech based on what is being said—the content of the speech. However, there are a few specific **categories** of speech that can be punished based on content: obscenity, defamation, and "fighting words." Advertising can also be regulated to some extent.

category a division within a system of classification

Imagine that you are a police officer and you are assigned to work at a controversial rally in your town. Your job is to keep everyone safe during the rally and keep any riots or violence from breaking out. During the rally, one of the speakers talks about taking up arms against the government. He urges the attendees to protest if they disagree with government policies, and suggests that they have a responsibility to fight the government if change does not come quickly. You can see the crowd getting excited, shouting and chanting. You are worried that the crowd might become violent.

Understanding Perspectives

How would you respond? Would you attempt to get the speaker off the stage, even arresting him if you need to? Or would you focus on the people in the crowd and try to contain them if things get out of hand?

obscenity anything that treats sex or nudity in an offensive or lewd manner, violates recognized standards of decency, and lacks serious literary, artistic, political, or scientific value

defamation false expression that injures a person's reputation

slander false speech that damages a person's reputation

libel false written or published statements that damage a person's reputation

"fighting words" words spoken face-to-face that are likely to cause immediate violence

commercial speech speech where the speaker is more likely to be engaged in commerce and the intended audience is commercial, actual, or potential consumers

seditious speech speech urging the resistance to lawful authority or advocating the overthrow of the government

Obscenity **Obscenity** is anything that treats sex or nudity in an offensive or lewd manner, violates recognized standards of decency, and lacks serious literary, artistic, political, or scientific value. In 1957 the U.S. Supreme Court ruled that obscenity is not speech protected by the Constitution. It also said that standards for what is considered obscene may be different from one community to the next. This has allowed some cities to pass zoning ordinances that restrict the locations of stores or theaters that feature pornography. Determining what the community standards are on the Internet presents additional challenges. In 1997, in a case called *Reno* v. *ACLU*, the Supreme Court ruled that a law prohibiting the distribution of indecent material online was unconstitutional. The Court said the law was too broad—it did not specifically target obscene material and did not define "indecent."

Defamation A false expression about a person that damages that person's reputation is called **defamation**. When defamation is spoken, it is called **slander**. Defamation published in a more lasting form—for example, a book, article, movie, audio recording, or blog—is called **libel**. However, if a statement—written or spoken, no matter how damaging or embarrassing—is proven to be true, then it is not defamation. The First Amendment does not protect defamation, so someone who commits slander or libel may be sued and ordered to pay money damages to the person harmed by the false statements.

The value placed on freedom of speech in the United States makes it difficult for public officials or public figures to win defamation suits. There is a concern that holding speakers, which includes the press, responsible for comments about matters of public importance will "chill" or discourage expression. In *New York Times Co.* v. *Sullivan* (1964), the Supreme Court determined that even if a newspaper story about an Alabama police commissioner was false, it was protected speech unless the statement was made with the knowledge that it was false or with reckless disregard for whether or not it was false.

"Fighting Words" The First Amendment also does not protect you if you use words that are so abusive or threatening that they amount to what the U.S. Supreme Court calls **"fighting words."** These are words spoken face-to-face that are likely to cause immediate violence. Fighting words are like a verbal slap in the face. They are not protected by the First Amendment. Their value is outweighed by society's interest in maintaining order. Still, courts very rarely use the "fighting words" doctrine today. Even offensive, provocative speech that makes its listeners very angry is generally protected and not considered to be fighting words.

Commercial Speech Most advertising is considered **commercial speech**, as distinguished from individual speech. At one time, commercial speech was not protected by the First Amendment at all. More recently, however, courts have ruled that commercial speech is protected, though not to the extent that political speech is.

Governments can ban or regulate commercial speech that is false or misleading or provides information about illegal products. Governments may also place restrictions on other forms of commercial speech if they have a good reason. For example, a government can prohibit advertising about cigarettes to children or can restrict distracting billboards along roads.

Seditious Speech At various times, Congress and state legislatures have outlawed **seditious speech**, which is speech urging the resistance to lawful authority or advocating the overthrow of the government. In different eras, the courts have taken different views about the constitutionality of such laws.

If a conflict occurs between free expression and public safety, judges often look at whether the speech presents an immediate danger. This standard was set out in a 1919 case called *Schenck* v. *United States*. A member of the Socialist Party was convicted of violating the 1917 Espionage Act by printing leaflets that urged draftees to obstruct the World War I effort. The Court ruled that Schenk's conviction was constitutional because his actions took place during wartime when there was a "clear and present danger" that they would bring about "substantive evils."

A few years later, the Supreme Court gave the government more leeway in regulating "dangerous" speech. In *Gitlow* v. *New York* (1925), the Court ruled that speech could be restricted even if it only had a tendency to lead to illegal action. In the same year but in a different case, the Court said the government could prohibit speech that threatened to overthrow the government by unlawful means (*Whitney* v. *California*, 1927). Those standards shifted a bit as the courts ruled that First Amendment freedoms are fundamental. Since the 1940s, the government has been able to restrict such speech only when absolutely necessary. For example, in a case called *Brandenburg* v. *Ohio* (1969), the Supreme Court said speech that generally advocates violence is protected. Only speech directed toward "inciting immediate lawlessness" and likely to produce such behavior could be punished. Therefore, it is not illegal to merely say that the government should be overthrown. In *Brandenburg*, a man had given a speech at a Ku Klux Klan rally where he advocated violence but did not incite it.

☑ **READING PROGRESS CHECK**

Summarizing What types of speech may be restricted under the First Amendment?

Though commercial speech is protected, it is not protected to the same level as political speech.

▲ **CRITICAL THINKING**
Identifying What kind of speech is advertising? What kinds of restrictions—if any—can be placed on this type of speech?

Time, Place, and Manner Regulations

GUIDING QUESTION *What time, place, and manner restrictions may be placed on free speech in our democracy?*

As a general rule, government cannot regulate the content of expression, except in special situations, as noted in the preceding sections. However, government may make reasonable regulations governing the time, place, and manner of speech. Towns and cities may **require** citizens to obtain permits to hold a march; to use sound trucks; or to stage protests in parks, on streets, or on other public property. They may also regulate the time during which loudspeakers may be used, the places political posters may be displayed, and the manner in which political demonstrations may be conducted. Such laws control when, where, and how expression is allowed. However, these regulations must be viewpoint neutral; that is, they cannot promote or censor a particular point of view. They also must be enforced even-handedly—officials cannot deny permits to groups they disagree with.

There are some special places where the rules about free speech are different than in the general public, including prisons, schools, and the military. These are places in which the government has "compelling interests" in making sure that the purpose of the institution is not compromised.

require to claim or ask for by right and authority

Free Speech in Special Places Enlisted military personnel are protected by the Constitution, but are also subject to a special set of laws called the Uniform Code of Military Justice. Members of the military are prohibited, for example, from using contemptuous words against the president.

One of the most common explanations for restrictions of free speech in the military has to do with the need for respecting the chain of command. Speech that mocks the president could create a clear and present danger to discipline and morale within the armed forces.

Prisoners also have basic rights to free expression. However, the Court has ruled that free speech may be limited in prisons if that speech could endanger inmates and staff, or if prison authorities believe limited speech serves legitimate correctional purposes.

Free Speech in Public Schools Public schools—which are run by the government—present special First Amendment problems. The rights of public school students may at times conflict with the rights of others or interfere with the need to maintain a good learning environment.

As a general rule, courts allow greater expression rights in public parks and on street corners than in schools. Courts sometimes speak of these places where First Amendment rights are traditionally exercised as public forums. For the most part, however, students in public schools have more limited First Amendment freedoms than in public forums. In *Tinker* v. *Des Moines* (1969), for example, the Supreme Court said that students have free speech rights in school as long as exercise of that right does not result in a substantial disruption in the educational process or violate the rights of others. Later rulings have clarified the authority school officials have to regulate student speech consistent with First Amendment rights. In *Bethel* v. *Fraser* (1986), for instance, the Court ruled that schools can punish lewd or indecent speech, even though that same speech would be protected outside school. In *Hazelwood* v. *Kuhlmeier* (1988), the Court ruled that school officials can regulate student speech in school-sponsored activities, like the school newspaper and theater productions.

In addition, courts consider the age of the student and the precise educational setting when deciding these cases: a student at a public university is likely to have greater expression rights than a middle school student.

☑ **READING PROGRESS CHECK**

Synthesizing Why is speech more restricted in prisons, the military, and public schools?

LESSON 1 REVIEW

Reviewing Vocabulary
1. *Making Connections* How are the terms *defamation*, *slander*, and *libel* related?

Using Your Graphic Organizer
2. *Constructing Arguments* Choose an example from your graphic organizer where you disagree with the Supreme Court's current interpretation of the First Amendment. Write an essay arguing why this form of speech should or should not be protected under the First Amendment.

Answering the Guiding Questions
3. *Analyzing* Why is free speech essential in a democracy?

4. *Describing* What content restrictions may be placed on the freedom of speech?

5. *Discussing* What time, place, and manner restrictions may be placed on free speech in our democracy?

Writing About Government
6. *Informative/Explanatory* Write an essay explaining why the First Amendment's protection of free speech is central to democracy in the United States. Provide at least two reasons and illustrative examples in your essay.

Should our democracy limit hateful speech?

DEBATING DEMOCRATIC PRINCIPLES

In recent years, there has been an effort to punish those who express views motivated by bigotry or racism. Such speech is called *hate speech*. Some states and cities have passed laws prohibiting the display of symbols that are hateful on the basis of race, gender, or religion. Others have enacted laws that increase criminal punishments for bias-motivated violence and intimidation. Sometimes, these laws come into conflict with the First Amendment's protection of free speech. Some laws have been ruled unconstitutional, while others have been upheld.

YES

TEAM A — Hate Speech Should Be Outlawed

Hate speech should be outlawed. Certain symbols and expressions are clearly hateful and have no meaningful social benefit. Our freedom of speech is important, but it is not an absolute guarantee. The government should balance freedom of expression with other democratic values, such as respect, equality, and tolerance.

Hateful speech is particularly dangerous when it is directed against minority groups. Such people already lack power in our society. Prohibiting hateful speech against these groups prevents hateful ideas from turning into discriminatory actions. History shows us that the first act of persecution of minorities is frequently speech that condemns or abuses those minorities.

NO

TEAM B — Hate Speech Should Be Protected

Hate speech is regretful and upsetting, but it should not be illegal. Exposure to offensive speech is one small price to pay to ensure our freedom to speak. It is better to counter hate speech with positive speech, or to ignore it, than to make it illegal. In an open "marketplace of ideas," hateful and offensive ideas will be denounced by other speech.

Additionally, hate speech laws are unworkable. They require the government to determine the intent of the speaker. Once we give the government the power to punish some forms of expression based on the speaker's intent, the government will soon be able to punish other speech as well. The government should only ban actions, not what people say or believe.

EXPLORING THE ESSENTIAL QUESTION

Analyzing Americans disagree about whether our democracy should limit hateful speech. Read the evidence provided, and prepare to debate one side or the other.

1. Identify the best reasons to support your side of the debate question.
2. Draft a compelling opening statement that sets out your position in the debate and summarizes your argument.
3. Anticipate the strongest arguments to support the other position. How could you respond to those points?

Reading Help Desk

Academic Vocabulary

- presume
- outcome

Content Vocabulary

- censorship
- prior restraint
- gag order
- sequester
- petition

TAKING NOTES:

Key Ideas and Details

SUMMARIZING As you read, list the ways in which the government regulates the freedoms of press, assembly, and petition.

Regulations		
Press	Assembly	Petition

LESSON 2
Freedoms of Press, Assembly, and Petition

ESSENTIAL QUESTION

What restrictions, if any, should be placed on our constitutional rights and freedoms?

Read the following hypothetical situations. Do you consider the government's actions fair or unfair? Make note of your answers, reasons, and the criteria you used to make each decision.

a. The government prevents a newspaper from publishing information about a recent murder for fear of not being able to find impartial jury members in a few weeks.

b. The government denies a permit to an environmental group that planned to hold a peaceful protest that would block the path of construction crews about to build an oil pipeline.

c. The government prevents a reporter from publishing leaked information about an upcoming military strike in a current war.

d. The White House asks reporters not to announce that the president is visiting a country where U.S. troops are fighting until after he lands there—for his safety and theirs.

e. The government prohibits the publication of news about a campaign finance scandal that involves a state senator who is up for reelection in two weeks.

f. A county's charter requires its lawmakers to hold an open (public) hearing for community input before it passes any law. For one contentious issue, more than 60 people sign up to speak. The meeting starts late and due to time constraints, the moderator allows only two people to testify before a vote is taken.

Freedom of the Press

GUIDING QUESTION *In what instances may the freedom of the press be limited?*

The First Amendment to the U.S. Constitution guarantees freedom of the press. It protects us from government censorship of newspapers, magazines, books, radio, television, and film. **Censorship** occurs when governments prohibit the use of publications or productions they find offensive or contrary to their own interests. Traditionally, courts have protected the press from government censorship. In addition to providing information about news events, the press subjects all our political and legal institutions to public scrutiny and criticism.

However, freedom of the press sometimes clashes with other rights, such as a defendant's right to a fair trial or a citizen's right to privacy. Sometimes, freedom of the press also clashes with the government's interests. When can the government reasonably prevent the press from obtaining or publishing information or force the press to disclose information? Are special limits on the press needed during wartime?

Prior Restraint
In many nations, **prior restraint**—censorship of information before it is published—is a common way for government to control information and limit freedom. In the United States, attempts at prior restraint are **presumed** unconstitutional by the courts, unless publication would cause a certain, serious, and irreparable harm, and stopping publication would prevent the harm, but no lesser means would do so.

Two Supreme Court decisions illustrate these principles. In a 1931 case called *Near* v. *Minnesota*, a newspaper had called local officials "gangsters" and "grafters." A state law prohibited the publication of any "malicious, scandalous, or defamatory" newspapers or magazines. Acting under the state's law, officials obtained a court order to prevent the paper from being published. By a 5 to 4 vote, the Supreme Court ruled that the state law was an unconstitutional limitation on the press.

The Supreme Court reaffirmed its position in *New York Times Co.* v. *United States* (1971)—widely known as the Pentagon Papers case. In 1971 a former Pentagon employee leaked to the *New York Times* a secret government report

censorship the act of governments prohibiting the use of publications or productions they find offensive or contrary to their own interests

prior restraint censorship of information before it is published

presume to take for granted, assume, or suppose

C·I·V·I·C PARTICIPATION IN A DIGITAL AGE

National Security and Freedom of the Press

Imagine you and four others are on the editorial team at a leading online and television news outlet. One of your top reporters came to you this morning with a story. Someone inside the state government gave the reporter a copy of a top-secret report. The report details multiple security lapses at a local electrical utility that make the facility vulnerable to a terrorist attack. It outlines the possible consequences of an attack and strongly recommends that the government immediately divert funds to fix the problems.

©2007 Getty Images, Inc.

The reporter's source said the state's elected leaders are ignoring the report and do not plan to make it public. The source is concerned that the safety of the community is in jeopardy and wants to make people aware. You contacted the government official who would be in charge of implementing the report's findings. The official confirms the report exists and asks you not to publish this information, because the report provides very specific details about the facility and its vulnerabilities. It is possible that potential terrorists or criminals could use the information in the report to plan and launch an attack.

outlining the history of American involvement in the Vietnam War. This report, which became known as the Pentagon Papers, contained many government documents, including secret cables and memos.

Believing the Pentagon Papers showed that government officials had lied about the ongoing war, the newspaper began to publish parts of the report. The government tried to stop publication of the papers, arguing that national security was at risk and that the documents had been stolen. The Court rejected the government's claims that prior restraint was reasonable. Justice William O. Douglas noted that "the dominant purpose of the First Amendment was to prohibit the widespread practice of governmental suppression of embarrassing information." Justice Hugo L. Black added: "The press [is] to serve the governed, not the governors. . . . The press was protected so that it could bare the secrets of government and inform the people."

Fair Trials Conflicts have also occurred between the First Amendment's freedom of the press and the Sixth Amendment's right to a fair trial. Can the press publish information that might influence the **outcome** of a trial? Can courts limit what can be published to increase the chances of a fair trial?

A case involving these questions went to the Supreme Court. In that case, a trial judge issued a **gag order**, which prohibited the news media from reporting on an upcoming murder trial. The judge feared the news coverage would make it impossible for a suspect in a multiple murder case to get a fair trial before an unbiased jury. The media challenged the gag order. The Supreme Court ruled in *Nebraska Press Association* v. *Stuart* (1976) that the gag order was too vague and said the trial judge could take other actions to protect the defendant's right to a fair trial. For example, the judge could keep the jury **sequestered**, or isolated from the public and media, during the trial.

New Media In writing the First Amendment, the Founders thought of the press as printed material like books, newspapers, and pamphlets. They could not have foreseen the growth of technology and mass communication. Modern media has created new issues regarding freedom of the press.

Even comparing news of today to 40 years ago, media and free press issues have become more complicated. Consider the dilemma of finding an unbiased jury for high-profile criminal trials like in the *Nebraska* case. Now imagine that a video clip showing the alleged murderer at the scene of the crime has gone viral on the Internet. How could a judge issue a gag order broad enough to cover any journalist who wants to cover the story? How can the defendant expect to find an unbiased jury?

The Internet has been the source of much debate when it comes to freedom of the press. Should we treat a blogger like a newspaper reporter? What do we do when an anonymous comment online is defamatory or fraudulent? The courts are still deciding cases about these new issues.

✔ **READING PROGRESS CHECK**

Specifying What are two actions a trial judge can take to protect a defendant's Sixth Amendment rights?

Freedoms of Petition and Assembly

GUIDING QUESTION *What restrictions can the government place on the freedoms of petition and assembly?*

The First Amendment guarantees "the right of the people peaceably to assemble, and to petition the Government for a redress of grievances." These are essential rights in a democracy because they offer people opportunities

outcome a final product or end result

gag order an order by a judge barring the press from publishing certain types of information about a pending court case

sequester to hold in isolation

Julian Assange challenged the limits of the freedom of speech and press by publishing leaked confidential information on WikiLeaks, a website he started in 2006.

▼ CRITICAL THINKING

Examining Should Internet posts receive the same protection as newspapers under the First Amendment? Why or why not?

©iStockphoto.com/EdStock2

PARTICIPATING
in Your Government

Petition

Find out when your city or county government is having its next meeting that is open to the public. Get a copy of the agenda so you can begin thinking about the topics they will be discussing or debating.

EXPLORING THE ESSENTIAL QUESTION

Option A

Creating Arguments If you have a strong opinion on one of the proposals, write up a petition that asks them to take a certain action and states the reasons they should. Ask friends, family, or neighbors if they will sign your petition. Make a copy for your teacher and submit your petition to your government officials at the meeting. Report back on their response.

Option B

Analyzing Arguments If you do not fully understand or have a strong opinion about the proposals, observe the meeting and take notes about what other members of the public say when they testify. What points do they make? Which presenters were most persuasive and what made them most effective? Write a news report about how members of your community exercised their right to petition.

A petition for woman suffrage from 1887

---

to join together to make their voices stronger when they want to send the government a message. When individuals **petition**, they ask the government to take action or refrain from taking a planned action, and to work for them.

petition to request

These rights are not guaranteed in totalitarian states, where a gathering of people—even in a private home—can arouse government suspicion. Because totalitarian governments serve the interests of their leaders, input from citizens is irrelevant.

Freedom of Petition The Constitution protects our right to petition the government for redress of grievances. Petition includes such things as signing a petition, filing a lawsuit, writing a letter or e-mail, testifying before tribunals, and collecting signatures for ballot initiatives. The right to petition has roots in the Magna Carta and English Bill of Rights. In fact, one of the reasons the colonists listed this right in the Declaration of Independence is that King George III failed to hear petitions from the colonies.

Freedom of Assembly The right to free assembly means people can participate in protests, parades, and other large events to show their unity and to show their support or opposition to a government policy. They are also free to meet with others in homes and other private places. However, the Constitution makes it clear that the gatherings must be peaceful.

At times in our history, assemblies have become violent riots. Like other First Amendment freedoms, the freedom of assembly must be balanced with the need to maintain order. For example, the government can require a group to get a permit before it stages a rally. It can deny a group from taking over a public space, which would deny others the use of the same public space. As with the freedom of speech, the government can reasonably regulate the time, place, and manner of assemblies, as long as it does so in the same way

Analyzing Some people claimed the purpose of the demonstration was to incite Skokie's Jewish residents and inflict emotional harm, rather than communicate ideas.

a. Do you agree or disagree? Should the motive of the speaker influence whether speech is protected by the Constitution?

b. Was the permit law in this case neutral in its viewpoint?

c. How do you think this case should have been decided? In what ways, if any, should the town be able to regulate the demonstration?

for all groups, regardless of their message. Some demonstrations could become violent because those with opposite views may launch counter-demonstrations. Opponents may engage in heated verbal or physical clashes.

A controversial example of balancing freedom of speech with freedom of assembly involved a Nazi Party rally in Skokie, Illinois. In 1977 the American Nazi Party, a small group patterned after Adolf Hitler's German Nazi Party, announced plans to hold a rally in Skokie, Illinois, a largely Jewish suburb of Chicago. Skokie residents were outraged. Many were survivors of the Holocaust, the mass extermination of Jews and other groups by the Nazis during World War II. Others were relatives of Jews who were killed in Nazi death camps.

Skokie officials, citizens, and many others argued that the Nazis should not be allowed to march. They claimed that the march would cause great pain to residents and would attract a counterdemonstration. To prevent the march, the city required the Nazis to post a $350,000 bond to get a parade permit. The Nazis claimed the high bond interfered with their rights to free speech and assembly. The courts sided with the demonstrators, ruling that the law requiring the high bond was intended to restrict speech based on its content.

Some new challenges in the freedom of assembly involve the organization of protests by social media. E-mail blasts or social media can be used to organize spontaneous assemblies, sometimes in a matter of minutes. These demonstrations present new challenges for the government. Detractors say that large gatherings with no prior authorization endanger protesters and bystanders and disrupt local communities. Supporters argue that spontaneous gatherings are sometimes necessary to respond to a breaking news story or an official decision.

In keeping with the freedoms of the First Amendment, the government cannot deny a demonstration permit simply because it does not like the message. If, for example, the government permits pro-government groups to rally in a public park, then it cannot deny the same rights to groups that protest the government's actions.

☑ **READING PROGRESS CHECK**

Making Connections Why was the freedom of petition important to the colonists? Why is it important today?

LESSON 2 REVIEW

Reviewing Vocabulary

1. *Explaining* How do some governments use prior restraint to control information?

Using Your Graphic Organizer

2. *Summarizing* Write a report summarizing the ways in which the government can limit the freedoms of press, assembly, and petition.

Answering the Guiding Questions

3. *Making Generalizations* In what instances may the freedom of the press be limited?

4. *Describing* What restrictions can the government place on the freedoms of petition and assembly?

Writing About Government

5. *Informative/Explanatory* How have the Internet and digital communications changed the press? How have they changed the way individuals assemble? What challenges does this present for understanding the freedoms of the press and assembly? Write an essay explaining how technology has affected these First Amendment freedoms.

Interact with these digital assets and others in lesson 3

✓ **INTERACTIVE CHART**
Prayer in Public Schools

✓ **INTERACTIVE IMAGE**
"In God We Trust"

✓ **SELF-CHECK QUIZ**

✓ **VIDEO**
Van Orden v. Perry

netw⊚rks
TRY IT YOURSELF ONLINE

LESSON 3
Freedom of Religion

ESSENTIAL QUESTION

Why are the freedoms in the Bill of Rights and later amendments essential to our democracy?

Read each scenario below. Do you think the actions described should be allowed in our democracy?

a. A group gets together once a week in a private home for prayer and religious study.

b. The federal government requires all citizens to donate 5 percent of their income to a religious organization of their choice.

c. A city government provides funding to a religious organization to run a homeless shelter.

d. A religious organization holds a pledge drive among its members to fund the construction of a new place of worship.

e. A school requires that students pray at the beginning of the day. The school does not specify what prayer students must use.

f. A woman wears an article of clothing, which is required by her religion, to work.

g. A town sponsors a religious holiday display in the city hall.

Reading Help Desk

Academic Vocabulary

- significant
- inhibit
- excessive

Content Vocabulary

- establishment clause
- secular
- free exercise clause
- graven image

TAKING NOTES:

Key Ideas and Details

CATEGORIZING Use the table to list the Supreme Court cases that are related to the establishment clause and the free exercise clause.

Establishment Clause	Free Exercise Clause

Religious Freedom

GUIDING QUESTION *Why is the freedom of religion essential to our democracy?*

The first 16 words of the First Amendment to the U.S. Constitution deal with freedom of religion.

❝❝ **PRIMARY SOURCE**
Congress shall make no law respecting an establishment of religion, or prohibiting the free exercise thereof . . ."

—The First Amendment

These words reflect the deep concern that the Founders of the United States had about the relationship between church and state and about the right of individuals to practice their religion freely. In addition, Article VI of the Constitution prohibits the government from requiring any religious test for public office.

The First Amendment prohibits the government from either endorsing or punishing religious belief or practice. Some people believe that the two clauses require the government to be neutral toward religion. This means that the government should not take actions or create laws that favor one religion over another, or favor religious activities over nonreligious activities. Other people believe that the First Amendment requires the government to accommodate religious belief and practice, as long as it does not establish or promote a particular state or national religion.

Between 1791 and 1940, the U.S. Supreme Court heard only five cases dealing with the separation of church and state and church-state relations. Since then, the Court has heard more than a hundred such cases. Based on data about religious affiliation and attendance, religion is a **significant** part of American life. About 85 percent of Americans identify with a religion. Many national traditions have religious overtones. For example, U.S. money includes the words "In God We Trust." Since 1954, the Pledge of Allegiance has contained a reference to God. Many state legislatures, Congress, and the Supreme Court begin their sessions with a brief prayer. Although these traditions are criticized by some people as violating the First Amendment, they have been upheld by the courts.

✓ READING PROGRESS CHECK

Analyzing Why did the Founders protect religious freedom in the United States?

The Establishment Clause

GUIDING QUESTION *How does the establishment clause of the First Amendment protect the freedom of religion?*

The first phrase in the First Amendment is called the **establishment clause**. It forbids state and federal governments from setting up churches, from passing laws aiding one or all religions, or from favoring one religion over another. In addition, the establishment clause forbids the government from passing laws requiring attendance at any church or belief in any religious idea.

Thomas Jefferson once referred to the establishment clause as a "wall of separation between church and state." That phrase is not used in the Constitution, however. Over time, the idea of a wall of separation has been expanded and become controversial. How high should the wall go? Does it mean that the government should have no contact with any religious group?

In practice, religion has long been a part of public life in the United States, and in some ways, the government encourages religion. Places of worship are indirectly aided by government in many ways. For example, houses of worship, such as churches, temples, and mosques, do not have to pay real estate taxes, even though they receive government services such as police and fire protection.

Cases involving the establishment clause have been among the most controversial to reach the U.S. Supreme Court. One of the first cases the Court decided on the establishment clause was *Everson* v. *Board of Education*. In 1947 the Supreme Court ruled that New Jersey was allowed to pay for busing students to religious private schools, even though opponents argued that it amounted to state support for religion. The law, the justices said, benefited students rather than aiding a religion directly.

Since then, the Supreme Court has decided several cases about public funding for religious private schools. Sometimes, they have upheld the funding as legal, while other times they say the aid is unconstitutional. For example, it has allowed states to provide bus transportation, computers, and

significant having or likely to have influence or effect

U.S. money includes the words "In God We Trust." While such traditions have been criticized as violating the First Amendment, they have been upheld by the courts.

▼ CRITICAL THINKING
Defending Is the motto "In God We Trust" on U.S. currency a violation of constitutional principles? Explain your answer.

Engel v. *Vitale* (1962)	The Court ruled that the prayer read every morning in New York public schools violated the establishment clause. The prayer acknowledged God, but was not tied to a specific religion. The ruling said that it is no "business of government to compose official prayers for any group of the American people to recite as part of a religious program carried on by government."
Abington v. *Schempp* (1963)	The Supreme Court banned school-sponsored Bible reading and recitation of the Lord's Prayer. Because these activities were conducted by government-paid teachers, the Court ruled that they violated the establishment clause.
Wallace v. *Jaffree* (1985)	The Court struck down an Alabama law requiring teachers to observe a moment of silence for "meditation or voluntary prayer" at the start of each school day. The Court said that this law had a religious purpose, and that the state failed to maintain absolute neutrality toward religion and instead endorsed it.
Santa Fe v. *Doe* (2000)	The Supreme Court ruled that public school districts cannot let students lead stadium crowds in prayer before football games.

◄ **CRITICAL THINKING**

Researching Choose one of the Supreme Court cases and research the public reaction to the Court's decision. Write a brief summary of what you have learned.

loans of certain textbooks to students in religious schools. It refused to allow state-supported bus transportation for field trips, though. Why the difference? Since 1971, the justices have used a three-part evaluation to decide whether such government aid to schools violates the establishment clause.

Known as "The Lemon Test," because it was first set out in the case of *Lemon* v. *Kurtzman* (1971), the Court said that a law or government action must:

- have a **secular**, or nonreligious, purpose;
- in its main effect neither advance nor **inhibit**, or hold back, religion; and
- avoid **excessive** entanglement of government with religion.

In 2002 the Court approved a program from Ohio that provided vouchers to low-income parents to help pay tuition at a variety of schools, including religiously affiliated schools (*Zelman* v. *Simmons-Harris*).

Many states have provisions in their constitutions that ban government aid to any school with a religious affiliation. These are known as Blaine Amendments, after a similar federal constitutional amendment that was proposed in 1875 but failed to gain enough votes in Congress.

School Prayer Establishment clause cases are particularly controversial when they involve prayer in public schools. Because they are funded and run by the government, public schools are part of the government. In cases such as *Engel* v. *Vitale*, the Supreme Court has held that public school-sponsored prayer violates the establishment clause.

Many Americans disagree with the Supreme Court's decisions in prayer-in-school cases. Congress has considered several constitutional amendments to allow prayer in public schools, but none have received enough votes in Congress or the states to be ratified.

Despite restrictions on school-led or school-endorsed prayer, public school students may still study religion, and may even meet in religious groups. Schools are allowed to teach about the history of religion and the religions of the world as long as they do not endorse any particular belief. Student-initiated and -led groups, including student prayer groups, are allowed to use school space to meet outside school hours, just like any other club.

establishment clause the First Amendment guarantee that prohibits state and federal governments from setting up churches, passing laws aiding one or all religions or favoring one religion over another, or passing laws requiring attendance at any church or belief in any religious idea

secular nonreligious; not associated with any faith-based organization

inhibit to prohibit from doing something

excessive going beyond the usual, necessary, or proper limit or degree

FREEDOM
OF RELIGION

The Universal Declaration on Human Rights proclaims the freedom of religion. Protections for religious freedom and their day-to-day implementation vary from country to country.

(t to r) Getty Images/Comstock Images; Getty Images/Comstock Images; Tetra Images/Getty Images

JAPAN
Religious Affiliations
52% Shinto
42% Buddhist
4% Other
1% Christian

CHILE
Religious Affiliations
70% Roman Catholic
15% Protestant
10% Unaffiliated
5% Other

SAUDI ARABIA
Religious Affiliations
85 to 90 % Sunni Muslim
10 to 15 % Shia Muslim

Church and state are officially separate, and religious freedom is protected by law and in practice. According to Japan's Agency for Cultural Affairs, approximately 183,000 religious groups were certified by the government as religious organizations with corporate status. The government does not observe any religious holidays as national holidays.

Church and state are officially separate, and religious freedom is generally protected by law and in practice. Publicly subsidized schools are required to offer religious education during two teaching hours per week through high school. Parents may decide to have their children excused from any religious education. The majority of religious instruction in public schools is Catholic, although the Ministry of Education has approved curricula for 14 other religious groups. The government observes several religious holidays as national holidays.

Sunni Islam is the official religion, and there is no separation between state and religion. Saudi Arabia does not recognize freedom of religion and prohibits the public practice of any religion other than Islam. Some Muslims who do not adhere to the government's interpretation of Islam face significant political, economic, legal, social, and religious discrimination. All public schools provide religious instruction. The Committee for the Promotion of Virtue and Prevention of Vice is a government agency that monitors social behavior and enforces morality according to the government's interpretation of Islam.

▲ CRITICAL THINKING

1. *Comparing and Contrasting* Compare the religious composition and protections of these countries. In what ways are the protections similar and different?

2. *Applying* Choose one of your countries of origin (a country your relatives left to come to the U.S.) or the United States. Research that country's religious composition and level of religious freedom, and write a profile of that country.

Religious Displays by Governments Not all establishment clause issues concern education. For example, the establishment clause also prohibits some religious displays by the government. Generally, the Supreme Court has ruled that in instances where governments display symbols of a variety of religions, or do so with a secular (nonreligious) purpose, such displays are constitutional.

For example, when a Kentucky courthouse displayed a copy of the Ten Commandments by itself, the Supreme Court said that it violated the establishment clause (*McCreary Co.* v. *ACLU*, 2005). However, a Texas monument on the state capitol grounds that was donated by a private organization and included the Ten Commandments and accompanied by many other monuments and statues was found to be constitutional (*Van Orden* v. *Perry*, 2005). The city of Pawtucket, Rhode Island, was allowed to display a nativity scene with secular items like a Christmas tree, sleigh, and reindeer (*Lynch* v. *Donnelly*, 1984). Allegheny County, Pennsylvania, however, was prevented from displaying a publicly funded nativity scene on its own (*Allegheny County* v. *ACLU*, 1989).

✓ READING PROGRESS CHECK

Summarizing How has the Supreme Court ruled on school prayer cases? Explain.

The Free Exercise Clause

GUIDING QUESTION *How does the free exercise clause of the First Amendment protect the freedom of religion?*

The **free exercise clause** protects the right of individuals to worship as they choose. However, when an individual's right to free exercise of religion conflicts with other important interests, the First Amendment claim does not always win. As a rule, religious belief is protected, yet actions based on those beliefs may be restricted if they violate an important secular government interest. In 1878 the U.S. Supreme Court upheld the conviction of a Mormon man who had violated the criminal law against polygamy—having multiple spouses—even though his religion encouraged this practice at that time in history (*Reynolds* v. *United States*).

Difficulties arise when the government passes a law that happens to punish religious practice or forces people to act in a way that violates their religious beliefs. For example, many states have laws requiring that children be in school until age 16. In 1972 some Amish parents challenged one state's law, arguing that children should not be required to attend school past eighth grade. In *Wisconsin* v. *Yoder*, the Supreme Court ruled in their favor.

Two of the most discussed free exercise cases have to do with whether children could be forced to salute the American flag. In 1935 William and Lillian Gobitis were expelled from school for refusing to salute the flag. The family believed this violated the religious commandment against worshiping **graven images**. In *Minersville School District* v. *Gobitis* (1940), the Court upheld the school regulation. It said that the state legislature was democratically elected, had control over schools, and had a reasonable purpose for promoting patriotism—all of which outweighed the Gobitis family's claim.

After the *Gobitis* decision, the West Virginia board of education directed all students and teachers to salute the flag and recite the Pledge of Allegiance as part of regular school activities. When this state requirement was challenged, the Court overturned the *Gobitis* decision and said such laws are unconstitutional interferences with the free exercise of religion. The Court concluded in *West Virginia State Board of Education* v. *Barnette* (1943) that patriotism could be achieved without forcing people to violate their religious beliefs. It also said the right to free speech also means the government cannot compel speech, like requiring someone to recite the pledge.

free exercise clause the First Amendment guarantee that prohibits government from unduly interfering with the free exercise of religion

graven image an idol or physical object of worship

☑ READING PROGRESS CHECK

Analyzing Why did the Court rule that students and teachers cannot be required to salute the flag and recite the Pledge of Allegiance?

LESSON 3 REVIEW

Reviewing Vocabulary
1. *Comparing* What do the terms *secular* and *religious* mean?

Using Your Graphic Organizer
2. *Categorizing* Write a summary of the types of cases the Supreme Court has held regarding the establishment and free exercise clauses.

Answering the Guiding Questions
3. *Determining Importance* Why is the freedom of religion essential to our democracy?

4. *Explaining* How does the establishment clause of the First Amendment protect the freedom of religion?

5. *Explaining* How does the free exercise clause of the First Amendment protect the freedom of religion?

Writing About Government
6. *Argument* Choose one of the Supreme Court cases discussed in this lesson where you disagree with the Court's ruling. Write a blog post or letter to the editor explaining why you disagree with the Court's decision.

ReadingHelp Desk

Academic Vocabulary
- **guarantee**

Content Vocabulary
- **Jim Crow laws**
- **substantive due process**
- **equal protection clause**
- **rational basis**
- **strict scrutiny**
- **substantial relationship**
- **incorporation doctrine**
- **selective incorporation**

TAKING NOTES:
Key Ideas and Details

SUMMARIZING Use the table to take notes about the Fourteenth Amendment.

Citizenship	Due Process	Equal Protection

LESSON 4
The Fourteenth Amendment

ESSENTIAL QUESTION

Why are the freedoms in the Bill of Rights and later amendments essential to our democracy?

The Supreme Court has ruled that some rights are "fundamental" and that any government law that affects these fundamental rights should be closely scrutinized.

a. Think about the concept of fundamental rights.

b. What does *fundamental* mean to you?

c. Which rights do you consider fundamental? Why?

The Context of the Fourteenth Amendment

GUIDING QUESTION *What historical conditions led to the passage of the Fourteenth Amendment?*

After the Civil War, three amendments to the Constitution were ratified almost immediately. The Thirteenth Amendment outlawed slavery, and the Fifteenth Amendment said that the right to vote could not be restricted based on race or color. The Fourteenth Amendment was the longest and most complex of the three. It did three very important things:

1. Granted citizenship to all persons born in the United States.
2. **Guaranteed** due process of law from all state governments.
3. Guaranteed equal protection of the laws from all state governments.

Citizenship Just before the Civil War, the Supreme Court ruled that African Americans, whether enslaved or free, were not citizens. In this case, *Dred Scott* v. *Sandford* (1857), the Supreme Court said that an enslaved man could not sue in federal court because African Americans were not U.S. citizens when the Constitution was adopted. This decision, regarded today as one of the worst decisions the Court ever made, caused great outrage at the time. After the Civil War, the Fourteenth Amendment clearly established what constitutes citizenship: Anyone born or naturalized in the United States is a citizen, as long as he or she is subject to U.S. jurisdiction. Diplomats and foreign officials, for example, are not subject to U.S. jurisdiction.

The Fourteenth Amendment was a major milestone. For the first time, people of all races (excluding Native Americans) who were born in the U.S. were citizens and states could not deprive anyone of that citizenship.

Native American Citizenship The Fourteenth Amendment, however, did not grant citizenship to Native Americans. That came later. In 1887 Congress passed the General Allotment Act, which came to be known as the Dawes Act, for its champion, Henry Dawes. Seen in a positive light, the Dawes Act aimed to give individual Native Americans all the benefits of land ownership and education. The government would pay for schools where Native Americans could learn how to integrate into mainstream American society, which would ultimately lessen the burden of the government to oversee Native American welfare.

Seen in a negative light, the Dawes Act had the effect of breaking up reservations and cultural loyalty. In order to receive U.S. citizenship and a parcel of land, Native Americans had to agree to live separately from their own cultures and to give up their traditional ways. After all the allotments of land were given out, much of the remaining reservation land was sold to white settlers at a very low cost.

In 1919 Congress passed a law that made it possible, but not guaranteed, that those Native Americans who had fought during World War I and had been honorably discharged could become U.S. citizens. Finally, in 1924 the Indian Citizenship Act granted citizenship to all Native Americans born in the United States.

History of the Fourteenth Amendment At the time of the Civil War, the Fifth Amendment already ensured that the federal government could not deprive anyone of "life, liberty, or property, without due process of law." However, since the Bill of Rights limited only the federal government, this right to due process was not guaranteed by the states.

In theory, states already had such protections built into their constitutions. In practice, however, some state governments had ignored individual rights even after the Civil War. Many denied voting rights to African Americans, restricted their movement, prohibited them from accessing the courts, or discriminated in other ways. An amendment to the national Constitution would ensure that states could not continue to treat African Americans as second-class citizens. Or would it?

guarantee an assurance for the fulfillment of a condition

The Constitution

"All persons born or naturalized in the United States, and subject to the jurisdiction thereof, are citizens of the United States and of the state wherein they reside. No State shall make or enforce any law which shall abridge the privileges or immunities of citizens of the United States; nor shall any State deprive any person of life, liberty, or property without due process of law; nor deny to any person within its jurisdiction the equal protection of the laws."

—The Fourteenth Amendment

DBQ Read and analyze the Fourteenth Amendment of the U.S. Constitution, and answer the document-based questions below.

1. *Analyzing* Which part of this text guarantees citizenship to people born in the United States?

2. *Specifying* Which words say that state governments have to provide due process of law?

3. *Analyzing* Which part guarantees equal protection of the laws from state governments?

Library of Congress Prints & Photographs Division [LC-DIG-ppmsca-03095]

In *Brown* v. *Board of Education* (1954), the Supreme Court ruled that separate facilities for African Americans and whites were inherently unequal.

▲ **CRITICAL THINKING**

Explaining How did the Supreme Court justify segregation by race in the 1896 *Plessy* v. *Ferguson* case, in light of the Fourteenth Amendment? How did the Court find differently in the 1954 *Brown* v. *Board of Education* case?

Jim Crow laws any of the laws requiring racial segregation in places like schools, hotels, and public transportation in the South between the end of the Reconstruction period to the beginning of the civil rights movement in the 1950s

substantive due process the principle requiring that a government action not unreasonably interfere with a fundamental or basic right

equal protection clause prohibits government actions from unreasonably discriminating between different groups of people

rational basis a standard of judicial review that examines whether a legislature had a reasonable and not an arbitrary reason for enacting a particular statute

Shortly after ratification, the Fourteenth Amendment was used to overturn several laws that overtly discriminated against a specific racial group, such as a ban on African Americans serving on a jury. Unfortunately, these early moves toward equality were short-lived. By the late 1800s, about half of the states had adopted **Jim Crow laws** requiring racial segregation in places like schools, hotels, and public transportation. In the 1896 case *Plessy* v. *Ferguson*, the Supreme Court ruled that states were allowed to segregate by race so long as the state provided similar facilities to all. The justices said that such segregation did not violate the Fourteenth Amendment's requirements about fair laws.

Over time, the members of the Supreme Court changed and Americans' ideas about discrimination began to change, too. In 1954 the Supreme Court unanimously ruled that separate facilities for African Americans and whites were *inherently unequal*. This decision came in the landmark case of *Brown* v. *Board of Education*. The Supreme Court said that segregated public schools did, in fact, violate the Fourteenth Amendment's protections.

Today, almost 150 years of court rulings have informed our understanding of the Fourteenth Amendment. The Supreme Court has decided many cases that clarify what the Fourteenth Amendment permits and prohibits. There are two key provisions of the Fourteenth Amendment that guarantee fair laws: due process and equal protection.

☑ **READING PROGRESS CHECK**

Determining Importance Why is the Fourteenth Amendment important to our democracy?

Due Process

GUIDING QUESTION *How does due process protect individual rights and limit the powers of government?*

The text of the Fourteenth Amendment has been interpreted to include both procedural and substantive due process protection.

Procedural Due Process Procedural due process means the government must follow fair procedures if it is going to deprive someone of life, liberty, or property. The law cannot be enforced arbitrarily, and there must be reasonable safeguards to make sure that people are treated fairly.

Procedural due process guarantees that anyone who goes to court will go through a fair process and have the opportunity to assert his or her legal rights. Today, this is most often seen in criminal law, where all suspects have the right to an attorney, the right to be tried by a jury, and the right to have their attorney cross-examine any witnesses who have testified against the suspect. No matter where you go in the United States, procedural due process ensures that the fundamental procedures that make a trial fair should be present.

Substantive Due Process Substantive due process means that the laws themselves have to be fair. A law or government action cannot unreasonably interfere with a fundamental or basic right.

What is a fundamental right? Fundamental rights go to the heart of the American system and are indispensable to justice. The Supreme Court has ruled that the freedom of speech, freedom of the press, right to a fair trial, right to marry, right to travel, and right to educate one's children are all fundamental rights. Some of these rights are stated in the Constitution, and others are not specifically listed but are deeply rooted in American society.

A law will not necessarily be declared unconstitutional simply because it affects a fundamental right. If the government does want to take action that affects a fundamental right, it must show that it has a very strong, or compelling, interest. Sometimes, the government can prove this compelling interest and a court will uphold a law that infringes on someone's fundamental right. For example, the right to vote is a fundamental one. However, the government has a compelling interest in preventing voter fraud, so states may set reasonable residency and registration requirements for voters.

✓ **READING PROGRESS CHECK**

Contrasting What is the difference between procedural due process and substantive due process?

EXPLORING THE ESSENTIAL QUESTION

Categorize the following Supreme Court cases by whether they address procedural or substantive due process.

a. *Miranda* v. *Arizona* (1966) ruled that people accused of crimes must be informed of their right to remain silent and to avoid self-incrimination.

b. *in re Gault* (1967) ruled that juveniles accused of crimes are entitled to many of the same due process rights as adults.

c. *Engel* v. *Vitale* (1962) ruled that school prayer violated the establishment clause.

d. *Loving* v. *Virginia* (1967) ruled that a state law criminalizing marriage between people of different races violated the fundamental right to marry.

Equal Protection

GUIDING QUESTION *How does the equal protection clause protect individual rights and limit the powers of government?*

Equal protection means that laws must apply equally to all people who are in similar situations unless the state has a very good reason. The government cannot draw unreasonable distinctions. The key word is *unreasonable*. As with setting a minimum age for driver's licenses, governments must draw some distinctions between different groups of people.

When a law or government action is challenged as violating the **equal protection clause**—that is, unfairly discriminating between different groups of people—judges must determine whether or not the law is constitutional. To determine whether a law or government practice meets the equal protection standard, courts use one of three different tests, depending upon the type of discrimination involved.

Rational Basis In most discrimination cases that go to court, judges use the **rational basis** test. Using this test, judges will uphold a law or practice that treats some people differently than others if there is a rational basis for the different treatment. A rational basis exists when there is a logical relationship between the treatment or classification of some group of people and the purpose of the law. This test is used when the group of people being discriminated against is not part of a group that has been historically mistreated by the government.

For example, states require their citizens to be a certain age before they can marry. This discriminates against people below that age. However, this ensures that those who do marry are capable of accepting the respon-sibilities of marriage. In general, people become more responsible as they get older, so there is a rational relationship between the classification and the purpose of the law.

The Supreme Court used a test called strict scrutiny to make its decision in the case of *Loving* v. *Virginia* (1967), ruling that a racial classification did not serve a compelling state interest. This photograph shows Mildred and Richard Loving at a press conference after the ruling.

▲ CRITICAL THINKING

Assessing What is the relationship between substantive due process and the Supreme Court's ruling in *Loving* v. *Virginia*?

strict scrutiny a standard of judicial review for a challenged policy in which the court presumes the policy to be invalid unless the government can demonstrate a compelling interest to justify the policy

substantial relationship a standard of judicial review that examines whether there is a close connection between the law or practice and its purpose; specifically, laws that classify based on gender must serve an important governmental purpose

Strict Scrutiny Because some groups have historically faced severe discrimination in our society, laws that discriminate based on race, national origin, or citizenship status of people are judged more strictly. In these cases, the courts use a test called **strict scrutiny**. Judges applying strict scrutiny will find the law or practice constitutional if the state can show that the discriminating classification serves a compelling, or very important, interest. For example, a state law in Virginia prohibited marriage between persons of different races. When *Loving* v. *Virginia* (1967) came to the U.S. Supreme Court for review, it presented a clear situation where a state law created a classification based on race. The Court was unanimous in overturning this law because the racial classification did not serve a compelling state interest. The strict scrutiny test is also used when a law infringes on a fundamental right, as described above.

Substantial Relationship In gender discrimination cases, courts use the **substantial relationship** test—a middle ground between rational basis and strict scrutiny. By this standard, there must be a close connection—not just a rational relationship—between the law or practice and its purpose. In addition, laws that classify based on gender must serve an important governmental purpose.

Equal protection cases are complicated and controversial. Some people have argued, for example, that when the Fourteenth Amendment was ratified in 1868, Congress intended it to protect only against racial discrimination. Others argue that it was intended to protect only African Americans—not women, other racial minorities, or whites—against discrimination. Still others contend that the amendment embodies the national commitment to the fundamental value of equality; therefore, all unfair forms of government discrimination should be prohibited by the equal protection clause.

✓ READING PROGRESS CHECK

Applying What standards has the Court used to determine when the equal protection clause has been violated?

EXPLORING THE ESSENTIAL QUESTION

In a 1979 Supreme Court case, Justice Potter Stewart wrote "the Fourteenth Amendment guarantees equal laws, not equal results."

The case, *Personnel Administrator of Massachusetts* v. *Feeney*, was about a state law that gave preference to military veterans for government jobs. A woman who applied for a government job scored high on the civil service exam, but was ranked lower than several veterans who had also applied and not done as well on the exam. She protested against the law, claiming that the law unfairly discriminated against women because the overwhelming number of veterans at that time were men. The government defended the law, arguing that the veterans' preference was available for both men and women, and both male and female non veterans were equally disadvantaged. The Court ruled that the law was not discriminatory against women.

a. **Discussing** How does this case illustrate a guarantee of equal laws, rather than equal results?

b. **Evaluating** Do you believe that the law unconstitutionally discriminated against women? Why or why not?

JUDICIAL ANALYSIS OF 14th AMENDMENT CASES

TESTS:

DESCRIPTION:

USED WHEN:

When judges decide whether a law or government action unfairly discriminates, they look at the law usually using one of three tests.

Strict Scrutiny

The law (or government action) must serve a compelling government interest in a narrowly tailored way.

The law treats people differently based on race, color, national origin, or religion.

Regardless of who the case involves, this test is also used if the case involves fundamental rights, like those listed in the Bill of Rights, the right to travel, and the right to privacy.

Substantial Relationship

There must be a close connection or substantial relationship between the law (or government action) and an important government purpose.

The law treats people differently based on characteristics like their sex or the marital status of their parents.

Rational Basis

There must be a logical relationship between the treatment or classification of people and the purpose of the law.

The law impacts rights that are not fundamental, such as the right to practice a trade or profession, the right to welfare benefits, the right to education, etc.

AND when people are being treated differently based on characteristics like age, disability, wealth, or political affiliation.

EXPLORING THE ESSENTIAL QUESTION

Applying Which test would a judge use to evaluate the constitutionality of :

a. a city law that says that women cannot be firefighters? The city says its purpose is to make sure that the firefighters can carry people out of burning houses.

b. a state's practice of funding of its public schools by property taxes? This means that wealthier communities with more expensive homes will have much more money available for schools than poorer communities.

Do you believe these laws or actions violate the Fourteenth Amendment? Why or why not?

Incorporation of the Bill of Rights

GUIDING QUESTION *How has the selective incorporation of the Bill of Rights expanded due process and affected federalism?*

Originally, the Bill of Rights was intended to limit only the national government's power. In the 1833 case of *Barron* v. *Baltimore*, the Supreme Court affirmed this intention by ruling that the Bill of Rights applied only to the national government. It said the Constitution was silent on how the states could treat their citizens. When the Fourteenth Amendment was ratified in 1868, many thought that it would require the states to abide by all of the protections in the Bill of Rights. Until the turn of the century, however, the Court repeatedly ruled that the Fourteenth Amendment did not bind states with respect to the Bill of Rights.

In 1925, however, the Court began to shift its position when it ruled the Fourteenth Amendment required states to protect freedom of speech (*Gitlow*

v. *New York*). The justices said free speech was one of the liberties protected by the Fourteenth Amendment's promise that no one could be deprived of liberty without due process of law. This was the first step in the development of the **incorporation doctrine**, an interpretation of the Constitution that means the due process clause of the Fourteenth Amendment requires state and local governments to guarantee their citizens the rights stated in the Bill of Rights. To that end, the Court in the 1931 *Near* v. *Minnesota* ruling held that the amendment also required states to protect freedom of the press.

But did all the Bill of Rights apply to every state action? In 1937 the Court said in *Palko* v. *Connecticut* that incorporation applied to what it called fundamental rights, those rights so essential to order, liberty, and justice "as to be ranked fundamental." Using this standard, the Court began following a process called **selective incorporation**, whereby it decided on a case-by-case basis which federal rights also applied to the states.

Eventually selective incorporation came to mean that almost all of the Bill of Rights now apply to the states. In 2010 the right to bear arms (Second Amendment) was incorporated in the case of *McDonald* v. *City of Chicago* when the Court said the right to keep a handgun in your home was a "fundamental" right. Today, only three rights have not been incorporated by the states: the right to a grand jury (part of the Fifth Amendment), the unanimity requirement in a criminal jury (part of the Sixth Amendment), and the right to a civil jury trial (part of the Seventh Amendment).

The process of incorporation has greatly expanded the scope of constitutional rights. It gives people the opportunity to take their cases to federal court if they believe a state or local government is refusing to protect their fundamental liberties. At the same time, by doing this incorporation, it has altered the balance of power between the states and the national government in our federal system. The power of the national government to overrule or modify state government actions through the federal courts has expanded at the expense of the states.

incorporation doctrine the process by which the Bill of Rights was extended to the states and localities

selective incorporation the process by which the Supreme Court decided on a case-by-case basis which federal rights also applied to the states

☑ **READING PROGRESS CHECK**

Explaining How have the Court's decisions requiring states to uphold the Bill of Rights affected the balance of power between states and the national government?

LESSON 4 REVIEW

Reviewing Vocabulary
1. ***Explaining*** How did Jim Crow laws undermine the Fourteenth Amendment?

Using Your Graphic Organizer
2. ***Summarizing*** Use your completed graphic organizer to summarize the different parts of the Fourteenth Amendment.

Answering the Guiding Questions
3. ***Analyzing*** What historical conditions led to the passage of the Fourteenth Amendment?

4. ***Explaining*** How does due process protect individual rights and limit the powers of government?

5. ***Explaining*** How does the equal protection clause protect individual rights and limit the powers of government?

6. ***Understanding Relationships*** How has the selective incorporation of the Bill of Rights expanded due process and affected federalism?

Writing About Government
7. ***Informative/Explanatory*** Return to the questions at the beginning of this lesson. How do your choices compare to the list of rights the Supreme Court has called fundamental? Create a chart that compares and contrasts the two. Then write a few paragraphs explaining the rights the Court has called fundamental.

Interact with these digital assets and others in lesson 5

✓ **INTERACTIVE INFOGRAPHIC**
Gender Pay Gap

✓ **INTERACTIVE TIME LINE**
Civil Rights Legislation

✓ **SELF-CHECK QUIZ**

✓ **VIDEO**
Gratz and Grutter

networks
TRY IT YOURSELF ONLINE

LESSON 5
Equal Protection and Discrimination

Reading Help Desk

Academic Vocabulary

- diverse
- sphere

Content Vocabulary

- discrimination
- civil rights movement
- sit-in
- picket
- disability
- affirmative action
- racial quota

TAKING NOTES:

Key Ideas and Details

IDENTIFYING Use the chart to list different types of discrimination and the constitutional protections and civil rights legislation that prohibit this discrimination.

Discrimination Based On	Constitutional Protections and Laws
Race	
National Origin	
Gender	
Other	

ESSENTIAL QUESTION

What restrictions, if any, should be placed on our constitutional rights and freedoms? How have citizen movements and social movements brought about political and social change?

The following situations involve some form of discrimination. For each, decide whether the discrimination is reasonable and should be allowed or is unreasonable and should not be allowed. Explain your reasons.

a. An airline requires its pilots to retire at age 60.

b. A child with a disability is not permitted to play at a public playground.

c. Veterans receive preference in applying for government jobs.

d. Girls are not allowed to try out for positions on an all-boy baseball team at a public high school.

e. Auto insurance rates are higher for young, unmarried drivers.

f. An expensive seafood restaurant requires that its servers wear tuxedos. The restaurant hires only male wait staff.

g. Latinos and African Americans are charged higher interest rates for home loans compared to Caucasians with the same credit scores.

Select one example where you think the discrimination described is unreasonable. What actions could be taken to prevent future discrimination?

Protection from Unfair Discrimination

GUIDING QUESTION *When is discrimination unconstitutional?*

The promise of equality is set out in the Declaration of Independence: "We hold these truths to be self-evident, that all men are created equal, that they are endowed by their Creator with certain unalienable rights…" But what does *equality* mean? Does it mean that every American receives the same treatment? That everyone has equal opportunities? Or something else?

Discrimination occurs when some people are treated differently than others because of their membership in a group based on some shared characteristic—like their race, age, gender, religion, or appearance. Sometimes, the government must treat different groups of people differently. For example, we require people to be a certain age before we allow them to drive. Those laws discriminate on the basis of age, but it is reasonable and legal to do so. Other laws or government actions discriminate in a way that is unconstitutional. For example, in the 1950s, some public school districts did not allow children of different races to go to school together. That kind of discrimination violates the U.S. Constitution, specifically the Fourteenth Amendment.

☑ READING PROGRESS CHECK

Defining What is discrimination?

Discrimination Based on Race

GUIDING QUESTION *How do the Constitution and federal legislation protect people from discrimination based on race?*

Even though the Thirteenth Amendment ended slavery in 1865 and the Fifteenth Amendment guaranteed the right to vote for all citizens regardless of race, segregation and discrimination based on color persisted. In the decades after the Civil War, many states passed Jim Crow laws, which allowed segregation of people of different races. The laws also limited opportunities and legal protections for African Americans. These types of laws were upheld by the Supreme Court in the case of *Plessy* v. *Ferguson* (1896). Then, in 1954 the Supreme Court made a decision that would change everything and become a milestone in the long struggle for civil rights.

Brown v. Board of Education (1954) In the 1950s, the schools of Topeka, Kansas, were racially segregated. Linda Carol Brown, an eight-year-old African American, was denied admission to an all-white school near her home and had to attend an all African American school further from her home. With the help of the National Association for the Advancement of Colored People (NAACP), Linda's family sued the Topeka Board of Education.

At the time, the head lawyer for the NAACP was Thurgood Marshall. He and his team had already successfully argued several discrimination cases before the courts, including cases about segregated juries, law schools, and graduate schools. The *Brown* v. *Board of Education of Topeka* case would be the first to challenge segregated elementary, middle, and high schools.

In what many consider one of the most important Supreme Court decisions in U.S. history, the Court unanimously ruled that segregated schools could never be equal and were, therefore, unconstitutional. In doing so, the Court overturned the "separate but equal" doctrine from the *Plessy* case and set a precedent that guided numerous later decisions. In 1967 President Johnson appointed Marshall associate justice on the Supreme Court, where he became the first African American justice.

The Civil Rights Movement The *Brown* decision reflected decades of work to reduce discrimination. It also was a powerful catalyst to expand the **civil rights movement**. Courageous men and women of many races fought

discrimination treatment or consideration of, or making a distinction in favor of or against, a person or thing based on the group, class, or category to which that person or thing belongs rather than on individual merit

LANDMARK LAWS
THE CIVIL RIGHTS ACT OF 1964

The Civil Rights Act of 1964 empowered the federal government to:

★ Prohibit discrimination based on race, religion, sex, and national origin in employment, which includes hiring, firing, working conditions, and promotion

★ Ban discrimination in public accommodations and in government services

★ Establish the Equal Employment Opportunity Commission (EEOC) to enforce the law and investigate complaints

▲ CRITICAL THINKING
Making Connections Think of an example where the Civil Rights Act of 1964 has protected you or someone you know from discrimination.

We the People: Making a Difference

Dr. Martin Luther King, Jr.

National Archives and Records Administration [542068]

Following in the footsteps of his grandfather and father, Martin Luther King, Jr. became a minister. In 1954 King became pastor of Dexter Avenue Baptist Church in Montgomery, Alabama, and soon emerged as a central figure in the civil rights movement, leading a boycott that ended with a Supreme Court ruling against bus segregation. As president of the Southern Christian Leadership Conference, King focused on fighting racial injustice. His massive protest campaign in Birmingham in 1963 increased support across the nation for civil rights. That same year King delivered his "I Have a Dream" speech to 250,000 peaceful marchers in Washington, D.C.

Though successful, King's work provoked violent opposition. His home was bombed, he was assaulted, and authorities arrested him twenty times. Despite these challenges, he remained committed to peaceful protest. King's effective use of nonviolent tactics led to a Nobel Peace Prize in 1964. King continued using nonviolent methods to fight injustice until his assassination in April 1968.

CRITICAL THINKING

1. Analyzing How do you think King's background helped prepare him to lead the civil rights movement?

2. Assessing Do you agree with the style of protest tactics King used to promote civil rights? Why or why not?

---

segregation and discrimination through actions across the country. Many individuals and groups worked tirelessly, organized nonviolent protests, and risked their lives to stand up to entrenched discrimination.

Dr. Martin Luther King, Jr., who was a Baptist minister, led nonviolent marches and demonstrations against segregation. He understood the importance of the courts in trying to win equal rights and sought to stir the nation's conscience. King, John Lewis, Rev. Fred Shuttlesworth, Rosa Parks, and other leaders coordinated the actions of groups like the NAACP, the Montgomery Improvement Association, and the Southern Christian Leadership Conference (SCLC). These leaders and countless less famous Americans held sit-ins at restaurant lunch counters that served only whites. When arrested for breaking the law, they were almost always found guilty. They could then appeal, challenging the constitutionality of the laws. Other groups organized boycotts, Freedom Schools, or marches.

In some cases, people across the country saw news footage of police violence in response to nonviolent protests. Slowly, public opinion about segregation and racial discrimination changed, and Congress began to act. After intense debates and filibustering by some, Congress passed two landmark civil rights and voting rights laws: the Civil Rights Act of 1964 and the Voting Rights Act of 1965. They prohibited discrimination based on race, gender, religion, and national origin in employment, public accommodations, government services, and voting. The Civil Rights Acts of 1968, 1974, and 1988 expanded these protections to housing discrimination.

civil rights movement the struggle by African Americans in the mid-1950s to late 1960s to be free of racial discrimination and to achieve rights, freedoms, and opportunities equal to those of whites

sit-in organized demonstration tactic in which participants seat themselves in a significant location and refuse to move; a form of peaceful protest

☑ **READING PROGRESS CHECK**

Determining Cause and Effect What led to the case of *Brown* v. *Board of Education* and what effects did the ruling have on the civil rights movement?

▲ The Voting Rights Act of 1965 allowed the federal government to ensure qualified voters can exercise their voting rights. The act was amended in the 1970s and 1980s and extended for another 25 years in 2006.

Discrimination Based on National Origin

GUIDING QUESTION *How does the Constitution protect people from discrimination based on national origin?*

In 1954 the Supreme Court made it clear that the Fourteenth Amendment protects people based on national origin as well as race. The case was *Hernandez* v. *Texas*. Pete Hernandez, a Mexican American, was convicted of murder by an all-white jury. His lawyer appealed, noting that a significant number of Mexican Americans were eligible for jury service where Hernandez was tried but had been systematically barred from jury service for more than 25 years. The Court agreed that the systematic exclusion of Mexican Americans on juries deprived defendants such as Hernandez of equal protection.

Latinos made significant advances in the 1960s and 1970s. Leaders such as Cesar Chavez and Dolores Huerta formed the National Farmworkers Association, which became the United Farm Workers. Together they worked for equal rights and fair pay for farmworkers, many of whom were Latino. Committed to the same philosophy of nonviolent protest as Martin Luther King, Jr., and Mohandas Gandhi, these activists held rallies and voter registration drives and organized boycotts aimed at pressuring famers to stop using dangerous pesticides on fruit being picked by farmworkers.

Their work continues, as does the work of many other groups working to end discrimination based on national origin such as the Asian American Justice Center and the National Congress of American Indians.

Civil rights laws protect against employment discrimination based on national origin. This means that employers cannot treat people less favorably in hiring or on the job because of their place of origin, ethnicity, or accent.

In 1981 undocumented immigrants challenged a Texas law that refused funding to local school districts for the education of undocumented children. In the case of *Plyler* v. *Doe*, the Supreme Court said this was unconstitutional because undocumented immigrants are protected by the Fourteenth Amendment. The state law severely disadvantaged these children by denying them the right to an education. Since Texas could not prove there was a compelling interest for the law, the Court said it was unconstitutional.

✓ READING PROGRESS CHECK

Examining What strategies were used by Latinos in their struggle for civil rights?

Discrimination Based on Sex and Gender

GUIDING QUESTION *How do the Constitution and federal legislation protect people from discrimination based on sex and gender?*

The movement to secure equal rights for women has a long history. The first women's rights convention was held in 1848. The most controversial issue to come out of the convention was demand for the right to vote.

Women in Wyoming, Colorado, Idaho, and Utah gained the right to vote by the end of the 1800s. Elsewhere, women and men who supported their cause **picketed** the White House, marched, petitioned, staged hunger strikes, and were arrested to draw attention and support to their cause. Women finally won full voting rights with the ratification of the Nineteenth Amendment in 1920.

picket demonstrate, as against a government's policies or actions

The Equal Rights Amendment (ERA) has been introduced in every congressional session (every two years) since 1923. It would amend the Constitution to specifically prohibit federal, state, and local governments from passing discriminatory laws or unequally enforcing laws based on gender. It passed the Congress in 1972 and was sent to the states for ratification. Supporters succeeded in getting 35 states to ratify it, but fell three states short of the required number of states by the deadline. While there is still no federal ERA, at least 22 states had passed specific protection laws against gender discrimination by 2012.

A variety of state and federal laws protect women and girls from discrimination. This includes the 1963 Equal Pay Act, which bans wage discrimination, and Title VII of the 1964 Civil Rights Act, which prohibits discrimination based on race and sex, including sexual harassment. Title IX of the Education Amendments Act of 1972, which also protects women and girls from discrimination, says: "No person in the United States shall, on the basis of sex, be excluded from participation in, be denied the benefits of, or be subjected to discrimination under any education program or activity receiving federal financial assistance." While Title IX is best known for protecting female athletes from discrimination, it also requires fair treatment for pregnant and parenting students and greatly expands the opportunities for females pursuing educational opportunities in math and science.

Despite many advances, women continue to earn less money than men. In 2014 the Bureau of Labor Statistics reported that women earn an average of 82 cents for every $1 white non-Hispanic men are paid. The pay gap typically widens as women age. The gap was generally even larger for women of color, with African American women earning 68 cents and Latino women earning 63 cents compared to white non-Hispanic men. There are many explanations for these pay gaps and perspectives about what, if anything, should be done to close them. The women's movement continues to fight for equal pay for equal work.

☑ READING PROGRESS CHECK

Describing What federal laws protect women and girls from discrimination?

Combating Other Forms of Discrimination

GUIDING QUESTION *How has protection against discrimination been extended to other categories of people?*

Federal discrimination laws have expanded to include age discrimination and discrimination against those living with disabilities. However, there are no federal laws that prohibit discrimination on the basis of sexual orientation.

Discrimination Based on Sexual Orientation Public opinion polls show that in the past two decades, American attitudes toward gays and lesbians have become more tolerant. Today, millions of people are campaigning for laws that would give gay, lesbian, and bisexual people equal rights. However, gay rights remain a controversial issue, and many people oppose specific laws that protect gays and lesbians.

In 2010 Congress passed a bill repealing a ban on openly gay people serving in the military. Under the ban, any service member who revealed he or she was gay or lesbian, or who was discovered, could be discharged from the armed services. A number of states, cities, and towns have passed laws that provide some protection from discrimination for people who are gay, lesbian, or bisexual. These laws vary and may protect individuals in the areas of employment,

▼ Title IX of the Education Act of 1972 prohibited gender discrimination in most school activities, including curriculum, faculty hiring, and student athletic programs.

State Civil Rights Laws

When the U.S. Supreme Court makes a decision regarding the Constitution, it determines the minimum protection that governments must extend to their citizens. However, state and local governments may offer greater protection than the Constitution requires. For example, federal civil rights laws prohibit certain forms of discrimination based on race, national origin, citizenship, gender, age, and disability. In addition, some state and local governments have passed their own antidiscrimination laws that cover discrimination based on marital status, personal appearance, sexual orientation, political affiliation, and more.

CRITICAL THINKING

Researching Investigate the laws in your state.

a. What types of discrimination are outlawed in your state?

b. How do residents report discrimination?

c. What agency or commission investigates and resolves complaints of discrimination?

disability a physical or mental condition that causes a person to have difficulty seeing, hearing, talking, walking, or performing basic activities of daily living

affirmative action policies that give preference to women or minorities for jobs, promotions, admission to schools, or other benefits, in order to make up for past or current discrimination

housing, education, family matters, and public accommodation. In 2013 the Supreme Court ruled that the federal government was required to recognize valid same-sex marriages for the purpose of federal law and benefits. By 2014, 11 states had passed laws legalizing same-sex marriages. Another 21 states allowed same-sex marriages despite a law or state constitutional amendment prohibiting it, because a state or federal court had ruled that the states' law violated the U.S. Constitution. Eighteen states had laws or state constitutional amendments still in force prohibiting same-sex marriage.

In the United States, many people oppose legal recognition of same-sex couples, arguing that it is inconsistent with the country's mainstream religious teachings, core traditions, and the morality of many people. Others see the protection of gay and lesbian people from discrimination as a moral issue and as part of the long history of civil rights movements.

Discrimination Based on Age Under the federal Age Discrimination in Employment Act of 1967, it is illegal for employers to discriminate against people over age 40. This means that employers cannot refuse to hire or promote someone simply because he or she is older. The law has several important exceptions, including if there is a valid reason to consider age.

Age discrimination is not limited to older people. Many laws and practices also discriminate against youth. However, restrictions based on age as it relates to voting, running for public office, making a will, driving, and drinking alcoholic beverages are generally upheld by the courts as being reasonable.

Discrimination Based on Disability According to the U.S. Census Bureau, about one in five Americans has some kind of **disability**. One in ten has a severe disability. A person is considered to have a disability if he or she has difficulty performing certain basic functions such as seeing, hearing, talking, or walking or has regular difficulty performing basic activities of daily living.

Many people with disabilities regularly suffer discrimination in certain areas of daily life. Since the 1970s, a number of laws have been passed to prohibit discrimination against people with disabilities, most notably the Americans with Disabilities Act (ADA) and the Individuals with Disabilities Education Act (IDEA). These laws require consideration of a person's special needs in education, employment, building design, and transportation.

✓ **READING PROGRESS CHECK**

Listing What federal laws prevent discrimination based on a person's age or disability?

Affirmative Action

GUIDING QUESTION *How has the Supreme Court ruled on affirmative action?*

Affirmative action involves governments and private employers taking steps to remedy past and current discrimination in employment and education. It goes beyond merely stopping or avoiding discrimination. For example, a university might take affirmative action by starting a program to attract more applications from students who are members of minority groups. Some affirmative action is required by governments, but many businesses use it voluntarily.

Affirmative action is controversial, and people in several states have voted to ban or limit these programs. Opponents of affirmative action say that it is a form of reverse discrimination. They argue that race should not be used as a basis for classification, because special treatment for some means discrimination against others. Supporters of affirmative action say that preferential treatment in educational programs and in employment is needed to overcome the effects of past discrimination.

The affirmative action issue in education was presented to the U.S. Supreme Court in the case of *Regents of the University of California* v. *Bakke* (1978). A white male student named Allan Bakke sued because he was twice rejected for medical school. He claimed the University of California had practiced reverse discrimination because a certain number of slots were guaranteed to minorities.

The Supreme Court found the medical school's special admissions program unconstitutional and ordered that Bakke be admitted to the university. The Court said that while **racial quotas** (reserving a certain number of spots for minorities) were illegal, race could be considered as one of the factors—but not the single deciding factor—in the admissions process in order to obtain a **diverse** student body.

After the *Bakke* decision, many colleges did use race as one of the factors in admissions to achieve a diverse student body. In two cases from Michigan, *Grutter* v. *Bollinger* and *Gratz* v. *Bollinger* (2003), the Court distinguished between types of admission preferences. The Court said universities could treat race as a "plus factor" in admitting students. However, it was unconstitutional to use a system that automatically gave a certain number of extra admission points to minorities. The Court said that universities serve a special role because they make it possible for people of all backgrounds to compete at all levels of society.

Outside of the educational **sphere**, the use of affirmative action has also been mixed. In a 1987 trucking industry case, the Supreme Court upheld a plan by a state transportation agency to take account of gender in promotions if the candidates for a position were equally qualified. Then in 1995, in *Adarand Constructors, Inc.* v. *Peña*, the Court overturned earlier decisions by saying that federal agencies could not automatically favor minority-based companies for federal contracts.

racial quotas a certain number of spots reserved for minorities

diverse of various kinds or forms

sphere the place or environment within which a person or thing exists

✓ **READING PROGRESS CHECK**

Discussing What are some arguments for and against the use of affirmative action in education and employment?

LESSON 5 REVIEW

Reviewing Vocabulary

1. ***Describing*** How did the civil rights movement use sit-ins in its struggle for African American civil rights?

Using Your Graphic Organizer

2. ***Identifying*** Use your organizer to describe groups of people that have been the subject of discrimination and the laws and constitutional rights protecting them.

Answering the Guiding Questions

3. ***Stating*** When is discrimination unconstitutional?

4. ***Interpreting*** How do the Constitution and federal legislation protect people from discrimination based on race?

5. ***Explaining*** How does the Constitution protect people from discrimination based on national origin?

6. ***Interpreting*** How do the Constitution and federal legislation protect people from discrimination based on sex and gender?

7. ***Making Connections*** How has protection against discrimination been extended to other categories of people?

8. ***Summarizing*** How has the Supreme Court ruled on affirmative action?

Writing About Government

9. ***Narrative*** Write a personal narrative about a time you experienced discrimination. Was it legal or unlawful discrimination? What did you do, if anything, to fight the discrimination? Is there something you wish you had done? Explain.

Grutter  Bollinger (2003)

FACTS OF THE CASE In 1997 Barbara Grutter, a resident of Michigan, applied for admission to the University of Michigan Law School. Grutter, who is white, had a 3.8 undergraduate GPA and scored well on the Law School Admission Test (LSAT). She was denied admission to the law school. She then sued, claiming that her rights to equal protection under the Fourteenth Amendment had been violated.

At the time, the law school had an admissions policy that used race as a factor in the admissions process. In selecting students, the law school considered the applicant's academic ability, including undergraduate GPA, standardized test scores, the applicant's personal statement, and letters of recommendation. The school also considered factors such as the applicant's experience and the degree to which the applicant would contribute to law school life and the diversity of the community, including the applicant's race.

ISSUE

Does a public university's use of race as a factor in admissions policies violate the Fourteenth Amendment?

ARGUMENTS

GRUTTER In this case, the university was discriminating on the basis of race, and the Constitution's prohibition against racial discrimination protects whites as well as minorities. While diversity was an important interest, there are other ways to achieve a diverse student body without looking at the race of each individual applicant. It is not acceptable to discriminate based on race when other methods would achieve the same government interest. In the 1970s, the Supreme Court ruled in case called *Bakke* that quotas—or numerical requirements that minority students make up a certain portion of the class—were unacceptable. In this case, the university's attempt to achieve a "critical mass" is essentially a quota.

BOLLINGER Diversity among the student body is a "compelling state interest" and therefore some consideration of applicants' race should be allowed. A critical mass of students of different racial backgrounds enhances everyone's education, breaks down racial stereotypes, and prepares a diverse workforce. Furthermore, the admission policy in this case is flexible because it individually assessed each applicant, and race was only one of several criteria. Universities are the training ground for many of our nation's leaders. The country will be best served by making sure that those universities and the path to leadership is visibly open to qualified applicants of all races and ethnicities.

EXPLORING THE ESSENTIAL QUESTION

Moot Court You will be assigned to one of three groups: lawyers for Barbara Grutter, lawyers for the University of Michigan Law School, and Supreme Court justices. You will prepare for a moot court of this case. The lawyers for each side should develop arguments to present during oral argument and prepare to answer questions from the justices. The justices should prepare questions to ask the lawyers during oral argument. When you argue the case, each team will have five minutes to present its side, and the justices will be allowed to ask the lawyers questions throughout their five minutes. The justices will then vote and announce their decision, explaining their reasons. After the moot court is complete, write a persuasive essay or blog that reflects your personal opinion about this issue.

LESSON 6
The Rights to Bear Arms and to Privacy

Reading Help Desk

Academic Vocabulary

- monitor
- expand

Content Vocabulary

- militia
- surveillance
- wiretap

TAKING NOTES:

Key Ideas and Details

LISTING Use the chart to list the major laws and Supreme Court cases regarding the right to bear arms and to privacy.

	Laws	Supreme Court Cases
Right to Bear Arms		
Right to Privacy		

ESSENTIAL QUESTION

What restrictions, if any, should be placed on our constitutional rights and freedoms?

Like most constitutional freedoms, the courts have allowed some reasonable restrictions on the right to bear arms and the right to privacy. Think about the principles of democracy and the purposes of government. Do you think the government should be able to:

a. limit the number of weapons a law-abiding citizen can purchase? If so, to what number? If not, why not?

b. keep a national database of anyone with a history of mental health issues, give gun sellers access to it, and make it illegal to sell a gun to a person on the list? Why or why not?

c. perform full-body scans of all individuals for security reasons before they board an airplane? Why or why not?

d. keep track of everyone's health conditions and genetic predispositions to diseases in a database? Explain your reasoning.

The Second Amendment

GUIDING QUESTION *In what circumstances may the government limit the right to keep and bear arms?*

In colonial times and through the American Revolution, it was common for groups of men in one town or region to form **militias**. These were groups of people who owned guns and were ready to defend the town, even though they were not professional soldiers. Without these well-armed militias, America could not have won the war against the British and gained independence.

The Constitution and Bill of Rights were written at a time when many people were concerned that a strong national government might suppress their freedoms. The Second Amendment expresses their concerns this way:

PRIMARY SOURCE
A well-regulated militia, being necessary to the security of a free state, the right of the people to keep and bear arms, shall not be infringed."

Today, many Americans disagree about exactly what the Second Amendment means. The Supreme Court has clearly ruled that it protects an individual's right to keep a gun. Beyond that, does it give individuals the right to keep, carry, and use all types of guns? Can or should the government reasonably restrict gun ownership? What level of government should decide these questions—national, state, or local?

Gun Control Efforts by the government to regulate firearms are very controversial. Most Americans who own firearms own them legally and use them lawfully. They believe that "guns don't kill people, people do"; so to them, limiting gun ownership is misguided. They believe passionately that their liberty and perhaps their safety will be at risk if gun ownership is restricted. Supporters of gun control laws believe that the relatively easy availability of firearms contributes to violent crime, accidental shootings, and suicide. They point out that the United States has the highest rate of civilian gun ownership in the world.

The primary federal gun-control law is the Gun Control Act of 1968. It prohibits certain people—such as convicted felons, minors, and illegal immigrants—from buying or possessing guns. It also regulates how and where guns can be sold and sets penalties for carrying and using firearms in crimes of violence or drug trafficking.

Many states have also enacted their own legislation about guns. Some states have given people more freedom to own and carry guns. For example, in Alaska and Vermont, adults without a felony conviction can carry a concealed weapon without having to first obtain a permit. Other states have passed laws making it harder to own, carry, and use guns. Some states require background checks, fingerprinting, firearms training, and other application requirements to purchase a gun.

In 1976 the city government of Washington, D.C., passed a law that made it a crime to carry an unregistered firearm and prohibited the registration of handguns in the district. It further mandated that all registered (legal) firearms be kept unloaded and disassembled or trigger locked. Several D.C. residents tried to fight the law in court, claiming it violated the Second Amendment.

militia a local group of armed citizens

In a landmark case called *District of Columbia* v. *Heller* (2008), the Supreme Court ruled that D.C. law was unconstitutional. In its written opinion, the justices explored the history and language of the Second Amendment. A five-justice majority ruled that people have a constitutional right to keep guns in their homes. The justices said, "the inherent right of self-defense has been central to the Second Amendment right." The Court said that the scope of the right to bear arms is not unlimited, however. The government can choose to regulate the possession of guns, or to ban certain groups, like convicted felons, from possessing guns.

Four justices dissented from this ruling. They also examined the language and history of the amendment, and came to the opposite conclusion. In their dissent, they wrote that the purpose and intent of the Second Amendment was to protect the right of the people to maintain a well-regulated militia. They also argued that in reviewing firearms laws, the Court should balance protection of constitutional rights against the interest of public safety.

✔ READING PROGRESS CHECK

Explaining Why did the Supreme Court rule that Washington, D.C.'s gun law was unconstitutional? Explain.

C·I·V·I·C PARTICIPATION IN A DIGITAL AGE

Gun Rights

Americans for Responsible Solutions is an advocacy group and political action committee that supports stricter gun-control laws to limit the sale of assault weapons and to require criminal background checks for all gun buyers and other measures to protect people from gun owners who are criminals or who are mentally ill. The organization was started in 2013 by former U.S. Representative Gabrielle Giffords. In 2010 Giffords was severely injured herself by a man who fired 33 bullets from a semiautomatic pistol into a crowd listening to her speak. Twelve others were injured and another six people died.

The National Rifle Association's Institute for Legislative Action describes itself as America's premier defender of the Second Amendment. It advocates for preserving the right of all law-abiding individuals to purchase, possess, and use firearms for legitimate purposes. It lobbies to prevent gun-control laws and to enact pro-gun legislation. The NRA was founded in 1871 to promote rifle practice and improve the marksmanship of potential American soldiers.

CRITICAL THINKING

Exploring Issues Look at the websites of Americans for Responsible Solutions and the National Rifle Association's Institute for Legislative Action. Both websites feature a section called "take action." Using both websites, look for petitions you could sign, polls you could take, volunteer opportunities, and other ways you can add your voice to the debate about what gun control, if any, is best for America. Write a summary of what you found.

Right to Privacy

GUIDING QUESTION *In what circumstances may the government limit privacy rights?*

Although the words "right to privacy" or "right to be let alone" do not appear anywhere in the U.S. Constitution, many people contend that privacy is a basic right that should be protected against unreasonable interference from the government.

The Supreme Court has issued several rulings that relate to privacy, citing the First, Third, Fourth, Fifth, and Ninth Amendments. They have said that, taken together, the freedom of speech and association, the right to have one's home free of soldiers during peacetime, the freedom from unreasonable search and seizure, the right to remain silent, and the unspecified rights kept by the people create a "zone of privacy."

Like other constitutional freedoms, however, the government may limit privacy rights. Sometimes the right to privacy conflicts with important government interests. For example, the police may obtain a search warrant to examine the contents of a computer that it believes may have been used by a suspected criminal.

Some states have passed privacy laws or added a right to privacy to their state constitutions. Others believe that the Supreme Court has gone too far in recognizing a right to privacy, arguing that that right does not appear anywhere in the Constitution.

Reproductive Rights and Privacy The Supreme Court first recognized a right to privacy in the mid-1960s. In a case called *Griswold* v. *Connecticut*, the Court examined whether a state could outlaw access to contraception. In reading the entire Bill of Rights, the justices found that several implied a right to privacy. The Court ruled that Connecticut could not outlaw contraception, because it would violate the privacy of married couples.

Perhaps the most controversial rulings about a right to privacy come from cases about the right to an abortion. Before the 1970s, states had a wide variety of laws relating to abortion. Some permitted it. Others outlawed it. Others made it illegal unless the life of the mother was at stake.

This photograph shows pro-life and pro-choice activists holding signs outside the U.S. Supreme Court during the "March for Life" event in 2005.

▲ **CRITICAL THINKING**
Summarizing Briefly summarize the Supreme Court's 1973 *Roe* v. *Wade* decision.

monitor to watch, keep track of, or check

In 1973 the landmark *Roe* v. *Wade* decision established a woman's right to get an abortion during the first six months of her pregnancy but said that individual states could prohibit abortion in the last three months. The Court noted that it was necessary to balance a woman's right to privacy of her body with the rights of the unborn child. It also noted that there was no clear agreement among medical and philosophical experts on exactly when life begins.

Since the 1970s, abortion has remained very controversial. Some people argue that abortion is wrong in all situations. They believe human life begins at conception and must be protected from that moment on. Others argue that whether or not to have an abortion is a private matter. They believe that a woman must be allowed to control her own body and that abortion is a right protected by the Constitution.

In a 1992 case, for example, the Court ruled that Pennsylvania could require a woman who wants an abortion to first get counseling—even counseling that is aimed at persuading her against having an abortion. In 2003 Congress passed a federal law banning a particular medical procedure used for abortions when the fetus is more developed, and in 2007 the Court upheld the law.

Abortion has been an important and controversial issue in elections and in judicial nominations. As long as the American public and the Supreme Court remain divided over abortion issues, advocacy groups on both sides will closely **monitor** elections and nominations to the Supreme Court and other federal courts.

Information Gathering and Privacy Telecommunications has changed the way we live, work, and play. Advances in technology have allowed businesses, organizations, individuals, and the government to collect and store information in ways that America's Founders never imagined. Often, personal data is collected without the knowledge or consent of the individuals concerned.

Online privacy is also threatened by websites and hackers who gather information on people who use the Internet. By monitoring—some call it "spying on"—your online activity, companies can develop targeted advertisements that show they know your income, recent purchases, music preferences, political party, etc. More and more, personal information is being collected in data warehouses where it is for sale to businesses, current or potential employers, or nearly anyone else willing to pay for it. These actions of private businesses or individuals do not violate the Constitution (which applies only to government actions). Private businesses and individuals are affected by state and federal laws regulating data collection and online privacy.

Government Surveillance War and the threat of terrorism create tension in a democracy between citizens' privacy rights and national security needs. Since the terrorist attacks of September 11, 2001, the U.S. government has had more power to conduct **surveillance** against everyone. Currently, two laws lay down the guidelines for government surveillance in national security cases: the 1978 Foreign Intelligence Surveillance Act (FISA) and the 2001 USA Patriot Act. FISA requires federal agents to get a warrant from a special FISA court before tapping domestic phone and computer lines. FISA court records and rulings are kept completely secret.

surveillance a watch kept over a person, group, etc., especially over a suspect or prisoner

The Patriot Act and its revisions broadened the definition of who could be seen as a terrorist and expanded the government's power to detain, investigate, and prosecute suspected terrorists. The FISA court can approve **wiretaps** to monitor an individual's telephone and Internet communications, even if the government has not met the standards of proof that would be required by a non-FISA court. Evidence that was authorized secretly by the FISA court can now also be used in criminal trials. In some cases, the government can delay notifying people that their houses or apartments have been searched until long after the search has taken place.

wiretap an act or instance of tapping telephone or telegraph wires for evidence or other information

Most citizens supported the Patriot Act when it was passed. However, these **expanded** powers raised key questions for Americans: Do these measures infringe on citizens' rights? How much freedom and privacy should be given up in order to be more secure? Some members of Congress and the public have criticized the expanded surveillance powers and use of secret wiretaps by the government. Others argue that these powers keep us safer and that some loss of freedom is the appropriate price to pay for safety.

expand to increase in extent, size, volume, or scope

✓ **READING PROGRESS CHECK**

Specifying Which laws regulate government surveillance in national security? What do these laws do?

EXPLORING THE ESSENTIAL QUESTION

On a scale from 1 to 5, with 1 meaning that you strongly agree, and 5 meaning that you strongly disagree, indicate where you stand on the following statement:

"In a time of heightened concern about domestic terrorism and national security, the government should be allowed to do whatever it believes is necessary to find and arrest terrorists."

Using the same scale, take a stand on each of the following statements. In each case, assume that Congress has proposed laws giving the federal government the power to take the following actions:

   a. Look at everyone's e-mail at work

   b. Look at everyone's social network posts

   c. Install surveillance cameras on all public streets

   d. Plant small cameras in the homes of suspected terrorists

   e. Check the travel records of people coming into the country

LESSON 6 REVIEW

Reviewing Vocabulary

1. ***Explaining*** Why are wiretaps used as a form of government surveillance? Be sure to define both *wiretaps* and *surveillance* in your response.

Using Your Graphic Organizer

2. ***Gathering Information*** Review your completed graphic organizer and choose a law or Supreme Court ruling you would like to know more about. Conduct Internet research about the topic and write a paragraph explaining what you have learned.

Answering the Guiding Questions

3. ***Analyzing*** In what circumstances may the government limit the right to keep and bear arms?

4. ***Interpreting*** In what circumstances may the government limit privacy rights?

Writing About Government

5. ***Argument*** Write a persuasive speech, create a script for a political commercial, or draw a political cartoon that advocates for your stance on gun control. What elements of persuasion did you use?

STUDY GUIDE

FIRST AMENDMENT PROTECTIONS
LESSONS 1, 2, and 3

Freedom of Speech	Protects the right to free speech—verbal expression and the use of action and symbols
Freedom of the Press	Protects against government censorship of newspapers, magazines, books, radio, television, and film
Freedom of Petition	Protects the right to petition the government for redress of grievances
Freedom of Assembly	Protects the right to join with others in peaceful gatherings
Freedom of Religion	Protects against government interference in religious practice and establishment of religion

RESTRICTIONS ON FREE SPEECH
LESSON 1

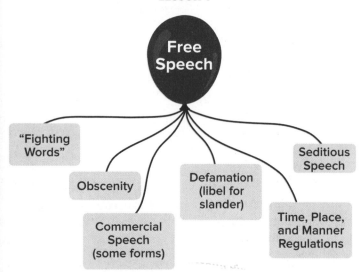

Free Speech
- "Fighting Words"
- Obscenity
- Commercial Speech (some forms)
- Defamation (libel for slander)
- Time, Place, and Manner Regulations
- Seditious Speech

FOURTEENTH AMENDMENT
LESSON 4

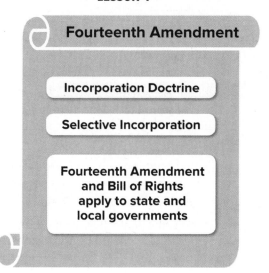

Fourteenth Amendment
- Incorporation Doctrine
- Selective Incorporation
- Fourteenth Amendment and Bill of Rights apply to state and local governments

ADVANCING EQUAL PROTECTION
LESSON 5

Discrimination based on...	Key Protections
Race	• *Brown* v. *Board of Education* • Civil Rights Acts of 1964, 1968, 1974, 1988 • Voting Rights Act of 1965
National Origin	• *Hernandez* v. *Texas* • *Plyler* v. *Doe*
Gender	• Nineteenth Amendment • Equal Pay Act of 1963 • Title VII of Civil Rights Act of 1964 • Title IX of Education Amendments Act of 1972
Sexual Orientation	• some state and local laws • end of "don't ask, don't tell" policy
Disability	• Age Discrimination in Employment Act of 1967 • Americans with Disabilities Act • Individuals with Disabilities Education Act

FINDING A BALANCE
LESSON 6

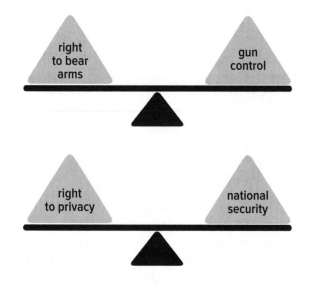

right to bear arms — gun control

right to privacy — national security

Directions: On a separate sheet of paper, answer the questions below. Make sure you read carefully and answer all parts of the questions.

Lesson Review

Lesson 1

1 *Categorizing* Identify three categories of speech that can be punished based on the content of the speech.

Lesson 2

2 *Identifying* What part of the Constitution protects the freedom to ask the government for a "redress of grievances"?

Lesson 3

3 *Examining* Why did the Founders protect religious freedom in the United States? Why did they guarantee its free exercise in the First Amendment?

Lesson 4

4 *Explaining* What does the Fourteenth Amendment's guarantee of "equal protection of the laws" mean?

Lesson 5

5 *Identifying Cause and Effect* How did the outcome of *Hernandez* v. *Texas* affect the interpretation of the Fourteenth Amendment?

Lesson 6

6 *Analyzing* Describe the historical context that underscored the importance of including the Second Amendment rights in the Constitution.

ANSWERING THE ESSENTIAL QUESTIONS

Review your answers to the introductory questions at the beginning of each lesson. Then answer the following Essential Questions based on what you learned in the chapter. Have your answers changed?

7 *Exploring Issues* What restrictions, if any, should be placed on our constitutional rights and freedoms?

8 *Making Connections* Why are the freedoms in the Bill of Rights and later amendments essential to our democracy?

9 *Analyzing Cause and Effect* How have citizen movements and social movements brought about political and social change?

DBQ Interpreting Political Cartoons

Use the political cartoon to answer the following questions.

10 *Interpreting Visuals* What does the lady in the cartoon represent? What is the significance of the scale?

11 *Making Inferences* What is this cartoon saying about the application of the First Amendment?

Critical Thinking

12 *Analyzing* Why are conflicts involving freedom of expression among the most difficult ones that courts are asked to resolve?

13 *Interpreting Significance* Why are the First Amendment rights of speech, press, assembly, and petition important in a democracy?

14 *Analyzing* How did the Supreme Court rule in *Texas* v. *Johnson* (1989)? Why? Do you agree or disagree? Explain your viewpoint.

Need Extra Help?

If You've Missed Question	**1**	**2**	**3**	**4**	**5**	**6**	**7**	**8**	**9**	**10**	**11**	**12**	**13**	**14**
Go to page	443	450	453	461	468	473	443	440	465	443	443	441	441	443

Directions: On a separate sheet of paper, answer the questions below. Make sure you read carefully and answer all parts of the questions.

15 *Comparing and Contrasting* Discuss the similarities and differences between these two phrases: "Congress shall make no law respecting an establishment of religion, or prohibiting the free exercise thereof" and "separation of church and state."

16 *Synthesizing* Explain the process of selective incorporation, using the outcomes of these Court cases: *Gitlow* v. *New York*, *Palko* v. *Connecticut*, *McDonald* v. *City of Chicago*. Analyze the effects of these cases on the scope of fundamental rights and federalism.

17 *Analyzing* What right did the Supreme Court establish in *Roe* v. *Wade*, and why does this issue continue to be controversial?

DBQ Analyzing Primary Sources

Read the excerpts and answer the questions that follow.

PRIMARY SOURCE

"The most stringent protection of free speech would not protect a man in falsely shouting fire in a theatre and causing a panic. . . . The question in every case is whether the words used are used in such circumstances and are of such a nature as to create a clear and present danger."
—Justice Oliver Wendell Holmes (1919), *Schenck* v. *United States*

18 *Analyzing Primary Sources* What limit did the Supreme Court place on free speech in the case *Schenck* v. *United States*?

PRIMARY SOURCE

"Freedoms of speech and press do not permit a State to forbid advocacy of the use of force or of law violation except where such advocacy is directed to inciting or producing imminent lawless action and is likely to incite or produce such action."
—Unanimous Supreme Court decision in *Brandenburg* v. *Ohio* (1969)

19 *Interpreting* According to the Court's decision in *Brandenburg* v. *Ohio*, what type of speech is protected?

20 *Finding the Main Idea* In *Brandenburg* v. *Ohio*, what limit did the Court place on this type of speech?

Social Studies Skills

21 *Sequencing* Create a chronological chart of the Supreme Court decisions regarding the freedom of religion discussed in Lesson 3. Include the year, a short summary of the facts, and the basic court ruling. Why do you think so many of these Supreme Court cases are about religion in public schools?

22 *Explaining Continuity and Change* Research the movement to expand rights for African Americans or Latinos. Create a time line of key events in the movement and their significance.

Research and Presentation

23 *Analyzing* Analyze the Supreme Court's interpretation of freedom of religion in *Engel* v. *Vitale*. Do research to find out more about the case. Then write a position paper supporting your point of view, using facts from the case.

24 *Researching* Do research on the meaning of affirmative action today. Prepare an electronic slideshow explaining how the key cases *Regents of the University of California* v. *Bakke*, *Grutter* v. *Bollinger*, and *Gratz* v. *Bollinger* shaped the practice of affirmative action.

25 *Defending* Work with a small group of students to prepare for a debate on one of these issues: gun control, government surveillance, or reproductive rights. One group should prepare to argue in favor of more restrictions and another group against more restrictions. Research your group's position and stage a debate.

Need Extra Help?

If You've Missed Question	**15**	**16**	**17**	**18**	**19**	**20**	**21**	**22**	**23**	**24**	**25**
Go to page	453	463	476	444	445	445	453	465	455	470	473

Constitutional Right to a Fair Trial

networks
www.connected.mcgraw-hill.com
There's More Online about the constitutional right to a fair trial.

CHAPTER 16

ESSENTIAL QUESTIONS

- How does our democracy protect the rights of individuals suspected, accused, convicted, or acquitted of crimes? • How does our democracy balance the rights of the defendant and the search for truth?

◄ One of the responsibilities of a judge is to ensure that every accused person is given the right to a fair trial as promised in the Constitution.

Photographer's Choice/Getty Images

481

BEYOND A REASONABLE DOUBT

Many of the protections in the Bill of Rights were designed to ensure that people accused of crimes are treated fairly and receive a fair trial. Yet tension has always existed between the rights of the accused and the community's interest in keeping its citizens safe. Can that tension be resolved? Think about that question as you examine the sources provided here.

PRIMARY SOURCE A

"Justice is incidental to law and order."

—J. Edgar Hoover, Director of the Federal Bureau of Investigation, 1935–1972

PRIMARY SOURCE B

"It is better that ten guilty persons escape than that one innocent suffer."

—William Blackstone, eighteenth-century English judge and legal scholar, in *Commentaries on the Laws of England*

PRIMARY SOURCE C

"Privileges so fundamental as to be inherent in every concept of a fair trial that could be acceptable to the thought of reasonable men will be kept inviolate and inviolable, however crushing may be the pressure of incriminating proof. But justice, though due to the accused, is due to the accuser also. The concept of fairness must not be strained till it is narrowed to a filament. We are to keep the balance true."

—Justice Benjamin Cardozo, writing for the Supreme Court in *Snyder* v. *Massachusetts* (1934)

SECONDARY SOURCE D

This graph compares the number of federal crimes committed each year to the number of arrests, people charged, convictions, and offenders sent to prison.

368,000 **Total Federal Crimes Committed (estimated)**

184,000 **Number of Suspects Arrested**

85,000 **Number of Suspects Charged with a Crime**

76,500 **Number of Defendants Found Guilty**

Number of Offenders Sent to Prison 67,500

*All figures are rounded. **Source:** Bureau of Justice Statistics, *National Crime Victimization Survey*

WHAT WILL YOU DO?

There are many ways for an average American to influence our nation's balance between the rights of the accused and community safety. Which of the following organizations would you be more likely to work for: a victims' rights organization, a group that uses DNA evidence to free wrongly convicted prisoners, a citizen-based crime-fighting organization, or a citizens' group established to review police work?

DBQ DOCUMENT-BASED QUESTIONS

1. **Identifying** How do the three quotations illustrate the tension between the rights of the accused and community safety?

2. **Interpreting** What stage in the criminal justice process is represented by each point on the graphic? What protections provided in the Bill of Rights are relevant at each stage? Do you think these protections influence how many people leave the process at each stage?

3. **Explaining** What is the cartoonist's point of view? Do you agree or disagree with the point being made?

4. **Evaluating** Do you think the United States has found a "true balance" between the rights of the accused and community safety? Explain your answer.

EXPLORE the interactive version of the analyzing primary sources feature on Networks.

networks *TRY IT YOURSELF* ONLINE   www.connected.mcgraw-hill.com   *Constitutional Right to a Fair Trial* **483**

Interact with these digital assets and others in lesson 1

✓ **INTERACTIVE CHART**
Applying the Exclusionary Rule

✓ **INTERACTIVE IMAGE**
Evidence

✓ **SELF-CHECK QUIZ**

✓ **VIDEO**
Miranda Rights

netw⊙rks
TRY IT YOURSELF ONLINE

Reading Help Desk

Academic Vocabulary

- retain
- voluntary

Content Vocabulary

- criminal justice process
- evidence
- prosecute
- search warrant
- probable cause
- contraband
- arrest
- exclusionary rule
- interrogation
- self-incrimination
- Miranda rights

TAKING NOTES:

Key Ideas and Details

LISTING Use the table to record the rights that individuals have during searches, seizures, and interrogations.

Searches	Seizures	Interrogations

LESSON 1
Constitutional Rights Before Trial

ESSENTIAL QUESTION

How does our democracy protect the rights of individuals suspected, accused, convicted, or acquitted of crimes?

The Constitution and Bill of Rights protect the rights of people suspected, accused, convicted, or acquitted of crimes. For each example below, decide whether the person should have the right or freedom described.

a. An inmate serving five years for an arson conviction wants the right to send letters to his family.

b. A woman was accused of shoplifting at a local mall. The police want to search her home, but she wants them to get a search warrant from a judge before they search.

c. A person was arrested on suspicion of participating in a robbery. The police are holding him in jail while they finish gathering evidence. He has been in jail for two weeks now, but has not been charged with a crime yet. He wants to be able to leave the jail.

d. The FBI has been monitoring your family's e-mail and phone conversations for three months. When your family finds out, they want the FBI to stop.

e. Two American citizens are flying from an airport in Wisconsin to one in Florida. The Transportation Security Administration (TSA) agents want to x-ray their luggage, but the couple does not want their belongings searched.

f. Two police officers are questioning a teenager near the scene of a drive-by shooting. The teenager wants to call a lawyer before answering any more questions.

Rights of the Accused in a Democracy

GUIDING QUESTION *How does the criminal justice process protect the rights of the accused?*

In our democracy, all people have constitutionally protected rights and freedoms, even if they have been charged with or convicted of a crime.

Our government has a duty to protect society against criminals. However, in the process of investigating and prosecuting crimes, the government may not infringe on anyone's fundamental rights. Since possible consequences of being convicted of a crime include loss of liberty or even loss of life, individuals accused of crimes **retain** important rights.

The federal and state governments must use fair procedures to accuse and prosecute someone of a crime. The Fifth and Fourteenth Amendments to the Constitution say that the government may not deprive anyone of "life, liberty, or property, without due process of law." In criminal cases, this right is known as *procedural due process*, or fair procedures for handling cases. At the most basic level, procedural due process requires:

- Notifying a person that he or she is accused of wrongdoing and the government intends to take action against that person.

- Giving the affected person the right to respond to the accusation.

The **criminal justice process** includes everything that happens to a person who commits a crime, from arrest through prosecution and conviction to release from prison. There are rights that people retain at different stages in the criminal justice process. For example, the government must convince a judge or jury beyond a reasonable doubt that the person accused committed the crime. Several safeguards are in place to ensure that trials are fair and impartial. These include the right to have a trial that takes place in public, the right to have an attorney, and the right not to testify against oneself, among others.

retain to continue to hold or have

criminal justice process
everything that happens to a person who commits a crime, from arrest through prosecution and conviction to release from prison

☑ **READING PROGRESS CHECK**

Determining Importance Why is it important that our democracy protects those accused of crimes?

Searches and Seizures

GUIDING QUESTION *How does the Fourth Amendment protect Americans from unreasonable searches and seizures?*

Americans have always valued their privacy. They expect to be left alone, to be free from unreasonable snooping or spying, and to be secure in their

The
Constitution

"The right of the people to be secure in their persons, houses, papers, and effects, against unreasonable searches and seizures, shall not be violated, and no Warrants shall be issued, but upon probable cause, supported by oath or affirmation, and particularly describing the place to be searched, and the persons or things to be seized."

—The Fourth Amendment

DBQ
1. ***Paraphrasing*** Make a list of the uncommon words in the Fourth Amendment. Use the glossary or other resources to define those words. Use your definitions to rewrite the Fourth Amendment in a way a fifth-grader could understand.

2. ***Contrasting*** Describe a search you think would be "unreasonable" and a search that would be "reasonable." How are the two examples different?

Police can show that a search is reasonable by getting a search warrant that explains where they plan to look and what they are looking for.

▲ CRITICAL THINKING
Identifying What Constitutional amendment is being followed when the police obtain a search warrant from a court official before searching for evidence?

evidence an outward sign; something that furnishes proof

prosecute to conduct criminal proceedings in court against

search warrant an order signed by a judge describing a specific place to be searched for specific items

probable cause a reasonable basis to believe a person or premises are linked to a crime

contraband anything prohibited by law from being imported, exported, or possessed

homes. The Fourth Amendment to the U.S. Constitution protects Americans from unreasonable government searches and seizures.

The police need **evidence** to investigate and **prosecute** crimes, but getting evidence often requires searching people or their homes, cars, offices, or electronic records. The Fourth Amendment does not mean that the government (or agents of the government, like police officers) cannot ever invade someone's privacy to look for evidence of crimes. It does mean, however, that the government cannot engage in unreasonable searches. The exact meaning of the word *unreasonable* has been the subject of debate.

©Mikael Karlsson

EXPLORING THE ESSENTIAL QUESTION

Making Connections Imagine that you are a detective on the police force in your city. Your supervisors believe that a local shipping and delivery business is really a front for moving and selling drugs in your state and beyond. They think that the business receives large shipments of illegal drugs disguised as car parts. It then distributes them around town using a fleet of delivery trucks.

As an investigator, what would you want to examine to learn more about this case and gather evidence? Make a list of the places you would want to look, records you would want to see, and evidence you might look for. How might your investigation violate the privacy of people associated with the shipping and delivery business?

One way that police can show that a search is reasonable is by getting a **search warrant** before making the search. A warrant is an official legal document issued by a judge. To get a warrant, the police must state under oath that they have **probable cause** (a reasonable belief) to suspect that someone has committed a crime. The warrant explains where the police plan to look and what they are looking for.

Searches Without a Warrant Police usually need a warrant to search a private home. There are some instances, however, when police are allowed to search without a warrant.

In situations where the police officer's safety is at risk, for example, the officer can search without a warrant. Police may stop and frisk someone who is behaving suspiciously to check for weapons in order to protect themselves and bystanders. They are not allowed to thoroughly search the person. Instead, they can perform a "pat down" to see if the individual is concealing a weapon. Police are also allowed to search a lawfully arrested person to make sure that that person does not have any hidden weapons, means to escape, or evidence that might be destroyed.

Another exception to the warrant requirement occurs when police enter a building during an emergency or when chasing a criminal suspect. Police often do not need warrants to search vehicles, either. If the police have probable cause to believe that a vehicle contains **contraband**, they may search the entire vehicle.

Police are also allowed to search a person or their belongings if the person voluntarily consents to the search. Similarly, government officials may search people's belongings at international borders and in airports. In those cases, police do not need any cause to search. At international borders and in airports, people have a reduced expectation of privacy and accept a certain amount of government intrusion into their privacy.

Finally, police are allowed to seize an item that can be seen in plain view from a place that an officer has a right to be. For example, if an officer legally stops a car for a traffic violation and sees a gun lying on the car seat next to the driver, he or she may seize it without a warrant.

In general, when evaluating whether a warrantless search violates the Fourth Amendment, courts look at the circumstances of the case and ask whether the person concerned had a "reasonable expectation of privacy." Generally, people have the greatest expectation of privacy inside their homes. In one case, the Supreme Court decided that a person did not have a reasonable expectation of privacy in garbage left in a plastic bag for pickup outside his house. In that case, police were allowed to search the person's garbage without obtaining a warrant.

Seizures An arrest is considered a seizure under the Fourth Amendment, which requires seizures be reasonable. An **arrest** takes place when a person suspected of a crime is taken into custody. Someone who is taken into custody under circumstances in which a reasonable person would not feel free to leave is considered to be under arrest, whether or not he or she is told that.

A person can be arrested under a warrant issued by a judge, or without a warrant if a law enforcement officer has probable cause. Probable cause means having a reasonable belief that a person has committed a crime.

A police officer does not need probable cause to stop and question an individual on the street, but the officer must have reasonable suspicion to believe that the individual is involved in criminal activity. Reasonable suspicion is based on less evidence than probable cause but still must be more than a mere hunch. Even without reasonable suspicion, a police officer may go up to any individual and ask to speak to him or her. The person may decline and continue his or her activity.

The Exclusionary Rule If a court decides that evidence in a case was gained through an illegal search, then the evidence cannot be used at trial against the defendant. This principle is called the **exclusionary rule**.

The Fourth Amendment does not mention the exclusionary rule. However, the Supreme Court has ruled that the exclusionary rule is necessary to give the amendment force. In *Mapp* v. *Ohio* (1961), the Supreme Court ruled that the exclusionary rule applies to both state and federal governments.

The exclusionary rule does not prevent the arrest or trial of a suspect. However, in some cases, it does mean that people who committed a crime might go free. This could happen when the prosecutor cannot obtain a conviction without evidence that has been excluded from trial.

The exclusionary rule is very controversial. Many people claim that it is a legal loophole that allows dangerous criminals to go free. They also point out that many other countries have no such rule; instead, those countries punish the police for violating citizens' rights. Others say the rule is necessary to safeguard our rights and to prevent police misconduct. They argue that the exclusionary rule maintains judicial integrity by making sure that courts are not parties to lawbreaking by the police. They also believe that police will be less likely to violate a citizen's rights if they know that illegally seized evidence will be thrown out of court.

EXPLORING THE
ESSENTIAL QUESTION

Making Visuals Imagine that you are teaching a class on search and seizure at the police academy. Your students are confused about when they can search without a warrant. Create a graphic organizer that summarizes when searches can be conducted without a warrant. Try to show the information in a way that will help police officers make good decisions when investigating cases.

arrest to take or keep in custody by authority of law

exclusionary rule a rule that forbids the introduction of illegally obtained evidence in a criminal trial

If a court decides that evidence in a case was gained through an illegal search, it cannot be used at trial.

▼ CRITICAL THINKING
Summarizing What is the exclusionary rule? What are some arguments in favor of the rule? Against it?

APPLYING THE EXCLUSIONARY RULE

The exclusionary rule says that evidence gathered in violation of the law cannot be used in court. But the exclusionary rule does not apply in every case. Read the examples and decide whether you think the evidence in the case should be admitted or excluded at trial.

CRITICAL THINKING

Explaining Write an explanation of why you admitted or excluded the evidence in each of the cases.

Case	Evidence
1. The police, armed with a search warrant, execute a search at a home where they find evidence of illegal gambling. Later, the search warrant is thrown out because the judge had issued the wrong type of warrant.	Should the evidence of illegal gambling be excluded?
2. Believing a bombing suspect may be hiding in Ms. Draper's home, police ask her if they can search the house. She refuses. Later, they return, waving a piece of paper and saying they have a warrant. They do not find the alleged bomber, but they do find evidence of drug crimes. But the paper was not a warrant.	Should the evidence of drug crimes be excluded?
3. Jim's girlfriend gives the police permission to search his home. They find evidence implicating Jim in a string of burglaries. However, Jim's girlfriend did not live in the house and could not legally authorize a search.	Should the evidence be excluded?

In recent years, the U.S. Supreme Court has decided several cases that have established a "good faith" exception to the exclusionary rule. This means that evidence gathered in violation of the Fourth Amendment may be allowed at trial if the police were acting in good faith and believed they had a valid warrant.

✓ **READING PROGRESS CHECK**

Analyzing Under what circumstances can a lawful search be conducted without a warrant? Explain.

Special Issues in Search and Seizure

GUIDING QUESTION *What are some special issues in our right to be protected from unreasonable searches and seizures?*

Fourth Amendment rights are not the same in every situation. Locations such as public schools or international borders create special issues. So too does the use of racial profiling.

Searches in Public Schools Students have limited Fourth Amendment rights in schools. In *New Jersey* v. *T.L.O.* (1985), the Supreme Court ruled that school officials do not need warrants or probable cause to search students or their property. They do, however, need reasonable suspicion that a student has violated the law or broken a school rule.

Suspicionless Searches Usually, police officers must have suspicion that a specific person has committed a crime in order to conduct a search. For example, the police could not search everyone standing on a street corner if they suspect that someone in the group possesses evidence of a crime. However, in some circumstances, police may search everyone without individual suspicion. In situations like fixed-point searches at international borders and highway sobriety checkpoints, police may search everyone who comes through. These searches support a special need beyond ordinary law enforcement.

Racial Profiling Racial profiling is the inappropriate use of race as a factor in identifying people who may break or have broken the law. Profiling occurs, for example, when an airport security guard selects an "Arab-looking" person to be searched solely because of his or her appearance. In some situations, officers may consider appearance when deciding whom to stop. For example, if an eyewitness describes the robber as an Asian American male of medium height who is running from a specific location, a police officer may use this description, which includes race as a factor, in deciding to stop an Asian American man of medium height she sees running from the scene of the crime.

☑ **READING PROGRESS CHECK**

Applying In what special instances are a warrantless or suspicionless search constitutional?

PARTICIPATING
🅝 Your Government

Persuasive Speaking

Imagine a committee of state legislators is holding a hearing on the issue of racial profiling. The state's data show that drivers who are African American, Latino, or of Middle Eastern descent are more likely to be stopped and searched by police than are people of other ethnic groups. At this hearing, citizens will be invited to present their views on how to solve this problem.

Imagine the following ideas have been presented by members of the committee:

Rep. Gomez:	Some police officers have stereotypes of people of other races or cultures. All police should receive training on diversity and cultural sensitivity.
Rep. Amici:	Each time a driver is stopped, the officer should be required to fill out a form describing the time and date, driver's age, probable race, gender, and the reasons for the stop. This data will keep police officers accountable to the public.
Rep. Reynolds:	The U.S. Constitution and state laws already prohibit searches that are unreasonable. The police department has procedures for filing complaints. This is enough to protect citizens.
Rep. Dubois:	We need to have a board made up of ordinary citizens to hear complaints about racial profiling. The board should have the authority to take disciplinary actions against officers.

EXPLORING THE ESSENTIAL QUESTION

Problem Solving Decide which of these proposals you support. Prepare a two-minute statement advocating for that position. Open by clearly stating which proposal(s) you support. Then give evidence and arguments to support your view. Relevant personal stories can be effective, but keep them short. Close by restating your position.

Interrogations

GUIDING QUESTION *How and why are individuals protected from unlawful interrogations?*

After an arrest is made, it is standard police practice to question, or interrogate, the accused. These **interrogations** may result in confessions or admissions of guilt that are later used in court. The Fifth Amendment protects people from **self-incrimination**, and the Sixth Amendment ensures the right to an attorney. Police must balance their interest in gathering information about a crime with the rights of the people in custody.

interrogation a formal or official questioning

self-incrimination testifying against oneself

voluntary proceeding from the will or from one's own choice or consent

Forced Confessions A confession cannot be used in court if it is not **voluntary** and trustworthy. This means that using physical force, torture, or threats to force a person to confess is prohibited. In the case of *Escobedo* v. *Illinois* (1964), the Supreme Court said that even a voluntary confession is inadmissible if it has been obtained after denying the accused person's request to talk to an attorney.

Miranda Rights The Supreme Court also ruled in *Miranda* v. *Arizona* (1966) that the Fifth Amendment requires police to inform suspects in custody of their rights before questioning them. This protects the rights of suspects who might not be aware of this right. The Court said that the Fifth Amendment right against self-incrimination is fundamental to our system of justice, and is "one of our Nation's most cherished principles." If a defendant is not informed of his or her rights, any statements he or she makes cannot be used in court. These rights include:

- The right to remain silent. Any statement made may be used as evidence against the defendant.
- The right to the presence of an attorney, either hired by the defendant or appointed by the court.

Miranda rights the right for a defendant being taken into police custody to remain silent (to avoid self-incrimination) and the right to an attorney; the police must inform a defendant of these rights before questioning, or anything learned from the interrogation cannot be used against the defendant at trial

These protections are commonly known as **Miranda rights**. The Miranda rights apply only to custodial interrogations. This kind of interrogation means that the person must be in custody (not free to leave) and being questioned by law enforcement.

☑ **READING PROGRESS CHECK**

Explaining Why are forced confessions inadmissible in court?

LESSON 1 REVIEW

Reviewing Vocabulary
1. ***Explaining*** What is the exclusionary rule and why is it controversial?

Using Your Graphic Organizer
2. ***Making Connections*** Use your completed graphic organizer to summarize the rights of the accused during searches, seizures, and interrogations. Then explain which constitutional amendments guarantee these protections.

Answering the Guiding Questions
3. ***Identifying*** How does the criminal justice process protect the rights of the accused?

4. ***Describing*** How does the Fourth Amendment protect Americans from unreasonable searches and seizures?

5. ***Exploring Issues*** What are some special issues in our right to be protected from unreasonable searches and seizures?

6. ***Explaining*** How and why are individuals protected from unlawful interrogations?

Writing About Government
7. ***Informative/Explanatory*** Locate a news article about a case where evidence was ruled inadmissible in court. Write a summary explaining why this was so and which constitutional rights and amendments apply.

Yarborough v Alvarado (2004)

FACTS OF THE CASE The police investigating a murder and robbery decided to question 17-year-old Michael Alvarado. The detective contacted Michael's mother, who agreed to bring him into the police station for questioning. When they arrived, Michael's parents asked to remain with their son during the interview, but the detective denied this request. Michael had no prior arrest record. While his parents waited in the lobby, Michael was questioned alone for two hours. He was never told that he was under arrest. He was given several bathroom breaks and was allowed to leave after the questioning ended. At no time was Michael advised that he had the right to remain silent, to consult an attorney, or to leave the police station whenever he wanted. Later, Michael Alvarado was convicted, largely because of incriminating statements he made during the interview with the detective. He appealed his conviction, arguing that he should have been read his Miranda rights and that his statements were therefore inadmissible in court.

ISSUE

Did the police violate the Fifth and Sixth Amendments by not reading Michael Alvarado his *Miranda* rights?

ARGUMENTS

Arguments in a Supreme Court case are often based on precedents—previous cases the Court has decided about similar issues. Both sides argue that a particular precedent does or does not apply to the present case. The Supreme Court of the United States has decided previous cases about interrogation:

1. ***Miranda* v. *Arizona* (1966)** Ernesto Miranda was arrested for kidnapping and rape. He was questioned for two hours without a lawyer or being told about his right to remain silent. Miranda confessed. The Supreme Court said that the right against self-incrimination is fundamental to our system of justice, and is "one of our Nation's most cherished principles." If a suspect is in police custody, he must be informed of his rights before he is questioned.

2. ***Oregon* v. *Mathiason* (1977)** A police officer questioned a suspect at the police station. The officer informed the suspect that he was not under arrest but that he was a suspect in a burglary. During a 30-minute interview, he confessed. The Supreme Court ruled that the suspect's rights were not violated, because he was not in custody. The suspect had come voluntarily to the station, was told he was not under arrest, and was allowed to leave at the end.

3. ***Thompson* v. *Keohane* (1995)** The Supreme Court said that in order to decide whether or not someone is "in custody," courts must determine whether a reasonable person would have felt he or she could end the interrogation and leave. A person can be "in custody" even if he has not been arrested, but only if a reasonable person would not have felt free to leave.

EXPLORING THE ESSENTIAL QUESTION

Analyzing Take on the role of a Supreme Court justice to determine whether these precedents apply to the case of *Yarborough* v. *Alvarado*. Think carefully about whether the fact that Michael Alvarado was under age 18 matters. For each precedent listed, answer these questions:

1. How is this precedent similar to the current case?
2. How is this precedent different from the current case?
3. In your opinion, does this precedent apply to the current case?

Interact with these digital assets and others in lesson 2

✓ INTERACTIVE IMAGE
  Gideon's Petition

✓ SELF-CHECK QUIZ

✓ VIDEO
  Gideon v. Wainwright

✓ WE THE PEOPLE
  Clarence Earl Gideon

networks
TRY IT YOURSELF ONLINE

Reading Help Desk

Academic Vocabulary

- bias
- solely
- equip

Content Vocabulary

- presumption of innocence
- plea bargain
- counsel
- acquittal
- indigent
- cross-examination
- status offense

TAKING NOTES:
Key Ideas and Details

EXAMINING List the constitutional rights of individuals at trial, explain what they mean, and examine in what ways they can be limited.

Rights at Trial

	Explanation	Limits
Right to a Jury		
Right to an Attorney		
Other Rights at Trial		

LESSON 2
Constitutional Rights at Trial

ESSENTIAL QUESTION

How does our democracy balance the rights of the defendant and the search for truth?

The starting point for every trial is the presumption of innocence, a long-standing principle of criminal law. Think about the phrase "innocent until proven guilty."

- What do these words mean to you?

- Why might it be important in a democracy to presume that defendants are innocent until proven otherwise?

- What are some possible consequences of this feature of our criminal justice system?

Presumption of Innocence

GUIDING QUESTION *Why is the presumption of innocence an important protection in our criminal justice system?*

The **presumption of innocence** means that the deciders of fact in a trial—the judge or jury—must regard the defendant as innocent until the government proves that he or she is guilty. This means that the government has the burden of proof in a criminal trial.

In order to prove a defendant's guilt in a criminal trial, each element of the crime must be proven beyond a reasonable doubt. The defendant does not need to prove that he or she did not commit the crime. The defendant does have the opportunity to respond to the government's claims and to introduce evidence that casts doubt on the government's claims. The reason for this strict standard of proof in a criminal trial is that the defendant's liberty, and in some cases life, are in jeopardy.

Many of the rights afforded to people being tried in the criminal justice system are protected by the Fifth and Sixth Amendments.

☑ **READING PROGRESS CHECK**

Defining What is a *burden of proof*? What does it mean that the government has the burden of proof in a criminal trial?

The Constitution

"No person . . . shall be compelled in any criminal case to be a witness against himself, nor deprived of life, liberty, or property, without due process of law . . ."

—Fifth Amendment

"In all criminal prosecutions, the accused shall enjoy the right to a speedy and public trial, by an impartial jury of the State and district wherein the crime shall have been committed . . . ; to be confronted with the witnesses against him; to have compulsory process for obtaining Witnesses in his favor; and to have the assistance of counsel for his defense."

—Sixth Amendment

DBQ

1. **Understanding Relationships** Create a two-column chart. In the left column, list the specific rights guaranteed in the Fifth and Sixth Amendments. In the right column, explain how each right can be related to the presumption of innocence. If you see no relationship, write NA in the right column.

2. **Constructing Arguments** When your chart is complete, decide which of the rights in the Fifth and Sixth Amendments is most important to ensuring the presumption of innocence. Explain why.

Right to a Jury

GUIDING QUESTION *What is the right to an impartial jury trial?*

Defendants in felony criminal cases in all state and federal courts have a right to a jury trial. The Sixth Amendment provides for a trial "by an impartial jury of the State and district wherein the crime shall have been committed." Juries consist of citizens from the community in which the trial is taking place. The jury is chosen by the attorneys for both sides of the case. The lawyers ask potential jurors questions to determine possible **bias**, and either lawyer can request that a potential juror be eliminated. The Supreme Court has ruled in a number of cases that attorneys may not exclude prospective jurors from serving on a jury **solely** because of their race, gender, or national origin. Criminal trials with juries selected in a discriminatory manner harm the defendant, injure the persons removed from the jury for discriminatory reasons, and damage society in general.

However, juries are not used very often. Many cases are settled by **plea bargains** before trial. This is a process whereby the defendant pleads guilty to a lesser crime than the crime he or she was originally charged with in order to avoid a trial. Plea bargaining is widely used as a way to handle the tremendous volume of criminal cases the court must handle each year.

Supporters of the process claim that it is efficient and saves the state the cost of a trial in situations where guilt is obvious, as well as those where the government's case may have weaknesses. Some opponents, however, argue that "copping a plea" allows criminals to get off lightly; others say that it encourages people to give up their rights to a fair trial. The Supreme Court in several decisions has approved the process of plea bargaining as constitutional. In *Santobello* v. *New York* (1971), the Court said plea bargaining was "an essential component of the administration of justice. Properly administered, it is to be encouraged."

presumption of innocence the principle that one is considered innocent until proven guilty; the government has the burden of proof in a criminal trial

bias information and ideas that support only one point of view on an issue; the distortion of a set of statistical results

solely to the exclusion of all else

plea bargain an agreement whereby a defendant pleads guilty to a lesser crime than the one with which a defendant was originally charged and in return the government agrees not to prosecute the defendant for the more serious crime

In cases that do go to trial, many defendants waive their right to a jury trial and proceed to a bench trial before a judge. Bench trials are faster and less expensive, and some defendants who are being tried for a crime that is morally distasteful to society feel that they will face less bias in a bench trial than they would in a jury trial decided by members of their community.

☑ **READING PROGRESS CHECK**

Discussing How does the criminal justice process ensure that juries are impartial?

Right to an Attorney

GUIDING QUESTION *How does the criminal justice system provide for the right to an attorney?*

The Sixth Amendment provides that "In all criminal prosecutions, the accused shall enjoy the right to . . . have the Assistance of Counsel for his defence." What happens, however, when a defendant cannot afford to employ **counsel**? At one time, except in cases involving the death penalty or life imprisonment, a defendant had the right to an attorney only if he or she could afford one. Defendants who could afford the best lawyers stood a better chance of **acquittal**. Poorer defendants were often convicted because they could not adequately argue their own cases in court.

However, in 1938 the U.S. Supreme Court ruled that federal courts must appoint attorneys for **indigent** defendants—those without financial means—in all federal felony cases. Twenty-five years later, in the case of *Gideon* v. *Wainwright*

counsel an attorney providing legal advice or representation

acquittal judicial deliverance from a criminal charge on a verdict or finding of not guilty

indigent suffering from extreme poverty

 We the People: Making a Difference

Clarence Earl Gideon was charged with unlawful breaking and entering in Florida. He could not afford to hire a lawyer to assist him at his trial. He asked the trial court to provide him with a free lawyer. The state court refused to do so because the state law provided free attorneys only to defendants charged with capital crimes (those crimes that carry a penalty of death or life imprisonment). Gideon had to defend himself at his trial and was convicted. From his jail cell, he wrote to the U.S. Supreme Court, asking them to take his case. The Supreme Court agreed to hear his case, to decide whether an indigent (poor) defendant in a felony case in a state court had a right to free legal counsel under the Constitution. Federal courts and some states required that people being prosecuted for felonies receive free legal counsel, while others, including Florida, did not. This is an example of a case that presented a conflict among lower courts.

In a unanimous decision, the Court decided that states must provide and pay for attorneys for indigent defendants in a felony case. Justice Hugo Black said in the decision that "lawyers in criminal courts are necessities, not luxuries."

CLARENCE EARL GIDEON

AP Images

EXPLORING THE ESSENTIAL QUESTION

1. **Interpreting** Based on your understanding of the law and court procedures, do you agree that "lawyers in criminal courts are necessities, not luxuries"? Give reasons for your answer.

2. **Evaluating** Like Clarence Gideon, litigants in cases that ask the Supreme Court to rule on important constitutional issues make a difference in our democracy. Review the Supreme Court cases you have studied in this course or visit a website that reports on Supreme Court cases. Select a case of particular interest to you. Write a profile of the litigant in the case, highlighting how that person made a difference.

(1963), the Court extended this right to felony defendants in state courts as well. Today, governments are required to provide attorneys for defendants who cannot afford them in any case where a jail sentence could be imposed.

The right to the assistance of counsel is basic to the idea of a fair trial. In a criminal trial, the state (the people) is represented by a prosecutor who is a lawyer. In addition, the prosecutor's office has other resources, including investigators, to help prepare the case against the accused. At a minimum, the defendant needs a skillful lawyer to ensure a fair trial.

Criminal defendants who cannot afford an attorney have one appointed to them free of charge by the government. These attorneys may be either public defenders or private attorneys. A public defender's office is funded by the government. In some counties and cities, the government hires private lawyers, either on a contract or case-by-case basis, to handle criminal cases for indigent defendants. Both public defenders and contracted private attorneys are typically paid less than private lawyers hired directly by a defendant. In addition, many counties' and states' indigent defense systems are overloaded and lack the funds to effectively represent everyone who needs a lawyer.

Some people criticize the overall quality of representation that poor criminal defendants still receive in this country. These critics say that criminal defendants with money to hire their own lawyers have a much better chance of being found not guilty than do economically disadvantaged defendants.

☑ **READING PROGRESS CHECK**

Making Inferences Do you think that defendants who have court-appointed attorneys are at a disadvantage? Why or why not?

Other Rights at Trial

GUIDING QUESTION *What rights at trial are protected by the Fifth and Sixth Amendments?*

In addition to the rights to a jury and an attorney, there are several other rights at trial that are covered in the Fifth Amendment and Sixth Amendment.

Speedy and Public Trials The Sixth Amendment provides a right to a *speedy* and public trial in all criminal cases. Without this, an innocent person could await trial—in jail—for years. The Constitution, however, does not define *speedy*, so the federal government and some states have set specific time limits within which a case must be brought to trial. If a person does not receive a speedy trial, the case may be dismissed. However, defendants often waive their right to a speedy trial because an important witness is not available or because their attorneys need more time to prepare their cases.

Confrontation of Witnesses The Sixth Amendment provides people accused of crimes with the right to confront (be face-to-face with) the witnesses against them and to ask them questions by way of **cross-examination**. Defendants also have the right to call their own witnesses, and to get a court order requiring witnesses to testify.

Freedom from Self-Incrimination Freedom from self-incrimination means that you cannot be forced to testify against yourself in a criminal trial. This right comes from the Fifth Amendment and can be exercised in all criminal cases. The protection against self-incrimination is also usually available to witnesses who appear before a congressional committee or grand jury. If Congress grants an individual immunity from prosecution, that person will often testify.

GOVERNMENT *in your* **COMMUNITY**

Public Defender System

While they are required to provide free attorneys to most indigent criminal defendants, states and counties are free to choose the type of system they use to grant this legal assistance. Research the system used by your city or county. The website for your state's bar association is a good place to start. Interview someone in the system to find out

- how criminal defense services are delivered to low-income people facing criminal charges.

- whether the indigent defense system in your community is facing any challenges and, if so, what they are.

cross-examination the examination of a witness who has already testified in order to check or discredit the witness's testimony, knowledge, or credibility

This is sometimes referred to as "taking the Fifth." Defense attorneys may counsel their clients not to take the stand at trial for their own protection. In addition, the prosecutor is forbidden to make any statement drawing the jury's attention to the defendant's refusal to testify, and the jury is instructed by the judge not to draw any conclusions based on a refusal to testify.

✓ READING PROGRESS CHECK

Explaining What is the freedom from self-incrimination?

The Juvenile Justice System

GUIDING QUESTION *In what ways is the juvenile justice system different from the adult criminal justice system?*

In the United States, juveniles in trouble with the law are treated differently from adults. Juveniles may be taken into custody for committing crimes that are also illegal for adults. However, juveniles can also be taken into custody for **status offenses**—acts that would not be crimes if they were committed by adults. These include running away from home and truancy from school.

> **status offense** any act that a juvenile can be lawfully detained for, but which is not a crime if committed by an adult

Most of the constitutional protections and safeguards that are present in the adult courts are also required in juvenile systems. Exceptions include the right to a public trial and the right to a jury trial. The Supreme Court ruled that neither public nor jury trials are required in juvenile cases because they could destroy the privacy of juvenile hearings. If incarcerated, juveniles are required to be housed separately from the adult inmate population.

In most states, young people under age 17 are prosecuted in juvenile courts. Eleven states end juvenile court jurisdiction at age 15 or 16. However, all states have processes that allow some juveniles to be tried in adult court in certain circumstances. Some people believe that the juvenile system is not **equipped** to deal with youth who commit serious crimes. Opponents of trying juveniles in adult courts argue that young people's brains are still developing and they are less culpable for their actions than adults are.

> **equip** to make ready

✓ READING PROGRESS CHECK

Comparing Advantages and Disadvantages What are some reasons to support and oppose trying juveniles in adult courts for serious crimes?

LESSON 2 REVIEW

Reviewing Vocabulary

1. *Defining* What are some other ways of saying *indigent defendant*?

Using Your Graphic Organizer

2. *Summarizing* Use your completed graphic organizer to create a one-page summary explaining what constitutional rights the accused have at trial.

Answering the Guiding Questions

3. *Interpreting* Why is the presumption of innocence an important protection in our criminal justice system?

4. *Describing* What is the right to an impartial jury trial?

5. *Explaining* How does the criminal justice system provide for the right to an attorney?

6. *Specifying* What rights at trial are protected by the Fifth and Sixth Amendments?

7. *Contrasting* In what ways is the juvenile justice system different from the adult criminal justice system?

Writing About Government

8. *Argument* In this lesson, there are several examples of rights guaranteed to defendants on trial. Provide several examples from the text. Then write a persuasive speech explaining which you think is more important in a democracy: protecting all defendants or putting more criminals behind bars.

Should terrorist detainees have access to domestic courts and basic constitutional protections?

DELIBERATING DEMOCRATIC PRINCIPLES

After the terrorist attacks on the United States on September 11, 2001, the United States began a "war on terrorism." During fighting in Afghanistan, the U.S. military captured many prisoners. In early 2002, the United States began transporting some of these foreign captives to the U.S. military base located in Guantanamo Bay, Cuba. Guantanamo Bay is leased to the United States by Cuba on a long-term basis.

More than 700 individuals are imprisoned at Guantanamo Bay. These prisoners are labeled as "enemy combatants" rather than "prisoners of war." These enemy combatants have been held at Guantanamo Bay for many years without being charged with a crime. Some people argue that prisoners at Guantanamo should have access to courts and basic constitutional protections. Others argue that enemy combatants are dangerous terrorists who should be held in a military prison until the threat of war has passed.

YES

TEAM A | **Guantanamo Detainees Should Be Granted Constitutional Protections**

Many detainees at Guantanamo are being held illegally because they have not been charged with a crime, have no access to lawyers, and have no access to a court to plead their cases. This violates the constitutional protections for people who have been accused of crimes. At the very least, a court should review their cases to determine whether these detainees are actually enemy combatants and not just innocent people being held indefinitely. Our courts are capable of conducting trials for dangerous people like terrorists. Even though Guantanamo Bay is in Cuba, it is basically a U.S. territory. It is a long-term U.S. military base, and the protections of the U.S. Constitution should apply there.

NO

TEAM B | **Guantanamo Detainees Should Not Be Granted Constitutional Protections**

The prisoners at Guantanamo should be detained until the end of the war on terrorism. This is a special situation—because these people have direct ties to terrorist organizations and were captured in battle, they can be held until the end of the war. In times of war, the military should be the ones to establish who is an enemy combatant, not a court. Federal courts should not hear the detainees' cases because the prisoners are not American citizens and are not being held in the United States. In addition, trials in the United States could endanger Americans and could result in sensitive information being made public, harming the war effort.

EXPLORING THE ESSENTIAL QUESTION

Deliberating With a partner, review the main arguments for either side. Decide which points are most compelling. Then paraphrase those arguments to a pair of students who were assigned to the other viewpoint. Listen to their strongest arguments. Switch sides and repeat the best arguments and add another compelling argument the other pair may not have thought about or presented. Then drop your roles and have a free discussion about which policy you support and why. Can you find any areas of common ground among the two views? How might a sensible policy address that common ground? What do you think is the best answer? Why?

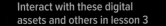

Interact with these digital assets and others in lesson 3

✓ **INTERACTIVE GRAPH**
Executions Around the World

✓ **INTERACTIVE IMAGE**
Three Strikes

✓ **SELF-CHECK QUIZ**

✓ **VIDEO**
Death Penalty Age

netwⓞrks
TRY IT YOURSELF ONLINE

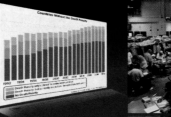

LESSON 3
Constitutional Rights After Trial

Reading Help Desk

Academic Vocabulary

- **file**
- **suspend**

Content Vocabulary

- **sentence**
- **ex post facto clause**
- **three-strikes laws**
- **capital punishment**
- **treason**
- **espionage**
- **double jeopardy**

TAKING NOTES:

Key Ideas and Details

IDENTIFYING Use the graphic organizer to record an individual's constitutional rights after trial.

Rights After Trial

ESSENTIAL QUESTION

How does our democracy protect the rights of individuals suspected, accused, convicted, or acquitted of crimes?

Once a trial is over, if the defendant was found guilty, the next step is deciding on the punishment. Imagine that you are a judge. At trial in your courtroom, a 20-year-old babysitter has just been convicted of child endangerment. What will be the purpose or purposes of the sentence you will issue?

- Incapacitation (preventing the person from doing the same thing again)
- Deterrence (discouraging others from committing similar crimes)
- Restitution (helping the injured parties recover)
- Retribution (getting back at the person for the harm done)
- Rehabilitation (helping the person become a better citizen)

Which purpose would be most important to you? How would it influence your decision?

Purposes and Types of Punishment

GUIDING QUESTION *What are the purposes of punishment in our criminal justice system?*

When a defendant is found guilty, a judge usually decides the **sentence**, or punishment. Most criminal laws set out basic sentencing structures, but judges generally have considerable freedom in choosing the type, length, and conditions of the sentence. Sentences may require time in prison, a fine, community service, or probation. In many states, judges have the option of handing down the death penalty for the most serious offenses. In a few states, jurors play a role in sentencing.

Criminal sentences serve a number of different purposes, including retribution, deterrence, rehabilitation, restitution, and incapacitation. The type of sentence given might depend in part on the court's purpose in punishing the person convicted. For example, if the goal is to keep the criminal from threatening the safety of the community (incapacitation), a prison sentence might be the best fit. If the goal is to help the criminal change his or her behavior (rehabilitation), then probation, community service, or counseling might be appropriate.

Ex Post Facto Clause The **ex post facto clause** in the U.S. Constitution prevents the government from punishing anyone for doing something that was not a crime when the act was committed. For example, if Joe sells a legal drug in 2012 and then in 2013 the state legislature makes that drug illegal, Joe cannot be punished for having sold the drug before it was illegal.

Disproportionate Incarceration A significant issue in the criminal justice system is the disproportionate percentage of racial minorities in prisons. In 2010 African American males were incarcerated at a rate more than six times that of white males. Many things contribute to this difference—from more contact with law enforcement to poverty to sentencing laws. Some data show evidence of discriminatory sentencing: minorities were given relatively longer sentences than whites for the same types of crimes.

Disproportionate incarceration challenges the basic assumption that everyone receives equal justice under the law. Moreover, if people perceive unfair treatment by the criminal justice system, they may be less likely to cooperate with the process by testifying as a witness or serving on a jury. The federal government and many states have attempted to study this problem and develop solutions to make the system fairer.

☑ **READING PROGRESS CHECK**

Making Generalizations What evidence is there of discriminatory sentencing?

sentence the punishment to be imposed on an offender after a guilty verdict

ex post facto clause the clause in the U.S. Constitution that prevents the government from punishing someone for doing something that was not a crime when the act was committed

three-strikes laws laws that typically impose an automatic minimum sentence of 25 years or life imprisonment when a person is convicted of a serious offense for the third time

Cruel and Unusual Punishment

GUIDING QUESTION *What is and is not considered "cruel and unusual punishment" under the Eighth Amendment?*

The Eighth Amendment prohibits "cruel and unusual punishment." It is the only place in the Constitution where criminal penalties are specifically limited. Courts have ruled that the Eighth Amendment also means that punishments must be proportionate to the crime committed. Most punishments handed down by courts today are not considered "cruel and unusual."

Three-Strikes Laws In the 1990s, many citizens became frustrated with the short sentences some serious criminals were receiving and with the number of repeat offenders. Beginning with the state of Washington in 1993, many states passed **three-strikes laws**—a nickname referring to the baseball phrase "three strikes, you're out."

These laws typically impose an automatic minimum sentence of 25 years or life imprisonment when a person is convicted of a serious offense for the third time.

Three-strikes laws are controversial. Opponents argue that they can be unfair. For example, what happens if one of the three offenses is serious but not violent? (A violent felony would be murder, robbery, or rape.) People who support the three-strikes laws argue that states that have adopted this approach have seen a drop in serious crime.

A prominent court case challenging California's three-strikes law involved Gary Ewing, a man who stole three golf clubs from a pro shop in El Segundo, California. Because of Ewing's many previous crimes, the judge in the case stated

Three-strikes laws typically impose an automatic minimum sentence of 25 years to life imprisonment for a person who is convicted of a serious offense for the third time. This photograph illustrates one of the drawbacks of the three-strikes laws: crowded prisons.

▼ **CRITICAL THINKING**

Defending Do overcrowded prison conditions constitute "cruel and unusual punishment" for the prison population? Explain your answer.

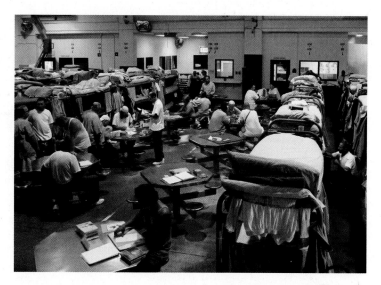

that stealing the clubs was a third strike, and Ewing was sentenced to 25 years to life. In *Ewing* v. *California*, the U.S. Supreme Court decided that the three-strikes law was constitutional.

Capital Punishment **Capital punishment**, or the death penalty, is the most controversial sentence given to defendants. Capital punishment was once used for a variety of crimes, but today it is reserved only for murder and crimes against the nation, such as **treason** and **espionage**.

Capital punishment is also the area where the Supreme Court has been most active in applying the Eighth Amendment. The Court has ruled that the death penalty is unconstitutional in certain situations. In the 1970s, executions in the United States were halted for 10 years while courts studied the legality of capital punishment. In 1972 the Supreme Court ruled the death penalty was unconstitutional. In the case of *Furman* v. *Georgia*, the Court said that judges had too much discretion in assigning a death penalty sentence and the sentence was applied inconsistently. States rewrote their laws about capital punishment.

Later that decade, the Supreme Court ruled that the death penalty was constitutional as long as judges considered all factors that might suggest the defendant deserved a more severe or more lenient sentence, such as previous convictions, crimes involving children, or the defendant's age.

Since the 1970s, the Supreme Court has restricted the use of the death penalty. People who are mentally disabled and people who were under age 18 when they committed their crimes may not be executed. The Court has reasoned that these people have reduced culpability for their crimes because of their age or mental capacity.

Many states have chosen to abolish the death penalty. As of 2013, 18 states and the District of Columbia did not have the death penalty.

capital punishment execution of an offender sentenced to death after conviction by a court of law of a criminal offense

treason the offense of acting to overthrow one's government or to harm or kill its leader

espionage the use of spies by a government to discover the military and political secrets of other nations

---

GRAPH

The number of countries that have abolished the death penalty has increased steadily since the 1980s.

▶ **CRITICAL THINKING**

Making Generalizations Find out which countries still allow the death penalty and see if their locations follow any pattern. What do you think the significance of the pattern might be?

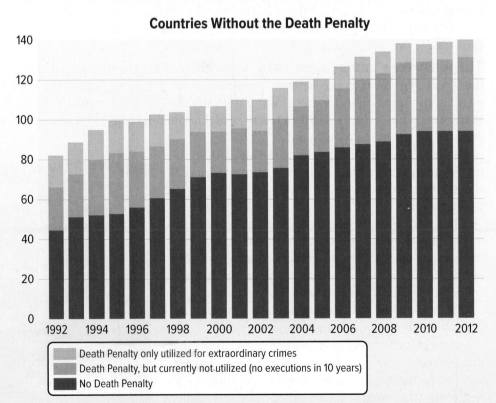

Countries Without the Death Penalty

Death Penalty only utilized for extraordinary crimes
Death Penalty, but currently not utilized (no executions in 10 years)
No Death Penalty

Source: Amnesty International, *Death Penalty Trends*

Juvenile Sentencing In *Graham* v. *Florida* (2010), the Supreme Court decided that juveniles cannot be given life without parole for a crime other than murder. In *Miller* v. *Alabama* (2012), the Court ruled that mandatory sentences of life in prison without parole are unconstitutional for juveniles. Mandatory sentences do not take into account serious differences between children and adults. Judges can still order sentences of life in prison without parole so long as they have considered in the individual juvenile case those factors that differentiate adults from juveniles.

☑ **READING PROGRESS CHECK**

Identifying What are three-strikes rules and why are they controversial?

Rights After a Conviction or Acquittal

GUIDING QUESTION *How does the Constitution protect an individual's rights after he or she is convicted or acquitted?*

The Fifth Amendment's protection against **double jeopardy** means that a defendant cannot be prosecuted a second time for the same offense. If a defendant believes he or she was wrongly convicted because of an error of law during the trial, the defendant can appeal the decision to a higher court.

Habeas Corpus Habeas corpus is a way for people who are imprisoned to challenge their confinement. A defendant can apply to a court for a writ of habeas corpus, asking the court to determine whether his or her imprisonment is unlawful. Someone else can also **file** this writ on behalf of a prisoner.

Habeas corpus is a legal principle with a long history in English law. It serves as an important safeguard against arbitrary or unjustified imprisonment. Article I, Section 9, of the Constitution says that habeas corpus cannot be **suspended**, except in cases of rebellion or invasion.

Habeas corpus was used by the prisoners detained at Guantanamo Bay during the war on terrorism. The Supreme Court ruled that all the Guantanamo Bay prisoners, including foreigners, have a constitutional right to seek a writ of habeas corpus in federal court.

☑ **READING PROGRESS CHECK**

Applying What steps can a person convicted of a crime take to challenge his or her conviction?

▲ Hundreds of wrongly convicted prisoners have been released with the aid of DNA evidence, new witnesses, and other technology.

CRITICAL THINKING
Researching Visit the Innocence Project's website to learn more about their work. Why does the Innocence Project believe that reforms are necessary to ensure fair criminal trials? Who might be opposed to these reform efforts, and why?

double jeopardy the subjecting of a person to a second trial or punishment for the same offense for which the person has already been tried or punished

file to initiate through proper formal procedure

suspend to defer to a later time on specified conditions

LESSON 3 REVIEW

Reviewing Vocabulary
1. *Defining* What is the meaning of the term *double jeopardy* in the context of our criminal justice system?

Using Your Graphic Organizer
2. *Summarizing* Use your completed graphic organizer to write a guide to an individual's constitutional rights after trial.

Answering the Guiding Questions
3. *Identifying* What are the purposes of punishment in our criminal justice system?

4. *Interpreting* What is and is not considered "cruel and unusual punishment" under the Eighth Amendment?

5. *Explaining* How does the Constitution protect an individual's rights after he or she is convicted or acquitted?

Writing About Government
6. *Argument* The Supreme Court has upheld the use of capital punishment in some situations. Do you agree with the Court's interpretation of the Eighth Amendment? Write an essay in which you defend your belief that capital punishment constitutes "cruel and unusual punishment" in some, all, or no cases.

STUDY GUIDE

RIGHTS BEFORE TRIAL
LESSON 1

FOURTH AMENDMENT

Protection from unreasonable search and seizure

- Searches and seizures require probable cause and a search warrant.
- There are some situations where no warrant is needed.

Important Court Rulings:
- *Mapp* v. *Ohio*
  - exclusionary rule applies to both state and federal government
- *New Jersey* v. *T.L.O.*
  - covers searches in public schools

FIFTH AMENDMENT

Protection from self-incrimination

- Cannot be compelled to testify against oneself
- Procedural due process

Important Court Rulings:
- *Escobedo* v. *Illinois*
  - confession must be voluntary and trustworthy
- *Miranda* v. *Arizona*
  - inform suspect of rights before questioning
  - right to remain silent
  - right to an attorney

JUVENILE JUSTICE SYSTEM
LESSON 2

Most adult protections apply

May be tried as adults for serious crimes

Juvenile Justice System

Privacy protected— neither public nor jury trials required

Jailed juveniles housed separately from adults

RIGHTS AT TRIAL
LESSON 2

FIFTH AMENDMENT

- Freedom from self-incrimination
- Due process of law

SIXTH AMENDMENT

- Speedy and public trial
- Impartial jury
- Confrontation of witnesses
- Right to call own witnesses
- Right to attorney

RIGHTS AFTER TRIAL
LESSON 3

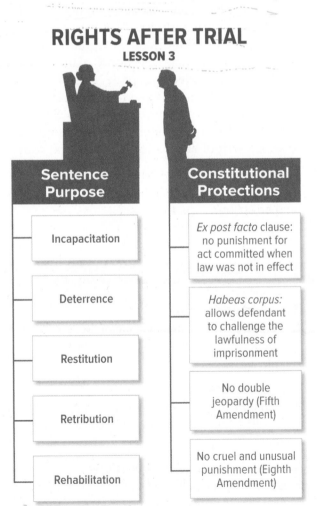

Sentence Purpose

- Incapacitation
- Deterrence
- Restitution
- Retribution
- Rehabilitation

Constitutional Protections

- *Ex post facto* clause: no punishment for act committed when law was not in effect
- *Habeas corpus:* allows defendant to challenge the lawfulness of imprisonment
- No double jeopardy (Fifth Amendment)
- No cruel and unusual punishment (Eighth Amendment)

Directions: On a separate sheet of paper, answer the questions below. Make sure you read carefully and answer all parts of the questions.

Lesson Review

Lesson 1

1 ***Identifying Central Issues*** Why was the decision in *Mapp* v. *Ohio* important?

2 ***Specifying*** What must the police do to obtain a search warrant? When can the police make a search without a warrant?

Lesson 2

3 ***Specifying*** In a criminal trial, what standard of proof is required for a defendant to be found guilty?

4 ***Making Connections*** What is cross-examination, and what Sixth Amendment right does it fulfill?

Lesson 3

5 ***Applying*** In criminal sentencing, what is "restitution"? Give an example of a sentence that imposes restitution.

6 ***Specifying*** For what crimes can capital punishment be applied in the United States today?

ANSWERING THE ESSENTIAL QUESTIONS

Review your answers to the introductory questions at the beginning of each lesson. Then answer the following Essential Questions based on what you learned in the chapter. Have your answers changed?

7 ***Identifying Central Issues*** How does our democracy protect the rights of individuals suspected, accused, convicted, or acquitted of crimes?

8 ***Explaining*** How does our democracy balance the rights of the defendant and the search for truth?

DBQ Interpreting Political Cartoons

Use the political cartoon to answer the following questions.

9 ***Drawing Inferences*** Who does the batter represent in the cartoon?

10 ***Interpreting Significance*** What is the significance of the third strike?

Critical Thinking

11 ***Making Connections*** How did the Supreme Court interpret Fifth Amendment rights in *Miranda* v. *Arizona*?

12 ***Analyzing*** Is it ever appropriate for police to use race as a factor in deciding who to stop and search? Explain.

13 ***Making Connections*** How does the *Gideon* v. *Wainwright* case relate to the Sixth Amendment?

14 ***Analyzing*** Explain how the jury selection process helps to ensure an impartial jury.

15 ***Interpreting*** What does the Fifth Amendment protection against double jeopardy mean for a criminal defendant who is acquitted?

16 ***Analyzing*** A significant issue in the criminal justice system is the disproportionate percentage of racial minorities in prisons. How do you explain this disparity?

Need Extra Help?

If You've Missed Question	1	2	3	4	5	6	7	8	9	10	11	12	13	14	15	16
Go to page	487	486	492	495	498	500	485	485	499	499	490	489	494	493	501	499

Directions: On a separate sheet of paper, answer the questions below. Make sure you read carefully and answer all parts of the questions.

DBQ Analyzing Primary Sources

Read the excerpts and answer the questions that follow.

PRIMARY SOURCE

"... *in our adversary system of criminal justice, any person haled [sic] into court, who is too poor to hire a lawyer, cannot be assured a fair trial unless counsel is provided for him. ... From the very beginning, our ... constitutions and laws have laid great emphasis on ... safeguards designed to assure fair trials. ... This noble ideal cannot be realized if the poor man charged with crime has to face his accusers without a lawyer to assist him. ... [Citing Justice Sutherland in* Powell v. Alabama*] 'Even the intelligent and educated layman has small and sometimes no skill in the science of law. ... Without [a lawyer's help], though he be not guilty, he faces the danger of conviction because he does not know how to establish his innocence.'*"

—Justice Hugo Black,
opinion in *Gideon* v. *Wainwright*, March 18, 1963

17 *Finding the Main Idea* According to Justice Black, what individual right is violated if a poor person facing trial for a crime has no lawyer?

18 *Interpreting* What reason did Justice Sutherland give for why every person accused of a crime should have a lawyer?

PRIMARY SOURCE

"*If an obscure Florida convict named Clarence Earl Gideon had not sat down in his prison cell with a pencil and paper to write a letter to the Supreme Court, and if the Court had not taken the trouble to look for merit in that one crude petition ... the vast machinery of American law would have gone on functioning undisturbed. But Gideon did write that letter, the Court did look into his case ... and the whole course of American legal history has been changed.*"

—Attorney General Robert F. Kennedy,
November 1, 1963

19 *Identifying Central Issues* According to Robert Kennedy, what would have happened if Clarence Gideon had not written his petition?

20 *Making Connections* How did Gideon's petition change "the whole course of American legal history"?

Social Studies Skills

21 *Sequencing* Conduct research to create a multimedia flowchart showing each step in the criminal justice process. Include a brief description of what occurs at each step.

22 *Analyzing Arguments and Drawing Conclusions* Conduct research to learn more about plea bargaining. Construct a chart showing advantages and disadvantages. Then draw your own conclusion about whether the process works as it is or needs to change in some way. Explain.

Research and Presentation

23 *Questioning* Write five questions about the juvenile justice system in your state to which you would like answers. Then do online research to find the answers. Be prepared to share your questions and answers in a class discussion.

24 *Exploring Issues* Capital punishment is a highly controversial issue. Read online articles in favor of and opposed to the death penalty. Then decide how you stand. Prepare for a class debate on the issue.

25 *Analyzing* Do online research to find statistics about the prison population either in your state or in the nation. Choose a table, chart, or graph that interests you and capture it electronically. Analyze what the statistics say about the prison population and present your analysis to the class.

Need Extra Help?

If You've Missed Question	17	18	19	20	21	22	23	24	25
Go to page	494	495	494	494	485	493	496	500	494

UNIT 5
Participating in Government

IT MATTERS BECAUSE . . .

There are many ways you can participate in your government. Citizens in the United States can vote for candidates in elections, volunteer for a political party or election campaign, join interest groups to affect issues that matter to them, contact their elected representatives, and follow the news about government in their state or community. Social media makes it easier than ever for you to contact your elected representatives. To participate in government effectively, citizens must be well informed about candidates and issues. Consequently, you have a responsibility to stay on top of current events from a variety of credible news and information sources. Participation in government is in your own self-interest. By participating in your government, you can make your voice heard at all levels of government, influence policies, and improve the success of American democracy.

How to
Debate and Deliberate

Debating and deliberating skills help you to analyze and defend a point of view on a political or policy issue. These skills will also allow you to practice presenting in front of an audience. Debating or deliberating an issue will give you greater insight into a political or policy issue. Doing so will allow you to use problem-solving and decision-making processes to devise solutions to and make decisions about complex issues or problems in American government. When debating or deliberating an issue, follow these steps:

1. Work in teams to identify a political problem or issue. Gather information about the issue and conduct outside research as necessary to identify and develop arguments and evidence for both sides of the issue. Consider advantages and disadvantages about the various options.

2. Debate or deliberate the issue as a whole class or in small groups.

2a. In a debate, each side will present a prepared speech to the class, followed by time for questions and rebuttals. An in-class debate will often conclude with a class vote to determine the winner.

2b. In a deliberation, work with a partner to review each side and present those arguments to another pair of students. Listen to their arguments. Then switch sides and repeat the process. Conclude by having a free discussion and searching for common ground among the two points of view. Consider which solution to the problem you would choose to implement and the probable effectiveness of that solution.

3. After the debate or deliberation, reflect on the issue area and follow with a written presentation or product to further your understanding of the issue or topic.

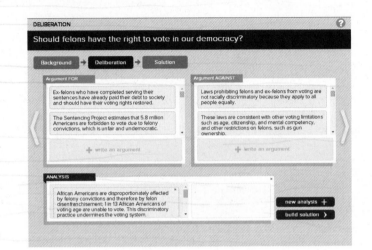

4. Another option is to use a decision-making process to extend your understanding. Now that you have learned more about a particular problem or issue, identify a situation at the local, state, or national level that needs to be remedied. Gather information about the situation, identify options, and predict the consequences of each. Think of ways you could take action to implement this decision.

netw⊙rks   *TRY IT YOURSELF* ONLINE

Go online to interact with these digital activities and more in each chapter.

Chapter 17 Political Parties

Chapter 18 Voting and Elections

Chapter 19 Public Opinion and Interest Groups

Chapter 20 Mass Media in the Digital Age

✓ **VIDEO**
CONVENTION SPEECHES

✓ **INFOGRAPHIC**
POLITICAL PARTY PLATFORMS

✓ **INTERACTIVE GRAPH**
HOW INTEREST GROUPS MAY INFLUENCE CONGRESS

✓ **ANALYZING PRIMARY SOURCES**
CONSUMING THE NEWS

Political Parties

networks
www.connected.mcgraw-hill.com
There's More Online about political parties.

CHAPTER 17

ESSENTIAL QUESTION

How does the two-party system influence American democracy?

▲ President Barack Obama and Republican challenger Mitt Romney faced off in a 2012 presidential debate.

Carolyn Kaster/AP Images

POLITICAL POLARIZATION

Americans have disagreed on political issues since the nation's founding. Recently, however, some political observers have noted that the political parties and Americans themselves are becoming increasingly polarized. That is, they are moving toward the extreme ends of the political spectrum, leaving no middle ground where people can talk, compromise, and learn to be tolerant of other views—to agree to disagree. Recently, stronger party commitments—sometimes called hyper-partisanship—have combined with polarization to create a stalemate in the national government. Explore the sources to learn more about political polarization.

PRIMARY SOURCE and B

In October 2013, the federal government shut down for more than two weeks because Congress did not pass a continuing resolution to fund the government. Some Republicans in the House of Representatives wanted to defund the Affordable Care Act (ACA). Democrats in the Senate said they would not vote for a resolution that defunded the ACA. Both parties blamed the other.

"My simple message today is: Call a vote. Call a vote. Put it on the floor. Take a vote, stop this farce and end this shutdown right now. The only thing that's keeping the government shut down . . . is that Speaker John Boehner won't even let the bill get a yes or no vote because he doesn't want to anger the extremists in his party."

—President Barack Obama

"They will not negotiate. We had a nice conversation, a polite conversation, but at some point we've got to allow the process that our founders gave us to work out."

—House Speaker John Boehner

PRIMARY SOURCE C

Former Republican Senate Leader Trent Lott was critical of the way the 2013 Congress handled budget negotiations:

"Now you've got—I hate to say it this way—the far right in the Republican Party and the far left in the Democratic Party and, as (William Butler) Yeats would say in his poem, the center would not hold. The fact that the Senate has not passed a budget in four years—how could that happen? The fact that they don't even do appropriations bills anymore?"

—Former Senate Republican leader Trent Lott, co-chairman of the Bipartisan Policy Center Commission on Political Reform

SECONDARY SOURCE D

In 2013 *USA Today* and the Bipartisan Policy Center conducted a survey of public opinions about partisanship. It found:

- 76% of Americans believed that American politics is more divided than ever.

- About three-fourths of respondents said this deeper division is bad for the country.

- 20% said the partisan divide is good because it gives voters real choices.

These cartograms represent the 2012 presidential election. These cartograms are maps in which the sizes of states are rescaled according to their electoral votes. The first map shows the electoral vote—the blue areas are states that awarded their electoral votes to Barack Obama, while the red sections awarded votes to Mitt Romney. The second map shows the division of the vote by counties, with colors ranging from blue (strongly Democrat) to red (strongly Republican) across various shades of purple, indicating counties where the vote was more evenly divided.

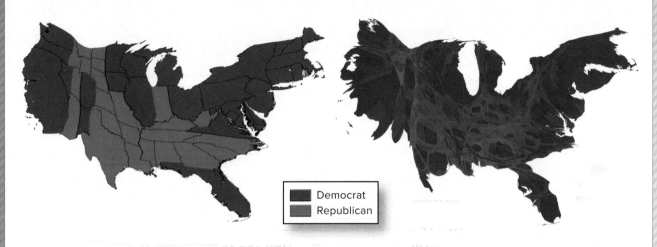

Democrat
Republican

SOURCE: U.S. Census, 2012; Mark Newman, Department of Physics and Center for the Study of Complex Systems, University of Michigan, 2012

DBQ DOCUMENT-BASED QUESTIONS

1. **Identifying** According to these sources, what factors contribute to polarization and hyper-partisanship? How are these phenomena seen by the American public?

2. **Analyzing** Which cartogram suggests greater polarization in the electorate? Is there a geographic basis to this polarization? How does the second cartogram refine your understanding of this polarization?

3. **Making Connections** What problems has polarization caused in government? Do you think polarization has any positive effects? Explain your answer.

WHAT WILL YOU DO?

What will you do to decrease political polarization and hyper-partisanship? Think about everyday solutions (e.g., talking to people who disagree with you) and political solutions (e.g., voting only for candidates with a proven record of problem solving and compromise).

EXPLORE the interactive version of the analyzing primary sources feature on Networks.

 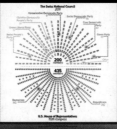 

Interact with these digital
assets and others in lesson 1

✓ **INTERACTIVE IMAGE**
   Divided Government

✓ **INTERACTIVE INFOGRAPHIC**
   Political Parties in the United States

✓ **SLIDE SHOW**
   Third Parties

✓ **VIDEO**
   Federalists and
   Democratic-Republicans

netw⊙rks
TRY IT YOURSELF ONLINE

LESSON 1
Development of Political Parties

Reading Help Desk

Academic Vocabulary

- stability
- range

Content Vocabulary

- political party
- patronage
- one-party system
- two-party system
- coalition government
- third party
- single-issue party
- ideological party
- splinter party
- single-member district
- proportional representation

TAKING NOTES:

Integrating Knowledge and Ideas

LISTING Use the graphic organizer to list the functions of political parties and party systems.

Functions of Political Parties	Party Systems

ESSENTIAL QUESTION

How does the two-party system influence American democracy?

Think about your favorite team sport and what it takes to win a national or world championship. What things are most important to winning? Work with one other student to rank each of the following factors from most to least important.

___ Recruiting the most talented players

___ Having the best strategies on the field or court

___ Having the hardest-working athletes

___ Having the most inspiring coaches

___ Having the best feeder team (like a minor league baseball team)

___ Having the most money to advertise game-day information to fans and potential fans

___ Having the best scouts to discover the other teams' strategies and weaknesses

___ Having the most loyal fans

Functions of Political Parties

GUIDING QUESTION *What functions do political parties serve in government?*

A **political party** is a group of people with broad common interests who organize to win elections, control government, and thereby influence government policies. When trying to elect candidates, parties need some of the same things as a winning sports team. For example, parties need hard-working candidates, money to spread information about their positions on issues, and lots of fans.

The most successful political parties win on Election Day when more of their "fans" come to the polls. However, once party candidates win elections, their work has just begun. Then they have to govern, often with members of the other team; they must work to implement the policies they campaigned for, while also preparing for the next election.

The Constitution does not provide for political parties or even mention them, yet political parties are an integral part of the American democratic system. Political parties perform several important functions that no other body or institution in American politics does.

Electing Candidates Political parties recruit men and women to run for office who appear to have a good chance of being elected. Parties raise money for campaigns and organize rallies and meetings to generate enthusiasm for their candidates. They also manage "Get Out the Vote" events to remind their supporters to vote on Election Day. They might even offer transportation services to make sure loyal supporters can get to the polls.

Educating the Public Political parties bring important issues to the public's attention. Each party publishes its position on important issues such as inflation, military spending, taxes, pollution, energy, and the environment. Candidates present these views in pamphlets, press conferences, speeches, and television, radio, newspaper, and online advertisements. Candidates in the 2012 election used information such as supporters' Facebook likes, location, and photos to tailor their advertising. Candidates' websites, social network pages, and Twitter feeds all push information about their views out to the public and seek to engage supporters.

Unfortunately, many Americans are not very well-informed about the backgrounds of candidates or their views on important issues. Political parties simplify elections by helping such people decide how to vote. By supporting a candidate just because he or she is a Democrat or a Republican, the voter knows generally how the candidate stands on key issues. In this way, political party affiliation helps voters assess which candidate will be more acceptable.

Involving People in the Political Process Political parties provide numerous opportunities for people to affect government, even people who have no interest in getting elected themselves. Through local political parties, people can become involved in campaigns by helping to register other voters, posting signs, donating money, and so on. On Election Day, political parties need people to serve as election judges and poll watchers to make sure that all election laws are followed. Political parties set their goals by listening to what people say they want from their government.

Operating the Government Political parties also play a key role in running and staffing the executive and legislative branches of government. Congress and the state legislatures are organized and carry on their work on the basis of party affiliation. Party leaders in the legislatures make every effort to see that their members support the party's position when considering legislation.

A party also acts as a link between a legislature and a chief executive. A chief executive works through his or her party leaders in the legislature to promote the administration's programs. For most of the past 30 years, however, one party has controlled the White House and the other has controlled one or both houses of Congress—this is known as divided government. In recent years, the same situation has developed between governors and legislatures in more than half the states.

Republican Governor Rick Scott of Florida meeting with Democratic State Senator Arthenia Joyner before the governor's state of the state address in 2012.

▼ CRITICAL THINKING
Speculating Some polls have indicated that Americans prefer divided government. Why do you think that might be the case?

ZUMA Press, Inc./Alamy

political party a group of individuals with broad common interests who organize to nominate candidates for office, win elections, conduct government, and determine public policy

patronage the practice of granting favors to reward party loyalty

Dispensing Patronage Political parties also dispense **patronage**, or favors given to reward party loyalty, to their members. These favors often include jobs, contracts, and appointments to government positions. Business executives or labor unions that contribute heavily to a political party, for example, may expect government to be sympathetic to their problems if that party comes to power. They might be awarded contracts to provide government with goods or services. Loyal party workers might be placed in government jobs. Although laws and court decisions limit patronage, the practice remains a way for parties to control and reward their supporters.

On the one hand, patronage may be unseemly if inexperienced people get key jobs as a reward just because they donated a lot of money to a winning candidate. On the other hand, patronage allows the party in power to be sure there are at least some very loyal people in government to carry out the party's visions for public policy.

Developing and Implementing Policy After winning an election, a political party works to implement its key policy initiatives. Elected officials and party leaders set goals for government action and articulate those goals to the American people. Through the legislatures, they work to pass laws to address pressing issues. Through the executives, they work to implement government programs in line with their beliefs and priorities.

Government Watchdog The party that is out of power in the legislative or executive branch assumes the role of "watchdog" over the government. It observes the party that is in power, criticizes it, and offers solutions to political problems. If the opposition party does this successfully, public opinion might swing in its favor and return it to power in a future election. Concern about this makes the party in power more sensitive to the will of the people.

stability remaining steady

Providing Stability Parties contribute to political **stability**. When one party loses control of the government, the transfer of power takes place peacefully. No violent revolutions occur after elections, as they do in some nations. In the United States, the losing party accepts the outcome of elections because it knows that the party will continue to exist as the opposing party and someday will return to power.

✓ **READING PROGRESS CHECK**

Explaining How do political parties help educate the public about major issues? How do they assist in the operation of the government?

EXPLORING THE ESSENTIAL QUESTION

Categorizing Review this list of political party activities and categorize each into one or more of the functions described in the text.

a. High school students volunteer at the party headquarters to call people to remind them to vote for the Green Party candidate on Election Day.

b. Republicans in the House of Representatives hold an election to choose their leader, the Speaker of the House.

c. Democrats from across the state meet to debate and decide the party's official positions and plans to solve various public policy problems.

d. The Libertarian Party issues a press statement that the $32 billion tax cuts are "so small you need a microscope to find them."

e. The Constitution Party sends a pamphlet to every home in a certain zip code just before Election Day. It highlights five issues important to people in that area and why their party's candidate is best.

f. The Republican Party gives out political buttons and bumper stickers at a country music concert.

PARTY SYSTEMS

This activity compares two-party systems to multi-party systems. The graph contrasts the Swiss National Council and the U.S. House of Representatives.

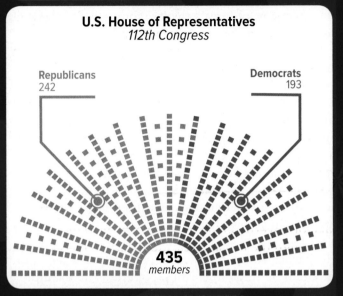

U.S. House of Representatives
112th Congress

Republicans
242

Democrats
193

435
members

TWO-PARTY SYSTEMS

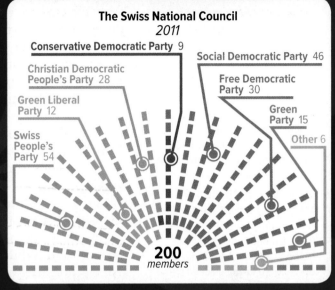

The Swiss National Council
2011

Conservative Democratic Party 9

Christian Democratic People's Party 28

Social Democratic Party 46

Green Liberal Party 12

Free Democratic Party 30

Swiss People's Party 54

Green Party 15

Other 6

200
members

MULTI-PARTY SYSTEMS

In the United States, a person runs for the House or Senate from a particular state or district. Whoever gets the most votes in that state or district wins. So a candidate who wins 51 percent of the vote in a district represents the entire district, winning the only seat available.

This "winner-take-all" method favors the two major parties, because parties who garner only 10 or 15 percent of the vote will never be elected to office.

This system can provide stability. Both main parties are relatively centrist so that they will appeal to a wide array of voters. When a party gains control over Congress or the presidency—or even some level of state government—the government does not undergo radical change.

Multi-party systems often award representation proportionately. That is, parties are awarded seats in the legislature based on the percentage of votes they receive in each district. If one party gets 51 percent of the votes, that party gets 51 percent of the seats for that district. The other seats go to the other parties who received votes.

Supporters say this allows more points of view to be heard. A broader spectrum of views is represented. The chance to be heard encourages more people to vote.

In this system, it is more likely that no party will hold a majority in the legislature. Parties must collaborate to form coalition governments. Two or more parties work together to run the parliament and choose a prime minister.

Party Systems

GUIDING QUESTION *How does the two-party system in the United States compare to other party systems?*

While the United States has two major parties, not all countries do. Most nations have one or more political parties, but their number and role differ with each nation's political system.

One-Party Systems **One-party systems** are usually found in nations with authoritarian governments. Only one political party exists, often because the government tolerates no opposition. In these nations, the party is the government. The party leaders run the government and set all policy. Such governments are formed when political parties or the military take power by force. Today, Cuba, Vietnam, North Korea, and China are all one-party Communist governments.

Some nations are de facto one-party states. While the government might allow other parties to participate, they have no realistic chance of winning. After briefly experimenting with democratic elections in the

▲ CRITICAL THINKING

1. *Evaluating* Citizen participation and majority rule with minority rights are two principles of democracy. Do you think two-party or multi-party systems are more likely to embody these principles? Explain your answer.

2. *Analyzing* Which system, if either, do you think would make a legislature operate more efficiently? More collaboratively?

one-party system a system in which only one political party exists, often because the government tolerates no other opposition; usually in authoritarian governments

Many political parties throughout American history have challenged the Democrats and Republicans, yet none have been very successful.

▼ **CRITICAL THINKING**

1. *Exploring Issues* Identify the sections on the time line where there is turmoil and movement between parties. What historical events were taking place at the same time?

2. *Constructing Arguments* Is it a good thing for our democracy that the two parties have been relatively stable for so long? Why or why not?

mid-1990s, Russia has created an authoritarian system in which no political parties are able to effectively compete against Vladimir Putin's United Russia Party.

Two-party and Multi-party Systems Only about a dozen nations have systems in which two major political parties compete for power, although minor parties exist. Like the United States, these are known as **two-party systems**.

Far more common among political systems today is the multi-party system. For example, France and Italy each have more than 15 political parties that exert influence on government, with 5 to 7 typically having a significant number of seats in the parliament. In such countries, voters have a wide **range** of choices on Election Day. These systems are more common in countries with parliamentary governments.

In some cases, multi-party systems do not allow for as much opposition as it may appear. For example, in Iran, many parties exist, but religious conservatives control the country, which makes it difficult for reformist opposition parties to participate in government.

In other cases, some multi-party systems operate essentially as a one-party system. While many parties compete in elections, one party tends to win election after election, often by huge majorities. Nigeria is an example. Nigeria gained its independence in 1960; since then, it has had periods of democracy, as well as periods of military rule. Its current democracy has been in place since 1999. While Nigeria currently has nearly 30 political parties, every president since 1999 has been a member of the People's

TIME LINE OF POLITICAL PARTIES

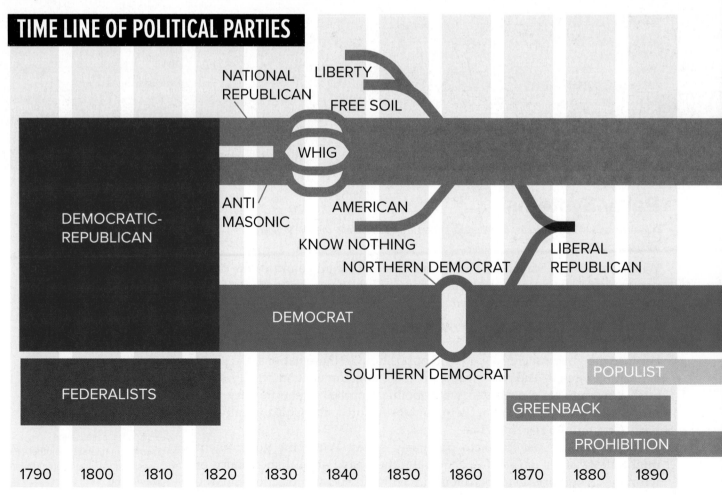

NATIONAL REPUBLICAN

LIBERTY

FREE SOIL

WHIG

ANTI MASONIC

AMERICAN

KNOW NOTHING

NORTHERN DEMOCRAT

LIBERAL REPUBLICAN

DEMOCRATIC-REPUBLICAN

DEMOCRAT

SOUTHERN DEMOCRAT

POPULIST

FEDERALISTS

GREENBACK

PROHIBITION

| 1790 | 1800 | 1810 | 1820 | 1830 | 1840 | 1850 | 1860 | 1870 | 1880 | 1890 |

Democratic Party (PDP); 345 of the 469 members of the National Assembly are members of the PDP. With this kind of dominance, the PDP can enact whatever policies it wants.

In a multi-party system, one party rarely gets enough support to control the government. Several parties often combine forces to obtain a majority and form a **coalition government**. When groups with different ideologies share power, disputes sometimes arise and coalitions often break down. Sometimes, the coalition is not able to govern effectively, and new elections may be called.

coalition government one formed by several parties who combine forces to obtain a majority

☑ **READING PROGRESS CHECK**

Contrasting How do one-party and two-party systems differ?

Evolution of American Parties

GUIDING QUESTION *How has the American two-party system evolved?*

Many of the Founders distrusted factions, or groups with differing political views. In his Farewell Address of 1796, President George Washington warned against the "baneful [very harmful] effects of the spirit of party." Even so, by the end of his second term, two political parties had organized in opposition to one another. Over time, some parties disintegrated and others began. At some times, there were several major political parties in the United States; after the Civil War, however, two strong parties emerged that remain the dominant players to this day: the Democratic Party and the Republican Party.

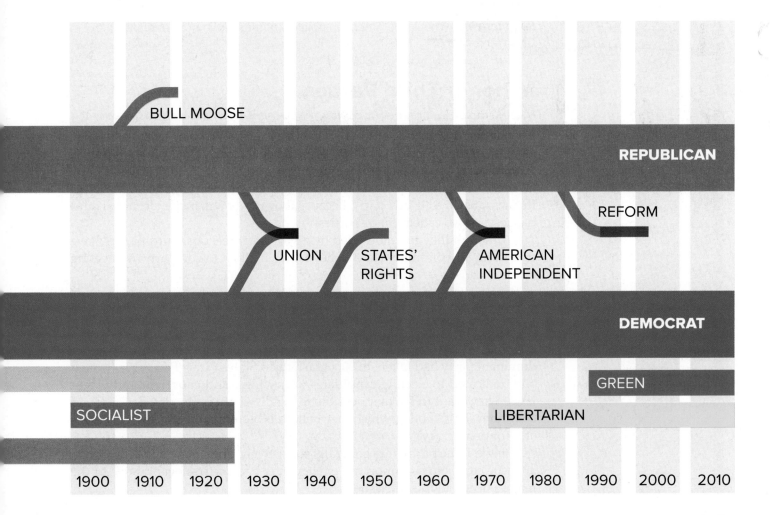

Parties Before the Civil War In the late 1700s, the two original parties were the Federalists, who called for a strong central government, and the Democratic-Republicans, who believed that the states should have more power. After Federalist John Adams became president in 1796, the party's power quickly declined. The Democratic-Republicans dominated politics into the 1820s. Conflicts over banking, tariffs, and slavery later shattered the party. By 1828, the Democratic-Republicans were splitting into two parties. Then-president Andrew Jackson aligned with the group called Democrats. The other group called itself the National Republicans, or the Whigs.

By the 1850s, the debate over slavery had created divisions within both parties. The Free Soil and Know-Nothing parties arose. The Democrats split into Northern and Southern factions. Many Whigs joined a new party that opposed the spread of slavery—the Republican Party.

Parties After the Civil War By the end of the Civil War, two major parties dominated the national political scene. The Republicans generally represented the Northern states and controlled the presidency and both houses of Congress. The Democrats tended to be from the Southern states. Democrats held the presidency for only four terms between 1860 and 1932. In 1932 the Democratic Party won the White House and assumed control of Congress. For most of the next 60 years, Democrats were the majority party. A variety of minor parties existed throughout these years, but none usurped the role of the two major parties. Since 1968, these two parties have often split control of the presidency and Congress.

✔ **READING PROGRESS CHECK**

Summarizing What were American political parties like before and after the Civil War?

Minor or Third Parties

GUIDING QUESTION *What role do third parties, or minor parties, play in the United States government?*

Despite the dominance of the two major parties, third parties have been an element of the American political scene since the early days of the Republic. A **third party** is any party other than one of the two major parties. In any election, more than one party may run against the major parties, yet each of them is labeled a "third" party. Because they rarely win major elections, third parties are also called minor parties.

Although they are motivated by a variety of reasons, third parties have one thing in common: They believe that neither major party is meeting certain needs.

Types of Third Parties Minor parties generally fall into one of three categories. **Single-issue parties** focus exclusively on one major social, economic, or moral issue. For example, in the 1840s, the Liberty Party and the Free Soil Party formed to take stronger stands against slavery than either dominant party had taken. In 2006 the United States Pirate Party was formed and dedicated to electing candidates who will reform copyright and patent laws. They want to make it possible to legally share online movies, art, and computer source codes, which they believe is better for creative professionals and for democracy.

Single-issue parties are generally short-lived. They may fade away when an issue ceases to be important, or they may become irrelevant if one of the major parties adopts the issue.

third party any political party other than one of the two major parties

single-issue party a political party that focuses exclusively on one major social, economic, or moral issue

THIRD PARTIES

Third parties believe that the major parties are not addressing certain issues or meeting certain needs.

GREEN PARTY

LIBERTARIAN PARTY

CONSTITUTION PARTY

Green Party presidential candidate Cynthia McKinney holds a rally in 2008 in New York City to raise support for her campaign.

Former New Mexico governor Gary Johnson holds a press conference in Santa Fe in 2011 to announce he is leaving the Republican Party to join the Libertarian Party and seek that party's nomination for president.

Constitution Party presidential candidate Virgil Goode speaks to a group at a Virginia public library in 2012.

Another type of third party is the **ideological party**, which has a particular set of ideas about how to change society overall rather than focusing on a single issue. Ideological parties such as the Socialist Labor Party and the Communist Party USA advocate government ownership of factories, transportation, resources, farmland, and other means of production and distribution. The Libertarian Party calls for drastic reductions in the size and scope of government in order to increase personal freedoms.

The third type of minor party is the **splinter party**, which splits away from one of the major parties because of some disagreement, like the failure of a popular figure to gain the major party's presidential nomination. Splinter parties typically fade away with the defeat of their candidate.

For example, in 1912 former president Theodore Roosevelt led a group out of the Republican Party to form the Progressive Party, also known as the Bull Moose Party. The party dissolved after Roosevelt lost the election. In 1948, when the Democratic Party endorsed an end to segregation, presidential candidate Strom Thurmond formed his own "States Rights Democratic Party," also known as the "Dixiecrats." This short-lived party dissolved after the 1948 election, where Thurmond won only four states.

The Impact of Third Parties Minor parties have influenced the outcome of national elections. Theodore Roosevelt's Bull Moose Party drew so many Republican votes from President William Howard Taft in 1912 that Democratic candidate Woodrow Wilson was elected. In 1968 the American Independent Party won 13.5 percent of the vote, and some think this helped the Republican candidate Richard Nixon to win. In 2000 Green Party candidate Ralph Nader earned more than 2 million votes. Some analysts believe he drew votes from Democrat Al Gore, allowing Republican George W. Bush to win.

Perhaps the most successful third-party candidate in a presidential election was Ross Perot, a member of the Reform Party, who won 19 percent of the popular vote in 1992. Even though Bill Clinton won the election, Perot's influence was significant. Perot brought voters' attention to urgent problems

▲ CRITICAL THINKING
Assessing Do you think voting for a minor party candidate is a "wasted vote"? Explain.

ideological party a political party that has a particular set of ideas about how to change society overall rather than focusing on a single issue

splinter party a political party that splits away from a major party because of some disagreement

caused by the federal budget deficit. Clinton was compelled to tackle the deficit because it was clear voters expected him to.

Third parties often influence politics by promoting new ideas. If they gain support, the major parties adopt their issues. For example, Socialists were the first to popularize the woman suffrage movement in the late 1800s. They, along with the Populist Party, were also the first to propose laws against child labor, and the 40-hour workweek in the early 1900s. These issues were later adopted by the Democrats.

Obstacles for Third Parties As a result of the two-party tradition, minor parties face difficulties in getting on the ballot in all 50 states. The names of Republicans and Democrats are automatically on the ballot in many states, but third-party candidates are required to obtain a large number of voter signatures in a short time.

Another difficulty for third-party candidates is that nearly all elected officials in the United States are selected by **single-member districts**. Under this system, no matter how many candidates compete in a district, only one will win. Because most voters support a major party, the winner has almost always been a Democrat or a Republican. By contrast, many nations use an election system based on **proportional representation**. In this system, several officials are elected to represent voters in an area. Offices are filled in proportion to the votes that each party's candidates receive. Such a system encourages minority parties.

Third parties often have problems with financing campaigns. Candidates from the major political parties can choose to get government funding to help pay for their campaigns. However, the rules state that government funding is available only to political parties that received a certain percentage of votes in the previous election. Because of these rules, most third parties have not qualified for public financing. Third-party candidates also tend to get less media coverage, which limits their fundraising and their ability to convince voters to choose them. Another problem is that voters may prefer a third-party candidate to the others, but if they do not think he or she can win, they are less likely to contribute to their campaigns or vote for them.

single-member district an electoral district in which only one candidate is elected to each office

proportional representation a system in which several officials are elected to represent the same area in proportion to the votes each party's candidate receives

☑ **READING PROGRESS CHECK**

Explaining Explain the differences between single-issue, ideological, and splinter parties. Which tend to be short-lived and why?

LESSON 1 REVIEW

Reviewing Vocabulary
1. *Contrasting* What is the difference between a one-party system and a two-party system?

Using Your Graphic Organizer
2. *Summarizing* Use your completed graphic organizer to write a summary of the functions of political parties.

Answering the Guiding Questions
3. *Analyzing* What functions do political parties serve in government?

4. *Explaining* How does the two-party system in the United States compare to other party systems?

5. *Comparing* How has the American two-party system evolved?

6. *Evaluating* What role do third parties, or minor parties, play in the United States government?

Writing About Government
7. *Informative/Explanatory* Choose an American political party from before the Civil War. Research the party's history. Include how the party was founded, prominent leaders, how the party evolved over time, and an analysis of the impact of political changes brought about by this political party. Write a report with your findings.

Arkansas Educational Television Commission v Forbes (1997)

FACTS OF THE CASE The Arkansas Educational Television Commission, a state-owned public broadcaster, sponsored debates between the Republican and Democratic candidates in an election to choose the next representative for the Third Congressional District. Ralph Forbes, an Independent, sought permission to participate in the debate. The television station's staff determined that the Forbes campaign had not generated enough enthusiasm from voters and did not include him in the debate. Forbes sued, contending that his exclusion violated his First Amendment rights.

ISSUE

Does the exclusion of a third-party candidate from a debate televised by a public broadcaster violate the candidate's right to free speech?

ARGUMENTS

OPINION A The television station was owned by the state. Therefore, the station's decisions about who is and who is not a viable candidate were actually the government's decisions. This kind of decision must be left to the voters. Forbes had previously been a candidate for lieutenant governor and won a majority of the counties in the Third Congressional District in that election. He was a viable candidate, and voters would have been better served by having heard his views in the debate. The government should not be in the business of deciding who voters hear from before an election. All candidates should have an equal chance to persuade voters of their positions.

OPINION B It is true that the government cannot restrict speech it disagrees with. However, the television commission did not base its decision on Forbes's political views. Rather, it made a journalistic decision that was viewpoint-neutral. The station staff did not invite Forbes because he lacked serious voter support, which was the criterion for who was eligible to participate in the debate. A television station cannot be expected to give airtime to any person who runs for office; it is in the business of attracting viewers. Forbes had plenty of other ways to make his views known, from giving speeches to printing campaign brochures to buying advertisements.

EXPLORING THE ESSENTIAL QUESTION

Analyzing Read the facts of the case and each of the two sample opinions in this case. Analyze the arguments made in Opinion A and Opinion B. What do you think? Does the exclusion of a third-party candidate from a debate televised by a public broadcaster violate the candidate's right to free speech? Decide which one you think should be the majority (winning) opinion and which one you think should be the dissenting opinion. Explain your choice.

interact with these digital
assets and others in lesson 2

✓ **INTERACTIVE IMAGE**
  The Donkey and the Elephant

✓ **INTERACTIVE INFOGRAPHIC**
  Political Party Demographics

✓ **SELF-CHECK QUIZ**

✓ **VIDEO**
  American Young Voters

netw⚬rks
TRY IT YOURSELF ONLINE

LESSON 2
Party Ideology and Identification

to r) Kean Collection/Archive Photos/Getty Images; © Blend Images/Alamy;
Kean Collection/Archive Photos/Getty Images

Reading Help Desk

Academic Vocabulary

- **ideology**
- **symbol**

Content Vocabulary

- **liberal**
- **conservative**
- **moderate**
- **Democratic Party**
- **Republican Party**
- **platform**
- **party identification**
- **independent**
- **polarize**
- **centrist**

TAKING NOTES:

Integrating Knowledge and Ideas

DESCRIBING Use the graphic organizer to list the major and minor political parties in the United States and then describe the viewpoints of those political parties.

Political Party	Viewpoints
Republican	
Democratic	
Green	
Libertarian	
Constitution	

ESSENTIAL QUESTION

How does the two-party system influence American democracy?

In your view, what is the proper role of government? Your beliefs about the size and function of government are the foundation of your political philosophy or ideology. Consider the following pairs of positions that help identify political ideology. In each pair, choose the statement closest to your view.

Government needs to be big enough to provide the services people need.	The best government is the smallest government.
Taxes should be high enough to fund government programs; rich people should pay higher taxes to help people in need.	Taxes should be kept as low as possible for everyone so that people have money to invest in business.
The government must act to meet the needs of people who are struggling economically.	Most needs can be met through the free market and charities.
The government should not interfere with people's right to live as they wish, as long as they do not hurt anyone else.	The government should protect society against behavior that violates traditional beliefs about right and wrong.
The government should rely more on diplomacy than military power to keep us safe.	A strong military and willingness to use it are necessary to our nation's security.

Summarize your responses by explaining your political philosophy in two sentences.

Political Ideology

GUIDING QUESTION *How are political ideology and political party affiliation related?*

An **ideology** is a set of basic beliefs about life, culture, government, and society. Generally, people on the left of the political spectrum have a **liberal** ideology, while people on the right of the political spectrum have a **conservative** ideology. Most Americans fall somewhere along a spectrum between those two ends.

Liberals typically believe that the proper role of government is to promote health, education, and justice. They are usually willing to curtail economic freedom in order to increase equality. They believe the government should not restrict most individual freedoms. On the other hand, conservatives typically believe in limiting the government's role—that citizens can better solve their problems without government intervention. They also typically support "traditional family values" and may support a government role in protecting what they see as a moral lifestyle.

Most people do not wholeheartedly embrace either of these ideologies. Many are **moderates**, falling somewhere in between liberal and conservative. Some are liberal on certain issues and conservative on others. This might be most obvious when distinguishing between economic and social issues. For example, some people believe in strong free markets and reduced government regulation of the economy, while also supporting liberal social causes, like affirmative action.

A political ideology can give a person a framework for looking at government and public policy. It can also give a person clues about which political party they identify with. In recent decades, the **Democratic Party** has been more associated with liberals and moderate-liberals, while the **Republican Party** is more associated with conservatives and moderate-conservatives. These are simple labels for complex arrangements of different viewpoints on different issues, however. It might be more accurate to think of political ideology and party positions as a web of connections and beliefs, rather than a simple line.

✓ READING PROGRESS CHECK

Differentiating What is the difference between a liberal ideology and a conservative ideology?

Party Platforms

GUIDING QUESTION *What are the major differences in viewpoints between the Republican Party and the Democratic Party?*

Republicans are sometimes referred to as the GOP ("Grand Old Party") and are often represented by the color red and the **symbol** of an elephant. Democrats are often associated with the color blue and the symbol of a donkey. These two parties agree on some foundational beliefs and values—they both believe America should have a mixed capitalist economy, support the Constitution and Bill of Rights, believe in the value of private property, and emphasize individual achievement.

Despite these shared values, the two parties disagree on many key social, economic, and business issues. Each party sets out a **platform**, or statement of its beliefs on issues. The platforms are adopted in party conventions. We can look at the party platforms as a guide to each party's philosophy. Of course, many party members disagree with some aspect of the official party platforms described as follows.

Republican Party The Republican Party supports "individuals' rights in opposition to a large, intrusive government." The party opposes too much government intervention in the economy. It does not believe government should burden businesses with excessive regulation. Republicans generally prefer lower taxes and oppose taxing wealthy people at significantly higher rates than poorer people. Republicans support restrictions on public employee unions.

ideology a set of basic beliefs about life, culture, government, and society

liberal the belief that the proper role of government is to actively promote health, education, and justice

conservative the belief that the government should play a limited role in citizens' lives; also the belief in "traditional family values" and what is viewed as a moral lifestyle

moderate the belief in both liberal and conservative viewpoints

POLITICAL CARTOON

The elephant and the donkey are well-known political symbols that date back to the nineteenth century.

▲ CRITICAL THINKING

Analyzing Visuals What animal do you think would be a good symbol for one of the minor parties, such as the Libertarian or Green parties? Explain your answer.

Democratic Party the party more associated with liberal and moderate-liberals

Republican Party the party more associated with conservative and moderate-conservatives

symbol something that stands for something else

platform a statement of a political party's principles, beliefs, and positions on vital issues

In its 2012 platform, the Republican Party argued that marriage should be limited to one man and one woman. The party also restated its opposition to abortion. While the party supports Medicare, it believes this government health care program for the elderly is unsustainable and would replace it with a plan to pay some or all of older Americans' premiums in private health insurance plans.

The party believes that environmental protection is needed but is best accomplished by private landowners, rather than the government. The 2012 party platform does not mention climate change or global warming, except to say that the Republicans oppose a "cap and trade" system to reduce greenhouse gases. The Republican Party encourages use of all energy sources but believes the free market should drive choices about which energy to use. Republicans generally advocate for strong coal, oil, and gas industries and promote exploration and development of those resources on American lands and in the oceans. They typically want federal lands open for timber harvesting, mining, or other resource extraction.

The Republican Party believes that America occupies a unique place in human history and that it is America's responsibility to take a significant role in world affairs. This philosophy is known as American exceptionalism. It leads Republicans to prefer increased military spending, reduced reliance on the United Nations, strong counterterrorism measures, and significant presidential power to maintain our national security.

Democratic Party The Democratic Party says that it believes that "we're greater together than we are on our own—that this country succeeds when everyone gets a fair shot, when everyone does their fair share." The Democrats believe that the government should generally take a bigger role in providing social services and security to Americans. Democrats would prefer to increase taxes on the wealthy and reduce taxes on poorer Americans. They encourage a variety of government regulations to protect consumers in the financial, housing, health care, and energy industries.

The 2012 Democratic Party platform argued for an increase in the federal minimum wage and expressed strong support for unions, including the right to unionize for public employees. The Democrats articulated support for same-sex marriage and for women's rights to access a variety of reproductive services, including abortion. They support legislation to ban employment discrimination against gay and lesbian people and to prevent wage discrimination based on gender. The Democratic Party opposes the Republican suggestion that Medicare should be privatized.

The Democratic platform identifies climate change as a significant threat and prefers policies like fuel efficiency standards and carbon pollution limits for power plants to address the problem. They are also more likely to prefer conserving publicly owned lands and limiting resource extraction from those areas.

The Democratic Party is less likely than the Republicans to want to become involved in military conflicts around the world. The Democrats supported the removal of troops from Iraq and Afghanistan and support the United Nations as a centerpiece of international order. They generally want to reduce military spending and reduce stockpiles of nuclear weapons. The Democratic Party still supports strong counterterrorism measures, creating a cyber security command within the military and aggressively hunting down leaders of terrorist groups.

Minor Parties The Green Party, the Libertarian Party, and the Constitution Party are the most prominent third parties. These three parties generally have significant ideological differences with the major parties.

The Green Party is generally more liberal than the Democratic Party. Founded to focus on environmental issues, the Green Party has developed a full issue platform addressing major topics like foreign policy, civil rights, economics, education, criminal justice, and political reforms. The Green Party advocates nonviolence, environmental sustainability, alternative energy, universal health care, and electoral reform.

The Libertarian Party believes in personal responsibility and minimal government intrusion into Americans' lives. Libertarians believe that the government should not interfere at all with the free market or with individuals' liberties. They oppose regulation of wages, prices, guns, marriage, abortion, and the media. They oppose the criminalization of drugs and would phase out Social Security. They believe the only role for American military force is in response to aggression.

The Constitution Party is generally more conservative than the Republican Party. The Constitution Party advocates abolishing most federal taxes, including the income tax, and dismantling several federal agencies. The party opposes abortion in all cases and opposes same-sex marriage. It would limit immigration, make English the official language, phase out Social Security, and end social programs like welfare.

☑ **READING PROGRESS CHECK**

Defining What is American exceptionalism? How does it influence Republican foreign policy?

PARTICIPATING
ⓘ Your Government

Conducting and Analyzing Surveys

Create a survey to learn about how people in your school, family, or community identify themselves politically. Start by carefully writing the questions. The first question should be about whether they identify with the Democrats, the Republicans, or neither party. The next set of questions could ask if they agree with five positions typically held by the Democrats and then five positions typically held by Republicans. (Do not tell them which are associated with either party.) You may also want to collect data about the respondents' age, race, religion, and education level. Promise your respondents that you will keep their individual views anonymous.

©Blend Images/Alamy

EXPLORING THE ESSENTIAL QUESTION

a. **Interpreting** What can you deduce about how uniform self-identified party members are in their views? Did respondents who identified as independent lean toward one party or the other in their responses?

b. **Hypothesizing** How could the two major parties capitalize on the views of these independent voters?

c. **Making Generalizations** What can you deduce about which demographic groups tend to support which political party?

Republicans and Democrats draw their support from different demographics.

▶ CRITICAL THINKING
Identifying What percentage of each party are non-Caucasian?

POLITICAL PARTY BASES, 2012

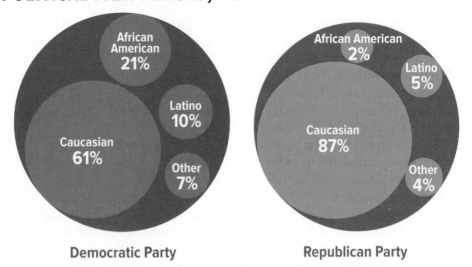

Democratic Party

African American 21%
Latino 10%
Caucasian 61%
Other 7%

Republican Party

African American 2%
Latino 5%
Caucasian 87%
Other 4%

Party Identification

GUIDING QUESTION *What are the demographic differences between voters who identify as Republicans and voters who identify as Democrats?*

party identification loyalty to a political party

Party identification measures a voter's sense of psychological attachment to a political party. Voting, however, is a behavior. In any election, voters who identify with one party may vote for a candidate from another party. Overall, in 2013, 32 percent of voters identified themselves with the Democratic Party, 24 percent identified with the Republican Party, and 38 percent identified with no particular party—that is, they were **independents**. A very small percentage of Americans identified with one of the minor parties.

independent a voter who does not support any particular party

The Republican Party tends to have more white, male, educated, and religious members than the population at large. Generally, the Democratic Party has more women, minorities, and young members than the population at large. In 2012, 34 percent of Democrats identified themselves as working class, and 50 percent identified themselves as middle class or upper middle class. Among Republicans in 2012, 33 percent said they were a member of the working class, while 62 percent said they were middle class or upper middle class.

When compared to the country as a whole, Democrats are somewhat over-represented in the Northeast, while Republicans are over-represented in the South and mountain West. Both parties are represented in proportion to the population in the Midwest. The Democratic Party tends to have more supporters in cities and along both coasts, while people in rural areas and the suburbs are more likely to be Republicans.

☑ **READING PROGRESS CHECK**

Describing In which parts of the United States do people tend to be members of the Republican Party? The Democratic Party?

Political Party Polarization

GUIDING QUESTION *How does political polarization affect political parties and vice versa?*

polarize to divide into opposing groups

In recent years, Americans have become increasingly **polarized**. Both parties have become more ideologically homogenous. This means that party members and elected officials are more likely to agree on all points with the party platform and less likely to cross party lines on key issues. The parties are also more dominated by people with strong ideological beliefs. For example, in the Republican Party, there are twice as many conservatives as moderates.

As voters become more entrenched in their positions and insistent that their elected officials toe the party line, the parties are more likely to nominate ideological, rather than **centrist**, candidates. States have redrawn district boundaries in ways that often protect incumbents, as well. This means that seats are often "safely" Democratic or Republican. In these instances, primary elections become hotly contested by people within the same party.

In 2009 conservative Americans who were dissatisfied with the positions of the major parties formed grassroots "Tea Party" organizations. These groups organized local meetings and protests and supported strongly conservative candidates in the 2010 Republican primaries. Some of those nominees went on to win the general election, while others lost to Democrats in the general election. Overall, the Tea Parties' activism and participation helped to move the ideology of the Republican Party to the right.

Sometimes, more ideological challengers win the party's nomination and the general election. Legislative bodies are then composed of fewer moderates. If the more extreme members of the party are unwilling to compromise or break with the party on some issues, gridlock can result. A review of congressional voting records in 2012 showed a decline of moderates.

Some Americans are independents—unaffiliated with any political party—either because they became disillusioned and left one of the major parties or because they were always unaffiliated. The number of independents has increased in recent years, but many independents still lean strongly toward one of the two major parties.

A variety of strategies have been proposed to reduce polarization: from encouraging more Americans to vote to moving toward proportional representation to increasing the influence of third parties. Some argue that this period of partisanship will peak and then pass. Others say that partisanship shows multiple viewpoints and is good for our democracy.

centrist a person whose views tend to be moderate

☑ **READING PROGRESS CHECK**

Applying What led to the formation of Tea Party organizations?

LESSON 2 REVIEW

Reviewing Vocabulary

1. *Explaining* What is a centrist candidate? Why are parties more likely to nominate ideological candidates?

Using Your Graphic Organizer

2. *Summarizing* Use your completed graphic organizer to write a summary describing the viewpoints of the major and minor political parties in the United States.

Answering the Guiding Questions

3. *Understanding Relationships* How are political ideology and political party affiliation related?

4. *Contrasting* What are the major differences in viewpoints between the Republican Party and the Democratic Party?

5. *Identifying* What are the demographic differences between voters who identify as Republicans and voters who identify as Democrats?

6. *Explaining* How does political polarization affect political parties and vice versa?

Writing About Government

7. *Argument* Choose a contemporary political issue that interests you. Research the points of view of at least two different political parties on this issue. In your view, which political party presents the most compelling argument? Explain.

Should it be U.S. policy to promote renewable sources of energy?

DEBATING DEMOCRATIC PRINCIPLES

One issue Democrats and Republicans typically approach from different perspectives is the proper role of the government in regulating activities that may impact the environment. How to respond to global climate change, or global warming, has been a controversial issue for years. Our sources of energy—fossil fuels like coal, oil, and natural gas, and renewable resources like solar and wind power—are central to this debate. Our country depends on having readily available and affordable sources of energy to power our businesses and lives. However, we are dependent on non renewable energy sources that often pollute and that we must import from other countries.

 YES

TEAM A | **We Should Promote Renewable Energy and Reduce Fossil Fuels**

The damage being done to our environment could be irreversible. We should invest in new technologies so that we do not pass on a dire situation to our children. The free market does not recognize the costs that come with using fossil fuels. While these sources seem less expensive than renewable sources of energy, we are not accounting for the billions of dollars to repair the damage they do. It is better to implement a tax or emissions cap on fossil fuel emissions. This makes cleaner, renewable energy more affordable.

Our economy is too dependent on unreliable energy imports. We should reduce the amount of energy we consume as a low-cost way to import less. We can create new, green jobs by making our homes and businesses more energy efficient and by developing new renewable energy technologies.

 NO

TEAM B | **We Should Let the Free Market Decide Which Energy Sources to Use**

We should not implement an additional burden of new taxes on already struggling businesses. Any move to set up a carbon credit system or a carbon tax will harm businesses and slow the economy. Government should not be in the business of choosing winners and losers when it comes to energy technologies. The best ideas will win in the free market.

Our national security can be threatened when we import oil from the Middle East, an unstable area of the world. The best way to ensure that we are not dependent on foreign energy sources is to develop our own. We have vast oil and gas resources, and we should allow exploration and drilling. We have hundreds of years of coal under the ground, and innovative companies are developing technology that will make this energy source cleaner than ever.

EXPLORING THE ESSENTIAL QUESTION

Evaluating Consider each proposal below. How would you balance the need for energy with the need to protect the environment? Draw a line across your paper. Label one end BECOME LAW and the other end NOT A LAW. Place the number of each proposal along your line to indicate how much you want the proposal to become law. Note the reasons to support your position. Be prepared to debate these proposals:
1. Drill for oil and gas in protected wilderness areas; **2.** Import less foreign oil; **3.** Build more nuclear power plants; **4.** Require manufacturers to use less energy; **5.** Tax carbon emissions; **6.** Offer government subsidies for alternative energy sources like solar and wind power; and **7.** Develop technologies to make coal cleaner.

Interact with these digital assets and others in lesson 3

✓ **INTERACTIVE CHART**
Political Party Organization

✓ **INTERACTIVE IMAGE**
Primaries and Caucuses

✓ **SELF-CHECK QUIZ**

✓ **VIDEO**
Convention Speeches

netw⊙rks
TRY IT YOURSELF ONLINE

ReadingHelp Desk

Academic Vocabulary
- distribute
- assemble

Content Vocabulary
- canvass
- petition
- caucus
- direct primary
- closed primary
- open primary
- plurality
- ticket

TAKING NOTES:
Key Ideas and Details

LISTING Use the graphic organizer to list the ways that candidates are selected to run for office.

Candidates
1.
2.
3.
4.

LESSON 3
Party Organization and Nominating Candidates

ESSENTIAL QUESTION

How does the two-party system influence American democracy?

Regular free and fair elections are an important principle of democracy. But the political parties, as private organizations, use various methods to select their candidates, which may or may not seem democratic.

These statements describe the way the major parties select their candidates for president and vice president. Label each as democratic or undemocratic.

- Voters in the states that have the first caucus (Iowa) and primary (New Hampshire) have more influence on the nomination than voters in states with later caucuses or primaries.

- Turnout is usually lower at caucuses than in primaries. The people who come to a caucus are generally less moderate than the average voter. Thus, more conservative or more liberal candidates often do well in caucus states.

- The presidential nominee picks the vice-presidential nominee.

- Who is allowed to vote in presidential party primaries varies from state to state.

Based on your analysis, is the selection of presidential candidates a democratic process? Do you think it should be?

Party Organization and Membership

GUIDING QUESTION *How are political parties organized and how can citizens participate in political parties?*

Democrats and Republicans are organized into 50 state parties and thousands of local parties that operate independently of the national organization. Although the three levels generally cooperate, separate authority exists at each level. Local, state, and national parties select their own officers and raise their own funds. The national party cannot give orders to the state or local parties.

Party Organization To be successful, a political party needs strong leadership and good organization at every level. Both major parties employ small paid staffs in permanent party offices at the county, state, and national levels.

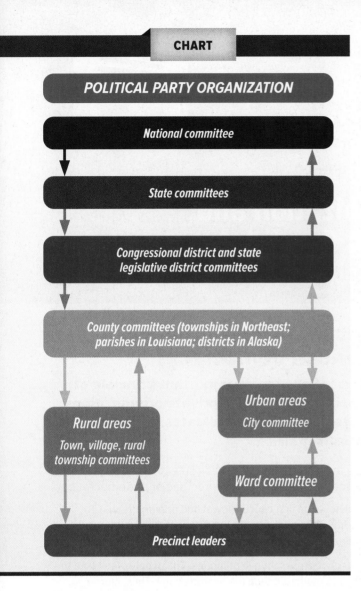

POLITICAL PARTY ORGANIZATION

National committee

State committees

Congressional district and state legislative district committees

County committees (townships in Northeast; parishes in Louisiana; districts in Alaska)

Rural areas
Town, village, rural township committees

Urban areas
City committee

Ward committee

Precinct leaders

▲ CRITICAL THINKING
Reading Charts At the local level, what is the basic component of political organization?

At the local level, parties choose which candidates to run under the party's name and **distribute** information about the party and its candidates to attract voters to the polls. Sometimes local party officials will pass on recommendations for judicial or executive appointments to the state or national elected officials from their party.

At the state level, the main function of a political party is to help elect the party's candidates for state government offices. In addition, the state party may provide assistance to local parties and candidates and may help coordinate the activities of the local parties. The state party also works hard at raising money.

The national party organization consists mainly of representatives from the 50 state party organizations. The national committee raises money for the party; touts its achievements; and promotes national, state, and local party cooperation. Both the Democrats and the Republicans have independent campaign committees for the House of Representatives and the Senate. These committees provide assistance to party members who are running for election to Congress. Every four years, the national parties hold conventions to nominate presidential and vice-presidential candidates.

Party Membership In many states, citizens must declare their party preference when they register to vote or when they vote in certain elections. People who belong to a political party generally do so because they support most of its ideas and candidates. Party membership involves no duties or obligations beyond voting. Joining a political party, however, is not required in the United States. A voter may declare that he or she is an independent, not supporting any particular party.

Some people choose to become more involved in the political process. They might support a party by contributing money or by doing volunteer work for the party or its candidates. In most states, one must be a party member in order to hold an office in a party or to be its candidate for a public office. Thus, party membership provides a way for citizens to increase their influence on government.

In order to succeed, a political party must have a dedicated core of willing volunteers. The parties depend on volunteers to perform many tasks—from obtaining campaign contributions and publicizing candidates to **canvassing** voters.

✓ READING PROGRESS CHECK

Explaining Why is party organization and membership important to government?

Selecting Candidates to Represent the Party

GUIDING QUESTION *What role do political parties play in the electoral process at the national, state, and local levels?*

One of the vital functions of political parties is to nominate candidates for elected office. The parties want to nominate candidates that share the party's values and will work to promote and implement its preferred policies.

GOVERNMENT *in your* COMMUNITY

Political Parties in Your Community

Choose one political party to learn more about its activities in your community. Call, e-mail, or check out the party's website or Facebook page to get answers to the following questions:

a. What are the party's goals or beliefs?

b. What volunteer opportunities does the party offer? (Which appeal to you?)

c. Are candidates from this party running for local election soon? If so, who?

d. Does this party make it easy for citizens to register to vote?

e. When and where is the next scheduled meeting or social event? Are non party members welcome?

f. How does this party inform its members about what is going on? Does it have a presence on Twitter, Facebook, Google+, or a different social media?

g. Does this group have a student chapter that you could join at your school? If not, does it offer suggestions about how to start one?

h. Does the party make it easy to donate money?

▲ CRITICAL THINKING
Summarizing Write a fact sheet summarizing your research.

Members of the parties weigh in to help decide who should be nominated for different offices. The process used to collect this input varies from state to state. Some states hold primary elections, while others hold a series of meetings (called *caucuses*) or one large meeting—a convention. Some states use a combination of these methods.

Petitions Candidates cannot win election if their names are not on the ballot. To get their name on the ballot, most candidates must pay a small filing fee—usually 1 to 3 percent of the salary they would make if they win election. Candidates who want to avoid paying the fee can use the **petition** method, which means they must collect a certain number of signatures from people who live in the district. If they get enough signatures, usually about 3 percent of registered voters in that district, their names will appear on the ballot. Some states require all candidates to file petitions.

Caucuses Early in our nation's history, **caucuses**—private meetings of party leaders—chose nearly all candidates for office. Today, caucuses are more open and all party members can attend. The caucus process involves a series of meetings. Beginning at the local level, attendees discuss candidates and party positions, elect local party leaders, and choose delegates to represent them at regional caucuses. Regional caucuses (often based on the county, state legislative district, or congressional district boundaries) choose candidates for local and state legislative offices, as well as delegates to send to the state meeting. At the state level, delegates choose candidates for statewide office and select delegates to attend the party's national convention.

Iowa traditionally holds the first presidential caucus in early January of a presidential election year. Candidates often spend a lot of time campaigning in Iowa so that they will have a strong showing at the very beginning of the presidential race. In 2012, 13 states, Puerto Rico, and four territories chose their delegates to the national party conventions through caucuses. The number of states holding caucuses has actually risen slightly in recent years, in large part because caucuses are less expensive than primary elections.

distribute to give out or disburse to clients, customers, or members of a group

canvass to solicit votes and determine opinions

petition an appeal

caucus a private meeting of party leaders to choose candidates for office

Nominating Conventions Under this nominating system, local party organizations send representatives to a county nominating convention that selects candidates for county offices and chooses delegates to go to a state nominating convention. The state convention selects candidates for statewide office and chooses delegates to go to the national convention. The delegates at the national convention then choose the party's presidential candidate.

Primary Elections The method most commonly used today to nominate candidates is the **direct primary**, an election in which party members select people to run in the general election. Two major types of primary elections are held. Most states hold a **closed primary**, in which only members of a political party can vote. Thus, only Democrats pick Democratic candidates for office, and only Republicans can vote in the Republican primary. In an **open primary**, all voters may participate, even if they do not belong to the party, but they can vote in only one party's primary. California has recently instituted a new type of primary, in which all parties' candidates appear on one ballot. The top two vote-getters, whether two Democrats, two Republicans, or two people from different parties, face off in the general election. The idea behind this reform is to get more moderate candidates on the ballot.

The Constitution gives power to the states to establish their own election laws. Primary elections are conducted according to state law and are held at regular polling places just as general elections are. In most states, a primary candidate does not need a majority (50 percent plus one vote) to win, but only a **plurality** (more votes than any other candidate). In a few states, if no one receives a majority, a runoff primary is held. The runoff is a second primary election between the two candidates who received the most votes in the first primary. In most states today, candidates for governor and for the House, Senate, other state offices, and most local offices are selected in primary elections.

Presidential Primaries Presidential primaries operate under a variety of state laws. In addition, each party frequently changes its rules regarding delegate selection. Even in the same state, the two parties' primaries may operate under different procedures and be held on different days. A primary may be binding—that is, delegates to the convention must vote according to the results of the primary. Primaries in a few states are nonbinding, meaning they simply show voters' preference but do not determine for whom delegates will vote. In some primaries, the candidate who wins the primary gets all the state's convention delegates (called *winner-take-all*). In others, each candidate gets delegates based on how many popular votes he or she receives in the primary (called *proportional representation*). The Democrats use proportional representation. The Republicans allow both winner-take-all and proportional systems.

Criticisms of Presidential Primaries While most people agree that the presidential primary system is a great improvement over the previous methods of selecting convention delegates, it has its critics. A major criticism is that the primaries extend too long in an election year. With the first primary held in January or February and the last in June, seeking a party's nomination is a very long,

---

direct primary an election in which party members select people to run in the general election

closed primary an election in which only members of a political party can vote

open primary an election in which all voters may participate

plurality the largest number of votes in an election

Presidential primaries operate under a wide variety of state laws, and each party often changes its rules regarding delegate selection. This photograph shows ballots being counted at a 2012 Iowa caucus voting site by citizens hoping to pick the next Republican presidential candidate.

▼ CRITICAL THINKING
Describing How does the caucus process work?

Jewel Samad/AFP/Getty Images

Political observers have discussed many ways of improving the process by which presidential candidates are chosen. Read the three proposals below and decide which you would support. Be sure you can give reasons for your choice.

Rotating Regional Primary System. Under this plan, the United States would be divided into four regions: West, Midwest, South, and Northeast. Each region would have a primary in a different month. The order would rotate from year to year, giving each state a chance to be an "early state" every fourth presidential election. This system would lower campaign costs by allowing candidates to travel to one region at a time. A major disadvantage would be the need for significant campaign funds to launch a campaign. Also, if the first primary were held in a region with a strong political bias, that could hurt some candidates.

National Primary. All state primaries and caucuses would be held on a single day. This system would ensure that all votes count equally. No one would be voting after the nomination has already been secured. However, it would not acknowledge the role of states in our federal system. Also, it could eliminate any chance for a candidate with little money to pick up momentum through early success.

Keep the System We Have. The current system allows candidates having little money to campaign locally in early states. As they pick up votes there, they can raise more money to help them in the larger states. This system gives states an important role, which is part of our federalist system. However, it undercuts the idea of "one person, one vote." Some votes are more important—and those votes may be in states that do not represent the United States as a whole.

◀ **CRITICAL THINKING**
Decision Making Which of the proposals do you support? Explain your reasoning. Which of the proposals do you not support? Why?

costly, and exhausting process. Another criticism is that relatively few people vote in primaries or attend caucuses. Thus, the winner of a primary might not be as popular as the victory would indicate.

Candidates who win the early primaries capture the media spotlight. Often the other candidates are saddled with a "loser" image that makes it difficult for them to raise campaign contributions and win in states that have later primaries. Some candidates are forced to drop out before the majority of voters in either party have the chance to cast their ballots. This gives voters in states with later primaries less say in who the candidate will be. In recent elections, many states have moved their presidential caucuses or primaries forward in hopes they will play a more important role in determining who gets the nomination. Earlier primaries put even greater pressure on candidates to raise money quickly and to do well at the very start of the process.

✓ **READING PROGRESS CHECK**

Comparing What is a caucus? How is a caucus different from a primary?

National Party Conventions

GUIDING QUESTION *How do political parties nominate presidential candidates?*

Every four years, each major party gathers during July or August in a national convention. Elected or appointed delegates representing the 50 states, Guam, Puerto Rico, the Virgin Islands, American Samoa, and the District of Columbia attend the convention. The task of the delegates is to select a **ticket**—candidates for president and vice president—to run against the other party's candidate in the November general election. From January to June, the candidates crisscross the country competing for delegate support.

ticket a party's candidates for president and vice president

C·I·V·I·C PARTICIPATION IN A DIGITAL AGE

Using Technology to Nominate a Presidential Candidate

In 2012 a nonpartisan group calling itself Americans Elect tried to use the Internet to give voters a greater voice in selecting a presidential ticket. The idea was to conduct an online primary and convention so people vote directly on the nomination of a presidential candidate. That presidential candidate would then run in the general election, providing another option for voters.

Americans Elect set up a process for taking part in the online primary. Individuals who met a list of qualifications could announce their candidacy. Citizens could also draft candidates. Candidates needed to get a significant number of "clicks" from at least 10 states to qualify for the primary. By the deadline, however, no candidate had enough clicks. Americans Elect announced that it would not be holding its online primary and convention in 2012.

Sarah Phipps/AP Images

EXPLORING THE ESSENTIAL QUESTION

Applying Why do you think this effort to use technology to let the people nominate a candidate failed? Could you devise a better plan? Work with two other students to develop ideas for employing the technology you use every day to nominate a presidential candidate. When you have some ideas, share your thoughts with another group of three. In your group of three, agree on a plan or some specific strategies to present to the class.

---

assemble to gather together

Assembling the Convention
Thousands of delegates **assemble** in the convention city, accompanied by a mass of spectators, protesters, and news media representatives. When the delegates arrive, many are already pledged to a candidate, but others are not. The candidates woo these uncommitted delegates. Sometimes the presidential nomination is still in doubt, and the candidates are still competing for votes.

On the first evening, the keynote speech is delivered. It is an address by an important party member that is intended to unite the party for the coming campaign. The delegates then approve the convention's four standing committees—rules and order of business, credentials, permanent organization, and platform and resolutions. The convention spends two or more days listening to reports from committees and to speeches about them.

The Platform Committee
The platform committee writes the party's platform, a statement of its principles, beliefs, and positions on vital issues. It also spells out how the party intends to deal with these issues. The party must try to adopt a platform that appeals to all factions at the convention.

Part of the difficulty in getting platforms accepted is that individual parts of the platform, called *planks*, may divide the delegates. In 1968, for example, a pro-Vietnam War plank angered Democrats who wanted the United States to withdraw from that conflict. In 1980 the Republican platform contained a plank opposing the Equal Rights Amendment. Although this plank was controversial, the platform passed. The danger is that a platform fight might divide the party. If the fight is bitter, as it was for Democrats in 1968, the party could become so divided that it loses the election.

Nominating the Presidential and Vice-Presidential Candidates
After the committee reports are adopted, it is time to select the party's candidate for president. The clerk reads an alphabetical roll call of the states and the chairperson of each state delegation calls out the delegates' votes.

The candidate who receives a majority becomes the nominee. If no candidate wins the majority, then further roll calls are taken until a candidate drops out or delegates change their votes.

While this roll call can be dramatic, by the time of the convention, there is rarely a mystery about who will be nominated. This is partly because the way primary elections are staggered before the convention makes it clear who is the most popular candidate from that party.

Party leaders benefit from the early victory of one candidate, having more time to plan the convention and unify the party. The convention can usually then become a scripted television event and ceremonial function.

The vice-presidential candidate is also nominated at the convention. Usually, the party's presidential nominee selects a running mate, and the convention automatically nominates the person chosen. Sometimes, a presidential candidate chooses a running mate who has done very well in the primaries. A vice-presidential candidate is often selected to balance the ticket, meaning that he or she has a personal, political, and geographic background that is different from the presidential nominee. This balance is designed to make the ticket appeal to as many voters as possible.

In 1960 John F. Kennedy, a senator from Massachusetts, chose Lyndon B. Johnson, a senator from Texas, as his running mate, adding geographic diversity to the ticket. In 1984 Democratic candidate Walter F. Mondale made Representative Geraldine Ferraro the first female vice-presidential major party candidate. Barack Obama's choice of Senator Joe Biden brought foreign policy expertise to the ticket. In 2008 long-time Republican Senator John McCain's choice of Sarah Palin brought youth, gender diversity, and a more conservative ideology into the ticket. In 2012 Republican candidate Mitt Romney's choice of Paul Ryan appealed to Tea Party conservatives.

Adjournment After being nominated, the presidential and vice-presidential nominees appear before the delegates and make their acceptance speeches. These speeches are intended to bring the party together, to attack the opposition party, to sound a theme for the upcoming campaign, and to appeal to a national television audience. The convention then adjourns. And the general election—the competition between the two parties—begins in earnest.

☑ **READING PROGRESS CHECK**

Explaining What role do delegates play in nominating the president and vice president?

LESSON 3 REVIEW

Reviewing Vocabulary
1. *Defining* What is a plurality vote?

Using Your Graphic Organizer
2. *Summarizing* Use your completed graphic organizer to summarize the ways that candidates are selected to run for public office.

Answering the Guiding Questions
3. *Explaining* How are political parties organized and how can citizens participate in political parties?

4. *Analyzing* What role do political parties play in the electoral process at the national, state, and local levels?

5. *Examining* How do political parties nominate presidential candidates?

Writing About Government
6. *Informative/Explanatory* Find your state's Democratic Party and Republican Party websites. Identify opportunities for you and your classmates to participate in these political parties at the state level and the national level. Write a brief report that summarizes this information.

STUDY GUIDE

PARTY SYSTEMS
LESSON 1

One-Party System	Two-Party System	Multi-Party System
authoritarian governments: Cuba, Vietnam, North Korea, China	about a dozen nations, including the United States	coalition governments: most nations, including France

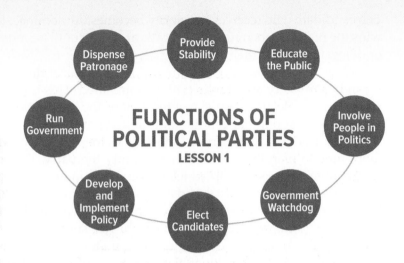

FUNCTIONS OF POLITICAL PARTIES
LESSON 1

Dispense Patronage · Provide Stability · Educate the Public · Run Government · Involve People in Politics · Develop and Implement Policy · Elect Candidates · Government Watchdog

COMPARISON OF MAJOR PARTIES LESSON 2

Democratic Party

Ideology

More liberal

Platform

- Larger government role in providing social services
- Favor government regulations to protect consumers
- Favor increase in minimum wage
- Support unions, including public employee unions
- View climate change as a threat; support fuel efficiency standards and carbon pollution limits
- Prefer limits on resource extraction from public lands
- Less likely to support military involvement in conflicts
- Support the United Nations

Demographics

women, minorities, young people, working class and middle/upper middle class in about even proportions, strongly supported in Northeast

Republican Party

Ideology

More conservative

Platform

- Favor smaller government role in providing social services
- Less government regulation
- Favor lower taxes
- Support restrictions on public employee unions
- Oppose "cap and trade" to reduce greenhouse gases
- Free market should drive choices about energy use
- Promote coal, oil, and gas extraction on public lands
- Increased military spending
- Reduced reliance on the United Nations

Demographics

white, men, religious, more middle/upper middle class than working class, strongly supported in South and mountain West

SELECTING CANDIDATES TO RUN FOR OFFICE LESSON 3

Petition	Candidates collect enough signatures to get on ballot
Caucuses	Candidates selected in series of meetings open to all party members
Nominating Conventions	Party representatives select candidates at county, state, and national conventions
Direct Primary	**Closed:** Election open to only the party members **Open:** Election open to all, regardless of party
Presidential Primary	**Binding:** Convention delegates must vote according to primary results **Nonbinding:** Convention delegates may vote as they wish **Winner-take-all:** Winner gets all the state's convention delegates **Proportional:** Each candidate gets convention delegates based on percentage of votes received
National Party Convention	State delegates select candidates for president and vice president

Directions: On a separate sheet of paper, answer the questions below. Make sure you read carefully and answer all parts of the questions.

Lesson Review

Lesson 1

1 *Specifying* Think about the two-party tradition in elections. What must third-party candidates do to get on the ballot?

2 *Identifying* What are three ways that you could participate in local campaigns with your favorite political party?

Lesson 2

3 *Contrasting* Contrast the political ideology of liberals and conservatives on the proper role of government.

4 *Hypothesizing* Julie is a 19-year-old college student living in New York City. With which party does Julie most likely identify? Explain your reasoning.

Lesson 3

5 *Describing* How do parties use nominating conventions to select candidates to run for local, state, and national offices?

6 *Differentiating* In presidential primaries, what is the difference between a binding and a nonbinding primary?

ANSWERING THE ESSENTIAL QUESTIONS

Review your answers to the introductory questions at the beginning of each lesson. Then answer the following Essential Question based on what you learned in the chapter. Has your answer changed?

7 *Analyzing* How does the two-party system influence American democracy?

DBQ Interpreting Political Cartoons

Use the political cartoon to answer the following questions.

8 *Interpreting* What does the snake represent?

9 *Drawing Inferences* What comment is the cartoonist making about the relative strength of two political parties?

Critical Thinking

10 *Analyzing Cause and Effect* What processes do political parties use to affect public policy?

11 *Hypothesizing* Suppose a splinter party broke off from the Republican Party and ran its own candidate for president. How might this affect the outcome of the election?

12 *Classifying* Where would you place the Libertarian Party on the liberal-conservative political spectrum? Explain.

13 *Making Connections* How does political polarization lead to gridlock in Congress?

14 *Evaluating* What are some drawbacks of the presidential primary system?

15 *Drawing Inferences* Describe one advantage and one disadvantage that you see in using an open primary instead of a closed primary.

Need Extra Help?

If You've Missed Question	**1**	**2**	**3**	**4**	**5**	**6**	**7**	**8**	**9**	**10**	**11**	**12**	**13**	**14**	**15**
Go to page	518	511	521	524	530	530	514	518	518	511	517	523	525	530	530

Directions: On a separate sheet of paper, answer the questions below. Make sure you read carefully and answer all parts of the questions.

DBQ Analyzing Primary Sources

Read the excerpt and answer the questions that follow.

As President George Washington prepared to retire at the end of his second term, he reflected on his fledgling nation and expressed his thoughts in a letter to the American people. The following is a passage from this letter.

PRIMARY SOURCE

"*Let me now . . . warn you in the most solemn manner against the baneful effects of the spirit of party . . . . This spirit, unfortunately, is inseparable from our nature, having its root in the strongest passions of the human mind . . . . The alternate domination of one faction over another, sharpened by the spirit of revenge, natural to party dissension, . . . is itself a frightful despotism. But this leads at length to a more formal and permanent despotism . . . . Sooner or later the chief of some prevailing faction . . . turns this disposition to the purposes of his own elevation, on the ruins of public liberty.*"

—George Washington, Farewell Address, 1796

16 *Identifying Central Issues* What is the subject of this passage?

17 *Identifying Perspectives* What is Washington's frame of reference? What is Washington's view of his subject?

18 *Analyzing* List descriptive words from the passage that show Washington's attitude toward his subject.

19 *Interpreting* Rewrite the last sentence in your own words to show its meaning.

Social Studies Skills

20 *Evaluating Secondary Sources* Search online for an opinion article about a current political issue. In a sentence or two, summarize the writer's point of view on the issue. Does this article reflect a conservative, moderate, or liberal frame of reference? Explain.

21 *Comparing and Contrasting* Find an opinion article about the same current political issue as for question 20, but with a different point of view. Compare and contrast the point of view and frame of reference (conservative, moderate, or liberal) for both pieces. Which opinion do you consider most valid? Defend your choice.

22 *Evaluating Primary Sources* Find an online video advertisement for both presidential candidates in a recent election. Identify ads that present counterarguments to the other candidate's claims. How do these ads try to influence voter opinion? Which ad do you consider most valid? Why? Present the advertisements and your analysis to the class.

Research and Presentation

23 *Identifying Perspectives* Research one of these third-party candidates: Theodore Roosevelt (Bull Moose Party), Ralph Nader (Green Party), or Ross Perot (Reform Party). Create a multimedia presentation about your candidate's platform and the candidate's effect on the presidential election.

24 *Making Decisions* Go to the websites of the Republican National Committee and the Democratic National Committee. Compare their positions on current issues. For each issue, note which party's position most closely fits your beliefs. Then decide whether you identify most as a Democrat or Republican. Prepare to explain why.

25 *Gathering Information* Do research to learn how your state selects candidates for office. Create a fact sheet that answers these questions: Caucus or primary? Open, closed, or other (describe)? Binding or nonbinding? Majority or plurality to win? Does your state hold runoffs? Include other relevant facts.

26 *Making Inferences* Think about political boundaries and political party polarization in voters. How is the distribution of political power related to both of these?

Need Extra Help?

If You've Missed Question	16	17	18	19	20	21	22	23	24	25	26
Go to page	536	536	536	536	520	520	511	523	521	529	524

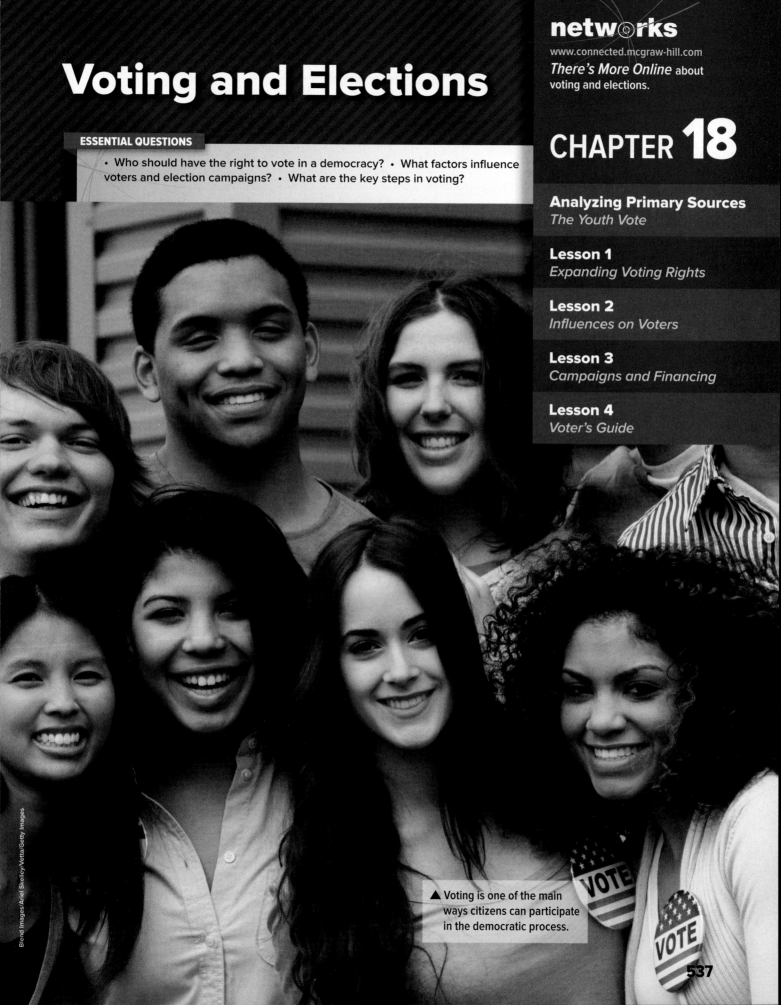

Voting and Elections

networks

www.connected.mcgraw-hill.com
There's More Online about voting and elections.

ESSENTIAL QUESTIONS

• Who should have the right to vote in a democracy? • What factors influence voters and election campaigns? • What are the key steps in voting?

CHAPTER 18

▲ Voting is one of the main ways citizens can participate in the democratic process.

Blend Images/Ariel Skelley/Vetta/Getty Images

THE YOUTH VOTE

Young people—especially those 18 to 24 years old—have lower rates of voter registration and turnout than the general population. Why do you think this is so? Do you know how many young people vote? Why should young people vote? Read and analyze the primary and secondary sources and answer the questions that follow.

PRIMARY SOURCE A

"The findings of the non-partisan group HeadCount found that seven out of 10 young voters changed residence in the past four years, and 43 percent of those potential voters have yet to update their voter registration. The so-called 'youth vote' is the estimated 15.5 million U.S. citizens who are 18 to 24 years old, according to the Census Bureau."

—FoxNews.com, "Report: Roughly half of the 2008, first-time youth vote now unsure of registration status," September 23, 2012

PRIMARY SOURCE B

Polls conducted prior to the 2012 presidential elections found that youth were less likely to plan to vote than any other age group.

"Colorado State University political scientist Robert Duffy says negative campaigning and pronounced partisan differences in Washington may be exacerbating the historic electoral passivity among young voters. 'Younger people are more susceptible to the trends that affect all voters,' he says. 'They get frustrated at lack or pace of change.'"

—Marissa Alioto, "The Youth Vote 2012: Once Again, With Enthusiasm?" NPR, August 5, 2012

SECONDARY SOURCE C

Comparing Youth and Total Voter Registration and Voting in the 2008 and 2012 Presidential Elections

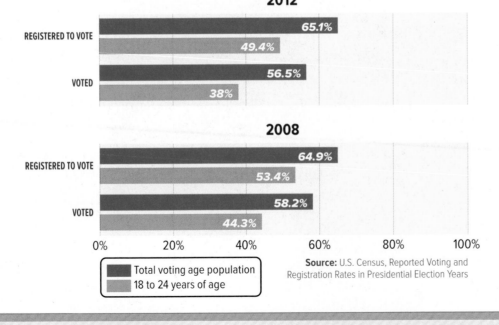

Youth Voter Registration and Turnout

2012

REGISTERED TO VOTE — 65.1% / 49.4%
VOTED — 56.5% / 38%

2008

REGISTERED TO VOTE — 64.9% / 53.4%
VOTED — 58.2% / 44.3%

0% 20% 40% 60% 80% 100%

Total voting age population
18 to 24 years of age

Source: U.S. Census, Reported Voting and Registration Rates in Presidential Election Years

Senator Edward Kennedy supported the constitutional amendment to lower the voting age to 18, which was ratified in 1971.

"Our young people today are far better equipped—intellectually, physically, and emotionally—to make the type of choices involved in voting than were past generations of youth . . . Indeed, in many cases, 18 to 21 year-olds already possess a better education than a large proportion of adults among our general electorate. And, they also possess a far better education than the vast majority of the electorate in all previous periods of our history. The statistics are dramatic:

In 1920, just fifty years ago, only 17% of Americans between the ages of 18 and 21 were high school graduates. Only 8% went on to college. Today [in 1970], by contrast 79% of Americans in this age group are high school graduates. 47% go on to college.

. . . on the basis of our broad experience with 18 to 21 year-olds: as a class, I believe they possess the requisite maturity, judgment, and stability for responsible exercise of the franchise. They deserve the right to vote and the stake in society it represents."

—Senator Edward M. Kennedy, Testimony Before the Senate Subcommittee on Constitutional Amendments, March 9, 1970

SECONDARY SOURCE **E**

DBQ **DOCUMENT-BASED QUESTIONS**

1. **Specifying** How many 18- to 24-year-olds vote in comparison to other age groups?

2. **Synthesizing** What obstacles do youth face in registering to vote and voting?

3. **Analyzing** Why did Senator Kennedy believe that 18- to 21-year-olds should have the right to vote? Do those same reasons apply today?

4. **Explaining** Why should young people vote?

WHAT WILL YOU DO?

Will you vote when you are eligible? Why or why not? What will you need to know in order to vote?

EXPLORE the interactive version of the analyzing primary sources feature on Networks.

(l to r) Archive Photos/Getty Images, ... Ken Basant, McGraw-Hill Education, Blend Images/Ariel Skelley/Vetta/Getty Images, Library of Congress Prints & Photographs Division [LC-DIG-ppmsca-02919]

Interact with these digital assets and others in lesson 1

✓ **INTERACTIVE IMAGE**
The Youth Vote

✓ **INTERACTIVE POLITICAL CARTOON**
African American Suffrage

✓ **SELF-CHECK QUIZ**

✓ **VIDEO**
Voting Rights Act

netw🌐rks
TRY IT YOURSELF ONLINE

ReadingHelp Desk

Academic Vocabulary
- device
- minimum

Content Vocabulary
- election
- voting
- suffrage
- disenfranchise
- grandfather clause
- literacy test
- poll tax

TAKING NOTES:
Key Ideas and Details

LISTING Use the graphic organizer to list some of the laws, customs, and procedures by which suffrage was restricted and expanded over the course of American history.

Restricted Suffrage	Expanded Suffrage

LESSON 1
Expanding Voting Rights

Who should have the right to vote in a democracy?

Read each of the examples below and decide whether each person should have the right to vote in our democracy. List your reasons for each decision.

a. Sue is 16 and very smart. She has taken a civics class in school and studied issues in the upcoming election.

b. Mary is 92 years old. She uses a wheelchair and has trouble reading small print.

c. Kavna is 48 years old. She dropped out of school at age 10 and cannot read or write well.

d. Jeff has been diagnosed with schizophrenia and is currently living in a mental health hospital.

e. Stan was convicted of a felony drug crime. He has served his time and was released from prison one month ago.

f. Raul, now 22, was born in South America and moved to the U.S. with his parents when he was young. He is not a U.S. citizen.

g. Marty is currently homeless. He has not had a permanent address in the past year and splits his time between shelters and parks in his city.

Voting Limitations in Early America

GUIDING QUESTION *Who could and could not vote in early America?*

An **election** is an orderly process for making group decisions. Free and fair elections are the hallmark of democracy. **Voting** is making a choice among alternatives in an election.

Like other rights, the right to vote is not absolute but subject to regulations and restrictions. During periods of American history, law, custom, and even violence have prevented certain groups of people from voting.

Before the American Revolution, the colonies placed many restrictions on who had the right to vote. Women and most African Americans were not allowed to vote; neither were white males who did not own property or pay taxes. In some colonies, only members of the dominant religious group could vote.

As a result, only about five or six percent of the adult population was eligible to vote. These restrictions existed because educated white men of the time believed that voting was best left to wealthy, white, property-owning males, whom they assumed would make wiser choices. As John Jay, who served on the U.S. Supreme Court as the first chief justice of the United States, put it: "The people who own the country ought to govern it."

After the Constitution was adopted, the states were allowed to set the time, place, and manner of elections. Each state could have its own rules about who could vote in national elections as long as these rules did not violate the U.S. Constitution. Despite having the power to do so, Congress did not make many laws regulating elections until after the Civil War.

During the first half of the 1800s, state legislatures gradually abolished property requirements and religious restrictions for voting. By the mid-1800s, the country achieved nearly universal white adult male **suffrage**, or the right to vote. Still, the vast majority of African Americans and all women could not vote.

✔ **READING PROGRESS CHECK**

Describing What restrictions prevented most white males from voting in early America?

election an orderly process for making group decisions

voting making a choice among alternatives in an election

suffrage the right to vote

African American Suffrage

GUIDING QUESTION *How was African American suffrage restricted and extended in the nineteenth and twentieth centuries?*

When the Constitution went into effect in 1789, African Americans, both enslaved and free, made up about 20 percent of the U.S. population. Yet enslaved persons were not permitted to vote anywhere, and free African Americans who were allowed to vote could do so in only a few states.

The Fifteenth Amendment The first effort to extend suffrage to African Americans nationwide came shortly after the Civil War, when the Fifteenth Amendment was ratified in 1870. The amendment provided that no state could deprive any citizen of the right to vote on account of race, color, or previous condition of servitude. This amendment marked the first time that the U.S. Constitution dictated rules to the states about who they must allow to vote.

The Grandfather Clause Although the Fifteenth Amendment was an important milestone on the road to full suffrage, it did not result in complete voting rights for African Americans. Political leaders in Southern states set up a number of roadblocks to **disenfranchise** and discourage the participation of African American voters.

One such practice was the **grandfather clause**. It was incorporated in the constitutions of some Southern states. The grandfather clause provided that only voters whose grandfathers had voted before 1867 were eligible to vote without paying a certain tax or passing a test. The grandfathers of most African American Southerners had been enslaved and were not permitted to vote, so this clause prevented most of them from voting. In 1915 the Supreme Court declared the grandfather clause unconstitutional (*Guinn* v. *United States*). Even so, state governments throughout the South developed a range of additional rules that prevented the vast majority of African Americans in the South from voting.

POLITICAL CARTOON

An African American votes as President Andrew Johnson and his associates watch disapprovingly.

Analyzing Visuals Do you think the cartoonist supported African American suffrage? Why or why not?

The Literacy Test and Poll Tax Until the 1960s, many states required citizens to pass a **literacy test** to qualify to vote. In many cases, white voters were judged literate if they could write their names, but African American voters were often required to do much more. For example, they were often asked to explain a complicated part of the state or national constitution.

Another **device** that was designed to discourage African American suffrage was the poll tax. Usually amounting to a dollar or two, citizens had to pay a **poll tax** before they could vote. The poll tax had to be paid not only for the current year but also for previous unpaid years. It was a financial burden for poor people of all ethnic and racial backgrounds. In addition, the tax had to be paid well in advance of Election Day, and the poll-tax payer had to present a receipt showing payment before voting. Voters who did not have their receipts were barred from voting. Thousands of African Americans in the states with poll taxes were excluded from the polls.

In 1964, the Twenty-fourth Amendment outlawed the poll tax in national elections. The use of the poll tax in state elections was not eliminated until a 1966 Supreme Court decision (*Harper* v. *Virginia Board of Election*).

The Voting Rights Acts Despite gains, many discriminatory practices still prevented African Americans from voting into the mid-twentieth century, particularly in the South. One key pillar of the civil rights movement of the 1960s was the fight for voting laws that would prohibit this discrimination. With the passage of the Voting Rights Act of 1965, the federal government took new steps to directly regulate state-controlled election procedures. The act allowed the federal government to register voters and send poll watchers on Election Day in states and localities that discriminated against African American voters.

Voting rights laws of 1970, 1975, and 1982 also broadened the federal role in elections. Literacy tests were abolished. The laws also required that ballots be printed in Spanish for Spanish-speaking communities or in other minority languages where appropriate. The Voting Rights Acts resulted in a dramatic increase in African American voter registration. In 1960 only 29 percent of all African Americans in the South were registered. By 2000, the figure had risen to more than 65 percent.

Within a few years of the passage of the 1965 Voting Rights Act, more than 1,000 African Americans were elected to political office. Within a decade, about 200 African American mayors served in cities of all sizes.

In 2006 Congress reauthorized the Voting Rights Act for another 25 years. The vote was nearly unanimous and bipartisan. After reviewing thousands of pages of evidence, lawmakers determined that racial discrimination in voting persisted in many areas. While obvious forms of discrimination, like literacy tests, had disappeared, more subtle forms of discrimination were still in place. For example, some states redrew their district boundaries in a way to spread minority voters out so they did not form a majority in any district. Other times, district boundaries were drawn to pack all the minority voters into one district. Both of these strategies amounted to gerrymandering and meant that these voters had a disproportionately small amount of political power.

Until 2013 the Voting Rights Acts still placed special regulations on states with a history of voter discrimination. Those states had to ask for permission from the federal government before changing any of their voting laws.

LANDMARK LAWS
THE VOTING RIGHTS ACT OF 1965

The Voting Rights Act of 1965 empowered the federal government to:

★ register voters in any district where less than 50 percent of African American adults were on the voting lists.

★ register voters in districts where it appeared that local officials were discriminating against African Americans.

★ prevent states from dividing election districts in order to diminish the impact of minority voters.

★ appoint poll watchers to see that all votes were properly counted.

▲ CRITICAL THINKING
Determining Cause and Effect Choose one of the provisions in the table above and explain why it might have increased the number of African American voters.

However, in a 2013 case called *Shelby Co. v. Holder*, the Supreme Court ruled that the formula Congress used to decide which states had to follow these special regulations was unconstitutional because the formula was based on discrimination in place over 40 years ago. The Court said that Congress needed to develop a new way to decide which state and local governments would have all changes to their voting laws reviewed by the federal government. This decision ended the use of this special federal review of certain states' voting laws. However, states and districts can still be sued for laws and actions that discriminate against minority voters on a case-by-case basis.

Supporters believe it is good that local and state governments have more control over their own election and voting procedures. Critics are concerned that it "guts" the Voting Rights Act and makes it easier for state and local governments to enact laws that discriminate against some voters.

Other recent efforts at voting reform include the Help America Vote Act of 2002. Under this act, states must meet federal requirements to reform the voting process and make it as consistent and inclusive as possible.

✓ **READING PROGRESS CHECK**

Comparing and Contrasting How were the literacy test, poll tax, and grandfather clause similar? How were they different?

Suffrage for Women and Youth

GUIDING QUESTION *How was suffrage extended to women and 18- to 21-year-olds?*

It was not until the twentieth century that both universal adult woman suffrage and 18- to 21-year-old suffrage were achieved.

Woman Suffrage Beginning in the mid-1800s, women organized to fight for their right to vote. Groups of women suffragists held meetings, gave lectures, wrote articles and pamphlets, marched, and lobbied for a constitutional amendment that would recognize their right to vote.

Early Voting on a **College Campus**

For the March 2008 primary, some 1,000 students from Texas A&M University at Prairie View marched 7.3 miles from campus to the polls at the Waller County courthouse. They carried "Register to Vote" signs and their T-shirts read "It's 2008. We will vote." The students were protesting the failure of officials to provide an early voting site on campus. Freshman Brittney Veasey, a first-time voter, commented: "Instead of making it inconvenient, students should be encouraged to vote." Prairie View Mayor Frank Johnson praised the students. "Until they spoke up, there was only one early voting place in the entire county."

"Instead of making it inconvenient, students should be encouraged to vote."

—Freshman Brittney Veasey

EXPLORING THE ESSENTIAL QUESTION

Solving Problems Young people over the age of 18 have the right to vote, but many do not. What limits young people's ability to vote, and what solutions could remedy these problems?

©Ken Basart

The Twenty-sixth Amendment, which was ratified in 1971, lowered the voting age to 18 in every state.

▲ CRITICAL THINKING
Defending Would you favor lowering the voting age in the United States to 16? Explain.

EXPLORING THE ESSENTIAL QUESTION

Making Connections Why do you think that once they could vote, women did not experience the same voter suppression laws and tactics as African Americans?

minimum the least number possible

Women held vigils and hunger strikes and practiced civil disobedience by unlawfully registering and voting. By 1914, they had won the right to vote in 11 states, all of them west of the Mississippi.

During World War I, women suffragists continued the fight for the right to vote. In 1917 the National Women's Party, led by its founder Alice Paul, began picketing outside the White House and distributing leaflets. One read:

PRIMARY SOURCE

We women of America tell you that America is not a democracy. Twenty million women are denied the right to vote.... Tell our government that it must liberate its people."

—from leaflet written by Alice Paul, 1917

The cause of woman suffrage gained momentum during the war. In 1918 President Woodrow Wilson reversed his position and announced his support for a woman suffrage amendment to the Constitution.

Not until after World War I, when the Nineteenth Amendment was ratified, was woman suffrage put into effect nationwide. While the struggle to get the vote was significant, once the Nineteenth Amendment passed, women did not face the cultural or legal barriers to voting that many African Americans were forced to hurdle well into the mid-twentieth century.

Suffrage for 18- to 21-Year-Olds For many years, the **minimum** voting age in most states was 21. In the 1960s, many young Americans were fighting in Vietnam, and many others became involved in protests and politics. They also started a movement to lower the voting age to 18. The basic argument was that if individuals were old enough to be drafted and fight for their country, they were old enough to vote. The Twenty-sixth Amendment, which was ratified in 1971, lowered the voting age to 18 in every state. More than 10 million citizens between the ages of 18 and 21 gained the right to vote. In 1972 many young people exercised their right to vote for the first time.

✔ **READING PROGRESS CHECK**

Summarizing What were some of the arguments for allowing women to vote and lowering the voting age to 18?

LESSON 1 REVIEW

Reviewing Vocabulary
1. *Defining* How are the terms *suffrage* and *disenfranchise* related?

Using Your Graphic Organizer
2. *Sequencing* Use your graphic organizer to create a time line of the history of the expansion of suffrage in the United States.

Answering the Guiding Questions
3. *Summarizing* Who could and could not vote in early America?

4. *Explaining* How was African American suffrage restricted and extended in the nineteenth and twentieth centuries?

5. *Describing* How was suffrage extended to women and 18- to 21-year-olds?

Writing About Government
6. *Informative/Explanatory* Compare and contrast the movements to gain suffrage for women and for 18- to 21-year-olds. Research the two movements' strategies, supporters, and timing. Write two paragraphs noting the similarities and differences. Who supported each movement? What arguments did they make to gain the right to vote? What tactics did they use? How long did each campaign take to realize change?

Should felons have the right to vote in our democracy?

DELIBERATING DEMOCRATIC PRINCIPLES

Some states permanently ban people who have been convicted of a felony from ever voting again. Other states allow felons to have their voting rights restored after serving their sentences. A few others allow felons to vote even while in prison.

YES

NO

TEAM A — Felons Should Have the Right to Vote

The Sentencing Project estimates that 5.8 million Americans are forbidden to vote because of state laws that disenfranchise people with a felony conviction. These laws are unfair and undemocratic.

Ex-felons (people who have finished serving their sentence for committing a felony) have paid their debt to society by completing their sentences and should have their voting rights restored. Voting is a fundamental right and prohibiting convicted felons of this right curtails their citizenship. The ability to participate in our democracy gives ex-felons a meaningful way to reenter society and will promote good behavior. Felon disenfranchisement creates political outcasts of taxpaying, law-abiding citizens who are ex-felons. It undermines citizenship for the individual and the communities to which the ex-felon belongs.

Because African Americans are disproportionally affected at every level of the criminal justice system, they are also disproportionally affected by felon disenfranchisement. One of every 13 African Americans of voting age is disenfranchised, a rate more than four times greater than non-African Americans. Continuing this discriminatory practice will marginalize the African American community and undermine our voting system.

TEAM B — Felons Should Not Have the Right to Vote

Serious lawbreakers should not have the right to be lawmakers. Convicted felons have proven bad judgment and should not be allowed to vote. Felons have shown that they do not meet the minimum standard of morality required of those participating in self-government. They have violated the public trust and do not have the right to help make decisions in the communities they have harmed. According to the Florida Department of Corrections, nearly 40 percent of offenders commit another crime within three years of release and 45 percent do so within five years. Recent ex-felons are not law-abiding, responsible citizens.

Laws prohibiting felons and ex-felons from voting are not racially discriminatory—they apply equally to all felons. These restrictions are also consistent with other voting limitations, such as age, citizenship, and mental competency, as well as other felon restrictions, such as gun restrictions for violent offenders. These laws are not a new invention—they have existed for a very long time and have served their purpose well. Laws that disenfranchise felons and ex-felons help uphold the integrity of our democratic government.

EXPLORING THE ESSENTIAL QUESTION

Deliberating With a partner, review the main arguments for either side. Decide which points are most compelling. Then paraphrase those arguments to a pair of students who were assigned to the other viewpoint. Listen to their strongest arguments. Switch sides and repeat the best arguments and add another compelling argument the other pair may not have thought about or presented. Then drop your roles and have a free discussion about which policy you support and why. Can you find any areas of common ground among the two views? How might a sensible policy address that common ground? What do you think is the best answer? Why?

Interact with these digital
assets and others in lesson 2

✓ INTERACTIVE INFOGRAPHIC
Political Party Platforms

✓ INTERACTIVE MAP
Electing the President

✓ SELF-CHECK QUIZ

✓ VIDEO
Young Voters

networks
TRY IT YOURSELF ONLINE

LESSON 2
Influences on Voters

Reading Help Desk

Academic Vocabulary

- occupation
- predict

Content Vocabulary

- midterm election
- legislative referendum
- popular referendum
- initiative
- cross-pressured voter
- straight party ticket

TAKING NOTES:

Key Ideas and Details

EXPLAINING Use this graphic
organizer to identify the major
influences on voting choices.

Influences on Voting Choices

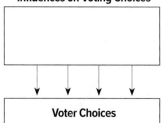

Voter Choices

ESSENTIAL QUESTION

What factors influence voters and election campaigns?

To cast an informed vote, you need to know how to choose your elected officials and how candidates and campaigns attempt to persuade you and other voters. What qualities, skills, or experiences do you look for in a candidate? Rank the following qualifications.

- Job experience in government or specific fields
- Age
- Gender
- Education level

- Health
- Party affiliation
- Personality
- Stance on specific issues
- Chance of winning

Discuss and compare your rank order with several of your classmates. Based on your discussion, would you change the order? If so, what persuaded you to switch your priorities?

The Structure of Elections

GUIDING QUESTION *How do election cycles, term limits, and ballot issues influence voting?*

Both federal and state guidelines structure the U.S. electoral system. Election cycles, term limits for elected officials, and ballot issues all influence voter choices at the polls.

Election Cycles The Constitution dictates the length of the terms of members of Congress, the president, and the vice president. Members of the House of Representatives serve two-year terms. Senators have a six-year term and the president serves a four-year term.

The federal election cycle ensures that the entire government will not turn over at the same time. Federal elections are held every two years for members of Congress, when every house member and one-third of the U.S. senators are up for election. Every four years, we have a presidential election. Congressional elections held in the middle of a president's term are called **midterm elections**.

The Constitution says that states may prescribe the time, place, and manner of elections, but Congress may, at any time, make or alter those regulations. Since 1845, Election Day has been on the Tuesday after the first Monday in November.

States determine the dates of their elections. Most states hold their state general elections on the first Tuesday after the first Monday in November, in keeping with the federal election cycle. Doing so helps save states money and is more convenient for voters, which improves voter turnout. States also have the power to determine the lengths of terms for their governor, legislators, and other state officials.

Term Limits The Twenty-second Amendment limits a president to two terms. The Constitution does not limit the number of terms a member of Congress can serve. There have been proposals to limit their terms, but efforts to amend the Constitution to impose term limits have failed.

On the state and local level, governors in 36 states are limited in the number of terms they may serve; in some states, legislators and a few locally elected officials also face term limits. In some cases, officials may serve more than one term if the terms are not consecutive.

Supporters say term limits reduce corruption, eliminate the advantages incumbent candidates have in reelection campaigns, and reduce the burden of campaigning on people in elected positions. Opponents say the more experience an elected leader has in office, the better he or she can do the job. They also say corruption can occur just as easily in a system with term limits and that if voters think someone has been in office too long or has too much power, they can choose another candidate in the next election.

Ballot Questions Many states also allow citizens to vote directly on issues or laws, in the form of a popular referendum, legislative referendum, or an initiative. All of these measures are examples of direct democracy, where voters have a more direct say in their own laws.

In a **legislative referendum**, the legislature refers a measure to the voters for their approval. In a **popular referendum**, voters gather signatures to put specific laws passed by the legislature on the ballot. Citizens can vote to approve or repeal the laws. In an **initiative**, voters who secure enough signatures can place their own proposed laws or state constitutional amendments on the ballot. If successful, initiatives can either force a state legislature to consider an issue or can bypass the legislature completely. In various states, voters have approved or rejected bans on abortion, same-sex marriage, tax increases, and collective bargaining by public employee unions via the initiative or referendum process.

☑ **READING PROGRESS CHECK**

Explaining What are some arguments in favor of term limits? What are some arguments against term limits?

A voter and her daughter proudly wear their "I voted" stickers.

▶ **CRITICAL THINKING**

Discussing Do the adults in your family vote regularly? Do members of your family consider voting an important responsibility? How much will your future as a voter be influenced by what you have learned about voting at home?

Design Pics/Ron Nickel

EXPLORING THE ESSENTIAL QUESTION

Applying Find out the term lengths of officeholders in your state. Are there limits on the number of terms a candidate can serve? Which offices are being contested in the next election? Who are the incumbents in those offices?

midterm election a Congressional election that takes place halfway through the president's term in office

legislative referendum a special election in which the legislature refers a measure to the voters for their approval

popular referendum a special election in which voters can vote to approve or repeal the laws passed by the legislature

initiative a method by which citizens propose a constitutional law or amendment

occupation a job; a vocation

predict to tell in advance of an event

cross-pressured voter a voter who is caught between conflicting elements in his or her identity

Voters' Election Choices

GUIDING QUESTION *How do personal backgrounds, party loyalty, candidate image, and campaign issues influence voters?*

There are four major factors that tend to drive voters' election choices: the personal background of the voter, the degree of loyalty to a political party, issues in the campaign, and the voter's perception of the candidates. These factors help determine whether a citizen will vote and who he or she will vote for.

Personal Background Voters' personal backgrounds affect their decisions. A person's background includes such things as family, age, education, religion, **occupation**, income level, where they live, and general outlook on life.

Consider how a person's age might affect his or her vote. A 68-year-old senior citizen might favor a candidate who promised an increase in Social Security payments. On the other hand, a voter who is 23 might not want more money deducted from her paycheck for Social Security and vote against this candidate.

Similarly, geography may affect how someone votes. People who live in cities may be more likely to vote for a candidate who wants to invest in public transportation than people who live in more rural areas. As the U.S. population shifts to become more urban and suburban, this could affect voting patterns.

Individuals may have multiple traits that align them with different positions on issues or candidates, which make **predicting** how they would vote difficult. These **cross-pressured voters** face conflicting pressures from different elements of their identity—religion, ethnicity, income level, or peer group. For example, Latino Catholics are generally more inclined to vote

MAP

ELECTING the PRESIDENT

Barack Obama and Mitt Romney received their strongest support in different areas of the country.

▶ **CRITICAL THINKING**

Analyzing Maps In which areas of the country did Obama receive the strongest support? In which did Romney?

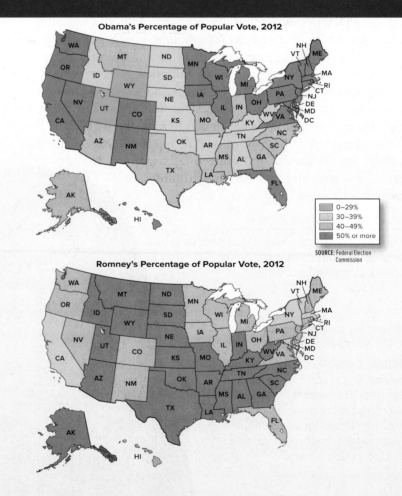

Obama's Percentage of Popular Vote, 2012

0–29%
30–39%
40–49%
50% or more

SOURCE: Federal Election Commission

Romney's Percentage of Popular Vote, 2012

PLATFORMS	DEMOCRATIC PARTY	REPUBLICAN PARTY
Roe v. *Wade*	👍 Believes *Roe* v. *Wade* was correctly decided and opposes placing additional restrictions on abortion.	👎 Believes *Roe* v. *Wade* was wrongly decided and supports placing additional restrictions on abortion.
Gun Regulation	👍 Supports placing additional restrictions on firearms.	👎 Opposes placing additional restrictions on firearms.
Environmental Regulation	👍 Believes government investment should aid environmental efforts.	👎 Believes that private ownership of natural resources leads to better conservation than government ownership.
Same-Sex Marriage	👍 Supports allowing same-sex marriages and equal treatment under law for same-sex couples.	👎 Supports a constitutional amendment defining marriage as "the union of one man and one woman."
Tax Cuts	👎 Supports raising taxes on the wealthiest and eliminating some deductions for large corporations.	👍 Supports reducing taxes for all income levels and eliminating certain types of taxes.
Affordable Care Act	👍 Supports the Affordable Care Act and opposes its repeal.	👎 Opposes the Affordable Care Act and supports its repeal.
Voter ID	👎 Opposes voter ID laws.	👍 Supports voter ID laws.
Immigration	👍 Supports providing amnesty and a path to citizenship for those who entered the country illegally.	👎 Opposes providing amnesty and a path to citizenship to people who entered the country illegally.

Democratic than Republican. Suppose that a Latino Catholic voter is strongly opposed to same-sex marriage, which is a position often taken by Republicans. How might this person vote? Can you think of any cross pressures that you might be faced with when voting?

Party Loyalty Another influence on voters' decisions is their loyalty—or lack of it—to one of the political parties. The majority of American voters consider themselves either Republicans or Democrats, and most vote for their party's candidates.

Strong party voters are those who select their party's candidates regardless of the specific issues or candidates in any given election. They typically vote a **straight party ticket**, meaning that they choose all candidates affiliated with their party on the ballot.

Unlike strong party voters, weak party voters are more likely to switch their votes based on the issues or candidates at hand. People who choose not to identify with a specific party are known as *independent voters*. Independent party voters factor importantly in presidential elections because strong party voters from both major parties tend to balance each other out. Because of this, candidates often try to tailor their messages to attract independent voters.

Candidate Qualifications and Image Voters look for a variety of qualifications in candidates for local, state, or national office. Some voters are concerned with whether candidates have specific experience in government, as an entrepreneur, or as a business leader. Other voters are looking for a fresh face or someone with a new perspective. It might be important to some that a presidential candidate has experience in the military or that a candidate for statewide office has a long history of living and working in that state. Some might want a candidate with impressive academic accomplishments; others prefer a candidate whose experiences more closely mirror their own.

Candidates do their best to portray an image they believe voters value. Candidates want to appear to be strong and trustworthy leaders. At the same time, they may want their opponents to appear weak or otherwise unprepared for the job. Campaigns, aided by political parties and interest groups, help candidates cultivate their messages and images to appeal to potential voters.

Issues Due to advances in education and access to new media technology, today's voters have more opportunities to become better informed about a

The Republican and Democratic parties tailor their party platforms to highlight the issues that will be most appealing to their voters.

▲ **CRITICAL THINKING**
Making Connections Which political party platform more closely aligns with your views and values? Why?

straight party ticket a ticket where a voter has selected candidates of his or her own party only

candidate's stance on issues than the voters of earlier years. Despite this, many voters are still not informed about all of the issues in a campaign. Voters are typically most concerned with issues that directly affect them. Important issues have included Social Security, health care, taxes, education, affirmative action, abortion, gun rights, and the environment. Different issues are important to different constituencies and geographic areas, too. For example, voters in the West might be much more concerned with water rights and resource management, and rural voters might be more concerned with aid to farmers.

✓ **READING PROGRESS CHECK**

Assessing Compare the influence of party loyalty and candidate image on voters' choices. Which do you think is more important? Why?

Voter Participation

GUIDING QUESTION *Who votes in U.S. elections?*

The percentage of Americans voting in presidential elections declined from about 69 percent in 1964 to 56 percent in 2012. Even fewer Americans vote in congressional, state, and local elections. For example, in the 2014 midterm elections approximately 37 percent of the voting eligible population cast a ballot. Voter participation in the United States is quite low compared to other democracies.

Why People Don't Vote Why is it that so many eligible Americans do not go to the polls? One major reason is our complicated registration practices. In most European nations, the government automatically registers every eligible citizen to vote. In the United States, the burden of registering falls entirely on the citizen, and voters must re-register if they move.

Another reason few people vote is the changing role of political parties. Parties used to be very involved in helping people find jobs and interact with government agencies. Without those close connections, parties may be less successful in their voter registration and get-out-the-vote efforts.

PARTICIPATING
ⓘⓃ Your Government

Acquiring, Organizing, and Using Information to Choose a Candidate

Create a table like the one to the right that lists the issues you most care about and the names of candidates competing in the upcoming election. You can choose any local, state, or national election that interests you. If there is not an election in the near future, consider a recent election.

ISSUES	CANDIDATE #1	CANDIDATE #2

Research each candidate's position on the issues you chose. Find information to help you complete your table by examining media sources such as television, radio, newspapers, magazines, and the websites of candidates or parties. You may also want to look for information from interest groups or in blogs written by analysts. You can also learn about a candidate's views by attending or watching a debate.

EXPLORING THE ESSENTIAL QUESTION

When it is complete, share your table with a family member or a classmate and answer the following questions:

a. **Evaluating** Which candidate most shares your views or your concerns?
b. **Analyzing Primary and Secondary Sources** Which sources of information gave you facts or opinions you trust? Why did you trust them?
c. **Identifying Bias** How do you assess bias in information about candidates?

The sheer number of elections we hold can contribute to low voter turnout. The United States holds twice as many national elections as other Western democracies and even more at the state and local level. In addition to national elections, we might vote for governors, lieutenant governors, state treasurers, public utility commissioners, judges, sheriffs, school board members, and more. All this voting requires a lot of time and attention.

Future voter turnout may be impacted by new laws passed in several states that require voters to show photo ID. These laws are surrounded by partisan controversy. Many Republican lawmakers argue that the laws are needed to prevent voter fraud and that photo ID is necessary for many parts of modern life. Many Democrats argue that voter impersonation is a miniscule problem, and the laws make it much harder for people without a photo ID—often poor, minority, and elderly people who vote Democratic—to exercise their right to vote.

The Voting Rights Act designated certain states and communities where voter discrimination had occurred in the past as requiring special attention. Under the law, the federal government had authority to approve or disapprove changes in voting laws or procedures in these designated places. Because of this, the federal government prevented some state and local voter ID laws from being implemented, saying they burdened poor, minority voters.

In 2013 the Supreme Court declared the part of the Voting Rights Act that determined which places needed federal pre-approval to be unconstitutional. In effect, it removed the requirement that states seek permission before changing voting laws. Several previously covered states put voter ID laws into effect.

Increasing Voter Turnout Citizens who vote regularly have positive attitudes toward government and citizenship. Education, age, and income are important factors in predicting which citizens will vote. The more education a citizen has, the more likely it is that he or she will vote regularly. Middle-aged citizens have the highest voting turnout of all age groups.

People who are concerned about the low percentage of people who vote have called for reforms to make voting more convenient. One suggestion is to shift Election Day from Tuesday to Saturday or Sunday; another is to leave the polls open for several days and for longer hours. Yet another idea is to have a national registration system so that people's registrations would follow them when they moved to a new state. Some areas are already experimenting with early voting or making absentee balloting easier in order to encourage participation.

Georgia was one of the first states to require citizens to show a photo ID in order to vote.

▲ **CRITICAL THINKING**
Making Connections Is a photo ID required to vote in your state?

☑ **READING PROGRESS CHECK**

Summarizing What are some of the barriers to voting in the United States?

LESSON 2 REVIEW

Reviewing Vocabulary
1. ***Applying*** What are referenda and initiatives? Provide at least two reasons they are important to democracy that are not located in the text.

Using Your Graphic Organizer
2. ***Summarizing*** Use your graphic organizer to explain what influences voter choices at the polls.

Answering the Guiding Questions
3. ***Explaining*** How do election cycles, term limits, and ballot issues influence voting?

4. ***Evaluating*** How do personal backgrounds, party loyalty, candidate image, and campaign issues influence voters?

5. ***Specifying*** Who votes in U.S. elections?

Writing About Government
6. ***Argument*** The text refers to several attempts people have made to increase voter turnout. Can you think of other ways to increase turnout? Which options would be the most effective? Explain your reasons.

Interact with these digital assets and others in lesson 3

✓ **INTERACTIVE CHART**
Common Propaganda Techniques

✓ **INTERACTIVE TIME LINE**
Campaign Finance Reform

✓ **SELF-CHECK QUIZ**

✓ **VIDEO**
Inside Obama's Reelection Campaign

netw⊙rks
TRY IT YOURSELF ONLINE

ReadingHelp Desk

Academic Vocabulary

- **strategy**
- **distribute**

Content Vocabulary

- **campaign manager**
- **propaganda**
- **corruption**
- **hard money**
- **political action committee (PAC)**
- **soft money**
- **SuperPAC**

TAKING NOTES:
Integration of Knowledge and Ideas

COMPARING AND CONTRASTING Use a Venn diagram to compare and contrast the use of television with that of the Internet and social media in modern-day election campaigns.

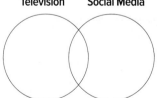

Television   Internet and Social Media

LESSON 3
Campaigns and Financing

ESSENTIAL QUESTION

What factors influence voters and election campaigns?

Which of the following do you think most influences a candidate's chance of winning an election? Once you have read this lesson, reevaluate your responses.

a. He is an incumbent.

b. He has a well-financed campaign.

c. He has the endorsement of large, powerful interest groups.

d. He has more television ads than his opponent.

e. He has the most support on social media.

f. He has many well-financed SuperPACs supporting his campaign.

Campaign Strategies

GUIDING QUESTION *How are campaigns run and how do they try to influence voters?*

Elections are a continuing part of American life. Understanding how campaigns work and how they are paid for can help you make more informed choices when you vote.

Candidates for major national office begin organizing their campaigns more than a year before elections. To win, campaign staffers need to make sure that every move the candidate makes is in line with the campaign strategy and that the public is paying attention to the "right issues." This requires strong organization as well as a clear, consistent message.

Campaign Organization The **campaign manager** is responsible for overall **strategy** and planning. In a campaign office, staff members handle media relations with journalists from television, radio, print, and digital media. Others manage finances, fundraising, advertising, opinion polls, and campaign materials. For state and local elections, state and local party officials may help coordinate the campaigns. Party officials and field workers contact voters, hold local rallies, and **distribute** campaign literature. These field workers, who are usually volunteers, ring doorbells, canvass voters by telephone, drive voters to polling places, and do whatever they can to make sure voters turn out for their candidate on Election Day.

In presidential races, campaign strategies are guided to some extent by the Electoral College. Presidential candidates need 270 of the 538 available electoral votes to win an election. In most cases, a candidate who wins the popular vote in a state receives all of that state's electoral votes. Candidates must therefore appeal to a broad range of voters in different states. They might spend a lot of time campaigning in states where polls show a tight race. In 2012 these "swing" states included Ohio, Virginia, Florida, Nevada, Colorado, Wisconsin, and Iowa. Federal congressional elections receive less national attention than presidential elections, but running for Congress is still quite expensive. Senate candidates are typically more well-known than candidates for the House of Representatives as they are more likely to have held a high-profile state or city office before running for Senate. Often, a House candidate's biggest campaign challenge is gaining name recognition among voters.

Propaganda and Advertising One of the largest expenditures for election campaigns is advertising. Candidates use advertising to inform voters of their position on issues, to portray themselves in an appealing light, and to criticize their opponents. Political parties and interest groups also use advertising in a variety of media to send messages to the American people. Many of these messages could be classified as propaganda. **Propaganda** involves using ideas, information, or rumors to influence opinion. It is not necessarily lying or deception, but it is not objective either.

There are many propaganda techniques, most of which rely on arguments that may sound convincing but that are not necessarily valid. Associating a candidate with a symbol, using negative words and labels to describe an opponent's positions, pretending that an opponent supports a position that he

campaign manager the person responsible for the overall strategy and planning of a campaign

strategy a plan or method for achieving a goal

distribute to give out or disburse to clients, customers, or members of a group

propaganda the use of ideas, information, or rumors to influence opinion

COMMON PROPAGANDA TECHNIQUES

Ad Hominem	Attacking the person instead of the issue.
Appeal to Authority	Citing a prominent figure to support an idea or candidate.
Appeal to Fear	Attempts to build support by instilling panic in the population.
Bandwagon	Urging voters to support a candidate because everyone else is.
Black and White	Presenting only two choices, with the desired selection presented as the only reasonable one to make.
Card Stacking	Giving only one side of the facts to support a position.
Common Man (or "Plain Folks") Appeal	An attempt to convince the audience that the candidate's position reflects the common sense of the people.
Glittering Generality	An unsupported statement that makes a candidate look good or virtuous.
Labeling	Identifying candidates with negative terms such as "un-American."
Testimonial	Having a well-known or highly regarded person urge voters for their support.
Transfer	Associating a positive or negative symbol with a candidate to make the candidate more acceptable or to discredit the candidate.

EXPLORING THE ESSENTIAL QUESTION

Applying Research a local candidate for an upcoming election and come up with four different campaign slogans. Design each one to appeal to a different group of people. If you are using propaganda, identify the type of strategy you used.

COMPARING
CAMPAIGN
COMMERCIALS

These television campaign commercials have become famous for their powerful impact and have been credited with turning the tide in an election.

"DAISY" (1964)
Produced by President
Lyndon B. Johnson

"ANY QUESTIONS?" (2004)
Produced by Swift Boat
Veterans for Truth

"WEEKEND PASSES" (1988)
Produced by
Americans for Bush

As a little girl counts petals off a flower, a voice counts down a missile launch. When the count reaches zero, the screen goes black and a mushroom cloud appears. This advertisement, aired only once, used an appeal to fear of nuclear attack in order to encourage support for President Johnson.

A series of men who said they served with presidential candidate John Kerry use labeling and card stacking to present him as unfit to lead America. The men claim he lied about military honors and events while serving in Vietnam. "Swiftboating" has become a common expression for attacking a candidate's credibility.

This advertisement convinced voters to vote for George H.W. Bush by using transfer and associating opponent Michael Dukakis with prisoner Willie Horton, who committed rape while on a prison furlough program that Dukakis supported.

▲ **CRITICAL THINKING**

1. Defining Define the propaganda techniques that were used in each of these television commercials.

2. Analyzing Watch one or more of these campaign commercials. Do you find them to be persuasive? Why or why not?

or she does not, and quoting only favorable statistics are some examples of the types of propaganda that have played a part in every campaign since the 1800s.

When political propaganda becomes obviously misleading, people become skeptical of politicians. Attack ads and name calling can override the important issues of a campaign and make voters weary. In some surveys, voters say they do not appreciate these negative ads, and some analysts believe this can result in reduced voter participation. Other research finds that while individuals say they do not like negative ads, negative ads are often persuasive, which is why many candidates continue to use them.

Television The most important communication tool for a presidential candidate is television. Watching television is the main way that many citizens find out about a candidate and his or her position on issues. Appearances on television news shows are vitally important for campaigns in order to remain in the public consciousness, and campaigns will routinely stage newsworthy events with their candidates in order to get favorable airtime. Televised debates, often occurring late in a campaign, can have an impact on undecided voters.

In the weeks and months before an election, television viewers can be deluged by commercials produced by the campaign or by a separate group supporting the candidate. You can tell whether an ad was produced by a campaign or by a supporting group by whether or not the candidate being supported states during the advertisement that he or she approves of the message. This is a requirement of the Bipartisan Campaign Reform Act of 2002, written with the idea that fewer negative ads would be created if candidates had to actively affirm the language in their advertisements. Other political commercials known as "issue ads" can be harder to trace back to their funders because issue groups are not bound by the same law. Just in time for the 2012 presidential election, an election watchdog group developed a cell phone application that allows a user to point his or her phone at the television and then be automatically linked to a database containing information about the group sponsoring the ad.

Internet and Social Media Candidates running for nearly every office from the president to county clerk use the Internet as some part of their campaign. Howard Dean, Democratic presidential candidate in 2004, was the first to raise significant contributions through his campaign website. President Barack Obama's 2008 campaign broke campaign fundraising records and raised over $700 million, in part by making it even easier for individual donors to give and volunteer through his campaign websites.

It is no longer enough for candidates to have just one campaign website as their Internet presence. Campaigns tweet to supporters, are active on Facebook and other social media sites, maintain blogs, send e-mail blasts to their supporters, and use targeted advertising across the web. Targeted advertising is the practice of using messages specifically designed to appeal to a type of person who is known to use certain products, belong to certain groups, or access certain websites.

Social media can be a powerful and cost-effective campaign tool. Campaign supporters generate new content and spread this content to their friends and connections through the use of social media. Campaign managers must work to ensure a consistent online message, even when their supporters are generating their own content about the candidate and the campaign.

☑ **READING PROGRESS CHECK**

Describing What are some of the roles and functions of a campaign organization?

C·I·V·I·C PARTICIPATION IN A DIGITAL AGE

Presidential Campaigns

Find two online examples of an official campaign promotion for any local or national political campaign or candidate. They can be a paid advertisement, blog post, tweet, video, or anything else that the campaign has produced. You can find these on Facebook, YouTube, or any pop-up or banner ad. Then find two online examples of a campaign promotion posted by supporters of the same candidate or campaigns. Blog posts, tweets, videos, and Facebook posts are again likely sources. For example, these images show the official 2012 presidential campaign Twitter accounts of Barack Obama and Mitt Romney.

EXPLORING THE ESSENTIAL QUESTION

a. **Analyzing** For both the official campaign promotion and the campaign promotion posted by supporters, explain where you found it, how you know whether it was produced by the campaign, the audience it is trying to reach, and whether or not it is employing any propaganda techniques.

b. **Comparing and Contrasting** Are there any discrepancies between how the campaign promotes itself and how its supporters promote the campaign? If so, what are they?

Campaign Finance

GUIDING QUESTION *What types of limitations, if any, should be placed on campaign donations and spending?*

Running for political office is very expensive. In the 2011–2012 election cycle, presidential and congressional candidates spent more than $7 billion on election campaigns. Candidates need money for office space, staff salaries, travel, and advertising, among other things. In addition, unions, corporations, and other groups spend huge sums of money to independently advertise on behalf of the candidates and issues that they support.

Fundraising for campaigns takes a lot of time—one member of Congress said he spent 10 hours each week "working the phones for cash" and that some members spend half their time fundraising for their next election. Many worry that the fundraising interferes with lawmakers' job responsibilities.

Efforts to regulate money in campaigns are controversial. Those favoring strict regulation believe unlimited spending can have a corrupting influence on politics and gives an unfair advantage to those with a lot of money. They argue that, once elected, candidates will feel the need to give favors to those who contributed heavily to their campaign. When a candidate seems to be motivated by specific monetary interests rather than by the good of the country as a whole, people accuse that candidate of **corruption**. Opponents of regulation believe money contributes to a broader political debate. They argue that giving and spending money in elections is a form of speech and thus protected by the First Amendment.

corruption impairment of integrity, virtue, or moral principle

Efforts to Regulate Campaign Finance Since 1908, Congress has tried to set limits on campaign funding in order to reduce corruption. This has proven to be a difficult balancing act, as limiting spending and donations can also be seen as limiting free speech. The early campaign finance laws

---

TIME LINE

CAMPAIGN FINANCE REFORM

▶ **CRITICAL THINKING**

1. Analyzing Based on the information in the time line, how would you characterize the role the Supreme Court has played in campaign finance reform?

2. Comparing and Contrasting Compare and contrast the campaign finance reform legislation of the 1970s and the first decades of the 2000s.

→ 1970

1971
- The Federal Election Campaign Act (FECA) required
- public disclosure of each candidate's spending,
- prohibited direct contributions from unions and
- business organizations to campaigns, and limited how
- much individuals, groups, and the candidates
- themselves could contribute.

1974
- Public funding was established for presidential candidates whose party received at least 5 percent of the popular vote in a previous election and agreed to limit campaign spending.

→ 1980

1976
- In *Buckley* v. *Valeo*, the Supreme Court ruled
- that limits on campaign contributions are
- permitted. However, campaign spending
- cannot be limited, because such spending is
- an expression of free speech. Candidates
- may contribute as much as they want to
- their own campaigns. Since *Buckley*, the
- idea that spending money is a form of
- speech has been central to court rulings on
- campaign finance.

James L. Buckley

The Washington Post/Getty Images

tried to limit both how much individuals and businesses could donate to campaigns and how much campaigns could spend. These laws were challenged in court. The Supreme Court said laws that restrict how much individuals and groups can donate directly to campaigns are constitutional. It also upheld rules that say that donors' names must be public. On the other hand, the Court struck down laws that restrict how much money a candidate can spend, or the amount individuals or groups can donate to political organizations unaffiliated with specific campaigns. The Court said those restrictions infringed on the First Amendment.

These campaign finance laws are for federal elections; states have their own campaign finance regulations. In 1975 the Federal Election Commission (FEC) was created to administer federal election laws.

Public Financing Federal funding for presidential elections was established as part of a 1974 amendment of the Federal Election Campaign Act (FECA). Candidates that qualify can receive campaign funds from the federal government if they promise to limit the amount their campaigns spend to a specific amount. The purpose of this initiative was to limit campaign spending and also to reduce the influence of large donors.

From 1976 to 2004, all major party candidates accepted these funds. In 2008, however, Barack Obama elected not to receive public financing while Republican nominee John McCain chose to receive it. As a result, Obama was able to outspend McCain by a factor of two to one. In 2012, neither presidential candidate used public funding.

Direct Funding Private direct funding comes from direct contributions to a candidate by individuals, political parties, corporations, and special interest groups and from the candidate's own money. Direct contributions are called **hard money** and are limited based on regulations set out in FECA.

hard money direct contributions to a candidate's political campaign

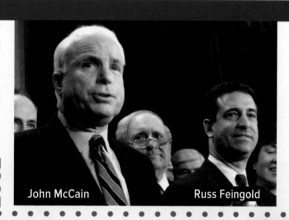

The Bipartisan Campaign Reform Act (BCRA), also known as McCain-Feingold, banned "soft money" donations and also prohibited groups from running issue ads within 30 days of primary elections and 60 days of general elections.

John McCain   Russ Feingold

1990 · · 2000 · · 2002

2010

The Supreme Court ruled in Citizens United that several of the restrictions of BCRA, including the prohibition on running ads at certain times and a limit on indirect corporate campaign spending, are violations of free speech.

Analyzing Free speech, privacy, transparency, and civic participation in government all are valued in democracies. Sometimes, in the area of campaign finance, these principles can compete with one another. For each of these following questions, share your opinion and the most compelling reasons for your opinions.

a. Do you think a person should be able to donate to a political campaign anonymously?

b. Do you think people have a First Amendment right to keep their political donations anonymous?

c. Do you think citizens of other countries should be able to donate to American elections? What about foreign governments?

political action committee (PAC) an organization formed to collect money and provide financial support for political candidates

soft money money raised by a political party for general purposes; money not designated for a candidate

SuperPAC a political action committee that does not coordinate with election campaigns and thus is eligible to receive unlimited donations

In 2013 individual supporters could donate $2,600 to a presidential candidate; national and local party committees could give $5,000. **Political action committees (PACs)**, which are groups established by interest groups to raise money to support candidates or parties, could donate $2,600. A candidate, however, can spend unlimited sums of money on his or her own campaign.

Indirect Funding Indirect funding includes contributions to issue groups and political organizations that are independent from and not coordinating with a campaign. In the past, money given to these organizations was often funneled to national parties and used to advertise for candidates, hold voter registration drives, or stage get-out-the-vote campaigns. In 2002 Senators John McCain and Russ Feingold sponsored a bill to rein in this spending. The Bipartisan Campaign Reform Act (BCRA) banned these **soft money** transactions. It also prohibited PACs, unions, and corporations from running issue ads that specifically supported or denounced a national candidate within 30 days of a primary election and 60 days of a general election.

In 2010 the Supreme Court struck down these advertising limits in *Citizens United v. FEC*. PACs that do not coordinate with campaigns can receive unlimited donations from individuals, corporations, unions, and other groups. PACs that take advantage of this new freedom are now commonly referred to as **SuperPACs**. These powerful groups collect and spend unlimited amounts of money to support or defeat a candidate. Many advertisements aired during the 2012 elections came from SuperPACs. These organizations are supposed to be independent and not coordinated with any candidate's campaign, but in reality, the SuperPACs are often run by the candidate's allies who already know what message the candidate wants to get out.

Any PAC that spends more than $5,000 during any campaign year must report all donors who give more than $100. Some PACs get around this by setting up other tax-free groups to receive donations for them. Donors who give money to these social welfare groups do not have to be disclosed, and the social welfare organization can then give the money to a PAC.

The Supreme Court's decision in the *Citizens United* ruling—that noncoordinating groups producing political "issue" advertisements can receive unlimited donations—has extended to state elections. In 2012 a Montana law banning corporations from making donations to groups advocating for or against a candidate was struck down by the Supreme Court under the same logic of *Citizens United*.

☑ **READING PROGRESS CHECK**

Contrasting How are rules governing PACs and SuperPACs different?

LESSON 3 REVIEW

Reviewing Vocabulary
1. *Explaining* What purpose can propaganda serve in a television commercial or debate performance?

Using Your Graphic Organizer
2. *Comparing* Use your organizer to write a paragraph explaining the similar functions that television and the Internet and social media play in campaigns.

Answering the Guiding Questions
3. *Explaining* How are campaigns run and how do they try to influence voters?

4. *Analyzing* What types of limitations, if any, should be placed on campaign donations and spending?

Writing About Government
5. *Informative/Explanatory* Write an essay explaining your views about the potential for campaign contributions leading to corruption. Is it a serious issue, in your opinion? Do you believe campaign contributions are a form of free speech?

Shelby County, Alabama V Holder (2013)

FACTS OF THE CASE Because the Fifteenth Amendment's promise that no person may be denied the right to vote was being violated, Congress passed the Voting Rights Act of 1965 (VRA) to stop discrimination against African American voters. Section 5 of the VRA required state and local governments with a history of voting discrimination to ask the federal government to approve any change to their voting laws to ensure that the change would not harm an individual's right to vote.

Another part of the law described the districts to which Section 5 applies: any local government that used discriminatory voting practices between 1965 and 1972. Once a district could prove it had not discriminated for 10 years, it could stop being monitored by the federal government. If other districts began discriminating, they could be added into Section 5 monitoring. In 2006 a nearly unanimous Congress believed that discrimination was still occurring and voted to extend the VRA for 25 years.

Shelby County, Alabama, was included in Section 5 because voting discrimination was taking place there in 1965. It has been covered ever since. In 2011 Shelby County sued the federal government because it believed that Section 5 of the VRA was unconstitutional.

ISSUE

Did Congress exceed its power to regulate voting when it reauthorized Section 5 of the Voting Rights Act in 2006?

ARGUMENTS

The following is a list of arguments made in the case of *Shelby County, Alabama* v. *Holder*. Read each argument and categorize each based on whether it supports Shelby County's side or Holder's side.

1. The Fifteenth Amendment gives Congress the authority to regulate voting in order to prevent discrimination.

2. Congress made a nearly unanimous decision to reauthorize the VRA in 2006. The Supreme Court should defer to the will of the people as represented by Congress.

3. Congress's power to regulate voting under the Fifteenth Amendment is not unlimited. Most aspects of election law are given to the states in Article 1, Section 4, of the Constitution. This law is too intrusive on the states' rights.

4. The VRA's formula for deciding which states are covered is based on discrimination that occurred more than 40 years ago. It was written to target only the use practices like poll taxes or literacy tests. Because these tactics are no longer used, the law is outdated.

5. Even though older methods of discrimination have stopped, local governments still discriminate in different ways. They make voting practice changes that the federal government reviews and rejects because they will have the effect of discriminating against minority voters.

6. This law is applied unequally among the states. Only a few must get the federal government to approve every voting law change they want to make. Other places discriminate, too, and the way the law is applied is unfair.

EXPLORING THE ESSENTIAL QUESTION

Categorizing After you have categorized the arguments, choose one that you think is the most persuasive and explain why you found that argument compelling.

YOU BE the JUDGE

LESSON 4
Voter's Guide

ReadingHelp Desk

Academic Vocabulary
- register
- margin

Content Vocabulary
- compulsory voting
- recall
- polling place
- precinct
- early voting
- absentee ballot
- canvassing board

TAKING NOTES:
Key Ideas and Details

SEQUENCING Use the flowchart to explain the steps that one must go through to vote.

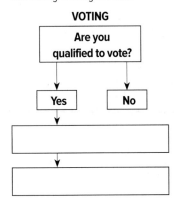

VOTING

| Are you qualified to vote? |

| Yes | No |

What are the key steps in voting?

Summarize what you already know about the voting process in your community and make a list of questions about what you do not know or understand. Then, create a personal voter's guide. It should include these categories:

1. Registration
   - Where
   - How
   - When
2. Preparing to Vote—Researching, Evaluating, and Deciding about...
   - Candidates
   - Ballot Issues
3. Voting
   - Where
   - When
   - Type of Ballot

As you read through this lesson, add or correct information for each category. Where general procedures are mentioned, research to learn the specific guidelines in your community. When the guide is complete, share it with a friend and keep it to use when you are ready to vote.

Voting Qualifications and Voter Registration

GUIDING QUESTION *Who can vote, and how can one register to vote?*

The Constitution gives each state authority to set its own rules about who can vote. However, federal law and several constitutional amendments set a basic standard that prohibits states from excluding U.S. citizens from voting based on gender, religious beliefs, income level, race, ethnicity, or for those aged 18 or older. Every state requires voters to be U.S. citizens and to be residents of the state for a certain period of time before they are eligible to vote.

Why Register to Vote? You cannot vote unless you have **registered**, or enrolled with your local government first. The processes and requirements to register vary by state. State boards of elections require you to register before you vote to prevent voter fraud; states want to be sure that voters are who they say they are and that they have met the eligibility requirements. Registration became common in the late 1800s as a way to stop voting fraud. In those days, the slogan "Vote Early and Often" was not a joke. In Denver in 1900, for example, one man confessed to having voted 125 times on Election Day! Reformers saw registration as a way to stop such abuses and clean up elections by giving officials a list of who could legally vote.

How and Where to Register? You must complete a registration form in order to become eligible to vote. In some states, you can complete the form online; in other states, you must sign and mail it to the board of elections. Contact your state board of elections to download or request a copy of your state's registration form.

In 1993 Congress passed The National Voter Registration Act to make registration easier, with the hope that more people would register and vote. As a result, you can also find registration forms at your post office, motor vehicle department, and some other government offices, including those that serve people who are disabled and people who receive welfare. The law also requires that government public agencies must make it clear that voting and registering to vote are optional and will not affect the amount of public assistance a person receives.

Who Can Help You Register? Political parties and campaign staff are eager to help people register to vote, especially people who they believe will support their candidates. They tend to focus their registration strategies in communities and demographic groups that traditionally vote for their parties.

We the People: Making a Difference

FREEDOM SUMMER
ACTIVISTS

Frank Hurley/NY Daily News via Getty Images

In 1964 several civil rights organizations conducted a voting and civil rights campaign called Freedom Summer. Thousands of volunteers—many of them white and black college students—worked together to teach African American children about civil and voting rights. They publicized obstacles to voting rights and hosted "Freedom Days" to register African Americans to vote. They faced serious obstacles, too—more than 30 African American churches and many homes were set afire that summer by opponents, and three young activists were murdered. In the end, though, their actions raised awareness and helped lead to the passage of the Voting Rights Act in 1965. Since then, other racial, ethnic, and minority groups have launched voter registration drives to increase their group's voice in elections.

EXPLORING THE ESSENTIAL QUESTION

a. **Analyzing** Why do you think voter registration efforts are so important to civil rights movements?

b. **Explaining** How does an increase in the number of registered voters improve democracy?

c. **Applying** If you wanted to increase voter registration among a group of people, what steps could you take?

register to enroll one's name with the appropriate local government in order to participate in elections

Many nonpartisan groups are dedicated to helping people register to vote as part of their mission to improve the democratic process. Groups like the League of Women Voters, Rock the Vote, and Kids Voting USA will be happy to help you register.

When Can You Register? Check your state's registration deadline by contacting your state board of elections. Most states require you to register to vote 15 to 30 days prior to an election. Nine states and the District of Columbia offer Election Day Registration (EDR). Studies have shown that states with EDR have higher turnouts than states without it. The biggest increase in voters with EDR is among the middle class.

✓ **READING PROGRESS CHECK**

Describing What are the steps that a person must take to register to vote?

Voting

GUIDING QUESTION *What are the procedures for voting?*

Many elections around the world—and at every level of government—have been won or lost by a miniscule **margin**. Your vote and every vote matters.

margin the limit or bare minimum

Deciding to Vote Democracy depends on informed and active citizens, and voting is one action you can take to get the democracy you want. Voting gives you a voice in your government and, therefore, in the laws and quality of life in your country, state, and community. The decision is yours to make, though. Voting is optional in the United States and in all but 16 democratic nations. In other countries, especially those with authoritarian governments, **compulsory voting** is enforced. In those countries, people who do not vote can be sanctioned with fines, jail time, or other penalties.

compulsory voting mandatory voting

GRAPH

COMPARING
VOTER TURNOUT

Peru is one of 16 democratic nations that make voting in national elections compulsory. Peruvians who are eligible to vote but fail to vote may face sanctions. The fine is equivalent to about 7 dollars. Nonvoters in Peru can also be denied bank loans and can be prohibited from receiving government goods and services.

Voting-Age Population Who Voted in Recent Presidential Elections

100% — 0%
81.4 — 2001
87.7 — 2006
82.5 — 2011

PERU

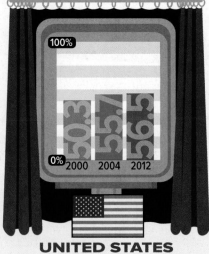

100% — 0%
50.3 — 2000
55.7 — 2004
56.5 — 2012

UNITED STATES

Sources: U.S. Census and IDEA

EXPLORING THE ESSENTIAL QUESTION

Analyzing Graphs Compare and contrast the bar graphs and answer these questions.

a. In your opinion, does mandatory voting increase voter turnout?

b. What other factors may explain this data?

c. What are advantages and disadvantages to compulsory voting?

d. Are there better ways to increase voter participation? If so, what would be better?

COMPARING BALLOT TYPES

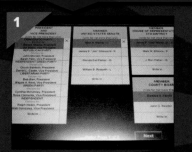

A touch screen ballot

A paper ballot

A paper ballot in Angola

EXPLORING THE ESSENTIAL QUESTION

Analyzing Visuals Compare and contrast the three ballots and answer these questions.

a. Compare ballots 1, 2, and 3. How are they the same? How are they different?

b. Locate a sample ballot from your local board of elections or online. How is the sample ballot similar to or different from those here? Which do you prefer? Why?

Preparing to Vote It is important to become informed about the issues and candidates that will be on the ballot. Everyone has different reasons for supporting one candidate over another. For many voters, a candidate's stance on certain issues or plans to solve problems is a key consideration.

Remember, elections are often about more than picking leaders. Some ballots also contain referenda, initiatives, or **recalls**. In some cases, these ballot questions may seem like minor changes to technical or legal language; in other cases, voters may be asked big questions such as whether students attending state colleges may receive in-state tuition if they are unable to prove they are U.S. citizens or if their county can raise tax rates. Be sure to find out if your ballot will contain such proposals. If so, consider your answers before the day you vote.

recall the procedure by which an elected official may be removed from office by popular vote

When and Where to Vote You may vote in person on Election Day, like many Americans. If so, you will go to the polling place near your home, typically at a school or library. Your **polling place** will be in a particular **precinct** or voting district. Each city or county is usually divided into precincts containing between 200 and 1,000 voters. You may receive a notice from your state board of elections telling you the location and hours for your polling place.

polling place the location in a precinct where people vote

precinct a voting district

Some people cannot vote in person on Election Day. If you live in one of the 33 states or the District of Columbia that allow **early voting**, you can cast a ballot in person during a designated period, usually for about three weeks prior to Election Day. No excuse or justification is required.

early voting provision that allows a person to vote in person for a specified period of time prior to Election Day

If you do not live in one of these early voting states, and you will be out of town, in the hospital, observing a religious holiday, or working on Election Day, you may vote early via an **absentee ballot**. This type of ballot allows you to vote without going to the polls. Military personnel and their family members who are stationed outside their home city and state are also entitled to vote absentee.

absentee ballot a ballot that allows a person to vote without going to the polls on Election Day

You may obtain an absentee ballot from your board of elections. In most states, you can request one in person at the office of your board of elections or you can request that one is sent to you. Deadlines for requesting an absentee ballot vary by state. Currently, 27 states and the District of Columbia do not require you to give an excuse—you can simply ask for an absentee ballot.

GOVERNMENT *in your* COMMUNITY

Becoming a Poll Worker

Have you ever considered becoming a poll worker? Poll workers are essential to the proper administration of elections. They help set up the voting equipment, verify registrations, provide ballots to voters, and help ensure ballots are delivered to the elections office. The requirements for becoming a poll worker vary by state. It is likely that you can find most of the information you need by doing a search on the Internet for poll worker information for your state. Also, the U.S. Election Assistance Commission website maintains a list of poll worker requirements by state that you can download. Consider contacting your local elections office to see if you qualify and to make an application. The chart provides some of the questions you'll need to answer before you apply.

◀ **CRITICAL THINKING**
Stating Would you be interested in being a poll worker in your community? Why or why not?

Poll Worker Requirements for Your State	
a. Do I need to be a registered voter to be a poll worker?	
b. Do I need to have a political party affiliation?	
c. What is the minimum age requirement?	
d. What is the residency requirement?	
e. What hours do I need to work on election day?	
f. Is a training session required?	
g. What are the specific duties of a poll worker?	
h. Does my state have a program for student election assistant volunteers?	

In other states, you must explain why you need to vote absentee. Once you receive your ballot, you can complete it at home and return it before Election Day (usually by mail).

How to Vote Voting procedures and ballots vary from state to state. If you vote in person, when you arrive at your polling place, you may see campaign workers or political party volunteers trying to persuade undecided voters. State laws restrict electioneering at polling places.

Inside, you will find several election officials and volunteers who work to make sure the election is fair and legal. These will include representatives of both political parties. Your first stop will be at a table where one of the election officials will ask your name, find it on the official list of registered voters, and ask you to sign your name on the registry list. In some states, you may have to present identification. Another official will provide you with your ballot, direct you to the voting booth, and ask if you understand how to cast your vote.

Inside the voting booth, you will be able to vote in secret. Different states offer different types of ballots. All ballots will contain instructions. Next you will choose the candidates and submit your completed paper or electronic ballot.

For many years, most votes were cast using a punch card system, which requires voters to insert a card into a machine, line it up next to candidate names, and punch a hole next to the name of their chosen candidate. In 2000, the presidential election was so close that votes had to be recounted.

In Florida, the recount was made more difficult because many cards were punched incorrectly or incompletely. Some voters said the voting machines and cards did not line up correctly, so they worried they may have voted for the wrong candidate. Since 2000, many states have modernized their voting machines to make them touch screens. However, problems can occur with any method. In 2008, the manufacturer of the touch-screen voting machines admitted that a source-code error had led to votes being dropped in some counties' elections.

Special Assistance Any voter who needs help voting is entitled to receive it. In the case of voters with disabilities, some states allow you to pick the person to assist you. Other states require that only officials at the polling place can help. To protect voters with disabilities from pressure, some states require that two election officials from opposite parties be present during voting. Non-English speaking voters are also entitled to special assistance under the Voting Rights Act of 1975. In many parts of Florida, Texas, and California, election materials are available in both Spanish and English. In Hawaii, election materials have been printed in Cantonese, Ilocano, Japanese, and English.

After You Vote As you leave the polling place, you may see reporters surveying people who have voted. This enables the media to project winners, even in close races, before all votes are counted and even before all polls close.

A voter with a disability receives assistance at her polling place.

▲ CRITICAL THINKING
Summarizing What types of assistance are available to voters with disabilities?

> **EXPLORING THE ESSENTIAL QUESTION**
>
> **Drawing Conclusions** Should media be able to announce projections of winners and losers before polls close everywhere? Give reasons for your answer.

As soon as the polls close, all the ballots from your precinct will be forwarded to your city or county **canvassing board**. This official group has representatives from both political parties and is in charge of counting votes, called *returns*. These local boards bundle all the returns together and send them to the state canvassing authority. Within days of the election, this state authority certifies the election of the winner. Through television and radio, people usually know the winners before canvassing boards certify them. In close elections, the result might depend upon the official vote count and certification.

canvassing board the official body that counts votes and certifies the winner

✓ **READING PROGRESS CHECK**

Explaining What are the different ways that a person can cast his or her ballot? Which method, if any, do you prefer? Why?

LESSON 4 REVIEW

Reviewing Vocabulary
1. *Defining* What are precincts, and where are polling places located?

Using Your Graphic Organizer
2. *Summarizing* Use your graphic organizer to describe the specific steps you must take to prepare for voting.

Answering the Guiding Questions
3. *Explaining* Who can vote, and how can one register to vote?

4. *Describing* What are the procedures for voting?

Writing About Government
5. *Informative/Explanatory* Find out your state's requirements for absentee voting and if it offers early voting, same-day registration, or Election Day registration. Write an informative article about your findings for your school newspaper.

STUDY GUIDE

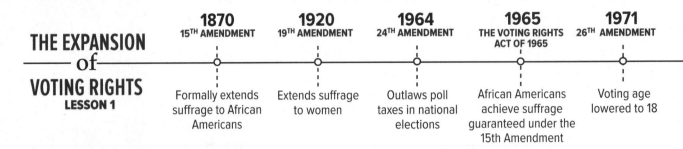

THE EXPANSION —of— VOTING RIGHTS
LESSON 1

1870
15TH AMENDMENT

Formally extends suffrage to African Americans

1920
19TH AMENDMENT

Extends suffrage to women

1964
24TH AMENDMENT

Outlaws poll taxes in national elections

1965
THE VOTING RIGHTS ACT OF 1965

African Americans achieve suffrage guaranteed under the 15th Amendment

1971
26TH AMENDMENT

Voting age lowered to 18

INFLUENCES ON VOTERS
LESSON 2

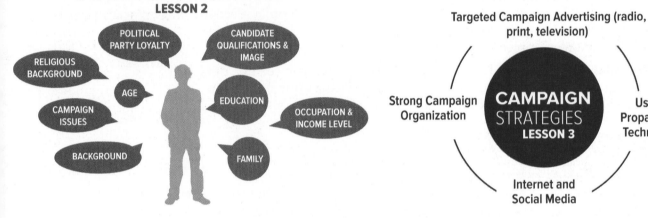

POLITICAL PARTY LOYALTY

CANDIDATE QUALIFICATIONS & IMAGE

RELIGIOUS BACKGROUND

AGE

EDUCATION

CAMPAIGN ISSUES

OCCUPATION & INCOME LEVEL

BACKGROUND

FAMILY

Targeted Campaign Advertising (radio, print, television)

CAMPAIGN STRATEGIES
LESSON 3

Strong Campaign Organization

Use of Propaganda Techniques

Internet and Social Media

VOTER PARTICIPATION
LESSON 2

POSSIBLE REASONS FOR **low voter turnout**	PROPOSALS TO **increase voter turnout**
• Complicated registration practices	• Moving election day to Saturday or Sunday
• Ineffective registration and voter drives	• Open polls for several days or longer hours
• Too many elections	• Early voting
• Photo ID laws	• Making absentee balloting easier
	• Create a national registration system

FINANCING CAMPAIGNS
LESSON 3

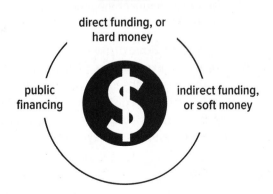

direct funding, or hard money

public financing

indirect funding, or soft money

VOTING
LESSON 4

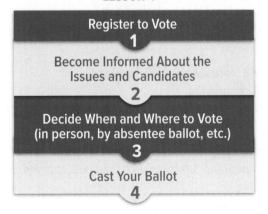

Register to Vote
1

Become Informed About the Issues and Candidates
2

Decide When and Where to Vote (in person, by absentee ballot, etc.)
3

Cast Your Ballot
4

Directions: On a separate sheet of paper, answer the questions below. Make sure you read carefully and answer all parts of the questions.

Lesson Review

Lesson 1

1 *Explaining* How did the Voting Rights Act of 1965 affect African Americans?

2 *Identifying* Which group of Americans gained the right to vote under the Nineteenth Amendment? The Twenty-sixth Amendment?

Lesson 2

3 *Contrasting* How are a popular referendum, a legislative referendum, and an initiative different?

4 *Explaining* Why is voter turnout so low? Suggest at least three ways of increasing it.

Lesson 3

5 *Describing* What are some common propaganda techniques? Which ones do you think are most effective?

6 *Differentiating* How are direct sources of campaign funding different from indirect sources?

Lesson 4

7 *Specifying* What two qualifications does every state require to vote?

8 *Drawing Conclusions* Why do you think it is important in a democracy that all eligible voters vote?

ANSWERING THE ESSENTIAL QUESTIONS

Review your answers to the introductory questions at the beginning of each lesson. Then answer the Essential Questions based on what you learned in the chapter. Have your answers changed?

9 *Identifying Central Issues* Who should have the right to vote in a democracy?

10 *Synthesizing* What factors influence voters and election campaigns?

11 *Sequencing* What are the key steps in voting?

DBQ Interpreting Political Cartoons

Use the political cartoon to answer the following questions.

12 *Interpreting* What does the ladder represent, and why is one step in the ladder drawn larger than others?

13 *Drawing Conclusions* What is this cartoon saying about the roles of women in society?

Critical Thinking

14 *Defending* Election Day was set during a very different time in our history. Do you think that Election Day should be on a Tuesday? Why or why not? If not, what day or days would you propose? Explain your reasons.

15 *Drawing Inferences* Sometimes presidential candidates who qualify to receive campaign funds from the federal government choose not to accept this money. Why do you think this is so?

16 *Identifying Central Issues* Write instructions for a friend who is about to vote for president for the first time. How should your friend research the candidates? What should your friend consider as he or she decides whom to vote for?

Need Extra Help?

If You've Missed Question	**1**	**2**	**3**	**4**	**5**	**6**	**7**	**8**	**9**	**10**	**11**	**12**	**13**	**14**	**15**	**16**
Go to page	542	544	547	550	553	557	560	562	541	548	560	543	543	550	557	548

Directions: On a separate sheet of paper, answer the questions below. Make sure you read carefully and answer all parts of the questions.

DBQ Analyzing Primary Sources

Read the excerpts and answer the questions that follow.

Anne Moody participated in the Freedom Summer of 1964.

PRIMARY SOURCE

"Sometimes out of twenty or twenty-five [African Americans] who went to register, only one or two would pass the test. Some of them were flunked because they used a title (Mr. or Mrs.) on the application blank; others because they didn't. And most failed to interpret a section of the Mississippi constitution to the satisfaction of Foote Campbell, the Madison County circuit clerk."

—Anne Moody, *Coming of Age in Mississippi*, 1968

17 *Drawing Inferences* How was the determination made as to whether someone met the requirements to register?

18 *Analyzing* Based on this account, why was it difficult for African Americans to register to vote?

PRIMARY SOURCE

"18. WRITE AND COPY IN THE SPACE BELOW SECTION— OF THE CONSTITUTION OF MISSISSIPPI [Instruction to registrar: You will designate the section of the Constitution and point out same to applicant]:

19. WRITE IN THE SPACE BELOW A REASONABLE INTERPRETATION (THE MEANING) OF THE SECTION OF THE CONSTITUTION OF MISSISSIPPI WHICH YOU HAVE JUST COPIED:"

—*Mississippi Voter Application & Literacy Test*, 1955

19 *Analyzing Historical Documents* How might these questions be used to discriminate against African American voters?

Social Studies Skills

Use the table to answer questions 20 and 21.

Year	Turnout	Year	Turnout
1964	61.4%	1988	50.3%
1968	60.7%	1992	55.2%
1972	55.1%	1996	49.0%
1976	53.6%	2000	50.3%
1980	52.8%	2004	55.7%
1984	53.3%	2008	57.1%

SOURCE: Statistical Abstract of the United States, 2012

20 *Using Tables* In which election year shown in the table was voter turnout highest? What was the percentage difference between the highest and lowest turnout?

21 *Understanding Relationships Among Events* Shortly before the 2008 election, the economy slipped into a deep recession. Many people lost their jobs and homes. How might this situation help explain the change in voter turnout from the previous election? Explain why.

22 *Creating a Chart* Create a graphic organizer that explains which categories of people are and are not allowed to vote in your state today. Consider any relevant facts such as age, length of residence, mental health, felony status.

23 *Sequencing* Research and create a time line of some major events in the woman suffrage movement in the United States. Include events from the mid-1800s to passage of the Nineteenth Amendment. Write a brief description of each event on the time line.

Research and Presentation

24 *Posing Questions* Write three questions that you would like to ask about the mechanics of voting at the polls on Election Day. Then ask an adult these questions. Prepare to share the answers in a class discussion.

25 *Exploring Issues* After the Supreme Court's decision in *Shelby Co*. v. *Holder* (2013), some states passed stricter voter identification laws. Research the kinds of identification that states now require at the polls. Find out if student IDs are acceptable under the new laws. As you research, take notes on the arguments both for and against the new voter ID requirements. Decide how you stand on the issue and prepare for a class debate.

26 *Geography Skills* How have recent changes in the U.S. population affected voting patterns? Create a multimedia presentation showing your results. You may want to include maps and graphs in your presentation.

Need Extra Help?

If You've Missed Question	**17**	**18**	**19**	**20**	**21**	**22**	**23**	**24**	**25**	**26**
Go to page	541	541	541	550	550	544	543	563	551	550

Public Opinion and Interest Groups

networks
www.connected.mcgraw-hill.com
There's More Online about public opinion and interest groups.

CHAPTER 19

ESSENTIAL QUESTIONS

- In what ways can public opinion affect government policy?
- How do special interest groups seek to influence U.S. public policy?

▲ Demonstrators hope to affect public policy by marching through Washington, D.C., during a rally.

Erkan Avci/Anadolu Agency/Getty Images

COLLABORATION & CIVIL SOCIETY

Since its earliest days as a nation, the United States has benefited from an active civil society. Civil society is made up of all the organizations and associations that people join voluntarily—from clubs and amateur sports groups to charitable organizations and advocacy groups. Why is civil society important in a democracy? How could one prepare to take part in civil society? Analyze the sources to find out.

PRIMARY SOURCE A

President Barack Obama began his career working with a civil society organization dedicated to giving poor communities in Chicago a voice. His commitment to that kind of grassroots group remained strong after he began working in government.

"... it is my firm belief that a country's strength ultimately comes from its people and that as important as government is—and laws—what makes a country democratic and effective in delivering prosperity and security and hope to people is when they've got an active, thriving civil society. ..."

—Barack Obama, "Remarks by the President to Civil Society Leaders," November 12, 2013

PRIMARY SOURCE B

Research conducted by the National Conference on Citizenship in 2012 found that communities with better civic health weathered the recent recession better than other communities. They described the causes:

"When civic health is higher, people seem to have more affection and optimism for their own communities and put more trust in their neighbors. When investors, employers, and consumers feel greater commitment to the places they live, they may be more likely to make economic decisions that generate or protect local jobs. Furthermore, being engaged with fellow citizens and participating with nonprofits can build local allegiance that makes individuals more likely to spend, invest, collaborate, and address problems in their own communities. These small choices can have ripple effects for a community's ability to remain strong during a crisis."

—National Conference on Citizenship, *Civic Health and Unemployment II: The Case Builds*, 2012

SECONDARY SOURCE C

Volunteering in America

64.3 million volunteers in **2011** an **increase** of **1.5 million** from **2010**

Americans **volunteered 8 billion** hours, with an economic **value** of **$171** billion

More than **1/3** of all **Americans** participated in a **civic, religious,** or **school group**

Source: Corporation for National & Community Service, 2012

PRIMARY SOURCE D

Professor Peter Levine believes our civil society, and by association, our democracy, is strongest when people from a variety of backgrounds participate.

"The business leader who enters public debates having struggled to meet a payroll while paying taxes speaks from authentic experience. So does the soup kitchen volunteer who has faced a long line of homeless people with insufficient welfare benefits. Civil society functions best when both kinds of people (and many others) bring their experience into a common conversation and then take what they learn from discussions back to their work, in an iterative cycle."

—Peter Levine, "Education in a Civil Society," 2012

SECONDARY SOURCE F

Nearly every U.S. state has at least one nonprofit service center to help civil society organizations be more successful. Here are some of the skills the Center for Participatory Change in North Carolina helps leaders of civil society organizations develop:

- Fundraising
- Public speaking
- Running a good meeting
- Facilitating workshops effectively
- Organizational planning
- Setting goals and evaluating projects

SOURCE: Center for Participatory Change, 2013

PRIMARY SOURCE E

The U.S. Department of State publishes *The NGO Handbook* to help people starting non-governmental organizations (NGOs) in countries around the world. The Handbook's advice applies equally well to civil society groups in the United States.

"Starting an NGO requires many kinds of support. You need volunteers, people who provide resources and advocates who believe in your efforts. Launching projects and activities demands multiple skills and forms of support. You need to make plans, reach out to the community, recruit volunteers, raise funds, monitor projects and evaluate results. Sustaining an NGO over time demands an even greater level of commitment, skills, systems, support and resources."

—U.S. State Department, *The NGO Handbook*

DBQ DOCUMENT-BASED QUESTIONS

1. **Analyzing** According to the sources, why are civil society organizations good for communities? Do you think Americans are adequately involved in groups, clubs, and organizations?

2. **Interpreting** According to Professor Levine, why is broad community participation good for civil society organizations? What data would you need to evaluate how diverse civil society groups are?

3. **Identifying** Use sources E and F to start a list of skills necessary to be a good member or leader of a civil society organization. What additional skills might leaders need?

WHAT WILL YOU DO?

What civil society organizations do you belong to? What organizations do you think you will join in the future? Write a letter to yourself, outlining the skills you need to develop to be an effective member of a civil society organization—or even a leader. Plan to read the letter a year from now to assess the progress you have made.

EXPLORE the interactive version of the analyzing primary sources feature on Networks.

Interact with these digital assets and others in lesson 1

✓ **INTERACTIVE IMAGE**
The Influence of Peer Groups

✓ **SELF-CHECK QUIZ**

✓ **SLIDE SHOW**
Waiting in Line

✓ **VIDEO**
Congressional Approval Rating

netw⊕rks
TRY IT YOURSELF ONLINE

LESSON 1
Shaping Public Opinion

Reading Help Desk

Academic Vocabulary

- **factor**
- **communicate**

Content Vocabulary

- **political socialization**
- **peer group**
- **mass media**
- **political culture**
- **political efficacy**
- **interest group**
- **public opinion**

TAKING NOTES:

Integration of Knowledge and Ideas

LISTING Create a web diagram similar to the one below. In each of the smaller circles, list examples of factors that influence an individual's political attitudes.

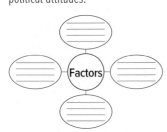

ESSENTIAL QUESTION

In what ways can public opinion affect government policy?

Think about two or three current issues on which you have strong views. Which of the following factors helped to shape your views on these issues? Give each factor a score from 1 to 5, with 1 representing no influence and 5 representing a major influence.

___ Views of your family

___ Views of your friends

___ Views of influential adults you know well

___ What you learned about the issues in your classes or through your own research

___ Views of government leaders

___ Personal experience with the issues

___ Personal philosophy about government

___ Religious beliefs

___ Media

___ Information or advertising by interest groups

Overall, which of these factors do you think is the biggest influence on your opinions about political issues? How might other people answer differently? Explain.

Public Opinion and Democracy

GUIDING QUESTION *Why is being responsive to public opinion important in a democracy?*

The Framers of the Constitution sought to create a representative democracy that would meet two goals. The first was to provide for popular rule—to give the people an active voice in government. The people were supposed to have control over the lawmakers who represented them. The Framers' second goal was to insulate government from the shifting whims of an ill-informed public.

The system the Framers created has worked well. Research shows that the government is responsive to public opinion—the wishes of the people. At the same time, public opinion is not the only influence on public policy. Interest groups, political parties, the mass media, government institutions, and activists and public officials themselves also help shape policy. Because public opinion does influence government, it is important for citizens and public officials alike to understand how opinions are formed.

✓ READING PROGRESS CHECK

Paraphrasing In your own words, what were the two goals the Framers of the Constitution wanted to meet by creating a representative democracy?

Political Socialization

GUIDING QUESTION *What factors influence an individual's political attitudes?*

Individuals learn their political beliefs and attitudes through a complex process called **political socialization**. This process begins early in life, continues throughout adulthood, and has a major influence on opinion formation.

Family and Home Influence Political socialization begins within the family. Children learn many of their early political opinions from their parents. In most cases, the political party of the parents becomes the party of their children. A study of high school seniors showed that only a small minority differed in party loyalty from their parents. As adults, more than two-thirds of all voters continue to favor the political party their parents supported.

Schools and Peer Groups School also plays an important part in the political socialization process. In the United States, all students learn about their nation, its history, and its political system. Civic values are also learned in school clubs and through school rules and regulations.

An individual's close friends, religious group, clubs, and work groups—called **peer groups**—are yet another factor in the political socialization process. A person's peer groups often influence and shape opinions. For example, a member of a labor union whose closest friends belong to the same union is likely to have political opinions similar to theirs.

Personal Experiences Individuals' personal experiences—the way they interact with the political and economic systems—also influence their political views. Because economic and social statuses affect these experiences, they play a role in political socialization. Whether a person is young or old, rich or poor, rural or urban, from the East Coast or from the South, African American or white, or male or female may affect personal political opinions.

The Mass Media The Internet, television, radio, newspapers, magazines, movies, and books—the **mass media**—play an important role in political socialization. Both the Internet and television provide political information and images that can directly influence political attitudes. For example, broadcasts of a rally against a Supreme Court decision or videos on the Internet of a riot outside an American embassy can help shape viewers' opinions.

political socialization a process by which individuals learn their political beliefs and attitudes from family, school, friends, coworkers, and other sources

peer group an individual's close friends, religious group, clubs, and work groups

mass media all the means for communicating information to the general public, such as newspapers, magazines, radio, television, and the Internet

An individual's peer groups are an important factor in the process of political socialization. This photograph shows young supporters of Representative Michelle Bachmann at a straw poll at Iowa State University in 2011.

▼ CRITICAL THINKING
Speculating Which factors of political socialization do you think most shape young people's views on issues that affect them?

Chip Somodevilla/Getty Images News/Getty Images

Movies, recordings, novels, and television entertainment also affect opinions. Showing police as heroes or as criminals, for example, can shape attitudes toward authority. The way the media depict different groups—men, women, African Americans, Asian Americans, Latinos, or immigrants—can discredit or reinforce stereotypes.

Other Influences Government leaders, interest groups, and religious organizations also play important roles in political socialization. The president especially has a tremendous influence on people's opinions. The news media provides almost continuous reports on the president's activities and policy proposals. The president also tries to reach the American people directly through e-mail and social networking communications.

Like the president, members of Congress try to influence opinions. They frequently go to their home states or home districts to talk to their constituents. Many legislators send newsletters or write personal letters to voters. They also appear on television programs and give news interviews on timely issues. Lawmakers who come across as sincere, personable, and intelligent are particularly effective in influencing opinions on major issues. At the state and local levels, lawmakers also use the media to gain public support for their views.

At the same time, interest groups try to shape public opinion. If an interest group can win enough support, public opinion might pressure legislators to accept the group's goals. Churches, synagogues, mosques, and other religious organizations also affect people's political opinions.

✔ **READING PROGRESS CHECK**

Speculating Why does mass media have a greater impact on political socialization today than at any other time in history?

Political Culture

GUIDING QUESTION *In what ways does America's political culture influence public opinion?*

Political socialization is not just a process of developing one's views on political issues. It is also a process of absorbing the political culture of one's nation. A **political culture** is a set of basic values and beliefs about a nation and its government that most citizens share. For example, one of the key elements of American political culture is a shared belief in liberty and freedom, as reflected in many patriotic songs, including "America," which is also known as "My Country 'Tis of Thee":

❝❝ **PRIMARY SOURCE**

My country, 'tis of thee,

Sweet land of liberty,

Of thee I sing;

Land where my fathers died,

Land of the pilgrims' pride,

From every mountainside

Let freedom ring."

—"America," Samuel F. Smith

Additional examples of widely shared political values include support for the Constitution and Bill of Rights, commitment to the idea of political equality, belief in the value of private property, and an emphasis on individual achievement. The American political culture helps shape public opinion in the United States in two ways.

political culture a set of basic values and beliefs about a nation and its government that most citizens share

America's unique political culture sets the boundaries within which citizens develop and express their opinions. This poster was created in the late 1930s for the Works Progress Administration, a government program.

▼ CRITICAL THINKING

1. *Analyzing Primary Sources* Make a list of adjectives and phrases that come to your mind as you analyze the poster. What political values does it promote? Do you share those values?

2. *Making Connections* Find a modern-day stamp, song, flag, or poster that represents the same values. Or, create one of your own. Why do you think the government creates images like these? Do you think they shape public opinion? Explain your reasons.

The political culture sets the general boundaries within which citizens develop and express their opinions. For example, Americans will disagree over how much the federal government should regulate the airline industry. Very few Americans, however, would urge that government eliminate regulations altogether or, conversely, that it take over and run the industry.

A nation's political culture also influences how its citizens interpret what they see and hear every day—the political culture colors how Americans see the world. An American citizen and a Russian citizen probably would interpret the same event quite differently. If shown a photo of people in line outside a grocery store, the Russian citizen might think there was a food shortage, but an American citizen might conclude there was a sale.

☑ **READING PROGRESS CHECK**

Identifying What are some examples of political values or viewpoints widely shared by American citizens?

Political Efficacy

GUIDING QUESTION *What factors influence an individual's political actions?*

Most people are unaware that political socialization occurs in their lives because it is a slow process that begins in childhood and continues over a lifetime. People may not realize that this socialization directly affects their opinions on public issues, as well as their feelings of political efficacy.

Political efficacy refers to a person's belief that he or she can have an impact on government and policy. Some people are socialized to believe that they cannot impact the system. Others are brought up to believe that their actions can be effective and lead to changes that are important to them. Some people join **interest groups**—groups of people who share common goals and organize to influence government and policy—because they believe being part of a group will increase their political efficacy.

> **EXPLORING THE ESSENTIAL QUESTION**
>
> **Making Connections** Do you believe you can be effective in influencing government? Rate your feelings of political efficacy on a scale of 1 to 5, with 1 being very low and 5 being very high. Write your rating on a piece of paper and hold it up so other students can see it. Pair up with a student whose rating is different from yours. With your partner, discuss why each of you chose the rating that you did and what you could do to become more confident that you can make a difference. Based on your conversation, what aspects of political socialization seem to be most significant in determining feelings of political efficacy?

Feelings of political efficacy are vital in a democracy. Without citizen participation, democracies would be unable to realize the concept of government "of the people, by the people, and for the people."

☑ **READING PROGRESS CHECK**

Explaining Why is it important for citizens of a democracy to act upon their feelings of political efficacy?

Igor Gavrilov/Time Life Pictures/Getty Images

A nation's political culture influences how its citizens see the world. For example, an American citizen and a Russian citizen may interpret the same event quite differently.

▲ CRITICAL THINKING

Analyzing Visuals How might an American interpret the photo of Russian people in line? Think about what kinds of lines Americans participate in. How would a Russian interpret them?

political efficacy a person's belief that he or she can have an impact on government and policy

interest group a group of people who share a common goal and organize to influence government and policy

The Nature of Public Opinion

GUIDING QUESTION *What is public opinion?*

People's opinions emerge as part of the process of political socialization. Most Americans have opinions or preferences about many matters that affect their lives. These range from preferences about the best baseball players to favorite television programs. Few such opinions, however, have much effect on government and public policy. Yet one form of opinion, called public opinion, has an enormous influence on government. **Public opinion** refers to the ideas and attitudes that a significant number of Americans hold about government and political issues. Three **factors** describe the nature of public opinion: diversity, communication, and significant numbers.

public opinion the ideas and attitudes that a significant number of Americans hold about government and political issues

factor part of a product or concept

communicate to convey information; to make known

Diversity Public opinion is varied. In a nation as vast as the United States, it is unlikely that all people will think the same way about any political issue. Because of our nation's history and the diversity of American society, different groups of people hold different opinions on almost every issue.

Communication People's ideas and attitudes must in some way be expressed and **communicated** to government. Unless Americans make their opinions on important issues clear, public officials will not know what people are thinking. Accordingly, officials will not be able to weigh public opinion when making decisions. Interest groups communicate the opinions of many individuals. Officials also rely on public opinion polls, letters and e-mails from constituents, and social networking to learn what people are thinking.

Significant Numbers The phrase "a significant number of Americans" in the definition of public opinion means that one or a few people's ideas do not constitute public opinion. Public opinion is the aggregate or combination of many people's views. Enough people—significant numbers—must hold a particular opinion to make government officials listen to them.

☑ **READING PROGRESS CHECK**

Making Inferences If public officials were unable to communicate with the American people, what might they use as a basis for making policy decisions?

LESSON 1 REVIEW

Reviewing Vocabulary
1. *Summarizing* What is political socialization and how might it influence a citizen's participation in the democratic process?

Using Your Graphic Organizer
2. *Determining Importance* Of the factors you listed in your web diagram, which do you think has the most powerful influence on political socialization? Explain your answer.

Answering the Guiding Questions
3. *Explaining* Why is being responsive to public opinion important in a democracy?

4. *Describing* What factors influence an individual's political attitudes?

5. *Determining Cause and Effect* In what ways does America's political culture influence public opinion?

6. *Describing* What factors influence an individual's political actions?

7. *Defining* What is public opinion?

Writing About Government
8. *Informative/Explanatory* Use library resources or the Internet to find examples of situations in which public opinion has caused an elected official to change his or her position on an issue. Present your findings in the form of a poster along with a written summary to your classmates.

Interact with these digital assets and others in lesson 2

✓ **INTERACTIVE CHART**
Analyzing Polls and Poll Data

✓ **INTERACTIVE IMAGE**
Straw Poll in Iowa

✓ **SLIDE SHOW**
Interpreting Opinion Polls

✓ **VIDEO**
Exit Polling

netw🌐rks
TRY IT YOURSELF ONLINE

LESSON 2
Measuring Public Opinion

Reading Help Desk

Academic Vocabulary

- indication
- variation

Content Vocabulary

- straw poll
- biased sample
- universe
- representative sample
- random sampling
- sampling error
- push polling
- exit poll

TAKING NOTES:

Integration of Knowledge and Ideas

ORGANIZING Create a table similar to the one below. Organize information from the lesson by recording it in the appropriate section of the table.

Measuring Public Opinion	
Nonscientific Methods	**Scientific Methods**

In what ways can public opinion affect government policy?

"What I want," Abraham Lincoln once declared, "is to get done what the people desire to have done, and the question for me is how to find that out exactly." Lincoln, of course, did not have access to the information sources currently available to the president and other leaders. With television, radio, and the Internet, public officials today can gain perspectives on the opinions of ordinary citizens quickly and efficiently.

The benefits are obvious. Are there any disadvantages to having so many opinions available to policymakers? Think about the question both from a citizen's perspective and a policymaker's viewpoint.

Nonscientific Methods

GUIDING QUESTION *What nonscientific methods are commonly used to gauge public opinion?*

Americans express their opinions at the ballot box. Between elections, officials want to know what the public is thinking. Over the years, the methods and technology used to access and tabulate public opinion have changed. Elected officials use a number of sources or channels to stay in touch with public opinion:

- political parties and interest groups,
- mass media,
- letters and e-mails or faxes,
- straw polls, and
- political websites, social networking sites, and blogs.

Party Organizations Party organizations have long been a reliable source of information about public opinion. In the past, party officials were in close touch with voters in their hometowns, cities, counties, and states. Local party leaders could provide information to national leaders. Interest groups, too, provide elected officials with an easy way to find out about the opinions of concerned citizens. Interest groups, however, often represent the attitudes of a vocal minority concerned with specific issues such as gun control, health care, or auto safety. They are not a good measure of broader public opinion.

Mass Media The mass media often reflect public attitudes fairly well because they speak to a broad audience. Newspapers, magazines, and television and radio programs reflect the interests of the public. For example, if a news program gets higher audience ratings by covering a certain issue or if a particular news story goes viral, those are **indications** of strong public interest in those issues. Elected officials keep an eye on headlines, magazine cover stories, editorials, radio talk shows, the "lead story" on television newscasts, and which news goes viral on the Internet.

These sources of information, however, may give a distorted view of public opinion. The mass media's focus on news that has visual appeal or shock value, such as stories about violent crime, distorts the public perception of reality. People who watch television news as their only source of news, for example, tend to be more pessimistic about the nation than those who also use other sources for information.

Constituent Views One time-honored way that officials gauge public opinion is by the volume of letters, e-mails, calls, and faxes they receive on different issues. The first major letter-writing campaign convinced George Washington to seek a second term as president in 1792. Letter writing increases in times of national crisis when major government decisions are being made. The president might even request that the public contact lawmakers to indicate support for a policy. Lawmakers may do the same. Today, interest groups often stage massive e-mail campaigns, where people can sign up online to send a standardized e-mail to their elected officials. Many officials give such letters less attention than personal letters from constituents. In general, people are more likely to contact legislators by e-mail than by written letter. This allows citizens to react almost immediately on an issue; legislators, too, can use electronic means to quickly respond to citizen concerns via Twitter, Facebook, or other social networking sites.

indication something that tells or points out, such as a sign or symbol

Because the people who take the poll self-select, straw polls are always a biased sample of the population.

▼ CRITICAL THINKING
Assessing Is this a scientific, unbiased measure of opinion? Why or why not?

Chip Somodevilla/Getty Images News/Getty Images

C·I·V·I·C PARTICIPATION IN A DIGITAL AGE

Straw Polls

ProCon.org is a website that provides opposing views on controversial issues. It also takes straw polls on the issues. Go to ProCon.org (http://www.procon.org/) and select an issue that interests you. Read some of the arguments on both sides of the issue and then cast your vote (look for the link for "comments").

Take a closer look at the reasons people who voted in the straw poll gave for their votes. Are their reasons clear? Do they provide evidence to support their views? Do they maintain a civil tone?

EXPLORING THE ESSENTIAL QUESTION

Evaluating Do you think online straw polls and discussions among people who vote in these polls are a good source for gauging public opinion? Explain your reasons.

Straw Polls Another method of gauging opinion is the **straw poll**. This is an unscientific attempt to measure public opinion. Newspapers, TV shows, radio stations, and websites ask their audiences to vote on different questions—"Should the mayor run for reelection?"—and publish the results. Members of Congress often send their constituents questionnaires. Straw polls do not use scientific procedures to choose the respondents. Instead, the people who respond to a straw poll have chosen to respond voluntarily. Because the people who take the poll self-select, straw polls are always a **biased sample** of the population.

Finally, elected officials and their staff keep track of opinions about current issues expressed on political websites and blogs, as well as social networking sites. Reviewing the discussions on such sites helps officials gauge what an important segment of the public thinks about issues and can alert leaders to emerging problems that have yet to be covered by the traditional mass media.

> **straw poll** an unscientific attempt to measure public opinion

> **biased sample** in polling, a group that does not accurately represent the larger population

☑ **READING PROGRESS CHECK**

Identifying What media resources could a citizen use to react very quickly to an issue or event?

Scientific Polling

GUIDING QUESTION *How does the process of scientific polling work?*

Almost everyone involved in politics today uses scientific polls to measure public opinion. Scientific polling involves three basic steps: selecting a sample of the group to be questioned, presenting carefully worded questions to the individuals in the sample, and interpreting the results.

Sampling In conducting polls, the group of people to be studied is called the **universe**. A universe might be all the seniors in a particular high school, all the people in Texas, or all women in the United States. It is not possible to actually interview every Texan or every woman in the United States,

> **universe** the group of people that is to be studied

representative sample a small group of people who are typical of the larger group being studied

so pollsters question a **representative sample**, a small group of people who are typical of that universe.

Most pollsters are able to use samples of only 1,200 to 1,500 adults to measure the opinions of all adults in the United States, which is more than 240 million people. Such a small group is representative because pollsters use **random sampling**, a technique in which everyone in that universe has an equal chance of being selected.

random sampling a technique in which everyone in a group has an equal chance of being selected

Telephone interviews are used in many national polls. To create a random sample, pollsters use random digit dialing: They select an area code and the first three local digits. Then a computer randomly chooses and dials the last four digits. The drawbacks to telephone interviews are that pollsters might fail to reach the person being called and that people might refuse to answer the questions. The rapidly growing use of cell phones has complicated these procedures and, according to some experts, has made such polls less reliable.

sampling error a measurement of how much the sample results might differ from the sample universe

A **sampling error** is a measurement of how much the sample results might differ from the sample universe. Sampling error decreases as the sample size becomes larger. If a poll says that 65 percent of Americans favor tougher pollution laws, with a 3 percent sampling error, that means between 62 and 68 percent of the entire population favor such laws.

variation difference; change

At times, pollsters adjust or weight the results of a poll to overcome defects in sampling. Pollsters may adjust a poll to take into account **variations** in race, gender, age, or education. For example, if pollsters found that not enough Americans over the age of 65 were interviewed, they might give extra weight to the opinions of the senior citizens who were interviewed.

PARTICIPATING
(IN) Your Government

Gauging Popular Opinion Through Polls

Poll results help government officials and party leaders develop policy. Work with two or three other students to develop and conduct a poll about an issue that is important to you.

1. Choose an issue that is important in your state. Do some research to identify details about the issue that will help you frame your questions.

2. Develop eight to ten questions to gauge public opinion in your community. Make sure your questions are clearly worded and will produce results you can easily interpret.

3. Discuss the best way to get a random sampling of opinions in your community. Should you interview people in person at a local supermarket or park? Should you randomly select phone numbers from the community?

4. Conduct the poll, tally the results, and express your findings in a bar graph that shows the questions along the horizontal axis and the number of each type of response along the vertical axis.

5. Make some conclusions about public opinion regarding your chosen issue and share them with the class.

Asking Questions The way a question is phrased can greatly influence people's responses and, in turn, poll results. For example, in 1971 the Gallup Poll asked whether people favored a proposal "to bring home all American troops from Vietnam before the end of the year." Two-thirds of those polled answered "yes." Then the Gallup Poll asked the question differently: "Do you agree or disagree with a proposal to withdraw all U.S. troops by the end of the year regardless of what happens there [in Vietnam] after U.S. troops leave?" When the question was worded this way, fewer than half the respondents agreed.

First, poll questions must be clearly worded so there is no confusion. Each question should ask only one thing; questions that include too many elements produce results that are hard to interpret. For example, a poll might include the question "Do you think the current tax laws are fair and easy to understand?" If the respondent answers "no," the pollster does not know whether the respondent thinks the tax code is unfair, hard to understand, or both.

Polling questions take many forms. In a common type of question, the pollster reads a statement such as "I agree with the president's views about raising taxes on wealthy people." The pollster then asks the respondent to choose one of the following responses: strongly agree, disagree, strongly disagree, or no answer.

Interpreting Results Scientific polling has improved since its first use in the 1930s. Polling is never completely accurate, however. Pollsters cannot be sure that the people they are interviewing are being honest. There may also be unanticipated sampling errors. Still, major polling organizations have learned how to conduct polls that are generally reliable within a few percentage points.

When one interprets a poll, it is important to know the sampling error. During the 1976 presidential race, for example, one poll said Jimmy Carter was behind Gerald Ford by 48 percent to 49 percent. With a sampling error of plus or minus 3 percent, Carter could have been ahead. As it turned out, Carter won the election. Similarly, in the 2012 presidential election, a Gallup poll conducted the night before the election showed Romney ahead by a single percentage point, but Obama ultimately won the election by close to 4 percentage points.

Other important factors in interpreting poll results are who paid for or sponsored the poll, who responded, and how well the questions were written. Sponsors of polls might ask the pollsters to focus on surveying people with a particular bias. For example, a poll of dog owners is likely to result in less favorable opinions of leash laws than a poll of the general population. Sometimes, political parties or interest groups intentionally write questions that they hope will produce the results they want. For example, respondents might be asked: "If you knew that Candidate X, who is running for mayor, had 72 unpaid parking tickets, would that change your opinion of the candidate?" When the wording of questions "push" respondents toward a particular answer or view, it is called **"push polling."** Push polls are not regarded as legitimate polls by reputable pollsters. However, the results of push polls are often presented as if the polls were legitimate. Thus, it is important to look behind results to the questions and sponsor.

push polling method of polling in which the wording of questions "push" respondents toward a particular answer or view

☑ **READING PROGRESS CHECK**

Listing What are the three basic steps involved in scientific polling?

INTERPRETING **OPINION POLLS**

Read the information about the two hypothetical public opinion polls and then answer the questions that follow.

Poll No. 1: Public Opinion About Priorities for Congress

Which ONE of the following do you think is the most important thing for Congress to concentrate on right now: the economy, the federal budget deficit, health care, education, illegal immigration, the environment, abortion, or something else?

The economy	40%
The federal budget deficit	16%
Health care	15%
Education	12%
Illegal immigration	8%
The environment	3%
Abortion	2%
Something else	2%
Unsure/No answer	2%

This poll sampled 1,036 adults nationwide and had a margin of error of ± 3.

Poll No. 2: Public Opinion About Candidate X

Overall, do you have a favorable or unfavorable impression of Candidate X?

Favorable	26%
Unfavorable	25%
No opinion	49%

This poll sampled 1,010 adults nationwide and had a margin of error of ± 3.5.

CRITICAL THINKING

Analyze the information from the public opinion polls and answer these critical thinking questions.

a. ***Interpreting Information*** Look at the question asked in the first poll. Does this give you a complete picture of the issues that concern Americans? Why or why not? What can you learn from the first poll?

b. ***Drawing Inferences*** What information does the second poll give you? What challenges might Candidate X face?

c. ***Applying*** Imagine Candidate X has hired you to work on her new campaign. Using this polling data as a guide, develop a slogan and a script for a television advertisement for the candidate.

Uses of Polling Data

GUIDING QUESTION *How do public officials and the media use polling data?*

Public officials use polls in a variety of ways. Polls that show constituents hold strong views on one side of an issue may prompt a lawmaker to introduce a bill on the issue or may sway a lawmaker's vote on a related bill. Candidates use polls to help them decide where to campaign and where to advertise most heavily. Poll results may also help candidates tailor their messages to appeal directly to voters' specific needs and concerns.

Considering public opinion when making decisions is a good idea, but government officials can go too far in their use of polling data. For example, if lawmakers change positions as public opinion changes, they may be criticized for waffling—failing to have any principles that guide their work. Similarly, a presidential candidate will be criticized if his or her message changes too much from place to place in response to polling data.

The media also use polling data. They report poll results as news, especially during election season. Citizens who enjoy following the campaigns in the same way they follow sports teams closely track poll results in the months leading up to major elections. While other media consumers may complain about the constant reporting of poll results, their own views might be shaped by what they see and hear via the media. Some citizens may even decide not to vote if polls indicate that one candidate has an insurmountable lead.

Exit polls involve interviewing voters as they leave the polling place and asking them for whom they voted. In presidential elections, the television networks have used exit polls to predict who has won a particular state. Often, these projections are made before the polls close in western states. If the projections suggest that one candidate is well on the way to victory, voters in the West may decide not to vote. When some projections based on exit polls turn out to be wrong, as they were in 2000, criticism of the media's use of exit polls increases.

exit poll polling that involves interviewing voters as they leave the polling place and asking them for whom they voted

☑ **READING PROGRESS CHECK**

Summarizing How might a political candidate use polling data during his or her campaign?

LESSON 2 REVIEW

Reviewing Vocabulary
1. *Explaining* Why are straw polls always a biased sample of the population?

Using Your Graphic Organizer
2. *Expressing* Of all the polling methods listed in your table, which do you believe to be the most accurate and effective way to measure public opinion?

Answering the Guiding Questions
3. *Summarizing* What nonscientific methods are commonly used to gauge public opinion?

4. *Explaining* How does the process of scientific polling work?

5. *Analyzing* How do public officials and the media use polling data?

Writing About Government
6. *Informative/Explanatory* Find a public opinion poll in a newspaper or newsmagazine. Analyze the poll by focusing on the following questions: How many people were contacted? Does the poll include a random or representative sampling? What is the sampling error? Are the questions presented in an unbiased and effective way? Present your answers in a well-organized informative paragraph.

Interact with these digital
assets and others in lesson 3

✓ **INTERACTIVE IMAGE**
   Interest Groups

✓ **PARTICIPATING IN YOUR GOVERNMENT**
   Interviewing

✓ **SELF-CHECK QUIZ**

✓ **VIDEO**
   Influencing Public Policy

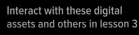
netw⊙rks
TRY IT YOURSELF ONLINE

ReadingHelp Desk

Academic Vocabulary

- **sufficient**
- **commodity**

Content Vocabulary

- **interest group**
- **civil society**
- **public interest group**

TAKING NOTES:

Key Ideas and Details

CATEGORIZING Use the graphic organizer to categorize and take notes about different interest groups.

Types of Interest Groups	Description	Examples

LESSON 3
Interest Groups and Their Roles

ESSENTIAL QUESTION

How do special interest groups seek to influence U.S. public policy?

Make a list of all the formal groups to which you belong. (For example, if you play soccer, include your soccer team but not the friends you sometimes kick a ball around with.) Now think of a way of categorizing these groups. For example, some groups might be school-related, while others might be community- or faith-based.

This lesson looks at a particular kind of group called an *interest group*—a group of people who share common goals and organize to influence government and policy.

- Are any of the groups to which you belong interest groups?

- If so, what policies do they want to influence? If not, can you think of a group in your community that could be classified as an interest group?

- What policies does this group want to influence?

Power of Interest Groups

GUIDING QUESTION *What are interest groups and are they an effective way for American citizens to participate in the political process?*

Mothers Against Drunk Driving, Associated Builders and Contractors, the Club for Growth, the Sierra Club, and the League of Women Voters— these are just a few of the countless interest groups in the United States that seek to influence public policy. An **interest group** is a group of people who share common goals and organize to influence government. Why do people join interest groups? Often they do so to increase their political efficacy; by joining with other like-minded individuals, they believe they can have a greater impact on government policy. Interest groups allow Americans to be represented according to their economic, social, or occupational interests.

Interest groups are an important component of American **civil society**. This is the network of voluntary associations that exist outside of government in any free society. These associations can include gardening clubs, a local church, organizations like the American Red Cross, and

584

interest groups such as the National Rifle Association. Private citizens—not government officials—organize and run such groups.

Interest groups have long been a feature of American political life, but many early leaders in the United States believed that interest groups could make governing difficult. In *The Federalist* No. 10, James Madison referred to "factions" as groups of people who are united to promote special interests that were "adverse to the rights of other citizens, or to the permanent and aggregate interests of the community." Madison believed that the Constitution would be a **sufficient** safeguard against the potential abuses of these interest groups. Whether he was right is a question still debated today.

Another view of the role of interest groups was expressed by Alexis de Tocqueville, a French visitor to the United States around 1830. In his classic book *Democracy in America*, de Tocqueville described the many civic groups in the United States as a positive for American democracy:

❝ PRIMARY SOURCE

In no country of the world has the principle of association been more successfully used, or applied to a greater multitude of objects, than in America. . . . In the United States associations are established to promote the public safety, commerce, industry, morality, and religion."

—Alexis de Tocqueville, 1835

Associations, de Tocqueville argued, engage Americans in causes larger than themselves and provide a means of helping people influence government.

Today there are interest groups to pressure all levels of government. These groups spend much time and money trying to influence government to take actions that they believe will be beneficial. Do these groups endanger the rights of other citizens, as Madison thought they might? Or do they play an important role in helping people interact with their government?

Comparing Interest Groups and Political Parties Political parties and interest groups have some similarities, but there are critical differences. Parties nominate candidates for office and try to win elections to gain control of the government. Interest groups may support candidates who favor their ideas, but they do not nominate candidates for office. Instead, interest groups try to influence government officials to support certain policies.

Another difference between interest groups and political parties is that interest groups are usually concerned with only a few issues or specific problems. They do not try to attract members with different points of view. Parties, on the other hand, are broad-based organizations. While they have contrasting ideas about government—ideologies—they must attract the support of people with varied ideas to win elections. They also must consider conflicting issues and problems that affect all Americans, not just certain groups. Interest groups also have ideologies. In fact, because they do not have to create broad-based memberships, their ideologies may be less flexible than those of political parties.

interest group a group of people who share common goals and organize to influence government and policy

civil society the complex network of voluntary associations that exist outside of government

sufficient enough; satisfactory in amount

Interest groups try to influence government officials to support certain policies. This photograph shows members of the AARP attending a rally in support of a Medicare bill.

▼ CRITICAL THINKING
1. *Identifying* What can you tell about the AARP from the picture? With what issue is this group concerned?
2. *Discussing* How would a public demonstration help an interest group achieve its goals?

COMPARING GOVERNMENTS

One component of a strong democracy is a vibrant civil society. A strong civil society "can discipline the state, ensure that citizens' interests are taken seriously, and foster greater civic and political participation." Freedom House, an interest group that works to expand freedom around the world, tracks nations' support for the freedom of association. This feature provides snapshots of the organization's reports on three countries' civil societies.

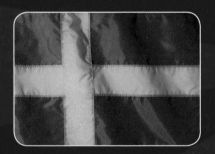

SWEDEN

RUSSIA

ZIMBABWE

Sweden respects the freedom of association, both in law and in practice. There are many civil society organizations, and they are allowed to operate free of government interference. Labor unions are protected by law, as is the right to strike. Trade union federations, which represent about 80 percent of the workforce, are strong and well organized.

The Russian government requires non-governmental organizations (NGOs) to meet difficult reporting requirements, decides which groups are allowed, and tightly controls these groups' use of foreign funds. The state restricts NGO activities it deems unacceptable. Trade union rights are legally protected, but they are limited in practice. Employers often ignore collective-bargaining rights and strikes are put down.

Zimbabweans must obtain police permission to hold public meetings and demonstrations. In 2011 police raided a meeting of civil society activists, arresting 46 people and charging them with treason (though the charges were eventually dropped). NGOs are active, but face legal restrictions and harassment. Human rights groups are explicitly prohibited from receiving foreign funds. Some trade unions are repressed and harassed.

EXPLORING THE ESSENTIAL QUESTION

1. **Comparing** How do these countries' civil societies compare?

2. **Making Inferences** How are the government actions listed related to the health of civil society?

3. **Evaluating** What things would you look for as indicators of a strong civil society?

Finally, most interest groups are organized on the basis of common values, rather than on geographic location. Political parties nominate officials from geographic areas to represent the people in those areas to the larger group. National interest groups unite people with common concerns from every region of the country.

The Purpose of Interest Groups Interest groups help bridge the gap between people and the government. Through interest groups, people communicate their "wants," or policy goals, to government leaders, such as the president, Congress, city council, or state legislators. When lawmakers begin to address the vital concerns of an interest group, its members swing into action. Interest groups also act as watchdogs and protest government policies that harm their members.

Most interest groups do not exist solely to influence public policy. They also have many other goals, including influencing business practices, educating their members and the public, supporting or conducting research, and providing services to people in need.

Political Power Interest groups follow the old principle "There is strength in numbers." By representing more than one individual, an interest group has a stronger bargaining position with leaders in government. The number of members needed to influence government leaders varies with the size of the community involved. Officials in a small community, for example, will listen to a 100-member group of citizens that has organized into a Local Safety Association, but officials in a large city might not be influenced by that number of people.

On the state and national levels, an interest group draws from the financial resources and expertise of its many members. Organized and equipped with sufficient resources, an interest group can exert influence far beyond the power of its individual members.

☑ **READING PROGRESS CHECK**

Explaining How are individuals able to influence government actions through participation in interest groups?

Leadership and Membership

GUIDING QUESTIONS *Why do people join interest groups?*

Interest group leaders strengthen the political power of the group by unifying its members. They keep members informed of the group's activities through e-mail blasts, newsletters, mailings, and telephone calls. They act as speakers for their group and try to improve its image in the media. They plan the group's strategy, raise money to run the organization, and oversee all financial decisions of the group.

Why do people join an interest group? Some people join interest groups to protect or promote their economic self-interest. A labor union works for higher union wages and other job benefits, while business associations work to ensure favorable tax laws. People join to get their beliefs translated into policy or into direct action to help others. They may also join interest groups for social reasons; socializing promotes a group unity that is vital to achieving political goals.

☑ **READING PROGRESS CHECK**

Listing List three reasons why individuals choose to join interest groups.

PARTICIPATING
IN Your Government

Interviewing

Identify an interest group that deals with a topic in which you are interested. Find out if it has a local chapter or branch in your community. Set up an interview with a member of the group to explore the reasons he or she decided to join this particular interest group.

Plan your questions carefully in advance. As with poll questions, interview questions should be clear. Unlike poll questions, interview questions should be open-ended, inviting the interview subject to provide details rather than a yes/no answer. Be sure to ask about individual and group goals, as well as the strategies the group uses to achieve those goals.

▶ **CRITICAL THINKING**

Summarizing Use the results of your interview to write a profile of the person you interviewed and share it with your classmates.

Types of Interest Groups

GUIDING QUESTION *What are the different ways that interest groups can be categorized?*

There are many thousands of interest groups in the United States. These groups can be categorized according to the size of their membership, the methods and relative effectiveness of those methods, or their goals. Most interest groups fall into one of the following categories. Some may even fall into two or more categories.

Economic Interest Groups Nearly all Americans have economic interests and concerns about taxes, food prices, housing, inflation, and unemployment. As a result, many interest groups are concerned with economic issues. These interest groups seek to convince public officials to support policies that they believe will strengthen the economy generally, as well as serve their own economic interests.

Business-related interest groups are among the oldest and largest in the nation. The National Association of Manufacturers (NAM) works to lower individual and corporate taxes and to limit government regulation of business, especially manufacturing. The U.S. Chamber of Commerce is a powerful interest group that represents more than 3 million businesses of all sizes and types. A third group is the Business Roundtable, which consists of executives from the largest and most powerful corporations. Specific industries, such as the oil and gas industry, also have associations that represent their interests to policy makers.

Labor unions are interest groups formed to advance the rights of workers. The American Federation of Labor and Congress of Industrial Organizations (AFL-CIO) is the largest and most powerful labor organization today. Among the many unions in the AFL-CIO are the United Auto Workers (UAW), United Mine Workers (UMW), and the International Brotherhood of Teamsters. A separate organization called the Committee on Political Education (COPE) directs the AFL-CIO's political activities. COPE's major goals include fundraising, holding voter-registration drives, and providing support for political candidates.

Three major interest groups represent almost 6 million American farmers. The largest of these agricultural groups is the American Farm Bureau Federation, which speaks for larger farmers and is closely associated with the federal Department of Agriculture.

The National Farmers' Union (NFU) draws its membership from smaller farmers and favors higher price supports for crops and livestock. The group also has supported laws protecting migrant farmworkers. The oldest farm group is the Patrons of Husbandry, known as The Grange. Although this group is more of a social organization than an interest group, it has been very outspoken in advocating price supports for crops. Also important are the **commodity** associations representing such groups as dairy farmers and potato growers.

commodity a product or good that is sold for profit, such as an agricultural product

The U.S. Chamber of Commerce is a powerful interest group that represents more than 3 million businesses of all sizes and types.

▼ **CRITICAL THINKING**
Identifying What kind of interest group is the U.S. Chamber of Commerce?

©Mandel Ngan/AFP/Getty Images

Public Interest Groups Some interest groups, called **public interest groups**, focus their work on influencing policies that they believe affect the general public, not just their own members. These groups might be concerned about issues relating to the environment, consumer protection, public health, families, education, community development, protecting the rights of children and the elderly, or government reform.

Concerns about the environment and the impact of environmental regulation have led to the founding of many environmental interest groups, both liberal and conservative. Their goals vary widely from conserving resources, protecting wildlife, and reversing the trend toward global warming to advancing the free market as the appropriate way to protect the environment. Among these interest groups are the Sierra Club, the National Wildlife Federation, the Environmental Defense Fund, and the Competitive Enterprise Institute.

One well-known public interest group is Common Cause, founded in 1970. This public interest group focuses on trying to reform campaign financing, elections, and other aspects of government accountability. The group In the Public Interest is concerned with making the public aware of the benefits and costs of privatizing services that were once government-run, such as prisons, transit systems, public hospitals, and so forth.

Civil Rights Groups Throughout U.S. history, interest groups have been formed to gain or protect the rights of various groups. Examples of civil rights groups include the National Association for the Advancement of Colored People (NAACP), National Council of La Raza, League of United Latin American Citizens (LULAC), National Organization of Women (NOW), and the Human Rights Campaign. While many of these groups trace their origins to the civil rights movement of the 1960s, NAACP and LULAC were founded in 1909 and 1929, respectively. The NAACP's mission is to end all race-based discrimination, and it works toward this mission by raising awareness and advocating for federal, state, and local antidiscrimination laws. LULAC works to improve the economic condition, political influence, and health of Hispanic Americans. Some civil rights groups, such as Amnesty International and Human Rights Watch, also work internationally.

Single-Issue Groups Some of the most effective interest groups are those that are dedicated to one particular issue such as advocating for the rights of the elderly, preventing homelessness, immigration reform, support for injured veterans, drunk driving prevention, gun rights, or gun control. The National Rifle Association (NRA) and the Brady Campaign are two opposing groups concerned about gun laws.

Ideological Interest Groups Some interest groups promote broad policies based on their core political or religious beliefs. For example, the Americans for Democratic Action and the American Conservative Union are two large interest groups that promote politics that reflect their liberal or conservative philosophies.

Throughout U.S. history, interest groups have formed to gain or protect the rights of various groups. This photograph shows thousands of people in a peaceful demonstration during the March on Washington in 1963.

▲ **CRITICAL THINKING**
Determining Importance At the end of the march, a group of civil rights leaders took a list of demands to the White House, to present them to President Kennedy. Conduct research to find out what specific demands were presented to the president. Did the government meet or try to meet those demands in the two or three years after the march? Based on your research, would you judge the march to have been a successful effort to influence government?

Faith-Based Interest Groups The number of religious interest groups has grown nearly fivefold in the last 40 years. Some of these groups are based in specific religious traditions, such as the American Jewish Committee or the Muslim American Society. Others, such as the Christian organizations Bread for the World and Focus on the Family, are concerned with broader issues such as hunger, education, or marriage rights and advocate for policies from their members' religious perspectives. In addition, some interest groups such as the Secular Coalition for America exist to keep religious bias out of public policy discussions.

Professional Interest Groups The American Bar Association (ABA) and the American Medical Association (AMA) are examples of interest groups that represent specific professions. Professional associations also represent bankers, teachers, college professors, police officers, and hundreds of other professions. These associations are concerned primarily with the standards of their professions, but they also provide their members with resources such as professional development and networking services. Many professional interest groups also work to influence government policy on issues important to them.

public interest group a type of interest group whose members focus their work on influencing policies that they believe affect the general public, not just themselves

Government Interest Groups Workers and leaders in American government at all levels—federal, state, and local—also act as interest groups. Examples of interest groups made up of government leaders are the National Governors' Association, the U.S. Conference of Mayors, and the National School Boards Association. Public employee unions include the American Postal Workers Union and the American Federation of Government Employees.

Government interest groups often try to influence Congress or the president because they want to receive more federal funds. They also advocate for action on state and local problems that require national solutions, such as immigration. Public sector unions often focus on improving working conditions, negotiating for fair wages, and securing benefits such as health insurance for workers.

✓ **READING PROGRESS CHECK**

Understanding Relationships What is the relationship between participation in interest groups and First Amendment rights?

LESSON 3 REVIEW

Reviewing Vocabulary

1. ***Applying*** Use the terms *civil society* and *public interest group* in a sentence.

Using Your Graphic Organizer

2. ***Listing*** What are the categories of interest groups?

Answering the Guiding Questions

3. ***Evaluating*** What are interest groups and are they an effective way for American citizens to participate in the political process?

4. ***Making Generalizations*** Why do people join interest groups?

5. ***Explaining*** What are the different ways that interest groups can be categorized?

Writing About Government

6. ***Argument*** Describe an interest group that you would like to see formed to address an interest or concern that you have. In the first paragraph, describe the goals of the group, the kinds of people likely to be members of the group, and the methods your group would use to attain its goals. In the second paragraph, write an argument for why your interest group would be more effective than groups mentioned in the lesson.

Interact with these digital assets and others in lesson 4

✓ **INTERACTIVE GRAPH**
PAC and SuperPAC Spending

✓ **INTERACTIVE IMAGE**
Letter-Writing Campaign

✓ **SELF-CHECK QUIZ**

✓ **VIDEO**
The NAACP

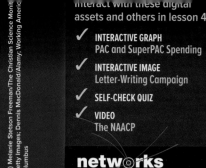

netw⊙rks
TRY IT YOURSELF ONLINE

LESSON 4
Affecting Public Policy

ReadingHelp Desk

Academic Vocabulary

- technique
- abstract

Content Vocabulary

- lobby
- lobbyist
- grassroots lobbying

TAKING NOTES:

Integration of Knowledge and Ideas

COMPARING AND CONTRASTING Use the Venn diagram to identify characteristics of PACs and SuperPACs.

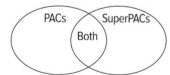

PACs SuperPACs
Both

ESSENTIAL QUESTION

How do special interest groups seek to influence U.S. public policy?

Interest groups could possibly use each of the strategies listed here to try to influence government policy.

Imagine that you are on the board of directors of an interest group with limited funds. Write a memo to the other board members advocating that the interest group use two of the strategies you think would be the most affordable, effective, and ethical. Explain your reasons.

- E-mail your mailing list, asking them to contact lawmakers and providing statements they can use in their e-mails or letters.

- Give expensive gifts to government administrators so they will consider your group's needs when deciding how to implement laws that you care about.

- Advertise on television and the Internet, presenting your group's position on two important bills currently being considered by the state legislature.

- Hire an attorney to prepare an amicus curiae (friend of the court) brief about a case before the Supreme Court that would affect the people your interest group serves.

- Donate money to the campaigns of candidates who agree with your positions.

Would the strategies you selected change if your group had huge sums in its bank account? What if it had 1 million members instead of 1,000? Why or why not?

Lobbying

GUIDING QUESTION *What impact do lobbyists have on public policy?*

Interest groups seek to influence public policy, wherever it is made—in all branches of government and at all levels. They use many strategies to achieve their goals—from using advertising to create public support for their causes to suing in court or seeking a constitutional amendment.

Lobbyists meet with elected officials to persuade them to make certain laws or policies. This example shows Senator Kelly Ayotte meeting with lobbyists outside the Senate chamber in the U.S. Capitol.

▲ CRITICAL THINKING
Making Generalizations Why are many Americans critical of the work of lobbyists?

lobby to make direct contact by lobbyists to persuade government officials to support the policies their interest group favors

lobbyist a paid representative of an interest group who contacts government officials on behalf of the interest group

grassroots lobbying political advocacy efforts carried out by the general public and members of interest groups, sometimes under the guidance of their professional lobbyists

technique method of accomplishing a desired aim

Meeting with elected officials to persuade them to make certain laws or policies is one way that interest groups influence public policy. This direct contact is called **lobbying** because of the practice of approaching senators and representatives in the lobby of a capitol building. Anyone can lobby by contacting their elected officials. However, some people are professional **lobbyists**—they are paid representatives of interest groups. Professional lobbyists contact government officials on behalf of the interest groups that are their clients. **Grassroots lobbying** refers to political advocacy efforts carried out by the general public and members of interest groups, sometimes under the guidance of professional lobbyists.

Lobbyists work to influence legislators at all levels of government—federal, state, and local. Sometimes the most effective way to reach lawmakers is through their staff, so lobbyists cultivate good relationships with the people who work for elected officials. Lobbyists also seek to influence government officials in the executive branch, such as the president, governors, and employees at state and federal agencies and regulatory bodies. Lobbying is one of the most widely used and effective **techniques** used by interest groups to bring about the laws and policies they seek.

Providing Useful Information One of the important ways that lobbyists make their cases is by providing government officials and their staff with facts and data about the policy the interest group wants enacted. When they do this, lobbyists will often try to meet face-to-face with members of Congress and other government officials—at the Capitol, in a member's office, over lunch, or even on a golf course. The information lobbyists provide legislators comes in many forms—pamphlets, reports, and statistical and trend data.

Lobbyists may pay for lunch or give government officials something else of value. Congressional rules, however, restrict the gifts lobbyists can give to federal lawmakers. Senators and their staff cannot accept any gift (including meals and entertainment) of more than $50 from a lobbyist. The Senate and House also have $100 limits on gifts from any single source. The president is able to set rules about lobbying in the executive branch. In 2009 President Obama issued an executive order banning all political appointees in the executive branch from accepting any gifts from lobbyists. Each state makes its own rules about lobbying in that state, and most states place some limit on the gifts lobbyists can give.

Members of Congress do rely on information presented by lobbyists. Legislators realize, however, that lobbyists are representing a particular interest. A lobbyist who intentionally misrepresents the facts runs the risk of losing a legislator's trust and permanently losing access to him or her.

Besides personally contacting legislators and other officials, lobbyists provide information in congressional testimony. Usually when Congress is considering a bill, various interest groups are invited to testify because of their expertise and lobbyists may testify. For example, a representative of the oil industry might be invited to testify before a committee considering a law to tax oil profits.

Drafting Bills Lobbyists and interest groups sometimes help write bills. Many well-organized interest groups have research staff who help members of Congress draft proposed laws. Studies have shown that interest groups and their lobbyists often draft parts of or entire bills for legislation. Lobbyists also submit comments on proposed federal regulations and rules to the executive branch agencies implementing the relevant law.

Who Are Lobbyists? By federal law, a lobbyist is anyone who:

- is employed or retained by a client to contact government officials about federal legislation or policy,
- makes more than one contact for the client, and
- spends more than 20 percent of his or her time serving the clients.

At the federal level, professional lobbyists must register with the government so that their professional activities can be monitored. The goal is to prevent illegal influence on members of Congress and the executive branch. Under current law, registered lobbyists must file semiannual reports with the Clerk of the House and the Secretary of the Senate. These reports must reveal the issues or laws being lobbied, the government branches and agencies being contacted, and an estimate of the money the client paid to the lobbyist.

These rules are all part of the 1995 Lobbying Disclosure Act. This law was intended to close loopholes in an older law that allowed most lobbyists to avoid registering with Congress. From the late 1990s to 2007, lobbying in Washington grew rapidly, but the number of active lobbyists has dropped slightly since then. In recent years, more than 12,000 people were active as lobbyists. The money spent on lobbying activities—including lobbyists' salaries, political donations, and more—grew dramatically, increasing from about $800 million in 1996 to $3.31 billion in 2012.

What kinds of people are lobbyists? Many are former government officials. They usually have friends in Congress and the executive branch and know the intricacies of Washington politics. Lobbying has proved to be an attractive second career for many members of Congress. In the 1980s, one national newsmagazine reported that many in Congress were cashing in on their connections: "For many, public service has become a mere internship

The Boston
Student Advisory Council

Heaven Reda was concerned about the quality of her education, so she joined the Boston Student Advisory Council, a citywide body of students who are elected to represent most high schools in Boston, Massachusetts. The BSAC members developed a student feedback form to help capture what students thought about the teaching and learning taking place in their schools. The students encouraged teachers who were supportive of their efforts to allow the forms to be used to evaluate their classes. They worked with the superintendent of the teachers' union to have the form used throughout their school district. But they had their sights set on the entire state of Massachusetts. They started lobbying their state board of education by attending meetings, holding rallies, and gathering support from parents, teachers, and students. And their efforts paid off: The Massachusetts Board of Elementary and Secondary Education voted to make student feedback a mandatory component of the educator evaluation policy.

"Let a student teach for a day, or help them build a curriculum or a strong student government."

—Heaven Reda

EXPLORING THE ESSENTIAL QUESTION

Making Connections Is there a similar student group in your community? How do students join this group? What issues is the group working on now? If you were going to meet with one of your state legislators about an issue you care about, how would you prepare for the meeting?

Dennis MacDonald/Alamy

for a lucrative career as a hired gun for special interests." Congress placed a limit on how soon former senators and representatives may become lobbyists; representatives must wait one year and senators two years after retirement.

Besides former government officials or members of Congress, lobbyists are often lawyers or public relations experts. Understanding the government and how it works is vital for a lobbyist to be successful and effective.

☑ **READING PROGRESS CHECK**

Speculating Do you think all professional lobbyists believe in the causes of the interest groups they represent? Explain your answer.

Interest Groups Seek Support

GUIDING QUESTION *How do interest groups use media to gain support for their issues?*

Interest groups run publicity campaigns to win support for their policies, both from members of the public and policy makers. Numerous techniques are available to interest groups in their efforts to influence people.

Media Campaigns Interest groups use the mass media—television, radio, newspapers, magazines, and the Internet—to inform the public and to create support for their views. For example, when Congress considered immigration reform in 2013, a group started by executives from tech companies in Silicon Valley used television advertising to support the reform bill. Environmentalists have run television and magazine ads to

GRAPH

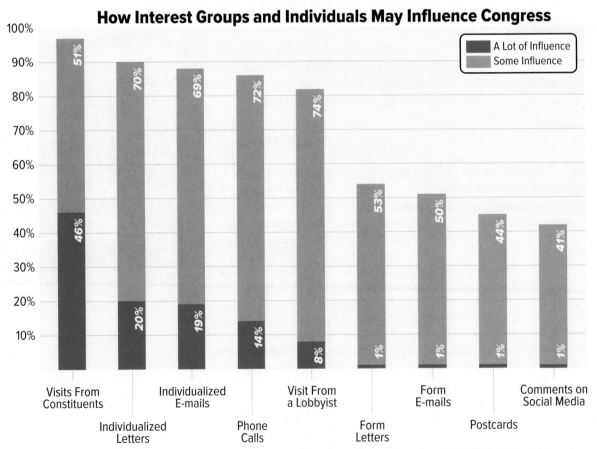

How Interest Groups and Individuals May Influence Congress

Legend: A Lot of Influence / Some Influence

- Visits From Constituents: 51% / 46%
- Individualized Letters: 70% / 20%
- Individualized E-mails: 69% / 19%
- Phone Calls: 72% / 14%
- Visit From a Lobbyist: 74% / 8%
- Form Letters: 53% / 1%
- Form E-mails: 50% / 1%
- Postcards: 44% / 1%
- Comments on Social Media: 41% / 1%

Source: *Communicating with Congress: Perceptions of Citizen Advocacy on Capitol Hill*, The Partnership for a More Perfect Union at the Congressional Management Foundation

dramatize pollution and the hazards it poses, just as senior citizens advertise their views when Congress considers changes in Social Security.

Beyond advertising, interest groups offer policy experts to civic and news organizations that cover their issues of concern. So, for example, if a group organizing a town hall meeting or a new program wants to showcase a pro/con discussion, interest group experts represent their views.

Digital media have offered new opportunities for seeking support and attempting to wield influence. Nearly all interest groups have websites and a presence on social media through which they can spread information and attempt to influence policy. They post ads supporting their views to video-sharing sites like YouTube and use Twitter to raise awareness. In January 2013, for example, the Robert Wood Johnson Foundation launched a month of tweets to stimulate discussion of disparities in health care.

Letter-Writing or E-mail Campaigns Many interest groups urge their members to call, fax, or send e-mails to government officials to demonstrate broad support for or against a policy. For example, the National Rifle Association (NRA) can deliver hundreds of thousands of letters, e-mails, and phone calls from its members. At the same time, however, groups taking the opposing position, such as Stop Handgun Violence, can also motivate letter-writers to contact policy makers.

Such campaigns make officials aware of an issue, but they do not always produce results. Officials may already have made up their minds on an issue. Others take into account the views of groups on both sides of the issue. In addition, congressional staffers report that, when legislators are undecided on an issue, e-mails and letters from individual citizens are more persuasive than form letters or e-mails sent by members of interest groups.

Limitations The public tends to believe that interest groups are well financed and carry a great deal of weight with Congress. Does this public perception match reality? Do lobbyists determine public policy?

Several factors limit the effectiveness of interest groups. Different interest groups compete for power and influence, keeping any single group from controlling lawmakers and other public officials. Generally, the larger the group, the more diverse the interests of its members are. This diversity has meant that nationally organized interest groups may be unable to adopt broad policy goals. As a result, smaller interest groups or single-issue interest groups—those that unite people who have narrower aims—have been most effective in shaping policy.

While large interest groups have membership that provides an impressive financial base, most interest groups struggle to pay small staffs. In recent years, the greatest concern about the power of interest groups has been their financial contributions to political campaigns.

☑ READING PROGRESS CHECK

Stating How have digital media affected the way interest groups operate?

Some interest groups send staff members or volunteers outside public areas to raise awareness, gather signatures, and even sign letters to send to their elected representatives in support for or against a policy.

▲ CRITICAL THINKING

Examining What are some reasons why a letter-writing campaign such as this one might fail to bring about the desired results of the sponsoring group?

The Rise of Political Action Committees

GUIDING QUESTION *What role do political action committees (PACs) and SuperPACs play in the U.S. political system?*

Some interest groups also provide a large percentage of the funds used in candidates' election campaigns. Most of these funds come from political action committees (PACs), organizations that are specifically designed to collect money and provide financial support for a political candidate.

PAC Fundraising and Spending The first national political action committee was formed in 1944 to reelect President Franklin D. Roosevelt. After 1974, when Congress passed new laws limiting donations to federal candidates, PACs became popular. PACs became a way for companies and labor unions to spend money to influence elections. While the law prevented companies and labor unions from donating directly to political candidates, the groups' political action committees could do so with the money the PACs raise from contributions from the company's executives or shareholders.

The Federal Election Commission (FEC) controls PAC activities with regard to federal elections. By law, a PAC is any group that spends more than $1,000 to influence a federal election and all PACs must register with the federal government. PACs that work to influence federal elections can receive donations of up to $5,000 from individuals, companies, or interest groups. PACs can give $5,000 directly to each candidate per election. States have their own rules about what constitutes a PAC and how much money they can raise and donate directly to campaigns.

However, there is no limit to how much PACs can spend indirectly—that is, independently of a candidate's campaign. Federal law established guidelines for when spending is "independent" and when it is "coordinated" with a campaign. In 1996 the Supreme Court ruled in *Colorado Republican Committee* v. *Federal Election Commission* that national, state, and local committee spending in support of federal candidates is a form of free speech that could not be limited.

Some PACs are tied to corporations, labor unions, trade groups, or health organizations—these are called *affiliated PACs*. Independent PACs organize around a cause but are not connected to a company, union, or trade group.

527 Organizations In the 2004 election, a new kind of political influence group appeared: the 527 organization, named for the part of the tax code that gives an exemption to certain groups. While these groups can have a PAC wing, the term is usually defined as a group that does not directly urge citizens to vote for a specific candidate. Instead, they focus on advocating an issue. For example, they may advocate for tax reform rather than advocate for a specific candidate who supports tax reform. The issue may be associated with a candidate, but by avoiding any mention of a candidate, 527s escape regulation.

SuperPACs Prior to 2010, federal laws like the Bipartisan Campaign Reform Act of 2002 (commonly known as the McCain-Feingold Act) placed limits on how and when corporate and labor money could be spent in federal elections. Several groups challenged the constitutionality of those reforms, however, and in 2010 the Supreme Court decided an important case.

In *Citizens United* v. *FEC* (2010), an independent PAC challenged the laws that limited corporations' and unions' political spending. The Supreme Court ruled that corporations, labor unions, and interest groups can then spend money to influence elections when and how they want, as long as they are doing so "independently," that is, as long as they do not coordinate their spending with specific candidates.

Other court rulings in 2010 said that PACs could be formed with an unlimited amount of contributions from U.S. citizens, corporations, unions, or interest groups. These new entities, which receive unlimited donations and can spend unlimited sums as long as they do not coordinate with candidates, became known as SuperPACs. Unlike traditional PACs (which

PACs and SuperPACs Total Dollars Raised

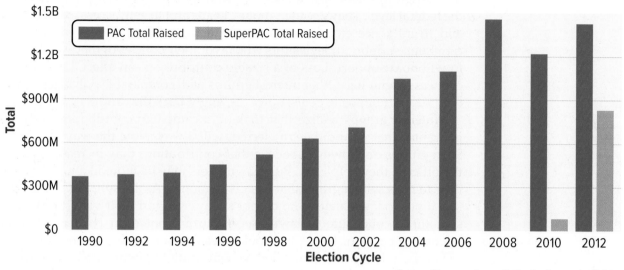

Source: Opensecrets.org: Center for Responsive Politics

cannot accept unlimited donations), SuperPACs cannot donate directly to candidates' campaigns.

Anyone can donate to a SuperPAC. Some are financed by very wealthy Americans making large donations of $1 million or more; others raise large amounts of money through smaller individual donations. Current laws require PACs and SuperPACs to disclose their lists of donors, but several provisions in the law allow PACs to maintain some secrecy about their donors.

▲ **CRITICAL THINKING**
Explaining How might a presidential campaign year affect the amount of money spent by a PAC?

☑ **READING PROGRESS CHECK**

Discussing What are 527 organizations and how do they get involved in political campaigns?

EXPLORING THE ESSENTIAL QUESTION

Making Decisions Should donor disclosure be required? Some people argue that spending money to elect candidates is the equivalent of free speech and must be protected. Others say that large donations have a corrupting influence and at the very least the names of those donors should be made public. What do you think? Examine each of the situations below. Do you think these donors should be required to disclose who they are and how much money they gave?

a. someone donates the maximum allowed amount ($2,600) directly to a presidential candidate

b. someone donates $2,000 to a labor union's PAC

c. someone donates $4 million to a SuperPAC opposing an incumbent senator

d. someone donates $50 to a PAC dedicated to immigration reform

e. someone donates $100 to a nonprofit organization focused on educating Americans about the federal budget

f. a registered lobbyist makes a $1,500 campaign contribution to a member of Congress on behalf of a client

What criteria did you use to evaluate the examples?

Strategies of PACs

GUIDING QUESTION *How effective are the methods used by PACs and SuperPACs to influence political campaigns?*

Interest groups generally follow two strategies to influence public policy at the federal level. They use their money to attempt to gain access to lawmakers and to influence election outcomes directly. Interest groups can promise campaign support for legislators who favor their policies or they can threaten to withhold support. Loss of a sizable contribution can affect a candidate's chances of winning. Other interest groups with comparable political strength who support opposite goals, however, might back the candidate.

Interest groups realize that making a campaign contribution does not guarantee that a candidate, if elected, will always vote the way they wish. Such groups do, however, believe that contributions may increase access to the officials they help elect. Busy lawmakers may be more likely to set aside time to meet with a group that has given money. As a result, PACs may give donations to lawmakers who do not always support their views. PACs also sometimes contribute to lawmakers who are not even challenged in an upcoming election. Joan Claybrook, president of Public Citizen, Inc. said: "That these PACs feel compelled to contribute to lawmakers who have no opponent shows that what is being sought is access and influence."

PACs also spend money to influence election outcomes. With SuperPACs, more money than ever is being spent to support or oppose candidates. SuperPACs can spend unlimited amounts on advertising as long as they do not coordinate with or donate to a candidate's campaign. In practice, SuperPACs are often run by close associates of the candidates. They support voter registration drives and get-out-the-vote efforts, too.

Some members of Congress admit to the power of the PACs. Former Representative Barney Frank (D-Mass.) once said: "We are the only human beings in the world who are expected to take thousands of dollars from perfect strangers and not be affected by it." Others disagree. Former Representative Dan Glickman (D-Kan.) said: "I do not think any member of Congress votes because of how a PAC gives him money on El Salvador, or the MX missiles, or . . . broader, **abstract** national issues."

abstract dealing with a subject in its theoretical aspects; not concrete

✓ READING PROGRESS CHECK

Identifying What are two ways interest groups can exercise power over political candidates?

LESSON 4 REVIEW

Reviewing Vocabulary

1. *Paraphrasing* Rewrite the definition of *grassroots lobbying* in your own words.

2. *Differentiating* What is the difference between a lobbyist and a volunteer?

Using Your Graphic Organizer

3. *Comparing and Contrasting* What are the similarities and differences between PACs and SuperPACs?

Answering the Guiding Questions

4. *Summarizing* What impact do lobbyists have on public policy?

5. *Explaining* How do interest groups use media to gain support for their issues?

6. *Interpreting* What role do political action committees (PACs) and SuperPACs play in the U.S. political system?

7. *Discussing* How effective are the methods used by PACs and SuperPACs to influence political campaigns?

Writing About Government

8. *Informative/Explanatory* Members of Congress rely on lobbyists to provide them with information. Write a job description for a professional lobbyist. Include the skills and experience required for the position and explain the responsibilities and duties involved.

Citizens United v Federal Election Commission (2010)

FACTS OF THE CASE In 2008 Citizens United, a nonprofit organization funded partially by corporate donations, produced *Hillary: The Movie*, a film created to dissuade voters from choosing Hillary Clinton as the 2008 Democratic presidential nominee. At the time, it was against the law to use corporate donations to air commercials directly supporting or opposing a national political candidate within 30 days of a primary. Citizens United said that this law infringed their First Amendment rights because it restricted corporations' ability to engage in political speech.

ISSUE

Does a law that limits indirect campaign support by corporations and labor unions violate the First Amendment's guarantee of free speech?

ARGUMENTS

CITIZENS UNITED Citizens United argued that companies, unions, and other organizations should be allowed to spend as much as they want on political advertising in the days leading up to an election. They said that the First Amendment applies equally to speech by individuals and speech by groups. Freedom of political speech is vital to our democracy, and spending money on advertisements is one way of spreading speech. A corporation's spending on political ads is therefore speech as well. Though some people or organizations have more money and can therefore speak more, the First Amendment does not allow for making some forms of speech illegal in order to make things "fair." Finally, Citizens United argued that merely spending money to support a candidate does not create or even suggest the corruption that campaign finance reform was originally created to address.

THE FEDERAL ELECTION COMMISSION The Federal Election Commission argued that the law limiting corporate and union spending on political advertising near elections did not violate the First Amendment. The FEC said that indirect campaigning—like this film—needed to be regulated because corruption is not limited to bribes and direct transactions. By being allowed to give unlimited sums of money in support of a candidate, corporations and unions will have a certain amount of access to, if not power over, that candidate. Further, even if no corruption takes place, there may be a public perception of corruption that could cause many voters to stop voting. Most importantly, they argued, the First Amendment does not apply to corporations because the Constitution was established for "We the People" and was set up to protect individual, rather than corporate, liberties.

EXPLORING THE ESSENTIAL QUESTION

Moot Court You will be assigned to one of three groups: lawyers for Citizens United, lawyers for the FEC, and Supreme Court justices. You will prepare for a moot court of this case. The lawyers for each side should develop arguments to present during oral argument and prepare to answer questions from the justices. The justices should prepare questions to ask the lawyers during oral argument. When you argue the case, each team will have five minutes to present its side, and the justices will be allowed to ask the lawyers questions throughout their five minutes. The justices will then vote and announce their decision explaining their reasons. After the moot court is complete, write a persuasive essay or blog that reflects your personal opinion about this issue.

YOU BE the JUDGE

STUDY GUIDE

POLITICAL SOCIALIZATION
LESSON 1

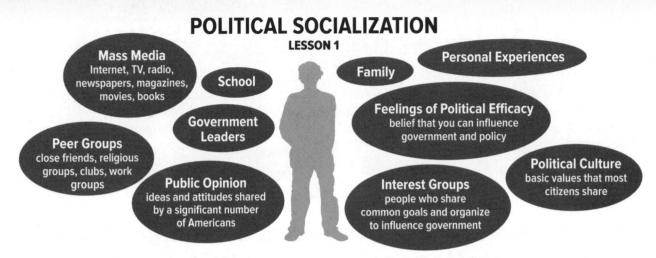

Mass Media
Internet, TV, radio, newspapers, magazines, movies, books

School

Family

Personal Experiences

Feelings of Political Efficacy
belief that you can influence government and policy

Government Leaders

Peer Groups
close friends, religious groups, clubs, work groups

Public Opinion
ideas and attitudes shared by a significant number of Americans

Interest Groups
people who share common goals and organize to influence government

Political Culture
basic values that most citizens share

SCIENTIFIC POLLING
LESSON 2

1. Select a sample.
- representative of universe
- randomly selected

2. Carefully word questions.
- clear wording
- each question asks only one thing

3. Interpret the results.
- know the sampling error
- identify bias

Polling data are used by:

Lawmakers
- to craft bills
- to decide how to vote

Campaign Staff
- to decide where to campaign and advertise
- to shape their messages

Media
- to broadcast as news
- to predict election winners

TYPES OF INTEREST GROUPS
LESSON 3

Economic	promote economic growth and their own economic interests
Public	focus on policies that affect the general public, not just their members
Civil Rights	gain and protect rights of the group
Single-Issue	dedicated to one particular issue
Ideological	promote broad policies based on their core political or religious beliefs
Faith-Based	form around a religious perspective
Professional	represent specific professions
Government	workers and leaders in all levels of government

HOW DO INTEREST GROUPS INFLUENCE PUBLIC POLICY?
LESSON 4

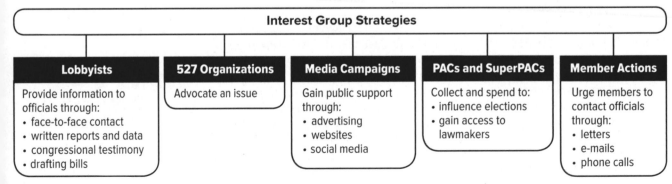

Interest Group Strategies

Lobbyists
Provide information to officials through:
- face-to-face contact
- written reports and data
- congressional testimony
- drafting bills

527 Organizations
Advocate an issue

Media Campaigns
Gain public support through:
- advertising
- websites
- social media

PACs and SuperPACs
Collect and spend to:
- influence elections
- gain access to lawmakers

Member Actions
Urge members to contact officials through:
- letters
- e-mails
- phone calls

Directions: On a separate sheet of paper, answer the questions below. Make sure you read carefully and answer all parts of the questions.

Lesson Review

Lesson 1

1 *Applying* Give three examples of elements of U.S. political culture.

2 *Specifying* At what time in a person's life does political socialization occur?

Lesson 2

3 *Analyzing* Interest groups provide information to public officials, but this information often presents a distorted view of public opinion. Explain why.

4 *Explaining* Why is "push polling" unreliable?

Lesson 3

5 *Categorizing* Based on the name "National Rifle Association," in what category would you place this interest group? Explain why.

6 *Identifying Perspectives* What are the missions of the League of United Latin American Citizens and the National Association for the Advancement of Colored People? Based on their missions, in what category do these interest groups belong?

Lesson 4

7 *Making Inferences* Why do you think limits are placed on the value of gifts lobbyists can give to lawmakers?

8 *Interpreting* The Supreme Court ruled that corporations, labor unions, and interest groups can spend unlimited amounts to influence elections as long as they do so "independently." What did the Court mean by "independently"?

ANSWERING THE ESSENTIAL QUESTIONS

Review your answers to the introductory questions at the beginning of each lesson. Then answer the following Essential Questions based on what you learned in the chapter. Have your answers changed?

9 *Identifying Cause and Effect* In what ways can public opinion affect government policy?

10 *Analyzing* How do special interest groups seek to influence U.S. public policy?

DBQ Interpreting Political Cartoons

Use the political cartoon to answer the following questions.

11 *Drawing Inferences* What do the balls represent, and why are they drawn as different types?

12 *Drawing Conclusions* What is the cartoon saying about members of Congress and public opinion?

Critical Thinking

13 *Making Connections* How are feelings of political efficacy related to interest groups?

14 *Making Inferences* Why do you think public officials may pay more attention to personal letters and e-mails from individual constituents than to standardized mass e-mails?

15 *Analyzing* Why do large interest groups have political power?

16 *Making Inferences* Why might a PAC donate to lawmakers who do not always support the PAC's views?

Need Extra Help?

If You've Missed Question	**1**	**2**	**3**	**4**	**5**	**6**	**7**	**8**	**9**	**10**	**11**	**12**	**13**	**14**	**15**	**16**
Go to page	574	573	577	581	589	589	592	596	572	584	577	577	575	595	596	596

Directions: On a separate sheet of paper, answer the questions below. Make sure you read carefully and answer all parts of the questions.

DBQ **Analyzing Primary Sources**

Read the excerpt and answer the questions that follow.

Congress began placing limits on political spending in 1907. The 2002 Bipartisan Campaign Reform Act limited how and when corporations and labor unions could spend on federal elections. A PAC, Citizens United, challenged this limit. In *Citizens United* v. *FEC* (2010), the Supreme Court ruled that spending by corporations and labor unions on independent political messages is speech protected by the First Amendment and cannot be limited. In the following excerpt, President Barack Obama comments on this decision.

PRIMARY SOURCE

"With all due deference to separation of powers, last week the Supreme Court reversed a century of law that I believe will open the floodgates for special interests—including foreign corporations—to spend without limit in our elections. (Applause.) I don't think American elections should be bankrolled by America's most powerful interests, or worse, by foreign entities. (Applause.) They should be decided by the American people."
—Barack Obama, State of the Union Address, 2010

17 *Identifying Perspectives* What is President Obama's opinion of the Supreme Court decision in *Citizens United* v. *FEC*?

18 *Interpreting* What reasons does he give for his opinion?

19 *Drawing Inferences* Why do you think President Obama chose to make this comment in his State of the Union Address?

Social Studies Skills

20 *Identifying Central Issues* Select two national interest groups that are focused on important contemporary issues, such as Mothers Against Drunk Driving, Club for Growth, Sierra Club, United Auto Workers, or the National Rifle Association. Create a graphic organizer that lists the purpose of the interest group, how it attracts members to its cause and spreads current information about the issue, and what groups would oppose its goals.

21 *Identifying Perspectives* Write a paragraph from the point of view of one of the interest groups discussed in this chapter, identifying why its perspective on an issue is appropriate and how it furthers public interest.

22 *Analyzing* Write a short essay discussing the methods used by one of the interest groups mentioned in this chapter to change or maintain public policy concerning the issue it focuses on. Then analyze the effectiveness of those methods.

Research and Presentation

23 *Exploring Issues* Locate a political cartoon about a contemporary political issue. Prepare a presentation explaining the cartoonist's viewpoint on the issue and how he or she uses elements in the cartoon to sway public opinion toward this viewpoint.

24 *Posing Questions* Choose a topic or issue about which you have a strong opinion. Write three survey questions that would influence respondents to agree with your opinion. Then rewrite the same questions in an unbiased way. Share your questions in a class discussion about how the wording of survey questions can bias the results.

25 *Simulating* In the Lesson 3 Review, you described an interest group that you would like to see formed. Create a mock website for this group. Design the home page and show links to other content on your site. Look at websites of similar interest groups online for ideas. Present your website to the class.

26 *Analyzing* Compare and contrast different ways individuals can participate in the political process at the national, state, and local levels. Then evaluate the effectiveness of each of the methods you identified.

Need Extra Help?

If You've Missed Question	**17**	**18**	**19**	**20**	**21**	**22**	**23**	**24**	**25**	**26**
Go to page	596	596	574	588	588	594	577	581	588	578

Mass Media in the Digital Age

ESSENTIAL QUESTIONS

- What role does the mass media play in the U.S. political system?
- How do the Internet and social media affect the U.S. political process?

netw⊙rks
www.connected.mcgraw-hill.com
There's More Online about
mass media in the digital age.

CHAPTER 20

Analyzing Primary Sources
Consuming the News

Lesson 1
How Media Impact Our Government

Lesson 2
Regulating Print and Broadcast Media

Lesson 3
The Internet and Democracy

▲ All forms of media can
have an impact on the
political system of the
United States.

ANALYZING PRIMARY SOURCES

CONSUMING THE NEWS

For most of America's history, the public received news in print—by newspaper, pamphlet, or magazine. In the mid-twentieth century, radio and then television revolutionized the way Americans learn about current events. Similarly, the advent of the Internet and mobile technology at the turn of the twenty-first century has radically impacted how we consume news. Increasingly, people are getting their news online. How does the new media affect our civic participation? Explore the sources here as you think about that question.

PRIMARY SOURCE A

Journalist James Fallows reflected on the impact of the Internet and social media on how Americans learned about unfolding events during Egypt's democratic protests in 2011. He remarked on the speed of the coverage and the diversity of voices that would have been impossible just a few years earlier.

"Within hours of the first protests in Egypt, American and world audiences read dispatches from professional correspondents—on Web sites, rather than waiting until the next day, as they had to during the fall of the Berlin Wall. They saw TV news footage—including Al Jazeera's, which was carried by few U.S. broadcasters but was available on computers or mobile apps. Then the Twitter feeds from and about Egypt, the amateur YouTube videos from the streets, the commentary of contending analysts—all of it available as the story took place. "

—James Fallows, "Learning to Love the (Shallow, Divisive, Unreliable) New Media," *The Atlantic,* February 24, 2011

SECONDARY SOURCE B

The Pew Research Center reports:

- Americans under age 25 get substantially more news digitally than from traditional news sources (60% vs. 43%).
- Almost 30% of those younger than 25 said they got no news the previous day.
- Interviewees aged 18–29 spent an average of 45 minutes watching, listening to, or reading news on a typical day. Older Americans spent between 62 and 83 minutes doing so.

—Pew Research Center for People & the Press, "In Changing News Landscape, Even Television is Vulnerable," 2012

PRIMARY SOURCE C

The television network Comedy Central conducted a study of Millennials' (the generation born between 1983 and the present) news habits as they relate to humor. Comedy Central airs the popular political satire show *The Daily Show with Jon Stewart*. The research report concluded:

"[Millenials] say that they get facts and insights from a variety of mainstream news sources; however Millennials are going to political comedies/satires to gain perspective on the issues. While conventional media continues to play an important role in keeping Millennials informed, fully half say they frequently use political satire shows to follow politics and the election. When it comes to political comedy/satires, Millennials don't watch to get informed; they watch because they are informed."

—Comedy Central Press Release, October 12, 2012

Lee Hamilton is a former member of the U.S. House of Representatives and the Director of the Center on Congress at Indiana University.

"The truth is, for our democracy to work it needs not just an engaged citizenry, but an informed one. We've known this since this nation's earliest days. . . . In the end, the burden lies with each of us as citizens. A lot of powerful groups and interests in this country try to manipulate public opinion, and they're very good at it. Yet a democratic society depends on its citizens separating the wheat from the chaff, forming good judgments, and putting pressure on their representatives to act accordingly. If ordinary people can't do this or don't want to devote the time and energy, the country suffers. No matter how good our leadership, if we don't have discriminating citizens, this nation will not work very well."

—Lee Hamilton, "Why We Need An Informed Citizenry," The Center on Congress at Indiana University

DBQ DOCUMENT-BASED QUESTIONS

1. **Drawing Conclusions** What conclusions can you draw from these sources about how young people interact with the news? Does it matter if young people consume news differently from older Americans?

2. **Analyzing** What is the point of view of the cartoonist? Do you think the cartoonist is biased? Why or why not?

3. **Explaining** How is civic participation influenced by our consumption of the news?

WHAT WILL YOU DO?

How will you stay informed about current events in the United States and around the world? What sources will you turn to? How will you judge the news you hear or read?

EXPLORE the interactive version of the analyzing primary sources feature on Networks.

netw⊙rks *TRY IT YOURSELF* ONLINE

Mass Media in the Digital Age **605**

Interact with these digital assets and others in lesson 1

✓ **INTERACTIVE CHART**
Styles of Journalism

✓ **INTERACTIVE IMAGE**
Fireside Chats

✓ **SELF-CHECK QUIZ**

✓ **VIDEO**
Infamous Scribblers

netw⊚rks
TRY IT YOURSELF ONLINE

LESSON 1
How Media Impact Our Government

Reading Help Desk

Academic Vocabulary

- **expose**
- **commentator**

Content Vocabulary

- **mass media**
- **journalist**
- **news release**
- **news briefing**
- **press conference**
- **leak**
- **media event**
- **horse-race coverage**
- **front-runner**
- **spot advertising**

TAKING NOTES:

Integrating Knowledge and Ideas

COMPARING Use the table to organize your notes about the role of the media in each of the three branches of government in the past and today.

	Executive/President	Congress	Courts
Past			
Present			

ESSENTIAL QUESTION

What role does the mass media play in the U.S. political system?

Since the founding of the United States, journalists have served a watchdog role, keeping a close eye on government officials to keep the public informed and to guard against corruption and the abuse of power. Today the media environment has changed drastically: Several television networks broadcast news 24 hours a day, sometimes with a very particular slant or bias.

Read the three scenarios below. What do these stories suggest about the media and government today? Is the press in each case performing a watchdog role? Explain your answer.

- At the U.S. Capitol, a senator complains about being "ambushed" by a young reporter. Television cameras had been limited to agreed-upon areas of the building, where lawmakers would go to talk to the press. This reporter is using a smartphone to record video away from the TV cameras.

- A TV network decides to air the trial of a mother accused of killing her young daughter. The trial becomes a "media circus," with reporters vying to interview the attorneys in the case and everyone associated with the victims and suspect. Talk shows devote entire hours to the case.

- In a series of investigative reports, a newspaper reveals that the governor has accepted expensive gifts from a businessman. An editorial writer calls for the governor to resign.

The Mass Media

GUIDING QUESTION *How has the relationship between the mass media and government changed over time?*

The **mass media** include all the means for communicating information to the general public. Media have covered the government since George Washington was president. Newspapers had the field to themselves until they were challenged by magazines, radio, television, and the Internet. Each additional medium has influenced the way news is reported. What once took days and weeks to reach readers can now reach them in seconds. News is available around the clock, and people with no experience or training as journalists have outlets for publishing their videos, photos, and stories.

The news media—the parts of the mass media that deliver news to the public—fill several roles in American society. The public relies on reporters to condense and clarify complicated stories. They also count on the media to alert them to important issues and to uncover problems in government.

News media use a variety of vehicles to fill these roles. Hard news stories are written by reporters and share only facts, not the author's opinion. Commentary provides analysis of the news, while editorials convey a person or group's opinion. Features take a deeper look at a topic, and columns are stories, usually including both news and opinion, written by the same person on a regular basis.

Print, broadcast, and electronic forms of mass media use sophisticated communications technology, but individual journalists, including reporters, columnists, editors, editorial writers, editorial cartoonists, photojournalists, correspondents, commentators, and news directors are still the heart of the media.

Journalism Today, citizens have access to more media than ever before. However, all news is not alike. Digital media have enabled citizens to act as amateur journalists and professional journalists to be on the job anytime and everywhere. Some people are reexamining the definition of **journalist**. Are journalists only trained reporters working in media companies? Are bloggers journalists because they comment on the news on their websites? As advertisers see the rising popularity of digital news consumption, they invest more in online sources of news. Newspapers and newsmagazines struggle to survive.

Even with all this news, are citizens paying attention? Perhaps not. Many Americans think they are too busy to watch the news or read newspapers—but many also have lost respect for the media. A 2013 poll revealed that only 28 percent of American adults think that journalists contribute "a lot" to our nation's well-being. Observers suggest that media bias and overemphasis on violence and stories about celebrities may explain this loss of public approval.

Relationship Between Media and Government Reporters cultivate sources within the government that can provide them with information and insights. The more highly placed these sources, the more exclusive the news. To win the confidence of their sources, reporters agree to some restrictions in what they can include in their stories. Some meetings are "off the record," meaning the reporter agrees not to print or broadcast the information. These meetings can still be useful because officials often establish valuable connections, and journalists receive tips to assist them during their reporting.

mass media all the means for communicating information to the general public, such as newspapers, magazines, radio, television, and the Internet

journalist professional media communicator, including reporter, columnist, editor, editorial writer, editorial cartoonist, photojournalist, correspondent, commentator, and news director

▼CRITICAL THINKING
Differentiating What is the difference between a hard news story and an editorial?

STYLES OF JOURNALISM

Type	Characteristics	Sample Headline
Hard News Story	Based on facts, these stories describe newsworthy events at the local, national, or international level.	"Winter Storm Buries New England, Millions Stranded Without Power"
Commentary	Commentaries provide in-depth analysis of events or developments. Rather than reporting just the facts, these articles seek to explain why something happened or the significance of a certain event.	"Why New England Was Unprepared for the Winter Storm"
Editorial	Editorials reflect the opinions of the writer. They may address events and trends in the news, but these articles are not considered factual news stories.	"Winter Storm Proves that Global Warming is a Myth"
Feature	Features focus on a specific topic. Features are often "softer" news articles, such as a human-interest story, a profile of a local resident, or a group with an unusual hobby.	"Boston Girl Rescues Lost Puppy During Winter Storm"
Column	Written by the same person at regular intervals, these articles reflect the interests and perspective of the writer. Some columnists seek to inform, such as a technology expert who writes about the latest gadgets. Other columnists seek to entertain, such as a humorist who shares her comic take on recent events.	"Mr. Handy's Tips on How to Prepare for the Next Winter Storm"

Some interviews are on "deep background," where the reporter will tell the story but agrees not to identify the source of the story. Reporters will make this kind of information public by saying, "Government sources said . . ." or "A senior White House official said. . . ." Backgrounders give government officials the opportunity to test new ideas or to send unofficial messages to other policy makers or even foreign governments.

Sometimes, government officials will prohibit sound and video recordings of meetings with journalists. Reporters for the new digital media have been less likely to accept such restrictions, however, and politicians have found comments they thought were made in private broadcast publicly.

The relationship between journalists and government officials can become adversarial. Politicians want to use the media to help them reach their goals. Government officials would like the media to pass on their messages just as the officials present them. Journalists, however, see their job as informing the public, not passing along politicians' messages.

☑ **READING PROGRESS CHECK**

Drawing Conclusions What are some ways the relationship between the mass media and government has not changed?

The Executive Branch and the Media

GUIDING QUESTION *What is the relationship between the mass media and the executive branch of the U.S. government?*

Executive branch leaders from mayors and governors to the president try to use the mass media to their advantage to convey information and gain support for their proposals. Advisers to executive branch leaders at all levels

PARTICIPATING
ⒾⓃ **Your Government**

Analyzing Media Coverage for Bias

Is the media biased? One way to answer that question is by comparing different news sources' coverage of the same event. Find at least two different accounts of the same event. (Make sure you are looking at news coverage, rather than editorial or opinion articles.) Think about the following questions as you analyze the news accounts:

- What aspects of the event are highlighted in the headline? Does the headline suggest a negative or positive take on the story? (The headline was probably not written by the reporter who wrote the article, but it can still reflect bias.)
- Are the same facts presented in all the accounts? What facts are omitted? Are the facts presented in a way that suggests a particular conclusion? Is enough context provided for the story to make sense?
- Does the reporter use value-laden language? For example, instead of describing someone as a "Republican from North Carolina," or a "Democrat from California," does the reporter refer to the person as a "right-wing Southerner" or a "West Coast leftie"?
- Are about the same number of people with different perspectives on the event quoted or do most of the quotes reflect only one perspective?

State Department Photo

▲ CRITICAL THINKING

Analyzing Secondary Sources Do you think any of the sources you analyzed were biased? What was the most important evidence of bias?

of government try to manage relations with the mass media by controlling the daily flow of information. To do so, they use news releases and briefings, press conferences, background stories, leaks, and media events.

News Releases and Briefings A government **news release** is a ready-made story prepared by officials for members of the press. Also called a press release, it can be printed or broadcast word-for-word or used as background information. A news release usually has a dateline that states the earliest time it can be published.

During a **news briefing**, a government official makes an announcement or explains a policy, a decision, or an action. Briefings give reporters the chance to ask officials about news releases or follow up on leads they have developed in their research. The president's press secretary meets daily with the press to answer questions, and the State Department also provides a daily press briefing. Governors and other state-level officials also issue news releases and hold briefings, but less frequently than their federal counterparts.

Press Conferences A **press conference** involves the news media's questioning of a high-level government official. Mayors, governors, and leaders of executive agencies all have media strategies that include giving the media certain access.

Presidents have held press conferences since the days of Theodore Roosevelt. Over the years, most presidential press conferences have been carefully planned events. In preparation for a press conference, the president often studies briefing books that identify potential questions. In addition, the White House can limit questions to certain topics, and aides may have friendly reporters ask specific questions that they want the president to address.

Other Means of Sharing Information Another way top officials try to influence the flow of information to the press is through a **leak**, or the release of secret information to the media by anonymous government officials. These officials might be seeking public support for a policy that others in the government do not like. Top officials do not control all leaks, however. Sometimes low-level officials leak information to **expose** corruption or to get top officials to pay attention to a problem. When the information leaked is classified, the person who leaked that information can be prosecuted.

Modern presidents often stage a **media event**, a visually interesting event designed to reinforce the president's position on some issue. A president who takes a strong stand against pollution, for example, makes a stronger statement by standing in front of a state-of-the-art, administration-supported solar cell energy plant than by remaining in the Oval Office.

The President and Television The president and the mass media, especially television, have a mutually beneficial relationship. As one of the most powerful government officials in the world, the president is a great source of news. Most television coverage of U.S. government officials focuses on the president.

Franklin D. Roosevelt was the first president to master the use of broadcast media. Broadcast television did not exist at the time of his presidency, and most newspaper owners did not support him. Therefore, Roosevelt presented his ideas directly to the people with "fireside chats" over the radio. In 1979, journalist David Halberstam described the impact of a Roosevelt fireside chat: "He was the first great American radio voice. . . . Most Americans in the previous 160 years had never even seen a President; now almost all of them were hearing him, in their own homes. It was . . . electrifying."

Franklin D. Roosevelt was the first president to master the use of broadcast media. This photograph shows him broadcasting his first "fireside chat" from the White House.

▲ CRITICAL THINKING
Explaining How did Franklin Roosevelt use broadcast media to help win support for his ideas?

horse-race coverage news coverage of presidential election campaigns in which the media treat the campaign as if it were a sporting event, generating excitement by focusing on who is ahead, who is making a comeback, and so on

front-runner label given to the candidate who wins an early primary, even if by a very small margin

National Archives and Records Administration

The era of television politics really began with the 1960 presidential debates between Richard Nixon and John F. Kennedy. Although radio listeners thought Nixon had won their first debate, he had been ill and looked haggard on television. Kennedy looked well and appealed more to the larger television audience. Reporters who covered the debate regarded it as the moment when television passed newspapers and radio as the primary communications medium. No presidential candidates agreed to another televised debate until 1976, and all presidents since then have paid great attention to their television image and their use of the medium.

Television and Presidential Campaigns Television has greatly influenced who runs for president, how candidates are nominated, and how election campaigns are conducted. Television has influenced the types of candidates who run for office in several ways. Candidates for major offices must be "telegenic"—that is, they must project a pleasing appearance and performance on camera. John F. Kennedy and Ronald Reagan were examples of good candidates for the television age. They had strong features and projected the cool, low-key style that goes over well on television.

Television has also made it much easier for people who are political unknowns to gain exposure and quickly become serious candidates for major offices. Barack Obama's televised speech at the 2004 Democratic convention catapulted him to national prominence.

The mass media have fundamentally changed the nomination process for president through **horse-race coverage** of elections, especially primaries. Horse-race coverage treats the campaign as if it were a sporting event, generating excitement by focusing on who is ahead, who is making a comeback, and so on. Exploring issues and policy positions is secondary in this type of coverage.

The media declare a candidate who wins an early primary, even if by a very small margin, a **front-runner**, or early leader. The press largely determines the weight attached to being a front-runner. The label carries great significance, however, because it is much easier for front-runners to attract the millions of dollars in loans and campaign contributions as well as the volunteer help they need to win the long, grueling nominating process.

Television also affects how presidential candidates communicate with the voters. The first presidential candidates in American history did little campaigning; they left such work to political supporters. Andrew Jackson's election started the "torchlight era," in which candidates gave stump speeches and provided parades and expensive entertainment for voters and supporters.

Around 1900, candidates began using advertisements in newspapers and magazines and mass mailings of campaign literature. In 1924 candidates began radio campaigning, and in 1952 the Eisenhower campaign began television advertising. Television has continued to be a major vehicle for advertising, but actual news coverage on television now involves only brief opportunities for politicians to share their views. In the 20 years between 1968 and 1988, the average length of a sound bite—the actual words of a candidate or elected leader included in a news story—shrank from 43 seconds to 9 seconds, where it has remained since.

✓ READING PROGRESS CHECK

Determining Importance How has television changed presidential campaigning?

The Legislative Branch and the Media

GUIDING QUESTION *What is the relationship between the legislative branch and the mass media?*

One of the ways reporters become experts is to focus on a particular branch of government or level of government. Reporters often specialize in "covering" local, state, and national lawmakers.

Covering Congress Thousands of reporters have press credentials to cover the House and Senate. Nearly every member of Congress has a press secretary to prepare press releases, arrange interviews, and give out television tapes. Most important congressional work takes place in committees and subcommittees over long periods of time. Congress's slow, complicated work rarely meets television's requirements for dramatic, entertaining news.

For that reason, the media usually focuses its attention on congressional leaders such as the speaker of the House and the majority and minority leaders. But of course, no single congressional leader can speak for all 535 members of Congress. Nationally known lawmakers often are seen as spokespersons for their political parties rather than for Congress. Most members of Congress devote their efforts to attracting local coverage, which helps them gain recognition among their constituents. Some members, especially those in seniority or leadership positions, work to get national coverage to help promote their goals. Most bills get little or no coverage. Coverage of individuals tends to be neutral or slightly positive, while coverage of Congress as an institution tends to be negative, focused on conflict and deadlock.

In addition to covering big congressional debates and bills, the media also report on controversial confirmation and oversight hearings. While most confirmation hearings are ignored in the media, if a reporter uncovers damaging information about a presidential appointee or a nominee holds views unpopular with members of Congress, hearings may suddenly become major news. Similarly, oversight is usually handled through routine hearings. Scandals involving lawmakers attract media attention as well.

C-SPAN In the late 1970s, when the cable industry was in its early stages, many people realized the contribution cable stations could play in educating the public about government. Cable-Satellite Public Affairs Network (C-SPAN) began as a "gavel-to-gavel" coverage of the speeches, debates, and votes on the floor of the House of Representatives. Since then, C-SPAN has expanded its coverage to include the Senate and major national events. Like other media, C-SPAN's format has expanded, too. C-SPAN can now be found on radio, satellite radio, and on the web.

Television and Legislative Campaigns Similar to presidential politics, television has impacted who runs for legislative office. The exposure provided by television helps candidates gain recognition, and television has encouraged celebrities—from actors and astronauts to professional athletes and television **commentators**—to enter politics. Since voters are familiar with such people from seeing them on television, these candidates have instant name recognition, which often aids them greatly in getting elected.

Candidates for Congress employ television advertising as a major campaign strategy. Television campaigns use **spot advertising**, the same basic technique used to sell other products. Spot advertisements are brief

POLITICAL CARTOON

Television has continued to be a major vehicle for advertising, but actual news coverage on television now involves only brief opportunities for politicians to share their views.

▲ **CRITICAL THINKING**

Analyzing Who are the two central figures in the cartoon? What are they doing? How does the cartoonist use irony, the contrast between what is said and what is real, to make a point? What is the cartoonist's thesis? Do you agree or disagree? Explain your answers.

commentator person who reports and discusses news on radio or television

spot advertising brief (30 seconds to 2 minutes), frequent, positive descriptions of the candidate or the candidate's major platform points, and/or negative depictions of the opposing candidate

Andrea Seabrook worked at National Public Radio (NPR) for 14 years. Covering Congress for a respected radio network sounds like a great job for a journalist, but Seabrook found it immensely frustrating. "There is so little genuine discussion going on with the reporters. . . . To me, as a reporter, everything is spin."

In 2012 Seabrook quit her job at NPR to start a website/podcast that would cover Congress in a new way. Her aim with DecodeDC, Seabrook says, is to spend the time needed to "break through the stale left/right political narrative and engage people in the search for solutions."

▶ **CRITICAL THINKING**

1. *Analyzing* Explore DecodeDC. What does Seabrook's work tell you about the relationship between Congress and the press?

2. *Explaining* What are the difficulties of covering Congress? How is the information available to citizens affected by those difficulties?

Andrea Seabrook

(30 seconds to 2 minutes), frequent, positive descriptions of the candidate or the candidate's major platform points. Advertisements also might present negative images of the opposing candidate.

The television advertising that has become such a necessary part of a political campaign is not cheap. Candidates rely on extensive fund-raising efforts to afford the huge fees needed to pay for sophisticated television advertising campaigns. One 30-second commercial in a medium-sized market can cost several thousand dollars. It has been estimated that a senator must raise close to $30,000 per week for six years to pay for a reelection campaign.

✓ **READING PROGRESS CHECK**

Identifying What types of congressional events receive press coverage?

The Judiciary and the Media

GUIDING QUESTION *What is the relationship between the Supreme Court and the mass media?*

Much of the media's coverage of the judiciary is related to criminal trials. Generally, journalists have access to trials, in part because the Sixth Amendment guarantees a defendant's right to a public trial. Courts are sometimes concerned, however, that intense media coverage could bias jurors. In those instances, the judge will order that the jury be sequestered, or isolated from the public and media, during the trial. In some cases, the trial will be moved to a different jurisdiction if media exposure in the local community may have influenced the potential juror pool. Some criminal trials attract huge public interest, and the media capitalize on this interest and provide extensive coverage of these trials. This is true particularly of cable news broadcasters, who might provide hours of coverage every day during a trial.

Covering the Supreme Court The Supreme Court and other appellate courts receive less media coverage than trial courts as well as less coverage than Congress or the president. The nature of these courts' work—their appellate jurisdiction—means that they are deciding issues of law, not ruling on whether or not a crime was committed. These issues are sometimes very technical and abstract, sometimes of little interest to the general public.

The media typically cover the Supreme Court cases that deal with issues of nationwide importance. They will report when the Court decides to hear a case, on oral argument in the case, and on the decision in the case. They work to simplify and distill the complex legal arguments for a lay audience.

Many news outlets do not have a full-time reporter at the Court. Instead, they publish news from a wire service or send a reporter to the Court for major cases only. Broadcast media are even less likely to report Supreme Court decisions than newspapers because broadcast news does not allow time to explain issues in depth, and television news must be highly visual. That said, major Supreme Court decisions, which set law and shape policy, receive wide media coverage.

Covering the courts differs substantially from covering the legislative and executive branches. Judges and justices rarely give interviews or discuss cases and never hold press conferences. They let the opinions, or rulings, speak for themselves. All reporters generally have access to the same information—the court filings and audiotapes of what takes place in the courtroom. They seldom have secret sources or big scoops. The Supreme Court, in particular, is known for being leak-proof. No one knows when a certain case will be handed down, and the staff in the building avoid speaking with reporters. Finally, some courts, including the Supreme Court, restrict the use of video cameras or recording devices inside. Without footage of the Supreme Court in action, broadcast media struggle to provide image and video to accompany their reporting. Many journalists are proponents of allowing cameras into the Supreme Court, arguing that such access is fundamental to an educated and informed public. Critics, including most Supreme Court justices, worry that the lawyers and the justices themselves might pander to the cameras and that sound bites will be presented by the media, which will not accurately portray complex legal issues.

☑ **READING PROGRESS CHECK**

Analyzing Why does the Supreme Court receive less media coverage than the other branches of government?

Media and the Public Agenda

GUIDING QUESTION *What role does the mass media play in setting the public agenda?*

The mass media play an important role in setting the public agenda, the collection of societal issues and problems that both political leaders and citizens agree need government attention. The wars in Iraq and Afghanistan, aid to the homeless, long-term health care for children and the elderly, teenage substance abuse, and high crime rates are all problems that have been part of the public agenda.

The media's role in setting the public agenda is not to determine how these social problems will be solved—although editorial writers and commentators may add their views to the conversation—but to bring these issues to the attention of the public and the government.

The media cover Supreme Court cases when they deal with issues that concern many citizens. This photograph shows journalists awaiting a decision by the U.S. Supreme Court on the constitutionality of the Affordable Care Act.

▼ CRITICAL THINKING
Summarizing Why do some courts, including the Supreme Court, restrict the use of cameras or recording devices inside?

Saul Loeb/AFP/Getty Images

When editors, news directors, and reporters decide which topics to cover and which stories to give prominence, they are highlighting the importance of some problems over others. For example, printed newspaper stories that appear on the front page above the fold on the right are generally considered to be the most important stories that day. Online, the process can be different. The flexible format allows editors to change where stories appear on the home page throughout the day or week. They can track how many times a particular story gets "shared" on social media and they can reposition stories based on what is "trending" as popular among readers.

Networks and the Issues How do the media decide what to cover? Of course, journalists' professional judgment plays a role. Reporters, editors, and news directors have views of what issues are most important, informed by their experience covering the news. Most media are businesses, however, and business considerations also play a part. The likely size of the audience is part of the answer. This is especially true for television. Each network competes to attract the biggest audience in a viewing market since a larger audience allows it to charge higher advertising rates. Thus, a network might cover a high-profile political scandal instead of the federal budget because they know most people will quickly switch to another channel if they report on budget details at length.

In turn, the extent of media coverage influences how the public ranks the importance of an issue to the nation. Maxwell McCombs, one of the leading scholars studying media influence, looked at all the research on how the media help to set the public agenda. He concluded, "Through their day-by-day selection and display of the news, editors and news directors focus our attention and influence our perceptions of what are the most important issues of the day." Furthermore, he noted, the more news people consume, the more likely they are to agree with others—regardless of age, race, and other demographics—on what issues are most important.

☑ **READING PROGRESS CHECK**

Explaining How do the mass media decide what issues to cover?

LESSON 1 REVIEW

Reviewing Vocabulary
1. *Discussing* How does the government use news releases and news briefings to communicate with the press and the public?

Using Your Graphic Organizer
2. *Comparing* Use your completed graphic organizer to explain the way the media interacted with government in the past. Compare that with how it interacts with the media today. Conclude by describing what you see as the most significant changes.

Answering the Guiding Questions
3. *Analyzing* How has the relationship between the mass media and government changed over time?

4. *Understanding Relationships* What is the relationship between the mass media and the executive branch of the U.S. government?

5. *Understanding Relationships* What is the relationship between the legislative branch and the mass media?

6. *Understanding Relationships* What is the relationship between the Supreme Court and the mass media?

7. *Finding the Main Idea* What role does the mass media play in setting the public agenda?

Writing About Government
8. *Argument* Research an example of how print or television news coverage has led to a political change. Did coverage raise awareness of a social problem or provide information about government corruption or news about a personal scandal of a public official? Then write a brief argument essay summarizing the political change and whether the media involvement was positive, negative, or neutral. What impact did the media have on the political process?

Interact with these digital assets and others in lesson 2

✓ **INTERACTIVE CHART**
Freedom of Information Act

✓ **INTERACTIVE IMAGE**
Protecting Confidential Sources

✓ **SELF-CHECK QUIZ**

✓ **VIDEO**
Protecting Sources

netw⊙rks
TRY IT YOURSELF ONLINE

Reading Help Desk

Academic Vocabulary

• **source**

Content Vocabulary

• **prior restraint**
• **libel**
• **defamation**
• **Freedom of Information Act (FOIA)**
• **shield law**
• **fairness doctrine**
• **embedded journalist**

TAKING NOTES:

Key Ideas and Details

IDENTIFYING Use the table to identify the ways that the FCC regulates the mass media.

Regulating the Mass Media

LESSON 2
Regulating Print and Broadcast Media

ESSENTIAL QUESTION

What role does the mass media play in the U.S. political system?

The First Amendment and many laws protect the rights of the press—the people and institutions who gather and publish or broadcast news. This protection has made it easier for journalists to fulfill their role as government watchdogs. Today, however, defining who is a journalist is challenging. Which of the following would you call a journalist?

• A reporter for the *Dallas Morning News* or *New York Times*

• A news anchor at your local television station who simply reads the script written for him

• A news producer at your local radio station who decides how much time each story will get and the order of stories in the newscast

• A father of four who blogs about the challenges of being a stay-at-home dad

• A mother of four who blogs about public policies that affect her family

• The webmaster for an interest group

• A person who starts attending a trial because she is interested in the case and then decides to make a documentary film about it

• A student who tweets about happenings at your school

Based on your selections, write a definition of a journalist for the twenty-first century.

Media Protections

GUIDING QUESTION *How do the First Amendment and other laws protect the mass media?*

The First Amendment says in part that "Congress shall make no law . . . abridging the freedom . . . of the press." The guarantee of this freedom is fundamental to democracy. A free and independent press can provide citizens with a variety of information and opinions about government policies. Even if a government is completely transparent, average citizens do not have the time or expertise to locate all the information they would need to make sure the government is being accountable. The press is, in essence, the tool citizens need to ensure that their government is both transparent and accountable. Thomas Jefferson described the importance of a free press when he argued:

 PRIMARY SOURCE

The people are the only censors of their governors. . . . The only safeguard of the public liberty . . . is to give them full information of their affairs through the channel of the public papers & to contrive that those papers should penetrate the whole mass of the people."

—Thomas Jefferson, 1787

In the United States, the First Amendment means that print media are free from **prior restraint**, or government censorship of information before it is published. Prior restraint on a publication is allowed only if publication of the information would cause certain, serious, and irreparable harm to our national security, and the prior restraint would be effective in avoiding this harm while no lesser means could do so. This means that, in almost every case, editors and reporters have freedom to decide what goes in or stays out of their publications.

Freedom of the press, however, is not absolute. False written statements intended to damage a person's reputation are called **libel**. If a publication damages someone's reputation with false statements, that person can sue the publication and recover damages. The value placed on our freedom of speech makes it difficult for public officials to win **defamation** lawsuits. The press must be free to criticize public officials without fear of being sued. Therefore, public officials must prove that the publisher acted with malice or a reckless disregard for the truth in order to win a libel suit. Public officials also generally have access to the media to tell their side of the story and correct false conceptions about themselves.

Freedom for the media to publish whatever they want means little if they cannot collect information about government actions and decisions. If government officials tell lies, hold secret meetings, or try to limit reporters' access to information in other ways, the media may not be able to provide the information citizens need. Does the First Amendment give the media special rights of access to courtrooms or government offices? Further, does it give reporters special protection for their news **sources**—the people they consult to get information?

The Right of Access to Information Sometimes the government tries to control the press by denying access to certain information. In 1966 Congress passed the **Freedom of Information Act (FOIA)**, which requires federal agencies to release files to the public, unless the material falls into certain exceptions for national security or other confidential information. Members of the press often file "FOIA requests" to force the government to release information. Many states have laws similar to FOIA that apply to state agencies.

The press has gone to court many times to fight for its right of access to information on government decisions. The results have been mixed. Generally, the Supreme Court has rejected the idea that the media have special rights of access above and beyond public access. For example, in the 1972 case *Branzburg* v. *Hayes*, the Court said that "the First Amendment does not guarantee the press a constitutional right of special access to information not available to the public generally." Authorities do not have to give the

prior restraint censorship of information before it is published

libel false written or published statements that damage a person's reputation

defamation false expression that injures a person's reputation

source person a reporter consults to get information

Freedom of Information Act (FOIA) requires federal agencies to release files to the public, unless the material falls into certain exceptions for national security or other confidential information

PROTECTING CONFIDENTIAL SOURCES

The press and the U.S. government have fought many battles over the media's right to keep sources secret. This chart shows famous cases in which reporters were in conflict with the courts for refusing to testify about confidential sources.

▲ **CRITICAL THINKING**

Defending Should reporters be forced to disclose the sources for their stories? Construct an argument for or against the proposition.

Reporter	Outcome
Vanessa Leggett	Leggett spent four years researching the 1997 murder of a Houston socialite for a book she planned to write. A federal grand jury subpoenaed the tape recordings of Leggett's interviews with her sources, as well as all transcript copies. When Leggett refused to turn over this information, a federal judge found her in contempt and sentenced her to jail. Leggett was released after six months when the grand jury that issued the subpoena expired.
Judith Miller	In 2003 the identity of covert CIA operative Valerie Plame was leaked to certain members of the press. *New York Times* reporter Judith Miller was one of the journalists who received this information. During an investigation into who leaked Plame's identity, Miller refused to reveal her source to the grand jury. Found guilty of contempt of court, Miller spent 85 days in jail.
James Risen	*New York Times* reporter James Risen published a book in 2006 that contained a chapter describing a failed CIA operation in Iran. The federal government launched an investigation of a CIA official believed to have leaked classified information to Risen. When subpoenaed, Risen refused to reveal his sources and appealed to a federal court to overturn his order to testify.
Jana Winter	Winter, a Fox News reporter, wrote an article in 2012 about a suspect charged with killing 12 people at a theater in Aurora, Colorado. After refusing to reveal the law enforcement officials who provided information for her article, Winter faced the prospect of going to prison. In December 2013, the New York Court of Appeals ruled that Winter did not have to disclose her sources.

media special right of access to crime or disaster sites if the general public is excluded, although they usually do. Reporters may be kept out of legislative sessions that are closed to the general public. Neither do reporters have special access to grand jury proceedings.

Protection of Sources Reporters often need secret informants when investigating abuse of power, scandals involving public officials, or crimes. Success in gathering news may depend on getting information from people who do not want their names made public. However, the government sometimes wants to know what journalists were told or who gave them information, in order to prosecute crimes. If the courts, the police, or legislatures force reporters to name their sources, these sources of information may vanish.

The press and the U.S. government have fought many battles over the media's right to keep sources secret. Forty-nine states and the District of Columbia have **shield laws** to protect reporters from having to reveal their sources. While no federal shield law exists, the Privacy Protection Act of 1980 prevents all levels of government from searching for and seizing source documentation, except in a few circumstances.

shield law a state law that protects reporters from having to reveal their sources

☑ **READING PROGRESS CHECK**

Determining Importance Why is the right of access to information about government crucial to the media's role?

Regulating Media

GUIDING QUESTION *How does the government regulate the mass media?*

Despite the regulatory powers of the federal government, the mass media in the United States have a great deal of freedom. Such freedom has given rise to many diverse avenues of expression. Of these, Internet communications and cable television are among the fastest growing. The goal of government regulations is to provide order, fairness, and access to the mass media.

In the United States, most mass media are private, money-making businesses. Like other businesses, they are subject to some government regulation. The federal government has more power to regulate the broadcast media than the print media largely because the airwaves that transmit broadcast media belong to the public. There is a limited amount of broadcast spectrum, so the government decides who gets a license to broadcast and for what use. In exchange, broadcasters are required to serve some public goals.

The Federal Communications Commission The Federal Communications Commission (FCC) is a government agency with authority to regulate interstate and international communications by radio, television, telephone, telegraph, cable, and satellite. The FCC has five commissioners appointed by the president with Senate approval.

The FCC has broad powers to make rules that require television and radio stations to operate in the public interest. The most important power is the power to grant licenses to all radio and television stations in the country. The FCC's two major regulatory activities deal with the content of broadcasts and with ownership of the media.

Content Regulation Over the years, the extent of FCC content regulation has varied in response to developments in technology, court rulings, and changes in political ideas about the proper role of government. Originally, the FCC set rules that broadcasters must cover issues of interest in the community and present contrasting viewpoints. Broadcasters were given wide leeway in deciding what counts as community issues and how to

GOVERNMENT *in your* COMMUNITY

Media Ownership

What media outlets—television or radio stations, newspapers, local websites—are important to people in your community? Who owns those outlets? List as many newspapers, radio stations, television stations, and websites in your community as you can. Use the Internet to find out who owns each outlet; this information can generally be found on the websites of the media outlets, although you may have to search for it. Make a list or chart showing each outlet you researched and the owner.

- Are any of the outlets owned by individual people rather than companies? How, if at all, might outlets owned by individuals be different from outlets owned by companies?

- Are multiple outlets owned by the same company? Why might this be important in terms of the news available?

Next, research the owners to find out if they also own media outlets in other communities.

▲ CRITICAL THINKING

Creating Maps Map the information you find on a map of the United States. What does your map show about media ownership in the United States? What effect might the patterns of media ownership you identified have on the news available to Americans?

provide contrasting views. This was known as the **fairness doctrine**. The doctrine was supposed to discourage one-sided coverage of issues and encourage stations to present a range of issues.

The Supreme Court had upheld the fairness doctrine as constitutional; however, some broadcasters and political activists claimed that the fairness doctrine was actually censorship. They argued that it caused stations to avoid reporting on any type of controversy. In 1987 the FCC decided to drop the fairness doctrine. Congress then passed a law requiring the FCC to keep it, but President Reagan vetoed the bill. Reagan said the growth of cable television had added many new outlets for different ideas and the fairness doctrine was no longer needed. Ending the fairness doctrine led to a burst of syndicated radio talk shows in which commentators expressed strident political opinions. Although often extreme and one-sided in their views, these commentators argued their points of view offered listeners an alternative to the mainstream media.

The FCC does still regulate broadcast content in other ways. For example, broadcasters can never air obscene programming, and indecent programming is limited to certain hours. While the FCC cannot censor broadcasts, it can issue fines and can threaten not to renew a station's license.

Ownership Regulation Given the power of the press, the federal government is also concerned with who owns media outlets. Owners can influence the message their outlets present.

Shortly after its creation, the FCC began setting rules to prevent the ownership of media from being concentrated in the same hands. It limited the number of radio stations that one company could own in the same large market like Chicago or New York. It also limited cross-ownership of media by stating that companies could no longer own a newspaper and a television or radio station in the same market.

By the 1990s, attitudes about media ownership had changed dramatically. Emerging technologies made new business relationships in telecommunications possible. Telephone lines could carry the same signals that cable companies carried, and cable companies could offer phone service. Both could offer Internet service, videoconferencing, and other services. Both the phone companies and broadcasters sought changes in the federal law.

Telecommunications Act of 1996 In 1996 Congress passed the Telecommunications Act, which ended or relaxed many FCC limits on media ownership. The law removed limits on how many stations a company could own as long as the company did not control more than 35 percent of the national market. It also allowed cross-ownership of cable and broadcast systems.

A key objective to the law was to increase competition, yet, contrary to what many predicted, even greater concentration of media ownership followed. Several media companies merged to create communications giants. For instance, before the law, a company could not own more than 40 radio stations nationwide; now a single company, Clear Channel, owns 850 stations.

Policy makers and interest groups often disagree whether the consequences of a new law are good or bad. Has consolidation in the radio broadcasting business given listeners more variety? Some say yes because companies that buy several stations eliminate duplication in reaching many different audiences. Others claim listeners have fewer choices and that more programming comes from outside the local community.

fairness doctrine rule that required broadcasters to provide opportunities for the expression of opposing views on issues of public importance

✓ **READING PROGRESS CHECK**

Explaining How does the FCC regulate television, radio, and the Internet?

Media and National Security

GUIDING QUESTION *Why are there restrictions on the media's coverage of national security issues?*

Tension often arises between the government's need for secrecy in national security matters and citizens' need for information. This is most obvious in foreign and military affairs. The government tries to control intelligence information by classifying some information as secret. During the Vietnam War, the *New York Times* and other papers published a secret Defense Department study on how the United States became involved in the war. The government tried to stop the publication, commonly called the Pentagon Papers. In *New York Times* v. *United States* (1971), the Supreme Court felt that the potential harm to national security was outweighed by values in the First Amendment.

Government restriction on media coverage during wartime has varied. During the Vietnam War, there were few limits. Reporters roamed freely across combat zones and learned that soldiers had doubts about the way the war was being fought. To prevent negative reports during the 1991 Persian Gulf War, the Defense Department limited coverage to a small group of reporters with most having to depend on official briefings for information.

embedded journalist a reporter who travels with and accompanies troops into battle, then reports live about what they experience

When the war in Iraq began in 2003, the Pentagon allowed 500 reporters to accompany troops into battle. These **embedded journalists** reported live, but they did not have complete freedom: they could not announce their exact location. Critics worried that reporters who shared military life and grew close to the troops would not want to write anything negative about the war.

In 2010 a website called WikiLeaks provided thousands of U.S. State Department documents to news media around the world. A U.S. Army private was charged with providing many of the documents, which dealt with the wars in Iraq and Afghanistan. The government believed that the leaks had jeopardized American lives. But when government prosecutors sought legal action, they found that prosecution would be difficult because of the First Amendment's protection of a free press. The Army private was, however, convicted of espionage charges in a military court.

In 2013 a computer expert who had worked at the National Security Agency (NSA) told a reporter that the NSA was spying on U.S. citizens using computer programs that can monitor cell phones, e-mail, and Internet traffic. The leaker, Edward Snowden, fled the United States to escape prosecution.

☑ **READING PROGRESS CHECK**

Describing How has government restriction of media coverage during wartime varied over time?

LESSON 2 REVIEW

Reviewing Vocabulary
1. ***Identifying Cause and Effect*** What was the fairness doctrine, and what have been the effects of its demise?

Using Your Graphic Organizer
2. ***Identifying*** Use your completed graphic organizer to identify ways the FCC regulates the mass media.

Answering the Guiding Questions
3. ***Explaining*** How do the First Amendment and other laws protect the mass media?

4. ***Identifying*** How does the government regulate the mass media?

5. ***Analyzing*** Why are there restrictions on the media's coverage of national security issues?

Writing About Government
6. ***Argument*** How has U.S. media coverage of wars and international conflicts affected national security policy? What do you think is the proper balance between access to information and national security? Write a letter to the editor explaining your point of view. Reference at least two wars or conflicts.

Interact with these digital assets and others in lesson 2

✓ **INTERACTIVE GRAPH**
   Federal Receipts by Source as Share of Total Receipts

✓ **INTERACTIVE IMAGE**
   Paystub

✓ **SELF-CHECK QUIZ**

✓ **VIDEO**
   Taxes

netw⊙rks
TRY IT YOURSELF ONLINE

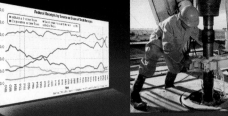

LESSON 2
Raising Revenue

ReadingHelp Desk

Academic Vocabulary

- **impose**
- **subsidy**
- **corporation**

Content Vocabulary

- **tax**
- **excise tax**
- **protective tariff**
- **progressive tax**
- **regressive tax**
- **marginal tax rate**
- **taxable income**
- **dependent**
- **withholding**
- **security**

TAKING NOTES:

Key Ideas and Details

IDENTIFYING Take notes on the various kinds of taxes using the graphic organizer.

Types of Taxes

ESSENTIAL QUESTION

How does the government raise and allocate money?

Taxes are used to raise money for government programs. Taxes can also promote or discourage behavior and activities. For example, if we added a $50 tax to every movie ticket, fewer people might go to the movies. If we offered a tax break for every round of golf, more people might become golfers. Look at the different tax policies listed here. What kind of behavior do you think each tax policy would encourage or discourage? Who might benefit from each tax? Who would have to pay this tax?

 a. a tax on every gallon of gasoline

 b. a tax on hotel rooms

 c. an income tax break for people who pay a mortgage on a house

 d. a tax on cigarettes

 e. a sales tax break on food and clothing

 f. an income tax break for people who have children

Taxes and the Economy

GUIDING QUESTION *What are the U.S. government's main sources of revenue?*

Taxes are payments made by individuals and businesses to support government activities and provide government services. As you will learn, decisions about how to raise and spend government funds are almost always political. Every time a tax law is changed or created, someone wins and someone loses. Government officials, political parties, business leaders, and average citizens all have different ideas about taxes.

Taxes in American History When you think of taxes today, the individual income tax likely comes to mind. The individual income tax as we know it today is a relatively recent addition to our government, however. Until the 1890s, the federal government relied on tariffs, or taxes levied on imported goods, for revenue. These are also called *customs duties* or *import duties*. There are excise taxes on many goods. **Excise taxes** are taxes on the manufacture, transportation, sale, or consumption of goods and services.

"The Congress shall have power to lay and collect Taxes, Duties, Imposts and Excises, and to pay the debts and provide for the common Defense and general Welfare of the United States."

—Article I, Section 8

▲ **DBQ** *Paraphrasing* Rewrite this excerpt from the Constitution using your own words.

Gas and cigarette taxes are excise taxes, for example. Early targets included taxes on horse carriages, snuff (smokeless tobacco), and liquor. The federal government **imposes** excise taxes to raise revenue or to protect domestic business and agriculture from foreign competition.

The Constitution places some limits on Congress's power to tax, however. These limits meant that Congress could not institute an income tax until the Sixteenth Amendment was ratified. In the early years, the income tax applied only to wealthy people. Most Americans were not required to pay an income tax until World War II, when the government desperately needed funds to pay for the war. By the middle of the twentieth century, the income tax was firmly entrenched as a large source of government revenue. As income tax revenue rose, customs duties made up a much less significant portion of the government's revenue streams.

Taxes Today In 2012 the federal government took in about $2.45 trillion in revenues—an average of $7,617 for each person in the nation. In the post-World War II period, the government's revenue has not kept up with its spending. So the federal government has had to borrow money to make up the difference. While income taxes on individuals and corporations make up the largest part of government revenue, they are not the only source.

There are five main types of federal taxes today—excise taxes, customs duties, estate and gift taxes, income taxes, and social insurance taxes. Excise taxes were an important source of revenue in early America, but they are much less important today. Today, excise taxes are imposed on gas, tobacco, liquor, airline tickets, and some luxury goods. Customs duties, also called tariffs, are taxes on imported goods. Congress determines which imports will be taxed and at what rate. Congress has also given the president authority to revise tariff rates through executive orders. In doing so, the president takes international trade agreements into account. High customs duties, called **protective tariffs**, are often popular with business, labor, and farm groups.

An estate tax is a tax on property and money left to others after someone has died. In 2013 the estate tax applied to estates worth more than $5,250,000. People have tried to avoid the estate tax by giving money to family and friends before they died. To prevent this, Congress passed the gift tax, which requires donors to pay taxes on money and property they give to others while they are still living. In 2013 the gift tax applied to gifts worth more than $14,000. Critics of the estate tax say it discourages savings and prevents families from passing on small businesses and farms to their heirs. Others argue that an estate tax is structured to apply only to the super rich.

The final two types of taxes—income and social insurance or Social Security taxes—bring in the largest share of government revenue. Almost all working Americans pay income and social insurance taxes.

✓ **READING PROGRESS CHECK**

Comparing and Contrasting What are the similarities and differences between income taxes and excise taxes?

Income and Social Insurance Taxes

GUIDING QUESTION *What determines who should pay income taxes and how much they should pay?*

Both income and social insurance taxes are levied as a percentage of a taxpayer's income, so people with no income do not pay these taxes. Income taxes go to the government's general fund, while social insurance taxes are reserved to pay for social insurance programs like Social Security and Medicare.

tax payment made by individuals and businesses to support government activities

excise tax a tax on the manufacture, transportation, sale, or consumption of goods and the performance of services

impose to establish or apply by authority

protective tariff a high customs duty

progressive tax tax whereby people with higher incomes pay a larger share of their income in taxes than people with lower incomes

regressive tax tax whereby people with lower incomes pay a larger share of their income in taxes than people with higher incomes

Federal Receipts by Source as Share of Total Receipts

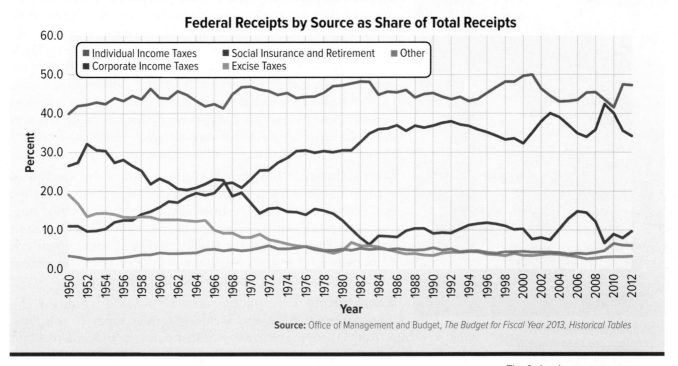

Source: Office of Management and Budget, *The Budget for Fiscal Year 2013, Historical Tables*

Individual Income Tax

The income tax is a **progressive tax**. This means that people with higher incomes pay a larger share of their income in tax than do people with lower incomes. A **regressive tax** would make people with lower incomes pay a larger share of their income in taxes than people with higher incomes. For example, a car registration fee of $100 is regressive, because that $100 is a larger share of a poor person's income than a rich person's income. Even though tax rates rise as income rises, people do not lose money to taxes if they start earning more. A higher tax rate applies only to income over a certain threshold. For example, in 2013, the first $8,925 a single person earned was taxed at 10 percent whether that person earned $50,000 or $500,000. The next highest rate, 15 percent, applied to income over $8,925 but less than $36,250. The top tax rate of 39.6 percent applied only to income over $400,000 for a single person. These brackets are known as **marginal tax rates**.

Income tax is calculated based on a person's **taxable income**. It includes wages (or salary), tips, commission, investment income, lottery or gambling winnings, and more. Tax laws allow people to reduce their total taxable income through a variety of deductions and exemptions, such as donations to charity. The most common exemption is for taxpayers' **dependents**—someone who depends on another person for basic needs such as food, clothing, and shelter. Usually, dependents are children under the age of 18.

Throughout the year, employers take money out of workers' paychecks and send it to the federal government. This **withholding** pays the anticipated taxes owed. Nearly everyone who earns an income must file a yearly report with the government—a tax return. The deadline for filing is April 15. If the withholding was too small, the taxpayer will owe the government money. If it was too large, the taxpayer must file for a refund. Self-employed people who do not receive regular salaries must file estimates of their income four times per year and make tax payments based on the estimate. In this way, these taxpayers avoid making one large payment for the year on April 15, while the government receives a steady flow of income.

The federal government uses revenue from a variety of sources to provide the services expected by citizens.

▲ **CRITICAL THINKING**

1. *Identifying* What are the largest sources of federal revenue? The smallest?

2. *Making Inferences* What has changed since 1950 in terms of different taxes as a proportion of federal revenue? What historical events or government programs might be related to those changes?

marginal tax rate the percentage of income taxes an individual pays increases as his or her income increases; the rate of taxation applies to incomes within defined ranges or brackets

taxable income the total income of an individual minus certain deductions and personal exemptions

dependent one who relies primarily on another person for basic needs such as food, clothing, and shelter

withholding the money an employer holds back from workers' wages as payment of anticipated income taxes

A tax break on oil exploration encourages people to invest in businesses that search for new energy sources.

▲ CRITICAL THINKING

Defending Some people have called the practice of giving tax breaks to large corporations a form of "corporate welfare." Do you agree? Defend your position.

subsidy a grant or gift of money

The Internal Revenue Service (IRS), a bureau of the U.S. Treasury Department, collects taxes. IRS staff members may do a quick computer check on some returns, while auditing a small percentage of the returns more closely. Each year, the IRS investigates many suspected criminal violations of the tax laws.

When the individual income tax was created in 1913, the tax code was less than 30 pages long. By 2013 it was more than 5,000 pages. The tax code includes rules about who must pay taxes and who can take a variety of exemptions, deductions, and credits to lower their taxes. Many Americans hire professionals to complete their annual tax returns, given the complexity of the system.

Deductions Income tax deductions reduce the amount of income that is subject to tax. For example, people who own homes and pay mortgage loans can deduct the interest they pay from their total income. People who receive health insurance through their employer can deduct some premiums from their total income. Some types of savings for retirement can be deducted from a person's total taxable income.

Exemptions Exemptions are a privilege granted by government that legally excludes certain types of property, sales, or income from taxpaying obligations. Most states, for example, exempt educational and religious groups from paying property taxes. Over the years, railroads, airlines, farmers, businesses, builders, defense contractors, the unemployed, the elderly, and veterans have received tax exemptions.

Tax Credits Tax credits directly reduce the amount of tax owed. Some credits are for people with dependents, child care expenses, or educational expenses. Certain older and retired people may also be entitled to a tax credit, depending on the amount of their income. One tax credit, the earned-income credit, will even return more money than a low-income family owed in taxes.

Taxes and Public Policy Tax deductions, exemptions, and credits function as a government **subsidy** to encourage a type of behavior or activity. Tax deductions for home mortgage interest, for example, encourage people to buy homes. That, in turn, helps the construction industry and promotes stable communities. A tax exemption on oil exploration encourages people to invest their money in businesses that search for new energy sources.

Each exemption or deduction favors some people or activities at the expense of others. In these examples, people who own homes are given a tax break not available to those who rent. Oil exploration outfits are given a break not available to other energy sector businesses. Sometimes exemptions granted to one group negatively affect another group. Tax subsidies for the airline industry, for example, might adversely affect the railroad industry.

Finally, every tax break "costs" the government money in lost revenue. For example, the government misses out on all the money it would have collected if contributions to retirement accounts were taxed.

Since exemptions, deductions, and credits result in lost government revenue, some economists think of these items as a form of government spending. Many exemptions and deductions were added to the tax code at the urging of special interest groups or lobbyists. In general, wealthy Americans often benefit more from deductions and exemptions. First, wealthy people are more likely to hire accountants and tax attorneys who can identify special exemptions they qualify for. Second, wealthy people pay higher income tax rates. So if a person who has a taxable income of

©Lloyd Sutton/Alamy

$50,000 per year donates $1,000 to charity, they could save $250 in taxes, because that $1,000 would have been taxed at 25 percent. If a person who makes $5 million donates $1,000 to charity, they save $396 in taxes for the same size donation, due to the higher tax rate. Even though people with higher incomes often take advantage of deductions that lower their taxes, the top 10% of taxpayers pay about two-thirds of all income taxes.

Income Tax Reforms Today, the federal income tax is a complicated maze of rates, exemptions, and deductions. Critics of the income tax system believe that exemptions are unfair and argue that only **corporations** or the wealthy take full advantage of them. Some economists and politicians have proposed reforming the tax system to remove most deductions and exemptions so that overall tax rates can be lowered. Calls for comprehensive tax reform have failed to gain traction in Congress, however.

The tax code has been reformed in the past. In 1986 President Reagan and Congress reduced deductions, credits, tax shelters, and the number of tax brackets or rates. In 2001 President George W. Bush and Congress enacted massive temporary tax cuts and in 2003 moved to make them permanent. This included a cut in the tax rate paid on a type of investment income called capital gains. Meant to encourage investment in new businesses, lower capital gains rates often favor wealthier people with money to invest. In 2012 President Obama and Congress compromised to raise the income and capital gains rates on high-income individuals making over $400,000.

Corporate Income Tax Corporations must also pay income taxes. The federal government taxes all a corporation's income beyond its expenses and deductions. Nonprofit organizations such as colleges, labor unions, and religious organizations are exempt from this tax. Corporate tax rates are also progressive—companies with larger profits are taxed at a higher rate. However, the rate that companies actually pay varies greatly. Due to various exemptions, tax credits, and accounting techniques, the actual tax rate many large companies pay is about 13 percent. Some corporations set up subsidiary companies in other countries with very low tax rates and send their profits overseas to reduce their taxes.

Social Insurance Taxes The federal government collects huge sums of money each year to pay for Social Security, Medicare, and unemployment compensation programs. The taxes collected to pay for these social programs are called *social insurance taxes*. People who work pay these taxes regardless of their income, and almost everyone pays the same rate. Income above a certain amount—$113,700 in 2013—is not taxed for Social Security but is taxed for Medicare.

Employees and employers share equally in paying the tax for Social Security and Medicare. Employers deduct it directly from each worker's paycheck, add an equal amount, and send the total to the federal government. All these

corporation a large legal business group with its own duties, powers, and liabilities

Both income and social insurance taxes are levied as a percentage of a taxpayer's income. Income taxes go to the government's general fund, while social insurance taxes are reserved to pay for social insurance programs like Social Security and Medicare. Use this sample paystub to learn more about taxes and deductions.

▼ CRITICAL THINKING

1. Calculating Over the course of the year, how much will this taxpayer have withheld?

2. Creating Graphs Create a graph that shows the percentage of the earned wages that is deducted in each category.

3. Summarizing Write a paragraph summarizing the different taxes deducted from the paycheck.

ConglomoCorp, Inc.
2504 Ubiquitous Ave.
Anywhere, USA
40000-1234

Pay Period: 2/17/2014 to 3/02/2014
Pay Date: 3/02/2014

Mike Mikkelson
6500 Any St.
Anywhere, USA
40000-1246

Hours and Earnings			Taxes and Deductions	
Hours	Rate	Earnings	Description	Amount
80	$27.00	$2160.00	Federal Tax	$296.75
			State Tax	$97.38
			Social Security	$81.41
			Medicare	$28.10

Gross Year-to-Date	Gross This Pay Period	Total Deductions	Net Pay
$8640.00	$2160.00	$503.64	$1656.36

social insurance taxes are often called *payroll taxes*. The revenue raised from these taxes then goes directly to the social insurance programs and pays the benefits for the people who are currently collecting Social Security or unemployment or are insured by Medicare. Only people who paid into the system are eligible for benefits. These taxes are considered regressive, because people with lower incomes pay a larger percentage of their incomes for these taxes than people with higher incomes.

✓ **READING PROGRESS CHECK**

Analyzing What are the arguments in support of and opposed to cutting the capital gains tax?

Borrowing for Revenue

GUIDING QUESTION *How does Congress try to control the national debt?*

If the government spends more than it collects, as it has done in most recent years, it runs a budget deficit. To make up the difference, the government borrows money by having the Treasury Department issue **securities** in the form of bonds, notes, and treasury bills. Anyone can buy these securities, in effect lending money to the government. The government then pays the money back, with interest, over time. Because the federal government has borrowed so much money in the past, today it pays a huge amount of interest.

security a financial instrument, including a bond, note, and certificate, that is sold as a means of borrowing money with a promise to repay the buyer with interest after a specific time period

Government borrowing to fund annual budget deficits over time creates the public, or national, debt. About half of the public debt is held by foreign investors and other countries that buy U.S treasury bonds. Congress has tried to control the size of the debt by setting a debt ceiling, or legal limit to the amount the federal government can borrow. The debt ceiling has not been very effective in the past, because the government would have to shut down if the Treasury was unable to borrow enough money to pay its bills. As a result, the debt ceiling has been raised many times and has become a contentious issue as concerns about the size of the national debt have grown. Economists generally agree that too much debt can be bad for the country, but no one knows exactly how much debt is too much.

✓ **READING PROGRESS CHECK**

Defining What are the U.S. national debt and the U.S. national debt ceiling?

LESSON 2 REVIEW

Reviewing Vocabulary

1. *Differentiating* What is the difference between progressive taxes and regressive taxes?

Using Your Graphic Organizer

2. *Applying* Write a short explanation of why each source of revenue is important to the U.S. government.

Answering the Guiding Questions

3. *Identifying* What are the U.S. government's main sources of revenue?

4. *Summarizing* What determines who should pay income taxes and how much they should pay?

5. *Explaining* How does Congress try to control the national debt?

Writing About Government

6. *Informative/Explanatory* Analyze how different federal taxes affect the U.S. economy. Then research several proposals to reform the U.S. tax code. Select one that you think would be most effective and write a brief fact sheet that summarizes the proposal and predicts how it would affect individual taxpayers, corporations, the U.S. government, and the U.S. economy overall.

Interact with these digital assets and others in lesson 3

✓ INTERACTIVE CHART
Key Economic Indicators

✓ INTERACTIVE MAP
The Federal Reserve System

✓ SELF-CHECK QUIZ

✓ VIDEO
Janet Yellen

netw⊙rks
TRY IT YOURSELF ONLINE

ReadingHelp Desk

Academic Vocabulary

- **index**
- **reluctant**

Content Vocabulary

- **economic indicators**
- **fiscal policy**
- **monetary policy**
- **gross domestic product (GDP)**
- **Federal Reserve System**
- **discount rate**
- **open-market operations**
- **reserve requirement**

TAKING NOTES:

Key Ideas and Details

ORGANIZING Complete the table to organize information about fiscal and monetary policies.

	Fiscal Policy	Monetary Policy
Who makes the policy?		
How can it influence the economy?		
What goals does it address?		
How quickly can it be changed?		

LESSON 3
Managing the Economy

ESSENTIAL QUESTION

What role does the government play in managing the economy?

Consider the following situations. How much control do you believe the president and Congress should have over the economic trends described in each situation? Give each one a ranking of "a lot," "some," or "none." Explain your reasons.

- You want to buy your first car. To do so, you will need a loan. When your older sister bought her car, she received an interest rate of 5 percent. Today, the best interest rate you can get is 9 percent.

- You are looking for a part-time job after school. You apply to more than 20 stores and restaurants, but no one is hiring.

- You want to go on vacation to a city about 200 miles away. This summer, gas costs 50 percent more than it did last spring. You are not sure you can afford the higher cost.

- A carton of milk and a dozen eggs used to cost $4 at your neighborhood store. Now the same products cost $5.

What types of things do you think lawmakers could do to affect these activities? Make a list, and then compare your list to another student's.

Influencing the Economy

GUIDING QUESTION *How much influence does the government have over the nation's economy?*

As candidates, politicians often set out economic plans—actions they want to take to improve some sector of the economy. The amount of influence they can actually have as lawmakers however, varies widely. There are many ways that federal government actions influence the economy—from what programs money is spent on to how revenue is raised and taxes are assessed to how much debt is carried and how much money and credit is available to borrowers. Many Americans disagree on what role the government should play in managing the economy. Our modified free enterprise system—sometimes called a *mixed economy*—means that the control over the economy is divided between government and the private sector. Yet most Americans expect the federal government to play a significant role in moderating the economy's ups and downs and in promoting economic growth.

Unemployment Rate: This is the number of Americans who are not working but are looking for work. It is published every month by the Bureau of Labor in the Employment Situation Summary, which also details average hours worked and average wages.

Dow Jones Industrial Average (the Dow), S&P 500, and NASDAQ: These are three stock indices. The Dow includes the stock prices of 30 large companies, while the S&P and NASDAQ represent much broader cross-sections of publicly traded American companies.

Consumer Price Index (CPI): This is a measure of the average change over time for the prices Americans pay for a list of set goods and services. It is one indication of the inflation rate.

Existing Home Sales: The National Association of Realtors reports on the number of already-built homes that are sold each month.

Consumer Confidence Index: This is a survey of 5,000 ordinary Americans to gauge how they feel about current economic conditions and their expectations for the future.

▲ CRITICAL THINKING

Creating Graphs Choose a month and research information about at least three of these indices for that month over the past three years. Draw a graphic or chart comparing the same month in different years. What do the numbers tell you about the relative health of the economy?

economic indicators markets, scales, reports, or figures that give information about how different areas of the economy are performing

index a list of companies and their stock prices

fiscal policy a government's use of spending and taxation to influence the economy

monetary policy the Federal Reserve System's actions to control the supply of money and cost of credit to influence the economy

Economic Indicators The American economy is massive, involving hundreds of millions of people and trillions of dollars. It can be difficult to know whether the overall economy is healthy or faltering from each individual person's perspective. In order to get a sense of how things are going, government officials and the public refer to a variety of **economic indicators**. These are market conditions, reports, or figures that give information about how the economy is performing. They include things like stock market **indices**, reports about employment levels, surveys about how consumers feel about the economy, information about construction and purchase of homes, reports on changing prices for goods and services, and more. If one or more of these indicators behave in an alarming manner, the government might want to take action to try to change economic conditions.

Since the 1930s the federal government has played an increasing role in managing the nation's economy. The government can influence the economy in two main ways: by using fiscal policy or monetary policy. **Fiscal policy** involves using government spending and taxation to influence the economy. **Monetary policy** involves controlling the supply of money and credit. However, U.S. monetary policy is exercised by the Federal Reserve System, which is an independent agency of the federal government.

Fiscal Policy The federal budget is a major tool of fiscal policy because it shapes how much money the government plans to spend and how much it plans to collect through taxes and borrowing. The president and Congress can use the budget to pump money into the economy to stimulate it or to take money out of the economy to slow it down.

To stimulate the economy, the government could spend money on various projects. Through increased spending, the government tries to put more people to work and increase economic activity. The government can also buy things—labor, equipment, materials, or services for government programs. Instead of spending more, the government could also reduce taxes. Lower taxes give consumers and investors more purchasing power. People would have more money in their pockets and be able to buy more goods and services. Either increased spending or reduced taxes or both at the same time can increase overall demand for goods and services in the economy.

There are several problems with fiscal policy. It can be difficult for Congress and the president to enact fiscal policy quickly enough to have an impact on an economic downturn. Spending to stimulate the economy usually leads to deficits and increases in the national debt. This is because the government must borrow the money it plans to spend. Finally, government spending is difficult to scale back when the economy recovers, especially if people become accustomed to having new services or programs. Tax cuts are politically popular, and are partially responsible for the federal budget deficits in the post-World War II period. Deficit spending has led to a growing national debt that could threaten future economic growth.

Demands for cutting the deficit and balancing the budget have grown even though experts disagree on what levels of debt and deficit are sustainable. Many economists believe that deficits are necessary if the government is going to use fiscal policy to shape the economy. Others say that the deficit as a percentage of the **gross domestic product (GDP)**, the market value of all final goods and services produced in the nation in a year, is more important than the actual size of the deficit. While there are merits to both positions, in 2013 the deficit represented about 6 percent of GDP. This is higher than the historical average but is much less than in recent times of financial stress.

Monetary Policy The American economy is based on a system of competitive markets that make extensive use of money and credit. The amount of money and credit available at any given time impacts the amount of borrowing and spending that businesses and individuals are able to do. Money is so important that the Constitution gave the national government authority to "coin money [and] regulate the value thereof." This means the federal government can create money and put it into circulation. This also means that the government can create an independent institution like the Federal Reserve System to manage the money supply and conduct monetary policy.

Monetary policy involves managing the supply of money and the cost of borrowing to meet the needs of the economy. In the United States, these responsibilities have been delegated to the Federal Reserve System.

✓ **READING PROGRESS CHECK**

Summarizing What do the executive and legislative branches of government hope to accomplish by implementing fiscal and monetary policies?

The chair of the Federal Reserve System, Janet Yellen, and its seven-member Board of Governors make economic decisions largely independent of political pressure.

▲ CRITICAL THINKING
Explaining What does it mean to say the Federal Reserve operates "independently" of the president and Congress?

gross domestic product (GDP) the market value of all final goods and services produced in a country in a year

The Federal Reserve System

GUIDING QUESTION *What role does the Federal Reserve play in the U.S. economy?*

The **Federal Reserve System**, also known as the Fed, is the central banking system of the United States. Created by Congress, the Fed operates independently. When people or corporations need money, they borrow from a bank. When banks need money, they borrow from the Fed. This is why the Fed is often called a "banker's bank," but the Fed has other responsibilities as well. The Fed's mandate is "to promote sustainable growth, high levels of employment, stability of prices to help preserve the purchasing power of the dollar, and moderate long-term interest rates." What does this mean? The Fed uses a variety of strategies aimed at keeping the inflation rate (the increase in consumer prices over time) low while helping the economy produce jobs for everyone who wants to work.

Organization of the Fed When the Federal Reserve System was established in 1913, it was organized as a privately owned stock corporation. The largest banks in the country were required to contribute a portion of their financial capital to build the Fed, and in return they received shares of stock ownership. This meant that the Fed was technically owned by private commercial banks, which, as owners, received dividends on their

Federal Reserve System the central banking system of the United States

POLITICAL CARTOONS

▲ Should the government spend money to stimulate the economy? Prominent economists, government officials, and ordinary Americans disagree.

EXPLORING THE ESSENTIAL QUESTION

Exploring Issues What is your opinion about whether government spending stimulates the economy? What additional information do you need to answer this question confidently? How and where might you find the answers and information you need?

discount rate the interest rate the Federal Reserve charges member banks for loans

open-market operations the means the Federal Reserve System uses to affect the economy by buying or selling government securities on the open market

reserve requirement the percentage of money member banks must keep in their vaults or on deposit with the Federal Reserve Banks as a reserve against their deposits

reluctant hesitant, unwilling, disinclined

stock ownership shares. To make sure that the Fed operated in the public interest, a Board of Governors was established in Washington, D.C.

The seven-member Board of Governors supervises the entire Federal Reserve System. The president selects these members whose appointments must be ratified, or approved, by the Senate. The president then selects one of the board members to chair the Board of Governors for a four-year term. Once appointed, board members and the chair are independent of the rest of the government. This allows the Board of Governors to make economic decisions largely independent of political pressure. Because of the unique nature of ownership and management, the Fed is often said to be a "privately-owned, publicly-controlled institution."

Making Monetary Policy The Board of Governors has two major responsibilities in forming monetary policy. First, and most important, it determines the general money and credit policies of the United States. Second, it supervises the operations of the Federal Reserve Banks in the 12 districts across the country.

The Fed uses three tools to control the nation's monetary policy and ensure the health of the economy. First, the Fed can raise or lower the **discount rate**. The discount rate is the rate of interest the Fed charges member banks for loans. Low discount rates encourage banks to borrow money from the Fed to make loans to their customers. High discount rates mean banks will borrow less money from the Fed, charge higher rates to their customers, and make fewer loans. When the economy is growing too slowly, the Fed will usually lower discount rates to stimulate the economy. If the economy is growing too fast and inflation is rising, the Fed will increase the discount rate to "cool off" lending.

Second, the Fed can put money into the economy by buying government bonds on the open market. These **open-market operations** stimulate and help expand the economy. The hope is that the increase of money in the economy will lower interest rates and increase consumer spending. If the Fed believes that inflation is growing too fast, it can stop buying or even sell government securities to decrease the supply of money entering the economy. As investors buy these securities, money is taken out of the economy, causing it to slow down.

Finally, the Fed can raise or lower the **reserve requirement** for member banks. Member banks must keep a certain percentage of their customers' deposits in their vaults or on deposit with the Federal Reserve Banks as a reserve against withdrawals. If the Fed raises the reserve requirement, banks must leave more money with the Fed. Thus, they have less money to lend. The Fed has been **reluctant** to use the reserve requirement as a policy tool because other monetary policy tools work better. However, the reserve requirement can be powerful should the Fed decide to use it.

☑ **READING PROGRESS CHECK**

Using Context Clues What is the meaning of the sentence *"Because of the unique nature of ownership and management, the Fed is often said to be a 'privately-owned, publicly-controlled institution'"*?

Impacts of Fiscal and Monetary Policy

GUIDING QUESTION *How do fiscal and monetary policies affect the U.S. economy?*

Government decisions about taxes and spending affect us in obvious ways. But these government decisions also impact us in more indirect ways, through their impact on the overall economy. Government policy might create more demand for goods and services, either if the government is purchasing more or if consumers have more money to spend. Demand can impact the costs of goods and services, the degree to which businesses grow, and employment levels. Fiscal policy can also impact the rate of foreign investment in the U.S. economy, which might make U.S. exports cheaper or more expensive. This can change how much Americans sell in other countries.

The Federal Reserve Board's decisions have a major impact on the economy and on the daily lives of nearly every American. If the Fed raises interest rates, buying a home or a car could become more expensive. If the Fed lowers interest rates and the reduction encourages businesses and people to borrow money and make investments, companies might hire more workers to meet increased demand or expand their business. If the Fed cuts back on buying securities, thereby lowering the amount of money circulating in the economy, consumers might spend less. Too much money circulating can create inflation and lower the purchasing power of each dollar.

Federal monetary policy affects the economy at the national, state, and local levels. Research has shown that monetary policies influence states and localities differently. For example, personal incomes in states with extractive industries are generally less affected by changes in the federal funds interest rate.

Because the Fed's actions can have such a strong impact on interest rates and the economy overall, investors watch the Fed's reports and meetings carefully. Statements by the Fed chair can cause rapid changes in the stock market as investors speculate about future Fed actions.

The Fed is an independent policy-making institution. While the president and Congress largely control taxing and spending, they have little control over the Fed. Sometimes, when conflicting economic policies arise, the president or Congress might complain that the Fed is interfering with their programs.

Because of conflicts like these, some would like to limit the Fed's role and make it less independent. Others maintain that the nation needs an institution that is removed from political pressures to watch over monetary policy.

☑ **READING PROGRESS CHECK**

Identifying Cause and Effect What causes inflation?

LESSON 3 REVIEW

Reviewing Vocabulary

1. ***Describing*** What are economic indicators and how do they influence government actions?

Using Your Graphic Organizer

2. ***Outlining*** Write a paragraph about how the government's monetary and fiscal policies influence the U.S. economy at the national level.

Answering the Guiding Questions

3. ***Summarizing*** How much influence does the government have over the nation's economy?

4. ***Describing*** What role does the Federal Reserve play in the U.S. economy?

5. ***Explaining*** How do fiscal and monetary policies affect the U.S. economy?

Writing About Government

6. ***Informative/Explanatory*** Think about how fiscal policy and monetary policy are different. Then write a comparative essay that considers how each can affect individuals, groups, and businesses differently.

Interact with these digital assets and others in lesson 4

✓ **INTERACTIVE GRAPH**
Sources of Local Government Revenue

✓ **INTERACTIVE IMAGE**
Assessing Property Values

✓ **SELF-CHECK QUIZ**

✓ **VIDEO**
State Budget Crises

netw⊙rks
TRY IT YOURSELF ONLINE

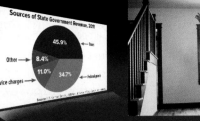

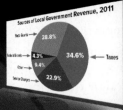

LESSON 4
Financing State and Local Governments

Reading Help Desk

Academic Vocabulary

• **welfare**

Content Vocabulary

• **severance tax**
• **block grant**
• **bond**
• **real property**
• **personal property**
• **market value**
• **special assessment**

TAKING NOTES:

Key Ideas and Details

LISTING Use the graphic organizer to list the ways state and local governments collect revenue.

Sources of Revenue

ESSENTIAL QUESTION

How does the government raise and allocate money?

Imagine that you are a state legislator. Your state's roads and highways are in dire need of repair, but the state does not have enough money in the budget to do the work. Consider the following options for raising additional revenue. List at least one advantage and disadvantage for each. Then decide which option you think would be best.

• Raise income tax rates slightly.

• Make two of the busier state highways toll roads.

• Raise the tax on gasoline and diesel fuel.

• Borrow money by selling highway bonds.

• Charge businesses that operate trucks in your state a highway repair fee.

Can you think of another solution?

Do you know if your state uses any of these revenue sources? If so, which one(s)?

State Revenue

GUIDING QUESTION *What are state governments' main sources of revenue?*

State governments raise revenue in a variety of ways. Taxes—usually including sales taxes, income taxes, property taxes, and license fees—account for the majority of the general revenue of the 50 states. However, the federal Constitution limits a state's taxing powers in three ways:

• A state cannot tax imports or exports. These make up interstate and foreign commerce that only Congress can tax or regulate.

• A state cannot tax federal property.

• A state cannot use its taxing power to deprive people of "equal protection of the law," nor can it use its taxing power to deprive people of life, liberty, or property without "due process of the law."

Individual state constitutions also limit state taxing powers. For instance, some state constitutions prevent states from taxing property used for educational, charitable, or religious purposes. Others prohibit or limit certain taxes such as the sales tax and the income tax.

Taxes cannot provide all the funds state governments need. The next largest source of revenue to the states is federal grants, which provide more than one-third of all state revenue. Charges for services provide about 10 percent of state revenue; other sources, like lotteries and payments into state retirement, account for less than 10 percent.

Sales Tax State governments began using the sales tax during the Great Depression in the 1930s. Sales tax is calculated as a percentage of dollars spent to buy goods. For example, if the sales tax is 5 percent and you spend $100, the tax is $5. Almost all states now have a sales tax, which accounts for about one-third of their tax revenue. Sales taxes are of two types: the general sales tax and the selective sales tax.

The general sales tax is imposed on items such as cars, electronics, household products, and other types of merchandise. In some states, food and drugs are not subject to this tax.

The selective sales tax is imposed on a narrower range of items, such as gasoline, liquor, or cigarettes. A selective sales tax is also called an *excise tax*.

People have strongly criticized the sales tax as a regressive tax. A regressive tax is a tax in which the percentage of income that is paid in taxes drops as incomes rise. Because basic, necessary goods are a larger portion of a poor person's income than a wealthy person's, sales taxes also represent a higher percentage of a low-income earner's income.

Traditionally, sales taxes have applied only to goods purchased. Today, however, some states are considering levying taxes on services as well. This means that getting a haircut, having your house cleaned, or taking a dancing lesson could all be taxed. Hawaii, New Mexico, and South Dakota already have such taxes in place on all services. Some states tax only certain services; for example, Texas taxes janitorial services.

State Income Tax Most states now have individual income taxes and corporate income taxes. Some policy makers believe that states should keep corporate tax rates low to attract businesses and therefore jobs to their states. Other policy makers consider that they need to raise revenue from a variety of sources that can afford to pay. Despite much opposition, the state income tax on individuals now accounts for more than 30 percent of all state tax revenues, compared to 10 percent in 1956. Many states impose an income tax on the earnings of both individuals and corporations.

Other Taxes States also raise revenue from several other sources. Many of these are imposed in the form of licensing fees. States require professionals to pay for licenses to do business in the state. For example, in order to practice as a doctor, realtor, or lawyer, a person must be licensed by the state, a process that often entails passing an exam and paying a fee. States also require licenses for hunting and fishing within their borders, as well as licenses to operate bus lines, amusement parks, and other businesses. By far, the most tax revenue from licenses comes from driver's licenses and motor vehicle registration.

Some states impose **severance taxes** on the removal of natural resources such as oil, gas, coal, uranium, and fish from land or water. Severance taxes are good sources of revenue in oil- and gas-producing states, such as Oklahoma, Texas, and Alaska. For Kentucky, a severance tax on coal brings in significant revenues.

severance tax a tax imposed by a state for the extraction of nonrenewable natural resources

C·I·V·I·C PARTICIPATION IN A DIGITAL AGE

Collecting Delinquent Taxes

Catching people who do not pay taxes is a problem for all levels of government. Many state governments are using the Internet to help collect delinquent taxes. More than 18 states have websites that post the names of people and businesses that have not paid their taxes. This "Internet shaming" has been very effective. In one year, Georgia collected more than $19 million in back taxes. When Wisconsin first implemented a new law requiring the names of those with unpaid taxes to be posted on the Internet, 913 people responded to warning letters and paid $8 million in taxes.

Top Ten States for Delinquent Taxpayers					
State	**Total Returns**	**Returns with Income Tax Liability**	**Returns with No Income Tax Liability**	**Nonpayers**	**Rank**
Mississippi	1,283,495	712,035	571,460	44.5%	1
Georgia	4,589,611	2,639,561	1,950,050	42.5%	2
Alabama	2,102,251	1,254,979	847,272	40.3%	3
Florida	9,631,252	5,879,430	3,751,822	39.0%	4
Arkansas	1,224,333	748,945	475,388	38.8%	5
South Carolina	2,051,823	1,255,957	795,866	38.8%	6
New Mexico	913,001	560,068	352,933	38.7%	7
Idaho	663,291	407,579	255,712	38.6%	8
Texas	10,995,576	6,760,829	4,234,747	38.5%	9
Utah	1,134,626	699,598	435,028	38.3%	10

CRITICAL THINKING

Evaluating Find out if your state publishes the names of people and companies who have not paid their taxes. If so, do you think this is good policy for your state? If not, do you think your state should implement such a policy? Explain your reasons.

---

welfare concerned with the well-being of disadvantaged social groups

Intergovernmental Revenue The federal government currently provides about one-quarter of all state revenues. Federal funds often come to states in the form of federal grants. These grants, also called *grants-in-aid*, are monies given to the states for specific purposes.

By stipulating how federal money is supposed to be used, these grants influence the states in a number of ways. First, grants supply funds for programs that states might not otherwise decide to support. Grants also promote programs and goals that reflect national goals. Finally, because grants come with certain guidelines and requirements, they often set minimum standards for a service in the states. For example, the federal government provides grants to make sure that all states provide a minimum public **welfare** program.

There are several kinds of categorical grants. Some are formula grants—federal funds go to all the states on the basis of a formula. Different amounts go to different states, often depending on factors such as the relative population size or wealth. These grants usually require states to provide matching funds. Others are project grants—state or local agencies or individuals may apply for funds for specific purposes: to fight crime, to improve a city's subway system, or to control air and water pollution, among other things.

block grant a grant of money to a state or local government to be used for a general purpose

State governments usually prefer block grants over categorical grants as a form of federal aid. A **block grant** is a large grant of money to a state or local government to be used for a general purpose, such as public health or crime control. Block grants have fewer guidelines, and state officials have considerably more choice over how the money will be spent.

Federal Mandates Between 1980 and 1990, the federal government increased the number of mandated programs for which state and local governments had to raise their own revenues. A mandate is a formal order given by a higher authority, in this case by the federal government. State and local officials complained about the rising cost of federal mandates in areas such as health and the environment. Some believed that the federal government had intruded on state sovereignty. In 1995 Congress passed the Unfunded Mandate Reform Act (UMRA), which required Congress to describe the costs to the state, local, or tribal governments, or private companies. By 2003, the law had reduced the burden on state governments.

Service Charges States also raise revenue by charging for services they provide. The largest part of revenue generated by charging for services comes from higher education (tuition paid to state colleges and universities) and health care services provided at state hospitals.

Other Revenue Sources More than 40 states run public lotteries to raise revenue. The states spend over half the lottery income on prizes and 5 percent on administering the lottery. Despite the high profile of state lotteries, they generate a rather small part of states' overall revenue—when prizes and administrative costs are subtracted, the net proceeds from lotteries provide only about 1 percent of the total revenue in the states that have lotteries.

Payments by workers into public employees' retirement funds and such insurance programs as unemployment and workers compensation are another source of revenue. Another revenue stream is provided through the interest earned on the accounts where this money is deposited. Unfortunately, recent years have seen low interest rates and higher expenses for retirement and unemployment compensation.

Borrowing States borrow money, often to pay for large, long-term expenditures such as highway construction or other building projects. State governments borrow by selling bonds. A **bond** is a contractual promise on the part of the borrower to repay a certain sum plus interest by a specified date. In most states, voters must be asked to approve new bond issues. As of 2011, the states owed about $1.1 trillion.

bond a government security

☑ **READING PROGRESS CHECK**

Explaining How do states sell bonds to pay for large, long-term projects?

GOVERNMENT *in your* COMMUNITY

State Government Revenue

State government revenue comes from taxes, federal grants, service charges, and other smaller sources, such as insurance trusts and utility revenue. The circle graph shows the averages for all states.

EXPLORING THE ESSENTIAL QUESTION

1. **Comparing** Investigate the sources of revenue for your state. Figure out how the exact figures in your state compare to this graph of the average.

2. **Creating Graphs** Draw or create a similar graph using computer software. Make a list of the taxes that go into the Taxes section of the graph.

Sources of State Government Revenue, 2011

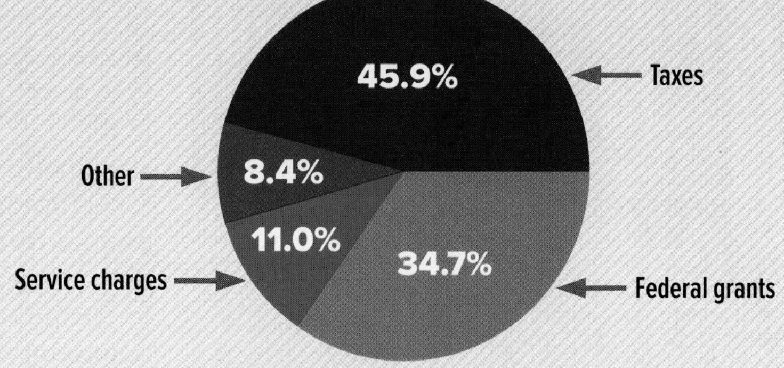

- Taxes — 45.9%
- Federal grants — 34.7%
- Service charges — 11.0%
- Other — 8.4%

Source: U.S. Census Bureau, 2011 Annual Survey of State Government Finances.

Financing Local Government

GUIDING QUESTION *What are local governments' main sources of revenue?*

Local governments provide services such as mass transit, airports, parks, water, sewage treatment, education, welfare, and correctional facilities. The costs for these services are enormous, and taxes—property taxes, sales taxes, income taxes, and fees—provide most of the revenues necessary to supply these services. Local governments also receive funds from state and federal government and borrow money in the form of municipal bonds.

Property Tax One of the oldest taxes—property taxes—once provided revenue for all levels of government. Property taxes are now the most important source of revenue for local governments, accounting for about three-quarters of all tax revenues.

Property taxes are collected on **real property** and **personal property**. Real property includes land and buildings. Personal property consists of such things as stocks and bonds, jewelry, furniture, automobiles, and works of art. Most local governments tax only real property. If personal property is taxed at all, the rate is usually very low.

How do local governments determine what the property tax rate will be? A government tax assessor first calculates the **market value** of the homes and other real property in the community. The market value of a house or a factory is the amount of money the owner could expect to receive if the property were sold.

Most local governments tax property on its assessed value, which is usually only a percentage of its market value. For example, a house that has an appraised value of $200,000 may have an assessed value of 80 percent of that figure, or $160,000. The homeowner would then pay a percentage (often 1 to 2 percent) of that assessed value as the property tax.

Public opinion surveys indicate that most Americans view the property tax as unfair. A major complaint against the tax is that it is regressive: It places a heavier burden on people with lower incomes than on those with higher incomes. The property tax also weighs heavily on retired homeowners with fixed incomes who cannot afford constantly rising taxes. The second criticism of the property tax is that it is often very difficult to determine property values on a fair and equal basis. Standards may vary with each tax assessor.

A third criticism is that reliance on the property tax results in unequal public services. A wealthy community with a large tax base can afford better public services than a less wealthy community with a small tax base. Based on this criticism, some state supreme courts have ruled against using the property tax to pay for local schools. They have held that using property taxes to support schools is a violation of the Fourteenth Amendment's guarantee of equal protection of the law.

Finally, government property and property used for educational, religious, or charitable purposes are exempt from the property tax. Some communities also give tax exemptions to new businesses and industries to encourage them to relocate there. As a result, the nonexempt property owners must bear a heavier share of the tax burden.

---

real property land and buildings

personal property movable belongings such as furniture and jewelry, as well as intangible items such as stocks and bonds

market value the amount of money a property owner could expect to receive if the property were sold

Local governments collect property taxes on real property, which includes land and buildings.

▼ **CRITICAL THINKING**

1. *Defining* What is an assessment?

2. *Evaluating* Walter purchased his home 50 years ago for $15,000. He believes that the property tax he pays should be based on the purchase price of his home. Evaluate his argument.

Sources of Local Government Revenue, 2011

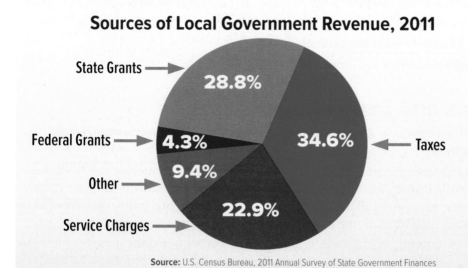

State Grants → 28.8%

Federal Grants → 4.3%

Other → 9.4%

Service Charges → 22.9%

34.6% ← Taxes

Source: U.S. Census Bureau, 2011 Annual Survey of State Government Finances

Local governments receive revenues from a variety of sources to provide services to the community.

◀ CRITICAL THINKING

Reading Graphs What portion of local revenue is represented by the combined contributions of the state and federal governments?

Other Local Revenue Sources Local governments sometimes impose local income taxes, sales taxes, and fines and fees, or operate government-owned businesses to raise additional revenue.

The local income tax is a tax on personal income. If the state and the local community each have an income tax, the taxpayer pays three income taxes: federal, state, and local. The sales tax is a tax on most items sold in stores; many states allow their local governments to use this tax.

Fines paid for traffic and other violations and fees for special services provide some of the income for local governments. **Special assessments** are fees that property owners must pay for services that benefit them—for example, an assessment to a homeowner when the city improves the sidewalk in front of the owner's home. Some cities also earn revenue through housing projects and parking garages.

States permit local governments to borrow money in the form of bonds—certificates that promise to repay the borrowed money with interest by a certain date. Some investors consider local government bonds to be good investments because their earned interest is not subject to federal income taxes. Municipal bonds raise money for large, expensive projects such as building a sports stadium, school buildings, or government office buildings. Local government debt is higher than state government debt—local governments owed $1.8 trillion in 2011 compared to $1.1 trillion for states.

Intergovernmental Revenue In addition to local sources of revenue, most local governments receive economic aid from state and federal governments. This aid often comes in the form of grants.

When local governments carry out state laws or provide state programs, such as constructing highways or matching welfare payments, they receive state aid. State governments also grant funds to localities for specific functions such as providing recreation and education services. Today, states are providing about one-third of the general revenue of local governments. Most state aid comes in the form of support for specific programs such as those designated for schools, highways, public welfare, and health and hospitals.

special assessment a fee that a property owner must pay for services that benefit them

Federal financial aid comes to cities in two forms: categorical grants and block grants. Usually Congress includes guidelines for how categorical grants should be spent—for example, to pay for new highway or new police equipment. Like state officials, local officials tend to prefer block grants.

✅ **READING PROGRESS CHECK**

Explaining What are property taxes and how are they calculated?

Tax and Expenditure Limits

GUIDING QUESTION *How do limits on taxes and expenditures influence the economy at state and local levels?*

Over half of the states and many local governments must adhere to statutory or constitutional limits on taxes levied and/or expenditures. Some of these limits were put in place through citizen initiative, but more were enacted by state legislatures. Some examples of tax and expenditure limits:

- Growth of revenue is tied to growth in personal income, inflation, and/or population growth. Excess funds collected must be returned to taxpayers unless voters vote to let government keep them.
- Growth in expenditures is tied to growth of the economy. Government spending cannot grow by a greater percentage than the state's economy grows.
- Expenditures cannot be greater than a certain percentage (usually 95 to 99 percent) of the revenue the state or local government expects to take in.
- All tax increases must be approved by voters.

Tax and expenditure limits have been supported primarily by conservatives who believe in smaller government. They believe keeping taxes low will keep the economy healthy by leaving more money in the private sector. Most liberals have opposed such limits, believing that some government programs are essential. They argue that higher taxes are sometimes necessary to keep government running and meet the needs of the people.

✅ **READING PROGRESS CHECK**

Applying What are some arguments for and against keeping taxes low?

LESSON 4 REVIEW

Reviewing Vocabulary

1. ***Explaining*** Why do state government officials often prefer block grants over other types of federal aid?

2. ***Categorizing*** Categorize each of the following types of property as either personal property or real property: car, laptop, apartment building, vacant lot, motorcycle, jewelry, farm, and furniture factory.

Using Your Graphic Organizer

3. ***Using Context Clues*** Using your graphic organizer, explain which sources of revenue are the most important to state and local governments.

Answering the Guiding Questions

4. ***Identifying*** What are state governments' main sources of revenue?

5. ***Identifying*** What are local governments' main sources of revenue?

6. ***Understanding Relationships*** How do limits on taxes and expenditures influence the economy at state and local levels?

Writing About Government

7. ***Informative/Explanatory*** Using the Internet or other library resources, find out what bond issues were on the ballot in the most recent local election. Write a short essay explaining the purpose of these bonds, whether or not voters approved them, and the current status of the projects or goals financed by these bonds.

Should states use lotteries to raise revenue?

DEBATING DEMOCRATIC PRINCIPLES

In 1964 New Hampshire became the first state to authorize a state-run lottery. By 2013, more than 40 states, the District of Columbia, Puerto Rico, and the U.S. Virgin Islands were using lotteries to raise revenue. In 2011 alone, Americans bought $54.7 billion worth of lottery tickets. Prizes totaled $33.8 billion. After the costs of running the lottery were subtracted, state lotteries brought in a combined $18.3 billion in revenue that year. Although this is a lot of money, it is a relatively small percentage of all state revenue, which totaled $2.3 trillion in 2011.

 YES

TEAM A — States Should Use Lotteries to Raise Revenue

Lotteries are a recession-proof source of state funds. People voluntarily buy lottery tickets even in a bad economy. Lotteries have also been called a "painless" tax. In fact, the public tends to be very supportive of lotteries. Citizens in only one state have voted against a lottery, and since 1964, no state has started and then abolished its lottery.

If legal gambling is not available, people will take part in illegal games run by criminals. A state lottery can actually reduce crime while raising funds for the state. In many states, those funds are designated for programs that improve local communities, such as education or parks. States cannot afford to lose any revenue source. While opponents say lottery revenue comes disproportionately from the poorest citizens, lower- and middle-income citizens spend about the same amount on lottery tickets.

 **NO**

TEAM B — States Should Not Use Lotteries to Raise Revenue

The lottery is a form of gambling. When a state runs a lottery, it legalizes gambling and encourages people to gamble. For those morally opposed to gambling, this is a problem. In addition, some people will become addicted, causing financial disaster for their families. The lottery is a regressive tax—it takes a larger percentage of poor people's income than wealthy people's income. Because of budget problems, states add new and more addictive lottery games and advertise heavily. This does not support the public interest.

Often, when states designate lottery funds for a specific program, they cut funding for that program from the general fund. If people understood this, lotteries might not be so popular. Lotteries can also lead to corruption.

EXPLORING THE ESSENTIAL QUESTION

Analyzing Should states use lotteries to raise revenue? Debate this question using these procedures:

- Form teams of three. Match up with another team and designate one team as "A" and the other as "B."
- Team A will have three minutes to present the arguments in support of state-run lotteries. No speaker can talk for more than one minute; before the minute is up, the speaker must "tag" another team member to pick up the arguments. Teammates who have something to add should hold out a hand to be tagged.
- Team B will have three minutes to present arguments against state-run lotteries, using the procedure.
- Next, each team has two minutes to rebut or "cross-examine" the other team's arguments. Again, no one person can speak for more than 60 seconds without tagging out.
- Finally, each team will summarize its position in one minute.

STUDY GUIDE

FEDERAL BUDGET PROCESS
LESSON 1

Executive Branch
- Prepares budget based on president's priorities
- Transmits budget proposal to Congress

Legislative Branch
- Revises president's budget proposal
- Negotiates compromises with executive branch and between House and Senate
- Approves final budget

SOURCES OF GOVERNMENT REVENUE
LESSON 2

Individual Income Taxes
- On taxable income
- Progressive
- Deductions, exemptions, credits

Gift Taxes
On money given to others while alive

Excise Taxes
On certain goods and services

Corporate Income Taxes
On taxable income of corporations

Government Borrowing
- By selling Treasury securities
- Creates national debt

Estate Taxes
On property of person who has died

Customs Duties
On imported goods

Social Insurance Taxes (Payroll Taxes)
- For Social Security, Medicare, unemployment compensation
- Regressive
- Employer shares cost

MANAGING THE ECONOMY
LESSON 3

Stimulating the Economy

Fiscal Policy Actions:
- Increase government spending
- Decrease taxes

Monetary Policy Actions:
- Lower discount rate
- Buy back government bonds on open market
- Lower reserve requirement

Fiscal Policy Actions:
- Reduce government spending
- Increase taxes

Monetary Policy Actions:
- Increase discount rate
- Sell government bonds on open market
- Raise reserve requirement

Slowing the Economy

FINANCING STATE AND LOCAL GOVERNMENTS
LESSON 4

Sources of Revenue (vary across states and localities)	
State Governments	**Local Governments**
Taxes	**Taxes**
• Sales tax	• Sales tax
• General sales tax	• Income tax
• Selective sales tax	• Individual income tax
• Income tax	• Corporate income tax
• Individual income tax	• Property tax
• Corporate income tax	• Real property
• Property tax	• Personal property
• License fees	• Fees
• Business licenses	• Special assessments
• Hunting and fishing licenses	• Housing projects
• Driver's licenses	• Parking garages
• Motor vehicle registrations	• Fines
• Severance tax	• Traffic violations
Federal Government	**Federal and State Governments**
• Formula grants	• State grants for specific programs
• Project grants	• Federal grants
• Block grants	• Categorical grants
	• Block grants

Directions: On a separate sheet of paper, answer the questions below. Make sure you read carefully and answer all parts of the questions.

Lesson Review

Lesson 1

1 *Identifying Cause and Effect* When the federal government has a budget deficit, what does it do to pay the bills?

2 *Explaining* Why are entitlements considered uncontrollable expenditures?

Lesson 2

3 *Differentiating* How does a tax credit differ from a tax deduction?

4 *Analyzing Cause and Effect* How does a tax deduction for home mortgage interest affect the economy?

Lesson 3

5 *Identifying Cause and Effect* If the federal government increases corporate taxes, how might this affect private enterprise?

6 *Explaining* Explain how the Fed can use the discount rate to slow an overheated economy.

Lesson 4

7 *Explaining* What are federal mandates, and why have state and local officials complained about them?

8 *Contrasting* Contrast the views of conservatives and liberals on regulatory limits that keep state and local taxes low.

ANSWERING THE ESSENTIAL QUESTIONS

Review your answers to the introductory questions at the beginning of each lesson. Then answer the following Essential Questions based on what you learned in the chapter. Have your answers changed?

9 *Analyzing* What role does the government play in managing the economy?

10 *Analyzing* How does the government raise and allocate money?

DBQ Interpreting Political Cartoons

Use the political cartoon to answer the following questions.

11 *Analyzing* What is the cartoonist's bias, and what elements in the cartoon reveal the bias?

12 *Evaluating* Is the cartoon a valid representation of the Tea Party and its position on the budget? Explain your answer.

Critical Thinking

13 *Contrasting* Suppose Congress is considering a bill to stop payday lenders from charging exorbitant interest rates. Which lawmakers would most likely support this bill: liberals or conservatives? Explain.

14 *Making Inferences* Why might a farm group support a protective tariff on grain?

15 *Analyzing Cause and Effect* Explain how fiscal policy actions affect the national debt.

16 *Making Connections* Why have some state supreme courts held that using property taxes to support local schools violates the Fourteenth Amendment's guarantee of equal protection of the law?

Need Extra Help?

If You've Missed Question	**1**	**2**	**3**	**4**	**5**	**6**	**7**	**8**	**9**	**10**	**11**	**12**	**13**	**14**	**15**	**16**
Go to page	639	643	648	648	652	654	659	662	638	645	638	638	662	646	652	660

Directions: On a separate sheet of paper, answer the questions below. Make sure you read carefully and answer all parts of the questions.

DBQ Analyzing Primary Sources

Read the excerpts and answer the questions that follow.

The 2008 election pitted Democrats Barack Obama and Joe Biden against Republicans John McCain and Sarah Palin. During a debate, the vice-presidential candidates addressed a question about taxes. Below are excerpts from that debate.

PRIMARY SOURCE

"BIDEN: The economic engine of America is middle class. It's the people listening to this broadcast. When you do well, America does well. Even the wealthy do well. . . . John [McCain] wants to add . . . new tax cuts . . . for corporate America and the very wealthy while giving virtually nothing to the middle class. We have a different value set. . . . They [the middle class] deserve the tax breaks, not the super wealthy. . . . They don't need any more tax breaks."

"PALIN: [W]hen you talk about Barack's plan to tax increase affecting only those making $250,000 a year or more, you're forgetting millions of small businesses that are going to fit into that category. So they're going to be the ones paying higher taxes thus resulting in fewer jobs being created and less productivity. . . . [G]overnment [should] lessen the tax burden . . . and get out of the way and let the private sector and our families . . . prosper."
—2008 Vice-Presidential Debate

17 *Finding the Main Idea* What tax policy is the Obama/Biden ticket proposing? What reasons does Biden give to support this proposal? What is Biden's frame of reference?

18 *Identifying Frame of Reference* What counter-argument does Palin give? Does her point of view suggest a liberal or conservative frame of reference? Explain.

19 *Evaluating Arguments and Counterarguments* Which person's argument do you consider most valid? Explain your point of view.

Social Studies Skills

Use the graph to answer questions 20 and 21.

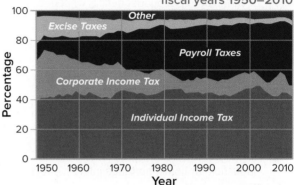

Sources of Federal Revenue,
fiscal years 1950–2010

Source: Budget of the United States Government, Fiscal Year 2012, Historical Tables: Table 2.1; http://www.whitehouse.gov/omb/budget/Historicals

20 *Identifying Continuity and Change* Describe the trend in payroll taxes compared to individual income taxes from 1950 to 2010.

21 *Creating Charts* Use the graph to determine the approximate percentages for each type of tax in 2010. Then use these percentages and software to create a circle graph.

22 *Using Tables* Go to the IRS website and bring up the individual income tax table for the current year. Assume that you are a single taxpayer who earned a taxable income of $35,369 for the year. How much federal tax would you owe?

Research and Presentation

23 *Comparing and Contrasting* Compare and contrast the roles of the executive and legislative branches in making fiscal policy. Summarize the information in a graphic organizer.

24 *Explaining* How do fiscal policies affect the economy at the national, state, and local levels? How do monetary policies affect the economy at the national, state, and local levels? Be sure to address similarities and differences among the three levels in your response.

Need Extra Help?

If You've Missed Question	**17**	**18**	**19**	**20**	**21**	**22**	**23**	**24**
Go to page	648	648	648	646	646	646	640	652

Making Social and Domestic Policy

networks
www.connected.mcgraw-hill.com
There's More Online about making social and domestic policy.

CHAPTER **22**

ESSENTIAL QUESTIONS

- How is social and domestic policy created and implemented?
- How do citizens influence government social and domestic policy?
- How do social and domestic policies affect U.S. society and culture?

▲ New citizens recite the Oath of Allegiance as part of their naturalization ceremony.

NPS Photo by Michael Quinn

PUBLIC POLICY PROBLEMS & SOLUTIONS

Public policies seek to address problems in our community that require coordinated action. People who develop and implement public policies can solve problems in two ways. They can try to minimize the problem or they can try to address the underlying causes of the problem. Take the issue of truancy. A policy can try to reduce the number of truant students at a particular school or try to address the underlying reasons why students do not attend school. These sources discuss some underlying reasons for infant mortality, hunger, and greenhouse gas emissions. As you read the sources, think about the underlying causes of these issues and some possible solutions to address them.

PRIMARY SOURCE

"Identifying genuine solutions to a problem means knowing what the real causes of the problem are. Taking action without identifying what factors contribute to the problem can result in misdirected efforts, and that wastes time and resources. However, by thoroughly studying the cause of the problem, you can build ownership, that is, by experiencing the problem you will understand it better, and be motivated to deal with it."

—The Community Toolbox, a program of the University of Kansas Work Group for Community Health and Development

PRIMARY SOURCE

Unlike in other parts of the world where food shortages are common, hunger in the United States is caused mainly by poverty and lack of money to purchase food. Bread for the World is a nonprofit organization that works in the United States and around the world to address food insecurity. The organization sees how food insecurity and hunger in the United States are closely related.

"The United States has done a much better job fighting hunger than it has poverty. Hunger is a simpler issue in some ways. The Food Stamp Program, the Special Supplemental Nutrition Program for Women, Infants and Children (WIC), the National School Lunch Program, and 12 other nutrition programs run by the U.S. Department of Agriculture (USDA) serve millions of U.S. residents every day."

—Bread for the World, "Causes of Hunger in the U.S."

PRIMARY SOURCE

Every year in the United States, thousands of babies die before their first birthday. This is known as infant mortality and is one of the highest priorities for agencies and organizations working to improve health outcomes in the United States. The Central Harlem Healthy Start, Northern Manhattan Perinatal Partnership (NMPP) is a program that works to lower infant mortality rates in New York City. In 1990 in central Harlem the infant mortality rate was 27.7 infant deaths per 1,000 live births. In 2004 the rate fell to 5.2 infant deaths per 1,000 live births.

"NMPP embarked on a campaign to reduce the number of bus depots in the Harlem community because of the established correlation between the type of air quality and diesel engine fumes emitted by buses with low birth weight. It likewise supported the building of supermarkets that provide healthier foods to its constituents while ensuring that the bid of the New York City government to construct 165,000 affordable housing [units] is realized. A number of its Healthy Start consumers have availed of the over 82,000 units that had been built so far and are now raising their families in a decent and secure environment."

—Julius Dasmarinas, "Spaces of Hope in Harlem," Association of Maternal and Child Health Programs, 2008

PRIMARY SOURCE D

Many Americans are concerned about increasing greenhouse gases in the atmosphere, which can trap energy in the atmosphere and cause the earth to warm, affecting human health and welfare. The EPA tracks the sources of greenhouse gas emissions in the United States.

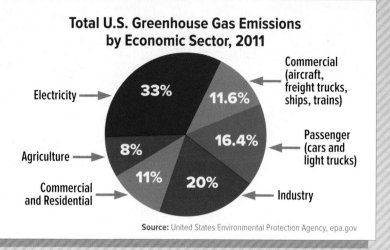

Total U.S. Greenhouse Gas Emissions by Economic Sector, 2011

- Electricity — 33%
- Commercial (aircraft, freight trucks, ships, trains) — 11.6%
- Passenger (cars and light trucks) — 16.4%
- Industry — 20%
- Commercial and Residential — 11%
- Agriculture — 8%

Source: United States Environmental Protection Agency, epa.gov

SOURCE E

A graphic organizer like this can be used to identify both consequences and underlying causes of a problem. If you need help identifying the consequences, ask yourself, "So what?" To find causes, think about the problem and ask, "why?"

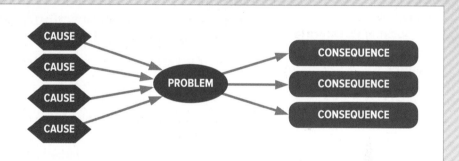

CAUSE · CAUSE · CAUSE · CAUSE → PROBLEM → CONSEQUENCE · CONSEQUENCE · CONSEQUENCE

DBQ DOCUMENT-BASED QUESTIONS

1. **Using Visuals** Use the graphic organizer in Source E to map out the information provided in Source B, C, or D. What is the central problem described? What does the source identify as consequences and as causes?

2. **Identifying Cause and Effect** For almost any social problem, different people and different groups will identify different causes. Do you have others ideas about what might cause infant mortality, hunger, or greenhouse gas emissions?

3. **Making Connections** When a problem has many root causes, how should policy makers prioritize which approach they will use and fund?

WHAT WILL YOU DO?

Think about a problem in your community or in the country. Then choose one of the underlying causes. What actions could or will you take to address that underlying cause?

EXPLORE the interactive version of the analyzing primary sources feature on Networks.

netw⚙rks
TRY IT YOURSELF ONLINE

LESSON 1
Business and Labor Policy

Reading Help Desk

Academic Vocabulary

- investor
- restore

Content Vocabulary

- mixed economy
- tariff
- subsidy
- trust
- monopoly
- interlocking directorate
- oligopoly
- security
- collective bargaining
- closed shop
- right-to-work law

TAKING NOTES:

Key Ideas and Details

SUMMARIZING Use the graphic organizer to summarize key business and labor legislation in chronological order.

Business Laws	Labor Laws

ESSENTIAL QUESTION

How is social and domestic policy created and implemented?

How involved should government be in solving various problems in our country? That is an enduring issue in the United States.

For each of the examples, decide whether the hypothetical problem should be solved by (a) government, (b) government and the private sector acting together, or (c) the private sector (business and/or charity). Give your reasons for each.

- A few ships have crashed near a harbor because it lacks a working lighthouse.
- Americans' health is declining due to poor nutrition.
- Many high school graduates do not have the skills needed to be successful in the workforce.
- Sometimes, farmers or ranchers lose an entire crop or herd to bad weather. Such a loss can bankrupt a small farm.
- An alarming number of people have been injured while using chainsaws.
- Home prices fell sharply in some cities and many homeowners could not afford to pay their mortgages.
- Fast-food workers complain that their pay—generally the federal minimum wage—is not enough to support their families.
- A business cannot market its products effectively because it does not have current information about the demographics of the community.

Promoting and Protecting Business

GUIDING QUESTION *How does the government promote and protect U.S. businesses?*

One of the most important responsibilities of government is to manage its nation's economy. Although free enterprise is the foundation of the American economic system, ours is really a **mixed economy** in which the government promotes, protects, and regulates private enterprise. For example, by placing tariffs on foreign cars, the federal government protects the U.S. auto industry and its workers' jobs. By requiring that all cars have certain safety features like airbags, the government protects people who ride in cars and lowers costs associated with accidents.

Free Trade The United States supports business by promoting free trade and providing subsidies and assistance to U.S. businesses. It also plays a leading role in promoting free trade around the world. Free trade is the selling of products between countries without **tariffs** (import taxes) or other trade barriers, such as limits on the amount of goods that can be imported. Although current tariff rates are at an all-time low, tariffs are still used to protect American industries from foreign competition. The government also restricts some products through quotas, or limits on the number that may be imported.

The United States has many regional and bilateral trade agreements. The North American Free Trade Agreement (NAFTA), signed by Canada, Mexico, and the United States in 1992, was designed to gradually eliminate trade restrictions among the trading partners. More recently in 2012, the United States entered into a free trade agreement with South Korea.

Federal Subsidies Today, the federal government provides at least four types of **subsidies**, or forms of aid to business. Tax incentives allow businesses to deduct certain expenses from their annual tax returns. Government loans, or credit subsidies, provide funds for businesses at low interest rates. Another type of subsidy is free services, such as weather information, census reports, and other information that is valuable to U.S. businesses. Finally, the government provides direct cash payments to businesses whose products or services are considered vital to the general public.

Assistance from Federal Agencies The United States Department of Commerce exists to "foster, promote, and develop the foreign and domestic commerce of the United States." The main functions of the Commerce Department are to provide information services, financial assistance, and research and development services. Several agencies within the Commerce Department supply businesses with valuable information and subsidies, particularly the Bureau of the Census, which provides important economic data to businesses.

Competition is important to the free enterprise system, so federal, state, and local governments try to help small businesses. The Small Business Administration (SBA) is an independent federal agency that gives free advice and information to small business firms.

mixed economy a system in which the government regulates private enterprise

tariff a tax placed on an import to increase its price in the domestic market

subsidy a grant or gift of money

CHART

Imagine you work for a company that designs and builds homes in San Antonio, Texas. You are interested in information that will help you decide how to approach your business over the next few years. Evaluate this information from the U.S. Census Bureau.

San Antonio, Texas, Statistics	
Average household size	2.75 people
Percentage of households with children under 18	32%
Vacancy rate for rentals	9.8%
Vacancy rate for owner-occupied homes	2.1%
Percentage of homes that are single-family detached houses	64%
Percentage of homes that are apartment buildings with 10 or more units	21%
Percentage of households with 1 or 2 cars	over 75%
Median household income	approximately $52,000

Source: *U.S. Census Bureau*

CRITICAL THINKING
Making Inferences What inferences can you make from this information? What type of homes might your company build over the next few years? What other factors would you need to consider as you make business decisions? Prepare a memo for the company's leaders explaining this information and how it might inform your business decisions.

Regional offices of the SBA offer government-sponsored classes on sound management practices for owners of small businesses. Businesses also may seek advice from the SBA on how to overcome their problems. In addition, the SBA conducts programs to help women and minorities in business.

✓ **READING PROGRESS CHECK**

Describing What are some of the roles that the Commerce Department and the Small Business Administration fulfill?

Regulating Business

GUIDING QUESTION *How does the government regulate U.S. businesses?*

Some Americans believe that government regulation of the economy is at best a mixed blessing. They think that the proper role of the government is to interfere as little as possible in the free market. Too much regulation can restrict private enterprise by, for example, raising the barriers to starting a business. Others believe that regulations play an important role in protecting the public interest. In many vital industries, including transportation, food, communications, and energy, regulations keep products safe and maintain a reliable supply.

The Constitution grants Congress the power to "lay and collect taxes" for the general welfare and to "regulate commerce . . . among the several states." Most regulatory laws are based upon these two powers. Many federal regulations are applied to businesses that operate across state lines or goods that travel in interstate commerce. Two laws based on this power have a major role in business regulation.

Sherman and Clayton Antitrust Acts In the late 1800s, many industries became dominated by monopolistic trusts. In a **trust**, several corporations combined their stock and operated as one giant enterprise, often forcing smaller companies out of business. The trustees could set production quotas, fix prices, and control the market, thereby creating a monopoly. A **monopoly** is a single producer that controls so much of a product, service, or industry that little or no competition exists. The government wants to prevent monopolies so that one company cannot gain an absolute hold over any one product or service—which could result in unreasonably high prices or a catastrophe in the market if that company went out of business.

Congress passed two important laws to break up monopolies. The first, the Sherman Antitrust Act of 1890, stated: "Every contract, combination in the form of trust or otherwise, or conspiracy, in restraint of trade or commerce among the several states, or with foreign nations is hereby declared to be illegal. . . . Every person who shall monopolize, or attempt to monopolize, or combine or conspire with any other person or persons to monopolize any part of the trade or commerce among the several states . . . shall be guilty of a misdemeanor."

Today, violating this part of the Sherman Antitrust Act is a felony. In 1911 the Standard Oil Company, a trust that controlled the production and sale of 90 percent of the oil refined in the United States, was convicted of violating the first two sections of the act. For the first time in the nation's history, the government declared a major trust illegal.

The Sherman Act proved difficult to enforce, and Congress followed it with the 1914 Clayton Antitrust Act, which prohibited charging high prices in an area where little competition existed, while at the same time charging lower prices in an area with strong competition. The act also said businesses could not buy stock in other corporations in order to reduce competition. Finally, the act

trust a form of business consolidation in which several corporations combine their stock and allow a board of trustees to operate as a giant enterprise

monopoly a business that controls so much of an industry that little or no competition exists

addressed the control of companies by outlawing **interlocking directorates**—a circumstance in which the same people served on the boards of directors of competing companies. Antitrust laws are enforced by the Department of Justice. While this department has the authority to bring suit against suspected violators of antitrust laws, relatively few cases are brought against companies—and those that are often are settled out of court.

Despite additional antitrust legislation passed since the Clayton Act, a few large corporations dominate several industries. Today, instead of trusts and monopolies, economic power belongs to oligopolies. An **oligopoly** exists when a few firms dominate a particular industry. The U.S. airline, wireless phone service, and video game console markets are examples. As of 2011, four companies—Verizon, AT&T, Sprint, and T-Mobile—controlled nearly 90 percent of the wireless phone service market in the United States.

Enforcing Antitrust Laws The Federal Trade Commission (FTC) is an independent regulatory agency that works to prevent unfair trading practices. The commission may define unfair competitive practices and issue orders to halt these practices, examine corporate purchases of stock, and regulate the packaging and labeling of certain consumer goods. It may determine whether an advertisement for a product is false or unfair. If it is, the FTC can order a company to change the ad to comply with FTC standards. As a result of one FTC ruling, cigarette manufacturers must place a health warning on cigarette packages. According to another FTC regulation, all manufacturers must clearly list the contents of packaged products on the label.

Consumer Protection Laws Shortly after the turn of the century, Upton Sinclair published a novel called *The Jungle*, in which he exposed the horrific conditions in a meatpacking house. In addition to Sinclair's stinging condemnation, magazine articles about similar conditions aroused public anger. Many corporations failed to make their products healthful or safe—foods were sometimes mislabeled or contaminated by additives or tainted by unsanitary conditions. Consumers were often duped into buying medicines that were often worthless and sometimes dangerous.

In response, Congress passed many federal consumer protection laws. The Pure Food and Drug Act and Meat Inspection Act, passed in 1906, were among the earliest. These laws made it illegal for a company engaged in interstate commerce to sell contaminated, unhealthful, or falsely labeled foods or drugs and provided for federal inspection of all meatpacking companies that sold meats across state lines.

Enforcing Consumer Protection Laws Congress also has established independent regulatory agencies that protect consumers or regulate certain economic activities.

The Food and Drug Administration (FDA) protects the public from poorly processed and improperly labeled foods and drugs. Scientists at FDA laboratories inspect and test prepared food, cosmetics, drugs, and thousands of other products every year. Agents from the FDA inspect factories, food-processing plants, and drug laboratories and check labels for accuracy. If a product fails to meet FDA standards, the FDA may force it off the market.

Congress created the Consumer Financial Protection Bureau (CFPB) in 2010 after the recession of 2007–2008 exposed issues in the banking and consumer finance sectors. The CFPB enforces federal consumer financial protection laws, educates Americans about financial services, and restricts unfair or deceptive practices. Congressional Republicans strongly opposed the way this new agency was structured, arguing that it would have too much unchecked regulatory power.

The U.S. cell phone industry is an oligopoly because a few firms dominate the industry.

▲ **CRITICAL THINKING**

Identifying In addition to the cell phone industry, name some other types of businesses that operate as oligopolies in the United States.

interlocking directorate the same people serving on the board of directors of competing companies

oligopoly situation in which only a few firms dominate a particular industry

Read and compare the two excerpts that outline consumer issues relating to two different industries.

THE JUNGLE (1906)

UNSAFE AT ANY SPEED (1965)

"There would be meat stored in great piles in rooms; and the water from leaky roofs would drip over it, and thousands of rats would race about it. . . . These rats were nuisances, and the packers would put poisoned bread out for them; they would die, and then rats, bread, and meat would go into the hoppers together."

—Upton Sinclair

"Highway accidents were estimated to have cost this country in 1964, $8.3 billion in property damage, medical expenses, lost wages, and insurance overhead expenses. Add an equivalent sum to comprise roughly the indirect costs and the total amounts to over two per cent of the gross national product. But these are not the kind of costs which fall on the builders of motor vehicles (excepting a few successful lawsuits for negligent construction of the vehicle) and thus do not pinch the proper foot."

— Ralph Nader

▲ CRITICAL THINKING

Making Connections Upton Sinclair's novel and Ralph Nader's book aroused public sentiment and prompted consumers to advocate for increased regulation. How do consumers become informed about business practices today? What types of media would spark consumer outrage and action now?

security a financial instrument, including a bond, note, and certificate, that is sold as a means of borrowing money with a promise to repay the buyer with interest after a specific time period

investor someone who puts money to a particular use in order to receive a profitable return

Books and articles about how consumers are cheated and deceived have always been popular. The book that really propelled consumer activism was Ralph Nader's *Unsafe at Any Speed*, published in 1965. Nader accused auto manufacturers of caring more about style than safety and neglecting to design cars to withstand crashes. Nader became a leader in the consumer movement.

As a result of this movement, Congress created the Consumer Product Safety Commission (CPSC) in 1972. It was set up to protect consumers from "unreasonable risk of injury from hazardous products." The CPSC establishes safety standards for a wide range of products; when products fail to meet the standards, the CPSC can order them off the market. In a global economy, the CPSC faces new challenges to screen products from abroad that do not meet American safety standards. In 2008 toys from China were a special concern because they contained lead-based paint.

Regulating the Sale of Stocks Since its creation during the Great Depression, the Securities and Exchange Commission (SEC) has regulated the trading of **securities**, or stocks and bonds. Stocks are ownership shares in a company. Bonds are essentially IOUs that companies or governments issue to people who loan them money.

Today, the SEC regulates securities issued by public utility companies and requires all corporations that issue public stock to file regular reports on their assets, profits, sales, and other financial data. These reports must be made available to **investors** so they can judge the true value of a company's stock offerings.

In 2001 the SEC learned that several large companies were using fraudulent accounting to inflate stock value to hide the firms' weaknesses and to create the appearance of corporate success. Unfortunately, the SEC discovered this only once the Enron Corporation declared bankruptcy. This was, at the time, the largest single bankruptcy in American history. Thousands of employees lost their jobs, and billions of dollars in stock investment disappeared.

The failure of the Securities and Exchange Commission to catch this problem in advance led to the passage of the Sarbanes-Oxley Act of 2002. The act required chief executive officers and chief financial officers of publicly traded companies to personally sign SEC reports and pay penalties if improper accounting is later discovered.

✓ **READING PROGRESS CHECK**

Determining Cause and Effect What events led to the creation of the CFPB and CPSC?

Government and Labor

GUIDING QUESTION *How has the U.S. labor movement evolved?*

As large-scale businesses multiplied in the late 1800s, the relationship between employer and employee became strained. Workers toiled long hours in unsafe conditions for poor wages. Child labor was common, with children as young as 7 working 12 to 18 hours a day in mines or factories.

Workers organized unions and elected leaders to represent them in negotiations with employers for labor contracts that specified wages, hours, and working conditions. The practice of negotiating labor contracts is known as **collective bargaining**.

Protecting Unions and Workers The first successful national labor organization, the American Federation of Labor, was founded in the 1880s. For decades, employers refused to negotiate with unions, and government generally favored business. Federal troops and state militia broke up some strikes. The courts even used the Sherman Antitrust Act, originally intended to regulate business, to prohibit union activities that restrained trade.

In the early 1900s, the government's attitude toward labor began to change. Before the 1930s, employers were often successful in challenging laws that regulated wages and working conditions. They won cases by arguing that workers and employers had the freedom to agree on the terms of employment without interference from the government, known as freedom of contract. In a 1937 case called *West Coast Hotel* v. *Parrish*, a hotel owner who was paying less than minimum wage claimed that the law deprived the employer of freedom of contract. However, the Supreme Court upheld the minimum wage set by the Industrial Welfare Committee of the state of Washington.

Today, federal laws set minimum wages and maximum working hours and prohibit child labor. In addition, the Department of Labor helps people find jobs, trains workers for new jobs, collects data, and offers unemployment insurance. States may pass laws requiring a higher minimum wage in their states. As of 2014, 23 states and the District of Columbia had done so. States also offer a variety of services to workers, including training and help with job placement.

Labor Laws of the 1930s The greatest gains of organized labor occurred in the 1930s during the Great Depression. Labor laws enacted at the time seemed revolutionary. Passed as part of President Franklin D. Roosevelt's New Deal, they guaranteed labor's right to bargain collectively and to strike, and they generally strengthened labor unions.

The National Labor Relations Board (NLRB) was created to enforce these laws. The board had power to supervise elections to determine which union a group of workers wanted to represent it. The NLRB could also hear labor's complaints and issue "cease and desist" orders to end unfair labor practices.

collective bargaining the practice of negotiating labor contracts

closed shop a workplace where only members of a union may be hired

restore to return to original condition, rebuild

right-to-work law state labor law that requires that all workplaces be open shops where workers may freely decide whether or not to join a union

People wait in line for bread during the Great Depression in the 1930s.

▼ **CRITICAL THINKING**
Making Connections How did the Great Depression shape business and labor laws in the United States?

Regulating Unions In the 1940s, business leaders began protesting that unions were becoming too powerful. Critics said that many workers were being forced to join unions and that employers were being prevented from hiring nonunion employees. To avoid strikes, employers had to agree to establish a closed shop. In a **closed shop**, only members of a union can be hired.

Responding to these criticisms, Congress tried to **restore** some balance between labor and management by passing the Taft-Hartley Act. This law aimed to limit the power and activities of unions. For example, unions were required to give advance notice before calling a strike—time for labor and management to settle their differences. The act also allowed the president to stop strikes that endanger the nation for up to 80 days.

While federal law prohibited the closed shop, it permitted the union shop where workers are required to join a union soon after they have been hired. Union shops can be formed if a majority of workers vote for them. They cannot be formed, however, in any state that has passed a right-to-work law. **Right-to-work laws** are state labor laws that prohibit both closed shops and union shops. They allow workers to freely decide whether or not to join a union. Proponents of right-to-work laws argue that workers should have the freedom to choose whether to join a union. They say such laws attract businesses to the state. Opponents say the laws are designed to weaken unions, because all the workers benefit from the union, but some will choose not to pay dues if they are not required to do so. They point out that workers in states with right-to-work laws earn less than those in states without.

Protecting Union Workers At some periods in our history, a few labor unions were corrupt. In 1957, for example, a Senate investigating committee found that some leaders of the Teamsters union misused or stole union funds. These scandals led to passage of the Landrum-Griffin Act of 1959. It made it a federal crime to misuse union funds and also protected union members from being intimidated by union officials. It also helped eliminate fraud in union elections. The act included a bill of rights for union members. This guaranteed the right of members to nominate and vote by secret ballot in union elections, to participate and speak freely at union meetings, to sue their union for unfair practices, and to examine union records and finances.

✓ **READING PROGRESS CHECK**

Describing Why was the National Labor Relations Board (NLRB) created? What is its role?

LESSON 1 REVIEW

Reviewing Vocabulary
1. *Contrasting* What is the difference between a closed shop and a union shop?

Using Your Graphic Organizer
2. *Sequencing* Use your completed graphic organizer to create an annotated time line of key business and labor legislation in the United States.

Answering the Guiding Questions
3. *Explaining* How does the government promote and protect U.S. businesses?

4. *Explaining* How does the government regulate U.S. businesses?

5. *Finding the Main Idea* How has the U.S. labor movement evolved?

Writing About Government
6. *Argument* The U.S. government plays an important role in both promoting and protecting U.S. businesses, and regulating them. There is a tension between these roles because too much regulation can restrict private enterprise, while not enough regulation can be harmful to consumers. What do you think is the right balance between the two? Write an essay in which you explain and argue your position.

Interact with these digital assets and others in lesson 2

✓ **INTERACTIVE INFOGRAPHIC**
Farming in the United States

✓ **INTERACTIVE TIME LINE**
Agriculture, Environment, and Energy

✓ **SELF-CHECK QUIZ**

✓ **VIDEO**
EPA Proposes Ozone Reductions

netw⊙rks
TRY IT YOURSELF ONLINE

ReadingHelp Desk

Academic Vocabulary

• environmental
• extract

Content Vocabulary

• price supports
• citizen suit
• renewable energy

TAKING NOTES:

Integration of Knowledge and Ideas

UNDERSTANDING CONTINUITY AND CHANGE Use the graphic organizer to compare and contrast agricultural, environmental, and energy policies in the past and present.

Policy Arena	Then	Now
Agriculture		
Environment		
Energy		

LESSON 2
Agriculture, the Environment, and Energy

ESSENTIAL QUESTION

How do citizens influence government social and domestic policy?

Some states have considered issuing new regulations for so-called factory farms. These farms raise huge numbers of chickens, hogs, and cattle in relatively small spaces. The farms are structured to make production of milk, eggs, and meat more efficient—thereby lowering consumer prices and maximizing profit. However, residents and activists have complained about the environmental effects of the vast quantities of manure, the overuse of antibiotics in animals, and the poor condition of the animals. Some small farmers believe that they cannot compete with these gigantic farms.

• Make a list of the different people, companies, organizations, and interests that would be affected by new regulations on factory farms.

• Choose two of the entries on your list and hypothesize how those players might feel about the regulation of factory farms. Then explain how they might respond in order to influence this policy.

Farmers and Government

GUIDING QUESTION *How has U.S. agricultural policy changed over time?*

The United States is an urban nation with more than 80 percent of Americans living in towns and cities and only 2 percent working in agriculture; nevertheless, the government continues to support agriculture because farming is vital to the nation. Over the past several decades, food production has been consolidated. By 2007, less than 10 percent of the nation's farms produced more than 60 percent of agricultural products for sale. Fewer farms have been able to produce more food due to large machinery, new varieties of crops, and industrial fertilizers and pesticides.

At the federal level, much farm policy is administered by the U.S. Department of Agriculture (USDA). Its chief functions are to help farmers market their produce, stabilize farm prices, conserve land, and promote research in agricultural science.

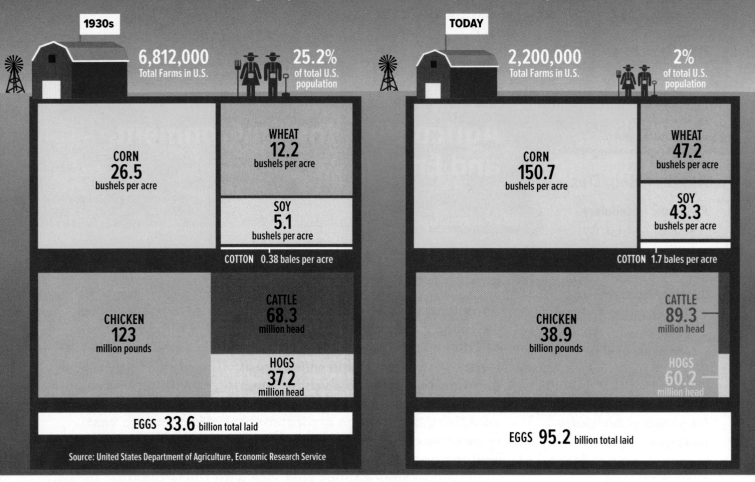

Changes in U.S. Farming: 1930s to Now

There have been many changes to the farm industry in the United States from the 1930s to today. Although the number of farms and farmers has greatly declined, farmland is more productive today than in the 1930s.

1930s

6,812,000
Total Farms in U.S.

25.2%
of total U.S. population

CORN
26.5
bushels per acre

WHEAT
12.2
bushels per acre

SOY
5.1
bushels per acre

COTTON 0.38 bales per acre

CHICKEN
123
million pounds

CATTLE
68.3
million head

HOGS
37.2
million head

EGGS 33.6 billion total laid

Source: United States Department of Agriculture, Economic Research Service

TODAY

2,200,000
Total Farms in U.S.

2%
of total U.S. population

CORN
150.7
bushels per acre

WHEAT
47.2
bushels per acre

SOY
43.3
bushels per acre

COTTON 1.7 bales per acre

CHICKEN
38.9
billion pounds

CATTLE
89.3
million head

HOGS
60.2
million head

EGGS 95.2 billion total laid

▲ CRITICAL THINKING

1. Using Visuals Write a sentence describing what each graphic shows. Taken together, what do these graphics tell you about how agriculture has changed in the United States?

2. Hypothesizing What explanation would you offer for why agriculture has changed?

3. Posing Questions What questions do you have about how changes in agriculture might affect agricultural policy?

price supports the program under which Congress buys farmers' crops if the market price falls below the support price

Agriculture Policy

Much of our modern farm policy originated in the 1930s after a decade of serious problems faced by the nation's farmers during the Great Depression. President Roosevelt's New Deal programs set out to raise the price of farm products by limiting the production of certain crops that were in oversupply. The government paid farmers for not producing their usual amounts of corn, wheat, hogs, and other commodities. It also provided loans to help farmers keep their land.

Today, most agricultural policy is legislated through omnibus Farm Bills. The Farm Bill is debated and passed every five to seven years. Each one has its own name—the first was the Agricultural Adjustment Act in 1933—but they are often just called the "Farm Bill."

Programs for Stabilizing Prices

The federal government coordinates several programs intended to keep crop prices from falling too low. Farms depend on seasonal weather conditions that can cause a crop yield to vary greatly from year to year. This could cause the price of those crops to also vary wildly. The government has a special interest in keeping food prices stable and ensuring a continued food supply. The government therefore intervenes in stabilizing prices for the agricultural industry in a way it does not in other industries.

Under the program of **price supports**, Congress establishes a support price for a particular crop. The government then lends the farmer money equal to the support price for the crop. If the actual market price falls below the support price, the farmer does not sell his or her crop on the market and instead repays the loan by sending his or her crop to the government. The government holds the surplus crops in storage facilities until the market price goes up and the crop can be sold. It also uses surplus crops for welfare programs, school lunches, and famine relief overseas. Even so, from time to time, huge surpluses of some products have accumulated.

To avoid large surpluses every year, the government restricts the amount of support farmers receive for certain crops. The government also allows farmers to control supply by setting a limit on how much they will sell. For example, farmers in California might meet and agree to release only 75 percent of that year's raisin crop to keep the supply somewhat limited and prices higher. In other industries, such price-setting practices may be illegal under antitrust law. In agriculture, however, the practice is not only legal but is widespread.

Not all observers agree with the government practices of supporting prices and providing subsidies. Critics claim that these subsidies are relics from decades ago—while they once supported small farmers, most subsidies now go to corporations or wealthy farmers. They say that the subsidies encourage the production of large-scale commodity crops, which results in a limited American diet focused on meat, corn, wheat, and soy at the expense of other healthy fruits and vegetables. They also argue that subsidies encourage environmentally unfriendly farming practices and cost taxpayers too much. Supporters of these government programs argue that the subsidies work and that variable growing conditions are still as much of a factor in a farm's success or failure as they were in the 1930s. Many farmers still struggle to make a profit, and more will leave farming if it becomes less lucrative.

☑ **READING PROGRESS CHECK**

Comparing Advantages and Disadvantages What are the advantages and disadvantages of using price controls and subsidies to support American agriculture?

PARTICIPATING
ⓘⓝ Your Government

Evaluating Policy Alternatives

Usually a new Farm Bill is passed every five years. The Farm Bill typically addresses a wide variety of issues—some of which are only indirectly related to agricultural policy. Many groups lobby Congress to make sure their interests are represented in the bill. Interest groups like the National Cotton Council and the American Soybean Association lobby to keep and expand commodity price supports. Food companies like Kraft or PepsiCo lobby to reduce regulations related to labeling foods and to keep commodity prices lower. Monsanto and other seed and fertilizer companies lobby to encourage crop production.

Photo by David Nance/USDA

EXPLORING THE ESSENTIAL QUESTION

Making Decisions Which of the following policy goals would you support in a Farm Bill? Explain your choices.

- **a.** SNAP benefits (formerly called food stamps) for 40 million Americans, averaging $130 each per month
- **b.** Funding to promote the sale of American specialty goods like olive oil
- **c.** Set standards that require a certain amount of American-grown corn to be made into ethanol fuel for cars
- **d.** Subsidies for farmers who grow soybeans rather than other crops
- **e.** Subsidies for insurance premiums that will pay farmers if their yields are lower than usual
- **f.** Funding to pay farmers not to grow crops on some land

GOVERNMENT
in your
COMMUNITY

Water Issues and Policies

Everyone needs water to survive. All levels of government often work together to address issues related to water use and pollution. Learn more about water issues and policies in your community:

- What bodies of water are near your community?

- What is that water used for—drinking, irrigation, recreation, industrial, or other uses?

- Has this body of water faced pollution challenges in the past?

- What state or local policies were enacted to address those challenges, and how did they work?

- What regulations must residents and businesses comply with regarding this water?

Create a water resources map of your community that illustrates your findings.

environmental having to do with air, water, land, and other natural resources

citizen suit a lawsuit by a private citizen to require a business or a government agency to enforce a law

Protecting the Environment

GUIDING QUESTION *How has U.S. environmental policy changed over time?*

For many years, the federal government did not set **environmental** policy. State and local governments also had few controls over air, water, land, and other natural resources. Until the 1970s, most Americans were not familiar with terms like *energy crisis, environmental pollution,* or *ecology.*

Awareness about the declining quality of the environment, combined with concerns about energy costs in the 1970s, inspired the government to put environmental issues higher on its policy agenda. The federal government began passing legislation to clean up the air and water and created the Environmental Protection Agency (EPA), which was charged with enforcing a host of new regulations aimed at protecting our environment.

Air Pollution Policies The Clean Air Act, passed in 1963 and amended several times since, has become the federal government's major tool for controlling air pollution on a national level. The law gives the EPA the power to set and enforce air quality standards for a wide variety of pollutants. In 1970 the Clean Air Act was the first major environmental law to allow **citizen suits**. This is a lawsuit by a private citizen to require polluters or a government agency to enforce an environmental law. Today, most environmental laws have provisions for citizen suits; such suits have become a major means of ensuring compliance with anti-pollution laws.

Water Pollution Policies As with the early air pollution laws, the first clean water laws passed in 1948 were weak. In the 1970s, Congress began taking stronger steps to prohibit the discharge of pollutants into American waterways.

Under the Water Pollution Control Act of 1972, all polluters, whether they were cities, industries, or farmers, needed a permit to dump waste into waterways. The EPA was required to monitor dumping locations for compliance. Many lawsuits resulted. Environmentalists sued because they thought the EPA was too permissive. Industries sued the EPA because they thought the agency's standards were unreasonably strict.

In the decades since the act's passage, the law has been changed and amended so it remains effective. Separate laws have also impacted the government's efforts to ensure pollution-free water. For example, in 1990 an agreement between the United States and Canada ensured better water quality in the Great Lakes.

Unfunded Mandates The EPA has issued hundreds of regulations to implement environmental laws. As implementation costs grew each year, state and local leaders began to complain about these unfunded mandates— programs ordered but not paid for by federal legislation. Pressured by state and local governments and by businesses, Congress in 1995 passed the Unfunded Mandates Reform Act. The Reform Act aimed at limiting the ability of the federal government to impose additional requirements on governments without providing funds to pay for them. The problem has not been solved, however, since existing mandates remain in place and many new mandates are not covered by the law. Since 2001, the federal government has imposed more than $100 billion in new, unfunded mandates to the states.

☑ **READING PROGRESS CHECK**

Summarizing What legislation to reduce air and water pollution was enacted in the 1970s?

Energy Policy

GUIDING QUESTION *What has been a major focus of U.S. energy policy and why?*

Energy policy deals with issues related to how energy is produced, distributed, and used by people. Ensuring that the United States has a secure and continuing source of oil has been a major focus of federal energy policy since 1973. In the winter of 1973–1974, Americans found themselves in an energy crisis. Arab countries cut off shipments of oil because the United States supported Israel during the Arab-Israeli war. Industries that depended on oil laid off workers. Many gas stations closed, and long lines formed at the ones that were open. States lowered speed limits, and people set thermostats lower to save energy.

Since then, the federal government has tried to fashion a new energy policy that will avoid such problems while not damaging the environment. The twin goals of increased production and environmental sustainability often come into conflict as Americans disagree about the best policies to pursue. Oil companies, for example, wanted to drill for more offshore oil, while environmentalists believed that drilling posed too great of a risk to the marine environment. Lately, the procedure used to **extract** fuel from shale deposits—known as hydraulic fracturing, or fracking—has raised environmental concerns. At the same time, in 2013 the U.S. became the world's leading oil producer, in large part because of fracking.

Recently, policy fights between environmentalists and business groups have intensified. First, there is a fear that terrorists or unfriendly governments might restrict access to Middle Eastern oil. Second, many people now worry that Americans' high consumption of oil contributes to global climate change. They argue that finding new energy sources will protect the environment, while business activists argue that making the nation less dependent on foreign oil must remain our most important goal.

The Obama administration has worked to support the development of renewable sources of energy. President Obama pledged to double the use of wind, solar, and geothermal energy by 2020. The government has provided loans to renewable start-up companies and devoted some public lands to **renewable energy** production. Some conservatives, oil and gas industry groups, and wildlife advocates have opposed these policies.

☑ **READING PROGRESS CHECK**

Explaining Why do environmentalists and business groups sometimes conflict over U.S. energy policy?

U.S. Coast Guard photo

Environmentalists believe that offshore oil drilling in ecologically sensitive areas poses too great a risk to the marine environment. This photograph shows fireboat response crews battling the blazing remnants of the oil rig Deepwater Horizon.

▲ **CRITICAL THINKING**
Considering Advantages and Disadvantages What are some potential advantages to the banning of offshore oil drilling? Are there any disadvantages to this policy?

extract to pull or draw out

renewable energy wind, solar, and geothermal sources of energy

---

LESSON 2 REVIEW

Reviewing Vocabulary
1. *Explaining* How does the U.S. government use price supports for the agricultural industry?

Using Your Graphic Organizer
2. *Analyzing* Select one of the policy areas in your completed graphic organizer and write an essay that analyzes current policy issues and debates.

Answering the Guiding Questions
3. *Discussing* How has U.S. agricultural policy changed over time?

4. *Discussing* How has U.S. environmental policy changed over time?

5. *Examining* What has been a major focus of U.S. energy policy and why?

Writing About Government
6. *Narrative* Choose a conservation project that you can do in your community. You might adopt a park, a pond, or a roadside to clean up and to keep attractive. Share your ideas with the class in the form of a proposal or presentation.

Should the U.S. require that GE foods be labeled as such?

DELIBERATING DEMOCRATIC PRINCIPLES

By inserting genes from one organism into the DNA of another, scientists can change the genetic makeup of plants and animals. Genetic engineering allows scientists to pinpoint the exact traits they want an organism to exhibit. For example, crops are engineered to have built-in defenses against pests and diseases. Scientists are also experimenting with crops that can resist frost, drought, and salt water. Such crops could allow farmers to grow food in new places. Some agricultural companies have made large profits on genetically engineered (GE) products.

 **YES**

 NO

TEAM A	The U.S. Should Require Labeling of GE Foods

Consumers have a right to know what is in their food. Many Americans are worried that GE foods could cause health problems. These foods have not been around long enough for long-term studies to prove they are safe. Other people believe human interference in natural processes could have unintended consequences. For example, crops that are resistant to herbicide (weed killer) can pass the trait on to weeds. Such "super weeds" can take over entire fields, requiring farmers to spray more and stronger chemical herbicides. Some of these herbicides contain toxic chemicals that may pollute the land, water, and air. GE products can also crowd out other plant varieties, threatening biodiversity and leaving farmers with fields more susceptible to a single disease. In addition, some people do not want to consume animal DNA. Americans who want to avoid GE foods should be able to see them clearly labeled in the grocery store. More than 20 countries and the European Union have established mandatory labeling out of concern for their citizens. This issue is about giving consumers a choice and helping them become informed.

TEAM B	The U.S. Should Not Require Labeling of GE Foods

Labeling GE products would be expensive and misleading. About 70 percent of processed American food contains at least one GE ingredient. Food producers will have to implement costly labeling, packaging, and record-keeping operations to label these foods, which will raise consumer prices. Labeling GE foods may suggest to consumers that they have something to worry about. The U.S. government tests and approves GE foods, and major scientific organizations have concluded that GE foods are safe. Also, no health differences between GE and conventional foods have been detected in scientific studies. Moreover, genetic engineering has been used for decades. It is an advancement that has the potential to reduce world hunger. GE foods can be enriched with vitamins, nutrients, and medicines. They can be designed to withstand drought and poor growing conditions. GE foods can be good for the environment if they reduce the land needed to grow crops or the chemicals used to protect them. If Americans want to avoid GE crops, they can buy certified organic foods, which, by definition, cannot include GE ingredients.

EXPLORING THE ESSENTIAL QUESTION

Deliberating With a partner, review the main arguments for either side. Decide which points are most compelling. Then paraphrase those arguments to a pair of students who were assigned to the other viewpoint. Listen to their strongest arguments. Switch sides and repeat the best arguments and add another compelling argument the other pair may not have thought about or presented. Then drop your roles and have a free discussion about which policy you support and why. Can you find any areas of common ground between the two views? How might a sensible policy address that common ground? What do you think is the best answer? Why?

Interact with these digital assets and others in lesson 3

✓ **INTERACTIVE IMAGE**
Scientific Research

✓ **PARTICIPATING IN YOUR GOVERNMENT**
Identifying Solutions

✓ **SELF-CHECK QUIZ**

✓ **VIDEO**
Children's Health Insurance Program

netw⊙rks
TRY IT YOURSELF ONLINE

LESSON 3
Income Security and Health Care

ReadingHelp Desk

Academic Vocabulary

• component

Content Vocabulary

• income security program
• unemployment insurance
• Medicare

TAKING NOTES:
Key Ideas and Details

DESCRIBING Use the chart to describe the government programs and agencies that are used to provide Americans with income security and health care.

Income Security	Health Care

ESSENTIAL QUESTION

How do social and domestic policies affect U.S. society and culture?

Read two presidents' comments about government programs for the poor ("relief" and "the war on poverty") and explain what they mean. Do you agree with either of the sentiments expressed? Why or why not?

". . . continued dependence upon relief induces a spiritual and moral disintegration fundamentally destructive to the national fiber. To dole out relief in this way is to administer a narcotic, a subtle destroyer of the human spirit. . . . Work must be found for able-bodied but destitute workers."

—President Franklin D. Roosevelt, 1935

"The war on poverty . . . is a struggle to give people a chance. It is an effort to allow them to develop and use their capacities, as we have been allowed to develop and use ours, so that they can share, as others share, in the promise of this nation. We do this, first of all, because it is right that we should."

—President Lyndon B. Johnson, 1964

The Effects of the Great Depression

GUIDING QUESTION *What were the effects of the Great Depression on income security and health care programs?*

Well into the 1900s, the federal government played almost no role in helping people find food and pay for health care and other basic needs. State and local governments provided some types of assistance, and many people in need depended on their family, place of worship, or a few private charities.

The Great Depression in the 1930s changed everything. After the stock market crash of 1929, the American economy continued to slump badly month after month for the next several years. Unemployment increased from about 3 percent of the nation's workforce in 1929 to almost 25 percent in 1933. Almost overnight, hunger and poverty became massive national problems.

As the Depression deepened, private charities and local and state governments could not cope with the problems of the poor. To ease the nation's suffering, President Franklin D. Roosevelt proposed and Congress passed the Social Security Act in 1935. This law marked the beginning of federal government social policy aimed at providing at least some economic security for all Americans.

Today, federal government social policy is centered on two types of programs: income security programs and health care programs. **Income security programs**, like Social Security, aim to protect people against loss of income due to retirement, disability, unemployment, or the absence of a family breadwinner. These programs are also known as social insurance or public assistance. Health care programs provide medical insurance and seek to protect the nation against diseases ranging from AIDS to cancer and obesity.

☑ **READING PROGRESS CHECK**

Defining What are some other terms used to describe income security programs?

Income Security

GUIDING QUESTION *What are the major U.S. income security programs, and who do they benefit?*

The Social Security Act and its later amendments became the foundation for the development of the federal government's income security policy. The Act created a social insurance system with three main **components**: (1) old-age insurance, now called Social Security; (2) public assistance for aged, blind, and disabled people (called Supplemental Security Income); and (3) **unemployment insurance**. Since 1935, the Act has been amended and expanded.

Social Security More than 90 percent of American workers participate in Social Security—most workers are required to. As our national pension plan, it provides a lifetime of retirement income to people who have paid into the system. Employers and employees both contribute to the Social Security system; retirees who have paid into the system for at least 10 years and are over age 62 may receive benefits. There are also benefits for people with disabilities, surviving spouses, and children of people who contributed to the system before they died. The amount retirees receive from Social Security is calculated based on their retirement ages and how much they earned and paid into the system.

The Social Security Administration is an independent executive agency with local offices around the country. Many experts are worried about the ability of the Social Security system to stay afloat financially—the number of workers who are retiring is putting a strain on the capacity of the system to pay out benefits. Unless it is changed, the system will probably run out of money at some point. Congress passed a law in 1983 that gradually raised the retirement age to 67 by the year 2027. Many other solutions have been proposed as well, including privatizing the system (allowing people to invest the contributions they would have made to Social Security into stocks and bonds instead). Other proposals are to reduce benefits, raise the retirement age, or require people to increase their contributions.

Unemployment Insurance The 1935 Social Security Act also set up unemployment insurance programs for people who are out of work. Overseen by the Department of Labor, federal and state governments cooperate to provide assistance.

Workers in every state are eligible to receive unemployment payments if their employers dismiss them from their jobs. To fund the program, employers pay a tax to the federal government. Then, when workers are involuntarily laid off, they may apply for weekly benefits. State governments administer this program; as a result, benefits may vary greatly from state to state.

---

income security program a government program designed to help elderly, ill, and unemployed citizens

component a part

unemployment insurance programs in which the federal and state governments cooperate to provide help for people who are out of work

EXPLORING THE ESSENTIAL QUESTION

Analyzing Different societies use different methods to care for older people who have stopped working. Who do you believe should pay for Americans' retirement? Look at the following categories and assign a percentage that each should contribute toward Americans' retirement.

1. individual savings or family support

2. pensions or retirement contributions from employers

3. government benefits

Then find two older Americans— one who is working and one who is retired—to answer this question and assign percentages. Compare their answers to yours.

PARTICIPATING
Your Government

Identifying Solutions

Explore these facts and opinions about Social Security: More than 53 million people (about 17 percent of all U.S. residents) collect Social Security benefits. For millions of people, Social Security constitutes 90 percent of their income during retirement.

"The current Social Security system is neither self-sustaining nor a true anti-poverty insurance program. These flaws could be fixed by indexing Social Security's eligibility and benefits to changes in factors such as life expectancy and wages and by limiting benefits to those who need them most."

—Rachel Greszler, The Heritage Foundation

"Because Social Security benefits are so modest and because benefits have been cut and will be cut some more, I believe that most of the imbalance should be closed by increasing payroll taxes."

—Henry J. Aaron, Brookings Institution

"If workers who retired in 2011 had been allowed to invest the employee half of the Social Security payroll tax over their working lifetime, they would retire with more income than if they relied on Social Security. Indeed, even in the worst-case scenario—a low-wage worker who invested entirely in bonds—the benefits from private investment would equal those from traditional Social Security. While there are limits and caveats to this type of analysis, it clearly shows that the argument that private investment is too risky compared with Social Security does not hold up."

—Michael D. Tanner, the Cato Institute

EXPLORING THE ESSENTIAL QUESTION

Decision Making List the various modifications that these statements suggest for ensuring the continued solvency of the Social Security system. Gather information by conducting some of your own research to learn what other solutions have been proposed. Next, consider the advantages and disadvantages for each solution. Which solutions seem most promising to you? What else would you need to know to evaluate their potential effectiveness?

Supplemental Security Income (SSI) Set up by Congress in 1974, this program brought all state programs for low-income persons who are elderly, blind, or disabled under federal control. Under the original Social Security Act, the states administered these programs, and benefits and procedures varied greatly from state to state. Today, the federal government provides primary funding and sets minimum benefit levels. Nearly all states supplement this with additional money.

The Social Security Administration runs the program, making a monthly payment to Americans who are 65 or older, or blind or disabled, and also have little or no regular income.

SNAP Program Commonly known as food stamps, President Kennedy started this program by executive order in 1961; it is now called the Supplemental Nutrition Assistance Program (SNAP). Its purpose was to increase the food-buying power of low-income families and to help dispose of America's surplus agricultural production. When the program started, about 367,000 people received food stamps. In 2013 about 47 million Americans received SNAP benefits.

EXPLORING THE ESSENTIAL QUESTION

Evaluating Choose one of the programs described in this section. Imagine that you work for an agency that has been asked to review the effectiveness of this public assistance program. What criteria will you use to determine whether the program is effective? What data will you need to collect to measure those criteria? What are some possible sources of that data?

Family Assistance During the Depression, the government designed a program to help poor families when the main wage earner died, was disabled, or left the family. This program lasted until 1996. Many people were frustrated by this welfare system. After more than 30 years of increasing program costs, the level of poverty remained high. Much of the public frustration over the welfare system stemmed from reports of welfare fraud and the cycle of dependence that developed among many welfare recipients. Many single parents on welfare had few strong incentives to work. Minimum-wage jobs provided less income than the welfare system, and working often meant paying additional day care expenses.

In the early 1990s, both President Clinton and congressional Republicans proposed broad welfare changes. After two years of negotiating, Congress and the president agreed on compromise legislation. On July 31, 1996, President Clinton announced:

PRIMARY SOURCE

Today we have an historic opportunity to make welfare what it was meant to be: a second chance, not a way of life. . . . I believe we have a duty to seize the opportunity it gives us to end welfare as we know it."

—President Bill Clinton

The new program was Temporary Assistance for Needy Families (TANF). TANF provides lump-sum payments to the states and gives states wide authority to design and operate their own welfare programs. TANF's goal was to make this aid a temporary solution until permanent work and self-sufficiency were reestablished. The program established work requirements for welfare recipients and set a time limit for how long a family could remain eligible for assistance. The bill cut back on the food stamp program and limited the amount of food stamps available for people without children.

☑ **READING PROGRESS CHECK**

Summarizing Who participates in the Social Security system, and how does it operate?

Health Care Programs

GUIDING QUESTION *How does the federal government work to promote public health?*

In 2009, with encouragement and pressure from the Obama administration, the House and Senate debated health care reforms for more than 18 months. Policy makers debated different reforms to attack spiraling health care costs and help the more than 45 million uninsured people in America. Suggested solutions included a government-run public insurance plan that people could opt into, reforms to allow insurance companies to compete across state lines, state-run websites to allow Americans to compare insurance plans, and reforms to the medical malpractice system.

Affordable Care Act In 2010, after months of debate, Congress passed the Affordable Care Act (ACA). The ACA was a blend of several suggestions. It has four major components: expanding Medicaid, preventing insurance companies from denying coverage to sick people or charging them more than others, requiring all Americans to buy health insurance, and requiring large employers to provide health insurance to their employees. The law requires all Americans to purchase health care insurance and provides financial support for low-income people to do so. Those who do not buy insurance are subjected to a fine, which is collected by the IRS. People who earn less than a certain amount are not required to pay the fine.

The law was controversial from the start. It passed Congress on a strict party-line vote: No Republicans voted for the bill. Several people sued the federal government arguing that the law was unconstitutional. In 2012 the Supreme Court ruled that the ACA's requirement that everyone buy insurance (the "individual mandate") was constitutional but that some components of the Medicaid expansion were not. The federal government could not condition all of the states' Medicaid funding on their acceptance of the expansion. Republican opposition continued, and the House voted to repeal the law more than 40 times. Many Republican governors refused to set up their states' health care exchanges, leaving it to the federal government. And several rejected federal funding to expand Medicaid. Additional challenges to implement the law included problems with the federally operated healthcare.gov website that enabled individuals in states without their own insurance exchanges to shop for and buy health insurance.

COMPARING
HEALTH CARE
AROUND THE WORLD

As you read the information about the health care systems of Denmark, Germany, and Pakistan, think about the health care system in the United States.

DENMARK

GERMANY

PAKISTAN

- System run by government
- All residents entitled to health care, bills paid by government
- Funded by a tax—8 percent of a person's taxable income
- System pays for primary-care doctors, hospital services, mental health services, long-term care
- Residents pay some co-pays for prescription drugs, dental care, and vision services; financial assistance available to people who cannot afford co-pays
- All health care free for children under 18
- Government authorities make decisions about types of services and treatments to offer
- Residents can also buy voluntary health insurance to cover co-pays and access to private treatment facilities

- All residents required to have health insurance
- About 90 percent insured by public system, where workers and employers each pay into the system (around 8 percent of income; income over about $60,000 not taxed). They choose from one of many non-profit, non governmental health insurance funds.
- Contribution covers an individual and dependents; long-term unemployed people do not pay
- Health insurance funds must cover doctor visits, hospital stays, mental health care, dental care, prescription drugs, and more
- Adults pay small co-pays for some doctor visits and for some prescription drugs
- The government sets caps on the prices of doctors' fees and prescription drug prices

- Has a network of government-funded hospitals, but there are not enough to serve everyone; some do not have resources to offer advanced medical treatment
- Government-run hospitals provide very basic care; further treatment must be approved by government health officials
- Most health care is therefore delivered by private institutions
- About 78 percent of the population pay health care expenses themselves
- No national health insurance system and most low-income residents have no health insurance
- Many of the country's poorest residents have no access to health care

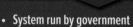

EXPLORING THE ESSENTIAL QUESTION

Comparing and Contrasting Think about what you know about health care in the United States, including Medicare, Medicaid, and the Affordable Care Act. In what ways is the United States system similar to each of these countries? In what ways is our system different? Which do you think is best? Why?

Medicare In 1965 the federal government started funding health insurance programs for seniors and the poor. The basic **Medicare** program is voluntary (though most people participate) and generally available to people over age 65. The program pays a major share of hospital bills for enrollees. For those who choose to pay an extra amount, Medicare also helps pay doctors' bills and the costs of X-rays, surgical dressings, and so on. The Centers for Medicare and Medicaid Services, an agency within the Department of Health and Human Services, manages the Medicare program.

Medicaid and CHIP Medicaid is designed to help pay hospital, doctor, and other medical bills for persons with low incomes. General federal, state, and local taxes fund this program that aids more than 71 million people at a cost of more than $414 billion each year. States administer their own Medicaid programs. Medicaid recipients are able to choose their own doctors, as long as those providers are enrolled with the Medicaid system. The health care provider submits the bill to Medicaid, where staff review and pay it. Health care providers are paid set rates that are established by the government. In some states, Medicaid recipients must pay part of their costs.

The Children's Health Insurance Program (CHIP) provides coverage to about 8 million children whose families earn too much to receive Medicaid but still cannot afford private insurance. Some observers argued that both Medicaid and Medicare contribute to rising hospital and medical costs. The government pays the medical bills, so the patients, doctors, and hospitals have no incentive under this program to keep costs down. Others say that Medicaid does a far better job of controlling costs than private insurers do, because private insurers also pay medical bills without patients ever seeing the true cost.

Public Health In addition to Medicare and Medicaid, the federal government operates several programs designed to promote and protect public health. The Department of Defense, for example, provides hospital and other medical care for active and retired American military personnel and their families. In addition, the Department of Veterans Affairs (VA) operates medical, dental, and hospital care programs for veterans.

The Public Health Service, part of the Department of Health and Human Services (HHS), promotes citizens' health by supporting research and health programs. Federal agencies, such as the Centers for Disease Control (CDC), focus on controlling the spread of infectious diseases like AIDS, flu, and tuberculosis. In 2009 the CDC identified and reported a new H1N1 flu virus (commonly called swine flu), and tracked the spread of the disease and effectiveness of vaccines. The agency estimated that 80 million Americans were vaccinated against the disease, preventing more than a million cases and 15,000 hospitalizations. The government also requires children attending public schools to be vaccinated against polio and measles.

Through a federal program called the Children's Health Insurance Program (CHIP), individual states and the federal government provide health insurance coverage to many low-income children.

▼ CRITICAL THINKING

Speculating What steps could states take to inform residents about CHIP and other programs to provide health care?

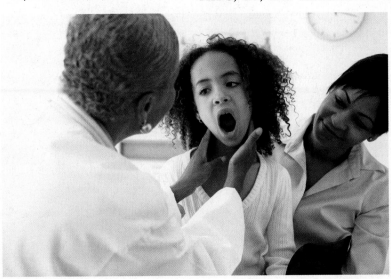

✔ READING PROGRESS CHECK

Considering Advantages and Disadvantages What are advantages and disadvantages of Medicare and the Children's Health Insurance Program?

Scientific Research

GUIDING QUESTION *How does the federal government work to promote scientific research?*

The federal government funds some scientific research. In 2009 the federal government provided about 30 percent of all the funding spent on scientific research and development in the United States. Private industry provided about 62 percent of the total spent, while the remainder came from colleges and universities, nonprofits, and state and local governments.

Support for scientific research is an important part of government social policy, especially in medicine. Public policy can encourage research in one field compared to another. The federal government provides research funds in the form of grants. Scientists can apply to agencies like the National Science Foundation (NSF) or the National Institutes of Health (NIH) to receive funding to conduct their research. Basic scientific breakthroughs can help society as a whole by leading to new medicines, treatments, technologies, and products. Every day, the NSF creates new technological innovations and makes discoveries that impact human life around the world. For example, NSF scientists are currently testing a promising new treatment for brain cancer using patients' own white blood cells to destroy tumors. Other current NSF studies and programs include work to reduce air pollution in Africa, methods to address environmental problems such as global climate change, research to learn more about human brain function, and training programs to prepare young people for careers using emerging technologies. The government funds research before direct connections are made to technological advances that might result from them.

The federal government also funds research performed by its own scientists. For example, NASA has scientists exploring space, the Department of Homeland Security develops new ways to detect bombs, and the National Oceanic and Atmospheric Administration (NOAA) has scientists monitoring coastal wetlands. More than half the federal government's science budget is spent on national defense.

The National Eye Institute (NEI) is part of the federal government's National Institutes of Health (NIH).

▲ **CRITICAL THINKING**
Explaining Why is federal funding of scientific and technological research important?

☑ **READING PROGRESS CHECK**

Analyzing Why does the federal government fund scientific research?

LESSON 3 REVIEW

Reviewing Vocabulary
1. ***Comparing and Contrasting*** What are the differences between Medicare and Medicaid?

Using Your Graphic Organizer
2. ***Describing*** Use your completed graphic organizer to create a slideshow explaining the work of three of the government agencies described in this lesson.

Answering the Guiding Questions
3. ***Determining Cause and Effect*** What were the effects of the Great Depression on income security and health care programs?

4. ***Summarizing*** What are the major U.S. income security programs, and who do they benefit?

5. ***Explaining*** How does the federal government work to promote public health?

6. ***Explaining*** How does the federal government work to promote scientific research?

Writing About Government
7. ***Informative/Explanatory*** Interview three elderly persons who have used Medicare. Ask the following: How does the Medicare system benefit you? What problems have you had with the system? What improvements could be made to Medicare? Compare your answers with your classmates'.

(l to r) Tony Linck/Time Life Pictures/Getty Images; Official White House Photo by Pete Souza; Tim Sloan/AFP/Getty Images; FEMA/Todd Swain; Library of Congress Prints and Photographs Division [LC-USZ62-19261]

Interact with these digital assets and others in lesson 4

✓ **INTERACTIVE GRAPH**
Funding for Public Higher Education

✓ **INTERACTIVE TIME LINE**
Education, Housing, and Transportation Acts

✓ **SELF-CHECK QUIZ**

✓ **VIDEO**
No Child Left Behind

netw⊙rks
TRY IT YOURSELF ONLINE

Reading Help Desk

Academic Vocabulary

• **undertaking**
• **subsequent**

Content Vocabulary

• **public housing**

TAKING NOTES:

Key Ideas and Details

SUMMARIZING Use the table to summarize the role of different federal programs for education, housing, and transportation.

Education	Housing	Transportation

LESSON 4
Education, Housing, and Transportation

ESSENTIAL QUESTION

How do citizens influence government social and domestic policy?

Make a list of the most basic goods and services that people need to survive and to thrive, such as water, food, and shelter. Compare your list to that of a partner. Next, look at your lists and think about the federal government. What role do you think the federal government should play in helping Americans to obtain the things on your list? Categorize them as large role, small role, or no role.

How do your ideas about the proper role of the federal government influence the way you evaluate government performance? How do your ideas influence your involvement in your community?

Public Education Programs

GUIDING QUESTION *How has U.S. education policy changed over time?*

Since the first modern public school system was set up in Indiana in 1816, states have had more authority over public education than the national government. States decide how their schools will be funded, set graduation standards, and choose how to license teachers. Most states have given the day-to-day responsibility for education to local governments, which decide how to spend funds, which courses to offer, and which teachers to hire.

Starting during World War II and continuing in the decades since, the federal government has taken a larger role in trying to strengthen public schools. Between 1990 and 2010, the federal share of overall education funding in the United States rose from 5.7 percent to 10.8 percent. Federal initiatives have been aimed at two major goals: (1) equal access to quality education for all students regardless of race, gender, socioeconomic status, or disability and (2) excellence, often motivated by a desire to maintain U.S. competitiveness with other nations.

Federal Aid to Primary and Secondary Education Congress began providing aid for specific educational activities about a hundred years ago—beginning with matching grants to the states for teaching courses in agriculture and home economics. Since then, Congress has passed several laws directed toward other aspects of elementary and secondary education.

Two recent programs illustrate how the federal government uses funding to shape educational policy. In 2002 a bipartisan effort led by Senator Edward Kennedy and President George W. Bush created the No Child Left Behind (NCLB) law. Its goal was to close the "achievement gap" between white and minority students, as well as between rich and poor. NCLB rewarded schools whose students showed improved test scores and punished schools whose students continued to fail. NCLB provided federal grants only to states that demonstrated steady improvement.

President Barack Obama issued waivers to exempt some states from NCLB requirements. His administration also initiated a competitive grant program called Race to the Top. States could compete for large federal grants, but to enter the competition, they had to first make several changes to align with federal policy. For example, states had to use students' scores on standardized tests as part of their system for evaluating teachers.

Aid to Higher Education Until 1862 higher education in the United States was a private **undertaking**. Then Congress passed the Morrill Act, which granted the states more than 13 million acres of public land for the endowment of colleges to teach agriculture and the mechanical arts. States established 69 of these so-called land-grant colleges under this act and a second similar law.

undertaking a task or project

Congress has also passed several G.I. bills of rights that gave veterans of World War II, the Korean War, and the Vietnam War grants to attend college. In 2008 Congress updated the laws to apply to veterans with active duty service on, or after, September 11, 2001. The Department of Education also offers federally subsidized and unsubsidized student loans, which borrowers must repay after college, and grants, which students do not repay.

Federal Education Policy Debates The policy of providing federal aid to public schools and colleges is controversial. Opponents say that education should be a state and local concern and worry that federal aid leads to federal control of what is taught and how it is taught. For example, many educational experts claimed NCLB relied too heavily on learning by repetition and teaching only to take a test. Other critics cautioned that reducing funding for failing schools was a bad idea.

School reformers often point to studies that show students in other countries outperform American students on standardized tests. In 2011 international standardized test comparisons revealed that U.S. fourth- and eighth-grade students were scoring above average but still lagged behind many east Asian countries on math, reading, and science tests.

One response has been to add national and state standards and develop tests to measure student progress toward those standards. For example, in 2009 the National Governors Association and the Council of Chief State School Officers, representing states across the country, decided to take a new approach to standards. They worked together to develop a single set of standards for English/Language Arts and Math, known as the Common Core State Standards. As of 2013, 45 states and the District of Columbia had voluntarily adopted the standards. While some observers see this as a creative state response to federal requirements, others worry that the Common Core is undermining state and local control over education policy.

Some states and the federal government have promoted school choice programs as another possible solution. These programs allow students to attend any school, even private and parochial schools, at the state's expense.

EXPLORING THE ESSENTIAL QUESTION

Evaluating If you were tasked with measuring success in your school—in terms of educating students, keeping them safe and healthy, and meeting the community's expectations—how would you go about it? Make a list of information that would help you determine whether the school is successful, then compare your list to that of a partner. Together, identify possible sources of the information you would need—student, parent, or teacher surveys, class observation, tests, academic records, community interviews, and so forth. Which items on your lists relate to students' academic progress and which relate to other measures of school success?

Official White House Photo by Pete Souza

President Obama initiated a program called Race to the Top that has provided billions of education dollars to states that strive to improve standards and teacher effectiveness. This photograph shows President Obama visiting a pre-kindergarten classroom.

▲ CRITICAL THINKING

Summarizing Why do some people oppose federal aid to public schools and colleges?

Some states have also promoted the development of public charter schools, which receive government funding but operate outside of normal state and local regulations. Proponents see school choice as a way for students to leave failing schools. Opponents of these programs argue that they take funding away from public schools that desperately need it while simultaneously leaving the public schools with the most challenged students.

☑ **READING PROGRESS CHECK**

Explaining What are No Child Left Behind and Race to the Top? Explain what they have in common and how they are different.

Housing and Urban Programs

GUIDING QUESTION *How does the Department of Housing and Urban Development implement U.S. policy?*

Adequate housing is a basic requirement for the welfare of any society. All levels of government work to ensure that Americans have decent housing. They have encouraged the construction and purchase of homes, created affordable housing for low-income residents, and discouraged housing discrimination. Despite these programs, homelessness and substandard housing remain problems across the United States.

Promoting Home Buying The federal government has developed several programs to promote building and purchasing houses, most administered by the Department of Housing and Urban Development (HUD). The best-known program is the Federal Housing Administration (FHA). The FHA guarantees banks and other private lenders against losses on loans they make to those who want to build or buy homes. By acting as an insurer for these mortgages, the FHA has allowed many low- and middle-income families who might not have qualified for private loans to purchase their own homes. HUD also offers rent assistance to low-income families.

In addition, the federal government also sponsors two mortgage corporations, known as Fannie Mae and Freddie Mac. For decades, Fannie Mae and Freddie Mac were privately owned companies, but they were protected by the federal government. They were exempt from state and local income taxes and regulated by HUD. There was an implicit assumption that if either ran into financial trouble, the U.S. government would bail them out. This made both companies attractive to investors, and they raised most of their funds from foreign governments, pension funds, and mutual funds that were willing to loan money to them at low interest rates. This, in turn, allowed them to give low-interest mortgages to low-income people. Fannie Mae and Freddie Mac earned enormous profits until the mid-2000s.

In 2007 and 2008, the housing market collapsed and many homes were quickly worth tens of thousands of dollars less than they had been. Fannie Mae and Freddie Mac held hundreds of billions of dollars in mortgage loans that were unlikely to be paid back. Suddenly, the two companies were in crisis, facing bankruptcy. To prevent the two companies from collapsing, the federal government took temporary control of them in late 2008. Congress debated ways to end the bailout and prevent such taxpayer-funded bailouts from happening again but disagreed on what approach to take instead.

Public Housing Programs Since 1937 and especially after passage of the Housing Act in 1949, the federal government has given aid to local governments to construct and operate **public housing** for low-income

public housing government-subsidized housing for low-income families

families. To implement the program, a city first sets up a "public housing authority" to which the federal government can make low-interest loans that may cover up to 90 percent of the housing construction costs. The government also grants subsidies to these agencies to allow them to operate by charging very low rents. Income from the rents is used to repay the federal loan. About 1.2 million households live in public housing. Over the years, public housing projects have faced serious problems and opposition from many groups. Local authorities have mismanaged some public housing projects. Many such projects have turned into high-rise slums and centers for crime.

A major alternative to public housing is the housing choice voucher program. Also known as Section 8, it is now the largest low-income housing program in the country. Lower-income families receive vouchers from their local public housing agency and use them to rent homes or apartments from private landlords. Tenants generally pay about 30 percent of their incomes in rent plus utilities, and the housing agency pays the rest, using funds from the federal government.

Some state and local governments are working to encourage mixed-income housing over large tracts of low-income housing. The federal government has provided some support for these initiatives. Supporters hope that such developments will contribute to the diversity and stability of communities.

☑ **READING PROGRESS CHECK**

Specifying What programs are implemented by the FHA?

PARTICIPATING
Ⓝ Your Government

Considering Different Perspectives

Should the federal government promote the goal of home ownership? While many Americans have a personal goal to own their own homes, others would prefer to rent for any number of reasons. For decades the federal government has employed policies that are intended to encourage home ownership. In the wake of the 2007–2008 financial crisis, many began to question that goal. Read these two perspectives.

"Owning a home insulates families from rent increases, which often outpace wage growth, and gives families a stake in the nation's prosperity. Homeownership offers them a way to participate in the growth of their community, and in so doing, it gives them an incentive to participate in their community. Studies show that homeowners tend to be more involved in civic institutions than renters."

—Professor of real estate and finance Susan M. Wachter

"Yet the evidence is weak that homeownership leads to this social outcome. And there is no evidence that owning larger homes leads to more stable communities. There also should be no doubt that U.S. housing policy benefits the rich much more than the poor and leads to greater, not less, inequality."

—Professor of applied economics Matthew P. Richardson

EXPLORING THE ESSENTIAL QUESTION

Comparing Advantages and Disadvantages Make a list of reasons why the government should spend money to encourage home ownership and a second list of reasons why it should not. Which list seems more persuasive to you? In a small group, explain your reasons to your peers and listen to their reasoning. Did any of their contributions sway your opinion?

Transportation Programs

GUIDING QUESTION *Which government departments and agencies implement U.S. transportation policy?*

In 1811, the national government built the National Road, which ultimately ran from Maryland to Illinois. Over the years, the federal government continued to contribute, usually through subsidies, to the building of channels, locks, dams, canals, ports, highways, railroads, and airports. Today, the Department of Transportation (DOT) coordinates national transportation policies and programs.

Building and Maintaining Highways Under the Federal Aid Highway Act of 1956 and **subsequent** amendments, states receive billions of dollars every year to build and improve the Interstate Highway System. This system consists of more than 45,000 miles of 4- to 8-lane superhighways connecting nearly all of the nation's major cities. While the federal government provides financial aid, the states construct and improve the highways. When the work has been completed, the interstate roads belong to the state or local governments, which have the responsibility of maintaining them.

Today, the Federal Highway Administration (FHWA) oversees federal highways and their funding, applies federal safety standards to trucks and buses, and plans and researches highway construction and maintenance.

Mass Transit The federal government helps cities build mass-transit systems and pay for improvements in transportation systems. Efforts are underway to upgrade existing bus service, promote car and van pooling, and think of ways to use existing rail systems. Laws passed in 2012 hope to improve safety in all forms of mass transit, develop passenger ferry systems in urban areas, and improve mobility of elderly and disabled persons.

Other Agencies Agencies outside the Department of Transportation also provide important services. The Federal Aviation Administration works to ensure safety in aviation; it licenses pilots and enforces safety rules for air traffic. The Federal Railroad Administration promotes and regulates the nation's railroad transportation. The National Highway Traffic Safety Administration is responsible for enforcing laws to protect drivers and promote highway safety.

✓ **READING PROGRESS CHECK**

Summarizing What role does the federal government play in building and maintaining highways?

The I-35 bridge collapse in 2007 in Minneapolis, Minnesota, was a tragedy. It prompted many conversations about whether state and federal governments were devoting enough money and time to maintaining aging infrastructure.

▲ **CRITICAL THINKING**
Specifying Which level of government should be responsible for maintenance of the interstate highway system?

subsequent following, coming after

LESSON 4 REVIEW

Reviewing Vocabulary
1. *Defining* What is public housing and how is it different from Section 8 housing?

Using Your Graphic Organizer
2. *Analyzing* Select one of the policy areas from your completed graphic organizer and analyze the current policies and programs that address that policy area.

Answering the Guiding Questions
3. *Understanding Continuity and Change* How has U.S. education policy changed over time?

4. *Explaining* How does the Department of Housing and Urban Development implement U.S. housing policy?

5. *Specifying* Which government departments and agencies implement U.S. transportation policy?

Writing About Government
6. *Informative/Explanatory* The federal government has developed several programs to ensure adequate housing for the people living in the United States. Research programs in your community that build or remodel homes for low-income families. Find out how the programs operate and who administers them. Write a summary of your findings.

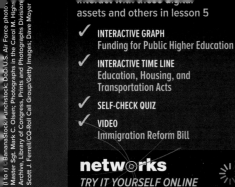

assets and others in lesson 5

✓ **INTERACTIVE GRAPH**
Funding for Public Higher Education

✓ **INTERACTIVE TIME LINE**
Education, Housing, and Transportation Acts

✓ **SELF-CHECK QUIZ**

✓ **VIDEO**
Immigration Reform Bill

networks
TRY IT YOURSELF ONLINE

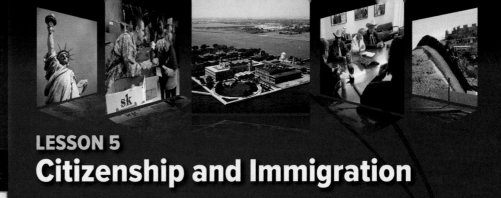

LESSON 5
Citizenship and Immigration

Reading Help Desk

Academic Vocabulary

- **status**

Content Vocabulary

- **citizen**
- **citizenship**
- **naturalization**
- **collective naturalization**
- **quotas**
- **amnesty**
- **visa**
- **green card**
- **asylum**
- **refugee**

TAKING NOTES:
Key Ideas and Details

LISTING Use the graphic organizer to create a list of the major immigration legislation discussed in this lesson and summarize the basic features of the law.

Major Immigration Legislation	Basic Features of the Law

ESSENTIAL QUESTION

How do social and domestic policies affect U.S. society and culture?

Recall the principles of democracy such as citizen participation, regular free and fair elections, the rule of law, majority rule with minority rights, limited government, equality, and individual rights.

- Make a list of at least ten actions people should take to demonstrate they are good citizens or positive members of our democratic society.

- Make a list of at least four character traits or values you think civic-minded people should possess in our democratic society.

- In your opinion, how does our democracy depend on people taking these responsibilities and duties seriously?

- How can or should government encourage civic participation and civic virtue?

Citizenship

GUIDING QUESTION *What are the responsibilities, duties, and obligations of citizenship?*

Citizens are members of a political society—a nation. American citizens have certain rights, responsibilities, obligations, and duties whether they are born here or become citizens after they arrive. Some of our rights are protected in the Constitution; others are protected by law. Citizens have certain legal obligations and duties that include observing the laws, paying taxes, serving on a jury if asked, and being loyal to the nation. In addition, sometimes citizenship requires individuals to serve the public good rather than their own personal desires and interests. These civic obligations, like voting, are important but not required by law.

Citizens have the obligation to respect the rights and opinions of others since multiple viewpoints and minorities' rights are important in a democracy. Democracy also depends on citizen involvement: choosing elected leaders and participating in government. As participants in government, citizens have the responsibility to be well informed about civic affairs and public issues. Citizens should be willing to take actions that benefit their communities and their country. These civic responsibilities are different from personal responsibilities such as taking care of oneself, accepting personal responsibility, and behaving kindly toward others.

The term *good citizen* describes all people who are civic-minded and who participate positively in their community's well-being. Global citizenship means that people are engaged in caring for people and issues beyond their own national borders.

Citizenship by Birth Every country has rules prescribing how to gain **citizenship**. In the United States, citizenship issues and other immigration matters are governed by federal law. People born in the United States (other than those born to foreign diplomats) are citizens regardless of the citizenship **status** of their parents. This rule comes from the Fourteenth Amendment. Even children born to parents who are not in the country legally are citizens. In addition, a child born outside the country to a parent who is a U.S. citizen is automatically a citizen.

Citizenship by Naturalization The Constitution provides that Congress sets the rules and requirements for citizenship. People born in other countries can become U.S. citizens through **naturalization**—a legal process by which applicants who meet certain qualifications may be granted citizenship. The requirements to apply for naturalization include:

- Legal residency in the United States for at least five years (with some exceptions),
- Physical presence in the United States during at least half of the past five years,
- Being at least 18 years of age,
- Having good moral character,
- The ability to speak, read, and write in English,
- Passing a citizenship test about U.S. history and government, and
- Swearing allegiance to the U.S. Constitution and loyalty to the United States.

The spouse of a citizen may apply for citizenship after having permanent residence in the United States for only three years and satisfying other naturalization requirements. A child who is a permanent resident may acquire citizenship automatically if a parent naturalizes before the child turns 18.

Citizens of another country can apply for dual citizenship allowing them to be U.S. citizens as long as the other country allows it. However, the U.S. government does not look favorably on U.S. citizens voluntarily applying for citizenship in another country. In such a case, their U.S. citizenship may be taken away. Citizenship can also be taken away if someone commits a serious federal crime such as treason or has obtained their naturalization through fraud.

☑ READING PROGRESS CHECK

Contrasting How do citizenship by birth and by naturalization differ?

Congress and Immigration Policy

GUIDING QUESTION *How has U.S. immigration law and policy changed over time?*

America has been a land of immigrants for more than 500 years. Since our nation's founding, laws, policies, and attitudes regarding immigration have changed many times. These changes reflect a persistent tension between the view that immigration should be restricted and the view that immigrants should be welcomed and celebrated.

The Powers of Congress Congress has sole power over naturalization. This means no state can give U.S. citizenship to anyone nor can a state take it away. It also means Congress can make laws limiting or expanding who can

citizen a member of a political society

citizenship the expected qualities that a person should have as a member of a community

status the condition of a person in the eyes of the law

naturalization the legal process by which a person is granted citizenship

EXPLORING THE ESSENTIAL QUESTION

Assessing People who want to become naturalized citizens must pass an oral test about U.S. history and government. Work with three classmates to develop three history questions and three government questions that you think all citizens should be able to answer. Swap your questions with students in two other groups. Can you answer your own questions and theirs?

Then, visit the website of the U.S. Citizenship and Immigration Services, the government agency that administers the naturalization test. Look at the study guides and sample test questions. How do your questions compare to the actual test questions? What is your assessment of the test and the support applicants are given to pass the test?

be naturalized. Congress, subject to Supreme Court rulings, can also restrict the rights of naturalized citizens.

Early in the nation's history, Congress declared a preference for immigrants from Europe. According to law in the 1790s, citizenship was possible only for someone who was "a free white person of good moral character."

In the early 1800s, Congress outlawed the importation of enslaved persons—immigrants who did not immigrate by their own choice. However, throughout that century, laws made it clear that African Americans would not be eligible for citizenship regardless of how long they lived here. African Americans were not given citizenship until after the Civil War and the passage of the Fourteenth Amendment.

Early immigration policies also restricted Asian immigrants. The California gold rush attracted people from many countries, especially from Japan and China. In 1882 Congress responded to this growing influx by passing the Chinese Exclusion Act. It barred Chinese laborers from entering the country and was not repealed until World War II. In the early 1900s, the United States also drastically limited the number of Japanese people that could immigrate to the U.S. mainland.

Congress also has the power to naturalize whole groups of people; this process is known as **collective naturalization**. Congress used collective naturalization to grant citizenship to people who had been living in the territory that is now Texas. That area was ceded by Mexico following the Mexican-American war in the mid-1800s. Congress used the same power to grant citizenship to all people living in Hawaii in 1900 and to residents of Puerto Rico in 1917. In 2000 it gave automatic citizenship rights to all minor children adopted abroad if one adoptive parent is an American citizen.

Quotas and Other Criteria In the late 1800s and early 1900s, as our country experienced rapid industrialization, millions of immigrants came to the United States, mainly from Russia and southern and eastern Europe.

collective naturalization a process by which a group of people become American citizens through an act of Congress

▼ CRITICAL THINKING

1. *Analyzing* What does each pair of images and quotes indicate about the views Americans hold on immigration?

2. *Making Connections* In your opinion, which pair most accurately describes the U.S. government's laws and policies about immigration today? Explain your reasons.

3. *Assessing* Which pair best reflects your own thinking about what our laws and policies should be about immigration? Why?

COMPARING
PRIMARY
SOURCES

Compare these two points of view on immigration.

(l to r) © BananaStock/Punchstock; Dave Moyer

"Give me your tired, your poor, Your huddled masses yearning to breathe free, The wretched refuse of your teeming shore. Send these, the homeless, tempest-tossed, to me: I lift my lamp beside the golden door!"

—Excerpt from "The New Colossus", by Emma Lazarus (1849–1887)

"Border security remains one of our nation's top priorities and we need to ensure that our families and communities are not threatened by terrorism and criminal activity. Of all the border security efforts currently underway, one of the most reliable and effective resources we have is the existing portion of the . . . border fence . . ."

—Rep. Duncan Hunter (1948–)

From 1892 to 1954, about 12 million immigrants came to America through the immigration screening station at Ellis Island. The quota system established in 1924 reduced the flow of immigrants, and Ellis Island was closed in 1954.

▲ CRITICAL THINKING

Contrasting What was the major difference between the Immigration and Nationality Act of 1965 and previous immigration policy?

quotas numerical limits on how many immigrants are allowed in from each country

amnesty a presidential order that pardons a group of people who have committed an offense against the government

Photographs in the Carol M. Highsmith Archive, Library of Congress, Prints and Photographs Division.

In the 1920s, the government passed two laws that set **quotas**, numerical limits on how many people would be allowed in from each country. The quotas were based on how many people from each country had already been here by a certain date. These laws favored immigrants from northern and western Europe and limited immigration from Asia and southern and eastern Europe. During the next 40 years, immigration dropped sharply.

In 1965 Congress passed the Immigration and Nationality Act, abolishing the quota system based on national origin. This law led to an increase of migrants from regions that had been restricted. The new law was driven by two principles: reunifying families and giving priority to people with certain skills. The law gives top priority to spouses, unmarried children under age 21, and parents of U.S. citizens older than 21. After that, preference is given to spouses and unmarried children of legal permanent residents, and adult children and siblings of U.S. citizens. Even those with top priority must often wait years to immigrate. The law also gives preference to refugees and to highly skilled workers, such as doctors and lawyers.

Federal Efforts to Control Illegal Immigration In the 1980s, immigration policy began to focus on curbing illegal immigration. The Immigration Reform and Control Act (IRCA) of 1986 tried to limit undocumented immigration by requiring employers to verify that potential employees were qualified to work in the United States. The law penalized employers who knowingly hired undocumented immigrants. Critics pointed out that the penalties were not severe enough and enforcement was lax.

The law also established a way for some undocumented immigrants to receive **amnesty**. They could become legal residents, and eventually citizens, after paying a fee, proving they had been continuous residents for four years, were of "good moral character," and spoke English. An estimated 2.7 million people became eligible for amnesty, including one million farmworkers.

By 1990, Congress had passed the Immigration Act, which said that no country could account for more than 7 percent of total immigrants in a given year. In 1996 and 2006, Congress passed new laws to increase the border patrol. It also authorized the construction of a fence along portions of the border with Mexico.

Many immigration laws, policies, and procedures changed after the attacks of September 11, 2001. Even though the perpetrators had entered the United States legally, terrorism and immigration became linked in the minds of some Americans. Spending on staffing for border patrol, fencing, and related technology more than tripled in the ten years after the attacks. In addition, the number of removals (deportations) has more than doubled since that time.

Immigration and Federalism In our federal system, the national and state governments often compete for power. This is true in the case of immigration policy. While the Constitution gives the national government supreme authority over naturalization, a growing number of state governments have passed their own laws aimed at identifying and deporting illegal immigrants. Supporters of such laws argue that the Tenth Amendment gives states the authority to enact immigration policy since the national government is failing to do so.

Debates About Immigration Reform Many people agree that current immigration policy should be reformed, even though they might not agree on what those reforms should be. Many of the controversies and proposed solutions involve whether and how to reduce illegal immigration and how to treat children of immigrants who came to the country illegally.

As of 2013, there were an estimated 12 million people living in the United States without proper visas or documentation. Some people believe that the priority of U.S. immigration policy should be preventing people from entering the United States illegally or from staying longer than they are permitted. They are worried about the strain on resources in communities that both absorb large numbers of undocumented immigrants and experience high rates of cross-border crime. Many solutions have been proposed—increasing border patrols, building a more secure fence along the border, using new forms of technology to identify undocumented immigrants, and increasing penalties on employers who hire undocumented workers. Opponents of these reforms have suggested that these solutions will cost too much money and that as long as people can find a better life in the United States, they will risk everything to cross the border. Some reformers want to focus on improving living conditions in the countries undocumented immigrants come from. Others propose making it easier for people to get a legal path to citizenship.

Some policy makers would like to make it easier for children brought to this country by their undocumented parents to gain legal status. Supporters of this reform argue that these young people came here through no fault of their own, contribute positively to the economy and to their communities, and pose no risk to national security. Opponents of this policy argue that all people who are in the United States illegally have broken the law and should not be rewarded with legal status or citizenship.

☑ **READING PROGRESS CHECK**

Analyzing How does federalism impact U.S. immigration policy?

PARTICIPATING
IN Your Government

Scott J. Ferrell/CQ-Roll Call Group/Getty Images

Finding Agreement

Several immigration reforms have been suggested, including stronger border protection, accelerated removal of undocumented immigrants, a pathway to citizenship for undocumented people, and increased seasonal and farmworker visas. You will act as a member of Congress or interest group leader to debate this issue and agree on an immigration reform bill. Review the reform proposals and your assigned role. You will represent one of these districts or interest groups:

a. A congressional district with many high-tech businesses and universities. Business leaders have said the success of their businesses depend on recruiting more high-tech workers from overseas. Universities want jobs for their graduates at home and to recruit the best professors from around the world.

b. A congressional district whose economy relies on agriculture. The farmers need people to pick their crops; they follow rules that require them to try to hire U.S. workers first but have trouble recruiting Americans. Many vocal constituents are opposed to looser immigration standards, however.

c. An urban district with high rates of unemployment. Many families have lived there for generations—and many others are newcomers, born in other countries. The majority of immigrants are living here legally, though some are unauthorized.

d. An interest group consisting of business leaders who want easier access to foreign workers.

e. An interest group representing "Dreamers"—young undocumented Americans who came to the U.S. as children and want to stay.

f. An interest group with members from border states who are concerned about increased crime and human trafficking and want an impenetrable southern border.

EXPLORING THE ESSENTIAL QUESTION

Simulating Make a preliminary decision about which reforms you might support (as a member of Congress) or how to advocate for your desired reform (as a member of an interest group). Be prepared to explain and defend your position and listen to the other elected officials and interest group representatives. Attempt to find proposals that can "pass" a vote from the majority of elected officials.

Immigration Procedures

GUIDING QUESTION *What different types of visas are available to immigrants who visit or stay in the United States?*

As of 2010, there were nearly 40 million foreign-born people living in the U.S., or 13 percent of the total population. Of those, roughly 66 percent are in the country legally. Nearly 44 percent have become naturalized citizens. Twenty-two percent have legal permanent resident status or are holding **visas**, special documents issued by the U.S. government giving them permission to enter and to stay for a specific period of time.

Visas There are more than 30 types of visas for visitors. For example, tourist visas allow people to visit for pleasure or on short business trips; student visas allow people to study at American schools. Visitors holding these types of visas cannot work in the United States.

Visitors who want to work in the United States for a specified period of time can apply for a temporary work visa. Once their work is completed and the deadline listed on their visa is reached, they must leave.

Immigrant visas are available for people who can stay in the United States indefinitely. These people become legal permanent residents (LPRs); the government gives them a document commonly known as a **green card** that shows they have permission to live and work in the United States.

Congress sets a limit on the number of immigrant visas each year. The vast majority of immigrant visas are issued in the category of family-sponsored visas. The second-largest number are issued to people who are sponsored by employers. A majority of these visas go to highly educated and skilled professionals.

Asylum and Refugees Every year, thousands of people come to the United States who are fleeing persecution or who are unable to return to their homeland due to life-threatening or extraordinary circumstances. The United States provides refuge or humanitarian protection through two programs: an **asylum** program for people who are already in the United States and their immediate relatives, and a **refugee** program for people outside the United States and their immediate relatives. Immigrants who are given refugee or asylum status may eventually become U.S. citizens.

✓ READING PROGRESS CHECK

Summarizing How are visas used to manage immigration to the United States?

visa a special document, required by certain countries, issued by the government of the country that a person wishes to enter

green card a document issued by the government that shows a person has permission to live and work in the United States

asylum refuge or humanitarian protection given by a country

refugee a person fleeing a country to escape persecution or danger

---

LESSON 5 REVIEW

Reviewing Vocabulary
1. *Understanding Relationships* What is the relationship between naturalization and citizenship?

Using Your Graphic Organizer
2. *Summarizing* Use your completed graphic organizer to summarize the provisions of the Immigration and Nationality Act of 1965 and the Immigration Reform and Control Act of 1986. How did these laws bring about changes in American culture?

Answering the Guiding Questions
3. *Explaining* What are the responsibilities, duties, and obligations of citizenship?

4. *Describing* How has U.S. immigration law and policy changed over time?

5. *Specifying* What different types of visas are available to immigrants who visit or stay in the United States?

Writing About Government
6. *Argument* Write an essay arguing for or against the following statement: "Citizenship requires that personal desires and interests be subordinated to the public good." If you think that it depends on the circumstances, be sure to include an explanation of when considerations of the public good should trump personal interests.

Plyler v Doe (1982)

FACTS OF THE CASE In 1975 the state of Texas passed a law that denied school districts money for educating students who could not prove they were living in the United States legally. The same law authorized local school districts to deny enrollment to such children. Two years later, a school district adopted a policy requiring foreign-born students to pay tuition to attend its public school. The fees would apply to students who could not prove they were in the country legally or students who could not get a federal judge's confirmation that they were in the process of getting legal documentation. A group of students who could not prove their legal status brought a class action lawsuit claiming that the law denied equal protection under the law, as required by the Fourteenth Amendment.

ISSUE

Does a state law violate the Equal Protection Clause of the Fourteenth Amendment if it denies a free public education to school-aged children who cannot prove they are in the country legally?

ARGUMENTS

OPINION A The Fourteenth Amendments says that "No state shall . . . deny to any person within its jurisdiction the equal protection of the laws." This principle should be applied literally to all persons, even the children of undocumented parents. While our past decisions have allowed states to treat undocumented individuals differently from those legally admitted, the idea of punishing innocent children for the misconduct of their parents does not fit with our country's basic idea of fairness. Although there is no federal constitutional right to an education, we recognize that economic opportunity is severely limited for those who are unable to obtain one. This law unconstitutionally places a lifetime of hardship on the children of undocumented parents. It can also place social and economic costs onto other citizens if these children grow up to be unproductive members of society.

OPINION B Undocumented individuals, as opposed to legal residents, are not receiving special judicial protection according to our past decisions, and this Court has never held that education is a fundamental right. Therefore, when we look at this new law, we should not be tempted to substitute our wisdom for that of the representatives elected by the state's citizens. Our precedents require only that state laws not violate the Constitution. In this case, the law must have a rational basis. It is certainly not irrational for the state to conclude, as it apparently has, that it does not have the responsibility to provide benefits for persons whose presence in this country is illegal. The state law in question does not violate the federal Constitution. The children of undocumented parents need to address their problem to their state legislature.

EXPLORING THE ESSENTIAL QUESTION

Making Decisions Read each of the two sample opinions in this case, and think about whether the Fourteenth Amendment guarantees a free public education to school-aged children who are undocumented. Decide which opinion you think should be the majority (winning) opinion and which one you think should be the dissenting opinion. Explain your choice.

STUDY GUIDE

BUSINESS AND LABOR POLICY
LESSON 1

Government Promotes and Protects Business	Government Regulates Business
• Free trade • Protective tariffs • Subsidies • Commerce Department • Bureau of the Census • Small Business Administration	• Federal Trade Commission • Food and Drug Administration • Consumer Financial Protection Bureau • Consumer Product Safety Commission

INCOME SECURITY AND HEALTH CARE
LESSON 3

Income Security

Social Security
• Retirees over age 62 who paid into system for at least 10 years, surviving spouses and children of deceased retirees, people with disabilities

Unemployment Insurance
• Workers laid off involuntarily

Supplemental Nutrition Assistance Program (SNAP)
• Helps low-income families buy food

Temporary Assistance for Needy Families (TANF)

Health Care

Affordable Care Act (ACA)
• All Americans must buy health insurance or pay a fine
• Provides subsidies to buy insurance
• Federal funds help states expand Medicaid

Medicare
• Helps pay medical expenses for people over age 65

Medicaid
• Helps pay medical expenses for people with low incomes

Children's Health Insurance Program (CHIP)
• Insurance for families with children who do not qualify for Medicaid

Public Health
• Research and health programs

Scientific Research

• Grants to private research scientists
• Supports research by scientists employed by federal agencies

AGRICULTURE, THE ENVIRONMENT, AND ENERGY
LESSON 2

Agricultural Policy
• Policy arose from hardships of Great Depression
• Goals: stabilize prices and ensure continued food supply

Environmental Policy
• Policy arose from concern about declining environment and rising energy costs in 1960s and 1970s

Energy Policy
• Goals: increased production and environmental sustainability
• Goals often conflict

EDUCATION, HOUSING, AND TRANSPORTATION
LESSON 4

Education Policy
• Ensure equal access to quality education
• Maintain U.S. competitiveness

Housing Policy
• Insure mortgages to encourage home ownership
• Help low-income families afford housing

Transportation Policy
• Build and maintain highways
• Help build and improve mass transit
• Regulate aviation and railroads

U.S. CITIZENSHIP
LESSON 5

By Birth	By Naturalization
• Born in U.S., regardless of citizenship or immigration status of parents • Born outside U.S. if one or both parents are U.S. citizens	• Legal resident at least 5 years • Live in U.S. at least half of last 5 years • Age 18 or older • Good moral character • Speak, read, and write English • Pass citizenship test • Swear allegiance to U.S. and Constitution

Directions: On a separate sheet of paper, answer the questions below. Make sure you read carefully and answer all parts of the questions.

Lesson Review

Lesson 1

1 *Describing* How did U.S. labor policy change in the 1940s?

Lesson 2

2 *Explaining* What is the significance of citizen suits in U.S. environmental policy?

Lesson 3

3 *Specifying* What are the four major components of the Affordable Care Act?

Lesson 4

4 *Interpreting Significance* In what way did construction of the National Road mark a turning point in transportation policy?

5 *Considering Advantages and Disadvantages* How does the Federal Housing Administration (FHA) benefit home buyers? What are possible pitfalls of the FHA's actions?

Lesson 5

6 *Explaining* What is the difference between personal and civic responsibility?

7 *Making Inferences* How do you think the terrorist attacks of September 11, 2001, influenced public views on immigration?

ANSWERING THE ESSENTIAL QUESTIONS

Review your answers to the introductory questions at the beginning of each lesson. Then answer the following Essential Questions based on what you learned in the chapter. Have your answers changed?

8 *Analyzing* How is social and domestic policy created and implemented?

9 *Analyzing Cause and Effect* How do citizens influence government social and domestic policy?

10 *Explaining* How do social and domestic policies affect U.S. society and culture?

DBQ Interpreting Political Cartoons

Use the political cartoon to answer the following questions.

"IN ITS MAJESTIC EQUALITY, THE LAW FORBIDS RICH AND POOR ALIKE TO SLEEP UNDER BRIDGES, BEG IN THE STREETS AND STEAL LOAVES OF BREAD."
—ANATOLE FRANCE

11 *Interpreting* Who do the characters in this cartoon represent?

12 *Analyzing* What is the quote in the cartoon saying about equality under the law?

Critical Thinking

13 *Analyzing Cause and Effect* What are likely consequences for consumers if monopolies were allowed to flourish in our economy?

14 *Making Inferences* Why does government intervene to stabilize prices in the agriculture industry?

15 *Identifying Cause and Effect* How did the Temporary Assistance for Needy Families legislation reform the welfare system?

16 *Identifying Perspectives* What are the Common Core Standards and what are some arguments for and against these standards?

17 *Analyzing* What education policy did the government implement through the G.I. bills of rights? How do you think this policy affected the American culture after World War II?

Need Extra Help?

If You've Missed Question	**1**	**2**	**3**	**4**	**5**	**6**	**7**	**8**	**9**	**10**	**11**	**12**	**13**	**14**	**15**	**16**	**17**
Go to page	676	680	686	694	692	695	698	670	680	683	683	683	672	678	686	691	691

Directions: On a separate sheet of paper, answer the questions below. Make sure you read carefully and answer all parts of the questions.

DBQ Analyzing Primary Sources

Read the excerpt and answer the questions that follow.

PRIMARY SOURCE

"But when workers get higher wages and more civilized working conditions through the free market, when they get them by firms competing with one another for the best workers, by workers competing with one another for the best jobs, those higher wages are at nobody's expense. They can only come from higher productivity, greater capital investment, more widely diffused skills. The whole pie is bigger, there is more for the worker, but there's also more for the employer, the investor, the consumer and even the tax collector."
—Milton Friedman, *Free to Choose: A Personal Statement*
(Mariner Books, 1990)

18 *Identifying Frame of Reference and Bias* What is Friedman's frame of reference? Does this passage reflect a liberal or conservative bias? Explain.

19 *Drawing Inferences* Based on the views expressed in this passage, would Friedman support or oppose right-to-work laws? Explain.

Social Studies Skills

Use the graph to answer the following questions.

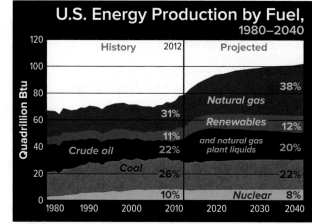

Source: U.S. Energy Information Administration

20 *Using Graphs* The graph shows coal at 26 percent in 2012. What does this figure mean?

21 *Identifying Continuity and Change* Describe the expected trend in coal production from 2012 to 2040 in terms of quantity produced and percentage.

22 *Comparing and Contrasting* Compare the expected trends for natural gas and for renewables from 2012 to 2040. How are the trends similar? How are they different?

Research and Presentation

23 *Problem Solving* Identify a problem you have faced as a consumer. The problem might involve product quality, product availability, or service issues. Gather information about the problem and devise a list of solutions, including possible government regulations. What are advantages and disadvantages of these government regulations or other solutions for businesses and consumers? Select the best solution. How would you implement it? How effective would it be?

24 *Evaluating Information, Arguments, and Counterarguments* Go online to find primary and secondary sources advocating for and against fracking. Identify the bias and propaganda in each source. Then analyze the validity of the information and arguments presented. Take a position and prepare to defend it in a class debate.

25 *Synthesizing* What does "global good citizenship" mean to you? Go online to find images that illustrate acts of global good citizens. Use the images to create three electronic slides. Add captions to explain how each image relates to global good citizenship. Combine your slides with those of other students to create a class slide show. As a class, compose a definition of global good citizenship.

26 *Analyzing* Research a policy issue and find examples of how individual citizens, political parties, interest groups, and the mass media have tried to affect the policy area.

Need Extra Help?

If You've Missed Question	18	19	20	21	22	23	24	25	26
Go to page	670	676	681	681	681	673	681	695	670

Making Foreign and Defense Policy

networks
www.connected.mcgraw-hill.com
There's More Online about making foreign and defense policy.

CHAPTER 23

ESSENTIAL QUESTIONS

• How does U.S. foreign policy affect other countries and regions? • How is foreign policy made and implemented? • How is foreign policy affected by the separation of powers?

HERE RESTS IN
HONORED GLORY
AN AMERICAN
SOLDIER

◀ The Tomb of the Unknowns is an important tribute to those who have fought to defend our nation.

U.S. Army photo by Myles D. Cullen

ANALYZING PRIMARY SOURCES

THE NATIONAL SECURITY AGENCY AND U.S. SURVEILLANCE

In 2013, Edward Snowden, a former government contractor, leaked thousands of classified documents that described U.S. surveillance on targets around the world. Some of the United States's extensive international intelligence gathering programs came to light. Those programs include monitoring and mining data, social media networks, and communications of Americans and citizens of other countries. For example, starting in 2011, the U.S. National Security Agency (NSA) collected 1.1 billion cellphone records each day from American service providers. The NSA also conducted surveillance of at least 35 foreign leaders.

PRIMARY SOURCE A

"The National Security Agency and the FBI are tapping directly into the central servers of nine leading U.S. Internet companies, extracting audio and video chats, photographs, e-mails, documents, and connection logs that enable analysts to track foreign targets, according to a top-secret document obtained by *The Washington Post*.

The program, code-named PRISM, has not been made public until now. It may be the first of its kind."

—Barton Gellman and Laura Poitras, "U.S., British intelligence mining data from nine U.S. Internet companies in broad secret program," *The Washington Post*, June 6, 2013

PRIMARY SOURCE B

German Chancellor Angela Merkel made the following statement in response to reports that the NSA had eavesdropped on her personal cellphone calls and communications involving German citizens.

"This is not just about me, but it's about all German citizens. Partnerships are based on trust and we now have to rebuild trust. I repeat that spying among friends is not at all acceptable against anyone, and that goes for every citizen in Germany."

—German Chancellor Angela Merkel, October 2013

PRIMARY SOURCE C

"NSA conducts all of its activities in accordance with applicable laws, regulations, and policies—and assertions to the contrary do a grave disservice to the nation, its allies and partners, and the men and women who make up the National Security Agency. . . . Seventy years ago, the communications links were shortwave radio transmissions between two points on the globe. Today's communications flow over technologies like satellite links, microwave towers, and fiber optic cables. Terrorists, weapons proliferators, and other valid foreign intelligence targets make use of commercial infrastructure and services. When a validated foreign intelligence target uses one of those means to send or receive their communications, we work to find, collect, and report on the communication."

—U.S. National Security Agency, "NSA's Activities: Valid Foreign Intelligence Targets Are the Focus," October 31, 2013

PRIMARY SOURCE D

"To be perfectly clear, this is not information that we collected on European citizens. It represents information that we, and our NATO allies, have collected in defense of our countries and in support of military operations . . . [This program has saved lives] not only here but in Europe and around the world."

—Army General Keith Alexander, NSA Director, testimony before House Intelligence Committee hearing, October 29, 2013

Headlines showing the international response to the NSA surveillance program:

"Leaders of Mexico and Brazil Rebuke U.S. for NSA Snooping"

—*Time*, September 6, 2013

"French president says U.S. spying allegations threaten trade"

—*Fox News*, July 2, 2013

"Outrage Over NSA Spying Spreads to Asia: More information about the NSA's operations in Asia has come to light, sparking widespread outrage"

—*The Diplomat*, October 13, 2013

"NSA whistleblower Edward Snowden offered asylum by Venezuela, Nicaragua and now Bolivia"

—*The Independent*, November 22, 2013

Results of a September 2013 poll conducted by the German Marshall Fund, a U.S.-based program whose goal is to support cooperation between the United States and Europe.

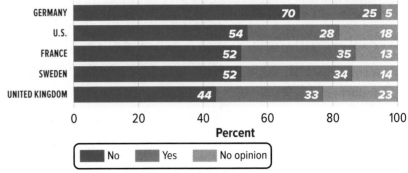

Is a Government's Collection of the Internet and Telephone Data of Its Own Citizens Justified?

Country	No	Yes	No opinion
GERMANY	70	25	5
U.S.	54	28	18
FRANCE	52	35	13
SWEDEN	52	34	14
UNITED KINGDOM	44	33	23

Percent

Source: The German Marshall Fund of the United States

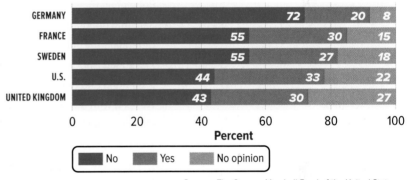

Is a Government's Collection of the Internet and Telephone Data of Allied Nations' Citizens Justified?

Country	No	Yes	No opinion
GERMANY	72	20	8
FRANCE	55	30	15
SWEDEN	55	27	18
U.S.	44	33	22
UNITED KINGDOM	43	30	27

Percent

Source: The German Marshall Fund of the United States

DBQ DOCUMENT-BASED QUESTIONS

1. **Explaining** What is the purpose of the National Security Agency's surveillance program? How does the NSA collect and use data?

2. **Applying** What principles of democracy and purposes of government are in tension with surveillance programs like the NSA's?

3. **Analyzing** Do you think the government is justified when it monitors communications between private individuals to protect the nation from terrorism?

WHAT WILL YOU DO?

If you were in charge of foreign intelligence gathering for the United States, which targets would you allow surveillance of and using what techniques? How would you respond to criticism of your choices?

EXPLORE the interactive version of the analyzing primary sources feature on Networks.

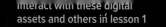

l to r) USAID Indonesia; U.S. Navy photo by Eric J. Tilford; Getty Images Sport/Getty Images; George Silk/Time Life Pictures/Getty Images

ReadingHelp Desk

Academic Vocabulary

- **fundamental**
- **maintain**

Content Vocabulary

- **foreign policy**
- **national security**
- **isolationism**
- **containment**
- **terrorism**

TAKING NOTES:

Key Ideas and Details

SEQUENCING INFORMATION Use the time line to sequence and record information from the lesson about major events and turning points in U.S. foreign policy.

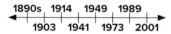

1890s 1914 1949 1989
◄—————————————————►
1903 1941 1973 2001

LESSON 1

Goals and Development of Foreign Policy

ESSENTIAL QUESTION

How does U.S. foreign policy affect other countries and regions?

For each of these foreign policy goals, decide if it is (N) not important, (S) somewhat important, or (V) very important to you.

- Preventing future acts of international terrorism
- Preventing the spread of weapons of mass destruction
- Securing adequate supplies of energy for the U.S.
- Defending the security of our allies
- Promoting trade policies that benefit Americans and American companies
- Promoting and defending human rights in other countries
- Working with the United Nations to bring about world cooperation
- Helping other countries build democracies
- Promoting economic development in other countries

Compare your answers to those of two other students. Then, together, discuss these questions:

1. Can you think of a hypothetical or real situation that illustrates competing goals?

2. Pursuing foreign policy costs money and has risks. Choose one goal and imagine a situation in which the American people have a lot to gain or a lot to lose.

Goals of U.S. Foreign Policy

GUIDING QUESTION *How do the U.S. government's foreign policy goals affect political, economic, and security interests at home and abroad?*

Foreign policy consists of the goals and strategies that guide a nation's relations with other countries and groups in the world. Even while the strategies may change from year to year, the long-term goals of that policy remain constant, reflecting both the nation's ideals and its self-interest.

Security Interests The principal goal of American foreign policy is to preserve the security of the United States. **National security** means protection of a nation—its lands and people—from foreign threats, whether from governments, organized groups, or individual terrorists. This goal is **fundamental** because no nation can achieve other aims such as improving its education system or providing better health care if it is under attack.

Economic Interests **Maintaining** trade with other nations and promoting America's economic interests are basic goals of U.S. foreign policy. American factories and farms depend on people in foreign countries to buy and sell their goods. The United States also works to preserve access to the natural resources that we import. For example, countries in the Middle East are of strategic importance because of the large amount of oil reserves in the region. While the United States supports trade that is free from both export and import restrictions, it does limit trade in some ways to protect its own domestic industries and workers from foreign competition. Some people argue that a policy of supporting free and open trade harms people in poorer parts of the world.

World Peace American leaders work for peace because they believe it helps the nation avoid outside conflicts and aids national security. The United States tries to help other nations settle disputes and has also supplied economic aid to at-risk countries, in part to prevent uprisings and revolutions. The United States helped organize the United Nations to promote world peace. We also work with many other international organizations such as the North Atlantic Treaty Organization (NATO) to prevent regional conflicts.

Promoting Democracy The United States has often been a democratic model for other countries. Even when the United States falls short of its democratic aspirations, the nation still believes that democracy is the best system of government.

foreign policy the strategies and goals that guide a nation's relations with other countries and groups in the world

national security protection of a nation—its lands and people—from foreign threats, whether from governments, organized groups, or individual terrorists

fundamental a basic and necessary component of something; original, primary, and essential

maintain to continue, uphold, sustain, or defend

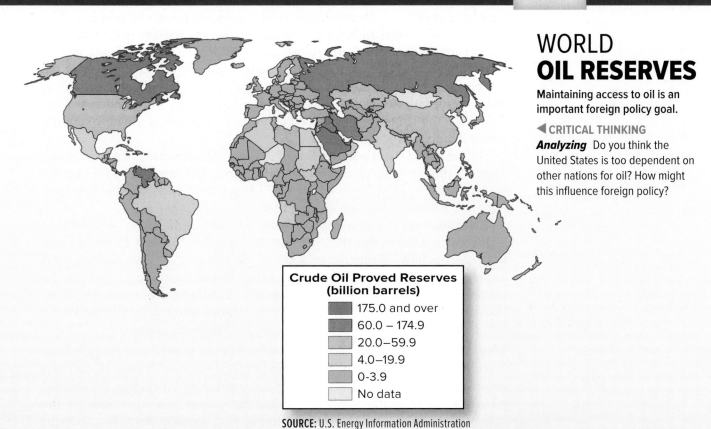

WORLD **OIL RESERVES**

Maintaining access to oil is an important foreign policy goal.

◀ **CRITICAL THINKING**
Analyzing Do you think the United States is too dependent on other nations for oil? How might this influence foreign policy?

Crude Oil Proved Reserves (billion barrels)
- 175.0 and over
- 60.0 – 174.9
- 20.0 – 59.9
- 4.0 – 19.9
- 0 - 3.9
- No data

SOURCE: U.S. Energy Information Administration

The United States often demonstrates its concern for others and helps maintain political stability by providing food and medical supplies after natural disasters. This photograph shows earthquake victims in Indonesia receiving assistance from USAID.

▲ **CRITICAL THINKING**

Explaining How does providing foreign aid help the U.S. meet its long-term foreign policy goals?

isolationism avoiding involvement in world affairs

Most U.S. leaders say democracy aligns with our fundamental values and helps to create a more secure and stable global arena and good trade partners. Democracy, they argue, helps people around the world because it protects people's rights, combats international terrorism and crime, and promotes human health. However, some believe that the United States should not intervene in other countries because the costs are too great and the outcomes uncertain.

Concern for Humanity Victims of natural disasters or starvation have looked to the United States for help, and the United States has often responded by providing food, medical supplies, and technical assistance for humanitarian reasons. At the same time, this aid serves the strategic interests of the United States by maintaining political stability in the world.

☑ **READING PROGRESS CHECK**

Listing What are the basic goals of U.S. foreign policy?

Development of U.S. Foreign Policy

GUIDING QUESTION *How have isolationism and internationalism affected U.S. foreign policy over time?*

Until the late 1800s, U.S. foreign policy was based on **isolationism**—avoiding involvement in world affairs. During the twentieth century, however, the nation shifted toward internationalism. Internationalists believed that involvement in world affairs was necessary to pursue many national goals such as national security and promoting democracy.

Moving Toward Internationalism In the 1890s, the United States became an industrial power and needed world markets for its products as well as sources for raw materials. Many leaders believed that the United States needed to play an active role in the world and even to expand and acquire a colonial empire. Wars and political maneuvers around the turn of the twentieth century resulted in American colonies in the Philippine Islands, Guam, Puerto Rico, Hawaii, and Samoa; the United States was now a major power in the Caribbean as well as in the Pacific region and East Asia. In 1903, after providing military support to Panamanian rebels who wanted independence from Colombia, the United States gained control of a portion of the new country, where it built the Panama Canal.

When World War I began in Europe in 1914, America did not get involved. Then Germany sank neutral ships—including U.S. ships—and Congress declared war against Germany in 1917. American troops went overseas to fight in a European war for the first time.

Disillusioned by the terrible cost of war, Americans returned to isolationism. During the 1920s and 1930s, however, ruthless dictators came to power in Italy, Germany, and Japan. By the 1930s, these nations used military force to invade other nations. When World War II began in 1939, the United States officially remained neutral. The Japanese attack on Pearl Harbor in 1941, however, drew the United States into the war. Since World War II, U.S. foreign policy has been based on internationalism.

The Cold War The Cold War was a war of words and ideologies— primarily between the United States and the Soviet Union. It was also a clash of power and interests. Both countries emerged from World War II as world powers, and American leaders viewed the power and ambitions of the communist Soviet Union as a threat to national security. Between 1945 and 1949, the Soviet Union imposed a communist system of government on the nations of Eastern Europe. Meanwhile, in 1949 Chinese Communists seized control of China. These events convinced U.S. leaders that they needed to halt Communist aggression.

The United States employed a policy of **containment**: The goal was to avoid war with the Soviet Union but to keep communism from spreading. American leaders hoped that eventually the Soviet Union would collapse from its own internal problems. The policy of containment did lead to military action elsewhere, however. One approach was to give aid to nations that appeared to be in danger of communist revolution or had been threatened by communist countries. Under the Marshall Plan, the United States gave war-torn nations of Western Europe more than $13 billion in aid between 1947 and 1951. The U.S. also provided overt and covert aid to anticommunist resistance movements in Afghanistan, Nicaragua, Angola, Cambodia, and other countries. In some instances, the U.S. intervened militarily in countries that were threatened by communist forces. The U.S. got involved in the Korean War and the Vietnam War as a result of containment.

Cold War tensions and fears also led to an arms race. The Soviet Union's development of nuclear weapons and large missiles that could reach the United States prompted the U.S. to build more weapons. Both sides promised to respond to the use of nuclear weapons with their own such strikes. This threat deterred outright war but led to large stockpiles of nuclear weapons.

containment the Cold War policy of keeping the Soviet Union from expanding its power

The Korean and Vietnam Wars In the Korean War, the United States aided pro-U.S. South Korea when it was invaded by communist North Korea. After three years of fighting, an armistice was signed in 1953 restoring a border between communist North Korea and democratic South Korea.

In the Vietnam War, the United States committed troops for many years to fight on the side of the South Vietnamese government against communist North Vietnam. After almost ten years of involvement in combat operations, Americans were weary of the Vietnam War and public support plummeted. President Nixon withdrew most American troops from Vietnam in 1973; in 1975 South Vietnam became part of communist North Vietnam.

The Cold War Ends By 1989, the Soviet Union was growing weaker. In 1990 communist East Germany and democratic West Germany reunited. Soon, Poland, Czechoslovakia, Hungary, Romania, and Bulgaria—all parts

CHART

Analyzing Foreign Policy Actions

Analyze each of these foreign policy actions. Which goal(s) do you think the action was intended to achieve?

ACTION	GOAL(S)
In 1954, the U.S. Central Intelligence Agency funded, trained, and assisted rebels in a military coup that removed the democratically elected president of Guatemala. Prior to the coup, the Guatemalan government had begun an aggressive land reform program that took land from wealthy landowners to give to poorer people. The landowner that lost the most land was United Fruit Company, a corporation based in the United States.	
In 1980, President Carter decided that the U.S. would not participate in the Olympics. The boycott was in protest of the Soviet Union's invasion of Afghanistan.	
Voice of America (VOA) began as a U.S.-funded radio program in 1942 to broadcast anti-Nazi messages to the German people in their native language. During the Cold War, VOA broadcast anti-communist messages to people living in Soviet-controlled countries where news was censored by their own governments. Since the 1960s, VOA's mission has been to promote freedom and democracy through accurate, objective, and balanced news about America to the world.	

of the Soviet empire—overthrew their communist governments. Then in 1991 the Soviet Union finally collapsed. It split into Russia and 14 other nations; the Cold War was over.

A multipolar system emerged with several major powers, including the United States, the European Union, China, India, Japan, and Russia. As the United States dealt with international crises, no new strategic doctrine emerged to guide foreign policy. Instead, U.S. troops were sent to hot spots across the globe, while policy makers called for the United States to protect American trade interests, encourage democracy, and advance human rights.

The largest conflict of the period involved Iraq. In August 1990, the dictator of Iraq, Saddam Hussein, decided to invade the tiny nation of Kuwait to gain control of its oil supplies. President George H.W. Bush quickly assembled a coalition of 34 nations and won approval from the UN Security Council for action against Iraq. In early 1991, coalition troops, led by an American force, expelled Iraqi forces from Kuwait.

Throughout the 1990s, President Clinton sent U.S. forces to several places to maintain political order and protect humanitarian interests. In 1992 American troops joined a multinational force in Somalia to protect relief organizations during a civil war. In 1994 American troops preserved order in Haiti when the elected president was forced to flee the country. In 1995 American forces and NATO allies intervened to end ethnic warfare amongst Croats, Serbs, and Muslims resulting from the breakup of the former Yugoslavia. Then in 1999, American and NATO air power and troops forced Serbian troops to withdraw from the Yugoslavian province of Kosovo.

☑ **READING PROGRESS CHECK**

Naming Throughout its history, the focus of the United States's foreign policy has shifted between two different geopolitical concepts. Name them both.

Foreign Policy Since September 11, 2001

GUIDING QUESTION *How did the events of September 11, 2001, affect the goals and development of U.S. foreign policy?*

Terrorism is the use of violence by nonstate actors, such as al-Qaeda, against civilian targets to achieve political goals. On September 11, 2001, terrorists hijacked commercial jetliners and crashed them into the World Trade Center in New York City and the Pentagon in Washington, D.C. Another plane intended for a similar attack crashed in Pennsylvania. These attacks killed nearly 3,000 people. Since then, stopping international terrorism has become a major goal of American foreign policy. President George W. Bush quickly announced a focus on a war on terror. He outlined a new foreign policy strategy—preemption. Instead of waiting for an attack, the United States would strike first to prevent nations that support terrorism from developing weapons of mass destruction. Supporters of preemption argued that older policies did not work in a world of suicide bombers and outlaw nations. Critics claimed that preemption ignored international law and might lead to a series of wars.

The War in Afghanistan U.S. intelligence agencies soon discovered the al-Qaeda leaders were based in Afghanistan. The Taliban, the militant Islamic government of Afghanistan, had refused to surrender al-Qaeda leaders there. In 2001 the United States and its NATO allies invaded Afghanistan. In a few months, Taliban leaders were driven from power and retreated to the south. The United States helped the Afghani people elect a new government, but Taliban guerrillas continued to fight. In 2009 President Obama committed

terrorism the use of violence against civilians to achieve political goals

The September 11 attacks influenced many of the foreign policy decisions that have been made since 2001.

▼ **CRITICAL THINKING**
Describing What was the foreign policy strategy that was announced following the attacks? How was it implemented?

U.S. Navy photo by Eric J. Tilford

34,000 additional troops to Afghanistan while NATO troops equipped and trained Afghan forces to take control of the country's security. However, operations were marred by insurgent attacks. Finally, in 2013 the main combat role was handed from American and NATO troops to the Afghan army. Most U.S. troops were scheduled to depart Afghanistan by 2014.

The War in Iraq President Bush applied preemption in March 2003 when the United States, with help from Great Britain and several other nations, invaded Iraq and removed the government of Saddam Hussein. The Bush administration claimed that Iraq had developed weapons of mass destruction and that overthrowing Iraq's dictator would help stabilize the Middle East and reduce terrorism. The coalition forces quickly defeated the Iraqi army but never found weapons of mass destruction.

Iraqi insurgents launched a guerrilla war. Some insurgents supported Saddam Hussein, while others were affiliated with terrorist groups and wanted to establish a religious state. Still others belonged to tribal militias.

From 2003 to 2008, U.S. troops fought the insurgents, and billions of dollars in aid was spent to rebuild Iraq. Iraqis voted for a new constitution and held their first free multiparty elections in 50 years, but the fighting continued. By 2007, more than 3,000 American soldiers had been killed, most Americans no longer supported the war, and many coalition partners had withdrawn from the country. President Obama withdrew U.S. combat forces in 2010 and all troops in 2011. In 2014 violence still plagued the country.

A Multilateral Approach President Obama continued to pursue the war on terror. Drone strikes increased, and the United States killed a large number of top terrorist leaders, including Osama bin Laden. However, the Obama administration's foreign policy was less focused on military power alone. It aimed to deal with multiple foreign policy challenges, including wars in Iraq and Afghanistan, terrorism and terrorist groups such as the so-called Islamic State (ISIS), a global economic recession, problems with illegal immigration, unrest in the Middle East, and efforts by Iran and North Korea to build nuclear weapons.

✓ **READING PROGRESS CHECK**

Paraphrasing Using your own words, explain the basic arguments for and against the strategy of preemption.

Shah Marai/AFP/Getty Images

In 2006 NATO took over command in southern Afghanistan from the U.S.-led coalition.

▲ CRITICAL THINKING
Describing How did U.S. military involvement in Afghanistan change from 2001 to 2014?

LESSON 1 REVIEW

Reviewing Vocabulary
1. *Understanding Relationships* How are the terms *foreign policy* and *national security* related to one another? Be sure to define each in your response.

Using Your Graphic Organizer
2. *Sequencing Information* The aftermath of what event listed on your time line prompted the United States's return to isolationism?

Answering the Guiding Questions
3. *Summarizing* How do the U.S. government's foreign policy goals affect political, economic, and security interests at home and abroad?

4. *Explaining* How have isolationism and internationalism affected U.S. foreign policy over time?

5. *Analyzing Cause and Effect* How did the events of September 11, 2001, affect the goals and development of U.S. foreign policy?

Writing About Government
6. *Argument* How should the United States decide which foreign policy goals to prioritize? Write a newspaper editorial about this topic describing how you would prioritize American foreign policy goals.

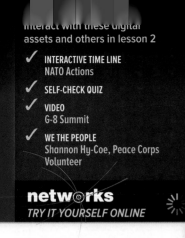

(l to r) DoD photo by Sgt. Brendan Stephens, U.S. Army;
Peace Corps photo; Shah Marai/AFP/Getty Images

LESSON 2
Foreign Policy Tools

ReadingHelp Desk

Academic Vocabulary

- nuclear

Content Vocabulary

- bilateral agreement
- multilateral agreement
- sanction
- alliance
- regional security pact
- collective security
- bilateral treaty
- blockade

TAKING NOTES:

Key Ideas and Details

LISTING Use the graphic organizer to list the foreign policies the U.S. government uses to ensure the nation's security.

National Security

ESSENTIAL QUESTION

How is foreign policy made and implemented?

In November 2013, the BBC reported that Pakistan was considering giving nuclear weapons to Saudi Arabia. According to the report, the Saudis wanted to have a counter-threat if Iran develops nuclear weapons. Saudi Arabia has signed the Treaty on the Non-Proliferation of Nuclear Weapons. In this treaty, countries that do not have nuclear weapons, like Saudi Arabia, promised never to acquire them. The United States does not think arming Saudi Arabia with nuclear weapons is a good idea. What should the United States do?

In a group of three, brainstorm as many responses to this situation as possible. Remember: In a brainstorm, all ideas are valid. The goal is to generate as many ideas as you can without evaluating or editing your work.

Diplomatic Foreign Policy Tools

GUIDING QUESTION *What are the federal government's main foreign policy responsibilities for national defense?*

The United States uses many different tools to achieve its foreign policy goals. To minimize the danger to national security, the U.S. tries to settle conflicts and work toward its goals peacefully. Sometimes, however, the U.S. resorts to using military force.

Relationships with other countries are often facilitated using a range of diplomatic strategies—from the dissemination of information and ideas to cultural exchanges to formal diplomatic recognition and treaties. Much of this diplomatic work takes the form of direct discussions. Journalist Edward R. Murrow once said, "The real crucial link in the international exchange is the last three feet, which is bridged by personal contact, one person talking to another."

Negotiations and Agreements Discussions between U.S. diplomats and those in foreign countries often lead to different types of formal agreements. In these agreements, countries might agree on joint health and welfare programs, trade policies, territorial boundaries, or many other topics. Diplomats must be focused and skillful to conduct successful negotiations—they must have a clear goal and strategy, must listen carefully to what the other side says, and must be able to find ways to compromise. In negotiating, diplomats often use positive and negative incentives—promises about future trade, aid, or other support—to persuade their counterparts.

While diplomatic staff conduct many of the negotiations that lead to agreements between countries, national leaders speak directly about the most important issues. The U.S. Secretary of State or the president will represent American interests in direct talks with foreign leaders. For example, every year the Group of 8 (G8) holds a summit for the heads of government for eight of the world's largest economies. The leaders discuss the major issues of the day.

Membership in International Organizations The United States participates in dozens of international organizations. These organizations are groups of countries that address a range of global issues, including peace and security, **nuclear** nonproliferation, human rights, economic development, climate change, global health, and much more. The most familiar is the United Nations, which counts more than 190 countries among its members. Similarly, the Organization of American States (OAS) includes the United States and our Latin American neighbors. The OAS countries meet to resolve conflict and promote economic, social, and cultural development.

The United States is also part of several economic organizations, including the International Monetary Fund (IMF) and the World Trade Organization (WTO). The United States works on global health and humanitarian issues through the World Health Organization (WHO), collaborates to fight global crime with other countries in Interpol, and works

nuclear being a weapon whose destructive power comes from a nuclear reaction

We the People: Making a Difference

SHANNON HY-COE

Peace Corps photo

The Peace Corps began in 1961, an outgrowth of President John F. Kennedy's challenge to young people to serve their country by living and working in developing countries. The Peace Corps works to help the people of developing countries, to promote a better understanding of Americans by others, and to promote a better understanding of other peoples by Americans.

Shannon Hy-Coe is one of the more than 210,000 volunteers of all ages and backgrounds who have served in the Peace Corps. She worked in youth development and with Special Olympics in Paraguay—leading workshops, teaching English, and establishing youth groups. Of her experience in the Peace Corps, Shannon has said, "I joined the Peace Corps because I always wanted to give back to society. I grew up in a developing country and understand the lack of resources, especially for people with disabilities. I've grown and changed and learned throughout this whole experience. It has taught me patience and the need to be flexible."

As a person with a disability, Shannon believes her participation changed attitudes towards those with disabilities in Paraguay.

CRITICAL THINKING
1. *Applying* What goals of foreign policy does the Peace Corps address?
2. *Classifying* Would you classify the Peace Corps as a tool of public diplomacy? Why or why not?
3. *Explaining* How did Shannon Hy-Coe's participation in the Peace Corps benefit her, the people of Paraguay, and the United States?

Analyzing Foreign policy tools can be positive incentives to encourage other countries' behavior, or negative incentives to "punish" countries that act against U.S. interests. Imagine you are the Undersecretary for Public Diplomacy and Public Affairs. Which of these incentives do you think would be most effective? Rank the strategies according to which you would be most likely to use (1 = most likely, 8 = least likely).

_____ Sponsoring exchange programs that bring foreign professionals to the United States to learn about our country and send American professionals abroad

_____ Offering Massive Online Open Courses (MOOCs) on topics related to democracy, the free enterprise system, and American culture

_____ Providing "American Spaces" around the world— welcoming environments where people can learn about the United States and meet and interact with Americans

_____ Countering anti-American propaganda and misinformation in digital environments created by terrorist groups

_____ Producing videos and publications about U.S. culture

_____ Sending musical ambassadors abroad to perform concerts and teach people of other cultures about American music

_____ Broadcasting news with an American perspective in the native languages of countries around the world

_____ Your own idea:

bilateral agreement a free trade agreement that is between the U.S. and one other government

to promote safe and secure nuclear technologies as a member of the International Atomic Energy Agency (IAEA). A bureau in the State Department coordinates U.S. involvement in these organizations.

Public Diplomacy Most diplomacy occurs between two governments. But governments also appeal directly to the people of other countries. This process is called *public diplomacy*. Every U.S. embassy and consulate has staff that work with media, cultural, and educational leaders in the host country to publicize the domestic and international policies and programs of the United States.

The United States also sponsors educational activities and cultural exchanges to share information about America with people in other countries. Participating in the Olympic Games is a form of public diplomacy. The United States also disseminates news and information about America around the world through the multimedia broadcaster Voice of America.

✓ **READING PROGRESS CHECK**

Identifying Which two individuals represent the United States in direct diplomatic talks with other world leaders?

Economic Foreign Policy Tools

GUIDING QUESTION *How does the U.S. government use economic resources in foreign policy?*

The United States is the world's largest trading nation—the biggest importer and exporter of goods and services. The U.S. frequently employs trade-related tools in executing foreign policy. These include agreements to facilitate trade with other countries, monetary aid to countries, and policies to restrict trade in the form of economic sanctions.

International Trade Agreements The United States has free trade agreements in effect with 20 countries. Many of our free trade agreements are between the United States and one other government. These are called **bilateral agreements**. But some, like the North American Free Trade Agreement (NAFTA) and the Dominican Republic-Central America-United States Free Trade Agreement, are **multilateral agreements** among several parties. When the United States wants to signal its displeasure with a country, it may restrict trade with them.

Foreign Aid Every year, the U.S. gives billions of dollars of aid to other countries. This aid helps establish friendly relations with other nations and helps them emerge as eventual economic partners. It can also save lives and create conditions for democracy to flourish. The United States gives economic aid to countries that need help feeding, housing, and educating their citizens. This aid often comes with specific requirements for its use—like which programs it may be used for or what the foreign government must do to receive the aid. Sometimes, aid comes in the form of food, medicine, or technical advice.

Today, the Agency for International Development (USAID), an agency of the State Department, administers economic aid. USAID dispenses loans and technical assistance to countries throughout the world. Critics of American foreign aid spending argue that it is taken by corrupt recipient governments and rarely reaches poor people who actually need it.

The United States also distributes humanitarian aid through our participation in international organizations like the UN. Along with contributions from other countries, American funds at the UN help pay for refugee settlements, removing landmines from former war zones, vaccinating people against disease, and protecting World Heritage sites, as well as many other things.

The United States also offers military aid—funds to support the purchase of American armaments. This aid can benefit the foreign government that receives it and also benefits the American businesses that build such weapons. The Foreign Assistance Act mandates that aid be frozen or cut off to countries if an elected leader is overthrown in a coup. For example, in 2013, the U.S. government froze some military aid to Egypt after President Mohamed Morsi was ousted.

Economic Sanctions The withdrawal or denial of benefits is another diplomatic strategy. American policy makers sometimes use it to show that they oppose another nation's policies and to pressure the other nation's governments to make changes.

multilateral agreement a trade agreement among several parties

PARTICIPATING
IN Your Government

Analyzing Policy Options

International piracy is a serious problem for all seafaring nations. Pirates are outlaws who commandeer commercial and recreational vessels and take hostages, holding them for ransom. Over the past 15 years, piracy increased in major shipping channels off the coast of East Africa and in the Indian Ocean. In 2012, more than 500 people were taken hostage. It is estimated that piracy cost governments and private industry more than $5 billion that year. Many pirates come from war-torn Somalia, where there is virtually no functioning government and residents have bleak prospects for a safe and productive life. Many people have suggested tactics to fight maritime piracy:

INTERNATIONAL PIRACY IN SOMALIA		
DIPLOMATIC	ECONOMIC	MILITARY

- deploy U.S. Navy destroyer ships to afflicted areas to scare and deter pirates
- prosecute captured pirates in U.S. courts
- provide aid to stabilize the Somali government
- allow commercial ships to carry armed security guards
- form an alliance to communicate with other countries' navies and chase down pirate ships
- give money to Middle Eastern countries to strengthen their navies
- collaborate with other countries to create a special international court to try piracy cases

EXPLORING THE ESSENTIAL QUESTION

1. **Categorizing** Examine each of these actions and categorize them as diplomatic, economic, or military tools and place them in the graphic organizer.
2. **Researching** Next decide which two strategies you think are most promising. Conduct additional research to learn whether these strategies have been deployed and, if so, how well they have worked.

sanction an action such as withholding loans, arms, or economic aid to force a foreign government to stop certain activities

One way of withdrawing benefits is by applying sanctions. **Sanctions** are measures such as withholding loans, arms, or economic aid to force a foreign government to cease certain activities. During the last century, the United States has employed sanctions more than 90 times.

✓ **READING PROGRESS CHECK**

Explaining How does the U.S. government use economic and humanitarian aid as foreign policy tools?

Military Tools

GUIDING QUESTION *What roles do military alliances and military action play in U.S. foreign policy?*

In some cases, peaceful diplomacy and economic incentives do not deliver the desired results; consequently, the U.S. turns to military tools, such as displays of military power or influence as well as the use of actual military force. Americans are sometimes sharply divided about military force: Under what conditions should military force be used? In what ways should it be deployed?

alliance a voluntary relationship between different nations in which they agree to support one another in case of an attack

regional security pact a mutual defense treaty among multiple nations within a world region

collective security a system by which member nations agree to take joint action against a nation that attacks any one of them

Military Alliances Throughout history, when nations felt a common threat to their security, they came together to negotiate mutual defense **alliances**. Nations that form such alliances usually agree to support one another in case of an attack. The United States has signed mutual defense treaties with nations in three regions. Through such alliances, the United States has committed itself to defending Western Europe; the North Atlantic, Central and South America; and the island nations of the South Pacific. The treaties that protect these areas are referred to as **regional security pacts**.

The goal of these treaties is to provide **collective security** for the United States and its allies. Collective security is a system by which member nations agree to take joint action against a nation that attacks any one of them.

The North Atlantic Treaty Organization In 1945 the United States and leaders of the war-torn nations in Western Europe agreed to protect each other from domination by the Soviet Union. They formed the North Atlantic Treaty Organization (NATO), which committed its members to consider an attack on one country to be an attack against them all.

By providing this framework of military security, NATO gave the nations of Western Europe time to establish solid democratic governments and strong, free market economies. While primarily a military alliance, NATO also served as a useful place for American and European policy makers to meet regularly and discuss mutual problems. Since the major military threat to its members ended in the early 1990s, NATO has expanded its mission to include crisis intervention and peacekeeping in other areas of the world.

Many European leaders believe that the United States is now less concerned with cooperating with its allies and more willing to act on its own when it deals with global threats to American security. They note that the United States is becoming more concerned with threats to its national security that arise outside Europe. Further, they note that in recent years, the United States has spent more than twice as much on national defense than all of the other NATO members combined.

A massive NATO bombing campaign followed by the insertion of NATO peacekeeping troops halted Serbian aggression in the province of Kosovo.

▼ **CRITICAL THINKING**
Describing Describe how being a part of NATO has helped the United States achieve its foreign policy goals over time.

Other Military Alliances In 1947 the United States and its Latin American neighbors signed the Inter-American Treaty of Reciprocal Assistance, commonly called the Rio Pact. By signing this treaty, member states agreed to aid one another in the event of any foreign attack. Most Latin American nations (except Cuba) and the United States have participated in the Rio Pact.

The United States also has a regional security pact with Australia and New Zealand. The ANZUS Pact, signed in 1951, obliged Australia, New Zealand, and the United States to come to one another's aid in case of attack. In 1984 New Zealand adopted a policy that excluded nuclear weapons and nuclear-powered ships from the nation's ports and waters. In response, the United States announced in 1986 that it would no longer guarantee New Zealand's security under the ANZUS treaty.

The United States has also signed bilateral treaties of alliance. A **bilateral treaty** is an agreement that involves only two nations (as opposed to a multilateral treaty, which includes several nations).

The United States has alliances with more than 50 nations. These nations can count on the military support of the United States in case of an attack.

bilateral treaty an agreement that involves only two nations

The Use of Military Force Using military force, or threatening to use force, has always been an important tool of foreign policy. Some argue that using force represents a complete breakdown of diplomacy. Others counter that using force, including covert operations, can be an effective way to avoid larger wars, ward off an impending attack, or protect human rights in other countries from brutal dictators. Today, American military force includes secret paramilitary operations and drone strikes as well as traditional troop mobilizations, **blockades**, and armed interventions.

The Constitution divides the war power between the president and Congress. Nevertheless, in the last 50 years, presidents have sent U.S. troops into battle on numerous occasions without asking Congress for a formal declaration of war. International law governs the conduct of armed conflict under the Geneva Conventions. As a signatory to these treaties, the United States pledges to follow specific rules about the treatment of prisoners of war, wounded enemy soldiers, and medical personnel.

blockade obstruction for the purpose of isolating an area; during military conflicts, a blockade may be used to prevent troops, weapons, or supplies from entering a specific area

☑ **READING PROGRESS CHECK**

Considering Advantages and Disadvantages What are some possible advantages and disadvantages of joining a mutual defense alliance?

LESSON 2 REVIEW

Reviewing Vocabulary
1. *Classifying* What type of trade agreement is the North American Free Trade Agreement (NAFTA)?

Using Your Graphic Organizer
2. *Summarizing* Using your completed graphic organizer, write a brief summary of the tools used by the United States government to promote U.S. national security.

Answering the Guiding Questions
3. *Summarizing* What are the federal government's main foreign policy responsibilities for national defense?

4. *Explaining* How does the U.S. government use economic resources in foreign policy?

5. *Identifying* What roles do military alliances and military action play in U.S. foreign policy?

Writing About Government
6. *Informative/Explanatory* Do research on some of the U.S. foreign aid programs, agencies, or organizations of the past 50 years. Which do you think has been the most effective? Write a short essay explaining your answer.

Kiobel Ⓥ Royal Dutch Petroleum (2013)

FACTS OF THE CASE In 1789, during its first session, Congress passed a law called the Alien Tort Statute. This law says that individuals who are not U.S. citizens can file a lawsuit in federal court for an action that violates either international law or a treaty that the U.S. has signed. The law does not specify what types of wrongdoing can be the subject of a lawsuit, who can be sued, or where the violation of law must have taken place.

Twelve Nigerians filed a lawsuit in U.S. federal court against Royal Dutch Petroleum, a Dutch oil company, and several other British, Dutch, and Nigerian companies. They claimed that these companies violated international laws by convincing the government of Nigeria to commit human rights abuses against them. They say that between 1992 and 1995, the Nigerian military violently put down protests against oil exploration.

Before anyone could decide whether the companies being sued were responsible for the harm caused to these 12 people, the U.S. Supreme Court had to first decide whether a U.S. court could even hear this case.

ISSUE

Does the Alien Tort Statute allow U.S. courts to rule on cases where the violation of international law happened in another country?

ARGUMENTS

OPINION A The Alien Tort Statute does allow this lawsuit. Crimes against humanity, violations of the laws of war, and other human rights abuses are of universal concern. Every nation has a responsibility to hold accountable those who commit such acts. The Alien Tort Statute should certainly allow cases where the wrongdoing occurred in the United States and cases where the entity being sued is American. However, the law should also allow cases where the wrongdoing seriously affects an important American national interest. It is in our national interest to prevent the United States from becoming a safe harbor for torturers, war criminals, or others who abuse human rights. This case is not about whether these companies are guilty—it is only about whether U.S. courts should be able to decide that question. People who have suffered human rights abuses turn to American courts for justice when they are unlikely to receive it elsewhere. The United States has an obligation to hear such cases, and the Alien Tort Statute allows it.

OPINION B The Alien Tort Statute does not permit this type of lawsuit—where foreign nationals sue foreign companies over alleged wrongdoing that happened in a foreign country. Neither the people claiming to be harmed nor the businesses they allege caused the harm were American. The United States cannot be the moral custodian of the world, sweeping in to resolve disputes that happen elsewhere. It would be a serious blow to all countries' sovereignty if foreign courts began hearing cases that involve noncitizens and incidents that happened elsewhere. In fact, if the U.S. courts started overreaching like this, we run the risk that U.S. citizens would be similarly hauled into foreign courts to answer for events that happened in the United States. As long as a foreign country has a legitimate, functioning government, we must let them handle their own court cases. The protesters should file suits in either Nigeria, where the harm happened, or in the Netherlands, where Royal Dutch Petroleum is headquartered.

EXPLORING THE ESSENTIAL QUESTION

Making Decisions Read each of the two sample opinions in this case. Decide which one you think should be the majority (winning) opinion and which one you think should be the dissenting opinion. Explain your choice.

YOU BE the JUDGE

Interact with these digital assets and others in lesson 3

✓ **INTERACTIVE GRAPH**
   U.S. Spending on Foreign Affairs

✓ **INTERACTIVE IMAGE**
   Central Intelligence Agency

✓ **SELF-CHECK QUIZ**

✓ **VIDEO**
   Military Action in Syria

netw⊙rks
TRY IT YOURSELF ONLINE

LESSON 3
Foreign Policy Powers

ReadingHelp Desk

Academic Vocabulary

- military
- consult

Content Vocabulary

- ambassador
- treaty
- executive agreement

TAKING NOTES:

Key Ideas and Details

LISTING Use the graphic organizer to list the ways Congress can influence foreign policy.

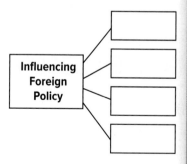

ESSENTIAL QUESTION

How is foreign policy affected by the separation of powers?

Find a news story about the U.S. government interacting with another country.

- What country besides the United States is mentioned in the story? What issue is involved?

- Who is mentioned in the story? What is their official position in government? Include both U.S. officials and those from the other country.

- How are the officials working on the issue? Are they negotiating an agreement? Are they appealing to the people of the two countries for support? Are they working through an international organization?

How well do you understand the issue based on one story? Try to find another story about the same interaction but from a different medium (newspaper, magazine, television, blog, podcast, etc.). Does using more than one source enhance your understanding?

Presidential Powers and Responsibilities

GUIDING QUESTION *Which powers and responsibilities for foreign policy are reserved for the executive branch of government?*

The Framers of the Constitution balanced the responsibility for foreign policy between the president and Congress. The judicial branch plays a more limited role in foreign affairs—although the courts sometimes hear cases involving foreign parties or decide the constitutionality of U.S. laws or actions regarding foreign policy.

The Constitution grants the president the power to be the commander in chief of the nation's **military** forces. As such, the president may send troops, ships, and planes or even use nuclear weapons anywhere in the world, without congressional approval. However, the power to formally declare war is reserved for Congress. The Constitution also grants the president certain diplomatic powers. The president appoints **ambassadors**, the government officials who represent the nation. The president also receives ambassadors from foreign governments.

By receiving an ambassador or other diplomat from a country, the president formally recognizes that government. Conversely, by refusing to do so, the president can withhold diplomatic recognition of a government. Formal recognition is vital because it qualifies a foreign government for economic and other forms of aid. The Constitution also empowers the president to make treaties. A **treaty** is a formal agreement between the governments of two or more nations.

As head of state, the president plays an important part in controlling foreign policy. He or she represents the nation and stands as a symbol to the world for its policies. In an international crisis, Americans look to their president for leadership.

Before making foreign policy decisions, presidents usually **consult** advisers. Generally, they rely upon the information and advice of the cabinet members, the White House staff, and officials in specialized agencies dealing with foreign policy. At times, presidents also go outside the government and seek advice from private individuals who have specialized knowledge in foreign affairs.

Key Officials and Advisers In their specialized fields, all cabinet members bring international problems to the president's attention and recommend how to deal with them. For two cabinet departments, however—the Department of State and the Department of Defense—foreign affairs are a full-time concern.

The secretary of state supervises all the diplomatic activities of the U.S. government. In the past, most presidents have relied heavily on their secretary of state, who is generally considered the most important cabinet official. Normally, the secretary of state carries on diplomacy at the highest level. The secretary frequently travels to foreign capitals for important negotiations with heads of state and represents the United States at major international conferences.

The secretary of defense supervises the government's military activities. He or she also informs and advises the president on the nation's military forces, weapons, and bases. The national security advisor—who is also the director of the National Security Council (NSC)— is responsible for giving

military referring to the armed forces

ambassador an official of the government who represents the nation in diplomatic matters

treaty a formal agreement between the governments of two or more nations

consult to ask for advice

The greatest source of congressional power in foreign policy derives from the control that Congress has over government spending.

▼ CRITICAL THINKING
Reading Graphs How much of the 2013 fiscal year budget is spent on foreign assistance? Do you think this is too much or too little? Explain.

GRAPH

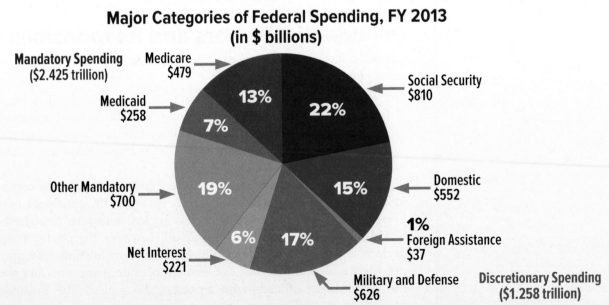

Major Categories of Federal Spending, FY 2013
(in $ billions)

Mandatory Spending ($2.425 trillion)

Medicare $479 — 13%

Medicaid $258 — 7%

Other Mandatory $700 — 19%

Net Interest $221 — 6%

Social Security $810 — 22%

Domestic $552 — 15%

Foreign Assistance $37 — 1%

Military and Defense $626 — 17%

Discretionary Spending ($1.258 trillion)

Source: Historical Tables, Office of Management and Budget, http://www.whitehouse.gov/omb/budget/Historicals

Central Intelligence Agency

the president information and advice related to national security. This adviser also coordinates some foreign policies among executive branch agencies.

Intelligence Agencies To make decisions about foreign affairs, the president and the president's advisers need timely information about the activities of other nations along with data on nonstate terrorist groups like al-Qaeda. The Central Intelligence Agency (CIA) was created in 1947 to gather and coordinate intelligence data for the president from across the world.

Today, the CIA is only one of 17 intelligence agencies in the federal government. The largest, the National Security Agency (NSA), is responsible for code breaking and electronic spying. Different executive departments—including Defense, State, Energy, Treasury, and Homeland Security—also have their own intelligence groups. Taken together, all of these agencies are known as the "intelligence community." More than 100,000 people work in these various intelligence agencies. The Director of National Intelligence coordinates the work of these different agencies.

Making Foreign Policy After reviewing information and intelligence and listening to trusted advisers, the president formulates an approach to world issues and informs officials in the executive branch to act accordingly. The president is ultimately responsible for the policies the executive branch works to implement. As President Ronald Reagan wrote, only the president can "respond quickly in a crisis or formulate a coherent and consistent policy in any region of the world." However, a president's foreign policy goals and strategies are sometimes foiled by Congress, which can disrupt the president's actions by refusing to appropriate money, confirm key officials, or authorize military actions.

☑ **READING PROGRESS CHECK**

Naming What are the titles of the three most important foreign policy advisers to the president?

The Central Intelligence Agency (CIA) was created in 1947 to gather and analyze intelligence data. This photograph shows the courtyard of CIA headquarters in Langley, Virginia.

▲ CRITICAL THINKING

Speculating In 2004 Congress created the cabinet-level position of Director of National Intelligence to coordinate the work of the government's various intelligence agencies. Why do you think such a position was needed?

Hypothesizing Official recognition of a country is an important diplomatic tool. As of 2013, the United States does not have diplomatic relations with Iran, North Korea, Bhutan, Cuba, or the Republic of China (Taiwan). Why might the United States withhold recognition from these countries? Find out if your hypotheses are correct.

Collaborating Form a group with two other students. Each student should take one of the following portions of the Constitution: Article I, Article II, or Article III. Investigate your Article and make a list of all the sections that refer to foreign affairs. What powers do those sections grant? To which branch of government do they grant these powers? Compare your list with the other two students in your group. Based on these lists, which branch appears to have the most power related to foreign affairs? Do you think that division of power holds true in practice?

Powers of Congress

GUIDING QUESTION *What role does the U.S. Congress play in making and implementing foreign policy?*

The Constitution balances the president's powers as commander in chief by granting Congress the power to declare war. Although the president may send troops anywhere in the world, only Congress may declare war. Congress has not declared war very often, and the U.S. has been involved in many military conflicts without a declaration of war. Often the president asks Congress for an authorization of the use of military force. This happened with the Vietnam, Persian Gulf, Afghanistan, and Iraq wars.

By far the greatest source of congressional power in foreign policy derives from the control that Congress has over government spending. Only Congress can appropriate the funds to equip American armed forces and to build new weapons. In a similar fashion, Congress may refuse to provide funds for aid to other nations. Congress may decide not only the sum to be granted but also the conditions that a foreign country must meet to be eligible for aid.

The Constitution also gives the Senate the power of advice and consent on all treaties. The president may make treaties with foreign governments, but a two-thirds vote of the Senate must ratify them. Increasingly, presidents have turned to **executive agreements** to avoid potential Senate rejection of treaties. These are legally binding pacts between the president and the head of a foreign government that do not require Senate approval. Today, executive agreements make up more than 90 percent of all U.S. international agreements. The Senate also must confirm presidential appointments to diplomatic posts. Usually the Senate is willing to accept these appointments.

International Trade and Commerce The U.S. Constitution gives Congress more power than the executive branch in the international trade arena. Article I, Section 8, grants Congress the authority to regulate foreign commerce, while the Constitution is silent when it comes to executive branch powers over international trade. However, Congress has delegated away much of its power over international trade to the president and the executive branch. Congress has given presidents the authority to negotiate trade agreements and have them considered in Congress under expedited rules allowing for no amendments and an up-or-down vote. Still, Congress exercises oversight of international trade policy by approving trade agreements negotiated by the executive branch and overseeing the implementation of these policies and agreements.

executive agreement legally binding pact between the president and the head of a foreign government that does not require Senate approval

Intelligence Agency and the National Geospatial-Intelligence Agency. In addition, the DOD provides top military leaders with advice on foreign policy. These functions give the secretary of defense a chance to rival the secretary of state for influence with the president.

Civilian Control of the Military In the United States, the DOD's influence over foreign policy is tempered by the fact that the Founders wanted to ensure that the military would always be subordinate to the civilian leaders of the government. As a result, the ultimate authority for commanding the armed forces rests with the civilian commander in chief, the president of the United States. Congress also exercises **considerable** authority over military matters. Because of its power over appropriations, Congress determines how much money the Department of Defense will spend each year.

Structure and Staffing of the DOD The major divisions within the DOD are the Departments of the Army, Navy, and Air Force. A civilian secretary heads each branch. The United States Marine Corps, under the jurisdiction of the Navy, maintains separate leadership, identity, and traditions.

The president, the National Security Council, and the secretary of defense rely on the Joint Chiefs of Staff (JCS) for military advice. This group is made up of the top-ranking officers of the armed forces as well as the Chairperson and Vice Chairperson of the Joint Chiefs of Staff.

The United States has used two methods of staffing its armed forces—by **conscription**, or compulsory military service, and by using volunteers. Conscription was first used during the Civil War and was implemented during World War I and World War II.

By executive order, President Richard Nixon suspended conscription, or the draft, in 1973. Since then, membership in the military has been voluntary. Nixon's order, however, did not repeal the law that created the Selective Service System that administered the draft. For that reason, males between the ages of 18 and 25 could be required to serve if conscription is reinstated.

All young men who have passed their eighteenth birthdays are required to register their names and addresses with local draft boards. Though women are not eligible to be drafted, they may volunteer to serve in any branch of the armed services—including in combat roles.

The Pentagon, located in Arlington, Virginia, is the headquarters of the Department of Defense. The Department of Defense provides the president and Congress with information that helps to shape their foreign policy decisions.

▲ CRITICAL THINKING
1. Stating What is the function of the Joint Chiefs of Staff?
2. Explaining How did the Founders ensure that the military would always be subordinate to the civilian leaders of government?

considerable of substantial size or importance

conscription compulsory military service

☑ **READING PROGRESS CHECK**

Naming What are some ways that the DOD is directly involved in making foreign policy?

LESSON 4 REVIEW

Reviewing Vocabulary
1. Contrasting What is the major difference between an *embassy* and a *consulate*?

2. Using Context Clues Based on the context in which the vocabulary word *conscription* is used in the lesson, what does *compulsory* mean?

Using Your Graphic Organizer
3. Summarizing Use your notes from the outline to write a short summary of what you learned about the Department of State and the Department of Defense.

Answering the Guiding Questions
4. Listing What are the Department of State's responsibilities for implementing foreign policy?

5. Explaining How is the Department of Defense vital to national security?

Writing About Government
6. Informative/Explanatory How do the roles of the Department of State and the Department of Defense differ? How are they similar? Write a one-page fact sheet explaining the role of each in creating U.S. foreign policy.

STUDY GUIDE

FOREIGN POLICY GOALS
LESSON 1

U.S. Foreign Policy Goals
- ☑ Protect national security
- ☑ Maintain trade
- ☑ Promote U.S. economic interests
- ☑ Preserve access to imported natural resources
- ☑ Work for a peaceful international environment
- ☑ Promote democracy
- ☑ Provide humanitarian aid

FOREIGN POLICY TOOLS
LESSON 2

Diplomatic Tools
- Negotiations
- International Organizations
- Public Diplomacy

Economic Tools
- Trade Agreements
- Foreign Aid
- Sanctions

Military Tools
- Mutual Defense Alliances
- Regional Security Pacts
- Threat of Military Force
- Use of Military Force

FOREIGN POLICY POWERS
LESSON 3

Executive Branch

President
- Commander in chief of military
- May send forces and weapons anywhere without congressional approval
- Appoints ambassadors
- Receives foreign ambassadors
- Formally recognizes foreign governments
- Makes treaties
- Issues executive agreements
- Grants most-favored-nation status

Executive Agencies
- Department of State
- Department of Defense
- National Security Council
- Central Intelligence Agency
- National Security Agency

Legislative Branch

Congress
- Sole power to declare war
- Appropriates money to carry out foreign policy
- Can decide amount of aid to grant
- Can set conditions for receiving aid
- Can overturn most-favored-nation status with two-thirds vote

Senate
- Power of advice and consent on all treaties
- Two-thirds vote to ratify treaties
- Confirms diplomatic appointments

STATE AND DEFENSE DEPARTMENTS
LESSON 4

Department of State

Functions
- Informs president on international issues
- Maintains diplomatic relations
- Negotiates treaties
- Protects interests of Americans traveling or doing business abroad

Embassies
- Facilitates diplomatic communication
- Headed by ambassadors
- Specialists help resolve disputes in their area of expertise

Consulates
- Promotes American business interests
- Safeguards American travelers

Department of Defense

Functions
- Supervises the armed forces
- Influences foreign policy regarding use of military
- Implements foreign assistance in natural disasters
- Provides intelligence to president and Congress

Structure
- Each service branch headed by civilians
- Joint Chiefs of Staff made up of top-ranking officers of each service branch
- Selective Service System administers conscription, if needed

Directions: On a separate sheet of paper, answer the questions below. Make sure you read carefully and answer all parts of the questions.

Lesson Review

Lesson 1

1 *Explaining* Why are countries in the Middle East of strategic importance to the United States?

2 *Identifying Cause and Effect* Why did industrialization in the 1890s push the United States toward internationalism?

Lesson 2

3 *Describing* What personal qualities do diplomats need to conduct successful negotiations?

4 *Specifying* What is the main purpose of the North Atlantic Treaty Organization (NATO)? What other purposes does it serve?

Lesson 3

5 *Making Connections* How can the president control what countries are eligible for U.S. economic aid?

6 *Identifying Cause and Effect* How did public opinion influence U.S. foreign policy in Syria during the crisis over chemical weapons?

Lesson 4

7 *Differentiating* How does a passport differ from a visa?

8 *Identifying* What important role does the Defense Department play in foreign assistance programs?

ANSWERING THE ESSENTIAL QUESTIONS

Review your answers to the introductory questions at the beginning of each lesson. Then answer the following Essential Questions based on what you learned in the chapter. Have your answers changed?

9 *Analyzing Cause and Effect* How does U.S. foreign policy affect other countries and regions?

10 *Identifying Central Issues* How is foreign policy made and implemented?

11 *Analyzing Cause and Effect* How is foreign policy affected by the separation of powers?

DBQ Interpreting Political Cartoons

Use the political cartoon to answer the following questions.

12 *Interpreting* What is the cartoonist saying about national security?

13 *Analyzing Visuals* Do you agree with the point of view of the cartoonist? Why or why not?

Critical Thinking

14 *Differentiating* In your own words, explain the difference between the preemption policy of President George W. Bush and the multilateral approach of President Barack Obama. Which approach has worked better?

15 *Analyzing* How does the United States use foreign aid to promote foreign policy goals?

16 *Identifying Central Issues* How can Congress use its appropriations power to affect foreign policy?

17 *Making Inferences* Why do you think the Founders wanted to ensure that the military would always be subordinate to the civilian leaders of the government?

Need Extra Help?

If You've Missed Question	1	2	3	4	5	6	7	8	9	10	11	12	13	14	15	16	17
Go to page	709	710	714	718	722	726	729	730	708	714	721	733	733	712	716	724	731

Directions: On a separate sheet of paper, answer the questions below. Make sure you read carefully and answer all parts of the questions.

DBQ Analyzing Primary Sources

Read the excerpt and answer the questions that follow.

After the terrorist attacks of September 11, 2001, President George W. Bush addressed the nation, as shown below.

PRIMARY SOURCE

"*Today, our fellow citizens, our way of life, our very freedom came under attack. . . . The pictures of airplanes flying into buildings, fires burning, huge structures collapsing, have filled us with disbelief, terrible sadness, and a quiet, unyielding anger. . . . Our military is powerful, and it's prepared. . . . Our first priority is to get help to those who have been injured, and to take every precaution to protect our citizens at home and around the world from further attacks. . . . The search is underway for those who are behind these evil acts. I've directed the full resources of our intelligence and law enforcement communities to find those responsible and to bring them to justice. We will make no distinction between the terrorists who committed these acts and those who harbor them.*"
—President George W. Bush, September 11, 2001

18 *Finding the Main Idea* What principal goal of American foreign policy does President Bush emphasize in this excerpt?

19 *Analyzing Primary Sources* How does this excerpt reflect the emotions of that day? Cite specific words from the excerpt.

20 *Hypothesizing* What possible effects might come from carrying out the foreign policy stated in the last sentence?

Social Studies Skills

21 *Identifying Perspectives and Differing Interpretations* With a partner, identify a cross-border disagreement between insurgents and a national government or between two nations. Find secondary sources describing the viewpoints and biases of both sides. Write a script dramatizing a negotiation between the two parties and perform it for the class. Then, as a class, discuss the validity of the arguments and counterarguments based on each negotiator's frame of reference.

22 *Economics* Select one of the international economic organizations mentioned in the chapter: IMF, World Bank, or the WTO. Go to the organization's website to find out what it does. Create an annotated poster summarizing its major functions.

Research and Presentation

23 *Researching* In the 1990s, U.S. forces intervened in Kuwait (1990), Somalia (1992), Haiti (1994), Bosnia (1995), and Kosovo (1999). Divide into five groups, with each group taking one of these interventions. Do research and create an oral presentation analyzing U.S. policy in the region, including why the U.S. intervened, what policy goals the intervention served, and the effects on the region.

24 *Decision Making* Identify a current foreign policy problem that requires a decision. The problem might involve an armed conflict, a trade dispute, a humanitarian crisis, or something else. Gather information about the problem, identify options, and predict the consequences of each option. What decision would you make? How would you implement it? Present your findings.

25 *Exploring Issues* Imagine that you are a Foreign Service officer (FSO). In what country would you like to serve? Do research to learn about the country's difficulties and U.S. interests in that region. Write a report describing how you could help as an FSO there. Be sure to use standard grammar, spelling, sentence structure, and punctuation in your report.

26 *Analyzing* What is the role of Congress in creating and implementing international trade policy? What is the role of the president and executive branch? Which do you think has greater power and influence in setting international trade policy? Why?

Need Extra Help?

If You've Missed Question	18	19	20	21	22	23	24	25	26
Go to page	712	712	713	714	715	713	714	728	724

Comparing Political and Economic Systems

netw⦵rks
www.connected.mcgraw-hill.com
There's More Online about comparing political and economic systems.

ESSENTIAL QUESTIONS

- What are the advantages and disadvantages of different types of political systems? • How do nations and citizens interact in the global political and economic arenas? • What is the role of government in different economic systems?

▲ In the global economy, nations around the world engage in international trade and commerce.

Robert Mandel/Vetta/Getty Images

ANALYZING PRIMARY SOURCES

GLOBAL STUDENT VOICES: ACTIVISM AROUND THE WORLD

Young people living in democracies around the world use their democratic freedoms to speak up for the issues they are passionate about. Under other systems of government, making your voice heard may be difficult or even dangerous. Whether activism is safe or risky, however, its purpose is the same: to improve communities, nations, and even the world.

PRIMARY SOURCE A

Malala Yousafzai, Pakistan

Malala became an advocate at age 11, when the Taliban, an Islamic fundamentalist group, closed schools to girls in her native region of Swat in Pakistan. Malala began writing a blog, arguing that girls had a right to an education. In 2012, a member of the Taliban shot Malala in the head. She was taken to Great Britain for treatment. Following her recovery, she has continued her advocacy for education, writing a memoir about her life and work. On her sixteenth birthday, she spoke at the United Nations:

"I did not write that speech only with the UN delegates in mind, I wrote it for every person around the world who could make a difference. I wanted to reach all people living in poverty, those children forced to work and those who suffer from terrorism or lack of education. Deep in my heart I hoped to reach every child who could take courage from my words and stand up for his or her rights."

—Malala Yousafzai, *I Am Malala: The Girl Who Stood Up for Education and Was Shot by the Taliban*, 2013

PRIMARY SOURCE B

Mauricio Ruiz, Brazil

Mauricio Ruiz was 15 when he resolved to do something about deforestation in Brazil. Fifteen years later, the organization he started, the Instituto Tera de Preservacao Ambiental, had more than 100 employees and had planted hundreds of thousands of trees. Ruiz reflected on his inspiration:

"We were on a boat on the Amazon. It was a long trip, and de Mello read out a poem he was writing. It was about a dialogue between two great rain forests. I was very impressed. I told him where I came from, and he said I should go back and help my forest to recover."

—Mauricio Ruiz, 2012

SECONDARY SOURCE C

Khetam Bneyan, Syria

During the anti government demonstrations in Syria in 2013, 19-year-old Khetam Bneyan protested peacefully. She carried a sign saying, "Only in Syria, the thinking mind is imprisoned." She was arrested and spent nearly three weeks in jail. She reported that another young woman imprisoned with her was sexually assaulted by guards. Another woman had a stroke and died in her cell. Journalist Kristin Deasy interviewed Khetam for *The Daily Beast*:

"'What we want after the revolution is something that can be simply described in three words, freedom, equality, dignity,' Bneyan said. She was willing to put herself in great danger for that very reason. Her detainment seems to have strengthened her determination. 'When I think about what I saw in there [prison], it makes my outrage at the regime increase,' she said."

—Interview of Khetam Bneyan, 2013

PRIMARY SOURCE D

Girls Empowerment Network Malawi

The Girls Empowerment Network Malawi is a nongovernmental organization (NGO) that fights for the rights of girls and women. One of the practices they are fighting is child marriage, which causes girls to drop out of school and subjects them to the dangers of pregnancy and childbirth before their bodies are mature. GENET's plan is to turn survivors of child marriage into activists. Maria Nkomera is one of the survivors working with GENET. She says:

> "I started visualizing a bright future when committee members of Girls Empowerment Network visited and encouraged me about the importance of education over Child Marriage."

—Maria Nkomera

PRIMARY SOURCE E

Cao Yuan, China

Youth around the world have organized to address issues of climate change. Chinese activist Cao Yuan speaks of the advantages youth have as advocates:

> "They [people collaborating on climate change issues] are more likely to trust the youth. And in this way we are better communicators for the NGOs amongst all kinds of players.
>
> When we want to do promotional activities, youth are very good at influencing others I think, as we care about our future and when we talk about this from our view and our own perspective people are more likely to think yes this is the youth's future."

—Cao Yuan, Interview for the website Responding to Climate Change, September 12, 2012

PRIMARY SOURCE F

As of September 2013, Spain's unemployment rate for people under the age of 24 was 56 percent. While some young Spaniards emigrated to look for work, others, who call themselves *indignados,* protested government policies they blamed for the problem.

Students protest unemployment in Madrid, 2011

DBQ DOCUMENT-BASED QUESTIONS

1. **Comparing** How are these young activists similar to one another? How are they similar to the young people you have read about in the "Student Voices" features in this program? Think beyond the obvious (their ages and involvement in civic affairs).

2. **Identifying** What inspires these young activists? Do any of these young people inspire you? Explain your answer.

3. **Analyzing** Explain Cao Yuan's views on the effectiveness of youth as advocates. Do you agree or disagree? What evidence supports your position?

4. **Building Coalitions** How might you try to build an international coalition on an issue in which you are interested?

WHAT WILL YOU DO?

The young people you have read about here are already active citizens. In what ways are you currently exercising the responsibilities, duties, and obligations of a citizen? What are you willing to do today to strengthen your community, the nation, or the world?

EXPLORE the interactive version of the analyzing primary sources feature on **Networks.**

Interact with these digital assets and others in lesson 1

✓ **INTERACTIVE CHART**
Comparing Presidential and Parliamentary Systems

✓ **INTERACTIVE IMAGE**
Vatican City

✓ **SELF-CHECK QUIZ**

✓ **VIDEO**
The Arab Spring in Egypt

netw○rks
TRY IT YOURSELF ONLINE

LESSON 1
Political Systems in Action

ESSENTIAL QUESTION

What are the advantages and disadvantages of different types of political systems?

"To rule is easy, to govern difficult."

—**Johann von Goethe**

"Government, even in its best state, is but a necessary evil; in its worst state, an intolerable one . . ."

—**Thomas Paine**

What does each of these quotes mean to you? Rewrite each quote in your own words. Then think about how each quote applies to these different systems of government:

- Dictatorship, in which one person has all the power
- Monarchy, in which power is vested in a family and is hereditary
- Republic, in which representatives hold power on behalf of the population at large
- Democracy, where the citizens hold the power

ReadingHelp Desk

Academic Vocabulary

- **presume**

Content Vocabulary

- **parliamentary government**
- **prime minister**
- **presidential government**

TAKING NOTES:

Key Ideas and Details

SEQUENCING INFORMATION Use the flowchart to list the steps in the process by which officials in a parliamentary government are chosen.

Parliamentary Government

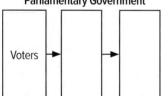

Voters → □ → □ → □

Democratic Governments

GUIDING QUESTION *What are the advantages and disadvantages of presidential and parliamentary systems of government?*

No two democracies function in the exact same way. The key factor that defines a democracy is that government is by the people. Most democratic governments try to balance legislative, executive, and judicial functions in such a way that no branch can abuse the power given to it by the people. Today, there are two main types of democratic governments: parliamentary and presidential.

Parliamentary Government The most widespread type of democratic government is the **parliamentary government**. In this form, the elected assembly (often called a parliament) holds both executive and legislative powers.

The leader of the majority party in the parliament becomes the **prime minister**, the head of the government. The prime minister, along with other party leaders, chooses the leaders of executive departments who serve as cabinet members.

Most ministers are members of the majority party. If no party has a majority in the parliament, which can happen in countries with more than two parties, then two or more parties must work together to form a coalition government.

Elections for the parliament are required periodically, but there is no fixed date for elections. The prime minister decides when to hold elections, within a period specified by law. If public support for the majority party is high, they may hold new elections sooner, believing that they will gain seats and power in the parliament.

The prime minister and the cabinet are accountable to the elected representatives. If the parliament no longer supports them, it might hold a "no confidence" vote. Such a vote means that the legislature no longer believes the leaders are governing effectively. It triggers new general elections for all members of parliament and, therefore, prime minister.

Political scientists say that it is easier to pass legislation in a parliamentary system, because the prime minister has no veto power. They also argue that parliamentary systems are less likely to break down than presidential systems, citing evidence that new democracies succeed more often with parliamentary systems than presidential systems. However, others remain concerned that in a parliamentary system there is no real check on the legislature's power. Because the head of the government is not elected, no one in the system is tasked with representing the interests of the nation as a whole. In addition, the ability to dissolve the government and call for new elections at any time makes the system more unpredictable.

Great Britain Many countries' parliamentary systems are adapted from the British model. In Great Britain, Parliament is a bicameral, or two-house, legislature, consisting of the House of Commons and the House of Lords.

parliamentary government form of democratic government in which the elected assembly (often called a parliament) holds both executive and legislative powers

prime minister leader of the majority party in the parliament; the head of government in the parliamentary system

▼ CRITICAL THINKING
1. Contrasting Which of these differences do you think is the most significant? Why?
2. Researching Research a country that has a parliamentary system of government and prepare a very brief report about it that includes a map, names the head of state and the prime minister, and describes when and how the prime minister was most recently elected to office.

CHART

Comparing Presidential and Parliamentary Systems

The United States and about 40 other countries have presidential governments. But even more countries—approximately 75—have parliamentary systems, with the government headed by a prime minister. The chart shows some of the key differences between a president and a prime minister.

President	Prime Minister
Elected by the people (or by the Electoral College in the United States).	Usually elected to parliament (legislature) and chosen by the parliament to be the head of government.
Serves as both head of government and head of state.	Usually serves only as head of government; head of state may be a monarch or an elected president with few real powers.
Heads the executive branch, which is separate from the legislative branch.	Heads both the executive branch and the legislative branch, which overlap.
Appoints heads of the executive departments; most are members of the president's political party.	Works with others to name heads of departments, often other members of parliament.
Usually has a set term of office, after which he/she must run for reelection.	Usually does not have a set term of office; a new election can be called when the parliament votes to do so or when the prime minister thinks an election would strengthen his/her party.

Both have a role in enacting legislation, but the House of Commons has much greater power than the House of Lords. Members of the House of Commons are elected by the people. Known as Members of Parliament (MPs), these representatives serve five-year terms. Their terms may be shorter if Parliament is dissolved for new elections.

The other half of Parliament is the House of Lords. For centuries, only the first sons of noble families and bishops of the Church of England sat in the House of Lords. The system has been reformed now, so that most members are appointed for life by the king or queen. The House of Lords's power is limited. It cannot propose finance bills, and, if it votes down a bill, the House of Commons can override it and pass the bill the following year.

The prime minister has considerable power. However, he or she must answer—literally—to the Members of Parliament. Weekly, the prime minister goes into the House of Commons to answer questions from MPs.

India Canada, Israel, India, Australia, and Japan are examples of parliamentary democracies—and all have different variations of this system of government. India, a former British colony, differs from Great Britain's government because it is a federal system. Its states have their own governments. The Indian Parliament has a bicameral parliament with an upper and lower house. But the members of the upper house are elected by legislatures in India's states. In addition, India's Parliament elects a president who heads the executive branch.

Presidential Government The type of democracy most familiar to Americans is **presidential government**. In a presidential system of government, executive, legislative, and judicial powers are separated. The people choose the president to head the executive branch and representatives to form the legislative branch. Some nations directly elect a president but also have a prime minister (sometimes called a premier). In these semi-presidential systems, the president and prime minister share some executive functions.

In France, for example, the president maintains contact with the legislative branch through a premier, whom the president appoints. The premier, in turn, names the ministers who form the government. Together they conduct day-to-day government affairs. The premier and cabinet ministers answer to both the president and the legislature, which includes the Assembly and the Senate.

The French president is unusually powerful and has the right to exercise dictatorial powers in a national emergency. The president can dissolve the National Assembly (the lower house of the legislature) and call for new elections. This power can be used to persuade the legislators, called deputies, to accept the president's leadership.

Mexico also has a presidential form of government with three branches: executive, legislative, and judicial. The president heads the executive and is directly elected for one six-year term. The president exercises strong governmental control and is the dominant figure in politics. Like the United States, Mexico has a two-chamber legislature consisting of the Senate and the Chamber of Deputies. Senators are elected to six-year terms and deputies serve for three years.

☑ READING PROGRESS CHECK

Distinguishing Fact From Opinion Is the following statement a fact or an opinion? *The key factor that defines a democracy is government by the people.*

presidential government form of democratic government in which executive, legislative, and judicial powers are separated

Walter Sisulu

Sunday Times/Brian Hendler/Avusa Media Ltd/Gallo Images via Getty Images

In 1940 Walter Sisulu became active in the African National Congress, an organization dedicated to winning equal rights for black South Africans, working with Nelson Mandela. At the time, South Africa was ruled under a system of apartheid, which kept people of different races separate and denied black South Africans the right to vote and many other freedoms.

In a letter sent to the South African prime minister in February 1952, Sisulu and ANC president Dr. J.S. Moroka wrote, "With reference to the campaign of mass action which the African National Congress intends to launch, we would point out that as a defenceless and voteless people, we have explored other channels without success. The African people are left with no alternative but to embark upon the campaign referred to above. We desire to state emphatically that it is our intention to conduct this campaign in a peaceful manner."

After the peaceful protests against apartheid began, Sisulu was arrested seven times in ten years. The peaceful protests were met with a violent government response. The government also banned the ANC. By 1961, the ANC had taken up arms against the government. Soon, Sisulu, Mandela, and many other ANC leaders were in prison. Sisulu was released from prison in 1989. In 1990 Nelson Mandela was released, and in 1994 South Africa held its first democratic elections, where South Africans of all races were allowed to vote.

EXPLORING THE ESSENTIAL QUESTION

Analyzing Under apartheid, the government banned Sisulu's political party, the ANC. However, its members continued to work for democratic reforms. What risks did ANC members take to bring about change? Do you agree with their strategies?

Emerging Democracies

GUIDING QUESTION *What are some of the challenges and successes of relatively new democracies in Africa, Asia, and Latin America?*

In the past century, democracy has spread around the world, becoming the dominant form of government. Since the collapse of communism beginning in 1989, many countries in Eastern Europe began to establish democratic governments. Countries in Latin America, Africa, Asia, and the Middle East have also experienced transitions to more democratic governments.

Ghana provides a good example of a transition to democracy. Ghana gained its independence in 1957 under the leadership of Kwame Nkrumah. Over the next 35 years, Ghana experienced a series of coups. Since 1992, however, Ghana has been a stable democracy operating under a constitution written in that year. In 2000 it experienced a peaceful transfer of power from one democratically elected president to another, a mark of a stable democracy. In 2012 it weathered a very closely contested presidential election in which the losing candidate sued over the election results. When its supreme court ruled against him, he accepted its ruling, another positive indicator of the system's stability. Another positive sign is the high voter turnout in 2012—80 percent of eligible voters went to the polls.

The Arab Spring In 2010 anti government protesters in Tunisia began calling for the resignation of the president and his regime, which the people viewed as autocratic. Soon, protests had spread to other countries in North Africa. This wave of protests became known as the Arab Spring.

In China, government critics use Weibo, a microblogging site similar to Twitter, to expose government corruption and criticize the government's response to natural and human-made disasters. China has worked to block such criticism in social media.

▲ CRITICAL THINKING
Applying Given the nature of technology, do you think it is possible for an authoritarian government to restrict citizens' use of digital tools over an extended period of time?

Within two years, the governments of Tunisia, Egypt, Yemen, and Libya—all ruled by long-time dictators—had been overthrown. Other protests resulted in significant changes to the ruling government in countries throughout the region. One of the largest changes brought about by the Arab Spring was an increase in fair and open elections.

The effects of the Arab Spring are still being felt around the world. Though many countries had free elections for the first time in decades, some struggled to implement democratic reforms. In Egypt, the first popularly elected president following the Arab Spring, Mohammed Morsi, faced a wave of protests less than a year after his election. Morsi was overthrown by the Egyptian military in July of 2013.

☑ **READING PROGRESS CHECK**

Specifying What is the dominant form of government in the world today?

Authoritarian Governments

GUIDING QUESTION *In what ways do authoritarian governments differ from the democratic government of the United States?*

The number of democratic nations is increasing, but many authoritarian governments still exist. Governments such as those in the People's Republic of China, Cuba, and North Korea present a stark contrast to democracies.

China During World War II, China suffered greatly. This weakened the Nationalist Party and allowed Communists, led by Mao Zedong, to win an ongoing civil war. In 1949 Mao and the Chinese Communist Party (CCP) took control of all major industries, including agriculture. It forced peasants to work on collective farms that were run by the government. Following Mao's death, reformers within the CCP gained power. They moved China toward a more capitalistic system while still retaining central government authority. Some small steps toward democratization have also been taken, but they have been limited to local government.

Authoritarian governments tolerate little criticism of their policies. In China, a dramatic example of this intolerance occurred in 1989 when Chinese military forces massacred hundreds of unarmed, pro-democracy students who were demonstrating in Beijing's Tiananmen Square. The government continues today to suppress criticism and marginalize minorities.

To control freedom of expression on the Internet, China has developed an extensive system of Internet censorship. The government regularly denies local users access to many websites. Still, advocates for change find ways to get their message out, risking their own freedom to do so.

North Korea While China merely has totalitarian characteristics, North Korea provides a prime example of a pure totalitarian state. After World War II, the Korean peninsula was divided into North and South Korea. With U.S. aid, South Korea became a democracy with a strong free market economy. North Korea became a communist nation supported by the Soviet Union and led by a dictator. The same family—the Kims—has held power for more than 50 years.

North Korea controls all aspects of people's lives. North Koreans are almost completely cut off from outside sources of information. The government controls the production and distribution of all food. About 70 percent of North Korea's children are severely malnourished. In the 1990s, more than 2 million North Koreans starved to death.

North Korea's economy is weak, but its military is strong. In the early 1990s, the country began to develop chemical, biological, and nuclear weapons. Few experts believe North Korea would use such weapons directly against the United States, but it could sell the weapons to terrorists. As a result, the United States seeks to limit North Korea's development of nuclear weapons.

✔ **READING PROGRESS CHECK**

Contrasting What are the differences between the governments of North Korea and South Korea?

Theocracies

GUIDING QUESTION *What basic principle sets theocracies apart from all other forms of government?*

A theocracy is a government based on religion. In a pure theocracy, the leader of the government is thought to lead the country based on guidance from the divine. This is different from a state that simply has an official religion. The leader of a theocracy is **presumed** to speak on behalf of the deity or at least draw his or her authority from the deity. For example, the pope is both the spiritual leader of the Catholic Church and the official political leader of Vatican City, one of the only true theocracies currently in existence.

Islamic States Today, the most visible theocracy-like governments are in the Middle East. While not pure theocracies, they are Islamic states that base their law, known as Sharia, on the Quran, Islam's holy book. The Quran provides guidance on issues such as the duties of citizens and rulers, rights citizens have, and how the government should exercise power.

Iran Iran provides a good example of how modern Islamic theocracies work. Iran is best described as a theocratic republic. That is, its constitution requires that all laws be interpreted by religious courts that are headed by a "Supreme Leader." The Supreme Leader has immense power over most of the important positions in government, but there is also a popularly elected president and a popularly elected legislature (both from an approved list of candidates) that give the people of Iran some voice in their own governance.

✔ **READING PROGRESS CHECK**

Stating Where do leaders of theocratic governments claim to get their power?

EXPLORING THE ESSENTIAL QUESTION

Evaluating Social scientists have developed criteria for measuring the effectiveness of democracies. These include examining the principles of democracy, like a country's election transparency, freedom of the press, guaranteed liberties, and corruption. How would you evaluate whether a government is doing a good job for its people? Identify five factors you think are most important in evaluating whether a government is doing a good job. Then choose one factor and develop a strategy for evaluating it. What would you look for? What questions would you ask people inside and outside the country?

presume to believe, assume, or imagine to be true

LESSON 1 REVIEW

Reviewing Vocabulary

1. *Identifying* In what form of government does an elected body of officials handle both executive and legislative responsibilities?

Using Your Graphic Organizer

2. *Comparing* Using your completed flowchart, compare the steps in the process by which officials in parliamentary governments are chosen to the steps by which members of the U.S. Congress are chosen.

Answering the Guiding Questions

3. *Considering Advantages and Disadvantages* What are the advantages and disadvantages of presidential and parliamentary systems of government?

4. *Describing* What are some of the challenges and successes of relatively new democracies in Africa, Asia, and Latin America?

5. *Specifying* In what ways do authoritarian governments differ from the democratic government of the United States?

6. *Applying* What basic principle sets theocracies apart from all other forms of government?

Writing About Government

7. *Informative/Explanatory* In a brief paragraph, identify the advantages and disadvantages of the presidential system. Then hypothesize as to why there are more parliamentary than presidential democracies.

interact with these digital
assets and others in lesson 2

✓ **INTERACTIVE IMAGE**
  The United Nations

✓ **SELF-CHECK QUIZ**

✓ **SLIDE SHOW**
  International NGOs

✓ **VIDEO**
  NATO

netw⊚rks
TRY IT YOURSELF ONLINE

Reading Help Desk

Academic Vocabulary

- **undertake**
- **violation**

Content Vocabulary

- **intergovernmental organization (IGO)**
- **nongovernmental organization (NGO)**

TAKING NOTES:

Key Ideas and Details

SUMMARIZING Use the table to summarize information about the international organizations described in the lesson.

Organization	Membership	Goals

LESSON 2

International Organizations and Global Issues

ESSENTIAL QUESTION

How do nations and citizens interact in the global political and economic arenas?

In 2008 the Colombian government sent special forces to rescue hostages being held by FARC, a rebel group fighting the Colombian government. They convinced FARC that an international organization such as the Red Cross or the United Nations was coming to see the hostages. One of the Colombian soldiers, nervous about entering the situation with no weapons, put on a Red Cross shirt. The 15 hostages were rescued without a shot being fired.

Afterwards, the Colombian government was accused of violating the rules of war. Soldiers cannot pretend to be members of the Red Cross. This rule exists because the international community wants combatants to be able to trust certain organizations, like the Red Cross.

Do you think the Colombian government should be punished for the soldier's action? Why or why not? How would your view change if a) you were one of the rescued hostages, b) you were a member of FARC, which claims to be fighting for the poor people of Colombia, or c) you were an official with the Red Cross or United Nations, and the Colombian government had ordered the soldiers to wear Red Cross shirts?

The United Nations

GUIDING QUESTION *What are the structure and functions of the United Nations?*

In the aftermath of World War II, the United States and other nations established the United Nations (UN) to provide a forum for nations to settle their disputes peacefully. The Charter of the UN identifies three major goals. One is to preserve world peace and security. The second is to encourage nations to deal fairly with one another. The third is to help nations cooperate in trying to solve their social and economic problems. UN membership is open to all "peace-loving states." Today, 193 nations from around the world are members of the UN.

Structure of the UN The UN is a large and complex organization, with more than 50,000 employees working at the headquarters in New York City and around the world. The UN's two deliberative bodies are the General Assembly and the Security Council. In the General Assembly, each member nation has one vote. The Security Council has only 15 members, five of which are permanent members. The permanent members are the United States, Russia, the People's Republic of China, France, and Great Britain. The General Assembly elects the other 10 members for two-year terms.

The Secretary General is the chief administrative officer for the UN and the International Court of Justice is its judicial branch. Member nations may voluntarily submit disputes over international law to this court.

The United Nations also has units that carry out many of the organization's humanitarian activities. These specialized agencies include the World Health Organization (WHO), the United Nations Children's Fund (UNICEF), and the United Nations Educational, Scientific, and Cultural Organization (UNESCO). The UN also has regional agencies such as the Organization of American States (OAS), which includes all 35 independent countries in the Americas.

EXPLORING THE ESSENTIAL QUESTION

Researching UNESCO runs the UN's World Heritage program. This program works to preserve sites that represent the world's natural and cultural heritage. Sites selected for the program must be "of outstanding value to humanity." These sites are all on the World Heritage List.

- The Namib Sand Sea in Namibia, the world's only coastal desert with extensive sand fields influenced by fog
- Levuka Historical Port Town in Fiji, which shows the integration of local building traditions with those of a colonial naval power
- Mount Fuji in Japan, a place regarded as sacred by the Japanese and an inspiration to artists for many generations

Think of a natural or cultural site near you that fits the criteria of the World Heritage program. Create a multimedia presentation aimed at convincing UNESCO to add your site to the World Heritage List.

---

undertake to take on, accept, or begin a project or responsibility

In the aftermath of World War II, the United States and other nations established the United Nations (UN) to provide a forum for nations to settle their disputes peacefully.

▼ CRITICAL THINKING

Making Inferences Why might the permanent members of the Security Council find it hard to agree on issues of peace and security?

Peacekeeping Activities In addition to promoting alternatives to armed conflict, the UN has a limited ability to use military force for peacekeeping. The UN acts as a peacekeeper when its member states have approved a mission, volunteered troops, and agreed to pay for the mission.

UN peacekeeping often involves inserting an international force of troops between combatants as a way to calm an explosive situation or to monitor a negotiated cease-fire. Sometimes lightly armed peacekeeping forces will **undertake** other missions, such as overseeing elections or providing humanitarian aid to help starving people in a war-torn country.

✔ **READING PROGRESS CHECK**

Identifying What are the three major goals stated in the Charter of the United Nations?

Negotiating

The Arctic ice cap is melting, and accessing its resources—gas, oil, and rare minerals—is becoming easier. Ships can pass through parts of the Arctic Ocean previously covered by ice. Using this shortcut between Asia and Europe could save businesses millions of dollars. This poses challenges for countries that claim Arctic territory: the United States, Canada, Russia, and several northern European countries.

China's Role China has no Arctic claims, but it sees Arctic resources as "the inherited wealth of all mankind." China has asked to become an official observer of the Arctic Council, a transnational group that studies and makes decisions regarding development of the Arctic. China has also begun investing in companies that hope to mine or drill for Arctic resources. The United States is concerned about taking any actions that would strengthen Chinese influence or dilute its own Arctic claims. At the same time, China is the second-biggest U.S. trading partner.

Topics	Starting Point: What Is Your Ideal Outcome?	Bottom Line: What Points Are Non-negotiable?	Room to Negotiate: Where Is There Flexibility?
1. Role of China			
2. Development vs. Environment and Public Health			
3. Security			

Protecting the Arctic Environment and Arctic Peoples Development of Arctic resources may harm the environment and threaten the health and safety of Arctic peoples. Some people argue for an international treaty putting strict limits on Arctic development. Others say the United Nations Convention on the Law of the Sea already provides workable environmental guidelines. (The U.S. Senate has never ratified that convention.) The United States wants access to the resources in the area, but it also is committed to environmental protection.

Security The Arctic is a non militarized area. However, the United States must be able to defend its interests in the region, including the ability to navigate through the area. A large American military presence might, however, be upsetting to other countries.

EXPLORING THE ESSENTIAL QUESTION

Organizing You are part of a group helping the president plan for a meeting of the Arctic Council. All of these issues will come up at the meeting. With your group, identify what you think U.S. policy should be. Then consider which points you are willing to negotiate and where you will draw the line—the point at which you cannot compromise further. Use the chart to plan a negotiating strategy.

Global Organizations

intergovernmental organization (IGO) type of international organization made up of groups of national governments and created through agreements negotiated by member states; an IGO's powers are established and limited by its members

nongovernmental organization (NGO) type of international organization made up of individuals and groups that are not part of any government

GUIDING QUESTION *What are intergovernmental organizations and international nongovernmental organizations, and what issues do they work to solve?*

In the twenty-first century, the Nobel Peace Prize has been awarded to five international organizations, highlighting the key role such organizations play in world politics. One way of categorizing international organizations is by their members. The members of **intergovernmental organizations (IGOs)** are national governments, while the members of **nongovernmental organizations (NGOs)** are individuals and groups that are not part of any government. IGOs are created through agreements, usually treaties, negotiated by the member states. The powers of an IGO are established and limited by its members, and IGOs are generally funded by their member nations. NGOs are funded largely by donations from private individuals and charitable foundations.

Other Intergovernmental Organizations While the UN is the most well-recognized IGO, many other organizations have been created to serve regional interests or to address very specific purposes.

The North Atlantic Treaty Organization (NATO) is an IGO for military cooperation between the United States, Canada, and countries in Europe. Created to provide a unified front against the countries allied with the Soviet Union, NATO continues to fight in military engagements around the world if doing so is seen as being in the interests of its member nations.

OPEC, the Organization of the Petroleum Exporting Countries, is a group of oil-producing states such as Iraq, Kuwait, Saudi Arabia, and Venezuela. OPEC regulates the production of oil across the globe, and OPEC has an enormous impact on oil prices. In 1973 OPEC stopped shipments of oil to the U.S. and parts of Europe because of their support of Israel during the Yom Kippur War. The result was an oil crisis that changed views about the use of oil and also resulted in the creation of the U.S. Department of Energy.

International NGOs International NGOs vary widely in their sizes, scopes, effectiveness, and missions. Some international NGOs, like Amnesty International, advocate for change, while others, like the Red Cross, provide direct assistance to those in need. Some are large and work in many global regions, while others focus in a particular geographic area. Some focus on just a particular issue—such as global health, literacy, human rights, or disaster relief—while others focus on a wide range of issues. Some NGOs, such as Catholic Relief Services (CRS) or World Vision, are faith-based; others are secular in orientation. The following examples suggest the variety of organizations working around the world.

International Red Cross and Red Crescent Movement The largest and perhaps most well-known global humanitarian NGO is composed of the International Committee of the Red Cross (ICRC), the International Federation of Red Cross and Red Crescent Societies, and 189 member Red Cross and Red Crescent Societies, such as the American Red Cross, the Magen David Adom in Israel, and the Turkish Red Crescent. The ICRC monitors the treatment of prisoners during war. The American Red Cross is perhaps best known for its disaster relief work in the United States but also does international relief and development work.

BRAC Most Americans have never heard of BRAC. But, based on the criteria of impact, innovation, and sustainability, the *Global Journal* in 2013 ranked BRAC as the top NGO in the world. Headquartered in Bangladesh, BRAC (formerly named Bangladesh Rural Advancement Committee) started as a microfinance organization, providing small loans to entrepreneurs in developing countries to get their businesses off the ground. BRAC has expanded its work to include agriculture and food security, legal aid, children's health, and more.

Doctors Without Borders (Médecins Sans Frontières) Doctors Without Borders won the Nobel Peace Prize in 1999 for its work providing medical aid in war-torn areas and preventing the spread of epidemics. The organization also speaks out about neglected international crises, inadequacies or abuses of the foreign aid system, and the need for improved medical treatments and protocols.

Doctors Without Borders provides a significant amount of aid, specifically in the field of health care, to people who live in areas where they do not have regular access to the care they need, including war-torn regions and areas of international crisis.

▼ CRITICAL THINKING
Researching Research to learn more about the work of Doctors Without Borders. Create a presentation explaining when the organization was founded, the countries in which it works, and some of its current programs.

✓ READING PROGRESS CHECK

Speculating Why are NGOs important to millions of people around the world?

Francesco Zizola/Noor

Global Issues

GUIDING QUESTION *Which of the world's current issues must be solved by cooperative action?*

In today's interdependent world, many problems that affect significant numbers of people cannot be solved by a single nation. Cooperative action is required to solve a variety of global issues, including terrorism, human trafficking, and environmental issues, among others.

Global issues can pose a challenge to a nation's sovereignty—its ability to rule its own borders without interference from other nations. Responding effectively to global issues sometimes means accepting the decisions or rules of an international organization, even when those decisions or rules might be different from what a nation would decide on its own.

International Terrorism Terrorism is the use of violence by nongovernmental groups against civilians to achieve a political goal. Prior to 1968, terrorists and their targets were generally within the same country. While domestic terrorism is still common, international terrorism has become a serious problem in the global era. For Americans, the terrorist attacks of September 11, 2001, brought this problem home. On that day, terrorists launched a devastating attack on the United States, hijacking commercial airliners and crashing them into the World Trade Center towers in New York City and the Pentagon in Washington, D.C. Another plane intended for a similar attack crashed in Pennsylvania. Since 2001, terrorists have launched major attacks in India, Russia, Great Britain, Jordan, Egypt, Iraq, Pakistan, Afghanistan, and many other nations.

The response to terrorism can also create new issues. For example, the United States has used targeted killings and drone strikes against terrorists

PARTICIPATING
IN Your Government

Taking Action

There are more than 30 million enslaved persons around the world, including many living in conditions of modern slavery in the United States. Imagine that you have just bought a pair of jeans you have been wanting for quite a while. Then one of your friends shows you an article that says the jeans were made by the labor of enslaved persons. What would you do, if anything, in response?

- Boycott the company that makes the jeans
- Boycott the store that sells the jeans
- Start a campaign in your school to have students cut the labels off their jeans and attach them to a letter to be sent to the company that makes the jeans
- Organize a rally to raise awareness of the issue of forced labor/human trafficking
- Start a petition asking the local, state, and federal governments to take more aggressive action against forced labor/human trafficking
- Write a letter to the editor of your school newspaper
- Other (describe what action/nonaction you would take)

EXPLORING THE ESSENTIAL QUESTION

Defending Describe the actions you would take, using the list provided as a guide. Then write a statement explaining your decision.

around the world. Sometimes they have entered countries to conduct strikes without notifying the government. Many see this action as a **violation** of national sovereignty. Drone strikes have also killed civilians, which NGOs such as Amnesty International and Human Rights Watch see as violations of the rules of war.

Human Trafficking Human trafficking is the trade in human beings. It involves holding people captive, usually for the purpose of sexual slavery, forced labor, or as the source of organs or tissues for transplanting. Those who take part in this illegal business make a lot of money—approximately $32 billion each year worldwide. Often, human traffickers lure victims by promising them good jobs. Victims are then taken to distant cities or even to foreign countries where they cannot speak the language. They are held against their will and forced into slavery. Today, millions of people worldwide are victims of human trafficking. Many of them are women or children.

> **violation** an act of disregard or disrespect

International organizations have fought human trafficking for decades by advocating for treaties and special initiatives. In 2007 the UN began a new effort to address trafficking. Called the Global Initiative to Fight Human Trafficking (UN.GIFT), the initiative aims to coordinate the efforts of national and local governments, IGOs and NGOs, and other stakeholders.

Protecting the Environment Because the environment is a basic part of our daily lives, it is easy to take the air, water, and land upon which all life depends for granted. Yet the political issues and technical questions resulting from exploding population growth, increasing consumption of natural resources, and the growing discharge of pollution into the environment raise many difficult global issues. Policy makers and scientists recognize that dealing effectively with such issues requires transnational programs that depend upon international cooperation.

The United States occupies a unique place in international debates and negotiations regarding the environment. As one group of scholars explains: "The United States is at the same time one of our world's leading promoters of environmental concerns and because of our size and extensive industrial wealth one of its major polluters."

☑ **READING PROGRESS CHECK**

Determining Importance Which of the global issues described in this section do you believe is the most urgent or important? Why?

LESSON 2 REVIEW

Reviewing Vocabulary
1. ***Differentiating*** In what ways is terrorism different from combat attacks that happen during declared wars?

Using Your Graphic Organizer
2. ***Comparing and Contrasting*** Using your notes from the table, compare and contrast the membership and goals of three of the organizations discussed in this lesson.

Answering the Guiding Questions
3. ***Identifying*** What are the structure and functions of the United Nations?

4. ***Explaining*** What are intergovernmental organizations and international nongovernmental organizations, and what issues do they work to solve?

5. ***Specifying*** Which of the world's current issues must be solved by cooperative action?

Writing About Government
6. ***Informative/Explanatory*** Choose one of the following international NGOs to research: Room to Read, Water for People, or Friends of the Earth Middle East. Visit the NGO's website to learn more about the organization. Create a poster explaining the group's work to other students in your school.

Medellín v Texas (2008)

FACTS OF THE CASE The United States ratified an international treaty that says that countries must inform any foreigners they arrest that they have the right to have their home country's embassy notified. In 1993 Jose Medellín, a Mexican citizen, was arrested for murder in Texas. He was not informed of his right to contact his embassy, and he was later found guilty and sentenced to death. He later appealed his sentence. By that time, the International Court of Justice (ICJ) found that Medellín and 50 other Mexican citizens incarcerated in America were entitled to have their cases reviewed because they had not been informed of their right to contact their consulate. President George W. Bush ordered Texas to review Medellín's case, but Texas refused.

ISSUE

Are U.S. states required to follow provisions of a ratified international treaty or decisions of the International Court of Justice?

ARGUMENTS

MEDELLÍN U.S. states should be required to enforce international treaties because, by signing the treaty, the United States was agreeing to inform foreign citizens of their rights upon their arrest. No additional law needed to be passed by Congress to require states to inform these foreigners of their rights because the requirement was plainly written in the treaty that had been signed and ratified by the president and Congress. In addition, states should be required to follow International Court of Justice (ICJ) rulings because the ICJ is a part of the United Nations, of which the United States is a member.

International treaties and rulings of the ICJ would become meaningless if all states within the United States are not required to abide by them. What meaning does signing and ratifying a treaty even have if the state courts—which handle the overwhelming majority of cases in the United States— are not required to follow the provisions of those treaties?

TEXAS Treaties and rulings by the International Court of Justice create obligations on the part of the United States, but those obligations do not require the states themselves to take any action under U.S. law. If Congress passes a law to enforce the international treaties in Texas, then they would have to comply, but Congress did not do so. Though it would have been nice for Texas to follow the treaty, no state must follow the directions of an international organization unless there is a domestic law that requires them to do so.

It is the responsibility of the legislative branch to transform international treaties into binding national law. If we were to automatically rule that state courts must follow ICJ rulings and treaty provisions, we would take away that authority from Congress, upsetting the checks and balances between the branches.

EXPLORING THE ESSENTIAL QUESTION

Moot Court You will be assigned to one of three groups: lawyers for Medellín, lawyers for Texas, and Supreme Court justices. You will prepare for a moot court of this case. The lawyers for each side should develop arguments to present during oral argument, and prepare to answer questions from the justices. The justices should prepare questions to ask the lawyers during oral argument. When you argue the case, each team will have 5 minutes to present its side, and the justices will be allowed to ask the lawyers questions throughout their 5 minutes. The justices will then vote and announce their decision, explaining their reasons. After the moot court is complete, write a persuasive essay or blog that reflects your personal opinion about this issue.

YOU BE the JUDGE

Interact with these digital assets and others in lesson 3

✓ **EXPLORING THE ESSENTIAL QUESTION**
Economic Systems in Action

✓ **INTERACTIVE IMAGE**
Chinese Labor Unrest

✓ **SELF-CHECK QUIZ**

✓ **VIDEO**
Entrepreneurs Create New Jobs

netw⊙rks
TRY IT YOURSELF ONLINE

LESSON 3
Economic Systems in Action

ESSENTIAL QUESTION

What is the role of government in different economic systems?

Make a list of words, phrases, or ideas that you associate with each of these words: capitalism, communism, and socialism. Use your list to create a visual representation of each word. What do your images indicate about your views about each economic system?

Reading Help Desk

Academic Vocabulary
• migrate

Content Vocabulary
• **communism**
• **capitalism**
• **socialism**
• **entrepreneur**
• **profit**
• **patent**
• **mixed economy**

TAKING NOTES:
Key Ideas and Details

CLASSIFYING Use the graphic organizer to write notes about the three main economic systems discussed in the lesson.

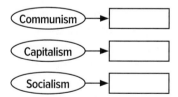

Economic Systems

GUIDING QUESTION *What are the three major economic systems used in the world today?*

We live in a world with limited food, land, energy, and other resources. Different societies allocate those resources in different ways. For example, in some societies, farms are privately owned. Farms produce food, and people can buy food from farmers. In other societies, the government owns the farms and produces food and then distributes it to the people.

We can categorize countries into three major forms of economic organization: capitalism, socialism, or communism. These labels describe the type of economic system a country uses and how its government interacts with the economy. **Communism** is a command system in which the central government directs all major economic decisions. Under **capitalism**, private citizens own and use the basic factors of production in free markets to earn profits. Under **socialism**, the government owns the basic factors of production and plays a major role in the distribution of wages and output. A socialist system also has some elements of free markets.

☑ READING PROGRESS CHECK

Stating What purposes do economic systems serve?

Capitalism

GUIDING QUESTION *What are the characteristics of capitalist economies?*

Capitalism is an economic system that relies on the private ownership of the land, tools, and materials required to produce goods and services, which are then allocated by free market forces. Capitalist economic systems are often called *free market* or *free enterprise* systems.

There are several characteristics of a capitalist economy. First, most property and resources are privately owned, and the law protects this private ownership. Second, competition and freedom of choice are present in a capitalist economy. Businesses compete with each other for customers—and no one business controls the market for a product. Consumers can choose which products to buy, and businesses can choose which to make and sell. Workers can choose which jobs to work at and can switch jobs when they want to. Companies can choose who to hire. Third, capitalist systems depend on individual initiative and **entrepreneurs**, or risk-taking individuals who start new businesses or invent new products in hopes of making a profit. The law does not prevent anyone from trying to be an entrepreneur. These businesses are motivated by the ability to make money, or **profit**. With the potential to make a profit, however, also comes the risk of a loss.

In pure capitalism, the government would stay almost entirely out of the economy. Few countries are purely capitalist, however—most have some government involvement in the economy, though they differ somewhat in the government's role. Generally, in mixed capitalist economies, the government provides some services that the private sector would not; it also regulates and taxes the private sector.

United States The United States's mixed capitalist economy illustrates the main components of capitalism. The private sector owns most property and resources, but the government owns some land (about 30 percent of the country), as in the case of national parks. Local, state, or federal governments provide services that the private sector is unlikely to provide or that are deemed to be essential to fundamental rights. For example, the government provides roads for transportation, libraries and schools for general education, and water purification systems for drinking. It protects the consumer, regulates manufacturers and businesses of all kinds, and is sometimes a direct producer of goods and services.

The United States respects private property—in fact, the Fifth Amendment to the Constitution guarantees that the government shall not deprive people of their property "without due process of law; nor shall private property be taken for public use, without just compensation."

The U.S. government also supports and encourages private business and entrepreneurship. U.S. law protects inventors' rights. People who invent something can receive a **patent** from the government, guaranteeing them the exclusive right to own or sell that product for 20 years. In return, inventors must make the plans for their invention public, and others can copy their invention after 20 years. This law is very important and is intended to encourage and reward innovation. To help ensure competition, the government restricts monopolies, or companies with enough control over one type of good that they could exploit customers or single-handedly crash the economy.

Sweden In the post-war period, Sweden was a democratic socialist country. Sweden is now a capitalist **mixed economy** with more social welfare support than the United States. Sweden encourages private business by maintaining fairly simple regulation of business, making it easy to start a business, and by having a relatively low corporate income tax.

In comparison to the United States, however, Sweden offers many more government services to the people. For example, almost all education and health care is paid for by the government. The Swedish government also pays for new parents to take more than a year off work and gives parents a monthly child care allowance until the child turns 16. To afford all these services, Swedes pay much higher taxes than in the United States—almost twice as high. Paying higher taxes for more services results in less disposable income for average Swedes but also provides a greater safety net for everyone in the country.

Singapore Singapore, a very small nation in Asia, has an economy much larger than its geographic size would suggest. After the country gained its independence from Great Britain in the mid-1960s, the government adopted a pro-business, pro-foreign investment economic policy. Starting a business is easy in Singapore, and the government encourages international trade.

Residents of Singapore pay significantly lower taxes than people in the United States or Sweden. However, the government also provides less in the way of social services. The culture places a lot of importance on personal responsibility, and only the very poorest residents receive welfare support from the government. Workers who have been laid off do not receive unemployment pay. The people are generally expected to rely on their own savings and family support in their old age.

☑ **READING PROGRESS CHECK**

Differentiating Explain the difference between pure capitalism and mixed capitalism, and describe which economic system is used in the United States today.

Socialism

GUIDING QUESTION *What is the basic goal of a socialist economy, and how do socialist governments meet this goal?*

Under socialism, the government controls production in basic industries, determines the use of resources, and provides significant welfare for the people. The basic goal of a socialist economy is to share wealth more equally in a society. Since socialists believe that wealth should be distributed as equally as possible, their policies are directed at making essential goods and basic social services available more or less equally to all.

Major industries—like energy, transportation, and natural resource extraction—are generally publicly owned. Other industries, like food and clothing production, may be privately owned and operated. Socialist governments also provide a wide array of benefits for their citizens—including free or low-cost medical care and education, including college, along with generous retirement and unemployment benefits.

Venezuela The Venezuelan government dominates its economy. The government controls several industries and uses revenues to subsidize food, housing, health care, and education. Many residents remain very poor, however, and government mismanagement has led to food and energy shortages.

Venezuela's leaders have undertaken a campaign of nationalization, in which the government takes control of formerly privately owned industries. Venezuela has nationalized some or all of the oil, electricity, telecommunications, cement, steel, chemical, tourism, banking, and agribusiness industries. In some cases, the government has taken over companies or assets owned by U.S. companies, sometimes providing little or no compensation to the private owners of businesses in these industries. This trend has made foreign companies and investors wary of doing business in Venezuela.

☑ **READING PROGRESS CHECK**

Identifying What is the socialist attitude toward wealth?

Singapore's service sector, including banking, finance, and insurance, is about 80 percent of the economy.

▲ **CRITICAL THINKING**
Classifying How would you classify the economy of Singapore—capitalist, socialist, or communist? Explain.

patent the exclusive right of an inventor to manufacture, use, and sell his or her invention for a specific period, currently 20 years, after which a patent may be renewed

mixed economy economic system that combines elements of capitalism and socialism; in a mixed economy, the government regulates private enterprise

Communism

GUIDING QUESTION *What aspects of the economy do communist governments control?*

The ultimate goal of communism is to create a classless society. Like socialism, under communism, the government has the power to command or direct the economy. The government owns all factors of production and decides what, how, and for whom to produce, usually with a detailed plan.

A five-year plan would tell factory heads in every part of the country precisely how many units to manufacture and where these goods would be delivered. The government also controls labor unions, wages, and prices. In these systems, workers often have little incentive to work hard, and inefficiency can be widespread.

Communism differs from socialism in political ways, too. In a communist country, such as the former Soviet Union or Cuba, only one party exists, and the people have no control over the economic decisions. North Korea and Cuba are two of the few modern examples of a communist country. On the other hand, some nations are transitioning from communism toward free market economies. The two most significant nations in this group are Russia and China.

Cuba While largely state-controlled and centrally planned, Cuba's economy does have some private enterprise. Cuba is a one-party state, ruled by the Communist Party. The government sets prices and determines who will receive which goods and services and in what quantities. The vast majority of working Cubans are employed by the government—approximately 80 percent. The Cuban government has occasionally taken some steps to broaden the economy, by opening the country to tourism, allowing for the sale of some private property or used cars or allowing some people to become self-employed.

The Cuban government provides education and health care for its citizens. However, a vibrant informal economy, or black market, exists, where people sell goods and services outside of the state-run economy. Sometimes the goods sold are smuggled or stolen. The United States has embargoed (banned all trade with) Cuba since 1962, to pressure the government to become a democracy and protect human rights. Some argue that the embargo has not helped achieve these goals. Others argue that the embargo is necessary to continue to pressure Cuba.

Russia In the Soviet Union, the Communist Party closely controlled the government and made almost all the economic decisions. With few exceptions, enterprises were state owned and state operated. For example, the government owned almost all the farmland and directed the production and distribution of food.

The huge state bureaucracy that managed every detail of production bred economic stagnation. By 1991, a combination of political and cultural forces, pressure from foreign governments, and economic decline led to the collapse of the Soviet Union. Since then, Russian leaders have been attempting to build a more competitive system that can compete effectively in the global economy.

Its leaders have broken up the huge, state-owned industries, created a stock market, and initiated other reforms, but progress has been slow. A lack of significant political change has resulted in one party, and one leader in particular (Vladimir Putin), controlling Russia for more than a decade.

China After World War II, Communists won a civil war in China and began implementing a command economy. Private ownership of property was banned, and the government took control of all production of goods, employment, and distribution of goods and services. Over time, however, China found itself unable to compete economically with the market-based economies of its neighbors such as Taiwan, South Korea, Japan, Hong Kong, and Singapore. In the late 1970s, China's Communist leaders began dismantling the centrally controlled economy and encouraging private enterprise.

Recently, China's economy has been growing relatively fast. With low wages and government promotion of manufacturing, many foreign companies have located factories in China. China's government gives foreign companies tax breaks and cheap land and has invested heavily in upgrading highways, ports, and communications systems to assist manufacturers. Millions of Chinese citizens have **migrated** from rural farming communities to booming cities to work in these factories. They work long hours for low wages. However, this shift away from a communist economy has come without real political change. Thus, Communist Party officials have been the ones most able to reap the benefits of economic gains.

With low wages and government promotion of manufacturing, many foreign companies have located factories in China.

▲ CRITICAL THINKING

1. Drawing Conclusions Has the growth of the Chinese economy been good or bad for the United States? Explain.

2. Speculating Do you think the economic changes in China will eventually lead to a change in the country's political system? Why or why not?

migrate to move from one geographic area to another

☑ **READING PROGRESS CHECK**

Activating Prior Knowledge Based on your prior knowledge, what is a "classless society"?

EXPLORING THE ESSENTIAL QUESTION

Identifying Central Issues Revisit your lists and graphic from the opening exercise. How do your initial impressions compare with the information you learned in this lesson? Revise your list and image accordingly.

LESSON 3 REVIEW

Reviewing Vocabulary

1. Comparing and Contrasting In what ways are communism and socialism alike and different?

Using Your Graphic Organizer

2. Questioning Use your notes from the graphic organizer to write one question you have about each of the three major economic systems. Then use library resources to find the answers to your questions.

Answering the Guiding Questions

3. Listing What are the three major economic systems used in the world today?

4. Identifying What are the characteristics of capitalist economies?

5. Explaining What is the basic goal of a socialist economy, and how do socialist governments meet this goal?

6. Describing What aspects of the economy do communist governments control?

Writing About Government

7. Informative/Explanatory Write an essay explaining the connection between economic freedom and political freedom. As you write, integrate your answer to the following question into your essay: Can democratic freedoms such as freedom of speech exist in a nation without economic freedom?

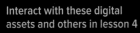

LESSON 4
The Global Economy

(l to r) Kent Knudson/PhotoLink/Getty Images;
Richard Ellis/Hulton Archive/Getty Images; Lionel
Healing/AFP/Getty Images

Reading Help Desk

Academic Vocabulary

- instance
- regional

Content Vocabulary

- tariff
- quota
- trading bloc
- developing nation

TAKING NOTES:

Key Ideas and Details

LISTING Use the graphic organizer to list the ways in which governments may restrict international trade.

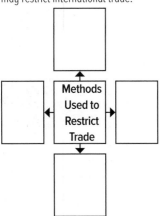

Methods Used to Restrict Trade

ESSENTIAL QUESTION

How do nations and citizens interact in the global political and economic arenas?

Look around you and make a list of at least 10 items that you see. Next try to figure out where those items came from— where were they made? Many items have this information printed on them. For others, you might need to do a little Internet research. Which item was made the farthest from you, and which was the closest? How do you think all of these things came to you? Draw a map or a graphic that illustrates the origins of your everyday things.

International Trade

GUIDING QUESTION *How does international trade affect the way different governments interact?*

In today's interdependent world, many forms of international economic activity take place. Participants range from individuals to giant multinational corporations that employ tens of thousands of workers. Global economic activities include investments in factories, banking and financial services, and transactions on foreign currency exchanges.

Purpose of Trade Nations engage in international trade for several reasons. One is to obtain goods and services that they cannot produce themselves. For example, the United States imports, or buys, industrial diamonds from other countries because we do not have deposits of such minerals. The United States exports, or sells, computers and complex weapons to countries that do not have the technology to make their own.

Another reason nations trade is comparative advantage—the ability of a country to produce a good more efficiently than can other countries. When nations specialize in goods they can produce most efficiently and purchase the rest from others, total world production is greater. This means that while more products are produced, the average cost of each product is less, which benefits all consumers.

Finally, international trade creates jobs. For **instance**, the global market for automobiles is much larger than the market in the United States alone. More jobs will exist for American autoworkers if American automakers can sell their products abroad. The same is true for industries in other countries that sell to the United States.

Barriers to International Trade Unfortunately, unrestricted international trade can threaten some domestic industries and the jobs of workers in those industries. As a result, policy makers in every nation are often under pressure to limit or control some international trade. National governments then may want to use one of several trade barriers to restrict international trade.

One trade barrier is a **tariff**, or a tax placed on an imported item to increase its price in the domestic market. Another barrier is a **quota**, a limit on the quantity of a foreign product that can be imported. If a country can impose either a tariff or a quota on a good, the imported item will become more expensive and consumers will be less likely to buy it—thereby protecting domestic jobs.

Countries also can use nontariff barriers (NTBs) to limit or control unwanted imports. These are very strict health, safety, or other regulations that must be met before a foreign product can be imported. Finally, countries may use an embargo to legally ban all trade with a specific country. The use of an embargo is considered an extreme measure, so embargoes are often employed more for political than economic reasons. For example, the United States has a long-standing embargo against Cuba.

Besides these barriers, countries sometimes engage in unfair trade practices. The most common is dumping, or the practice of selling a product in another country below its manufacturing cost, or below its "fair" market value. Dumping by a foreign firm can drive domestic producers out of their home market if they cannot match the low price. After the domestic producers are gone, the price of the goods being dumped is raised and the foreign producer has the market all to itself.

Some nations have agreed to lower or eliminate barriers to trade with each other. These nations have signed agreements and created organizations to monitor them. These country groupings are called **trading blocs**. The European Union (EU) is one such trading bloc because the nations have a mutual agreement to reduce internal trade barriers.

instance example; as an illustration of a concept

tariff a tax placed on an import to increase its price in the domestic market

quota a limit on the quantities of a foreign product that can be imported

trading bloc agreement and organization created by a group of nations that want to limit trade barriers with one another

---

EXPLORING THE ESSENTIAL QUESTION

Categorizing Consider these examples of trade practices. Categorize each as a tariff, quota, nontariff barrier, embargo, or unrestricted trade. For each barrier to trade, explain who or what the policy might protect.

- The United States increased the tax it charges on Chinese-made car tires.
- Japan required very strict fuel efficiency and exhaust emission standards on all cars. Japanese carmakers met these standards, but many American carmakers did not.
- Greece banned all trade with the Republic of Macedonia because it believed the new country would try to claim Greek territory.
- Canola oil from plants grown in Canada is imported into the United States and blended with gasoline to make biofuels.
- During the Great Depression, the United States set a maximum amount of raw sugar it would import so that U.S. growers would receive higher prices.
- Japan refuses to import beef from regions with mad cow disease (Bovine Spongiform Encephalopathy). Mad cow disease has been found in Scotland, so Japan will not buy any beef from Scotland.

WTO The World Trade Organization (WTO) was created to enforce the provisions of trade treaties signed by more than 149 nations. In these treaties, countries have pledged to limit trade barriers and avoid unfair trade practices. The WTO calls these agreements "the legal ground rules for international commerce."

The WTO hears complaints from member countries and has the authority to assess penalties against nations that violate the terms. Critics of the WTO argue that its policies often favor businesses in wealthy countries. They also argue that the WTO frequently overlooks environmental laws or promotes trade that has significant environmental or human health impacts.

Tariffs, import quotas, and subsidies for agriculture are major issues in the WTO. For example, a group of developing nations may say that the United States and Europe are hurting the economies of developing nations by subsidizing their own farmers, thus making it impossible for farmers in poorer countries to compete.

regional involving or related to a specific geographic area

The European Union The European Union (EU) has become one of the world's largest and most important **regional** trading blocs with 28 European member nations. The gross national product (GNP) of the EU is almost as large as that of the United States, and its population is much larger. No trade barriers exist among the EU nations, so goods, services, and workers can move freely among member countries. Many of the EU countries use a common currency, the euro.

The EU's cohesion has been rocked by the global recession and financial crisis, however. For years, some countries like Greece, Italy, and Portugal had been spending far more money than they took in, and their public debt skyrocketed. When investors became skeptical of their economic strength during the recession, these governments were in danger of defaulting on their debt. This could have meant an economic crisis for the EU, which decided to bail out the troubled countries by giving or loaning them money. The citizens of some of the EU's wealthier countries didn't want to fund what they saw as excessive, irresponsible spending in other nations. By 2013, the economy in Europe seemed to be slowly improving. One bailed-out country, Ireland, was on track to repay the funds it had borrowed on time. Two others, Portugal and Greece, were on much shakier ground.

North American Free Trade Agreement The nations of North America constitute another large trading bloc. The United States, Canada, and Mexico are part of the North American Free Trade Agreement (NAFTA), which pledges to remove all trade barriers among the three countries.

Since the start of NAFTA, trade among the United States, Canada, and Mexico has expanded rapidly. At the same time, NAFTA has been controversial. In the United States, opponents of NAFTA fear that American workers will lose jobs as businesses move from the United States to Mexico

CHART

Annual Trade Balances, 2013

Trade imbalances often exist between nations or trading partners. A trade deficit occurs when a nation imports more from a trading partner than it exports to that partner. A trade surplus occurs when a nation exports more to a partner than it imports from that trading partner.

U.S. Trade Balance With Brazil
Exports to Brazil $44.1 billion
$27.6 billion
Imports from Brazil

U.S. Trade Balance With China
$121.7 billion
Exports to China
Imports from China
$440.4 billion

U.S. Trade Balance With the European Union
$262.2 billion
Exports to the European Union
Imports From the European Union
$387.6 billion

Source: U.S. Census Bureau, http://www.census.gov/foreign-trade/balance/

▲ CRITICAL THINKING

Analyzing Graphics Which countries in this graphic have a trade deficit with the United States? Which have a trade surplus? What could these numbers tell us about the health of the U.S. economy?

to take advantage of lower labor costs and less strict environmental and workers' rights laws. Supporters of NAFTA argue that the agreement provides an increase in lower-cost goods for Americans to buy and thereby decreases their cost of living.

Debates About Trade Trade policies range from totally free trade to protectionism. Completely free trade means that businesses in different nations could buy and sell goods with no tariffs, quotas, or limitations. Protectionism, on the other hand, involves trade barriers to protect domestic industries from foreign competition. The compromise between the two systems is known as managed trade, a compromise that features government intervention in some issues to achieve a specific result.

In theory, free trade would allow all trading nations to produce those things that they produce more efficiently than other countries. Advocates of free trade argue that it will promote prosperity, by making available the largest number of markets for American goods. In their view, this will eventually create new jobs for American workers. Advocates also argue that foreign competition is good for the American economy. Competition spurs American manufacturers to modernize their production techniques to stay competitive. In the process, American consumers are offered better products at lower costs. Finally, free traders argue that free trade policies have a beneficial effect on international relations: promoting economic interdependence, they say, reduces the chances of military conflict or all-out war.

Protectionists remind us that most countries, including the United States, have never followed a pure free-trade policy. This is because governments are always under pressure to protect domestic workers and industries from foreign competition. Protectionists believe that it is possible for foreign producers to influence the American economy if they are not regulated. They also believe that international trade agreements erode American sovereignty. Protectionists are worried about rules made by organizations like the WTO, rules they fear will be detrimental to American interests.

Managed trade does not conflict with comparative advantage. If a firm or an industry can produce a product at a lower relative cost, then the good will still be competitive internationally. American consumers will benefit from having new and varied products at lower prices. Also, limited protection of some firms or industries may be beneficial if these products are needed for national defense. After all, in times of conflict, foreign sources may well be cut off. Third, managed trade still allows trade policy to serve as a foreign policy tool. For example, the United States embargoed most trade with Iran to punish the country for attempting to develop nuclear weapons. America also used some trade restrictions against Russia in retaliation for the seizure and annexation of Crimea in 2014.

The globalization of the economy has brought many benefits to American consumers, including new and more varied products and lower prices for goods. Yet globalization has also brought its share of challenges. American workers must now compete with a much wider labor pool for some jobs, and economic and political decisions are now far more complicated for the federal policy makers and the U.S. Congress.

Opponents of the North American Free Trade Agreement (NAFTA) in the United States are concerned that American workers are losing jobs as businesses move from the United States to Mexico in pursuit of lower labor costs.

▲ CRITICAL THINKING
Summarizing Many Americans are wary of NAFTA. Summarize their opposition to NAFTA in one sentence.

☑ **READING PROGRESS CHECK**

Discussing Would international trade be stronger and better for everyone if all trade barriers were removed?

GOVERNMENT *in your* COMMUNITY

The World Trade Organization

In 2002 Brazil filed a dispute at the World Trade Organization (WTO) over American cotton. The U.S. government subsidizes cotton farmers when market prices fall below a certain threshold. Brazil argued that this was a violation of world trade rules because it made it harder for Brazilian cotton farmers to sell their product at a high price. In 2004 the WTO agreed. That organization does not have a way to make countries comply with its rulings, though, and the United States refused to end the subsidy program. Brazil then threatened economic sanctions, including higher tariffs on many goods like cars, textiles, medicines, and wheat. Brazil also threatened to stop enforcing U.S. patents and copyrights. The sanctions would have cost American businesses around $800 million each year. To avert the sanctions, the United States and Brazil negotiated an agreement. The United States would pay Brazil about $150 million a year and keep the cotton subsidies in place until the next Farm Bill was passed.

Kent Knudson/PhotoLink/Getty Images

EXPLORING THE ESSENTIAL QUESTION

Making Connections Almost half of America's cotton is grown in Texas. What products does your community grow or make for export? Where are these products sold? Visit the WTO's website to learn more about trade disputes. Have there been trade disputes regarding the types of products your community exports to other countries?

Global Economic Issues

GUIDING QUESTION *What are the causes and effects of the world's current economic issues?*

Several organizations exist to deal with global economic issues. The International Monetary Fund (IMF) and the World Bank were created after World War II to stabilize the international economy. The IMF provides policy advice and loans to member nations with temporary economic difficulties. The World Bank focuses on development and support of poor countries by providing low-interest loans, grants, and advice for development projects.

Both the IMF and the World Bank have become the target of protests. Critics dislike these institutions because they believe both impose Western-style capitalism on poor countries without regard for social or environmental concerns. The IMF has been criticized over the conditions it attaches to loans. Governments in economic crisis that receive IMF money are often required to drastically trim spending, sometimes on health and welfare programs. The World Bank has been faulted for funding development projects that caused significant environmental damage.

developing nation nation with little or no industry; many developing nations are former colonies of Western European powers

Economic Development **Developing nations** are countries with relatively low per capita incomes, little or no significant industry, poorly developed infrastructure, and inadequate health and educational systems. Industrialized, or developed, nations have highly developed economies and advanced infrastructure. Many developing nations are former colonies of Western European nations and gained independence only after World War II. Many are located in Africa, Central and South America, and southern Asia, often referred to as the "Global South." How to best support developing nations—where many of the world's poorest people live—is a matter of ongoing debate.

Some argue that developing nations need cash from the developed world to help lift their people out of poverty and develop infrastructure. Others argue that cash support should be limited, and instead these governments should open their economies to foreign capital investment. Still others argue that the developing world needs support in the form of expertise—highly skilled experts to help governments design and implement programs to grow the economy and create vibrant local businesses.

Twentieth-century development programs left many developing nations—most in the Global South—with tremendous debt. Many countries in sub-Saharan Africa borrowed money from foreign governments and banks to fund infrastructure and industrial development. Beginning in the 1970s, droughts, growing populations, lack of capital, and falling world prices for their exports weakened most African economies. Some countries' corrupt governments misspent the money. These countries were carrying enormous debt loads—paying $1.30 toward debt for every $1.00 received in aid. A movement to cancel Africa's staggering debt has gained momentum around the world. Supporters argue that most African nations' current debt is so large that they will continue to pay more toward paying interest and principal on the debt than for health care and development unless their debt is canceled. Opponents argue that unless these nations end corruption, debt cancellation will only continue the cycle.

Global Economic Downturns In 2008 many of the world's economies experienced a deep recession and a crisis in the financial sector. In the United States and other countries, the crisis began in the home mortgage industry. American homebuyers were being offered cheap loans, often without meeting minimum income standards. Investors all over the world then bought bonds that used these risky home mortgage loans as collateral, thinking they were solid investments. When the homeowners could not pay back the loans, many of the bonds that the investors bought became worthless, and the system unraveled. Investors lost trillions of dollars and stocks plunged everywhere. Similar housing "bubbles" were experienced in other countries and the economic downturn was global. Governments in Europe even had to rescue their banks that had purchased mortgage-backed securities from American banks. Stock markets around the world plunged.

The world economy was well on the road to recovery by 2013, but the severity of the 2008 financial crisis showed how interconnected world economies had become.

✓ READING PROGRESS CHECK

Defining What is the meaning of the term "Global South"?

Diamond sales have helped to fund civil wars and conflicts in Africa.

▲ CRITICAL THINKING

1. Applying What steps could the diamond industry take to reassure consumers that their diamonds do not fund wars? Research to find out whether any of the steps you suggest have been taken.

2. Researching Which IGOs and NGOs are working on this issue? Create a flyer that a jewelry store could use to inform customers about the issue and address potential concerns.

LESSON 4 REVIEW

Reviewing Vocabulary

1. Contrasting What is the difference between tariffs and quotas?

Using Your Graphic Organizer

2. Defining Using your notes from the graphic organizer, write the definition of each term referring to international trade restrictions.

Answering the Guiding Questions

3. Describing How does international trade affect the way different governments interact?

4. Identifying Cause and Effect What are the causes and effects of the world's current economic issues?

Writing About Government

5. Informative/Explanatory Trade is becoming more international, and more countries are now linking their economic fortunes with trade agreements. However, barriers to international trade exist. Review these barriers and prepare a written plan for helping nations overcome these barriers as a means to build their international trade opportunities.

STUDY GUIDE

POLITICAL SYSTEMS IN ACTION
LESSON 1

Democratic Governments

Parliamentary Government

- Elected assembly holds both executive and legislative powers
- Prime minister, leader of majority party, heads government
- Prime minister decides when to hold elections within set period
- Parliament can trigger new elections with "no confidence" vote
- Examples: Great Britain, India, Canada, Israel, Australia, Japan

Presidential Government

- Executive, legislative, and judicial powers separated
- President, popularly elected, heads executive branch
- Representatives popularly elected to legislature
- President shares some executive functions with premier in some nations
- Examples: United States, France, Mexico

Authoritarian Governments

- Controlled by elected or nonelected rulers who restrict popular participation in government
- Examples: Cuba, China, North Korea, Saudi Arabia

Theocracies

- Religion-based government
- Examples: Vatican City, Islamic states such as Iran

INTERNATIONAL ORGANIZATIONS
LESSON 2

Intergovernmental Organizations (IGOs)
are made up of groups of national governments. Examples include:
- **UN**
- **NATO**
- **OPEC**

Nongovernmental Organizations (NGOs)
are not part of any government. Examples include:
- **Amnesty International**
- **BRAC**
- **Doctors Without Borders**

ECONOMIC SYSTEMS IN ACTION
LESSON 3

Economic Systems			
	Capitalism	Socialism	Communism
Who owns the factors of production?	Private owners	Government with some private ownership	Government
Who decides the allocation of resources?	Free market forces	Government mostly and a few free markets	Government
Who makes the economic decisions?	Individual businesses and consumers	Government	Government
Characteristics	• Individual initiative • Entrepreneurship	Government provides for the people's welfare	Government controls labor unions, wages, and prices

THE GLOBAL ECONOMY
LESSON 4

Barriers to International Trade

Tariffs

Quotas

Nontariff Barriers

Embargoes

Dumping

Free Trade versus Managed Trade

Arguments for Free Trade

- Allows all nations to produce things they can produce most efficiently
- Opens the most markets for American goods, creating American jobs
- Foreign competition good for overall health of U.S. economy
- Foreign competition spurs U.S. manufacturers to modernize
- U.S. consumers get better products at lower costs
- Promotes peaceful relations

Arguments for Managed Trade

- Protects American jobs and industries from foreign competition
- Prevents foreign investors from gaining undue influence in U.S. economy
- Protects public health and safety
- Free trade erodes sovereignty by requiring U.S. to accept rules made by organizations like WTO
- Trade restrictions can be powerful foreign policy tool to promote American interests

Directions: On a separate sheet of paper, answer the questions below. Make sure you read carefully and answer all parts of the questions.

Lesson Review

Lesson 1

① *Comparing* What aspects of India's government are like those of the United States?

② *Contrasting* How is the form of government in North Korea different from the U.S. form of government?

Lesson 2

③ *Specifying* What are three major goals of the United Nations?

④ *Identifying Cause and Effect* What new issues have U.S. actions against terrorism created for the world community?

Lesson 3

⑤ *Explaining* What affect do patents have on competition and entrepreneurship?

⑥ *Finding the Main Idea* What does a society's economic system do?

Lesson 4

⑦ *Explaining* Why do nations form trading blocs?

⑧ *Analyzing Cause and Effect* How does free trade affect products and prices for consumers?

ANSWERING THE ESSENTIAL QUESTIONS

Review your answers to the introductory questions at the beginning of each lesson. Then answer the following Essential Questions based on what you learned in the chapter. Have your answers changed?

⑨ *Considering Advantages and Disadvantages* What are the advantages and disadvantages of different types of political systems?

⑩ *Analyzing* How do nations and citizens interact in the global political and economic arenas?

⑪ *Comparing and Contrasting* What is the role of government in different economic systems?

DBQ Interpreting Political Cartoons

Use the political cartoon to answer the following questions.

⑫ *Identifying Point of View* Is the cartoonist expressing an argument for or against NAFTA? Explain. Then write a counterargument expressing a contrasting point of view.

⑬ *Evaluating* Is the cartoonist's argument valid? Explain.

Critical Thinking

⑭ *Comparing and Contrasting* Compare and contrast the government systems of Iran and the United States.

⑮ *Making Inferences* The Obama administration adopted a policy to promote the development of alternative forms of energy. How might the existence of OPEC have influenced the administration to make this policy?

⑯ *Analyzing* Nations with a communist economic system often experience shortages of consumer goods. Why do you think this is so?

⑰ *Considering Advantages and Disadvantages* How do the International Monetary Fund and World Bank help developing countries? How might they harm developing nations, according to critics?

Need Extra Help?

If You've Missed Question	①	②	③	④	⑤	⑥	⑦	⑧	⑨	⑩	⑪	⑫	⑬	⑭	⑮	⑯	⑰
Go to page	740	742	744	748	752	751	757	758	738	744	751	758	758	743	747	754	760

Directions: On a separate sheet of paper, answer the questions below. Make sure you read carefully and answer all parts of the questions.

DBQ Analyzing Primary Sources

Study the North Korean poster and answer the questions that follow.

Tony Wheeler/Lonely Planet Images/Getty Images

18 *Identifying Bias* This poster demonstrates bias toward a particular political and economic system. Which one? How do you know?

19 *Interpreting* How does this poster fit the definition of propaganda?

20 *Analyzing Primary Sources* Analyze the validity of the information and arguments portrayed in this poster as counterarguments to capitalism.

Social Studies Skills

21 *Economics* Draw a continuum with capitalism at one extreme, communism at the other, and socialism in the middle. Place these countries on the continuum based on what you have learned about their economic systems: United States, Russia, Venezuela, Cuba, Sweden, China, Singapore, North Korea. Be prepared to explain your choices.

22 *Problem Solving* Suppose a baseball costs $4 to manufacture in Mexico. The Mexican company adds 10 percent to the price for profit before exporting it to the United States. Suppose the U.S. tariff on baseballs is 20 percent. How much will a Mexican baseball cost the American buyer? Suppose a U.S. manufacturer charges $5 for its baseballs. How will the tariff benefit the domestic manufacturer?

Research and Presentation

23 *Acquiring Information* With a partner, select one of the nations affected by the Arab Spring: Tunisia, Egypt, Yemen, or Libya. Do research to learn about the country's progress toward democracy. Present your findings in an oral report.

24 *Synthesizing* Go to the United Nations website and select one of its specialized agencies, such as the WHO or UNICEF. Each student should select a different agency. Create three electronic slides that use pictures and annotations to describe what the agency does. Put your slides together with those of other students to create a class slideshow.

25 *Exploring Issues* Select a developing nation in the Global South. Do research to find out the main problems impeding this nation's progress. Write a report describing these problems and ways that you think the world community could help this nation develop.

Need Extra Help?

If You've Missed Question	**18**	**19**	**20**	**21**	**22**	**23**	**24**	**25**
Go to page	742	742	742	751	759	741	745	760

CONTENTS

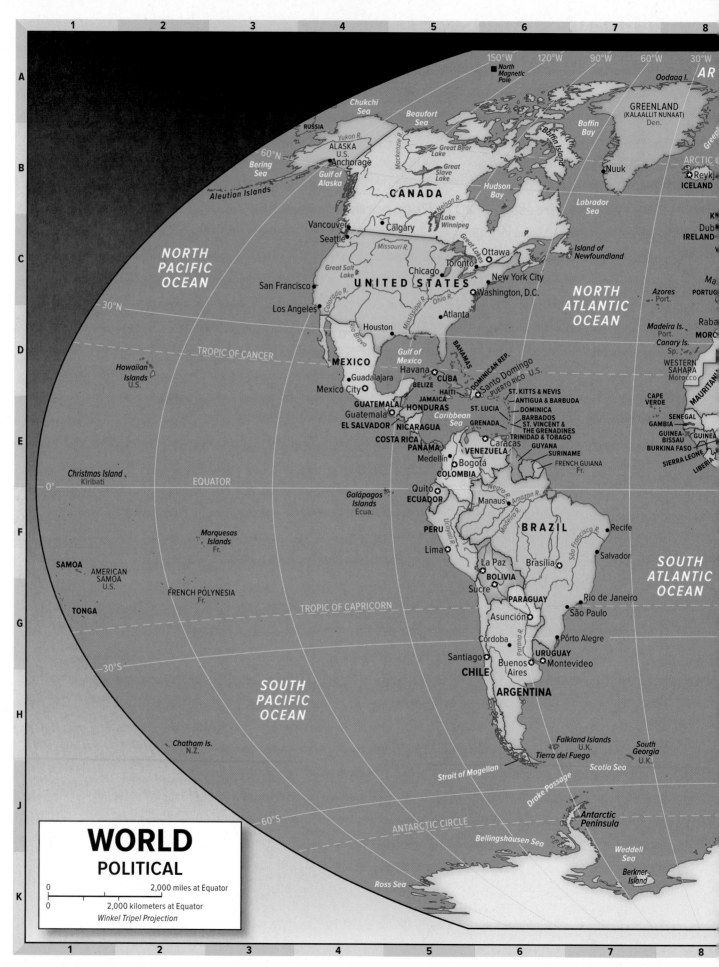

WORLD
POLITICAL

0   2,000 miles at Equator

0   2,000 kilometers at Equator
Winkel Tripel Projection

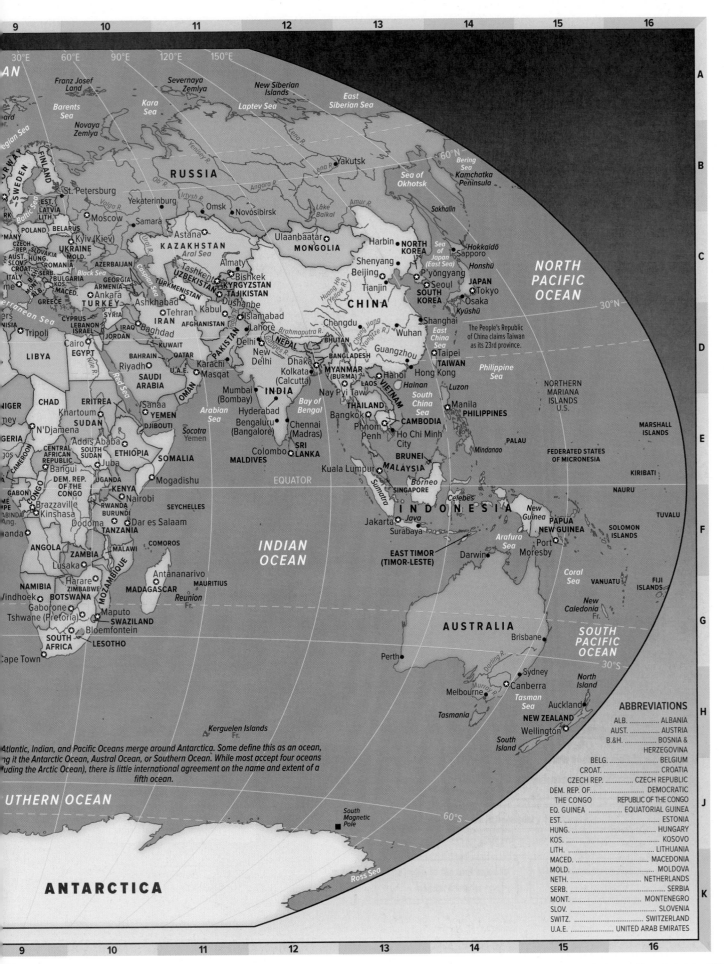

ABBREVIATIONS

ALB.	ALBANIA
AUST.	AUSTRIA
B.&H.	BOSNIA & HERZEGOVINA
BELG.	BELGIUM
CROAT.	CROATIA
CZECH REP.	CZECH REPUBLIC
DEM. REP. OF THE CONGO	DEMOCRATIC REPUBLIC OF THE CONGO
EQ. GUINEA	EQUATORIAL GUINEA
EST.	ESTONIA
HUNG.	HUNGARY
KOS.	KOSOVO
LITH.	LITHUANIA
MACED.	MACEDONIA
MOLD.	MOLDOVA
NETH.	NETHERLANDS
SERB.	SERBIA
MONT.	MONTENEGRO
SLOV.	SLOVENIA
SWITZ.	SWITZERLAND
U.A.E.	UNITED ARAB EMIRATES

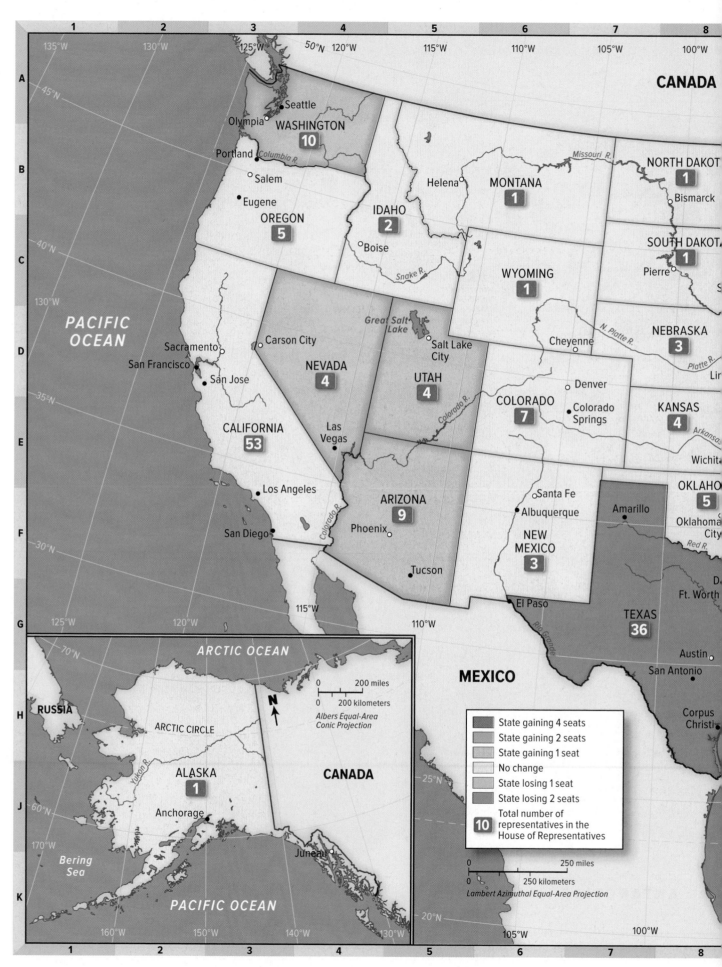

| 1 | 2 | 3 | 4 | 5 | 6 | 7 | 8 |

135°W 130°W 125°W 50°N 120°W 115°W 110°W 105°W 100°W

A

CANADA

Seattle
Olympia **WASHINGTON** **10**
Portland *Columbia R.*

B

Helena **MONTANA** **1**

NORTH DAKOT **1**
Bismarck

Salem
Eugene
OREGON **5**

IDAHO **2**
Boise

Snake R.

SOUTH DAKOT **1**
Pierre

C

WYOMING **1**

Great Salt Lake

NEBRASKA **3**

PACIFIC OCEAN

Sacramento Carson City
San Francisco
San Jose

NEVADA **4**

Salt Lake City
UTAH **4**

Cheyenne *N. Platte R.*
Platte R.

D

CALIFORNIA **53**

Las Vegas

Colorado R.

Denver
COLORADO **7** Colorado Springs

KANSAS **4**
Arkansas
Wichit

E

Los Angeles

Colorado R.

ARIZONA **9**
Phoenix

Santa Fe
Albuquerque

Amarillo

OKLAHO **5**
Oklahoma City

F

San Diego

Tucson

NEW MEXICO **3**

El Paso

Red R.

D.
Ft. Worth

TEXAS **36**

Austin
San Antonio

G

115°W 110°W 105°W

MEXICO

Corpus Christi

H

ARCTIC OCEAN

0 ___ 200 miles
0 ___ 200 kilometers
Albers Equal-Area Conic Projection

N

RUSSIA ARCTIC CIRCLE

Yukon R.

ALASKA **1**

CANADA

25°N

J

60°N 170°W

Anchorage

Juneau

Bering Sea

	State gaining 4 seats
	State gaining 2 seats
	State gaining 1 seat
	No change
	State losing 1 seat
	State losing 2 seats
10	Total number of representatives in the House of Representatives

K

PACIFIC OCEAN

160°W 150°W 140°W 130°W

20°N

0 ___ 250 miles
0 ___ 250 kilometers
Lambert Azimuthal Equal-Area Projection

105°W 100°W

| 1 | 2 | 3 | 4 | 5 | 6 | 7 | 8 |

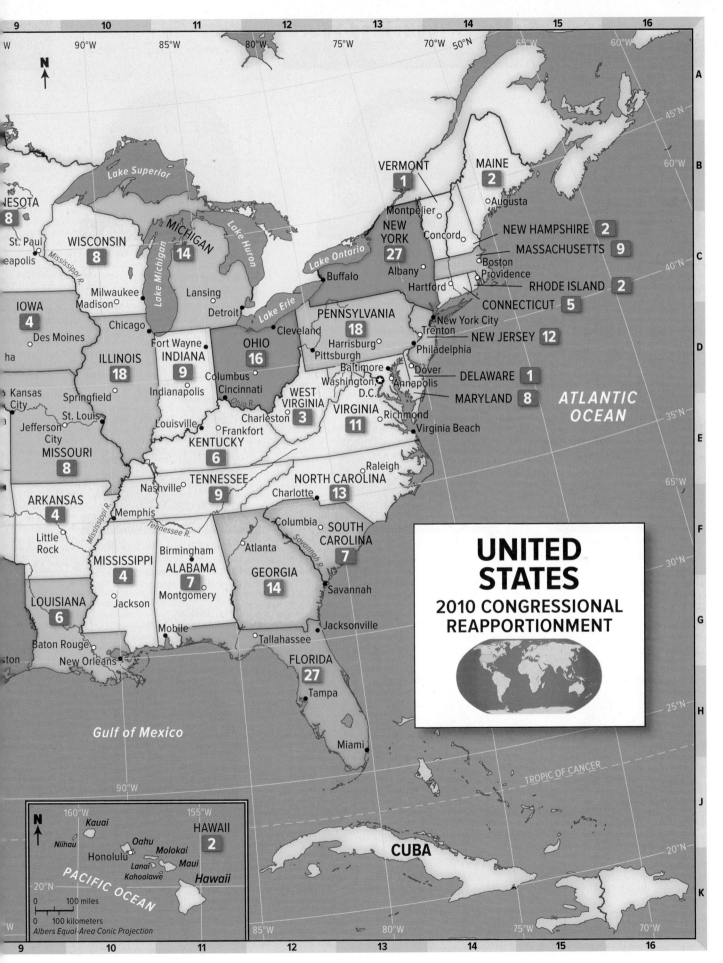

UNITED STATES
2010 CONGRESSIONAL REAPPORTIONMENT

PRESIDENTS OF THE UNITED STATES

**The first Republican Party became today's Democratic Party. Today's Republican Party began in 1854.

1 GEORGE WASHINGTON

Presidential term: 1789–1797
Lived: 1732–1799
Born in: Virginia
Elected from: Virginia
Occupations: Soldier, Planter
Party: None
Vice President: John Adams

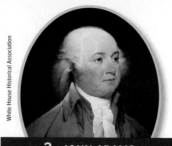

2 JOHN ADAMS

Presidential term: 1797–1801
Lived: 1735–1826
Born in: Massachusetts
Elected from: Massachusetts
Occupations: Teacher, Lawyer
Party: Federalist
Vice President: Thomas Jefferson

3 THOMAS JEFFERSON

Presidential term: 1801–1809
Lived: 1743–1826
Born in: Virginia
Elected from: Virginia
Occupations: Planter, Lawyer
Party: Republican**
Vice Presidents: Aaron Burr, George Clinton

4 JAMES MADISON

Presidential term: 1809–1817
Lived: 1751–1836
Born in: Virginia
Elected from: Virginia
Occupation: Planter
Party: Republican**
Vice Presidents: George Clinton, Elbridge Gerry

5 JAMES MONROE

Presidential term: 1817–1825
Lived: 1758–1831
Born in: Virginia
Elected from: Virginia
Occupation: Lawyer
Party: Republican**
Vice President: Daniel D. Tompkins

6 JOHN QUINCY ADAMS

Presidential term: 1825–1829
Lived: 1767–1848
Born in: Massachusetts
Elected from: Massachusetts
Occupation: Lawyer
Party: Republican**
Vice President: John C. Calhoun

7 ANDREW JACKSON

Presidential term: 1829–1837
Lived: 1767–1845
Born in: South Carolina
Elected from: Tennessee
Occupations: Lawyer, Soldier
Party: Democratic
Vice Presidents: John C. Calhoun, Martin Van Buren

8 MARTIN VAN BUREN

Presidential term: 1837–1841
Lived: 1782–1862
Born in: New York
Elected from: New York
Occupation: Lawyer
Party: Democratic
Vice President: Richard M. Johnson

9 WILLIAM H. HARRISON

Presidential term: 1841
Lived: 1773–1841
Born in: Virginia
Elected from: Ohio
Occupations: Soldier, Planter
Party: Whig
Vice President: John Tyler

10 JOHN TYLER

Presidential term: 1841–1845
Lived: 1790–1862
Born in: Virginia
Elected as V.P. from: Virginia
Succeeded Harrison
Occupation: Lawyer
Party: Whig
Vice President: None

11 JAMES K. POLK

Presidential term: 1845–1849
Lived: 1795–1849
Born in: North Carolina
Elected from: Tennessee
Occupation: Lawyer
Party: Democratic
Vice President: George M. Dallas

12 ZACHARY TAYLOR

Presidential term: 1849–1850
Lived: 1784–1850
Born in: Virginia
Elected from: Louisiana
Occupation: Soldier
Party: Whig
Vice President: Millard Fillmore

13 MILLARD FILLMORE

Presidential term: 1850–1853
Lived: 1800–1874
Born in: New York
Elected as V.P. from: New York
Succeeded Taylor
Occupation: Lawyer
Party: Whig
Vice President: None

14 FRANKLIN PIERCE

Presidential term: 1853–1857
Lived: 1804–1869
Born in: New Hampshire
Elected from: New Hampshire
Occupation: Lawyer
Party: Democratic
Vice President: William R. King

15 JAMES BUCHANAN

Presidential term: 1857–1861
Lived: 1791–1868
Born in: Pennsylvania
Elected from: Pennsylvania
Occupation: Lawyer
Party: Democratic
Vice President: John C. Breckinridge

16 ABRAHAM LINCOLN

Presidential term: 1861–1865
Lived: 1809–1865
Born in: Kentucky
Elected from: Illinois
Occupation: Lawyer
Party: Republican
Vice Presidents: Hannibal Hamlin, Andrew Johnson

17 ANDREW JOHNSON

Presidential term: 1865–1869
Lived: 1808–1875
Born in: North Carolina
Elected as V.P. from: Tennessee
Succeeded Lincoln
Occupation: Tailor
Party: Democratic; National Unionist
Vice President: None

18 ULYSSES S. GRANT

Presidential term: 1869–1877
Lived: 1822–1885
Born in: Ohio
Elected from: Illinois
Occupations: Farmer, Soldier
Party: Republican
Vice Presidents: Schuyler Colfax, Henry Wilson

Presidents of the United States **771**

19 RUTHERFORD B. HAYES

Presidential term: 1877–1881
Lived: 1822–1893
Born in: Ohio
Elected from: Ohio
Occupation: Lawyer
Party: Republican
Vice President: William A. Wheeler

20 JAMES A. GARFIELD

Presidential term: 1881
Lived: 1831–1881
Born in: Ohio
Elected from: Ohio
Occupations: Laborer, Professor
Party: Republican
Vice President: Chester A. Arthur

21 CHESTER A. ARTHUR

Presidential term: 1881–1885
Lived: 1830–1886
Born in: Vermont
Elected as V.P. from: New York
Succeeded Garfield
Occupations: Teacher, Lawyer
Party: Republican
Vice President: None

22 GROVER CLEVELAND

Presidential term: 1885–1889
Lived: 1837–1908
Born in: New Jersey
Elected from: New York
Occupation: Lawyer
Party: Democratic
Vice President: Thomas A. Hendricks

23 BENJAMIN HARRISON

Presidential term: 1889–1893
Lived: 1833–1901
Born in: Ohio
Elected from: Indiana
Occupation: Lawyer
Party: Republican
Vice President: Levi P. Morton

24 GROVER CLEVELAND

Presidential term: 1893–1897
Lived: 1837–1908
Born in: New Jersey
Elected from: New York
Occupation: Lawyer
Party: Democratic
Vice President: Adlai E. Stevenson

25 WILLIAM MCKINLEY

Presidential term: 1897–1901
Lived: 1843–1901
Born in: Ohio
Elected from: Ohio
Occupations: Teacher, Lawyer
Party: Republican
Vice Presidents: Garret Hobart, Theodore Roosevelt

26 THEODORE ROOSEVELT

Presidential term: 1901–1909
Lived: 1858–1919
Born in: New York
Elected as V.P. from: New York
Succeeded McKinley
Occupations: Historian, Rancher
Party: Republican
Vice President: Charles W. Fairbanks

27 WILLIAM H. TAFT

Presidential term: 1909–1913
Lived: 1857–1930
Born in: Ohio
Elected from: Ohio
Occupations: Lawyer
Party: Republican
Vice President: James S. Sherman

28 WOODROW WILSON

Presidential term: 1913–1921
Lived: 1856–1924
Born in: Virginia
Elected from: New Jersey
Occupation: College Professor
Party: Democratic
Vice President: Thomas R. Marshall

29 WARREN G. HARDING

Presidential term: 1921–1923
Lived: 1865–1923
Born in: Ohio
Elected from: Ohio
Occupations: Newspaper Editor, Publisher
Party: Republican
Vice President: Calvin Coolidge

30 CALVIN COOLIDGE

Presidential term: 1923–1929
Lived: 1872–1933
Born in: Vermont
Elected as V.P. from: Massachusetts, Succeeded Harding
Occupation: Lawyer
Party: Republican
Vice President: Charles G. Dawes

31 HERBERT C. HOOVER

Presidential term: 1929–1933
Lived: 1874–1964
Born in: Iowa
Elected from: California
Occupation: Engineer
Party: Republican
Vice President: Charles Curtis

32 FRANKLIN D. ROOSEVELT

Presidential term: 1933–1945
Lived: 1882–1945
Born in: New York
Elected from: New York
Occupation: Lawyer
Party: Democratic
Vice Presidents: John N. Garner, Henry A. Wallace, Harry S. Truman

33 HARRY S. TRUMAN

Presidential term: 1945–1953
Lived: 1884–1972
Born in: Missouri
Elected as V.P. from: Missouri Succeeded Roosevelt
Occupations: Clerk, Farmer
Party: Democratic
Vice President: Alben W. Barkley

34 DWIGHT D. EISENHOWER

Presidential term: 1953–1961
Lived: 1890–1969
Born in: Texas
Elected from: New York
Occupation: Soldier
Party: Republican
Vice President: Richard M. Nixon

35 JOHN F. KENNEDY

Presidential term: 1961–1963
Lived: 1917–1963
Born in: Massachusetts
Elected from: Massachusetts
Occupations: Author, Reporter
Party: Democratic
Vice President: Lyndon B. Johnson

36 LYNDON B. JOHNSON

Presidential term: 1963–1969
Lived: 1908–1973
Born in: Texas
Elected as V.P. from: Texas Succeeded Kennedy
Occupation: Teacher
Party: Democratic
Vice President: Hubert H. Humphrey

PRESIDENTS OF THE UNITED STATES

37 RICHARD M. NIXON

Presidential term: 1969–1974
Lived: 1913–1994
Born in: California
Elected from: New York
Occupation: Lawyer
Party: Republican
Vice Presidents: Spiro T. Agnew, Gerald R. Ford

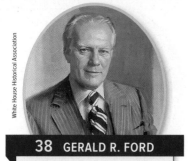

38 GERALD R. FORD

Presidential term: 1974–1977
Lived: 1913–2006
Born in: Nebraska
Appointed as V.P. upon Agnew's resignation; succeeded Nixon
Occupation: Lawyer
Party: Republican
Vice President: Nelson A. Rockefeller

39 JAMES E. CARTER, JR.

Presidential term: 1977–1981
Lived: 1924–
Born in: Georgia
Elected from: Georgia
Occupations: Business, Farmer
Party: Democratic
Vice President: Walter F. Mondale

40 RONALD W. REAGAN

Presidential term: 1981–1989
Lived: 1911–2004
Born in: Illinois
Elected from: California
Occupations: Actor, Lecturer
Party: Republican
Vice President: George H.W. Bush

41 GEORGE H.W. BUSH

Presidential term: 1989–1993
Lived: 1924–
Born in: Massachusetts
Elected from: Texas
Occupation: Business
Party: Republican
Vice President: J. Danforth Quayle

42 WILLIAM J. CLINTON

Presidential term: 1993–2001
Lived: 1946–
Born in: Arkansas
Elected from: Arkansas
Occupation: Lawyer
Party: Democratic
Vice President: Albert Gore, Jr.

43 GEORGE W. BUSH

Presidential term: 2001–2009
Lived: 1946–
Born in: Connecticut
Elected from: Texas
Occupation: Business
Party: Republican
Vice President: Richard B. Cheney

44 BARACK OBAMA

Presidential term: 2009–
Lived: 1961–
Born in: Hawaii
Elected from: Illinois
Occupation: Lawyer
Party: Democratic
Vice President: Joseph R. Biden, Jr.

Chief Justices of the United States

Name and Years of Service	State From Which Appointed	President by Whom Appointed
John Jay (1789–1795)	NY	Washington
John Rutledge (1795)*	SC	Washington
Oliver Ellsworth (1796–1800)	CT	Washington
John Marshall (1801–1835)	VA	John Adams
Roger B. Taney (1836–1864)	MD	Jackson
Salmon P. Chase (1864–1873)	OH	Lincoln
Morrison R. Waite (1874–1888)	OH	Grant
Melville W. Fuller (1888–1910)	IL	Cleveland
Edward D. White (1910–1921)	LA	Taft
William Howard Taft (1921–1930)	CT	Harding
Charles Evans Hughes (1930–1941)	NY	Hoover
Harlan F. Stone (1941–1946)	NY	F.D.Roosevelt
Fred M. Vinson (1946–1953)	KY	Truman
Earl Warren (1953–1969)	CA	Eisenhower
Warren E. Burger (1969–1986)	D.C.	Nixon
William H. Rehnquist (1986– 2005)	AZ	Reagan
John C. Roberts, Jr. (2005–)	D.C.	Bush

* Rutledge was appointed Chief Justice on July 1, 1795, while Congress was not in session. He presided over the August 1795 term of the Supreme Court, but the Senate rejected his appointment on December 15, 1795.

Senate Majority Leaders

Congress	Years	Leaders
62nd	1911–13	Shelby M. Cullom, R–IL
63rd–64th	1913–17	John W. Kern, D–IN
65th	1917–19	Thomas S. Martin, D–VA
66th–67th	1919–24	Henry Cabot Lodge, R–MA
68th–70th	1924–29	Charles Curtis, R–KS
71st–72nd	1929–33	James E. Watson, R–IN
73rd–75th	1933–37	Joseph T. Robinson, D–AR
75th–79th	1937–47	Alben W. Barkley, D–KY
80th	1947–49	Wallace H. White, Jr., R–ME
81st	1949–51	Scott W. Lucas, D–IL
82nd	1951–53	Ernest W. McFarland, D–AZ
83rd	1953–55	Robert A. Taft, R–OH William F. Knowland, R–CA
84th–86th	1955–61	Lyndon B. Johnson, D–TX
87th–94th	1961–77	Mike Mansfield, D–MT
95th–96th	1977–81	Robert C. Byrd, D–WV
97th–98th	1981–85	Howard H. Baker, Jr., R–TN
99th	1985–87	Robert Dole, R–KS
100th	1987–89	Robert C. Byrd, D–WV
101st–103rd	1989–95	George J. Mitchell, D–ME
104th	1995–96	Robert Dole, R–KS
104th–107th	1996–01	Trent Lott, R–MS
107th	2001–03	Tom Daschle, D–SD
108th–109th	2003–07	William H. Frist, R–TN
110th	2007-	Harry Reid, D–NV

Speakers of the House of Representatives

Congress	Years	Speaker	Congress	Years	Speakers
1st	1789–91	Frederick A.C. Muhlenberg, F–PA	41st–43rd	1869–75	James G. Blaine, R–ME
2nd	1791–93	Jonathan Trumbull, F–CT	44th	1875–76	Michael C. Kerr, D–IN
3rd	1793–95	Frederick A.C. Muhlenberg, F–PA	44th–46th	1876–81	Samuel J. Randall, D–PA
4th–5th	1795–99	Jonathan Dayton, F–NJ	47th	1881–83	Joseph Warren Keifer, R–OH
6th	1799–1801	Theodore Sedgwick, F–MA	48th–50th	1883–89	John G. Carlisle, D–KY
7th–9th	1801–07	Nathaniel Macon, D–NC	51st	1889–91	Thomas Brackett Reed, R–ME
10th–11th	1807–11	Joseph B. Varnum, D–MA	52nd–53rd	1891–95	Charles F. Crisp, D–GA
12th–13th	1811–14	Henry Clay, R–KY	54th–55th	1895–99	Thomas Brackett Reed, R–ME
13th	1814–15	Langdon Cheves, D–SC	56th–57th	1899–1903	David B. Henderson, R–IA
14th–16th	1815–20	Henry Clay, R–KY	58th–61st	1903–11	Joseph G. Cannon, R–IL
16th	1820–21	John W. Taylor, D–NY	62nd–65th	1911–19	James B. Clark, D–MO
17th	1821–23	Philip P. Barbour, D–VA	66th–68th	1919–25	Frederick H. Gillet, R–MA
18th	1823–25	Henry Clay, R–KY	69th–71st	1925–31	Nicholas Longworth, R–OH
19th	1825–27	John W. Taylor, D–NY	72nd	1931–33	John Nance Garner, D–TX
20th–23rd	1827–34	Andrew Stevenson, D–VA	73rd	1933–34	Henry T. Rainey, D–IL*
23rd	1834–35	John Bell, W–TN	74th	1935–36	Joseph W. Byrns, D–TN
24th–25th	1835–39	James K. Polk, D–TN	74th–76th	1936–40	William B. Bankhead, D–AL
26th	1839–41	Robert M.T. Hunter, D–VA	76th–79th	1940–47	Sam Rayburn, D–TX
27th	1841–43	John White, W–KY	80th	1947–49	Joseph W. Martin, Jr., R–MA
28th	1843–45	John W. Jones, D–VA	81st–82nd	1949–53	Sam Rayburn, D–TX
29th	1845–47	John W. Davis, D–IN	83rd	1953–55	Joseph W. Martin, Jr., R–MA
30th	1847–49	Robert C. Winthrop, W–MA	84th–87th	1955–61	Sam Rayburn, D–TX
31st	1849–51	Howell Cobb, D–GA	87th–91st	1962–71	John W. McCormack, D–MA
32nd–33rd	1851–55	Linn Boyd, D–KY	92nd–94th	1971–77	Carl B. Albert, D–OK
34th	1855–57	Nathaniel P. Banks, R–MA	95th–99th	1977–87	Thomas P. O'Neill, Jr., D–MA
35th	1857–59	James L. Orr, D–SC	100th–101st	1987–89	Jim C. Wright Jr., D–TX**
36th	1859–61	William Pennington, R–NJ	101st–103rd	1989–95	Thomas S. Foley, D–WA
37th	1861–63	Galusha A. Grow, R–PA	104th–105th	1995–99	Newt Gingrich, R–GA
38th–40th	1863–68	Schuyler Colfax, R–IN	106th–109th	1999–07	J. Dennis Hastert, R–IL
40th	1868–69	Theodore M. Pomeroy, R–NY	110th–111th	2007–2011	Nancy Pelosi, D–CA
			112th–	2011–	John Boehner, R–OH

Party abbreviations: (D) Democrat, (F) Federalist, (R) Republican, (W) Whig

The following case summaries explain the significance of important Supreme Court cases mentioned in the text narrative.

Abington School District v. *Schempp* **(1963)** struck down a Pennsylvania statute requiring public schools in the state to begin each school day with Bible readings. The Supreme Court ruled that the business of government is not to craft and mandate religious exercises. It held that the establishment clause leaves religious beliefs and practices to each individual's choice and commands that government not intrude into this decision-making process.

Abrams v. *United States* **(1919)** sought to decide whether amendments to the Espionage Act were in violation of the First Amendment right to free speech. The defendants were convicted for distributing leaflets that denounced the United States' action in sending troops into Russia and urged citizens to stop the production of materials essential for war. The majority opinion upheld the guilty verdict, deciding that the right to free speech was not violated in this case.

Adarand Constructors, Inc. v. *Peña* **(1995)** announced a major shift in the way the Court viewed federal affirmative action programs. Before this case, courts did not give the same level of scrutiny to federal programs as was given to state and local programs. After this case, all government affirmative action programs must be justified by a compelling interest.

Alden v. *Maine* **(1999)** decided that a group of probation officers may not sue the state that employed them over a matter of violations to the 1938 Fair Labor Standards Act. The Eleventh Amendment gives provisions for states' immunity from being prosecuted in a federal court. In a close decision, the Court held that the immunity could be extended to state courts, meaning that a state could not be sued in its own state court.

Allegheny County v. *ACLU* **(1989)** held that a crèche (a Nativity scene) by a banner reading "Glory to God in the Highest" and centrally displayed in a city/county building violated the establishment clause because it endorsed a particular religious viewpoint.

Arkansas Educational Television v. *Forbes* **(1998)** held that the decision of a state-owned public television broadcaster to deny a third party candidate participation in a televised debate did not violate the candidate's First Amendment right to free speech. The Court maintained that, because the broadcasters reserved participation for candidates within a certain district, the debate could not be viewed as a public forum and therefore did not impinge upon Forbes's right to free speech.

Austin v. *Michigan Chamber of Commerce* **(1990)** decided that the Michigan Campaign Finance Act, which specified that corporations may not use general funds to support or promote a candidate for state office but may set up an independent fund for that purpose, did not violate the First Amendment right to free speech. It also ruled that the Michigan Chamber of Commerce was not exempt from the provisions of the Act on the grounds of being a "nonprofit ideological corporation" since it functioned as a business and interacted closely with business corporations.

Baker v. *Carr* **(1962)** established that federal courts can hear suits seeking to force a state to redraw electoral districts. In this case, the plaintiffs wanted the population of each district to be roughly equal to the population in all other districts. They claimed that where district populations differ, such an imbalance denied them equal protection of the laws. Before this case, it was thought that federal courts had no authority under the Constitution to decide issues of malapportionment.

Barron v. *Baltimore* **(1833)** held that the Fifth Amendment's provision that the government must pay if it takes private property did not apply to state governments. At the time, the decision supported the view that the Bill of Rights applied only to the federal government. However, the Supreme Court established that most of the rights contained in the

Bill of Rights apply to all levels of government—states, counties, cities, towns, and agencies such as local school boards. This case has been effectively overruled by cases that apply Fourteenth Amendment protections to the Bill of Rights.

***Bethel School District v. Fraser* (1986)** retreated from the expansive view of the First Amendment rights of public school students found in *Tinker* v. *Des Moines School District*. Here the Supreme Court held that a public high school student did not have a First Amendment right to give a sexually suggestive speech at a school-sponsored assembly and upheld the three-day suspension of the student who made the speech. In deciding the case, the Court made it clear that students have only a limited right of free speech. According to the Court, a school does not have to tolerate student speech that is inconsistent with its educational mission, even if the same speech would be protected elsewhere.

***Betts* v. *Brady* (1942)** refused to extend the holding of *Powell* v. *Alabama* to noncapital, i.e., nondeath penalty, cases. The Supreme Court held that poor defendants in noncapital cases are not entitled to an attorney at government expense. This case was overturned by *Gideon* v. *Wainright*.

***Board of Education* v. *Earls* (2002)** held that the Tecumseh, Oklahoma, School District's requirement of drug testing for all students wishing to participate in an extracurricular activity did not violate Fourth Amendment protections from unreasonable search and seizure, even if the district did not have evidence to suggest a particular drug problem among the student population. The decision maintained that the right to privacy is limited for students and that the school district's actions were a reasonable means of attaining its goal of detecting and deterring drug use among its students.

***Boumediene* v. *Bush* (2008)** addressed the rights of foreigners detained as terrorist suspects at Guantanamo Bay military base. The Court ruled that such suspects have the same habeas corpus rights under the Constitution as citizens; that is, they have the right to challenge their detention in American courts. Specifically, the Court ruled that operation of the military tribunals set up by the 2006 Military Commissions Act does not suspend their habeus corpus rights.

***Brandenburg v. Ohio* (1969)** overruled *Whitney* v. *California*. In this case, the Supreme Court held that laws that punish people for advocating social change through violence violate the First Amendment. The Court explained that advocacy of an idea, even an idea of violence, is protected by the First Amendment. What is not protected is inciting people to engage in immediate lawless conduct. The Court then reversed the conviction of a member of the Ku Klux Klan for holding a rally and making strong derogatory statements against African Americans and Jews.

***Branzburg* v. *Hayes* (1972)** established that the press may be required to give information in its possession to law enforcement authorities. In this case, the Supreme Court upheld findings of contempt against three journalists who refused to testify before grand juries investigating criminal activity. The Court recognized that an effective press must be able to keep the identity of news sources confidential but concluded that news-source confidentiality must yield to the needs of law enforcement.

***Brown v. Board of Education* (1954)** overruled *Plessy* v. *Ferguson* (1896) and abandoned the "separate but equal" doctrine in the context of public schools. In deciding this case, the Supreme Court rejected the idea that truly equivalent but separate schools for African American and white students would be constitutional. The Court then held that racial segregation in public schools violates the equal protection clause because it is inherently unequal. In practical terms, the Court's holding in this case has been extended beyond public education to virtually all public accommodations and activities.

***Buckley* v. *Valeo* (1976)** clarified the bearing that campaign finance laws had on the First Amendment's protection of free speech and association. In 1975 Congress attempted to eliminate sources of political campaign corruption with a law regulating and limiting campaign funds. The Court ruled that limiting the dollar amount contributed by individuals was allowable because the Court said it strengthened the "integrity of our system of representative democracy." The Court decided that other restrictions, such as limiting the total amount of money spent on a campaign, were not enough of a threat to government interests to justify limiting free speech.

Supreme Court Case Summaries

Bush v. Gore (2000) found that a manual recount of disputed presidential ballots in Florida lacked a uniform standard of judging a voter's intent, thus violating the equal protection clause of the Constitution. The court also ruled that there was not enough time to conduct a new manual recount that would pass constitutional standards. The case arose when Republican candidate George W. Bush asked the Court to stop a hand recount. This decision ensured that Bush would receive Florida's electoral votes and win the election.

Bush v. Palm Beach Canvassing Board (2000) was the first time the Supreme Court agreed to hear a case involving a presidential election. The Court reviewed a decision by the Florida Supreme Court to extend the deadline for recounting votes and returned the case to the Florida court for a better explanation of its reasoning.

Chisholm v. Georgia (1793) stripped the immunity of the states to lawsuits in federal court. The Supreme Court held that a citizen of one state could sue another state in federal court without that state consenting to the suit. The Court's decision created a furor and led to the adoption of the Eleventh Amendment, which protected states from federal court suits by citizens of other states. In 1890, in *Hans* v. *Louisiana*, the Court extended this immunity; unless a state agreed, it could not be sued in federal court by its own citizens.

Citizens United v. Federal Election Commission (2010) dealt with the issue of free speech as it applies to spending money by a corporation to advocate for or against a candidate. Citizens United created a film that portrayed Hillary Clinton as an unfit candidate for president. The Bipartisan Campaign Reform Act (BCRA) said that such electioneering advertisements could not be aired in close proximity to an election. Citizens United argued that the BCRA should not apply to their film, and said parts of the act were unconstitutional. The Supreme Court upheld the constitutionality of BCRA's donor disclosure requirement, but also held that the First Amendment barred restrictions on corporate funding of independent political broadcasts.

Clinton v. City of New York (1998) consolidated two challenges to line-item vetoes President Bill Clinton issued in 1997. The Court ruled 6 to 3 in favor of New York City hospitals and Idaho's Snake River Potato Growers, who challenged separate vetoes. Justice John Stevens said Congress could not endow the president with power to alter laws without amending the Constitution.

Colorado Republican Federal Campaign Committee v. Federal Election Commission (1996) ruled that the Party Expenditure Provision of the Federal Election Campaign Act of 1971 (FECA), which limits spending by a political party on the campaign of a particular candidate, violated the First Amendment on its face and as it applied to this case. Because the Colorado Republican Committee used its funds in opposition of a Democratic candidate but was not affiliated with any specific candidate's campaign, the provision of FECA should not apply.

Coyle v. Smith (1911) held that Congress had overreached its power when, in admitting Oklahoma to the Union, it set a temporary location for the state capital and determined that the change to another location could not occur until 1913. The Court determined that the state had the right to set its own capital at the time of its own choosing.

Cox v. New Hampshire (1941) upheld the convictions of 68 Jehovah's Witnesses for marching on a public sidewalk without a permit. The Court stressed that the defendants were not being punished for distributing religious leaflets or inviting passersby to a meeting of the religious group. The Court explained that local government officials have the authority to establish time, place, and manner restrictions on the use of public property for expressive purposes and that requiring a permit is a reasonable way for local officials to ensure that marching is not disruptive.

Crawford v. Marion County Election Board (2008) dealt with the constitutionality of I.D. requirements for voters in Indiana. While opponents argued that this requirement would be a particular burden on low-income and minority voters who historically tend to vote with the Democratic Party, the Supreme Court's majority decision ruled that the law was not discriminatory and the burden on voters was insignificant. It held that the I.D. requirement was an acceptable means for the state of Indiana to accomplish its goal of preventing voter fraud.

De Jonge v. *Oregon* **(1937)** reinforced earlier Supreme Court holdings that the First Amendment's protection of peaceable assembly and association must be honored by the states. In this case, Dirk De Jonge, a member of the Communist Party, was convicted and sentenced to a seven-year prison term for speaking at a public meeting of the party. In reversing the conviction, the Court held that merely speaking at a meeting of the Communist Party was protected by the First Amendment.

District of Columbia v. *Heller* **(2008)** held that a 1975 law banning handguns for most Washington, D.C., residents was unconstitutional. It was the first time that the Court ruled a law unconstitutional because it violated the Second Amendment. The Court said that the Second Amendment right to bear arms applies to individuals, not just to state militias. The Court said that, while the right to bear arms is not unlimited, the District law tried to ban an entire class of firearms that Americans often choose for the lawful purpose of self-defense.

Dred Scott v. *Sandford* **(1857)** was decided before the Fourteenth Amendment was added to the Constitution. (The Fourteenth Amendment provides that anyone who is born or naturalized in the United States is a citizen of the nation and of his or her state of residence.) In this case, the Supreme Court held that an enslaved person was property, not a citizen, and thus had no rights under the Constitution. The Court's decision was met with outrage in the North and was a prime factor precipitating the Civil War.

Engel v. *Vitale* **(1962)** held that the establishment clause (U.S. Const., Amend. I, cl. 1) was violated by a public school district's practice of starting each school day with a prayer that began: "Almighty God, we acknowledge our dependence upon Thee." The Supreme Court explained that under the establishment clause, religion is a personal matter to be guided by individual choice. In short, the Court concluded that the establishment clause was intended to keep government out of religion, thus making it unacceptable for government to compose prayers for anyone to recite.

Escobedo v. *Illinois* **(1964)** was the forerunner of *Miranda* v. *Arizona*. In this case, the Supreme Court reversed the murder conviction of Danny Escobedo, who gave damaging statements to police during questioning. Throughout the questioning, Escobedo repeatedly but unsuccessfully asked to see his attorney. In holding that Escobedo's Sixth Amendment right to counsel had been violated, the Court explained that an attorney could have assisted Escobedo in invoking his Fifth Amendment privilege against self-incrimination. In other words, an attorney could have told Escobedo when to keep quiet.

Everson v. *Board of Education* **(1947)** concluded that a New Jersey township had not violated the establishment clause when it reimbursed parents for the cost of sending their children to school on public transportation. The reimbursement was made to all parents even if their children attended religious schools. The Supreme Court explained that the practice served the public purpose of getting children to school safely; was neutrally administered, neither favoring nor disfavoring anyone on the basis of their religious views; and was not intended to advance religion.

Ewing v. *California* **(2003)** addressed the constitutionality of three-strikes laws. Gary Ewing was convicted of stealing three golf clubs while on parole from a 9-year prison term. California's three-strike law meant that Ewing would receive a sentence of 25 years to life in prison, but Ewing believed this an unreasonable punishment for his crime and appealed the case, citing the Eighth Amendment right of protection from cruel and unusual punishment. The Supreme Court, however, upheld California's three-strike law. It determined that such laws are acceptable means for states to deter and incapacitate repeat felons.

Ex parte Endo **(1944)** arose out of the detainment of Japanese Americans living on the West Coast during World War II when Japan was an enemy of the United States. The case began when a citizen of Japanese descent, whose loyalty to the United States was never in doubt, asked to be released from a relocation camp. In this case, the Supreme Court held that the federal government has no constitutional basis to detain a loyal citizen.

Ex parte Milligan **(1866)** established the primacy of the judicial branch in the absence of a bona fide national emergency. The case concerned the military trial of Lambdin Milligan, who was accused by the Army of conspiring to liberate Confederate prisoners from Union prisons during the Civil War. The Supreme Court held that the Constitution prohibits the federal government from trying a civilian in a military court as long as civilian courts are open and available.

Furman v. *Georgia* **(1972)** invalidated imposition of the death penalty under state laws then in place. The Supreme Court explained that existing death penalty statutes did not give juries enough guidance in deciding whether or not to impose the death penalty; the result was that the death penalty in many cases was imposed arbitrarily, i.e., without a reasonable basis in the facts and circumstances of the offender or the crime.

Gibbons v. *Ogden* **(1824)** made it clear that the authority of Congress to regulate interstate commerce (U.S. Const., Art. I, sec. 8, cl. 3) includes the authority to regulate intrastate commercial activity that bears on, or relates to, interstate commerce. Before this decision, it was thought that the Constitution would permit a state to close its borders to interstate commercial activity—which, in effect, would stop such activity in its tracks. This case says that only Congress can regulate commercial activity that has both intrastate and interstate dimensions.

Gideon v. *Wainwright* **(1963)** overruled *Betts* v. *Brady* (see above) and held for the first time that poor defendants in criminal cases have the right to a state-paid attorney under the Sixth Amendment. This rule has been refined to apply when the defendant, if convicted, can be sentenced to more than six months in jail.

Gitlow v. *New York* **(1925)** upheld a conviction for publishing articles that advocated the violent overthrow of democratic governments, in general, and the U.S. government, in particular. In upholding the defendant's conviction under New York's so-called criminal anarchy law, the Court again rejected a free-speech defense while recognizing that the right of free speech is fundamental and that a state legislature is entitled to take steps to prevent public disorder.

Graham v. *Florida* **(2010)** overturned the decision of a lower court to sentence a minor to life imprisonment without parole for a nonhomicidal crime. The defendant was a repeat offender, but he claimed that such a sentence for an armed robbery conviction was a cruel and unusual punishment that violated his Eighth Amendment rights. The Court's ruling followed the precedent of earlier cases that determined juvenile offenders to be less culpable. It therefore held that a life sentence for a nonhomicidal crime must be considered a violation of the Eighth Amendment as it applies to juveniles.

Gratz v. *Bollinger* **(2003)** ruled that the use of an admission system that gave points to applicants based on their race violated the Equal Protection Clause of the Fourteenth Amendment and Title VI of the 1964 Civil Rights Act. (Compare this with the *Grutter* v. *Bollinger* ruling discussed below.)

Gregg v. *Georgia* **(1976)** specifically held that the death penalty is not necessarily unconstitutional. The Supreme Court went on to uphold the Georgia death penalty statute, explaining that the law provided sufficient safeguards to ensure that the penalty was imposed only as a rational response to the facts of the crime and the circumstances of the offender.

Griswold v. *Connecticut* **(1965)** established the idea that, while the Constitution does not explicitly provide for the protection of privacy within the marital relationship, provisions within the Bill of Rights collectively form a given right to privacy. Griswold, the director of the Planned Parenthood League of Connecticut, was originally prosecuted for counseling married couples on the use of contraceptives, which was at that time against Connecticut Law. The Supreme Court ruled that the Bill of Rights did provide for the right to privacy within marital relationships, making the Connecticut law null and void.

Grutter v. *Bollinger* **(2003)** upheld the University of Michigan Law School's consideration of race as a holistic factor in its admissions policy. The Court ruled that the procedure's narrow focus did not violate the Equal Protection Clause of the Fourteenth Amendment.

Guinn v. *United States* **(1915)** decided that the grandfather clause, which said that only those whose grandfathers had voted before 1867 would be allowed to vote without paying a poll tax or passing a literacy test, was unconstitutional. Such laws were found to be in direct violation of the Fifteenth Amendment, which extended suffrage to African Americans, almost none of whom would be able to vote under the grandfather cause.

Hamdan v. *Rumsfeld* **(2006)** ruled that the executive branch did not have the authority to set up special military commissions to try terrorist suspects without the authorization of Congress. As a result, Congress passed the Military Commissions Act, which provided for special military tribunals to try these suspects. The law, however, stated that noncitizens would not have the right to file writs of habeas corpus. (See *Boumediene* v. *Bush* for the Court's later ruling on that provision.)

Hamdi v. *Rumsfeld* **(2004)** dealt with the case of an American citizen who was held without trial after being charged as an "enemy combatant" in Afghanistan. Hamdi's attorney filed a habeas corpus petition, arguing that the imprisonment violated Hamdi's Fifth Amendment right to due process. After a district court ruled in Hamdi's favor, the Fourth Circuit Court of Appeals reversed the decision, stating that the executive and legislative branches have power over the judicial branch in wartime matters. The Supreme Court, however, disagreed, finding the imprisonment of a U.S. citizen without due process to be unconstitutional regardless of the involvement of other branches of government in this case.

Harper v. *Virginia Board of Elections* **(1966)** decided that poll taxes were unconstitutional. The Court ruled that a poll tax, which made voter affluence a prerequisite to voting, violated equal protection under the Fourteenth Amendment. In this decision, the Court also found that what constituted "equal protection" could change over time.

Hazelwood School District v. *Kuhlmeier* **(1988)** held that public school officials are in control of the editorial content of a student newspaper published as part of the school's journalism curriculum. Students' First Amendment rights do not include deciding what will and will not be published in a student newspaper that is tied to the school's curriculum.

Heart of Atlanta Motel, Inc. v. *United States* **(1964)** upheld the Civil Rights Act of 1964, which prohibits racial discrimination by those who provide goods, services, and facilities to the public. The Georgia motel in the case drew its business from other states but refused to rent rooms to African Americans. The Supreme Court explained that Congress had the authority to ban such discrimination under both the equal protection clause (U.S. Const., Amend. XIV, sec. 1) and the commerce clause (U.S. Const., Art. I, sec. 8, cl. 3).

Hernandez v. *Texas* **(1954)** decided by a unanimous vote that Mexican Americans must receive equal protection under the Fourteenth Amendment and must be treated as a special class when evidence showed a clear history of discrimination against them. Until that time it was commonly held that Mexican Americans were a "white" race, and therefore not a special class. When Hernandez was convicted of murder by an all-white jury, he appealed the case, arguing that Mexican Americans had not served on a jury in his county in the past 25 years, proving that they were being purposely excluded as a group. The Supreme Court agreed, concluding that the Fourteenth Amendment must apply to all groups and not adhere to a "two-class" theory.

Hutchinson v. *Proxmire* **(1979)** articulated the limits of the speech and debate clause (U.S. Const., Art. I, sec. 6), which provides that members of Congress cannot be held criminally or civilly liable for statements made in either house. In this case, however, the Supreme Court held that the clause did not protect Wisconsin Senator William Proxmire from being sued for libel. In a press release, at a news conference, and on television news programs, Proxmire claimed that federal funds were wasted in paying for a study of aggressive behavior in animals. Had the senator limited his remarks to a speech on the Senate floor, the speech and debate clause would have protected him from the libel suit; he lost the protection of the clause by making his remarks outside of Congress.

In re Gault **(1967)** ruled that juveniles have the same right to due process as adults under the Fourteenth Amendment. Gault was arrested and held in juvenile detention after being accused of making an obscene phone call. His parents did not receive notice of his arrest. Gault was sentenced to six years in detention, much more than the maximum sentence for an adult convicted of the same crime. When the case was appealed, the Supreme Court deliberated over whether a juvenile had the same rights as an adult in the criminal justice system and decided that the Fourteenth Amendment did indeed extend these rights, making Gault's previous trial and sentencing unconstitutional.

INS v. *Chadha* **(1983)** held that legislative action by Congress must comply with the Constitution. In this case, the Supreme Court concluded that the Constitution did not permit one house, acting unilaterally, to override the decision of the attorney general allowing an alien, Chadha, to remain in the United States. The Court said that the attorney general's decision could be set aside only by legislation passed by both houses and signed into law by the president or passed a second time by a two-thirds vote of both houses in the event of a presidential veto.

Kelo v. *City of New London* **(2005)** considered the meaning of "public use" under the Fifth Amendment concerning seizure of private property by the local government. The city of New London, Connecticut, used eminent domain to take private property with the intention of selling the land to private developers as part of a plan to help the struggling local economy. The owners of the property sued, arguing that selling the land to private developers could not qualify as "public use," which was specified in the takings clause of the Fifth Amendment as a condition that must be met for the government to take the property. The Supreme Court ruled in favor of New London, finding that the purpose of the property seizure did not need to be public in a literal sense if it was part of a larger plan to benefit the public as a whole.

Kiobel v. *Royal Dutch Petroleum* **(2013)** dealt with an issue of jurisdiction: whether U.S. courts could decide a case in which neither party is a U.S. citizen or corporation and the infraction did not occur in U.S. territory. The petitioners sought to sue the Royal Dutch Petroleum Company on the grounds that they believed the company was complicit in human rights violations by the Nigerian government. They believed they had a right to a trial in the United States under the Alien Tort Statute. After several dismissals and appeals, the Supreme Court heard the case and ultimately concluded that the United States cannot hear cases of this kind under the Alien Tort Statute, because it has no jurisdiction to decide cases of international justice. This set a new precedent under which the United States would not seek to become involved in settling international

human rights disputes in which the United States has no specific interest. However, three concurring opinions indicate that some issues in the case may be open to further consideration in the future.

Korematsu v. *United States* **(1944)** upheld the federal government's authority to exclude Japanese Americans, many of whom were citizens, from designated military areas that included almost the entire West Coast. The government defended the so-called exclusion orders as a necessary response to Japan's attack on Pearl Harbor, which widened World War II from a war against Germany to one against Japan as well. However, in upholding the exclusion orders, the Supreme Court established that courts will subject government actions that discriminate on the basis of race to the most exacting scrutiny, often referred to as strict scrutiny.

Lau v. *Nichols* **(1974)** held that the Civil Rights Act of 1964 was violated when San Francisco's public school district refused to instruct children of Chinese ancestry in English. The Supreme Court explained that the Chinese students in the case were not receiving the same education as non-Chinese students as required by the Civil Rights Act, which the school district had agreed to abide by in exchange for receiving federal funds.

League of United Latin American Citizens v. *Perry* **(2006)** examined the constitutionality of a state legislature redrawing electoral boundaries in a way that citizens viewed as discriminatory. In 2003 the Texas legislature redrew electoral boundaries based on population data from the 2000 census. The new districts decreased minority voting strength, and the League of United Latin American Citizens sued, arguing that the rights of minority citizens under the Voting Rights Act had been violated. The Supreme Court agreed that the redrawing of boundaries in this case violated the Voting Rights Act by making it impossible for minority citizens to elect a candidate of their choosing. However, they found no breech in the constitutionality of a state legislature redrawing electoral boundaries as often as it sees fit, so long as it does so at least every ten years.

Lemon v. *Kurtzman* **(1971)** established a three-part test for determining if a particular government action violates the establishment clause (U.S. Const., Amend. I, cl. 1). First, the test asks if the government action has a primary *purpose* of advancing religion; second, if the action has a primary *effect* of advancing religion; and third, if the action risks entangling government in religious affairs or vice versa. The establishment clause is violated if the action fails any one of these tests.

Loving v. *Virginia* **(1967)** argued that Virginia's antimiscegenation statute, which made the interracial marriage of Mildred Jeter and Richard Loving illegal in their state, was unconstitutional. The Supreme Court ruled that this law had no purpose other than to discriminate based on race and that such laws should be subject to "rigid scrutiny." The Court further argued that under the protections of the Fourteenth Amendment, the Constitution grants the freedom of an individual to marry a person of another race if he or she so chooses and that this right may not be infringed upon by the state.

Lynch v. *Donnelly* **(1984)** held that a city-owned crèche (a Nativity scene) included in a Christmas display that also included reindeer, a Santa Claus, and a Christmas tree did not endorse a particular religious viewpoint and thus did not violate the establishment clause (U.S. Const., Amend. I, cl. 1). In the Supreme Court's view, the display was a secular holiday display.

Mapp v. *Ohio* **(1961)** extended the exclusionary rule announced in *Weeks* v. *United States* to state and local law-enforcement officers. After this case, evidence seized in violation of the Fourth Amendment could not be used by the prosecution as evidence of a defendant's guilt in any court—federal, state, or local.

Marbury v. *Madison* **(1803)** established one of the most significant principles of American constitutional law. In this case, the Supreme Court held that it is the Court itself that has the final say on what the Constitution means. It is also the Supreme Court that has the final say in whether or not an act of government—legislative or executive at the federal, state, or local level—violates the Constitution.

McCreary County v. *ACLU* **(2005)** found that the display of the Ten Commandments at courthouses in Kentucky violated the First Amendment's establishment clause. The Court held that the displays could not considered to serve any purpose other than the furthering of a particular

religion and would therefore give the impression that the government was endorsing that religion.

McCulloch v. *Maryland* **(1819)** established the foundation for the expansive authority of Congress. The Supreme Court held that the necessary and proper clause (U.S. Const., Art. I, sec. 8, cl. 18) allows Congress to do more than the Constitution expressly authorizes it to do. This case says that Congress can enact nearly any law that will help achieve any of the ends set forth in Article I, Section 8. For example, Congress has the express authority to regulate interstate commerce; the necessary and proper clause permits Congress to do so in ways not specified in the Constitution.

McDonald v. *City of Chicago* **(2010)** upheld the decision *of District of Columbia* v. *Heller*, which found a handgun ban in the District of Columbia to be a violation of the Second Amendment. In this case, the Court decided that the protections of the Second Amendment also extend to the states, although the justices voting in McDonald's favor disagreed on which clause of the Fourteenth Amendment granted this protection.

Medellín v. *Texas* **(2008)** held that the Vienna Convention was not binding upon state courts, as Congress had not enacted it as law. In this case, Medellín appealed his conviction and death sentence, arguing that the court had violated terms of the Vienna Convention by not allowing him to contact his consulate. The International Court of Justice ruled that the United States had violated the treaty and that the case must be reconsidered, and the president instructed the courts to comply with this ruling. The Supreme Court, however, found that the president had no authority in this matter and that the Constitution does not require states to comply with treaty obligations of the United States when the treaty is not self-executing.

Miller v. *Alabama* **(2012)** argued that a mandatory life sentence without the possibility of parole was a cruel and unusual punishment when applied to a fourteen-year-old child. Two companion cases were considered, addressing the sentencing of both defendants who were charged with capital murder at the age of fourteen. The Supreme Court ruled that sentencing for children is different from sentencing for adults and that a mandatory lifetime prison sentence without parole was a mandatory violation of the Eighth Amendment when applied to children.

***Minersville School District* v. *Gobitis* (1940)** held that a state could require public school students to salute the American flag. The Supreme Court explained that a general law (the flag-salute law in this case), not intended to restrict or promote religious views, must be obeyed. This decision did not last long; it was overruled three years later by *West Virginia State Board of Education* v. *Barnette*, discussed below.

***Miranda* v. *Arizona* (1966)** held that a person in police custody cannot be questioned unless told that: 1) he or she has the right to remain silent, 2) he or she has the right to an attorney (at government expense if the person is unable to pay), and 3) that anything the person says after acknowledging that he or she understands these rights can be used as evidence of guilt at trial. These advisements constitute the well-known *Miranda* warnings and operate to ensure that a person in custody will not unknowingly give up the Fifth Amendment's protection against self-incrimination.

***Morse* v. *Frederick* (2007)** outlined the limits of free speech in a school setting. The Court ruled that schools have a reasonable right to ban student speech that promotes drugs, because it undermines the schools' mission to discourage drug use. This decision emphasized that the right to free speech, like other rights, is limited as it applies to students.

***Myers* v. *United States* (1926)** overturned an 1876 law that said that postmasters of the first, second, and third classes shall be appointed to and may be removed from office by the president only with the approval of the Senate. When President Woodrow Wilson removed Myers from his position as postmaster first class without Senate approval, Myers sued, but the Supreme Court ruled that the 1876 law was unconstitutional. The Court found that intention of the First Congress was to give the president alone the power to appoint and remove officials.

***National Federation of Independent Business* v. *Sebelius* (2012)** upheld the power of Congress to enact the Affordable Healthcare Act, one of the most controversial laws in history. Plaintiffs argued that the law, which would require most Americans to purchase some form of health insurance by 2014, exceeded the enumerated powers of Congress and interfered with states' sovereignty. The Court ruled that the law was not constitutional under the commerce clause, but upheld it as an exercise of Congress's power to tax. However, the Court invalidated the law's Medicaid expansion provision because it was unconstitutionally coercive.

***Near* v. *Minnesota* (1931)** established the prior restraint doctrine. The doctrine protects the press (broadly defined to include newspapers, television and radio, filmmakers and distributors, etc.) from government attempts to block publication. Except in extraordinary circumstances, the press must be allowed to publish. If what is published turns out to be unprotected by the First Amendment, the government can take appropriate action.

***Nebraska Press Association* v. *Stuart* (1976)** struck down a judge's order that the press covering a mass murder case could not report any facts that strongly implicated the defendant. The Supreme Court held that the press cannot be prohibited from reporting what transpires in a courtroom and that, in this case, there were no facts suggesting that press coverage would infringe upon the defendant's Sixth Amendment right to a fair trial.

***New Jersey* v. *T.L.O.* (1985)** held that public school officials can search a student's property, such as a purse, for evidence of wrongdoing (i.e., violating the school's no-smoking policy) without having probable cause to believe that the student did anything wrong. It is enough, said the Supreme Court, if school officials have reason to believe that the student violated a rule and that the search will confirm or dispel that suspicion. The Court agreed, however, that the Fourth Amendment protects public school students from unreasonable searches and seizures but not to the degree that adults are protected.

***New York Times Co.* v. *Sullivan* (1964)** extended the protections afforded to the press by the free press clause (U.S. Const., Amend. I). In this case, the Supreme Court held that a public official or public figure suing a publisher for libel (i.e., defamation) must prove that the publisher published a story that he or she knew was false or published the story in reckless disregard of its truth or falsity, which means that the publisher did not take professionally adequate steps to determine the story's truth or falsity.

New York Times Co. v. United States (The Pentagon Papers Case) (1971) reaffirmed the prior restraint doctrine established in *Near* v. *Minnesota* (see above). In this case, the Supreme Court refused to halt publication of the Pentagon Papers, which gave a detailed critical account of the United States's involvement in the Vietnam War. There was, however, considerable disagreement on the Court with four dissenting justices voting to halt publication temporarily to allow the president to show that the documents jeopardized the war effort.

Oregon v. Mathiason (1977) ruled that incriminating evidence obtained during an informal interview may be used against a suspect even if the Miranda rights have not been read to the suspect prior to the questioning. The decision in *Miranda* v. *Arizona* required law enforcement officers to read a citizen his rights only if he was being "deprived of his freedom of action in any significant way." The Court held that, even if Mathiason was coercively pressured by police during his interview, he came to the station under his own free will and was free to leave at any time, so the Miranda rights did not apply.

Palko v. Connecticut (1937) held that protection against double jeopardy did not apply in the case of Frank Palko, who was found charged with first-degree murder and found guilty of second-degree murder, but then convicted of first-degree murder when the state of Connecticut appealed the case, changing his sentence from life imprisonment to the death sentence. The Supreme Court ruled that the due process clause of the Fourteenth Amendment did not apply, as it was intended only to extend to the states the most basic rights guaranteed in the Bill of Rights and did not include protection from double jeopardy. This case was later overturned by *Benton* v. *Maryland* (1969).

Parents Involved in Community Schools v. Seattle School District No. 1, et al (2007) held that public schools could not assign students purely for the purpose of achieving racial integration. In the Court's 5–4 ruling, the majority opinion argued that any school assignment plan that used race as a factor had to be very narrowly tailored and that

factors besides race are involved in achieving a diverse student body.

Personnel Administrator of Massachusetts v. Feeney (1979) found a Massachusetts law that gave hiring preference for civil service positions to veterans who had been honorably discharged to be constitutional. The plaintiff was a female who had scored higher on civil service examinations than many males with veteran service and believed that the law therefore discriminated unfairly against women. The Court decided that the purpose of the law was "legitimate and worthy" and that veteran status did not preclude women, so the distinction was between veterans and nonveterans, not between sexes. Therefore the law could not be construed as discriminating against women, as men who were not veterans were at an equal disadvantage.

Plessy v. Ferguson (1896) upheld the "separate but equal" doctrine used by Southern states to perpetuate segregation after the Civil War officially ended it. At issue was a Louisiana law requiring passenger trains to have "equal but separate accommodations for the white and colored races." The Court held that the Fourteenth Amendment's equal protection clause required only equal public facilities for the two races, not equal access to the same facilities. This case was overruled by *Brown* v. *Board of Education* (1954) (see above).

Plyler v. Doe (1982) ruled that a Texas education law withholding funds from school districts for educating children of illegal aliens was unconstitutional. Under the Fourteenth Amendment, the Court reasoned, people, including illegal aliens and their children, are afforded protection. As such, the state of Texas had no right to withhold funding for the education of these children. Further, the Court could not find evidence that the law was serving any "compelling state interest," and it struck down the regulation.

Powell v. Alabama (1932) established that the due process clause of the Fourteenth Amendment guarantees the defendant in any death penalty case the right to an attorney. Accordingly, states are required to provide an attorney to poor defendants who face the death penalty if convicted. Since *Gideon* v. *Wainright* and *Argersinger* v. *Hamlin* (1972), the right of free counsel has been expanded to anyone facing possible jail time.

Regents of the University of California v. Bakke (1978) was the first Supreme Court decision to suggest that an affirmative action program could be justified on the basis of diversity. The Supreme Court explained that racial quotas were not permissible under the equal protection clause (U.S. Const., Amend. XIV, sec. 1) but that the diversity rationale was a legitimate interest that would allow a state medical school to consider an applicant's race in evaluating his or her application for admission.

Reno v. American Civil Liberties Union (1997) tested the Communications Decency Act that made it a crime to distribute "indecent" material over computer online networks. The Court said that protecting children from pornography did not supersede the right to freedom of expression, adding that the act was unenforceable with the current technology.

Reynolds v. Sims (1964) extended the one-person, one-vote doctrine announced in *Wesberry v. Sanders* to state legislative elections. The Court held that the inequality of representation in the Alabama legislature violated the equal protection clause of the Fourteenth Amendment.

Reynolds v. United States (1879) was the first major Supreme Court case to consider the impact of neutral laws of general application on religious practices. (A neutral law of general application is one that is intended to protect the public health and safety and applies to everyone regardless of religious belief or affiliation. Such a law is not intended to affect adversely any religious belief or practice but may have indirect adverse effects.) The case presented a free-exercise challenge by a Mormon to a federal law making it unlawful to practice polygamy (marriage in which a person has more than one spouse). The Mormon religion permitted a male to have more than one wife. The Court upheld the statute, saying that Congress did not have the authority to legislate with respect to religious beliefs but did have the authority to legislate with respect to actions that subvert good order.

Roe v. Wade (1973) held that females have a constitutional right under various provisions of the Constitution—most notably, the due process clause (Amend. XIV, sec. 1)—to decide whether to terminate a pregnancy. The Supreme Court's decision in this case was the most significant in a long line of decisions over a period of 50 years that recognized a constitutional right of privacy, even though the word *privacy* is not found in the Constitution.

Roper v. Simmons (2005) overturned the 1989 ruling of *Stanford v. Kentucky*, which held that the death penalty for a minor was not a cruel or unusual punishment. In this case, the Court found that the execution of the seventeen-year-old defendant would be a violation of the Eighth Amendment. It was the opinion of the Court that public opinion had changed and now viewed execution as a disproportionate punishment for minors.

Salazar v. Ramah Navajo Chapter (2012) ruled that the government was obligated to cover all costs associated with contracts under the Indian Self-Determination and Education Assistance Act, under which the Ramah Navajo Chapter agreed to administer federal programs in exchange for payment to cover the costs of operating these programs. The funds were to be appropriated for each contract and Congress placed a statutory cap on these apportionments. When the Chapter did not receive the funding needing to cover their costs due to insufficient funds appropriated, they sued, arguing that the government was contractually obligated to cover these costs. The Court agreed, deciding that the case should be handled as any other contractual agreement and that the costs of running the programs must be paid in full, despite any statutory caps.

Santa Fe School District v. Doe (2000) ruled that the Santa Fe School District violated the establishment clause of the First Amendment when it allowed a student council member to deliver a prayer over the intercom before varsity football games.

Santobello v. New York (1971) put the Supreme Court's stamp of approval on plea bargaining. The Supreme Court explained that plea bargaining is an essential component in the administration of justice. The Court's decision established that a prosecutor must live up to the terms of a plea agreement, although the Court also made it clear that a defendant does not have an absolute right to have the trial judge accept a guilty plea or a plea agreement.

***Schenck* v. *Pro-Choice Network of Western New York* (1997)** upheld parts of an injunction aimed at antiabortion protesters and regulating the manner in which they could conduct their protests. The Supreme Court upheld the creation of a fixed 15-foot buffer zone separating protesters from the entrance to abortion clinics, their parking lots, or their driveways; the Court also upheld a cease-and-desist order under which a protester must move away from any person who indicates that he or she does not want to hear the protester's message. But the Court struck down the "floating buffer zone" that had prevented protesters from coming within fifteen feet of patrons and employees.

***Schenck* v. *United States* (1919)** upheld convictions under the Federal Espionage Act. The defendants were charged with distributing leaflets aimed at inciting draft resistance during World War I; their defense was that their antidraft speech was protected by the free speech clause (U.S. Const., Amend. I, cl. 2). The Supreme Court explained that whether or not speech is protected depends on the context in which it occurs. Here, said the Court, the context was the nation's war effort. Because the defendants' antidraft rhetoric created a "clear and present danger" to the success of the war effort, it was not protected speech.

***Shaw* v. *Reno* (1993)** supported the claim of North Carolina residents that the reapportionment plan creating a second district with an African American majority raised a valid constitutional issue under the Fourteenth Amendment. The unusual shape of the newly added district made it clear to the Court that its creation was an example of racial gerrymandering. The Court remanded the case to the District Court to decide whether there was compelling government interest to support this redistricting plan.

***Shelby County, Alabama* v. *Holder* (2013)** held that Section 4 of the Voting Rights Act was unconstitutional. The provision was meant to guard against discriminatory practices in areas that had a history of preventing minorities from voting, but the Court ruled that these procedures are no longer necessary. Furthermore, the Court ruled that Section 4 violated the Tenth Amendment and Article 4 of the Constitution by taking away the right of states to make their own election laws and that Congress had exceeded its authority when it continued to renew the conditions of the Voting Rights Act past the original five-year term.

***Sheppard* v. *Maxwell* (1966)** made it clear that a criminal defendant's Fourteenth Amendment right to due process can justify restrictions on the press's First Amendment rights. The Supreme Court, however, was careful to explain that any restrictions on the press must be no broader than necessary to ensure that the defendant is tried in court and not in the press.

***The Slaughterhouse Cases* (1873)** upheld Louisiana laws regulating the butcher trade. This decision was rendered shortly after the Civil War. It narrowly interpreted the privileges and immunities clause, as well as the due process and equal protection clauses. At the time, the Court saw these provisions as securing the rights of newly freed enslaved persons, not protecting the ordinary contract rights of businesspeople.

***Stanford* v. *Kentucky* (1989)** upheld the decision of local courts to impose death sentences on capital offenders under the age of 18. The Court's decision was based on insufficient evidence proving a national consensus on the matter. The case included an examination of state policies on capital punishment for minors, but too much variation existed for the Court to rule that the death sentence would be considered a cruel and unusual punishment in violation of the Eighth Amendment. The Court ruled that local courts had the final decision on whether they saw fit to impose such a punishment on the defendants. This case was later overturned by *Roper* v. *Simmons*.

***Stromberg* v. *California* (1931)** ruled that a California law banning the display of red flags, then considered a symbol of communism and opposition to the government, was unconstitutional. This landmark case was one of the first cases in which the Fourteenth Amendment was extended to cover the protections of the First Amendment, including symbolic speech. While the Court upheld the intention of portions of the law meant to punish those who incited violence or the overthrow of government by unlawful means, it found the law as a whole too broad, leading to the conviction of citizens who expressed their views in a peaceful and lawful manner.

Sweatt v. *Painter* **(1950)** held that the rejection of an African American man, Sweatt, from the University of Texas Law School based on race alone was a violation of the Fourteenth Amendment. After Sweatt asked a state court to order his admission, the school attempted to create a "separate but equal" law school for African American students. The Supreme Court struck down the attempt, finding that the separate school would be unequal to the main law school and that separating African American students from other law students would be a major impediment as they competed in the legal arena. The Court required that Sweatt be admitted to the law school.

Texas v. *Johnson* **(1989)** held that burning an American flag is expressive conduct protected by the First Amendment. Expressive conduct, the Supreme Court explained, is conduct that is intended by the actor to convey a message, and the message that the actor intends to convey is one that observers likely would understand. The Court applied the O'Brien test (see *United States* v. *O'Brien*) under which the government can punish a person for conduct that might have an expressive component as long as the punishment advances an important government interest that is unrelated to the content of speech. The Court then reversed the conviction of Gregory Johnson for desecrating a venerated object—burning an American flag at the 1984 Republican National Convention to protest the policies of the Reagan administration. The Court explained that Johnson was convicted solely because of the content of his speech.

Texas v. *White* **(1869)** held that Texas continued to be a state in the Union throughout the war of rebellion, ruling that states did not have the right to unilaterally secede from the Union. The case involved bonds that were given to Texas by Congress before the war to be redeemable at a later date. In 1862, an insurgent Texas legislature approved the use of the bonds to buy war supplies. After the war was over, the reconstructed government wanted to reclaim the bonds. The Supreme Court ruled that the bonds were still redeemable as the insurgent government was unconstitutional, even if ratified by a majority of Texans, and had no valid right to the bonds.

Thompson v. *Keohane* **(1995)** ruled that 28 U.S. Code Section 2254, which says that federal courts must assume state courts to be correct in factual questions, did not apply to cases of Miranda rights. In this case, the defendant had been interrogated and confessed to murder without being read his Miranda rights, but there was disagreement over whether he was in police custody at the time. The Supreme Court sent the case back to District Court to decide whether Thompson had in fact been in custody.

Tinker v. *Des Moines School District* **(1969)** extended First Amendment protection to public school students in the now-famous statement that "it can hardly be argued that either students or teachers shed their constitutional rights of freedom of speech or expression at the schoolhouse gate." The Supreme Court then held that a public school could not suspend students who wore black armbands to school to symbolize their opposition to the Vietnam War. In so holding, the Court likened the students' conduct to pure speech and decided it on that basis.

United States v. *American Library Association* **(2003)** upheld the Children's Internet Protection Act (CIPA), which required libraries to install Internet filtering software on their computers as a requirement for getting federal funding. The American Library Association believed the law to be a violation of the First Amendment rights of library patrons. The Court ruled that Internet filtering did not infringe upon First Amendment rights of library patrons, making the law constitutional. It further ruled that the stipulation was an acceptable exercise of Congress's spending power.

United States v. *Carolene Products Co.* **(1938)** upheld a 1923 act of Congress that banned the shipment of "filled milk" across state lines. Within the Court's opinion, Justice Stone established the idea that the Court should give deference to Congress in economic matters. However, he suggested that the Court should take a closer look at statutes involving fundamental rights or those directed at religious, national, or racial minorities.

United States v. *Jones* **(2012)** held that the warrantless tracking of a car via GPS device violated the Fourth Amendment. The Court said that the placing of the device on the car without a warrant was a trespass to property and as such was automatically unreasonable. The Court ruled that this was a violation of the Fourth Amendment protections from unreasonable search and seizure and that such protections extend to a reasonable expectation of privacy, particularly in an era when surveillance is easily maintained without a physical intrusion.

***United States v. Lopez* (1995)** struck down the 1990 Gun-Free School Zones Act. A twelfth-grade student, Alfonzo Lopez, was charged with carrying a concealed weapon into his high school, but the state charges against him were dropped and he was instead convicted of violating this federal statute. The Supreme Court ruled, however, that the statute was unconstitutional because it exceeded Congress's power under the Commerce Clause. The Court ruled that possessing a firearm within a school zone had nothing to do with economic activities.

***United States v. Nixon* (1974)** made it clear that the president is not above the law. In the early 1970s, President Richard Nixon was named as an unindicted coconspirator in the criminal investigation that arose in the aftermath of a break-in at the offices of the Democratic Party in Washington, D.C. A federal judge ordered President Nixon to turn over tapes of conversations he had with his advisers. Nixon resisted the order, claiming that the conversations were entitled to absolute confidentiality by Article II of the Constitution. The Supreme Court disagreed and held that only those presidential conversations and communications that relate to performing the duties of the office of president are confidential and protected from a judicial order of disclosure.

***United States v. O'Brien* (1968)** upheld the conviction of David Paul O'Brien for burning his draft card to dramatize his opposition to the Vietnam War, in violation of a regulation requiring a draft registrant to keep his card in his possession at all times. The Court held that symbolic speech was not a defense to a draft-card burning charge because the regulation: 1) served a valid government interest unrelated to the suppression of speech; 2) was narrowly drawn to serve the identified government interest; and 3) left open alternative channels of sending the same message.

***United States v. Thind* (1923)** denied an Indian man, Bhagat Singh Thind, the right to become a U.S. citizen through naturalization. Thind argued that, under the Naturalization Act of 1906, naturalization was permitted for "white persons" and attempted to prove that his heritage should classify him as part of the Aryan race. The Court denied his claim, finding that Thind was not Caucasian by common standards, and upholding the 1917 act of Congress that prohibited the naturalization of natives of Asia, which geographically included all of India.

***United States v. Virginia* (1996)** found the creation of a women's-only academy as an alternative to admitting women to the Virginia Military Institute unconstitutional. The United States brought a case against the school, finding its policy of male-only admittance to be discriminatory while females were allowed to serve in the military. The school attempted to form a separate institution for women to offer comparable educational benefits, but the Supreme Court ruled that VMI could not produce convincing evidence of justification for its gender-based admission policy. The Court ruled that the policy and the creation of a women's-only institution violated the Fourteenth Amendment's Equal Protection clause.

***United States v. Windsor* (2013)** held that, even though the executive branch and the defendant agreed with a lower court's ruling, there was still a valid controversy that allowed the Court to rule on the merits of the case. The Court ruled that, DOMA did in fact violate the Fifth Amendment rights of same-sex couples who had been legally married under their state law. The original case in question would decide whether Windsor, the beneficiary of her wife's estate, would have to pay substantial taxes on the inheritance due to not being recognized as legally married under federal law, although the marriage was legal in her state. The Court ruled in Windsor's favor, finding DOMA in violation of rights extended to her by the state of New York.

***U.S. Term Limits v. Thornton* (1995)** struck down an amendment to the Arkansas State Constitution that set a limit on how many times representatives or senators may be reelected to represent Arkansas. The Court ruled that states do not have the power to change or further restrict the qualifications for members of Congress as set forth in the U.S. Constitution.

***Van Orden* v. *Perry* (2005)** found that the presence of a monument displaying the Ten Commandments on the grounds of the Texas state capitol building was not in violation of the First Amendment's establishment clause. The Court ruled that the display was meant to show the historical traditions of the Ten Commandments' meaning and did not seek to advance or establish any particular religion.

***Vernonia School District 47J* v. *Acton* (1995)** held that the Fourth Amendment's prohibition of unreasonable searches and seizures was not violated by a public school district's policy of conducting random, suspicionless drug tests of all students participating in interscholastic athletics. The Supreme Court explained that the district's interest in combating drug use outweighed the students' privacy interests.

***Wallace* v. *Jaffree* (1985)** held that an Alabama law authorizing teachers to lead students in prayers or religious activities during the school day was unconstitutional. The Court found the law in violation of the First Amendment's establishment clause, since the religious activities could not be proven to have any purpose other than to endorse religion and deviated from the duty of states to maintain neutrality toward religion.

***Watkins* v. *United States* (1957)** limited the authority of congressional committees to hold witnesses in contempt for refusing to answer questions. The Supreme Court explained that a witness can be required to answer questions posed by a committee of Congress, but only if the questions are relevant to the committee's purpose. The Court also held that a witness before a congressional committee can invoke the Fifth Amendment's privilege against self-incrimination.

***Weeks* v. *United States* (1914)** created the exclusionary rule as the remedy for an unconstitutional search or seizure (U.S. Const., Amend. IV). Under the exclusionary rule, evidence seized as a result of an unconstitutional search or seizure cannot be used as evidence of guilt at a later criminal trial. The Supreme Court applied the rule only against federal officers because, at that time, the Bill of Rights was thought to apply only to the federal government.

***Wesberry* v. *Sanders* (1964)** established the one-person, one-vote doctrine in elections for the U.S. House of Representatives. The doctrine ensures that the vote of each voter has the same weight as the vote of every other voter. This decision means that the voting population of each congressional district within a state must be as nearly equal as possible.

***West Coast Hotel Co.* v. *Parrish* (1937)** upheld a Washington state statute that authorized a state commission to fix the minimum wages of women and minors. The statute was challenged as a violation of the right to contract. The Supreme Court explained that the right to contract, like most of the rights protected by the due process clause (U.S. Const., Amend. XIV, sec. 1), is not absolute. The Court held that the right to contract was outweighed by the state's interest in protecting the health, safety, and security of vulnerable workers.

***West Virginia State Board of Education* v. *Barnette* (1943)** made it clear that the free exercise clause (U.S. Const., Amend. I) forbids the government from requiring a person to swear to a belief. The Supreme Court struck down a state law requiring public school students to salute the American flag and recite the Pledge of Allegiance. Parents and students of the Jehovah's Witness faith claimed that the law violated their free exercise rights because their religion prohibits them from pledging allegiance to anything other than God. The Court agreed and held that the state had no interest compelling enough to justify the law.

***White* v. *Regester* (1973)** upheld the decision of the District Court ordering the state of Texas to redraw boundaries in multimember districts in two counties and instead to create single-member districts. This issue arose after Texas attempted to redraw electoral boundaries for its state House of Representatives and state Senate, the result of which were districts in which the minority population would be significantly underrepresented. The Supreme Court agreed that Texas could use the current districts for a limited period until boundaries could be redrawn to remedy the issue.

***Whitney* v. *California* (1927)** upheld the California Criminal Syndicalism Act against a claim that the statute violated First Amendment rights of speech and association. The statute made it a crime for anyone to become a member of any group known to espouse political change, particularly change that would affect the distribution of wealth in the country. This case was overturned by *Brandenburg v. Ohio*.

Wickard v. *Filburn* **(1942)** ruled that Filburn, an Ohio farmer, violated an amendment by Congress that limited the acreage on which he was allowed to produce wheat. Filburn claimed the excess production was all for local use on his farm. The Court found that such use was illegal because it affected interstate commerce, even if only in an indirect way. Congress's limitations on the farmer's production was found constitutional.

Wisconsin v. *Yoder* **(1972)** ruled that Wisconsin's compulsory education laws must yield to the concerns of Amish parents that sending their children to public school after the eighth grade exposed the children to influences that undermined their religious faith and religious practices.

Worcester v. *Georgia* **(1832)** struck down a Georgia state law that sought to regulate the interactions between citizens of its state and members of the Cherokee Nation. Worcester was convicted of residing within Cherokee territory under this law but appealed his case, claiming that the state of Georgia had no right to make rulings in this matter. The Supreme Court agreed, finding that Georgia's law violated the Constitution, laws, and treaties of the United States, which mandated that Native American territories be treated separately from the states in which they are located and not as part of the state. The state laws, therefore, were ruled void within the Cherokee territory.

Yarborough v. *Alvarado* **(2004)** held that an officer did not necessarily have to take into account a person's age and history with law enforcement when determining whether or not that person was "in custody" and therefore whether Miranda warnings were required. The Court said that reasonable judges could disagree as to whether the defendant was actually in custody in this situation and that the state court's determination that he was not in custody was reasonable since the Supreme Court had never held that age was a factor to consider in a custody analysis.

Youngstown Sheet & Tube Co. v. Sawyer (the Steel Seizure Case) **(1952)** arose when a nationwide strike of steelworkers threatened to shut down the industry at the height of the Korean War. (Steel production was essential to the war effort.) To avert the strike, President Harry S. Truman ordered the secretary of commerce to take over the steel mills and to keep them running. The Supreme Court held that the president must relinquish control of the mills because he had exceeded his constitutional authority. The Court specifically held that the president's authority as commander in chief did not justify his action. The Court explained that only Congress could "nationalize" an industry; if Congress did so, the president, who is constitutionally required to execute the law, would be authorized to seize and operate the mills.

Zelman v. *Simmons-Harris* **(2002)** found that an Ohio voucher program that granted aid to families based on financial need to cover the tuition at a public or private institution of each family's choice was not in violation of the First Amendment's Establishment clause. The plaintiff argued that because a majority of the schools to which aid was being routed had religious affiliation, the government could be seen as endorsing the religious cause. The Court ruled that the government was neutral to any religious endorsements, because the choice of where to spend the aid money lay entirely with the individuals, not with the government. The basis of providing aid was financial need only and did not serve to promote or disapprove of any particular religion or institution.

Zemel v. *Rusk* **(1965)** placed a national-security limitation on a citizen's right to travel abroad. In this case, a citizen tried to get a visa to travel to Cuba, a Communist country with very tense relations with the United States in the early to mid-1960s. The State Department denied the visa request, and the Supreme Court affirmed, citing the "weightiest considerations of national security" as illustrated by the Cuban missile crisis of 1962 that had the United States on the brink of war with the Soviet Union.

JULY 4, 1776

DELEGATES AT THE SECOND CONTINENTAL CONGRESS faced an enormous task. The war against Great Britain had begun, but to many colonists the purpose for fighting was unclear. As sentiment increased for a complete break with Britain, Congress decided to act. A committee was appointed to prepare a document that declared the thirteen colonies free and independent from Britain. More important, the committee needed to explain why separation was the only fitting solution to long-standing disputes with Parliament and the British Crown. Thomas Jefferson was assigned to write a working draft of this document, which was then revised. It was officially adopted on July 4, 1776. More than any other action of Congress, the Declaration of Independence served to make the American colonists one people.

Architect of the Capitol

Preamble

When in the Course of human events, it becomes necessary for one people to dissolve the political bands which have connected them with another, and to assume among the powers of the earth, the separate and equal station to which the Laws of Nature and of Nature's God entitle them, a decent respect to the opinions of mankind requires that they should declare the causes which impel them to the separation.—

Declaration of Natural Rights

We hold these truths to be self-evident, that all men are created equal, that they are endowed by their Creator with certain unalienable Rights, that among these are Life, Liberty, and the pursuit of Happiness.—

That to secure these rights, Governments are instituted among Men, deriving their just powers from the consent of the governed,—

That whenever any Form of Government becomes destructive of these ends, it is the Right of the People to alter or to abolish it, and to institute new Government, laying its foundation on such principles and organizing its powers in such form, as to them shall seem most likely to effect their Safety and Happiness. Prudence, indeed, will dictate that Governments long established should not be changed for light and transient causes; and accordingly all experience hath shewn, that mankind are more disposed to suffer, while evils are sufferable, than to right themselves by abolishing the forms to which they are accustomed. But when a long train of abuses and usurpations, pursuing invariably the same Object evinces a design to reduce them under absolute Despotism, it is their right, it is their duty, to throw off such Government, and to provide new Guards for their future security.—

List of Grievances

Such has been the patient sufferance of these Colonies; and such is now the necessity which constrains them to alter their former Systems of Government. The history of the present King of Great Britain is a history of repeated injuries and usurpations, all having in direct object the establishment of an absolute Tyranny over these States. To prove this, let Facts be submitted to a candid world.—

He has refused his Assent to Laws, the most wholesome and necessary for the public good.—

He has forbidden his Governors to pass Laws of immediate and pressing importance, unless suspended in their operation till his Assent should be obtained; and when so suspended, he has utterly neglected to attend to them.—

He has refused to pass other Laws for the accommodation of large districts of people, unless those people would relinquish the right of Representation in the Legislature, a right inestimable to them and formidable to tyrants only.—

He has called together legislative bodies at places unusual, uncomfortable, and distant from the depository of their public Records, for the sole purpose of fatiguing them into compliance with his measures.—

The printed text of the document shows the spelling and punctuation of the parchment original. To aid in comprehension, selected words and their definitions appear in the side margin, along with other explanatory notes.

impel to force

endowed provided

People create governments to ensure that their natural rights are protected.

If a government does not serve its purpose, the people have a right to abolish it. Then the people have the right and duty to create a new government that will safeguard their security.

Despotism unlimited power

usurpations unjust uses of power

Each paragraph lists alleged injustices of George III.

relinquish to give up
inestimable priceless

He has dissolved Representative Houses repeatedly, for opposing with manly firmness his invasions on the rights of the people.—

He has refused for a long time, after such dissolutions, to cause others to be elected; whereby the Legislative powers, incapable of Annihilation, have returned to the People at large for their exercise; the State remaining in the meantime exposed to all the dangers of invasion from without, and convulsions within.—

He has endeavoured to prevent the population of these States; for that purpose obstructing the Laws for Naturalization of Foreigners; refusing to pass others to encourage their migrations hither, and raising the conditions of new Appropriations of Lands.—

He has obstructed the Administration of Justice, by refusing his Assent to Laws for establishing Judiciary powers.—

He has made Judges dependent on his Will alone, for the tenure of their offices, and the amount and payment of their salaries.—

He has erected a multitude of New Offices, and sent hither swarms of Officers to harass our people, and eat out their substance.—

He has kept among us, in times of peace, Standing Armies without the Consent of our legislatures.—

He has affected to render the Military independent of and superior to the Civil power.—

He has combined with others to subject us to a jurisdiction foreign to our constitution, and unacknowledged by our laws; giving his Assent to their Acts of pretended Legislation:—

For quartering large bodies of troops among us:—

For protecting them, by a mock Trial, from punishment for any Murders which they should commit on the Inhabitants of these States:—

For cutting off our Trade with all parts of the world:—

For imposing Taxes on us without our Consent:—

For depriving us in many cases, of the benefits of Trial by Jury:—

For transporting us beyond Seas to be tried for pretended offences:—

For abolishing the free System of English Laws in a neighbouring Province, establishing therein an Arbitrary government, and enlarging its Boundaries so as to render it at once an example and fit instrument for introducing the same absolute rule into these Colonies:—

For taking away our Charters, abolishing our most valuable Laws, and altering fundamentally the Forms of our Governments:—

For suspending our own Legislatures, and declaring themselves invested with power to legislate for us in all cases whatsoever.—

He has abdicated Government here, by declaring us out of his Protection and waging War against us.—

He has plundered our seas, ravaged our Coasts, burnt our towns, and destroyed the Lives of our people.—

He is at this time transporting large Armies of foreign Mercenaries to compleat the works of death, desolation and tyranny, already begun with circumstances of Cruelty & perfidy scarcely paralleled in the most barbarous ages, and totally unworthy the Head of a civilized nation.—

He has constrained our fellow Citizens taken Captive on the high Seas to bear Arms against their Country, to become the executioners of their friends and Brethren, or to fall themselves by their Hands.—

He has excited domestic insurrections amongst us, and has endeavoured to bring on the inhabitants of our frontiers, the merciless

Annihilation destruction

convulsions violent disturbances

Naturalization of Foreigners process by which foreign-born persons become citizens

tenure term

Refers to the British troops sent to the colonies after the French and Indian War.

Refers to the 1766 Declaratory Act.

quartering lodging

Refers to the 1774 Quebec Act.

render to make

abdicated given up

perfidy violation of trust

Indian Savages, whose known rule of warfare, is an undistinguished destruction of all ages, sexes and conditions.

In every stage of these Oppressions We have Petitioned for Redress in the most humble terms: Our repeated Petitions have been answered only by repeated injury. A Prince, whose character is thus marked by every act which may define a Tyrant, is unfit to be the ruler of a free people.

Nor have We been wanting in attentions to our British brethren. We have warned them from time to time of attempts by their legislature to extend an unwarrantable jurisdiction over us. We have reminded them of the circumstances of our emigration and settlement here. We have appealed to their native justice and magnanimity, and we have conjured them by the ties of our common kindred to disavow these usurpations, which would inevitably interrupt our connections and correspondence. They too have been deaf to the voice of justice and of consanguinity. We must, therefore, acquiesce in the necessity, which denounces our Separation, and hold them, as we hold the rest of mankind, Enemies in War, in Peace Friends.—

Resolution of Independence by the United States

We, therefore, the Representatives of the united States of America, in General Congress, Assembled, appealing to the Supreme Judge of the world for the rectitude of our intentions, do, in the Name, and by Authority of the good People of these Colonies, solemnly publish and declare, That these United Colonies are, and of Right ought to be Free and Independent States; that they are Absolved from all Allegiance to the British Crown, and that all political connection between them and the State of Great Britain, is and ought to be totally dissolved; and that as Free and Independent States, they have full Power to levy War, conclude Peace, contract Alliances, establish Commerce, and to do all other Acts and Things which Independent States may of right do.—

And for the support of this Declaration, with a firm reliance on the protection of divine Providence, we mutually pledge to each other our Lives, our Fortunes and our sacred Honour.

insurrections rebellions

Petitioned for Redress asked formally for a correction of wrongs

unwarrantable jurisdiction unjustified authority

consanguinity originating from the same ancestor

rectitude rightness

The signers, as representatives of the American people, declared the colonies independent from Great Britain. Most members signed the document on August 2, 1776.

John Hancock
  President from
  Massachusetts

Georgia
Button Gwinnett
Lyman Hall
George Walton

North Carolina
William Hooper
Joseph Hewes
John Penn

South Carolina
Edward Rutledge
Thomas Heyward, Jr.
Thomas Lynch, Jr.
Arthur Middleton

Maryland
Samuel Chase
William Paca
Thomas Stone
Charles Carroll
  of Carrollton

Virginia
George Wythe
Richard Henry Lee
Thomas Jefferson
Benjamin Harrison
Thomas Nelson Jr.
Francis Lightfoot
  Lee
Carter Braxton

Pennsylvania
Robert Morris
Benjamin Rush
Benjamin Franklin
John Morton
George Clymer
James Smith
George Taylor
James Wilson
George Ross

Delaware
Caesar Rodney
George Read
Thomas McKean

New York
William Floyd
Philip Livingston
Francis Lewis
Lewis Morris

New Jersey
Richard Stockton
John Witherspoon
Francis Hopkinson
John Hart
Abraham Clark

New Hampshire
Josiah Bartlett
William Whipple
Matthew Thornton

Massachusetts
Samuel Adams
John Adams
Robert Treat Paine
Elbridge Gerry

Rhode Island
Stephen Hopkins
William Ellery

Connecticut
Samuel Huntington
William Williams
Oliver Wolcott
Roger Sherman

The Constitution
of the United States

The Constitution of the United States is a truly remarkable document. It was one of the first written constitutions in modern history. The entire text of the Constitution and its amendments follow. For easier study, those passages that have been set aside or changed by the adoption of amendments are printed in blue. Also included are explanatory notes that will help clarify the meanings of important ideas presented in the Constitution.

Preamble

We the People of the United States, in Order to form a more perfect Union, establish Justice, insure domestic Tranquility, provide for the common defence, promote the general Welfare, and secure the Blessings of Liberty to ourselves and our Posterity, do ordain and establish this **Constitution** for the United States of America.

Article I

Section 1

All legislative Powers herein granted shall be vested in a Congress of the United States, which shall consist of a Senate and House of Representatives.

Section 2

[1.] The House of Representatives shall be composed of Members chosen every second Year by the People of the several States, and the Electors in each State shall have the Qualifications requisite for Electors of the most numerous Branch of the State Legislature.

[2.] No person shall be a Representative who shall not have attained the Age of twenty five Years, and been seven Years a Citizen of the United States, and who shall not, when elected, be an Inhabitant of that State in which he shall be chosen.

[3.] Representatives and direct Taxes shall be apportioned among the several States which may be included within this Union, according to their respective Numbers, which shall be determined by adding to the whole Number of free Persons, including those bound to Service for a Term of Years, and excluding Indians not taxed, three fifths of all other Persons. The actual **Enumeration** shall be made within three Years after the first Meeting of the Congress of the United States, and within every subsequent Term of ten Years, in such Manner as they shall by Law direct. The Number of Representatives shall not exceed one for every thirty Thousand, but each State shall have at Least one Representative; and until such enumeration shall be made, the State of New Hampshire shall be entitled to chuse three; Massachusetts eight, Rhode-Island and Providence Plantations one, Connecticut five, New-York six, New Jersey four, Pennsylvania eight, Delaware one, Maryland six, Virginia ten, North Carolina five, South Carolina five, and Georgia three.

[4.] When vacancies happen in the Representation from any State, the Executive Authority thereof shall issue Writs of Election to fill such Vacancies.

[5.] The House of Representatives shall chuse their Speaker and other Officers; and shall have the sole Power of **Impeachment**.

The Preamble introduces the Constitution and sets forth the general purposes for which the government was established. The Preamble also declares that the power of the government comes from the people.

The printed text of the document shows the spelling and punctuation of the parchment original.

Article I. The Legislative Branch

The Constitution contains seven divisions called articles. Each article covers a general topic. For example, Articles I, II, and III create the three branches of the national government—the legislative, executive, and judicial branches. Most of the articles are divided into sections.

Section 1. Congress

Lawmaking The power to make laws is given to a Congress made up of two chambers to represent different interests: the Senate to represent the states and the House to be more responsive to the people's will.

Section 2. House of Representatives

Division of Representatives Among the States The number of representatives from each state is based on the size of the state's population. Each state is entitled to at least one representative. The Constitution states that each state may specify who can vote, but the Fifteenth, Nineteenth, Twenty-fourth, and Twenty-sixth Amendments have established guidelines that all states must follow regarding the right to vote. *What are the qualifications for members of the House of Representatives?*

Vocabulary

preamble: *introduction*
constitution: *principles and laws of a nation*
enumeration: *census or population count*
impeachment: *bringing charges against an official*

Section 3. The Senate

Voting Procedure Originally, senators were chosen by the legislators of their own states. The Seventeenth Amendment changed this so that senators are now elected by their state's people. There are 100 senators, 2 from each state.

What Might Have Been

Electing Senators South Carolina delegate Charles Pinckney suggested during the Convention that the members of the Senate come from four equally proportioned districts within the United States and that the legislature elect the executive every seven years.

Section 3. The Senate

Trial of Impeachments One of Congress's powers is the power to impeach—to accuse government officials of wrongdoing, put them on trial, and, if necessary, remove them from office. The House decides if the offense is impeachable. The Senate acts as a jury, and when the president is impeached, the Chief Justice of the United States serves as the judge. A two-thirds vote of the members present is needed to convict impeached officials. *What punishment can the Senate give if an impeached official is convicted?*

Vocabulary

president pro tempore: *presiding officer of the Senate who serves when the vice president is absent*

Section 3

[1.] The Senate of the United States shall be composed of two Senators from each State, chosen by the Legislature thereof, for six Years; and each Senator shall have one Vote.

[2.] Immediately after they shall be assembled in Consequence of the first Election, they shall be divided as equally as may be into three Classes. The Seats of the Senators of the first Class shall be vacated at the Expiration of the second Year, of the second Class at the Expiration of the fourth Year, and of the third Class at the Expiration of the sixth Year, so that one third may be chosen every second Year; and if Vacancies happen by Resignation, or otherwise, during the Recess of the Legislature of any State, the Executive thereof may make temporary Appointments until the next Meeting of the Legislature, which shall then fill such Vacancies.

[3.] No Person shall be a Senator who shall not have attained to the Age of thirty Years, and been nine Years a Citizen of the United States, and who shall not, when elected, be an Inhabitant of that State for which he shall be chosen.

[4.] The Vice President of the United States shall be President of the Senate, but shall have no Vote, unless they be equally divided.

[5.] The Senate shall chuse their other Officers, and also a **President pro tempore**, in the Absence of the Vice President, or when he shall exercise the Office of the President of the United States.

[6.] The Senate shall have the sole Power to try all Impeachments. When sitting for that Purpose, they shall be on Oath or Affirmation. When the President of the United States is tried, the Chief Justice shall preside: And no Person shall be convicted without the Concurrence of two thirds of the Members present.

[7.] Judgment in Cases of Impeachment shall not extend further than to removal from Office, and disqualification to hold and enjoy any Office of honor, Trust or Profit under the United States: but the Party convicted shall nevertheless be liable and subject to Indictment, Trial, Judgment and Punishment, according to Law.

Section 4

[1.] The Times, Places and Manner of holding Elections for Senators and Representatives, shall be prescribed in each State by the Legislature thereof; but the Congress may at any time by Law make or alter such Regulations, except as to the Places of chusing Senators.

[2.] The Congress shall assemble at least once in every Year, and such Meeting shall be on the first Monday in December, unless they shall by Law appoint a different Day.

Section 5

[1.] Each House shall be the Judge of the Elections, Returns and Qualifications of its own Members, and a Majority of each shall constitute a **Quorum** to do Business; but a smaller Number may **adjourn** from day to day, and may be authorized to compel the Attendance of absent Members, in such Manner, and under such Penalties as each House may provide.

[2.] Each House may determine the Rules of its Proceedings, punish its Members for disorderly Behaviour, and, with the **Concurrence** of two thirds, expel a Member.

[3.] Each House shall keep a Journal of its Proceedings, and from time to time publish the same, excepting such Parts as may in their Judgment require Secrecy; and the Yeas and Nays of the Members of either House on any question shall, at the Desire of one fifth of those Present, be entered on the Journal.

[4.] Neither House, during the Session of Congress, shall, without the Consent of the other, adjourn for more than three days, nor to any other Place than that in which the two Houses shall be sitting.

Section 6

[1.] The Senators and Representatives shall receive a Compensation for their Services, to be ascertained by Law, and paid out of the Treasury of the United States. They shall in all Cases, except Treason, Felony and Breach of the Peace, be privileged from Arrest during their Attendance at the Session of their respective Houses, and in going to and returning from the same; and for any Speech or Debate in either House, they shall not be questioned in any other Place.

[2.] No Senator or Representative shall, during the Time for which he was elected, be appointed to any civil Office under the Authority of the United States, which shall have been created, or the **Emoluments** whereof shall have been encreased during such time; and no Person holding any Office under the United States, shall be a Member of either House during his Continuance in Office.

Section 7

[1.] All Bills for raising **Revenue** shall originate in the House of Representatives; but the Senate may propose or concur with Amendments as on other **Bills**.

[2.] Every Bill which shall have passed the House of Representatives and the Senate, shall, before it become a Law, be presented to the President of the United States; If he approve he shall sign it, but if not he shall return it, with his Objections to that House in which it shall have originated, who shall enter the Objections at large on their Journal, and proceed to reconsider it. If after such Reconsideration two thirds of that House shall agree to pass the Bill, it shall be sent,

Section 6. Privileges and Restrictions

Pay and Privileges To strengthen the federal government, the Founders set congressional salaries to be paid by the United States Treasury rather than by members' respective states. Originally, members were paid $6 per day. In 2011, all members of Congress received a base salary of $174,000.

Section 7. Passing Laws

Revenue Bill All tax laws must originate in the House of Representatives. This ensures that the branch of Congress that is elected by the people every two years has the major role in determining taxes.

together with the Objections, to the other House, by which it shall likewise be reconsidered, and if approved by two thirds of that House, it shall become a Law. But in all such Cases the Votes of both Houses shall be determined by yeas and Nays, and the Names of the Persons voting for and against the Bill shall be entered on the Journal of each House respectively. If any Bill shall not be returned by the President within ten Days (Sundays excepted) after it shall have been presented to him, the Same shall be a Law, in like Manner as if he had signed it, unless the Congress by their Adjournment prevent its Return, in which Case it shall not be a Law.

[3.] Every Order, **Resolution**, or Vote to which the Concurrence of the Senate and House of Representatives may be necessary (except on a question of Adjournment) shall be presented to the President of the United States; and before the Same shall take Effect, shall be approved by him, or being disapproved by him, shall be repassed by two thirds of the Senate and House of Representatives, according to the Rules and Limitations prescribed in the Case of a Bill.

Section 8

[1.] The Congress shall have the Power to lay and collect Taxes, Duties, Imposts and Excises, to pay the Debts and provide for the common Defence and general Welfare of the United States; but all Duties, Imposts and Excises shall be uniform throughout the United States;

[2.] To borrow Money on the credit of the United States;

[3.] To regulate Commerce with foreign Nations, and among the several States, and with the Indian Tribes;

[4.] To establish an uniform Rule of **Naturalization**, and uniform Laws on the subject of Bankruptcies throughout the United States;

[5.] To coin Money, regulate the Value thereof, and of foreign Coin, and fix the Standard of Weights and Measures;

[6.] To provide for the Punishment of counterfeiting the Securities and current Coin of the United States;

[7.] To establish Post Offices and post Roads;

[8.] To promote the Progress of Science and useful Arts, by securing for limited Times to Authors and Inventors the exclusive Right to their respective Writings and Discoveries;

[9.] To constitute Tribunals inferior to the supreme Court;

[10.] To define and punish Piracies and Felonies committed on the high Seas, and Offences against the Law of Nations;

[11.] To declare War, grant Letters of Marque and Reprisal, and make Rules concerning Captures on Land and Water;

[12.] To raise and support Armies, but no Appropriation of Money to that Use shall be for a longer Term than two Years;

[13.] To provide and maintain a Navy;

[14.] To make Rules for the Government and Regulation of the land and naval Forces;

Section 7. Passing Laws

How Bills Become Laws A bill may become a law only by passing both houses of Congress and being signed by the president. The president can check Congress by rejecting—vetoing—its legislation. *How can Congress override the president's veto?*

Section 8. Powers Granted to Congress

Powers of Congress Expressed powers are those powers directly stated in the Constitution. Most of the expressed powers of Congress are listed in Article I, Section 8. These powers are also called enumerated powers because they are numbered 1–18. *Which clause gives Congress the power to declare war?*

Vocabulary

resolution: *legislature's formal expression of opinion*

naturalization: *procedure by which a citizen of a foreign nation becomes a citizen of the United States*

[15.] To provide for calling forth the Militia to execute the Laws of the Union, suppress Insurrections and repel Invasions;

[16.] To provide for organizing, arming, and disciplining, the Militia, and for governing such Part of them as may be employed in the Service of the United States, reserving to the States respectively, the Appointment of the Officers, and the Authority of training the Militia according to the discipline prescribed by Congress;

[17.] To exercise exclusive Legislation in all Cases whatsoever, over such District (not exceeding ten Miles square) as may, by Cession of particular States, and the Acceptance of Congress, become the Seat of Government of the United States, and to exercise like Authority over all Places purchased by the Consent of the Legislature of the State in which the Same shall be, for the Erection of Forts, Magazines, Arsenals, dock-Yards, and other needful Buildings; And

[18.] To make all Laws which shall be necessary and proper for carrying into Execution the foregoing Powers, and all other Powers vested by this Constitution in the Government of the United States, or in any Department or Officer thereof.

Section 9

[1.] The Migration or Importation of such Persons as any of the States now existing shall think proper to admit, shall not be prohibited by the Congress prior to the Year one thousand eight hundred and eight, but a Tax or duty may be imposed on such Importation, not exceeding ten dollars for each Person.

[2.] The Privilege of the Writ of Habeas Corpus shall not be suspended, unless when in Cases of Rebellion or Invasion the public Safety may require it.

[3.] No Bill of Attainder or ex post facto Law shall be passed.

[4.] No Capitation, or other direct, Tax shall be laid, unless in Proportion to the Census or Enumeration herein before directed to be taken.

[5.] No Tax or Duty shall be laid on Articles exported from any State.

[6.] No Preference shall be given by any Regulation of Commerce or Revenue to the Ports of one State over those of another: nor shall Vessels bound to, or from, one State, be obliged to enter, clear, or pay Duties in another.

[7.] No Money shall be drawn from the Treasury, but in Consequence of Appropriations made by Law; and a regular Statement and Account of the Receipts and Expenditures of all public Money shall be published from time to time.

[8.] No Title of Nobility shall be granted by the United States: And no Person holding any Office of Profit or Trust under them, shall, without the Consent of the Congress, accept of any present, Emolument, Office, or Title, of any kind whatever, from any King, Prince, or foreign State.

Section 10.
Powers Denied to the States

Limitations on Powers Section 10 lists limits on the states. These restrictions were designed, in part, to prevent an overlapping in functions and authority with the federal government.

Article II.
The Executive Branch

Article II creates an executive branch to carry out laws passed by Congress. Article II lists the powers and duties of the president, describes qualifications for office and procedures for electing the president, and provides for a vice president.

What Might Have Been

Term of Office Alexander Hamilton also provided his own governmental outline at the Constitutional Convention. Some of its most distinctive elements were that both the executive and the members of the Senate were "elected to serve during good behaviour," meaning there was no specified limit on their time in office.

Section 1.
President and Vice President

Former Method of Election In the election of 1800, the top two candidates received the same number of electoral votes, making it necessary for the House of Representatives to decide the election. To eliminate this problem, the Twelfth Amendment, added in 1804, changed the method of electing the president stated in Article II, Section 3. The Twelfth Amendment requires that the electors cast separate ballots for president and vice president.

Section 10

[1.] No State shall enter into any Treaty, Alliance, or Confederation; grant Letters of Marque and Reprisal; coin Money; emit Bills of Credit; make any Thing but gold and silver Coin a Tender in Payment of Debts; pass any Bill of Attainder, ex post facto Law, or Law impairing the Obligation of Contracts, or grant any Title of Nobility.

[2.] No State shall, without the Consent of the Congress, lay any Imposts or Duties on Imports or Exports, except what may be absolutely necessary for executing its inspection Laws: and the net Produce of all Duties and Imposts, laid by any State on Imports and Exports, shall be for the Use of the Treasury of the United States; and all such Laws shall be subject to the Revision and Controul of the Congress.

[3.] No State shall, without the Consent of Congress, lay any Duty of Tonnage, keep Troops, or Ships of War in time of Peace, enter into any Agreement or Compact with another State, or with a foreign Power, or engage in War, unless actually invaded, or in such imminent Danger as will not admit of delay.

Article II

Section 1

[1.] The executive Power shall be vested in a President of the United States of America. He shall hold his Office during the Term of four Years, and, together with the Vice President, chosen for the same Term, be elected, as follows.

[2.] Each State shall appoint, in such Manner as the Legislature thereof may direct, a Number of Electors, equal to the whole Number of Senators and Representatives to which the State may be entitled in the Congress: but no Senator or Representative, or Person holding an Office of Trust or Profit under the United States, shall be appointed an Elector.

[3.] The Electors shall meet in their respective States, and vote by Ballot for two Persons, of whom one at least shall not be an Inhabitant of the same State with themselves. And they shall make a List of all the Persons voted for, and of the Number of Votes for each; which List they shall sign and certify, and transmit sealed to the Seat of the Government of the United States, directed to the President of the Senate. The President of the Senate shall, in the Presence of the Senate and House of Representatives, open all the Certificates, and the Votes shall then be counted. The Person having the greatest Number of Votes shall be the President, if such Number be a Majority of the whole Number of Electors appointed; and if there be more than one who have such Majority, and have an equal Number of Votes, then the House of Representatives shall immediately chuse by Ballot one of them for President; and if no person have a Majority, then from the five highest on the List the said House shall in like Manner chuse the President. But in chusing the President, the Votes shall be taken by States, the Representation from each State having one Vote; A quorum for this Purpose shall consist of a Member or Members from two thirds of the States, and a Majority of all the States shall be necessary to a Choice. In every Case, after the Choice of the President, the Person having the greatest Number of Votes of the Electors shall be the Vice President. But if there should remain two or more who have equal Votes, the Senate shall chuse from them by Ballot the Vice President.

[4.] The Congress may determine the Time of chusing the Electors, and the Day on which they shall give their Votes; which Day shall be the same throughout the United States.

[5.] No Person except a natural born Citizen, or a Citizen of the United States, at the time of the Adoption of this Constitution, shall be eligible to the Office of President; neither shall any Person be eligible to that Office who shall not have attained to the Age of thirty five Years, and been fourteen Years a Resident within the United States.

[6.] In Case of the Removal of the President from Office, or of his Death, Resignation, or Inability to discharge the Powers and Duties of the said Office, the Same shall devolve on the Vice President, and the Congress may by Law provide for the Case of Removal, Death, Resignation or Inability, both of the President and Vice President, declaring what Officer shall then act as President, and such Officer shall act accordingly, until the Disability be removed, or a President shall be elected.

[7.] The President shall, at stated Times, receive for his Services, a Compensation, which shall neither be encreased nor diminished during the Period for which he shall have been elected, and he shall not receive within that Period any other Emolument from the United States, or any of them.

[8.] Before he enter on the Execution of his Office, he shall take the following Oath or Affirmation:—"I do solemnly swear (or affirm) that I will faithfully execute the Office of President of the United States, and will to the best of my Ability, preserve, protect and defend the Constitution of the United States."

Section 2

[1.] The President shall be Commander in Chief of the Army and Navy of the United States, and of the Militia of the several States, when called into the actual Service of the United States; he may require the Opinion, in writing, of the principal Officer in each of the executive Departments, upon any Subject relating to the Duties of their respective Offices, and he shall have Power to grant Reprieves and Pardons for Offences against the United States, except in Cases of Impeachment.

What Might Have Been

Qualifications At the Constitutional Convention, the New Jersey Amendments, sponsored by the smaller states, raised the possibility of making the executive a committee of people rather than a single individual. Also, executives were not allowed to run for a second term of office under this plan.

Section 1.
President and Vice President

Qualifications The president must be a citizen of the United States by birth, at least 35 years of age, and a resident of the United States for 14 years.

Section 1.
President and Vice President

Vacancies If the president dies, resigns, is removed from office by impeachment, or is unable to carry out the duties of the office, the vice president becomes president. (see Amendment XXV)

Section 1.
President and Vice President

Salary Originally, the president's salary was $25,000 per year. The president's current salary is $400,000 plus a $50,000 nontaxable expense account per year. The president also receives living accommodations in two residences—the White House and Camp David.

Section 2.
Powers of the President

Cabinet Mention of "the principal officer in each of the executive departments" is the only suggestion of the president's cabinet to be found in the Constitution. The cabinet is an advisory body, and its power depends on the president. Section 2, Clause 1, also makes the president the head of the armed forces. This established the principle of civilian control of the military.

Section 2.
Powers of the President

Treaties The president is responsible for the conduct of relations with foreign countries. *What role does the Senate have in approving treaties?*

Section 3.
Powers of the President

Executive Orders An important presidential power is the ability to issue executive orders. An executive order is a rule or command the president issues that has the force of law. Only Congress can make laws under the Constitution, but executive orders are considered part of the president's duty to "take care that the laws be faithfully executed." This power is often used during emergencies. Over time, the scope of executive orders has expanded. Decisions by federal agencies and departments are also considered to be executive orders.

Section 4. Impeachment

Reasons for Removal From Office This section states the reasons for which the president and vice president may be impeached and removed from office. Only Andrew Johnson and Bill Clinton have been impeached by the House. Richard Nixon resigned before the House could vote on possible impeachment.

Article III.
The Judicial Branch

The term *judicial* refers to courts. The Constitution set up only the Supreme Court but provided for the establishment of other federal courts. The judiciary of the United States has two different systems of courts. One system consists of the federal courts, whose powers derive from the Constitution and federal laws. The other includes the courts of each of the 50 states, whose powers derive from state constitutions and laws.

[2.] He shall have Power, by and with the Advice and Consent of the Senate, to make Treaties, provided two thirds of the Senators present concur; and he shall nominate, and by and with the Advice and Consent of the Senate, shall appoint Ambassadors, other public Ministers and Consuls, Judges of the supreme Court, and all other Officers of the United States, whose Appointments are not herein otherwise provided for, and which shall be established by Law: but the Congress may by Law vest the Appointment of such inferior Officers, as they think proper, in the President alone, in the Courts of Law, or in the Heads of Departments.

[3.] The President shall have Power to fill up all Vacancies that may happen during the Recess of the Senate, by granting Commissions which shall expire at the End of their next Session.

Section 3

He shall from time to time give to the Congress Information of the State of the Union, and recommend to their Consideration such Measures as he shall judge necessary and expedient; he may, on extraordinary Occasions, convene both Houses, or either of them, and in Case of Disagreement between them, with Respect to the Time of Adjournment, he may adjourn them to such Time as he shall think proper; he shall receive Ambassadors and other public Ministers; he shall take Care that the Laws be faithfully executed, and shall Commission all the Officers of the United States.

Section 4

The President, Vice President and all civil Officers of the United States, shall be removed from Office on Impeachment for, and Conviction of, Treason, Bribery, or other high Crimes and Misdemeanors.

Article III

Section 1

The judicial Power of the United States, shall be vested in one supreme Court, and in such inferior Courts as the Congress may from time to time ordain and establish. The Judges, both of the supreme and inferior Courts, shall hold their Offices during good Behaviour, and shall, at stated Times, receive for their Services, a Compensation, which shall not be diminished during their Continuance in Office.

Section 2

[1.] The judicial Power shall extend to all Cases, in Law and Equity, arising under this Constitution, the Laws of the United States, and Treaties made, or which shall be made, under their Authority;—to all Cases affecting Ambassadors, other public Ministers and Consuls;—to all Cases of admiralty and maritime Jurisdiction;—to Controversies to which the United States shall be a Party;—to Controversies between two or more States;—between a State and Citizens of another State;—between Citizens of different States,—between Citizens of the same State claiming Lands under Grants of different States, and between a State, or the Citizens thereof, and foreign States, Citizens or Subjects.

[2.] In all Cases affecting Ambassadors, other public Ministers and Consuls, and those in which a State shall be Party, the supreme Court shall have **original Jurisdiction**. In all the other Cases before mentioned, the supreme Court shall have **appellate Jurisdiction**, both as to Law and Fact, with such Exceptions, and under such Regulations as the Congress shall make.

[3.] The Trial of all Crimes, except in Cases of Impeachment, shall be by Jury; and such Trial shall be held in the State where the said Crimes shall have been committed; but when not committed within any State, the Trial shall be at such Place or Places as the Congress may by Law have directed.

Section 3

[1.] Treason against the United States, shall consist only in levying War against them, or in adhering to their Enemies, giving them Aid and Comfort. No Person shall be convicted of Treason unless on the Testimony of two Witnesses to the same overt Act, or on Confession in open Court.

[2.] The Congress shall have Power to declare the Punishment of Treason, but no Attainder of Treason shall work Corruption of Blood, or Forfeiture except during the Life of the Person attainted.

Article IV

Section 1

Full Faith and Credit shall be given in each State to the public Acts, Records, and judicial Proceedings of every other State. And the Congress may by general Laws prescribe the Manner in which such Acts, Records and Proceedings shall be proved, and the Effect thereof.

Section 2

[1.] The Citizens of each State shall be entitled to all Privileges and Immunities of Citizens in the several States.

[2.] A Person charged in any State with **Treason**, Felony, or other Crime, who shall flee from Justice, and be found in another State, shall on Demand of the executive Authority of the State from which he fled, be delivered up, to be removed to the State having Jurisdiction of the Crime.

[3.] No Person held to Service of Labour in one State, under the Laws thereof, escaping into another, shall, in Consequence of any Law or Regulation therein, be discharged from such Service or Labour, but shall be delivered up on Claim of the Party to whom such Service or Labour may be due.

Section 2. Jurisdiction

General Jurisdiction Federal courts deal mostly with "statute law," or laws passed by Congress, treaties, and cases involving the Constitution itself.

Section 2. Jurisdiction

The Supreme Court A court with "original jurisdiction" has the authority to be the first court to hear a case. The Supreme Court generally has "appellate jurisdiction" in that it hears mostly cases appealed from lower courts.

Section 2. Jurisdiction

Jury Trial Except in cases of impeachment, anyone accused of a crime has the right to a trial by jury. The trial must be held in the state where the crime was committed. Jury trial guarantees were strengthened in the Sixth, Seventh, Eighth, and Ninth Amendments.

Vocabulary

original jurisdiction: *authority to be the first court to hear a case*

appellate jurisdiction: *authority to hear cases appealed from lower courts*

treason: *violation of the allegiance owed by a person to his or her own country, for example, by aiding an enemy*

Article IV. Relations Among the States

Article IV explains the relationship of the states to one another and to the national government. This article requires each state to give citizens of other states the same rights as its own citizens, addresses the admission of new states, and guarantees that the national government will protect the states.

Section 1. Official Acts

Recognition by States This provision ensures that each state recognizes the laws, court decisions, and records of all other states. For example, a marriage license issued by one state must be accepted by all states.

Section 3. New States and Territories

New States Congress has the power to admit new states. It also determines the basic guidelines for applying for statehood. Two states, Maine and West Virginia, were created within the boundaries of another state. In the case of West Virginia, President Lincoln recognized the West Virginia government as the legal government of Virginia during the Civil War. This allowed West Virginia to secede from Virginia without obtaining approval from the Virginia legislature.

Article V. The Amendment Process

Article V explains how the Constitution can be amended, or changed. All of the 27 amendments were proposed by a two-thirds vote of both houses of Congress. Only the Twenty-first Amendment was ratified by constitutional conventions of the states. All other amendments have been ratified by state legislatures.
What is an amendment?

Vocabulary

amendment: *a change to the Constitution*
ratification: *process by which an amendment is approved*

Article VI. Constitutional Supremacy

Article VI contains the "supremacy clause." This clause establishes that the Constitution, laws passed by Congress, and treaties of the United States "shall be the supreme Law of the Land." The "supremacy clause" recognizes the Constitution and federal laws as supreme when in conflict with those of the states.

Section 3

[1.] New States may be admitted by the Congress into this Union; but no new State shall be formed or erected within the Jurisdiction of any other State; nor any State be formed by the Junction of two or more States, or Parts of States, without the Consent of the Legislatures of the States concerned as well as of the Congress.

[2.] The Congress shall have Power to dispose of and make all needful Rules and Regulations respecting the Territory or other Property belonging to the United States; and nothing in this Constitution shall be so construed as to Prejudice any Claims of the United States, or of any particular State.

Section 4

The United States shall guarantee to every State in this Union a Republican Form of Government, and shall protect each of them against Invasion; and on Application of the Legislature, or of the Executive (when the Legislature cannot be convened) against domestic Violence.

Article V

The Congress, whenever two thirds of both Houses shall deem it necessary, shall propose **Amendments** to this Constitution, or, on the Application of the Legislatures of two thirds of the several States, shall call a Convention for proposing Amendments, which, in either Case, shall be valid to all Intents and Purposes, as Part of this Constitution, when ratified by the Legislatures of three fourths of the several States, or by Conventions in three fourths thereof, as the one or the other Mode of **Ratification** may be proposed by the Congress; Provided that no Amendment which may be made prior to the Year One thousand eight hundred and eight shall in any Manner affect the first and fourth Clauses in the Ninth Section of the first Article; and that no State, without its Consent, shall be deprived of its equal Suffrage in the Senate.

Article VI

[1.] All Debts contracted and Engagements entered into, before the Adoption of this Constitution, shall be as valid against the United States under this Constitution, as under the Confederation.

[2.] This Constitution, and the Laws of the United States which shall be made in Pursuance thereof; and all Treaties made, or which shall be made, under the Authority of the United States, shall be the supreme Law of the Land; and the Judges in every State shall be bound thereby, any Thing in the Constitution or Laws of any State to the Contrary notwithstanding.

[3.] The Senators and Representatives before mentioned, and the Members of the several State Legislatures, and all executive and judicial Officers, both of the United States and of the several States, shall be bound by Oath or Affirmation, to support this Constitution; but no religious Test shall ever be required as a Qualification to any Office or public Trust under the United States.

Article VII

The Ratification of the Conventions of nine States, shall be sufficient for the Establishment of this Constitution between the States so ratifying the Same.

Done in Convention by the Unanimous Consent of the States present the Seventeenth Day of September in the Year of our Lord one thousand seven hundred and Eighty seven and of the Independence of the United States of America the Twelfth. In witness whereof We have hereunto subscribed our Names,

Article VII. Ratification

Article VII addresses ratification and states that, unlike the Articles of Confederation, which required approval of all thirteen states for adoption, the Constitution would take effect after it was ratified by nine states.

Signers

George Washington,
President and Deputy from Virginia

New Hampshire
John Langdon
Nicholas Gilman

Massachusetts
Nathaniel Gorham
Rufus King

Connecticut
William Samuel Johnson
Roger Sherman

New York
Alexander Hamilton

New Jersey
William Livingston
David Brearley
William Paterson
Jonathan Dayton

Pennsylvania
Benjamin Franklin
Thomas Mifflin
Robert Morris
George Clymer
Thomas FitzSimons
Jared Ingersoll
James Wilson
Gouverneur Morris

Delaware
George Read
Gunning Bedford, Jr.
John Dickinson
Richard Bassett
Jacob Broom

Maryland
James McHenry
Daniel of St. Thomas Jenifer
Daniel Carroll

Virginia
John Blair
James Madison, Jr.

North Carolina
William Blount
Richard Dobbs Spaight
Hugh Williamson

South Carolina
John Rutledge
Charles Cotesworth Pinckney
Charles Pinckney
Pierce Butler

Georgia
William Few
Abraham Baldwin

Attest: William Jackson, Secretary

Amendment I

Congress shall make no law respecting an establishment of religion, or prohibiting the free exercise thereof; or abridging the freedom of speech, or of the press; or the right of the people peaceably to assemble, and to petition the Government for a redress of grievances.

Amendment II

A well regulated Militia, being necessary to the security of a free State, the right of the people to keep and bear Arms, shall not be infringed.

The Amendments

This part of the Constitution consists of changes and additions. The Constitution has been amended 27 times throughout the nation's history.

The Bill of Rights

The first 10 amendments are known as the Bill of Rights (1791). These amendments limit the powers of the federal government. The First Amendment protects the civil liberties of individuals in the United States. The amendment freedoms are not absolute, however. They are limited by the rights of other individuals. *What freedoms does the First Amendment protect?*

Vocabulary

quarter: *to provide living accommodations*
warrant: *document that gives police particular rights or powers*

Amendment 5

Rights of the Accused This amendment contains protections for people accused of crimes. One of the protections is that government may not deprive any person of life, liberty, or property without due process of law. This means that the government must follow proper constitutional procedures in trials and in other actions it takes against individuals. *According to Amendment V, what is the function of a grand jury?*

Amendment 6

Right to Speedy and Fair Trial
A basic protection is the right to a speedy, public trial. The jury must hear witnesses and evidence on both sides before deciding the guilt or innocence of a person charged with a crime. This amendment also provides that legal counsel must be provided to a defendant. In 1963, in *Gideon* v. *Wainwright*, the Supreme Court ruled that if a defendant cannot afford a lawyer, the government must provide one to defend him or her. *Why is the right to a "speedy" trial important?*

Vocabulary

common law: *law established by previous court decisions*

Amendment III

No Soldier shall, in time of peace be **quartered** in any house, without the consent of the Owner, nor in time of war, but in a manner to be prescribed by law.

Amendment IV

The right of the people to be secure in their persons, houses, papers, and effects, against unreasonable searches and seizures, shall not be violated, and no **Warrants** shall issue, but upon probable cause, supported by Oath or affirmation, and particularly describing the place, to be searched, and the persons or things to be seized.

Amendment V

No person shall be held to answer for a capital, or otherwise infamous crime, unless on a presentment or indictment of a Grand Jury, except in cases arising in the land or naval forces, or in the Militia, when in actual service in time of War or public danger; nor shall any person be subject for the same offence to be twice put in jeopardy of life or limb; nor shall be compelled in any criminal case to be a witness against himself, nor be deprived of life, liberty, or property, without due process of law; nor shall private property be taken for public use without just compensation.

Amendment VI

In all criminal prosecutions, the accused shall enjoy the right to a speedy and public trial, by an impartial jury of the State and district wherein the crime shall have been committed, which district shall have been previously ascertained by law, and to be informed of the nature and cause of the accusation; to be confronted with the witnesses against him; to have compulsory process for obtaining Witnesses in his favor, and to have the assistance of counsel for his defence.

Amendment VII

In Suits at common law, where the value in controversy shall exceed twenty dollars, the right of trial by jury shall be preserved, and no fact tried by a jury, shall be otherwise reexamined in any Court of the United States, than according to the rules of **common law**.

Amendment VIII

Excessive **bail** shall not be required, nor excessive fines imposed, nor cruel and unusual punishments inflicted.

Amendment IX

The enumeration in the Constitution, of certain rights, shall not be construed to deny or disparage others retained by the people.

Amendment X

The powers not delegated to the United States by the Constitution, nor prohibited by it to the States, are reserved to the States respectively, or to the people.

Amendment XI

The Judicial power of the United States shall not be construed to extend to any suit in law or equity, commenced or prosecuted against one of the United States by Citizens of another State, or by Citizens or Subjects of any Foreign State.

Amendment XII

The electors shall meet in their respective states and vote by ballot for President and Vice-President, one of whom, at least, shall not be an inhabitant of the same state with themselves; they shall name in their ballots the person voted for as President, and in distinct ballots the person voted for as Vice-President, and they shall make distinct lists of all persons voted for as President, and of all persons voted for as Vice-President, and of the number of votes for each, which lists they shall sign and certify, and transmit sealed to the seat of the government of the United States, directed to the President of the Senate;—The President of the Senate shall, in the presence of the Senate and House of Representatives, open all the certificates and the votes shall then be counted;—The person having the greatest number of votes for President, shall be the President, if such number be a **majority** of the whole number of Electors appointed; and if no person have such majority, then from the persons having the highest numbers not exceeding three on the list of those voted for as President, the House of Representatives shall choose immediately, by ballot, the President. But in choosing the President, the votes shall be taken by states, the representation from each state having one vote; a quorum for this purpose shall consist of a member or members from two-thirds of the states, and a majority of all the states shall be necessary to a choice. And if the House of Representatives shall not choose a President whenever the right of choice shall devolve upon them, before the fourth day of March next following, then the Vice-President shall act as President, as in the case of the death or other constitutional disability of the President. The person having the greatest number of votes as Vice-President, shall be the Vice-President, if such number be a majority of the whole number of Electors appointed, and if no person have a majority, then from the two highest numbers on the list, the Senate shall choose the Vice-President; a quorum for the purpose shall consist of two-thirds of the whole number of Senators, and a majority of the whole number shall be necessary to a choice. But no person constitutionally ineligible to the office of President shall be eligible to that of Vice-President of the United States.

Amendment 9

Powers Reserved to the People
This amendment prevents government from claiming that the only rights people have are those listed in the Bill of Rights.

Amendment 10

Powers Reserved to the States
This amendment protects the states and the people from the federal government. It establishes that powers not given to the national government and not denied to the states by the Constitution belong to the states or to the people. These are checks on the "necessary and proper" power of the federal government, which is provided for in Article I, Section 8, Clause 18.

Amendment 11

Suits Against the States The Eleventh Amendment (1795) provides that a lawsuit brought by a citizen of the United States or a foreign nation against a state must be tried in a state court, not in a federal court. The Supreme Court had ruled in *Chisholm* v. *Georgia* (1793) that a federal court could try a lawsuit brought by citizens of South Carolina against a citizen of Georgia.

Vocabulary

bail: *money that an accused person provides to the court as a guarantee that he or she will be present for a trial*
majority: *more than half*

Amendment 12

Election of President and Vice President The Twelfth Amendment (1804) corrects a problem that had arisen in the method of electing the president and vice president, which is described in Article II, Section 1, Clause 3. This amendment provides for the Electoral College to use separate ballots in voting for president and vice president. *If no candidate receives a majority of the electoral votes, who elects the president?*

Amendment 13

Abolition of Slavery Amendments Thirteen (1865), Fourteen, and Fifteen often are called the Civil War or Reconstruction amendments. The Thirteenth Amendment outlaws slavery.

Amendment 14

Rights of Citizens The Fourteenth Amendment (1868) originally was intended to protect the legal rights of the freed slaves. Its interpretation has been extended to protect the rights of citizenship in general by prohibiting a state from depriving any person of life, liberty, or property without "due process of law." In addition, it states that all people have the right to equal protection of the laws in all states.

Vocabulary

abridge: *to reduce*

Amendment 14. Section 2

Representation in Congress This section reduced the number of members a state had in the House of Representatives if it denied its citizens the right to vote. Later civil rights laws and the Twenty-fourth Amendment guaranteed the vote to African Americans.

Amendment 14. Section 3

Penalty for Engaging in Insurrection The leaders of the Confederacy were barred from state or federal offices unless Congress agreed to remove this ban. By the end of Reconstruction, all but a few Confederate leaders were allowed to return to public service.

Amendment XIII

Section 1

Neither slavery nor involuntary servitude, except as a punishment for crime whereof the party shall have been duly convicted, shall exist within the United States, or any place subject to their jurisdiction.

Section 2

Congress shall have power to enforce this article by appropriate legislation.

Amendment XIV

Section 1

All persons born or naturalized in the United States, and subject to the jurisdiction thereof, are citizens of the United States and of the State wherein they reside. No State shall make or enforce any law which shall **abridge** the privileges or immunities of citizens of the United States; nor shall any State deprive any person of life, liberty, or property, without due process of law; nor deny to any person within its jurisdiction the equal protection of the laws.

Section 2

Representatives shall be apportioned among the several States according to their respective numbers, counting the whole number of persons in each State, excluding Indians not taxed. But when the right to vote at any election for the choice of electors for President and Vice President of the United States, Representatives in Congress, the Executive and Judicial officers of a State, or the members of the Legislature thereof, is denied to any of the male inhabitants of such State, being twenty-one years of age, and citizens of the United States, or in any way abridged, except for participation in rebellion, or other crime, the basis of representation therein shall be reduced in the proportion which the number of such male citizens shall bear to the whole number of male citizens twenty-one years of age in such State.

Section 3

No person shall be a Senator or Representative in Congress, or elector of President and Vice President, or hold any office, civil or military, under the United States, or under any State, who, having previously taken an oath, as a member of Congress, or as an officer of the United States, or as a member of any State legislature, or as an executive or judicial officer of any State, to support the Constitution of the United States, shall have engaged in insurrection or rebellion against the same, or given aid or comfort to the enemies thereof. But Congress may by a vote of two-thirds of each House, remove such disability.

Section 4

The validity of the public debt of the United States, authorized by law, including debts incurred for payment of pensions and bounties for service in suppressing **insurrection** or rebellion, shall not be questioned. But neither the United States nor any State shall assume or pay any debt or obligation incurred in aid of insurrection or rebellion against the United States, or any claim for the loss or emancipation of any slave; but all such debts, obligations and claims shall be held illegal and void.

Section 5

The Congress shall have power to enforce, by appropriate legislation, the provisions of this article.

Amendment XV

Section 1

The right of citizens of the United States to vote shall not be denied or abridged by the United States or by any State on account of race, color, or previous condition of servitude.

Section 2

The Congress shall have power to enforce this article by appropriate legislation.

Amendment XVI

The Congress shall have power to lay and collect taxes on incomes, from whatever source derived, without **apportionment** among the several States and without regard to any census or enumeration.

Amendment XVII

Section 1

The Senate of the United States shall be composed of two Senators from each State, elected by the people thereof, for six years; and each Senator shall have one vote. The electors in each State shall have the qualifications requisite for electors of the most numerous branch of the State legislatures.

Section 2

When **vacancies** happen in the representation of any State in the Senate, the executive authority of such State shall issue writs of election to fill such vacancies: *Provided,* That the legislature of any State may empower the executive thereof to make temporary appointments until the people fill the vacancies by election as the legislature may direct.

Section 3

This amendment shall not be so construed as to affect the election or term of any Senator chosen before it becomes valid as part of the Constitution.

Amendment XVIII

Section 1

After one year from ratification of this article, the manufacture, sale, or transportation of intoxicating liquors within, the importation thereof into, or the exportation thereof from the

---

Amendment 14. Section 4

Public Debt The public debt acquired by the federal government during the Civil War was valid and could not be questioned by the South. However, the debts of the Confederacy were declared to be illegal. *Could former slaveholders collect payment for the loss of their slaves?*

Amendment 15

Voting Rights The Fifteenth Amendment (1870) prohibits the government from denying a person's right to vote on the basis of race. Despite the law, many states denied African Americans the right to vote by such means as poll taxes, literacy tests, and white primaries.

Amendment 16

Income Tax The origins of the Sixteenth Amendment (1913) date back to 1895, when the Supreme Court declared a federal income tax unconstitutional. To overturn this decision, this amendment authorizes an income tax that is levied on a direct basis.

Vocabulary

insurrection: *rebellion against the government*

apportionment: *distribution of seats in House based on population*

vacancy: *an office or position that is unfilled or unoccupied*

Amendment 17

Direct Election of Senators The Seventeenth Amendment (1913) states that the people, instead of state legislatures, elect United States senators. *How many years are in a Senate term?*

United States and all territory subject to the jurisdiction thereof for beverage purposes is hereby prohibited.

Section 2

The Congress and the several States shall have concurrent power to enforce this article by appropriate legislation.

Section 3

This article shall be inoperative unless it shall have been ratified as an amendment to the Constitution by the legislatures of the several States, as provided in the Constitution, within seven years from the date of the submission hereof to the States by the Congress.

Amendment XIX

Section 1

The right of citizens of the United States to vote shall not be denied or abridged by the United States or by any State on account of sex.

Section 2

Congress shall have power by appropriate legislation to enforce the provisions of this article.

Amendment XX

Section 1

The terms of the President and Vice President shall end at noon on the 20th day of January, and the terms of the Senators and Representatives at noon on the 3d day of January, of the years in which such terms would have ended if this article had not been ratified; and the terms of their successors shall then begin.

Section 2

The Congress shall assemble at least once in every year, and such meeting shall begin at noon on the 3rd day of January, unless they shall by law appoint a different day.

Section 3

If, at the time fixed for the beginning of the term of the President, the **President elect** shall have died, the Vice President elect shall become President. If a President shall not have been chosen before the time fixed for the beginning of his term, or if the President elect shall have failed to qualify, then the Vice President elect shall act as President until a President shall have qualified; and the Congress may by law provide for the case wherein neither a President elect nor a Vice President elect shall have qualified, declaring who shall then act as President, or the manner in which one who is to act shall be selected, and such person shall act accordingly until a President or Vice President shall have qualified.

Section 4

The Congress may by law provide for the case of the death of any of the persons from whom the House of Representatives may choose a President whenever the right of choice shall have devolved upon them, and for the case of the death of any of the persons from whom the Senate may choose a Vice President whenever the right of choice shall have devolved upon them.

Section 5

Section 1 and 2 shall take effect on the 15th day of October following the ratification of this article.

Section 6

This article shall be inoperative unless it shall have been ratified as an amendment to the Constitution by the legislatures of three-fourths of the several States within seven years from the date of its submission.

Amendment XXI

Section 1

The eighteenth article of amendment to the Constitution of the United States is hereby repealed.

Section 2

The transportation or importation into any State, Territory, or possession of the United States for delivery or use therein of intoxicating liquors, in violation of the laws thereof, is hereby prohibited.

Section 3

This article shall be inoperative unless it shall have been ratified as an amendment to the Constitution by conventions in the several States, as provided in the Constitution, within seven years from the date of the submission hereof to the States by the Congress.

Amendment XXII

Section 1

No person shall be elected to the office of the President more than twice, and no person who had held the office of President, or acted as President, for more than two years of a term to which some other person was elected President shall be elected to the office of the President more than once. But this Article shall not apply to any person holding the office of President when this Article was proposed by the Congress, and shall not prevent any person who may be holding the office of President, or acting as President, during the term within which this Article becomes operative from holding the office of President or acting as President during the remainder of such term.

Section 2

This article shall be inoperative unless it shall have been ratified as an amendment to the Constitution by the

---

Amendment 20. Section 3

Succession of President and Vice President This section provides that if the president elect dies before taking office, the vice president elect becomes president.

Amendment 21

Repeal of Prohibition The Twenty-first Amendment (1933) repeals the Eighteenth Amendment. It is the only amendment ever passed to overturn an earlier amendment. It is also the only amendment ratified by special state conventions instead of state legislatures.

Amendment 22

Presidential Term Limit The Twenty-second Amendment (1951) limits presidents to a maximum of two elected terms. The amendment wrote into the Constitution a custom started by George Washington. It was passed largely as a reaction to Franklin D. Roosevelt's election to four terms between 1933 and 1945. It also provides that anyone who succeeds to the presidency and serves for more than two years of the term may not be elected more than one more time.

legislatures of three-fourths of the several States within seven years from the date of its submission to the States by the Congress.

Amendment XXIII

Section 1

The District constituting the seat of Government of the United States shall appoint in such manner as the Congress may direct:

A number of electors of President and Vice President equal to the whole number of Senators and Representatives in Congress to which the District would be entitled if it were a State, but in no event more than the least populous State; they shall be in addition to those appointed by the States, but they shall be considered, for the purposes of the election of President and Vice President, to be electors appointed by a State; and they shall meet in the District and perform such duties as provided by the twelfth article of amendment.

Section 2

The Congress shall have power to enforce this article by appropriate legislation.

Amendment XXIV

Section 1

The right of citizens of the United States to vote in any primary or other election for President or Vice President, for electors for President or Vice President, or for Senator or Representative in Congress, shall not be denied or abridged by the United States or any State by reason of failure to pay any poll tax or other tax.

Section 2

The Congress shall have power to enforce this article by appropriate legislation.

Amendment XXV

Section 1

In case of the removal of the President from office or his death or resignation, the Vice President shall become President.

Section 2

Whenever there is a vacancy in the office of the Vice President, the President shall nominate a Vice President who shall take the office upon confirmation by a majority vote of both Houses of Congress.

Section 3

Whenever the President transmits to the President pro tempore of the Senate and the Speaker of the House of Representatives his written declaration that he is unable to discharge the powers and duties of his office, and until he

---

Amendment 23

D.C. Electors The Twenty-third Amendment (1961) allows citizens living in Washington, D.C., to vote for president and vice president, a right previously denied residents of the nation's capital. The District of Columbia now has three presidential electors, the number to which it would be entitled if it were a state.

Amendment 24

Abolition of the Poll Tax
The Twenty-fourth Amendment (1964) prohibits poll taxes in federal elections. Prior to the passage of this amendment, some states had used such taxes to keep low-income African Americans from voting. In 1966, the Supreme Court banned poll taxes in state elections as well.

transmits to them a written declaration to the contrary, such powers and duties shall be discharged by the Vice President as Acting President.

Section 4

Whenever the Vice President and a majority of either the principal officers of the executive departments or of such other body as Congress may by law provide, transmit to the President pro tempore of the Senate and the Speaker of the House of Representatives their written declaration that the President is unable to discharge the powers and duties of his office, the Vice President shall immediately assume the power and duties of the office of Acting President.

Thereafter, when the President transmits to the President pro tempore of the Senate and the Speaker of the House of Representatives his written declaration that no inability exists, he shall resume the powers and duties of his office unless the Vice President and a majority of either the principal officers of the executive department or of such other body as Congress may by law provide, transmit within four days to the President pro tempore of the Senate and the Speaker of the House of Representatives their written declaration that the President is unable to discharge the powers and duties of his office. Thereupon Congress shall decide the issue, assembling within forty-eight hours for that purpose if not in session. If the Congress, within twenty-one days after receipt of the latter written declaration, or, if Congress is not in session, within twenty-one days after Congress is required to assemble, determines by two-thirds vote of both Houses that the President is unable to discharge the powers and duties of his office, the Vice President shall continue to discharge the same as Acting President; otherwise, the President shall resume the power and duties of his office.

Amendment XXVI

Section 1

The right of citizens of the United States, who are eighteen years of age or older, to vote shall not be denied or abridged by the United States or by any State on account of age.

Section 2

The Congress shall have power to enforce this article by appropriate legislation.

Amendment XXVII

No law, varying the compensation for the services of Senators and Representatives, shall take effect, until an election of representatives shall have intervened.

Amendment 25

Presidential Disability and Succession The Twenty-fifth Amendment (1967) established a process for the vice president to take over leadership of the nation when a president is disabled. It also set procedures for filling a vacancy in the office of vice president.

This amendment was used in 1973, when Vice President Spiro Agnew resigned from office after being charged with accepting bribes. President Richard Nixon then appointed Gerald R. Ford as vice president in accordance with the provisions of the Twenty-fifth Amendment. A year later, President Nixon resigned during the Watergate scandal, and Ford became president. President Ford then had to fill the vice presidency, which he had left vacant upon assuming the presidency. He named Nelson A. Rockefeller as vice president. Thus, individuals who had not been elected held both the presidency and the vice presidency. *Whom does the president inform if he or she cannot carry out the duties of the office?*

Amendment 26

Voting Age of 18 The Twenty-sixth Amendment (1971) lowered the voting age in both federal and state elections to 18.

Amendment 27

Congressional Salary Restraints The Twenty-seventh Amendment (1992) makes congressional pay raises effective during the term following their passage. James Madison offered the amendment in 1789, but it was never adopted. In 1982 Gregory Watson, then a student at the University of Texas, discovered the forgotten amendment while doing research for a school paper. Watson made the amendment's passage his crusade.

Contents

The Code of Hammurabi

Hammurabi, a Mesopotamian ruler, developed his code of laws around 1700 B.C. This development of written law was a major advance toward justice and order.

Anu and Bel called by name me, Hammurabi, the exalted prince, who feared God, to bring about the rule of righteousness in the land, to destroy the wicked and the evil-doers; so that the strong should not harm the weak; so that I should . . . further the well-being of mankind. . . .

2. If any one bring an accusation against a man, and the accused go to the river and leap into the river, if he sink in the river his accuser shall take possession of his house. But if the river prove that the accused is not guilty, and he escape unhurt, then he who had brought the accusation shall be put to death, while he who leaped into the river shall take possession of the house that had belonged to his accuser. . . .

8. If any one steal cattle or sheep, or an ass, or a pig or a goat, if it belong to a god or to the court, the thief shall pay thirtyfold therefor; if they belonged to a freed man of the king he shall pay tenfold; if the thief has nothing with which to pay he shall be put to death. . . .

21. If any one break a hole into a house (break in to steal), he shall be put to death before that hole and be buried.

22. If any one is committing a robbery and is caught, then he shall be put to death.

23. If the robber is not caught, then shall he who was robbed claim under oath the amount of his loss; then shall the community, and . . . on whose ground and territory and in whose domain it was compensate him for the goods stolen. . . .

53. If any one be too lazy to keep his dam in proper condition, and does not so keep it; if then the dam break and all the fields be flooded, then shall he in whose dam the break occurred be sold for money, and the money shall replace the corn which he has caused to be ruined. . . .

117. If any one fail to meet a claim for debt, and sell himself, his wife, his son, and daughter for money or give them away to forced labor: they shall work for three years in the house of the man who bought them, or the proprietor, and in the fourth year they shall be set free. . . .

136. If any one leave his house, run away, and then his wife go to another house, if then he return, and wishes to take his wife back: because he fled from his home and ran away, the wife of this runaway shall not return to her husband. . . .

142. If a woman quarrel with her husband . . . the reasons for her prejudice must be presented. If she is guiltless, and there is no fault on her part, but he leaves and neglects her, then no guilt attaches to this woman, she shall take her dowry and go back to her father's house.

143. If she is not innocent, but leaves her husband . . . this woman shall be cast into the water. . . .

195. If a son strike his father, his hands shall be hewn off.

196. If a man put out the eye of another man, his eye shall be put out.

197. If he break another man's bone, his bone shall be broken. . . .

200. If a man knock out the teeth of his equal, his teeth shall be knocked out. . . .

202. If any one strike the body of a man higher in rank than he, he shall receive sixty blows with an ox-whip in public. . . .

215. If a physician make a large incision with an operating knife and cure it, or if he open a tumor (over an eye) with an operating knife, and saves the eye, he shall receive ten shekels in money. . . .

218. If a physician make a large incision with the operating knife, and kill him, or open a tumor with the operating knife, and cut out the eye, his hands shall be cut off. . . .

229. If a builder build a house for some one, and does not construct it properly, and the house which he built fall in and kill its owner, then that builder shall be put to death. . . .

The Magna Carta

The Magna Carta, signed by King John in 1215, marked a decisive step forward in the development of constitutional government in England. Later it served as a model for colonists who carried its guarantees of legal and political rights to America.

John, by the grace of God, king of England, lord of Ireland, duke of Normandy and Aquitaine, and count of Anjou: to the archbishops, bishops, abbots, earls, barons, justiciaries, foresters, sheriffs, reeves, ministers, and all bailiffs and others his faithful subjects, greeting. . . .

1. We have, in the first place, granted to God, and by this our present charter confirmed for us and our heirs forever that the English church shall be free. . . .

9. Neither we nor our bailiffs shall seize any land or rent for any debt so long as the debtor's chattels are sufficient to discharge the same. . . .

12. No scutage [tax] or aid [subsidy] shall be imposed in our kingdom unless by the common counsel thereof . . . .

14. For obtaining the common counsel of the kingdom concerning the assessment of aids . . . or of scutage, we will cause to be summoned, severally by our letters, the archbishops, bishops, abbots, earls, and great barons; we will also cause to be summoned generally, by our sheriffs and bailiffs, all those who hold lands directly of us, to meet on a fixed day . . . and at a fixed place. . . .

20. A free man shall be amerced [punished] for a small fault only according to the measure thereof, and for a great crime according to its magnitude. . . . None of these amercements shall be imposed except by the oath of honest men of the neighborhood.

21. Earls and barons shall be amerced only by their peers, and only in proportion to the measure of the offense. . . .

38. In the future no bailiff shall upon his own unsupported accusation put any man to trial without producing credible witnesses to the truth of the accusation.

39. No free man shall be taken, imprisoned, disseised [seized], outlawed, banished, or in any way destroyed, nor will we proceed against or prosecute him, except by the lawful judgment of his peers and by the law of the land.

40. To no one will we sell, to none will we deny or delay, right or justice. . . .

42. In the future it shall be lawful . . . for anyone to leave and return to our kingdom safely and securely by land and water, saving his fealty to us. Excepted are those who have been imprisoned or outlawed according to the law of the land. . . .

61. Whereas we, for the honor of God and the amendment of our realm, and in order the better to allay the discord arisen between us and our barons, have granted all these things aforesaid. . . .

63. Wherefore we will, and firmly charge . . . that all men in our kingdom shall have and hold all the aforesaid liberties, rights, and concessions . . . fully, and wholly to them and their heirs . . . in all things and places forever . . . . It is moreover sworn, as well on our part as on the part of the barons, that all these matters aforesaid will be kept in good faith and without deceit. Witness the abovenamed and many others. Given by our hand in the meadow which is called Runnymede. . . .

The English Bill of Rights

In 1689 William of Orange and his wife, Mary, became joint rulers of England after accepting what became known as the Bill of Rights. This document assured the people of certain basic civil rights.

An act declaring the rights and liberties of the subject and settling the succession of the crown. Whereas the lords spiritual and temporal and commons assembled at Westminster lawfully fully and freely representing all the estates of the people of this realm did upon the thirteenth day of February in the year of our Lord one thousand six hundred eight-eight [-nine] present unto their majesties . . . William and Mary prince and princess of Orange . . . a certain declaration in writing made by the said lords and commons in the words following viz

Whereas the late king James the second by the assistance of divers evil counsellors judges and ministers employed by him did endeavor to subvert and extirpate the protestant religion and the laws and liberties of this kingdom.

By assuming and exercising a power of dispensing with and suspending of laws and the execution of laws without consent of parliament. . . .

By levyng money for and to the use of the crown by pretence of prerogative for other time and in other manner than the same was granted by parliament.

By raising and keeping a standing army within this kingdom in time of peace without consent of parliament and quartering soldiers contrary to law. . . .

By violating the freedom of election of members to serve in parliament. . . .

And excessive bail hath been required of persons committed in criminal cases to elude the benefit of the laws made for the liberty of the subjects.

And excessive fines have been imposed.

And illegal and cruel punishments inflicted. . . .

And thereupon the said lords spiritual and temporal and commons . . . do . . . declare

That the pretended power of suspending of laws or the execution of laws by regal authority without consent of parliament is illegal. . . .

That levying money for or to the use of the crown . . . without grant of parliament for longer time or in other manner than the same is or shall be granted is illegal.

That it is the right of the subjects to petition the king and all commitments and prosecutions for such petitioning are illegal.

That the raising or keeping a standing army within the kingdom in time of peace unless it be with consent of parliament is against law. . . .

That election of members of parliament ought to be free. . . .

That excessive bail ought not to be required nor excessive fines imposed nor cruel and unusual punishments inflicted. . . .

The said lords . . . do resolve that William and Mary prince and princess of Orange be and be declared king and queen of England France and Ireland. . . .

The Mayflower Compact

On November 21, 1620, 41 men aboard the Mayflower *drafted this agreement. The* Mayflower Compact *was the first plan of self-government ever put in force in the English colonies. The original compact has been lost.* Mourt's Relation *(1622) is the earliest source of the text reprinted here.*

This day, before we came to harbor, observing some not well affected to unity and concord, but gave some appearance of faction, it was thought good there should be an association and agreement that we should combine together in one body, and to submit to such government and governors as we should by common consent agree to make and choose, and set our hands to this that follows word for word.

In the name of God, Amen. We whose names are underwritten, the loyal subjects of our dread sovereign lord, King James, by the grace of God, of Great Britain, France, and Ireland, King, Defender of the Faith, etc.

Having undertaken for the glory of God, and advancement of the Christian faith and honor of our king and country, a voyage to plant the first colony in the northern parts of Virginia, do by these present, solemnly and mutually, in the presence of God and one of another, covenant and combine ourselves together into a civil body politic, for our better ordering and preservation and furtherance of the ends aforesaid; and by virtue hereof to enact, constitute, and frame such just and equal laws, ordinances, acts, constitutions, offices from time to time as shall be thought most meet and convenient for the general good of the colony; unto which we promise all due submission and obedience. In witness whereof we have hereunder subscribed our names, Cape Cod, 11th of November, in the year of the reign of our sovereign lord, King James, of England, France, and Ireland 18, and of Scotland 54. Anno Domini 1620.

Fundamental Orders of Connecticut

In January 1639, settlers in Connecticut, led by Thomas Hooker, drew up the Fundamental Orders of Connecticut—America's first written constitution. It is essentially a compact among the settlers and a body of laws.

Forasmuch as it has pleased the Almighty God by the wise disposition of His Divine Providence so to order and dispose of things that we, the inhabitants and residents of Windsor, Hartford, and Wethersfield are now cohabiting and dwelling in and upon the river of Conectecotte and the lands thereunto adjoining; and well knowing where a people are gathered together the Word of God requires that, to maintain the peace and union of such a people, there should be an orderly and decent government established according to God, . . . do therefore associate and conjoin ourselves to be as one public state or commonwealth. . . . As also in our civil affairs to be guided and governed according to such laws, rules, orders, and decrees as shall be made, ordered, and decreed, as follows:

1. It is ordered . . . that there shall be yearly two general assemblies or courts; . . . The first shall be called the Court of Election, wherein shall be yearly chosen . . . so many magistrates and other public officers as shall be found requisite. Whereof one to be chosen governor . . . and no other magistrate to be chosen for more than one year; provided aways there be six chosen besides the governor . . . by all that are admitted freemen and have taken the oath of fidelity, and do cohabit within this jurisdiction. . . .

4. It is ordered . . . that no person be chosen governor above once in two years, and that the governor be always a member of some approved congregation, and formerly of the magistracy within this jurisdiction; and all the magistrates freemen of this Commonwealth. . . .

5. It is ordered . . . that to the aforesaid Court of Election the several towns shall send their deputies. . . . Also, the other General Court . . . shall be for making of laws, and any other public occasion which concerns the good of the Commonwealth. . . .

7. It is ordered . . . that . . . the constable or constables of each town shall forthwith give notice distinctly to the inhabitants of the same . . . that . . . they meet and assemble themselves together to elect and choose certain deputies to be at the General Court then following to [manage] the affairs of the Commonwealth; which said deputies shall be chosen by all that are admitted inhabitants in the several towns and have taken the oath of fidelity. . . .

10. It is ordered . . . that every General Court . . . shall consist of the governor, or someone chosen to moderate the Court, and four other magistrates, at least, with the major part of the deputies of the several towns legally chosen. . . . In which said General Courts shall consist the supreme power of the Commonwealth, and they only shall have power to make laws or repeal them, to grant levies, to admit of freemen, dispose of lands undisposed of to several towns or person, and also shall have power to call either Court or magistrate or any other person whatsoever into question for any misdemeanor. . . .

In which Court, the governor or moderator shall have power to order the Court to give liberty of speech, . . . to put all things to vote, and, in case the vote be equal, to have the casting voice. . . .

Two Treatises of Government

John Locke's Two Treatises of Government *was published in 1690. The "Second Treatise of Government" states his belief that government is based on an agreement between the people and ruler.*

Of the State of Nature.

To understand Political Power right, and to derive it from its Original, we must consider what State all Men are naturally in, and that is, a State of perfect Freedom to order their Actions, and dispose of their Possessions, and Persons as they think fit, within the bounds of the Law of Nature, without asking leave, or depending upon the Will of any other Man.

A State also of Equality, wherein all the Power and Jurisdiction is reciprocal, no one having more than another. . . .

Of the Beginning of Political Societies.

Men being, as has been said, by Nature, all free, equal and independent, no one can be put out of this Estate, and subjected to the Political Power of another, without his own Consent. The only way whereby any one divests himself of his Natural Liberty, and puts on the bonds of Civil Society is by agreeing with other Men to joyn and unite into a Community, for their comfortable, safe, and peaceable living one amongst another, in a secure Enjoyment of their properties, and a greater Security against any that are not of it. This any number of Men may do, because it injures not the Freedom of the rest; they are left as they were in the Liberty of the State of Nature. . . .

For when any number of Men have, by the consent of every individual, made a Community, they have thereby made that Community one Body, with a Power to Act as one Body, which is only by the will and determination of the majority. . . .

Whosoever therefore out of a state of Nature unite into a Community, must be understood to give up all the power, necessary to the ends for which they unite into Society, to the majority of the Community. . . .

Of the Dissolution of Government.

. . . Governments are dissolved from within . . . when the Legislative is altered. . . . First, that when such a single Person or Prince sets up his own Arbitrary Will in place of the Laws, which are the Will of the Society, declared by the Legislative, then the Legislative is changed. . . . Secondly, when the Prince hinders the legislative from . . . acting freely, pursuant to those ends, for which it was Constituted, the Legislative is altered. . . . Thirdly, When by the Arbitrary Power of the Prince, the Electors, or ways of Election are altered, without the Consent, and contrary to the common Interest of the People, there also the Legislative is altered. . . .

In these and the like Cases, when the Government is dissolved, the People are at liberty to provide for themselves, by erecting a new Legislative, differing from the other, by the change of Persons, or Form, or both as they shall find it most for their safety and good. For the Society can never, by the fault of another, lose the Native and Original Right it has to preserve itself. . . .

The Wealth of Nations

Adam Smith, a Scottish economist and philosopher, published An Inquiry into the Nature and Causes of the Wealth of Nations *in 1776. The book offered a detailed description of life and trade in English society. It also scientifically described the basic principles of economics for the first time.*

But it is only for the sake of profit that any man employs a capital in the support of industry; and he will always, therefore, endeavour to employ it in the support of that industry of which the produce is likely to be of the greatest value, or to exchange for the greatest quantity either of money or of other goods. . . .

As every individual, therefore, endeavours as much as he can both to employ his capital in the support of domestic industry, and so to direct that industry that its produce may be of the greatest value; every individual necessarily labours to render the annual revenue of the society as great as he can. He generally, indeed, neither intends to promote the public interest, nor knows how much he is promoting it. . . . By pursuing his own interest he frequently promotes that of the society more effectually than when he really intends to promote it. . . .

What is the species of domestic industry which his capital can employ, and of which the produce is likely to be of the greatest value, every individual, it is evident, can, in his local situation, judge much better than any statesman or lawgiver can do for him. . . .

To give the monopoly of the home-market to the produce of domestic industry, in any particular art or manufacture, is in some measure to direct private people in what manner they ought to employ their capitals, and must, in almost all cases, be either a useless or a hurtful regulation. If the produce of domestic can be brought there as cheap as that of foreign industry, the regulation is evidently useless. If it cannot, it must generally be hurtful. It is the maxim of every prudent master of a family, never to attempt to make at home what it will cost him more to make than to buy. The taylor does not attempt to make his own shoes, but buys them of the shoemaker. The shoemaker does not attempt to make his own clothes, but employs a taylor. The farmer attempts to make neither the one nor the other, but employs those different artificers. All of them find it in their interest to employ their whole industry in a way in which they have some advantage over their neighbours, and to purchase with a part of its produce . . . whatever else they have occasion for.

What is prudence in the conduct of every private family, can scarcely be folly in that of a great kingdom. If a foreign country can supply us with a commodity cheaper than we ourselves can make it, better buy it of them with some part of the produce of our own industry, employed in a way in which we have some advantage. . . . It is certainly not employed to the greatest advantage, when it is thus directed towards an object which it can buy cheaper than it can make.

Articles of Confederation

Articles of Confederation and Perpetual Union Between the States of New Hampshire, Massachusetts Bay, Rhode Island and Providence Plantations, Connecticut, New York, New Jersey, Pennsylvania, Delaware, Maryland, Virginia, North Carolina, South Carolina, and Georgia.

Article I. The style of this confederacy shall be "The United States of America."

Article II. Each state retains its sovereignty, freedom, and independence, and every power, jurisdiction, and right which is not by this confederation expressly delegated to the United States in Congress assembled.

Article III. The said states hereby severally enter into a firm league of friendship with each other, for their common defense, the security of their liberties, and their mutual and general welfare, binding themselves to assist each other against all force offered to, or attacks made upon them, or any of them, on account of religion, sovereignty, trade, or any other pretense whatever.

Article IV. The better to secure and perpetuate mutual friendship and intercourse among the people of the different states in this union, the free inhabitants of each of these states, paupers, vagabonds, and fugitives from justice excepted, shall be entitled to all privileges and immunities of free citizens in the several states; and the people of each state shall have free ingress and regress to and from any other state and shall enjoy therein all the privileges of trade and commerce, subject to the same duties, impositions, and restrictions as the inhabitants thereof respectively, provided that such restrictions shall not extend so far as to prevent the removal of property imported into any state, to any other state of which the owner is an inhabitant; provided also that no imposition, duties, or restriction shall be laid by any state on the property of the United States, or either of them.

If any person guilty of or charged with treason, felony, or other high misdemeanor in any state shall flee from justice, and be found in any of the United States, he shall, upon demand of the governor or executive power of the state from which he fled, be delivered up and removed to the state having jurisdiction of his offense.

Full faith and credit shall be given in each of these states to the records, acts, and judicial proceedings of the courts and magistrates of every other state.

Article V. For the more convenient management of the general interests of the United States, delegates shall be annually appointed in such manner as the legislature of each state shall direct, to meet in Congress on the first Monday in November, in every year, with a power reserved to each state to recall its delegates, or any of them, at any time within the year and to send others in their stead for the remainder of the year.

No state shall be represented in Congress by less than two nor by more than seven members; and no person shall be capable of being a delegate for more than three years in any term of six years; nor shall any person, being a delegate, be capable of holding any office under the United States for which he, or another for his benefit, receives any salary, fees, or emolument of any kind.

Each state shall maintain its own delegates in a meeting of the states and while they act as members of the Committee of the States.

In determining questions in the United States in Congress assembled, each state shall have one vote.

Freedom of speech and debate in Congress shall not be impeached or questioned in any court or place out of Congress, and the members of Congress shall be protected in their persons from arrests and imprisonments during the time of their going to and from, and attendance on, Congress, except for treason, felony, or breach of the peace.

Article VI. No state, without the consent of the United States in Congress assembled, shall send any embassy to, or receive any embassy from, or enter into any conference, agreement, alliance, or treaty with any king, prince, or state; nor shall any person holding any office of profit or trust under the United States, or any of them, accept of any present, emolument, office, or title of any kind whatever from any king, prince, or foreign state; nor shall the United States in Congress assembled, or any of them, grant any title of nobility.

No two or more states shall enter into any treaty, confederation, or alliance whatever between them without the consent of the United States in Congress assembled, specifying accurately the purposes for which the same is to be entered into and how long it shall continue.

No state shall lay any imposts or duties which may interfere with any stipulations in treaties entered into by the United States in Congress assembled with any king, prince, or state, in pursuance of any treaties already proposed by Congress, to the courts of France and Spain.

No vessels of war shall be kept up in time of peace by any state except such number only as shall be deemed necessary by the United States in Congress assembled for the defense of such state or its trade; nor shall any body of forces be kept up by any state in time of peace except such number only as in the judgment of the United States in Congress assembled shall be deemed requisite to garrison the forts necessary for the defense of such state; but every state shall always keep up a well-regulated and disciplined militia, sufficiently armed and accoutered, and shall provide and constantly have ready for use, in public stores, a due number of field pieces and tents and a proper quantity of arms, ammunition, and camp equipage.

No state shall engage in any war without the consent of the United States in Congress assembled unless such state be actually invaded by enemies, or shall have received certain advice of a resolution being formed by some nation of Indians to invade such state, and the danger is so imminent as not to admit of a delay till the United States in Congress assembled can be consulted; nor shall any state grant commissions to any ships or vessels of war, nor letters of marque or reprisal, except it be after a declaration of war by the United States in Congress assembled, and then only against the kingdom or state and the subjects thereof against which war has been so declared and under such regulations as shall be established by the United States in Congress assembled, unless such state be infested by pirates, in which case vessels of war may be fitted out for that occasion and kept so long as the danger shall continue or until the United States in Congress assembled shall determine otherwise.

Article VII. When land forces are raised by any state for the common defense, all officers of or under the rank of colonel shall be appointed by the legislature of each state respectively, by whom such forces shall be raised, or in such manner as such state shall direct, and all vacancies shall be filled up by the state which first made the appointment.

Article VIII. All charges of war and all other expenses that shall be incurred for the common defense or general welfare, and allowed by the United States in Congress assembled, shall be defrayed out of a common treasury, which shall be supplied by the several states in proportion to the value of all land within each state, granted to or surveyed for any person, as such land the buildings and improvements thereon shall be estimated according to such mode as the United States in Congress assembled shall from time to time direct and appoint. The taxes for paying that proportion shall be laid and levied by the authority and direction of the legislatures of the several states within the time agreed upon by the United States in Congress assembled.

Article IX. The United States in Congress assembled shall have the sole and exclusive right and power of determining on peace and war, except in the cases mentioned in the sixth article—of sending and receiving ambassadors—entering into treaties and alliances, provided that no treaty of commerce shall be made whereby the legislative power of the respective states shall be restrained from imposing such imposts and duties on foreigners as their own people are subjected to or from prohibiting the exportation or importation of any species of goods or commodities whatsoever—of establishing rules for deciding in all cases what captures on land or water shall be legal, and in what manner prizes taken by land or naval forces in the service of the United States shall be divided or appropriated—of granting letters of marque and reprisal in times of peace—appointing courts for the trial of piracies and felonies committed on the high seas and establishing courts for receiving and determining finally appeals in all cases of captures, provided that no member of Congress shall be appointed a judge in any of the said courts.

The United States in Congress assembled shall also be the last resort on appeal in all disputes and difference now subsisting or that hereafter may arise between two or more states concerning boundary, jurisdiction, or any other cause whatever. . . . Provided, also, that no state shall be deprived of territory for the benefit of the United States.

All controversies concerning the private right of soil claimed under different grants of two or more states, whose jurisdictions as they may respect such lands, and the states which passed such grants are adjusted, the said grants or either of them being at the same time claimed to have originated antecedent to such settlement of jurisdiction shall, on the petition of either party to the Congress of the United States, be finally determined as near as may be in the same manner as is before prescribed for deciding disputes respecting territorial jurisdiction between different states.

The United States in Congress assembled shall also have the sole and exclusive right and power of regulating the alloy and value of coin struck by their own authority or by that of the respective states—fixing the standard of weights and measures throughout the United States— regulating the trade and managing all affairs with the Indians not members of any of the states, provided that the legislative right of any state within its own limits be not infringed or violated— establishing or regulating post offices from one state to another, throughout all the United States, and exacting such postage on the papers passing through the same as may be requisite to defray the expenses of the said office—appointing all officers of the land forces in the service of the United States excepting regimental officers—appointing all the officers of the naval forces, and commissioning all officers whatever in the service of the United States—making rules for the government and regulation of the said land and naval forces, and directing their operations.

The United States in Congress assembled shall have authority to appoint a committee, to sit in the recess of Congress, to be denominated "A Committee of the States," and to consist of one delegate from each state; and to appoint such other committees and civil officers as may be necessary for managing the general affairs of the United States under their direction—to appoint one of their number to preside, provided that no person be allowed to serve in the office of President more than one year in any term of three years; to ascertain the necessary sums of money to be raised for the service of the United States, and to appropriate and apply the same for defraying the public expenses—to borrow money or emit bills on the credit of the United States, transmitting every half-year to the respective states an account of the sums of money so borrowed or emitted—to build and equip a navy—to agree upon the number of land forces, and to make requisitions from each state for its quota, in proportion to the number of white inhabitants in such state, which requisition shall be binding. . . .

Thereupon the legislature of each state shall appoint the regimental officers, raise the men and clothe, arm, and equip them in a soldier-like manner, at the expense of the United States; and the officers and men so clothed, armed, and equipped shall march to the place appointed and within the time agreed on by the United States in Congress assembled. . . .

The United States in Congress assembled shall never engage in a war, nor grant letters of marque and reprisal in time of peace, nor enter into any treaties or alliances, nor coin money, nor regulate the value thereof, nor ascertain the sums and expenses necessary for the defense and welfare of the United States, or any of them, nor emit bills, nor borrow money on the credit of the United States, nor appropriate money, nor agree upon the number of vessels of war to be built or purchased or the number of land or sea forces to be raised, nor appoint a commander in chief of the Army or Navy, unless nine states assent to the same; nor shall a question on any other point, except for adjourning from day to day, be determined unless by the votes of a majority of the United States in Congress assembled. . . .

Article XI. Canada acceding to this Confederation, and joining in the measures of the United States, shall be admitted into and entitled to all the advantages of this union; but no other colony shall be admitted into the same unless such admission be agreed to by nine states.

Article XII. All bills of credit emitted, moneys borrowed, and debts contracted by or under the authority of Congress, before the assembling of the United States, in pursuance of the present Confederation, shall be deemed and considered as a charge against the United States, for payment and satisfaction whereof the said United States and the public faith are hereby solemnly pledged.

The Federalist, No. 10

Among the numerous advantages promised by a well-constructed Union, none deserves to be more accurately developed than its tendency to break and control the violence of faction. The friend of popular governments never finds himself so much alarmed for their character and fate as when he contemplates their propensity to this dangerous vice. . . . The instability, injustice, and confusion introduced into the public councils have, in truth, been the mortal diseases under which popular governments have everywhere perished. . . .

By a faction I understand a number of citizens, whether amounting to a majority or minority of the whole, who are united and actuated by some common impulse of passion, or of interest, adverse to the rights of other citizens, or to the permanent and aggregate interests of the community.

There are two methods of curing the mischiefs of faction: the one, by removing its causes; the other, by controlling its effects.

There are again two methods of removing the causes of faction: the one, by destroying the liberty which is essential to its existence; the other, by giving to every citizen the same opinions, the same passions, and the same interests.

It could never be more truly said than of the first remedy that it was worse than the disease. Liberty is to faction what air is to fire, an aliment without which it instantly expires. But it could not be a less folly to abolish liberty, which is essential to political life, because it nourishes faction than it would be to wish the annihilation of air, which is essential to animal life, because it imparts to fire its destructive agency.

The second expedient is as impracticable as the first would be unwise. As long as the reason of man continues fallible, and he is at liberty to exercise it, different opinions will be formed. . . .

The latent causes of faction are thus sown in the nature of man; and we see them everywhere brought into different degrees of activity, according to the different circumstances of civil society. A zeal for different opinions concerning religion, concerning government, and many other points . . . ; an attachment to different leaders ambitiously contending for pre-eminence and power . . . have, in turn, divided mankind into parties, inflamed them with mutual animosity, and rendered them much more disposed to vex and oppress each other than to cooperate for their common good. . . . The regulation of these various and interfering interests forms the principal task of modern legislation and involves the spirit of party and faction in the necessary and ordinary operations of government. . . .

[Y]et what are many of the most important acts of legislation but so many judicial determinations, not indeed concerning the rights of single persons, but concerning the rights of large bodies of citizens? And what are the different classes of legislators but advocates and parties to the causes which they determine? . . .

It is in vain to say that enlightened statesmen will be able to adjust these clashing interests and render them all subservient to the public good. Enlightened statesmen will not always be at the helm. Nor, in many cases, can such an adjustment be made at all without taking into view indirect and remote considerations, which will rarely prevail over the immediate interest which one party may find in disregarding the rights of another or the good of the whole. . . .

If a faction consists of less than a majority, relief is supplied by the republican principle, which enables the majority to defeat its sinister views by regular vote. It may clog the administration, it may convulse the society; but it will be unable to execute and mask its violence under the forms of the Constitution. When a majority is included in a faction, the form of popular government, on the other hand, enables it to sacrifice to its ruling passion or interest both the public good and the rights of other citizens. To secure the public good and private rights against the danger of such a faction, and at the same time to preserve the spirit and the form of popular government, is then the great object to which our inquiries are directed. . . .

By what means is this object attainable? Evidently by one of two only. Either the existence of the same passion or interest in a majority at the same time must be prevented, or the majority, having such coexistent passion or interest, must be rendered, by their number and local situation, unable to concert and carry into effect schemes of oppression. If the impulse and the opportunity be suffered to coincide, we well know that neither moral nor religious motives can be relied on as an adequate control. They are not found to be such on the injustice and violence of individuals, and lose their efficacy in proportion to the number combined together. . . .

From this view of the subject it may be concluded that a pure democracy, by which I mean a society consisting of a small number of citizens, who assemble and administer the government in person, can admit of no cure for the mischiefs of faction. A common passion or interest will, in almost every case, be felt by a majority of the whole; a communication and concert results from the form of government itself; and there is nothing to check the inducements to sacrifice the weaker party or an obnoxious individual. Hence it is that such democracies have ever been spectacles of turbulence and contention; have ever been found incompatible with personal security or the rights of property; and have in general been as short in their lives as they have been violent in their deaths. . . .

A republic, by which I mean a government in which the scheme of representation takes place, opens a different prospect and promises the cure for which we are seeking. Let us examine the points in which it varies from pure democracy, and we shall comprehend both the nature of the cure and the efficacy which it must derive from the Union.

The two great points of difference between a democracy and a republic are: first, the delegation of the government, in the latter, to a small number of citizens elected by the rest; secondly, the greater number of citizens and greater sphere of country over which the latter may be extended.

The effect of the first difference is, on the one hand, to refine and enlarge the public views by passing them through the medium of a chosen body of citizens, whose wisdom may best discern the true interest of their country and whose patriotism and love of justice will be least likely to sacrifice it to temporary or partial considerations. Under such a regulation it may well happen that the public voice, pronounced by the representatives of the people, will be more consonant to the public good than if pronounced by the people themselves. . . . On the other hand, the effect may be inverted. Men of factious tempers, of local prejudices, or of sinister designs, may, by intrigue, by corruption, or by other means, first obtain the suffrages, and then betray the interests of the people. The question resulting is, whether small or extensive republics are most favorable to the election of proper guardians of the public weal; and it is clearly decided in favor of the latter . . .

In the first place it is to be remarked that however small the republic may be the representatives must be raised to a certain number in order to guard against the cabals of a few; and that however large it may be they must be limited to a certain number in order to guard against the confusion of a multitude. Hence, the number of representatives in the two cases not being in proportion to that of the constituents, and being proportionally greatest in the small republic, it follows that if the proportion of fit characters be not less in the large than in the small republic, the former will present a greater option, and consequently a greater probability of a fit choice.

In the next place, as each representative will be chosen by a greater number of citizens in the large than in the small republic, it will be more difficult for unworthy candidates to practise with success the vicious arts by which elections are too often carried; and the suffrages of the people being more free, will be more likely to center on men who possess the most attractive merit and the most diffusive and established characters. . . .

By enlarging too much the number of electors, you render the representative too little acquainted with all their local circumstances and lesser interests; as by reducing it too much, you render him unduly attached to these, and too little fit to comprehend and pursue great and national objects. The federal Constitution forms a happy combination in this respect; the great and aggregate interests being referred to the national, the local and particular to the State legislatures. . . .

In the extent and proper structure of the Union, therefore, we behold a republican remedy for the diseases most incident to republican government. And according to the degree of pleasure and pride we feel in being republicans ought to be our zeal in cherishing the spirit and supporting the character of federalists.

The Federalist, No. 39

The first question that offers itself is, whether the general form and aspect of the government be strictly republican. It is evident that no other form would be reconcilable with the genius of the people of America; with the fundamental principles of the Revolution; or with that honorable determination which animates every votary of freedom, to rest all our political experiments on the capacity of mankind for self-government. If the plan of the convention, therefore, be found to depart from the republican character, its advocates must abandon it as no longer defensible.

What, then, are the distinctive characters of the republican form? Were an answer to this question to be sought, not by recurring to principles, but in the application of the term by political writers, to the constitution of different States, no satisfactory one would ever be found.

If we resort for a criterion to the different principles on which different forms of government are established, we may define a republic to be, or at least may bestow that name on, a government which derives all its powers directly or indirectly from the great body of the people, and is administered by persons holding their offices during pleasure, for a limited period, or during good behavior. It is *essential* to such a government that it be derived from the great body of the society, not from an inconsiderable proportion, or a favored class of it; otherwise a handful of tyrannical nobles, exercising their oppressions by a delegation of their powers, might aspire to the rank of republicans, and claim for their government the honorable title of republic. It is *sufficient* for such a government that the persons administering it be appointed, either directly or indirectly, by the people; and that they hold their appointments by either of the tenures just specified; otherwise every government in the United States, as well as every other popular government that has been or can be well organized or well executed, would be degraded from the republican character.

On comparing the Constitution planned by the convention with the standard here fixed, we perceive at once that it is, in the most rigid sense, conformable to it. The House of Representatives, like that of one branch at least of all the State legislatures, is elected immediately by the great body of the people. The Senate, like the present Congress, and the Senate of Maryland, derives its appointment indirectly from the people. The President is indirectly derived from the choice of the people, according to the example in most of the States. Even the judges, with all other officers of the Union, will, as in the several States, be the choice, though a remote choice, of the people themselves, the duration of the appointments is equally conformable to the republican standard, and to the model of State constitutions The House of Representatives is periodically elective, as in all the States; and for the period of two years, as in the State of South Carolina. The Senate is elective, for the period of six years; which is but one year more than the period of the Senate of Maryland, and but two more than that of the Senates of New York and Virginia. The President is to continue in office for the period of four years; as in New York and Delaware, the chief magistrate is elected for three years, and in South Carolina for two years.

Could any further proof be required of the republican complexion of this system, the most decisive one might be found in its absolute prohibition of titles of nobility, both under the federal and the State governments; and in its express guaranty of the republican form to each of the latter.

"But it was not sufficient," say the adversaries of the proposed Constitution, "for the convention to adhere to the republican form. They ought, with equal care, to have preserved the *federal* form, which regards the Union as a *Confederacy* of sovereign states; instead of which, they have framed a *national* government, which regards the Union as a *consolidation* of the States." And it is asked by what authority this bold and radical innovation was undertaken? The handle which has been made of this objection requires that it should be examined with some precision.

On examining the first relation, it appears, on one hand, that the Constitution is to be founded on the assent and ratification of the people of America, given by deputies elected for the special purpose; but, on the other, that this assent and ratification is to be given by the people, not as individuals composing one entire nation, but as composing the distinct and independent States to which they respectively belong. It is to be the assent and ratification of the several States, derived from the supreme authority in each State, the authority of the people themselves. The act, therefore, establishing the Constitution, will not be a *national*, but a *federal* act.

The next relation is, to the sources from which the ordinary powers of government are to be derived. The House of Representatives will derive its powers from the people of America; and the people will be represented in the same proportion, and on the same principle, as they are in the legislature of a particular State. So far the government is *national*, not *federal*. The Senate, on the other hand, will derive its powers from the States, as political and coequal societies; and these will be represented on the principle of equality in the Senate, as they now are in the existing Congress. So far the government is *federal*, not *national*. The executive power will be derived from a very compound source. The immediate election of the President is to be made by the States in their political characters. The votes allotted to them are in a compound ratio, which considers them partly as distinct and coequal societies, partly as unequal members of the same society. The eventual election, again, is to be made by that branch of the legislature which consists of the national representatives; but in this particular act they are to be thrown into the form of individual delegations, from so many distinct and coequal bodies politic. From this aspect of the government it appears to be of a mixed character, presenting at least as many *federal* as *national* features.

If we try the Constitution by its last relation to the authority by which amendments are to be made, we find it neither wholly *national* nor wholly *federal*. Were it wholly national, the supreme and ultimate authority would reside in the *majority* of the people of the Union; and this authority would be competent at all times, like that of a majority of every national society, to alter or abolish its established government. Were it wholly federal, on the other hand, the concurrence of each State in the Union would be essential to every alteration that would be binding on all. The mode provided by the plan of the convention is not founded on either of these principles. In requiring more than a majority, and particularly in computing the proportion by *States*, not by *citizens*, it departs from the *national* and advances towards the *federal* character; in rendering the concurrence of less than the whole number of States sufficient, it loses again the *federal* and partakes of the *national* character.

The proposed Constitution, therefore, [even when tested by the rules laid down by its antagonists,][1] is, in strictness, neither a national nor a federal Constitution, but a composition of both. In its foundation it is federal, not national; in the sources from which the ordinary powers of the government are drawn, it is partly federal and partly national; in the operation of these powers, it is national, not federal; in the extent of them, again, it is federal, not national; and, finally, in the authoritative mode of introducing amendments, it is neither wholly federal nor wholly national.

---

1 This phrase appears in the Rossiter edition, but not the Cooke edition.

The Federalist, No. 51

To what expedient, then, shall we finally resort, for maintaining in practice the necessary partition of power among the several departments as laid down in the Constitution? . . .

In order to lay a due foundation for that separate and distinct exercise of the different powers of government, which to a certain extent is admitted on all hands to be essential to the preservation of liberty, it is evident that each department should have a will of its own; and consequently should be so constituted that the members of each should have as little agency as possible in the appointment of the members of the others. Were this principle rigorously adhered to, it would require that all the appointments for the supreme executive, legislative, and judiciary magistracies should be drawn from the same fountain of authority, the people. . . .

It is equally evident that the members of each department should be as little dependent as possible on those of the others for the emoluments [finances] annexed to their offices. Were the executive magistrate, or the judges, not independent of the legislature in this particular, their independence in every other would be merely nominal.

But the great security against a gradual concentration of the several powers in the same department consists in giving to those who administer each department the necessary constitutional means and personal motives to resist encroachments of the others. . . . Ambition must be made to counteract ambition. The interest of the man must be connected with the constitutional rights of the place. It may be a reflection on human nature that such devices should be necessary to control the abuses of government. But what is government itself but the greatest of all reflections on human nature? If men were angels, no government would be necessary. If angels were to govern men, neither external nor internal controls on government would be necessary. In framing a government which is to be administered by men over men, the great difficulty lies in this: you must first enable the government to control the governed; and in the next place oblige it to control itself. A dependence on the people is, no doubt, the primary control on the government; but experience has taught mankind the necessity of auxiliary precautions. . . .

But it is not possible to give to each department an equal power of self-defense. In republican government, the legislative authority necessarily predominates. The remedy for this inconveniency is to divide the legislature into different branches; and to render them, by different modes of election and different principles of action, as little connected with each other as the nature of their common functions and their common dependence on the society will admit. It may even be necessary to guard against dangerous encroachments by still further precautions. As the weight of the legislative authority requires that it should be thus divided, the weakness of the executive may require, on the other hand, that it should be fortified. An absolute negative [veto] on the legislature appears, at first view, to be the natural defense with which the executive magistrate should be armed. But perhaps it would be neither altogether safe nor alone sufficient. On ordinary occasions it might not be exerted with the requisite firmness, and on extraordinary occasions it might be perfidiously abused. May not this defect of an absolute negative be supplied by some qualified connection between this weaker department and the weaker branch of the stronger department, by which the latter may be led to support the constitutional rights of the former, without being too much detached from the rights of its own department? . . .

There are, moreover, two considerations particularly applicable to the federal system of America, which place that system in a very interesting point of view.

First. In a single republic, all the power surrendered by the people is submitted to the administration of a single government; and the usurpations are guarded against by a division of the government into distinct and separate departments. In the compound republic of America, the power surrendered by the people is first divided between two distinct governments, and then the portion allotted to each subdivided among distinct and separate departments. Hence a double security arises to the rights of the people. The different governments will control each other, at the same time that each will be controlled by itself.

Second. It is of great importance in a republic not only to guard the society against the oppression of its rulers, but to guard one part of the society against the injustice of the other part. Different interests necessarily exist in different classes of citizens. If a majority be united by a common interest, the rights of the minority will be insecure. There are but two methods of providing against this evil: the one by creating a will in the community independent of the majority—that is, of the society itself; the other, by comprehending in the society so many separate descriptions of citizens as will render an unjust combination of a majority of the whole very improbable, if not impracticable. The first method prevails in all governments possessing an hereditary or self-appointed authority. This, at best, is but a precarious security; because a power independent of the society may as well espouse the unjust views of the major as the rightful interests of the minor party, and may possibly be turned against both parties. The second method will be exemplified in the federal republic of the United States. Whilst all authority in it will be derived from and dependent on the society, the society itself will be broken into so many parts, interests and classes of citizens, that the rights of individuals, or of the minority, will be in little danger from interested combinations of the majority. In a free government the security for civil rights must be the same as that for religious rights. It consists in the one case in the multiplicity of interests, and in the other in the multiplicity of sects. The degree of security in both cases will depend on the number of interests and sects; and this may be presumed to depend on the extent of country and number of people comprehended under the same government. This view of the subject must particularly recommend a proper federal system to all the sincere and considerate friends of republican government, since it shows that in exact proportion as the territory of the Union may be formed into more circumscribed Confederacies, or States, oppressive combinations of a majority will be facilitated; the best security, under the republican forms, for the rights of every class of citizen, will be diminished; and consequently the stability and independence of some member of the government, the only other security, must be proportionally increased. Justice is the end of government. It is the end of civil society. It ever has been and ever will be pursued until it be obtained, or until liberty be lost in the pursuit. . . .

The Federalist, **No. 78**

Under the name of "Publius," Alexander Hamilton wrote many of the Federalist Papers. *Here he argues that an independent judiciary is critical to liberty. Two things are necessary to guarantee an independent judiciary, he said: Judges must be able to hold office for as long as they show good behavior, and the judiciary must be independent of other branches of government. It is no accident that two of his footnotes cite the French philosopher Baron de Montesquieu, the first thinker to theorize on the importance of separate branches of government.*

According to the plan of the convention, all judges who may be appointed by the United States are to hold their offices DURING GOOD BEHAVIOR; which is conformable to the most approved of the State constitutions and among the rest, to that of this State. . . . The standard of good behavior for the continuance in office of the judicial magistracy, is certainly one of the most valuable of the modern improvements in the practice of government. In a monarchy it is an excellent barrier to the despotism of the prince; in a republic it is a no less excellent barrier to the encroachments and oppressions of the representative body. And it is the best expedient which can be devised in any government, to secure a steady, upright, and impartial administration of the laws.

Whoever attentively considers the different departments of power must perceive, that, in a government in which they are separated from each other, the judiciary, from the nature of its functions, will always be the least dangerous to the political rights of the Constitution; because it will be least in a capacity to annoy or injure them. The Executive not only dispenses the honors, but holds the sword of the community. The legislature not only commands the purse, but prescribes the rules by which the duties and rights of every citizen are to be regulated. The judiciary, on the contrary, has no influence over either the sword or the purse; no direction either of the strength or of the wealth of the society; and can take no active resolution whatever. It may truly be said to have neither FORCE nor WILL, but merely judgment; and must ultimately depend upon the aid of the executive arm even for the efficacy of its judgments.

This simple view of the matter suggests several important consequences. It proves incontestably, that the judiciary is beyond comparison the weakest of the three departments of power;[1] that it can never attack with success either of the other two; and that all possible care is requisite to enable it to defend itself against their attacks. It equally proves, that though individual oppression may now and then proceed from the courts of justice, the general liberty of the people can never be endangered from that quarter; . . . . For I agree, that "there is no liberty, if the power of judging be not separated from the legislative and executive powers."[2] And it proves, in the last place, that as liberty can have nothing to fear from the judiciary alone, but would have every thing to fear from its union with either of the other departments.

Some perplexity respecting the rights of the courts to pronounce legislative acts void, because contrary to the Constitution, has arisen from an imagination that the doctrine would imply a superiority of the judiciary to the legislative power. It is urged that the authority which can declare the acts of another void, must necessarily be superior to the one whose acts may be declared void. As this doctrine is of great importance in all the American constitutions, a brief discussion of the ground on which it rests cannot be unacceptable.

If it be said that the legislative body are themselves the constitutional judges of their own powers, and that the construction they put upon them is conclusive upon the other departments, it may be answered, that this cannot be the natural presumption, where it is not to be collected from any particular provisions in the Constitution. It is not otherwise to be supposed, that the Constitution

---

1 The celebrated Montesquieu, speaking of them, says: "Of the three powers above mentioned, the judiciary is next to nothing." "Spirit of Laws," vol. i., page 186.

2 Idem, page 181.

could intend to enable the representatives of the people to substitute their WILL to that of their constituents. It is far more rational to suppose, that the courts were designed to be an intermediate body between the people and the legislature, in order, among other things, to keep the latter within the limits assigned to their authority. The interpretation of the laws is the proper and peculiar province of the courts. A constitution is, in fact, and must be regarded by the judges, as a fundamental law. It therefore belongs to them to ascertain its meaning, as well as the meaning of any particular act proceeding from the legislative body. If there should happen to be an irreconcilable variance between the two, that which has the superior obligation and validity ought, of course, to be preferred; or, in other words, the Constitution ought to be preferred to the statute, the intention of the people to the intention of their agents.

Nor does this conclusion by any means suppose a superiority of the judicial to the legislative power. It only supposes that the power of the people is superior to both; and that where the will of the legislature, declared in its statutes, stands in opposition to that of the people, declared in the Constitution, the judges ought to be governed by the latter rather than the former. They ought to regulate their decisions by the fundamental laws, rather than by those which are not fundamental.

If, then, the courts of justice are to be considered as the bulwarks of a limited Constitution against legislative encroachments, this consideration will afford a strong argument for the permanent tenure of judicial offices, since nothing will contribute so much as this to that independent spirit in the judges which must be essential to the faithful performance of so arduous a duty.

This independence of the judges is equally requisite to guard the Constitution and the rights of individuals from the effects of those ill humors, which the arts of designing men, or the influence of particular conjunctures, sometimes disseminate among the people themselves, and which, though they speedily give place to better information, and more deliberate reflection, have a tendency, in the meantime, to occasion dangerous innovations in the government, and serious oppressions of the minor party in the community. Though I trust the friends of the proposed Constitution will never concur with its enemies,[3] in questioning that fundamental principle of republican government, which admits the right of the people to alter or abolish the established Constitution, whenever they find it inconsistent with their happiness, yet it is not to be inferred from this principle, that the representatives of the people, whenever a momentary inclination happens to lay hold of a majority of their constituents, incompatible with the provisions in the existing Constitution, would, on that account, be justifiable in a violation of those provisions; . . . . Until the people have, by some solemn and authoritative act, annulled or changed the established form, it is binding upon themselves collectively, as well as individually; and no presumption, or even knowledge, of their sentiments, can warrant their representatives in a departure from it, prior to such an act. But it is easy to see, that it would require an uncommon portion of fortitude in the judges to do their duty as faithful guardians of the Constitution, where legislative invasions of it had been instigated by the major voice of the community.

PUBLIUS

---

3 Vide "Protest of the Minority of the Convention of Pennsylvania," Martin's Speech, etc.

Seneca Falls Declaration

One of the first documents to express the desire for equal rights for women is the Declaration of Sentiments and Resolution, issued in 1848 at the Seneca Falls Convention.

When, in the course of human events, it becomes necessary for one portion of the family of man to assume among the people of the earth a position different from that which they have hitherto occupied, but one to which the laws of nature and of nature's God entitle them, a decent respect to the opinions of mankind requires that they should declare the causes that impel them to such a course.

We hold these truths to be self-evident: that all men and women are created equal; that they are endowed by their Creator with certain inalienable rights; that among these are life, liberty, and the pursuit of happiness; that to secure these rights governments are instituted, deriving their just powers from the consent of the governed. Whenever any form of government becomes destructive of these ends, it is the right of those who suffer from it to refuse allegiance to it, and to insist upon the institution of a new government, laying its foundation on such principles, and organizing its powers in such form, as to them shall seem most likely to effect their safety and happiness. Prudence, indeed, will dictate that governments long established should not be changed for light and transient causes; and accordingly all experience hath shown that mankind are more disposed to suffer. while evils are sufferable, than to right themselves by abolishing the forms to which they are accustomed. But when a long train of abuses and usurpations, pursuing invariably the same object, evinces a design to reduce them under absolute despotism, it is their duty to throw off such government, and to provide new guards for their future security. Such has been the patient sufferance of the women under this government, and such is now the necessity which constrains them to demand the equal station to which they are entitled. The history of mankind is a history of repeated injuries and usurpations on the part of man toward woman, having in direct object the establishment of an absolute tyranny over her. To prove this, let facts be submitted to a candid world.

The history of mankind is a history of repeated injuries and usurpations on the part of man toward woman, having in direct object the establishment of an absolute tyrranny over her. To prove this, let facts be submitted to a candid world.

He has never permitted her to exercise her inalienable right to the elective franchise.

He has compelled her to submit to laws, in the formation of which she had no voice.

He has withheld from her rights which are given to the most ignorant and degraded men—both natives and foreigners.

Having deprived her of this first right of a citizen, the elective franchise, thereby leaving her without representation in the halls of legislation, he has oppressed her on all sides.

He has made her, if married, in the eye of the law, civilly dead.

He has taken from her all right in property, even to the wages she earns.

He has made her, morally, an irresponsible being, as she can commit many crimes with impunity, provided they be done in the presence of her husband. In the covenant of marriage, she is compelled to promise obedience to her husband, he becoming, to all intents and purposes, her master--the law giving him power to deprive her of her liberty, and to administer chastisement.

He has so framed the laws of divorce, as to what shall be the proper causes, and in case of separation, to whom the guardianship of the children shall be given, as to be wholly regardless of the happiness of women— the law, in all cases, going upon a false supposition of the supremacy of man, and giving all power into his hands.

After depriving her of all rights as a married woman, if single, and the owner of property, he has taxed her to support a government which recognizes her only when her property can be made profitable to it.

He has monopolized nearly all the profitable employments, and from those she is permitted to follow, she receives but a scanty remuneration. He closes against her all the avenues to wealth and distinction which he considers most honorable to himself. As a teacher of theology, medicine, or law, she is not known.

He has denied her the facilities for obtaining a thorough education, all colleges being closed against her.

He allows her in church, as well as state, but a subordinate position, claiming apostolic authority for her exclusion from the ministry, and, with some exceptions, from any public participation in the affairs of the church.

He has created a false public sentiment by giving to the world a different code of morals for men and women, by which moral delinquencies which exclude women from society, are not only tolerated, but deemed of little account in man.

He has usurped the prerogative of Jehovah himself, claiming it as his right to assign for her a sphere of action, when that belongs to her conscience and to her God.

He has endeavored, in every way that he could, to destroy her confidence in her own powers, to lessen her self-respect, and to make her willing to lead a dependent and abject life.

Now, in view of this entire disfranchisement of one-half the people of this country, their social and religious degradation—in view of the unjust laws above mentioned, and because women do feel themselves aggrieved, oppressed, and fraudulently deprived of their most sacred rights, we insist that they have immediate admission to all the rights and privileges which belong to them as citizens of the United States.

Fourth of July Address

As the city's most distinguished resident, Frederick Douglass was requested to address the citizens of Rochester on the Fourth of July celebration in 1852. The speech he delivered, under the title "What to the Slave Is the Fourth of July?" is excerpted below.

Fellow Citizens: Pardon me, and allow me to ask, why am I called upon to speak here today? What have I or those I represent to do with your national independence? Are the great principles of political freedom and of natural justice, embodied in that Declaration of Independence, extended to us? And am I, therefore, called upon to bring our humble offering to the national altar, and to confess the benefits, and express devout gratitude for the blessings resulting from your independence to us? . . .

I say it with a sad sense of disparity between us. I am not included within the pale of this glorious anniversary! Your high independence only reveals the immeasurable distance between us. The blessings in which you this day rejoice are not enjoyed in common. The rich inheritance of justice, liberty, prosperity, and independence bequeathed by your fathers is shared by you, not by me. . . . This Fourth of July is yours, not mine. You may rejoice, I must mourn. . . .

I do not hesitate to declare, with all my soul, that the character and conduct of this nation never looked blacker to me than on this Fourth of July. Whether we turn to the declarations of the past, or to the professions of the present, the conduct of the nation seems equally hideous and revolting. America is false to the past, false to the present, and solemnly binds herself to be false to the future. . . . I will, in the name of humanity, which is outraged, in the name of liberty, which is fettered, in the name of the Constitution and the Bible, which are disregarded and trampled upon, dare to call in question and to denounce, with all the emphasis I can command, everything that serves to perpetuate slavery—the great sin and shame of America! "I will not equivocate; I will not excuse"; I will use the severest language I can command, and yet not one word shall escape me that any man, whose judgment is not blinded by prejudice, or who is not at heart a slave-holder, shall not confess to be right and just. . . .

Would you have me argue that man is entitled to liberty? That he is the rightful owner of his own body? You have already declared it. Must I argue the wrongfulness of slavery? . . . There is not a man beneath the canopy of heaven who does not know that slavery is wrong for him.

What! Am I to argue that it is wrong to make men brutes, to rob them of their liberty, to work them without wages, to keep them ignorant of their relations to their fellow men, to beat them with sticks, to flay their flesh with the lash, to load their limbs with irons, to hunt them with dogs, to sell them at auction, to sunder their families, to knock out their teeth, to burn their flesh, to starve them into obedience and submission to their masters? . . . The feeling of the nation must be quickened; the conscience of the nation must be roused; the propriety of the nation must be startled; the hypocrisy of the nation must be exposed; and its crimes against God and man must be denounced. . . .

The Emancipation Proclamation

On January 1, 1863, President Abraham Lincoln issued the Emancipation Proclamation, which freed all slaves in states under Confederate control. The Proclamation was a significant step toward the Thirteenth Amendment (1865) that ended slavery in the United States.

Whereas, on the 22nd day of September, in the year of our Lord 1862, a proclamation was issued by the President of the United States, containing, among other things, the following, to wit:

> That on the 1st day of January, in the year of our Lord 1863, all persons held as slaves within any state or designated part of a state, the people whereof shall then be in rebellion against the United States, shall be then, thenceforward, and forever free; and the executive government of the United States, including the military and naval authority thereof, will recognize and maintain the freedom of such persons and will do no act or acts to repress such persons, or any of them, in any efforts they may make for their actual freedom.
>
> That the executive will, on the first day of January aforesaid, by proclamation, designate the states and parts of states, if any, in which the people thereof, respectively, shall then be in rebellion against the United States; and the fact that any state or the people thereof shall on that day be in good faith represented in the Congress of the United States by members chosen thereto at elections wherein a majority of the qualified voters of such states shall have participated shall, in the absence of strong countervailing testimony, be deemed conclusive evidence that such state and the people thereof are not then in rebellion against the United States.

Now, therefore, I, Abraham Lincoln, President of the United States, by virtue of the power in me vested as commander in chief of the Army and Navy of the United States, in time of actual armed rebellion against the authority and government of the United States, and as a fit and necessary war measure for suppressing said rebellion, do, on this 1st day of January, in the year of our Lord 1863, and in accordance with my purpose so to do, publicly proclaimed for the full period of 100 days from the day first above mentioned, order and designate as the states and parts of states wherein the people thereof, respectively, are this day in rebellion against the United States. . . .

And, by virtue of the power and for the purpose aforesaid, I do order and declare that all persons held as slaves within said designated states and parts of states are, and henceforward shall be, free; and that the executive government of the United States, including the military and naval authorities thereof, will recognize and maintain the freedom of said persons. . .

And upon this act, sincerely believed to be an act of justice, warranted by the Constitution upon military necessity, I invoke the considerate judgment of mankind and the gracious favor of Almighty God.

The Fourteen Points

On January 8, 1918, President Woodrow Wilson went before Congress to offer a statement of aims called the Fourteen Points.

We entered this war because violations of right had occurred. . . . What we demand in this war, therefore, is . . . that the world be made fit and safe to live in. . . . The only possible programme, as we see it, is this:

I. Open covenants of peace, openly arrived at, after which there shall be no private international understandings of any kind but diplomacy shall proceed always frankly and in the public view.

II. Absolute freedom of navigation upon the seas, outside territorial waters, alike in peace and in war. . . .

III. The removal, so far as possible, of all economic barriers and the establishment of an equality of trade conditions among all the nations. . . .

IV. Adequate guarantees given and taken that national armaments will be reduced to the lowest point consistent with domestic safety.

V. A free, open-minded, and absolutely impartial adjustment of all colonial claims, based upon a strict observance of the principle that in determining all such questions of sovereignty the interests of the populations concerned must have equal weight with the equitable claims of the government whose title is to be determined.

VI. The evacuation of all Russian territory and . . . opportunity for the independent determination of her own political development and national policy. . . .

VII. Belgium . . . must be evacuated and restored. . . .

VIII. All French territory should be freed and the invaded portions restored, and the wrong done to France by Prussia in 1871 in the matter of Alsace-Lorraine should be righted. . . .

IX. A readjustment of the frontiers of Italy should be effected along clearly recognizable lines of nationality.

X. The peoples of Austria-Hungary . . . should be accorded the freest opportunity of autonomous development.

XI. Rumania, Serbia, and Montenegro should be evacuated; occupied territories restored . . . the relations of the several Balkan states to one another determined by friendly counsel along historically established lines of allegiance and nationality. . . .

XII. The Turkish portions of the present Ottoman Empire should be assured a secure sovereignty. . . .

XIII. An independent Polish state should be erected which should include the territories inhabited by indisputably Polish populations. . . .

XIV. A general association of nations must be formed under specific covenants for the purpose of affording mutual guarantees of political independence and territorial integrity. . . .

The Four Freedoms

President Franklin D. Roosevelt delivered this address on January 6, 1941, in his annual message to Congress. Roosevelt called for a world founded on "four essential human freedoms": freedom of speech and expression, freedom of worship, freedom from want, and freedom from fear.

Just as our national policy in internal affairs has been based upon a decent respect for the rights and dignity of all our fellowmen within our gates, so our national policy in foreign affairs has been based on a decent respect for the rights and dignity of all nations, large and small. And the justice of morality must and will win in the end.

Our national policy is this:

First, by an impressive expression of the public will and without regard to partisanship, we are committed to all-inclusive national defense.

Second, by an impressive expression of the public will and without regard to partisanship, we are committed to full support of all those resolute peoples, everywhere, who are resisting aggression and are thereby keeping war away from our Hemisphere. . . .

Third . . . we are committed to the proposition that principles of morality and considerations for our own security will never permit us to acquiesce in a peace dictated by aggressors. . . .

Let us say to the democracies, "We Americans are vitally concerned in your defense of freedom. We are putting forth our energies, our resources, and our organizing powers to give you the strength to regain and maintain a free world. We shall send you, in ever increasing numbers, ships, planes, tanks, guns. This is our purpose and our pledge."

In fulfillment of this purpose we will not be intimidated by the threats of dictators that they will regard as a breach of international law and as an act of war our aid to the democracies which dare to resist their aggression. . . .

In the future days, which we seek to make secure, we look forward to a world founded upon four essential human freedoms.

The first is freedom of speech and expression everywhere in the world.

The second is freedom of every person to worship God in his own way everywhere in the world.

The third is freedom from want, which, translated into world terms, means economic understandings which will secure to every nation a healthy peacetime life for its inhabitants everywhere in the world.

The fourth is freedom from fear—which, translated into world terms, means a worldwide reduction of armaments to such a point and in such a thorough fashion that no nation will be in a position to commit an act of physical aggression against any neighbor—anywhere in the world. . . .

Charter of the
United Nations

The United Nations Charter was signed on June 26, 1945. It formally established the United Nations, a new international peace organization to succeed the League of Nations. The following excerpt contains Article I of the charter.

We the peoples of the United Nations determined

to save succeeding generations from the scourge of war, which twice in our lifetime has brought untold sorrow to mankind, and

to reaffirm faith in fundamental human rights, in the dignity and worth of the human person, in the equal rights of men and women and of nations large and small, and

to establish conditions under which justice and respect for the obligations arising from treaties and other sources of international law can be maintained, and

to promote social progress and better standards of life in larger freedom,

And for these ends

to practise tolerance and live together in peace with one another as good neighbours, and

to unite our strength to maintain international peace and security, and

to ensure, by the acceptance of principles and the institution of methods, that armed force shall not be used, save in the common interest, and

to employ international machinery for the promotion of the economic and social advancement of all peoples,

Have resolved to combine our efforts to accomplish these aims.

Accordingly, our respective Governments, through representatives assembled in the city of San Francisco, who have exhibited their full powers found to be in good and due form, have agreed to the present Charter of the United Nations and do hereby establish an international organization to be known as the United Nations. . . .

Article 1. The Purposes of the United Nations are:

1. To maintain international peace and security, and to that end: to take effective collective measures for the prevention and removal of threats to the peace, and for the suppression of acts of aggression or other breaches of the peace, and to bring about by peaceful means and in conformity with the principles of justice and international law, adjustment or settlement of international disputes or situations which might lead to a breach of the peace;

2. To develop friendly relations among nations based on respect for the principle of equal rights and self-determination of peoples, and to take other appropriate measures to strengthen universal peace;

3. To achieve international co-operation in solving international problems of an economic, social, cultural, or humanitarian character, and in promoting and encouraging respect for human rights and for fundamental freedoms for all without distinction as to race, sex, language, or religion; and

4. To be a centre for harmonizing the accusations of nations in the attainment of these common ends.

The Universal Declaration of Human Rights

Preamble. Whereas recognition of the inherent dignity and of the equal and inalienable rights of all members of the human family is the foundation of freedom, justice and peace in the world,

Whereas disregard and contempt for human rights have resulted in barbarous acts which have outraged the conscience of mankind, and the advent of a world in which human beings shall enjoy freedom of speech and belief and freedom from fear and want has been proclaimed as the highest aspiration of the common people,

Whereas it is essential, if man is not to be compelled to have recourse, as a last resort, to rebellion against tyranny and oppression, that human rights should be protected by the rule of law, . . .

Now, Therefore THE GENERAL ASSEMBLY proclaims THIS UNIVERSAL DECLARATION OF HUMAN RIGHTS as a common standard of achievement for all peoples and all nations, . . .

Article 1. All human beings are born free and equal in dignity and rights.They are endowed with reason and conscience and should act towards one another in a spirit of brotherhood.

Article 2. Everyone is entitled to all the rights and freedoms set forth in this Declaration, without distinction of any kind, such as race, colour, sex, language, religion, political or other opinion, national or social origin, property, birth or other status. Furthermore, no distinction shall be made on the basis of the political, jurisdictional or international status of the country or territory to which a person belongs, whether it be independent, trust, non-self-governing or under any other limitation of sovereignty.

Article 3. Everyone has the right to life, liberty and security of person.

Article 4. No one shall be held in slavery or servitude; slavery and the slave trade shall be prohibited in all their forms.

Article 5. No one shall be subjected to torture or to cruel, inhuman or degrading treatment or punishment.

Article 6. Everyone has the right to recognition everywhere as a person before the law.

Article 7. All are equal before the law and are entitled without any discrimination to equal protection of the law. All are entitled to equal protection against any discrimination in violation of this Declaration and against any incitement to such discrimination.

Article 8. Everyone has the right to an effective remedy by the competent national tribunals for acts violating the fundamental rights granted him by the constitution or by law.

Article 9. No one shall be subjected to arbitrary arrest, detention or exile.

Article 13. (1) Everyone has the right to freedom of movement and residence within the borders of each state. (2) Everyone has the right to leave any country, including his own, and to return to his country.

Article 17. (1) Everyone has the right to own property alone as well as in association with others. (2) No one shall be arbitrarily deprived of his property.

Article 18. Everyone has the right to freedom of thought, conscience and religion; this right includes freedom to change his religion or belief, and freedom, either alone or in community with others and in public or private, to manifest his religion or belief in teaching, practice, worship and observance.

Article 19. Everyone has the right to freedom of opinion and expression; this right includes freedom to hold opinions without interference and to seek, receive and impart information and ideas through any media and regardless of frontiers.

Article 23. (1) Everyone has the right to work, to free choice of employment, to just and favourable conditions of work and to protection against unemployment.

(2) Everyone, without any discrimination, has the right to equal pay for equal work.

(3) Everyone who works has the right to just and favourable remuneration ensuring for himself and his family an existence worthy of human dignity, and supplemented, if necessary, by other means of social protection.

(4) Everyone has the right to form and to join trade unions for the protection of his interests.

Gulf of Tonkin Resolution

The Gulf of Tonkin Resolution was a joint resolution passed overwhelmingly by Congress on August 7, 1964. It became the basis for President Johnson's escalation of the war in Southeast Asia. A 1968 U.S. Senate investigation questioned the alleged Gulf of Tonkin attacks, and the resolution was repealed in May 1970.

PUBLIC LAW 88—408; 78 STAT. 384
[H.J. Res 1145]
JOINT RESOLUTION

To promote the maintenance of international peace and security in southeast Asia.

Whereas naval units of the Communist regime in [North] Vietnam, in violation of the principles of the Charter of the United Nations and of international law, have deliberately and repeatedly attacked United States naval vessels lawfully present in international waters, and have thereby created a serious threat to international peace; and

Whereas these attacks are part of a deliberate and systematic campaign of aggression that the Communist regime in North Vietnam has been waging against its neighbors and the nations joined with them in the collective defense of their freedom; and

Whereas the United States is assisting the peoples of southeast Asia to protect their freedom and has no territorial, military or political ambitions in that area, but desires only that these peoples should be left in peace to work out their own destinies in their own way: Now, therefore, be it

Resolved by the Senate and House of Representatives of the United States of America in Congress assembled,

That the Congress approves and supports the determination of the President, as Commander in Chief, to take all necessary measures to repel any armed attack against the forces of the United States and to prevent further aggression.

Sec. 2. The United States regards as vital to its national interest and to world peace the maintenance of international peace and security in southeast Asia. . . . The United States is, therefore, prepared, as the President determines, to take all necessary steps, including the use of armed force, to assist any member or protocol state of the Southeast Asia Collective Defense Treaty requesting assistance in defense of its freedom.

Sec. 3. This resolution shall expire when the President shall determine that the peace and security of the area is reasonably assured by international conditions created by action of the United Nations or otherwise, except that it may be terminated earlier by concurrent resolution of the Congress.

Approved August 10, 1964.

George W. Bush's
Address to Congress, September 20, 2001

On September 11, 2001, terrorists destroyed the World Trade Center in New York City and damaged the Pentagon. President Bush responded in a message to Congress on September 20.

. . . Tonight we are a country awakened to danger and called to defend freedom. Our grief has turned to anger, and anger to resolution. Whether we bring our enemies to justice, or bring justice to our enemies, justice will be done.

. . . On September 11th, enemies of freedom committed an act of war against our country. Americans have known wars—but for the past 136 years, they have been wars on foreign soil, except for one Sunday in 1941. Americans have known the casualties of war—but not at the center of a great city on a peaceful morning. Americans have known surprise attacks—but never before on thousands of civilians. All of this was brought upon us in a single day—and night fell on a different world, a world where freedom itself is under attack.

. . . Americans are asking: Who attacked our country? The evidence we have gathered all points to a collection of loosely affiliated terrorist organizations known as al Qaeda. They are the same murderers indicted for bombing American embassies in Tanzania and Kenya, and responsible for bombing the USS *Cole*.

. . . This group and its leader—a person named Osama bin Laden—are linked to many other organizations in different countries.

. . . Americans are asking, why do they hate us? They hate what we see right here in this chamber—democratically elected government. . . . They hate our freedoms—our freedom of religion, our freedom of speech, our freedom to vote and assemble and disagree with each other.

. . . We are not deceived by their pretenses to piety. We have seen their kind before. They are the heirs of all the murderous ideologies of the 20th century. By sacrificing human life to serve their radical visions—by abandoning every value except the will to power—they follow the path of Nazism, and totalitarianism. And they will follow that path all the way to where it ends: in history's unmarked grave of discarded lies.

. . . We will direct every resource at our command—every means of diplomacy, every tool of intelligence, every instrument of law enforcement, every financial influence and every necessary weapon of war—to the disruption and to the defeat of the global terror network.

. . . Every nation, in every region, now has a decision to make. Either you are with us, or you are with the terrorists.

. . . This is not, however, just America's fight. And what is at stake is not just America's freedom. This is the world's fight. This is civilization's fight.

. . . We are in a fight for our principles, and our first responsibility is to live by them. No one should be singled out for unfair treatment or unkind words because of their ethnic background or religious faith.

. . . Great harm has been done to us. We have suffered great loss. And in our grief and anger we have found our mission and our moment. Freedom and fear are at war. The advance of human freedom—the great achievement of our time, and the great hope of every time—now depends on us. Our nation—this generation—will lift a dark threat of violence from our people and our future.

. . . I will not forget this wound to our country or those who inflicted it. I will not yield; I will not rest; I will not relent in waging this struggle for freedom and security for the American people.

- Content vocabulary are words that relate to United States government content.
- Words that have an asterisk (*) are academic vocabulary. They help you understand your school subjects.
- All vocabulary words are **boldfaced or highlighted in yellow** in your textbook.

ENGLISH — A — SPANISH

ENGLISH	SPANISH
absentee ballot a ballot that allows a person to vote without going to the polls on Election Day (p. 563)	**voto en ausencia** voto que permite que una persona vote sin tener que concurrir a los comicios el día de las elecciones (pág. 563)
***abstract** dealing with a subject in its theoretical aspects; not concrete (p. 598)	***abstracto** que trata sobre un tema en sus aspectos teóricos; no concreto (pág. 598)
***access** freedom or ability to obtain or make use of something (p. 275)	***acceso** libertad o capacidad de obtener o hacer uso de algo (pág. 275)
***accommodation** something supplied for convenience or to satisfy a need (p. 119)	***comodidade** lo que se suministra para utilidad o para satisfacer una necesidad (pág. 119)
acquittal judicial deliverance from a criminal charge on a verdict or finding of not guilty (p. 494)	**absolución** liberación judicial de una acusación criminal mediante un veredicto o dictamen de inculpabilidad (pág. 494)
action alert a message from an interest group to its members, calling upon them to respond immediately by phone, fax, or e-mail to public officials (p. 624)	**alerta para la acción** mensaje de un grupo de interés a sus miembros, pidiéndoles que respondan de inmediato por teléfono, fax o correo electrónico a funcionarios públicos (pág. 624)
***adjust** to adapt to or conform (p. 236)	***ajustarse** adaptarse o amoldarse (pág. 236)
***administer** to manage or supervise the execution, use, or conduct of (p. 115)	***administrar** dirigir o supervisar la ejecución, el uso o la conducta (pág. 115)
administrative assistant a member of a lawmaker's personal staff who runs the lawmaker's office, supervises the schedule, and gives advice (p. 162)	**auxiliar administrativo** miembro de los colaboradores personales de un legislador, que tiene a cargo la oficina del legislador, supervisa la agenda y proporciona consejos (pág. 162)
***administrator** one who performs executive duties or manages (p. 354)	***administrador** persona que realiza tareas ejecutivas o dirige (pág. 354)
adversarial system a trial system that is a contest between opposing sides (p. 391)	**sistema acusatorio** sistema de enjuiciamiento que consiste en el litigio entre partes contrarias (pág. 391)
advisory opinion a ruling on a law that has not yet been challenged in court (p. 415)	**dictamen consultivo** sentencia sobre una ley que aún no ha sido impugnada en un tribunal (pág. 415)
***advocate** to support or speak in favor of (p. 232)	***defender** apoyar o hablar a favor (pág. 232)
***affect** to influence (p. 71)	***afectar** influenciar (pág. 71)
affirmative action policies that give preference to women or minorities for jobs, promotions, admission to schools, or other benefits, in order to make up for past or current discrimination (p. 470)	**acción afirmativa** normas que dan preferencia a la mujer o las minorías en trabajos, promociones, admisiones a escuelas u otros beneficios para compensar por discriminaciones pasadas y actuales (pág. 470)
alliance a voluntary relationship between different nations in which they agree to support one another in case of an attack (p. 718)	**alianza** relación voluntaria entre distintas naciones en la cual acuerdan apoyarse mutuamente en caso de un ataque (pág. 718)
***allocate** to assign a portion of something (p. 111)	***adjudicar** asignar una porción de algo (pág. 111)

Glossary/Glosario

*alter to make different without changing into something else (p. 110)

*alternative a different option (p. 307)

ambassador an official of the government who represents the nation in diplomatic matters (pp. 326, 721)

*amend to change, alter (pp. 204, 431)

amendment a change to the Constitution (p. 70)

amicus curiae Latin for "friend of the court"; a written brief from an individual or group claiming to have information useful to a court's consideration of a case (p. 419)

amnesty a presidential order that pardons a group of people who have committed an offense against the government (pp. 270, 698)

anarchy a state without government and laws (p. 6)

*annual happening once per year (p. 279)

appellate jurisdiction authority held by a court to hear a case that is appealed by a lower court (p. 426)

appellate litigation a lawsuit occurring at the appeals level of the court system (p. 426)

appropriation approval of government spending (p. 210)

appropriations bill a proposed law to authorize spending money (pp. 175, 210)

*arbitrary existing or coming about seemingly at random or by chance (p. 398)

arrest to take or keep in custody by authority of law (p. 487)

article one of seven main divisions of the body of the Constitution (p. 69)

*assemble to gather together (p. 532)

*assembly a gathering (p. 16)

assessment the process of calculating the value of real property (p. 661)

*assign to appoint to a duty (p. 225)

*assistant a helper (p. 149)

*assurance full confidence, freedom from doubt (p. 83)

asylum refuge or humanitarian protection given by a country (p. 700)

at-large as a whole; for example, statewide (p. 136)

*alterar hacer que algo sea diferente sin convertirlo en otra cosa (pág. 110)

*alternativa una opción diferente (pág. 307)

embajador funcionario del gobierno que representa al país en asuntos diplomáticos (pp. 326, 721)

*enmendar cambiar, alterar (pág. 204, 431)

enmienda cambio a la Constitución (pág. 70)

amicus curiae "amigo del tribunal" en latín; alegato por escrito de una persona o un grupo en el cual aseguran poseer información útil para la consideración de un caso por parte de un tribunal (pág. 419)

amnistía decreto ley que indulta a un grupo de personas que han cometido un delito contra el gobierno (pág. 270, 698)

anarquía estado que no tiene gobierno ni leyes (pág. 6)

*anual que sucede una vez al año (pág. 279)

jurisdicción de apelaciones autoridad que posee un tribunal para ver una causa que es apelada por un tribunal inferior (pág. xxx)

recurso de apelación demanda que ocurre al nivel de apelaciones del sistema judicial (pág. 426)

asignación aprobación de gastos del gobierno (pág. 210)

proyecto de ley de asignación ley propuesta para autorizar gastos (pág. 175, 210)

*arbitrario que existe o sucede aparentemente al azar o por casualidad (pág. 398)

arrestar poner o mantener bajo arresto por la autoridad que confiere la ley (pág. 487)

artículo una de las siete divisiones principales del cuerpo de la Constitución (pág. 69)

*congregar reunir (pág. 532)

*asamblea reunión (pág. 16)

tasación proceso de cálculo del valor de bienes inmuebles (pág. 661)

*designar nombrar para alguna función (pág. 225)

*asistente ayudante (pág. 149)

*seguridad confianza total, ausencia de duda (pág. 83)

asilo refugio o protección humanitaria otorgada por un país (pág. 700)

en general en conjunto; por ejemplo, en todo el estado (pág. 136)

authoritarian controlling all aspects of citizens' economic, political, and social lives (p. 15)

autoritario que controla todos los aspectos de la vida social, política y económica de los ciudadanos (pág. 15)

*authority the right to command or lead (p. 104)

*autoridad derecho a mandar o dirigir (pág. 104)

authorization bill a bill that sets up a federal program and specifies how much money may be appropriated for the program (pp. 175, 210)

proyecto de ley de autorización proyecto de ley que establece un programa federal y especifica cuánto dinero puede asignarse para el programa (pp. 175, 210)

*aware knowing (p. 215)

*consciente que tiene conocimiento (pág. 215)

*bias information and ideas that support only one point of view on an issue; the distortion of a set of statistical results (p. 493)

*sesgo información e ideas que apoyan solo un punto de vista en un asunto; distorsión de un conjunto de resultados estadísticos (pág. 493)

biased sample in polling, a group that does not accurately represent the larger population (p. 579)

muestra sesgada en encuestas, grupo que no representa con exactitud la población mayor (pág. 579)

bicameral relative to a two-house legislative body (p. 56)

bicameral respecto a una legislatura que está compuesto de dos cámaras (pág. 56)

bicameral legislature a two-chamber legislature (pp. 132, 233)

poder legislativo bicameral poder legislativo que consta de dos cámaras (pp. 132, 233)

bilateral agreement a free trade agreement that is between the U.S. and one other government (p. 716)

acuerdo bilateral acuerdo de libre comercio entre Estados Unidos y algún otro país (pág. 716)

bilateral treaty an agreement that involves only two nations (p. 719)

tratado bilateral acuerdo que involucra solo a dos naciones (pág. 719)

bill a proposed law (p. 145)

proyecto de ley ley propuesta (pág. 145)

blanket primary a primary in which all candidates are placed on the same primary ballot, regardless of party (p. 235)

elecciones primarias indiscriminadas elecciones primarias en las cuales los nombres de todos los candidatos se ponen en la misma papeleta de votación, sin importar el partido (pág. 235)

block grant a grant of money to a state or local government to be used for a general purpose (pp. 370, 658)

subvención en bloque subvención de dinero otorgada a un estado o gobierno local para ser usada con fines generales (pág. 370, 658)

blockade obstruction for the purpose of isolating an area; during military conflicts, a blockade may be used to prevent troops, weapons, or supplies from entering a specific area (p. 719)

bloqueo obstrucción con el fin de aislar a un área; durante conflictos militares, un bloqueo puede usarse para evitar que tropas, armas o suministros entren a un área específica (pág. 719)

blog a personal "Web log," or online journal, in which an individual or group records their own thoughts, experiences, observations, opinions, and so on (p. 622)

blog registro personal en Internet, o diario en línea, en el cual una persona o un grupo anota sus pensamientos, experiencias, observaciones, opiniones, etc. (pág. 622)

*bond a government security (pp. 176, 659)

*bono título de deuda del gobierno (pág. 176, 659)

bourgeoisie capitalists who own the means of production (p. 27)

burguesía capitalistas que poseen los medios de producción (pág. 27)

boycott to refuse to have dealings with in order to express disapproval or to force acceptance of certain conditions (p. 45)

boicotear rehusarse a tratar con alguien con el fin de expresar desaprobación o para forzar la aceptación de ciertas condiciones (pág. 45)

brief a written statement setting forth the legal arguments, relevant facts, and precedents supporting one side of a case (p. 419)

alegato declaración por escrito que describe los argumentos legales, hechos relevantes y antecedentes que apoyan una parte de un caso (pág. 419)

budget a plan for how much revenue an individual or government expects to take in and how this money will be spent or allotted (p. 639)

presupuesto plan de la cantidad de ingresos que una persona o el gobierno espera recibir y cómo ese dinero se gastará o distribuirá (pág. 639)

Glossary/Glosario

budget deficit condition that occurs when the federal government spends more than it takes in (p. 639)

budget surplus extra money left in a budget after all spending takes place (p. 639)

bureaucrat one who works for a department or agency of the federal government; a civil servant (p. 338)

cabinet the president's closest advisers, consisting of the vice president, the secretaries of each of the 15 executive departments, and other top government officials that help the president make decisions and policy (p. 316)

calendar a schedule that lists the order in which bills will be considered in Congress (p. 146)

campaign manager the person responsible for the overall strategy and planning of a campaign (p. 552)

canvass to solicit votes and determine opinions (p. 528)

canvassing board the official body that counts votes and certifies the winner (p. 565)

capital punishment execution of an offender sentenced to death after conviction by a court of law of a criminal offense (p. 500)

capitalism an economic system in which private citizens own and use the factors of production in order to generate profits (pp. 23, 751)

casework the work a lawmaker does to help constituents with problems (p. 222)

caseworker a member of a lawmaker's personal staff who handles requests for help from constituents (p. 163)

*category a division within a system of classification (p. 443)

caucus an event held before an election where members of a political party select delegates to send to the national party convention, where they will also vote to nominate a candidate; a private meeting of party leaders to choose candidates for office (pp. 145, 304, 529)

censorship the act of governments prohibiting the use of publications or productions they find offensive or contrary to their own interests (p. 448)

censure a vote of formal disapproval of a member's actions (p. 137)

census complete count of a population, including place of residence (p. 134)

centrist a person whose views tend to be moderate (p. 525)

déficit presupuestario problema que ocurre cuando el gobierno federal gasta más de lo que recibe (pág. 639)

superávit presupuestario dinero que sobra en un presupuesto después de todo el gasto tiene lugar (pág. 639)

burócrata persona que trabaja para un departamento o un organismo del gobierno federal; servidor público (pág. 338)

gabinete consejeros más cercanos del presidente, que consiste en el vicepresidente, los ministros de cada uno de los 15 ministerios que forman parte del poder ejecutivo y otros funcionarios gubernamentales importantes, que ayudan al presidente a tomar decisiones y diseñar la política (pág. 316)

calendario agenda que enumera el orden en el cual los proyectos de ley serán considerados en el Congreso (pág. 146)

director de campaña persona responsable de la planificación y la estrategia general de una campaña (pág. 552)

sondear solicitar personalmente votos y determinar las opiniones (pág. 528)

comité de escrutinio cuerpo oficial que cuenta votos y certifica al ganador (pág. 565)

pena capital ejecución de un delincuente sentenciado a morir después de la condena de un tribunal por un delito penal (pág. 500)

capitalismo sistema económico en el cual los ciudadanos poseen y usan los factores de producción para lograr utilidades (pág. 23, 751)

trabajo social trabajo que hace un legislador para ayudar a los electores con problemas (pág. 222)

ayuda al constituyente miembro/a de los colaboradores personales de un legislador/a, que se encarga de las solicitudes de ayuda de los electores (pág. 163)

*categoría división dentro de un sistema de clasificación (pág. 443)

caucus evento que se lleva a cabo antes de una elección, en el cual miembros de un partido político eligen delegados para enviar a la convención nacional del partido, donde estos también votarán para nominar a un candidato; reunión privada de líderes del partido para que eligen candidatos a puestos (pág. 145, 304, 529)

censura acto de los gobiernos mediante el cual prohíben el uso de publicaciones o producciones que les parecen ofensivas o contrarias a sus propios intereses (pág. 448)

reprobación voto de desaprobación formal de las acciones de un miembro (pág. 137)

censo conteo completo de la población, incluyendo el lugar de residencia (pág. 134)

centrista persona cuyos puntos de vista suelen ser moderados (pág. 525)

charter a written instrument from the authorities of a society granting rights or privileges (p. 40)

carta instrumento escrito de las autoridades de una sociedad que otorga derechos o privilegios (pág. 40)

*circumstance a modifying or influencing factor (p. 400)

*circunstancia factor que influye o modifica (pág. 400)

citizen a member of a political society (p. 695)

ciudadano miembro de una sociedad política (pág. 695)

citizen suit a lawsuit by a private citizen to require a business or a government agency to enforce a law (p. 680)

demanda ciudadana demanda de un ciudadano privado para exigir que una empresa o un organismo del gobierno hagan cumplir una ley (pág. 680)

citizenship the expected qualities that a person should have as a member of a community (p. 696)

ciudadanía cualidades que se espera que una persona debería tener como miembro de una comunidad (pág. 696)

civil rights movement the struggle by African Americans in the mid-1950s to late 1960s to be free of racial discrimination and to achieve rights, freedoms, and opportunities equal to those of whites (p. 466)

movimiento pro derechos civiles lucha de los afroamericanos a mediados de la década de 1950 hasta finales de la de 1960 para liberarse de la discriminación racial y alcanzar derechos, libertades y oportunidades iguales a las de los blancos (pág. 466)

civil service system government employment based on competitive examinations and merit (p. 333)

sistema de servicio civil empleo gubernamental basado en mérito y pruebas por oposición (pág. 333)

civil society the complex network of voluntary associations that exist outside of government (p. 584)

sociedad civil red compleja de asociaciones voluntarias que existen por fuera del gobierno (pág. 584)

civil trial court hears cases where one person or group thinks another person or group should pay for causing harm (p. 391)

juzgado de lo civil ve casos en los que una persona o un grupo piensa que otra persona u otro grupo debería pagar por los daños causados (pág. 391)

civilian one not on active duty in the armed services or not on a police or firefighting force (p. 273)

civil persona que no se encuentra en servicio activo en las fuerzas armadas ni en la policía o los bomberos (pág. 273)

*clarify to make clear (p. 388)

*aclarar dejar claro (pág. 388)

client group individuals and groups who work with a government agency and are most affected by its decisions (p. 343)

grupo de clientes personas y grupos que trabajan con un organismo del gobierno y son los más afectados por sus decisiones (pág. 343)

closed primary an election in which only members of a political party can vote (p. 530)

elecciones primarias cerradas elecciones en las cuales solo miembros de un partido político pueden votar (pág. 530)

closed rule rule that forbids members of Congress to offer amendments to a bill from the floor (p. 209)

norma cerrada norma que prohíbe a los miembros del Congreso presentar enmiendas a un proyecto de ley cuando este ya está en una sesión del Congreso (pág. 209)

closed shop a workplace where only members of a union may be hired (p. 676)

empresa con sindicalización obligatoria lugar de trabajo donde solo miembros de un sindicato pueden ser contratados (pág. 676)

cloture resolution a procedure that allows each senator to speak only one hour on a bill under debate (p. 152)

resolución de clausura procedimiento que permite que cada senador hable solo durante una hora cuando se debate un proyecto de ley (pág. 152)

coalition government one formed by several parties who combine forces to obtain a majority (p. 515)

gobierno de coalición gobierno formado por varios partidos que combinan fuerzas para obtener una mayoría (pág. 515)

collective bargaining the practice of negotiating labor contracts (p. 675)

negociación colectiva práctica de la negociación de convenios de trabajo (pág. 675)

collective naturalization a process by which a group of people become American citizens through an act of Congress (p. 697)

naturalización colectiva proceso por el cual un grupo de personas se hacen ciudadanos estadounidenses mediante una ley del Congreso (pág. 697)

collective security a system by which member nations agree to take joint action against a nation that attacks any one of them (p. 718)

command economy an economic system in which the government controls the factors of production (p. 27)

*commentator person who reports and discusses news on radio or television (p. 611)

commercial speech speech where the speaker is more likely to be engaged in commerce and the intended audience is commercial, actual, or potential consumers (p. 444)

committee staff the people who work for House and Senate committees (p. 162)

*commodity a product or good that is sold for profit, such as an agricultural product; an article of commerce (p. 588)

*communicate to convey information; to make known (p. 576)

communism an economic system in which factors of production are collectively owned and the central government directs all major economic decisions (pp. 27, 751)

compensation something given or received as an equivalent for services (p. 298)

*complex involved, not simple (p. 161)

*component a part (p. 684)

compulsory voting mandatory voting (p. 562)

concurrent jurisdiction authority shared by both federal and state courts (p. 147)

concurrent powers powers that both the national government and the states have (p. 105)

concurrent resolution a resolution that cover matters requiring the action of the House and Senate but on which a law is not needed (p. 201)

concurring opinion a document issued by judges who agree with the majority opinion, but for different reasons than those used to support the majority opinion; the view expressed by justices who agree with the outcome, but not with all the reasoning (pp. 399, 420)

confederacy a loose union of independent states (p. 12)

conference committee a temporary joint committee set up when the House and the Senate have passed different versions of the same bill (p. 157)

conscription compulsory military service (p. 731)

---

seguridad colectiva sistema por el cual países miembros consienten en actuar conjuntamente contra un país que ataque a cualquiera de ellos (pág. 718)

economía planificada sistema económico en el cual el gobierno controla los factores de producción (pág. 27)

*comentarista persona que informa y discute noticias en la radio o la televisión (pág. 611)

discurso comercial discurso en el que el locutor es más probable que se ocupe del comercio y la audiencia prevista sea comercial, consumidores potenciales o reales (pág. 444)

personal de comités personas que trabajan en comités de la Cámara de Representantes y el Senado (pág. 162)

*mercancía producto o bien que se vende para obtener utilidades, como un producto agrícola; artículo comercial (pág. 588)

*comunicar transmitir información; dar a conocer (pág. 576)

comunismo sistema económico en el cual los factores de producción se poseen de modo colectivo y el gobierno central toma las decisiones económicas más importantes (pág. 27, 751)

retribución algo que se da o se recibe como equivalente por servicios (pág. 298)

*complejo enrevesado, no sencillo (pág. 161)

*componente parte (pág. 684)

voto obligatorio voto forzoso (pág. 562)

jurisdicción concurrente autoridad compartida por tribunales federales y estatales (pág. 147)

poderes concurrentes poderes que tienen ambos el gobierno nacional y los estados (pág. 105)

resolución concurrente resolución que abarca asuntos que requieren que actúen la Cámara de Representantes y el Senado, pero para los cuales no se necesita una ley (pág. 201)

opinión concurrente documento emitido por jueces que están de acuerdo con la opinión mayoritaria, pero por razones diferentes a las usadas para apoyar la opinión mayoritaria; el punto de vista expresada por jueces que están de acuerdo con el resultado, pero no con todas la razones (pág. 399, 420)

confederación unión imprecisa de estados independientes (pág. 12)

comité de conferencia comité mixto temporal constituido cuando la Cámara de Representantes y el Senado han aprobado versiones diferentes del mismo proyecto de ley (pág. 157)

conscripción servicio militar obligatorio (pág. 731)

*consent voluntary agreement by a people to organize a civil society and give authority to a government (p. 46)

*consenso acuerdo voluntario por parte de un pueblo para organizar una sociedad civil y dar autoridad a un gobierno (pág. 46)

*consequence something produced by a cause or action (p. 210)

*consecuencia algo producido por una causa o acción (pág. 210)

conservative the belief that the government should play a limited role in citizens' lives; also the belief in "traditional family values" and what is viewed as a moral lifestyle (p. 520)

conservador creencia de que el gobierno debería jugar un papel limitado en la vida de los ciudadanos; también la creencia en "valores familiares tradicionales" y lo que se considera un estilo de vida moral (pág. 520)

*considerable of substantial size or importance (p. 731)

*considerable de importancia o tamaño significativo (pág. 731)

constituent a person whom a member of Congress has been elected to represent (p. 143)

elector persona representada por un miembro del Congreso que ha sido elegido (pág. 143)

*constitute to make up, form, compose (p. 147)

*constituir dar forma legal, formar, componer (pág. 147)

constitution a plan that provides the rules for government (p. 13)

constitución plan que proporciona las reglas para el gobierno (pág. 13)

constitutional government a government in which a constitution has authority to place clearly recognized limits on the powers of those who govern (p. 14)

gobierno constitucional gobierno en el cual una constitución posee autoridad para poner límites claramente reconocidos a los poderes de quienes gobiernan (pág. 14)

consulate office functioning primarily to promote American business interests in foreign countries and to serve and safeguard American travelers in those countries (p. 729)

consulado oficina que funciona principalmente para promover los intereses comerciales de Estados Unidos en países extranjeros y para servir y amparar a los viajeros estadounidenses en esos países (pág. 729)

*consult to ask for advice (p. 722)

*consultar pedir consejo (pág. 722)

*consumer a person who purchases and uses goods and services (p. 23)

*consumidor persona que compra y usa productos y servicios (pág. 23)

containment the Cold War policy of keeping the Soviet Union from expanding its power (p. 711)

contención política durante la Guerra Fría que consistía en evitar que la Unión Soviética expandiera su poder (pág. 711)

*contemporary happening, existing, living, or coming into being during the same period of time (p. 262)

*contemporáneo que sucede, existe, vive o surge durante el mismo período (pág. 262)

contempt willful obstruction of justice (p. 185)

desacato obstrucción deliberada de la justicia (pág. 185)

contentious likely to cause disagreement or argument (p. 424)

polémico que probablemente causará discrepancias o debates (pág. 424)

continuing resolution a resolution that keeps the government open and operating under previous levels of appropriation during times when the House and Senate are controlled by different parties and cannot agree on an appropriation bill (p. 211)

resolución de continuidad resolución que mantiene abierto y funcionando al gobierno bajo los niveles previos de asignación durante los períodos en los que la Cámara de Representantes y el Senado son controlados por partidos diferentes y no se pueden poner de acuerdo en un proyecto de ley de asignación (pág. 211)

contraband anything prohibited by law from being imported, exported, or possessed (p. 486)

contrabando cualquier cosa que la ley prohíbe que se importe, se exporte o se posea (pág. 486)

*contradict to assert the contrary of, to imply the opposite of (p. 106)

*contradecir afirmar lo contrario, insinuar lo opuesto (pág. 106)

*contrast the difference between things that are of similar natures (p. 76)

*contraste diferencia entre cosas que tienen una naturaleza similar (pág. 76)

*contribute to give or supply in company with others (p. 216)

*contribuir dar o suministrar con otros (pág. 216)

convention a meeting held for the purpose of proposing and voting on amendments; a meeting where political party members who have been chosen as delegates from each state vote for the candidate supported by their state's voters (pp. 82, 304)

*coordinate to arrange and organize (p. 165)

copyright the exclusive right to publish and sell a literary, musical, or artistic work for a specified period of time (p. 179)

*corporation a large legal business group with its own duties, powers, and liabilities (p. 649)

corruption impairment of integrity, virtue, or moral principle (p. 556)

Council of Economic Advisers presidential advisers who study the economy and advise the president on domestic and international economic policies (p. 281)

counsel an attorney providing legal advice or representation (p. 494)

country a political community that occupies a definite territory and has an organized government (p. 9)

county the largest political subdivision of a state (p. 240)

county board the governing body of most counties (p. 240)

court-martial similar to criminal trials, but consists of judges and attorneys drawn from legal officers of the military branch in which the violation occurred (p. 407)

creditor one to whom a debt is owed (p. 51)

criminal justice process everything that happens to a person who commits a crime, from arrest through prosecution and conviction to release from prison (p. 485)

criminal trial court hears cases about crimes like burglary, murder, or driving under the influence of alcohol or drugs (p. 390)

cross-examination the examination of a witness who has already testified in order to check or discredit the witness's testimony, knowledge, or credibility (p. 495)

cross-pressured voter a voter who is caught between conflicting elements in his or her identity (p. 548)

currency a medium of exchange, a common example being paper money or coins (p. 51)

*data factual information used as a basis for reasoning, discussion, or calculation (p. 328)

convención reunión que se celebra con el fin de proponer y votar enmiendas; reunión en la cual miembros del partido político que han sido elegidos como delegados de cada estado votan por el candidato que apoyan los votantes de su estado (pág. 82, 304)

*coordinar ordenar y organizar (pág. 165)

derechos de autor derechos exclusivos a publicar y vender una obra literaria, musical o artística por un período específico (pág. 179)

*corporación gran grupo comercial legalmente constituido que tiene sus propios deberes, derechos y responsabilidades (pág. 649)

corrupción menoscabo de la integridad, la virtud o los principios morales (pág. 556)

Consejo de Asesores Económicos asesores presidenciales que estudian la economía y asesoran al presidente sobre políticas económicas nacionales e internacionales (pág. 281)

abogado representante legal que aconseja o representa (pág. 494)

país comunidad política que ocupa un territorio determinado y tiene un gobierno organizado (pág. 9)

condado la subdivisión más grande de un estado (pág. 240)

junta del condado cuerpo de gobierno de la mayoría de los condados (pág. 240)

corte marcial similar a un juicio penal, pero consistente en jueces y abogados provenientes de funcionarios judiciales de la rama de las fuerzas armadas en la cual ocurrió la transgresión (pág. 407)

acreedor alguien a quien se le debe una deuda (pág. 51)

proceso de justicia penal todo lo que le sucede a una persona que comete un delito, desde el arresto, pasando por el enjuiciamiento y la condena, hasta la excarcelación (pág. 485)

juzgado de lo penal ve casos sobre delitos como hurtos, asesinatos o conducción bajo la influencia del alcohol o las drogas (pág. 390)

contrainterrogatorio interrogatorio de un testigo que ya ha testificado con el fin de comprobar o poner en duda el testimonio, los conocimientos o la credibilidad del testigo (pág. 495)

votante bajo presión votante que se encuentra entre elementos conflictivos con respecto a su identidad (pág. 548)

moneda medio de cambio, siendo un ejemplo común el dinero en papel o metálico (pág. 51)

*datos información fundada en hechos que se usa como la base para el razonamiento, la discusión o el cálculo (pág. 328)

*decline to refuse to undertake (p. 297)

*rechazar declinar a emprender (pág. 297)

defamation false expression that injures a person's reputation (pp. 444, 616)

difamación expresión falsa que perjudica la reputación de una persona (pp. 444, 616)

defendant the person against whom a civil or criminal suit is brought in court (p. 392)

acusado persona contra la cual se entabla una demanda civil o penal en un tribunal (pág. 392)

delegated powers powers the Constitution grants or delegates to the national government (p. 104)

poderes delegados poderes que la Constitución cede o delega al gobierno nacional (pág. 104)

democracy government in which the people rule (p. 16)

democracia gobierno en el cual el pueblo gobierna (pág. 16)

Democratic Party the party more associated with liberal and moderate-liberals (p. 521)

Partido Demócrata partido más asociado con liberales y liberales moderados (pág. 521)

democratic socialist a socialist who is committed to democracy but wants government involvement in the distribution of wealth (p. 26)

socialista democrático socialista comprometido con la democracia pero que quiere la participación del gobierno en la distribución de la riqueza (pág. 26)

*deny to refuse to admit or acknowledge (p. 275)

*rechazar negarse a admitir o reconocer (pág. 275)

dependent one who relies primarily on another person for basic needs such as food, clothing, and shelter (p. 647)

dependiente persona que cuenta principalmente con otra persona para sus necesidades básicas, como la comida, la ropa y el alojamiento (pág. 647)

deregulate to remove regulation (p. 344)

desregular eliminar las regulaciones (pág. 344)

*desecrate to treat disrespectfully (p. 83)

*profanar tratar irrespetuosamente (pág. 83)

developing nation nation with little or no industry; many developing nations are former colonies of Western European powers (p. 760)

país en desarrollo país con poca o ninguna industria; muchos países en desarrollo son excolonias de potencias de Europa occidental (pág. 760)

*device a mechanism designed to serve a special purpose or perform a special function (p. 542)

*aparato mecanismo diseñado para servir para un fin especial o realizar una función especial (pág. 542)

*devote to commit to an activity (p. 150)

*dedicarse comprometerse a una actividad (pág. 150)

dictatorship a system of government in which power is in the hands of one person who has total control (p. 16)

dictadura sistema de gobierno en el cual el poder se encuentra en manos de una persona, quien tiene control total (pág. 16)

direct democracy a form of government wherein citizens rule themselves rather than electing representatives to govern on their behalf (p. 242)

democracia directa forma de gobierno en la cual los ciudadanos se gobiernan a sí mismos en vez de elegir representantes para que gobiernen por ellos (pág. 242)

direct primary an election in which party members select people to run in the general election (p. 530)

elecciones primarias directas elecciones en las cuales miembros del partido eligen a quienes serán candidatos en las elecciones generales (pág. 530)

disability a physical or mental condition that causes a person to have difficulty seeing, hearing, talking, walking, or performing basic activities of daily living (p. 470)

discapacidad estado mental o físico que causa que una persona tenga dificultades para ver, oír, hablar, caminar o realizar actividades básicas de la vida cotidiana (pág. 470)

*discontent displeased or unsatisfied (p. 53)

*descontento disconforme o insatisfecho (pág. 53)

discount rate the interest rate the Federal Reserve charges member banks for loans (p. 654)

tasa de descuento tasa de interés que la Reserva Federal cobra a bancos miembros por préstamos (pág. 654)

*discretionary left to choice or judgment (p. 643)

*discrecional que queda a elección o a criterio (pág. 643)

Glossary/Glosario

discrimination treatment or consideration of, or making a distinction in favor of or against, a person or thing based on the group, class, or category to which that person or thing belongs rather than on individual merit (p. 466)

disenfranchise to deprive of the right to vote (p. 541)

*disposal the act of getting rid of (p. 242)

dissenting opinion a document issued by judges who disagree with the majority opinion (pp. 399, 420)

*distribute to give out or disburse to clients, customers, or members of a group (pp. 528, 552)

*diverse of various kinds or forms (p. 471)

divided government when one party controls the White House and the other controls the House and Senate (p. 190)

divine right the idea that people are chosen by a god or gods to rule (p. 11)

double jeopardy the subjecting of a person to a second trial or punishment for the same offense for which the person has already been tried or punished (p. 501)

*draft the first form of any writing, subject to revision (p. 46)

*dynamic forceful, energetic (p. 71)

e-commerce the sales of goods and services online (p. 627)

early voting provision that allows a person to vote in person for a specified period of time prior to Election Day (p. 563)

earmark part of a funding bill that will go toward a certain purpose (p. 212)

economic indicators markets, scales, reports, or figures that give information about how different areas of the economy are performing (p. 652)

economics the study of how people and nations use their limited resources to attempt to satisfy wants and needs (p. 22)

elastic clause clause in Article I, Section 8, of the Constitution that gives Congress the right to "make all laws necessary and proper" to carry out the powers expressed in the other clauses of Article I (p. 74)

election an orderly process for making group decisions (p. 540)

elector a member of a political party chosen in each state to formally elect the president and vice president (p. 302)

discriminación tratamiento o consideración a favor o en contra de una persona o cosa, basándose en el grupo, la clase o la categoría a la que pertenece la persona o la cosa en vez de en méritos individuales (pág. 466)

inhabilitar para votar privar del derecho a votar (pág. 541)

*eliminación acto de deshacerse de algo (pág. 242)

opinión disidente documento emitido por jueces que no están de acuerdo con la opinión mayoritaria (págs. 399, 420)

*distribuir repartir o disponer entre clientes, compradores o miembros de un grupo (pág. 528, 552)

*diverso de varios tipos o formas (pág. 471)

gobierno dividido cuando un partido controla la Casa Blanca y el otro controla la Cámara de Representantes y el Senado (pág. 190)

derecho divino idea de que las personas son elegidas por un dios o dioses para gobernar (pág. 11)

cosa juzgada sometimiento de una persona a un segundo juicio o sanción por el mismo delito por el cual ya ha sido enjuiciada o castigada (pág. 501)

*borrador primera forma de cualquier escrito, sujeto a revisión (pág. 46)

*dinámico enérgico, vigoroso (pág. 71)

comercio electrónico venta de productos y servicios por Internet (pág. 627)

voto anticipado medida que permite a alguien votar en persona durante un período especificado antes del día de las elecciones (pág. 563)

asignar especialmente parte de una propuesta de ley de financiación destinada a un propósito específico (pág. 212)

indicadores económicos mercados, magnitudes, informes o cifras que proporcionan información acerca de cómo distintas áreas de la economía se están desempeñando (pág. 652)

economía estudio sobre cómo la gente y los países usan sus recursos limitados para intentar satisfacer deseos y necesidades (pág. 22)

cláusula flexible cláusula en el Artículo I, Sección 8, de la Constitución, que otorga al Congreso el derecho a "hacer todas las leyes necesarias y apropiadas" para llevar a cabo los poderes que se expresan en las otras cláusulas del Artículo I (pág. 74)

elección proceso ordenado para tomar decisiones en grupo (pág. 540)

compromisario a miembro/a de un partido político que está elegido/a en cada estado para elegir formalmente al presidente y el vicepresidente (pág. 302)

Electoral College the institution that is composed of a set of electors who are chosen to elect a president and vice president into office every four years (p. 302)

Colegio Electoral institución compuesta por un grupo de compromisarios que cada cuatro años se eligen para que voten por quienes asumirán los cargos de presidente y vicepresidente (pág. 302)

electronic mailing list an automated e-mail notification that provides subscribers with current information on a topic (p. 623)

lista de correo electrónico notificación automática por correo electrónico que proporciona información actual sobre un tema a los suscriptores (pág. 623)

electronic petition a message that asks the recipient to "sign" his or her name electronically to a request that will be sent to an official (p. 624)

petición electrónica mensaje que pide a quien lo recibe que "firme" su nombre electrónicamente en una solicitud que se enviará a un funcionario (pág. 624)

embargo an agreement prohibiting trade (p. 45)

embargo acuerdo que prohíbe comerciar (pág. 45)

embassy the official residence and offices of the ambassador and his or her staff; the primary function of an embassy is to make diplomatic communication between governments easier (pp. 326, 729)

embajada oficinas y residencia oficial del embajador y su personal; la función principal de una embajada es facilitar la comunicación diplomática entre los gobiernos (pág. 326, 729)

embedded journalist a reporter who travels with and accompanies troops into battle, then reports live about what they experience (p. 620)

periodista incorporado corresponsal que viaja acompañando a las tropas a la batalla, y luego informa en vivo acerca de sus experiencias (pág. 620)

eminent domain the power of government to take private property for public use (p. 85)

dominio eminente poder del gobierno de apropiarse de propiedad privada con fines de uso público (pág. 85)

enabling act an act that allows the people of a territory interested in becoming a state to prepare a constitution (p. 109)

ley habilitante ley que permite que las personas de un territorio interesadas en convertirse en estado preparen una constitución (pág. 109)

*ensure to make sure, certain, or safe (p. 282)

*asegurar verificar, cerciorarse o poner a salvo (pág. 282)

entitlement a required government expenditure that continues from one year to the next (pp. 212, 643)

título gasto necesario del gobierno que continúa de un año a otro (pág. 212, 643)

*entity something that has separate and distinct existence (p. 388)

*entidad algo que tiene existencia aparte y diferenciada (pág. 388)

entrepreneur a person who starts a new business (p. 752)

empresario persona que monta un nuevo negocio (pág. 752)

enumerated powers a list of items, found in Article I, Section 8, of the Constitution, that set forth the authoritative capacity of Congress (p. 74)

poderes enumerados lista de elementos que se encuentran en el Artículo I, Sección 8, de la Constitución y describen la capacidad autoritativa del Congreso (pág. 74)

*environmental having to do with air, water, land, and other natural resources (p. 680)

*medioambiental relacionado con el aire, el agua, el suelo y otros recursos naturales (pág. 680)

equal protection clause prohibits government actions from unreasonably discriminating between different groups of people (p. 461)

cláusula de protección igualitaria disposición que prohíbe que las acciones del gobierno causen discriminación entre los diferentes grupos de personas (pág. 461)

*equip to make ready; to prepare (p. 496)

*equipar dejar listo; preparar (pág. 496)

error of law a mistake by a judge as to the applicable law in a case (p. 398)

error de derecho error de un juez con respecto a la ley aplicable en un caso (pág. 398)

espionage the use of spies by a government to discover the military and political secrets of other nations (p. 500)

espionaje uso de espías por parte de un gobierno para descubrir secretos militares y políticos de otros países (pág. 500)

*establish to institute permanently by enactment or agreement (p. 37)

*establecer instituir permanentemente por medio de promulgación o acuerdo (pág. 37)

Glossary/Glosario

establishment clause the First Amendment guarantee that prohibits state and federal governments from setting up churches, passing laws aiding one or all religions or favoring one religion over another, or passing laws requiring attendance at any church or belief in any religious idea (p. 454)

evidence an outward sign; something that furnishes proof (p. 486)

ex post facto clause the clause in the U.S. Constitution that prevents the government from punishing someone for doing something that was not a crime when the act was committed (p. 499)

*excessive going beyond the usual, necessary, or proper limit or degree (p. 455)

excise tax a tax on the manufacture, transportation, sale, or consumption of goods and the performance of services (p. 645)

exclusionary rule a rule that forbids the introduction of illegally obtained evidence in a criminal trial (p. 487)

executive agreement legally binding pact between the president and the head of a foreign government that does not require Senate approval (pp. 276, 724)

executive order a rule issued by the president that has the force of law (p. 268)

executive privilege the right of the president and other high-ranking executive officers to refuse to testify before Congress or a court (p. 263)

exit poll polling that involves interviewing voters as they leave the polling place and asking them for whom they voted (p. 583)

*expand to increase in extent, size, volume, or scope (p. 477)

expenditure financial outlay (p. 642)

*expert a person who has special knowledge in an area (p. 162)

*expertise special skill or knowledge in a particular field (p. 406)

*exports products, goods, resources, or other materials that are sold and sent to another country as part of international trade (p. 58)

*expose to make known, reveal, or disclose the faults of (p. 609)

expressed powers powers directly stated in the Constitution (pp. 104, 173)

*extract to pull or draw out (p. 681)

extradite to return a fugitive who flees across state lines back to the original state (p. 116)

extralegal not sanctioned by law (p. 59)

cláusula de establecimiento garantía de la Primera Enmienda, que prohíbe a los gobiernos federal y estatales fundar iglesias, aprobar leyes que auxilien o favorezcan a cualquier religión, o aprobar leyes que exijan la asistencia a cualquier iglesia o idea religiosa (pág. 454)

evidencia manifestación; algo que aporta pruebas (pág. 486)

cláusula ex post facto cláusula de la Constitución de Estados Unidos, que evita que el gobierno castigue a alguien por hacer algo que no era un delito cuando lo hizo (pág. 499)

*excesivo que va más allá del límite o grado de lo apropiado, usual o necesario (pág. 455)

impuesto especial impuesto a la fabricación, el transporte, la venta o el consumo de bienes y la prestación de servicios (pág. 645)

regla de exclusión regla que prohíbe presentar evidencia obtenida ilegalmente en un juicio penal (pág. 487)

convenio ejecutivo pacto legalmente vinculante entre el presidente y el jefe de un gobierno extranjero que no requiere aprobación del Senado (pág. 276, 724)

decreto ley norma promulgada por el presidente, que tiene fuerza de ley (pág. 268)

inmunidad del poder ejecutivo derecho del presidente y otros funcionarios de alto rango a negarse a testificar ante el Congreso o un tribunal (pág. 263)

encuesta a boca de urna encuesta que implica entrevistar a votantes a medida que salen del lugar de votación y preguntarles por quién votaron (pág. 583)

*expandir aumentar en extensión, tamaño, volumen o alcance (pág. 477)

gasto desembolso financiero (pág. 642)

*experto persona que tiene conocimientos especiales en un área (pág. 162)

*pericia conocimientos o destreza especial en un campo en particular (pág. 406)

*exportaciones productos, bienes, recursos u otros materiales que se venden y envían a otro país como parte del comercio internacional (pág. 58)

*exponer dar a conocer, revelar o divulgar las faltas de alguien (pág. 609)

poderes expresados poderes directamente indicados en la Constitución (pág. 104, 173)

*extraer retirar o sacar (pág. 681)

extraditar devolver a su estado de origen a un fugitivo que huye atravesando límites estatales (pág. 116)

extralegal no autorizado por la ley (pág. 59)

extraordinary going beyond what is usual, regular, or customary

extraordinario que va más allá de lo usual, regular o acostumbrado

*factor part of a product or concept (p. 576)

*factor parte de un producto o concepto (pág. 576)

fairness doctrine rule requiring broadcasters to provide opportunities for the expression of opposing views on issues of public importance (p. 619)

norma de equidad norma que requiere que las emisoras proporcionen oportunidades para la expresión de puntos de vista opuestos en asuntos de importancia pública (pág. 619)

*federal pertaining to the union of states under a central government distinct from the individual governments of the separate states (p. 319)

*federal concerniente a la unión de estados bajo un gobierno central diferente a los gobiernos individuales de los estados por separado (pág. 319)

Federal Election Commission (FEC) an independent regulatory agency created by Congress to enforce federal election laws (p. 303)

Comisión Federal Electoral (FEC) organismo regulador independiente creado por el Congreso para hacer cumplir las leyes electorales federales (pág. 303)

federal grant a sum of money given to a state or local government for a specific purpose (p. 110)

subvención federal suma de dinero otorgada a un gobierno estatal o local para un propósito específico (pág. 110)

Federal Reserve System the central banking system of the United States (pp. 281, 653)

Sistema de la Reserva Federal sistema bancario central de Estados Unidos (pág. 281, 653)

federal system a government that divides the powers of government between the national government and state or provincial governments (p. 13)

sistema federal gobierno que divide los poderes gubernamentales entre el gobierno nacional y gobiernos estatales o provinciales (pág. 13)

federalism a system of government in which two or more governments exercise power over the same people and the same territory (p. 103)

federalismo sistema de gobierno en cual dos o más gobiernos ejercen poder sobre la misma gente y el mismo territorio (pág. 103)

"fighting words" words spoken face-to-face that are likely to cause immediate violence (p. 444)

"palabras de confrontación" palabras habladas cara a cara que es probable que provoquen violencia inmediata (pág. 444)

*file to initiate through proper formal procedure (p. 501)

*interponer iniciar mediante un procedimiento formal apropiado (pág. 501)

filibuster a method of defeating a bill in the Senate by stalling the legislative process and preventing a vote (p. 151)

obstruccionismo método para rechazar un proyecto de ley en el Senado al paralizar el proceso legislativo e impedir la votación (pág. 151)

*finance to provide necessary funds for; the management of revenues (p. 370)

*finanzas administración de los ingresos (pág. 370)

fiscal policy a government's use of spending and taxation to influence the economy (p. 652)

política fiscal uso que hace el gobierno de los gastos y las tributaciones para influir en la economía (pág. 652)

fiscal year a 12-month accounting period; the federal government's runs from October 1 to September 30 (p. 640)

año fiscal período contable de 12 meses; el del gobierno federal va del 1.° de octubre al 30 de septiembre (pág. 640)

*flexible capable of readily adapting to change (p. 149)

*flexible capaz de adaptarse rápidamente a un cambio (pág. 149)

foreign policy the strategies and goals that guide a nation's relations with other countries and groups in the world (p. 708)

política exterior estrategias y objetivos que guían las relaciones de un país con otros países y grupos en el mundo (pág. 708)

*format general plan of organization, arrangement, or choice of material

*formato plan general de organización, disposición o elección de material

*formulate to devise or develop (p. 133)

*formular concebir o desarrollar (pág. 133)

free enterprise the opportunity to control one's own economic decisions (p. 23)

libre empresa oportunidad de controlar las propias decisiones económicas (pág. 23)

Glossary/Glosario

free exercise clause the First Amendment guarantee that prohibits government from unduly interfering with the free exercise of religion (p. 457)

free market economic system in which buyers and sellers make free choices in the marketplace (p. 23)

Freedom of Information Act (FOIA) requires federal agencies to release files to the public, unless the material falls into certain exceptions for national security or other confidential information (p. 616)

front-runner label given to the candidate who wins an early primary, even if by a very small margin (p. 610)

***fund** financial capital (p. 268)

***fundamental** a basic and necessary component of something; original, primary, and essential (p. 709)

***furious** exhibiting anger (p. 53)

gag order an order by a judge barring the press from publishing certain types of information about a pending court case (p. 450)

general jurisdiction courts that are able to hear a wide variety of cases that deal with state or local law, the state constitution, or federal law or the federal constitution (p. 403)

***generate** to produce; to be the cause of (p. 293)

gerrymander to draw a district's boundaries to gain an advantage in elections (p. 135)

***global** worldwide; universal (p. 627)

***goal** aim, purpose (p. 79)

government an institution through which leaders exercise power to make and enforce laws affecting the people under its control (p. 7)

government corporation a business that the federal government runs (p. 330)

governor the leader of the executive branch of a state (p. 352)

grand jury a group that hears charges against a suspect and decides whether there is sufficient evidence to bring the person to trial (p. 395)

grandfather clause an exemption in a law for a certain group based on previous conditions (p. 541)

grassroots lobbying political advocacy efforts carried out by the general public and members of interest groups, sometimes under the guidance of their professional lobbyists (p. 592)

graven image an idol or physical object of worship (p. 457)

cláusula de ejercicio libre garantía de la Primera Enmienda, que prohíbe al gobierno interferir excesivamente en el ejercicio libre de la religión (pág. 457)

libre mercado sistema económico en el cual compradores y vendedores toman decisiones libres en el mercado (pág. 23)

Ley de Libertad de Información (FOIA) exige que los organismos federales den a conocer archivos al público, a menos que el material se incluya dentro de ciertas excepciones por seguridad nacional u otra información confidencial (pág. 616)

favorito término con que se nombra al candidato que gana una de las primeras elecciones primarias, aunque sea por un margen muy pequeño (pág. 610)

***fondo** capital financiero (pág. 268)

***fundamental** componente básico y necesario de algo; original, primario y esencial (pág. 709)

***furioso** que manifiesta ira (pág. 53)

orden de no divulgación orden de un juez que prohíbe a la prensa la publicación de ciertos tipos de información acerca de un caso pendiente en un tribunal (pág. 450)

jurisdicción general tribunales que pueden ver una gran variedad de casos relacionados con las leyes estatales o locales, la constitución estatal, la ley federal o la constitución federal (pág. 403)

***generar** producir; ser la causa (pág. 293)

gerrymander trazar los límites de un distrito para obtener una ventaja en las elecciones (pág. 135)

***global** mundial; universal (pág. 627)

***meta** objetivo, propósito (pág. 79)

gobierno institución mediante la cual los líderes ejercen poder para crear y hacer cumplir leyes que afectan a las personas que están bajo su control (pág.7)

corporación gubernamental empresa que opera el gobierno federal (pág. 330)

gobernador líder del poder ejecutivo de un estado (pág. 352)

gran jurado grupo que ve cargos contra un sospechoso y decide si hay evidencia suficiente como para llevar a la persona a un juicio (pág. 395)

cláusula de derechos adquiridos excepción en una ley para cierto grupo basada en condiciones previas (pág. 541)

cabildeo de las bases esfuerzos de incidencia política realizados por el público en general y miembros de grupos de interés, a veces bajo la dirección de sus cabilderos profesionales (pág. 592)

ídolo imagen u objeto físico de adoración (pág. 457)

green card a document issued by the government that shows a person has permission to live and work in the United States (p. 700)

tarjeta verde documento emitido por el gobierno que muestra que una persona tiene permiso para vivir y trabajar en Estados Unidos (pág. 700)

gross domestic product (GDP) the sum of all goods and services produced in a country in a year (p. 653)

producto interno bruto (PIB) suma de todos los bienes y servicios producidos en un país en un año (pág. 653)

*guarantee an assurance for the fulfillment of a condition (p. 458)

*garantía seguridad para el cumplimiento de una condición (pág. 458)

gubernatorial from the Latin *gubernare*, meaning of or relating to the governor (p. 353)

gubernativo del latín *gubernare*, que significa perteneciente o relativo al gobernador (pág. 353)

hard money direct contributions to a candidate's political campaign (p. 557)

dinero duro contribuciones directas a la campaña política de un candidato (pág. 557)

hearing a session at which a committee listens to testimony from people interested in the bill (p. 204)

audiencia sesión en la cual un comité escucha testimonios de personas interesadas en el proyecto de ley (pág. 204)

*highlight to center attention on (p. 640)

*resaltar hacer centrar la atención en algo (pág. 640)

hold a motion placed on a bill in the Senate that alerts party leaders that if unanimous consent were to be sought, they would object (p. 151)

mocion de bloqueo mocion presentada en el Senado para alertar a los líderes partidarios que si se buscara consentimiento unánime en un proyecto de ley, se opondrían (pág. 151)

horse-race coverage news coverage of presidential election campaigns in which the media treat the campaign as if it were a sporting event, generating excitement by focusing on who is ahead, who is making a comeback, and so on (p. 610)

cobertura de carrera de caballos cobertura de campañas para las elecciones presidenciales en la cual los medios de comunicación tratan las campañas como si fuesen eventos deportivos, generando entusiasmo al mostrar quién va delante, quién está recuperándose, etc. (pág. 610)

human rights rights regarded as belonging fundamentally to all persons (p. 47)

derechos humanos derechos considerados como intrínsecamente pertenecientes a todas las personas (pág. 47)

*ideological of or pertaining to the body of beliefs that guide an individual, political system, or nation (p. 425)

*ideológico perteneciente o relativo al conjunto de creencias que guían a una persona, un sistema político o una nación (pág. 425)

ideological party a political party that has a particular set of ideas about how to change society overall rather than focusing on a single issue (p. 517)

partido ideológico partido político que tiene un conjunto específico de ideas acerca de cómo cambiar la sociedad en general en vez de enfocarse en un solo asunto (pág. 517)

*ideology a set of basic beliefs about life, culture, government, and society (p. 520)

*ideología conjunto de creencias básicas acerca de la vida, la cultura, el gobierno y la sociedad (pág. 520)

*ignore to refuse to take notice of (p. 333)

*ignorar negarse a prestar atención a algo (pág. 333)

immunity freedom from prosecution for witnesses whose testimony ties them to illegal acts (p. 186)

inmunidad derecho a no ser procesado para testigos cuyo testimonio los relaciona a actos ilegales (pág. 186)

impartial unbiased (p. 389)

imparcial sin sesgo (pág. 389)

impeach to accuse a public official of misconduct in office (pp. 88, 264)

enjuiciar políticamente acusar a un funcionario público de mala conducta en sus funciones (pág. 88, 264)

impeachment the formal accusation of misconduct in office (p. 180)

impugnación acusación formal de mala conducta en un puesto (pág. 180)

*implement to put into effect and ensure fulfillment by concrete measures (p. 338)

*implementar llevar a cabo y asegurar el cumplimiento de algo por medio de medidas concretas (pág. 338)

implied powers powers the government requires to carry out its expressed constitutional powers (pp. 104, 173)

poderes implícitos poderes que el gobierno requiere para llevar a cabo sus poderes constitucionales (pág. 104, 173)

Glossary/Glosario

*impose to establish or apply by authority (p. 646)

impound to refuse to spend (p. 269)

impoundment the president's refusal to spend money Congress has voted to fund a program (p. 193)

*inadequate insufficient (p. 374)

income security program a government program designed to help elderly, ill, and unemployed citizens (p. 684)

*incorporate to blend into or combine (p. 247)

incorporation doctrine the process by which the Bill of Rights was extended to the states and localities (pp. 83, 464)

incumbent elected official who is already in office (p. 139)

independent a voter who does not support any particular party (p. 524)

*index a list of companies and their stock prices (p. 652)

*indication something that tells or points out, such as a sign or symbol (p. 578)

indictment a formal charge of criminal action by a grand jury (p. 395)

indigent suffering from extreme poverty (p. 494)

infrastructure the basic facilities of a city, such as roads, bridges, water and sewage pipes, and public buildings (p. 374)

inherent powers powers not described in the Constitution, but that have been claimed by presidents (p. 262)

*inhibit to prohibit from doing something (p. 455)

initiative a method by which citizens propose a constitutional law or amendment (p. 547)

injunction an order that will stop an action or enforce a rule or regulation (p. 340)

*innovative characterized by a new idea or method (p. 330)

inquisitorial system a trial system where the judge plays an active role in gathering evidence (p. 391)

*instance example; as an illustration of a concept (p. 756)

*institution establishment practice, or social organization (p. 18)

*integrity firm adherence to a code of moral values (p. 109)

*imponer establecer o aplicar por medio de la autoridad (pág. 646)

embargar rehusar un gasto (pág. 269)

confiscación negativa del presidente a gastar dinero que el Congreso ha aprobado para financiar un programa (pág. 193)

*inadecuado insuficiente (pág. 374)

programa de seguridad de ingreso programa gubernamental creado para ayudar a los ciudadanos ancianos, enfermos, y desempleados (pág. 684)

*incorporar integrar o combinar (pág. 247)

doctrina de incorporación proceso mediante el cual la Declaración de Derechos se extendió a los estados y localidades (pág. 83, 464)

titular funcionario electo que ya ejerce su cargo (pág. 139)

independiente votante que no apoya ningún partido en particular (pág. 524)

*índice lista de empresas y el precio de sus acciones (pág. 652)

*indicación algo que indica o señala, como un signo o un símbolo (pág. 578)

acusación cargo formal de una acción penal imputado por un gran jurado (pág. 395)

indigente que sufre de pobreza extrema (pág. 494)

infraestructura servicios básicos de una ciudad, como caminos, puentes, cañerías de agua corriente, emisarios de aguas residuales y edificios públicos (pág. 374)

poderes inherentes poderes no descritos en la Constitución pero que han sido reivindicados por presidentes (pág. 262)

*inhibir prohibir hacer algo (pág. 455)

iniciativa método por el cual los ciudadanos proponen una enmienda o ley constitucional (pág. 547)

medidas cautelares orden que impedirá una acción o hará cumplir una norma o un reglamento (pág. 340)

*innovador caracterizado por una nueva idea o un nuevo método (pág. 330)

sistema inquisitivo sistema de enjuiciamiento en el cual el juez juega un papel activo en la acumulación de evidencia (pág. 391)

*caso ejemplo; como ilustración de un concepto (pág. 756)

*institución establecimiento u organización social (pág. 18)

*integridad adhesión firme a un código de valores morales (pág. 109)

*interactive relating to a two-way electronic communication system (p. 204)

*interactivo relacionado con un sistema de comunicación electrónica en dos direcciones (pág. 204)

interest group a group of people who share common goals and organize to influence government and policy (pp. 219, 575, 584)

grupo de interés grupo de personas que comparten metas comunes y se organizan para influenciar en el gobierno y la política (pág. 219, 575, 584)

intergovernmental organization (IGO) type of international organization made up of groups of national governments and created through agreements negotiated by member states; an IGO's powers are established and limited by its members (p. 746)

organización intergubernamental tipo de organización internacional conformada por grupos de gobiernos nacionales y creada por medio de acuerdos negociados por los estados miembros; los poderes de una organización intergubernamental son establecidos y limitados por sus miembros (pág. 746)

interlocking directorate the same people serving on the board of directors of competing companies (p. 673)

junta directiva entrelazada las mismas personas que sirven en las juntas directivas de empresas rivales (pág. 673)

*interpretation explanation (p. 387)

*interpretación explicación (pág. 387)

interrogation a formal or official questioning (p. 490)

interrogatorio serie de preguntas formales u oficiales (pág. 490)

interstate commerce trade among states (pp. 58, 176)

comercio interestatal comercio entre estados (pág. 58, 176)

interstate compact a written agreement between two or more states (p. 117)

convenio interestatal acuerdo por escrito entre dos o más estados (pág. 117)

*investigation a systematic examination of related facts (p. 264)

*investigación examen sistemático de hechos relacionados (pág. 264)

*investor someone who puts money to a particular use in order to receive a profitable return (p. 674)

*inversionistas quienes ponen dinero para un uso en particular con el fin de recibir un rendimiento rentable (pág. 674)

*involve to engage as a participant (p. 222)

*involucrarse comprometerse como participante (pág. 222)

iron triangle a relationship formed among government agencies, congressional committees, and client groups that work together (p. 343)

triángulo de hierro relación formada para trabajar juntos entre organismos del gobierno, comités del Congreso y grupos de clientes (pág. 343)

isolationism avoiding involvement in world affairs (p. 710)

aislacionismo acto de evitar la participación en asuntos mundiales (pág. 710)

*issue an important topic or problem for debate or discussion (p. 154)

*asunto tema importante o problema que hay que debatir o discutir (pág. 154)

Jim Crow laws any of the laws requiring racial segregation in places like schools, hotels, and public transportation in the South between the end of the Reconstruction period to the beginning of the civil rights movement in the 1950s (p. 460)

leyes de Jim Crow cualquiera de las leyes que exigían segregación racial en lugares como escuelas, hoteles y transporte público en el Sur, desde el fin del período de la Reconstrucción hasta el comienzo del movimiento de los derechos civiles en la década de 1950 (pág. 460)

joint committee a committee that consists of members from both the House and Senate, formed to act as a study group that reports back to the House and Senate on a topic or bill (p. 157)

comité mixto comité conformado por miembros de ambas cámaras, la de Representantes y el Senado, creado para actuar como grupo de estudio que informa a la Cámara de Representantes y el Senado sobre un tema o un proyecto de ley (pág. 157)

joint resolution a resolution passed in the same form by both houses (p. 201)

resolución conjunta resolución aprobada de la misma forma por ambas cámaras (pág. 201)

journalist professional media communicator, including reporter, columnist, editor, editorial writer, editorial cartoonist, photojournalist, correspondent, commentator, and news director (p. 607)

periodista cualquier comunicador profesional de los medios de comunicación, incluyendo reporter, columnista, editor, escritor de editoriales, reportero gráfico, corresponsal, comentarista, y director de noticias (pág. 607)

Glossary/Glos

judicial activism the philosophy that courts must sometimes step into political and social controversies in order to protect Constitutional rights (p. 429)

judicial restraint the philosophy that courts should generally avoid overturning laws passed or actions taken by democratically elected bodies (p. 429)

judicial review the power of the Supreme Court to declare laws and actions of local, state, or national governments unconstitutional (pp. 76, 388)

jurisdiction the limits or territory within which authority may be exercised (p. 76)

jury a group of citizens who hear evidence during a trial and give a verdict (p. 392)

laissez-faire the philosophy that government should keep its hands off the economy (p. 23)

landslide a great majority of votes for one side (p. 293)

law the set of rules and standards by which a society governs itself (p. 387)

law clerk an attorney who assists a justice in reviewing cases (p. 418)

leak the release of secret information to the media by anonymous government officials (pp. 317, 609)

legislative assistant a member of a lawmaker's personal staff who makes certain that the lawmaker is well informed about proposed legislation (p. 162)

legislative oversight power of the legislative branch to review the policies, programs, and activities of the executive branch on an ongoing basis (p. 186)

legislative referendum a special election in which the legislature refers a measure to the voters for his or her approval (p. 547)

legislative veto a provision that Congress wrote into some laws that allowed it to review and cancel actions of executive agencies (p. 187)

***levy** to impose a tax (p. 37)

liaison officer an officer who develops relationships with the elected officials and congressional staff members who have authority over the work of his or her department (p. 338)

libel false written or published statements that damage a person's reputation (pp. 444, 616)

liberal the belief that the proper role of government is to actively promote health, education, and justice (p. 520)

activismo judicial filosofía según la cual los juzgados, en ocasiones, deben participar en controversias políticas y sociales para proteger los derechos constitucionales (pág. 429)

restricción judicial filosofía según la cual los juzgados deben, generalmente, evitar la anulación de leyes aprobadas o acciones llevadas a cabo por estamentos elegidos democráticamente (pág. 429)

revisión judicial poder de la Corte Suprema de declarar inconstitucionales a leyes y acciones de gobiernos locales, estatales o nacionales (pág. 76, 388)

jurisdicción límites o territorio dentro del cual puede ejercerse autoridad (pág. 76)

jurado grupo de ciudadanos que ven la evidencia durante un juicio y dan un veredicto (pág. 392)

laissez-faire filosofía que expresa que el gobierno debería evitar interferir en la economía (pág. 23)

victoria aplastante gran mayoría de votos para una de las partes (pág. 293)

ley conjunto de reglas y normas por las cuales una sociedad se gobierna (pág. 387)

secretario judicial abogado que ayuda a un juez a revisar casos (pág. 418)

filtración divulgación de información secreta a los medios de comunicación por parte de funcionarios gubernamentales anónimos (pág. 317, 609)

auxiliar legislativo miembro de los colaboradores personales de un legislador, que se asegura de que el legislador esté bien informado acerca de los proyectos de ley (pág. 162)

vigilancia legislativa facultad del poder legislativo regularmente a revisar las políticos, los programas, y las actividades del poder ejecutivo (pág. 186)

referéndum legislativo elección especial en la que la asamblea legislativa presenta una medida a los votantes para que la aprueben (pág. 547)

veto legislativo estipulación que incluyó el Congreso en algunas leyes que le permite revisar y cancelar acciones de los organismos del poder ejecutivo (pág. 187)

***gravar** imponer un impuesto (pág. 37)

funcionario de enlace funcionario que se relaciona con funcionarios elegidos y congresistas, que tienen autoridad en el departamento donde él trabaja (pág. 338)

libelo declaraciones publicadas o escritas falsas que dañan la reputación de una persona (pág. 444, 616)

liberal creencia en que el papel apropiado del gobierno es promover activamente la salud, la educación y la justicia (pág. 520)

*license to give official permission to operate in a certain occupation (p. 115)

*licencia permiso emitido por un organismo oficial (pág. 115)

lieutenant governor elected official serving as deputy to the governor (pp. 233, 353)

vicegobernador funcionario elegido que cumple la función de gobernador subrogante (pág. 233, 353)

limited government a system in which the power of the government is limited, not absolute (p. 37)

gobierno limitado sistema en el cual el poder del gobierno es limitado, no es absoluto (pág. 37)

limited jurisdiction courts that generally hear cases that raise questions about a federal law or the federal constitution (p. 404)

jurisdicción limitada tribunales que generalmente ven casos que plantean interrogantes acerca de una ley federal o la constitución federal (pág. 404)

line-item veto the power of an executive to reject one or more items in a bill without vetoing the entire bill (pp. 193, 355)

veto de partidas específicas poder de la persona al mando del poder ejecutivo de rechazar uno o más artículos en un proyecto de ley sin vetar todo el proyecto de ley (pág. 193, 355)

literacy test a test based on a person's ability to read or write (p. 542)

prueba de alfabetismo prueba basada en la capacidad de una persona de leer o escribir (pág. 542)

"living" constitution a concept that claims that the Constitution is dynamic and that modern society should be considered when interpreting key constitutional text (p. 431)

constitución viviente concepto que afirma que la Constitución es dinámica y que debería considerarse la sociedad moderna al interpretar algún texto constitucional clave (pág. 431)

lobby to make direct contact by lobbyists to persuade government officials to support the policies their interest group favors (p. 592)

cabildear hacer contacto directo por cabilderos con el fin de persuadir a los funcionarios gubermentales para apoyar las políticas favorecdio por su groupo de interés (pág. 592)

lobbying direct contact made by lobbyists to persuade government officials to support the policies their interest group favors (p. 219)

cabildeo contacto directo realizado por cabilderos para convencer a funcionarios del gobierno de que apoyen las políticas que su grupo de interés favorece (pág. 219)

lobbyist a paid representative of an interest group who contacts government officials on behalf of these interest groups (pp. 219, 592)

cabildero representante pagado de un grupo de interés, que se pone en contacto con funcionarios del gobierno en nombre de esos grupos de interés (pág. 219, 592)

*logic the science of the formal principles of reasoning (p. 95)

*lógica ciencia de los principios formales del razonamiento (pág. 95)

logrolling an agreement by two or more lawmakers to support each other's bills (p. 225)

sistema de concesiones mutuas acuerdo entre dos o más legisladores para apoyar mutuamente sus proyectos de ley (pág. 225)

*maintain to continue, uphold, sustain, or defend (p. 709)

*mantener continuar, sostener, sustentar o defender (pág. 709)

*maintenance the upkeep of property or equipment (p. 242)

*mantenimiento cuidado de propiedad o equipamiento (pág. 242)

*major prominent or significant in size, amount, or degree (p. 174)

*muy importante prominente o considerable en tamaño, cantidad o grado (pág. 174)

majority leader the Speaker's top assistant whose job is to help plan the majority party's legislative program and to steer important bills through the House (p. 145)

líder de la mayoría principal asistente del presidente de la Cámara de Representantes, cuyo trabajo consiste en ayudar a planificar el programa legislativo del partido mayoritario y encaminar proyectos de ley importantes a través de la Cámara de Representantes (pág. 145)

majority opinion states the decision of the court (pp. 399, 420)

opinión mayoritaria expresa la decisión del tribunal (pág. 399, 420)

Glossary/Glosario

mandate a formal order given by a higher authority; an authorization to act given to a representative (pp. 111, 263)

***margin** the limit or bare minimum (pp. 303, 562)

marginal tax rate the percentage of income taxes an individual pays increases as his or her income increases; the rate of taxation applies to incomes within defined ranges or brackets (p. 647)

market value the amount of money a property owner could expect to receive if the property were sold (p. 660)

mass media all the means for communicating information to the general public, such as newspapers, magazines, radio, television, and the Internet (pp. 573, 606)

mass transit a public transportation network, consisting of buses, trains, subways, or other forms of public transportation (pp. 249, 375)

mayor-council form a system in which executive power belongs to an elected mayor and legislative power belongs to an elected council; in this system, mayors may have extensive executive powers or few executive powers (p. 358)

***media** sources of information, such as radio, television, newspapers, magazines, and the Internet, that reach or influence people widely (p. 305)

media event a visually interesting event designed to reinforce a politician's position on some issue (p. 609)

Medicare a government program that pays the medical bills of over 30 million senior citizens (p. 688)

midterm election a Congressional election that takes place halfway through the president's term in office (p. 546)

***migrate** to move from one geographic area to another (p. 755)

***military** referring to the armed forces (p. 721)

military tribunal a military court designed to try members of enemy forces during wartime, operating outside the scope of conventional criminal and civil proceedings (p. 274)

militia a local group of armed citizens (pp. 84, 473)

***minimum** the least number possible (p. 544)

mandato orden formal dada por una autoridad superior; autorización para actuar dada a un representante (pág. 111, 263)

***margen** límite o lo indispensable (pág. 303, 562)

tasa impositiva marginal porcentaje de impuestos a la renta que paga una persona aumenta al aumentar sus ingresos; la tasa de tributación se aplica a ingresos dentro de rangos o niveles definidos (pág. 647)

valor de mercado cantidad de dinero que el dueño de una propiedad podría esperar recibir si la propiedad se vendiera (pág. 660)

medios masivos de comunicación todos los medios para comunicar información al público en general, como periódicos, revistas, radio, televisión e Internet (pág. 573, 606)

transporte público red para transportar grandes cantidades de personas, consistente en autobuses, trenes, metros u otras formas de transportar a grandes cantidades de personas (pág. 249, 375)

forma de gobierno alcalde-concejo sistema en el cual el poder ejecutivo está en manos de un alcalde electo y el poder legislativo está en manos de un concejo electo; en este sistema, los alcaldes pueden tener amplios poderes ejecutivos o pocos poderes ejecutivos (pág. 358)

***medios de comunicación** fuentes de información, como radio, televisión, periódicos, revistas e Internet, que llegan o influyen mucho en la gente (pág. 305)

acontecimiento periodístico evento visualmente interesante creado para reforzar la posición de un político en algún asunto (pág. 609)

Medicare programa gubernamental que paga los gastos médicos de más de 30 millones de ancianos (pág. 688)

elecciones a mitad del mandato elecciones para el Congreso que tienen lugar a la mitad del período del presidente en funciones (pág. 546)

***emigrar** mudarse de un área geográfica a otra (pág. 755)

***militar** referido a las fuerzas armadas (pág. 721)

tribunal militar corte militar creada para juzgar a miembros de las fuerzas enemigas durante períodos de guerra, que operan fuera del ámbito de los procesos convencionales penales y civiles (pág. 274)

milicia grupo local de ciudadanos armados (pág. 84, 473)

***mínimo** el menor número posible (pág. 544)

Miranda rights the right for a defendant being taken into police custody to remain silent to avoid self-incrimination and the right to an attorney; the police must inform a defendant of these rights before questioning or anything learned from the interrogation cannot be used against the defendant at trial (p. 490)

derechos Miranda derecho de un acusado que está siendo puesto bajo arresto policial a permanecer en silencio para evitar autoincriminarse y el derecho a tener un abogado; la policía debe informar al acusado de estos derechos antes de interrogarlo o cualquier cosa que se sepa durante el interrogatorio no podrá usarse contra el acusado en un juicio (pág. 490)

*misconduct deliberate violation of a law or standard especially by a government official (p. 365)

*mala conducta violación deliberada de una ley o una norma, especialmente por parte de un funcionario gubernamental (pág. 365)

mixed economy economic system that combines elements of capitalism and socialism; in a mixed economy, the government regulates private enterprise (pp. 25, 671, 752)

economía mixta sistema económico que combina elementos del capitalismo y el socialismo; en una economía mixta, el gobierno regula la empresa privada (pág. 25, 671, 752)

moderate the belief in both liberal and conservative viewpoints (p. 521)

moderado creencia en los puntos de vista liberal y conservador a la vez (pág. 521)

*modify to alter, change, or revise (p. 357)

*modificar alterar, cambiar o corregir (pág. 357)

monarchy a system of government in which a king, queen, or emperor exercises supreme powers of government (p. 16)

monarquía sistema de gobierno en el cual un rey, una reina o un emperador ejerce los poderes supremos del gobierno (pág. 16)

monetary policy a government's control of the supply of money and credit to influence the economy (p. 652)

política monetaria control por parte de un gobierno del suministro de dinero y crédito para influenciar en la economía (pág. 652)

*monitor to watch, keep track of, or check (p. 476)

*monitorizar vigilar, dar seguimiento, verificar (pág. 476)

monopoly a business that controls so much of an industry that little or no competition exists (p. 672)

monopolio empresa que controla tanto de una industria que existe poca o ninguna competencia (pág. 672)

multilateral agreement a trade agreement among several parties (p. 716)

acuerdo multilateral acuerdo comercial entre varias partes (pág. 716)

municipality an urban unit of government chartered by a state (pp. 241, 359)

municipio unidad urbana de gobierno dependiente de un estado (pág. 241, 359)

nation a group of people united by bonds of race, language, custom, tradition, and sometimes religion (p. 9)

nación grupo de personas unidas por lazos de raza, idioma, costumbres, tradición y, a veces religión (pág. 9)

national budget the yearly financial plan for the federal government (p. 192)

presupuesto nacional plan financiero anual del gobierno federal (pág. 192)

national debt the total amount of money the government has borrowed but not paid back (p. 639)

deuda pública cantidad total de dinero que el gobierno ha pedido prestado pero no ha devuelto (pág. 639)

National Guard a rapid-response military body responsible for maintaining order during state emergencies and civil disturbances and providing emergency relief during natural disasters (p. 356)

Guardia Nacional cuerpo militar de respuesta rápida responsable de mantener el orden durante crisis estatales y disturbios sociales, y de proporcionar ayuda de emergencia durante desastres naturales (pág 356)

national security protection of a nation—its lands and people—from foreign threats, whether from governments, organized groups, or individual terrorists (pp. 274, 708)

seguridad nacional protección de una nación—su tierra y su gente—contra amenazas del extranjero, ya sean gobiernos, grupos organizados o terroristas individuales (pág. 274, 708)

Glossary/Glosario

National Security Advisor the director of the National Security Council (NSC) (p. 321)

nationalist position a position that favors national action in dealing with problems (p. 120)

naturalization the legal process by which a person is granted citizenship (p. 696)

necessary and proper clause Article I, Section 8, of the Constitution, which gives Congress the power to make all laws that are necessary and proper for carrying out its duties (p. 173)

*neutral not favoring either side in a debate, contest, or war; not aligned with a political or ideological group (p. 335)

news briefing a media communication during which a government official makes an announcement or explains a policy, a decision, or an action (p. 609)

news release a ready-made story prepared by officials for members of the press; also called a press release (p. 609)

nongovernmental organization (NGO) type of international organization made up of individuals and groups that are not part of any government (p. 746)

*nuclear being a weapon whose destructive power comes from a nuclear reaction (p. 715)

obscenity anything that treats sex or nudity in an offensive or lewd manner, violates recognized standards of decency, and lacks serious literary, artistic, political, or scientific value (p. 444)

*obtain to get, acquire, or procure, as through an effort or by a request (p. 365)

*obvious easily discovered, seen, or understood (p. 393)

*occupation a job; a vocation (p. 548)

*occur to happen (p. 134)

oligarchy a system of government in which a small group holds power (p. 16)

oligopoly situation in which only a few firms dominate a particular industry (p. 673)

Asesor de Seguridad Nacional director del Consejo de Seguridad Nacional (NSC) (pág. 321)

posición nacionalista posición que favorece la acción nacional para ocuparse de los problemas (pág. 120)

naturalización proceso legal por el cual a una persona se le otorga ciudadanía (pág. 696)

cláusula necesaria y justa Artículo I, Sección 8 de la Constitución, que le da al Congreso el poder de crear todas las leyes que sean necesarias y justas para llevar a cabo sus obligaciones (pág. 173)

*neutral que no favorece a ninguno de los lados en un debate, una elección o una guerra; no alineado con un grupo ideológico o político (pág. 335)

reunión informativa comunicado a los medios de información durante el cual un funcionario del gobierno hace un anuncio o explica una política, una decisión o una acción (pág. 609)

comunicado de prensa artículo preparado por funcionarios para miembros de la prensa; también llamado nota de prensa (pág. 609)

organización no gubernamental (ONG) tipo de organización internacional compuesta por personas y grupos que no forman parte de ningún gobierno (pág. 746)

*nuclear armas cuyo poder destructivo proviene de una reacción nuclear (pág. 715)

obscenidad todo lo que trata al sexo o la desnudez de modo ofensivo o lascivo, viola estándares reconocidos de decencia y carece de valores literarios, artísticos, políticos o científicos serios (pág. 444)

*obtener conseguir, adquirir o procurar, por medio de un esfuerzo o a pedido (pág. 365)

*obvio fácil de descubrir, ver o entender (pág. 393)

*ocupación empleo; profesión (pág. 548)

*ocurrir suceder (pág. 134)

oligarquía sistema de gobierno en el cual un grupo pequeño tiene el poder (pág. 16)

oligopolio situación en la cual solo unas pocas empresas dominan una industria en particular (pág. 673)

Glossary/Glosario

one-party system a system in which only one political party exists, often because the government tolerates no other opposition; usually in authoritarian governments (p. 513)

sistema de partido único sistema en el cual solo existe un partido político, a menudo porque el gobierno no tolera la oposición; usualmente existe en gobiernos autoritarios (pág. 513)

open primary an election in which all voters may participate (p. 530)

elecciones primarias abiertas elecciones en las cuales todos los votantes pueden participar (pág. 530)

open rule rule that permits floor debate and the addition of amendments to the bill (p. 209)

norma abierta norma que permite debates en las sesiones del Congreso y agregar enmiendas a un proyecto de ley (pág. 209)

open-market operations the means the Federal Reserve System uses to affect the economy by buying or selling government securities on the open market (p. 654)

operaciones de mercado abierto medios que usa el Sistema de la Reserva Federal para influir en la economía al comprar o vender títulos del gobierno en el mercado abierto (pág. 654)

ordinance a law at the local level (p. 241)

ordenanza ley al nivel local (pág. 241)

original jurisdiction the authority of a trial court to be the first to hear a case (p. 391)

jurisdicción original autoridad de un tribunal para ser el primero en ver un caso (pág. 391)

originalism a judicial philosophy that interprets the Constitution by exploring understanding of the text that people had when they adopted the Constitution (p. 431)

originalismo filosofía judicial que interpreta la Constitución, explorando el entendimiento del texto que tenían las personas en la época en que adoptaron la Constitución (pág. 431)

*outcome a final product or end result (p. 450)

*resultado producto o consecuencia final (pág. 450)

*parallel to correspond to (p. 145)

*paralelo correspondiente (pág. 145)

pardon a presidential order that releases a person from legal punishment (p. 270)

indulto decreto ley que libera a una persona de la sanción legal (pág. 270)

parliamentary government form of democratic government in which the elected assembly (often called a parliament) holds both executive and legislative powers (p. 738)

sistema parlamentario forma de gobierno democrático en la cual la asamblea electa (a menudo llamada parlamento) tiene los poderes ejecutivo y legislativo (pág. 738)

party identification loyalty to a political party (p. 524)

identificación partidista lealtad a un partido político (pág. 524)

passport document issued by the State Department, with which an American citizen can expect to be granted entry into many countries; American travelers carrying passports are entitled to privileges and protections established by an international treaty (p. 729)

pasaporte documento emitido por el Departamento de Estado con el cual un ciudadano estadounidense puede entrar a muchos países; los viajeros estadounidenses que llevan pasaporte tienen derecho a privilegios y protecciones establecidos por un tratado internacional (pág. 729)

patent the exclusive right of an inventor to manufacture, use, and sell his or her invention for a specific period, currently 20 years (pp. 179, 752)

patente derecho exclusivo de un inventor a fabricar, usar y vender su invento por un período específico, actualmente de 20 años, después del cual una patente puede renovarse (pág. 179, 752)

patronage the practice of granting favors to reward party loyalty (p. 512)

favoritismo práctica de otorgar favores para recompensar la lealtad al partido (pág. 512)

peer group an individual's close friends, religious group, clubs, and work groups (p. 573)

grupo de pares amigos cercanos, grupo religioso, clubes y grupos de trabajo de una persona (pág. 573)

*period a series of events, as in time (p. 192)

*período serie de sucesos, como en el tiempo (pág. 192)

perjury lying under oath (p. 185)

perjurio mentir estando bajo juramento (pág. 185)

personal property movable belongings such as furniture and jewelry, as well as intangible items such as stocks and bonds (p. 660)

bienes muebles pertenencias movibles, como el mobiliario y las joyas, así como objetos intangibles, como acciones y bonos (pág. 660)

Glossary/Glosario

personal staff the people who work directly for individual senators and representatives (p. 162)

petition to request an appeal (pp. 451, 529)

*philosopher one who engages in the pursuit of wisdom (p. 11)

picket to demonstrate, as against a government's policies or actions (p. 468)

plaintiff in a civil trial, the person who brings suit in court (p. 392)

platform a statement of a political party's principles, beliefs, and positions on vital issues (p. 521)

plea bargain an agreement whereby a defendant pleads guilty to a lesser crime than the one with which a defendant was originally charged and in return the government agrees not to prosecute the defendant for the more serious crime (pp. 394, 493)

plurality the largest number of votes in an election (pp. 364, 530)

pocket veto when a president kills a bill passed during the last 10 days Congress is in session by simply refusing to act on it (p. 207)

polarize to break up into opposing groups (p. 524)

*policy a plan that includes general goals and procedures (p. 119)

Political Action Committee (PAC) an organization formed to collect money and provide financial support for political candidates (pp. 303, 558)

political culture a set of basic values and beliefs about a nation and its government that most citizens share (p. 574)

political efficacy a person's belief that he or she can have an impact on government and policy (p. 575)

political party a group of individuals with broad common interests who organize to nominate candidates for office, win elections, conduct government, and determine public policy (p. 510)

political patronage appointment to political office, usually as a reward for helping get a president elected (p. 282)

political socialization a process by which individuals learn their political beliefs and attitudes from family, school, friends, coworkers, and other sources (p. 573)

poll tax money paid in order to vote (p. 542)

colaboradores personales personas que trabajan directamente para senadores y representantes individuales (pág. 162)

petición solicitar una apelación (pág. 451, 529)

*filósofo persona que se ocupa de buscar la sabiduría (pág. 11)

hacer un piquete manifestarse, como contra acciones o políticas del gobierno (pág. 468)

demandante en un juicio civil, persona que entabla un pleito en un tribunal (pág. 392)

plataforma declaración de los principios, las creencias y las posiciones en asuntos vitales de un partido político (pág. 521)

declaración negociada acuerdo por el cual un acusado se declara culpable de un delito menor al de la acusación original, y a cambio el gobierno acepta no enjuiciar al acusado por el delito más grave (pág. 394, 493)

pluralidad mayor cantidad de votos en una elección (pág. 364, 530)

veto indirecto cuando el presidente echa abajo un proyecto de ley durante los últimos 10 días de sesión del Congreso, simplemente negándose a actuar de acuerdo al mismo (pág. 207)

polarizar dividir en grupos opuestos (pág. 524)

*política plan que incluye procedimientos y metas generales (pág. 119)

comité de acción política (PAC) organización creada para recaudar dinero y proporcionar apoyo financiero a candidatos políticos (pág. 303, 558)

cultura política conjunto de creencias y valores básicos acerca de una nación y su gobierno que comparte la mayoría de los ciudadanos (pág. 574)

eficacia política creencia de una persona en que puede tener un impacto en el gobierno y las políticas (pág. 575)

partido político grupo de personas con intereses comunes generales que se organizan para nominar candidatos a cargos públicos, ganar elecciones, dirigir el gobierno y determinar políticas públicas (pág. 510)

favoritismo político nombramiento a un puesto político, usualmente como recompensa por ayudar a que el presidente fuese electo (pág. 282)

socialización política proceso por el cual las personas aprenden sus actitudes y creencias políticas de la familia, la escuela, los amigos, los compañeros de trabajo y otras fuentes (pág. 573)

impuesto al sufragio dinero pagado para poder votar (pág. 542)

polling place the location in a precinct where people vote (p. 563)	**lugar de votación** lugar en un distrito electoral donde vota la gente (pág. 563)
popular referendum a special election in which voters can vote to approve or repeal the laws passed by legislatures (p. 547)	**referéndum** elección especial en la cual los votantes pueden votar para ratificar o derogar las leyes aprobadas por el poder legislativo (pág. 547)
***populous** comprised of a large number of inhabitants (p. 55)	***populoso** compuesto por una gran cantidad de habitantes (pág. 55)
pork-barrel legislation laws that are passed by Congress to appropriate money for local federal projects (p. 224)	**legislación por barril de tocino** leyes que se aprueban en el Congreso para asignar dinero a proyectos federales locales (pág. 224)
precedent a legal principle created by an appellate court decision that lower court judges must follow when deciding similar cases (p. 400)	**precedente** principio legal creado por una decisión de un tribunal de apelaciones que los jueces de tribunales inferiores deben seguir al decidir acerca de casos similares (pág. 400)
precinct a voting district (p. 563)	**distrito electoral** zona electoral (pág. 563)
***predict** to tell in advance of an event (p. 548)	***predecir** saber por adelantado sobre un suceso (pág. 548)
preemption the federal government's ability to take over a state government function (p. 111)	**prioridad** capacidad del gobierno federal de hacerse cargo de las funciones de un gobierno estatal (pág. 111)
***preliminary** something that precedes or is introductory or preparatory (p. 420)	***preliminar** algo que precede o es introductorio o preparatorio (pág. 420)
president pro tempore the Senate member, elected by the Senate, who stands in as president of the Senate in the absence of the vice president (p. 150)	**presidente pro témpore** miembro del Senado, elegido por el Senado, que sustituye al vicepresidente en la presidencia del Senado cuando el mismo está ausente (pág. 150)
presidential government form of democratic government in which executive, legislative, and judicial powers are separated (p. 740)	**sistema presidencial** forma democrática de gobierno en la cual los poderes ejecutivo, legislativo y judicial están separados (pág. 740)
presidential succession the order in which officials fill the office of president in case of a vacancy (p. 301)	**sucesión presidencial** orden en el cual funcionarios ocupan el cargo de presidente en caso de estar vacante (pág. 301)
press conference the news media's questioning of a high-level government official (p. 609)	**conferencia de prensa** serie de preguntas de los medios de comunicación a un funcionario del gobierno de alto nivel (pág. 609)
press secretary one of the president's top assistants who is in charge of media relations (p. 323)	**secretario de prensa** uno de los principales asistentes del presidente, quien está a cargo de las relaciones con los medios de comunicación (pág. 323)
***presume** to take for granted, assume, or suppose; to believe, assume, or imagine to be true (pp. 449, 743)	***presunto** dado por hecho, asumido o supuesto; presumir creer, suponer, o imaginar ser verdad (pág. 449, 743)
presumption of innocence the principle that one is considered innocent until proven guilty; the government has the burden of proof in a criminal trial (p. 492)	**presunción de inocencia** principio que establece que alguien se considera inocente hasta que se pruebe la culpabilidad; el gobierno tiene la carga de la prueba en un juicio penal (pág. 492)
price supports the program under which Congress buys farmers' crops if the market price falls below the support price (p. 678)	**ayuda en materia de precios** programa por el cual el Congreso compra las cosechas de los granjeros si el precio de mercado cae por debajo del precio mínimo garantizado (pág. 678)

Glossary/Glosario

primary an event held before an election where members of the party go to the polls and vote on which candidate they want to see earn their party's nomination; *first in order of time or development (pp. 304, 414)

prime minister leader of the majority party in the parliament; the head of government in the parliamentary system (p. 739)

***principle** an underlying doctrine or assumption (p. 357)

prior restraint censorship of information before it is published (pp. 449, 616)

private bill a bill dealing with individual people or places (p. 200)

probable cause a reasonable basis to believe a person or premises are linked to a crime (pp. 85, 486)

procedural due process the fair administration of justice (p. 398)

***professional** relating to job experience that requires special education, training, or skill (p. 424)

profit money earned or taken in by a business that is in excess of the funds invested in operating the business (p. 752)

progressive tax tax whereby people with higher incomes pay a larger share of their income in taxes than people with lower incomes (p. 647)

***prohibit** to forbid (p. 249)

proletariat workers who produce the goods (p. 27)

propaganda the use of ideas, information, or rumors to influence opinion (p. 553)

proportional representation a system in which several officials are elected to represent the same area in proportion to the votes each party's candidate receives (p. 518)

prosecute to conduct criminal proceedings in court against (p. 486)

prosecutor an attorney who represents the government in a criminal case (p. 392)

protective tariff a high customs duty (p. 646)

public bill a bill dealing with general matters and applying to the entire nation (p. 200)

public defender attorney who works for the state and defends people who cannot afford a private attorney (p. 393)

elecciones primarias evento que se realiza antes de las elecciones, en las cuales miembros del partido concurren a votar por el candidato que quieren que obtenga la nominación de su partido; primero en orden cronológico o de desarrollo (pág. 304, 414)

primer ministro líder del partido mayoritario en el parlamento; jefe de gobierno en el sistema parlamentario (pág. 739)

***principio** supuesto o doctrina subyacente (pág. 357)

censura previa censura de información antes de su publicación (pág. 449, 616)

proyecto de ley singular proyecto de ley que trata sobre lugares o personas en particular (pág. 200)

causa probable fundamento razonable para creer que una persona o un establecimiento están relacionados con un delito (pág. 85, 486)

garantías procesales administración imparcial de la justicia (pág. 398)

***profesional** persona que es experta en su trabajo; respecto a experiencia de trabajo que requiere educación, entrenamiento, o habilidad especial (pág. 424)

utilidades dinero ganado o cobrado por una empresa, que excede los fondos invertidos para la operación del negocio (pág. 752)

impuesto progresivo impuesto por el cual las personas con mayores ingresos pagan una porción mayor de sus ingresos a modo de impuestos que las personas con menores ingresos (pág. 647)

***prohibir** impedir (pág. 249)

proletariado trabajadores que producen los bienes (pág. 27)

propaganda uso de ideas, información o rumores para influir en la opinión (pág. 553)

representación proporcional sistema en el cual varios funcionarios son elegidos para representar la misma área en proporción a los votos que recibe el partido de cada candidato (pág. 518)

enjuiciar presentar acción penal en un tribunal contra una persona (pág. 486)

fiscal abogado que representa al gobierno en un caso penal (pág. 392)

arancel proteccionista arancel aduanero elevado (pág. 646)

proyecto de ley general proyecto de ley que trata sobre asuntos generales y se aplica a toda la nación (pág. 200)

defensor de oficio abogado que trabaja para el estado y defiende a personas que no pueden contratar a un abogado privado (pág. 393)

public housing government-subsidized housing for low-income families (p. 692)

public interest group a type of interest group whose members focus their work on influencing policies that they believe affect the general public, not just themselves (p. 589)

public opinion the ideas and attitudes that a significant number of Americans hold about government and political issues (p. 576)

public policy a plan of action adopted by government decision makers to solve a problem or reach a goal (pp. 119, 245, 338)

public utility an organization, either privately or publicly owned, that supplies such necessities as electricity, gas, telephone service, or transportation service (p. 372)

pure speech verbal expression before an audience that has chosen to listen (p. 442)

push polling method of polling in which the wording of questions "push" respondents toward a particular answer or view (p. 581)

quorum the minimum number of members who must be present to permit a legislative body to take official action (p. 147)

quota (economic) a limit on the quantities of a foreign product that can be imported (p. 757)

quota (immigration) a numerical limit on how many immigrants are allowed in from each country (p. 698)

racial quota a certain number of spots reserved for minorities (p. 471)

random sampling a technique in which everyone in a group has an equal chance of being selected (p. 580)

*range the extent of options (p. 514)

*ratify to approve (p. 50)

rational basis a standard of judicial review that examines whether a legislature had a reasonable and not an arbitrary reason for enacting a particular statute (p. 461)

*reaction a response to a situation or stimulus (p. 323)

real property land and buildings (p. 660)

reapportionment the process of reassigning representation based on population, after every census (p. 134)

reauthorize the act of passing legislation into law again (p. 274)

---

vivienda pública vivienda subvencionada por el gobierno para familias de bajos ingresos (pág. 692)

grupo de interés público un tipo de grupo de interés cuyos miembros concentran su trabajo en influenciar las políticas que creen que afectan al público en general, no solo a ellos mismos (pág. 589)

opinión pública ideas y actitudes que una cantidad importante de estadounidenses tienen acerca de asuntos políticos y del gobierno (pág. 576)

política pública plan de acción adoptado por quienes toman las decisiones en el gobierno para resolver un problema o alcanzar una meta (pág. 119, 245, 338)

empresa de servicios públicos organización pública o privada que suministra necesidades, como la electricidad, el gas, el servicio telefónico o el servicio de transporte (pág. 372)

discurso puro expresión verbal del pensamiento y la opinión ante una audiencia que ha elegido escuchar (pág. 442)

encuesta de empuje método de encuestar en el cual la redacción de las preguntas "empuja" a los encuestados hacia un punto de vista o una respuesta en particular (pág. 581)

quórum cantidad mínima de miembros que deben estar presentes para permitir que un cuerpo legislativo actúe oficialmente (pág. 147)

cuota (economía) límite de las cantidades de un producto extranjero que puede importarse (pág. 757)

cupo (inmigración) límite numérico de la cantidad de inmigrantes que se permite que vengan de cada país (pág. 698)

cuota racial cierta cantidad de lugares reservados para las minorías (pág. 471)

muestreo aleatorio técnica en la cual todos los miembros de un grupo tienen la misma probabilidad de ser elegidos (pág. 580)

*rango extensión de las opciones (pág. 514)

*ratificar aprobar (pág. 50)

fundamento razonable estándar de la revisión judicial que examina si un poder legislativo tuvo un motivo razonable y no arbitrario para promulgar un estatuto en particular (pág. 461)

*reacción respuesta a una situación o un estimulo (pág. 323)

bienes inmuebles tierra y edificios (pág. 660)

redistribución proceso de reasignar la representación basándose en la población después de cada censo (pág. 134)

reautorizar aprobar nuevamente una ley (pág. 274)

Glossary/Glosario

recall the procedure by which an elected official may be removed from office by popular vote (pp. 365, 563)

*recover to bring back to normal

recuse to remove oneself from participation to avoid a conflict of interest (p. 336)

red tape overly burdensome regulations and requirements (p. 345)

redistrict to set up new district lines after reapportionment is complete (p. 134)

refugee a person fleeing a country to escape persecution or danger (p. 700)

*regional involving or related to a specific geographic area (p. 758)

regional circuit the divisions under the United States Federal Courts system, grouped into 12 regional circuits, each of which has a federal court of appeals, also called a U.S. Circuit Court (p. 405)

regional security pact a mutual defense treaty among multiple nations within a world region (p. 718)

*register to enroll one's name with the appropriate local government in order to participate in elections (p. 561)

regressive tax tax whereby people with lower incomes pay a larger share of their income in taxes than people with higher incomes (p. 647)

*regulation rule or procedure that has the force of law (p. 22)

*reject to refuse to grant (p. 432)

*reluctant hesitant, unwilling, disinclined (p. 654)

renewable energy wind, solar, and geothermal sources of energy (p. 681)

repeal to revoke by legislative enactment (p. 82)

representative government a system of government in which people elect delegates to make laws and conduct government (p. 37)

representative sample a small group of people who are typical of the larger group being studied (p. 580)

reprieve a presidential order that postpones legal punishment (p. 270)

republic a government in which voters hold sovereign power; elected representatives, responsible to the people, exercise that power (p. 17)

referéndum de destitución procedimiento por el cual un funcionario electo puede ser apartado de su cargo por el voto popular (pág. 365, 563)

*recuperar volver a la normalidad

excusarse dejar uno de participar para evitar un conflicto de intereses (pág. 336)

trámites burocráticos requisitos y normas muy complicados (pág. 345)

reordenar establecer nuevos límites en los distritos después de que la redistribución se ha completado (pág. 134)

refugiado persona que huye de un país para escapar de la persecución o el peligro (pág. 700)

*regional perteneciente o relativo a un área geográfica específica (pág. 758)

circuito regional divisiones en el sistema de Tribunales Federales de Estados Unidos, agrupados en 12 circuitos regionales, cada uno de los cuales tiene un tribunal federal de apelaciones, también llamado Tribunal de Circuito de Estados Unidos (pág 405)

pacto de seguridad regional tratado de defensa mutua entre varios países dentro de una región del mundo (pág. 718)

*registrarse inscribirse en el gobierno local apropiado con el fin de participar en las elecciones (pág. 561)

impuesto regresivo impuesto por el cual las personas con menores ingresos pagan una porción mayor de sus ingresos a modo de impuesto que las personas con mayores ingresos (pág. 647)

*norma regla o procedimiento que tiene fuerza de ley (pág. 22)

*denegar rehusarse a otorgar (pág. 432)

*reacio renuente, reticente, poco dispuesto (pág. 654)

energía renovable fuentes de energía eólica, solar y geotérmica (pág. 681)

derogar dejar sin efecto por medio de una disposición legislativa (pág. 82)

gobierno representativo sistema de gobierno en el cual las personas eligen delegados para crear leyes y llevar el gobierno (pág. 37)

muestra representativa grupo pequeño de personas que son típicas del grupo más grande que se está estudiando (pág. 580)

aplazamiento decreto ley que pospone el castigo legal (pág. 270)

república gobierno en el cual los votantes tienen el poder soberano; representantes electos, responsables ante el pueblo, ejercen ese poder (pág. 17)

Republican Party the party more associated with conservative and moderate-conservatives (p. 521)	**Partido Republicano** partido más asociado con conservadores y conservadores moderados (pág. 521)
***require** to claim or ask for by right and authority (p. 445)	***exigir** reclamar o pedir por derecho y autoridad (pág. 445)
reservation a tract of public land set aside for use by Native Americans, on which most of these groups have their own tribal justice systems (p. 407)	**reserva** extensión de tierra pública destinada al uso por parte de indígenas americanos, donde la mayoría de estos grupos tienen sus propios sistemas de justicia tribal (pág. 407)
reserve requirement the percentage of money member banks must keep in their vaults or on deposit with the Federal Reserve Banks as a reserve against their deposits (p. 654)	**encaje legal** porcentaje de dinero que bancos miembros deben mantener en sus cajas fuertes o depositado en los bancos de la Reserva Federal como reserva por los depósitos recibidos (pág. 654)
reserved powers powers that belong strictly to the states (p. 104)	**poderes reservados** poderes que pertenecen estrictamente a los estados (pág. 104)
***residency** determined as where one lives and is legally eligible to vote (p. 116)	***residencia** determinada por el lugar donde una persona vive y tiene legalmente derecho a votar (pág. 116)
***resource** a source of supply or support; available goods or means (p. 353)	***recurso** fuente de suministros o apoyo; medios o bienes disponibles (pág. 353)
***restore** to return to original condition, rebuild (p. 676)	***restaurar** devolver la condición original, reconstruir (pág. 676)
restraint an act that limits a state's ability to regulate an area (p. 111)	**restricción** acción que limita la capacidad de un estado de regular un área (pág. 111)
***restrict** to limit (p. 249)	***restringir** limitar (pág. 249)
***restrictive** of or relating to a limitation on the use or enjoyment of property or a facility	***restrictivo** perteneciente o relativo a una limitación en el uso o disfrute de propiedad o una instalación
***retain** to continue to hold or have; to keep in one's pay or service (p. 485)	***retener** seguir manteniendo o teniendo; mantener al servicio o a sueldo (pág. 485)
***retention** the act of continuing to hold or have, as in a political position (p. 404)	***retención** acción de seguir manteniendo o teniendo, como un cargo político (pág. 404)
revenue the money a government collects from taxes or other sources (pp. 43, 639)	**rentas públicas** dinero que el gobierno recauda de impuestos u otras fuentes (pág. 43, 639)
revenue bill a proposed law for raising money (p. 175)	**proyecto de ley fiscal** ley propuesta para recaudar dinero (pág. 175)
***revise** to correct or improve; to alter something already written or printed, in order to make corrections, improve, or update (pp. 191, 421)	***corregir** modificar o mejorar; cambiar algo ya escrito o impreso, para que haga correciones, mejore, o actualize (pág. 191, 421)
rider a provision included in a bill on a subject other than the one covered in the bill (p. 201)	**cláusula añadida** estipulación incluida en un proyecto de ley sobre un asunto diferente al que trata el proyecto de ley (pág. 201)
right-to-work law state labor law that requires that all workplaces be open shops where workers may freely decide whether or not to join a union (p. 676)	**ley de derecho al trabajo** ley laboral estatal que exige que todos los lugares de trabajo sean sin sindicalización obligatoria, donde los trabajadores puedan decidir libremente si unirse o no a un sindicato (pág. 676)
rule of four an unwritten rule declaring that if four of the nine justices agree to hear a case, it will be scheduled for argument (p. 418)	**regla de los cuatro** regla no escrita que dice que si cuatro de los nueve jueces de la Corte Suprema están de acuerdo en ver un caso, este se agendará para ser debatido (pág. 418)

Glossary/Glosario

sampling error a measurement of how much the sample results might differ from the sample universe (p. 580)

sanction an action such as withholding loans, arms, or economic aid to force a foreign government to stop certain activities (p. 718)

*schedule to plan to occur at a specific time (p. 184)

*scheme a plan of action, especially a crafty or secret one (p. 184)

search warrant an order signed by a judge describing a specific place to be searched for specific items (p. 486)

secular nonreligious; not associated with any faith-based organization (p. 455)

security a financial instrument, including a bond, note, and certificate, that is sold as a means of borrowing money with a promise to repay the buyer with interest after a specific time period; *safety (pp. 650, 674, 727)

seditious speech speech urging the resistance to lawful authority or advocating the overthrow of the government (p. 444)

select committee a temporary committee formed to study one specific issue and report its findings to the House or Senate (p. 157)

selective incorporation the process by which the Supreme Court decided on a case-by-case basis which federal rights also applied to the states (p. 464)

self-incrimination testifying against oneself (p. 490)

seniority system a system that gives the member of the majority party with the longest uninterrupted service on a particular committee the leadership of that committee (p. 159)

sentence the punishment to be imposed on an offender after a guilty verdict (p. 498)

sequester to hold in isolation (p. 450)

session meeting (p. 133)

severance tax a tax imposed by state for the extraction of nonrenewable natural resources (p. 657)

shield law a state law that protects reporters from having to reveal their sources (p. 617)

*significant having or likely to have influence or effect (p. 454)

error muestral medida de cuánto difieren los resultados de la muestra del universo de la muestra (pág. 580)

sanción acción como retener préstamos, armas, o ayuda económica para forzar a un gobierno extranjero a dejar de hacer ciertas actividades (pág. 718)

*agendar planificar para que ocurra en un momento específico (pág. 184)

*trama plan de acción, especialmente uno ingenioso o secreto (pág. 184)

orden de registro orden firmada por un juez donde describe un lugar específico para ser registrado en busca de artículos específicos (pág. 486)

laico no religioso; no asociado con ninguna organización de carácter religioso (pág. 455)

título instrumento financiero, incluyendo bono, pagaré y certificado, que se vende con el fin de tomar dinero prestado con la promesa de reembolsar al comprador con intereses después de un período específico; *que es seguro (pág. 650, 674, 727)

discurso sedicioso discurso que insta a resistirse a la autoridad legal o aboga por el derrocamiento del gobierno (pág. 444)

comité de estudio comité temporal creado para estudiar un asunto en particular e informar sobre sus conclusiones a la Cámara de Representantes o el Senado (pág. 157)

incorporación selectiva proceso por el cual la Corte Suprema decidió, según cada caso, qué derechos federales también se aplicaban a los estados (pág. 464)

autoincriminación declaración en contra de uno mismo (pág. 490)

sistema de antigüedad sistema que otorga al miembro del partido mayoritario con el mayor servicio ininterrumpido en un comité en particular el liderazgo de ese comité (pág. 159)

sentencia sanción que se impone a un delincuente después de recibir un veredicto de culpabilidad (pág. 498)

secuestrar mantener en aislamiento (pág. 450)

sesione reunione (pág 133)

impuesto sobre el uso de recursos naturales impuesto aplicado por el estado para la extracción de recursos naturales no renovables (pág. 657)

ley de protección de fuentes ley estatal que protege a los periodistas de la obligación de revelar sus fuentes (pág. 617)

*significativo que tiene o es probable que tenga influencia o consecuencia (pág. 454)

simple resolution a statement adopted to cover matters affecting only one house of Congress (p. 201)

single-issue party a political party that focuses exclusively on one major social, economic, or moral issue (p. 516)

single-member district an electoral district in which only one candidate is elected to each office (p. 518)

sit-in organized demonstration tactic in which participants seat themselves in a significant location and refuse to move; a form of peaceful protest (p. 467)

slander false speech that damages a person's reputation (p. 444)

*so-called commonly named (p. 345)

social contract theory that by contract, people surrender to the state the power needed to maintain order and the state, in turn, agrees to protect its citizens (p. 11)

socialism an economic system in which the government owns the basic means of production, distributes the products and wages, and provides social services such as health care and welfare (pp. 26, 751)

soft money money raised by a political party for general purposes; money not designated for a candidate (p. 558)

*solely to the exclusion of all else (p. 493)

*source origin, point of procurement; one who supplies information; person a reporter consults to get information (pp. 225, 616)

sovereignty the supreme and absolute authority within territorial boundaries (p. 9)

special assessment a fee that a property owner must pay for services that benefit them (p. 661)

special district a unit of local government that deals with a specific function, such as education, water supply, or transportation (pp. 243, 358)

special session a specially called meeting of the legislature, typically to deal with pressing problems (p. 234)

*specific having distinct or particular characteristics (p. 148)

*sphere the place or environment within which a person or thing exists (p. 471)

splinter party a political party that splits away from a major party because of some disagreement (p. 517)

spoils system victorious politicians rewarding their supporters with government jobs (p. 333)

resolución simple declaración que se aprueba al tratar asuntos que afectan solo a una de las cámaras del Congreso (pág. 201)

partido con un solo propósito partido político que se concentra exclusivamente en un asunto social, económico o moral importante (pág. 516)

distrito uninominal distrito electoral en el cual solo un candidato se elige para cada puesto (pág. 518)

sentada táctica de manifestación organizada en la cual los participantes se sientan en un lugar significativo y se niegan a moverse; forma de protesta pacífica (pág. 467)

calumnia discurso falso que daña la reputación de una persona (pág. 444)

*llamada nombrado comúnmente (pág. 345)

contrato social teoría que dice que la gente cede por contrato al estado el poder necesario para mantener el orden, y el estado, como contrapartida, consiente en proteger a sus ciudadanos (pág. 11)

socialismo sistema económico en el cual el gobierno posee los medios básicos de producción, distribuye los productos y salarios, y proporciona servicios sociales como el cuidado de la salud y los beneficios sociales (pág. 26, 751)

dinero blando dinero recaudado por un partido político con fines generales; no es dinero asignado para un candidato (pág. 558)

*exclusivamente con exclusión de todo lo demás (pág. 493)

*fuente origen, punto de adquisición; persona que suministra información; persona que un periodista consulta para obtener información (pág. 225, 616)

soberanía autoridad suprema y absoluta dentro de los límites territoriales (pág. 9)

tasación especial tarifa que un propietario debe pagar por servicios que lo benefician (pág. 661)

distrito especial unidad del gobierno local que se encarga de una función específica, como la educación, el suministro de agua corriente o el transporte (pág. 243, 358)

sesión extraordinaria reunión del poder legislativo convocada especialmente, por regla general para tratar problemas urgentes (pág. 234)

*específico que tiene características determinadas o particulares (pág. 148)

*esfera lugar o ambiente dentro del cual una persona o una cosa existe (pág. 471)

partido disidente partido político que se escinde de un partido más grande debido a algún desacuerdo (pág. 517)

sistema de favoritismo práctica de políticos victoriosos que recompensan a sus partidarios con empleos en el gobierno (pág. 333)

Glossary/Glosario

spot advertising brief (30 seconds to 2 minutes), frequent, positive descriptions of the candidate or the candidate's major platform points, and/or negative depictions of the opposing candidate (p. 611)

anuncio publicitario descripciones breves (de 30 segundos a 2 minutos), frecuentes y positivas del candidato o de los principales puntos de la plataforma del candidato, y/o descripciones negativas del candidato de la oposición (pág. 611)

*stability remaining steady (p. 512)

*estabilidad permanencia estable (pág. 512)

stakeholder a private citizen or other who will be affected by potential rules and regulations (p. 339)

parte interesada ciudadanos particulares u otros que serán afectados por normas y reglamentos potenciales (pág. 339)

standing committee a permanent committee in Congress that oversees bills that deal with certain kinds of issues (p. 156)

comité permanente comité continuo en el Congreso que supervisa los proyectos de ley que tienen que ver con ciertos tipos de asuntos (pág. 156)

stare decisis a Latin term meaning "let the decision stand"; refers to the principle that courts should follow precedent (p. 400)

stare decisis término del latín que significa "atenerse a lo decidido"; se refiere al principio de que las cortes deben seguir un precedente (pág. 400)

state a political community that occupies a definite territory and has an organized government (p. 9)

estado comunidad política que ocupa un territorio determinado y tiene un gobierno organizado (pág. 9)

states' rights position a position that favors state and local action in dealing with problems (p. 120)

posición de derechos de los estados posición que favorece la acción estatal y local al tratar de resolver los problemas (pág. 120)

*status the condition of a person in the eyes of the law (p. 696)

*estatus situación de una persona a los ojos de la ley (pág. 696)

status offense any act that a juvenile can be lawfully detained for, but which is not a crime if committed by an adult (p. 496)

delito por causa de estatus cualquier acción por la cual un menor pueda ser detenido, pero la cual no es un crimen si la comete un adulto (pág. 496)

statute a federal law; a law written by a legislative branch (p. 403)

estatuto ley federal; ley escrita por una rama legislativa (pág. 403)

straight party ticket a ticket where a voter has selected candidates of his or her own party only (p. 549)

papeleta partidaria papeleta en la que un votante ha elegido candidatos de su propio partido solamente (pág. 549)

*strategy a plan or method for achieving a goal (pp. 212, 552)

*estrategia plan o método para alcanzar una meta (pág. 212, 552)

straw poll an unscientific attempt to measure public opinion (p. 579)

votación falsa intento no científico de medir la opinión pública (pág. 579)

strict scrutiny a standard of judicial review for a challenged policy in which the court presumes the policy to be invalid unless the government can demonstrate a compelling interest to justify the policy (p. 462)

examen estricto criterio estándar de revisión judicial para una política objetada en la cual el tribunal supone que la política es inválida a menos que el gobierno pueda demostrar un interés convincente para justificar la política (pág. 462)

strong-mayor system a mayoral system in which the mayor usually has the power to veto measures that the city council passes, appoint department heads, prepare the municipal budget, and propose legislation (p. 358)

sistema municipal de regalías sistema de alcaldía en el cual el alcalde, por lo general, tiene el poder para vetar medidas que aprueba el consejo municipal, designa jefes de departamento, prepara el presupuesto municipal y propone legislación (pág. 358)

subcommittee a group within a standing committee that specializes in a subcategory of its standing committee's responsibility (p. 156)

subcomité grupo dentro de un comité permanente que se especializa en una subcategoría de la responsabilidad de su comité permanente (pág. 156)

subpoena a legal order that a person appear or produce requested documents (p. 185)

citación orden legal para que una persona comparezca o presente documentos solicitados (pág. 185)

*subsequent following, coming after (p. 694)

*subsiguiente que viene a continuación, que viene después (pág. 694)

*subsidy a grant or gift of money (pp. 648, 671)

*subsidio subvención o donación de dinero (pág. 648, 671)

substantial relationship a standard of judicial review that examines whether there is a close connection between the law or practice and its purpose; specifically, laws that classify based on gender must serve an important governmental purpose (p. 462)

relación sustancial criterio estándar de revisión judicial que examina si hay una relación cercana entre la ley o el ejercicio y su finalidad; específicamente, leyes que se clasifican basándose en el sexo deben servir para una finalidad importante del gobierno (pág. 462)

substantive due process the principle requiring that a government action not unreasonably interfere with a fundamental or basic right (p. 460)

debido proceso fundamental principio que requiere que una acción del gobierno no interfiera injustificadamente con un derecho fundamental o básico (pág. 460)

suburb an outlying part of a city or town (p. 374)

suburbio parte periférica de una ciudad o un pueblo (pág. 374)

*succession the action or process of inheriting a title or office (p. 145)

*sucesión acción o proceso de heredar un título o un cargo (pág. 145)

*successor one that follows (p. 300)

*sucesor persona que sigue (pág. 300)

*sufficient enough to meet the needs of a situation or a proposed end; enough; satisfactory in amount (pp. 395, 585)

*suficiente bastante como para satisfacer las necesidades de una situación o un fin propuesto; satisfactorio en cantidad (pág. 395, 585)

suffrage the right to vote (p. 541)

sufragio derecho a votar (pág. 541)

sunset law a law that requires periodic checks of laws or of government agencies to see if they are still needed (p. 119)

ley con cláusula de caducidad ley que requiere controles periódicos de leyes u organismos del gobierno para ver si todavía es necesaria (pág. 119)

sunshine law a law prohibiting public officials from holding meetings not open to the public (p. 119)

ley de libertad de información ley que prohíbe a los funcionarios públicos tener reuniones no abiertas al público (pág. 119)

superPAC a political action committee that does not coordinate with election campaigns and thus is eligible to receive unlimited donations (p. 558)

comité de gastos independientes (superPAC) comité de acción política que no coordina con campañas electorales y que por lo tanto tiene derecho a recibir donaciones ilimitadas (pág. 558)

supremacy clause statement in Article VI of the Constitution establishing that the Constitution, laws passed by Congress, and treaties of the United States "shall be the supreme Law of the Land" (pp. 93, 106)

cláusula de supremacía declaración en el Artículo VI de la Constitución que establece que la Constitución, las leyes aprobadas por el Congreso y los tratados de Estados Unidos "serán las leyes supremas del país" (pág. 93, 106)

Supreme Court justice a member of the Supreme Court of the United States, the highest court in the nation (p. 423)

juez de la Corte Suprema miembro de la Corte Suprema de Estados Unidos, el tribunal más alto del país (pág. 423)

surveillance a watch kept over a person, group, etc., especially over a suspect or prisoner (p. 476)

vigilancia guardia que se mantiene sobre una persona, un grupo, etc., especialmente sobre un sospechoso o un prisionero (pág. 476)

*survey a poll; a collection of data (p. 293)

*encuesta sondeo; recopilación de datos (pág. 293)

*suspend to defer to a later time on specified conditions (p. 501)

*suspender diferir para más adelante con condiciones específicas (pág. 501)

*symbol something that stands for something else (p. 521)

*símbolo algo que representa otra cosa (pág. 521)

Glossary/Glosario

symbolic speech the use of actions and symbols, in addition to or instead of words, to express ideas (p. 442)

tariff a tax placed on an import to increase its price in the domestic market (pp. 51, 671, 757)

tax the money that people and businesses pay to support the activities of the government; payment made by individuals and businesses to support government activities (pp. 208, 645)

taxable income the total income of an individual minus certain deductions and personal exemptions (p. 647)

*technique method of accomplishing a desired aim (p. 592)

*technology digital tools used to record and share information (p. 627)

*temporary lasting a short amount of time (p. 157)

terrorism the use of violence against civilians to achieve political goals (p. 712)

*theory speculation based on study (p. 10)

third party any political party other than one of the two major parties (p. 516)

third-party candidate someone who represents a political party that is neither Democrat nor Republican (p. 306)

three-strikes laws laws that typically impose an automatic minimum sentence of 25 years or life imprisonment when a person is convicted of a serious offense for the third time (p. 499)

ticket a party's candidates for president and vice president (p. 531)

totalitarianism a system of government in which the government has total control (p. 15)

town meeting a meeting called by an elected official to get input from his or her constituents (p. 242)

township a unit of local government found in some states, usually a subdivision of a county (p. 241)

*trace to discover by going backward over the evidence (p. 136)

trading bloc agreement and organization created by a group of nations that want to limit trade barriers with one another (p. 757)

treason the offense of acting to overthrow one's government or to harm or kill its leader (p. 500)

discurso simbólico uso de acciones y símbolos, o incluso de palabras, para expresar ideas (pág. 442)

arancel impuesto recaudado sobre una importación con el fin de aumentar su precio en el mercado nacional (pág. 51, 671, 757)

impuesto dinero que las personas y las empresas pagan para financiar las actividades del gobierno; pago hecho por personas y empresas para apoyar las actividades gubernamentales (pág. 208, 645)

ingresos imponibles ingresos totales de una persona menos ciertas deducciones y exenciones personales (pág. 647)

*técnica método para alcanzar una meta deseada (pág. 592)

*tecnología herramientas digitales usadas para guardar y compartir información (pág. 627)

*temporal que dura poco tiempo (pág. 157)

terrorismo uso de violencia contra civiles para alcanzar metas políticas (pág. 712)

*teoría especulación basada en el estudio (pág. 10)

tercer partido cualquier partido político que no sea uno de los dos partidos principales (pág. 516)

candidato de un tercer partido alguien que representa a un partido político que no es el Demócrata ni el Republicano (pág. 306)

leyes de tres delitos leyes que usualmente imponen una sentencia mínima automática de 25 años o cadena perpetua cuando una persona es declarada culpable de un delito grave por tercera vez (pág. 499)

papeleta candidatos de un partido para presidente y vicepresidente (pág. 531)

totalitarismo sistema de gobierno en el cual el gobierno tiene control total (pág. 15)

reunión municipal reunión convocada por un funcionario electo para recibir aportes de sus electores (pág. 242)

municipio unidad de gobierno local que hay en algunos estados, usualmente una subdivisión de un condado (pág. 241)

*rastrear descubrir algo al revisar la evidencia (pág. 136)

bloque comercial acuerdo y organización creado por grupos de naciones que quieren limitar las barreras comerciales entre sí (pág. 757)

traición delito que se comete al obrar para derrocar el gobierno propio o para hacer daño o matar a su líder (pág. 500)

treaty a formal agreement between the governments of two or more countries (pp. 51, 275, 722)	**tratado** acuerdo formal entre los gobiernos de dos o más países (pág. 51, 275, 722)
tribal court a court that hears criminal and civil cases operating within the tribal justice system (p. 407)	**tribunal tribal** tribunal que ve casos civiles y penales operando dentro del sistema de justicia tribal (pág. 407)
trust a form of business consolidation in which several corporations combine their stock and allow a board of trustees to operate as a giant enterprise (p. 672)	**cartel** forma de consolidación empresarial por la cual varias corporaciones combinan sus acciones y permiten que una junta de fiduciarios lo dirijan como a una empresa gigante (pág. 672)
two-party system a system in which two major parties compete for power, although minor parties may exist (p. 514)	**sistema bipartidista** sistema en el cual dos partidos importantes compiten por el poder, aunque puedan existir partidos menores (pág. 514)
unanimous consent a motion by all members of the Senate who are present to set aside formal rules and consider a bill from the calendar (p. 151)	**consentimiento unánime** moción por parte de todos los miembros del Senado que están presentes para dejar de lado las normas formales y considerar un proyecto de ley del calendario (pág. 151)
unanimous ruling issued when the justices all agree on the outcome and the reasons for a decision in a case (p. 420)	**fallo unánime** se emite cuando los jueces están todos de acuerdo en el resultado y las razones para tomar una decisión en un caso (pág. 420)
unconstitutional not consistent with a nation's constitution (p. 388)	**inconstitucional** no consistente con la constitución de un país (pág. 388)
uncontrollable a government expenditure required by law or resulting from previous budgetary commitments (p. 643)	**no controlable** gasto del gobierno exigido por ley o resultado de previos compromisos presupuestales (pág. 643)
***undertake** to take on, accept, or begin a project or responsibility (p. 745)	***emprender** aceptar, iniciar o hacerse cargo de un proyecto o una responsabilidad (pág. 745)
***undertaking** a task or project (p. 691)	***emprendimiento** tarea o proyecto (p. 691)
unemployment compensation payments to people who lose their jobs (p. 372)	**subsidio por desempleo** pago que se hace a las personas que pierden el empleo (pág. 372)
unemployment insurance programs in which the federal and state governments cooperate to provide help for people who are out of work (p. 684)	**seguro de desempleo** programas en los cuales los gobiernos federal y estatal cooperan entre ellos para proporcionar ayuda a las personas que no tienen trabajo (pág. 684)
unfunded mandate program ordered but not paid for by federal legislation (p. 680)	**mandato sin financiación** programa ordenado pero no costeado por la ley federal (pág. 680)
unicameral relative to a single-chamber legislature (pp. 50, 233)	**unicameral** poder legislativo con una sola cámara (pág. 50, 233)
***uniform** consistent in conduct or opinion (p. 414)	***uniforme** coherente en conducta u opinión (pág. 414)
unitary system a government that gives all key powers to the national or central government (p. 12)	**sistema unitario** gobierno que otorga todos los poderes clave al gobierno nacional o central (pág. 12)
universe the group of people that is to be studied (p. 579)	**universo** grupo de personas que se ha de estudiar (pág. 579)
***variation** difference; change (p. 580)	***variedad** diferencia; cambio (pág. 580)
veto rejection of a bill by the president (p. 206)	**veto** rechazo de un proyecto de ley por parte del presidente (pág. 206)
***violation** an act of disregard or disrespect (pp. 93, 749)	***violación** acto de desacato o insolencia (pág. 93, 749)

Glossary/Glosario

visa a special document, required by certain countries, issued by the government of the country that a person wishes to enter (p. 700)

*vital necessary to the maintenance of life (p. 41)

*voluntary proceeding from the will or from one's own choice or consent (p. 490)

voting making a choice among alternatives in an election (p. 540)

weak-mayor system a mayoral system in which the mayor has limited powers and the city council makes most decisions (p. 359)

*welfare concerned with the well-being of disadvantaged social groups (p. 658)

whip an assistant to the party floor leader in the legislature (p. 145)

whistleblower a federal employee who reports corruption or wrongdoing by the government (p. 334)

White House chief of staff the president's most trusted adviser and the overseer of the work and operations of the White House and the Executive Office of the President (EOP) (p. 323)

winner-take-all system the system used by the Electoral College in almost every state in which the candidate who receives the most popular votes in a given state wins all the electoral votes for that state (p. 303)

wiretap an act or instance of tapping telephone or telegraph wires for evidence or other information (p. 477)

withholding the money an employer holds back from workers' wages as payment of anticipated income taxes (p. 647)

workers' compensation payments to people who are unable to work as a result of job-related injury or ill health (p. 372)

writ of certiorari an order from the Supreme Court to a lower court to send up the records on a case for review (p. 417)

zoning the means a local government uses to regulate the way land and buildings may be used in order to shape community development (p. 373)

zoning code a rule that specifies how land in particular parts of a city or county can be used (p. 240)

visa documento especial, exigido por ciertos países, emitido por el gobierno del país al que la persona desea entrar (pág. 700)

*vital necesario para el mantenimiento de la vida (pág. 41)

*voluntario que procede de la voluntad o del propio consentimiento o preferencia (pág. 490)

votar elegir entre alternativas en una elección (pág. 540)

sistema de alcalde débil sistema de alcaldías en el cual el alcalde tiene poderes limitados y el concejo municipal toma la mayor parte de las decisiones (pág. 359)

*bienestar interesado con mejora la situación de grupos sociales desfavorecidos (pág. 658)

jefe de disciplina asistente del líder del partido en el poder legislativo (pág. 145)

filtrador empleado del gobierno federal que divulga corrupción o acciones ilícitas (pág. 334)

Jefe de Gabinete de la Casa Blanca consejero de mayor confianza del presidente y supervisor del trabajo y las operaciones de la Casa Blanca y la Oficina Ejecutiva del Presidente (EOP) (pág 323)

sistema en el que el ganador se lleva todo sistema usado por el Colegio Electoral en casi todos los estados por el cual el candidato que recibe la mayoría de los votos populares en determinado estado gana todos los votos electorales para ese estado (pág. 303)

intervención telefónica acción o instancia de intervenir líneas de teléfono o telégrafo para obtener evidencia u otra información (pág. 477)

retención fiscal dinero que un empleador retiene del salario de los trabajadores como pago de impuestos sobre la renta pagados por anticipado (pág. 647)

subsidio por incapacidad pagos que se hacen a las personas que no pueden trabajar debido a mala salud o lesiones relacionadas con el trabajo (pág. 372)

auto de avocación orden de la Corte Suprema a un tribunal inferior de que envíe los archivos de un caso para revisión (pág. 417)

zonificación medios que usa un gobierno local para regular la manera como la tierra y los edificios pueden usarse para determinar el desarrollo de la comunidad (pág. 373)

código de zonificación norma que especifica cómo puede usarse la tierra en partes específicas de una ciudad o un condado (pág. 240)

Index

Index

Index

Index

Index

Index

Index

Index

Index

Index

Index